HANDBOOK OF EVIDENCE-BASED PRACTICE IN CLINICAL PSYCHOLOGY VOLUME 2

HANDBOOK OF EVIDENCE-BASED PRACTICE IN CLINICAL PSYCHOLOGY VOLUME 2

Adult Disorders

Edited by

PETER STURMEY
AND
MICHEL HERSEN

WILEY

John Wiley & Sons, Inc.

Published by John Wiley & Sons, Inc., Hoboken, New Jersey.
Published simultaneously in Canada.

For general information on our other products and services, please contact our Customer Care Department within the United States at (800) 762-2974, outside the United States at (317) 572-3993 or fax (317) 572-4002.

Wiley publishes in a variety of print and electronic formats and by print-on-demand. Some material included with standard print versions of this book may not be included in e-books or in print-on-demand. If this book refers to media such as a CD or DVD that is not included in the version you purchased, you may download this material at http://booksupport.wiley.com. For more information about Wiley products, visit www.wiley.com.

Library of Congress Cataloging-in-Publication Data:

Handbook of evidence-based practice in clinical psychology / edited by Peter Sturmey and Michel Hersen.
   v. ; cm.
Includes bibliographical references and index.
Contents: v. 1. Child and adolescent disorders – v. 2. Adult disorders.
ISBNs for Vol. 1: 978-0-470-33544-4 (cloth: alk. paper); 978-1-118-14471-8 (ebk); 978-1-118-14472-5 (ebk); 978-1-118-14470-1 (ebk)
ISBNs for Vol. 2: 978-0-47033546-8 (cloth: alk. paper); 978-1-118-14476-3 (ebk); 978-1-118-14475-6 (ebk); 978-1-118-14474-9 (ebk)
ISBN 978-1-118-15639-1 (eMRW)
ISBN 978-0-470-33542-0 (set)
   1. Clinical psychology–Practice.   2. Evidence-based psychotherapy.   I. Sturmey, Peter.   II. Hersen, Michel.
[DNLM: 1. Mental Disorders–therapy.   2. Evidence-Based Practice.   3. Psychology, Clinical–methods.   WM 400]
   RC467.95.H36 2012
   616.89—dc22
                                                                                            2011012039

Printed in the United States of America

10 9 8 7 6 5 4 3 2 1

Contents

Preface

Evidence-based practice in adult mental health has become a driving force for research, professional training, allocation of mental health resources, and service planning. It is also a lightning rod for debate among mental health professionals, researchers, service planners, and mental health economists. This volume brings together some of the leading researchers who have identified the professional, ethical, and economic issues related to evidence-based practice and adult mental health, and who have conducted systematic reviews, meta-analyses, and reviewed the existing literature on evidence-based practice for all the major adult mental health disorders.

Volume 2 is in two parts. Part I provides overview chapters that summarize the field of evidence-based practice in adult mental health, illustrate the application of principals to the planning of adult mental health services in the British National Health Service and professional training, and look at the economics of mental health that sometimes drives work in this area. Thomas Mauer's chapter offers a dissenting voice by highlighting the limits to evidence-based practice. Part II consists of more than 20 chapters that review the current status of evidence-based practice for all the major adult mental health disorders. The chapters differ tremendously in terms of the amount and quality of evidence available for each disorder. As one might expect, those disorders that are most common and have the

greatest economic impact have a very large evidence base—for example, there are hundreds of studies for tobacco-related disorders and for depression. These large literatures sometimes permit more confident answers as to "what works," as they are based on many studies with multiple independent replications. They also permit answers to questions that are more subtle than "Does this therapy work for this problem?," such as "Is this therapy more effective than another therapy?" A notable observation is that broadly defined cognitive-behavior therapy sweeps the board as an evidence-based practice whether or not one wishes to consider such diverse disorders as social anxiety disorder, sleep disorders, or personality disorders. There are, indeed, examples of other evidence-based practices, but they are much less frequent; there are examples of certain therapies that research has robustly shown to be ineffective or even harmful, such as brief psychological debriefing for posttraumatic stress disorder.

We believe this volume offers a comprehensive review of evidence-based practice in clinical psychology of adult mental health disorders that will be invaluable to students, teachers, and practitioners alike. Although this field is a rapidly changing one—as journals publish new evidence and reviewers reanalyze existing literatures—this volume offers one snapshot of the current status of what works in adult mental health.

Acknowledgments

We would first like to thank our authors. Many of them undertook an enormous task of summarizing sometimes hundreds of articles, systematic literature reviews, and consensus panels and sometimes reviewing the outcome literature for many different forms of treatment for one disorder. They faced the challenge of being accurate and fair in identifying those practices that the literature support, those that researchers had little convincing evidence to support them, and those that research has shown to be ineffective or harmful. We believe they all succeeded in doing so. We should both like to express our unending thanks to Carole Londeree's persistent and cheerful technical assistance throughout this project. Finally, we would like to express our thanks to the editorial staff at John Wiley & Sons who worked so hard to make this project a success.

Contributors

Jonathan S. Abramowitz is Associate Chair and Professor of Psychology at the University of North Carolina at Chapel Hill. He has published over 150 scholarly articles, book chapters, and books on anxiety disorders, including obsessive-compulsive disorder. He is associate editor of the *Journal of Cognitive Psychotherapy* and of *Behaviour Research and Therapy*.

Lesley A. Allen is Visiting Associate Professor of Psychology at Princeton University and Adjunct Associate Professor in the Department of Psychiatry at Robert Wood Johnson Medical School, University of Medicine and Dentistry of New Jersey. She has been awarded numerous grants from the National Institute of Mental Health to study the treatment of somatoform disorders and has published widely on this topic. She is the coauthor of *Treating Somatization: A Cognitive Behavioral Approach*.

Gerhard Andersson is Professor of Clinical Psychology at Linköping University, Linköping and the Karolinska Institute, Stockholm, Sweden. He has published widely on Internet delivered psychological treatments, tinnitus, depression, and anxiety disorders.

Martin M. Antony is Professor and Graduate Program Director in the Department of Psychology at Ryerson University in Toronto, where he also directs the Anxiety Research and Treatment Lab. He has published numerous books, scientific papers, and book chapters on anxiety disorders, perfectionism, cognitive behavior therapy, and psychological assessment.

John G. Arena is Psychology Executive at the Charlie Norwood Department of Veterans Affairs Medical Center, and Professor in the Department of Psychiatry and Health Behavior at the Medical College of Georgia in Augusta, Georgia. He is past president of the Association of Applied Psychophysiology and Biofeedback, and has published widely in the areas of psychological and psychophysiological assessment and treatment of chronic pain disorders, and medical psychology.

David C. Atkins is a Research Associate Professor in the Department of Psychiatry and Behavioral Sciences at the University of Washington. His research has focused on sociological and treatment studies of infidelity as well as treatment and process research on Integrative Behavioral Couple Therapy. He also is actively involved as a quantitative methodologist with particular interests in multilevel models and count regression methods.

Álvaro N. Atallah is full Professor and Head of the Emergency Department and Evidence-Based Medicine Division of Universidade Federal de São Paulo Brazil and Director of the Brazilian Cochrane Centre São Paulo.

Andrew J. Baillie is a Senior Lecturer in the Department of Psychology at Macquarie University in Sydney. He is the Director of Clinical Psychology Training and a member of the Centre for Emotional Health at Macquarie. He also holds an honorary appointment as a clinical psychologist at Drug Health Services, Royal Prince Alfred Hospital, in Sydney. He has published on anxiety disorders and comorbidity with alcohol use disorders from an assessment, treatment, and epidemiological perspective.

Anthony R. Beech is Chair of Criminological Psychology and a Fellow of the British Psychological Society. He is the Director of the Forensic and Criminological Psychology at the University of Birmingham. He has authored over 125 peer reviewed articles, 30 book chapters, and five books in the area of forensic science/criminal justice. He is the current recipient of the Senior Award for a significant lifetime contribution to Forensic Psychology in the United Kingdom, Division of Forensic Psychology, BPS, June 2009. He has also received the significant achievement award from the Association for the Treatment of Sexual Abusers in Dallas, Texas, October 2009.

Claudi Bockting is Associate Professor of Clinical Psychology at Groningen University in Groningen and works as a clinician in a mental health-care center, Symfora in Almere, the Netherlands. Her research focuses on long-term course of depression and anxiety disorders, processes that cause and maintain mood disorders, and development and evaluation of psychological interventions to prevent recurrence. In addition, she studies processes that cause and maintain mood disorders, as well as the treatment processes that reduce and prevent relapse and recurrence.

Stephanie Both is psychologist and Assistant Professor at the Department of Gynaecology at the Leiden University Medical Center in the Netherlands. She has published widely on male and female sexual functioning, and experimental research in sexual motivation and arousal.

Shawn P. Cahill is an Assistant Professor in the Psychology Department at the University of Wisconsin at Milwaukee. He received his PhD from Binghamton University, State University of New York in 1997. His research interests include understanding the nature and treatment of anxiety and other emotional reactions to stress, such as anger reactions. He has particular interest in posttraumatic stress disorder, obsessive-compulsive disorder, and panic in adults.

Hilary Cartwright co-wrote her chapter for this volume while she was a clinical psychologist and Assistant Professor in the Department of Clinical Health Psychology at the University of Manitoba. She is now a practicing clinician in Fredericton, New Brunswick, Canada. Her research and clinical interests are in child and adolescent psychology.

Linda Clare is Professor of Clinical Psychology and Neuropsychology at Bangor University, Wales, United Kingdom. Her interests focus primarily on the theoretical and clinical issues surrounding awareness and self-concept in dementia, the impact of progressive cognitive impairment on self and relationships, and the potential of neuropsychological rehabilitation for people with early-stage dementia. She has published numerous papers and Cochrane reviews and several books on these topics. She is coeditor of the *Handbook of the Clinical Psychology of Ageing* (2nd edition: John Wiley & Sons, 2008).

Roger Covin received his PhD in Clinical Psychology at the University of Western Ontario. He completed his residency training in Calgary, Alberta, Canada and is a former staff psychologist with the First Episode Mood and Anxiety Disorders Program in the Department of Psychology at London Health Sciences Centre, London, Canada. He has coauthored a number of journal articles and book chapters on a variety of topics such as cognitive behavior therapy outcomes for generalized anxiety disorder, normative data in clinical practice, and development of the Cognitive Distortions Scale. He currently operates a private practice in Montreal, Canada.

Pim Cuijpers is Professor of Clinical Psychology and Head of the Department of Clinical Psychology at the Vrije Universiteit University Amsterdam, the Netherlands. He is also Vice Director of the EMGO Institute for Health and Care Research of the Vrije Universiteit Amsterdam and Vrije Universiteit University Medical Center. He specializes in conducting randomized controlled trials and meta-analyses on prevention and psychological treatments of common mental disorders, especially depression and anxiety disorders.

Michelle E. Culang-Reinlieb is a fourth-year student in the doctoral subprogram in Neuropsychology at Queens College of the City University of New York. Her research interests focus on late-life depression with an emphasis on the role of executive dysfunction and change in cognitive functioning in antidepressant treatment trials.

Natasha Dagys is a doctoral student in School Psychology at the University of California, Berkeley. Her research interests focus on the consequences of sleep deprivation and on the role of sleep in social, emotional, and cognitive functioning, particularly during adolescence.

Mark R. Dixon is Professor of Behavior Analysis and Therapy at Southern Illinois University and a Board Certified Behavior Analyst. He has published over 90 papers and authored three books on a wide variety of topics including gambling addiction, weight loss interventions, treatment of children with autism, organizational behavior management, terrorism, and verbal behavior.

Michelle A. Doeden is a doctoral candidate at Fuller Graduate School of Psychology, Pasadena, California. She has been involved in couple therapy research throughout her graduate career, including work as a research fellow on an NIMH-funded grant, focused on language and couple therapy process.

David J. A. Dozois is Professor of Psychology and Director of the Clinical Psychology Graduate Program at the University of Western Ontario in London, Ontario, Canada. He is a Fellow of the Academy of Cognitive Therapy and a former Beck Institute Scholar at the Beck Institute for Cognitive Therapy and Research. Dr. Dozois's research focuses on cognitive vulnerability to depression and anxiety.

Ellen Driessen is a PhD candidate at the department of Clinical Psychology at Vrije Universiteit University Amsterdam, the Netherlands. Her research interest concerns the efficacy of psychotherapy in the outpatient treatment of depression.

Jon D. Elhai is Assistant Professor of Psychology at the University of Toledo. His research is on psychological trauma and post-traumatic stress disorder, exploring assessment, psychopathology, and treatment issues. He teaches undergraduate and graduate courses in clinical psychology. He also serves as an expert witness in his role as a forensic psychological evaluator and consultant.

Paul M. G. Emmelkamp is a licensed psychotherapist and clinical psychologist and full Professor of Clinical Psychology at the University of Amsterdam. Over the years, he has published widely on the etiology and treatment of anxiety disorders. He is involved in therapy-outcome studies on adults with work-related distress, substance abuse disorders, personality disorders, depression, anxiety disorders; on youth with attention-deficit/hyperactivity disorder, conduct disorder, and anxiety disorders; and on the elderly with anxiety disorders. He has written and coedited many books, and over 350 publications in peer reviewed journals or books. He has received a number of honors and awards, including a distinguished professorship ("Academy Professor") by the Royal Academy of Arts and Sciences.

Eric A. Fertuck is Associate Professor of Psychology at City College of New York and the Graduate Center of the City University of New York and a Research Scientist at Columbia University, New York State Psychiatric Institute. He investigates borderline personality disorder from many perspectives including the social, neurocognitive, physiological, and neural. His research is supported by the National Institute of Mental Health, the American Foundation for Suicide Prevention, the Neuropsychoanalysis Foundation, and the Fund for Psychoanalytic Research.

Jennifer Fidler is a Research Health Psychologist whose research focuses on smoking behavior, adolescent smoking, markers of smoking behavior and dependence, and the development of adolescent smoking behavior. Her current research examines the distribution of cotinine as a biological marker of nicotine intake and sociodemographic factors associated with this objective marker of smoking.

Edna B. Foa is a Professor of Clinical Psychology in Psychiatry at the University of Pennsylvania, where she serves as the Director of the Center for the Treatment and Study of Anxiety. She is an internationally renowned authority on the psychopathology and treatment of anxiety. Her research, aimed at determining causes and treatments of anxiety disorders, has been highly influential. She is an expert in the areas of posttraumatic stress disorders (PTSD) and obsessive-compulsive disorder. The program she has developed for rape victims is considered to be one of the most effective therapies for PTSD. She has published over 200 articles and book chapters, lectured extensively around the world, and received numerous awards and distinctions.

Julian D. Ford is Professor of Psychiatry at the University of Connecticut School of Medicine and Director of the University of Connecticut Health Center Child Trauma Clinic and the Center for Trauma Response Recovery and Preparedness (www.ctrp.org). He also conducts research on posttraumatic stress disorder, psychotherapy and family therapy, health services utilization, psychometric screening and assessment, and psychiatric epidemiology.

B. Christopher Frueh is Professor of Psychology and Director of the Division of Social Sciences at the University of Hawaii, Hilo, Hawaii. He also serves as the McNair Scholar and Director of Clinical Research at The Menninger Clinic in Houston, Texas. His research focuses on clinical trials, health services, epidemiological and qualitative studies relevant to the design and implementation of innovative treatments, and mental health service improvements in a variety of clinical settings.

James L. Furrow is Evelyn and Frank Freed Chair of Marital and Family Therapy at Fuller Graduate School of Psychology, Pasadena, California. He is author of a number of publications on the practice of Emotionally Focused Couple Therapy. He is a certified Emotionally Focused Therapy therapist, supervisor, and trainer.

Sidney Glina is the Director of the Instituto H. Ellis and Head of the Department of Urology in the Hospital Ipiranga, Sao Paolo, Brazil.

Brenna L. Greenfield is a graduate student in the Clinical Psychology PhD program at the University of New Mexico. She is interested in advanced statistical modeling techniques and collaborating with American Indian communities to develop and disseminate culturally appropriate alcohol use disorders treatment and prevention programs.

Anouk L. Grubaugh is Associate Professor in the Department of Psychiatry and Behavioral Sciences at the Medical University of South Carolina and a Research Health Scientist at the Charleston Veterans Affairs Medical Center. Her clinical and research interests include assessment and treatment of patients with posttraumatic stress disorder and severe mental illness, treatment adherence and attrition in public-sector settings, racial disparities in health outcomes, qualitative research methods, and mental health services methods.

Lisa H. Glynn is a doctoral candidate in Clinical Psychology at University of New Mexico. She has published in the areas of Motivational Interviewing, treatment mechanisms, and addictions. She is interested in processes of group-delivered alcohol treatment, coding of therapeutic interactions, and issues of diversity and multiculturalism.

Elizabeth A. Gordon is a doctoral student in clinical psychology at Temple University, Philadelphia, Pennsylvania. She is especially interested in examining the interplay of interpersonal processes and social anxiety disorder. Elizabeth received her BA in Human Biology from Stanford University and her MA in Clinical Psychology from Yeshiva University. Prior to studying clinical psychology, Elizabeth worked in the field of animal behavior and wildlife conservation.

Kevin A. Hallgren is a graduate student in clinical psychology at the University of New Mexico. He is interested in mechanisms of change in psychosocial treatments for alcohol use disorders, with a particular interest in methodologies for studying in-session behavior and changes in social networks as they relate to subsequent alcohol use.

Leigh Harkins is a Lecturer in Forensic Psychology at the University of Birmingham, United Kingdom. She has published a number of articles and chapters on sex offender treatment, risk assessment, and group aggression.

Allison G. Harvey is Professor of Psychology at University of California, Berkeley. She has published widely on sleep disorders, mood disorders, and empirically supported treatments.

Richard G. Heimberg is Professor and Distinguished Faculty Fellow in Psychology at Temple University, Philadelphia, Pennsylvania, where he directs the Adult Anxiety Clinic of Temple. He is Past President of the Association for Cognitive and Behavioral Therapies and Past Editor of its journal *Behavior Therapy*. He has published more than 325 articles and chapters, as well as 11 books, on the assessment and treatment of anxiety disorders and related topics, and his cognitive behavioral protocols for the treatment of social anxiety disorder have been implemented around the world.

Christopher Jones is a Consultant Clinical Psychologist and Senior Lecturer in Clinical Psychology at the University of Birmingham, United Kingdom. He is an active researcher, most notably in the area of engagement with assertive outreach services, evidence based practice, and clinical neuropsychology.

Rebecca L. Jump is a clinical psychologist at the Veterans Affairs Medical Center in Augusta, Georgia, and Assistant Professor at the Medical College of Georgia. She has clinical expertise in the areas of chronic pain, behavioral medicine, and sexual trauma/abuse.

Dora Kanellopoulos is a fifth year doctoral student in the doctoral subprogram in Neuropsychology at The Graduate Center, City University of New York. Her research interests focus on brain abnormalities related to depression and cognition in late life.

Martin Knapp is Professor of Social Policy and Director of the Personal Social Services Research Unit at the London School of Economics and Political Science. He is also

Professor of Health Economics and Director of the Centre for the Economics of Mental Health at King's College London, Institute of Psychiatry. In 2009, he was appointed by the National Institute for Health Research as the inaugural Director of the National School for Social Care Research. Martin's research activities are primarily in the mental health long-term care and social care fields, focusing particularly on policy analysis and economic aspects of practice.

Naomi Koerner is Assistant Professor in the Department of Psychology at Ryerson University in Toronto, Canada, where she also directs the Cognition and Psychopathology Lab. She has published scientific papers and book chapters on worry, worry-related cognitive processes, anxiety disorders, and psychological assessment.

Benjamin Ladd is a clinical psychology graduate student at the University of New Mexico. He is interested in the influence and impact of social support for change in the treatment and maintenance of treatment gains for alcohol use disorders. He is also interested in integrating the various areas of clinical knowledge, from the neurobiological to psychosocial, to develop comprehensive models of treatment for the spectrum of alcohol related problems.

Thomas Maier is head of the Psychiatric Services of the Canton St. Gallen North, Switzerland, and lecturer at Zurich University. He is a psychotraumatologist and has published on posttraumatic stress, obsessive compulsive disorders, and transcultural psychiatry, and also on complexity and nonlinear dynamics in psychiatry and on limitations of evidence based psychiatry.

Barbara S. McCrady is a Distinguished Professor of Psychology and the Director of the Center on Alcoholism, Substance Abuse, and Addictions at the University of New Mexico. Dr. McCrady has published widely on her research on couples therapy, cognitive behavior therapy, mutual help groups, and therapies for women with substance use disorders. She is a fellow of the American

Psychological Association (APA), past President of the Addictions Division of APA, and past member of the Board of Directors of the Research Society on Alcoholism. She has published more than 200 refereed papers, chapters, and books on her work.

David McDaid is Senior Research Fellow in health policy and health economics at both the Personal Social Services Research Unit and the European Observatory on Health Systems and Policies at the London School of Economics and Political Science. His primary research interests focus on comparative international analysis of mental health, health promotion, and public health-care policy and practice.

Dean McKay is Professor, Department of Psychology, Fordham University and Adjunct Professor of Psychiatry, Mount Sinai School of Medicine. He serves on the editorial boards of several journals including *Behaviour Research and Therapy* and *Journal of Anxiety Disorders*, and is Associate Editor of *Journal of Cognitive Psychotherapy*. He has published over 130 journal articles and book chapters, and is editor or coeditor of 10 published or forthcoming books. His research has focused primarily on obsessive-compulsive disorder (OCD), body dysmorphic disorder and health anxiety and their link to OCD, and the role of disgust in psychopathology. His research has also focused on mechanisms of information processing bias for anxiety states.

Mary McMurran is Professor of Personality Disorder Research at the University of Nottingham's Institute of Mental Health, United Kingdom. Her research interests include social problem solving as a model of understanding and treating people with personality disorders, the assessment and treatment of alcohol-related aggression and violence, and understanding and enhancing offenders' motivation to engage in therapy. She is a Fellow of the British Psychological Society, and recipient of the Division of Forensic Psychology's Lifetime Achievement Award in 2005.

Alan Meaden is a Consultant Clinical Psychologist who has specialized in the rehabilitation of those with schizophrenia and other psychoses for over 15 years. He is an active researcher, most notably in the area of cognitive therapy for command hallucinations alongside other research interests in engagement and staff factors.

Tamara Melnik is a researcher and Professor of Internal Medicine and Evidence-Based Medicine at the Universidade Federal de São Paulo (Unifesp) and Brazilian Cochrane Center.

Becky L. Nastally is a Visiting Assistant Professor in the Behavior Analysis and Therapy program at Southern Illinois University-Carbondale (SIUC). She was the 2009 SIUC Student Researcher of the Year and has authored 11 peer-reviewed journal articles, one book chapter, and 19 professional presentations. Her research interests lie in the area of nonsubstance-related behavioral addiction, verbal behavior, and cognitive behavior therapy.

Nisha Nayak is a postdoctoral fellow at the Center for the Treatment and Study of Anxiety at the University of Pennsylvania.

Brian P. O'Connor is a Professor of Psychology at the University of British Columbia Okanagan, in Kelowna, British Columbia, Canada. He conducts research on normal and abnormal personality, on personality disorders, and on interpersonal aspects of psychopathology. He also teaches advanced statistics and research methods courses and has written programs for a variety of specialty statistical procedures. Further information is available at https://people.ok.ubc.ca/brioconn/.

Allison J. Ouimet completed her master's degree in Clinical Psychology at The University of Western Ontario, in Ontario, Canada. She is currently in the Clinical Psychology doctoral program at Concordia University in Montreal, Canada. Her research at the Fear and Anxiety Disorders Laboratory focuses on the role played by basic cognitive processes in the etiology and maintenance of anxiety disorders.

Lorna Peters is a Lecturer in the Department of Psychology at Macquarie University, Sydney, Australia. She is a member of the Centre for Emotional Health at Macquarie and has published widely on adult anxiety mood disorders.

Stephen Pilling is Professor of Clinical Psychology and Clinical Effectiveness in the Research Department of Clinical, Health, and Educational Psychology, University College London, United Kingdom. He is the director of the National Collaborating Centre for Mental Health, which develops clinical practice guidelines for the National Institute for Health and Clinical Excellence. His research focuses on the evaluation of complex interventions for the treatment of severe mental illness, the development and evaluation of psychological treatments for depression, and the competences required to provide them effectively.

Lion Shahab is currently working as a lecturer in health psychology in the Department of Epidemiology and Public Health at the University College London. His expertise lies in epidemiology, tobacco control, public health, and health psychology. Current research interests focus on the detection of smoking-related diseases in the population, the use of smoking-related biomarkers to motivate smoking cessation, the development and impact of potential harm reduction strategies, and public attitudes to tobacco policy.

Joel R. Sneed is an Assistant Professor of Psychology at Queens College and an adjunct Assistant Professor of Medical Psychology in Psychiatry in the Division of Geriatric Psychiatry at Columbia University and the New York State Psychiatric Institute. He is Director of the Laboratory for Lifespan Development and Psychopathology and has published widely in the areas of geriatric, lifespan development, and personality disorders. His research on vascular depression is supported by the National Institute of Mental Health.

Sherry A. M. Steenwyk is a postdoctoral resident at Purdue University Counseling and

Psychological Services, West Lafayette, Indiana. Her clinical interests include working with couples, substance abuse issues, grief and loss, anxiety, and spirituality. Her research has focused on exploring the process of integrative behavioral couple therapy.

Patricia van Oppen is Associate Professor at the Department of Psychiatry, Vrije Universiteit Medical Center, Amsterdam, where she works as a clinical psychologist/behavior therapist. Her main research interest focuses on the evaluation of treatments of depression and anxiety disorders. She has published a substantial number of papers and has been an editor of several books on these topics.

Mark B. Powers is Assistant Professor and Codirector of the Anxiety Research and Treatment Program at Southern Methodist University, Dallas, Texas. He received his bachelor's degree in psychology at the University of California at Santa Barbara and his master's degree in psychology at Pepperdine, working with Dr. Joseph Wolpe on anxiety disorders. He received his PhD in clinical psychology from the University of Texas at Austin working with Dr. Michael J. Telch.

Annemieke van Straten is a psychologist and epidemiologist. She is Associate Professor in the department of Clinical Psychology at the Vrije Universiteit, Amsterdam, the Netherlands. Her research focuses on Internet interventions for common mental disorders in different settings and stepped care. She has published more than 60 international publications.

Steven Taylor is a professor and clinical psychologist in the Department of Psychiatry at the University of British Columbia, and editor in chief of the *Journal of Cognitive Psychotherapy*. He has published over 250 articles and book chapters, and 18 books on anxiety disorders and related topics. He is a Fellow of several scholarly organizations including the American and Canadian Psychological Associations and the Association for Psychological Science. His research interests include cognitive behavioral treatments and mechanisms of anxiety disorders, and related conditions, as well as the behavioral genetics of these disorders.

Moniek M. ter Kuile is Clinical Psychologist and Associate Professor at the Department of Gynaecology at the Leiden University Medical Center in the Netherlands. She has published widely on female sexual dysfunction, experimental research in sexual arousal and pain, and treatment outcome.

Jacques J. D. M. van Lankveld is Professor of Sexology at Maastricht University, the Netherlands. He has published widely on male and female sexual dysfunction, experimental research in sexual arousal, and treatment outcome.

Ellen Vedel is a cognitive behavior therapist and treatment manager at the Jellinek Addiction Treatment Centre in Amsterdam. As a senior researcher, she is currently involved in clinical trials testing integrated treatment protocols for substance abuse and posttraumatic stress disorder and for substance abuse and intimate partner violence. Together with Paul Emmelkamp, she is the coauthor of *Evidence-Based Treatments for Alcohol and Drug Abuse: A Practitioner's Guide to Theory, Methods and Practice.*

Valerie Vorstenbosch is a doctoral student in Clinical Psychology in the Department of Psychology at Ryerson University, Toronto, Canada. Her research interests are in the areas of obsessive-compulsive disorder, specific phobia, and cognitive behavior therapy. She has presented her research findings at several scientific meetings.

Monnica Williams is an Assistant Professor of Psychology at the University of Pennsylvania in the Center for the Treatment and Study of Anxiety. Dr. Williams completed her undergraduate studies at Massachusetts Institute of Technology and University of California at Los Angeles, and received her doctoral degree in clinical psychology from the University of Virginia. Dr. Williams's scholarly publications include scientific articles on racial/ethnic differences in anxiety disorders and obsessive-compulsive disorder (OCD). Her current research area includes African Americans with OCD, OCD treatment outcomes, and OCD symptom dimensions. Her clinical work is focused on anxiety disorders in adults.

Gill Windle is a Research Fellow in the Dementia Services Development Centre, Bangor University, Wales. Her published research has focused on resilience and well-being in older people, and the effects of exercise on well-being. Her current role includes providing academic support for research networks on aging and dementia in Wales.

Bob Woods is Professor of Clinical Psychology of Older People at Bangor University, Wales, United Kingdom, and Director of the Dementia Services Development Centre, Wales. His work on the development and evaluation of psychological interventions with people with dementia and their caregivers began over 30 years ago, and he has published widely on this and related topics, including several Cochrane reviews. He is coeditor of the *Handbook of the Clinical Psychology of Ageing* (2nd edition: John Wiley & Sons, 2008).

Judy Wong is a doctoral student in clinical psychology at Temple University, Philadelphia, Pennsylvania. Her interests focus on the influence of culture on the development and treatment of anxiety disorders. Judy received her BA in Psychology from the University of California, Berkeley.

Robert L. Woolfolk is Professor of Psychology and Philosophy at Rutgers University, New Jersey, and Visiting Professor of Psychology at Princeton University. He has published numerous papers and books on psychotherapy and psychopathology. A practicing clinician for over 30 years, he has sought in both his work with patients and his scholarly endeavors to integrate the scientific and humanistic traditions of psychotherapy. He is the coauthor of *Treating Somatization: A Cognitive-Behavioral Approach* and author of *The Cure of Souls.*

PART I

Overview and Foundational Issues

1

Evidence-Based Practice in Adult Mental Health

B. CHRISTOPHER FRUEH, JULIAN D. FORD, JON D. ELHAI, AND ANOUK L. GRUBAUGH

INTRODUCTION

There is widespread and growing awareness that behavioral and mental health care, like other sectors of health care, require rigorous practice standards and professional accountability (Institute of Medicine, 2001; Kazdin, 2008; President's New Freedom Commission on Mental Health, 2003). Evidence-based practice (EBP) and empirically supported treatments are a critical element of these standards for both child and adult populations (APA, 2006; Barlow, 2000; Spring, 2007; Spring et al., 2008; Torrey et al., 2001; Weisz, Hawley, Pilkonis, Woody, & Follette, 2000). Unfortunately, interventions used in clinical, behavioral, and mental health practice settings are often not carefully based on empirical evidence, resulting in a discrepancy between research and practice (Cook, Schnurr, & Foa, 2004; P. W. Corrigan, Steiner, McCracken, Blaser, & Barr, 2001; Ferrell, 2009; Frueh, Cusack, Grubaugh, Sauvageot, & Wells, 2006; Gray, Elhai, & Schmidt, 2007;

This work was partially supported by grants MH071168 from the National Institute of Mental Health, CD-70/015 from Veterans Affairs HSR&D, OHDP CL 535.35.35.35 from the Department of Justice, and awards from the McNair Foundation and Menninger Foundation.

Henggeler, Sheidow, Cunningham, Donohue, & Ford, 2008; Kazdin, 2008; Schoenwald & Hoagwood, 2001; Stewart & Chambless, 2007). In this chapter we provide an overview of EBP in adult mental health, including definitions, purpose, processes, and challenges.

DEFINING EVIDENCE-BASED PRACTICE

Evidence-based practice is an empirically based approach to identify and appraise the best available scientific data in order to guide the implementation of assessment and intervention practices. This entails making decisions about how to integrate scientific evidence with clinical practice, taking account of relevant practice setting, population, provider, and other contextual characteristics. Exact definitions of what constitutes an EBP have been proposed. Some have suggested that designation of an intervention as an EBP requires favorable empirical support from at least two randomized controlled trials (RCTs) conducted by independent researchers/labs (Chambless & Hollon, 1998), or seven to nine smaller experimental design studies each with at least three subjects conducted by at least two independent researchers (Chambless & Hollon, 1998; Lonigan, Elbert, & Johnson, 1998). These requirements were proposed in order to define specific treatment models as empirically supported treatments (ESTs). The ESTs are a subcategory of EBT that focuses on specific (usually manualized) treatment models for which substantial scientific evidence of efficacy or effectiveness has been accrued.

Others have proposed the value of expert consensus panels, meta-analyses, and/or Cochrane database reviews to overcome the potential biases of individual or critical reviews (Spring et al., 2008). Further, governments and health insurance companies have developed detailed EBP guidelines for specific psychiatric disorders, such as the UK's National Institute for Clinical Health and Excellence (NICE, 2005) and the United States' Institute of Medicine and National Research Council (IOM, 2007) guidelines for treating posttraumatic stress disorder (PTSD), in order to guide (or mandate) efficacious mental health-care practices.

EBP does not necessarily imply the designation of certain treatment models as "evidence based." An alternative way to conceptualize EBP is to place less emphasis on specific intervention protocols (e.g., manualized treatment models) and focus instead on empirically supported general content-domain practice elements (Chorpita, Daleiden, & Weisz, 2005; Rosen & Davison, 2003). For example, practice elements might include the development of a therapeutic working alliance and enhancing client motivation, teaching of skills for coping with symptoms, or facilitation of therapeutic processing of distressing emotions.

In addition, research evidence is not necessarily the only base for determining what constitutes EBP. The American Psychological Association Presidential Task Force on Evidence-Based Practice (2006) explicitly proposed requiring evidence from clinicians' real-world observations and from client values and preferences in addition to research evidence as a basis for establishing EBP. These added requirements reflect an attempt to ensure that EBP is not only likely to produce quantifiable outcomes (based on the results of scientific research), but will also have utility for clinicians (First et al., 2003) and will be acceptable to and respectful of the recipients of the services. Regardless of the specific evidentiary requirements that are defined as necessary to establish a mental or behavioral health practice as evidence-based, EBP must be defined in terms of behaviorally specific practices that can be readily and reliably taught to and followed by clinicians. Both treatment models and transtheoretical practice elements involve competencies that must be operationalized and replicable. Practitioner competencies for EBP fall into four broad areas, including: (1) assessment skills, (2) process skills (i.e., enhancing client motivation and the clinician-client working alliance), (3) communication skills for collaborative decision making, and (4) intervention skills (Spring et al., 2008).

Two other important concepts related to EBP require definition. *Dissemination* is the targeted distribution of synthesized scientific evidence and materials related to an intervention, practice, or clinical population to relevant key stakeholders (e.g., health-care administrators, clinicians, patients). *Implementation* is the use of specific strategies to ensure the successful adoption of disseminated EBPs and integration into practice patterns within clinical settings.

PURPOSE

The EBP in mental health care is important for several reasons. It allows for a shared vocabulary and conceptual framework to facilitate transdisciplinary research and high-quality practice in mental health care, providing a framework and process to ensure accountability and reduce the research-practice gap for the sake of the public health (IOM, 2001; Kazdin, 2008). Additionally, the conceptual framework provided by EBP allows for improved communication among professionals and disciplines, thus facilitating the dissemination and implementation of the very best available clinical practices with sufficient fidelity to ensure high-quality services.

THE PROCESS OF EVIDENCE-BASED PRACTICE

Because EBP is multifaceted and constantly evolving as empirical knowledge is accumulated, it requires an ongoing process. This process, a central tenet of EBP, involves several steps (as outlined by Spring 2007 and Spring et al., 2008).

1. *Ask* patient-centered questions relevant at the individual, community, or population level. For example, questions that have informed the development of EBP include: (a) Who are the patients who do *not* respond favorably to the best available treatments (e.g., those with Axis II personality disorders or more chronic symptoms), and how can adaptations of these treatments or alternative new treatments effectively address the barriers or problems that have limited these patients' ability to benefit? (b) What are the core symptoms or features of each disorder that must be addressed therapeutically in order to produce clinically significant change, and how can treatment be structured to directly address those symptoms or features? (c) What modifications in treatment models or practices can increase the pace at which change occurs, in order to relieve patients' suffering and increase their functioning in the most timely and least costly manner?

2. *Identify and acquire* the best available empirical evidence to address relevant questions. As noted earlier, the evidence should include the results of scientifically rigorous research, observations of how clinicians actually deliver services, and preferences expressed by patients that are relevant to effectively engaging and motivating them in treatment.

3. *Appraise the evidence critically* (see next section) in order to make appropriate implementation decisions.

4. *Apply the evidence in practice*, taking into account relevant factors such as limitations in the evidence base, clinical context, patient values and preferences, and available resources.

5. *Assess outcomes*, adjust in an iterative (and ongoing) manner, and disseminate when appropriate.

EVIDENCE APPRAISAL IN EVIDENCE-BASED PRACTICE

In order to make the most effective practice decisions, the best available empirical evidence must not only be identified and acquired, but also critically appraised and integrated. Relevant data can take many forms, including single case, time series, or open trials; randomized clinical trials; meta-analyses; consensus panels or agency guidelines.

Single case, time series, open trials. Smaller, nonrandomized treatment studies are typically an important early step in the development and evaluation of new interventions or applications of established interventions to new populations or via novel service delivery modes. Such studies can provide important information about intervention feasibility, acceptance of the intervention by patients and providers, and potential for efficacy. Alone, however, these trials rarely provide sufficient evidence to support an intervention as an EBP.

Randomized clinical trials (RCTs). Larger, randomized trials that are designed to carefully control for alternative factors that may account for what appear to be the outcomes of a treatment are usually the "gold standard" required for acknowledging an intervention as an EBP. There are a number of key elements to consider when evaluating the quality and applicability of an RCT (Borkovec & Castonguay, 1998; Chambless & Hollon, 1998). These include (1) study design, (2) methods and measures, (3) sample characteristics and size, (4) clinician characteristics, (5) dependent variable considerations, (6) data analyses, (7) results and effect sizes (statistical and clinical significance), and (8) potential side effects and adverse events, outcomes, and considerations. See also the

Consolidated Standards of Reporting Trials (CONSORT) statement, which was developed to improve the quality of reports of RCTs (Begg et al., 1996; CONSORT, 2009).

Clinical trials are often classified according to their phase (I to IV; NIH Guidelines, 2009) based on a system originally developed for medical outcome studies. A Phase I clinical trial involves testing a treatment model or practice with a relatively small number of recipients (in pharmacotherapy research this tends to range between 20 and 80) who are assessed before and after (and often during) the treatment in order to establish whether the treatment is safe and associated with sufficient benefits to warrant further testing. Phase I clinical trials may also test different variations of the treatment, such as fewer or more sessions (comparable to the dose of a medicine), and the mechanisms by which the treatment achieves outcomes (comparable to testing how a medicine is metabolized and affects the body). Phase II clinical trials test the efficacy of a treatment by rigorously comparing its outcomes versus those of usual clinical care or relatively innocuous alternative conditions that control for alternative possible sources of improvement (comparable to a placebo in medical research). Phase III clinical trials test the effectiveness of a treatment by administering it to much larger numbers of recipients (several hundred to thousands) in real-world circumstances that may include a comparison with the best available alternative treatment(s), careful monitoring of side effects, and follow-up assessments to determine if the benefits are sustained over time. Finally, Phase IV trials typically constitute postmarketing studies that are geared toward gathering more specific information about the risks, benefits, and optimal use of the intervention.

Critical reviews, meta-analyses, consensus panels, and agency guidelines: Reviews of empirical knowledge base can take a variety of forms, which can include objective efforts to quantifiably summarize and synthesize a large number of RCTs (e.g., meta-analyses).

Literature reviews can also help summarize what types of studies have been conducted and organize evidence to address a range of potentially important questions that extend beyond those addressed by a single RCT. These include questions regarding short- and long-term efficacy, efficacy for specific subgroups, effectiveness in practice settings, and comparisons across multiple interventions, limitations, and future directions for research and development.

Efficacy and effectiveness: Two conceptual forms of research studies represent two broad methods for evaluating outcomes, with efficacy study designs emphasizing internal validity (i.e., whether the intervention works in a controlled research setting) and effectiveness studies emphasizing external validity (whether the intervention works in real-world practice settings; Frueh, Monnier, Elhai, Grubaugh, & Knapp, 2004; Seligman, 1996). An RCT is a type of efficacy study that includes the use of manualized protocols with a fixed number of sessions and random assignment to different conditions. Although important for drawing inferences about causality, an inherent limitation of most RCTs is that they tend to emphasize laboratory rigor over real-world implementation. That is, RCTs generally include lengthy assessments that may or may not be practical in other settings, or they rely on interventions that may not easily translate to other settings due to varying provider and patient characteristics. Most RCTs to date have excluded patients with the most severe forms of the disorder being targeted, those with comorbid diagnoses, and those generally considered fragile or vulnerable. Additionally, most RCTs do not adequately represent ethnoracial minorities. These issues have raised questions among clinicians regarding the effectiveness of these interventions for the patients seen in their practice settings, many of whom have these characteristics.

Keeping up with the literature: Because scientific knowledge is constantly accumulating, EBP requires a continuous quality improvement perspective (IOM, 2001). New treatments or practices are under development constantly in the mental and behavioral health field, with research supporting their efficacy and effectiveness often emerging quite rapidly (despite the fact that clinical trials usually require several years to complete each phase). For example, only two medication treatments (sertraline, paroxetine) are considered sufficiently safe, efficacious, and effective for adults with PTSD to warrant approval by the U.S. Food and Drug Administration (which establishes federal guidelines for EBP for all pharmaceutical treatments), despite over 30 years of vigorous clinical trials since that diagnosis was formally recognized by the American Psychiatric Association in 1980 in the *Diagnostic and Statistical Manual* (3rd revision)—and no medication has been FDA approved for the treatment of PTSD with children. However, between 2000 and 2002 a series of Phase I clinical trials were reported suggesting that an antihypertensive medication (Prazosin) was associated with reduced nightmares in PTSD, and from 2003 to 2008 several large Phase II clinical trials confirmed the efficacy of Prazosin for PTSD nightmares and for some of the core daytime symptoms of PTSD as well (Raskind et al., 2007; F. Taylor et al., 2006; H. Taylor et al., 2008).

CULTURAL COMPETENCE IN EBP

Evidence-based practice by its very definition requires respect for diversity and knowledge about the limitations of EBPs as they pertain to various groups (Spring et al., 2008; Whaley & Davis, 2007). Because ethnoracial minorities are often not well represented in RCTs, concerns have been raised about the validity of EBPs for ethnoracial minorities and whether EBP standards are even relevant for many underserved/understudied groups. Certainly, more research needs to be conducted with such groups in a variety of practice settings, with a focus on effectiveness research. However, it is

not realistic to conduct efficacy or effectiveness trials for every possible configuration of intervention, comorbid condition, practice setting, and ethnoracial or socioeconomic status group. This alone is not reason enough to dismiss using theoretically sound and empirically supported interventions. Rather, it is important to follow the EBP process outlined earlier, reviewing, synthesizing, and adapting the best available empirical data to make contextualized practice decisions that take into account limitations of the existing knowledge base. In fact, the perspectives of cultural competence and EBP are complementary to each other in that they each emphasize the importance of thoughtfully adapting interventions from RCTs for use with specific populations and clinical contexts (Whaley & Davis, 2007). In this regard, extant empirical data can be used to tailor and refine interventions as needed to ensure that they are sensitive to and appropriate for specific clinical populations.

CHALLENGES TO DISSEMINATION AND IMPLEMENTATION OF EBP IN PRACTICE SETTINGS

Empirical evidence limitations: A major barrier to dissemination and implementation of EBP for many adult psychiatric disorders is that the empirical literature base remains undeveloped, especially with regard to co-occurring disorders and among underserved/understudied populations. We know very little about the efficacy of established interventions for patients with multiple psychiatric diagnoses, or with regard to the optimal timing of treating one disorder versus another among those with dual diagnoses. That is, for example, a clinician may rightly be hesitant to use a specific EBP intervention that has been shown in clinical trials to have efficacy for depressed patients with the clinicians' depressed and anxious patient, since it may be unclear how well the EBP's treatment effects generalize to patients with anxiety comorbidity. Also, the clinician working in an independent practice may be leery of adopting an EBP that proved efficacious in an academic medical center's RCT (since RCTs often have strict eligibility and exclusion criteria, as well as tending to provide treatments in a time-limited format that often is not sufficient to fully address complicated clinical problems). However, evidence actually suggests that private practice and community setting patients show comparable gains to those published in academic medical centers' RCTs despite RCT's strict inclusion criteria. And, evidence suggests that diagnostic complexity does not appear to substantially alter the effectiveness of EBPs tested on only a single disorder. Collaboration between researchers and clinicians has resulted in innovative adaptations of ESTs designed to enhance their applicability to clinicians and patients in real-world settings (e.g., Cook et al., 2004; Fava et al., 2006; Kazdin, 2001; Stroup et al., 2006).

Barriers to dissemination and implementation of EBP in practice settings: There is little evidence that EBPs are yet effectively disseminated or implemented in the vast majority of real-world practice settings, or that EBPs are implemented in ways that are likely to support wider dissemination efforts (Drake et al., 2001; Gold, Glynn, & Mueser, 2006; Mueser, Torrey, Lynde, Singer, & Drake, 2003; Shumway & Sentell, 2004). The literature on effective dissemination practices emphasizes the need to provide clinicians the training, tools, and ongoing supervision to deliver empirically validated treatments (P. W. Corrigan, Steiner, McCracken, Blaser, & Barr, 2001; Friedberg, Gorman, & Beidel 2009; Henggeler et al., 2008; Torrey et al., 2001). Although necessary, however, these strategies are recognized as insufficient to overcome clinical and administrative barriers to the implementation and maintenance of EBPs in most practice settings, public and private. These barriers generally include a lack of motivation and resistance to change by providers, lack of skills and inadequate training among providers, limited resources and incentives for providers, deficient incentives for providers and administrators, cost concerns regarding implementation and maintenance, lack of ongoing quality assurance or fidelity monitoring, limited involvement and commitment from key stakeholders, diffuse leadership, and insufficient accountability at multiple organizational levels (Addis & Waltz, 2002; P. W. Corrigan et al., 2001; P. Corrigan, McCracken, & Blaser, 2003; Drake et al., 2001; Frueh et al., 2009; Ganju, 2003; Mueser et al., 2003; Schoenwald & Henggeler, 2003; Schoenwald & Hoagwood, 2001; Torrey et al., 2001).

Practitioner beliefs and resistance: Practitioner beliefs about and resistance to EBP is a major concern. Clinicians often have concerns regarding the effectiveness of EBPs, including a possible compromised therapeutic relationship when using potentially "sterile" treatment manuals, when individual patient needs are not met, when treatment credibility is undermined by a formulaic lockstep approach, when there is contraindication in the most typical patients (e.g., those with comorbid conditions, ethnoracial minorities; see the aforementioned), when clinical innovation is hampered, and the belief that service innovations may reflect the interests and needs of administrators or payers of services rather than patients (Addis, 2002; Barlow, Levitt, & Bufka, 1999; Frueh, Cusack, Grubaugh, Sauvageot, & Wells, 2006; Gold et al., 2006; Hoagwood, Burns, Kiser, Ringeisen, & Schoenwald, 2001). Additionally, even with positive attitudes toward EBP, logistical challenges frequently hamper implementation efforts. These include difficulty in learning new skills, lack of infrastructure to provide clinicians with training, ongoing supervision and feedback (i.e., maintain fidelity of implementation), and lack of researcher-clinician partnerships (Cook et al., 2004; P. W. Corrigan et al., 2001; Schoenwald et al., 2003; Sullivan et al., 2005; Torrey et al., 2001). In fact, a survey of practicing psychologists demonstrates that fewer than half have a clear idea of treatment manuals, most mistakenly believing that they are cookbook approaches imposed by insurers (Addis & Krasnow, 2000).

Practitioner implementation: Even when practitioner beliefs and expectations regarding EBP are positive, this does not necessarily translate into actual or effective implementation. Studies evaluating attitudes toward and use of EBP among mental health professionals show that although only a minority of participants report negative views of EBPs, favorable EBP attitudes are not strongly correlated with reported clinical behaviors (e.g., Gray, Elhai, & Schmidt, 2007). Even respondents who tend to rely on treatments that are not empirically based report positive opinions about EBPs, suggesting that practitioners may hold widely varying evidentiary standards (Frueh et al., 2006).

Limited practice accountability at provider, facility, and system levels: Unfortunately, practice accountability, treatment quality, and outcomes are not systematically linked at all levels in most mental health clinics and systems (Gold et al., 2006). Performance standards usually focus on counting the number of patients treated (e.g., "billable hours"), general procedure categories administered, and medical record keeping tasks (e.g., progress notes completed). While these administrative criteria are important in terms of documenting that work is being accomplished, they do not ensure (and may actually shift the clinician's attention away from) the delivery of quality care and the attainment of meaningful benefits by patients. Some health care programs and systems (such as the U.S. Veterans Affairs health care system) also include measurement of patient attendance and drop out, scheduling of follow up appointments, and referrals, all of which are meaningful variables. However, mental health systems rarely monitor actual clinical outcomes at the individual patient or aggregate level, improvements in social and occupational functioning, or specific details of clinical practice behaviors (e.g., treatment fidelity monitoring) to ascertain whether EBP is used at all or used appropriately. Thus, frontline clinicians, facility directors, and system administrators are

rarely held accountable for using EBP. Without such accountability, large-scale adoption of EBP is unlikely to develop fully.

STRATEGIES FOR DISSEMINATION AND IMPLEMENTATION OF EBP IN PRACTICE SETTINGS

To effectively disseminate EBP in real-world practice settings, a multipronged effort targeted at every level of the organization (provider, facility, and system) is needed. Proposed strategies (Frueh et al., 2009) for overcoming such identified challenges are: set clear goals; nurture broad-based organizational commitment and key stakeholder involvement; implement specialty training efforts to provide information and change attitudes; provide ongoing technical assistance and clinical supervision; conduct fidelity and competence monitoring; and ensure accountability to the extent possible.

1. *Set clear goals*: It is important to set goals that are clear, specific, and realistic — and to then communicate these goals effectively to relevant change agents and key stakeholders. Goals should be objectively measurable so that progress in relevant domains can be empirically tracked, and goals can be revised accordingly. For example, a dissemination and implementation goal might be to train a cohort of clinicians to deliver an EST with 90% fidelity (or greater) to the model based on independent quality assurance review of videotaped treatment sessions, and to sustain this level of fidelity through weekly consultation meetings in which tapes are reviewed by the clinicians and expert supervisors. An outcomes goal might be to enable patients to reduce the severity of the symptoms of their primary disorder(s) to within the subclinical or nonclinical range when a sufficient "dose" (e.g., length of treatment or number of sessions) of the EST has been received.

2. *Nurture broad based organizational commitment and key stakeholder involvement*:

Successful dissemination and implementation of any new program within most large mental health agencies and practice settings requires broad-based organizational commitment, including representation and "buy-in" from the full range of key stakeholders, including patients (whose voices can be powerful and persuasive) (Cusack, Wells, Grubaugh, Hiers, & Frueh, 2007; Frueh et al., 2009; Gold et al., 2006). While administrators, clinicians, and other stakeholders are committed to improving patient outcomes, they must be convinced that proposed assessment procedures and interventions can do so cost effectively. After obtaining stakeholder buy-in, empirical data should guide decisions regarding how services will be implemented. These decisions should be flexible to ensure practices are appropriate and sensitive to the needs of both patients and providers within a particular facility. Similar to a bottom-up approach, provider feedback and concerns regarding the intervention should be solicited and appropriately addressed. Importantly, it has been proposed that making treatment manuals more user friendly and obtaining clinician input and refining treatment procedures to address high priority challenges (e.g., preventing and managing psychiatric crises; engaging and achieving progress with refractory patients) is key. Such feedback could alter aspects of the intervention but will ultimately increase the likelihood that the intervention will be successful by promoting a sense of ownership and collaboration among providers (Sullivan et al., 2005).

3. *Incorporate specialized training efforts to provide information and change attitudes:* Specialized training is necessary to help clinicians make the leap from learning new practices or treatments to actually incorporating the skills and knowledge into their clinical repertoire. Refresher training also is important to enable clinicians to keep up with refinements in the EBP as well as broader advances in their field, and to identify and address knowledge deficits. Available empirical data can be used to persuade stakeholders to accept the need for developing or changing clinical practices, and to provide direction on how those practices might be structured. For example, introducing specific measures or treatment manuals that are relatively user friendly and providing resources and instruction on their use can be extremely helpful to well-intentioned clinicians who want to change their practice but are unsure of where to begin. It is also important to include relevant instructional approaches that are tailored to specific audiences. Further, the use of multichannel approaches (e.g., video, Web-based, behavioral role plays) to clarify and reinforce key points is important to facilitate and consolidate learning. In combination, these training efforts can help to increase knowledge, expand skill sets, and dispel inaccurate practitioner beliefs.

4. *Provide ongoing supervision and peer review:* It is not sufficient to merely provide education and training to clinicians (Henggeler et al., 2008). The dissemination and implementation literatures suggest that single or compressed training sessions in practice settings seldom result in meaningful or lasting changes. Ongoing clinical supervision is an essential component of effective dissemination and implementation efforts, providing clinicians with role modeling and guidance by experts and assistance in competently adapting the EBP or EST to their setting and patients while maintaining fidelity to the model or practices (P. W. Corrigan, Steiner, McCracken, Blaser, & Barr, 2001; Torrey et al., 2001). Obstacles in training and supervision of EBPs have hampered real-world implementation in practice settings, requiring special attention and innovative models of dissemination (Friedberg, Gorman, & Beidel, 2009; Sudak, 2009).

5. *Conduct fidelity monitoring:* It is well-recognized that fidelity monitoring is essential to ensure effective long-term implementation of EBP (Backer, Liberman, & Kuehnel, 1986; McGrew, Bond, Dietzen, & Salyers, 1994). Without such monitoring, protocol deviations inevitably occur, including the introduction of theoretically incompatible, unsupported, or inert treatment strategies. For example, we found that clinicians being trained in the use of cognitive-behavioral treatment for PTSD were often tempted to fall back on old habits (e.g., avoiding discussion of trauma exposure details or PTSD symptoms) or to use elements of other incompatible interventions (Frueh et al., 2009). Fidelity efforts will be most effective if they are relatively quick, user friendly, and cost efficient (Schoenwald & Henggeler, 2003). Strategies include checklists to ensure session content areas are covered, peer review, and formal supervision in group or individual format. Optimally, actual observation of delivery of treatment by the supervisor (e.g., behind a one-way window) and the clinician (e.g., reviewing videotapes of treatment sessions) provides real-time samples of the patient-clinician interaction that can be discussed in terms of the clinician's successes in adhering to EBP as well as deviations that are opportunities for reexamining the purpose and benefits of the EBP and recommitting to it.

6. *Ensure accountability to the extent possible:* The final, and perhaps most difficult to incorporate, component of dissemination and implementation is accountability at all levels of the organization. Once an organization has made the decision to change, has implemented new procedures and services, and clinicians are trained and prepared to implement EBP, accountability is necessary. This requires: (a) ongoing assessment of protocol adherence (e.g., fidelity monitoring) and clinical outcomes, which can be used to help ensure accountability; and (b) ongoing training and supervision to maintain currency with EBP. Strategies must also be developed to incorporate goal obtainment accountability at provider, facility, and system levels. This should include both incentives for success and feedback, guidance, and ultimately consequences if goals are not met. This may be the most difficult challenge to surmount in most practice settings, and requires committed and creative leadership.

CONCLUSIONS

Widespread dissemination and implementation of EBP, including the conceptual framework and processes this entails, is critical to improving mental and behavioral health patient outcomes, yet is widely lacking in practice settings (Kazdin, 2008). Many clinicians still do not know that their jobs can be made easier and the benefits their patients accrue can be increased by incorporating EBP into their practice. Although EBP requires fidelity to a model of assessment and treatment and the tools for implementation (e.g., validated interview or questionnaire measures, replicable treatment strategies), the reality of clinical practice is that clinicians are using their own idiosyncratic implicit practice models. Utilizing EBP simply makes this explicit and open to thoughtful innovation, as opposed to the less desirable alternative of sporadic changes in practice or unquestioning adherence to practice as usual.

Thus, it is time that practitioners and mental health care systems align their clinical services with the best available empirical data. Ultimately, each clinician will choose her or his own practice model, but with an explicit EBP or set of ESTs the array of choices is enlarged and each choice about assessment or treatment strategy can be made on a more fully informed basis. It is essential that EBPs are defined, researched, taught, and supervised in a manner that facilitates rather than artificially constricts the clinician's ability to adapt practices to best suit the setting and each unique patient or cohort of patients. Schoenwald and Hoagwood (2001) noted the "process of moving efficacious treatments to usual care settings is complex and may require adaptations of treatments, settings, and service systems" (p. 1196). Accordingly, we have outlined a number of challenges to implementing EBP in clinical settings and suggested strategies for overcoming these challenges. These strategies include efforts at every level of the organization: clinician, facility, and system.

A great deal of change is still needed with regard to research and practice efforts. There is need to (a) enhance the empirical database on EBP for virtually all psychiatric disorders, especially with regard to comorbid conditions and understudied populations (e.g., ethnoracial minorities); (b) conduct and systematically evaluate related dissemination and implementation strategies and outcomes; (c) expand the empirical database on EBPs, as well as dissemination and implementation efforts for interventions in highly vulnerable populations (e.g., prisoners, veterans, low-income females, children, persons with substance abuse disorders); (d) examine and initiate widespread change efforts related to mental health practices in public-sector agencies; and (e) incorporate changes to graduate and medical training curricula to reflect the advances in EBP for adult psychopathology.

While this chapter has focused on the challenges and opportunities presented by the translation of scientific and clinical innovation into clinical practice, the true starting point for the widespread adoption of an EBP perspective to mental and behavioral health services is teaching EBP as a fundamental clinical practice framework in pregraduate and graduate education programs. When EBP is the rule and not the exception in clinical training across the mental and behavioral health professions, the dissemination and implementation of EBP in practice settings will be much closer to being the accepted and welcomed norm rather than a controversial externally imposed requirement. Precisely what EBP means in each setting and for each clinician will continue to be adaptable based on the best judgment of the clinician and the best interests of the patient, and as a result of utilizing an EBP framework those judgments and interests will be explicit and open to empirically guided enhancement. Considered in that light, EBPs provide a win-win opportunity for clinical innovation, if taught and applied in the spirit of humanistic empiricism that is their true foundation.

REFERENCES

Addis, M. E. (2002). Methods for disseminating research products and increasing evidence-based practice: Promises, obstacles, and future directions. *Clinical Psychology: Science and Practice, 9,* 367–378.

Addis, M. E., & Krasnow, A. D. (2000). A national survey of practicing psychologists' attitudes toward psychotherapy treatment manuals. *Journal of Consulting and Clinical Psychology, 68,* 331–339.

Addis, M. E., & Waltz, J. (2002). Implicit and untested assumptions about the role of psychotherapy treatment manuals in evidence-based mental health practice. *Clinical Psychology: Science and Practice, 9,* 421–424.

American Psychological Association Presidential Task Force on Evidence-Based Practice. (2006). Evidence-based practice in psychology. *American Psychologist, 61,* 271–285.

Backer, T. E., Liberman, R. P., & Kuehnel, T. G. (1986). Dissemination and adoption of innovative psychosocial interventions. *Journal of Consulting and Clinical Psychology, 54,* 111–118.

Barlow, D. H. (2000). Evidence-based practice: A world view. *Clinical Psychological: Science and Practice, 7,* 241–242.

Barlow, D. H., Levitt, J. T., & Bufka, L. F. (1999). The dissemination of empirically supported treatments: A view to the future. *Behaviour Research and Therapy, 37,* S147–S162.

Begg, C. B., Cho, M. K., Eastwood, S., Horton, R., Moher, D., Olkin, I., . . . Stroup, D. F. (1996). Improving the quality of reporting of randomized controlled trials: the CONSORT statement. *Journal of the American Medical Association, 276,* 637–639.

Borkovec, T. D., & Castonguay, L. G. (1998). What is the scientific meaning of empirically supported therapy? *Journal of Consulting and Clinical Psychology, 66,* 136–142.

Chambless, D. L., & Hollon, S. D. (1998). Defining empirically supported treatments. *Journal of Consulting and Clinical Psychology, 66,* 7–18.

Chorpita, B. F., Daleiden, E. L., & Weisz, J. R. (2005). Identifying and selecting the common elements of evidence-based interventions: A distillation and matching model. *Mental Health Services Research, 7,* 5–20.

Consolidated Standards for Reporting of Trials. (2009). Retrieved from http://www.consort-statement.org/

Cook, J. J., Schnurr, P. P., & Foa, E. B. (2004). Bridging the gap between posttraumatic stress disorder research and clinical practice: The example of exposure therapy. *Psychotherapy: Theory, Research, Practice, Training, 41,* 374–387.

Corrigan, P., McCracken, S., & Blaser, B. (2003). Disseminating evidence-based mental health practices. *Evidence-Based Mental Health, 6,* 4–5.

Corrigan, P. W., Steiner, L., McCracken, S. G., Blaser, B., & Barr, M. (2001). Strategies for disseminating evidence-based practices to staff who treat people with serious mental illness. *Psychiatric Services, 52*, 1598–1606.

Cusack, K. J., Wells, C. B., Grubaugh, A. L., Hiers, T. G., & Frueh, B. C. (2007). An update on the South Carolina Trauma Initiative. *Psychiatric Services, 58*, 708–710.

Drake, R. E., Goldman, H. H., Leff, H. S., Lehman, A. F., Dixon, L., Mueser, K. T., & Torrey, W. C. (2001). Implementing evidence-based practices in routine mental health service settings. *Psychiatric Services, 52*, 179–182.

Fava, M., Rush, A. J., Wisniewski, S. R., Nierenberg, A. A., Alpert, J. E., McGrath, P. J., . . . STAR*D Study Team. (2006). A comparison of mirtazapine and nortriptyline following two consecutive failed medication treatments for depressed outpatients: A STAR*D Report. *American Journal of Psychiatry, 163*, 1161–1172.

Ferrell, C. B. (2009). Reengineering clinical research science: A focus on translational research. *Behavior Modification, 23*, 7–23.

First, M., Pincus, H., Levine, J., Williams, J., Ustun, B., & Peele, R. (2003). Clinical utility as a criterion for revising psychiatric diagnoses. *American Journal of Psychiatry, 161*, 946–954.

Friedberg, R. D., Gorman, A. A., & Beidel, D. C. (2009). Training psychologists for cognitive-behavioral therapy in the raw world: A rubric for supervisors. *Behavior Modification, 33*, 104–123.

Frueh, B. C., Cusack, K. J., Grubaugh, A. L., Sauvageot, J. A., & Wells, C. (2006). Clinician perspectives on cognitive-behavioral treatment for PTSD among public-sector consumers with severe mental illness. *Psychiatric Services, 57*, 1027–1031.

Frueh, B. C., Grubaugh, A. L., Cusack, K. J., & Elhai, J. D. (2009). Disseminating evidence-based practices for adults with PTSD and severe mental illness in public-sector mental health agencies. *Behavior Modification, 33*, 66–81.

Frueh, B. C., Monnier, J., Elhai, J. D., Grubaugh, A. L., & Knapp, R. G. (2004). Telepsychiatry treatment outcome research methodology: Efficacy versus effectiveness. *Telemedicine Journal and E-Health, 10*, 455–458.

Ganju, V. (2003). Implementation of evidence-based practices in state mental health systems: Implications for research and effectiveness studies. *Schizophrenia Bulletin, 29*, 125–131.

Gold, P. B., Glynn, S. M., & Mueser, K. T. (2006). Challenges to implementing and sustaining comprehensive mental health service programs. *Evaluation & the Health Professions, 29*, 195–218.

Gray, M. J., Elhai, J. D., & Schmidt, L. O. (2007). Trauma professionals' attitudes towards and utilization of evidence-based practices. *Behavior Modification, 31*, 732–748.

Henggeler, S. W., Sheidow, A. J., Cunningham, P. B., Donohue, B. C., & Ford, J. D. (2008). Promoting the implementation of an evidence-based intervention for adolescent marijuana abuse in community settings: Testing the use of intensive quality assurance. *Journal of Clinical Child and Adolescent Psychology, 37*, 682–689.

Hoagwood, K., Burns, B. J., Kiser, L., Ringeisen, H., & Schoenwald, S. K. (2001). Evidence-based practice in child and adolescent mental health services. *Psychiatric Services, 52*, 1179–1189.

Institute of Medicine and National Research Council. (2001). *Crossing the quality chasm: A new health system for the 21st century.* Washington, DC: The National Academies Press.

Institute of Medicine and National Research Council. (2007). *Treatment of posttraumatic stress disorder: An assessment of the evidence.* Washington, DC: The National Academies Press.

Kazdin, A. (2001). Progression of therapy research and clinical application of treatment require better understanding of the change process. *Clinical Psychology: Science and Practice, 8*, 143–151.

Kazdin, A. (2008). Evidence-based treatment and practice: New opportunities to bridge clinical research and practice, enhance the knowledge base, and improve patient care. *American Psychologist, 63*, 146–159.

Lonigan, C. J., Elbert, J. C., & Johnson, S. B. (1998). Empirically supported psychosocial interventions for children: An overview. *Journal of Clinical Child Psychology, 27*, 138–145.

McGrew, J. H., Bond, G. R., Dietzen, L., & Salyers, M. (1994). Measuring the fidelity of implementation of a mental health program model. *Journal of Consulting and Clinical Psychology, 62*, 670–678.

Mueser, K. T., Torrey, W. C., Lynde, D., Singer, P., & Drake, R. E. (2003). Implementing evidence-based practices for people with severe mental illnesses. *Behavior Modification, 27*, 387–411.

National Institute for Health and Clinical Excellence. (2005). *The management of posttraumatic stress disorder in primary and secondary care.* London: NICE.

National Institute of Health. (2009). *Clinical trials.gov.* Retrieved from http://clinicaltrials.gov/ct2/info/understand

President's New Freedom Commission on Mental Health. (2003). *Achieving the promise: Transforming mental health care in America. Final report* (Department of Health and Human Services Report No. SMA 03-3832). Rockville, MD: Department of Health and Human Services.

Raskind, M., Peskind, E., Hoff, D., Hart, K., Holmes, H., Warren, D., . . . McFall, M. E. (2007). A parallel group placebo-controlled study of Prazosin for trauma nightmares and sleep disturbance in combat veterans with Posttraumatic Stress Disorder. *Biological Psychiatry, 61*, 928–934.

Rosen, G. M., & Davison, G. C. (2003). Psychology should list empirically supported principles of change (ESPs) and not credential trademarked therapies or other treatment packages. *Behavior Modification, 27,* 300–312.

Schoenwald, S. K., & Henggeler, S. W. (2003). Current strategies for moving evidence-based interventions into clinical practice: Introductory comments. *Cognitive & Behavioral Practice, 10,* 275–277.

Schoenwald, S. K., & Hoagwood, K. (2001). Effectiveness, transportability, and dissemination of interventions: What matters when? *Psychiatric Services, 52,* 1190–1197.

Seligman, M. E. (1996). Science as an ally of practice. *American Psychologist, 51,* 1072–1079.

Shumway, M., & Sentell, T. L. (2004). An examination of leading mental health journals for evidence to inform evidence-based practices. *Psychiatric Services, 55,* 649–653.

Spring, B. (2007). Evidence-based practice in clinical psychology: What it is, why it matters; and what you need to know. *Journal of Clinical Psychology, 63,* 611–631.

Spring, B., Walker, B., Brownson, R., Mullen, E., Newhouse, R., Satterfield, J., . . . Hitchcock, K. (2008). *Definition and competencies for evidence-based behavioral practice (EBBP).* Counsel for Training in Evidence-Based Behavioral Practice: Evanston, IL.

Stewart, R. E., & Chambless, D. L. (2007). Does psychotherapy research inform treatment decisions in private practice? *Journal of Clinical Psychology, 63,* 267–281.

Stroup, T. S., Lieberman, J. A., McEvoy, J. P., Swartz, M. S., Davis, S. M., Rosenheck, R. A., . . . CATIE Investigators. (2006). Effectiveness of olanzapine, quetiapine, risperidone, and ziprasidone in patients with chronic schizophrenia following discontinuation of a previous atypical antipsychotic. *American Journal of Psychiatry, 163,* 611–622.

Sudak, D. M. (2009). Training in cognitive behavioral therapy in psychiatry residency: An overview for educators. *Behavior Modification, 33,* 124–137.

Sullivan, G., Duan, N., Mukherjee, S., Kirchner, J., Perry, D., & Henderson, K. (2005). The role of health services researchers in facilitating intervention research. *Psychiatric Services, 56,* 537–542.

Taylor, F., Lowe, K., Thompson, C., McFall, M., Peskind, E, Kanter, E., . . . Raskind, M. A. (2006). Daytime prazosin reduces psychological distress to trauma specific cues in civilian trauma posttraumatic stress disorder. *Biological Psychiatry, 59,* 577–581.

Taylor, H., Freeman, M., & Cates, M. (2008). Prazosin for treatment of nightmares related to posttraumatic stress disorder. *American Journal of Health Systems in Pharmacy, 65,* 716–722.

Torrey, W. C., Drake, R. E., Dixon, L., Burns, B. J., Flynn, L., Rush, A. J., . . . Klatzker, D. (2001). Implementing evidence-based practices for persons with severe mental illness. *Psychiatric Services, 52,* 45–50.

Weisz, J. R., Hawley, K. M., Pilkonis, P. A., Woody, S. R., & Follette, W. C. (2000). Stressing the (other) three Rs in the search for empirically supported treatments: Review procedures, research quality, relevance to practice and the public interest. *Clinical Psychology: Science and Practice, 7,* 243–258.

Whaley, A. L., & Davis, K. E. (2007). Cultural competence and evidence-based practice in mental health services: A complementary perspective. *American Psychologist, 62,* 563–574.

2

Developing Clinical Guidelines for Adults

Experience From the National Institute for Health and Clinical Excellence

STEPHEN PILLING

INTRODUCTION

The National Institute for Health and Clinical Excellence (NICE) was established in 1999 to develop guidance for the National Health Service in England and Wales. It operates as an independent body within the state funded health care system, known as the National Health Service (NHS), but its funding and the remit for its work comes from the government. The central role of NICE is to provide recommendations on the best practices in health care and thereby set standards by which health care and health outcomes can be improved. It produces guidance in four areas: (1) Clinical Practice, that is, clinical guidelines, such as guidance focused primarily on a disorder or condition, such as depression or type I diabetes; (2) Technology Appraisals, which are cost effectiveness reviews of health technologies, usually, but not limited to, drugs. For example, in mental health technology, appraisals have covered novel hypnotics, Electroconvulsive Therapy (ECT), drugs for the treatment of attention-deficit/hyperactivity disorder (ADHD), and parent training in conduct

disorder; (3) Interventional Procedures, which are concerned primarily with the efficacy and safety of surgical procedures but do, on occasion, move outside this field to consider nonsurgical interventions for example, transmagnetic stimulation for the treatment of depression; and (4) Public Health Guidance, which is concerned with public health interventions, and its brief extends beyond health care to involve social care and the wider environment. These four elements constitute the largest single program for the development of clinical guidance in the world. This chapter will provide an introduction to the work of NICE in mental health, concentrating primarily on the clinical guidelines program for adults and its impact on the development of psychological treatments in the UK, but will also refer to other elements of the NICE program. Some of the guidelines cover disorders of both adults and children, for example, eating disorders (See Volume 1, Chapter 1, by Pilling and Fonagy for an account of NICE's work on children and adolescent mental health.)

Although NICE is probably the largest guideline development organization, it is not alone. The past 20 years have seen a major expansion in guidance development around the world. Some measure of the rate of expansion can be obtained from the following figures. Parry, Cape, and Pilling (2003) reported that the total number of guidelines concerned with the treatment of depression on the National Guidelines Clearinghouse, an international register of completed guidelines (www.guideline.gov), was 170. As of December 31, 2008, this figure had reached 487. Despite this proliferation of guidelines, relatively few have explicitly focused on psychological therapies although there are some exceptions; see, for example, the guideline on Treatment Choice in Psychological Therapies and Counselling (Department of Health, 2001). Despite this lack of explicit focus, psychological interventions have assumed an increasingly important role in a number of mental health guidelines, in particular the NICE mental health guidelines, where psychological interventions have been identified as key recommendations for implementation in 13 out of the 16 mental health guidelines so far produced (www.nccmh.org.uk). Indeed, the location of psychological interventions within broadly based diagnostic or condition-based guidelines has been important in establishing psychological therapies as mainstream treatment options.

DEVELOPING CLINICAL GUIDELINES

The focus of this chapter is on the development of clinical guidelines, particularly as they apply to psychological therapies for adults, and mental health more generally. It will first consider the rationale for their development; briefly review the methods by which they are produced, reviewing some of the particular problems in their development; consider the evidence for their effective implementation; briefly describe some major implementation initiatives in the NHS; and briefly consider future developments in clinical guidelines in mental health and psychological therapies. The chapter draws on the author's experience as the

joint director of the National Collaborating Centre for Mental Health, a British Psychological Society and Royal College of Psychiatrists joint initiative that develops clinical practice guidelines in mental health for NICE.

Rationale for Clinical Guidelines

Clinical guidelines are defined as "systematically developed statements to assist practitioner and patient decisions about appropriate healthcare for specific clinical circumstances" (Field & Lohr, 1990, p. 8). This definition, developed in the 1990 Institute of Medicine report, is the one adopted by the UK healthcare system (Department of Health, 1996). They differ from standard literature reviews and textbooks in the explicit methods used in their construction, which usually involves a representative guideline development group of professionals who use a systematic approach to identify and evaluate the evidence. Increasingly, patients and caregivers also participate in the development of guidelines. Evidence from secondary research, usually in the form of systematic reviews, is used in combination with the expertise and knowledge of the guideline development group to arrive at a set of recommendations for clinical practice. Guideline development groups increasingly follow standard methods for development of recommendations including, where appropriate, formal and informal consensus methods (NICE, 2009a). An important characteristic of high-quality clinical guidelines is that the method is transparent and well described so that the evidence supporting each recommendation is clearly identifiable.

A primary aim of clinical guidelines is to promote clinically cost-effective care; in order to achieve this, they need to be based on the best available evidence. In seeking to achieve this aim, guidelines set standards for interventions by health-care professionals that should guide professional behavior; however, they are not a substitute for the clinical judgment exercised by a health-care professional when determining the most effective care for an individual (NICE, 2009a). Because clinical guidelines are based on the needs of the hypothetical typical patient, and because patient needs inevitably vary from the average, recommendations may require adaptation to suit the needs of the individual. For example, this might mean varying the duration of the recommended treatment for patients with comorbid disorders, such as in the treatment of PTSD with comorbid personality disorder (NICE, 2005b). Typically, it might be expected that the recommendations contained in a guideline would apply to about 80% of the individuals with the condition or disorder covered by that particular guideline (Eddy, 1990). Clinical guidelines should also be distinguished from protocols. Protocols specify precisely what a health-care professional should do in a certain set of circumstances and should be based on good-quality evidence with a high degree of certainty about the benefits and/or risks of the intervention; for example, the means of administration of certain cytotoxic drugs, and opinions/options. In contrast, a synthesis of the evidence sets out a range of possible interventions and the evidence for their effectiveness without necessarily specifying in detail the circumstances in which they might be used, such as the empirically supported treatment approach adopted by the American Psychological Association (Chambless, 1993). Clinical guidelines can be particularly important when considerable uncertainty exists about the correct intervention for a particular disorder or problem, as is often the case in mental health.

The focus in clinical guidelines on setting standards for and improving patient outcomes has a number of direct and indirect consequences. In addition to improved quality of care, these include the allocation of resources toward more effective treatments and away from less effective treatments and improved access to effective care, particularly if the guidelines also make recommendations about the nature of service delivery systems. Clinical guidelines are also increasingly used to better

inform patients about the type of care they may expect. This requires that the guidance be presented in forms accessible to patients. NICE produces publications for all its guidance that specifically aim to inform patients and their caregivers about the guidance it has issued (NICE, 2009a). This means that guidelines cannot only help patients in making informed decisions about their care, but may also improve communication between patients and professionals. Guidelines may also be used by health-care commissioners and managers to guide the purchasing of services to: (a) develop the service structures needed to deliver effective health care, (b) develop the systems for effective monitoring, and (c) evaluate services. Finally, guidelines can also have a role in the education and training of health-care professionals and may assume an increasing prominence in the curricula of the undergraduate and postgraduate training of health-care professionals. The aim of clinical guidelines is to reduce existing uncertainties about which interventions are most likely to bring benefit for patients and generate greater cost effectiveness in the health care system, thereby ensuring that unacceptable variation in both clinical practice and the distribution of resources is reduced.

As can be seen from the previous discussion, NICE and other clinical guidelines are increasingly drawn into the discussion of the allocation of resources. This represents an engagement with issues beyond the simple identification of effective interventions and is a challenge that faces all health care systems where the demand for health care outstrips the system's capacity and resources to deliver, including those in the United States (Peterson, 2008; Steinbrook, 2008). While it is not the role of clinical guidelines or their developers to decide on what resources should be allocated by a community for the health care of its citizens, guidelines can have a role to play in determining the means by which those agreed resources are allocated. Therefore, it is important that the methods used are seen to be fair and transparent. This is particularly important if guidelines are to retain the support of the professional and patient communities whose practice and care is directly impacted by them. Inevitably, this requires that the values on which the guidelines are based are made explicit, as are the methods by which the guidelines are produced.

While guideline development methods have become increasingly transparent (Grilli, Magrini, Penna, Mura, & Liberati 2000), there are few guideline development organizations that make explicit the values that underpin their work. The NICE is one of the few guideline development organizations that has an explicit statement of its social value judgements (NICE, 2005c). These values include: (a) statements on recommending interventions where good evidence is available but not doing so where it is not available; (b) considering cost-effectiveness in the evaluation of interventions; (c) considering age, race, or gender only where it is an indicator of the likely effectiveness of an intervention that cannot be accounted for by any other means; and (d) not denying interventions because the condition that they aim to ameliorate may, in part, be self-inflicted (NICE, 2005c). This approach recognizes that it is extraordinarily difficult, if not impossible, to develop an agreed set of rules that could allow for the allocation of health-care resources on which all citizens could agree (Daniels & Sabin, 2002), but that it may be possible to obtain agreement on the process by which the decisions are reached. This approach, known as procedural justice (Daniels & Sabin, 2002), underpins the NICE program and requires a transparent and fair process in which all relevant stakeholders are actively involved. Guideline developers are not expected to satisfy everyone since this may well not be achievable, but they can be held to account for the reasonableness of their decision-making process (Rawlins & Dillon, 2005).

Methods for Developing Clinical Guidelines

There are a number of methods for the synthesis of evidence to support clinical decision making and the development of clinical guidelines. These include systematic reviews (Egger, Davey Smith, & Altman, 2001); meta-analysis or other methods of aggregating multiple data sets on the effects of an intervention (Egger et al., 2001); evidence briefings (see www.nta.nhs.uk for examples from the field of substance misuse), reviews of the cost or cost-effectiveness of health interventions (Whitten et al., 2002), and formal and informal consensus methods (Black et al., 1999). As will be seen from the following discussion, these approaches are not mutually exclusive. Systematic reviews are the building blocks of almost all high-quality evidence reviews and the methods for doing this, while not always followed, are the best developed. See Moher et al. (1999) for a statement on the methods to be adopted for high-quality systematic reviews.

In most cases clinical guidelines, including those from NICE, are condition- or problem-based. Thus, they may address diagnoses, such as depression or diabetes, or problems, such as violence in psychiatric settings. They focus on what should be done and less on how treatments might be delivered (Parry et al., 2003). The consequences of this approach for clinical guidelines in mental health and psychological therapies will be returned to later in this chapter; however, in most health-care systems the clinical guideline remains the most complete manifestation of evidence-based medicine, and one that may also include advice on the care pathways and service structures to support effective delivery of care.

Initially, most clinical guidelines were developed by specialist uniprofessional groups; for example, by groups of specialist physicians such as cardiologists or neurologists. In a systematic review of specialist guidelines developed by uniprofessional groups, Grilli et al. (2000) focused on three areas of guideline development: (1) professional and stakeholder involvement, (2) identification of primary evidence, and (3) appropriate grading of recommendations. They highlighted some of the potential problems with this specialist uniprofessional approach. For example, of the 431 specialty guidelines they reviewed, only 5% were rated as adequate in terms of the search strategies used, the structure of the guideline development groups, and the grading of recommendations. Grilli and collegues argued that this demonstrated the need for a multidisciplinary approach with explicit and transparent methods based on international standards of good practice. Recent trends in guideline development have supported this view and the recent significant international expansion of evidence-based medicine has often been based in multiprofessional development programs such as NICE in England and Wales, the Scottish Intercollegiate Guidelines Network (SIGN), and the Agency for Healthcare Research and Quality (AHRQ) in the United States (Parry et al., 2003). In addition, there have been recent and important advances in the methods for the evaluation of the quality of clinical guidelines. Perhaps the best developed, reliable, and most widely used method is the AGREE instrument (www.agreecollaboration .org). It was produced by an international group of guideline developers and methodologists (AGREE, 2003) to assess the quality of guideline development. It includes ratings of the scope and purpose of the guideline, the extent of stakeholder involvement, the rigor of development, the clarity and presentation, the applicability of the guideline, and the degree of editorial independence of the developers. For an example of its use in an international review of the quality of clinical guidelines in schizophrenia, see Gaebel, Weinmann, Sartorius, Rutz, and McIntyre (2005).

Clinical guidelines typically rely on two main methods for the identification and aggregation of data from primary research: systematic review and meta-analysis. Thus, the quality of these activities is central to the development of high-quality clinical guidelines. Systematic reviews usually summarize large bodies of evidence by synthesizing the results of multiple primary investigations using strategies designed to reduce bias and random error (Egger et al., 2001). In well-conducted systematic reviews, these methods are predefined and presented in a reliable, transparent, and reproducible manner (Egger et al., 2001). They clearly specify the means by which studies will be identified, selected for inclusion, appraised and their results aggregated, and include steps to minimize bias at each of these stages. In most systematic reviews of the efficacy of a clinical intervention, the randomized controlled trial (RCT)— regardless of the results—is the preferred building block (Starr & Chalmers, 2003). A systematic review usually, but not always, contains a quantitative synthesis of the results—a meta-analysis—but this might not always be possible. For example, when the designs of the studies included in the analysis are too different from each other for an average of their results to be appropriate. This may occur when: (a) combining data from individual or cluster randomized trials without data available to allow for adjustments to take into account the effects of clustering; (b) if the outcomes are not adequately reported; or (c) where the difference in the nature of the outcome measures is too great to allow for a direct comparison. A meta-analysis can also be performed without a systematic review simply by combining the results from more than one study, but considerable caution is often needed in the interpretation of the results.

One of the major difficulties that arises in the interpretation and use of systematic reviews in support of clinical decision making derives from the methods used to identify, select, and critically appraise the relevant studies. For most well-conducted systematic reviews, a well-designed electronically based search strategy is required, one that includes clearly specified search terms relevant to the subject under review and searches relevant databases such as Medline, EMBASE, and PsycINFO. The development of these strategies is well described in a number of publications (Egger et al., 2001) and any well-conducted review should report on the number of relevant studies identified at each stage of the search and appraisal process (Moher et al., 1999); however, even the best-designed search strategies have their limitations. When searching for efficacy studies these include the inability of the search strategies to fully compensate for the consequences of bias in publication. These biases include the presence or absence in the review of unpublished studies or the selective reporting of outcomes, limitations of the Medical Subject Headings terms used in the descriptions of some studies, and the delay in entering recently published studies onto relevant databases. Solutions to the latter two problems can be addressed to an extent by hand searching the references of identified studies and regularly updating the searches during the course of a review, but the problem of publication bias presents a much greater challenge.

The extent of the problems presented by unpublished studies is illustrated in the systematic review by Whittington et al. (2004) that compared the clinical recommendations that could be made about the use of selective serotonin reuptake inhibitors (SSRIs) for children and adolescents with depression, based on published and unpublished clinical trials of these drugs The analysis was performed in support of the NICE clinical guideline on Depression in Children (NICE, 2005a). They demonstrated that if published studies alone had been used, a systematic review would have supported the widespread use of these drugs with few concerns being raised about the potential increased incidence of suicidal ideation in this very vulnerable group. The addition of unpublished studies led to a very different outcome, with all but one of the SSRIs—fluoxetine—being identified as having an unacceptable harm/benefit ratio. This problem of selective reporting of trial outcomes has been confirmed in a number of studies, which demonstrated that the inclusion of previously unpublished data may significantly alter the outcomes of a systematic review. For example, Melander, Ahlqvist-Rastad, Meijer, & Beermann (2003), in a review of trials of SSRIs submitted

to the Swedish medicines regulatory authority, demonstrated that studies with significant results were more likely to be published than those with nonsignificant results.

Another source of bias may arise from investigator allegiance. This can be seen in a number of studies of pharmaceutical industry sponsorship, including Perlis et al. (2005) and Lexchin, Bero, Djulbegovic, and Clark (2003). Perlis et al. reported that company-sponsored trials were 4.9 times more likely to report a positive outcome for a particular drug than non-industry-sponsored studies. Lexchin et al. reported evidence of a systematic bias in favour of the products produced by the company funding the research and suggest that this may in part be accounted for by the use of inappropriate comparator and publication bias. Much of the focus of this work has been on the bias introduced into clinical research by the commercial interests of the pharmaceutical industry. Non-industry-sponsored trials, including trials of psychological or service interventions, are not free from publication bias. Jacobson and Hollon (1996), in a discussion of the Elkin et al. (1989) trial of pharmacological and psychological treatment for depression, also raised the possibility of investigator allegiance as a factor that may have influenced the outcome of the trial. In a well-conducted review, Chan, Hrobjartsson, Haahr, Gøtzsche, and Altman (2004) also demonstrated how the outcomes in final trial reports often differed from those set out in the original protocols, including many non-pharmacological trials, which resulted in a bias toward the publication of significant results. They suggested that this problem could be addressed by the registration of trial protocols when the trial is established and that subsequent publication of the trial outcomes be assessed against the original protocol. A more immediate solution to the problem of publication bias that is commonly used in systematic reviews where quantitative synthesis of data is undertaken is to use a funnel plot (Egger, Davey Smith, Schneider, & Minder, 1997). A funnel plot is a scatter plot of the effects of the intervention from individual studies against a measure of each study's size or precision. The term arises from the fact that precision of the estimated effects increase as the size of the study increases. Effect estimates from small studies will therefore scatter more widely at the bottom of the graph, with the spread narrowing among larger studies. Where no bias has occurred, the plot should approximate to a symmetrical (inverted) funnel. Where bias has occurred, for example, because of small non-significant unpublished studies, this will result in an asymmetrical plot. Such plots tend to be associated with an overestimation of the inter-vention effect. Most often asymmetry is assessed visually but there are doubts about researcher's capacity to do this and a number of statistics are now available to guide the assessment of asymmetry (Higgins & Green, 2008).

THE NATIONAL COLLABORATING CENTRE FOR MENTAL HEALTH

The National Collaborating Centre for Mental Health (NCCMH) is one of seven National Collaborating Centres (NCCs), originally established by NICE in April 2001 specifically, but not exclusively, to generate evidence based guidelines in mental health. In establishing the NCCs, NICE made an explicit decision to locate the groups outside of NICE and closely allied to the main health professional groups. Other NCCs originally covered primary care, nursing and supportive care, cancer, acute care, care of chronic conditions, and women and child health. In 2008 four of the centers, pri-mary care, nursing and supportive care, acute care, and care of chronic conditions merged into a single center, leaving four NCCs. Most of the NCCs are based in or have very strong links with the leading professional bodies in England and Wales, such as the medical Royal Colleges. The National Collaborating Centre for Mental Health (NCCMH) is a collaboration between the Royal College of Psychiatrists and the

British Psychological Society supported by a management board with representatives from the relevant professional bodies, social care organizations, patient organizations, and health services managers. The NCCMH has a joint university (University College London) and professional base (the Research Unit of the Royal College of Psychiatrists). It currently has just under 20 staff, including two part-time joint directors, who are both practicing clinicians, one center manager, two project managers, four systematic reviewers, one information scientist, three health economists, one editor and five research assistants, and has the capacity to develop six guidelines at any one time.

The topics selected for mental health guide-lines are identified by a consideration panel, which in turn advises the Department of Health with whom rests the final decision about which guidelines are to be developed. Suggestions for the development of new guidance can be made to NICE by professional bodies, the Department of Health, patient organizations and, through the NICE Web site, by individual health pro-fessionals or patients. Once a topic has been agreed on, a remit is sent to the NCC who uses it to develop a scope that sets out the specific aspects of the condition or disorder to be reviewed and identifies the key clinical ques-tions to be addressed. In keeping with the emphasis on consultation and transparency, a scoping meeting is held, all registered stake-holders are invited, and the scope is further developed before undergoing a period of formal public consultation. Registered stakeholders include professional bodies, patient and care giver organizations, the Department of Health, the pharmaceutical industry, health and social care provider organizations, and invited experts. There are few restrictions on register-ing, but individual professionals are encouraged to submit comment via the relevant professional bodies (NICE, 2009a). During this time the NCCMH, in conjunction with NICE, appoints an independent chair of the guideline develop-ment group who will usually be a respected senior clinician who may or may not have specific topic expertise; the key qualifications are an understanding of the process of evidence-based medicine, the process of clinical guideline development, and an ability to chair a large multiprofessional group. In turn, the chair and the NCCMH then appoint a guideline development group (GDG). These groups typically comprise 10 to 12 individuals. They are drawn from relevant professions such as physicians, nurses, psychologists, social workers, and patient and caregiver organizations; however, the professionals do not represent their professions. There are typically two patient and one caregiver representatives chosen for their knowledge and experience of the specific topic under consideration as well as an understanding of evidence-based medicine, guideline development, and ability to function in a multidisciplinary setting. They are supported by a technical team from the NCCMH comprising one of the joint directors, a systematic reviewer, a health economist, the information scientist, a project manager, and a research assistant. All individuals function as full members of the GDG contributing to the process of evidence identification, synthesis, and interpretation, which in turn leads to the development of clinical recommendations. The full method is set out in detail in the NICE Technical Manual (NICE, 2009a). The GDG are also provided with specific training in guideline development by the NCCMH with patient and caregiver representatives in receipt of additional support from a specialist unit within NICE (the Patient and Public Involvement Unit) that supports patient and caregiver members throughout the development process.

Agreeing to and/or refining the clinical questions set out in the scope is the first major task of the GDG. The majority of the questions are questions of efficacy. These questions are answered using a problem, intervention, comparator, outcome (PICO) approach and often draw on RCTs as the basis for the evidence. The NICE and the NCCMH do not rely solely on RCTs for evidence of efficacy; rather, the emphasis is on identifying the best available evidence, which may simply be defined as that which is "fit for purpose." The NICE has explicitly moved away from evidence hierarchies (Rawlins, 2008) and lays considerable emphasis on the GDG exercising its judgment on what kind of evidence is best placed to answer the important clinical questions facing the group. In this way, NICE has developed a different approach from that set out by authorities in the United States (for example, Chambless & Hollon, 1998). There are a number of reasons for this. For example, in rare disorders associated with recruitment problems such as patients with anorexia nervosa requiring inpatient care, well-designed cohort studies, small N designs or case series may be more informative. Another example is where case series have unequivocally established the effectiveness of an intervention, such as the use of acetylcysteine in the treatment of acetaminophen (also called paracetamol in the United Kingdom) overdose (Prescott et al., 1979). The RCTs in mental health often provide relatively little information on possible harms and, again, cohort studies or data mining studies are potentially better sources for such evidence. The NICE guidelines are also concerned with the other types of questions: (a) prognostic indicators, in which case cohort studies would usually be the best source of evidence; (b) problems evaluating harm where data mining studies may be the best source; and (c) patient experience where evidence from qualitative studies is of real value, and for questions concerned with service design a GDG may draw on all of the aforementioned. In addition, NICE recommendations often draw simultaneously from different sources of evidence; for example, efficacy drawn from RCTs and harm from cohort studies, and the privileging of one kind of evidence over another in a pre-determined hierarchy begins to make little sense. Nevertheless, when determining the efficacy of an intervention NICE often draws on the RCT or meta-analysis of RCTs.

Recognizing that all health decisions have cost implications and that all health-care systems face cost constraints, NICE guidelines are also concerned with matters of cost-effectiveness (Steinbrook, 2008). The preferred NICE approach to health economics is the Quality-Adjusted Life Year (QALY), which is widely accepted as the best developed metric for assessing cost-effectiveness (Drummond, Sculpher, Torrance, O'Brien, & Stoddart, 2005). The QALY is an incremental cost-effectiveness ratio that provides information on the relative cost of an additional quality life year achieved by one treatment compared to another treatment. The NICE currently sets an acceptable QALY at between £20,000 (approximately $32,000 in 2009) to £30,000 (approximately $49,000 in 2009) with costs beyond that usually seen as not cost-effective. Recent developments at NICE suggest that for certain end-of-life treatments these thresholds may be varied to reflect the different value that is placed on the quality of life when a person has a terminal illness and only a few months to live.

This threshold, which is often more problematic for the NICE technology appraisal program than for the clinical guidelines program, has been the subject of considerable controversy (Appleby, Devlin, & Parkin, 2007), but a detailed discussion is beyond the scope of this chapter.

Just as evidence of clinical efficacy alone does not determine clinical recommendations, neither does cost-effectiveness; both, along with other sources of evidence relevant to the clinical question, are considered alongside contextual evidence such as their potential impact or feasibility in the UK NHS. Examples of how contextual factors may modify recommendations include evidence for the efficacy of individual supported employment schemes in schizophrenia. A number of well-conducted RCTs were identified during the development of the NICE schizophrenia guidelines, however, all trials were conducted in the United States and, although the evidence was strong, the GDG was concerned about the transferability of the model from the United

States to the United Kingdom. Consequently, the recommendation was couched in suitability cautious terms.

The final products of a review include: (a) a full guideline produced by the NCC; (b) the NICE guideline, available only in electronic form; (c) the Quick Reference Guide, a digest sent out to the NHS; and (d) a patient guide. In addition to the consultation on the scope of the questions to be answered, these final products are also subject to a formal public consultation in which all registered stakeholders plus specialist methodological reviewers comment on the guideline (NICE, 2009a). The guideline developers are required to respond to all comments and have to satisfy NICE that the response is of a sufficient standard. This can lead to significant improvements in the guidelines; helpful comments often center on the interpretation of the evidence and the drafting of recommendations.

Another distinctive feature of NICE guidelines is the abandonment of a formal grading system of the strength of recommendations. These systems were originally developed in the United States (Agency for Health Care Policy and Research, 1993) and were intended to inform the clinician on the strength of the recommendation and, therefore, the confidence with which the clinician should act. They were supported by a system for grading the strength of the evidence that was based on a hierarchy with large-scale RCTs and meta-analyses at the top and case series at the bottom (Hadorn, Baker, Hodges, & Hicks, 1996). There are a number of significant limitations to this approach: (a) It does not take into account contextual issues such as the transferability of complex interventions between different health care systems. (b) Recommendations are often based on multiple sources of evidence, not all of which can easily fit within the evidence hierarchy. (c) It does not consider the offset between patient choice and treatment risk, for example, the decision to take anticoagulants following a deep venous thrombosis (DVT) where strong evidence of reduced recurrence of a DVT has to be offset against the increased risk of bleeding; (d) Important recommendations, such as the use of acetylcysteine in acetaminophen overdose, which are not supported by RCTs, inevitably receive lower grade recommendations that can lead to such recommendations being ignored; for example, in the United Kingdom one leading professional body would typically only evaluate or endorse to their members recommendations that were graded at level A or B.

The solution to these problems that have been considered by NICE has been twofold: first, exploration of the adoption of the Grades of Recommendation Assessment, Development, and Evaluation (GRADE) system (Guyatt et al., 2008) for the assessment of evidence, and, second, a move away from any grading of recommendations. The GRADE system aims to improve both the rating of the quality of the evidence and the strength of the recommendations by first introducing some rigorous and explicit criteria for the rating of evidence, including any study design limitations, the inconsistency of results, the indirectness of evidence, the imprecision of the results, and any evidence of reporting bias. The advantage of such a system is that it helps to make both explicit and transparent the move from evidence to recommendations. Second, the GRADE system separates the assessment of evidence from the grading of recommendations and allows for factors such as the quality of the evidence, uncertainty about the balance of positive and negative consequences of treatment, patient values and preferences, and uncertainty about effective resource use. The GRADE system proposes that recommendations be then classified as strong or weak; "conditional" or "discretionary" are also offered as alternative terms. While the NCCMH and NICE have explored the adoption of the GRADE system for assessing evidence, they have so far not adopted the strong/weak approach to grading recommendations. Currently, the NCCMH prefers to deal with this issue in the wording of the recommendations with the strength of the recommendation being

reflected in the language used. For example, a strong recommendation could be worded as:

> Drug services should introduce contingency management programmes to reduce illicit drug use and/or promote engagement with services for people receiving methadone maintenance treatment. (NICE, 2007b, p. 14)

A recommendation where there is less certainty might be worded as

> For people with antisocial personality disorder with a history of offending behaviour who are in community and institutional care, consider offering group-based cognitive and behavioural interventions (for example, programs such as Reasoning and Rehabilitation) focused on reducing offending and other antisocial behaviour. (NICE, 2009b, p. 27)

There is also considerable interest from the NCCMH in writing recommendations that reflect, as much as possible, the decisions clinicians and patients have to make in everyday practice. This inevitably leads to more complex recommendations where clinicians are asked to consider a range of options depending on a range of patient factors. For example,

> If a woman is taking an antidepressant and her latest presentation was a severe depressive episode, the following options should be discussed with the woman, taking into account her previous response to treatment, her preference, and risk: combining drug treatment with psychological treatment, but switching to an antidepressant with lower risk: switching to a psychological treatment (Cognitive Behavioural Therapy or Interpersonal Therapy). (NICE, 2007a, p. 28)

A further methodological challenge facing NICE is that of updating the guidelines. Currently NICE reviews all guidelines two years after publication to see if significant new evidence has emerged that would require some form of update and commits to an update at four years. To date, this has not happened for the NCCMH. Experience from the updates of the schizophrenia and depression guidelines suggests that this process can be as time consuming as the original production. This in part reflects methodological advances in the development of guidelines and to a lesser extent available new evidence, but the most significant challenge comes from disentangling the interrelated nature of many of the recommendations in the guideline. One solution to this problem is to distinguish: (a) what recommendations to make for which type of treatment, (b) how to make recommendations for what duration/intensity of treatment; and (c) where to make recommendations for what place in a stepped-care system the treatment should occupy. The adoption of such a system could make the process of updating somewhat more efficient.

THE NICE MENTAL HEALTH GUIDELINES

The NICE mental health guideline program has so far produced 16 guidelines with a further four in production and two currently being updated. A full list of the published guidelines is set out in Table 2.1. Nine are concerned with adult disorders and only one has focused exclusively on children, although the ADHD guideline is focused primarily on children with a small section on the treatment and management of adults with ADHD. The remaining five guidelines cover both adults and children, which reflects the remit that the NCCMH received from the Department of Health. In some cases this combining of adults and children makes good sense, for example, with eating disorders, where a peak age of onset in the midteens makes the traditional adult/child distinction unhelpful, or with antisocial personality disorder, where the evidence for the prevention of the disorder through intervention in childhood and adolescence is a good deal more compelling than for interventions with adults. For some disorders, such as obsessive-compulsive disorder, posttraumatic stress disorder (PTSD), and bipolar disorder, the rationale for combining child and adult

TABLE 2.1   NICE Guidelines in Mental Health

Guideline	Date published
Schizophrenia[1]	December 2002
Eating disorders[2]	January 2004
Self-harm[1]	July 2004
Depression[1]	December 2004
Anxiety (generalized anxiety disorder and panic disorder)[1]	December 2004
Management of violence[1]	February 2005
Posttraumatic stress disorder[2]	March 2005
Depression in children[3]	September 2005
Obsessive-compulsive disorder[2]	November 2005
Bipolar disorder[2]	July 2006
Dementia[1]	December 2006
Antenatal and postnatal mental health[2]	January 2007
Drug misuse psychosocial interventions[1]	July 2007
Drug misuse detoxification[1]	July 2007
Attention deficit/Hyperactivity disorder[2]	February 2008
Personality disorder borderline[1]	January 2009
Personality disorder antisocial[3]	January 2009

[1] Adult only
[2] Adults and children
[3] Children only

recommendations is less compelling, as the services are provided in very different settings and the comorbidity of disorders common in childhood and adolescence require a broader approach to care than one focused on a specific disorder. Further discussion of the challenges this presents for guideline development are discussed more fully in Volume 1, Chapter 4, by Pilling and Fonagy.

The remainder of this chapter will focus on adult disorders and will address three key issues in relation to NICE mental health guidelines. First, it will set out some of the key recommendations in relation to psychological therapies. Second, it will address some of the commonly made criticisms of the guideline program. Third, it will highlight some of the challenges and successes of the implementation program.

Key Aspects of NICE Recommendations

The number of recommendations in a NICE guideline can vary considerably but rarely falls below 50 and can exceed 100. Thus, clinicians and service mangers face a challenge in deciding what to implement. The NICE assists in this process by identifying key recommendations for implementation—usually between five and eight per guideline. The way these are chosen in the NCCMH essentially come down to two key criteria: (1) The likelihood that implementation will significantly reduce variation in practice across the NHS, and (2) that implementation will have a significant impact on clinical outcome. A major consequence of the application of these two criteria has been to see a significant number of psychological interventions featured in key recommendations for implementation. Table 2.2 gives examples of some of these recommendations. Table 2.2 is not exhaustive but the emphasis on psychological interventions, including for disorders such as schizophrenia, had a very significant impact on the NHS where historically the availability of psychological therapies had been limited (Lovell & Richards, 2000).

In addition to providing a much higher profile for psychological therapies, the guideline for common mental disorders such as depression and anxiety promoted a stepped-care model for their delivery based on the evidence that brief intervention, such as guided self-help, were effective interventions for mild to moderate disorders (Ekers, Richards, & Gilbody, 2008; Gellatly et al., 2007; Hirai & Clum, 2006; Kaltenthaler, Parry, Beverley, & Ferriter, 2008). An example of a stepped-care model in which psychological and other interventions are integrated can be seen in Figure 2.1, which is taken from the NICE Depression Guideline (NICE, 2004b). The development of the stepped-care model was also a recognition that, even with considerable increase in resources, the prevalence of disorders such as depression was so great that prompt accesses to effective interventions was necessary. The increased emphasis on psychological interventions in the guidelines also shifted the focus of treatment away from medications such as the SSRIs. For example, the Depression Guideline (NICE, 2004b) had an explicit recommendation that cautioned against the routine use of antidepressants in

TABLE 2.2   Some Examples of NICE Guidelines That Have Recommended Psychological Treatments

Guideline	Treatment
Schizophrenia	Family intervention and cognitive behavior therapy
Eating disorders	Family and psychological interventions for anorexia nervosa
	Cognitive behavior therapy for bulimia nervosa and binge eating disorders
Depression	Guided self-help based on cognitive behavioral principles for mild depression
	Cognitive behavior therapy, interpersonal therapy, and couples therapy for moderate to severe depression
Anxiety*	Cognitive behavior therapy for panic disorder and generalized anxiety disorder
PTSD	Cognitive behavior therapy and eye movement sensitization and reprocessing
Drug misuse	Contingency management, motivational interviewing, and behavioral couples' therapy

*Note: the NICE Anxiety Guideline (NICE, 2004a) covers panic disorder and generalized anxiety disorder.

Step 5: Inpatient care, crisis teams	Risk to life, severe self-neglect	Medication, combined treatments, ECT
Step 4: Mental health specialists including crisis teams	Treatment-resistant, recurrent, atypical and psychotic depression and those at significant risk	Medication, complex psychological interventions, combined treatments
Step 3: Primary care team, primary care mental health worker	Moderate or severe depression	Medication, psychological interventions, social support
Step 2: Primary care team, primary care mental health worker	Mild depression	Watchful waiting, guided self-help, computerized CBT, exercise, brief psychological interventions
Step 1: GP, practice nurse	Recognition	Assessment

Figure 2.1   The Stepped-Care Model

mild depression: "Antidepressants are not recommended for the initial treatment of mild depression, because the risk-benefit ratio is poor" (NICE, 2004b, p. 17).

Across the wider NHS, the recommendations were generally welcomed, but there were a number of criticisms. Family doctors were very concerned about an increased demand for psychological interventions since in the United Kingdom 90% of common mental disorders are treated in primary care (Lovell & Richards, 2000). There was also an increasing concern on the part of some psychopharmacologists that the importance of psychological interventions had been overplayed (D. Nutt & Sharpe, 2008). The first of these criticisms has real substance and it was not until the development of the Improving Access to Psychological Interventions Programme (IAPT) that it could be properly addressed (see later in the chapter). The second is unfortunate and, although the discussion has spilled out in the professional press (D. J. Nutt, 2008; Pilling, 2008a), it might best be seen as a simple misrepresentation of the NICE guidelines where medication and its use in combination with psychological intervention is given a prominent position. Some of the most strident criticism of the NICE program is that it has significant methodological limitations

and, as a result, had overemphasised certain psychological interventions, especially Cognitive Behavior Therapy (CBT), at the expense of others. This response can be seen as a reawakening of the "Dodo bird hypothesis" (Luborsky, Singer, & Luborsky, 1975; Wampold et al., 1997; Beutler, 2002). This criticism is dealt with in some more detail later, as it comes most prominently from other psychologists.

Limitations of Clinical Guidelines

One of the most common criticisms of clinical guidelines is that they draw their evidence base from populations that are unrepresentative of those encountered in routine clinical practice. This criticism will be considered later. Before addressing this criticism, it should be pointed out that the expectation is that NICE guidelines apply to about 80 to 85% of the patients with the disorder (Eddy, 1990), that is, about 15 to 20% of patients seen in routine practice may be outside the recommendations of the guideline. If this is the case then recommendations may require some adaptation if they are to be of value in helping determine a treatment plan for a particular patient. Further criticism has focused on the definition of outcomes, for example, symptoms rather than quality of life

Although there has been considerable criticism of the lack of recognition of common factors in driving therapeutic change (see earlier reference to the "Dodo bird hypothesis"), surprisingly little mention has been made of the role of therapist competence, which is a very significant factor in determining the outcome of treatment (Brown, Lambert, Jones, & Minami, 2005). These problems and a response to them have been discussed by Pilling (2008b) and Pilling and Price (2006); they are briefly summarized later.

Patient Population

Randomized controlled trials, particularly efficacy studies that constitute the vast majority of psychological RCTs, require high internal validity and therefore may include precisely specified populations with limited comorbidity. This may lead to trial participants unlike those encountered in routine practice. For example, in mental health disorders comorbidity of disorders is common with approximately 50% of people with a depressive disorder also having significant comorbid anxiety (Goldberg et al., 2005), and approximately 40% of people with PTSD also suffering from a depressive disorder (NICE, 2004b). This difference between trial and routine care populations is often cited as a reason by clinicians for the lack of uptake of evidence-based medicine (Sackett, Rosenberg, Gray, & Haynes, 1996); however, there are a number of reasons why differences in patient populations may not limit extrapolation to the extent that is often assumed. First, it must be remembered that the comparisons are relative since both experimental and comparator groups are from the same population (with or without associated comorbidities). In addition, comorbidities do not necessarily prevent patients from benefiting from particular interventions. For example, patients with comorbid Personality Disorder can benefit from psychological treatments for anxiety and depressive disorders, although treatments may need to be extended to produce reasonable outcomes

(Dreessen and Arntz, 1998; Mulder, 2002). Further, Franklin, Abramowitz, Kozak, Levitt, and Foa (2000), in a study of Obsessive-Compulsive Disorder, demonstrated that those patients who had been excluded from RCTs because of comorbidities and related problems benefited as much, if not more, than those in the original trials. Finally, Gillespie, Duffy, Hackmann, and Clark (2002) report a study of people suffering from PTSD following the Omagh bombing in Northern Ireland, which demonstrated that the provision of the same treatment as delivered in clinical trials produced comparable results in nonselected populations.

Outcomes Used and Follow-Up Duration

The current reporting of outcomes in RCTs presents several problems for guideline developers. One major concern is the reliance on symptomatic measures as primary outcome measures, often with little follow up beyond the end of treatment. Given the chronic and interpersonal nature of many mental disorders, there is a strong argument that measures of interpersonal, social, and occupational functioning should be given much more prominence as primary outcomes, but this is often not the case (Pilling & Price, 2006). This absence of long-term follow-up can also lead to an overestimation of treatment effects. For example, the meta-analysis by Westen and Morrison (2001) reviewed short- and long-term outcomes of psychological treatments for panic disorder, generalized anxiety disorder, and depression. They found that while good results were obtained in both the short- and long-term for panic disorder, this was often not the case for depression or generalized anxiety disorder.

Comparators Used in Trials

Assessing the efficacy of any intervention crucially depends on an understanding of the comparator condition. In some cases this can be straightforward, such as when the comparator is an alternative drug; however, in many trials the comparators are often inadequately described. Terms such as *treatment as usual* or *usual care* are often assumed to be equivalent, but such assumptions may mean that important differences are missed with a consequent misinterpretation of the results. For example, in the Elkin et al. (1989) trial of psychological and pharmacological interventions for depression, the antidepressant arm of the trial consisted of both antidepressants and clinical management. Clinical management consisted initially of weekly sessions with a psychiatrist lasting 20 minutes and the availability of 7-day-a-week, 24-hour-a-day crisis interventions. Such an intervention is very different from that routinely provided in either the United States or the United Kingdom, and it is possible that the regular contact with the psychiatrist and the access to crisis services would have a therapeutic benefit over and above that of the antidepressants.

Therapist Competence

This issue is often not referred to in discussion of the interpretation of clinical trials, but recent research suggests that it may be one of the most significant factors in accounting for variance in outcome. It is well illustrated by a series of studies from Lambert's group in the United States who have analyzed outcome data on large cohorts of individuals in psychological treatment and, importantly, also on a large number of therapists. For example, Brown et al. (2005), in a study of over 10,000 patients and 281 therapists, demonstrated that the most effective 25% of therapists had an overall 53% greater improvement that could not be explained by diagnosis, age, sex, severity, prior treatment history, length of treatment, or therapist training and experience. In a similar study of over 7,500 patients and 149 therapists, Okiishi, Lambert, Eggert, Nielsen, and Dayton (2006) showed that the most effective 25% of therapists had over 100% better recovery rates (22.40% vs. 10.61%) and, perhaps more worrisome, over 100% less deterioration (5.20% vs. 10.56%) than the least effective 25% of

therapists. This has lead to an increasing focus on therapist competence (Roth & Pilling, 2008), an issue that has yet to be properly addressed in clinical guidelines. As evidence of what constitutes competent practice becomes clearer, the evidence base on which guideline developers can draw will be expanded. Roth and Pilling (2009) examined the relationship of certain therapist competencies/behaviors to outcomes, drawing largely on the psychotherapy process—outcome literature. Although the data in this area are limited, a number of relevant findings have emerged. For example, there is evidence to suggest that a focus on the concrete aspects of CBT for depression, such as agenda setting, homework, or a focus on negative thoughts, (McGlinchey & Dobson, 2003) may be associated with improved efficacy. This research begins to point to the kind of recommendations that might bridge the gap between what should be done and how it might be done in clinical guidelines, an important distinction when the skill of the therapist is a key determinant in the outcome of an intervention.

Differences Between Therapeutic Modalities

Clinical guidelines have also been criticized for promoting certain treatments at the expense of others. One oft-repeated phrase is "the absence of evidence does not mean the absence of effect"; however, it is not possible in a guideline development program to recommend treatments for which no evidence can be found when good evidence for other interventions exists. A more substantial objection is that the supposed differences between treatments simply do not exist (Wampold et al., 1997). This approach, referred to as the Dodo Bird hypothesis (Luborsky et al., 1975), holds that there are really no important differences between psychotherapies and that variables such as common therapeutic factors or therapist competence accounts for far more of the variance than do differences in treatment models. A number of authors have responded critically to this assertion (Beutler, 2002). A review by Benish, Imel, and Wampold (2008) has extended this work and focused on the comparison of bona fide treatments. Bona fide treatments are treatments delivered by a competent therapist face-to-face, individualized, and containing psychologically valid components (Wampold et al., 1997). Benish et al. (2008) argued that all bona fide treatments for PTSD include not only eye movement desensitization retraining (EMDR) and trauma-focused CBT (NICE, 2005c), but also hypnotherapy and psychodynamic therapy, which he claimed were as effective as EMDR and trauma-focused CBT. This contrasts with Bisson et al.'s (2007) review that formed the basis of the recommendations for the NICE PTSD guidelines (NICE, 2006) and reported clinically significant differences between a number of different treatments including different forms of CBT for PTSD. They concluded that trauma-focused CBT was clinically and statistically significantly more effective than non-trauma-focused CBT. A review of the two papers reveals that they had different aims; Benish et al. sought to demonstrate the equal effectiveness of bona fide treatments and Bisson et al. sought to support recommendations for a clinical guideline. Of course, a finding of no difference between treatments does not mean they are equivalent. Benish et al.'s analyses were of efficacy trials and not equivalence trials. As such, they were neither designed nor powered to establish equivalence; see Piaggio, Elbourne, Altman, Pocock, and Evans (2006) for a fuller discussion of these issues. Consequently, Benish et al. were concerned with the relative effectiveness of treatments, a task in which they are hampered by the small number of studies, resulting in a number of their comparisons being based on just two studies. Bisson et al. were concerned with not just effectiveness, but also with the robustness of the findings. For example, they investigated whether the intervention had been tested in a number of different studies, by different investigators in different settings, and is the outcome of clinical significance. In addition, clinical guidelines are also concerned with cost-effectiveness and this can lead to recommendations based on differences in cost-effectiveness where no differences in clinical effectiveness are identified (see Simon, Pilling, Burbeck, & Goldberg, 2006).

What Has Been NICE's Impact on Mental Health Practice?

The impact of NICE guidelines on mental health practice has been considerable. This will be illustrated with a number of examples, which, while primarily focused on psychological interventions, show the range of methods that have been used across the NHS to support the implementation of the guidelines. Three examples from national programs have been chosen: (1) the IAPT program of the Department of Health; (2) the development of a national contingency management program for drug misuse services led the National Treatment Agency; and (3) the role of the Health Care Commission (HCC) in the audit of the NICE Schizophrenia Guidelines.

Before reviewing each of these areas, I will briefly review the general evidence for clinical guideline implementation, an area that has undergone considerable evaluation (for example, Grimshaw et al., 2004; Grol & Jones, 2000.) Perhaps the most important message to emerge from this literature is that the majority of interventions to support implementation have only small to moderate effects. Grimshaw et al. (2004) in a comprehensive review of 235 guideline implementation studies identified improvements in the desired direction in 86% of studies but the effects on improvements in care were modest, falling broadly within the range of 6% to 14% improvement in experimental versus comparator groups, although a small number of projects have reported larger effects between 30% to 60% improvement in care (Grol & Jones, 2000). Reminders to clinicians were consistently observed to be the most effective interventions with more limited effects reported for educational outreach, and variable but sometimes important effects for the dissemination of educational materials.

Multifaceted approaches, such as those associated with the chronic care model (Von Korff & Goldberg, 2001), were not necessarily more effective than single interventions. Audit and feedback, and the use of opinion leaders were usually less successful in bringing about positive change. One discouraging aspect of implementation research on clinical guidelines is that the overall improvement is often much the same for poorly performing clinicians as clinicians who performed well, with the result that guideline implementation programs may do little to reduce variation in practice.

Grol and Grimshaw (2003) reviewed a number of organizational interventions designed to improve patient care, including leadership, process redesign, organizational culture, and organizational learning interventions. They concluded that there was no consistent evidence that supported the use of any one of the interventions over any other, but that all could potentially bring about positive benefits in patient care; however, they raised questions about the sustainability of benefit if the interventions were not maintained. The guideline implementation literature indicates that there is a suggestion that organizational interventions, such as clinician specific reminders or educational interventions may be effective, as might the development of leadership programs and new professional roles and multidisciplinary teams; however, uncertainty about the sustainability, long-term benefits and cost effectiveness of the interventions remain. Multifaceted approaches and the use of quality management programs look less promising and this may arise from a lack of specificity or targeting of the change interventions in these programs or the failure to develop effective quality management technology so far.

A number of authors, including Wensing, Wollersheim, and Grol (2006), have argued that the lack of an agreed taxonomy for organizational interventions, including implementation guidelines, presents significant problems in both developing and evaluating them. The development of such a taxonomy requires not only

effective descriptions of the interventions but also ways of characterizing the environment in which the interventions are set. The importance of this can be seen in a UK-based evaluation of the implementation of NICE clinical guidance—the Technology Appraisal program (Sheldon, Cullum, Dawson, et al., 2004). They reported variable uptake of a range of health technologies, primary pharmaceuticals, and some surgical procedures, with the guidance more often being followed for pharmaceuticals, in particular drugs for cancer and obesity, but with a lower uptake for a range of surgical procedures. Organizational factors associated with successful implementation included: strong professional support, effective professional management structures, and good financial and clinical monitoring systems.

The lack of a taxonomy for characterizing change in organizational behavior referred to by Wensing and colleagues (2006) is also mirrored in the lack of a taxonomy for changing health professionals' behavior, despite the fact that many service improvement strategies focus on this area. Michie, Johnston, Abraham, et al. (2005) argued that this lack of a typology of health professionals' behavior has significantly held back the development of effective strategies to support implementation. They have developed a typology of health behaviors based on a systematic review of psychological theories of behavior change, which they argued should form the basis of a typology of future studies to change behavior. These behaviors include: knowledge, skills, social/professional role and identity, beliefs about capabilities, beliefs about consequences, motivation and goals, memory, attention and decision processes, environmental context and resources, social influences, emotion regulation, behavioral regulation, and the nature of the behavior. This approach has been used in a number of pilot studies, including work on the style in which clinical guidelines are written (Michie & Johnston, 2004; Michie & Lester, 2005) and also on clinicians' attitudes and intentions regarding the implementation of specific guidance (Michie, Pilling, Garety, et al., 2007). In their 2007 study, Michie et al. used the framework to examine the implementation of specific recommendations in the NICE schizophrenia guideline (NICE, 2002). The study demonstrated that the model cannot only serve as a framework for developing an intervention but can also lead to a more precise directing of resources onto the skill or support needs identified by staff who are required to implement the intervention.

Understanding what constitutes the effective elements of a complex organizational intervention is not only handicapped by the lack of appropriate typologies at the individual or organizational level but also by the absence of an overarching theoretical framework in which to integrate them. Ferlie and Shortell (2001) provided a multi-level framework in which it may be possible to begin to integrate the different levels of approach. They specified four levels: the individual health professional, the health-care team, the organization providing health care, and the larger health-care system, such as the NHS. They argued that change at any one level may require change at another level or, at a minimum, awareness of the change; therefore, the adoption of the framework can guide the selection of the appropriate interventions at each level. Such a framework may indeed prove helpful but to date few studies have focused on these wider organizational issues preferring to focus on individual health-professional behavior (Grimshaw et al., 2004).

The Improving Access to Psychological Interventions Program

The IAPT program, launched by the Department of Health in 2007 (Department of Health, 2007), is the single largest psychological therapies implementation program in the world. It aims, over the course of 6 years, to train an additional 7,200 psychological therapists in addition to those already completing clinical and counseling psychology training programs, who will treat an additional 1,800,000 patients

at a cost of £346 million (approximately $560 million in 2009). The program owes much to the work of Richard Layard, a noted labor economist, who with support from David Clark, a leading psychological treatment developer and evaluator, set out a series of arguments (Centre for Economic Performance, 2006) that made a powerful case for a significant expansion of psychological therapies. A central tenet of their argument was that the NICE guidelines for depression and anxiety disorders had made a strong, evidence-based case for increased psychological treatment but the lack of resources meant that this was being denied to people with consequent significant health and social care costs. This argument was won and, after the evaluation of two successful pilots in Doncaster and Newham (Clark, Layard, & Smithies, 2008), the UK government launched the program in 2007. Full details of the IAPT program can be found on www.iapt.nhs.uk. The program is delivered at a local level with specialist treatment centers being developed for populations of around 250,000. These services provide NICE-supported treatments within a stepped-care framework with so-called low-intensity interventions such as guided self-help, computerized cognitive behavior therapy, and psychoeducational groups, provided by a group of specifically trained and recruited paraprofessional staff and high-intensity interventions, such as formal psychological therapies, predominantly CBT but also including interpersonal therapy EMDR and couples therapy, provided by trained psychological therapists at master's and doctoral levels. In addition to the new resources made available, a significant number of the psychological therapy staff were provided by existing local services. Typically, a service comprises about 40% low-intensity and 60% high-intensity staff. Working within the stepped-care framework, about 60% of the patients are treated by low-intensity staff and about 40% by high-intensity staff. The stepped-care framework operates such that the majority of patients are first seen by the low-intensity worker; patients may then be treated or referred on for high-intensity treatment. This initial assessment process is closely monitored and supervised and referral is determined by a number of factors including the nature of the disorder. For example, there are currently no evidence-based low-intensity interventions for PTSD or depression. Failure to respond to a brief intervention will result in referral to high-intensity intervention. Current practice suggests that about 20% of patients may be stepped up and about 20% to 30% are referred directly for high-intensity interventions, but a clearer picture will emerge as the IAPT system becomes established. National guidance on the appropriate treatments for specific disorder has been issued by the IAPT program and can be found on the IAPT Web site (www.iapt.nhs.uk). It is expected that this will be reflected in local protocols.

For both high- and low-intensity staff there are also specifically designed training courses run at a regional level and typically covering five to eight treatment centers with around 50 trainees on any one course. The courses are of 1 year's duration with 1 day at the training institution for the low-intensity staff and 2 days for high-intensity staff. There is also a strong emphasis on careful supervision in the workplace. They have a nationally agreed curricula specifically developed for the IAPT program based on a competency framework for cognitive behavior therapy developed specifically for the IAPT program (Roth & Pilling, 2008). See again www.iapt.nhs.uk and www.ucl.ac.uk/CORE for further details.

The IAPT program has a number of other features that are not typical of what currently is provided in the NHS. These include the use of session by session outcome monitoring. The pilot sites demonstrated a very high completion rate of sessional monitoring through the use of specially designed software. The IAPT also includes the possibility of self referral (most referrals in the NHS to psychological treatments services are made by family doctors). This is important as evidence from the pilot sites showed that self referrals had

similar levels of morbidity to professional referrals but a higher proportion of people from minority ethnic groups. The outcome monitoring is essential because the aim of the programs is to obtain outcomes for patients equivalent to those in the NICE guidelines; that is, those typically obtained in well-conducted clinical trials.

The program is now well underway. The first 34 centers have opened and over 750 staff are in training. The program is under close scrutiny but the early indications are that it has been well received. Other countries are developing similar models; Scotland is rolling out a similar training model and a pilot of low intensity interventions are being developed across the province of British Columbia in Canada.

Contingency Management Program for Drug Misuse

In 2007 the NICE (2007c) guideline on psychosocial intervention in drug misuse identified the provision of contingency management as a key priority for implementation. The evidence reviewed in the development of the guideline showed some very strong effects for drug users, such as those on methadone maintenance programs. Contingency management interventions included reinforcing abstinent behavior, as indicated by a negative drug screen, or reinforcing compliance with hepatitis B vaccination programs. The majority of this evidence came from the United States, but also included some data from Europe and Australia. The GDG was acutely aware of the controversial nature of the intervention since it would be viewed by many, including clinicians, the general public, policy makers and politicians, as paying an undeserving group—intravenous drug users—public money to help them overcome a self-inflicted problem. After careful consideration, the GDG felt that the potential benefit warranted the risk. Not surprisingly, the recommendations met with considerable professional, public, and political opposition. With support from NICE—its independence from the Department of Health and its burgeoning international reputation certainly helped—the recommendation stood.

The National Treatment Agency (NTA) (www.nta.nhs.uk) is the agency responsible for drug treatment policy and implementation in England and has a direct connection to all drug misuse commissioning in the country. As such it is ideally placed to support the implementation of any new treatment program and, despite initial misgivings, the NTA agreed to sponsor and coordinate a series of national demonstration sites of contingency management programs as recommended in the NICE guideline. Despite some initial skepticism, the response from the field was extraordinarily positive and 16 sites were identified. The sites that were established in early 2008 were supported by a series of national seminars and will report in early 2009. Again, initial indications are of a very positive response to this NICE promoted initiative.

The Healthcare Commission Audit of NICE Schizophrenia Guidelines

Both examples described so far have been nationally led initiatives that have had considerable resources devoted to them. An alternative approach that has supported the implementation of NICE guidance has been through the use of national audit programs. The Healthcare Commission (HCC) (www.healthcarecommission .org.uk) is the body in the NHS in England charged with monitoring service standards. Among its activities are a series of thematic service reviews, and it has so far conducted two reviews of community mental health services. Community mental health services are specialist mental health services for those with severe mental illness. In both of these reviews, the HCC adopted the audit criteria from the NICE schizophrenia guidelines and focused specially on the provision of psychological interventions and the use of atypical antipsychotic medication. In the second review (2007/2008), the focus was explicitly on the NICE schizophrenia guideline. The consequences of this was to force

providers of services to place greater emphasis on the provision of psychological intervention for schizophrenia, as the rating and future funding of any health-care provider are significantly influenced by their evaluation by the HCC. It is increasingly likely that this form of audit will play a key part in supporting the implementation of NICE guidelines—the HCC role has recently been redefined and a new body, the National Audit Governance Group, with increased resources for audits, has been has been established (www.nagg.nhs.uk).

The examples given earlier all draw on national implementation programs, and it is one of the benefits of a national system of health care that this is possible; however, much of the implementation of NICE guidance happens at the local level and all health-care providers now have systems in place to support local implementation. They are helped in this task by a clear requirement from national government and local commissioners to see NICE guidance implemented. There is also an increasing focus within NICE on influencing commissioning decisions. For example, NICE has recently produced guidance specifically for commissioners on cognitive behavioral treatment for common mental disorders in adults based on the recommendations in existing NICE guidance (www .nice.nhs.uk). Changing the pattern of the allocation of health-care resources and the practice of health-care professionals takes time but the NICE guidelines have set out a compelling case for change driven by a strong evidence base. This has been achieved by working with the key professional bodies, patients' organizations and health-care managers. For example, the NCCMH has produced joint information sheets on NICE guidance with patients' groups. Effective implementation requires the support of a broad constituency and it takes time.

Future Developments in NICE Clinical Guidelines

The process and methods for developing guidelines are constantly evolving. Some of the more imminent challenges for NICE and the NCCMH include generating novel methods of guideline development to support more effective and efficient updating, improving the methods of decision making in GDGs, and developing service or clinical pathway-related guidance. There is considerable demand for these from the NHS but it presents a real challenge as the evidence base is weak. The achievements of the NICE mental health program to date though have been considerable and are most obviously seen in the massive expansion in the availability of evidence-based psychological interventions in the NHS. Yet, much remains to be done. The standards achieved need not only be met but improved on; the continuing support of the professions and patients needs to be further nurtured and encouraged, and there is a need for more careful scrutiny of the benefits that accrue to patients from the program.

REFERENCES

Agency for Healthcare Research and Quality. (1993). *Acute pain management: Operative or medical procedures and trauma*. United States Department of Health and Human Services. Rockville, MD: Author.

AGREE Collaboration. (2003). Development and validation of an international appraisal instrument for assessing the quality of clinical practice guidelines: The AGREE project. *Quality and Safety in Health Care 12*, 18–23.

Appleby, J., Devlin, N., & Parkin, D. (2007). NICE's cost effectiveness threshold. *British Medical Journal, 335*, 358–359.

Benish, S., Imel, Z., & Wampold, B. (2008). The relative efficacy of bona fide psychotherapies for treating post traumatic stress disorder: A meta-analysis of direct comparisons. *Clinical Psychology Review, 28*, 746–758.

Beutler, L. (2002). The Dodo bird is extinct. *Clinical Psychology: Science and Practice, 9*, 30–34.

Bisson, J., Ehlers, A., Matthews, R., Pilling, S., Richards, D., & Turner, S. (2007). Psychological interventions for PTSD: A meta-analysis. *British Journal of Psychiatry, 190*, 97–104.

Black, N., Murphy, M., Lamping, D., McKee, M., Sanderson, C., Askham, J., & Marteau, T. (1999). Consensus development methods: A review of best

practice in creating clinical guidelines. *Journal of Health Services Research and Policy, 4*, 236–248.

Brown, G. S., Lambert, M. J., Jones, E. R., & Minami, T. (2005). Identifying highly effective psychotherapists in a managed care environment. *American Journal of Managed Care 11*, 513–520.

Centre for Economic Performance. (2006). *The depression report: A new deal for depression and anxiety disorders*. London, England: London School of Economics.

Chambless, D. L. (1993). *Taskforce on promotion and dissemination of psychological procedures. A report adopted by the division 12 board, October 1993*. Washington, DC: American Psychological Association.

Chambless, D. L., & Hollon, S. D. (1998). Defining empirically supported therapies. *Journal of Consulting and Clinical Psychology, 66*, 7–18.

Chan, A. W., Hrobjartsson, A., Haahr, M. T., Gøtzsche, P. C., & Altman, D. G. (2004). Empirical evidence for selective reporting of outcomes in randomized trials: Comparison of protocols to published articles. *Journal of the American Medical Association, 291*, 2457–2465.

Clark, D. M., Layard, R., & Smithies, R. (2008). *Improving access to psychological therapy: Initial evaluation of the two demonstration sites*. (Centre for Economic Performance Working Paper No. 1648). London, England: London School of Economics.

Daniels, N., & Sabin, J. E. (2002). *Setting limits fairly: Can we learn to share medical resources?* New York, NY: Oxford University Press.

Department of Health. (1996). *Clinical guidelines: Using clinical guidelines to improve patient care within the NHS*. Leeds, England: NHS Executive.

Department of Health. (2001). *Treatment choice in psychological therapies and counselling: Evidence based clinical guideline*. London, England: Author.

Department of Health. (2007). *Commissioning a brighter future: Improving access to psychological therapies*. London, England: Author.

Dreessen, L., & Arntz, A. (1998). The impact of personality disorders on treatment outcome of anxiety disorders: Best-evidence synthesis. *Behaviour Research and Therapy, 36*, 483–504.

Drummond, M. F., Sculpher, M. J., Torrance, G. W., O'Brien, B. J., & Stoddart, G. L. (2005). *Methods for the economic evaluation of health care programmes* (3rd ed.). Oxford, England: Oxford University Press.

Eddy, D. M. (1990). Clinical decision making: From theory to practice. Resolving conflicts in practice policies. *Journal of the American Medical Association, 264*, 389–391.

Egger, M., Davey Smith, G., & Altman, D. G. (2001). *Systematic reviews in health care: Meta-analysis in context* (2nd ed.). London, England: BMJ Books.

Egger, M., Davey Smith, G., Schneider, M., & Minder, C. (1997). Bias in meta-analysis detected by a simple graphical test. *British Medical Journal, 315*, 629–634.

Ekers, D., Richards, D., & Gilbody, S. (2008). A meta-analysis of randomised trials of behavioural treatment of depression. *Psychological Medicine 38*, 611–623.

Elkin, I., Shea, M. T., Watkins, J. T., Imber, S. D., Sotsky, S. M., Collins, J. F., . . . Parloff, M. B. (1989). National Institute of Mental Health treatment of depression collaborative research programme. General effectiveness of treatments. *Archives of General Psychiatry, 46*, 971–982.

Ferlie, E. B., & Shortell, S. M. (2001). Improving the quality of health care in the United Kingdom and the United States: A framework for change. *The Milbank Quarterly, 79*, 281–315.

Field, M. J., & Lohr, K. N. (Eds.). (1990). *Clinical practice guidelines: Direction for a new program*. Washington, DC: National Academy Press.

Franklin, M. E., Abramowitz, J. S., Kozak, M. J., Levitt, J. T., & Foa, E. B. (2000). Effectiveness of exposure and ritual prevention for obsessive-compulsive disorder: Randomized compared with nonrandomized samples. *Journal of Consulting and Clinical Psychology, 68*, 594–602.

Gaebel, W., Weinmann, S., Sartorius, N., Rutz, W., & McIntyre, J. S. (2005). Schizophrenia practice guidelines: International survey and comparison. *British Journal of Psychiatry,187*, 248–255.

Gellatly, J., Bower, P., Hennessy, S., Richards, D., Gilbody, S., & Lovell, K. (2007). What makes self-help interventions effective in the management of depressive symptoms? Meta-analysis and meta-regression. *Psychological Medicine, 37*, 1217–1228.

Gillespie, K., Duffy, M., Hackmann, A., & Clark, D. M. (2002). Community based cognitive therapy in the treatment of posttraumatic stress disorder following the Omagh bomb. *Behaviour Research and Therapy, 40*, 345–57.

Goldberg, D., Pilling, S., Kendall, T., Ferrier, N., Foster, T., Gates, J., . . . Tylee, A. (2005). *Management of depression in primary and secondary care*. London, England: Gaskell.

Grilli, R., Magrini, N., Penna, A., Mura, G., & Liberati, A. (2000). Practice guidelines developed by specialty societies: The need for critical appraisal. *Lancet, 355*, 103–106.

Grimshaw, J. M., Thomas, R. E., MacLennan, G., Fraser, C., Ramsay, C. R., Vale, L., . . . Donaldson, C. (2004). Effectiveness and efficiency of guideline dissemination and implementation strategies. *Health Technology Assessment, 8*, 1–72.

Grol, R., & Grimshaw, J. (2003). From best evidence to best practice: Effective implementation of change in patients' care. *Lancet, 362*, 1225–1230.

Grol, R., & Jones, R. (2000). Twenty years of implementation research. *Family Practice, 17* (Suppl 1), S32–S35.

Guyatt, G. H., Oxman, A. D., Kunz, R., Falck-Ytter, Y., Vist, G. E., Liberati, A., & Schunemann, H. J. (2008).

Rating quality of evidence and strength of recommendations. Going from evidence to recommendations. *British Medical Journal 336*, 1049–1051.

Hadorn, D., Baker, D., Hodges, J., & Hicks. N. (1996). Rating the quality of evidence for clinical practice guidelines. *Journal of Clinical Epidemiology, 49*, 749–754.

Higgins, J. P. T., & Green, S. (Eds.). (2008). Cochrane handbook for systematic reviews of interventions Version 5.0.1 [updated September 2008]. *The Cochrane Collaboration, 2*. Retrieved from www.cochrane-handbook.org

Hirai, M., & Clum, G. A. (2006). A meta-analytic study of self-help interventions for anxiety problems. *Behavior Therapy, 37*, 99–111.

Jacobson, N. S., & Hollon, S. D. (1996). Cognitive-behavior therapy versus pharmacotherapy: Now that the jury's returned its verdict, it's time to present the rest of the evidence. *Journal of Consulting and Clinical Psychology, 64*, 74–80.

Kaltenthaler, E., Parry, G., Beverley, C., & Ferriter, M. (2008). Computerised cognitive-behavioural therapy for depression: Systematic review. *British Journal of Psychiatry, 193*, 181–184.

Lexchin, J., Bero, L. A., Djulbegovic, B., & Clark, O. (2003). Pharmaceutical industry sponsorship and research outcome and quality: Systematic review. *British Medical Journal, 326*, 1167–1170.

Lovell, K., & Richards, D. (2000). Multiple access points and levels of entry (MAPLE): Ensuring choice, accessibility and equity for CBT services. *Behavioural and Cognitive Psychotherapy, 28*, 379–391.

Luborsky, L., Singer, B., & Luborsky, E. (1975). Comparative studies of psychotherapies: Is it true that "Everybody has won and all must have prizes"? *Archives of General Psychiatry, 32*, 995–1008.

McGlinchey, J. B., & Dobson, K. S. (2003). Treatment integrity concerns in cognitive therapy for depression. *Journal of Cognitive Psychotherapy, 17*, 299–319.

Melander, H., Ahlqvist-Rastad, J., Meijer, G., & Beermann, B. (2003). Evidence b(i)ased medicine—selective reporting from studies sponsored by pharmaceutical industry: Review of studies in new drug applications. *British Medical Journal, 326*, 1171–1713.

Michie, S., & Johnston, M. (2004). Changing clinical behaviour by making guidelines specific. *British Medical Journal, 328*, 343–345.

Michie, S., Johnston, M., Abraham, C., Lawton, R., Parker, D., & Walker, A. (2005). Making psychological theory useful for implementing evidence based practice: Consensus approach. *Quality and Safety in Healthcare, 14*, 26–33.

Michie, S., & Lester, K. (2005). Words matter: Increasing the implementation of clinical guidelines. *Quality and Safety in Health Care, 14*, 367–370.

Michie, S., Pilling, S., Garety, P., Whitty, P., Eccles, M., Johnston, M., & Simmons, J. (2007). Factors influencing the implementation of a mental health guideline: An exploratory investigation using psychological theory. *Implementation Science, 1*, 2–8.

Moher, D., Cook, D. J., Eastwood, S., Olkin, I., Rennie, D., & Stroup, D. F. (1999). Improving the quality of reports of meta-analyses of RCTs: The QUOROM statement. *Lancet, 354*, 1896–1900.

Mulder, R. T. (2002). Personality pathology and treatment outcome in major depression: A review. *American Journal of Psychiatry, 159*, 359–371.

National Institute for Health and Clinical Excellence (NICE). (2002). *Core interventions in the treatment and management of schizophrenia in primary and secondary care. Clinical guideline 1.* Retrieved from www.nice.org.uk

National Institute for Health and Clinical Excellence (NICE). (2004a). *Anxiety: Management of anxiety (panic disorder, with or without agoraphobia, and generalised anxiety disorder) in adults in primary, secondary and community care. Clinical guideline 22.* Retrieved from www.nice.org.uk

National Institute for Health and Clinical Excellence (NICE). (2004b). *Depression guideline management of depression in primary and secondary care. Clinical guideline 23.* Retrieved from www.nice.org.uk

National Institute for Health and Clinical Excellence (NICE). (2005a). *Depression in children and young people. Clinical guideline 28.* London, England: Author. Retrieved from www.nice.org.uk

National Institute for Health and Clinical Excellence (NICE). (2005b). *Management of PTSD in adults in primary, secondary and community care.* Retrieved from www.nice.org.uk

National Institute for Health and Clinical Excellence (NICE). (2005c). *Social value judgments: Principles for the development of NICE's guidance.* Retrieved from www.nice.org.uk

National Institute for Health and Clinical Excellence (NICE). (2006). *Conduct disorder in children: Parent training/education programmes. Guidance TA102.* Retrieved from www.nice.org.uk

National Institute for Health and Clinical Excellence (NICE). (2007a). *Antenatal and postnatal mental health guideline. Clinical guideline 45.* London, England: Author. Retrieved from www.nice.org.uk

National Institute for Health and Clinical Excellence (NICE). (2007b). *Psychosocial interventions in drug misuse guideline. Clinical guideline 51.* London, England: Author. Retrieved from www.nice.org.uk

National Institute for Health and Clinical Excellence (NICE). (2009a). *The guidelines manual.* Retrieved from www.nice.org.uk

National Institute for Health and Clinical Excellence (NICE). (2009b). *Antisocial personality disorder*

guideline: Clinical guideline 77. London, England: Author. Retrieved from www.nice.org.uk

Nutt, D. (2008, April). Have psychotherapies been overhyped? *Pulse 20.* Retrieved from http://www.pulsetoday.co.uk/story.asp?storycode=4118734

Nutt, D. J., & Sharpe, M. (2008). Uncritical positive regard? Issues in the efficacy and safety of psychotherapy. *Journal of Psychopharmacology, 22*, 3–6.

Okiishi, J. C., Lambert, M. J., Eggert, D., Nielsen, L., & Dayton, D. D. (2006). An analysis of therapist treatment effects: Toward providing feedback to individual therapists on their clients' psychotherapy outcome. *Journal of Clinical Psychology, 62*, 1157–1172.

Parry, G., Cape, J., & Pilling, S. (2003). Clinical practice guidelines in clinical psychology and psychotherapy. *Clinical Psychology and Psychotherapy, 10*, 337–354.

Perlis, R. H., Perlis, C. S., Wu, Y., Hwang, C., Joseph, M., & Nierenberg, A. A. (2005). Industry sponsorship and financial conflict of interest in the reporting of clinical trials in psychiatry. *The American Journal of Psychiatry, 162*, 1957–1960.

Peterson, M. A. (2008). The truth about health care: Why reform is not working in America; The health care mess: How we got into it and what it will take to get out of it. *Journal of Health Politics, Policy and Law, 33*, 343–357.

Piaggio, G., Elbourne, D. R., Altman, D., Pocock, S. J., & Evans, S. J. W. (2006). Reporting of non inferiority and equivalence randomized trials: An extension of the CONSORT Statement. *Journal of the American Medical Association, 295*, 1152–1160.

Pilling, S. (2008a, April). Have psychotherapies been overhyped? *Pulse 20.* Retrieved from www.pulsetoday.co.uk/story.asp?storycode=4118734

Pilling, S. (2008b). History, context, process and rationale for the development of clinical guidelines. *Psychology and Psychotherapy: Theory, Research and Practice, 81*, 331–350.

Pilling, S., & Price, K. (2006). Developing and implementing clinical guidelines: Lessons from the NICE schizophrenia guideline. *Epidemiologia e Psichiatria Sociale, 15*, 109–116.

Prescott, L. F., Illingworth, R. N., Critchley, J. A., Stewart, M. J., Adam, R. D., & Proudfoot, A. T. (1979). Intravenous N-acetylcysteine: The treatment of choice for paracetamol poisoning. *British Medical Journal, 6198*, 1097–1100.

Rawlins, M. (2008). *De testimonio: On the evidence for decisions about the use of therapeutic interventions.* London, England: Royal College of Physicians.

Rawlins, M., & Dillon, A. (2005). NICE discrimination. *Journal of Medical Ethics, 31*, 683–684.

Roth, A. D., & Pilling, S. (2008). Using an evidence-based methodology to identify the competences required to deliver effective cognitive and behavioural therapy for depression and anxiety disorders. *Behavioural and Cognitive Psychotherapy*, 129–147.

Roth, A. D., & Pilling, S. (2009). *The impact of adherence and competence on outcome in CBT and psychological therapies*. Manuscript in preparation.

Sackett, D. L., Rosenberg, W. M. C., Gray, J. A., & Haynes, R. B. (1996). Evidence-based medicine: What is and what isn't. *British Medical Journal*, 312, 71–72.

Sheldon, T. A., Cullum, N., Dawson, D., Lankshear, A., Lowson, K., Watt, I., . . . Wright, J. (2004). What's the evidence that NICE guidance has been implemented? Results from a national evaluation using time series analysis, audit of patients' notes and interviews. *British Medical Journal*, 329, 999–1004.

Simon, J., Pilling, S., Burbeck, R., & Goldberg, D. (2006). Treating moderate and severe depression with antidepressants, psychological therapy or their combination: A decision analytic model of effectiveness and costs developed to support a clinical guideline. *The British Journal of Psychiatry*, 189, 494–501.

Starr, M., & Chalmers, I. (2003). *The evolution of the Cochrane Library, 1988–2003*. Oxford, England: Update Software. Retrieved from www.update-software.com/history/clibhist.html

Steinbrook, R. (2008). Saying no isn't NICE—The travails of Britain's National Institute for Health and Clinical Excellence. *New England Journal of Medicine, 359*, 1997–1981.

Von Korff, M., & Goldberg, D. (2001). Improving outcomes in depression. *British Medical Journal, 323*, 948–949.

Wampold, B. E., Mondin, G. W., Moody, M., Stich, F., Benson, K., & Ahn, H. (1997). A meta-analysis of outcome studies comparing bona fide psychotherapies: Empirically, "all must have prizes." *Psychological Bulletin 122*, 203–215.

Wensing, M., Wollersheim, H., & Grol, R. (2006). *Organizational interventions to implement improvements in patient care: A structured review of reviews*. Retrieved from www.implementationscience.com/content/1/1/2

Westen, D., & Morrison, K. (2001). A multidimensional meta-analysis of treatments for depression, panic, and generalized anxiety disorder: An empirical examination of the status of empirically supported therapies. *Journal of Consulting and Clinical Psychology, 69*, 875–899.

Whitten, P. S., Mair, F. S., Haycox, A., May, C., Williams, T. L., & Hellmich, S. (2002). Systematic review of cost effectiveness studies of telemedicine interventions. *British Medical Journal, 324*, 1434–1437.

Whittington, C. J., Kendall, T., Fonagy, P., Cottrell, D., Cotgrove, A., & Boddington, E. (2004). Selective serotonin reuptake inhibitors in childhood depression: systematic review of published versus unpublished data. *Lancet, 363*, 1341–1345.

3

Professional Training Issues in Evidence-Based Clinical Psychology

ANDREW J. BAILLIE AND LORNA PETERS

EVIDENCE-BASED PRACTICE IN CLINICAL PSYCHOLOGY

Evidence-based clinical psychology describes both clinical psychology interventions that have an evidence base, often termed *empirically supported treatments* (ESTs) (e.g., Chambless & Ollendick, 2001), and a specific set of skills using research evidence in clinical decision making that we and others call *evidence based practice* (EBP) skills (Hoge, Tondora, & Stuart, 2003; Spring, 2007; Walker & London, 2007). Much has been written about the benefits of EBP in psychology (American Psychological Association Presidential Task Force on Evidence Based Practice, 2006; Goodheart, Kazdin, & Sternberg, 2006) but there is relatively little about the specific skill set that is required (c.f. Hoge et al., 2003; Spring, 2007; Walker & London, 2007) and how to train clinical psychologists in EBP skills. This chapter reviews evidence about training in evidence based practice, describes

Thanks to our students in the clinical psychology program at Macquarie University for asking probing questions that encouraged us to think more clearly about our teaching.

the content and methods of such training, and reviews issues and future directions for training in EBP.

Practice as a clinical psychologist involves many questions and uncertainties, some of which may be resolvable, others may remain uncertain. What is the nature of this client's problems? What is the best treatment for this client? These may be examples of more common questions or *information needs* that emerge from a clinical encounter. Typical information needs are concerned with methods for diagnosis or assessment, the best therapy, the likely prognosis, what harms could occur from treatment, and the cost effectiveness of different interventions. The EBP skills set provides one specific way of addressing clinical information needs. Importantly, EBP skills are only one of many strategies in the clinician's toolkit. Broadly, the specific strategy derived from Gordon Guyatt, David Sackett, and colleagues' *Evidence Based Medicine* (Evidence Based Medicine Working Group, 1992; Sackett, Richardson, Rosenberg, & Haynes, 1997; Sackett, Strauss, Richardson, Rosenberg, & Haynes, 2000; Strauss, Richardson, Glasziou, & Haynes, 2005) involves the following steps:

1. Convert clinical information needs into answerable questions.

2. Track down the best evidence with which to answer them;
3. Critically appraise that evidence for its validity and applicability;
4. Apply the results of this appraisal in clinical practice; and
5. Evaluate performance (Strauss et al., 2005).

These skills are not about how to do a particular EST but are career-long skills to keep up to date with the literature. Importantly, EBP differs from recommendations that clinicians implement in ESTs and other clinical practice guidelines (e.g., Chambless & Ollendick, 2001) in that it is more individualized to both the client and clinician's needs and less "top-down" (Shlonsky & Gibbs, 2004). Training in current ESTs gives graduate students in clinical psychology practical knowledge in current best practices. While the evidence base of clinical practice guidelines ages and becomes out of date, searches conducted as needed to identify the best evidence for a clinical question are more up to date. In addition, the methods for arriving at clinical practice guidelines are not always transparent, leaving the reader unable to judge whether biases in methods may limit the quality or applicability of the guidelines. Thus, EBP skills provide an individualized "bottom-up" procedure driven by client and clinician needs for information rather than the one-size-fits-all approach of clinical practice guidelines (Shlonsky & Gibbs, 2004). Training in EBP skills adds specific skills in the selection of best practice at any point in the future and its application to the individual client.

Nonproprietary procedural interventions, like those employed in clinical psychology, are more difficult to implement than the proprietary pharmaceutical treatments that are a significant part of evidence-based medicine (EBM) (Andrews, 1984). Knowing the name, duration, and intensity of a procedural intervention is not enough to implement that intervention in the way that the name and dose of an approved medication can lead to prescribing treatment. Even if there is a treatment manual available that specifies the intervention, the clinical psychologist may not be competent in the specific procedures. Thus, additional training and supervision may be required before a new intervention can be implemented. Appraisal of resources to support implementation is one of the key developments in the application of EBM techniques to clinical psychology. Specification of psychological therapies is clearly aided by the publication of lists of treatment manuals for ESTs and lists of agencies providing training in ESTs (Klonsky, undated; Sanderson & Woody, 1995; Woody & Sanderson, 1998). Additional resources that the practitioner must expend to learn new procedures to improve competence is a barrier to the uptake of new techniques—and further work on ways to disseminate new ESTs is needed.

"Half of what you are taught as medical students will in ten years have been shown to be wrong. And the trouble is none of your teachers knows which half" (Burwell, 1956 in Strauss et al., 2005). Thus an important training issue for EBP is how, and when, do established clinical psychologists retrain themselves in emerging procedures. Despite the importance of continuing education to maintain, extend, and update the skills of qualified clinical psychologists, we know of only one survey of clinical psychologists (Chan & Tang, 1996) and no empirical studies of the effectiveness of continuing education. Later, we review evidence about the effectiveness of continuing education from other health professions as an indication of what might be the possible effects in clinical psychology. However, the importance of disseminating innovations to the profession means there is a clear and pressing need for more research to establish the best methods for practitioners to keep up to date.

Traditional scientist-practitioner training in clinical psychology is compatible with EBP, but scientist-practitioner training is not sufficient to ensure that practitioners are good consumers of research and continue to be so over their careers. EBP provides practical skills to achieve scientist-practitioner aspirations to be better consumers of research. EBP skills are specific technical skills for using research in clinical decision making. They are consistent with the scientist-practitioner model in that they provide specific steps that operationalize the use of research. However, Geddes (2000) points out that the emphasis of scientist-practitioner training is often on the *production* of research. The principles of research underlie the critical appraisal of existing research that is essential to be an evidence-based consumer of research. However, the student emerging from a scientist-practitioner clinical psychology program may have to generalize that learning to the specific tasks of EBP. Providing more direct training may make it easier for new clinical psychologists to practice EBP. Geddes (2000) also cites Richard Suinn's 1993 observation that *scientific purism* in scientist practitioner training may lead practitioners to dismiss the relevance of all research. By seeking the best evidence to guide specific questions about specific patients, the debate about the usefulness of research to practitioners (Persons & Silberschatz, 1998) becomes more specific how useful is this research for this question relating to this client.

In advocating for increased use of research findings in clinical practice, it is important to acknowledge that there is also a gap between the information needs of clinicians and the answers provided in the research literature. Over past years, there has been an increasing emphasis on the extent to which the research literature addresses issues of concern to clinicians with participants and methods that are representative and generalizable to clinical contexts. Before turning to training in EBP, a brief review of some developments that are likely to make research more relevant to clinical decisions is helpful. Shadish and colleagues have developed criteria to judge the clinical representativeness of published clinical trials and conducted meta-analyses (Shadish, Matt, Navarro, & Phillips, 2000; Shadish et al., 1997) in which they found little difference in the size

of treatment effects between more and less clinically representative research.

The development and wide promulgation of the Consolidated Standards of Reporting Trials (Moher, Schulz, & Altman, 2001) make the methods of clinical trials more transparent and hence it is easier to critically appraise their clinical representativeness. The requirement from many funding bodies and ethical review committees that clinical trials are entered into clinical trial registries (e.g., www.clinical trials.gov in the United States and www.who.int/ictrp from the World Health Organization [WHO]) before they can commence means trials that show nonsignificant differences will be more visible and publication bias in systematic reviews will likely be reduced. A novel service from the United Kingdom's National Health Service National Health Library, the Database of Uncertainties about the Effects of Treatments (DUETs) (National Health Service Institute for Innovation and Improvement, 2008) provides feedback to researchers about areas where clinician queries received by the National Health Library are not well addressed by the published literature. These and other developments have the potential to decrease the gap between the information needs of clinicians and the answers contained in the research literature.

It is important to stress that EBP does not, and indeed cannot, deliver answers to all clinical information needs. This is not solely because the research literature is uneven in its coverage of clinical issues. Rather, many clinical information needs are best addressed by other sources of information. Information about the local context of the clinical contact such as culture and society, about referrals and specialties, about the social, legal, ethical, financial, and political factors that impact on practice, about organization and funding of health systems, of agencies and practitioners to refer to, and access to training in the procedures. Clinical experience and the knowledge of peers and clinical supervisors can provide answers in many of these areas. Thus, while

EBP gives less emphasis to clinical experience and the opinions of peers, supervisors, and experts about which intervention is the best for an individual, these sources of information play a valuable role in how to implement specific interventions among other information needs.

In this chapter, we review the evidence that health professionals in general (and clinical psychologists by extrapolation) can be trained in EBP and discuss some of the issues that arise from the literature and our own teaching experience. Whether this practice leads to improvement in client outcomes remains an open empirical question.

DOES TRAINING IN EBP WORK?

We found no empirical studies of the outcomes of training in evidence-based practice in clinical psychology, so we provide a brief review of the outcomes of training in EBP in other health professions and of the evidence that professional training leads to outcome. Such research may be generalized to clinical psychology and may give us a sense of the possible outcomes of training in EBP. The Evidence-Based Medicine Working Group (1992) made the point that traditional methods of professional training were not well supported by empirical evidence and that perhaps EBP did not need much research to demonstrate better outcomes. A change in curriculae and teaching methods requires some resources; it is preferable to know ahead of time whether embracing EBP training will produce sufficient outcomes to justify the resources expended.

The most comprehensive review of the effects of training in EBP was conducted by Coomarasamy and Kahn (2004), who reviewed four randomized trials, seven nonrandomized controlled studies, and 12 pre-post evaluations of training in EBM for postgraduate medical practitioners. Teaching methods included stand-alone workshops, seminars, and journal clubs, and teaching methods that were more integrated into clinical settings such as clinical rounds or more direct interactions with patients.

The outcomes evaluated were changes in knowledge, skills, attitudes, and behaviors related to the practice of EBM. No studies of the effects of EBM on client outcome were found. A vote-count tabular review was used because of heterogeneity between the included studies, and this may rely on the adequacy of the statistical analyses conducted in each study compared to a more formal meta-analysis. Knowledge of EBM increased with both stand-alone and more integrated teaching. Coomarasamy and Kahn (2004) reported good evidence that integrated teaching improved skills, attitudes, and behavior with only weak evidence that stand-alone training effected these outcomes.

One argument is that EBP increases the use of interventions that have been demonstrated to work in clinical trials so it improves client outcomes. While this has some validity, more definitive conclusions can come from empirical evaluation of the outcomes of EBP training. Coomarasamy and Kahn (2004) point out that a shift in knowledge about EBM (and by extension EBP) is insufficient to argue for client outcome. They argue that shifts in skills and practice behavior toward greater use of interventions with support from systematic reviews and clinical trials is needed before assuming training in EBP improves client outcome.

Without direct evidence about the impact of training in EBP in clinical psychology, is there evidence that EBP could improve clinician skills and client outcomes? In other words, can clinical psychologists be trained to deliver evidence-based therapies and does that impact on client outcomes? There is a body of evidence that training can produce changes in knowledge, practice, and client outcomes. Atkins and Christensen (2001) report a review of studies comparing professional and paraprofessional counselors and the impact of psychotherapy training on client outcomes. Concerns about the methodological quality of the literature temper their conclusion that while paraprofessionals can produce good results, professional training leads to briefer therapy, greater retention, and better client outcomes in some specific areas.

O'Donovan, Bain, and Dyck (2005) compared the effect of clinical psychology training through the performance of 32 clinical psychology trainees and 38 graduates from 4-year psychology training in an intake interview with standardized clients. Those undergoing clinical training showed greater improvements in psychological knowledge (but not diagnostic knowledge) and working alliance but not client-rated relationship, nor therapist conceptualization of the case. Other common aspects of clinical training such as supervision may produce changes in knowledge, behavior, and outcomes (e.g., Milne & James, 2002).

Taken together, these studies may give prima facie evidence that successful training in empirically supported therapies could possibly deliver better patient outcomes. It is important to acknowledge the likely limited effects of traditional didactic teaching methods and the likely superiority of more interactive and perhaps problem-based learning approaches.

How effective is continuing professional education? O'Brien, Freemantle, Oxman, Wolf, Davis, and Herrin (2001) reviewed outcome studies of continuing medical education (CME) in a Cochrane Review and found that while didactic sessions had little impact, interactive workshops had moderately large changes in professional practice. Results from the studies included in this review were heterogeneous, suggesting that significant variation in the effects of CME is due to factors other than teaching methods. Results of this review show that it is possible for continuing education using interactive workshops to have an impact on the practice of health professionals.

The empirical literature on continuing education in clinical psychology is very sparse. Chan and Tang reported (1996) a survey of 57 clinical psychologists in Hong Kong and found that the majority were critical of the benefits of the continuing education they had received. There is a clear need for more empirical research in continuing education.

The journal club is one venue for training in EBM that may be applicable for practicing clinical psychologists who can meet with colleagues on a regular basis for professional discussions. Parkes, Hyde, Deeks, and Milne (2001) report a Cochrane Review of teaching critical appraisal skills in health-care settings. They found only one paper that met their methodological criteria (Linzer, DeLong, & Hupart, 1987) and no papers that reported client outcomes or changes in practice. In this randomized controlled trial of critical appraisal skills training in a journal club versus control in 44 internal medicine interns in a hospital setting, critical skills training lead to statistically significantly greater knowledge of critical appraisal.

Hoge, Tondora, and Stuart (2003) argue that traditional journal clubs that are driven by recently published literature may seem abstract from clinical encounters; participants may only appraise articles when it is their turn to present. While journal clubs may be a good venue to teach critical appraisal of literature, other EBP skills such as framing answerable questions and searching are not covered. Thus, there is a risk that teaching EBP in a traditional journal club will reinforce an academic rather than practical clinical approach. As an alternative, teaching EBM in clinical rounds or reviews may allow for modeling by senior clinicians, and retain the focus on the clinical issues. The EBM book (Strauss et al., 2005) includes suggestions, such as the random selection of cases for review in clinical rounds to stop staff consciously or otherwise selecting safer patients to discuss.

These studies may give some limited confidence that training in EBP could lead to improvements in knowledge, skills, practice, and outcomes. It is clear that experimental studies that randomly allocate to EBP training versus traditional training are required. It is likely that stand-alone didactic methods will not impact on attitudes or practice and hence are unlikely to impact on client outcome. Interactive teaching based around clinical encounters is more likely to change attitudes and practices and this has the possibility of improving client outcomes.

HOW TO TRAIN PROFESSIONALS IN EVIDENCE-BASED PRACTICE

We concur with Hoge et al. (2003) in recommending that anyone intending to teach EBP skills should consult the concise book by David Sackett and colleagues entitled *Evidence Based Medicine* now in its third edition (Straus et al., 2005) and its accompanying Web pages. We hope this chapter can add to the EBM book by interpreting and adapting that material for clinical psychology.

In the second edition, Sackett et al. (1997, p. 205) list seven mistakes made in teaching EBM:

1. Teaching learners how to do research rather than how to use it.
2. Teaching learners how to perform statistical analyses rather than how to interpret them.
3. Teaching a preset series of content topics rather than have content determined by a patient's problems.
4. Evaluating learners on the basis of their retention of facts rather than their skills in obtaining, appraising, and applying facts to patients.
5. Insisting on sticking to the teaching schedule when the clinical service is swamped.
6. Striving for closure at the end of every session rather than leaving plenty to think about between sessions.
7. Devaluing team members for asking "stupid" questions or providing "ridiculous" answers.

Training in EBP skills is often conducted around clinical cases, real or simulated, in small groups. In the following section we discuss issues in training clinical psychology graduate students in EBP before turning to continuing education in EBP and then to training issues with each of the specific skills of EBP.

ATTITUDINAL BARRIERS TO EBP

Both graduate and qualified clinical psychologists are likely to harbor some reservations about EBP. It is important to anticipate these issues at the beginning of training and address them as they arise. Some of these are legitimate questions for debate within the profession and the best a training program can hope for is that decisions about how to practice are based on careful consideration of the arguments. Shlonsky and Gibbs (2004) describe some of the attitudinal barriers from their experience in teaching EBP to graduate social work students.

Misinterpreting the aims of EBP: It is common for students to believe that EBP is solely concerned with applying clinical practice guidelines and on that basis they believe it does not account for individual differences between clients. EBP has been described as a three-legged stool—clinical experience, patient values and preferences, and the best evidence from the literature are the three legs upon which the EBP stool sits (Sackett, Rosenberg, Gray, Haynes, & Richardson, 1996).

Already doing it: Sometimes this belief can be addressed by demonstrating the specific EBP skills. Teaching of EBP is often done in accord with the principles of adult education and it is important to work with the skills and experience that trainees bring. In this way we propose to roll with resistance.

There is no additional information to be found in research: Again this may be addressed as a more specific question—is there anything in the literature that helps us with this specific question about this specific client's care? Without looking we may never find out.

POSTGRADUATE CLINICAL PSYCHOLOGY TRAINING IN EBP

Many topics covered in a clinical psychology program are good preparation for learning EBP skills. Training in research methods, assessment, theories of psychopathology, and empirically supported treatments is probably covered in most scientist-practitioner-based clinical psychology programs. EBP skills do not replace but rather complement existing curricula. The assumed knowledge that would most likely be taught in a scientist-practitioner-based clinical psychology program includes research design, theories of assessment, and of psychopathology. Most clinical psychology students will have sufficient training in psychometric theory and knowledge of resources like the *Mental Measurements Year Books* (e.g., Geisinger, Spies, Carlson, & Plake, 2007) and the Association for the Advancement of Behavior Therapy Clinical Assessment Series (Antony, Orsillo, & Roemer, 2007; Kelly, Reitman, & Noell, 2002; Nezu, Ronan, Meadows, & McClure, 2000) that they do not require additional training in searching and appraisal of assessment tools.

EBP may require a shift from the academic critique of study methods to the appraisal of the relevance of the results of those methods to a specific client. So while they may debate the usefulness of clinical trials for clinicians, the EBP approach asks more specifically about what the results of a specific clinical trial or meta-analysis can tell us about the care of this specific client.

EBP will reduce uncertainty for some clinical information needs. The practitioner using EBP needs to have knowledge of how to implement the chosen interventions and needs experience in the so-called nonspecifics of therapy because not all the therapeutic effects come from the specifics of particular intervention techniques. Because the literature does not cover every question a clinical psychologist may ask of it, clinical psychologists using EBP need skills in functional assessment and idiopathic case formulation and a broad knowledge of the science of psychopathology. These skills and knowledge base are required to judge the psychological plausibility of an intervention that is

appraised to be relevant to the client and are needed to develop interventions in the absence of assistance from the literature.

Clinical psychology students may require some didactic teaching in unfamiliar statistical methods for the evaluation of health interventions and technology. In our experience, some may be unfamiliar with the use of meta-analysis to systematically combine the results of clinical trials, receiver operating characteristic (ROC) analyses for the evaluation of screening and diagnostic tools (e.g., Wyshak, Barsky, & Klerman, 1991) and systematic reviews of such studies (Pai, McCulloch, Enanoria, & Colford, 2004), with economic evaluations such as cost-effectiveness analysis (e.g., Severens, Prins, Van Der Wilt, Van Der Meer, & Bleijenberg, 2004). Some didactic training about the key elements of these techniques assists in the critical appraisal of studies using these methods.

OUR OWN EXPERIENCE IN TEACHING EVIDENCE-BASED CLINICAL PSYCHOLOGY

Since 2004 we have taught EBP skills in six 2-hour workshops to groups of up to 15 clinical psychology master's and doctoral level students. We developed PSY967 Evidence-Based Clinical Psychology as an alternative to the traditional postgraduate training in advanced statistical analysis. The unit is made up of lectures on applied research methods for clinical practice and lectures and practical training in evidence-based practice. The EBP material contributes 1/32nd of the work of a master's degree in Clinical Psychology and 1/64th of a professional doctorate.

Assessment is the presentation of a written evidence-based treatment plan based on a case scenario used for teaching in other units on psychopathology and introductory cognitive behavior therapy. The specific literature searches and the evidence collected and critically appraised is included to show the justification for the treatment plan.

The majority of teaching EBP happens around clinical cases–some didactic material is necessary to introduce and give a broad description of the strategy, its history, and some of the alternatives (Isaacs & Fitzgerald, 1999). In the following section we describe issues with each of the steps in EBP from the literature and from our own teaching experience.

What Do I Need to Know?

In the interaction with a client, there are many questions that arise. For the clinical psychologist trainee starting out, the number of questions that they ask themselves is often daunting, let alone the questions that the client asks. Writings in EBM often group these questions into diagnosis, therapy, prognosis, risks, and cost-effectiveness. A key skill for health professionals is to organize, sort, and prioritize these questions so that they may be addressed. Traditional clinical training provides guidance in how to manage these questions. Clinical psychologist trainees need to develop heuristics to group and prioritize clinical questions. Persons's case formulation procedure (Persons, 2008) begins with a comprehensive problem list. Skills in the functional analysis of problems and a hierarchy of clinical issues such as that specified by Linehan (1993) are two key strategies.

A great many questions that arise in clinical encounters are not resolvable through the literature on empirical research, but instead require practical knowledge of the context of clinical practice. Who can monitor my client's suicide risk over the weekend? Where can I refer this client? What financial support can my client get access to while unemployed? How should I present a report for the judge who presides over my client's drunk driving charge? Other questions can be addressed through careful assessment. So, it is important for clinical psychologist trainees not to overestimate the value of EBP.

Clinical information needs are specific and unique to this particular client, this particular therapist, in this particular context.

On the other hand, we suspect that experienced clinical psychologists get out of the habit of using empirical evidence to answer their clinical information needs and may require assistance to see opportunities for evidence to inform their practice.

What Are My Client's Values and Preferences?

Directly asking clients is the obvious way to establish their values and preferences for intervention. Some knowledge and sensitivity to gender and cultural issues is also important. We are often surprised that both trainee and experienced clinical psychologists forget or minimize this source of information. It is unlikely that clients are going to adhere to an intervention that pays no attention to their beliefs about the nature of problems and their preferences for treatment (Foulks, Persons, & Merkel, 1986). Such a collaborative approach to therapy is a common feature of many forms of psychotherapy (c.f. Beck, Rush, Shaw, & Emery, 1987).

What Is the Question?

Turning information needs and client preferences into specific answerable questions is a crucial step in EBP (Geddes, 1999; Richardson, Wilson, Nishikawa, & Hayward, 1995). Specifying a question improves the possibility that there might be an answer in the literature. We teach the use of the PICO acronym. Specifying questions with PICO, Patient, the proposed Intervention, the Comparison intervention, and the desired Outcomes can assist in phrasing an answerable question.

Shlonsky and Gibbs (2004) identify poor questions as a stumbling point for social work students learning EBP. They describe how their students commonly phrase their questions too vaguely (e.g., What is the best treatment for chronic pain?) without adequate specification of the key elements. Other problems occur with selecting outcomes that are not relevant to the client's preferences or interventions that are not feasible in the context. A question should reflect a single issue and not confuse a number of concerns. Phrasing questions in terminology and language that is used in the search tools can also help. We encourage our students to become familiar with the controlled and regulated terminology of subject headings used in PsycINFO and MeSH.

Our students sometimes stumble with the need for a comparison intervention (the C in PICO). Our responses here are: If there are no real alternatives, there is no need to engage in the decision process as to what intervention should be provided! Second, we encourage them to consider doing nothing, nonspecific supportive counseling, or referral to less specialized services as the comparison as these may be realistic and require less resources to implement.

What Is the Best Source of Information to Address My Question and How Do I Find It?

Clinical psychologist trainees begin their postgraduate training with experience in searching literature from their undergraduate training. However, they may have had little formal training in the workings of the search tools and may be using them inefficiently, and the nature of searching to address a clinical information need is different. One key difference is the time available – it is not practical to conduct the exhaustive searches required for a research thesis in a typical clinical setting. Rather, we train our students to restrict their searching to 20 minutes based on the expectation that when they are carrying a large caseload the amount of time they will have to search for each clinical query will be even less. Thus, it is important to adapt existing skills to conducting much quicker searches. The specific skills required are first to select the search

tool that will give the best results in the shortest time and, second, to use optimal strategies within that search tool.

In our unit, we run two sessions of 2 hours each for searching in one of our university library's training rooms. It is equipped with a PC for each student and sufficient licenses for all to access relevant search tools. Using a clinical case for which we have previously worked up a specific question, we begin by demonstrating search techniques in the search tools listed in Table 3.1 and EBM journals (e.g., *Evidence-Based Mental Health* and *Clinical Evidence*). It is worth pointing out that new search tools will continue to be developed. Indeed, in researching this chapter we found that Walker and London (2007) described two new search tools that we had not previously included in our teaching!

When teaching searching, we encourage students to be aware of all the fields that are indexed and available to be searched, to know how to use Boolean operators (AND and OR) to limit searches, to use the controlled language of subject headings (MeSH in PubMed and Cochrane, Psychological index terms in PsycINFO), and to limit visual inspection of search results to no more than 20 references. The key technique to quick searching is to use filters with known sensitivity and specificity to identify research with potentially better quality methodology. Typically, search strategies begin with methodological filters to identify systematic reviews and if insufficient results are found the search strategy is to broaden out to randomized controlled trials. We provide some didactic material about the sensitivity and specificity of particular search strategies, and on this basis recommend the use of PubMed's Clinical Queries or the methodology and topic limits in PsycINFO to identify systematic reviews. Although recent versions of PsycINFO have introduced clinical queries limits for searches, there is apparently no evidence base like that available for the PubMed filters developed by Haynes (Haynes, McKibbon, Wilczynski,

TABLE 3.1   Search Tools for Evidence-Based Clinical Psychology

Search Tool	Web Address	Key Strengths	Key Weaknesses
U.S. Department of Health and Human Services, Agency for Healthcare Research and Quality, National Guidelines Clearing House	www.guideline.gov	Coverage restricted to Clinical Practice guidelines Free access to search	Guidelines may be out of date Access to content of guidelines may be restricted
The Cochrane Library	www3.interscience.wiley.com/cgi-bin/mrwhome/106568753	Comprehensive coverage of Cochrane Reviews and of clinical trials (via CENTRAL database) Links to content	Incomplete coverage of psychological literature Access may require subscription
The Campbell Collaboration's Campbell Library of Systematic Reviews	www.campbellcollaboration.org/campbell_library	Comprehensive coverage of educational and social programs	
U.S. National Library of Medicine, PubMed	www.pubmed.gov	Comprehensive coverage of primary literature Clinical queries to restrict searches on methodology and focus of study Freely accessible	Incomplete coverage of psychological literature
American Psychological Association, PsycINFO	*Through various providers* www.apa.org/psycinfo/	Comprehensive coverage of primary literature Comprehensive coverage of psychological literature	Access requires subscription Methodological and topic limits are available but of unknown sensitivity and specificity

Walter, & Werre, 2005). Eady, Wilczynski, and Haynes (2008) have developed and tested search strategies in PsycINFO that need to be entered by the user but have known sensitivity and specificity in identifying randomized controlled trials and systematic reviews.

Our students sometimes have difficulty limiting search time if they find very little. This seems to be driven by doubting their search strategy and believing there must be more literature available. Sometimes a reminder of the empirical evaluation of search strategies helps and, in other instances, developing confidence in their search abilities.

Another difficulty is finding too much information. We encourage students to return to their question and employ limits on study methods or from the PICO formulation of their information needs to reduce the information that they select for retrieval.

After we have demonstrated these search tools, students work by themselves or in small teams to try different search strategies for the

clinical questions they have been working to specify in previous classes. We end with a discussion of the strengths and weaknesses of each search tool.

How Valid Is the Information I've Found and Will It Generalize to My Client?

Our students come with well-developed skills in the appraisal of research for the purposes of academic writing and the learning objective is to generalize those skills to the task of deciding upon the most valid evidence and its applicability to their client.

Training in critical appraisal of search results thus begins with some didactic material on research design to reiterate the superiority of the RCT and meta-analysis to answer questions about optimal treatment, important features of RCTs and Systematic reviews that influence the validity of their results and the generalizability of those results to the specific client. Students use worksheets provided by the Section of General Practice and Primary Care at the University of Glasgow (undated) to evaluate one or more of the studies retrieved in previous weeks and discuss that appraisal around specific case material in small groups. They rejoin the wider class to reflect upon the content and process of the task.

How Do I Implement This Intervention?

After deciding on the most valid evidence that is applicable to their client, the next task is to decide how to employ that intervention with the client. Are there treatment manuals available and accessible? Are treatment manuals sufficiently detailed to enable implementation? Does the training and experience of the therapist in the clinical trials match up with that of the practitioner? Are there training resources that the practitioner can access such as knowledgeable peers and clinical supervisors? Are the procedures in the treatment manual sufficiently different from those the practitioner has demonstrated with competence and confidence? If there are client workbooks or self help manuals, are these suitable for the client in terms of reading ability? In short, these considerations all attempt to address the feasibility of the specific practitioner implementing the specific intervention with the specific client. The critical appraisal of the feasibility of a new intervention is the aspect of EBP that requires the greatest adaptation to clinical psychology.

How Do I Evaluate My Intervention?

From the client's values and preferences and knowledge about the realistic outcomes of the proposed intervention, select Patient Oriented Evidence that Matters (POEMs), such as functional outcomes and quality of life, rather than Disease oriented Evidence (DOEs), such as symptoms or the presence or absence of a disorder. Goal Attainment Scaling (Kiresuk & Sherman, 1968; Kiresuk, Smith, & Cardillo, 1994) may be one method for combining different aspects of the client's desired outcomes.

Evaluation of Our EBP Training

Our students respond well to most aspects of the EBP training. They give particularly positive feedback about the training in literature search skills. Material on appraisal of cost-effectiveness evaluations is rated the least positively, probably because it is novel and some consider such economic evaluations of little relevance when they anticipate a career in private practice.

In 2005 we presented the results of an uncontrolled pre-post evaluation of skills in EBP (Baillie & Peters, 2005). All 27 master's or doctor of clinical psychology students in the PSY967 Evidence-Based Clinical Psychology unit in 2004 (N = 12) and 2005 (N = 15) were asked to complete a modified version of the Fresno Medical Education Tool (Ramos, Schafer, & Tracz, 2003) in the first and last classes on EBP skills. Of the 27 students enrolled in the unit, 26 consented to participate and completed the modified Fresno during the first class, a response rate of 96.3%. Also, 14 completed the Fresno test at the end of the last class, giving a follow up rate of 51.9%.

The average modified Fresno score before the classes on EBP (mean = 72.2, SD = 22.5) showed a limited knowledge of EBP skills despite basic science training. Carrying the pre values forward for those who did not complete the post gave average post Fresno scores of 76.6 (SD = 26.9), again in the limited range. There was no significant difference on a paired samples t test (t(25) = 1.573, p = 0.128).

All our postgraduate clinical psychology students come to us with four or more years of training in the science of psychology. Despite this basic science training, EBP skills were at a low level prior to participation in the course. This may demonstrate that training in research methods may not easily generalize to the appraisal of research. Thus, one rationale for EBP is supported.

Participation in the new course led to non significant increases in EBP skills and EBP skills remained in the limited range. This course was not as effective at increasing EBM skills as other courses that have used similar methods and measures (Coomarasamy & Kahn, 2004). Our results are consistent with findings from training medical professionals (Coomarasamy & Kahn, 2004) in that a stand-alone coverage of EBP has not lead to improvements in knowledge. We believe that we can improve our training in EBP with greater focus on clinical cases and increased use of EBP techniques across our program (Hoge et al., 2003). Lack of resources to integrate EBP across our clinical program has been one barrier.

Advances in Information Technology and EBP

Evidence-based practice has become possible because of the growth in information technology. As undergraduates 20 years ago, a search of *Psychological Abstracts* by hand used two bookcases of paper indices and abstracts. Now we sit in our offices, pull up an Internet browser and link to the full text of many articles through our institutional library. These advances in IT make much of EBP possible and future advances in IT may enable other clinical innovations. Many currently practicing clinical psychologists are not trained in the best current search tools. If advances in IT continue as it has over the past years, it will be necessary to provide practicing clinical psychologists with training in how to use new search and appraisal tools for EBP.

Advances in IT may make more information available to practitioners and without careful consideration of how to manage that additional information practitioners may become overwhelmed (Williams, 2007). EBP skills to search and critically appraise information are helpful and there are some potential tools that may assist. Clinical practice guidelines may become embedded in tools (Muir Gray, 2005) so that instead of an effortful deliberate search, the clinician is prompted with suggestions based on guidelines. Stead (2007) provides an

example of how keywords in electronic health records may trigger suggestions from guidelines in much the same way as Google selects advertisements from keywords in searches and e-mail messages to provide advertising links alongside its popular e-mail program. Stead (2007) sees this as shift from the clinician as the integrator of clinical and research information to the clinician as the *pilot* of a clinical decision system. This specific example may or may not come to fruition but it seems clear that there will be advances in IT that may support and advance EBP.

SUMMARY

It is relatively easy to add didactic training in evidence-based clinical psychology to existing clinical psychology training programs and produce improvements in knowledge. To change clinical practice and client outcomes, it is likely that a more interactive approach across the curriculum that is integrated with real clinical contacts and case material and is based in the principles of adult learning is required.

Developments in the content of ESTs and in the tools to support searching for evidence require a substantial effort in continuing education. Practicing psychologists who rely on the treatment techniques they learned in graduate school or internships are likely to be using treatments that are out of date and providing their clients with suboptimal treatment. Practicing psychologists also need updates in the specific skills of evidence-based practice, particularly as advances in information technology has revolutionized literature searching. Continuing professional education based around didactic presentations may improve knowledge about ESTs and EBP but, as with postgraduate clinical psychology education, is unlikely to change attitudes, clinical practices, or clinical outcomes. Evidence from continuing medical education (O'Brien et al., 2001) indicates that interactive approaches based on principles of adult learning are more likely to lead to improvements in clinical practice and hence client outcomes. We found very little empirical evidence about continuing education in clinical psychology and, if correct, this is a large gap where research is needed.

There is limited evidence about the effects of training in evidence-based clinical psychology on changes in clinical practice or client outcomes. Most of the evidence comes from medical education that cannot completely generalize to clinical psychology. It is clear that given the effort and resources expended in postgraduate clinical psychology education that more high-quality empirical research is needed to justify the investment made by those seeking to become clinical psychologists and our broader communities.

Much work is being done in methods of training medical practitioners in evidence-based medicine that can generalize to clinical psychology. Those directors of clinical programs interested in including EBP in their programs will find many teaching resources available to them. We have argued earlier that there are additional training requirements for the use of nonproprietary procedural therapies like the majority of those employed by clinical psychologists. It is not sufficient to critically appraise clinical trial results and decide that the treatment with the best evidence that also generalizes to your client and is consistent with their values and preferences is best for your client. The clinical psychologist also needs to critically appraise whether they can deliver the chosen treatment by considering the availability of treatment manuals, training, and suitable supervision. The question here is: *Are they sufficiently similar to the therapists who delivered the treatment in the clinical trial(s) to be confident that they could produce the results obtained by the therapist in the literature?* Search tools with good coverage of psychological therapies are not as well developed as those that cover more medical literature so there are also additional training issues in teaching search skills.

In conclusion, training clinical psychologists to find the best empirical evidence and combine it with their knowledge of each specific client and their clinical experience may produce better client outcomes by increasing the use of treatments that have clinical trial support. Training in EBP is probably best embedded across the clinical psychology curricula and conducted in real clinical encounters with real clinical cases. In this way, EBP provides specific skills in the consumption of research. Training resources are well established in evidence based-medicine and are applicable to postgraduate clinical psychology education with some additions. High-quality empirical evaluations of training in evidence-based clinical psychology are required and there needs to be significant work to provide and evaluate such training as part of continuing education.

REFERENCES

Andrews, G. (1984). On the promotion of non drug treatments. *British Medical Journal*, 289(6450), 994-995.

Antony, M. M., Orsillo, S. M., & Roemer, L. (Eds.) (2001). *Practitioner's guide to empirically based measures of anxiety.* New York, NY: Kluwer Academic/Plenum Publishers.

American Psychological Association Presidential Task Force on Evidence Based Practice. (2006). Evidence based practice in psychology. *American Psychologist*, 61(4), 271-285.

Atkins, D. C., & Christensen, A. (2001). Is professional training worth the bother? A review of the impact of psychotherapy training on client outcome. *Australian Psychologist*, 36, 122-130.

Baillie, A. J., & Peters, L. (2005, October) *Does training in evidence based clinical psychology improve skills in evidence based clinical psychology?* Paper presented at the 13th Cochrane Colloquium. Abstract retrieved from www.cochrane.org/colloquia/abstracts/melbourne/P-130.

Beck, A. T., Rush, A. J., Shaw, B. F., & Emery, G. (1987). *Cognitive therapy of depression.* New York, NY: Guilford Press.

Chambless, D. L., & Ollendick, T. H. (2001). Empirically supported psychological interventions: Controversies and evidence. *Annual Review of Psychology*, 52, 685-716.

Chan, R. W., & Tang, C. S. K. (1996). A survey of Hong Kong clinical psychologists: Training and continuing education. *Bulletin of the Hong Kong Psychological Society, 36*, 39–46.

Coomarasamy, A., & Kahn, K. S. (2004). What is the evidence that postgraduate teaching in evidence based medicine changes anything? A systematic review. *British Medical Journal, 329*, 1017–1021.

Eady, A. M., Wilczynski, N. L., & Haynes, R. B. (2008). PsycINFO search strategies identified methodologically sound therapy studies and review articles for use by clinicians and researchers. *Journal of Clinical Epidemiology, 61*, 34–40.

Evidence-Based Medicine Working Group. (1992). Evidence-based medicine. A new approach to teaching the practice of medicine. *JAMA, 268*, 2420–2425.

Foulks, E. F., Persons, J. B., & Merkel, R. L. (1986). The effect of patient's beliefs about their illnesses on compliance in psychotherapy. *American Journal of Psychiatry, 143*, 340–344.

Geddes, J. (1999). Asking structured and focused clinical questions: Essential first step of evidence-based practice. *Evidence-Based Mental Health, 2*, 35–36.

Geddes, J. (2000). Evidence-Based Practice in Mental Health. In L. Trinder & S. Reynolds (Eds.), *Evidence-Based Practice: A Critical Appraisal* (pp. 66–88). Oxford, UK: Blackwell.

Geisinger, K. F., Spies, R. A., Carlson, J. F., & Plake, B. S. (2007). *The seventeenth mental measurements yearbook*. Lincoln, NE: Buros Institute of Mental Measurements.

Goodheart, C., Kazdin, A., & Sternberg, R. (2006). *Evidence-based psychotherapy: Where practice and research meet*. Washington, DC: American Psychological Association.

Haynes, R. B., McKibbon, K. A., Wilczynski, N. L., Walter, S. D., & Werre, S. R. (2005). Optimal search strategies for retrieving scientifically strong studies of treatment from Medline: Analytical survey. *British Medical Journal, 330*(7501), 1179.

Hoge, M. A., Tondora, J., & Stuart, G. W. (2003). Training in evidence-based practice. *Psychiatric Clinics of North America, 26*, 851–865.

Isaacs, D., & Fitzgerald, D. (1999). Seven alternatives to evidence based medicine. *British Medical Journal, 319*, 1618.

Kelly, M. L., Reitman, D., & Noell, G. H. (Eds.). (2002). *Practitioner's guide to empirically based measures of school behavior*. New York, NY: Kluwer Academic/Plenum.

Kiresuk, T. J., & Sherman, R. E. (1968). Goal attainment scaling: A general method for evaluating comprehensive community mental health programs. *Community Mental Health Journal, 4*, 443–453.

Kiresuk, T. J., Smith, A., & Cardillo, J. E. (1994). *Goal attainment scaling: Applications, theory and measurement*. Hillsdale, NJ: Erlbaum.

Klonsky, E. D. (n.d.). Website on Research Supported Psychological Treatments. Retrieved from www.psychology.sunysb.edu/eklonsky-/division12

Linehan, M. M. (1993). *Cognitive-behavioral treatment of borderline personality disorder*. New York, NY: Guilford Press.

Linzer, M., DeLong, E. R., & Hupart, K. H. (1987). A comparison of two formats for teaching critical reading skills in a medical journal club. *Journal of Medical Education, 62*, 690–692.

Milne, D. L., & James, I. A. (2002). The observed impact of training on competence in clinical supervision. *British Journal of Clinical Psychology, 41*, 55–72.

Moher, D., Schulz, K. F., & Altman, D. (2001). The CONSORT statement: Revised recomendations for improving the quality of reports of parallel-group randomised trials. *JAMA, 285*, 1987–1991.

Muir Gray, J. A. (2005, October). *Is evidence ever enough: How can evidence best contribute to global improvement in Health*. Paper presented at the 13th Cochrane Colloquium.

National Health Service Institute for Innovation and Improvement. (2008). Database of Uncertainties About the Effects of Treatments. Retrieved from www.library.nhs.uk/duets/

Nezu, A. M., Ronan, G. F., Meadows, E. A., & McClure, K. S. (Eds.). (2000). *Practitioner's guide to empirically based measures of depression*. New York, NY: Kluwer Academic/Plenum.

O'Brien, M. A., Freemantle, N., Oxman, A. D., Wolf, F., Davis, D. A., & Herrin, J. (2001). Continuing education meetings and workshops: Effects on professional practice and health care outcomes. *Cochrane Database of Systematic Reviews*, (1). Retrieved from www.mrw.interscience.wiley.com/cochrane/clsysrev/articles/CD003030/frame.html. doi:10.1002/14651858.CD003030

O'Donovan, A., Bain, J. D., & Dyck, M. J. (2005). Does clinical psychology education enhance the clinical competence of practitioners? *Professional Psychology-Research and Practice, 36*, 104–111.

Pai, M., McCulloch, M., Enanoria, W., & Colford, J. M. (2004). Systematic reviews of diagnostic test evaluations: What's behind the scenes? *Evidence-Based Medicine, 9*, 101–103.

Parkes, J., Hyde, C., Deeks, J., & Milne, R. (2001). Teaching critical appraisal skills in health care settings. *Cochrane Database of Systematic Reviews*, (3). Retrieved from www.mrw.interscience.wiley.com/cochrane/clsysrev/articles/CD001270/frame.html. doi:10.1002/14651858.CD001270

Persons, J. B. (2008). *The case formulation approach to cognitive-behavior therapy*. New York, NY: Guilford Press.

Persons, J. B., & Silberschatz, G. (1998). Are results of randomized controlled trials useful to psychotherapists?

Journal of Consulting and Clinical Psychology, 66, 126–135.

Ramos, K. D., Schafer, S., & Tracz, S. M. (2003). Validation of the Fresno test of competence in evidence based medicine. *British Medical Journal, 326,* 319–321.

Richardson, W. S., Wilson, M. C., Nishikawa, J., & Hayward, R. S. (1995). The well-built clinical question: A key to evidence-based decisions. *American College of Physicians Journal Club, 123,* A12–A13.

Sackett, D. L., Richardson, W. S., Rosenberg, W., & Haynes, R. B. (1997). *Evidence-based medicine: How to practice and teach EBM.* London, England: Churchill Livingstone.

Sackett, D. L., Rosenberg, W. M. C., Gray, J. A. M., Haynes, R. B., & Richardson, W. S. (1996). Evidence based medicine: What it is and what it isn't. *British Medical Journal, 312*(7023), 71–72.

Sackett, D. L., Straus, S. E., Richardson, W. S., Rosenberg, W., & Haynes, R. B. (2000). *Evidence based medicine: How to practice and teach EBM* (2nd ed.). London, England: Churchill Livingstone.

Sanderson, W. C., & Woody, S. R. (1995). Manuals for empirically validated treatments: A project of the Task Force on Psychological Interventions. *Clinical Psychologist, 48,* 7–11.

Section of General Practice and Primary Care, University of Glasgow. (n.d.). Evidence based practice check lists. Retrieved from www.gla.ac.uk/departments/generalpracticeprimarycare/ebp/checklists/

Severens, J. L., Prins, J. B., Van Der Wilt, G. J., Van Der Meer, J. W. M., & Bleijenberg, G. (2004). Cost effectiveness of cognitive behaviour therapy for patients with chronic fatigue syndrome. *Quarterly Journal of Medicine, 97,* 153–161.

Shadish, W. R., Matt, G. E., Navarro, A. M., & Phillips, G. (2000). The effects of psychological therapies under clinically representative conditions: A meta-analysis. *Psychological Bulletin, 126,* 512–529.

Shadish, W. R., Matt, G. E., Navarro, A. M., Siegle, G., Crits-Christoph, P., Hazelrigg, M. D., . . . Weiss, B. (1997). Evidence that therapy works in clinically representative conditions. *Journal of Consulting and Clinical Psychology, 65,* 355–365.

Shlonsky, A., & Gibbs, L. (2004). Will the real evidence-based practice please stand up? Teaching the process of evidence-based practice to the helping professions. *Brief Treatment & Crisis Intervention, 4,* 137–153.

Spring, B. (2007). Evidence-based practice in clinical psychology: What it is, why it matters; what you need to know. *Journal of Clinical Psychology, 63,* 611–631.

Stead, W. W. (2007). Clinicians and the electronic health record as a learning tool. In Institute of Medicine (Ed.), *The learning healthcare system: Workshop summary* (pp. 268–275). Washington, DC: National Academies Press.

Straus, S. E., Richardson, W. S., Glasziou, P., & Haynes, R. B. (2005). *Evidence based medicine: How to practice and teach EBM* (3rd ed.). London, England: Churchill Livingstone.

Walker, B. B., & London, S. (2007). Novel tools and resources for evidence based practice in psychology. *Journal of Clinical Psychology, 63,* 633–642.

Williams, M. V. (2007). Knowledge translation: Redefining continuing education around evolving evidence. In Institute of Medicine (Ed.), *The learning healthcare system: Workshop summary* (pp. 281–287). Washington, DC: National Academies Press.

Woody, S. R., & Sanderson, W. C. (1998). Manuals for empirically supported treatments. *Clinical Psychologist, 51,* 17–21.

Wyshak, G., Barsky, A. J., & Klerman, G. L. (1991). Comparison of psychiatric screening tests in a general medical setting using ROC analysis. *Medical Care, 29,* 775–785.

4

Limitations to Evidence-Based Practice

THOMAS MAIER

The promotion of *evidence-based medicine* (EBM) or, more generally, of *evidence-based practice* (EBP) has strongly characterized most medical disciplines over the past 15 to 20 years. Evidence-based medicine has become a highly influential concept in clinical practice, medical education, research, and health policy. Although the evidence-based approach has also been increasingly applied in related fields such as psychology, education, social work, or economics, it was and still is predominantly used in medicine and nursing.

Evidence-based practice is a general and nonspecific concept that aims to improve and specify the way decision makers should make decisions. For this purpose it delineates methods of how professionals should retrieve, summarize, and evaluate the available empirical evidence in order to identify the best possible decision to be taken in a specific situation. So EBP is, in a broader perspective, a method to analyze and evaluate large amounts of statistical and empirical information to understand a particular case. It is therefore not limited to specific areas of science and is potentially applicable in any field of science using statistical and empirical data.

Many authors often cite Sackett, Rosenberg, Muir Gray, Haynes, and Richardson's (1996) article entitled "Evidence based medicine. What it is and what it isn't" as the founding deed of

evidence-based practice. David L. Sackett (born 1934), an American-born Canadian clinical epidemiologist, was professor at the Department of Clinical Epidemiology and Biostatistics of McMaster University Medical School of Hamilton, Ontario, from 1967 to 1994. During that time, he and his team developed and propagated modern concepts of clinical epidemiology. Sackett later moved to England, and from 1994 to 1999, he headed the National Health Services' newly founded Centre for Evidence Based Medicine at Oxford University. During that time, he largely promoted EBM in Europe by publishing articles and textbooks as well as by giving numerous lectures and training courses. David Sackett is seen by many as the founding father of EBM as a proper discipline, although he would not at all claim this position for himself. In fact, Sackett promoted and elaborated concepts that have been described and used by others before, the origins of EBM are rooted back in much earlier times.

The foundations of clinical epidemiology were already laid in the 19th century mainly by French, German, and English physicians systematically studying the prevalence and course of diseases and the effects of therapies. As important foundations of the EBM movement, certainly the works and insights of the Scottish epidemiologist Archibald (Archie) L. Cochrane (1909–1988) have to be

mentioned. Cochrane, probably the true
founding father of modern clinical epidemiology, had long before insisted on sound epidemiological data, especially from RCTs, as the
gold standard to improve medical practice
(Cochrane, 1972). In fact, the evaluation of
epidemiological data has always been one of
the main sources of information in modern
academic medicine, and many of the most
spectacular advances of medicine are direct
consequences of the application of basic epidemiological principles such as hygiene, aseptic
surgery, vaccination, antibiotics, and the identification of cardiovasular and carcinogenic risk
factors. One of the most frequent objections
against the propagation of EBM is, "It's nothing
new, doctors have done it all the time."
Rangachari, for example, apostrophized EBM
as "old French wine with a new Canadian
label" (Rangachari, 1997, p. 280) alluding to the
French 19th century epidemiology pioneer
Pierre Louis, who was an influencing medical
teacher in Europe and North America, and to
David L. Sackett, the Canadian epidemiologist.

Even though the "conscientious, explicit and
judicious use of the current best evidence in
making decisions about the care of individual
patients" (Sackett et al., 1996, p. 71) seems to be a
perfectly reasonable and unassailable goal, EBM
has been harshly criticized from the very beginning of its promotion (Berk & Miles Leigh, 1999;
B. Cooper, 2003; Miles, Bentley, Polychronis,
Grey, and Price, 1999; Norman, 1999; Williams
& Garner, 2002). In 1995, for example, the edi-
tors of The Lancet chose to publish a rebuking
editorial against EBM entitled "Evidence-based
medicine, in its place" (The Lancet, 1995):

> The voice of evidence-based medicine has
> grown over the past 25 years or so from a
> subversive whisper to a strident insistence that
> it is improper to practise medicine of any
> other kind. Revolutionaries notoriously exag-
> gerate their claims; nonetheless, demands to
> have evidence-based medicine hallowed as
> the new orthodoxy have sometimes lacked
> finesse and balance, and risked antagonising
> doctors who would otherwise have taken

many of its principles to heart. The Lancet
applauds practice based on the best available
evidence–bringing critically appraised news
of such advances to the attention of clinicians
is part of what peer-reviewed medical journals
do–but we deplore attempts to foist evidence-
based medicine on the profession as a discipline in itself. (p. 785)

This editorial elicited a fervid debate carried
on for months in the letter columns of *The
Lancet*. Indeed, there was a certain doggedness
on both sides at that time, astonishing neutral
observers and rendering the numerous critics
even more suspicious. The advocates of EBM
on their part acted with great self-confidence and
claimed no less than to establish a new discipline
and to put clinical medicine on new fundaments;
journals, societies, conferences, and EBM
training courses sprang up like mushrooms;
soon academic lectures and chairs emerged;
however, this clamorous and pert appearance of
EBM repelled many. A somehow dogmatic,
almost sectarian, tendency of the movement was
noticed with discontent, and even the deceased
patron saint of EBM, Archie Cochrane, had to
be invoked in order to push the zealots back:

> How would Archie Cochrane view the
> emerging scene? His contributions are
> impressive, particularly to the development
> of epidemiology as a medical science, but
> would he be happy about all the activities
> linked with his name? He was a freethinking,
> iconoclastic individual with a healthy cynicism,
> who would not accept dogma. He brought an
> open sceptical approach to medical problems
> and we think that he would be saddened
> to find that his name now embodies a
> new rigid medical orthodoxy while the real
> impact of his many achievments might be
> overlooked. (Williams & Garner 2002, p. 10)

THE DEMOCRATIZATION
OF KNOWLEDGE

How could such an emotional controversy
arise about the introduction of a scientific

method (Ghali, Saitz, Sargious, & Hershman, 1999)? Obviously, the propagation and refusal of EBM have to be seen not only from a rational scientific standpoint but also from a sociological perspective (Miettinen, 1999; Norman, 1999): The rise of the EBM movement fundamentally reflects current developments in contemporary health care concerning the allocation of information, knowledge, authority, power, and finance (Berk & Miles Leigh, 1999), a process becoming more and more critical during the late 1980s and the 1990s. Medicine has, for quite some time, been losing its prestige as an intangible, moral institution. Its cost-value ratio is questioned more and more and doctors are no longer infallible authorities. We do not trust doctors anymore to know the solution for any problem; they are supposed to prove and to justify what they do and why they do it. These developments in medicine parallel similar tendencies in other social domains and indicate general changes in Western societies' self-conception. Today we are living in a *knowledge society*, where knowledge and information is democratized, available and accessible to all. There is no retreat anymore for secret expert knowledge and for hidden esoteric wisdom. The hallmarks of our time are free encyclopedic databases, open access, the World Wide Web, and Google©. In the age of information, there are no limitations for filing, storage, browsing, and scanning of huge amounts of data; however, this requires more and more expert knowledge to handle it. So, paradoxically, EBM represents a new specialized expertise that aims to democratize or even to abolish detached expert knowledge.

The democratization of knowledge increasingly questions the authority and self-sufficiency of medical experts and has deeply unsettled many doctors and medical scientists. Of course, this struggle is not simply about authority and truth, it is also about influence, power, and money. For all the unsettled doctors, EBM must have appeared like a guide for the perplexed leading them out of insecurity

and doubt. Owing to its paradoxical nature, EBM offers them a new spiritual home of secluded expertise allowing doctors to regain control over the debate and to reclaim authority of interpretation from bold laymen. For this purpose, EBM features and emphasizes the most valuable label of our time that is so believable in science: *science-* or *evidence-based*. In many areas of contention, terms like *evidence-based* or *scientifically proven* are used for the purpose of putting opponents on the defensive. Nobody is entitled to question a fact, which is declared evidence-based or scientifically proven. By definition, these labels are supposed to convey unquestioned and axiomatic truth. It requires rather complex and elaborate epistemological reasoning to demonstrate how even true evidence-based findings can at the same time be wrong, misleading, and/or useless.

All these accounts and arguments apply in particular to the disciplines of psychiatry and clinical psychology, which have always had a marginal position among the apparently respectable disciplines of academic medicine. Psychiatrists and psychologists always felt particularly pressured to justify their actions and are constantly suspected to practice quackery rather than rational science. It is therefore not surprising that among other marginalized professionals, such as the general practitioners, psychiatrists and psychotherapists made particularly great efforts over the last years to establish their disciplines as serious matters of scholarly medicine by diligently adopting the methods of EBM (Geddes & Harrison, 1997; Gray & Pinson, 2003; Oakley Browne, 2001; Sharpe, Gill, Strain, & Mayou, 1996). Yet, there are also specific problems limiting the applicability of EBP in these disciplines.

EMPIRICISM AND REDUCTIONISM

In order to understand the role and function of EBP within the scientific context, it may be helpful to give a brief overview of the theoretical backgrounds of science in general. What is science and how does it proceed? Science can be seen as a potentially endless human endeavour that aims to understand and determine reality. Not only are physical objects matters of science, but also immaterial phenomena like language, history, society, politics, economics, human behavior, thoughts, or emotions. Starting with the Greek scientists in the ancient world, but progressing more rapidly with the philosophers of the Enlightenment, modern science adopted defined rules of action and standards of reasoning that delineate science from nonscientific knowledge such as pragmatics, art, or religion. Unfortunately, notions like science, scientific, or evidence are often wrongly used in basically nonscientific contexts causing unnecessary confusion.

The heart and the starting point of any positive science is *empiricism*, meaning the systematic observation of phenomena. Scientists of any kind must start their reasoning with observations, possibly refined through supportive devices or experimental arrangements. Although positive science fundamentally believes in the possibility of objective perception, it also knows the inherent weaknesses of reliability and potential sources of errors. Rather than have confidence in single observations, science trusts repeated and numerous observations and statistical data. This approach rules out idiosyncratic particularities of single cases to gain the benefit of identifying the common characteristics of general phenomena (i.e., *reductionism*). This approach of comprehending phenomena by analytically observing and describing them has in fact produced enormous advancements in many fields of science, especially in technical disciplines; however, contrasting and confusing gaps of knowledge prevail in other areas such as causes of human behavior, mind–body problems, or genome–environment interaction. Some areas of science are apparently happier and more successful using the classical

approach of positive science, while other disciplines feel less comfortable with the reductionist way of analyzing problems. The less successful areas of science are those studying complex phenomena where idiosyncratic features of single cases can make a difference, in spite of perfect empirical evidence. This applies clearly to medicine, but even more to psychology, sociology, or economics. Medicine, at least in its academic version, usually places itself among respectable sciences, meeting with and observing rules of scientific reasoning; however, this claim may be wishful thinking and medicine is in fact a classical example of a basically atheoretical, mainly pragmatic undertaking pretending to be based on sound science. Inevitably, it leads to contradictions when trying to bring together common medical practice and pure science.

COMPLEXITY

Maybe the deeper reasons for these contradictions are not understood well enough. Maybe they still give reason for unrealistic ideas to some scientists. A major source of misconception appears to be the confused ontological perception of some objects of scientific investigation. What is a disease, a disorder, a diagnosis? What is human behavior? What are emotions? Answering these questions in a manner to provide a basis for scientific reasoning in a Popperian sense (see later) is far from trivial. Complex objects of science, like human behavior, medical diseases, or emotions, are in fact not concrete, tangible things easily accessible to experimental investigation. They are *emergent phenomena*, hence they are not stable material objects, but exist only as transitory, nonlocal appearances fluctuating in time. They continuously emerge out of indeterminable complexity through repeated self-referencing operations in complex systems (i.e., autopoietic systems). Indeterminable complexity or *deterministic chaos* means that a huge number of mutually interacting parameters autopoietically form a system, rendering any precise calculation of the system's future conditions impossible. Each single element of the system perfectly follows the physical rules of causality; however, the system as a whole is nevertheless unpredictable. Its fluctuations and oscillations can be described only probabilistically. In order to obtain reasonable and useful information about a system, many scientific disciplines have elaborated probabilistic methods of approaching their objects of interest. Thermodynamics, meteorology, electroencephalography, epidemiology, and macroeconomics are only a few such examples. Most structures in biological, social, and psychological reality can be conceived as emergent phenomena in this sense. Just as the temperature of an object is not a quality of the single molecules forming the object—a single molecule has no temperature—but a statistic description of a huge number of molecules, human behavior cannot be determined through the description of composing elements producing the phenomenon—for example, neurons—even if these elements are necessary and indispensable preconditions for the emergence of the phenomenon. The characteristics of the whole cannot be determined by the description of its parts. When the precise conditions of complex systems turn out to be incalculable, the traditional reaction of positive science is to intensify analytical efforts and to compile more information about the components forming the system. This approach allows scientists to constantly increase their knowledge about the system in question without ever reaching a final understanding and a complete determination of the function of the system. This is exactly what happens currently in neurosciences. Reductionist approaches have their inherent limitations when it comes to the understanding of complex systems.

A similar problem linked to complexity that is particularly important is the assumed comparability of similar cases. In order to understand an individual situation, science routinely compares defined situations to similar situations or, even better, to a large number of

similar situations. Through the pooling of large numbers of comparable cases, interfering individual differences are statistically eliminated, and only the common ground appears. The conceptual assumption behind this procedure is that similar—but still not identical—cases will evolve similarly under identical conditions. One of the most important insights from the study of complex phenomena is that in complex systems very small differences in initial conditions may lead to completely different outcomes after a short time—the so-called butterfly effect. This insight is well known to natural scientists; however, clinical epidemiologists do not seem to be completely aware of the consequences of the butterfly effect to their area of research.

FROM KARL POPPER TO THOMAS S. KUHN

Based on epistemological considerations, the Anglo-Austrian philosopher Karl Popper (1902–1994) demonstrated in the 1930s the limitations of logical empiricism. He reasoned that general theories drawn from empirical observations can never be proven to be true. So, all theories must remain tentative knowledge, waiting to be falsified by contrary observations. In fact, Popper conceived the project of science as a succession of theories to be falsified sooner or later and to be replaced by new theories. This continuous succession of new scientific theories is the result of natural selection of ideas through the advancement of science. According to Popper, any scientific theory must be formulated in a way to render it potentially falsifiable through empirical testing. Otherwise, the theory is not scientific. It may be metaphysical, religious, or spiritual instead. This requires that a theory must be formulated in terms of clearly defined notions and measurable elements.

Popper's assertions were later qualified as being less absolute by the American philosopher of science Thomas S. Kuhn (1922–1996),

Kuhn, originally a physicist, pointed out that in real science any propagated theory could be falsified immediately by contrary observations because contradicting observations are always present; however, science usually ignores or even suppresses observations dissenting with the prevailing theory in order to maintain the accepted theory. Kuhn calls the dissenting observations *anomalies*, which are—according to him—always obvious and visible to all, but nevertheless blinded out of perception in order to maintain the ruling paradigm. In Kuhn's view, science will never come to an end and there will never be a final understanding of nature. No theory will ever be able to integrate and explain consistently all the observations drawn from nature. At this point, even the fundamental limitations to logical scientific reasoning demonstrated by Gödel's incompleteness theorems become recognizable (cf. also Sleigh, 1995). Based on his considerations, Kuhn clear-sightedly identified science to be a social system, rather than a strictly logical and rational undertaking. Science, as a social phenomenon, functions according to principles of Gestalt psychology. It sees the things it wants to see and overlooks the things that do not fit. In his chief work *The Structure of Scientific Revolutions*, Kuhn (1962) gives several examples from the history of science supporting this interpretation. It is in fact amazing to see how difficult it was for most important scientific breakthroughs to become acknowledged by the contemporary academic establishment. Kuhn uses the notion *normal science* to characterize the established academic science and emphasizes the self-referencing nature of its operating mode. Academic teachers teach students what the teachers believe is true. Students have to learn what they are taught by their teachers if they want to pass their exams and get their degrees. Research is mainly repeating and retesting what is already known and accepted. Journals, edited and peer-reviewed by academic teachers, publish what conforms with academic teachers' ideas. Societies and associations—headed by the same academic teachers—ensure the purity of doctrine by sponsoring those who confirm the prevailing paradigms. Dissenting opinions are unwelcome. Based on Kuhn's view of normal science, EBP and EBM can be identified as classical manifestations of normal science. The EBP helps to ensure the implementation of mainstream knowledge by declaring to be most valid what is best evaluated. Usually the currently established practices are endorsed by the best and most complete empirical evidence; dissenting ideas will hardly be supported by good evidence, even if these ideas are right. Since EBP instructs its adherers to evaluate the available evidence on the basis of numerical rules of epidemiology, arguments like plausibility, logic consistency, or novelty are of little relevance.

AN EXAMPLE FROM RECENT HISTORY OF CLINICAL MEDICINE

When in 1982 the Australian physicians Barry Marshall and Robin Warren discovered Helicobacter pylori in the stomachs of patients with peptic ulcers, their findings were completely ignored and neglected by the medical establishment of that time. The idea that peptic ulcers are provoked by an infectious agent conflicted with the prevailing paradigm of academic gastroenterology, which conceptualized peptic ulcers as a consequence of stress and lifestyle. Although there had been numerous previous reports of helicobacteria in gastric mucosa, all these findings were completely ignored because they conflicted with the prevailing paradigm. As a consequence Marshall and Warren's discovery was ignored for years because it fundamentally challenged current scientific opinion. They were outcast by the scientific community, and only 10 years later their ideas slowly started to convince more and more clinicians. Now, 25 years later, it is common basic clinical knowledge that

Helicobacter pylori is one of the major causes of peptic ulcers, and eradication therapy is the accepted and rational therapy for gastric ulcers. Finally, in 2005 Barry Marshall and Robin Warren gained the Nobel Price for their discovery (Parsonnet, 2005).

BENEFITS AND RISKS OF EVIDENCE-BASED PRACTICE

The true benefits of EBP for patients and society in terms of outcomes and costs have not been proven yet—at least not through sound empirical evidence (B. Cooper, 2003; Geddes & Harrison, 1997). Nevertheless, there is no doubt that the method has a beneficial and useful potential. Many achievements of EBP are undisputable and undisputed, hence they are *evident*.

Owing to the spread of methodical skills in retrieving and evaluating the available epidemiological evidence, it has become much harder to apply any kind of obscure or idiosyncratic practices. The experts' community, as well as the customers and the general public, are much more critical toward pretended effects of treatments and ask for sound empirical evidence of effectiveness and safety. It is increasingly important not only to know the best available treatment, but also to prove it. The EBP is therefore a helpful instrument for doctors and therapists to justify and legitimate their practices to insurance, judiciary, politics, and society.

Furthermore, individual patients might be less at risk to wrong or harmful treatment due to scientific misapprehension. Of course, common malpractice owing to manity, negligence, or viciousness will never be eliminated, not even by the total implementation of EBP, however, treatment errors committed by diligent and virtuous doctors are minimized through careful adherence to rational guidelines.

In general, clinical decision making paths have become more comprehensible and rational, probably also due to the spread of EBP. As medicine is in fact not a thoroughly scientific matter (Ghali et al. 1999), continuous efforts are needed to enhance and renew rationality. The EBP contributes to this task and helps clinicians to maintain rationality in a job where inscrutable complexity is daily business. In current medical education, the algorithms of EBP are now instilled into students as a matter of course. Seen from that perspective, EBP is also an instrument of discipline and education, for it compels medical students and doctors to reflect continuously all their opinions and decisions scientifically (Norman, 1999). Today EBP has a great impact on the education and training of future doctors, and it thereby enhances the uniformity and transparency of medical doctrine. This international alignment of medical education with the principles of EBP will, in the long run, allow for better comparability of medical practice all over the world. This is an important precondition for the planning and coordination of research activities. Thus, the circle of normal science is perfectly closed through the widespread implementation of EBP.

GENERAL LIMITATIONS TO EVIDENCE-BASED PRACTICE

It has been remarked, not without reason, that the EBP movement itself has adopted features of dogmatic authority (B. Cooper, 2003; Geddes et al., 1996; Miles et al., 1999). This appears particularly ironic, because EBP explicitly aims to fight any kind of orthodox doctrine. The ferocity of some EBP adherents may not necessarily hint at conceptual weaknesses of the method, rather, it is more likely a sign of an iconoclastic or even patricidal tendency inherent to EBP. Young, diligent scholars, even students, possibly without any practical experience, are now entitled to criticize and rectify clinical authorities (Norman, 1999). This kind of insurgence must evoke resistance from authorities. If the acceptance of EBP among clinicians should be enhanced, it is advisable that the method is not only propagated by diligent theoreticians, but mainly by experienced practitioners.

One of the first and most important arguments against EBP is reductionism (see earlier, Welsby, 1999). Complex and maybe fundamentally diverse clinical situations of individual patients have to be condensed and aggregated to generalized questions in order to retrieve empirical statistical evidence. Important specific information about the individual cases is inevitably lost owing to this generalization. The usefulness of the retrieved evidence is therefore inevitably diluted to a very general and dim level. Of course, there are some frequently used standard interventions, which are really based upon good empirical evidence (Geddes et al., 1996).

EXAMPLES FROM CLINICAL MEDICINE

Scabies, a parasitic infection of the skin, is an important public health problem, mainly in resource-poor countries. For the treatment of the disease, two treatment options are recommended: topical permethrin and oral ivermectin. Both treatments are known to be effective and are usually well tolerated. The *Cochrane Review* concluded from the available empirical evidence that topical permethrin appears to be the most effective treatment of scabies (Strong & Johnstone, 2007). This recommendation can be found in up-to-date medical textbooks and is familiar to any well-trained doctor.

Acute otitis media in children is one of the most common diseases, one of the main causes for parents to consult a pediatrician, and a frequent motive for the prescription of antibiotics, even though spontaneous recovery is the usual outcome. Systematic reviews have shown that the role of antibiotic drugs for the course of the disease is marginal, and there is no consensus among experts about the

identification of subgroups who would potentially profit from antibiotics. In clinical practice, in spite of lacking evidence of its benefit, the frequent prescription of antibiotic drugs is mainly the consequence of parents' pressure and doctors' insecurity. A recent meta-analysis (Rovers et al., 2006) found that children younger than 2 years of age with bilateral acute otitis media and those with otorrhea benefited to some extent from antibiotic treatment; however, even for these two particular conditions, differences were moderate: After 3–7 days, 30% of the children treated with antibiotics still had pain, fever, or both, while in the control group the corresponding proportion was 55%. So, the available evidence to guide a clinician when treating a child with acute otitis media is not really significant and the decision will mostly depend on soft factors like parents' preferences or practical and economical considerations.

Evidently, clinicians choosing these interventions do not really need to apply the algorithms of EBP to make their decisions. They simply administer what they had learned in their regular clinical training. The opponents of EBP rightly argue that the real problems in clinical practice arise from complex, multimorbid patients presenting with several illnesses and other factors that have to be taken into account by the treating clinician. In order to manage such cases successfully there is usually no specific statistical evidence available to rely on. Instead, clinicians have to put together evidence covering some aspects of the actual case and hope that the resulting treatment will still work even if it is not really designed and tested for that particular situation. Good statistical evidence meeting the highest standards of EBP is almost exclusively derived from ideal monomorbid patients, who are rarely seen in real, everyday practice (Williams & Garner, 2002). It is not clear at all—and far from evidence-based—whether evidence from ideal cases can be transferred to more complex cases without substantial loss of validity.

Another argument criticizing EBP points at an epistemological problem. Because the EBP operates retrospectively by evaluating what was done in the past, it cannot directly contribute to developing new strategies and to finding new therapies. The EBP helps to consolidate well-known therapies, but cannot guide researchers toward scientific innovations. No scientific breakthrough will ever be made owing to EBP. On the contrary, if all clinicians strictly followed recommendations drawn from available retrospective evidence and never dared to try something different, science would stagnate in fruitless self-reference. There is a basically conservative and backward tendency inherent to the method. Although it cannot exactly be called anti-scientific on that account (B. Cooper, 2003; Miles et al., 1999), EBP is a classical phenomenon of normal science (Kuhn, 1962). It will not itself be the source of fundamental new insights.

Finally, there is an external problem with EBP, which is probably most disturbing of all: Production and compilation of evidence available to clinicians is highly critical and exposed to different nonscientific influences (Miettinen, 1999). Selection of areas of research is based more and more on economic interests. Large, sound, and therefore scientifically significant epidemiologic studies are extremely complex and expensive. They can be accomplished only with the support of financially potent sponsors. Compared with public bodies or institutions, private companies are usually faster and more flexible in investing important amounts of money into medical research. So, for many ambitious scientists keen on collecting publishable findings, it is highly appealing to collaborate with commercial sponsors. This has a significant influence on the selection of diseases and treatments being evaluated. The resulting body of evidence is necessarily highly unbalanced because mainly diseases and interventions

promising important profits are well evaluated. For this reason, more money is probably put into trials on erectile dysfunction, baldness, or dysmenorrhea than on malaria or on typhoid fever. So, even guidelines based on empirical evidence—considered to be the ultimate gold standard of clinical medicine—turn out to be arbitrary and susceptible to economical, political, and dogmatic arguments (Berk & Miles Leigh, 1999). So, EBP's goals to replace opinion and tendency by knowledge are in danger of being missed, if the relativity of available evidence is unrecognized. The uncritical promotion of EBP opens a clandestine gateway to those who have interests in controlling the contents of medical debates and have the financial means to do so. Biasing clinical decisions in times of EBP is probably no longer possible by false or absent evidence; however, the selection of what is researched in an EBP-compatible manner and what is published may result in biased clinical decisions (Miettinen, 1999). One of the most effective treatment options in many clinical situations—watchful waiting—is notoriously under-researched because there is no commercial or academic interest linked to that treatment option. Unfortunately, there will never be enough time, money, and workforce to produce perfect statistical evidence for all useful clinical procedures. So, even in the very distant future, clinicians will still apply many of their probably effective interventions without having evidence about their efficacy and effectiveness; thus, EBP is a technique of significant but limited utility (Green & Britten, 1998; The Lancet, 1995; Sackett et al., 1996).

EXAMPLE FROM CLINICAL MEDICINE

Lumbar back pain is one of the most frequent health problems in Western countries. About 5% of all low back problems are caused by prolapsed lumbar discs. The treatment is mainly nonsurgical and 90% of acute attacks of nerve root pain (sciatica) settle without surgical intervention; however, different forms of surgical treatments have been developed and disseminated. Usually these methods are considered for more rapid relief in patients whose recovery is unacceptably slow. The *Cochrane* reviewers criticize that "despite the critical importance of knowing whether surgery is beneficial for disc prolapse, only four trials have directly compared discectomy with conservative management and these give suggestive rather than conclusive results" (Gibson & Waddell, 2007, p. 1). They concluded:

> Surgical discectomy for carefully selected patients with sciatica due to lumbar disc prolapse provides faster relief from the acute attack than conservative management, although any positive or negative effects on the lifetime natural history of the underlying disc disease are still unclear. (p. 2)

Surgical treatments of low back pain hold an enormous commercial potential due to the worldwide frequency of the problem. It appears obvious that there are only a few trials comparing conservative treatment with surgery.

SPECIFIC LIMITATIONS TO EBP IN PSYCHIATRY, PSYCHOTHERAPY, AND CLINICAL PSYCHOLOGY

In psychiatry and psychotherapy, there is an ambivalent attitude toward EBP. Attempting to increase their scientific respectability, some psychiatrists and clinical psychologists zealously adopted EBP algorithms (Geddes & Harrison, 1997; Gray & Pinson, 2003; Oakley-Browne, 2001; Sharpe et al., 1996) and started *evidence-based psychiatry*. Others remain hesitant or doubtful about the usefulness of EBP in their field, and several authors have addressed different critical aspects of evidence-based psychiatry (Berk & Miles Leigh, 1999; Bilsker,

1996; Brendel, 2003; Geddes & Harrison, 1997; Goldner & Bilsker, 1995; Harari, 2001; Hotopf, Churchill, & Lewis, 1999; Lawrie, Scott, & Sharpe, 2000; Seeman, 2001; Welsby, 1999; Williams & Garner, 2002) with all of them fundamentally concerning practical and scientific particularities of psychiatry and clinical psychology. Next, we shall try to clarify these arguments.

The evidence-based approach to individual cases is critically dependent on the validity of diagnoses. This is an axiomatic assumption of EBP, which is rarely analysed or scrutinized in detail. If in a concrete case no diagnosis could be attributed, the case would not be amenable to EBP, and no evidence could support decisions in such a case. If the diagnosis is wrong, or—even more intricate—if cases labeled with a specific diagnosis are still not homogenous enough to be comparable in relevant aspects, EBP will provide useless results.

EXAMPLE FROM PSYCHIATRY

According to *DSM-IV*, eating disorders are classified in different categories: anorexia nervosa (AN), bulimia nervosa (BN), binge eating disorder (BED), and eating disorder not otherwise specified (EDNOS). These categories are clinically quite distinct and diagnostic criteria are clear and easily applicable. In spite of the phenomenological diversity of the disease patterns, there is a close relationship between the different forms of eating disorders. In clinical practice, switches between different diagnoses and temporary remissions and relapses are frequent. In the course of time, patients may change their disease pattern several times: At times they may not meet the criteria for a diagnosis anymore, although they are not completely symptom free, and later they may relapse to a full-blown eating disorder again or may be classified as having EDNOS.

Corresponding to these clinical impressions, longitudinal studies demonstrate that the stability of eating disorder diagnoses over time is low (Fichter & Quadflieg, 2007; Grilo et al., 2007; Milos, Spindler, Schnyder, & Fairburn, 2005). Based on systematic evaluation of the available evidence, however, treatment guidelines give specific recommendations for the different conditions (National Institute for Clinical Excellence [NICE], 2004). For patients with AN, psychological treatment on an outpatient basis is recommended. The treatment should be offered by "a service that is competent in giving that treatment and in assessing the physical risk of people with eating disorders" (p. 60). For patients with BN, the NICE guideline proposes as a possible first step to follow an evidence-based self-help program. As an alternative, a trial with an antidepressant drug is recommended, followed by cognitive behavior therapy for bulimia nervosa. In the absence of evidence to guide the treatment of EDNOS, the NICE guideline recommends pragmatically that "the clinician considers following the guidance on the treatment of the eating problem that most closely resembles the individual patient's eating disorder" (p. 60). So even though specific diagnoses of eating disorders are not stable and a patient with AN might be diagnosed with BN a few months later, treatment recommendations vary considerably for the two conditions. It becomes obvious that different treatment recommendations for seemingly different conditions reflect rather accidental differences in the availability of empirical evidence than real differences in the response of certain conditions to specific treatments. Hence, the guidance offered by the guideline is basically a rather unstable crutch, and of course, cognitive behavior therapy or an evidence-based self-help program might be just as beneficial in AN or in EDNOS than it is in BN, even though nobody has yet compiled the statistical evidence to prove this.

What does the *validity* of a diagnosis mean? The question concerns epistemological issues and requires a closer look to the nature of medical diagnoses with special regard to psychiatric diagnoses. R. Cooper (2004) questioned if mental disorders as defined in diagnostic manuals are *natural kinds*. In her thoughtful paper, the author concluded that diagnostic entities are in fact theoretical conceptions, describing complex cognitive, behavioral, and emotional processes (R. Cooper, 2004; Harari, 2001). Diagnostic categories are based upon observations, still they are strongly influenced by theoretical, social, and even economical factors. The ontological structure of psychiatric diagnoses is therefore not one of natural kinds. They are not something absolutely existing that can be observed independently. Rather they are comprehensive theoretical definitions serving as tools for communication and scientific observation. Kendell and Jablensky (2003) have also recently addressed the issue of diagnostic entities and concluded that the validity of psychiatric diagnoses is limited. They analysed whether diagnostic entities are sufficiently separable from each other and from normality by *zones of rarity*. They concluded that this was not the case; rather, they concluded that psychiatric diagnoses often overlap (R. Cooper, 2004; Welsby, 1999), shift over time within the same patient, and several similar diagnoses can be present in the same patient at the same time (comorbidity). Not surprisingly, diagnosis alone is a poor predictor of outcome (Williams & Garner, 2002). Acknowledging this haziness of diagnoses, one realizes these problems when trying to match individual cases to empirical evidence. When even the presence of a correctly assessed diagnosis does not assure comparability to other cases with the same diagnosis, empirical evidence about mental disorders is highly questionable (Harari, 2001). Of course, limited validity does not imply complete absence of validity, and empirical evidence on mental disorders is still useful to some extent, however, insight into the limitations is important and that insight points out that psychiatric diagnoses represent phenomenological descriptions rather than natural kinds. Several authors have treated the same issue when writing about the complexity of cases, the problem of subsyndromal cases, and of single cases versus statistical evidence (Harari, 2001; Welsby, 1999; Williams & Garner, 2002).

NONLINEAR DYNAMICS IN THE COURSE OF DISEASES

It might be fruitful to look at evidence-based psychiatry from another perspective and to address the issues of *complexity* and *nonlinear dynamics*. With regard to their physical and mental functioning, humans can be conceptualized as systems of high complexity (Luhmann, 1995). This means that they cannot be determined precisely, but only in a probabilistic manner; however, probabilistic determination is sufficient for most purposes in observable reality. Human life consists fundamentally in dealing with probabilities. Social systems and human communication are naturally designed to manage complexity more or less successfully. Medicine itself is a social system (Luhmann, 1995) trying to handle the effects of complexity (Harari, 2001), for example, by providing probabilistic algorithms for treatments of diseases. In most situations, medicine can ignore the particular effects emerging from the complex nonlinear structure of its objects, although such effects are always present. Only sometimes do these effects become obvious and irritating, as for example in fluctuations of symptoms in chronic diseases, variations in response to treatment, unexpected courses in chronic diseases, and so on. Such phenomena can be seen as manifestations of the butterfly effect (see earlier). This insight questions deeply the core principle of EBP that assumes that it is rational to treat similar cases in the same manner because similarity in the initial conditions will

predict similar outcomes under the identical treatment. The uncertainty of this assumption is particularly critical in psychiatry and psychotherapy. In these fields similar appearance is just a palliation for untraceable difference, and this exact difference may crucially influence the outcome.

Addressing such problems is daily business for psychiatrists and psychotherapists, so their disciplines have developed special approaches. Diagnostic and therapeutic procedures in these disciplines are much less focused on critical momentary decisions, but more on gradual, iterative procedures. Psychiatric treatments and even more psychotherapy are self-referencing processes, where assessments and decisions are constantly re-evaluated. Instead, EBP focuses primarily on decision making as the crucial moment of good medical practice. One gets the impression that EBM clinicians are constantly making critical decisions, and after having made the right decision, the case is solved. Maybe it is because of this misfit between the proposals of the method and real daily practice that many psychiatrists are not too attracted by EBP.

EXAMPLE FROM PSYCHIATRY

The diagnosis of posttraumatic stress disorder (PTSD) was first introduced in the third edition of the *Diagnostic and Statistical Manual of Mental Disorders (DSM-III)* in 1980. Before that time, traumatized individuals were either diagnosed with different nonspecific diagnoses (e.g., anxiety disorders, depression, neurasthenia) or not declared ill at all. Astonishingly, the newly discovered entity appeared to be a clinically distinct disorder and the corresponding symptoms (re-experiencing, avoidance, hyperarousal) were quite characteristic and easily identifiable. Within a short time after its invention (Summerfield, 2001), PTSD became a very popular disorder;

clinicians and even patients loved the new diagnosis (Andreasen, 1995). The key point for the success of the new diagnosis was that it is explicitly based on the assumption of an external etiology; that is, the traumatic experience. This conception makes PTSD so appealing for the attribution of cause, responsibility, and guilt is neatly separated from the affected individual. PTSD allows for the exculpation of the victim, a feature that was particularly important when caring for Holocaust survivors and Vietnam War veterans. But what was almost proscribed for some time after the introduction of PTSD is now evidence-based: Preexisting individual factors play an important role in the shaping of posttraumatic response. Whether or not an individual develops PTSD after a traumatic experience is not only determined by the nature and the intensity of the traumatic impact, but also by various pretraumatic characteristics of the affected individual. Furthermore, PTSD is not the only posttraumatic mental disorder. A whole spectrum of mental disorders is closely linked to traumatic experiences, although they lack the monocausal appearance of PTSD. Anyway, the most frequent outcome after traumatic experiences is recovery. In the second rank of frequency comes major depression. Borderline personality disorder is fully recognized now as a disorder provoked by traumatic experiences in early childhood. Dissociative disorders, chronic somatoform pain, anxiety disorders, substance abuse, and eating disorders are equally related to traumatic experiences. Not surprisingly, PTSD is often occurring as a comorbid condition with one or more additional disorder or vice versa. In clinical practice, traumatized patients usually present more complex than expected. This may explain to some extent why PTSD was virtually overlooked by clinicians for many decades before its introduction, a fact that is sometimes hard to understand by younger

therapists who are so familiar with the PTSD diagnosis. At any rate, the high-functioning, intelligent, monomorbid PTSD patient is indeed best evaluated in clinical trials, but rarely seen in everyday practice.

PTSD was right in the focus of research since its introduction. Also from a scientific point of view, the disorder is appealing because it is provoked by an external event. PTSD allows ideally for the investigation of the human-environment interaction, which is a crucial issue for psychiatry and psychology in general. The number of trials on diagnosis and treatment of PTSD is huge, and the disorder is now probably the best evaluated mental disorder. What is the benefit of the accumulated large body of evidence on PTSD for clinicians? There are several soundly elaborated guidelines on the treatment of PTSD (American Psychiatric Association, 2004; Australian Centre for Posttraumatic Mental Health, 2007; NICE, 2005), meta-analyses, and Cochrane Reviews providing guidance for the assessment and treatment of the disorder. When we look at the existing conclusions and recommendations, we learn that:

- Debriefing is not recommended as routine practice for individuals who have experienced a traumatic event.
- When symptoms are mild and have been present for less than 4 weeks after the trauma, watchful waiting should be considered.
- Trauma-focused cognitive behavior therapy on an individual outpatient basis should be offered to people with severe posttraumatic symptoms.
- Eye movement desensitization and reprocessing is an alternative treatment option.
- Drug treatment should not be used as a routine first-line treatment in preference to a trauma-focused psychological therapy.
- Drug treatment (Specific Serotonin Reuptake Inhibitors) should be considered

for the treatment of PTSD in adults who express a preference not to engage in trauma-focused psychological treatment.

- In the context of comorbid PTSD and depression, PTSD should be treated first.
- In the context of comorbid PTSD and substance abuse, both conditions should be treated simultaneously.

These recommendations are obviously clear, useful, and practical. They give real guidance to therapists and do not leave much room for doubts or insecurity. On the other hand, they are basically very simple, almost trivial. For trauma therapists, these recommendations are commonplace and serve mainly to endorse what they are practicing anyway. The main points of the guidelines for the treatment of PTSD could be taught in a 1-hour workshop. The key messages of the guidelines represent basic clinical knowledge on a specific disorder as it has been instructed in times before EBP. Through their standardizing impact on the therapeutic community, guidelines may in fact align and improve the general service quality offered to traumatized individuals, although this effect has not yet been demonstrated by empirical evidence.

The treatment of an individual patient remains a unique endeavor where interpersonal relationship, flexibility, openness, and cleverness are crucial factors. This challenge is not lessened by evidence or guidelines.

REFERENCES

American Psychiatric Association. (2004). *APA practice guidelines. Treatment of patients with acute stress disorder and posttraumatic stress disorder.* doi: 10.1176/appi.books.9780890423363.52257

Andreasen, N. C. (1995). Posttraumatic stress disorder: Psychology, biology, and the Manichaean warfare between false dichotomies. *American Journal of Psychiatry, 152,* 963–965.

Australian Centre for Posttraumatic Mental Health. (2007). *Australian guidelines for the treatment of adults with acute stress disorder and posttraumatic stress disorder.* Melbourne, Victoria.

Berk, M., & Miles Leigh, J. (1999). Evidence-based psychiatric practice: Doctrine or trap? *Journal of Evaluation in Clinical Practice, 5,* 149–152.

Bilsker, D. (1996). From evidence to conclusions in psychiatric research. *Canadian Journal of Psychiatry, 41,* 227–232.

Brendel, D. H. (2003). Reductionism, eclecticism, and pragmatism in psychiatry: The dialectic of clinical explanation. *Journal of Medicine and Philosophy, 28,* 563–580.

Cochrane, A. L. (1972). *Effectiveness and efficiency: Random reflections on health services.* London, England: Nuffield Provincial Hospitals Trust.

Cooper, B. (2003). Evidence-based mental health policy: A critical appraisal. *British Journal of Psychiatry, 183,* 105–113.

Cooper, R. (2004). What is wrong with the DSM? *History of Psychiatry, 15,* 5–25.

Fichter, M. M., & Quadflieg, N. (2007). Long-term stability of eating disorder diagnoses. *International Journal of Eating Disorders, 40*(Suppl.), 61–66.

Geddes, J. R., Game, D., Jenkins, N. E., Peterson, L. A., Pottinger, G. R., & Sackett, D. L. (1996). What proportion of primary psychiatric interventions are based on evidence from randomised controlled trials? *Quality in Health Care, 5,* 215–217.

Geddes, J. R., & Harrison, P. J. (1997). Closing the gap between research and practice. *British Journal of Psychiatry, 171,* 220–225.

Ghali, W., Saitz, R., Sargious, P. M., & Hershman, W. Y. (1999). Evidence-based medicine and the real world: Understanding the controversy. *Journal of Evaluation in Clinical Practice, 5,* 133–138.

Gibson, J. N. A., & Waddell, G. (2007). Surgical interventions for lumbar disc prolapse. *Cochrane Database of Systematic Reviews, Issue 1.* Art. No.: CD001350. doi: 10.1002/14651858.CD001350.pub4

Goldner, E. M., & Bilsker, D. (1995). Evidence-based psychiatry. *Canadian Journal of Psychiatry, 40,* 97–101.

Gray, G. E., & Pinson, L. A. (2003). Evidence-based medicine and psychiatric practice. *Psychiatric Quarterly, 74,* 387–399.

Green, J., & Britten, N. (1998). Qualitative research and evidence based medicine. *British Medical Journal, 316,* 1230–1232.

Grilo, C. M., Pagano, M. E., Skodol, A. E., Stanislow, C. A., McGlashan, T. H., Gunderson, J. G., & Stout, R. L. (2007). Natural course of bulimia nervosa and of eating disorder not otherwise specified: Five-year prospective study of remissions, relapses and the effects of personality disorder psychopathology. *Journal of Clinical Psychiatry, 68,* 738–746.

Harari, E. (2001). Whose evidence? Lessons from the philosophy of science and the epistemology of medicine. *Australian and New Zealand Journal of Psychiatry, 35,* 724–730.

Hotopf, M., Churchill, R., & Lewis, G. (1999). Pragmatic randomised controlled trials in psychiatry. *British Journal of Psychiatry, 175,* 217–223.

Kendell, R., & Jablensky, A. (2003). Distinguishing between the validity and utility of psychiatric diagnoses. *American Journal of Psychiatry, 160,* 4–12.

Kuhn, T. (1962). *The structure of scientific revolutions.* Chicago, IL: University of Chicago.

The Lancet. (1995). Evidence based medicine, in its place [Editorial]. *Elsevier Science, 346,* 785.

Lawrie, S. M., Scott, A. I., & Sharpe, M. C. (2000). Evidence based psychiatry—Do psychiatrists want it and can they do it? *Health Bulletin, 58,* 25–33.

Luhmann, N. (1995). *Social Systems.* Stanford, CA: Stanford University Press.

Miettinen, O. S. (1999). Ideas and ideals in medicine: Fruits of reason or props of power? *Journal of Evaluation in Clinical Practice, 5,* 107–116.

Miles, A., Bentley, P., Polychronis, A., Grey, J., & Price, N. (1999). Advancing the evidence based healthcare debate. *Journal of Evaluation in Clinical Practice, 5,* 97–101.

Milos, G., Spindler, A., Schnyder, U., & Fairburn, C. G. (2005). Instability of eating disorder diagnoses: A prospective study. *British Journal of Psychiatry, 187,* 573–578.

National Institute for Clinical Excellence (NICE) (2004). *Eating disorders: Core interventions in the treatment and management of anorexia nervosa, bulimia nervosa, and related eating disorders. National clinical practical guideline number CG9.* London, England: The British Psychological Society and Gaskell.

National Institute for Clinical Excellence (NICE) (2005). *Posttraumatic stress disorder (PTSD): The management of PTSD in adults and children in primary and secondary care. Clinical guideline 26.* Retrieved from www.nice.org.uk/CG026NICEguideline

Norman, G. R. (1999). Examining the assumptions of evidence-based medicine. *Journal of Evaluation in Clinical Practice, 5,* 139–147.

Oakley-Browne, M. A. (2001). EBM in practice: Psychiatry. *Medical Journal of Australia, 174,* 403–404.

Parsonnet, J. (2005). Clinician-discoverers—Marshall, Warren, and H. pylori. *New England Journal of Medicine, 353,* 2421–2423.

Rangachari, P. K. (1997). Evidence-based medicine: Old French wine with a new Canadian label? *Journal of the Royal Society of Medicine, 90,* 280–284.

Rovers, M. M., Glasziou, P., Appelman, C. L., Burke, P., McCormick, D. P., Damoiseaux, R. A., . . . Hoes, A. W. (2006). Antibiotics for acute otitis media: A meta-analysis with individual patient data. *The Lancet, 368,* 1429–1435.

Sackett, D. L., Rosenberg, W. M. C., Muir Gray, J. A., Haynes, R., & Richardson, W. S. (1996). Evidence based medicine: What it is and what it isn't. *British Medical Journal, 312,* 71–72.

Seeman, M. V. (2001). Clinical trials in psychiatry: Do results apply to practice? *Canadian Journal of Psychiatry, 46,* 352–355.

Sharpe, M., Gill, D., Strain, J., & Mayou, R. (1996). Psychosomatic medicine and evidence based treatment. *Journal of Psychosomatic Research, 41,* 101–107.

Sleigh, J. W. (1995). Evidence based medicine and Kurt Godel: Letter to the editor. *The Lancet, 346,* 1172.

Strong, M., & Johnstone, P. W. (2007). Interventions for treating scabies. *Cochrane Database of Systematic Reviews, Issue 3.* Art. No.: CD000320. doi: 10.1002/14651858.CD000320.pub2

Summerfield, D. (2001). The invention of post-traumatic stress disorder and the social usefulness of a psychiatric category. *British Medical Journal, 322,* 95–98.

Welsby, P. D. (1999). Reductionism in medicine: Some thoughts on medical education from the clinical front line. *Journal of Evaluation in Clinical Practice, 5,* 125–131.

Williams, D. D. R., & Garner, J. (2002). The case against "the evidence": A different perspective on evidence-based medicine. *British Journal of Psychiatry, 180,* 8–12.

5

Economics of Evidence-Based Practice and Mental Health

MARTIN KNAPP AND DAVID MCDAID

WHY ECONOMICS?

The primary concerns of anyone working in a mental health system are alleviation of symptoms, promotion of quality of life, support of family caregivers, and improvement of broad life chances. These should also be the primary concerns of those people with responsibility for the allocation of resources, whether it is deciding how many resources can be made available for part or the whole of the system, how they are shared between competing uses, or how to improve efficiency and fairness in their use. The common threads running through these concerns are that: (a) resources are scarce relative to the demands for them, and also scarce relative to the needs of the population, (b) therefore, careful choices have to be made about how to utilize them, and (c) the criteria employed in making those choices should be linked in some way to the aim of the system, which is to improve health and quality of life. Economics is essentially the study of these common threads. It is concerned with how resources are generated and utilized, how decisions are made about how to make use of those resources, and what criteria might be employed to inform those choices.

This chapter is structured around these three issues. First, we look at how resources are generated for a mental health system – how mental health treatment and support are financed. Before we turn to the processes of how decisions are made to allocate those resources between different, competing uses, it is helpful to consider the criteria that are used to inform such decisions, particularly efficiency and equity. We then look at the tool most commonly associated with economic analysis in the mental health field: cost effectiveness analysis. We then offer a brief introduction to the methods and a few examples of their application in studies of psychological therapies for people with mental health problems. Building on this, we then return to the decision making process in a mental health system and how this can be supported by economics evidence. A brief concluding section brings the chapter to a close.

FINANCING MENTAL HEALTH SERVICES

How is mental health care financed? How are the funds generated that are needed to invest in buildings to house clinics, hire skilled staff, or purchase equipment and medications?

Market Failure

To answer these questions, it is helpful to contrast mental health services with groceries. Individuals needing food use their own income to purchase groceries. The store owner purchases stocks of groceries from a wholesaler, and then through various links in the economic chain the funds reach the farmers who grow the ingredients. At each stage, the purchaser has the freedom to decide whether or not to make the purchase, primarily based on their assessment of product quality and price. If the quality is insufficient to justify the price, then they will go elsewhere until they find a product that is worth buying. In this way, the simple workings of a market economy, what the philosopher and economist Adam Smith, writing at the time of the American Revolution, referred to as the "invisible hand" (Smith, 1776/1977), generally function well enough to allocate grocery products to people who need or want them. Of course, there can be glitches. Many consumers might be dissatisfied with the quality of their purchases as price does not always act as a good proxy for quality; some people are too poor to be able to afford to buy the groceries they need, others are so wealthy they may not be bothered about the prices they pay, while some funding chains are so protracted or distorted that the farmers who grow the raw materials do not receive sufficient recompense. But the solutions to these glitches generally lie in some adjustments to market forces.

Mental health services differ from groceries in many ways, of course. They are much more complex products: It is relatively straightforward for a consumer to ascertain the quality of groceries, but it is much harder for a mental health service user to judge the quality of their treatment. Indeed, more fundamentally, while an individual usually has a fairly clear idea of the groceries they need, the individual with mental health needs will often have no idea

what treatments are available, nor will they know generally which are most likely to meet their needs. The stigma and prejudice that continues to surround mental health services may also mean that some consumers are unwilling to be seen purchasing products that best meet their needs for fear of being identified as having mental health problems.

Moreover, the risks of severe adverse effects through the consumption of poor quality products are generally much greater for mental health services than for groceries. To complicate matters further, those needs are not necessarily predictable: They can arise unexpectedly and irregularly, unlike the need for groceries. Another key difference is that a course of mental health treatment can be expensive and many people with mental health needs, especially those that are enduring, cannot afford to pay for the treatment they need from their own income, unless their mental health insurance covers all the costs of the services.

For all of these reasons, it is widely recognized that a mental health system cannot sensibly be constructed along simple market lines. Not only are mental health services quite complex products, but most people who need or use them are not experienced consumers and thus cannot easily decide what is good or bad, suitable or unsuitable. Needs are uncertain and the costs of meeting them can be extremely high. This is why most high- and middle-income countries rely on prepayment systems to generate the revenue to pay for mental health services (World Health Organization, 2005).

Prepayment Systems

Prepayment is organized through tax contributions, social insurance or private insurance, more accurately labeled voluntary insurance. Prepayment is widely held to be preferable to out-of-pocket payments as the main way to finance health care since an individual's risk of needing health care is very uncertain, but when the need arises the attendant costs of treatment and losses of earnings could be very high or even catastrophic. Prepayment contributions pool risks: The pooling mechanism collectively brings together all prepayments made by or on behalf of all individuals in society or signed up by an insurer. In all tax-based systems (and most social health insurance systems), the level of contributions is not influenced by an individual's preexisting health status or age. Thus, prepayment also has the potential to redistribute benefits toward people with greater health needs. If contribution rates increase according to ability to pay, as observed in many tax-based systems, then these arrangements can also be described as progressive, in the sense that poorer individuals pay less for equivalent health care than richer people. Out-of-pocket payment systems cannot achieve such pooling of risk or targeting on either needs or income groups unless they are accompanied by very carefully designed systems of payment exemptions that are closely monitored to ensure implementation and prevent abuse. For instance, the public purse may often cover co-payments for people registered as unemployed, as well as for individuals whose incomes, when means tested, are found to be below a specified income threshold. Without such adjustments, utilization of services by those with low incomes is unlikely to be below their need for services (Tamblyn et al., 2001).

Prepayment systems have their problems. If there is no charge at the point at which a service is used, then an individual may have a perverse incentive to use more of a service than he or she actually needs—something that health economists would refer to as a moral hazard. This might be countered by introducing co-payments at point of use. Another potential difficulty is adverse selection. High-risk individuals are denied coverage or face unaffordable premiums. Additionally, in attempts to cap expenditures, some insurance or managed care arrangements exclude mental health coverage, with predictable consequences for access, knock-on costs (such as the costs of poor

physical health problems that might have been avoided through earlier consultation or the impact of lost employment), and societal inefficiencies and inequity. Legal intervention, regulation, or subsidy may be needed as countermeasures, or universal coverage guaranteed by public financing through taxation or social insurance to provide a safety net.

The most common method of financing is tax-based (60%), followed by social insurance (19%), out-of-pocket payments (16%), external grants (3%), and voluntary insurance (2%) (Saxena, Sharan, & Saraceno, 2003). As far as mental health systems are concerned, almost every high- and middle-income country has a mix of public funding through taxation or social insurance, complemented by private funding through out-of-pocket payments and voluntary private insurance. In contrast, whatever the merits of prepayment systems, there are obstacles to their wider use in low-income countries, including the state of the economy, the lack of administrative infrastructure to collect taxes, and the informality of much employment. Consequently, out-of-pocket payments, sometimes supplemented by foreign donor aid, dominate funding structures in many of these countries (Dixon, McDaid, Knapp, & Curran, 2006).

Tax-Based Financing

Many health, education, and other systems are funded from national, regional, or local taxes. Income tax can be structured to capture progressively larger income shares from wealthier individuals. Indirect taxes such as sales tax tend to be regressive, as poorer individuals often contribute larger proportions of their incomes. Income tax-based systems of health financing are seen as the most progressive and equitable (Mossialos, Dixon, Figueras, & Kutzin, 2002). Payments are mandatory, and scale economies can be achieved in administration, risk management, and purchasing power (Savedoff, 2004). For those who advocate health as a right, taxation-based health systems fit the bill, while those with libertarian or conservative leanings tend to view such arrangements as an erosion of personal responsibilities and freedom.

Tax-based systems have limitations. Health-care funding levels often fluctuate with the state of the national economy: When an economy is not doing well, there may be a tendency to freeze or cut back on publicly funded programs, particularly in the area of mental health (Frank & Glied, 2006; Kavanagh & Knapp, 1995). Competing political and economic objectives also make a tax-based system less transparent, and bureaucracy can add to the inefficiency, reflected perhaps in long waiting lists, although these may also reflect underfunding. Patients tend to view tax-based systems as offering them less choice although, of course, uninsured individuals in a country with an alternative financing system might argue that they face no choice whatsoever.

The U.S. health system is obviously a mixture of public and private finance, with the tax-based part organized at the state level but delivered primarily through nongovernment providers. Medicaid supports low-income individuals, financed jointly by the federal government and the states, and covering a substantial proportion of all mental health expenditure across the country, while Medicare covers these needs for those over the age of 65, although in the case of the latter there are much higher co-payments for mental health compared with physical health needs (Frank & Glied, 2006). In addition to some very basic services provided in the emergency rooms and county hospitals, publicly funded mental health care in the U.S. is mostly delivered through privately owned/managed health maintenance organizations, preferred provider organizations, or physicians in private practice. An example of a contrasting system is the Swedish health-care system, which is tax-funded, with predominantly regionally organized financing and administration, and relies on provision through public rather than private institutions.

Social Health Insurance

Social health insurance schemes generate most of their revenues from salary-based contributions often administered and managed by quasi-public bodies. They are sometimes called sickness funds. Enrollment is usually mandatory, and premiums are usually risk-adjusted and allow for redistribution according to need. Employers also make contributions, and transfers are made from general taxation to sickness funds to provide cover for the unemployed, the retired, and other disadvantaged or vulnerable people. This is clearly pertinent for people with mental health problems.

Social insurance schemes sometimes do not provide cover for all psychiatric care services; in some cases these may be funded through general taxation, as is the case for some long-term care services in France and the Netherlands. In other cases, entitlement to services funded within the health system may be limited and arguably inequitable. This is particularly the case as services are shifted out of health to sectors such as social care, employment, and housing where entitlements to service may not be universal and often subject to means-testing, potentially hindering access to services (McDaid, Oliveira, Jurczak, Knapp, & the MHEEN Group, 2007). In Austria, for example, social health insurance excludes most mental health disorders on the grounds that they are chronic rather than curable, and as much as one third of social care expenditure for mental health is realized through private out-of-pocket payments (Zechmeister & Oesterle, 2006).

Voluntary Health Insurance

Voluntary health insurance (VHI)—sometimes called private health insurance—is taken up and paid for at the discretion of individuals or employers on behalf of individuals and offered by public, quasi-public, for-profit, or non-profit organizations. In some high-income countries, such as Germany or Spain, it can act as a substitute for statutory protection, while in others, such as France or Ireland, it provides supplemental coverage and can cover the costs of some out-of-pocket costs.

In the United States, more than 54% of total health-care expenditure was private in 2006. Two thirds of this expenditure was due to VHI (Organisation for Economic Co-operation and Development, 2008); however, treatment of chronic conditions, such as many mental health problems, have historically been squeezed out. Although the level of coverage across different states varies significantly, with 36 states having parity legislation in place by the end of 2005, at the federal level the Mental Health Parity Act of 1996 still allowed insurers to limit access to mental health either by narrowing their definition of what constituted mental health services or by substituting utilization limits for dollar limits (Glied & Frank, 2008). Around 80% of individuals with private, employer-sponsored health insurance had in- or outpatient visit limits on their coverage; 23% did not meet the benchmark level of 30 inpatient days, 20 outpatient visits, and prescription drug coverage, while another 3% had no mental health benefits at all (U.S. Surgeon General, 2006).

People individually purchasing insurance have low bargaining power, which affects the benefits that are covered. As we have just seen, inherent also in this financing system are disadvantages like adverse selection and the practice of *cream skimming* in which higher risk groups, such as those with long-term mental health problems, may find insurance unaffordable, especially as mental health problems are more prevalent among lower income groups; however, the Wellstone and Domenici Mental Health Parity and Addiction Equity Act signed into law by President Bush in October 2008 should, when implemented in late 2009, help to eliminate most of the loopholes found in the 1996 Mental Health Parity Act (Congress of the United States of America, 2008). It stated that health plans covering 50 or more employees have financial requirements and treatment limitations for mental health and

substance use disorder benefits that are no more restrictive than those placed on medical and surgical benefits. This equity in coverage applies to all financial requirements, including deductibles, co-payments, coinsurance, and out-of-pocket expenses, and to all treatment limitations, including frequency of treatment, number of visits, days of coverage, or other similar limits. The law protects state mental health parity laws, including state coverage mandates, provided they are stronger than federal law and do not interfere with it.

Out-of-Pocket Payments

In prepayment systems, out-of-pocket payments may be co-payments (specific amount to be paid), coinsurance (agreed percentage of expenses) or deductibles (agreed amount to be paid before insurance kicks in). Though the objectives for introducing out-of-pocket payments differ, the impact remains common everywhere in adversely affecting access and equity. Out-of-pocket payments are justified on the economic rationale that they discourage unnecessary service use and create price sensitivity that might help direct patients to more cost-effective and appropriate treatments; however, in the long run they might defeat the very purpose of cost efficiency, as delayed treatments might substantially increase ultimate costs. About half of all western European countries levy some out-of-pocket charges for specialist mental health services within their publicly funded health systems (Knapp & McDaid, 2007), while they are even more prevalent in parts of central and eastern Europe (Zaluska, Suchecka, Traczewska, & Paszko, 2005), and are often the only means of health finance in low income countries (Dixon et al., 2006).

The share of total funding coming from out-of-pocket payments for a privately insured adult with a mental health problem in the United States varied between 35% and 40% of all mental health expenditures over the decade to 2005. This can be contrasted with out-of-pocket payments by those with private insurance for physical health problems that were below 30% in 2005 (Glied & Frank, 2008). The higher burden of out-of-pocket payments remains for many families a regressive practice that discourages the use of both essential and nonessential services. Given the stigma associated with mental health problems, their chronicity, and the damage they can reap, including on an individual's ability to obtain and retain paid employment, heavy reliance on out-of-pocket funds is inadvisable. The new U.S. mental health parity legislation discussed earlier may help reduce the need for such out-of-pocket payments.

EFFICIENCY AND EQUITY

No matter how the financial resources are generated for a mental health system, there will never be enough to meet all mental health needs, whether those are the expressed or diagnosed needs of people already in contact with the system, or the underlying and partly unrecognized needs of the population. In the face of such scarcity, choices must be made about how to make best use of those resources. For example, should there be greater investment in the training and deployment of clinical psychologists or a bigger budget for medications? If there are more people needing to see clinical or other specialist staff than there are treatment sessions available, who should get priority? What proportion of a mental health budget should be diverted away from treating identified needs in order to instead uncover previously unrecognized needs? What investment should be made to support a broader health promotion strategy seeking to prevent some mental health problems from emerging in the first place? When does it make sense to stop or reduce the frequency of therapy to one particular patient and to use the time to initiate a treatment program for someone who has been newly referred? Should treatment be provided in groups, which are sometimes

suboptimal for individual patients, or should everyone be treated individually, even through sometimes only a minority of patients accrue additional symptom reduction through more expensive individual treatment?

None of these is first and foremost an economic question, but each stems from the inherent scarcity of resources relative to needs. More importantly, each generates questions about what resources get used and with what impacts in terms of what needs are prevented, identified, treated, and met. And those latter questions certainly are economic: They concern the relationship between the resources used, the services or support arrangements provided, and the outcomes achieved for individuals, families and society.

Consequently, decision makers—from those who control large, central budgets to those who actually deliver the services to patients—need to be clear about the basis upon which they choose one option over another. In a world that is increasingly seeking evidence-based approaches to policy and practice, while recognizing resource scarcity, a number of resource-related criteria are likely to be invoked to guide such decisions. These might include maximizing the therapeutic impact from available resources, integrating more people with long-term mental health problems into mainstream community life, broadening and equalizing access to effective therapies, improving fairness in the amount that individuals are required to pay for their treatment, and improving the targeting of available services on needs. These resource-related criteria can be summarized under two broad headings: efficiency and equity.

Efficiency

Efficiency means achieving the maximum effects in terms of services delivered or outcomes achieved such as needs met, symptoms alleviated, or quality of life improved, from a specified volume of resources such as an available budget or a fixed number of therapy sessions per week. Many factors might prevent a mental health system from achieving full efficiency (Knapp et al., 2006). It may be that too many resources are used up in the administration of the system itself. For example, are there too many managers supervising the frontline staff who actually deliver treatment? Another source of inefficiency could be that resources are used in inappropriate combinations of resources. For example, a clinical psychology service is likely to be more efficient if it has access to a range of therapies delivered by a team of therapists, perhaps with simple, routine, effective interventions (such as relaxation groups) supplied by cheaper staff, and more complex work (such as case formulation and difficult-to-treat problems) supplied by more expensive staff. Support from other professions such as social work would be expected to improve efficiency, as would a good administrative structure that allocates routine administrative tasks to cheaper staff. Alternatively, it could be that resources are poorly targeted if: (a) they are not provided to the people who need them or could benefit from them most, either because insufficient efforts are made to identify and prioritize needs, or to encourage individuals to come forward for treatment; or (b) because of the use of ineffective or suboptimal interventions when effective alternatives are available. The fragmented nature of many mental health systems, with multiple sources of funding and multiple service delivery mechanisms both within health care and across other sectors such as social care, can also contribute to inefficiencies if insufficient attention is paid to coordination and cooperation. This is particularly important given that as the balance of care shifts to the provision of more services, including the provision of psychological treatments, for individuals living in the community it might be expected that an appropriate level of resources would also shift to those budget holders responsible for community based services; however, intra agency rivalries, administrative bureaucracy, and a desire to protect existing budgets may mean that

resources do not always follow service users along the continuum of care.

Inefficiency might also simply be due to key decision makers having little or no understanding of the relative costs and effectiveness of treatment options. This is where cost-effectiveness analyses can contribute so valuably (see later in the chapter).

Equity

Equity relates to the fairness of the distribution of outcomes, access, and payments across individuals or parts of a society. Most mental health systems are inequitable: They do not distribute these benefits and burdens fairly, but instead— wittingly or unwittingly— allow social, economic, or underlying demographic characteristics to have an influence. Hence, access to, payment for, or impact of evidence-based treatments are unfairly distributed by gender, ethnicity, age, language, religion, income, socioeconomic group, or place of residence.

The challenge when discussing a criterion such as equity is in deciding what is meant by *fairly*. It would be seen by most people as unfair if everyone in the population had exactly the same amount of support or treatment from the mental health system because many people have no need for such support, while a few people have very considerable needs. Equity is therefore generally not the same as equal provision of services. An equitable allocation of mental health resources would usually mean giving more of those resources to people with greater needs, or ensuring that those with the least ability to pay for their treatment are charged lower amounts than those with higher incomes. The two most commonly discussed aspects of equity are: (1) whether individual financial contributions are linked to ability to pay and whether there should be a redistributive effort so that low income individuals contribute proportionately lower amounts, and (2) whether access to evidence based treatment is linked to type and level of need.

We have already highlighted how funding mechanisms can impact ability to access mental health-care services. One recent study reported that financial barriers, particularly for those on low incomes, were much more likely to limit utilization of mental health services in the United States compared with the situation in Ontario, Canada, and The Netherlands, where there are fewer copayments required for access to services (Sareen et al., 2007); however, even in systems where there are no financial barriers to service use, the majority of those with mental disorders do not come into contact with mental health services, let alone use evidence-based psychotherapeutic interventions. For instance, data from the World Mental Health Survey suggested that overall only around one third of those who could benefit from treatment for anxiety, mood, and substance abuse disorders use services (Wang et al., 2007).

Why do individuals with mental health needs not utilize services? In addition to financial barriers, one enduring reason for a lack of contact with services is the stigma widely associated with mental illness (Schomerus & Angermeyer, 2008). Individuals may be fearful of discrimination if they are labeled as having a mental health problem (Corrigan & Wassel, 2008). They may also incorrectly believe that they are unlikely to be treated effectively and/or that the problem may clear up on its own (Sareen et al., 2007).

Another factor is the low rate of needs identification. Rates of contact with mental health professionals differ by mental health problem. They are highest for severe psychotic conditions, such as schizophrenia, but much lower for conditions perceived to be less serious, such as depression (Wittchen & Jacobi, 2005). This might, in part, reflect a concentration of resources on the most visible mental health problems where individuals are more likely to become known to the mental health system.

Racial and ethnic differences also lead to differences in rates and patterns of treatment in mental health services. Minority groups have less access to appropriate high-quality care, yet are often at higher risk of a severe mental disorder (Chow, Jaffee, & Snowden, 2003; Fearon et al., 2006; McGuire & Miranda, 2008; McKenzie & Bhui, 2007; Tapsell & Mellsop, 2007; U.S. Surgeon General, 2001).

Rates of service utilization remain low and patterns of access are unevenly distributed. Many factors contribute to inequality and numerous solutions have been propounded, including actions to improve public awareness and reduce discrimination, redistributive financing arrangements that are less disadvantageous to poor families, and so on.

Of course, services can only be utilized if they exist and/or are eligible for reimbursement. The extent to which different mental health systems provide clinical psychology services varies considerably. Across the United Kingdom, for example, although there is recognition in policy documents that people with enduring mental health problems should have access to specialist clinical psychological services within the National Health Service (NHS), the number of psychologists, particularly those working in psychological rehabilitation, has been limited. In some parts of the United Kingdom, shortages in clinical psychology services have been even more acute, with staffing levels just 20% of those found elsewhere in the United Kingdom (Department of Health, Social Services and Public Safety, 2003). In England, the Improving Access to Psychological Therapies (IAPT) initiative was piloted in 2006 and launched nationally in 2007 to substantially expand the availability of such services (see later in the chapter).

Reimbursement policies also impact the availability and utilization of psychological therapies. In the United States, it has been reported that over a 10-year period the number of visits to office-based psychiatric practices that involved psychotherapy decreased from 44% to 29%. This decrease has been attributed in part to a shift to insurance reimbursement policies that favor short medication visits compared to fewer longer psychotherapy sessions. Thus, practices have a financial incentive to spend more of their practice time on brief medication management visits as reimbursement for one 45- to 50-minute outpatient psychotherapy session is 41% lower than reimbursement for three 15-minute medication management visits (Mojtabai & Olfson, 2008).

As we shall discuss in the next section, evidence from economic evaluation can be used as one input to decide whether or not to invest in evidence-based clinical psychology services. Concerns about equity also suggest that when assessing the cost-effectiveness of different interventions, including psychological services, it is important not simply to think about what mix of interventions deliver the greatest mental health gains within a given budget—the efficiency criterion—but also to take into account the level of mental health inequalities in specific high-risk population subgroups. This might include consideration of the cost-effectiveness of different strategies to engage with these populations and encourage appropriate utilization of services.

COST-EFFECTIVENESS ANALYSIS

Decision makers are looking for answers to two questions when considering whether to recommend, license, purchase, or use a particular mental health intervention. The first is the question "Does it work?" or "Is the intervention effective in alleviating behavioral, emotional, or other symptoms and generally improving health-related quality of life?" If the answer to this effectiveness question is "yes," then there is a second question "Is it worth it?" That is, does the intervention achieve the improved outcomes at a cost that is worth paying? This is the cost-effectiveness question. The meaning of the word *worth* in this second question is not necessarily straightforward, as we shall discuss in a moment. One reason why it is not straightforward is because the question must be set in context. We need to ask whether the intervention is worth it—not in

some absolute sense—but in comparison with what might otherwise have been done. These two questions define an economic evaluation, and the previous paragraphs set out the main ingredients: (a) two or more treatments or interventions or policies that are being compared, including do nothing or watchful waiting; (b) the outcomes of each of them, measured, for instance, in terms of changes in symptoms and quality of life over time; and (c) the associated costs of each, measured in terms of health system resources used to deliver the interventions, and perhaps also some measure of the wider resource implications (see later in the chapter). An evaluation that has all of these ingredients—two or more options compared in terms of their outcomes and costs—can provide decision makers with relevant insights into efficiency and, in some respects, also equity. An analysis that misses one or more of these ingredients, for example, one that looks only at comparative outcomes and ignores costs, or stacks up the costs of different policy options without assessing the outcome implications, could still be useful, but it cannot provide evidence on efficiency, and only a partial perspective on equity.

Economic evaluations come in different forms, but they have a lot in common. For instance, they tend to share a common approach to the conceptualization, definition, and measurement of costs. The pertinent differences between the types of economic evaluation relate to how they define and assess outcomes, and this is primarily because they seek to answer slightly different questions. We can describe these different evaluative approaches by discussing, first, the questions that a cost-effectiveness study might address, and, second, looking at the measurement of costs and outcomes, and how trade-offs are made between them. Two further subsections examine the slightly more technical issues of utility and benefit measurement, both of which are becoming increasingly relevant, not just in how health economic evaluations are conducted, but in how decision makers utilize the evidence that is generated.

Question and Perspective

If the question to be addressed by an economic evaluation is about improving health—what is the most appropriate treatment for someone with particular mental health needs in particular circumstances—information will be needed on the comparative costs of the different treatments available, including the no-treatment option, and the comparative outcomes measured in terms of symptom alleviation, improved functioning and quality of life, and so on. A cost-effectiveness analysis would then be an appropriate type of economic evaluation (see the subsection on *Effectiveness Measurement* further on). Labels attached to different types of economic evaluation are not always consistently used, but the term *cost-effectiveness* is the most widely used, generic term in the health field and the description of an analysis that looks at mental health-specific measures of well-being.

But the question might be broader. It may be that the decision maker has to choose whether to treat more people with depression rather than spending the funds elsewhere in the health system, say in cardiology or oncology. In these circumstances, decision makers need to know the costs of the different options, but they also now need some measure of outcome that allows them to compare the impact of depression treatment with breast cancer treatment. For this comparison they need a common metric that has validity across different health domains. The most common such metric is *utility* and a cost-utility analysis would be undertaken, as we explain in the later subsection on *Utility Measurement*.

An even wider decision-making perspective would be to ask whether it is better to increase expenditure in the health system to allow more ill people to be treated or whether to spend more money on improving school education or to invest in a country's transport infrastructure. In this case, an evaluation again needs to ask about the comparative costs and impacts of the different options, but now it needs to make sure that the definition and measurement of impact are relevant across all of these public policy areas. The usual choice for such a broad impact measure is money, leading to a form of evaluation that health economists call cost-benefit analysis. We come back to what this means in practice in the *Benefit Measurement*.

Thus, the question to be addressed influences the type of evaluation needed. But these choices are not mutually exclusive when deciding what kind of economic evaluation to carry out: A single study can support more than one approach if the right measures are used.

Linked to specification of the question that an evaluation has to address is the perspective adopted by the study. To give one example, is the evaluation needed to help resource allocation within a particular agency, such as a primary care clinic, or a particular system, such as the health-care system, across different government sectors, and hence looking at the impact on public expenditure, or across the whole of society? The perspective needed for a study will obviously determine the breadth of both cost and outcome measurement, as we shall illustrate later in the chapter.

Costs

Some costs are directly associated with a disorder or its treatment, such as the money spent on medications and other health services. Other costs are indirect, such as lost productivity because of ill health or family cost of unpaid care. How broadly the costs are measured will depend upon the purpose and perspective of the study.

An example can be given. Figure 5.1 summarizes data from a study of children with persistent antisocial behavior in London prior to their participation in a trial of parenting groups (Scott, Spender, Doolan, Jacobs, & Aspland, 2001b). The economic study found that only 5% of the total cost associated with supporting these children was carried by the health service. The remainder fell to (a) schools, especially special education; (b) social

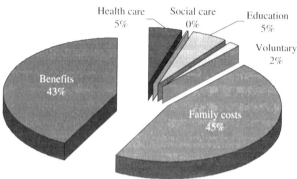

Total cost *excluding* benefits averaged £5,960 per
child per year, at 2000/01 prices (benefits = £4307)

Figure 5.1   Costs of Children With Persistent Antisocial Behavior
Source: Romeo et al. (2006).

care agencies; (c) community voluntary organizations; (d) families, through disrupted parental
employment, household damage, and so forth;
and (e) the welfare system, such as disability
and similar transfer payments (Romeo et al.,
2006). An earlier study found that adults who, as
children, had a conduct disorder generated costs
for a range of agencies that were significantly
higher than the costs for a nonmorbid control
group; most noticeable were the criminal justice
system costs, which were 18 times greater
(Scott, Knapp, Henderson, & Maughan, 2001a).

Finding the Data for Cost Measurement

When an evaluation is carried out, data are
needed on the services that individuals use.
Information on service use might come from
organizational billing systems, which record
amounts transferred between purchasers and
providers for services used, or from routine
computerized information systems that record
service contacts. Alternatively, or additionally,
data might be collected specifically for the
purposes of the research, perhaps through
interviews with service users, caregivers, or
service professionals. One instrument that
has been widely used is the Client Service
Receipt Inventory (Beecham & Knapp, 2001;
Chisholm et al., 2000).

The next task is to attach unit cost estimates
to these service use data. These are the average

costs for units of provision, such as the cost per
session of psychological therapy or the cost per
day for inpatient hospital stay. In England, an
excellent annual compendium of health and
social care unit costs provides just such figures
(Curtis, 2008); however, cost data are not
routinely available in many countries and so it
is often necessary for the economist to calculate unit costs anew. When carrying out cost
effectiveness evaluations in the mental health
field, the main cost categories that would need
to be included in calculating a unit cost would
include: (a) salaries of staff employed in prevention; (b) treatment and care services;
(c) facility operating costs, for example,
cleaning, catering; (d) overhead costs, for
example, personnel, finance; and (e) capital
costs for buildings and durable equipment. A
range of data sources could be used to build up
these cost measures, including government
statistics, health system expenditure figures,
and specific facility or organization accounts.

Effectiveness

The most appealing and intuitively familiar
type of economic evaluation is cost effectiveness analysis (CEA), which measures costs as
set out previously, and measures outcomes
along dimensions that would be recognized by
clinicians and other service professionals such
as changes in symptoms, behavior, and

functioning. A CEA can then help decision makers choose between interventions aimed at specific health needs, such as two different treatments for mild/moderate depression.

Strictly speaking, CEA looks at a single outcome dimension—such as change in depressive symptoms using, say, the Hamilton rating scale (Hamilton, 1960)—and then computes and compares the difference in costs between two interventions and the difference in this primary outcome. If one intervention is more effective in terms of improvement on the Hamilton scale and also less costly than the intervention with which it is compared, then it would clearly be seen as the more cost-effective of the two. But, if one intervention is more effective and more costly than the other, then a trade-off has to be made (see later in chapter).

Often the economist will compute cost differences and a range of effectiveness differences—one for each relevant outcome dimension. This approach, sometimes called cost-consequences analysis, has the advantage of breadth but poses a challenge if one intervention is found to be better on one outcome measure but worse on another when compared to an alternative intervention. It is then not immediately obvious which one of these two interventions is to be preferred, and the decision maker must weigh the strength of evidence. To some extent this will be a value judgment reflecting which outcome dimension they believe to be of most importance—for example, success in return to employment versus risk of contact with the criminal justice system. The recent Combined Pharmacotherapies and Behavioral Intervention (COMBINE) study of interventions for alcohol dependence (see Box 5.1) used three effectiveness measures: percentage point increase in percentage of days abstinent, avoiding heavy drinking, and achieving a good clinical outcome, assessed in part by using an attitudinal questionnaire (Zarkin et al., 2008). Fortunately, the outcomes all moved in the same

direction across the various interventions studied, but this will not always be the case. For this reason, attempts have been made to find summary outcome measures that can range across all of the dimensions (see the discussion of *Utility* further on).

BOX 5.1   COST-EFFECTIVENESS OF COMBINATION THERAPY FOR ALCOHOL DEPENDENCE

The COMBINE clinical trial compared (a) a combination of medications (naltrexone and acamprosate), medical management, and a combined behavioral intervention against (b) monotherapy, and (c) placebo therapies in outpatient treating of alcohol dependence (Zarkin et al., 2008). A total of 1,383 people across 11 U.S. sites were randomized into nine treatment groups and treated for 16 weeks. Cost data were collected alongside the effectiveness measures that included: (a) mean percentage of days abstinent; (b) proportion of patients not returning to heavy-drinking days; and (c) the proportion who maintained a good clinical outcome, including a questionnaire assessment of the social, physical, and psychological consequences of drinking. Three treatment options were more cost-effective than all others in all three cost-effectiveness analyses—one per outcome measure. Cost-effectiveness acceptability curves were plotted, showing the probability that each of the treatment options is the most cost-effective for alternative values of the willingness to pay for the outcomes. The choice of the most cost-effective intervention depended on what value might be placed on the outcomes by decision makers.

Making Trade-Offs

If an evaluation finds one intervention to be more effective but simultaneously more expensive than another intervention, which of them is the more cost-effective? A trade-off must be made between the better outcomes and the higher costs necessary to achieve them. The precise amount or threshold at which societies are willing to spend additional money for improved outcomes is a value judgment. It is not necessarily an arbitrary amount, but it is a value that comes from outside the evaluation context. As we describe later, NICE in England and Wales implicitly employs a threshold of \$46,300 (£30,000) per quality-adjusted life year (QALY) as a guide to deciding which health technologies to recommend for use in the NHS. (All prices are shown in 2007 International Dollars and original currencies at 2007 prices.) But even this is not the only consideration: NICE's decisions are influenced by other factors including issues of fairness and/or the need to target interventions at specific at-risk groups. This can allow some interventions with a higher cost per QALY to be recommended for use in the NHS.

The classical way of presenting the evidence from an economic evaluation so as to illustrate the nature of the trade off is to calculate the incremental cost effectiveness ratio (ICER). This ratio divides the extra cost associated with a new intervention by its additional effect. More recently, health economists have developed the net benefit approach to explicate the nature of the trade off. See the illustrative study summarized in Box 5.2 for an example. It is commonly seen today in the construction of cost effectiveness acceptability curves (CEACs). These curves show the probability that an intervention will be cost effective for each of a number of prespecified or implicit valuations of an outcome improvement by the decision maker. An example is given in Figure 5.2 for same study. The curved line shows the probability (on the vertical axis) that the experimental intervention (in this case, computerized cognitive behavior therapy) is more cost effective than the control intervention (in this case, treatment as usual in primary care) for each point on a

range of hypothetical societal values (along the horizontal axis) for a one-point reduction on the Beck Depression Inventory (BDI). It can be seen that, as a cost of £14.50 per session (which was the charge at the time of the evaluation), if society was prepared to pay as little as £21 for a one-point reduction on the BDI, then there would be a greater than 50% probability that the computerized CBT would be seen as the more cost-effective option.

BOX 5.2 COMPUTERIZED COGNITIVE BEHAVIOR THERAPY FOR DEPRESSION AND ANXIETY

Proudfoot et al. (2004) developed and tested a form of computerized cognitive behavior therapy (CCBT) for depression and anxiety in a randomized controlled trial. They found it to be better than standard primary care-based services in terms of symptom alleviation and work and social functioning at 8-month follow-up. In a linked economic evaluation, McCrone et al. (2004) computed the costs of all patient services and estimated the value of the productivity losses as a result of unemployment and absenteeism. The CCBT was more expensive in health service terms than standard primary care services, but more effective in reducing symptoms. The study therefore plotted cost-effectiveness acceptability curves in order to highlight the trade-offs facing decision makers. The fitted curves showed that, even if the value placed by society on a unit reduction in the Beck Depression Inventory – the primary clinical measure used in the trial – was as little as £40, there was an 81% probability that CCBT would be viewed as cost-effective. Similarly, assigning a societal value of just £5 to each additional depression free day would result in an 80% probability that CCBT would be cost effective.

The economic evaluation also included calculation of utility measures based on scores on the Beck Depression Inventory, following the approach developed by Lave, Frank, Schulberg, and Kamlet (1998). Although crude, this allowed the evaluation results to be viewed alongside findings from evaluations in other health-care areas, which subsequently supported the decision by NICE to include CCBT in its recommended clinical guidelines for depression.

Utility Measurement

One way to overcome the potential problem of different outcome dimensions pointing in different directions is to employ a single, overarching measure: A preference-weighted, health-related quality of life measure is the approach favored by most health economists. The value of the quality of life improvement is gauged in units of utility, usually expressed by a combined index of the mortality and quality of life effects of an intervention. The best known such index is the Quality Adjusted Life Year (QALY). Values are elicited from the public on the quality of life associated with different states of health, with 1 being time spent in perfect health and 0 representing death. In essence, the value of years of life lived is

then adjusted to take account of the quality of life experienced during that time period. For instance, if living with severe depression is valued by the public as being 0.8 of time spent in full health then an additional 5 years of life lived with severe depression would be equivalent to 4 quality-adjusted life years.

A cost-utility analysis (CUA) measures the outcome difference between two interventions in terms of QALY gain and compares this with the difference in costs. The CUAs have a number of attractions, including their use of a unidimensional, generic outcome measure that allows comparisons across diagnostic groups, based on an explicit methodology for weighting preferences and valuing health states. But the utility measure may be thought to be too reductionist and insufficiently sensitive to changes expected in a particular clinical area. This has been argued to be the case in respect to some mental health treatments (Ayuso Mateos, Salvador-Carulla, & Chisholm, 2006; Chisholm, Healey, & Knapp, 1997; Knapp & Mangalore, 2007). Disease-specific quality of life tools have in fact been developed, such as the McSad health state classification system for depression (Bennett, Torrance, Boyle, & Guscott, 2000), or the 55 health state instrument for Bipolar Disorder (Revicki et al., 2005).

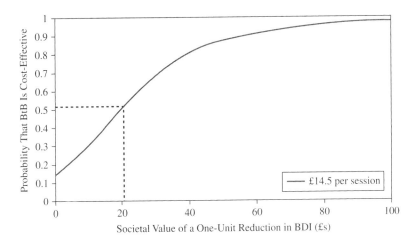

Figure 5.2   Cost-Effective Acceptability Curve for Computerized Cognitive Behavioral Therapy
Source: McCrone et al. (2004).

Another cruder approach is to estimate utility values from an established clinical scale, such as the Beck Depression Inventory (see Box 5.2 for an example).

If used, cost-utility analyses produce estimates of cost per QALY-gain from one therapy over another, which can then inform health-care resource allocation decisions, such as by NICE in England and Wales. More recently, NICE has also begun to use the QALY as an outcome measure for assessing the value of investing in mental well-being promotion initiatives, identifying the promotion of physical activity— for example, walking of health schemes— as one cost-effective approach (NICE, 2008b).

Monetary Benefits

Another approach to economic evaluation, cost-benefit analysis, values all costs and outcomes benefits in the same monetary units. If benefits exceed costs, the evaluation provides support for the intervention and vice versa. With two or more alternatives, the intervention with the greatest net benefit would be deemed the most efficient.

Cost benefit analyses are intrinsically quite attractive, as they can help decision makers to allocate resources across different sectors; for example, comparing investments in health care with those in housing, education, or transport. There have been only a few cost benefit analyses of mental health care interventions, including use of this approach in assessing the value of mental health prevention interventions, for example, suicide prevention (de Castro, Newman, Mills, & Sarr, 2004; Medoff, 1986; Zaloshnja et al., 2003).

DECISION MAKING SUPPORTED BY ECONOMIC EVIDENCE

Decision makers and other stakeholders in many mental health systems across the world

are increasingly turning to economics for evidence to help inform and support their actions. Some brief examples are given here to illustrate how information on costs and cost-effectiveness evidence in particular is being used in this way.

Interest Group Lobbying

It is common today to find studies that calculate the overall economic impact of a condition or disability. These cost-of-illness studies aim to sum all of the direct costs associated with treatment and support, as well as the indirect costs of reduced productivity because of interrupted employment and the unpaid support provided by family members. The outcome is usually a very considerable total cost that is then often quoted in order to lobby for more resources to be devoted to the area. One example is provided by the Dementia UK report, commissioned by the Alzheimer's Society in England (Knapp et al., 2007), which offered new data on the epidemiology of dementia, its treatment, policy trends, and its overall cost. The last of these pieces of evidence was widely quoted by lobbying groups when arguing for more resources to be allocated to the provision of dementia care services. The overall cost of £17 billion was dominated by expenditures on nursing home provision and the opportunity costs of informal care by family members. This report and a subsequent inquiry by the National Audit Office (2007), which also made great play of the economic evidence for treatment advances, contributed to the UK government's decision to develop its dementia strategy (Department of Health 2009), which was itself refined after completion of an economic impact assessment.

Marketing

Not far removed from the lobbying activities of patient and other interest groups are the marketing activities of pharmaceutical and other industries. Of course, the underlying motives are different—in one case, the primary concern is the promotion of better health and quality of life for a segment of the population, while in the other the bottom line is making profits, albeit in part to support ongoing and future research. Whatever the motivation, all such information seeks to draw attention to what is considered to be a neglected set of needs, and thus to encourage greater spending on meeting those unmet needs. In some countries there may be formal requirements, primarily for the manufacturers of new pharmaceuticals, to submit information on the cost-effectiveness of their medications to regulatory authorities (see evidence and appraisal later). Even where no such regulations exist, pharmaceutical companies may commission additional clinical and economic evidence to demonstrate that their product is more effective and cost-effective than other available treatments. Many economic evaluations have been commissioned by companies for this purpose—some of them of good quality and some not.

One consequence of this growing reliance on economic evidence to sell drugs is that non-proprietary treatments such as psychological therapies may lose out in the battle to convince budget holders how and where to spend their money. Psychological therapies are generally not owned by profit-seeking companies, although there may be some scope for revenue generation through the publication of training materials and manuals as well as in the accreditation process; thus, there has been much less demand to date for economic evaluation, and in the future, most evidence that will be generated about their effectiveness and cost-effectiveness will have to come from the profession or from government. This is why a number of governments in high-income countries now have systems for the careful appraisal of health technologies, including appropriate, financial support for economic appraisal, as well as policy development and monitoring (see later).

Policy Development and Monitoring

Evidence on economic impacts can also be used to inform the development of mental health services and then subsequently help monitor the consequences of policy change. Early examples are the studies that looked at the financial and economic impacts of rebalancing care by closing long-stay institutions and investing in alternative community-based services. In England the wide-ranging Team for the Assessment of Psychiatric Services project, funded by the National Health Service, evaluated the closure of two asylums in London and the transfer of over a thousand long-stay residents to a variety of community settings. *Inter alia*, the study looked at service configurations, staffing arrangements, public attitudes, patient outcomes and costs. Follow-up assessments 1 and 5 years after people moved out of the hospital showed that the former inpatients now had better quality lives, stable accommodation arrangements with almost no one homeless, better social networks, and few hospital readmissions (Leff, 1997). The comprehensive economic evaluation concluded that life in the community generated costs that were no higher than the costs of a hospital, suggesting that community care was the more cost-effective option (Beecham et al., 1997). Similar research in Indiana, commissioned by the state government, indicated that costs to the state mental health agencies decreased when individuals were transferred out of the central mental hospital to community-based care, while at the same time highlighting that there may be additional costs to be met, for example, for supported housing (Wright, 1999). A 13-year follow-up of individuals discharged from a long-stay institution in Pennsylvania in 1992 reported that costs of community care were no higher than hospital-based services for similar clients; moreover, this did not lead to any significant increase in homelessness or contact with the criminal justice system (Rothbard, Lee, Culnan, & Vasko, 2007).

We could point to many other areas where work has specifically been commissioned by governments to help inform policy, such as assessing the economic impacts of suicide and deliberate self-harm in Ireland as a precursor to the development of the national strategy on suicide prevention (Department of Health and Children, 2005), and analysis across a number of countries of the economic benefits of early intervention services for psychosis (McCrone & Knapp, 2007). A simple economic study described in Box 5.3 generated evidence that influenced the decision to launch the IAPT initiative, which is investing $278 million (£180 million) in psychological therapies in England (Department of Health, 2008). (See Chapter 4 in Volume 1 by Pilling and Fonagy and Chapter 2 by Pilling in this volume for descriptions of NICE and evidence-based practice and the British National Health Service.)

investment in psychological therapists would pay for itself many times over. Key to the argument was that, while the investment would be made by the health service, the economic benefits would principally accrue to the Department for Work and Pensions, which makes welfare payments to people unable to work. A cross-government funding strategy was agreed to in order to launch the Improving Access to Psychological Therapies initiative, and £180 million has been committed to allow expansion of CBT and other therapies (Department of Health 2008). The economics evidence, and Professor Lord Layard's good links with government decision makers, were key to this initiative.

Recently the European Commission and the EU member states endorsed a Mental Health Pact to help promote mental well being and address the needs of people with mental health problems. In developing the case for the Pact, the Commission put much emphasis on arguments highlighting the economic impacts of poor mental health (McDaid, 2008). Another international example of how economic evidence is used can be seen in the World Health Organization's (WHO) Choosing Interventions that are Cost Effective programe, which collates information for each of the 17 WHO subregions on the costs, impact on population health, and cost effectiveness of different health interventions (Hutubessy, Chisholm, Tan-Torres Edejer, & WHO CHOICE, 2003). Work to date has included identification of cost effective approaches combining drug and psychosocial interventions for the treatment of bipolar disorder (Chisholm, Van Ommeren, Ayuso-Mateos, & Saxena, 2005) and examination of psychotherapy and pharmaceutical interventions in the treatment of depression (Chisholm, Sanderson, Ayuso-Mateos, & Saxena, 2004).

BOX 5.3 MODELING THE NATIONAL COSTS AND BENEFITS OF COGNITIVE BEHAVIOR THERAPY

Many people with depression experience major difficulties with employment. Finding a job can be difficult, and absenteeism is common. These difficulties have impacts on the individual who suffers income losses, the employer through reduced productivity, and the state through higher social security payments. Layard, Clark, Knapp, & Mayraz (2007) carried out some very simple modeling to demonstrate the wide ranging costs of employment related difficulties for people with depression, the potential for treatment with CBT to alleviate symptoms and reduce absenteeism, and the economic payoffs that would result from investment to expand the availability of CBT within England's National Health Service. Data came from previous epidemiological, clinical, and economic research, and showed that a nationwide

Evidence Appraisal and Guideline Development

Cost-effective treatments for mental health problems may be underutilized within health systems (Vos et al., 2005). A growing number of countries, including much of Western Europe, Australia, Canada, New Zealand, and South Korea have established mechanisms to consider formally the cost-effectiveness of new technologies as part of reimbursement and coverage decision-making processes (Duckett, 2004; McDaid and Cookson, 2003; Tarride et al., 2008; Yang, Bae, & Kim, 2008). Although the explicit use of such information in systems such as Medicare and Medicaid in the United States remains limited, economic factors in the future increase pressure for greater consideration of cost in determining value for money of these programes in coverage decisions (Neumann et al., 2008; Orszag & Ellis, 2007).

Perhaps the best known mechanism is the NICE in England and Wales, which evaluates specific technologies and develops clinical guidelines. When technologies are appraised by NICE, not only does an expert committee look at a synthesis of information on the clinical effectiveness of the intervention under consideration, but it also receives an assessment of the potential cost-effectiveness to the NHS and personal social services of the intervention measured in terms of cost per QALY gained compared with current treatment. Effective interventions shown to have a cost per QALY gained of less than $46,300 (£30,000) are likely to be recommended for use within the NHS. For example, using this process, one type of computerized cognitive behavior therapy intervention for depression and anxiety disorders (see Box 5.2) was found to be highly cost-effective at $1,930 (£1250) per QALY gained (NICE, 2008a). If the costs per QALY gained of an intervention exceed $46,300 (£30,000) then it is only likely to be recommended if, as in the case of dialysis, not receiving treatment might have catastrophic consequences or if the technology fulfills some other important goal such as reducing inequalities in health.

Economic evidence can also be used to help develop clinical guidelines used by NICE and other bodies. For example, synthesizing information on both the effectiveness and costs of psychotherapy and pharmacotherapy in the treatment of depression, an economic model reported that there were costs per QALY gained of $9,895 (£6,412) and $24,904 (£16,138) for people with severe and moderate depression respectively. Solely taking account of the budgetary impact on the NHS and personal social services, subsequent guidelines from NICE recommended the front line use of combination therapy for severe depression and use as a second line therapy after pharmacotherapy for those with moderate depression (Simon, Pilling, Burbeck, & Goldberg, 2006). Economic evidence has also been considered in the development of clinical guidelines for depression used by a number of health plans in Minnesota. Again the guidelines recommend a combination of medication and psychotherapy (Institute for Clinical Systems Improvement, 2008).

Commissioning

Economic levers can also be used to help direct resources in the health system, for instance, to help implement clinical guidelines and/or to improve efficiency or equity. For example, specific bonus payments and other financial incentives might be awarded to practitioners seen to be adhering to clinical guidelines, as recently introduced for primary care doctors in the United Kingdom (Department of Health, 2004), while payments might also be made to those working in primary care who reach specific vulnerable population groups such as ethnic minorities.

The way revenues collected from taxes or insurance premiums flow to service providers also offer opportunities to influence resource allocation. Historically, fee-for-service arrangements have dominated financial flows, and although they encourage productivity, they also perversely encourage resource consumption through potentially unnecessary visits, diagnostic investigations and hospitalizations, and so increase costs. Consequently, prospective payments have increasingly been substituted, particularly as part of managed care developments, to encourage cost-consciousness among providers. Within Medicaid, for example, enrollment in some form of managed care increased from 10% of the covered population in 1991 to 58% in 2002 (Buck, 2003).

Different approaches include: (a) capitation, where a fixed payment is made for a defined set of benefits per individual in a set time period; and (b) diagnosis-related groups (DRGs), a case-mix classification system that groups patients with similar clinical diagnosis and treatment process to calculate allocated funds. One early calculation suggested that 20% of Medicare hospital costs were saved through the introduction of DRG-based pricing (Russell & Manning, 1989), although an ongoing challenge in using DRGs in both public and private health systems is to reduce opportunities for *DRG creep* or *up coding*, whereby there is a miscoding and misclassifying of patient data to receive higher reimbursements for services provided (Steinbusch, Oostenbrink, Zuurbier, & Schaepkens, 2007).

Given that many mental health services are funded and delivered outside the health care system, another area where economics can help is to look at improving collaboration and/or pooling budgets for mental health services between health, social care, employment, housing, and other sectors (McDaid et al., 2007). As part of a drive to help empower people with mental health problems, some health care systems have also evaluated the use of various forms of consumer-directed payment schemes, where consumers themselves can decide how to spend public resources on services that best meet their needs (Glendinning et al., 2008; Shen et al., 2008).

Conclusions

Economics starts from a recognition of the pervasive scarcity of resources relative to needs and demands, and hence the need for careful choices about how those resources are to be deployed. Economic analysis is primarily concerned with the efficiency with which resources are used: Achieving the maximum impact in terms of patient and other outcomes from a given volume of resources and/or minimizing the cost of achieving a particular effectiveness target. A second criterion is equity. This chapter concentrated on the various forms of cost-effectiveness analysis, describing how they are carried out, and how the evidence they generate can be used for practice and policy development. Among the uses discussed were interest group lobbying, marketing, policy development and monitoring, evidence appraisal and guideline development, and commissioning.

Even when there is an evidence base, many things can prevent the utilization of economics evidence (Knapp et al., 2006). One of the most insidious is resource scarcity itself: Mental health services are underfunded, especially in low income countries, although all mental health systems struggle with limited budgets, shortages of staff, and inadequate training opportunities. Increasing the resources available for mental health care would obviously help to overcome this difficulty, but even when resources are committed, the services funded might be poorly distributed, available at the wrong place or time relative to the distribution of needs. They may be concentrated in urban areas, or available only to people who can afford to pay for them. This distributional barrier often relates to the fundamental precepts of how a health system is financed and structured. In centrally coordinated systems, resources could perhaps be allocated according to need, while systems built on usually fragmented, voluntary health insurance financing have fewer opportunities.

A more general difficulty may be that available services do not match what is needed or preferred, perhaps being too rigidly organized, leaving service systems unable to respond to differences in individual patient needs or preferences, or to community circumstances. Such inflexibility is common when there is scant information on population or individual needs, when patients have limited opportunities to participate in treatment decisions, or when there is deep-rooted reluctance to move away from an established treatment model, such as hospital-based services. A related challenge is that services may be poorly coordinated, perhaps because health, social services, housing, and other professionals have few opportunities to work together, or because of stultifying bureaucratic or budgeting procedures preventing cross-agency collaboration.

Attitudes can put up another barrier. A population survey in Germany found that the general public were clearly less willing to safeguard spending on mental health compared with other health conditions (Matschinger & Angermeyer, 2004). The low priority accorded mental health was attributed to ignorance that conditions could be treated, beliefs that they were self-inflicted, and underestimation of individual susceptibility to psychiatric illness. Of course, people naturally want to give priority to treating life-threatening conditions, and most mental health problems are not seen in that light, but deep-rooted ignorance and stigma were probably hugely influential in shaping these attitudes.

The bottom line is, however, the bottom line: Decision makers within health systems across the world need to balance their budgets. But they need to do so while pursuing their primary objective, which is to maximize the impact that services and treatments can have on the health and quality of life of patients and families. This is an enormous challenge. Economic analysis certainly does not have all the answers, but what it can offer is a coherent framework and a set of empirical techniques that can provide decision makers with evidence to inform their responses to that challenge.

REFERENCES

Ayuso-Mateos, J. L., Salvador-Carulla, L., & Chisholm, D. (2006). Medida de la calidad de vida en el analisis economico de la atencion a la salud mental. [Measuring quality of life in the economic analysis of mental health]. *Actas Espana Psiquiatrica, 34*, 1–6.

Beecham, J., Hallam, A., Knapp, M., Baines, B., Fenyo, A., & Asbury, M. (1997). Costing care in the hospital and in the community. In J. Leff (Ed.), *Care in the community: Illusion or reality?* (pp. 93–108). Chichester, England: Wiley.

Beecham, J., & Knapp, M. (2001). Costing psychiatric interventions. In G. Thornicroft (Ed.), *Measuring mental health needs* (2nd ed.) (pp. 93–108). London, England: Gaskell.

Bennett, K. J., Torrance, G. W., Boyle, M. H., & Guscott, R. (2000). Cost-utility analysis in depression: The McSad utility measure for depression health states. *Psychiatric Services, 51*, 1171–1176.

Buck, J. B. (2003). Medicaid, health care financing trends, and the future of state-based public mental health services. *Psychiatric Services, 54*, 969–975.

Chisholm, D., Healey, A., & Knapp, M. (1997). QALYs and mental health care. *Social Psychiatry and Psychiatric Epidemiology, 32*, 68–75.

Chisholm, D., Knapp, M., Knudsen, H. C., Amaddeo, F., Gaite, L., van Wijngaarden, B., & the EPSILON Study Group. (2000). Client socio-demographic and service receipt inventory—EU version: Development of an instrument for international research. EPSILON Study 5. *British Journal of Psychiatry, 177*, 28–33.

Chisholm, D., Sanderson, K., Ayuso-Mateos, J. L., & Saxena, S. (2004). Reducing the global burden of depression. Population-level analysis of intervention cost effectiveness in 14 world regions. *British Journal of Psychiatry, 184*, 393–403.

Chisholm, D., van Ommeren, M., Ayuso-Mateos, J. L., & Saxena, S. (2005). Cost-effectiveness of clinical interventions for reducing the global burden of bipolar disorder. *British Journal of Psychiatry, 187*, 559–567.

Chow, J. C. C., Jaffee, K., & Snowden, L. (2003). Racial/ethnic disparities in the use of mental health services in poverty areas. *American Journal of Public Health, 93*, 792–797.

Congress of the United States of America. (2008). *Emergency economic stabilization act of 2008. H.R. 1424.* Washington, DC: Author.

Corrigan, P. W., & Wassel, A. (2008). Understanding and influencing the stigma of mental illness. *Journal of Psychosocial Nursing and Mental Health Services, 46*, 42–48.

Curtis, L. (2008). *Unit costs of health and social care 2008*. University of Kent, Canterbury, England: Personal Social Services Research Unit.

De Castro, S., Newman, F., Mills, G., & Sari, N. (2004). Economic evaluation of suicide prevention programs for young adults in Florida. *Business Review Cambridge, December*, 14–20.

Department of Health. (2004). *Quality and outcomes framework. Guidance*. London, England: Author.

Department of Health. (2008). *Improving access to psychological therapies: Implementation plan*. London, England: National Institute for Mental Health in England.

Department of Health. (2009). *Living with dementia: A national dementia strategy*. London, England: Author.

Department of Health and Children. (2005). *Reach out. National strategy for action on suicide prevention*. Dublin, Ireland: Author.

Department of Health, Social Services and Public Safety. (2003). *Social services and public safety. Clinical psychology services for older adults in Northern Ireland. A consultant document*. Belfast, Northern Ireland: Author.

Dixon, A., McDaid, D., Knapp, M., & Curran, C. (2006). Financing mental health: Equity and efficiency concerns for low and middle income countries. *Health Policy and Planning, 21*, 171–182.

Duckett, S. J. (2004). Drug policy down under: Australia's pharmaceutical benefits scheme. *Health Care Financing Review, 25*, 55–67.

Fearon, P., Kirkbride, J. B., Morgan, C., Dazzan, P., Morgan, K., Lloyd, T., . . . AESOP Study Group (2006). Incidence of schizophrenia and other psychoses in ethnic minority groups: Results from the MRC AESOP study. *Psychological Medicine, 36*, 1541–1550.

Frank, R. G., & Glied, S. A. (2006). *Better but not well. Mental health policy in the United States since 1950*. Baltimore, MD: Johns Hopkins University Press.

Glendinning, C., Challis, D., Fernandez, J. L., Jacobs, S., Jones, K., Knapp, M., . . . Wilberforce, M. (2008). *Evaluation of the individual budgets pilot programme. Final report*. University of York, York, England: Social Policy Research Unit.

Glied, S. A., & Frank, R. G. (2008). Shuffling towards parity. Bringing mental health care under the umbrella. *New England Journal of Medicine, 359*, 113–115.

Hamilton, M. (1960). A rating scale for depression. *Journal of Neurology, Neurosurgery and Psychiatry, 23*, 56–62.

Hutubessy, R., Chisholm, D., Tan-Torres Edejer, T., & WHO-CHOICE. (2003). Generalized cost-effectiveness analysis for national-level priority setting in the health sector. *Cost Effectiveness and Resource Allocation, 1*, 8.

Institute for Clinical Systems Improvement. (2008). *Major depression in adults in primary care: Health care guideline*. Bloomington, MN: Author.

Kavanagh, S., & Knapp, M. (1995). Market rationales, rationing and rationality? Mental health care reform in England. *Health Affairs, 14*, 260–268.

Knapp, M., Funk, M., Curran, C., Prince, M., Grigg, M., & McDaid, D. (2006). Economic barriers to better mental health practice and policy. *Health Policy and Planning, 21*, 157–170.

Knapp, M., & Mangalore, R. (2007). The trouble with QALYs . . . . *Epidemiologia e Psichiatria Sociale, 16*, 289–293.

Knapp, M., & McDaid, D. (2007). Financing and funding mental health care services. In M. Knapp, D. McDaid, E. Mossialos, & G. Thornicroft (Eds.), *Mental health policy and practice across Europe* (pp. 60–99). Buckingham, England: Open University Press.

Knapp, M., Prince, M., Albanesi, E., Banerjee, S., Dhanasiri, S., Fernandez, J. L., . . . Stewart, R. (2007). *Dementia UK*. London, England: Alzheimer's Society.

Lave, J., Frank, R. G., Schulberg, H. C., & Kamlet, M. S. (1998). Cost effectiveness of treatments for major depression in primary care patients. *Archives of General Psychiatry, 55*, 645–651.

Layard, R., Clark, D., Knapp, M., & Mayraz, G. (2007). Cost-benefit analysis of psychological therapy. *National Institute Economic Review, 202*, 90–98.

Leff, J. (Ed.). (1997). *Care in the community: Illusion or reality?* Chichester, England: Wiley.

Matschinger, H., & Angermeyer, M. (2004). The public's preference concerning the allocation of financial resources to health care: Results from a representative population survey in Germany. *European Psychiatry, 19*, 478–82.

McCrone, P., & Knapp, M. (2007). Economic evaluation of early intervention services. *British Journal of Psychiatry, 191*, s19–s22.

McCrone, P., Knapp, M., Proudfoot, J., Ryden, C., Cavanagh, K., Shapiro, D. A., . . . Tylee, A. (2004). Cost-effectiveness of computerised cognitive-behavioural therapy for anxiety and depression in primary care: Randomised controlled trial. *British Journal of Psychiatry, 185*, 55–62.

McDaid, D. (2008). Mental health reform: Europe at the crossroads. *Health Economics, Policy and Law, 3*, 219–228.

McDaid, D., & Cookson, R. (2003). Evaluating health care interventions in the European Union. *Health Policy, 63*, 133–139.

McDaid, D., Oliveira, M. D., Jurczak, K., Knapp, M., & the MHEEN Group. (2007). Moving beyond the mental health care system: An exploration of the interfaces between the health and non-health sectors. *Journal of Mental Health, 16*, 181–194.

McGuire, T., & Miranda, J. (2008). New evidence regarding racial and ethnic disparities in mental health: Policy implications. *Health Affairs, 27*, 393–403.

McKenzie, K., & Bhui, K. (2007). Institutional racism in mental health care. *British Medical Journal, 334*, 649–650.

Medoff, M. H. (1986). An evaluation of the effectiveness of suicide prevention centers. *Journal of Behavioral Economics, 15*, 43–55.

Mojtabai, R., & Olfson, M. (2008). National trends in psychotherapy by office based psychiatrists. *Archives of General Psychiatry, 65*, 962–970.

Mossialos, E., Dixon, A., Figueras, J., & Kutzin, J. (Eds.). (2002). *Funding health care: Options for Europe.* Buckingham, England: Open University Press.

National Audit Office. (2007). *Improving services and support for people with dementia.* London, England: The Stationery Office.

National Institute for Health and Clinical Excellence. (2008a). *Computerised cognitive behaviour therapy for depression and anxiety. Review of technology appraisal 51.* Technology Appraisal 97. London, England: Author.

National Institute for Health and Clinical Excellence. (2008b). *Occupational therapy interventions and physical activity interventions to promote the mental well-being of older people in primary care and residential care.* Public Health Guidance 16. London, England: Author.

Neumann, P. J., Palmer, J. A., Daniels, N., Quigley, K., Gold, M. R., & Chao, S. (2008). A strategic plan for integrating cost-effectiveness analysis into the US healthcare system. *American Journal of Managed Care, 14*, 185–188.

Organization for Economic Cooperation and Development. (2008). *Health data 2008.* Paris, France: Author.

Orszag, P., & Ellis, P. (2007). Addressing rising health care costs—A view from the Congressional Budget Office. *New England Journal of Medicine, 357*, 1885–1887.

Proudfoot, J., Ryden, C., Everitt, B., Shapiro, D. A., Goldberg, D., Mann, A. . . . Gray, J. A. (2004). Clinical efficacy of computerised cognitive-behavioural therapy for anxiety and depression in primary care: Randomised controlled trial. *British Journal of Psychiatry, 185*, 46–54.

Revicki, D. A., Hanlon, J., Martin, S., Gyulai, L., Nassir Ghaemi, S., Lynch, F. . . . Kleinman, L. (2005). Patient-based utilities for bipolar disorder-related health states. *Journal of Affective Disorders, 87*, 203–210.

Romeo, R., Knapp, M., & Scott, S. (2006). Children with antisocial behaviour: What do they cost and who pays? *British Journal of Psychiatry, 188*, 547–553.

Rothbard, A. B., Lee, S., Culnan, K., & Vasko, S. (2007). Service use and cost in 2002 among clients in community settings who were discharged from a state hospital in 1989. *Psychiatric Services, 58*, 1570–1576.

Russell, L. B., & Manning, C. L. (1989). The effect of prospective payment on Medicare expenditures. *New England Journal of Medicine, 16*, 439–444.

Sareen, J., Jagdeo, A., Cox, B. J., Clara, I., ten Have, M., Belik, S. . . . Stein, M. B. (2007). Perceived barriers to mental health service utilization in the United States, Ontario, and The Netherlands. *Psychiatric Services, 58*, 357–364.

Savedoff, W. (2004). *Tax-based financing for health systems: Options and experiences.* Geneva, Switzerland: World Health Organization.

Saxena, S., Sharan, P., & Saraceno, B. (2003). Budget and financing of mental health services: Baseline information on 89 countries from WHO's project atlas. *Journal of Mental Health Policy and Economics, 6*, 135–143.

Schomerus, G., & Angermeyer, M. C. (2008). Stigma and its impact on help-seeking for mental disorders: What do we know? *Epidemiologia e Psichiatrica Sociale, 17*, 31–37.

Scott, S., Knapp, M., Henderson, J., & Maughan, B. (2001a). Financial cost of social exclusion: Follow up study of antisocial children into adulthood. *British Medical Journal, 323*, 191–196.

Scott, S., Spender, Q., Doolan, M., Jacobs, B. & Aspland, H. (2001b). Multicentre controlled trial of parenting groups for childhood antisocial behaviour in clinical practice. *British Medical Journal, 323*, 194–198.

Shen, C., Smyer, M. A., Mahoney, K. J., Simon-Rusinowitz, L., Shinogle, J., Norstrand, J. . . . del Vecchio, P. (2008). Consumer-directed care for beneficiaries with mental illness: Lessons from New Jersey's Cash and Counseling program. *Psychiatric Services, 59*, 1299–1306.

Simon, J., Pilling, S., Burbeck, R., & Goldberg, D. (2006). Treatment options in moderate and severe depression: Decision analysis supporting a clinical guideline. *British Journal of Psychiatry, 189*, 494–501.

Smith, A. (1776/1997). *An inquiry into the nature and causes of the wealth of nations.* Chicago, IL: University of Chicago Press.

Steinbusch, P. J., Oostenbrink, J. B., Zuurbier, J. J., & Schaepkens, F. J. (2007). The risk of upcoding in casemix systems: A comparative study. *Health Policy, 81*, 289–299.

Tamblyn, R., Laprise, R., Hanley J. A., Abrahamowicz, M., Scott, S., Mayo, N. . . . Mallet, L. (2001). Adverse events associated with prescription drug cost-sharing among poor and elderly persons. *Journal of the American Medical Association, 285*, 421–429.

Tapsell, R., & Mellsop, G. (2007). The contributions of culture and ethnicity to New Zealand mental health research findings. *International Journal of Social Psychiatry, 53*, 317–324.

Tarride, J. E., McCarron, C. E., Lim, M., Bowen, J. M., Blackhouse, G., Hopkins, R. . . . Goeree, R. (2008). Economic evaluations conducted by Canadian health technology assessment agencies: Where do we stand? *International Journal of Technological Assessment in Health Care, 24*, 437–444.

U. S. Surgeon General. (2001). *Culture, race, and ethnicity, supplement to mental health: A report of the Surgeon General.* Rockville, MD: Center for Mental Health Services, Substance Abuse and Mental Health Services Administration.

Vos, T., Haby, M. M., Magnus, A., Mihalopoulos, C., Andrews, G., & Carter, R. (2005). Assessing cost-effectiveness in mental health: Helping policy-makers prioritize and plan health services. *Australian and New Zealand Journal of Psychiatry, 39*, 701–712.

Wang, P. S., Aguilar-Gaxiola, S., Alonso, J., Angermeyer, M. C., Borges, G., Bromet, E. J. . . . Wells, J. E. (2007). Use of mental health services for anxiety, mood, and substance disorders in 17 countries in the WHO world mental health surveys. *Lancet, 370*, 841–850.

Wittchen, H. U., & Jacobi, F. (2005). Size and burden of mental disorders in Europe—A critical review and appraisal of 27 studies. *European Neuropsycho pharmacology, 15*, 357–376.

World Health Organization. (2005). *Mental health atlas.* Geneva, Switzerland: Author.

Wright, E. R. (1999). Fiscal outcomes of the closing of Central State Hospital: An analysis of the costs to state government. *Journal of Behavioral Health Services and Research, 26*, 262–275.

Yang, B. M., Bae, E. Y., & Kim, J. (2008). Economic evaluation and pharmaceutical reimbursement reform in South Korea's national health insurance. *Health Affairs, 27*, 179–187.

Zaloshnja, E., Miller, T. R., Galbraith, M. S., Lawrence, B. A., DeBruyn, L. M., Bill, N. . . . Perkins, R. (2003). Reducing injuries among Native Americans: Five cost-outcome analyses. *Accident Analysis and Prevention, 35*, 631–639.

Zaluska, M., Suchecka, D., Traczewska, J. & Paszko, J. (2005). Implementation of social services for the chronically mentally ill in a Polish health district: Consequences for service use and costs. *Journal of Mental Health Policy and Economics, 8*, 37–44.

Zarkin, G. A., Bray, J. W., Aldridge, A., Mitra, D., Mills, M. J., Couper, D. J. . . . COMBINE Cost Effectiveness Research Group. (2008). Cost and cost-effectiveness of the COMBINE study in alcohol-dependent patients. *Archives of General Psychiatry, 65*, 1214–1221.

Zechmeister, I., & Oesterle, A. (2006). Distributional impacts of mental health care financing arrangements: A comparison of the UK, Germany and Austria. *Journal of Mental Health Policy and Economics, 9*, 35–44.

PART II

Specific Disorders

6

Dementia and Related Cognitive Disorders

BOB WOODS, LINDA CLARE, AND GILL WINDLE

OVERVIEW OF DEMENTIAS

Diagnostic Criteria

The two major internationally accepted diagnostic classification systems define dementia as an acquired global impairment of cognitive function sufficient to impinge on everyday activities, occurring in clear consciousness (World Health Organization, 1993; American Psychiatric Association, 1994 currently under review). Both systems have a rather limited view of globality, essentially requiring at least one area of ability to be impaired in addition to memory memory impairment being an essential component of the diagnosis of dementia. Change from a previous level is a key part of the definition, and dementias are usually expected to show progressive deterioration. At one time, the definition would specify that the condition is usually irreversible, but with increased optimism regarding therapeutic strategies, this aspect has tended to be dropped.

Several different types and variants of dementia have been identified, with three main disorders common in later life: Alzheimer's disease, vascular dementia, and Lewy body dementia (LBD). In order to be certain of the type of dementia present, a postmortem examination of the brain is required, and this has often been taken as the gold standard of diagnosis. During life, there are some differences in presentation between the dementias: In LBD, hallucinations often occur early, there are fluctuations in performance, and memory does not stand out as the primary impairment; Alzheimer's has an insidious onset and gradual progression, with memory and learning especially impaired; vascular dementia shows a more step-wise decline, with periods of stability and recovery before further decline, and a patchy picture of impairment. However, these textbook presentations are sometimes difficult to discern in real life, and the likelihood of mixed presentations may make diagnosis of dementia type during life a hit and miss exercise.

For many years, it has been recognized that there are a number of older people who show some degree of cognitive impairment, but not sufficient to meet the diagnostic criteria for a dementia either because only one area of cognition is impaired, or because the impairment does not have an impact on day to day life. Over the years, a variety of labels has been applied, with current terminology describing them as having Mild Cognitive Impairment (MCI). With the insidious onset of Alzheimer's disease, there must be a hinterland between normal ageing and clear cut Alzheimer's at a time when the presumed pathology is beginning to develop. Many individuals with MCI do indeed go on to develop a dementia (50% in 5 years in some studies), but some do not show further decline, or even improve on retesting. However, epidemiological studies clearly indicate that most people in their eighties will show some signs of pathological changes in the brain; these may be vascular changes, or the characteristic Alzheimer changes, or, more often than not, both (Snowdon, 2003). Mild Cognitive Impairment is attracting some research attention as an *at-risk* group, and any intervention that could prevent conversion from MCI to dementia would be invaluable.

Demographic Variables

Prevalence of the dementias has been the subject of numerous epidemiological studies internationally (e.g., Ferri et al., 2005). Age is the predominant risk factor, with dementia being relatively uncommon in those under 65 (approximately 0.1%), but very common in those aged over 80, at least 20% of whom may be affected.

Although cognitive changes are universal in dementia, other features, while not present in every case, are common enough to merit attention. Indeed, it is likely that it is these features that contribute more than cognitive deficits to caregiver strain (Donaldson, Tarrier, & Burns, 1998) and placement decisions. These non-cognitive features (often described as BPSD [Behavioral and Psychological Symptoms of Dementia]) include depression, anxiety, hallucinations, delusions, and challenging behaviors of various types (Burns, Jacoby, & Levy, 1990a,b,c). For example, delusions—often concerning theft—were reported by Burns et al. in about a sixth of their sample of people with Alzheimer's disease, with another fifth having shown some ideas of persecution since their dementia began. Thirty percent had misidentification syndromes, for instance, mistaking TV pictures or images in a picture or mirror for real people. Visual and auditory hallucinations were

each noted in around a tenth of the sample. Dementia and depression often present together, with 30% of people with dementia showing symptoms of anxiety and depression (Ballard, Bannister, & Oyebode, 1996; Ballard, Boyle, Bowler, & Lindesay, 1996).

Impact of Disorder

The dementias now present arguably the greatest challenge to health and social care systems around the world. As a consequence of increased longevity, more people than ever before are experiencing a significant degree of cognitive impairment, resulting in increased needs for care and support and increased demands on family members and other supporters. Projections of ageing populations worldwide suggest that, unless there were to be a dramatic breakthrough in prevention or treatment, the numbers will continue to grow, at a rate unprecedented in the history of the world. Ferri et al. (2005) estimated there would be 30 million people with dementia in 2008 across the world, with a projected increase to 59 million by the year 2030. The costs to society of dementia are massive—estimated as £17 billion in the United Kingdom alone per annum (Knapp & Prince, 2007).

There is a wide range of nonpharmacological interventions for people with dementia, offered by a range of practitioners and caregivers. In this chapter, we have focused on psychological therapies that might be seen as part of clinical psychology practice. Although several would not usually be delivered directly by a clinical psychologist, they might well be involved in training or supervising staff, or have been involved in the development of the intervention. Accordingly, we have omitted approaches such as sensory stimulation, aromatherapy, bright light therapy, and environmental design. We have also not provided here a detailed description of the values and principles of the person-centered approach that we see as underpinning good, humane clinical psychology practice in this area.

In selecting from the many consensus statements and guidelines regarding dementia care, we have focused on four that have a good coverage of psychological approaches, and have followed a clear, transparent methodology. The National Institute for Health and Clinical Excellence–Social Care Institute for Excellence (NICE-SCIE) guidelines (2006) from the United Kingdom, the Scottish Intercollegiate Guidelines Network (SIGN) guideline (2006) from Scotland, and the guidelines from the third Canadian Consensus Conference on the diagnosis and treatment of dementia (Hogan et al., 2008) are considered alongside a systematic review and recommendations made by a task group from the World Federation for Biological Psychiatry (Livingston, Johnston, Katona, Paton, & Lyketsos, 2005).

COGNITIVE-FOCUSED APPROACHES

Several psychological therapies have a focus on enhancing the cognitive function and performance of the person with dementia. Although they may aim to have broader effects, the expectation is that their mechanism of action will be through changes in cognition, whether on standardized tests or in everyday performance. These approaches have an extensive history, dating back at least 50 years, from the early attempts to implement reality orientation in Veterans' Administration Hospitals in the United States to the more recent use of computerized and Internet-based systems to provide practice in cognitive processes. Along the way, several terms have been coined to describe these approaches with little consistency in their usage, leading to some lack of clarity in the literature. In an attempt to provide a clear framework for reviews of this area, we have distinguished three types of approaches, defined as follows (Clare & R. T. Woods, 2004): (1) Cognitive *stimulation* involves a variety of general activities with a cognitive element, often in a social or group context; (2) cognitive *training* involves repeated practice at specific

structured cognitive tasks, which may be tailored to the person's ability level; and (3) cognitive *rehabilitation* assists the person to achieve individualized goals, using a variety of means, according to an understanding of the person's strengths and difficulties, which may include introducing memory aids and practical strategies or encouraging targeted new learning.

COGNITIVE STIMULATION

We have suggested (B. Woods, 2002) that this definition of *cognitive stimulation* should be taken to include the long-established reality orientation (RO) approach (Holden & Woods, 1995), which has probably the most extensive evaluative literature of all the psychosocial approaches used directly with people with dementia. Reality orientation, in fact, included another approach that will be considered elsewhere in this chapter. This was an approach to enhancing the spatial orientation of the person with dementia, typically through direct training in locating particular places, backed up by a number of changes to the environment, with clear sign posting of locations around the ward or home, extensive use of notices and other memory aids, and a consistent approach by all staff in interacting with the person with dementia. This was often referred to as 24-hour RO. It was the group or classroom aspect of RO that is seen as the forerunner of cognitive stimulation approaches. This comprised small, structured group sessions meeting regularly, often several times a week for half an hour or so, making use of a wide variety of activities and materials to engage the participants with their surroundings, to maintain contact with the wider world and to provide cognitive stimulation. A typical session would go over basic information (such as names of those in the group, day, date, time, and place), discuss a current relevant theme of interest, perhaps play a number of naming games, and finish with refreshments. Throughout there would be a tangible focus, a whiteboard for the current information, pictures or objects appropriate to the theme, and personal diaries and notebooks for those able to record information for later use. Spector, Orrell, Davies, and Woods (2001) report the development of a cognitive stimulation program from a systematic review of the literature at that time. The program comprises 14 sessions, to be held twice weekly for 60–90 minutes. It includes elements of RO and reminiscence, drawn from studies showing the most positive outcomes and comprising a range of activities encouraging cognitive activity in a social context (Spector, Thorgrimsen, Woods, & Orrell, 2006).

Consensus Panel Recommendations

Cognitive stimulation received strong support from the NICE-SCIE guidelines on dementia (NICE-SCIE, 2006), with a recommendation that all people with mild to moderate dementia should have the opportunity to participate in cognitive stimulation groups, irrespective of whether or not they were receiving acetylcholinesterase inhibiting medication (ACHEIs). The SIGN (2006) also recommended that "cognitive stimulation should be offered to individuals with dementia" (p. 8), suggesting it could be carried out at home by a caregiver with relatively little training. However, the studies on which this recommendation was based involved, in fact, by the definition we are adopting here, cognitive training, rather than cognitive stimulation. The SIGN (2006) also made a recommendation, graded at a lower level of evidence, regarding reality orientation, recommending that it "should be used by a skilled practitioner, on an individualized basis, with people who are disorientated in time, place, and person" (p. 11). The World Federation for Biological Psychiatry (Livingston et al., 2005) gives a relatively strong recommendation for cognitive stimulation in relation to its effects on neuropsychiatric symptoms, including mood, but notes there are some inconsistencies in the evidence on these outcomes. Finally, although

cognitive training and rehabilitation are discussed by the Canadian Consensus Conference (Hogan et al., 2008), cognitive stimulation does not appear to be considered specifically.

Meta-Analyses of Group Designs

Spector, Davies, Woods, and Orrell (2000) present a systematic review and meta-analysis of the RO literature, focusing on RO sessions. Six studies, including a total of 125 patients with dementia were included; there was a significant effect of RO on both cognitive function and behavioral function. A new Cochrane Review on cognitive stimulation (B. Woods, Spector, Prendergast, & Orrell, 2009) includes 15 RCTs; on specific commonly used measures of cognition, the meta-analysis indicates a significant benefit for cognitive stimulation over treatment as usual, with the comparisons involving over 600 participants in the case of the Mini Mental State Examination (MMSE). Importantly, in the two studies that have used a self-report measure of quality of life, the QOL-AD, the meta-analysis of over 200 participants again shows a significant benefit for cognitive stimulation.

Randomized Controlled Trials

Spector et al. (2003) report an RCT of this program with 201 older people with mild to moderate dementia, drawn from 23 care homes and day centers, who were randomized to standard care or to receive 14 biweekly sessions of the cognitive stimulation intervention. There were significant improvements in cognitive function and in self-reported quality of life for those participating. The size of the effect on cognition proved comparable to those reported in published studies on the most frequently used medications for people with Alzheimer's disease (the ACHEIs). Evidence is provided for the cost-effectiveness of this approach (Knapp et al., 2006) with preliminary data suggesting that weekly sessions maintain the benefits for at least six months (Orrell,

Spector, Thorgrimsen, & Woods, 2005). Improvements in quality of life appear to be mediated by improvements in cognition (B. Woods, Thorgrimsen, Spector, Royan, & Orrell, 2006). This suggests that enhanced well-being is not simply a result of the social context of the groups, but is linked to the cognitive improvements. This is in contrast to the general finding that cognitive function does not predict quality of life in people with dementia (Thorgrimsen et al., 2003).

Randomized controlled trials combining cognitive stimulation with ACHEIs are now appearing. Onder et al. (2005) showed improved cognitive function with a home-based stimulation program involving 137 family caregivers, half of whom were trained by a multidisciplinary team to carry out sessions with their relative with dementia. They were provided with a manual and specific schedules for each session; Chapman, Weiner, Rackley, Hynan, and Zientz (2004) report improved overall global performance, including reductions in apathy and irritability, following an 8 week group cognitive stimulation program. Olazaran et al. (2004) evaluated effects of cognitive stimulation together with a physical exercise program on people with cognitive impairment receiving ACHEIs. Cognitive and affective benefits were reported for those receiving the cognitive motor intervention. This study included 84 participants, 12 of whom had a diagnosis of MCI. There does then seem to be evidence that these approaches can add to any improvements associated with currently available medication.

Single-Case Experimental Designs

Several single-case designs were reported in the literature on reality orientation. Greene, Nicol, and Jameson (1979) report three single cases. They first used an ABABA design, with the intervention being an individual session where orientation items were practiced. Improvements in orientation were apparent during the intervention phases, with decline during

the return to baseline phases. Two further cases were evaluated using an ABAB design, and there were indications of improvements during intervention phases rated outside the sessions by raters blind to the treatment phase. Some generalization of improvements to items not specifically taught was noted. R. T. Woods (1983) examined the extent of generalization in more detail using a multiple baseline design with a participant diagnosed with Korsakoff's syndrome, and dividing the orientation and personal information material to be learned into three equivalent lists. Specificity of learning was noted, with generalization only occurring when the participant was encouraged to use a diary to recall information. Hanley and Lusty (1984) used an ABCBA design with an 84-year-old woman with dementia. She was provided with a diary and a watch during the B phases, but only when given training and encouragement to use these, during the C phases, did she show a marked increase in personal orientation. With the use of training to use memory aids, these latter cases may be seen as early examples of cognitive rehabilitation.

Conclusions

Evidence does appear to support the effectiveness of cognitive stimulation approaches in maintaining cognitive function and quality of life, leading to its recommendation for people with mild to moderate dementia in practice guidelines (e.g., NICE-SCIE, 2006). Although initially there was a view that only those orientation items specifically taught are learned, later reports (e.g., Breuil et al., 1994; Zanetti et al., 1995) have tended to support the notion that more wide ranging improvements in cognition may follow cognitive stimulation of this type. However, cognitive changes alone are of dubious utility, and so reports of enhanced quality of life and well being are especially important. Reality orientation fell out of favor in the United States and United Kingdom because it was seen as being administered in a mechanical, inflexible, insensitive, and confrontational manner (Dietch, Hewett, & Jones, 1989; Holden & Woods, 1995). Delivered in a person-centered context, offering choice and flexibility of approach, cognitive stimulation has a role to play in the range of available interventions, although there is little evidence that it has any effects on behavior and day-to-day function. Here, more focused, individualized, and tailored approaches will be required.

COGNITIVE TRAINING

As defined here, cognitive training involves guided practice on a range of standardized tasks reflecting particular domains of cognitive functioning, such as memory or problem solving or language or attention. The brain is viewed as similar to a muscle, in that regular mental exercise is seen as having the potential to improve or maintain functioning in a given domain, and even to generalize beyond the immediate training content. Cognitive training approaches used with healthy older people and older people with mild cognitive decline, variously defined and categorized, have demonstrated modest task-specific improvements but no generalization and very limited maintenance of gains (e.g., Ball et al., 2002; R. T. Woods & Clare, 2006).

A variety of cognitive training formats has been reported. These include: individual sessions with a therapist (e.g., Beck, Heacock, Mercer, Thatcher, & Sparkman, 1988; Davis, Massman, & Doody, 2001), home practice facilitated by the family caregiver (Quayhagen & Quayhagen, 2001) or group therapy sessions (e.g., Cahn-Weiner, Malloy, Rebok, & Ott, 2003). Tasks may be presented in paper-and-pencil (Davis et al., 2001; de Vreese et al., 1998; Quayhagen, Quayhagen, Corbeil, Roth, & Rodgers, 1995; Quayhagen et al., 2000) or computerized (Hofman, Hock, Kuhler, & Muller-Spahn, 1996; Schreiber, Schweizer, Lutz, Kalveram, & Jaencke, 1999) form, or may involve analogues of activities of daily living (Loewenstein, Acevedo, Czaja, & Durara, 2004; Zanetti, Magni, Binetti, Bianchetti, & Trabucchi, 1994; Zanetti et al., 1997; Zanetti et al., 2001). Usually, a range of difficulty levels is available within a standardized set of tasks to allow for selection of the level of difficulty that is most appropriate for a given individual. Some tasks may be personalized; for example, recall may be trained through practice in recalling items of personal information (Davis et al., 2001).

Consensus Panel Recommendations

As mentioned previously, although apparently a recommendation for cognitive stimulation, SIGN (2006) in fact supported implementation of cognitive training, to be delivered at home by caregivers with some minimal training. The Canadian Consensus Conference (Hogan et al., 2008), in contrast, concluded that there is insufficient evidence to draw any firm conclusions about the effectiveness of cognitive training in improving or maintaining cognitive and functional performance in people with mild to moderate dementia, and recommended further research. The World Federation for Biological Psychiatry (Livingston et al., 2005) and the NICE-SCIE guidelines (2006) do not specifically refer to cognitive training in their recommendations.

Meta-Analyses of Group Designs

The Cochrane Review of randomized controlled trials (RCTs) of cognitive training in dementia (Clare, Moniz-Cook, Orrell, Spector, & Woods, 2003, updated 2007) found no evidence that cognitive training produces improvements on standardized outcome measures of cognition, functioning, or well-being, although modest short-term improvements in performance on targeted tasks can sometimes be observed. Nine RCTs were included in the updated review, although the diversity of outcome measures reduced the possibilities for meta-analysis.

Sitzer, Twamley, and Jeste (2006), using broader inclusion criteria, included 17 studies in their meta-analysis of cognitive training in Alzheimer's disease. They conclude that there is a medium effect size (0.47) across all types of training across the whole range of outcome measures, making cognitive training a promising intervention. They distinguish restorative training strategies from compensatory strategies; the former involves general cognitive stimulation as well as repetitive memory drills, and the latter includes using external aids, mnemonics, and procedural learning (overlapping with our definition of cognitive rehabilitation). Restorative strategies appear to be associated in this review with larger effect sizes, with general stimulation techniques prominent in four of the five reports with the most beneficial results. It should be noted that in fact five of the 17 included studies here would be encompassed in our definition of cognitive stimulation. Other findings of interest from this analysis include larger effect sizes for individual interventions compared with group approaches, and lower effect sizes for studies judged to be of higher quality, in terms of design and execution. This appeared to reflect lower effect sizes where the comparison group received a placebo intervention, offering a control for the effects of attention rather than a wait list control group. Effect sizes varied across outcomes, with self-rated effect sizes being smaller than informant rated on measures of cognition and behavior. Large effect sizes were found, for example, on measures of verbal and visual learning and memory, especially using restorative strategies (1.16), and on performance-based Activities of Daily Living (ADLs) associated with compensatory procedural memory strategies (0.69).

Randomized Controlled Trials

Several of the RCTs included in the meta-analyses described previously have been able to demonstrate little or no benefit associated with cognitive training. For example, Heiss,

Kessler, Mielke, Szelies, and Herholz (1994) compared the effects of 26 weeks of twice-weekly 1-hour sessions of computerized training involving practice on memory, perceptual and motor tasks with a social support placebo condition involving in total 35 people with mild to moderate Alzheimer's disease (AD). After 26 weeks, no differences were found between the two groups on any measures. Cahn-Weiner et al. (2003) evaluated a 6-week group memory training program, comparing results with those of a group educational and support program. The memory training produced no significant benefits in terms of neuropsychological test performance or caregiver reports of memory functioning and activities of daily living. The 34 participants were all on AChEIs.

Other studies have shown some benefits on tasks directly targeted by the training, without generalization to other tasks or measures. For example, Davis et al. (2001) compared effects of an individual intervention consisting of five weekly 1-hour cognitive training sessions with a placebo therapy condition in 37 people with early-stage AD. The cognitive training sessions involved learning face-name associations and using the technique of spaced retrieval (Camp, Bird, & Cherry, 2000) to rehearse details of personal information. Following intervention, the trained group improved their scores compared to their own baseline performance on recall of face-name associations and personal details. Among a range of neuropsychological tests, there was only one significant difference, with the trained group performing better on one attentional task, and there were no between-group differences in levels of depression or self-rated quality of life. Loewenstein et al. (2004) were able to demonstrate significant benefits of cognitive training on a number of tasks designed to assess directly some of the skills targeted in their cognitive training intervention. These included face-name association recall, object recall, making change for a purchase, and balancing a checkbook.

Among studies appearing to show some effects on neuropsychological evaluations, Quayhagen et al. (1995) had family members engage the person with dementia in 1 hour per day of practice on tasks targeting memory, problem-solving and conversational fluency, comparing results with those of placebo and wait-list control groups, with 78 participants in total. Following intervention, the training group performed significantly better on some aspects of memory and verbal fluency, but not on other aspects of memory or problem solving. Caregiver ratings of behavior problems remained stable for the training group but declined for the other groups. However, aggregation of measures in reporting results makes the findings of this study difficult to interpret with certainty.

Two controlled trials enable some direct comparisons to be made between cognitive stimulation and cognitive training. Farina et al. (2006) compared two group programs, comprising 15 three-hour sessions over an 8-week period, involving 32 people with mild to moderate Alzheimer's disease. The first offered global stimulation, including recreational activities, similar to Spector et al.'s (2003) approach. The second program was described as cognitive specific and included procedural memory training on ADLs and training of residual functions, such as attention, memory, and language. Allocation to groups was sequential rather than randomized for pragmatic reasons. Participants in the global stimulation groups showed improvements in behavioral disturbances, improved function in everyday life and improved verbal fluency, whereas the cognitive specific groups showed only an improvement in ADL function. At 6-month follow-up, caregivers of those who had attended the global stimulation program reported less distress related to difficult behavior. The authors conclude that the global stimulation program, which could be delivered by staff with relatively little training, appeared to be at least as effective as the cognitive specific program, which was delivered by specialized staff. Tarraga et al. (2006) report an evaluation of multimedia therapy, a computerized system offering practice across cognitive domains including attention, language, and memory. Difficulty level was self-adjusting and tailored to the individual's performance level. Participants ($N = 15$) attended a day care center 5 days a week, where this system was available, alongside the other activities offered. Three computer sessions a week were offered, lasting from 15–25 minutes, over a 24-week period. Comparison participants ($N = 16$) did not have access to the computer system, but the other activities on offer, for 3.5 hours per day, constituted a global cognitive stimulation program, together with reinforcement of ADLs. The results of a comparison group not attending the day center are also presented, but it is only the comparison between computerized cognitive training plus cognitive stimulation and cognitive stimulation alone that involves random allocation. All participants had been taking ACHEIs for some time. Results indicated that the computerized system appeared to be associated with more sustained improvements on standard cognitive screening measures (the MMSE and ADAS-Cog) than the cognitive stimulation group, although the latter did show benefit compared with the untreated control group. However, most differences between the two types of intervention did not reach statistical significance.

Conclusions

Despite a good deal of research effort, there is an absence of clear support for efficacy of cognitive training with people with dementia. Some of the positive effects occasionally noted appear to be attributable to global stimulation rather than to specific training. However, studies have tended to have small sample sizes, and in some cases offered a relatively small dose of the intervention. Use of standardized neuropsychological tests as outcome measures in repeat testing sessions at relatively short intervals may contaminate the findings with general practice effects, thus obscuring possible effects of specific treatments.

Additionally, use of neuropsychological tests as outcome measures for cognition means, in effect, that what is being assessed is transfer of training effects, rather than specific effects on target tasks. This means there is a risk that some important effects, indicative of the potential of cognition-focused intervention to make a practical difference to functioning in everyday life, are missed. There are encouraging indications that short-term training-specific improvements may be achieved in some areas, and it will be important to harness the possible relevance of this to the person's everyday life. The use of analogues of real-life tasks as the focus of training is a useful development. Loewenstein et al. (2004) trained participants in tasks such as making change for a purchase and balancing a checkbook, demonstrating gains in targeted areas compared to control group performance. This is an important finding. Training effects may not automatically generalize to produce observable benefits in daily life, but if it is possible to support the ability to manage tasks of the kind that arise in daily life through cognitive training it may also be possible to demonstrate that this kind of approach does have an impact on functioning. However, at the present time, while cognitive training studies report some positive findings, the overall balance of evidence does not support the value of cognitive training for people with dementia.

COGNITIVE REHABILITATION

Cognitive rehabilitation is a more individualized approach, aiming to identify and tackle the difficulties that are most relevant to the person with dementia and his/her supporters (Clare, 2007). The emphasis is not on enhancing performance on cognitive tasks as such, but on improving functioning in the everyday context. Goals and needs are identified collaboratively, and reflect the impact of cognitive changes on daily life and well-being. These are then addressed directly in the real-life context in order to improve functioning, with no implicit assumption that changes instituted in one setting will necessarily generalize to another. Individual interventions are designed to address the identified goals. Interventions generally fall into one of three categories—restoration, compensation, or environmental modification. Aims may be to make the most of remaining memory abilities or enhance or maintain performance of everyday activities (for example, helping the person to remember important information so as to be able to continue with an enjoyed activity), to develop the use of compensatory aids and strategies in order to reduce demands on memory, for example, introducing a calendar so the person can find out what day it is, or to alter the surroundings so as to better support everyday functioning.

Several principles have been delineated that can assist in developing interventions to help with taking in and retaining information. These include the provision of extra support at encoding and retrieval, for example, by means of appropriate cues, mnemonics, or spaced retrieval (Camp et al., 2000; Hill, Evankovich, Sheikh, & Yesavage, 1987; Riley & Heaton, 2000), and encouraging rich and effortful processing of information during encoding, for example, through semantic elaboration, multimodal encoding, or subject performed tasks (Bird & Kinsella, 1996; Bird & Luszcz, 1991, 1993; Hutton, Sheppard, Rusted, & Ratner, 1996). While errorless learning, or the reduction of errors during learning, can produce good results (Clare & Jones, 2008), the most recent evidence finds no differences between errorless and errorful methods, suggesting that learning may be achieved through a variety of means (Dunn & Clare, 2007).

Attempts to enhance or maintain performance of everyday activities involve building on the relative preservation of procedural memory. Here again, subject-performed tasks may be used to good effect (Bird & Kinsella, 1996; Hutton et al., 1996). Provision of cues can assist in establishing performance, after which the cues can be gradually faded out. There is evidence that attention to procedural memory functioning can support activities of daily living (Josephsson et al., 1993), and similar approaches can be applied to the restoration of basic skills such as using a spoon to feed oneself (Camp et al., 1997).

Use of external memory aids can help to compensate for the impact of impaired memory functioning on everyday life. For the person with dementia it may be possible to build on existing strategies to adapt these and make them more efficient. A new memory aid may only be successful if appropriate support is given for learning to use it. Memory books or memory wallets can help to maintain social engagement, serving as prompts for conversation (Bourgeois, 1990). Signposts can help people find their way around an unfamiliar environment (Hanley, 1981).

Consensus Panel Recommendations

The Canadian Consensus Conference (Hogan et al., 2008) concluded that there is insufficient evidence to draw any firm conclusions about effectiveness of cognitive rehabilitation in improving or maintaining cognitive and functional performance in people with mild to moderate dementia and recommended further research on this topic. No specific recommendations are provided by the other guidelines considered.

Meta-Analyses of Group Designs

The Cochrane Review on cognitive training and cognitive rehabilitation in dementia (Clare et al., 2003, updated 2007) concluded that the absence of RCTs on cognitive rehabilitation made it impossible to draw any conclusions on its efficacy. Sitzer et al. (2006) did suggest that effect sizes for restorative strategies were higher than those for compensatory strategies, but few, if any, of the studies considered would be seen as encompassing the individualized approach to cognitive rehabilitation outlined earlier.

Randomized Controlled Trials

One RCT of way-finding in a new environment has been identified (McGilton, Rivera, & Dawson, 2003). Thirty-two nursing home residents with Alzheimer's disease were included, and the intervention comprised a location map and behavioral training, over a period of 1 month. Ability to find one location (out of several tested) was improved after the intervention, but the effects were not maintained 3 months later. These results were less promising than those reported in the reality orientation literature by Hanley, McGuire, and Boyd (1981), where ward orientation improved following a brief period of training.

Single-Subject Experimental Analyses

A number of case studies and case series has been reported, some using experimental analyses. Several of these have focused on identifying whether specific instructional techniques are beneficial in achieving improvement with identified goals. For example, in relation to making the most of remaining memory ability, two case studies are reported by Clare and colleagues. Clare, Wilson, Breen, and Hodges (1999) taught a participant with early-stage Alzheimer's disease the names of members of his social club to help maintain his confidence in participating. Names were taught using a multicomponent method incorporating mnemonics, the method of vanishing cues, and spaced retrieval. Recall improved from around 20% at baseline to almost 100% following intervention, which included generalization in the real-life setting, and gains were largely maintained up to two years later (Clare, Wilson, Carter, Hodges, & Adams, 2001). Clare, Wilson, Carter, and Hodges (2003) report a

66-year-old man with early-stage Alzheimer's disease. He was taught the names of 13 members of his support group using a mnemonic strategy coupled with either expanding rehearsal or repeated presentation, or both, within an errorless learning paradigm. Recall scores improved from a mean of 2.31% at initial baseline to 91.46% following intervention, and gains were largely maintained at follow-up. Clare, Wilson, Carter, Roth, and Hodges (2002) taught 12 people with mild Alzheimer's disease face-name associations using a similar paradigm. Results showed a significant group improvement in recall of trained, but not control, items, with gains largely maintained 6 months later without further practice. Individual differences in response to intervention suggested that participants who were more aware of their memory difficulties achieved better outcomes. No decline in well-being was evident. Dunn and Clare (2007) compared four different types of learning support for learning familiar and novel face-name associations with 10 people with Alzheimer's. It appeared that reducing errors was not a significant factor in improving performance, but that for novel associations, effortful strategies were more effective in supporting learning.

Bird (2001) describes the application of these strategies in addressing behavioral problems (see section on challenging behavior). Josephsson et al. (1993) evaluated the use of external memory aids and procedural memory training in supporting retrieval in everyday living tasks, such as making a drink or preparing a snack. Aids such as signs on drawers and cupboards were used, together with verbal guidance. Three of the four participants showed improvements, although two of these required continued support to maintain improved levels of function. The fourth participant was very anxious, and this interfered with learning. A recent case study describes the successful application of a cognitive rehabilitation approach with an individual meeting criteria for amnestic Mild Cognitive Impairment, whose individual goals

included increasing her level of social interaction (Clare et al., 2009).

Use of diaries and other memory aids was touched upon in the discussion of single-case studies in the area of cognitive stimulation. Clare et al. (2001) reported benefits arising from the introduction of simple memory aids as a means of addressing individual rehabilitation goals. Further work in this area has been undertaken by Bourgeois (1990, 1993), who has evaluated the effects of a prosthetic memory aid on conversational skills in six people with moderate to severe dementia. The aid consisted of photographs and pictures of past and more recent events, important people in the person's life, and so on, in a convenient, robust wallet or book format. The person's spouse and other visitors were encouraged to use the aid when talking with the person. The results suggest that its use was associated with less ambiguous utterances and more statements of fact. The quality of conversation was assessed by independent raters as being significantly improved with the use of the aid as a focus for conversation. The aid is also reported to have proved useful in improving the quality of interaction between pairs of people with dementia.

Finally, literature on signposting in reality orientation indicates the role of external memory aids. In several single-case studies, people with dementia have successfully been taught to find their way around a ward or care home environment (Gilleard, Mitchell, & Riordan, 1981; Hanley, 1981; Lam & Woods, 1986). Hanley (1981) showed that signs were more effective when combined with staff involvement, pointing out the signs and using them to orientate the person in simple, brief training sessions.

Conclusions

Evidence from single-case studies and series continues to be promising, but cognitive rehabilitation has faced several challenges in becoming an evidence-based intervention

These relate to its essence and strength as a fully individualized approach; it is not impossible to evaluate individualized interventions using the RCT design, but it does mean the treatment manual must build in the individualized assessment and goal planning required. Individualized outcome measures are also required. A recently completed RCT (Clare et al., 2010) involving 69 people with mild dementia identified significant improvements in achieving individualized goals, following eight sessions of individual cognitive rehabilitation, compared with no treatment and relaxation-based control groups, confirms that these difficulties are not insurmountable as well as the clinical efficacy of this approach.

REMINISCENCE THERAPY

Reminiscence-based approaches use photographs, music, and archive recordings and items from the past to prompt and stimulate a variety of personal memories. Reminiscence work with older people developed from psychotherapeutic considerations, emphasizing the place of life review in adaptation (Bornat, 1994; Coleman, 1986), and has been used extensively with older people who are depressed as well as those with dementia. There is substantial literature on the effectiveness of various types of reminiscence work in reducing depressive symptoms in older people (Bohlmeijer, Smit, & Cuijpers, 2003; Scogin & McElreath, 1994).

The terms *reminiscence* and *life review* have often been used interchangeably. Haight and Burnside (1993) propose that life review be used specifically to describe a therapeutic intervention where the goal is for the person to achieve a sense of integrity. This typically involves the older person recalling and evaluating events and experiences throughout their life, usually on a one-to-one basis with a therapist, who acts as a therapeutic listener (Garland, 1994). In view of the fact that life review therapy, as described here, is likely to

involve working through memories and experiences, which may at times be painful and difficult, it may be most useful in early-stage dementia (Haight et al., 2003), where it can be undertaken, with the person's consent and with a clear aim, in the context of a therapeutic relationship.

Reminiscence, on the other hand, typically has less specific goals and methods. It may aim to increase communication and socialization, and/or provide pleasure and entertainment. It may be individual or group-based; may be structured or free-flowing; may include more general memories than specific events or experiences; themes and prompts are frequently used; evaluation of memories is not specifically encouraged; and the focus is on a relaxed, positive atmosphere. Sad memories may emerge, but support is available from the group leader and other members, or from the worker in individual work, to contain any distress or pain associated with such memories. This approach is appropriate for people with a mild to moderate degree of dementia. There does need to be sensitivity to the possibility, particularly in a group setting, that events having traumatic connotations for certain individuals may be inadvertently raised by other members of the group. Awareness of participants' life histories can help to ensure appropriate support can be given if this does occur.

A popular development has been the production of life storybooks, often based on a life review, including photographs and incidents and events from the person's life (McKeown, Clark, & Repper, 2006). Increasingly, these are using modern technologies to store and present images, music, and so forth, and this can be on a personal basis, for life story work, or using more general images and sounds as triggers for individual or group reminiscence work.

Although reminiscence work originated from psychodynamic considerations, a cognitive basis for its use with people with dementia can also be identified. This is based on the apparent preservation of remote memory in dementia; the person appears to remember events from their childhood, while unable to recall what happened an hour previously. In fact, when this area has been systematically tested, recall for specific events from many years ago is not relatively preserved (Morris, 2008). People with dementia perform less well in retrieving memories from across the life span when compared with people without dementia, matched for age. People with dementia do recall more memories from early life, but so do normal older people. These memories may be overlearned or well rehearsed, or have particular personal and/or emotional significance for the person concerned. As Morris points out, research on autobiographical memory in dementia indicates there can typically be virtually no recall from the person's middle years. This may be seen as leading to a risk of discontinuity between past and present, which could be hypothesized as adding greatly to the difficulty of retaining a sense of identity (R. T. Woods, 1998). In this way, the cognitive process of autobiographical memory links with the person's sense of self, with potential implications for well being.

Consensus Panel Recommendations

Despite being a popular intervention in the dementia care field, reminiscence therapy has yet to figure strongly in consensus panel recommendations. The SIGN (2006) made no recommendation — not even based on expert opinion — concluding that there was a lack of evidence of clinical effectiveness for reminiscence therapy in the treatment of people with dementia. NICE SCIE (2006) included reminiscence therapy among a list of non-pharmacological interventions for people with dementia with comorbid depression and/or anxiety, along with exercise and multisensory stimulation. The Canadian Consensus Conference (Hogan et al., 2008) likewise places reminiscence therapy in a similar list in relation to behavioral and psychological symptoms in the setting of mild to moderate

dementia (recommendation 23b). The World Federation of Biological Psychiatry (Livingston et al., 2005) assigned their lowest grade of recommendation to reminiscence therapy, having identified five studies of reminiscence therapy interventions, but with inconsistent or inconclusive results, and generally having small numbers of participants.

Meta-Analyses of Group Designs

R. T. Woods, Spector, Jones, Orrell, and Davies (2005) carried out a Cochrane systematic review of reminiscence therapy for people with dementia. They were able to include five RCTs in the review, but only four, involving 144 participants, had extractable data that could be used in a meta-analysis. Each study used a different type of reminiscence work, including group and individual approaches and the involvement of families. Most had very small numbers of participants. There were some significant findings from the meta-analyses: Cognition and mood were improved at follow-up, and general behavioral function was improved at the end of the treatment period. There were indications of some positive changes for caregivers, with reduced strain and greater knowledge of the person with dementia reported. However, overall the review provided inconclusive evidence of the efficacy of reminiscence therapy for dementia.

Randomized Controlled Trials

Since publication of the Cochrane Review, several further RCTs have been published. Sixty people with dementia living in the community were randomized to attend 8-10 weekly reminiscence groups or treatment as usual, in each case at a day care facility (Tadaka & Kanagawa, 2004, 2007). For the group as a whole, significant improvements were reported on cognitive function, withdrawal and disorientation, with the improvements in withdrawal and disorientation being sustained at a 6 month follow-up evaluation

(Tadaka & Kanagawa, 2004). Participants diagnosed with vascular dementia tended to have better, more sustained outcomes than those with a diagnosis of Alzheimer's (Tadaka & Kanagawa, 2007).

Wang (2007) reports a RCT of reminiscence groups with 102 people with dementia living in institutional care in Taiwan. Eight weekly sessions were compared with usual treatment; assessors were blind to group allocation, and group leaders undertook extensive training. Significant improvements in both cognition, assessed with the MMSE (effect size 0.46), and depression rated by staff (effect size 0.59), were reported at the end of the treatment period.

In contrast to these group interventions, Haight, Gibson, and Michel (2006) evaluated an intervention involving the production of a life storybook, based on an individual structured life review. The intervention was delivered by care staff, who received training and weekly supervision. Randomization and evaluations were undertaken by researchers— it is not clear that those carrying out assessments were blind to group allocation. Thirty-one people with dementia participated, 16 of these being randomized to receive treatment as usual. Improvements favored the reminiscence group in terms of depression, communication, positive mood, and cognition (MMSE), with large effect sizes (e.g., 1.28 for cognition; 0.85 for depression).

Other studies have examined the immediate impact of involvement in a reminiscence group, with participants acting as their own controls. Head, Portnoy, and Woods (1990) found an increase in interaction in one group, compared with an alternative activity, but a group in another day center failed to show a differential benefit from involvement in reminiscence activities. Brooker and Duce (2000) showed higher levels of well-being during reminiscence groups, compared with other activities and unstructured time, in people with dementia attending 3-day hospitals. However, Baillon et al. (2004) showed no difference between the immediate effects of reminiscence and multisensory stimulation on agitation in people with dementia. Head et al. (1990) point out that whether reminiscence work will be more effective than a comparison activity will very much depend on the alternative activities on offer. This is illustrated by Politis et al. (2004), who compared kit-based one-to-one reminiscence sessions (involving quiz type questions) with resident-led one-to-one sessions in a nursing home. Apathy significantly reduced for residents receiving either intervention, with no difference between them. Again this emphasizes the variety of interventions encompassed by the reminiscence umbrella.

Single-Subject Experimental Analyses

An excellent example of the use of new technologies to support reminiscence work is reported by Massimi et al. (2008), with an 84-year-old man diagnosed with Alzheimer's disease. A Biography Theater was developed, presenting the person's digital life history in pictures and music, with video clips of his daughters talking about events in his life. The material was presented on what was essentially a digital picture frame on the man's kitchen table. Particular chapters could be selected, but in the absence of user input, the life history would run continuously (the volume could be turned down). The system was evaluated with a single-case ABC design (i.e., with no return to baseline or control condition), and the results were suggestive of a reduction in apathy and an increase in self-identity. There was some reduction in autobiographical memory overall, and no indication of depressed mood.

Conclusions

Moos and Bjorn (2006) have reviewed life story work in intervention studies for people with dementia in institutional care. They caution against overreliance on quantitative trials at this stage, arguing that there remains a great deal to learn regarding how best to provide interventions that are sensitive and individualized.

They suggest that life story work needs to translate into interactions with caregivers. Good examples of this would be care plans that are based on a full understanding of the person's life story, as a means of responding to challenging behavior (Gibson, 1994; Moniz-Cook, Stokes, & Agar, 2003), and the involvement of family caregivers in reminiscence groups for people with dementia (Gibson, 2004; Schweitzer & Bruce, 2008). There is scope here for studies using experimental single-case designs.

Clearly, as well as further development of intervention modalities, studies are needed delineating the outcomes of the different types of reminiscence work already available. The recent studies focusing on aspects such as well-being and autobiographical memory, where reminiscence work might be expected to have most impact, are especially welcome.

For the present, with the availability of a number of new RCTs, we can conclude that there is support from two small RCTs (one included in the Cochrane Review) from different research groups for life story books, based on a structured life review, having an effect on cognitive function and mood. There is also support from the meta-analysis and two additional RCTs for reminiscence groups having effects on cognition and aspects of mood and behavior. However, there is some inconsistency regarding at what point these improvements occur, and which aspects of behavior change; there are suggestions that people with different types of dementia may show less response than others. Further evaluation will be required here, particularly of the effects of involving family members in the group work, and the outcomes achieved for such caregivers.

PSYCHOLOGICAL APPROACHES WITH FAMILY CAREGIVERS

There is an extensive literature on psychological interventions with family caregivers

supporting people with dementia, recognizing that such caregivers frequently experience psychological distress and that depression and anxiety are common, especially in female spouses (Mahoney, Regan, Katona, & Livingston, 2005). Reducing such distress is, of course, worthy as a therapeutic target in its own right, but is likely to have the added value of enhancing the quality of life of the person with dementia, who may receive care at home for longer, and/or enjoy a better relationship with their caregiver, if they are less distressed and coping more effectively.

Early interventions tended to focus on group modalities, such as caregiver support groups, which varied in approach and emphasis from peer support, through psychoeducation, to a psychodynamic group. Although more individual-centered approaches are now apparent, there remain a variety of approaches, with multicomponent interventions being the norm. Among these components, the psychological approaches that can be identified include: (a) reducing the stressful aspects of caregiving, by using behavioral management techniques to reduce the impact of behaviors such as aggression, agitation, and so forth (Teri, McCurry, Logsdon, & Gibbons, 2005); (b) directly reducing symptoms of anxiety and negative affect through stress reduction techniques such as relaxation, anger management and/or therapy, including CBT, for depressed mood (Gallagher-Thompson & Steffen, 1994); (c) increasing knowledge and coping skills through education regarding dementia, symptoms, and management which would typically address attributions and perceptions regarding the problems experienced and aim to develop problem-solving skills and might take place in a peer support context, with a group of other family caregivers, sharing ideas and experiences (Brodaty & Berman, 2008); and (d) increasing social support by mobilizing family resources, enhancing existing social support and networks, and identifying and making use of possible sources of help (e.g., Zarit & Edwards, 2008).

Consensus Panel Recommendations

The World Federation of Biological Psychiatry (Livingston et al., 2005) does not address caregiver outcomes. The SIGN (2006) emphasizes importance of information for caregivers and people with dementia at every stage, and includes CBT, counseling, and stress management in a list of methods for disseminating appropriate information. NICE-SCIE (2006) provides a strong set of recommendations regarding interventions for family caregivers. Emphasis is on tailored interventions, with multiple components including: individual or group psychoeducation; peer support groups with other caregivers, tailored to the needs of individuals depending on the stage of dementia of the person being cared for and other characteristics; support and information by telephone and through the Internet; training courses about dementia, services, and benefits, and communication and problem solving in the care of people with dementia and involvement of other family members as well as the primary caregiver in family meetings (recommendation 1.11.2.2). Involvement of the person with dementia is to be encouraged wherever possible. A further recommendation (1.11.2.5) states that caregivers of people with dementia who experience psychological distress and negative psychological impact should be offered psychological therapy, including cognitive behavior therapy, conducted by a specialist practitioner.

The Canadian Consensus Conference (Hogan et al., 2008) makes a number of caregiver related recommendations (e.g., 24, 26). Relevant to the current discussion, referral to services that offer comprehensive treatment programs including caregiver support, education, and training is recommended. Assistance in developing skills in managing behavior problems through both support groups (extending over several months) and in-home psychoeducational interventions is also emphasized. Individual psychotherapy (or medication) from appropriate specialists is

recommended in response to identification of any mental health problems the caregiver may experience.

Meta-Analyses of Group Designs

Brodaty, Green, and Koschera (2003) report a meta-analysis of psychosocial interventions for caregivers of people with dementia. Thirty studies were included, with a positive effect size of 0.31 (CI 0.13–0.50) for psychological distress. Brodaty et al. point out that this small to moderate effect implies that, following the intervention, the average caregiver in a treatment group will be less depressed than 62% of caregivers in a control condition. Caregivers were very satisfied with all the interventions offered, and there was a moderate effect on caregiver knowledge, but a small effect size for caregiver burden. In four out of seven studies including time to nursing home placement as an outcome measure, placement was delayed by the intervention. The key elements of successful interventions could not be delineated, but it appeared that more intensive, flexible interventions and those where the person with dementia was also involved tended to be more effective.

Other systematic reviews have emphasized the diversity of results reported, but have examined in more detail the nature of interventions offered. Pusey and Richards (2001) concluded that individualized interventions utilizing problem solving and behavior management were most effective; Cooke, McNally, Mulligan, Harrison, and Newman (2001) similarly identified problem solving as important, but also highlighted the role of social support. Sorensen, Pinquart, and Duberstein (2002) report a meta-analysis of caregiver interventions, which was not specific to dementia, that found that the intervention effects for caregivers of people with dementia were less than those for other groups. They included 78 intervention studies and grouped interventions into six types, comparing results across a range of outcome domains. The six types were: (1) psychoeducation, (2) supportive interventions, (3) psychotherapy (including CBT), (4) respite/day care, (5) training of care recipient, and (6) multicomponent and miscellaneous. Psychoeducation and psychotherapy had the most consistent effect across outcomes, with multicomponent interventions having the biggest effect on burden. Longer interventions had more effect on depression, and individual interventions had more effect than those delivered in a group format. In general, spouse caregivers benefited less than adult children from the interventions reviewed.

A further review was undertaken for the NICE-SCIE guideline (2006), which identified 25 new dementia studies meeting the criteria for inclusion specified by Sorensen et al. (2002). Although the majority found an effect on at least some outcome measures, a quarter found no significant effects, suggesting that the effects of caregiver interventions can be elusive.

A meta-analysis of results from the multicenter REACH (Resources for Enhancing Alzheimer's Caregiver Health) project has been carried out (Gitlin et al., 2003). This involved six centers in the United States evaluating different interventions, but using a common set of measures and procedures. The main finding was that at a 6 month follow up assessment, active interventions (regardless of the type) were superior to control conditions in relation to caregiver burden. There were differences in response to treatment, with better results for females, caregivers with low education, Hispanics, and nonspouses. Gitlin et al. conclude that interventions should be multicomponent and tailored to the individual caregiver.

Randomized Controlled Trials

Most studies have included a variety of interventions, even when they are not presented as multicomponent. For example, Marriott, Donaldson, Tarrier, and Burns (2000) report a successful intervention program described as a cognitive behavioral family intervention, which appeared to include an educational component

as well as problem-solving skills and relaxation; and Mittelman et al. (1995) describe the impact of a comprehensive support program on depression in spouse caregivers, which included family counseling sessions and encouragement to join peer support groups.

The majority of studies have recruited any caregivers willing to take part, rather than targeting those with clinical levels of depression or anxiety, which may contribute to the mixed results obtained. Exceptions include the Marriott et al. (2000) study just mentioned, where caregivers were selected on the basis of psychiatric caseness, and a larger study reported by Gallagher-Thompson and Steffen (1994), who contrasted cognitive behavioral and brief psychodynamic treatments in 66 clinically depressed caregivers of frail, elderly relatives (some but not all had dementia). At posttreatment the two therapies were equally effective overall; 71% of patients no longer met clinical criteria for depression. However, there was an interaction between outcome and longevity of caretaking. Patients who had been caretakers for a shorter period had a greater response to psychodynamic therapy, while those who had been caring for their relative for more than 3.5 years responded better to CBT. This interaction was less evident at 3 and 12 month follow up. It is possible that more chronic caregivers have a greater need for a structured approach (which CBT offers) and a corresponding difficulty in exploring problems that may have left them emotionally depleted. Akkerman and Ostwald (2004) report an RCT of group CBT (nine sessions) for anxiety involving 38 caregivers of people with dementia, with a wait list control condition. Self report and clinician measures of anxiety were improved at the end of treatment and at a 6 week follow up, and improved sleep was also reported.

Mittelman's extensive series of studies in New York is of particular importance as an exemplar of a successful multicomponent approach. As mentioned previously, it involved family counseling and peer support, and 406 spouse caregivers participated in the RCT (Mittelman et al., 1995; Mittelman, Roth, Coon, & Haley, 2004). Six sessions of individual and family counseling were offered initially, backed up by availability of the counselor by telephone for the duration of the study. All participants (in control condition as well as in the intervention condition) agreed to attend peer support groups, and caregivers in the control condition could also access the counselors if desired. The main findings include both a reduced level of depression in caregivers and a marked reduction in rates of institutionalization of the person with dementia. These are sustained effects, with depression rates still lower 3 years later and at long-term follow-up (up to 17 years), a difference in median time to placement of 557 days between intervention and control groups (Mittelman, Haley, Clay, & Roth, 2006). The success of the program appears to be underpinned by enhanced social support networks over a 5-year period (Drentea et al., 2006) and changes in attributions regarding difficult behavior made by caregivers in the intervention condition (Mittelman, Roth, Haley, & Zarit, 2004). Benefits of the intervention persist in the period when the person with dementia is admitted to a nursing home; burden and depression were found to be less for caregivers in the intervention group following the admission, compared with caregivers in the control condition (Gaugler, Roth, Haley, & Mittelman, 2008).

Mittelman, Brodaty, Wallen, and Burns (2008) have now replicated this approach across three countries (United States, Australia, United Kingdom). A RCT included 158 spouse caregivers of people with dementia (all taking an acetylcholinetserase inhibitor, donepezil). Similar to the original study, five sessions of individual and family counseling were offered in the first 3 months, then ad hoc telephone counseling was available throughout a 24-month period. Caregivers' depression, assessed using the Beck Depression Inventory, reduced over the 2-year period, even though all the active intervention took place in the first 3 months. This could not be explained, for example, by any increased use of antidepressants in caregivers in the intervention condition.

Conclusions

Gallagher-Thompson and Coon (2007) identified psychoeducational programs (including behavior management, depression, and anger management approaches) and psychotherapy and multicomponent interventions as effective psychological approaches for caregivers, and there does appear to be widespread support for this view, albeit with a recognition that positive effects are not always identified. Behavior management approaches involving family caregivers are reviewed in the next section. Ensuring that interventions are tailored to individual caregiver needs, are of adequate intensity and duration, that outcome measures appropriate to the intervention are used, and that they are sensitive enough to show change (without floor or ceiling effects) in the population included, may increase the chances of success. It is of interest that these approaches often appear to have a greater effect than other social measures such as the provision of respite care or other community services, although it is these that are often seen as a greater priority.

CHALLENGING BEHAVIOR: BEHAVIORAL APPROACHES

Behavioral approaches have been used for many years in seeking to maintain the skills and independence of the person with dementia, for example, in dressing and toileting (R. T. Woods, 1999). From a psychological therapeutic perspective, the focus here is rather on attempts to reduce the frequency and severity of those challenging behaviors that contribute greatly to the difficulties and distress experienced by those in caregiving roles (e.g., Pinkston, Linsk, & Young, 1988). These areas of difficulty are sometimes described as behavior problems, disruptive behavior, behavioral disturbance, or behavioral and psychological symptoms of dementia (BPSD) or agitation. Specific positive behaviors, such as aggression, shouting, screaming, and other repeated vocalizations, sexual disinhibition, wandering and hoarding, and negative behaviors, such as withdrawal and apathy, are sometimes targeted.

Challenging behavior is our preferred term because it provides an implicit reminder that the problem lies in part with our reaction to the behavior, which of itself may not present a problem to the person with dementia. Challenging behavior is a function of a particular care environment; in a different care setting, the behavior in question may not be elicited, or may not be viewed as a problem by those providing care. This means that some interventions may have to involve changes in family caregiver/paid care-worker attributions, attitudes, and interactions.

It is tempting to attempt to identify the most effective therapeutic approach for each type of behavior problem. However, the same label, wandering or aggression, for example, may become attached to quite different behaviors, requiring quite different interventions (Bird & Moniz-Cook, 2008). Add to this the person's unique social environment, their particular profile of physical health, their life history, and so on, and it is clear that an individual assessment and analysis of each person's situation is needed. Often behavioral assessment follows the A-B-C model of antecedents, behavior, and consequences, set in a problem-solving framework (e.g., Teri et al., 2005). Bird and Moniz-Cook (2008) seek to place greater emphasis on the wider context and on antecedents that may not be observable (e.g., a flashback to a traumatic memory), and to include the caregiver response. They describe functional analysis, with an emphasis on the meaning of the behavior and response, as a basis for developing case-specific interventions. This can lead to hypotheses regarding the function of the behavior, which can be subject to testing and refinement (e.g., Moniz-Cook, Woods, & Richards, 2001).

Consensus Panel Recommendations

The SIGN (2006) describe behavior management as a structured, systematic intervention, carried out by family caregivers or care home staff under professional, expert supervision. While behavior management is recommended to reduce depression in people with dementia (see section on CBT for depression and anxiety further on), the conclusions regarding disruptive behavior in care homes or in the community are less positive, with no evidence of a significant reduction being identified.

The World Federation for Biological Psychiatry (Livingston et al., 2005) gives a fairly strong recommendation for the use of standard behavioral management techniques in dementia, but this is again influenced greatly by the impact on depressive symptoms (see section on CBT for depression and anxiety later).

The NICE-SCIE guideline (2006) emphasizes the importance of a thorough and careful assessment, including behavioral and functional analysis, but also the person's health status (including medication and pain), and environmental and biographical factors. The assessment should lead to an individually tailored care plan (recommendation 1.7.1.1), with a regular review and update procedure. It is emphasized that the behavioral and functional analysis should be undertaken by a professional with the appropriate skills, in conjunction with caregivers and care staff.

The Canadian Consensus Conference (Hogan et al., 2008) emphasizes the importance of considering nonpharmacological approaches first, but does not recommend any specific psychological therapies.

Randomized Controlled Trials

Systematic reviews (Livingston et al., 2005; Logsdon, McCurry, & Teri, 2007) have identified a number of relevant RCTs, but the results are mixed, in terms of indicating a clear benefit of behavioral approaches over control conditions.

Among studies failing to find a clear treatment effect, Gormley, Lyons, and Howard (2001) report results from a brief (four session) behavior management program taught to family caregivers, based on the A-B-C model, focused on aggression. Sixty-two people with dementia and their caregivers were randomly allocated to receive the intervention or to a control condition, involving four sessions with the therapist discussing other care-related issues. There was a trend toward reduced aggression in the intervention group. Burgio, Stevens, Guy, Roth, and Haley (2003) report a more intensive multicomponent intervention, involving a 3-hour workshop, 16 home visits over 2 months, and monthly follow-up for 10 months, compared with a control condition offering minimal support. The study was relatively large, involving 118 participants, but there were no significant differences in behavior problems between the conditions, with problems declining over time in both. Beck et al. (2002) also report a large study, with 179 nursing home residents. The interventions were complex, focusing on either activities of daily living or psychosocial activities, or a combination of both, but there were no significant reductions in disruptive behavior, compared with control conditions. Behavioral management was one of the interventions trialed in a rare study comparing psychological and pharmacological interventions in this field (Teri et al., 2000), targeting agitation. The behavioral management involved 11 sessions over 16 weeks with the family caregiver, and proved no less successful than commonly used medications in reducing agitation; however, placebo medication was equally effective.

More positive results have consistently been reported by Teri et al. in relation to their Seattle Protocols approach (Teri et al., 2005), which can be delivered by a range of health-care professionals with appropriate training, working with family caregivers. Relevant outcomes included significant reductions in both frequency and severity of behavior problems, and improved quality of life for the person with dementia. Caregivers were also less distressed by the behavior problems experienced. In relation to specific target behavior problems identified with caregivers at the outset of the intervention, all the caregivers receiving the intervention reported some improvement in at least one target behavior, and 57% of problems were reported to be less frequent. Pleasant event scheduling—a key aspect of the Seattle Protocols—was used by Lichtenberg, Kemp-Havican, MacNeill, and Johnson (2005) in a nursing home context, with a similar unit used as a comparison for that where the intervention took place. Reduced frequency of behavioral disturbance was noted in both units over a 3-month period, but severity significantly decreased in the behavioral treatment unit. Two studies have been based on the Progressively Lowered Stress Threshold Model (Gerdner, Buckwalter, & Reed, 2002; Huang, Shyu, Chen, Chen, & Lin, 2003) with family caregivers. Both involved problem solving, environmental modification, and building pleasant activities into the daily schedule, over four to six sessions at the person's home. Huang et al. (2003) involved 48 caregivers in total; they reported reduced behavior problems in the intervention group, compared with written educational materials. Gerdner et al. (2002) report reduced distress relating to behavioral problems in the intervention group ($N = 132$), with a significant reduction in problem frequency in those caregivers not providing care for a spouse, compared with routine care ($N = 105$).

Cohen-Mansfield, Libin, and Marx (2007) have developed an individualized approach to agitation, based on an assessment of the underlying causes of the behavior. The treatment plan is tailored accordingly, using a systematic algorithm, taking into account the person's remaining abilities and unique characteristics, including previous occupations, hobbies, and important relationships. Participants were 167 people with dementia living in 12 nursing home units. Residents in half the units received the individualized intervention, delivered by a member of the research team over 10 consecutive days, while in the other units staff attended a placebo educational intervention, describing the types and causes of agitation. The primary outcome measure was observed agitation. There was a significant reduction in agitation in participants in the intervention group, and also increases in observed pleasure and interest. It should be noted that it was not possible to allocate nursing home units to control and intervention conditions entirely at random, and the analyses reported do not appear to have taken into account clustering effects.

Single-Subject Experimental Analyses

Several single-case analyses are available, targeting a range of challenging behavior. Bird, Alexopoulos, and Adamowicz (1995) report the use of cued recall to decrease a range of difficult behaviors with people with dementia, including obsessive demands, inappropriate urinating, and intrusive aggressive behavior. Using A-B designs, the intervention appeared to be successful in four out of five cases. The intervention involved the person learning a response to a particular stimulus cue, taught by using spaced retrieval and a fading cues method. For example, a visual cue might indicate the location of the toilet, or mean "stop, do not enter," or an auditory cue (a beeper) might indicate when it was time to go to the toilet, depending on the behavior and its context. Written cues were used by Bourgeois, Burgio, Schulz, Beach, and Palmer (1997) with seven family caregivers each looking after a person with dementia who asked questions repeatedly. Using a multiple baseline design, and seven comparison caregivers, use of these cues was shown to reduce frequency of these repetitive verbalizations. Instead of answering the person's questions, the caregiver was trained to direct the person to make use of their written cues, to find the answer to the question for him/herself.

Functional analysis has been used in a number of single-case studies, using experimental designs. Baake et al. (1994) report a reduction in agitation in a 72-year-old man with probable Alzheimer's disease, during an occupational work program. The analysis indicated that his agitation was being reinforced by contingent attention, and so the intervention involved reinforcement of on-task behavior, additional breaks, more variety of activity, and so forth. Heard and Watson (1999) showed reduction in wandering in four people with dementia using ABAB designs. The intervention involved differential reinforcement of other behavior, using specific reinforcement in each case identified from the functional analysis. Buchanan and Fisher (2002) examined the effects of noncontingent reinforcement on two people with dementia with disruptive vocalizations. Attention and sensory stimulation (e.g., music or TV) were identified as reinforcers in these cases, and offering these noncontingently was effective in reducing the frequency of the target behavior, but in one case the resulting schedule required (of continuous attention) was impractical in a care setting. Noncontingent escape was used by Baker, Hanley, and Mathews (2006) with a 96-year-old woman with Alzheimer's who was hitting staff during personal care. The functional analysis indicated that the hitting served the function of escape, in that staff would back off when she hit out. By building in a 10-second break every 20 seconds during personal care, escape was no longer contingent on hitting, and the frequency of the hitting reduced. Such reduced frequency meant that the personal care routine took no longer than previously, despite the regular breaks. Moniz-Cook et al. (2001, 2003) have described 10 cases where functional analysis has been used to test hypotheses regarding the function of the behavior of people with dementia, including aggression, noise making, and refusal to cooperate with care. They have shown how long-standing culturally rooted beliefs and superstitions can shape the person's response to people and stimuli in their environment, and the importance of understanding the person's life story in evaluating the function of current behavior.

Conclusions

Guidelines often recommend that non-pharmacological approaches should be the first line of intervention in relation to challenging behavior. Howard et al. (2007) found that a brief four-session psychosocial intervention resulted in 14% of people with dementia referred because of agitation improving to the extent that their agitation was no longer a significant problem. Fossey et al. (2006) showed that staff training in person-centered care practices resulted in reduced use of anti-psychotic medication in nursing home residents. The evidence reviewed here—from RCTs and single case studies—suggests that there is even greater scope for individualized, tailored approaches to have an impact on challenging behavior in dementia. However, it is important to bear in mind the variety of factors leading to challenging behavior, including pain, physical health problems, environmental factors, and negative staff attitudes, so that a multidisciplinary, multicomponent approach, such as that described by Bird et al. (1998), will usually be required.

COGNITIVE BEHAVIOR THERAPIES FOR DEPRESSION AND ANXIETY IN DEMENTIA

Increased prevalence of symptoms of depression and anxiety in people with dementia, noted previously, raises issues of what therapeutic approaches might be feasible, especially as low mood appears to be a significant factor in reducing quality of life in people with dementia (Thorgrimsen et al., 2003). Widespread application of cognitive behavior therapy (CBT) for depression and anxiety in other

populations has led to consideration of its feasibility with people with dementia. It might be thought that intact cognitive abilities would be a prerequisite for participation in an approach that focuses on thinking patterns and their relationship to emotion and behavior. Indeed, suggestions were made (e.g., Church, 1983) that older people in general might lack the abstract ability to make use of this approach, but such concerns have proved ill-founded (e.g., James, 2008; Laidlaw, Thompson, Dick-Siskin, & Gallagher-Thompson, 2003). It is possible that the earlier diagnosis of dementia will mean that many more people receive a diagnosis of dementia at a point when they are able to engage in psychological therapy. Demonstration of feasibility and adaptation of approaches have been an important component of the literature in this area to date (Teri & Gallagher-Thompson, 1991; Thompson, Wagner, Zeiss, & Gallagher, 1990), with less emphasis on the cognitive and more on the behavioral in some applications.

Consensus Panel Recommendations

The SIGN (2006) recommends the use of behavior management to reduce depression in people with dementia, based on a study by Teri, Logsdon, Uomoto, and McCurry (1997). This involved family caregivers being taught to use either problem-solving approaches or pleasant-event scheduling to reduce depression in their relative with dementia, living with them in the community. Depression for the participants was improved for up to six months after both interventions.

NICE-SCIE (2006) makes a similar recommendation, also largely influenced by the work of Teri et al. (1997): "For people with dementia who have depression and/or anxiety, cognitive behavioral therapy, which may involve the active participation of their caregivers, may be considered as part of treatment" (recommendation 1.8.1.2).

The World Federation for Biological Psychiatry (Livingston et al., 2005) makes a less specific recommendation, recommending behavioral management techniques in a more general sense, but again largely based on the same group of studies from Teri et al. The Canadian Consensus Conference (Hogan et al., 2008) recommends nonpharmacological interventions as a general first line of intervention in relation to both anxiety and depression in dementia (recommendations 21 and 23), but does not specifically refer to CBT as a treatment modality.

Randomized Controlled Trials

As mentioned previously, the most influential RCT in this area has been that conducted by Teri et al. (1997). Three interventions were compared, in addition to a waiting-list control group. The interventions were undertaken primarily with the family caregiver, although the person with dementia was involved as much as possible. In each of the three conditions, there were nine weekly 1-hour sessions. The first intervention involved teaching the caregiver to identify and develop pleasant events for the person with dementia, and later for themselves, as well as strategies for managing challenging behavior. The second taught a more flexible problem-solving approach, focusing on specific depression behaviors of the person with dementia. A third condition offered a typical care control, with advice and support being offered, but no specific problem-solving or behavioral strategies being adopted. Seventy-two people with dementia and their caregivers, randomly allocated to the four treatment conditions, completed the study. Assessments were carried out blind to treatment allocation. Both the behavioral interventions were associated with reduced levels of depression, compared with the two control conditions. Effect sizes ranged from 0.9 to 1.7 on the depression rating scales used, with 60% of those in the active treatment conditions showing clinically significant improvement, compared with 20% of those in the control conditions. Improved caregiver mood was also

reported, with gains maintained at 6-month follow-up, with no differences between the two active treatments. The active involvement of the caregiver, who is potentially able to ensure regular between-session practice and to enable generalization of skills and activities to the person's everyday environment is a key element. More recently this approach has been described as the Seattle Protocols (Teri et al., 2005), and developed so it can be delivered by a range of health-care professionals with appropriate training. Teri et al. (2003) report a trial involving 153 people with dementia where this behavioral management approach was combined with an exercise program, aiming to achieve 30 minutes per day of structured exercise for the person with dementia. After the 3-month treatment period, there were reductions in depressed mood for the person with dementia, as well as improved physical functioning. A subgroup analysis of those entering this trial with significant levels of depression indicated that their scores on the Hamilton Depression Rating scale improved significantly (effect size 0.4), and that this effect was maintained at 2-year follow-up. McCurry, Gibbons, Logsdon, Vitiello, and Teri (2005) added advice for the caregiver regarding sleep hygiene, and increased daytime exercise and daylight exposure, and reported outcomes including improved sleep and, again, reduced depression (McCurry et al., 2005). In a UK study involving 120 care home residents, behavioral management training for care staff, delivered over seven 1-hour seminars, was associated with reduced depression in residents (Proctor et al., 1999).

Two studies have evaluated relaxation therapy for symptoms of anxiety in people with dementia. Welden and Yesavage (1982) reported improved ratings of behavioral function and less use of sleeping medication in those attending relaxation groups three times a week for 3 months, in comparison with a discussion group control condition. Suhr, Anderson, and Tranel (1999) report a RCT comparing progressive muscle relaxation (PMR) with imaginal relaxation. Thirty-four patients participated, with reduced clinician-rated anxiety and behavioral problems, and improvements on some tests of cognitive function in the group receiving training in PMR. Conceivably, the PMR group responded better as learning this form of relaxation, with its successive tensing and relaxing of muscle groups, relies more on procedural memory, which is relatively spared in dementia. Imaginal relaxation, on the other hand, places a greater demand on cognitive processes, and so may be less appropriate—and effective—with people with dementia.

Single-Subject Experimental Analyses

Four single-cases were reported by Teri and Uomoto (1991), reflecting development of their approach aimed at increasing the number and duration of pleasant events in people with dementia and comorbid depression. In this case series, caregivers met with the therapist for eight sessions, with the person with dementia being included in three of the sessions. The pleasant events schedule was used to identify activities that the person might enjoy, but was not engaging in; the therapist then worked with the caregiver to identify ways of increasing the frequency and duration of these activities. Often the challenge was to find ways of engaging in activities where reduced physical or cognitive function was a barrier; simplified or adapted activities were attempted. With one person with dementia, an ABAB design was used, with daily ratings of duration of pleasant activities and mood as the dependent variables. There was a clear treatment effect, and a clear association between mood and pleasant activities. This was supported by a further case, with a baseline/treatment/follow-up design, with clear increases in both activities and mood by the follow-up period. Two cases with pretest/posttest data are also reported, with improvements on depressed mood and significant increases in duration of pleasant events.

Scholey and Woods (2003) demonstrate the feasibility of individual CBT with people with dementia and comorbid depression, at least in early-stage dementia. In their case series of seven people with a mild degree of dementia, there was a significant overall improvement in depression following eight individual sessions of CBT. On average, there was a statistically significant 3.7-point improvement on the Geriatric Depression Scale (30 items), an effect size of 0.77. Two of the patients showed a significant Reliable Change Index. Adaptations required included more repetition, use of prompts and reminders and so forth, and more emphasis on behavioral activation, but checks were made to ensure adherence to essential CBT principles. Among the themes emerging from these cases were feelings of insecurity, loss of control, and a sense of hopelessness. Interpersonal issues were pertinent for many, and it was also noted that past memories of traumatic events became more difficult, as the coping strategies that had previously served well became weaker.

A small CBT group focusing on negative, unhelpful thoughts regarding memory difficulties, and including relaxation exercises, is described by Kipling, Bailey, and Charlesworth (1999). The three male participants attended seven weekly 1-hour sessions, and all reported reductions in anxiety, with two men also reporting improved mood. Husband (1999) similarly reports three cases where an individual CBT approach—addressing negative cognitions—was used to assist adaptation in the early stages of dementia. Banningh, Kessels, Olde-Rikkert, Geleijns-Lanting, and Kraaimat (2008) report an uncontrolled study of CBT groups with 22 people who had received a diagnosis of MCI and their significant others. The program comprised 10 weekly sessions, each lasting for 2 hours, with separate group sessions for people with MCI and significant others for the first 90 minutes, and all meeting together for the last half hour. The main finding was an increased level of acceptance for the people with MCI.

Koder (1998) described the adaptation of CBT for use with people with cognitive impairment, in relation to anxiety, illustrated by two cases with successful clinical outcomes.

Balasubramanyam, Stanley, and Kunik (2007) describe the adaptation of CBT for anxiety in people with dementia, and present a case example of a man with subcortical dementia, generalized anxiety disorder, PTSD, and major depression. Therapy included learning to self-monitor his anxiety symptoms, breathing skills to manage physiological symptoms, and the use of coping strategies such as coping self-state-ments that he could refer to as necessary. Improvements in worry and depression were reported. The same group (Kraus et al., 2008) reports a further two cases treated with this modified version of cognitive behavior therapy for anxiety in dementia (CBT-AD), including behavioral activation and exposure, with improvements noted in anxiety. Modifications were found to be necessary in the content and structure of CBT, as well as in the learning strategies employed, to take account of cognitive limitations. Family members, friends, or other caregivers were included in the treatment process.

Conclusions

Results from RCTs and several single cases (using AB designs) support the use of relaxation methods and CBT approaches for anxiety in people with mild to moderate dementia. There is promising evidence from the Seattle group regarding behavioral management of depression in people with dementia, from two RCTs and four single cases, which now requires replication by other research groups, with a specific focus on comorbid dementia and depression. Individual and group CBT are clearly feasible for people with mild dementia and depression, and there is some supportive single case evidence, which requires extension and replication.

PSYCHOTHERAPEUTIC APPROACHES

Here we consider a group of approaches that have an emphasis on the emotional world of the person with dementia, the significance of earlier experiences and relationships, and the (sometimes hidden) meanings of communication and behavior. More generally, being psychotherapeutic with people with dementia (Cheston, 1998) places importance on careful listening to the person with dementia, in a situation where, as dementia advances, rational connections may be difficult to discern, and communication becomes more symbolic and free-flowing.

Finnema, Droes, Ribbe, and van-Tilburg (2000) have reviewed studies evaluating emotion-oriented care, which includes such psychotherapeutic approaches used in the 24-hour care context, but has a slightly broader scope, including, for example, reminiscence, life review, and sensory stimulation approaches, as well as probably the best-known and most widely used of these approaches in dementia care, validation therapy (VT). This approach was developed, in part, as a response to the overconfrontational implementation of cognitive approaches, such as reality orientation (Feil, 1993). In VT the aim is to seek to understand attempts at communication made by the person with dementia, rather than simply correcting him or her. Confrontational correction was seen as producing negative emotional responses in the person with dementia ranging from withdrawal to hostility (Dietch et al., 1989).

Validation refers to the validation of the person's emotions, underlying the words expressed by the person with dementia, regardless of the apparent validity or reality of the words per se. Through listening empathically and nonjudgmentally, not challenging the person's view of reality, the aim is to maintain the person's dignity and prevent further withdrawal and decline. The person's current mental state is viewed as being influenced by unresolved issues from previous phases of life, and the person's efforts to deal with them. These issues may be accompanied by painful feelings from the past, which, if not expressed, acknowledged and validated are thought to increase in strength.

Validation therapy may be applied individually, as part of the overall practice of care, or in small group sessions (Morton & Bleathman, 1991). Music is used as a unifying activity in a VT group, and group members are encouraged to have a specific role, such as songleader, welcomer, and so forth. Discussion of a topic chosen to draw on the wisdom and experience of the group members takes up the largest part of the group (Bleathman & Morton 1992).

Validation therapy has typically been used with people across the severity range of dementia. The identification and diagnosis of many more people in the early stages of dementia has made possible a few attempts to apply more standard psychotherapeutic techniques to assist adjustment and adaptation, in both individual and group therapy contexts. Support groups for people with dementia have been described for some time (e.g., Yale, 1995), but there have been few attempts at rigorous evaluation of their effects.

Consensus Panel Recommendations

Emotion-oriented care and psychotherapy have yet to figure in the majority of the consensus panel recommendations reviewed, and the NICE-SCIE guideline did not, having considered the evidence, include VT in its recommendations. Similarly, VT was reviewed for the SIGN (2006) guidelines, but it was concluded that there were no statistically significant or clinically relevant effects from its use with people with dementia. Livingston et al. (2005) also concluded VT had no effect on neuropsychiatric symptoms in dementia.

The third Canadian Consensus Conference on the diagnosis and treatment of dementia (Hogan et al., 2008) recommended that "some people with dementia may benefit from . . . validation therapy . . . ," but noted that there was insufficient evidence to support its routine use in the management of behavioral and psychological symptoms of dementia (recommendation 23).

Livingston et al. (2005) reviewed self-maintenance therapy (Romero & Wenz, 2001), which incorporates techniques from validation, reminiscence, and psychotherapy and aims to help the person with dementia maintain a sense of personal identity, continuity, and coherence. There were positive outcomes in terms of reduced depression and difficult behavior, but this may have been attributable to the therapy being offered during a 3-week admission to a specialist unit with their family caregiver. Livingston et al. (2005) also note evidence indicating that training staff in emotion-oriented care had no effect in one evaluation (Schrijnemaekers et al., 2002).

Meta-Analyses of Group Designs

A Cochrane Review of validation therapy (Neal & Barton-Wright, 2007) identified only three studies—all involving group work—which could be included, with a total of 116 participants. The larger of these studies (Toseland, Diehl, Freeman, Manzanares, & McCallion, 1997) ensured that the validation approach was used appropriately, with training and supervision backed up by monitoring of the quality of the group sessions, which were tape-recorded. The results of the review were inconclusive, although a few positive findings favored validation.

Randomized Controlled Trials

Schrijnemaekers et al. (2002) report an extensive cluster-randomized trial of emotion-oriented care in the Netherlands, involving 151 people with dementia in 16 care homes for older people, over a 12-month follow-up period. Staff in half the homes received training, support, and supervision in implementing emotion-oriented care, including validation approaches, while care continued as usual in the other homes. There were no changes identified in behavior problems in the residents in the experimental homes, and the authors conclude there is insufficient evidence to implement emotion-oriented care more widely. However, it is not clear that the clustering effect was taken into account in determining sample size.

Also from the Netherlands, Finnema et al. (2005) describe an evaluation of integrated emotion-oriented care in 16 nursing home units, involving 146 people with dementia. The core aim of this approach was seen as aiding adaptation to the consequences of the dementia, to improve emotional and social functioning. Over a 7-month period, the results were not dramatic, but residents with mild to moderate dementia in the homes where emotion-oriented care was implemented showed less anxiety and less dissatisfaction than those in control homes. There were no differences attributable to emotion-oriented care for those with more advanced dementia. There was evidence that the extensive training provided for staff in the units where the intervention was implemented did make some difference to the care provided, particularly in relation to making use of knowledge about the resident's life in their care; however, the extent of difference that the training made in day-to-day care is difficult to quantify.

The only RCT identified of psychotherapy per se with people with dementia is reported by Burns et al. (2005). Participants were randomized to receive either six sessions of individual psychodynamic interpersonal psychotherapy or treatment as usual. Although there were no significant improvements on ratings of depression or function following the intervention, the approach proved feasible with, and appreciated by, people with early stage dementia. The therapy was carried out in the person's home, and the therapist spent 10 minutes after each session listening to the caregiver's needs and updating them on progress with the therapy; there was some evidence suggesting positive benefits for caregivers of people receiving the interpersonal therapy.

Single-Subject Experimental Analyses

Morton and Bleathman (1991) report results from a validation group in a residential home

involving five people with dementia. During a baseline period of 10 weeks, observations of behavior, mood, and interaction in the day-room of the home were made. These observations were continued for a further 20-week period, while participants were attending a weekly 1-hour validation group (Bleathman & Morton, 1992 provide a detailed description and selections of the group transcripts), and a further 10 weeks while the focus of the group shifted to reminiscence work. Three residents completed the study and their results were presented in relation to the A-B-C design; for two, interactions increased during the validation period, with a decline during the reminiscence phase, and the other resident showed the opposite pattern. It is noteworthy that these interactions were observed outside the group context — what is clear is that interaction levels were dramatically higher during the actual hour-long group sessions, whatever approach was adopted.

Conclusions

Research to date has failed to establish psychotherapy, validation therapy, and emotion-oriented care as effective therapies for people with dementia. In future research, further consideration needs to be given to the selection of appropriate outcome measures. Mood, quality of life, and engagement appear to be much more relevant than cognitive function, for example; reductions in problem behavior (which most likely has multifactorial causation) may be difficult to demonstrate in group studies. The effects on staff and caregivers and the impact of individual VT requires further study.

There is much scope for further work on psychotherapeutic support groups for people in the early stages of dementia. For example, Cheston, Jones, and Gilliard (2003) describe such groups, where participants were encouraged to share experiences and to discuss their emotional impact, while the group facilitators offered reflections upon the emotional significance of these experiences within the group context. Each group ran for 10 weekly sessions. Overall, participants in this uncontrolled study were significantly less depressed at the end of the group. Forgetfulness was the main theme of the groups, encompassing the experience of memory failure, but also the pain and distress of being forgotten about, and, conversely, the desire to be forgotten about and to be able to forget about oneself. The groups engendered a sense of togetherness, with one participant saying: "I now . . . know I am not the only one."

EVIDENCE-BASED PRACTICES

Table 6.1 summarizes the current state of evidence in relation to psychological therapies for people with dementia and their caregivers. It uses the criteria set out by Chambless and Hollon (1998) in relation to empirically supported therapies. Of the approaches reviewed, only cognitive training and psychotherapeutic approaches are not empirically supported. Cognitive behavior therapy for depression and anxiety in the context of dementia is possibly efficacious, and requires replication in other centers and with larger single-case series to be considered efficacious. Cognitive stimulation, cognitive rehabilitation, reminiscence therapy, caregiver interventions, individualized behavioral interventions, and functional analysis for challenging behavior and relaxation approaches for anxiety in dementia are all considered efficacious by these criteria. This summary indicates that consensus statements and guidelines need to be regularly updated to take into account the growing evidence-base on the efficacy of psychological therapies with people with dementia and their caregivers. It is notable that most of these approaches target people with mild to moderate dementia, and there is a need for continued development of approaches that will enhance the quality of life with people with severe dementia.

TABLE 6.1   Summary of Empirically Supported Psychological Therapies Using Chambless and Hollon (1998) Criteria

Psychological Therapy	Status	Justification
Cognitive stimulation	Empirically supported: efficacious	Several RCTs in independent research settings
Cognitive training	Not empirically supported	Efficacy not supported by the preponderance of RCTs
Cognitive rehabilitation	Empirically supported: efficacious	Single-case experiments with sample size 3+ in several independent research settings
Reminiscence therapy	Empirically supported: efficacious	Several RCTs in independent research settings
Caregiver interventions	Empirically supported: efficacious	Several RCTs in independent research settings
Challenging behavior: individualized behavioral approaches	Empirically supported: efficacious	Several RCTs in independent research settings
Challenging behavior: functional analysis	Empirically supported: efficacious	Single-case experiments with sample size 3+ in several independent research settings
CBT for depression and anxiety in dementia	Empirically supported: possibly efficacious	Several RCTs in one research setting; single-case experiments with small sample size
Relaxation for anxiety in dementia	Empirically supported: efficacious	Two RCTs in independent research settings
Psychotherapeutic approaches	Not empirically supported	RCTs do not indicate significant effects

REFERENCES

Akkerman, R. L., & Ostwald, S. K. (2004). Reducing anxiety in Alzheimer's disease family caregivers: The effectiveness of a nine-week cognitive-behavioral intervention. *American Journal of Alzheimer's Disease & Other Dementias, 19*, 117–123.

American Psychiatric Association. (1994). *Diagnostic and statistical manual of mental disorders* (4th ed.). Washington, DC: Author.

Baake, B. L., Kvale, S., Burns, T., McCarren, J. R., Wilson, L., Maddox, M., & Cleary, J. (1994). Multicomponent intervention for agitated behaviour in a person with Alzheimer's disease. *Journal of Applied Behavior Analysis, 27*, 175–176.

Baillon, S., Van Diepen, E., Prettyman, R., Redman, J., Rooke, N., & Campbell, R. (2004). A comparison of the effects of Snoezelen and reminiscence therapy on the agitated behaviour of patients with dementia. *International Journal of Geriatric Psychiatry, 19*, 1047–1052.

Baker, J. C., Hanley, G. P., & Mathews, R. M. (2006). Staff administered functional analysis and treatment of aggression by an elder with dementia. *Journal of Applied Behavior Analysis, 39*, 469–474.

Balasubramanyam, V., Stanley, M. A., & Kunik, M. E. (2007). Cognitive behavioral therapy for anxiety in dementia. *Dementia, 6*, 299–307.

Ball, K., Berch, D. B., Helmers, K. F., Jobe, J. B., Leveck, M. D., Marsiske, M., . . . Willis, S. L. (2002). Effects of cognitive training interventions with older adults: A randomized controlled trial. *Journal of American Medical Association, 288*, 2271–2281.

Ballard, C., Bannister, C., & Oyebode, F. (1996). Depression in dementia sufferers. *International Journal of Geriatric Psychiatry, 11*, 507–515.

Ballard, C., Boyle, A., Bowler, C., & Lindesay, J. (1996). Anxiety disorders in dementia sufferers. *International Journal of Geriatric Psychiatry, 11*, 987–990.

Bannerji, T. W. A., Kessels, R. P. C., Olde Rikkert, M. G. M., Geleijns-Lanting, C. E., & Kraaimat, F. W. (2008). A cognitive behavioural group therapy for patients diagnosed with mild cognitive impairment and their significant others: Feasibility and preliminary results. *Clinical Rehabilitation, 22*, 731–740.

Beck, C., Heacock, P., Mercer, S., Thatcher, R., & Sparkman, C. (1988). The impact of cognitive skills remediation training on persons with Alzheimer's disease or mixed dementia. *Journal of Geriatric Psychiatry, 21*, 73–88.

Beck, C., Vogelpohl, T. S., Rasin, J. H., Uriri, J. T., O'Sullivan, P., Walls, R., . . . Baldwin, B. (2002). Effects of behavioral interventions on disruptive behavior and affect in demented nursing home residents. *Nursing Research, 51*, 219–228.

Bird, M. (2001). Behavioural difficulties and cued recall of adaptive behaviour in dementia: Experimental and clinical evidence. *Neuropsychological Rehabilitation, 11*, 357–375.

Bird, M., Alexopoulos, P., & Adamowicz, J. (1995). Success and failure in five case studies: Use of cued recall to ameliorate behaviour problems in senile dementia. *International Journal of Geriatric Psychiatry, 10*, 305–311.

Bird, M., & Kinsella, G. (1996). Long-term cued recall of tasks in senile dementia. *Psychology & Aging, 11*, 45–56.

Bird, M., Llewellyn-Jones, R. H., Smithers, H., Andrews, C., Cameron, I., Cottee, A., . . . Russell, B. (1998). Challenging behaviours in dementia: A project at Hornsby/Ku-Ring-Gai Hospital. *Australasian Journal on Ageing, 17*, 10–15.

Bird, M., & Luszcz, M. (1991). Encoding specificity, depth of processing, and cued recall in Alzheimer's disease. *Journal of Clinical and Experimental Neuropsychology, 13*, 508–520.

Bird, M., & Luszcz, M. (1993). Enhancing memory performance in Alzheimer's disease: Acquisition assistance and cue effectiveness. *Journal of Clinical and Experimental Neuropsychology, 15*, 921–932.

Bird, M., & Moniz-Cook, E. (2008). Challenging behaviour in dementia: A psychosocial approach to intervention. In R. T. Woods & L. Clare (Eds.), *Handbook of the clinical psychology of ageing* (2nd ed., pp. 571–594). Chichester, England: Wiley.

Bleathman, C., & Morton, I. (1992). Validation therapy: Extracts from 20 groups with dementia sufferers. *Journal of Advanced Nursing, 17*, 658–666.

Bohlmeijer, E., Smit, F., & Cuijpers, P. (2003). Effects of reminiscence and life review on late life depression: A meta-analysis. *International Journal of Geriatric Psychiatry, 18*, 1088–1094.

Bornat, J. (Ed.). (1994). *Reminiscence reviewed: Perspectives, evaluations, achievements.* Buckingham, England: Open University Press.

Bourgeois, M. S. (1990). Enhancing conversation skills in patients with Alzheimer's disease using a prosthetic memory aid. *Journal of Applied Behavior Analysis, 23*, 29–42.

Bourgeois, M. S. (1993). Effects of memory aids on the dyadic conversations of people with dementia. *Journal of Applied Behavior Analysis, 26*, 77–87.

Bourgeois, M. S., Burgio, L. D., Schulz, R., Beach, S. R., & Palmer, B. (1997). Modifying repetitive verbalizations of community dwelling patients with AD. *Gerontologist, 37*, 30–39.

Breuil, V., De Rotrou, J., Forette, F., Tortrat, D., Ganansia-Ganem, A., Frambourt, A., . . . Boller, F. (1994). Cognitive stimulation of patients with dementia: Preliminary results. *International Journal of Geriatric Psychiatry, 9*, 211–217.

Brodaty, H., & Berman, K. (2008). Interventions for family caregivers of people with dementia. In R. T. Woods & L. Clare (Eds.), *Handbook of the clinical psychology of ageing* (2nd ed., pp. 550–569). Chichester, England: Wiley.

Brodaty, H., Green, A., & Koschera, A. (2003). Meta-analysis of psychosocial interventions for caregivers of people with dementia. *Journal of American Geriatrics Society, 51*, 657–664.

Brooker, D., & Duce, L. (2000). Wellbeing and activity in dementia: A comparison of group reminiscence therapy, structured goal-directed group activity and unstructured time. *Aging & Mental Health, 4*, 354–358.

Buchanan, J. A., & Fisher, J. E. (2002). Functional assessment and non-contingent reinforcement in the treatment of disruptive vocalization in elderly dementia patients. *Journal of Applied Behavior Analysis, 35*, 99–103.

Burgio, L. D., Stevens, A., Guy, D., Roth, D. L., & Haley, W. E. (2003). Impact of two psychosocial interventions on White and African American family caregivers of individuals with dementia. *The Gerontologist, 43*, 568–57.

Burns, A., Guthrie, E., Marino-Francis, F., Busby, C., Morris, J., Russell, E., . . . Byrne, J. (2005). Brief psychotherapy in Alzheimer's disease: Randomised controlled trial. *British Journal of Psychiatry, 187*, 143–147.

Burns, A., Jacoby, R., & Levy, R. (1990a). Psychiatric phenomena in Alzheimer's disease. I: Disorders of thought content. *British Journal of Psychiatry, 157*, 72–76.

Burns, A., Jacoby, R., & Levy, R. (1990b). Psychiatric phenomena in Alzheimer's disease. II: Disorders of perception. *British Journal of Psychiatry, 157*, 76–81.

Burns, A., Jacoby, R., & Levy, R. (1990c). Psychiatric phenomena in Alzheimer's disease. IV: Disorders of behaviour. *British Journal of Psychiatry, 157*, 86–94.

Cahn-Weiner, D. A., Malloy, P. F., Rebok, G. W., & Ott, B. R. (2003). Results of a randomised placebo-controlled study of memory training for mildly impaired Alzheimer's disease patients. *Applied Neuropsychology, 10*, 215–223.

Camp, C. J., Bird, M., & Cherry, K. E. (2000). Retrieval strategies as a rehabilitation aid for cognitive loss in pathological ageing. In R. D. Hill, L. Backman, & A. Stigsdotter-Neely (Eds.), *Cognitive rehabilitation in old age* (pp. 224–248). Oxford, England: Oxford University Press.

Camp, C. J., Judge, K. S., Bye, C., Fox, K., Bowden, J., Bell, M., . . . Mattern, J. (1997). An intergenerational program for persons with dementia using Montessori methods. *Gerontologist, 37*, 688–692.

Chambless, D. L., & Hollon, S. D. (1998). Defining empirically supported therapies. *Journal of Consulting & Clinical Psychology, 66*, 7–18.

Chapman, S. B., Weiner, M. F., Rackley, A., Hynan, L. S., & Zientz, J. (2004). Effects of cognitive-communication stimulation for Alzheimer's disease patients treated with donepezil. *Journal of Speech, Language & Hearing Research, 47*, 1149–1163.

Cheston, R. (1998). Psychotherapeutic work with people with dementia: A review of the literature. *British Journal of Medical Psychology, 71*, 211–231.

Cheston, R., Jones, K., & Gilliard, J. (2003). Group psychotherapy and people with dementia. *Aging & Mental Health, 7*, 452–461.

Church, M. (1983). Psychological therapy with elderly people. *Bulletin of the British Psychological Society, 36*, 110–112.

Clare, L. (2007). *Neuropsychological Rehabilitation and People with Dementia*. London, England: Psychology Press.

Clare, L., & Jones, R. S. P. (2008). Errorless learning in the rehabilitation of memory impairment: A critical review. *Neuropsychology Review, 18*, 1–23.

Clare, L., Linden, D. E., Woods, R. T., Whitaker, R., Evans, S. J., Parkinson, C. H., . . . Rugg, M. D. (2010). Goal-oriented cognitive rehabilitation for people with early-stage Alzheimer's disease: A single-blind randomized controlled trial of clinical efficacy. *American Journal of Geriatric Psychiatry, 18*, 928–939.

Clare, L., Moniz-Cook, E., Orrell, M., Spector, A., & Woods, B. (2003). Cognitive rehabilitation and cognitive training for early-stage Alzheimer's disease and vascular dementia [Updated 2007]. *The Cochrane Library*. Chichester, England: Wiley. doi:10.1002/14651858.CD003260

Clare, L., van Paasschen, J., Evans, S. J., Parkinson, C., Woods, R. T., & Linden, D. E. J. (2009). Goal-oriented cognitive rehabilitation for an individual with mild cognitive impairment: Behavioural and neuroimaging outcomes. *Neurocase, 15*, 318–331.

Clare, L., Wilson, B. A., Breen, K., & Hodges, J. R. (1999). Errorless learning of face-name associations in early Alzheimer's disease. *Neurocase, 5*, 37–46.

Clare, L., Wilson, B. A., Carter, G., & Hodges, J. R. (2003). Cognitive rehabilitation as a component of early intervention in Alzheimer's disease: A single case study. *Aging & Mental Health, 7*, 15–21.

Clare, L., Wilson, B. A., Carter, G., Hodges, J. R., & Adams, M. (2001). Long-term maintenance of treatment gains following a cognitive rehabilitation intervention in early dementia. *Neuropsychological Rehabilitation, 11*, 477–494.

Clare, L., Wilson, B. A., Carter, G., Roth, I., & Hodges, J. R. (2002). Relearning face-name associations in early Alzheimer's disease. *Neuropsychology, 16*, 538–547.

Clare, L., & Woods, R. T. (2004). Cognitive training and cognitive rehabilitation for people with early-stage Alzheimer's disease: A review. *Neuropsychological Rehabilitation, 14*, 385–401.

Cohen-Mansfield, J., Libin, A., & Marx, M. (2007). Non-pharmacological treatment of agitation: A controlled trial of systematic individualized intervention. *Journal of Gerontology: Medical Sciences, 62A*, 908–916.

Coleman, P. G. (1986). *Ageing and reminiscence processes: Social and clinical implications*. Chichester, England: Wiley.

Cooke, D. D., McNally, L., Mulligan, K. T., Harrison, M. G. J., & Newman, S. P. (2001). Psychosocial interventions for caregivers of people with dementia: A systematic review. *Aging & Mental Health, 5*(2), 120–135.

Davis, R. N., Massman, P. J., & Doody, R. S. (2001). Cognitive intervention in Alzheimer's disease: A randomized placebo-controlled study. *Alzheimer Disease and Associated Disorders, 15*, 1–9.

De Vreese, L. P., Verlato, C., Emiliani, S., Schioppa, S., Belloi, L., Salvioli, G., & Neri, M. (1998). Effect size of a three-month drug treatment in AD when combined with individual cognitive retraining: Preliminary results of a pilot study (Abstract). *Neurobiology of Aging, 19*(4S), S213.

Dietch, J. T., Hewett, L. J., & Jones, S. (1989). Adverse effects of reality orientation. *Journal of American Geriatrics Society, 37*, 974–976.

Donaldson, C., Tarrier, N., & Burns, A. (1998). Determinants of carer stress in Alzheimer's disease. *International Journal of Geriatric Psychiatry, 13*, 248–256.

Drentea, P., Clay, O. J., Roth, D. L., & Mittelman, M. S. (2006). Predictors of improvement in social support: Five year effects of a structured intervention for caregivers of spouses with Alzheimer's disease. *Social Science & Medicine, 63*, 957–967.

Dunn, J., & Clare, L. (2007). Learning face name associations in early-stage dementia: Comparing the effects of errorless learning and effortful processing. *Neuropsychological Rehabilitation, 17*, 735–754.

Farina, E., Mantovani, F., Fioravanti, R., Pignatti, R., Chiavari, L., Imbornone, E., . . . Nemni, R. (2006). Evaluating two group programmes of cognitive training in mild-to-moderate AD: Is there any difference between a "global" stimulation and a "cognitive specific" one? *Aging & Mental Health, 10*, 211–218.

Feil, N. (1993). *The validation breakthrough: Simple techniques for communicating with people with "Alzheimer's-type dementia."* Baltimore, MD: Health Professions Press.

Ferri, C. P., Prince, M., Brayne, C., Brodaty, H., Fratiglioni, L., Ganguli, M., . . . Scazufca, M. (2005). Global prevalence of dementia: A Delphi consensus study. *Lancet, 366*, 2112–2117.

Finnema, E., Droes, R.-M., Ettema, T., Ooms, M., Ader, H., Ribbe, M., & van Tilburg, W. (2005). The effect of integrated emotion-oriented care versus usual care on elderly persons with dementia in the nursing home and on nursing assistants: A randomized clinical trial. *International Journal of Geriatric Psychiatry, 20*, 330–343.

Finnema, E., Droes, R.-M., Ribbe, M., & van-Tilburg, W. (2000). The effects of emotion-oriented approaches in the care for persons suffering from dementia: A review of the literature. *International Journal of Geriatric Psychiatry, 15*, 141–161.

Fossey, J., Ballard, C., Juszczak, E., James, I., Alder, N., Jacoby, R., & Howard, R. (2006). Effect of enhanced psychosocial care on antipsychotic use in nursing home residents with severe dementia: Cluster randomised trial. *British Medical Journal, 332*, 756–758.

Gallagher-Thompson, D., & Coon, D. W. (2007). Evidence-based psychological treatments for distress in family caregivers of older adults. *Psychology & Aging, 22*, 37–51.

Gallagher-Thompson, D., & Steffen, A. M. (1994). Comparative effects of cognitive-behavioral and brief psychodynamic psychotherapies for depressed family caregivers. *Journal of Consulting & Clinical Psychology, 62*, 543–549.

Garland, J. (1994). What splendour, it all coheres: Life review therapy with older people. In J. Bornat (Ed.), *Reminiscence reviewed* (pp. 21–31). Buckingham, England: Open University Press.

Gaugler, J. E., Roth, D. L., Haley, W. E., & Mittelman, M. S. (2008). Can counseling and support reduce burden and depressive symptoms in caregivers of people with Alzheimer's disease during the transition to institutionalization? Results from the New York University caregiver intervention study. *Journal of American Geriatrics Society, 56*, 421–428.

Gerdner, L. A., Buckwalter, K. C., & Reed, D. (2002). Impact of a psychoeducational intervention on caregiver response to behavioral problems. *Nursing Research, 51*, 363–374.

Gibson, F. (1994). What can reminiscence contribute to people with dementia? In J. Bornat (Ed.), *Reminiscence reviewed: Evaluations, achievements, perspectives* (pp. 46–60). Buckingham, England: Open University Press.

Gibson, F. (2004). *The past in the present: Using reminiscence in health and social care*. Baltimore, MD: Health Professions Press.

Gilleard, C., Mitchell, R. G., & Riordan, J. (1981). Ward orientation training with psychogeriatric patients. *Journal of Advanced Nursing, 6*, 95–98.

Gitlin, L. N., Belle, S. H., Burgio, L. D., Czaja, S. J., Mahoney, D., Gallagher-Thompson, D., . . . Ory, M. G. (2003). Effect of multicomponent interventions on caregiver burden and depression: The REACH multisite initiative at 6-month follow-up. *Psychology & Aging, 18*, 361–374.

Gormley, N., Lyons, D., & Howard, R. (2001). Behavioural management of aggression in dementia: A randomized controlled trial. *Age & Ageing, 30*, 141–145.

Greene, J. G., Nicol, R., & Jamieson, H. (1979). Reality orientation with psychogeriatric patients. *Behaviour Research and Therapy, 17*, 615–617.

Haight, B. K., Bachman, D. L., Hendrix, S., Wagner, M. T., Meeks, A., & Johnson, J. (2003). Life review: Treating the dyadic family unit with dementia. *Clinical Psychology & Psychotherapy, 10,* 165–174.

Haight, B. K., & Burnside, I. (1993). Reminiscence and life review: Explaining the differences. *Archives of Psychiatric Nursing, 7,* 91–98.

Haight, B. K., Gibson, F., & Michel, Y. (2006). The Northern Ireland life review/life storybook project for people with dementia. *Alzheimer's and Dementia, 2*(1), 56–58.

Hanley, I. G. (1981). The use of signposts and active training to modify ward disorientation in elderly patients. *Journal of Behaviour, Therapy & Experimental Psychiatry, 12,* 241–247.

Hanley, I. G., & Lusty, K. (1984). Memory aids in reality orientation: A single-case study. *Behaviour Research & Therapy, 22,* 709–712.

Hanley, I. G., McGuire, R. J., & Boyd, W. D. (1981). Reality orientation and dementia: A controlled trial of two approaches. *British Journal of Psychiatry, 138,* 10–14.

Head, D., Portnoy, S., & Woods, R. T. (1990). The impact of reminiscence groups in two different settings. *International Journal of Geriatric Psychiatry, 5,* 295–302.

Heard, K., & Watson, T. S. (1999). Reducing wandering by persons with dementia using differential reinforcement. *Journal of Applied Behavior Analysis, 32,* 381–384.

Heiss, W. D., Kessler, J., Mielke, R., Szelies, B., & Herholz, K. (1994). Long-term effects of phosphatidylserine, pyritinol and cognitive training in Alzheimer's disease. *Dementia, 5,* 88–98.

Hill, R. D., Evankovich, K. D., Sheikh, J. I., & Yesavage, J. A. (1987). Imagery mnemonic training in a patient with primary degenerative dementia. *Psychology & Aging, 2,* 204–205.

Hofmann, M., Hock, C., Kuhler, A., & Muller-Spahn, F. (1996). Interactive computer-based cognitive training in patients with Alzheimer's disease. *Journal of Psychiatric Research, 30,* 493–501.

Hogan, D. B., Bailey, P., Black, S., Carswell, A., Chertkow, H., Clarke, B., . . . Thorpe, L. (2008). Diagnosis and treatment of dementia: 5. Nonpharmacologic and pharmacologic therapy for mild to moderate dementia. *Canadian Medical Association Journal, 179,* 1019–1026.

Holden, U. P., & Woods, R. T. (1995). *Positive approaches to dementia care* (3rd ed.). Edinburgh, Scotland: Churchill Livingstone.

Howard, R., Juszczak, E., Ballard, C., Bentham, P., Brown, R. G., Bullock, R., . . . Rodger, M. (2007). Donepezil for the treatment of agitation in Alzheimer's Disease. *New England Journal of Medicine, 357,* 1382–1392.

Huang, H.-L., Shyu, Y.-I. L., Chen, M.-C., Chen, S.-T., & Lin, L.-C. (2003). A pilot study on a home-based caregiver training program for improving caregiver self-efficacy and decreasing the behavioral problems of elders with dementia in Taiwan. *International Journal of Geriatric Psychiatry, 18,* 337–345.

Husband, H. J. (1999). The psychological consequences of learning a diagnosis of dementia: Three case examples. *Aging & Mental Health, 3,* 179–183.

Hutton, S., Sheppard, L., Rusted, J. M., & Ratner, H. H. (1996). Structuring the acquisition and retrieval environment to facilitate learning in individuals with dementia of the Alzheimer type. *Memory, 4,* 113–130.

James, I. (2008). Stuff and nonsense in the treatment of older people: Essential reading for the over-45s. *Behavioural & Cognitive Psychotherapy, 36,* 735–747.

Josephsson, S., Backman, L., Borell, L., Bernspang, B., Nygard, L., & Ronnberg, L. (1993). Supporting everyday activities in dementia: An intervention study. *International Journal of Geriatric Psychiatry, 8,* 395–400.

Kipling, T., Bailey, M., & Charlesworth, G. (1999). The feasibility of a cognitive behavioural therapy group for men with mild/moderate cognitive impairment. *Behavioural & Cognitive Psychotherapy, 27,* 189–193.

Knapp, M., & Prince, M. (2007). *Dementia UK.* London, England: Alzheimer's Society.

Knapp, M., Thorgrimsen, L., Patel, A., Spector, A., Hallam, A., Woods, B., & Orrell, M. (2006). Cognitive stimulation therapy for people with dementia: Cost-effectiveness analysis. *British Journal of Psychiatry, 188,* 574–580.

Koder, D. A. (1998). Treatment of anxiety in the cognitively impaired elderly: Can cognitive-behavior therapy help? *International Psychogeriatrics, 10,* 173–182.

Kraus, C., Seignourel, P., Balasubramanyam, V., Snow, A., Wilson, N., Kunik, M., . . . Stanley, M. (2008). Cognitive-behavioral treatment for anxiety in patients with dementia: Two case studies. *Journal of Psychiatric Practice, 14,* 186–192.

Laidlaw, K., Thompson, L. W., Dick-Siskin, L., & Gallagher-Thompson, D. (2003). *Cognitive behaviour therapy with older people.* Chichester, England: Wiley.

Lam, D. H., & Woods, R. T. (1986). Ward orientation training in dementia: A single-case study. *International Journal of Geriatric Psychiatry, 1,* 145–147.

Lichtenberg, P. A., Kemp-Havican, J., MacNeill, S. E., & Johnson, A. S. (2005). Pilot study of behavioral treatment in dementia care units. *Gerontologist, 45,* 406–410.

Livingston, G., Johnston, K., Katona, C., Paton, J., & Lyketsos, C. G. (2005). Systematic review of psychological approaches to the management of neuropsychiatric symptoms of dementia. *American Journal of Psychiatry, 162,* 1996–2021.

Loewenstein, D. A., Acevedo, A., Czaja, S. J., & Duara, R. (2004). Cognitive rehabilitation of mildly impaired

Alzheimer disease patients on cholinesterase inhibitors. *American Journal of Geriatric Psychiatry, 12,* 395–402.

Logsdon, R. G., McCurry, S. M., & Teri, L. (2007). Evidence-based psychological treatments for disruptive behaviors in individuals with dementia. *Psychology & Aging, 22,* 28–36.

Mahoney, R., Regan, C., Katona, C., & Livingston, G. (2005). Anxiety and depression in family caregivers of people with Alzheimer disease. *American Journal of Geriatric Psychiatry, 13,* 795–801.

Marriott, A., Donaldson, C., Tarrier, N., & Burns, A. (2000). Effectiveness of cognitive-behavioural family intervention in reducing the burden of care in carers of patients with Alzheimer's disease. *British Journal of Psychiatry, 176,* 557–562.

Massimi, M., Berry, E., Browne, G., Smyth, G., Watson, P., & Baecker, R. (2008). An exploratory case study of the impact of ambient biographical displays on identity in a patient with Alzheimer's disease. *Neuropsychological Rehabilitation, 18,* 742–765.

McCurry, S. M., Gibbons, L. E., Logsdon, R., Vitiello, M. V., & Teri, L. (2005). Nighttime insomnia treatment and education for Alzheimer's disease: A randomized controlled trial. *Journal of American Geriatrics Society, 53,* 793–802.

McGilton, K. S., Rivera, T. M., & Dawson, P. (2003). Can we help persons with dementia find their way in a new environment? *Aging & Mental Health, 7*(5), 363–371.

McKeown, J., Clarke, A., & Repper, J. (2006). Life story work in health and social care: Systematic literature review. *Journal of Advanced Nursing, 55,* 237–247.

Mittelman, M. S., Brodaty, H., Wallen, A. S., & Burns, A. (2008). A three country randomized controlled trial of a psychosocial intervention for caregivers combined with pharmacological treatment for patients with Alzheimer's disease: Effects on caregiver depression. *American Journal of Geriatric Psychiatry, 16,* 893–904.

Mittelman, M. S., Ferris, S. H., Shulman, E., Steinberg, G., Ambinder, A., Mackell, J. A., & Cohen, J. (1995). A comprehensive support program: Effect on depression in spouse caregivers of AD patients. *Gerontologist, 35,* 792–802.

Mittelman, M. S., Haley, W. E., Clay, O. J., & Roth, D. L. (2006). Improving caregiver well-being delays nursing home placement of patients with Alzheimer disease. *Neurology, 67,* 1592–1599.

Mittelman, M. S., Roth, D. L., Coon, D. W., & Haley, W. E. (2004). Sustained benefit of supportive intervention for depressive symptoms in caregivers of patients with Alzheimer's disease. *American Journal of Psychiatry, 161,* 850–856.

Mittelman, M. S., Roth, D. L., Haley, W. E., & Zarit, S. H. (2004). Effect of a caregiver intervention on negative caregiver appraisals of behavior problems in patients with Alzheimer's disease: Results of a randomized trial. *Journal of Gerontology: Psychological Sciences, 59B*(1), P27–P34.

Moniz-Cook, E., Stokes, G., & Agar, S. (2003). Difficult behaviour and dementia in nursing homes: Five cases of psychosocial intervention. *Clinical Psychology & Psychotherapy, 10,* 197–208.

Moniz-Cook, E., Woods, R. T., & Richards, K. (2001). Functional analysis of challenging behaviour in dementia: The role of superstition. *International Journal of Geriatric Psychiatry, 16,* 45–56.

Moos, I., & Bjorn, A. (2006). Use of life story in the institutional care of people with dementia: A review of intervention studies. *Ageing & Society, 26,* 431–454.

Morris, R. G. (2008). The neuropsychology of dementia: Alzheimer's disease and other neurodegenerative disorders. In R. T. Woods & L. Clare (Eds.), *Handbook of the clinical psychology of ageing* (2nd ed.) (pp. 161–184). Chichester, England: Wiley.

Morton, I., & Bleathman, C. (1991). The effectiveness of validation therapy in dementia: A pilot study. *International Journal of Geriatric Psychiatry, 6,* 327–330.

Neal, M., & Barton Wright, P. (2007). Validation therapy for dementia (Cochrane review). *The Cochrane Library, Issue 2.* Chichester, England: Wiley. doi:10.1002/14651858.CD001394

National Institute for Health and Clinical Excellence Social Care Institute for Excellence (NICE-SCIE). (2006). *Dementia: Supporting people with dementia and their carers in health and social care: Clinical Guideline 42.* London, England: Author.

Olazaran, J., Muniz, R., Reisberg, B., Pena-Casanova, J., del Ser, T., Cruz Jentoft, A. J., . . . Sevilla, C. (2004). Benefits of cognitive-motor intervention in MCI and mild to moderate Alzheimer disease. *Neurology, 63,* 2348–2353.

Onder, G., Zanetti, O., Giacobini, E., Frisoni, G. B., Bartorelli, L., Carbone, G., . . . Bernabei, R. (2005). Reality orientation therapy combined with cholinesterase inhibitors in Alzheimer's disease: Randomized controlled trial. *British Journal of Psychiatry, 187,* 450–455.

Orrell, M., Spector, A., Thorgrimsen, L., & Woods, R. (2005). A pilot study examining the effectiveness of maintenance cognitive stimulation therapy (CST) following CST for people with dementia. *International Journal of Geriatric Psychiatry, 20,* 446–451.

Pinkston, E. M., Linsk, N. L., & Young, R. N. (1988). Home-based behavioral family treatment of the impaired elderly. *Behavior Therapy, 19,* 331–344.

Politis, A., Vozzella, S., Mayer, L. S., Onyike, C. U., Baker, A. S., & Lyketsos, C. G. (2004). A randomized controlled clinical trial of activity therapy for apathy in patients with dementia residing in long-term care. *International Journal of Geriatric Psychiatry, 19,* 1087–1094.

Proctor, R., Burns, A., Stratton-Powell, H., Tarrier, N., Faragher, B., Richardson, G., . . . South, B. (1999). Behavioural management in nursing and residential homes: A randomised controlled trial. *Lancet, 354,* 26–29.

Pusey, H., & Richards, D. (2001). A systematic review of the effectiveness of psychosocial interventions for carers of people with dementia. *Aging & Mental Health, 5,* 107–119.

Quayhagen, M. P., & Quayhagen, M. (2001). Testing of a cognitive stimulation intervention for dementia caregiving dyads. *Neuropsychological Rehabilitation, 11,* 319–332.

Quayhagen, M. P., Quayhagen, M., Corbeil, R. R., Hendrix, R. C., Jackson, J. E., Snyder, L., & Bower, D. (2000). Coping with dementia: Evaluation of four non-pharmacologic interventions. *International Psychogeriatrics, 12,* 249–265.

Quayhagen, M. P., Quayhagen, M., Corbeil, R. R., Roth, P. A., & Rodgers, J. A. (1995). A dyadic remediation program for care recipients with dementia. *Nursing Research, 44,* 153–159.

Riley, G. A., & Heaton, S. (2000). Guidelines for the selection of a method of fading cues. *Neuropsychological Rehabilitation, 10,* 133–149.

Romero, B., & Wenz, M. (2001). Self-maintenance therapy in Alzheimer's disease. *Neuropsychological Rehabilitation, 11,* 333–355.

Scholey, K. A., & Woods, B. T. (2003). A series of brief cognitive therapy interventions with people experiencing both dementia and depression: A description of techniques and common themes. *Clinical Psychology & Psychotherapy, 10,* 175–185.

Schreiber, M., Schweizer, A., Lutz, K., Kalveram, K. T., & Jaencke, L. (1999). Potential of an interactive computer-based training in the rehabilitation of dementia: An initial study. *Neuropsychological Rehabilitation, 9,* 155–167.

Schrijnemaekers, V., van Rossum, E., Candel, M., Frederiks, C., Derix, M., Sielhorst, H., & van den Brandt, P. (2002). Effects of emotion-oriented care on elderly people with cognitive impairment and behavioral problems. *International Journal of Geriatric Psychiatry, 17,* 926–937.

Schweitzer, P., & Bruce, E. (2008). *Remembering yesterday, caring today: Reminiscence in dementia care: A guide to good practice.* London, England: Jessica Kingsley.

Scogin, F., & McElreath, L. (1994). Efficacy of psychosocial treatments for geriatric depression: A quantitative review. *Journal of Consulting & Clinical Psychology, 62,* 69–74.

Scottish Intercollegiate Guidelines Network (SIGN). (2006). *Management of patients with dementia: A national clinical guideline.* Edinburgh, Scotland: Author.

Sitzer, D., Twamley, E., & Jeste, D. (2006). Cognitive training in Alzheimer's disease: A meta-analysis of the literature. *Acta Psychiatrica Scandinavica, 114*(2), 75–90.

Snowdon, D. A. (2003). Healthy aging and dementia: Findings from the Nun study. *Annals of Internal Medicine, 139,* 450–454.

Sorensen, S., Pinquart, M., & Duberstein, P. R. (2002). How effective are interventions with caregivers? An updated meta-analysis. *Gerontologist, 42,* 356–372.

Spector, A., Davies, S., Woods, B., & Orrell, M. (2000). Reality orientation for dementia: A systematic review of the evidence for its effectiveness. *Gerontologist, 40,* 206–212.

Spector, A., Orrell, M., Davies, S., & Woods, B. (2001). Can reality orientation be rehabilitated? Development and piloting of an evidence-based programme of cognition-based therapies for people with dementia. *Neuropsychological Rehabilitation, 11,* 377–397.

Spector, A., Thorgrimsen, L., Woods, B., & Orrell, M. (2006). *Making a difference: An evidence-based group programme to offer cognitive stimulation therapy (CST) to people with dementia.* London, England: Hawker Publications.

Spector, A., Thorgrimsen, L., Woods, B., Royan, L., Davies, S., Butterworth, M., & Orrell, M. (2003). Efficacy of an evidence-based cognitive stimulation therapy programme for people with dementia: Randomised controlled trial. *British Journal of Psychiatry, 183,* 248–254.

Suhr, J., Anderson, S., & Tranel, D. (1999). Progressive muscle relaxation in the management of behavioural disturbance in Alzheimer's disease. *Neuropsychological Rehabilitation, 9,* 31–44.

Tadaka, E., & Kanagawa, K. (2004). A randomized controlled trial of a group care program for community-dwelling elderly people with dementia. *Japan Journal of Nursing Science, 1,* 19–25.

Tadaka, E., & Kanagawa, K. (2007). Effects of reminiscence group in elderly people with Alzheimer disease and vascular dementia in a community setting. *Geriatrics and Gerontology International, 7,* 167–173.

Tarraga, L., Boada, M., Modinos, G., Espinosa, A., Diego, S., Morera, A., . . . Becker, J. T. (2006). A randomised pilot study to assess the efficacy of an interactive, multimedia tool of cognitive stimulation in Alzheimer's disease. *Journal of Neurology, Neurosurgery & Psychiatry, 77,* 1116–1121.

Teri, L., & Gallagher-Thompson, D. (1991). Cognitive-behavioural interventions for treatment of depression in Alzheimer's disease. *Gerontologist, 31,* 413–416.

Teri, L., Gibbons, L. E., McCurry, S. M., Logsdon, R., Buchner, D. M., Barlow, W. E., . . . Larson, E. B. (2003). Exercise plus behavioral management in patients with Alzheimer disease: A randomized controlled trial. *Journal of American Medical Association, 290,* 2015–2022.

Teri, L., Logsdon, R. G., Peskind, E., Raskind, M., Weiner, M. F., Tractenberg, R. E., . . . Thal, L. J. (2000). Treatment of agitation in AD: A randomized, placebo-controlled clinical trial. *Neurology, 55*, 1271–1278.

Teri, L., Logsdon, R. G., Uomoto, J., & McCurry, S. M. (1997). Behavioral treatment of depression in dementia patients: A controlled clinical trial. *Journal of Gerontology, 52B*, P159–P166.

Teri, L., McCurry, S. M., Logsdon, R., & Gibbons, L. E. (2005). Training community consultants to help family members improve dementia care: A randomized controlled trial. *Gerontologist, 45*, 802–811.

Teri, L., & Uomoto, J. M. (1991). Reducing excess disability in dementia patients: Training caregivers to manage patient depression. *Clinical Gerontologist, 10(4)*, 49–63.

Thompson, L. W., Wagner, B., Zeiss, A., & Gallagher, D. (1990). Cognitive/behavioural therapy with early stage Alzheimer's patients: An exploratory view of the utility of this approach. In E. Light & B. D. Lebowitz (Eds.), *Alzheimer's disease: Treatment and family stress* (pp. 383–397). New York, NY: Hemisphere.

Thorgrimsen, L., Selwood, A., Spector, A., Royan, L., de Madariaga Lopez, M., Woods, R. T., & Orrell, M. (2003). Whose quality of life is it anyway? The validity and reliability of the Quality of Life Alzheimer's Disease (QoL-AD) scale. *Alzheimer Disease and Associated Disorders, 17*, 201–208.

Toseland, R. W., Diehl, M., Freeman, K., Manzanares, T., & McCallion, P. (1997). The impact of validation group therapy on nursing home residents with dementia. *Journal of Applied Gerontology, 16*, 31–50.

Wang, J. J. (2007). Group reminiscence therapy for cognitive and affective function of demented elderly in Taiwan. *International Journal of Geriatric Psychiatry, 22*, 1235–1240.

Welden, S., & Yesavage, J. A. (1982). Behavioral improvement with relaxation training in senile dementia. *Clinical Gerontologist, 1*, 45–49.

Woods, B. (2002). Editorial: Reality orientation: A welcome return? *Age & Ageing, 31*, 155–156.

Woods, B., Spector, A., Jones, C., Orrell, M., & Davies, S. (2005). Reminiscence therapy for people with dementia (review). *The Cochrane Database of Systematic Reviews*. Chichester, England: Wiley. doi:10.1002/14651858.CD001120.pub2

Woods, B., Spector, A., Prendergast, L., & Orrell, M. (2005). Cognitive stimulation to improve cognitive functioning in people with dementia (protocol). *The Cochrane Database of Systematic Reviews*.

Chichester, England: Wiley. doi:10.1002/14651858.CD005562

Woods, B., Thorgrimsen, L., Spector, A., Royan, L., & Orrell, M. (2006). Improved quality of life and cognitive stimulation therapy in dementia. *Aging & Mental Health, 10*, 219–226.

Woods, R. T. (1983). Specificity of learning in reality orientation sessions: A single-case study. *Behaviour Research and Therapy, 21*, 173–175.

Woods, R. T. (1998). Reminiscence as communication. In P. Schweitzer (Ed.), *Reminiscence in dementia care* (pp. 143–148). London, England: Age Exchange.

Woods, R. T. (1999). Promoting well-being and independence for people with dementia. *International Journal of Geriatric Psychiatry, 14*, 97–109.

Woods, R. T., & Clare, L. (2006). Cognition based therapies and mild cognitive impairment. In H. Tuokko & D. F. Hultsch (Eds.), *Mild cognitive impairment: International perspectives* (pp. 245–264). New York, NY: Taylor & Francis.

World Health Organization. (1993). *The ICD-10 classification of mental and behavioural disorders. Diagnostic criteria for research*. Geneva, Switzerland: Author.

Yale, R. (1995). *Developing support groups for individuals with early stage Alzheimer's disease: Planning, implementation and evaluation*. Baltimore, MD: Health Profession Press.

Zanetti, O., Binetti, G., Magni, E., Rozzini, L., Bianchetti, A., & Trabucchi, M. (1997). Procedural memory stimulation in Alzheimer's disease: Impact of a training programme. *Acta Neurologica Scandinavica, 95*, 152–157.

Zanetti, O., Frisoni, G. B., DeLeo, D., Buono, M. D., Bianchetti, A., & Trabucchi, M. (1995). Reality orientation therapy in Alzheimer's disease: Useful or not? A controlled study. *Alzheimer Disease and Associated Disorders, 9*, 132–138.

Zanetti, O., Magni, E., Binetti, G., Bianchetti, A., & Trabucchi, M. (1994). Is procedural memory stimulation effective in Alzheimer's disease? *International Journal of Geriatric Psychiatry, 9*, 1006–1007.

Zanetti, O., Zanieri, G., Di Giovanni, G., De Vreese, L. P., Pezzini, A., Metitieri, T., & Trabucchi, M. (2001). Effectiveness of procedural memory stimulation in mild Alzheimer's disease patients: A controlled study. *Neuropsychological Rehabilitation, 11*, 263–272.

Zarit, S. H., & Edwards, A. B. (2008). Family caregiving: Research and clinical intervention. In R. T. Woods & L. Clare (Eds.), *Handbook of the clinical psychology of ageing* (2nd ed., pp. 255–288). Chichester, England: Wiley.

7

Alcohol Use Disorders

KEVIN A. HALLGREN, BRENNA L. GREENFIELD, BENJAMIN LADD, LISA H. GLYNN,
AND BARBARA S. MCCRADY

OVERVIEW OF ALCOHOL USE DISORDERS

Diagnostic Criteria

Edwards and Gross (1976) characterized alcohol dependence as a syndrome of varying severity with both physical and psychological symptoms. The *DSM IV* diagnoses of alcohol dependence and abuse include many of these same elements (American Psychiatric Association, 2000). Fundamental to either approach is "a maladaptive pattern of substance use resulting in clinically significant impairment or distress" (p.199).

To receive a diagnosis of alcohol dependence, three or more of the following seven criteria must be met in a 12 month period: tolerance; withdrawal; drinking more and over longer periods than intended; spending significant amounts of time obtaining, consuming, and recovering from the effects of alcohol; an inability to control drinking; giving up activities not related to drinking; and continued drinking despite exacerbated psychological or physical problems. Alcohol dependence is further classified as occurring with or without physiological dependence. Its temporal course is specified as current, in remission (early or

sustained, partial or full), on agonist therapy, or in a controlled environment.

Alcohol abuse is considered less severe than alcohol dependence. It is diagnosed when one or more of the following occurs repeatedly in the 12 months prior to evaluation: drinking despite relationship problems worsened by the drinking; not meeting home, school, or work responsibilities; drinking in situations where it could be physically dangerous; and/or alcohol related legal trouble. Alcohol dependence precludes a diagnosis of alcohol abuse.

Demographic Variables

The 2001 2002 National Epidemiologic Survey on Alcohol and Related Conditions (NESARC) found a 30.3% lifetime prevalence of alcohol use disorders (AUDs) in the United States (Hasin, Stinson, Ogburn, & Grant, 2007). Lifetime prevalence for alcohol dependence was 12.5%, while lifetime prevalence of alcohol abuse was 17.8%. Over a 12 month period, the prevalence of alcohol dependence was 3.8% and the prevalence of alcohol abuse was 4.7%.

The U.S. lifetime prevalence for AUDs was 19.5% for women and 42.0% for men in 2001 2002 (Hasin et al., 2007). Worldwide, women are more likely to abstain from alcohol than men (World Health Organization [WHO], 2004). Ethnicity and culture also play a role in levels of alcohol consumption. For example, countries with Islam as the primary religion have higher alcohol abstinence rates (WHO, 2004). Data from NESARC suggested that in the United States, African Americans, Hispanics, and Asians all have a lower risk for past-year incidence of AUDs than Whites. For Asian Americans, genes that affect the metabolism of alcohol act as a protective factor and may be responsible for lower AUD rates (Cook et al., 2005). At 12.1%, Native Americans had significantly higher rates of past-year AUDs than other ethnic groups.

Younger individuals have a greater chance of having an AUD in the previous 12 months than older individuals (Hasin et al., 2007). In five of six European Union countries studied, young people had significantly higher rates of intoxication than their older counterparts (WHO, 2004).

Impact of AUDs

Alcohol use disorders are a significant public health issue. They tend to be chronic; in the United States the average length of alcohol dependence is almost four years (Hasin et al., 2007). Two billion people worldwide consume alcohol, and 76.3 million of them have AUDs (WHO, 2004). Over the past few decades global consumption of alcohol has swelled, largely because of increased drinking in developing countries where alcohol traditionally has not been consumed. These countries often have inadequate resources to deal with rising alcohol use.

On an individual and societal level, alcohol misuse can have multiple negative consequences. Yearly, an estimated 1.8 million deaths worldwide are alcohol-related. One-third of these deaths are the result of unintended injuries (WHO, 2004). The WHO's *Global Status Report on Alcohol 2004* noted, "Alcohol is estimated to cause about 20%–30% of esophageal cancer, liver cancer, cirrhosis of the liver, homicide, epileptic seizures and motor vehicle accidents worldwide" (p. 1).

Alcohol use disorders also impact social functioning. Problem drinkers and individuals with AUDs are more likely to miss work than their coworkers (WHO, 2004). Alcohol also plays a role in many domestic violence incidents. These and other alcohol-related social problems affect individuals beyond the drinker by decreasing productivity at work and taxing criminal justice and health-care resources.

In the United States, an estimated $275 billion is spent each year on substance abuse associated costs (McCarty, 2007). This figure contrasts with an annual $18 billion expended for drug and alcohol treatment. Most substance abuse treatment monies come from public funds. In a cost-benefit analysis, each dollar allocated toward substance abuse treatment yielded $7 in savings through increased employment and lower medical- and crime-related expenses.

These statistics affirm the cost savings of substance abuse treatment, but in 2001–2002 only 24.1% of those with a lifetime diagnosis of alcohol dependence in the United States had ever received treatment (Hasin et al., 2007). This treatment rate was slightly lower than the 1991–1992 rate, suggesting the need to identify and address individual and systemic factors that have reduced treatment utilization. As Hasin et al. (2007) noted, "*DSM-IV* alcohol abuse and dependence are highly prevalent, disabling disorders that go largely untreated in the United States" (p. 839).

Overview of Evidence-Based Alcohol Treatments and Sources of Evidence

A myriad of treatments exist for AUDs. Compared to other psychological disorders, the approach to alcohol treatment is not uniform, and no single treatment is considered vastly superior to others. For example, W. R. Miller and Wilbourne (2002) included 87 treatment modalities in their Mesa Grande review of AUD outcomes. The present chapter focuses on 10 treatments that have the strongest empirical support and demonstrated efficacy. They include cognitive behavior therapy, contingency management, cue-exposure therapy, the Community Reinforcement Approach, Behavioral Couples and Family Treatment, brief interventions, Motivational Interviewing/ Motivation Enhancement Therapy, 12-step-based therapies, and case management. Among these treatments, effects sizes are small to medium (Table 7.1). Because therapist and relationship factors play an overarching role in

all substance abuse treatments, a section on those factors also is included.

Several sources have provided reports of evaluations of multiple alcohol treatment modalities and will be discussed in more than one section of the chapter. To facilitate ease of understanding when they are mentioned, a brief overview of these sources is provided.

W. R. Miller and Wilbourne (2002) conducted a comprehensive review (titled Mesa Grande) of the alcohol outcome research literature grouped by treatment modality. In their review, 361 randomized clinical trials (RCTs)

TABLE 7.1   Summary of Evidence for Efficacy of Specific Treatments

| Treatment | Mesa Grande (W. R. Miller & Wilbourne, 2002) | | | | Endorsed By[1] | | | |
	No. of Studies	CES[2]	Rank	Effect Sizes	NREPP[3]	APA[4]	TIPS[5]	Cochrane Review
Cognitive behavior therapy				ds 0.20-0.94				
Social skills	25	85	5			✓		
Behavioral self control training	35	9	19					
Self management	3	4	22					
Contingency management				d 0.42		✓		
Cue exposure therapy[6]	2	0		r 0.33		✓		
Community Reinforcement Approach	4	80	6			✓		
Marital and family therapy/ Behavioral couple therapy	8	60	8	ds 0.36-0.58		✓ ✓		
Brief interventions	31	280	1	ds 0.06-0.67 ORs 0.95-1.94		✓		
Motivational Interviewing/ Motivational Enhancement Therapy	17	173	2	ds 0.19-1.05 pseudo R's 88-11%		✓	✓	
Twelve Step Facilitation	3	13	24.5	q 0.71		✓		✓
Alcoholics Anonymous	7	108	49.5					✓
Minnesota Model	3	3	20.5					
Case management	6	33	9	ds 0.21-0.93		✓		

[1] ✓ indicates positive endorsement; — indicates negative evaluation; blank indicates no evaluation of the treatment
[2] CES = cumulative evidence score; see text for details.
[3] NREPP = National Registry of Evidence Based Practices and Programs.
[4] APA = American Psychological Association.
[5] TIPS = Treatment Improvement Protocols.
[6] For Mesa Grande, cue exposure therapy was listed separately as it had less than three studies reporting results; no ranking information is available.

were identified and double-rated on 12 dimensions of methodological quality. Studies also were assigned a score based on the outcome and overall quality of the design. A cross-product of these two scores was computed to provide a cumulative evidence score (CES) (Table 7.1) by which treatment modalities were compared. Treatments also were rank ordered in efficacy.

The National Registry of Evidence-Based Practices and Programs (NREPP), sponsored by the Substance Abuse Mental Health Services Administration (SAMHSA), uses a standard set of criteria to identify substance abuse and mental health treatments as both efficacious and ready for dissemination to the practice community. Independent reviewers conduct reviews, and treatments are rated on 1 to 4 scales on each research and dissemination criterion (Table 7.2).

The American Psychological Association (APA) Task Force on Empirically Validated Treatments (EVT) was constituted in the early 1990s to identify psychosocial treatments with strong evidence for efficacy. The original task force produced three reports (Chambless et al., 1993, 1996, 1998); a 10-year follow-up update was reported recently (Woody, Weisz, & McLean, 2005). The original task force defined rigorous criteria for classification of treatments as *well-established* or *probably efficacious*, with the discrimination between the two being the number of supportive studies, the degree of replication across laboratories, and the nature of the experimental control/comparison group. The task force conclusions suggest, overall, that support for the efficacy of alcohol treatment has been demonstrated on several dimensions with different treatment modalities, but the evidence required to classify any of these treatments as well-established is lacking according to the task force standards, largely due to the lack of replication of treatment studies across laboratories.

Treatment Improvement Protocols (TIPs) comprise a series of publications that disseminate "best-practice guidelines for the treatment of substance use disorders" (Center for Substance Abuse Treatment [CSAT], 2006). The federally funded CSAT chooses an important and current topic, which is discussed by a consensus panel of peer-nominated experts in particular areas of substance-use research and practice. The resulting publications are available online at no charge to the public.

EVIDENCE-BASED TREATMENTS FOR ALCOHOL USE DISORDERS

Cognitive Behavior Therapy (CBT)

Treatment overview. Cognitive behavior therapy for AUDs includes several specific treatments, including behavioral self-control training (BSCT) (Hester, 2003), coping skills training (CST) (Monti & Rohsenow, 2003), social skills training (SST) (Chaney, O'Leary, & Marlatt, 1978), broad spectrum behavior therapy (BSBT) (P. M. Miller & Mastria, 1977), stress management (SM) (Alden, 1978), and relapse prevention (RP) (Marlatt & Gordon, 1985). All of these treatments are based on a social learning theory perspective on AUDs. Alcohol use is conceptualized as occurring in response to environmental stimuli, mediated by cognitive and affective processing, and maintained through principles of reinforcement. All CBT-based treatments help clients learn affective, cognitive, and behavioral coping skills, and typically introduce these skills gradually to enhance attainment of mastery in a widening set of situations. Behavioral self-control training focuses on drinking-specific skills and often allows clients to select their own drinking goals. Stress management focuses on skills to cope with general life problems. Coping skills training, social skills training, and broad spectrum behavior therapy typically are abstinence based and focus on a broader range of skills, including skills to attain and maintain abstinence as well as skills to cope with other life problems. Relapse prevention is similar,

TABLE 7.2 National Registry of Evidence-Based Practices and Programs (NREPP) Ratings

		Quality of Research						Readiness for Dissemination		
Program	Outcome Variable	Reliability – Outcome Measures	Validity – Outcome Measures	Intervention Fidelity	Missing Data and Attrition	Potential Confounding Variables	Appropriateness of Analyses	Implementation Materials	Training and Support Resources	Quality Assurance Procedures
		3.5	3.5	3.0	3.0	3.1	3.2	3.0	2.8	3.3
		4.0	4.0	3.3	2.9	3.0	3.0	3.5	3.5	2.5
		4.0	3.5	3.5	3.8	4.0	4.0	3.5	2.8	2.5
		3.5	2.8	4.0	2.0	1.5	2.5	3.5	4.0	4.0
		3.0	3.0	2.5	2.0	3.0	2.5	3.5	4.0	3.8
		3.5	3.5	2.9	4.0	3.0	3.0	4.0	3.3	3.8
		3.5	3.5	3.5	3.3	3.5	3.6	4.0	3.8	4.0
		3.5	3.5	3.5	4.0	3.0	4.0	3.0	3.0	3.0

but has an explicit focus on the prevention of relapses as well as initial skills acquisition.

Consensus panel recommendations. The third report of the APA Task Force on EVTs (Chambless et al., 1998) listed social skills training as a probably efficacious treatment. Surprisingly, there are no CBTs listed by NREPP, and CBT has not been the focus of a Cochrane Review.

Randomized clinical trials. Controlled studies of CBT approaches to the treatment of AUDs were first reported in the 1970s (e.g., Chaney et al., 1978; W. R. Miller, 1978); few other treatment approaches were the focus of as many RCTs in the 1970s and early-to-mid 1980s. As a result, CBT often has been used as the platform for the study of other research questions, such as patient-treatment matching, the effectiveness of evidence-based treatment for AUDs in community settings, the efficacy of pharmacotherapies, or mechanisms of change in psychosocial treatment. Two major studies have examined the efficacy or effectiveness of CBT. Project MATCH (Project MATCH Research Group, 1997, 1998a, 1998b) was a multisite, randomized clinical trial of outpatient treatments for AUDs, including CBT, Twelve-Step Facilitation Treatment (TSF), and Motivational Enhancement Therapy (MET). Project MATCH was designed to test a series of patient-treatment matching questions, tested in two populations—outpatients initiating treatment, and patients seeking aftercare treatment following inpatient or intensive outpatient treatment. The sample of 1,728 patients was randomly assigned to one of the three treatments, and was treated by clinicians with at least a master's level education and expertise in the specific treatment approach. All treatments were manual-guided, and patients were followed for 15 months from baseline (12 months from the end of the 3-month treatment). The CBT and TSF treatments were 12 sessions in length; MET was four sessions spread over a 12-week period. During the 1-year follow-up, the three treatments did not differ in continuous measures of alcohol use outcomes, although patients in the TSF condition were more likely to maintain continuous abstinence than were patients in the other two treatments. Patient-treatment matching hypotheses related to CBT were not supported in the original analyses. However, recent reanalyses of the MATCH data using catastrophe and growth mixture modeling found that CBT was more efficacious than the other two treatments for patients low in self-efficacy (Witkiewitz, van der Maas, Hufford, & Marlatt, 2007).

Ouimette, Finney, and Moos (1997) reported 1-year outcomes from a quasi-experimental study of CBT, 12-step, and eclectic inpatient treatment programs in the Veterans Administration (VA) system in the United States. The sample of 3,018 patients was heterogeneous in substances used, and most patients were male and relatively poor. Similar to Project MATCH, there were few differences in outcome among patients treated in the three types of treatment programs, although patients receiving 12-step treatment were more likely to be abstinent. No results favored the CBT programs; other results from this study are reported in the section of this chapter on 12-step-based therapies.

Morgenstern, Blanchard, Morgan, Labouvie, and Hayaki (2001) trained community-based substance abuse counselors in the use of the Project MATCH CBT manual, and then conducted an RCT comparing treatment as usual to high- or low-standardization CBT. Outcomes at 1 year suggested no differences among the three treatments.

Project COMBINE (Anton et al., 2006) was an RCT using a $2 \times 2 \times 2$ design that included two pharmacotherapies (naltrexone or acamprosate) and placebo controls for AUDs, as well as two psychosocial treatments (medical management, or combined treatment that included CBT along with elements of motivational interviewing and involvement with Alcoholics Anonymous [AA]). A ninth treatment condition provided the combined psychosocial treatment with no placebo medication. Patients receiving naltrexone in combination with the combined treatment had the most positive outcomes; those in the no medication, no placebo, combined psychosocial treatment had the poorest outcomes.

Meta-analyses of group designs. Meta-analyses have been conducted on BSCT and RP. The meta-analysis of BSCT (Walters, 2000) reviewed 17 RCTs. The aggregate effect size was small to medium ($d = 0.33$) across all studies. When compared to a no-contact control, the effect size was large ($d = 0.94$); it was small when compared to active treatment control groups ($d = 0.20$ to 0.28). Effect sizes were in the small-to-medium range, and similar for alcohol dependent ($d = 0.32$) and problem-drinking populations ($d = 0.34$). Irvin, Bowers, Dunn, and Wang (1999) conducted a meta-analysis of 26 studies of RP, including 13 RCTs with problem-drinking or alcohol-dependent populations. The effect size across the alcohol studies (weighted average correlation coefficient) was in the small to medium range ($r = 0.37$).

W. R. Miller and Wilbourne (2002) included three treatments, SST, BSCT, and SM, in their ratings of efficacious treatments (Table 7.1). Social skills training was ranked fifth, with a CES of 85. Behavioral self-control training was ranked 19th and the CES was 9. Stress management was ranked 22nd, with a CES of 4. Finney, Wilbourne, and Moos (2007) examined the efficacy of these treatments across four major quantitative reviews. Social skills training was ranked first or second in all four reviews; BSCT was ranked 2, 6, 8, and 10 in the four reviews; and SM was ranked 5, 5.5, 10, and 11.

Conclusions. On balance, there is strong evidence for the efficacy of specific forms of CBT for AUDs, particularly relapse prevention and social skills training. Evidence about BSCT is mixed, with one formal meta-analysis finding a small to medium effect size for the treatment. In contrast, W. R. Miller and Wilbourne's (2002) review did not rate either BSCT or SM among the top 10 treatments. In

general, when compared to other carefully delivered, credible treatments, CBT seems to yield similar, but not necessarily superior, results. To date, studies of the translation of CBT to community-based care have not suggested that using CBT improves outcomes beyond usual treatment. Unfortunately, CBT has been defined differently across studies, with many studies using very standardized treatment protocols, which are somewhat antithetical to a hallmark of CBT, which is individualized assessment and treatment planning.

Contingency Management

Treatment overview. Contingency management is based on the operant principle that behaviors that are reinforced are more likely to be repeated; in alcohol treatment the target behaviors usually are abstinence, reductions in alcohol use, or other actions inconsistent with continued alcohol use (e.g., Stitzer & Petry, 2006). Contingency management typically includes the use of a family of reinforcers, such as cash, prizes, or vouchers that are exchangeable for tangible goods or services (Stitzer & Petry, 2006). Reinforcers can be positive (e.g., winning a prize) or negative (e.g., removing restrictions on privileges), and it is important to note that, to be considered reinforcers, these prizes or restriction removals must be desirable enough to clients that they modify their subsequent behavior (CSAT, 2006).

Consensus panel recommendations. A consensus panel led by Forman and Nagy (CSAT, 2006) reviewed the strengths and challenges of contingency management. Their conclusion was that "abstinence . . . may not be sufficiently reinforcing to maintain a person's motivation to stop using drugs" (p. 149), and therefore that artificial reinforcers might be necessary to evoke behavior replacing alcohol use. The identified strengths of contingency management treatment included effectiveness in changing alcohol use behavior, evidence of efficacy alone and in combination with other alcohol treatments, potential low-cost implementation with community cooperation and donations, particular effectiveness for people with severe drug problems, and "extensive and robust" (p. 151) scientific support. However, they identified drawbacks of the method, including the potential cost of unsubsidized incentives (up to $1,200 per client), the need for highly reinforcing prizes, the frequency of testing required for alcohol (which is detectable in the body for only a short time after use), and the potential for relapse after contingencies are discontinued. Overall, Forman and Nagy (CSAT, 2006) reported favorable results for the efficacy of contingency management for treatment of AUDs.

The National Registry of Evidence-based Programs and Practices (2007c), concluded that outcomes regarding contingency management for substance-use treatment showed quality ratings of 3.5 to 4.0 and dissemination-readiness ratings of 2.5 to 3.5 (see Table 7.2).

Randomized clinical trials. Although many RCTs of contingency management have been conducted and have shown strong support for the treatment, nearly all contemporary studies have focused upon treatment for drugs other than alcohol (e.g., Higgins & Petry, 1999; Petry, Martin, Cooney, & Kranzler, 2000). However, a few recent trials, described later, have been informative for alcohol treatment.

The most notable study of contingency management for AUDs was conducted by Petry and colleagues (2000). In this study, 69% of participants in the condition combining contingency management with standard treatment were abstinent from alcohol posttreatment, compared to 39% abstinent in the standard-treatment-only condition. Furthermore, 84% in the contingency management condition, compared to just 22% in the standard-treatment condition, were retained through the 8 weeks of treatment. In this study, the average prize total was $200. Thus, the authors concluded that contingency management was efficacious for promoting treatment attendance and abstinence from alcohol use, and that it was a cost-effective intervention.

A multisite study (Alessi, Hanson, Wieners, & Petry, 2007), in which 50% of participants were diagnosed with AUDs, used a two-phase crossover design to compare contingency management to standard treatment plus attendance monitoring. Compared to the standard-treatment condition, contingency management participants showed lower rates of substance use (including alcohol use) at 6 and 9 months posttreatment (59% and 54% for contingency management, and 68% and 58% in standard treatment, respectively), as well as significantly greater "longest durations of abstinence."

By contrast, Litt, Kadden, Kabela-Cormier, and Petry's (2007) study of alcohol users that used contingency management as a control showed that contingency management did *not* add incremental utility over network support, but that both network-support conditions (with and without contingency management) were more effective than case management. The authors speculated that these findings might be due to already high adherence to treatment in their sample.

Meta-analyses of group designs. A single meta-analysis (Prendergast, Podus, Finney, Greenwell, & Roll, 2006) reviewed contingency management for substance use disorders (SUDs), including alcohol. In general, Prendergast and colleagues found that contingency management methods provide effective treatment for alcohol and other drugs—particularly for promoting engagement and participation in treatment—and named contingency management as one of the best methods for reinforcing abstinence during and following treatment. Effect sizes averaged $d = 0.42$, but it should be noted that only one study looked at alcohol specifically and most focused upon polydrug use. Also, the effects of contingency management therapy seemed to fade gradually after discontinuation of the contingencies. Finally, contingency management might be insufficient as a stand-alone therapy and preferably should be used in combination with other methods. The Mesa Grande panel (W. R. Miller & Wilbourne, 2002) also adopted this perspective, determining that contingency management was not a stand-alone treatment and therefore did not include it in their review.

Conclusions. With the exception of the Litt et al. (2007) study, contingency management generally has received strong support in the literature. Although the research focus on alcohol is limited, it might be possible to predict the results for alcohol based upon the results for drugs.

The literature is split somewhat in terms of the cost-effectiveness of contingency management. Olmstead, Sindelar, and Petry (2007) reported heterogeneity in cost-effectiveness for contingency management for drug use, Petry et al. (2006) noted an average cost of $200 per person, and CSAT (2006) reported costs up to $1,200 per person. Sindelar, Elbel, and Petry (2007) found that among cocaine users, greater-cost prizes actually led to lower per-unit costs — that is, high-cost prizes in contingency management added incremental effectiveness of contingency management.

Cue Exposure Therapy (CET)

Treatment overview. Cue exposure therapy is based on social learning and classical conditioning theories, positing that problem alcohol use arises from conditioned associations with alcohol-related stimuli and that disrupting those associations would result in better treatment outcomes. Studies of CET vary in the length of the intervention; however, the common element is direct exposure to salient alcohol cues while using techniques to reduce the urge to drink and craving. Often, coping skills and communication skills training are included in the intervention paradigm.

Consensus panel recommendations. The APA Division 12 Task Force on Promotion and Dissemination of Psychological Procedures listed cue exposure therapy as an adjunct to inpatient treatment as a probably efficacious intervention for alcohol dependence (Chambless et al., 1998). Thus, the panel found CET to be beneficial to patients, but there currently

was insufficient evidence to designate CET as an empirically validated treatment.

Randomized clinical trials. The RCTs examining the efficacy of CET have reported consistently favorable results. However, the specific CET intervention has varied considerably across studies. One of the earlier studies investigating CET looked at a sample of 40 male inpatients in a VA setting (Monti et al., 1993). All patients met *DSM-III-R* criteria for alcohol dependence. Participants were randomly assigned to receive either CET ($N = 22$) or a contrast condition (CC) ($N = 18$) in addition to the standard inpatient treatment. The CET consisted of six cue exposure sessions within a 2-week period. Participants' favorite alcoholic beverages were presented to elicit the highest urge to drink. Additionally, high-risk trigger situations were identified, imaginal cue exposure was used, and coping-skills training was included. The CC was the standard inpatient VA treatment, controlling for the amount of daily contact in the CET group. Results showed a significant decrease in self-reported urge to drink over time in both conditions. At the 3-month follow-up, there were no observed treatment condition effects on drinking outcomes. However, at 6 months posttreatment, significantly fewer participants reported any drinking in the CET group. Additionally, the CET group was found to have a significantly higher percentage of days abstinent (PDA) compared to the CC group. Although results support the efficacy of CET, the sample was relatively small and 15% of participants were not included in the analyses due to study attrition.

Another study examined a sample of 35 male patients meeting *DSM-III-R* criteria for alcohol dependence in a hospital alcohol clinic (Drummond & Glautier, 1994). Due to concerns about contamination of treatment groups, participants were assigned to conditions sequentially, with the first 20 participants enrolled assigned to CET and the next 15 assigned to the relaxation control condition (RC). The CET consisted of 10 cue exposure sessions. The relaxation control consisted of 10 sessions, using Progressive

Relaxation Training. Assessments were collected at 1-, 3-, and 6-month follow-ups. Logistic regression analyses suggested an advantage of CET over RC in latency to reinstatement of heavier drinking and alcohol dependence symptoms, as well as overall amount of alcohol consumed.

Sitharthan, Sitharthan, Hough, and Kavanagh (1997) investigated the effects of CET on outcome when the treatment goal was moderation instead of abstinence. Another major difference from prior RCTs of CET is that participants were excluded if they met criteria for alcohol dependence. Participants received six 90-minute sessions of CET ($N = 22$) or CBT ($N = 20$) provided in groups of three or four. A significant treatment condition by time interaction was observed, reflecting greater decreases in drinking frequency and drinks per occasion in the CET condition compared to CBT. Additionally, greater decreases in drinking problems were reported in the CET group. Although this study still had a relatively small sample size ($N = 42$), its strength lies in the comparison of CET to an active treatment, CBT, rather than to a more passive control group.

More recently, a larger study examined the effect of CET ($N = 63$) compared to an education and relaxation control ($N = 65$) (Monti et al., 2001). Both psychosocial interventions were provided daily for 90 minutes over the course of one to two weeks. In line with previous findings, no differences were observed at 3 months between conditions. However, a significantly larger percentage of the control group relapsed at 6 and 12 months compared to the CET group. The control group also had a larger percentage of heavy drinking days (PDH). The findings reported here were unaffected by medication status. Monti et al. (2001) also investigated the effect of naltrexone; however, the findings reported here were unaffected by medication status.

Another study by the same research group used a 2 × 2 design comparing random assignment to either CET or meditation/relaxation training control, as well as random assignment to either CST or education discussion (Rohsenow et al., 2001). Due to the delayed effect of CET observed in previous studies, drinking outcomes were examined separately in the first and second 6 months posttreatment. During the first 6 months, significant medium effect sizes were observed for PDH, with CET showing lower PDH than control, and CST showing lower PDH than education discussion. During the second 6 months, a significant interaction was found, showing a medium effect size ($f = 0.33$) in which the CET group receiving CST drank less than the CET group receiving education discussion and the control group receiving CST. The control group with education discussion had the poorest outcome. The Rohsenow et al. (2001) study is strong as it parsed out the effects of CET and CST independently and found that the combination of the two techniques provided incremental benefit over either independently.

Meta-analyses of group designs. At the time of publication, Mesa Grande (W. R. Miller & Wilbourne, 2002) only found two RCTs of CET. Evaluation of the two studies resulted in a CES of 32.

Conclusions. To date, studies examining the effects of CET on alcohol use outcome have reported consistent support for the efficacy of this intervention. Cue exposure therapy has been shown to provide better treatment outcomes across a variety of drinking measures. Additionally, the superiority of CET has been shown to persist when compared to multiple comparison treatments. Unfortunately, the number of CET studies is limited, and comprehensive reviews or meta-analyses of CET do not currently exist. Effect sizes were reported in only one study and sample sizes generally are small. Another potential weakness regarding the status of CET is that present studies have used different treatment protocols, making it difficult to generalize findings across studies. In fact, the earlier studies of CET used it only in addition to fairly intensive inpatient programs. In summary, the current evidence suggests the utility of CET and the need for further research, particularly on the long-term efficacy of this intervention and its generalizability to diverse populations.

Community Reinforcement Approach (CRA)

Treatment overview. The Community Reinforcement Approach (CRA) is based largely on behavioral conditioning theory, focusing particularly on the importance of an individual's interaction with his or her environment (E. J. Miller, 2001). The predominant goal in CRA is to build an environment that discourages substance use and reinforces sobriety (Meyers, Smith, & Lash, 2003). CRA has multiple components that aim to make nondrinking as positively reinforcing as drinking. Most commonly, these components include a functional analysis, behavioral skills training, relapse prevention, alcohol refusal training, and communication skills. In addition, job skills training, social/recreational counseling, and relationship counseling are offered to help promote positive experiences in career, social encounters, and family relationships as a drinking lifestyle graduates toward a non drinking one (Meyers, Villanueva, & Smith, 2005). Supportive monitoring of disulfiram by a significant other often is encouraged to help achieve abstinence during initial treatment periods (Meyers et al., 2005).

Consensus panel recommendations. The APA Task Force on EVTs listed CRA as a probably efficacious treatment for alcohol dependence (Chambless et al., 1998). CRA has not been evaluated in a Cochrane Review and is not listed by NREPP.

In a review evaluating RCTs with relation to their methodological quality, Roozen et al. (2004) concluded from consistent findings in multiple high quality RCTs that there was strong evidence that CRA reduces the number of drinking days compared to treatment as usual. These authors also concluded there was moderate evidence across both high and low quality RCTs that the number of drinking days

is reduced when disulfiram is added to CRA treatment. In terms of total abstinence, the authors concluded that there was conflicting evidence that CRA yields greater abstinence rates than treatment as usual.

Randomized clinical trials. The efficacy of CRA in the treatment of alcohol use disorders has been demonstrated through RCTs comparing CRA to placebo treatments in several populations. Initial RCTs with inpatients diagnosed with AUDs demonstrated that CRA treatment consisting of vocational, family, and social reinforcement counseling yielded less days drinking (14% vs. 79%), unemployed (5% vs. 62%), away from home and family (16% vs. 36%), and hospitalized (2% vs. 27%) compared to control participants (Hunt & Azrin, 1973). These results persisted at 6-month follow-up (Hunt & Azrin, 1973); however, the generalizability of this trial is limited by the small study size ($N = 16$). Expanding on these components to include situational alcohol refusal training, supportive monitoring of disulfiram, regular meeting with a supportive peer-advisor, and group counseling instead of individual counseling resulted in improvements similar to those in Hunt and Azrin (1973) (Azrin, 1976). These effects persisted over a 2 year follow up period. Moreover, while yielding better outcomes with the additional CRA components, clinicians spent less time with their patients than in the earlier study (Azrin, 1976), demonstrating a potentially stronger cost benefit ratio through the addition of these components.

In an RCT with rural outpatients seeking alcohol treatment, participants receiving CRA had fewer drinking days per month (0.9 vs. 16.4), consumed less alcohol per drinking episode (0.7 vs. 4.1 oz.), and were more compliant with disulfiram administration (24.8 vs. 0 days per month) than those receiving psychoeducational treatment (Azrin, Sisson, Meyers, & Godley, 1982). Improvements favoring CRA persisted throughout the 6 month follow up period.

A trial of 237 participants yielded several interesting findings in an examination of the combined effects of CRA and disulfiram

(W. R. Miller, Meyers, Tonigan, & Grant, 2001). Participants were randomly assigned to receive either CRA or treatment as usual that was similar to TSF. To examine the effects of supportive disulfiram monitoring, participants in both groups were further randomly assigned to receive or not receive both disulfiram and supportive monitoring. Although participants showed no difference in their likelihood of participating in either treatment type, CRA yielded fewer drinking days than did treatment as usual when participants did not receive disulfiram monitoring. Among participants who did receive disulfiram monitoring, CRA and treatment as usual yielded similar overall drinking rates; however, those receiving CRA showed lower rates of complete abstinence.

In an RCT of 106 alcohol-dependent homeless individuals, CRA showed better outcomes than those who received treatment as usual in number of drinking days, total alcohol consumption, and peak blood alcohol content over the 12-month follow-up (Smith, Meyers, & Delaney, 1998). Unexpectedly, CRA produced no differences in employment or homelessness in this alcohol-dependent homeless sample compared to the usual treatment. Using random assignment in a rural outpatient sample-seeking alcohol treatment, Mallams, Godley, Hall, and Meyers (1982) found that participants who were randomized to receive encouragement from counselors to attend weekly social club gatherings consumed significantly less alcohol, had less heavy alcohol consumption, and had less behavioral impairment than those not randomized to receive encouragement.

The use of disulfiram with supportive monitoring has been considered an active component to CRA, though experimental trials evaluating the contribution of disulfiram with supportive monitoring have had mixed findings. For married participants, the individual component of disulfiram monitoring by a family member or a friend without other components of CRA produced equal outcomes in sober days when compared to disulfiram monitoring with full CRA (30 vs. 30 days/month), both of which were higher than placebo treatment (17.4 days/month), suggesting that disulfiram monitoring alone had similar efficacy as full CRA among married individuals (Azrin et al., 1982). However, for unmarried participants, full CRA produced better outcomes in sober days than disulfiram monitoring alone, which showed little improvement compared to placebo treatment (28.3 vs. 8.0 vs. 6.8 days/month, respectively). A larger and more recent RCT yielded results suggesting limited efficacy of disulfiram monitoring, finding that among outpatients medically eligible for disulfiram, those assigned to receive disulfiram monitoring were only somewhat likely to administer disulfiram (56%), and unlikely to have a trained monitor (29%; W. R. Miller et al., 2001). This study also found that the efficacy of CRA did not increase with the addition of disulfiram monitoring.

Meta-analyses of group designs. In cost-benefit meta-analyses, CRA has been rated as having good evidence of effectiveness while having only a medium-to-low direct cost ($200 to $599 in 1987 dollars) over the entire course of treatment (Finney & Monahan, 1996; Holder, Longabaugh, Miller, & Rubonis, 1991). When effectiveness indices were adjusted to account for statistically expected values, CRA was ranked highest among psychosocial treatments in terms of total evidence for effectiveness (Finney & Monahan, 1996). In Mesa Grande (W. R. Miller & Wilbourne, 2002), CRA was ranked as having the sixth highest CES among pharmacotherapy- and psychosocial-based treatments with a score of 80.

Conclusion. CRA seeks to promote treatment for AUDs by helping clients build environments that positively reinforce abstinence. A number of RCTs have shown that CRA consistently demonstrates efficacy to reduce drinking in both inpatients and outpatients, as well as other groups such as homeless individuals. CRA has a high benefit-cost ratio; it is ranked consistently as one of the most efficacious treatments and is considered to have a medium-to-low cost to implement when compared to a range of inpatient and outpatient treatments (Holder, Longabaugh, Miller, & Rubonis, 1991). Supportive disulfiram administration with CRA has shown mixed results regarding an additive effect on treatment efficacy, and supportive monitoring may be especially helpful for individuals with a significant other; however, our understanding of the specific active ingredients and mechanisms of action in CRA is limited.

Behavioral Couples and Family Treatments

Treatment overview. Three related family-involved treatments for AUDs have strong evidence for their efficacy. Behavioral couple therapy (BCT) for AUDs (Epstein & McCrady, 1998) has the strongest evidence base. Behavioral couple therapy includes three major elements: (1) interventions to facilitate initial abstinence or to maintain continued abstinence, including behavioral contracts; (2) interventions to teach the partner skills to cope more effectively with alcohol use and abstinence; and (3) interventions to improve relationship functioning through reciprocity enhancement and improved skills in communication and problem solving. Treatments focused on intimate partners or others concerned about a person with an AUD include the Community Reinforcement Approach and Family Training (CRAFT) (W. R. Miller, Meyers, & Tonigan, 1999) and partner-focused coping skills training (Rychtarik & McGillicuddy, 2005). These treatments focus on coping skills for concerned significant others (CSOs), teaching them skills to cope more effectively with alcohol use and abstinence, self-care skills, and communication skills to encourage the drinker to seek help or decrease alcohol use without treatment. Family behavior therapy (FBT) (Azrin et al., 2001) combines elements of BCT with elements of CRA, including behavioral contracts, alcohol and drug-focused coping skills, communication skills, and job skills.

Consensus panel recommendations and consensus reviews. Five comprehensive reviews or consensus panels have identified various forms of BCT or FBT as efficacious treatments for AUDs. The National Registry of Evidence-based Programs and Practices (2006a, 2006b, 2009) lists three couples/family treatments for AUDs, including two different approaches to BCT. McCrady and Epstein's model of BCT, Alcohol Behavioral Couple Therapy (ABCT), was assessed as showing strong evidence for decreased alcohol use and increased relationship quality (NREPP, 2009). Studies compared different intensities of spouse-involved treatment (McCrady, Stout, Noel, Abrams, & Nelson, 1991) or compared individual therapy to ABCT (McCrady, Epstein, Cook, Jensen, & Hildebrandt, 2009). The NREPP reviewer ratings of the quality of the research evidence for ABCT for drinking outcomes were high, with a mean of 3.2. Readiness for dissemination ratings also were high, with a mean of 3.0. O'Farrell and Fals Stewart's model of BCT, BCT for alcoholism and drug abuse, also was assessed as showing strong evidence for decreased alcohol/drug use and intimate partner violence, and increased relationship quality, treatment compliance, and posttreatment child functioning. Most of the alcohol treatment studies reviewed (Fals Stewart, Birchler, & Kelley, 2006; Fals Stewart, Klostermann, Yates, O'Farrell, & Birchler, 2005; Kelley & Fals Stewart, 2002; O'Farrell, Murphy, Stephan, Fals Stewart, & Murphy, 2004; Winters, Fals Stewart, O'Farrell, Birchler, & Kelley, 2002) compared BCT with individual therapy in the context of an ongoing treatment program.[1] The NREPP reviewer

[1] Questions have been raised about the validity of research on BCT supported by grants to William Fals Stewart as Principal Investigator (Fals Stewart et al., 2005; Fals Stewart et al., 2006; Kelley & Fals Stewart, 2002; Winters et al., 2002); however, even without Fals Stewart's published studies, the body of work supporting BCT is strong and warrants its inclusion as an evidence-based treatment

ratings of the quality of the research evidence for positive substance-use outcomes were high, with a mean of 3.4. Readiness for dissemination ratings also were high, with a mean of 3.2. Table 7.2 provides ratings for each NREPP category.

Family behavior therapy showed strong evidence for decreases in alcohol and drug use, depression, and improvements in occupational functioning. Much of the research base for FBT focuses on adolescent treatment populations, but supportive evidence exists for adults as well (Azrin et al., 1994; Azrin et al., 1996; Azrin, Donohue, Besalel, Kogan, & Acierno, 1994; Azrin et al., 2001). The NREPP reviewer ratings of the quality of the research focusing on alcohol use were acceptable, ranging from 2.0 to 3.0 with a mean of 2.7. Readiness for dissemination ratings were stronger, ranging from 3.5 to 4.0 with a mean of 3.8. See Table 7.2 for more details.

The third report of the APA Task Force on EVTs (Chambless et al., 1998) listed BCT as meeting criteria for a "possibly efficacious treatment," based on two early studies by O'Farrell and his colleagues (O'Farrell, Cutter, Choquette, Floyd, & Bayog, 1992; O'Farrell, Cutter, & Floyd, 1985).

Randomized clinical trials. The majority of published studies of behavioral couples or family treatment for AUDs have been reviewed in meta-analyses, consensus panels, or comprehensive reviews described in the preceding paragraphs, and so are not further discussed here. Two studies tested relapse prevention (RP) techniques as add-ons to BCT. McCrady and colleagues (McCrady, Epstein, & Hirsh, 1999; McCrady, Epstein, & Kahler, 2004) tested BCT alone compared to BCT plus RP strategies and BCT plus AA involvement in a sample of 102 men with AUDs and their female partners. Length of treatment was 15 sessions across conditions, with up to four booster sessions available to the RP group. At 6 months, there were no treatment differences on PDA, but men in the RP condition had shorter length relapses; men in

the BCT condition had a longer time to their first drink (McCrady et al., 1999). No differences in alcohol use outcomes were observed 18 months posttreatment (McCrady et al., 2004). O'Farrell, Choquette, Cutter, Brown, and McCourt (1993) compared the efficacy of BCT to BCT plus an additional 15 sessions during the year posttreatment in a sample of 59 men with AUDs. One year after the index treatment (immediately posttreatment for those in the RP condition), results favored the RP condition on PDA and PDD; differences in alcohol use outcomes were not sustained at 30 month posttreatment follow-up (18 months for the RP condition), but wives in the RP condition were significantly happier than those in the BCT-only condition throughout the follow-up window.

McCrady et al. (2009) compared BCT to individual CBT in 102 women with AUDs, also testing the presence of other psychopathology as a moderator of treatment outcomes. Women receiving BCT had significantly greater PDA and fewer PDH than those in individual CBT. Moderator analyses found that BCT was more effective than CBT for women with Axis I and Axis II disorders.

One study has tested CRAFT for AUDs, comparing CRAFT to the Johnson Intervention and Al-Anon as methods to engage treatment-resistant identified patients (IPs) with AUDs into treatment (W. R. Miller et al., 1999). In a study of 130 CSOs, all three 12-session treatments resulted in similar improvements in CSO functioning, but treatment engagement for IPs was significantly higher for CRAFT (64%) than the Johnson Intervention (30%) or Al-Anon (13%). Rychtarik and McGillicuddy (2005) compared a CBT-based coping skills training to TSF for 171 wives of treatment-resistant men with AUDs. Both treatments were more effective than delayed treatment in reducing the women's depression and the men's drinking. However, men with a history of relationship violence had improved drinking outcomes with CBT but deteriorated outcomes with TSF.

Meta-analyses of group designs. One meta-analysis of BCT for AUDs has been reported (Powers, Vedel, & Emmelkamp, 2008). Studies were identified through exhaustive searches of PsycINFO, MEDLINE, and the Cochrane Central register, and were included if they reported randomized clinical trials of BCT compared to an active or inactive control and were published in the English language. Studies that included CSOs who were not intimate partners were excluded. The final sample for the meta-analysis included 12 published studies, with a total of 754 participants (Bowers & Al-Redha, 1990; Fals-Stewart et al., 2005; Fals-Stewart et al., 2006; Kelley & Fals-Stewart, 2002; McCrady et al., 1986; McCrady et al., 1991; O'Farrell et al., 1985; O'Farrell et al., 1992; Vedel, Emmelkamp, & Schippers, 2008; Walitzer & Derman, 2004). Eight of the 12 studies focused on AUDs; the balance reported studies of treatment for other substance use disorders. Results revealed an overall medium effect size favoring BCT (Cohen's d 0.54), medium effect sizes for consequences of use (d 0.52) and relationship satisfaction (d 0.58), and a small to medium effect size for frequency of use (d 0.36). There was no significant relation between publication year and effect size or number of treatment sessions and effect size; larger effect sizes were observed with larger samples.

Two systematic reviews of the alcohol treatment outcome literature have been published recently (Finney et al., 2007; W. R. Miller & Wilbourne, 2002). In the Mesa Grande report (W. R. Miller & Wilbourne, 2002), BCT received a CES of 60, and was rank ordered eighth. Finney et al. (2007), using W. R. Miller and Wilbourne as well as three earlier reviews, ranked BCT as between third and fifth in efficacy across the four reviews. Neither CRAFT nor FBT was rated in either review.

Conclusions. Behavioral couple therapy appears to be more efficacious than individual CBT in treating both men and women with AUDs. On average, the quality of research on BCT is very good, and results are fairly consistent across different research groups. Add-ons to BCT appear to enhance outcomes only if provided through a substantial number of additional treatment sessions. Newer research suggests that BCT may be particularly efficacious in the presence of other Axis I or Axis II disorders, but these results need to be replicated. Evidence supports FBT as well, although the evidence base for adults is more limited and distinctions between FBT and BCT are not well delineated. Single studies of two approaches to CSO-focused treatment have found improved outcomes for CSOs, and improved drinking outcomes or treatment engagement for IPs. Replication studies are needed for these treatments.

Brief Interventions

Treatment overview. Brief interventions (BIs) for problem alcohol use have garnered considerable attention and have created excitement about potential applications. Brief interventions are quick and easy to administer, and have been shown to be quite effective in a wide range of populations. Additionally, due to the ease with which such interventions can be delivered, BIs have been disseminated and implemented widely in general health care settings. Brief interventions also have been widely studied in college populations as a method to reduce high-risk drinking behavior. Brief interventions have two major goals: to reduce risky drinking and to facilitate referral to treatment (Bien, Miller, & Tonigan, 1993). Definitions of BIs vary, however, the critical characterization of a BI is in the relatively short duration of the intervention, although even this varies from a single session to up to five sessions (Moyer, Finney, Swearingen, & Vergun, 2002). Another common feature of BIs is that they rarely explicitly require a goal of abstinence, instead aiming to promote nonhazardous drinking. A third feature of treatments designated as BIs is that they typically are administered by nonaddiction specialists. Often, BIs incorporate aspects of Motivational Interviewing (MI) into the intervention framework.

Consensus panel recommendations. Recently, NREPP (2008a) concluded that the Drinker's Check-Up meets standards for an evidence-based practice. The Drinker's Check-Up is a computerized brief intervention designed to help people reduce their alcohol use. The overall ratings for the quality of research ranged from 2.7 to 2.8, while the ratings for readiness for dissemination ranged from 3.5 to 4.0.

Randomized clinical trials. Brief interventions are one of the most extensively studied alcohol treatment modalities. For example, one review (Moyer et al., 2002) identified 56 RCTs investigating the effects of BIs. As such, this section will not attempt to cover all studies examining the efficacy of BIs, especially since there are a number of thorough meta-analyses that summarize the findings of the RCTs. Instead, a few representative RCTs will be described to illustrate some of the diverse populations in which BIs have been investigated.

One of the most common settings in which BIs are utilized is medical care settings such as the emergency room. One study examined the effects of a brief motivational interview on 94 older adolescents (ages 18–19 years) who came into the ER for an alcohol-related event (Monti et al., 1999). Participants were randomly assigned to either the BI condition or to standard care (SC). The BI condition consisted of a brief motivational interview, informational handouts, and personalized feedback on alcohol use. The SC condition included a handout on drinking and driving as well as a list of local treatment agencies. During follow-up, the SC group was significantly more likely than the BI group to report drinking and driving. Additionally, the BI group was less likely to report alcohol-related injury and alcohol-related problems at 6-month follow-up. Thus, the findings suggest the effectiveness of BIs in emergency room settings.

Brief interventions often are utilized in college populations to reduce hazardous drinking behavior. One RCT examined the effect of a BI in a sample of college students (Marlatt et al., 1998). Students were contacted during the summer prior to their matriculation in college and those identified as high-risk drinkers were randomized to either a BI condition or an assessment only condition. The BI condition consisted of a brief motivational interview structured around personalized feedback during the winter term of students' first year in college. Participants in the BI condition also received personalized feedback forms in the mail the following winter. At 6 months, the BI group reported a significantly lower quantity and frequency of drinking. The observed effect size was small ($d = 0.15$), however. Similar patterns were observed at the 2-year follow-up, with similar effect sizes ($d = 0.14$–0.20).

Meta-analyses of group designs. W. R. Miller and Wilbourne (2002) found brief interventions to have the strongest empirical evidence of all alcohol treatment modalities (see Table 7.1). Thirty-one RCTs involving BIs yielded a cumulative evidence score of 280, more than 100 points higher than the second highest-rated treatment.

One of the earlier meta-analyses of the efficacy of BIs looked at 32 studies enrolling a total of 6,000 problem drinkers across 14 nations (Bien et al., 1993). Out of 12 studies examining the effects of BIs on referral rates in general health-care settings, 11 found that the BI condition increased referrals more than control conditions. Seven out of eight RCTs reported significant reductions in drinking in the BI condition in the same setting compared to a control. In self-referred drinkers, of 13 RCTs comparing BIs to more extensive treatment only two found the extended treatment to be more effective. Bien et al. (1993) found a mean effect size of 0.38 for BI over control. Studies comparing BI to extended therapy yielded a mean effect size of 0.06, suggesting no clear advantage of extended treatment over BI. A few methodological issues of studies were identified in this meta-analysis. First, roughly a third of outcome studies had sample sizes of 20 or less, thus reducing the power to detect significant effects. Additionally, the selection bias in these studies often was problematic. Finally, reactivity to assessment was identified as a possible confound that may have served to reduce differences observed between BIs and control conditions.

A more recent meta-analysis examined 56 studies comparing BI to control conditions in treatment-seeking populations ($N = 2$), non-treatment-seeking populations ($N = 34$), and extended treatment in treatment-seeking populations ($N = 20$) (Moyer et al., 2002). Aggregate effect sizes were calculated for alcohol consumption and a composite of drinking-related consequences. These effect sizes were calculated by time to follow-up in 3-month increments up to 1 year. In studies comparing BI to control in nontreatment-seeking samples, significant effect sizes ranged from 0.14 to 0.67. In studies comparing BI to extended treatment in treatment-seeking samples, a significant effect size was found only at 3 to 6 months for alcohol consumption ($d = 0.42$). The two studies comparing BI to controls in treatment-seeking samples could not be combined meta-analytically, but evidence suggested small to moderate effect sizes favoring BIs. Additionally, gender effects were examined based on suggestions of previous literature. No evidence for systematic differences between males and females was found. Of the studies identified in this meta-analysis, 37 excluded participants with alcohol dependence or severe drinking. Thus, findings on BIs from RCTs may not generalize to general populations of persons with AUDs, because the drinkers most at risk often have been excluded from participation.

Another meta-analysis calculated odds ratios for 13 studies assessing BIs in primary care settings using only intention-to-treat (ITT) analyses (Ballesteros, Duffy, Querejeta, Arino, & Gonzalez Pinto, 2004). Consideration also was given to the intensity (i.e., length) of the intervention, as brief interventions were

divided into three categories based on intensity: minimal intervention (3–5 minutes), brief intervention (10–15 minutes), and extended brief intervention (EBI) (10–15 minutes at initial assessment and again at follow-up). Odds ratios for BIs (1.6) and EBIs (1.5) were significantly higher than controls while not differing from each other. Minimal interventions (0.95) did not differ significantly from control conditions. After combining BIs and EBIs, an improvement of 11% in success rate was observed compared to control. Interestingly, BIs were found to be better suited to nontreatment-seeking samples (OR 2.19) than to treatment seekers (OR 1.41). Additionally, BIs appeared to work better for heavy drinkers (OR 1.94) than moderate drinkers (OR 1.42). This finding is of particular interest due to questions of generalizability to more severe samples raised by Moyer et al. (2002). Overall, the findings of this meta-analysis mirror previous meta-analyses, although a slightly lower efficacy of BIs was reported due to the ITT analysis methods. One potential issue to consider when interpreting the findings of Ballesteros et al. (2004) is the fact that 16 studies were determined to be ineligible due to insufficient data for ITT analyses, which is a larger number of studies than were actually included in the meta-analysis.

Conclusions. Brief interventions have an advantage over traditional treatment modalities because they do not need to be conducted by addiction specialists and can be completed in a short amount of time. Thus, health care workers can provide BIs to people in almost any setting, even if the person is resistant to full treatment. Not only can BIs be administered to a much larger population than many other alcohol interventions, but evidence for the efficacy of BIs is quite strong. Research consistently has shown BIs to be effective in both reducing alcohol use and in increasing subsequent participation in further treatment. The body of literature regarding BIs is relatively extensive, especially in comparison to many other alcohol treatments. However, the body of evidence is not without its caveats. Questions still remain about the generalizability of BIs to drinkers with more severe problems. However, when one takes into account how economical BIs are and their ability to reach a wide range of problem drinkers, the advantages of BIs are apparent.

Motivational Interviewing and Motivational Enhancement Therapy

Treatment overview. Motivational interviewing (MI) is a "client-centered, directive method for enhancing intrinsic motivation to change by exploring and resolving ambivalence" (W. R. Miller & Rollnick, 2002, p. 25) that originated in the field of substance abuse treatment. Unlike many traditional treatments for AUDs, MI is viewed as *nonconfrontational* (e.g., Moyers, Martin, Manuel, Hendrickson, & Miller, 2005), meaning that the goal of the provider is to allow the client to build a case for change (W. R. Miller & Rollnick, 2002). Motivational Enhancement Therapy (MET) is a four-session adaptation of MI that initially was tested in Project MATCH (see CBT section for more information about Project MATCH; W. R. Miller, Zweben, DiClemente, & Rychtarik, 1994; Project MATCH Research Group, 1997).

Consensus panel recommendations. Several expert panels have reviewed MI and MET (CSAT, 1999, 2006; NREPP, 2007a, 2007b). A panel chaired by Miller (CSAT, 1999) provided an in-depth view of the MI/MET approach, reviewing the research evidence, suggesting clinical guidelines, speculating on future directions for research, and including several screening and assessment tools. They concluded that motivation is a dynamic state that is strongly related to the client's likelihood of making a change, and as such clinicians should foster a "therapeutic partnership." A panel chaired by Forman and Nagy (CSAT, 2006) highlighted the perceived strengths and challenges of the MI/MET approach. Calling it

"evidence based" (p. 15), they identified the strengths as being client-centered, focusing upon attainable goals, encouraging self-efficacy, and maintaining a positive and empathic stance. Challenges included the need for clients to be self-aware, incongruence with some assessments and treatment approaches, unspecified session content, requirements for extensive provider training and supervision, and relatively untested outcomes in group formats.

The National Registry of Evidence-based Programs and Practices (2007a, 2007b) ranked highly the research quality and readiness for dissemination of both MI (3.3–3.6 and 3.8–4.0) and MET (2.9–4.0 and 2.8–3.5, Table 7.2).

Randomized clinical trials. Numerous RCTs have evaluated the use of MI/MET compared to other established treatments and to no treatment or placebo controls. Because many of these studies are included in the meta-analyses described later, only alcohol-related RCTs published between 2003 and 2007 (i.e., more recently than those included in the meta-analyses) and listed in the current MI Bibliography (Wagner & Connors, 2008) are summarized here.

Multiple studies showed support for MI/MET in adult samples. A multisite study by Carroll et al. (2006) compared MI plus standard treatment to standard treatment alone, finding that participants in the MI condition showed better treatment retention at 28 days ($d = 0.24$), but no differences in substance use; therefore, use of MI early in treatment might improve early treatment retention. Morgenstern and colleagues (2007) compared four sessions of MI to 12 sessions of CBT + MI using a sample of men with AUDs who have sex with men. During treatment, both groups showed a reduction in drinks per drinking day ($d = 0.78$ for MI and .60 for MI + CBT), with significantly lower mean drinking levels for the MI group (pseudo-R^2's = 8.8% to 14.5%); however, there were no significant posttreatment differences between groups. Hester, Squires, and Delaney (2005) compared a brief computer-delivered MI intervention to a waitlist control. The MI participants reduced their alcohol use by 50% and showed continued reductions at a 1-year follow-up, and effect sizes were large ($d = 0.93$ to 1.05). Thus, computer interventions might be an efficacious alternative to in-person MI-based interventions.

Murphy et al. (2004) compared personalized drinking feedback (PDF) alone to PDF + MI at 6 months posttreatment in a sample of college student alcohol users. Although both groups reduced their drinking significantly ($d_w = 0.42$ for PDF; $d_w = 0.48$ for PDF + MI), addition of the MI component did not provide additional benefit over PDF. Emmen, Schippers, Woller-sheim, and Bleijenberg (2005) compared a brief MI intervention to "care as usual" (p. 219) in a sample of hospital outpatients with problematic alcohol use. Although both groups showed reduced alcohol use (3.9 vs. 3.11 U/day of alcohol; 1 U = 10g ethanol) at a 6-month follow-up, they did not differ significantly on alcohol consumption or motivation to change. These studies offer contrasting results to the bulk of MI/MET studies, suggesting that the MI/MET approach is effective but not necessarily more so than other established treatments.

Motivational interviewing and MET also have been tested in combination with the drug naltrexone (Anton et al., 2005; Davidson, Gulliver, Longabaugh, Wirtz, & Swift, 2007; Kranzler, Wesson, & Billot, 2004) with mixed results. Together, these studies suggest that MET might allow naltrexone to be more effective, but that MET offers less additional benefit when combined with naltrexone than do other psychotherapies; however, several weaknesses of the studies should be considered in evaluating these findings.

When only psychotherapies are considered, RCTs show that MI/MET is equally beneficial to other psychotherapeutic interventions and more efficacious than no treatment or than standard medical care. Motivational interviewing and MET have received much support for improving treatment retention, increasing readiness to change, and reducing alcohol use during and after treatment. However, MI/MET

might not offer additional benefit when combined with other interventions, and if naltrexone pharmacotherapy is used, then MI/MET might be less effective than other treatments. Other measures of efficacy (such as cost-effectiveness and relative length of treatment) should be explored further.

Meta-analyses of group designs. Five recent reviews and meta-analyses have examined the effectiveness and efficacy of MI/MET interventions. Dunn, Deroo, and Rivara (2001) reviewed brief MI-based interventions and found that 73% of studies about substance use (including alcohol) showed significant effect sizes for the use of MI; for substance use studies (including alcohol) specifically, unit-free effect sizes ranged from 0.30 to 0.95. Because evidence for brief MI as a stand-alone treatment was limited, they concluded that the effects of MI might be strongest when used as a prelude to other treatments for SUDs. Burke, Arkowitz, and Menchola (2003) conducted a meta-analysis of controlled clinical trials of Adaptations of MI (AMIs), which they defined as drinking feedback delivered in an MI style, combinations of MI and other techniques, or interventions intended for use by non-specialists. They found medium effect sizes ($d = 0.25$–0.53) for AMIs for alcohol and a 56% reduction in client drinking, and concluded that AMIs are comparable to other treatments for AUDs and better than no treatment or placebo controls. Hettema, Steele, and Miller (2005) examined studies on MI for various health behavior changes, including 32 trials of MI for AUDs. These 32 studies yielded a mean Cohen's d of 0.41 posttreatment and 0.26 for all follow-up time points, suggesting that the effects of MI might fade gradually with time. Higher effect sizes were reported for ethnic minority clients and when MI treatments were not manual-guided. A 2006 meta-analysis (Vasilaki, Hosier, & Cox) reviewed 22 RCTs of brief MI treatments. Brief MI showed an average effect size of 0.19 overall but 0.60 within 3 months postintervention, for an average of 0.43. They concluded that brief MI is effective for reducing alcohol use, but that the effects of MI tend to fade over time. Lastly, for Motivational Enhancement, the Mesa Grande panel (W. R. Miller & Wilbourne, 2002) reported a CES of 173, a rank of 2, and a 71% positive rating (Table 7.1).

These meta-analytic studies lend strong support for the use of brief MI, adaptations of MI, MET, and standard MI for treating AUDs. The effects of MI treatments are likely to diminish with time, raising the question of what the proper effective dose and dosing schedule of MI might be. Similarly, stronger results for nonmanual-guided than manual-guided treatments suggest that MI/MET consists of more than a set of specified procedures.

Conclusions. Motivational interviewing and MET are interventions with extensive research support. Moreover, at $75 to $100 per person (NREPP, 2007a, 2007b), MI/MET appears to be a cost-effective treatment method. Although further research is needed to clarify the active ingredients and causal mechanisms of MI/MET, as well as the implications for use of MI/MET with pharmacotherapy, the approach can be used with confidence to improve several client outcomes.

12-Step-Based Therapies

Treatment overview. The disease concept of alcoholism and principles of Alcoholics Anonymous (AA) are the foundations of 12-step-based therapies. Individuals are encouraged to acknowledge their loss of control over alcohol, commit to complete abstinence from alcohol, read AA literature, find a sponsor, work the 12 steps, and attend AA meetings. One example of an AA-based treatment is the Minnesota Model, an approach that combines major principles of the AA program of recovery with professionally delivered treatment services to help clients initiate pervasive changes in their lives to support abstinence. The Project MATCH Research Group (1997) created a manual-guided version of 12-step-based therapy known as Twelve-Step Facilitation (TSF).

Consensus panel recommendations and consensus reviews. In 2006, the Cochrane Collaboration reviewed the evidence for AA and other 12-step programs. They concluded that such programs were no more effective than other treatments for alcohol dependence (Ferri, Amato, & Davoli, 2006). Kaskutas (2008) raised concerns about the quality of the Cochrane Review, calling it an incorrect interpretation of Project MATCH data. She also disagreed with the Cochrane conclusion that, "people considering attending AA . . . should be made aware that there is a lack of experimental evidence on the effectiveness of such programmes" (p. 12).

Morgenstern and McKay (2007) reviewed the literature on 12-step-based therapies and found no previous comprehensive reviews. They identified RCTs that compared 12-step-based therapy with another treatment, although not all of the studies dealt solely with alcohol use. Six of the studies found no difference in treatment outcomes, while two comparing 12-step-based therapies with CBT found mixed results.

Randomized clinical trials. Project MATCH (1997) was a seminal RCT comparing the effectiveness of TSF, MET, and CBT. At 1 and 3 months posttreatment, those in the TSF outpatient condition had higher rates of abstinence than did those in the other treatment groups. However, all groups decreased their posttreatment levels of drinking. At 3 years posttreatment, those in the TSF group had significantly higher PDA than those in the CBT group (Project MATCH, 1998a).

A secondary analysis of the Project MATCH data (Longabaugh, Wirtz, Zweben, & Stout, 1998) considered outcomes for individuals whose networks were supportive of drinking. At the 3-year follow-up, PDA was significantly higher in the TSF and CBT group than the MET group for those who had networks supportive of drinking ($\eta^2 = .74, p = .0058$). In addition, those who had networks supportive of drinking and were in the TSF group were more likely to attend AA meetings, which also was associated with better 3-year alcohol use outcomes.

Holder et al. (2000) considered the costs of medical care (from pre- to posttreatment) for the three Project MATCH treatment modalities at two of the nine Project MATCH sites. For patients with little network support for drinking, few psychiatric symptoms, and less severe alcohol dependence, MET had the lowest costs. In contrast, CBT and TSF were more cost-effective than MET for those with more severe symptoms.

Another large-scale study compared 12-step-based therapies to CBT programs at multiple 1-month inpatient substance abuse treatment programs in the VA system (Ouimette et al., 1997). Although the study used a quasi-experimental design, it still warrants inclusion because of its large sample size ($N = 3,018$) and methodological rigor. Measures were administered at baseline and 1- and 2-year follow-ups. Both groups showed substantial decreases in alcohol use at 1 year, although patients in the 12-step-based therapy programs were somewhat more likely to be completely abstinent. At 2 years, CBT and 12-step-based therapies resulted in similar remission rates (Ritscher, Moos, & Finney, 2002). Additionally, patients in the 12-step-based therapy programs had higher abstinence rates and were more involved with AA whereas the CBT group used mental health services more frequently. Because of this difference in patterns of service utilization, costs were 30% lower (a difference of $2,440) over the 2-year period for those in the 12-step-based therapies group (Humphreys & Moos, 2007).

Brown et al. (2006) also compared CBT with TSF for substance-dependent veterans, but focused on those who also had depressive disorders ($N = 66$). Each individual was randomly assigned to TSF or integrated cognitive behavioral therapy (ICBT). Both therapies were based on the Project MATCH manuals, but ICBT included a depression-focused component. The format was 24 group sessions over 12 weeks followed by 12 weekly refresher

sessions. Follow-up occurred at 3 and 6 months posttreatment. Both groups had similar decreases in substance use and depression scores during treatment, but only the ICBT group maintained those decreases over the 6-month follow-up period. Although further research is needed, these findings suggest that depression may impede involvement with AA and subsequent benefits of the program.

A Finnish study (Keso & Salaspuro, 1990) compared a 12-step-based program with a traditional Finnish model. The alcohol-dependent, largely male sample was randomly assigned to one of two groups ($N = 141$). The 12-step program consisted of 28 days of structured residential care focusing on abstinence and connections with AA members. The traditional model was less structured and focused on rehabilitation through therapy. Those in the 12-step program attended significantly more AA meetings posttreatment than those in the traditional model, who attended significantly more outpatient therapy after treatment. Amount of alcohol consumed did not differ between groups at any of the follow-ups, but those in the 12-step program were significantly more likely to be abstinent over the entire year.

McCrady et al. (2004) compared BCT outpatient treatment for men with alcohol problems ($N = 90$) in an RCT that added relapse prevention, AA, or no treatment to BCT. The 6-month outcomes favored other conditions over the AA/BCT condition. At the 18-month follow-up, there were no differences in drinking or happiness with their marriage for the three groups. However, those in the AA/BCT condition went to more AA meetings and their drinking outcomes were more strongly related to their meeting attendance.

Meta-analyses of group designs W. R. Miller and Wilbourne (2002) included the Minnesota model, 12-step facilitation, and Alcoholics Anonymous in their evaluation of treatment modalities for alcohol dependence. All modalities had negative CES ratings (-3, -13, and -108, respectively)

The National Registry of Evidence-based Programs and Practices (2008b) ratings of 12-step facilitation therapy ranged from 3.5 to 4.0 for research quality, and were a constant 3.0 for readiness for dissemination. These ratings were based on Project MATCH. The size and design of the study were noted as strengths, while the lack of a no treatment control group was identified as a drawback.

Conclusions. In effectiveness and efficacy, 12-step-based therapies yield outcomes similar to other treatments for alcohol dependence. However, 12-step-based therapies yield more positive outcomes in certain areas, typically resulting in higher levels of posttreatment abstinence and AA meeting attendance. These findings coincide with the treatment goals of 12-step-based therapies. In addition, 12-step-based therapies may be a good option for those who have networks supportive of drinking and more severe alcohol dependence. One study (Brown et al., 2006) suggested that TSF is less effective for individuals with active depression, a finding that needs to be replicated. Because AA meetings are free, the low cost of aftercare is an additional strength of 12-step-based therapies.

Case Management

Treatment overview. The Substance Abuse and Mental Health Services Administration (CSAT, 1998) defines case management as "a coordinated approach to the delivery of health, substance abuse, mental health, and social services, linking clients with appropriate services to address specific needs and achieve stated goals." It typically is an adjunct to other forms of substance abuse treatment, addressing life issues beyond alcohol or drug use. Vanderplasschen, Wolf, Rapp, and Broekart (2007) identified four primary models of case management. These include brokerage and generalist models, assertive community treatment and intensive case management, clinical and rehabilitation models, and strengths-based case management. Although these models differ in the level of services offered as well as case manager and client involvement, all types include assessment, planning, linkage, monitoring, and advocacy.

Consensus panel recommendations. A consensus panel convened by SAMHSA (CSAT, 1998) identified two key elements of case management that make it an especially effective addition to substance abuse treatment. The first is a focus on treatment engagement. This emphasis facilitates increased retention in treatment, which is associated with better treatment outcomes. Second, case management addresses many of an individual's needs, which also is related to more successful treatment outcomes.

Randomized clinical trials. The majority of case management studies have been conducted with homeless individuals. This demographic group benefits particularly from the multiple services that case management provides. Conrad et al. (1998) randomized a group of homeless male drug- and alcohol-dependent veterans (mainly African American) to a 2- to 3-week residential VA substance abuse hospital program or a case-managed 3- to 6-month residential program that included elements of CBT ($N = 358$). Following the residential program, the case management group participated in 6 months of community living with ongoing case management.

Both groups improved significantly on measures of homelessness, alcohol and drug use, medical problems, and employment. Approximately 45% of participants reported no alcohol or drug use at the follow-up, although the case management group reported less overall alcohol use. There was a main effect of case management on homelessness, but this effect was reversed at 24 months. Overall, the experimental group initially had better outcomes than the control group (partly because they were still in treatment), but these results leveled out over time. The small between-group differences may be explained by infrequent contact with case managers after discharge, which was a flaw in study design.

Additionally, the control group was in a treatment-rich environment and had adequate access to services. This suggests that case management may be most appropriate in settings where service availability is limited.

Essock et al. (2006) compared two subtypes of case management, Assertive Community Treatment and standard case management. For 2 years, they tracked a sample of 198 urban, mostly homeless individuals with co-occurring mental and substance use disorders. The two case management variations had similar outcomes, although decreases in substance use were greater than could be expected without treatment. This study failed to provide evidence for greater efficacy of one form of case management over another.

Cox et al. (1998) conducted an RCT with what they termed "chronic public inebriates" individuals who used detoxification facilities often and were usually homeless. The mostly male sample ($N = 298$) was randomized to intensive case management or a no treatment control group. Follow-up was scheduled to occur at 6 month intervals over the course of 2 years. However, follow-up data collection was not completed at 24 months because funding was discontinued. The case management intervention focused on finances, housing, and reduced substance use. An average of 110 case management activities occurred per person in the case management group. There was a significant difference between groups in favor of the case management group as measured by amount of public income, drinking days, and nights spent in own residence. At the 18 month follow-up, days drinking in the last month dropped from 24 for both groups to 15 for the control group and 11 for the case management group. Admissions for detoxification decreased from eight in 6 months to five for the control group and two and a half for the case management group. Overall, case management was beneficial, although the effect sizes for days drinking were small, $d = 0.02-0.32$ at 18 months. Number of months engaged in case management was

related to lower PDA, suggesting that extended case management is helpful.

Several other RCTs with homeless substance dependent individuals (Braucht et al., 1995; Lapham, Hall, & Skipper, 1995; Stahler, Shipley, Bartelt, DuCette, & Shandler, 1995) have found small or no between-group differences when case management was compared to treatment as usual. However, significant within-group differences from baseline to follow-up assessments were observed.

One of the few case management studies focusing on women examined the effects of intensive case management (ICM) on outcomes (Morgenstern et al., 2008). All of the women qualified for federal welfare; 22.4% of the women had alcohol dependence as their primary diagnoses. Each of the women ($N = 302$) was randomly assigned to either ICM or usual care (UC). Women in the ICM group were given the option of 12 weeks of treatment with 15 months of follow-up that included case management and vouchers for treatment attendance during the first 12 weeks. The UC group was referred to community treatment services. The ICM group was significantly more likely to be abstinent at the follow-ups occurring four to 15 months after the baseline interview. The impact of case management was greatest for women who attended the least amount of substance abuse treatment. This suggests that case management may provide an alternate path to sobriety for women who have trouble engaging in traditional substance abuse treatment. The mediating variables for the ICM group were greater contact with their case manager, engagement in treatment, and attending self-help groups. One drawback to the study was the contingency management component. It is unclear whether the effects of case management would be as strong if this component were absent. However, case management is generally an adjunct to other treatments, so this may be a particularly helpful combination, especially for women with lower SES.

Meta-analyses of group designs. W. R. Miller and Wilbourne (2002) ranked case management as ninth among treatments that had been the subject of three or more studies. The Mesa Grande review included six studies evaluating case management. Four of the studies found positive results for case management, and the CES was 33.

Conclusions. Case management appears to be as beneficial as, if not slightly better than, other AUD treatments in reducing substance use and affecting other quality of life variables. The most significant results were found for substance-dependent women on welfare (Morgenstern et al., 2008). Further research is needed to delineate whether case management is more helpful for women than men, and if an optimal length of case management maximizes outcomes.

Case management is best suited for settings where improved access to resources is needed. One of its strengths is the provision of an array of services that focuses on the whole person. Hence it is particularly valuable for individuals who have additional needs, such as those facing mental illness, AIDS, or homelessness (CSAT, 1998). Although case management is expensive, its costs may be offset for certain populations. For example, in their sample of 298 homeless chronic public inebriates, participants accrued a total of $2.5 million in medical charges over a 3-year period, which could offset case management costs (Cox et al., 1998).

Relationship and Therapist Factors

Overview. Although it is important to conduct alcohol treatments using techniques with empirical evidence for efficacy, there also are evidence-based therapist and relationship factors that have a significant impact on treatment outcomes. The importance of therapist and relationship factors should not be underestimated; in fact, some reviews of general psychotherapy literature have found that therapist-specific factors such as empathy, warmth, and therapeutic alliance contribute more to the prediction of client outcomes than

do technique-specific factors such as treatment modality (Lambert & Barley, 2001). Therapist- and relationship-specific factors have been shown to contribute to client outcomes in alcohol treatments as well (Crits-Christoph, Baranackie, Kurcias, & Beck, 1991; Saarnio, 2002; Valle, 1981). Therapist-specific factors are important across treatment modalities and theoretical frameworks (Crits-Christoph et al., 1991), and in light of the significant impact they have on alcohol-use outcomes, it is important that these factors be included in a discussion of evidence-based treatments.

Results of several studies have highlighted the importance of therapist and relationship factors on outcomes in alcohol treatments; however, given that most RCTs have evaluated the efficacy of technique-specific factors and used random assignment to treatment conditions (e.g., Treatment A vs. Treatment B), most studies of relationship factors have relied on secondary analyses to draw their conclusions. Thus, although relationship factors contribute substantially to the variance in treatment outcomes, until more RCTs are conducted that directly test the causal relationship involved in these factors, we must draw largely on secondary analyses and quasi-experimental studies for our findings. Specific factors addressed in the AUD treatment literature include therapeutic alliance, empathy, directiveness, and confrontation.

Randomized clinical trials and secondary analyses. The largest body of research on therapist and relationship factors in alcohol treatment focuses on the therapeutic alliance, conceptualized as collaboration and consensus between the therapist and client regarding the goals and process of therapy (Rychtarik, Prue, Rapp, & King, 1992). Ratings of therapeutic alliance have shown that higher alliance is often associated with better outcomes, including increased participation in treatment and reduced alcohol use (Connors, Carroll, DiClemente, Longabaugh, & Donovan, 1997; Dundon et al., 2008; M. A. Ilgen, McKellar, Moos, & Finney, 2006; M. Ilgen, Tiet, Finney,

& Moos, 2006). Positive alliance may play a particularly important role for clients with low pretreatment self-efficacy for abstinence. Clients with low self-efficacy typically have higher posttreatment alcohol use than those with higher self-efficacy (Rychtarik et al., 1992); however, when low self-efficacy clients maintain strongly allied therapeutic relationships, they fare as well as clients with high pretreatment self-efficacy for abstinence (Ilgen et al., 2006). In other words, a strong therapeutic alliance may compensate for the predisposition toward worse outcomes for clients with low self-efficacy.

The impact of therapeutic alliance on drinking outcomes has been shown to vary across treatment settings and modalities. It was a modest predictor of drinks per drinking day (r 0.102) and percent abstinent days (r 0.169) for outpatients, but not aftercare clients, in Project MATCH (Connors et al., 1997), and was unrelated to alcohol-use outcomes among inpatients and day-patients receiving CBT (Long, Williams, Midgley, & Hollin, 2000). Additionally, there is evidence that therapeutic alliance is related to alcohol-use outcomes in medication compliance interventions but not in CBT plus medication, psychodynamic, or multimodal behavior treatments (Dundon et al., 2008; Ojehagen, Berglund, & Hansson, 1997). In light of these variable findings, it has been suggested that therapeutic alliance may play a less prominent role in substance use outcomes with treatments that are more structured (e.g., CBT) and a more prominent role in treatments built on common therapy elements (Carroll, Nich, & Rounsaville, 1997).

Therapist empathy can be a strong predictor of posttreatment alcohol use in CBT (W. R. Miller, Taylor, & West, 1980). Ritter and colleagues (2002) found that client gains in self-efficacy were correlated with therapists' ratings of empathy and positive regard (rs 0.30 and 0.19, respectively). The study further demonstrated the importance of empathy, finding that therapist empathy was negatively correlated with clients' level of alcohol dependence (r 0.36), negative consequences from alcohol use

($r = -0.31$), and alcohol-related psychosocial consequences ($r = -0.40$) at 3-month follow-ups; these relationships persisted even when controlling for skills acquisition. Ritter et al. (2002) also found that clients with high levels of anxiety or low levels of cognitive functioning perceived therapists as less empathic. It should be noted, however, that low follow-up rates in this study may reduce the generalizability of the results. Accurate empathy corresponds with greater client disclosure, cooperation, and engagement in alcohol treatment using motivational interviewing (Moyers, Miller, & Hendrickson, 2005), and, more generally, may facilitate stronger therapeutic alliance that leads to better outcomes across treatment modalities (Watson & Geller, 2005).

Therapist levels of directiveness and confrontation also are important factors in treatment outcomes. An RCT found that confrontational-directive therapy produced more client resistance compared to nonconfrontational client-centered counseling, and client resistance predicted higher alcohol consumption at 1-year follow-ups (W. R. Miller, Benefield, & Tonigan, 1993). Furthermore, more frequent confrontation was strongly associated with higher quantities of alcohol consumption (r 0.65). Clients with higher levels of reactance (a characteristic similar to resistance) also fared worse when matched with therapists who were highly directive (Karno, Beutler, & Harwood, 2002; Karno & Longabaugh, 2005). Among these clients, the frequency of therapist initiation of new topics (a measure of therapist directiveness) and use of confrontation were predictive of higher quantity and frequency of alcohol use (Karno & Longabaugh, 2005). There is some evidence that the therapist directiveness leads to reduced frequency and quantity of alcohol consumption with clients that are low in reactance (Karno et al., 2002), and that directiveness and confrontation may have some benefit when conducted in a manner that is empathic and serves to enhance the therapeutic alliance (Moyers et al., 2005), though the role of these factors is not yet completely understood.

Conclusions. In addition to treatment modality, therapist and relationship factors contribute significantly to AUD treatment outcomes, although most studies of these factors rely on secondary analyses. High levels of therapeutic alliance and empathy often are linked with better treatment outcomes, though the importance of the former may vary among treatment settings and modalities. Confrontation often leads to increased resistance in clients, which can lead to higher levels of alcohol use, especially among clients who are highly reactive. Clients with high levels of reactance also fare worse in drinking outcomes when therapists are highly directive, although directiveness may actually benefit clients with lower levels of reactance, particularly if the directiveness functions to enhance therapeutic alliance.

DISCUSSION AND CONCLUSIONS

The approaches reviewed in this chapter have demonstrated efficacy for the treatment of AUDs for adult populations and stem from a variety of theoretical orientations. Several treatments for AUDs have been tested—in fact, one meta-analysis listed more than 80 existing treatment modalities (W. R. Miller & Wilbourne, 2002). The treatments we selected for the chapter as evidence-based were those with the strongest available evidence for improved alcohol use outcomes based on RCTs, meta-analyses, reviews, and consensus panel recommendations.

Of the practices not covered in this chapter, there is a large selection of treatments that have been found either to be ineffective or to lack the necessary research to assess their efficacy for improving AUD outcomes. Yet, despite the lack of evidence, many unsupported and unspecified treatments continue to be used in practice (McGovern, Fox, Xie, & Drake, 2004). Further, while all treatments selected for inclusion in this chapter were selected because they have demonstrated efficacy in studies with good methodological quality, it is important to note that the overall evidence base and specific outcomes associated with each of treatment modality are not equal.

A strong evidence base for a specific treatment is demonstrated through multiple RCTs that consistently demonstrate improved outcomes, as well as the extent to which research has been conducted by different researchers across laboratories (e.g., Chambless et al., 1998). The treatments listed in this chapter vary in each of these factors, so that each treatment has varying levels of evidence base to support it. For example, brief interventions have a relatively large evidence base, with dozens of RCTs that have tested their efficacy for improving alcohol consumption outcomes, whereas other treatments such as cue exposure therapy, the Community Reinforcement Approach, 12-step-based therapies, and nonspecific therapist and relationship factors have had relatively fewer RCTs. Similarly, the extent in which alcohol treatments have been tested across laboratories also varies substantially across treatments.

Study sample demographics and methodological controls used in many RCTs may limit the overall generalizability of observed treatment outcomes. Many treatment studies for AUDs are conducted in samples that are predominantly composed of men, Whites, and non-Hispanic individuals, and thus some outcomes studies may not account for treatment effects specific to women or to racial and ethnic minorities. Thus, many treatments listed in this chapter may generalize poorly to individuals within these demographics, or to individuals with underrepresented cultural and religious backgrounds; elderly individuals; or lesbian, gay, bisexual, and transgender individuals. Further, the strict inclusion and exclusion criteria used in many treatment studies to strengthen internal validity may concurrently limit the generalizability of treatment efficacy to real-world treatment settings. For example, many alcohol treatment studies exclude potential participants with other nonalcohol-related problems such as psychosis, severe cognitive impairment, and other use of other drugs other than alcohol (e.g., Project MATCH Research Group, 1997). Thus, treatment effects for populations with these co-occurring conditions are under-represented in the literature, even though clients with these conditions may be fairly common in clinical settings. Although conclusions drawn from studies with restricted participant pools can be used to show efficacy, they do not guarantee the effectiveness of a treatment in real-world treatment settings.

Several factors may influence a practitioner's choice of alcohol-treatment modality. This choice largely may be determined by clients' specific treatment goals, because each treatment modality has a different evidence base for outcomes regarding alcohol use and psychosocial variables. When a significant other (such as a spouse, family member, or friend) is available, treatment modalities such as behavioral couple therapy or the Community Reinforcement Approach may be optimal, because they are designed to address the needs of the client, the significant other, and the relationship. When treatment goals focus on complete abstinence outcomes, practitioners may wish to choose 12-step based therapies. When clients are highly angry or resistant to treatment, motivational interviewing/MET, brief interventions, and therapist use of non-confrontational and nondirective techniques may work best. When clients have multiple service needs, case management should be combined with other treatment strategies.

Treatments listed in this chapter also have demonstrable efficacy in improving psychosocial outcomes related to AUDs. When treatment goals include support for lifestyle changes related to housing, financial planning, or employment, both case management and the Community Reinforcement Approach may be used to improve these outcomes. When clients lack social networks that are supportive of abstinence, behavioral couple therapy, the Community Reinforcement Approach, and

12-step-based therapies may be used to help clients establish such social networks. However, although several treatment-specific strengths have been identified, it should be noted that large-scale studies have found only limited evidence for efficacy of client-treatment matching (Ouimette, et al., 1997; Project MATCH Research Group, 1998b).

The length of time and monetary costs associated with specific treatments may strongly influence a practitioner's choice of treatment modality. Many briefer treatments have demonstrated efficacy that is comparable to that of extended treatments. In addition to having a strong evidence base, brief interventions and motivational interviewing have demonstrated improved alcohol-use outcomes in treatment periods as short as one or a few sessions. Shorter treatment interventions may be more practical in real-world settings, as they increase practitioners' availability to see additional clients and often require fewer resources and less funding. Briefer treatments that return similar results can be more desirable than extended treatments and may even be mandated for insurance reimbursements.

Treatments for AUDs are largely imperfect, and even the best evidence-based practices generally result in only modest improvements in outcomes. Despite the difficulty in developing efficacious treatments for AUDs, several methods have shown promise through RCTs, meta-analyses, and consensus panel recommendations. With a growing number of treatments, practitioners ought to use the best supported methods available. Future research will further elucidate which treatments should be used in which contexts.

REFERENCES

Alden, L. (1978). Evaluation of a preventive self-management programme for problem drinkers. *Canadian Journal of Behavioural Science, 10,* 258–263.

Alessi, S. M., Hanson, T., Wieners, M., & Petry, N. M. (2007). Low-cost contingency management in community clinics: Delivering incentives partially in group therapy. *Experimental and Clinical Psychopharmacology, 15,* 293–300.

American Psychiatric Association. (2000). *Diagnostic and statistical manual of mental disorders* (4th ed., text rev.). Washington, DC: Author.

Anton, R. F., Moak, D. H., Latham, P., Waid, L. R., Myrick, H., Voronin, K., . . . Woolston, R. (2005). Naltrexone combined with either cognitive behavioral or motivational enhancement therapy for alcohol dependence. *Journal of Clinical Psychopharmacology, 25,* 349–357.

Anton, R. F., O'Malley, S. S., Ciraulo, D. A., Cisler, R. A., Couper, D., Donovan, D. M., . . . COMBINE Study Research Group. (2006). Combined pharmacotherapies and behavioral interventions for alcohol dependence: The COMBINE study: A randomized controlled trial. *Journal of the American Medical Association, 295,* 2003–2017.

Azrin, N. H. (1976). Improvements in the community-reinforcement approach to alcoholism. *Behaviour Research and Therapy, 14,* 339–348.

Azrin, N. H., Acierno, R., Kogan, E. S., Donohue, B., Besalel, V. A., & McMahon, P. T. (1996). Follow-up results of supportive versus behavioral therapy for illicit drug use. *Behaviour Research and Therapy, 34,* 41–46.

Azrin, N. H., Donohue, B., Besalel, V. A., Kogan, E. S., & Acierno, R. (1994). Youth drug abuse treatment: A controlled outcome study. *Journal of Child & Adolescent Substance Abuse, 3,* 1–15.

Azrin, N. H., Donohue, B., Teichner, G. A., Crum, T., Howell, J., & DeCato, L. A. (2001). A controlled evaluation and description of individual-cognitive problem solving and family-behavior therapies in dually diagnosed conduct-disordered and substance-dependent youth. *Journal of Child & Adolescent Substance Abuse, 11,* 1–41.

Azrin, N. H., McMahon, P. T., Donohue, B., Besalel, V. A., Lapinski, K. J., Kogan, E. S., . . . Galloway, E. (1994). Behavior therapy for drug abuse: A controlled treatment outcome study. *Behaviour Research and Therapy, 32,* 857–866.

Azrin, N. H., Sisson, R. W., Meyers, R., & Godley, M. (1982). Alcoholism treatment by disulfiram and community reinforcement therapy. *Journal of Behavior Therapy and Experimental Psychiatry, 13,* 105–112.

Ballesteros, J., Duffy, J. C., Querejeta, I., Ariño, J., & González-Pinto, A. (2004). Efficacy of brief interventions for hazardous drinkers in primary care: Systematic review and meta-analyses. *Alcoholism: Clinical and Experimental Research, 28,* 608–618.

Bien, T. H., Miller, W. R., & Tonigan, J. S. (1993). Brief interventions for alcohol problems: A review. *Addiction, 88,* 315–336.

Bowers, T. G., & Al-Redha, M. R. (1990). A comparison of outcome with group/marital and standard/individual therapies with alcoholics. *Journal of Studies on Alcohol, 51,* 301–309.

Braucht, G. N., Reichardt, C. S., Geissler, J. J., Bormann, C. A., Kwaitkowski, C. F., & Kirby, M. W. (1995). Effective services for homeless substance abusers. *Journal of Addictive Diseases, 14,* 87–109.

Brown, S. A., Glasner-Edwards, S. V., Tate, S. R., McQuaid, J. R., Chalekian, J., & Granholm, E. (2006). Integrated cognitive behavioral therapy versus twelve-step facilitation therapy for substance-dependent adults with depressive disorders. *Journal of Psychoactive Drugs, 38,* 449–460.

Burke, B. L., Arkowitz, H., & Menchola, M. (2003). The efficacy of motivational interviewing: A meta-analysis of controlled clinical trials. *Journal of Consulting and Clinical Psychology, 71,* 843–861.

Carroll, K. M., Ball, S. A., Nich, C., Martino, S., Frankforter, T. L., Farentinos, C., . . . Woody, G. E. (2006). Motivational interviewing to improve treatment engagement and outcome in individuals seeking treatment for substance abuse: A multisite effectiveness study. *Drug & Alcohol Dependence, 81,* 301–312.

Carroll, K. M., Nich, C., & Rounsaville, B. J. (1997). Contribution of the therapeutic alliance to outcome in active versus control psychotherapies. *Journal of Consulting and Clinical Psychology 65,* 510–514.

Center for Substance Abuse Treatment. (1998). *Comprehensive case management for substance abuse treatment.* (Treatment Improvement Protocol Series 27). Rockville, MD: Substance Abuse and Mental Health Services Administration. Retrieved from www.ncbi.nlm.nih.gov/books/NBK14516/

Center for Substance Abuse Treatment. (1999). *Enhancing motivation for change in substance abuse treatment.* (Treatment Improvement Protocol Series 35). Rockville, MD: Substance Abuse and Mental Health Services Administration.

Center for Substance Abuse Treatment. (2006). *Substance abuse: Clinical issues in intensive outpatient treatment* (Treatment Improvement Protocol Series 47). Rockville, MD: Substance Abuse and Mental Health Services Administration. Retrieved from www.ncbi.nlm.nih.gov/books/NBK14448/

Chambless, D. L., Baker, M. J., Baucom, D. H., Beutler, L. E., Calhoun, K. S., Crits-Christoph, P., . . . Woody, S. R. (1998). Update on empirically validated therapies, II. *Clinical Psychologist, 51,* 3–16.

Chambless, D. L., Gilson, M., Babich, K., Montgomery, R., Crits-Christoph, P., Rich, R., . . . Weinberger, J. (1993, October). *Task force on the promotion and dissemination of psychological procedures.* Retrieved from www.apa.org/divisions/div12/est/chamble2.pdf

Chambless, D. L., Sanderson, W. C., Shoham, V., Johnson, S. B., Pope, K. S., Crits-Christoph, P., . . . McCurry, S. (1996). An update on empirically validated therapies. *Clinical Psychologist, 49,* 5–18.

Chaney, E. F., O'Leary, M. R., & Marlatt, G. A. (1978). Skill training with alcoholics. *Journal of Consulting and Clinical Psychology, 46*, 1092–1104.

Connors, G. J., Carroll, K. M., DiClemente, C. C., Longabaugh, R., & Donovan, D. M. (1997). The therapeutic alliance and its relationship to alcoholism treatment participation and outcome. *Journal of Consulting and Clinical Psychology, 65*, 588–598.

Conrad, K. J., Hultman, C. I., Pope, A. R., Lyons, J. S., Baxter, W. C., Daghestani, A. N., . . . Manheim, L. M. (1998). Case managed residential care for homeless addicted veterans: Results of a true experiment. *Medical Care, 36*, 40–53.

Cook, T. A. R., Luczak, S. E., Shea, S. H., Ehlers, C. L., Carr, L. G., & Wall, T. L. (2005). Associations of ALDH2 and ADH1B genotypes with response to alcohol in Asian Americans. *Journal of Studies on Alcohol, 66*, 196–204.

Cox, G. B., Walker, D., Freng, S. A., Short, B. A., Meijer, L., & Gilchrist, L. (1998). Outcome of a controlled trial of the effectiveness of intensive case management for chronic public inebriates. *Journal of Studies on Alcohol, 59*, 523–32.

Crits-Christoph, P., Baranackie, K., Kurcias, J. S., & Beck, A. T. (1991). Meta-analysis of therapist effects in psychotherapy outcome studies. *Psychotherapy Research, 1*, 81–91.

Davidson, D., Gulliver, S. B., Longabaugh, R., Wirtz, P. W., & Swift, R. (2007). Building better cognitive-behavioral therapy: Is broad spectrum treatment more effective than motivational enhancement therapy for alcohol-dependent patients treated with naltrexone? *Journal of Studies on Alcohol, 68*, 238–247.

Drummond, D. C., & Glautier, S. (1994). A controlled trial of cue exposure treatment in alcohol dependence. *Journal of Consulting and Clinical Psychology, 62*, 809–817.

Dundon, W. D., Pettinati, H. M., Lynch, K. G., Xie, H., Varillo, K. M., Makadon, C., & Oslin, D. W. (2008). The therapeutic alliance in medical-based interventions impacts outcome in treating alcohol dependence. *Drug and Alcohol Dependence, 95*, 230–236.

Dunn, C., Deroo, L., & Rivara, F. P. (2001). The use of brief interventions adapted from motivational interviewing across behavioral domains: A systematic review. *Addiction, 96*, 1725–1742.

Edwards, G., & Gross, M. (1976). Alcohol dependence: Provisional description of a clinical syndrome. *British Medical Journal, 1*, 1058–1061.

Emmen, M. J., Schippers, G. M., Wollersheim, H., & Bleijenberg, G. (2005). Adding psychologist's intervention to physicians' advice to problem drinkers in the outpatient clinic. *Alcohol and Alcoholism, 40*, 219–226.

Epstein, E. E., & McCrady, B. S. (1998). Behavioral couples treatment of alcohol and drug use disorders: Current status and innovations. *Clinical Psychology Review, 18*, 689–711.

Essock, S. M., Mueser, K. T., Drake, R. E., Covell, N. H., McHugo, G. J., Frisman, L. K., . . . Swain, K. (2006). Comparison of ACT and standard case management for delivering integrated treatment for co-occurring disorders. *Psychiatric Services, 57*, 185–196.

Fals-Stewart, W., Birchler, G. R., & Kelley, M. L. (2006). Learning sobriety together: A randomized clinical trial examining behavioral couples therapy with alcoholic female patients. *Journal of Consulting and Clinical Psychology, 74*, 579–591.

Fals-Stewart, W., Klostermann, K., Yates, B. T., O'Farrell, T. J., & Birchler, G. R. (2005). Brief relationship therapy for alcoholism: A randomized clinical trial examining clinical efficacy and cost-effectiveness. *Psychology of Addictive Behaviors, 19*, 363–371.

Ferri, M. M. F., Amato, L., & Davoli, M. (2006). Alcoholics Anonymous and other 12-step programmes for alcohol dependence. *Cochrane Database of Systematic Reviews, 3*, Art. No. CD005032.

Finney, J. W., & Monahan, S. C. (1996). The cost-effectiveness of treatment for alcoholism: A second approximation. *Journal of Studies on Alcohol, 57*, 229–243.

Finney, J. W., Wilbourne, P. L., & Moos, R. H. (2007). Psychosocial treatments for substance use disorders. In P. E. Nathan & J. M. Gorman (Eds.), *A guide to treatments that work* (3rd ed., pp. 179–202). New York, NY: Oxford University Press.

Hasin, D. S., Stinson, F. S., Ogburn, E., & Grant, B. F. (2007). Prevalence, correlates, disability, and comorbidity of DSM-IV alcohol abuse and dependence in the United States: Results from the National Epidemiologic Survey on Alcohol and Related Conditions. *Archives of General Psychiatry, 64*, 830–842.

Hester, R. K. (2003). Behavioral self-control training. In R. K. Hester & W. R. Miller (Eds.), *Handbook of alcohol treatment approaches: Effective alternatives* (3rd ed., pp. 152–160). Boston, MA: Allyn & Bacon.

Hester, R. K., Squires, D. D., & Delaney, H. D. (2005). The Drinker's Check-up: 12-month outcomes of a controlled clinical trial of a stand-alone software program for problem drinkers. *Journal of Substance Abuse Treatment, 28*, 159–169.

Hettema, J., Steele, J., & Miller, W. R. (2005). Motivational interviewing. *Annual Review of Clinical Psychology, 1*, 91–111.

Higgins, S. T., & Petry, N. M. (1999). Contingency management: Incentives for sobriety. *Alcohol Research & Health, 23*, 122–127.

Hodder, H. D., Crider, R. A., Longabaugh, R., Stout, R. L., Treno, A. J., & Zweben, A. (2000). Alcoholism treatment and medical care costs from Project MATCH. *Addiction, 95*, 999–1013.

Hodder, H., Longabaugh, R., Miller, W. R., & Rubonis, A. V. (1991). The cost-effectiveness of treatment for alcoholism: A first approximation. *Journal of Studies on Alcohol, 52*, 517–540.

Humphreys, K., & Moos, R. H. (2007). Encouraging posttreatment self-help group involvement to reduce demand for continuing care services: Two-year clinical and utilization outcomes. *Alcoholism: Clinical and Experimental Research, 31,* 64–68.

Hunt, G. M., & Azrin, N. H. (1973). A community-reinforcement approach to alcoholism. *Behaviour Research and Therapy, 11,* 91–104.

Ilgen, M. A., McKellar, J., Moos, R., & Finney, J. W. (2006). Therapeutic alliance and the relationship between motivation and treatment outcomes in patients with alcohol use disorder. *Journal of Substance Abuse Treatment, 31,* 157–162.

Ilgen, M., Tiet, Q., Finney, J., & Moos, R. H. (2006). Self-efficacy, therapeutic alliance, and alcohol-use disorder treatment outcomes. *Journal of Studies on Alcohol, 67,* 465–472.

Irvin, J. E., Bowers, C. A., Dunn, M. E., & Wang, M. C. (1999). Efficacy of relapse prevention: A meta-analytic review. *Journal of Consulting and Clinical Psychology, 67,* 563–570.

Karno, M. P., Beutler, L. E., & Harwood, T. M. (2002). Interactions between psychotherapy procedures and patient attributes that predict alcohol treatment effectiveness: A preliminary report. *Addictive Behaviors, 27,* 779–797.

Karno, M. P., & Longabaugh, R. (2005). Less directiveness by therapists improves drinking outcomes of reactant clients in alcoholism treatment. *Journal of Consulting and Clinical Psychology, 73,* 262–267.

Kaskutas, L. A. (2008). Comments on the Cochrane review on Alcoholics Anonymous effectiveness [Letter to the editor]. *Addiction, 103,* 1402–1403.

Kelley, M. L., & Fals-Stewart, W. (2002). Couples- versus individual-based therapy for alcohol and drug abuse: Effects on children's psychosocial functioning. *Journal of Consulting and Clinical Psychology, 70,* 417–427.

Keso, L., & Salaspuro, M. (1990). Inpatient treatment of employed alcoholics: A randomized clinical trial on Hazelden-type and traditional treatment. *Alcoholism: Clinical and Experimental Research, 14,* 584–589.

Kranzler, H. R., Wesson, D. R., & Billot, L. (2004). Naltrexone depot for treatment of alcohol dependence: A multicenter, randomized, placebo-controlled clinical trial. *Alcoholism, Clinical and Experimental Research, 28,* 1051–1059.

Lambert, M. J., & Barley, D. E. (2001). Research summary on the therapeutic relationship and psychotherapy outcome. *Psychotherapy: Theory, Research, Practice, Training, 38,* 357–361.

Lapham, S. C., Hall, M., & Skipper, B. J. (1995). Homelessness and substance use among alcohol abusers following participation in project H&ART. *Journal of Addictive Diseases, 14,* 41–55.

Litt, M. D., Kadden, R. M., Kabela-Cormier, E., & Petry, N. (2007). Changing network support for drinking: Initial findings from the Network Support Project. *Journal of Consulting and Clinical Psychology, 75,* 542–555.

Long, C. G., Williams, M., Midgley, M., & Hollin, C. R. (2000). Within-program factors as predictors of drinking outcomes following cognitive-behavioral treatment. *Addictive Behaviors, 25,* 573–578.

Longabaugh, R., Wirtz, A. Z., Zweben, A., & Stout, R. L. (1998). Network support for drinking, Alcoholics Anonymous and long-term matching effects. *Addiction, 93,* 1313–1333.

Mallams, J. H., Godley, M. D., Hall, G. M., & Meyers, R. J. (1982). A social-systems approach to resocializing alcoholics in the community. *Journal of Studies on Alcohol, 43,* 1115–1123.

Marlatt, G. A., Baer, J. S., Kivlahan, D. R., Dimeff, L. A., Larimer, M. E., Quigley, L. A., . . . Williams, E. (1998). Screening and brief intervention for high-risk college student drinkers: Results from a 2-year follow-up assessment. *Journal of Consulting and Clinical Psychology, 66,* 604–615.

Marlatt, G. A., & Gordon, J. (1985). *Relapse prevention.* New York, NY: Guilford Press.

McCarty, D. (2007, May). *Substance abuse treatment benefits and costs: Knowledge assets policy brief.* Greensboro, NC: Robert Wood Johnson Foundation, Substance Abuse Policy Research Program.

McCrady, B. S., Epstein, E. E., Cook, S., Jensen, N. K., & Hildebrandt, T. (2009). A randomized trial of individual and couple behavioral alcohol treatment for women. *Journal of Consulting and Clinical Psychology, 77,* 243–256.

McCrady, B. S., Epstein, E. E., & Hirsch, L. (1999). Maintaining change after conjoint behavioral alcohol treatment for men: Outcomes at six months. *Addiction, 94,* 1381–1396.

McCrady, B. S., Epstein, E. E., & Kahler, C. W. (2004). Alcoholics Anonymous and relapse prevention as maintenance strategies after conjoint behavioral alcohol treatment for men: 18-month outcomes. *Journal Consulting and Clinical Psychology, 72,* 870–878.

McCrady, B. S., Noel, N. E., Stout, R. L., Abrams, D. B., Fisher-Nelson, H., & Hay, W. (1986). Comparative effectiveness of three types of spouse involvement in outpatient behavioral alcoholism treatment. *Journal of Studies on Alcohol, 47,* 459–467.

McCrady, B. S., Stout, R., Noel, N., Abrams, D., & Nelson, H. F. (1991). Effectiveness of three types of spouse-involved behavioral alcoholism treatment. *British Journal of Addiction, 86,* 1415–1424.

McGovern, M. P., Fox, T. S., Xie, H., & Drake, R. E. (2004). A survey of clinical practices and readiness to adopt evidence-based practices: Dissemination research in an addiction treatment system. *Journal of Substance Abuse Treatment 26,* 305–312.

Meyers, R. J., Smith, J. E., & Lash, D. N. (2003). The community reinforcement approach. *Recent Developments in Alcoholism, 16*, 183–195.

Meyers, R. J., Villanueva, M., & Smith, J. E. (2005). The community reinforcement approach: History and new directions. *Journal of Cognitive Psychotherapy, 19*, 247–260.

Miller, E. J. (2001). Practice and promise: The Azrin studies. In R. J. Meyers & W. R. Miller (Eds.), *A community reinforcement approach to addiction treatment* (pp. 8–27). New York, NY: Cambridge University Press.

Miller, P. M., & Mastria, M. A. (1977). *Alternatives to alcohol abuse: A social learning model.* Champaign, IL: Research Press.

Miller, W. R. (1978). Behavioral treatment of problem drinkers: A comparative outcome study of three controlled drinking therapies. *Journal of Consulting and Clinical Psychology, 46*, 74–86.

Miller, W. R., Benefield, R. G., & Tonigan, J. S. (1993). Enhancing motivation for change in problem drinking: A controlled comparison of two therapist styles. *Journal of Consulting and Clinical Psychology, 61*, 455–461.

Miller, W. R., Meyers, R. J., & Tonigan, J. S. (1999). Engaging the unmotivated in treatment for alcohol problems: A comparison of three strategies for intervention through family members. *Journal of Consulting and Clinical Psychology, 67*, 688–697.

Miller, W. R., Meyers, R. J., Tonigan, J. S., & Grant, K. A. (2001). Community reinforcement and traditional approaches: Findings of a controlled trial. In R. J. Meyers & W. R. Miller (Eds.), *A community reinforcement approach to addiction treatment* (pp. 79–103). New York, NY: Cambridge University Press.

Miller, W. R., & Rollnick, S. (2002). *Motivational interviewing: Preparing people for change* (2nd ed.). New York, NY: Guilford Press.

Miller, W. R., Taylor, C. A., & West, J. C. (1980). Focused versus broad spectrum behavior therapy for problem drinkers. *Journal of Consulting and Clinical Psychology, 48*, 590–601.

Miller, W. R., & Wilbourne, P. L. (2002). Mesa Grande: A methodological analysis of clinical trials of treatments for alcohol use disorders. *Addiction, 97*, 265–277.

Miller, W. R., Zweben, A., DiClemente, C. C., & Rychtarik, R. G. (1994). *Motivational enhancement therapy manual: A clinical research guide for therapists treating individuals with alcohol abuse and dependence* (Vol. 2, Project MATCH Monograph Series). Rockville, MD: National Institute on Alcohol Abuse and Alcoholism.

Monti, P. M., Colby, S. M., Barnett, N. P., Spirito, A., Rohsenow, D. J., Myers, M., . . . Lewander, W. (1999). Brief intervention for harm reduction with alcohol-positive older adolescents in a hospital emergency department. *Journal of Consulting and Clinical Psychology, 67*, 989–994.

Monti, P. M. & Rohsenow, D. J. (2003). Coping skills training and cue exposure treatment. In R. K. Hester & W. R. Miller (Eds.), *Handbook of alcohol treatment approaches: Effective alternatives* (3rd ed., pp. 213–236). Boston, MA: Allyn & Bacon.

Monti, P. M., Rohsenow, D. J., Rubonis, A. V., Niaura, R. S., Sirota, A. D., Colby, S. M., . . . Abrams, D. B. (1993). Cue exposure with coping skills treatment for male alcoholics: A preliminary investigation. *Journal of Consulting and Clinical Psychology, 61*, 1011–1019.

Monti, P. M., Rohsenow, D. J., Swift, R. M., Gulliver, S. B., Colby, S. M., Mueller, T. I., . . . Asher, M. K. (2001). Naltrexone and cue exposure with coping and communication skills training for alcoholics: Treatment process and 1-year outcomes. *Alcoholism: Clinical and Experimental Research, 25*, 1634–1647.

Morgenstern, J., Blanchard, K. A., Kahler, C., Barbosa, K. M., McCrady, B. S., & McVeigh, K. H. (2008). Testing mechanisms of action for intensive case management. *Addiction, 103*, 469–477.

Morgenstern, J., Blanchard, K. A., Morgan, T. J., Labouvie, E., & Hayaki, J. (2001). Testing the effectiveness of cognitive behavioral treatment for substance abuse in a community setting: Within treatment and posttreatment findings. *Journal of Consulting and Clinical Psychology, 69*, 1007–1017.

Morgenstern, J., Irwin, T. W., Wainberg, M. L., Parsons, J. T., Muench, F., & Bux Jr., D. A., . . . Schulz-Heik, J. (2007). A randomized controlled trial of goal choice interventions for alcohol use disorders among men who have sex with men. *Journal of Consulting and Clinical Psychology, 75*, 72–84.

Morgenstern, J., & McKay, J. R. (2007). Rethinking the paradigms that inform behavioral treatment research for substance use disorders. *Addiction, 102*, 1377–1389.

Moyer, A., Finney, J. W., Swearingen, C. E., & Vergun, P. (2002). Brief interventions for alcohol problems: A meta-analytic review of controlled investigations in treatment-seeking and non-treatment-seeking populations. *Addiction, 97*, 279–292.

Moyers, T. B., Martin, T., Manuel, J. K., Hendrickson, S. M., & Miller, W. R. (2005). Assessing competence in the use of motivational interviewing. *Journal of Substance Abuse Treatment, 28*, 19–26.

Moyers, T. B., Miller, W. R., & Hendrickson, S. M. J. (2005). How does motivational interviewing work? Therapist interpersonal skill predicts client involvement within motivational interviewing sessions. *Journal of Consulting and Clinical Psychology, 73*, 590–598.

Murphy, J. G., Benson, T. A., Vuchinich, R. E., Deskins, M. M., Eakin, D., Flood, A. M., . . . Torrealday, O. (2004). A comparison of personalized feedback for college student drinkers delivered with and without a motivational interview. *Journal of Studies on Alcohol,* 65, 200–203.

National Registry of Evidence-based Programs and Practices. (2006a). *Behavioral couples therapy for alcoholism and drug abuse.* Retrieved from www.nrepp.samhsa.gov/programfulldetails.asp?PROGRAM_ID=70

National Registry of Evidence-based Programs and Practices. (2006b). *Family behavior therapy.* Retrieved from www.nrepp.samhsa.gov/programfulldetails.asp?PROGRAM_ID=73

National Registry of Evidence-based Programs and Practices. (2007a). *Motivational enhancement therapy.* Retrieved from www.nrepp.samhsa.gov/programfulldetails.asp?PROGRAM_ID=182

National Registry of Evidence-based Programs and Practices. (2007b). *Motivational interviewing.* Retrieved from www.nrepp.samhsa.gov/programfulldetails.asp?PROGRAM_ID=183

National Registry of Evidence-based Programs and Practices. (2007c). *Prize incentives contingency management for substance abuse.* Retrieved from www.nrepp.samhsa.gov/programfulldetails.asp?PROGRAM_ID=136

National Registry of Evidence-based Programs and Practices. (2008a). *Drinker's Check-Up.* Retrieved from www.nrepp.samhsa.gov/programfulldetails.asp?PROGRAM_ID=165

National Registry of Evidence-based Programs and Practices. (2008b). *Twelve step facilitation therapy.* Retrieved from www.nrepp.samhsa.gov/programfulldetails.asp?PROGRAM_ID=219

National Registry of Evidence-based Programs and Practices. (2009). *Alcohol behavioral couples therapy for alcoholism and drug abuse.* Retrieved from www.nrepp.samhsa.gov/programfulldetails.asp?PROGRAM_ID=152

O'Farrell, T. J., Choquette, K. A., Cutter, H. S., Brown, E. D., & McCourt, W. F. (1993). Behavioral marital therapy with and without additional couples relapse prevention sessions for alcoholics and their wives. *Journal of Studies on Alcohol,* 54, 652–666.

O'Farrell, T. J., Cutter, H. S. G., Choquette, K. A., Floyd, F. J., & Bayog, R. D. (1992). Behavioral marital therapy for male alcoholics: Marital and drinking adjustment during the two years after treatment. *Behavior Therapy,* 23, 529–549.

O'Farrell, T. J., Cutter, H. S. G., & Floyd, F. J. (1985). Evaluating behavioral marital therapy for male alcoholics: Effects on marital adjustment and communication before to after treatment. *Behavior Therapy,* 15, 147–168.

O'Farrell, T. J., Murphy, C. M., Stephan, S. H., Fals-Stewart, W., & Murphy, M. (2004). Partner violence before and after couples-based alcoholism treatment for male alcoholic patients: The role of treatment

involvement and abstinence. *Journal of Consulting and Clinical Psychology,* 72, 202–217.

Öjehagen, A., Berglund, M., & Hansson, L. (1997). The relationship between helping alliance and outcome in outpatient treatment of alcoholics: A comparative study of psychiatric treatment and multimodal behavioural therapy. *Alcohol and Alcoholism,* 32, 241–249.

Olmstead, T. A., Sindelar, J. L., & Petry, N. M. (2007). Clinic variation in the cost-effectiveness of contingency management. *American Journal on Addictions,* 16, 457–460.

Ouimette, P. C., Finney, J. W., & Moos, R. H. (1997). Twelve-step and cognitive-behavioral treatment for substance abuse: A comparison of treatment effectiveness. *Journal of Consulting and Clinical Psychology,* 65, 230–240.

Petry, N. M., Kolodner, K. B., Li, R., Peirce, J. M., Roll, J. M., Stitzer, M. L., & Hamilton, J. A. (2006). Prize-based contingency management does not increase gambling. *Drug and Alcohol Dependence,* 83, 269–273.

Petry, N. M., Martin, B., Cooney, J. L., & Kranzler, H. R. (2000). Give them prizes and they will come: Contingency management for treatment of alcohol dependence. *Journal of Consulting and Clinical Psychology,* 68, 250–257.

Powers, M. B., Vedel, E., & Emmelkamp, P. M. G. (2008). Behavioral couples therapy (BCT) for alcohol and drug use disorders: A meta-analysis. *Clinical Psychology Review,* 28, 952–962.

Prendergast, M., Podus, D., Finney, J., Greenwell, L., & Roll, J. (2006). Contingency management for treatment of substance use disorders: A meta-analysis. *Addiction,* 101, 1546–1560.

Project MATCH Research Group. (1997). Matching alcoholism treatments to client heterogeneity: Project MATCH posttreatment drinking outcomes. *Journal of Studies on Alcohol,* 58, 7–29.

Project MATCH Research Group. (1998a). Matching alcoholism treatments to client heterogeneity: Project MATCH three-year drinking outcomes. *Alcoholism: Clinical and Experimental Research,* 22, 1300–1311.

Project MATCH Research Group. (1998b). Matching patients with alcohol disorders to treatments: Clinical implications from project MATCH. *Journal of Mental Health,* 7, 589–602.

Ritscher, J. B., Moos, R. H., & Finney, J. W. (2002). Relationship of treatment orientation and continuing care to remission among substance abuse patients. *Psychiatric Services,* 53, 595–601.

Ritter, A., Bowden, S., Murray, T., Ross, P., Greeley, J., & Pead, J. (2002). The influence of the therapeutic relationship in treatment for alcohol dependency. *Drug and Alcohol Review,* 21, 261–268.

Rohsenow, D. J., Monti, P. M., Rubonis, A. V., Gulliver, S. B., Colby, S. M., Binkoff, J. A. & Abrams, D. B.

(2001). Cue exposure with coping skills training and communication skills training for alcohol dependence: 6- and 12-month outcomes. *Addiction, 96*, 1161–74.

Roozen, H. G., Boulogne, J. J., van Tulder, M. W., van den Brink, W., De Jong, C. A. J., & Kerkhof, A. (2004). A systematic review of the effectiveness of the community reinforcement approach in alcohol, cocaine and opioid addiction. *Drug and Alcohol Dependence, 74*, 1–13.

Rychtarik, R. & McGillicuddy, N. (2005). Coping skills training and 12-step facilitation for women whose partner has alcoholism: Effects on depression, the partner's drinking, and partner physical violence. *Journal of Consulting and Clinical Psychology, 73*, 249–261.

Rychtarik, R. G., Prue, D. M., Rapp, S. R., & King, A. C. (1992). Self-efficacy, aftercare and relapse in a treatment program for alcoholics. *Journal of Studies on Alcohol, 53*, 435–440.

Saarnio, P. (2002). Factors associated with dropping out from outpatient treatment of alcohol other drug abuse. *Alcoholism Treatment Quarterly, 20*, 17–33.

Sindelar, J., Elbel, B., & Petry, N. M. (2007). What do we get for our money? Cost effectiveness of adding contingency management. *Addiction, 102*, 309–316.

Sitharthan, T., Sitharthan, G., Hough, M. J., & Kavanagh, D. J. (1997). Cue exposure in moderation drinking: A comparison with cognitive behavior therapy. *Journal of Consulting and Clinical Psychology, 65*, 878–882.

Smith, J. E., Meyers, R. J., & Delaney, H. D. (1998). The community reinforcement approach with homeless alcohol dependent individuals. *Journal of Consulting and Clinical Psychology, 66*, 541–548.

Stahler, G. J., Shipley, T. E., Bartelt, D., DuCette, J. P., & Shandler, I. W. (1995). Evaluating alternative treatments for homeless substance abusing men: Outcomes and predictors of success. *Journal of Addictive Diseases, 14*, 151–167.

Stitzer, M., & Petry, N. (2006). Contingency management for treatment of substance abuse. *Annual Review of Clinical Psychology, 2*, 411–434.

Valle, S. K. (1981). Interpersonal functioning of alcoholism counselors and treatment outcome. *Journal of Studies on Alcohol, 42*, 783–790.

Vanderplasschen, W., Wolf, J., Rapp, R. C., Broekart, E. (2007). Effectiveness of different models of case management for substance-abusing populations. *Journal of Psychoactive Drugs, 39*, 81–95.

Vasilaki, E. I., Hosier, S. G., & Cox, W. M. (2006). The efficacy of motivational interviewing as a brief intervention for excessive drinking: A meta-analytic review. *Alcohol and Alcoholism, 41*, 328–335.

Vedel, E., Emmelkamp, P. M., & Schippers, G. (2008). Individual cognitive-behavioral therapy and behavioral couple therapy in alcohol use disorder: A comparative evaluation in community-based addiction treatment centers. *Psychotherapy and Psychosomatics, 77*, 280–288.

Wagner, C., & Connors, W. (2008). *Motivational interviewing bibliography 1983–2007*. Retrieved from www.motivationalinterview.org/library/biblio.html

Walitzer, K. S., & Dermen, K. H. (2004). Alcohol focused spouse involvement and behavioral couples therapy: Evaluation of enhancements to drinking reduction treatment for male problem drinkers. *Journal of Consulting and Clinical Psychology, 72*, 944–955.

Walters, G. D. (2000). Behavioral self-control training for problem drinkers: A meta-analysis of randomized control studies. *Behavior Therapy, 31*, 135–149.

Watson, J. C. & Geller, S. M. (2005). The relation among the relationship conditions, working alliance, and outcome in both process experiential and cognitive behavioral psychotherapy. *Psychotherapy Research, 15*, 25–33.

Winters, J., Fals-Stewart, W., O'Farrell, T., Birchler, G., & Kelley, M. (2002). Behavioral couples therapy for female substance abusing patients: Effects on substance use and relationship adjustment. *Journal of Consulting and Clinical Psychology, 70*, 344–355.

Witkiewitz, K., van der Maas, H. L. J., Hufford, M. R., & Marlatt, G. A. (2007). Nonnormality and divergence in posttreatment alcohol use: Reexamining the Project MATCH data "another way." *Journal of Abnormal Psychology, 116*, 378–394.

Woody, S., Weisz, J., & McLean, C. (2005). Empirically supported treatments: 10 years later. *Clinical Psychologist, 58*, 5–11.

World Health Organization. (2004). *Global status report on alcohol 2004*. Geneva, Switzerland: Author.

8

Tobacco-Related Disorders

LION SHAHAB AND JENNIFER FIDLER

OVERVIEW OF TOBACCO-RELATED DISORDERS: NICOTINE DEPENDENCE AND DIAGNOSTIC CRITERIA

Development of Nicotine Dependence

Dependence on cigarettes, be they manufactured or in various hand-rolled forms, is by far the most common form of tobacco dependence and arguably also the most dangerous (Jha & Chaloupka, 1999). While there exist many more tobacco products such as pipes or cigars, they all have one common element crucial in the development of dependence: nicotine, an alkaloid that affects brain neurochemistry (Jarvis, 2004). The reason why cigarette use is more prevalent than other forms of tobacco use may be due to their design as a very efficient nicotine delivery device. Following a puff on a cigarette, nicotine is rapidly absorbed into the bloodstream through lung alveoli, reaching the brain in less than 20 seconds (Hemingfield, Stapleton, Benowitz, Grayson, & London, 1993). The design of cigarettes means that smokers have *fingertip control* over the dose of nicotine they receive by adjusting the intensity and frequency of puffing to suit their personal preferences (Russell & Feyerabend, 1978).

Over time, operant conditioning leads to dependence on nicotine as smoking is positively and negatively reinforced and abstinence is punished (West & Shiffman, 2007). Positive reinforcement occurs because nicotine binds to

nicotinic acetylcholine receptors in the brain, which leads to dopamine release in the nucleus accumbens shell and other brain areas that are associated with hedonic emotional effects (Watkins, Koob, & Markou, 2000). Negative reinforcement occurs due to changes in the dopaminergic system following chronic nicotine exposure, experienced as unpleasant withdrawal symptoms that smokers learn to avoid by smoking (West & Shiffman, 2007). There are also a number of sociocultural factors, such as peer smoking, that influence smoking (Tyas & Pederson, 1998). Moreover, nicotine can influence various levels of the motivational system thereby creating dependence in interaction with psychological, social, and environmental factors (West, 2006a).

Assessment of Nicotine Dependence

According to the *Diagnostic and Statistical Manual* (4th ed.) (*DSM-IV*) of the American Psychiatric Association (American Psychiatric Association, 1995), which is closely mirrored by the *International Classification of Diseases* (10th ed.) (*ICD-10*) (World Health Organization [WHO], 1992), generic substance dependence is present if at least three of the following symptoms are present at any time in a given 12-month period: (a) tolerance (need for an increase in the amount of substance used and diminished effect of same amount), (b) withdrawal (dysphoric/depressed mood, insomnia, irritability/frustration/anger, anxiety, difficulty concentrating, restlessness, decreased heart rate, increased appetite/weight gain) or use of substance to relieve withdrawal; (c) substance use persists for longer and in larger amounts than was intended; (d) persistent desire to cut down/control substance use; (e) a lot of time spent on obtaining substance, using substance, or recovering from its effect; (f) substance use results in reduction/giving up of important social, occupational, or recreational activities; and (g) substance use despite knowledge of persistent/recurrent physical or psychological consequences caused or exacerbated by substance. The consequences of tobacco use meet most of these diagnostic criteria for substance use disorders; however, *DSM-IV* and *ICD-10* definitions of dependence have low utility, are laborious to apply, and do not differentiate well between smokers (Woody, Cottler, & Cacciola, 1993). It is therefore better to classify smokers along a dependence continuum, and more convenient assessment methods to do so exist (Jarvis & Sutherland, 1998).

Arguably the most ubiquitously used tool to assess nicotine dependence is the Fagerstrom Test of Nicotine Dependence (FTND) (Heatherton, Kozlowski, Frecker, & Fagerstrom, 1991), which scores smokers on a scale from 0–10 based on six questions (see Table 8.1). The FTND has good reliability and validity; predicts a smoker's ability to stop smoking, and is a good correlate of biochemical measures of dependence (Breslau & Johnson, 2000). A shorter version of the FTND, the Heaviness of Smoking Index also has good reliability and validity (Kozlowski, Porter, Orleans, Pope, & Heatherton, 1994).

As smokers often compensate by smoking fewer cigarettes with greater intensity (Benowitz, 2001), cigarette consumption is an invalid dependence measure. There also exist a number of multidimensional instruments to assess nicotine dependence that are used to a lesser degree such as the Nicotine Dependence Syndrome Scale (Shiffman, Waters, & Hickcox, 2004).

TABLE 8.1 Fagerstrom Test for Nicotine Dependence

Question	Score*
1. How soon after you wake up do you smoke your first cigarette?[#]	After 60 minutes (0) 31–60 minutes (1) 6–30 minutes (2) Within 5 minutes (3)
2. Do you find it difficult to refrain from smoking in places where it is forbidden?	No (0) Yes (1)
3. Which cigarette would you hate most to give up?	First in the morning (1) Any other (0)
4. How many cigarettes per day do you smoke?[#]	10 or less (0) 11–20 (1) 21–30 (2) 31 or more (3)
5. Do you smoke more frequently during the first hours after awakening than during the rest of the day?	No (0) Yes (1)
6. Do you smoke even if you are so ill that you are in bed most of the day?	No (0) Yes (1)

* 0–2 Very low dependence; 3–4 Low dependence; 5 Medium dependence; 6–7 High dependence; 8–10 Very high dependence
[#] Used for Heaviness of Smoking Index (HSI)

Besides questionnaire measures, tobacco use and dependence can be detected by biochemical analysis of exhaled air, sputum, saliva, blood, skin, hair, or urine (Davis & Curvall, 1999). The most inexpensive and easily obtained biomarker is expired-air carbon monoxide (CO) measured with breathalyzers, which is a good marker of smoke exposure (Jarvis, Tunstall-Pedoe, Feyerabend, Vesey, & Saloojee, 1987); however, it is not specific to tobacco smoke since other unrelated sources of CO exposure exist, such as vehicle exhaust emissions (Sonnenworth & Jarrett, 1980). Moreover, it only assesses recent exposure due to its short half-life (Coburn, Forster, & Kane, 1965), is influenced by physical activity, lung disease, and gender, and does not detect use of smokeless forms of tobacco (Benowitz et al., 2002). Cotinine, the major metabolite of nicotine measured in plasma, saliva, and urine, has a substantially longer half-life and is therefore more frequently used (Benowitz et al., 2002). It is sensitive and specific to tobacco use, predictive of successful smoking cessation attempts (Stapleton et al., 1995), but cannot distinguish smoking from nicotine replacement therapy (NRT) use (Benowitz, Kuyt, Jacob, Jones, & Osman, 1983). Other more costly, inconvenient, and thus less commonly used biomarkers of nicotine exposure exist. In conclusion, tobacco dependence is a serious drug addiction that can be assessed with a simple set of criteria and its use verified with reliable exposure biomarkers.

TOBACCO USE AND INDIVIDUAL DIFFERENCES

With the invention of the manufactured cigarette in the late nineteenth century, smoking became a mass phenomenon (Royal College of Physicians, 2000). Cigarette consumption steadily increased from then onward; in the United States, for instance, around 55% of men and 34% of women smoked at the height of the tobacco epidemic in the 1950s (Mackay, Eriksen, & Shafey, 2006). Currently 23.9% of men and 18.0% of women smoke in the United States (Rock et al., 2007) though prevalence differs greatly by state (Kahende, Teplinskaya, Malarcher, Husten, & Maurice, 2007). In most of the developed world tobacco use prevalence peaked in the mid twentieth century and has steadily decreased ever since, in contrast to most developing nations or nations in transition where prevalence has been increasing over the latter part of the twentieth century (WHO, 1997). Indeed, of the worldwide 1.3 billion smokers, 1 billion live in the developing world (Mackay et al., 2006) and it is predicted that there will be 1.7 billion people worldwide, or 1.9 billion if an increase in income is assumed, who will use tobacco products by 2020 (Guindon & Boisclair, 2003).

Smoking is more common among men than women; 47% of men and 12% of women smoke worldwide (Shafey, Dolwick, & Guindon,

2003). Men smoke more cigarettes but women may be more dependent than men (Perkins, Donny, & Caggiula, 1999). While still present, the gender gap is reducing in the developed world (Mackay et al., 2006). In the developing world 5 times more men than women smoke, most likely due to social and cultural stigma attached to female smoking, though smoking among women is on the increase here, too (Shafey, Dolwick, & Guindon, 2003).

Tobacco use starts early; the overwhelming majority of smokers will have initiated the habit before the age of 18 years (Global Youth Tobacco Survey Collaborative Group, 2002). Over the lifetime, smoking prevalence takes a bell-shaped form as smoking rates are low in both young and old age and peak somewhere before middle age, around the mid-twenties in the United States (Rock et al., 2007). This pattern is primarily determined by two factors; after initiation into smoking due to peer pressure and other environmental influences, less dependent smokers begin to stop smoking as they grow older while those people who are more dependent and continue to smoke start to die as old age approaches.

In the United States, tobacco use varies by ethnic group. Notably American Indian and Alaska Natives have higher smoking rates, while Hispanics and Asians have a lower smoking prevalence than the population at large (Rock et al., 2007). Ethnic minority groups also have different gender biases for smoking. In the Asian community smoking prevalence is 3 times, and in the Hispanic community 2 times, higher among men than women, whereas gender differences in smoking rates are less pronounced in people with a White, African American, American Indian, or Native Alaskan ethnic background (Rock et al., 2007).

Smoking prevalence is strongly associated with markers of socioeconomic status (SES) but the direction of this relationship differs from country to country. Where less is known about the health consequences of smoking, consumption is primarily influenced by income and a positive correlation between smoking and

SES is observed (Lopez, Collishaw, & Piha, 1994). In countries with greater awareness of the negative impact of smoking, those that are better off financially are more successful at stopping smoking than more economically deprived smokers, resulting in a negative relationship between smoking and SES. In the United States, for instance, smoking rates among those living below the federal poverty level is 1.5 times higher than among those at or above this level (Rock et al., 2007). Such differences in cessation rates are likely to exist because disadvantaged smokers more commonly experience a lack of financial, emotional, and environmental resources to aid smoking cessation (Kotz & West, 2008). Other psychosocial factors such as greater dependence and a greater likelihood of having a partner who smokes will also undermine attempts to stop smoking in this group (Kenkel & Chen, 2000).

Tobacco use is strongly linked with mental disorders and exhibits a dose-response relationship with the disorder severity (West & Jarvis, 2005). Tobacco use is significantly more common among people with psychotic disorders, panic disorders, obsessive-compulsive disorders, phobias, depression and generalized anxiety disorders (Breslau, Kilbey, & Andreski, 1994), as well as eating disorders (Welch & Fairburn, 1998). Moreover, smokers are nearly twice as likely as nonsmokers to show signs of mental illness irrespective of the precise condition (Farrell et al., 2001). The relationship between smoking prevalence and mental disorders is even stronger in institutionalized individuals, particularly in schizophrenics: Nearly four out of five inpatients with schizophrenia smoke (De, 1996).

IMPACT OF DISORDER

Health Effects: Impact on Smokers

Tobacco use is commonly acknowledged to be the single most important preventable public health problem of modern society, killing more people than HIV, illicit drugs, and alcohol combined (Ezzati, Lopez, Rodgers, Vander, & Murray, 2002). In the United States it accounts for more than 435,000 deaths per year (Armour, Malarcher, Pechacek, & Husten, 2005), and approximately 5 million deaths globally in 2000 (Ezzati & Lopez, 2003). Cigarette smoke contains a dangerous mix of noxious and toxic compounds, exposure to which results in the development of various illnesses (Doll, Peto, Wheatley, Gray, & Sutherland, 1994; see Table 8.2). This risk is determined by the duration of tobacco use and the amount used, though it appears that the length of time of tobacco use has a greater impact on disease occurrence (Jarvis, 2003). On average, a lifelong smoker's life expectancy is reduced by 10 years and longitudinal studies show that more than one in two continuing smokers eventually dies from smoking (Doll, Peto, Boreham, & Sutherland, 2004).

The diseases that contribute most to smoking-related deaths are lung cancer, chronic obstructive pulmonary disease (COPD), and cardiovascular disease (CVD), which together make up 70% of all smoking-related deaths (Ezzati & Lopez, 2004). Smoking causes 70% of COPD-related deaths, 20%–40% of all cancer deaths, and around 20% of CVD-related deaths (Jarvis, 2003). Tobacco use is also a major cause of global morbidity: There are 20 times as many smokers who suffer from comorbid, disabling diseases, generally COPD, CVD, or cancer than smokers who die in a given year (Hyland et al., 2003). In addition, tobacco use is implied in a number of other nonfatal diseases (see Table 8.2). Moreover, smoking may also increase susceptibility to develop mental illnesses (West & Jarvis, 2005). Smoking has been implicated as both a consequence and cause of the development of psychiatric disorders such as depression in longitudinal studies (Choi, Patten, Gillin, Kaplan, & Pierce, 1997).

TABLE 8.2   Disorders and Diseases Linked to Tobacco Use Adapted From West (2006b)

Smoking

Cancer of the lung	Chronic obstructive pulmonary disease	Infertility
Cancer of the larynx	Pneumonia	Spontaneous abortion
Cancers or the oral cavity	Asthma attacks	Stillbirth
Cancer of the nasopharynx	Coronary heart disease	Low birth weight
Cancer of the oropharynx and nasopharynx	Aortic aneurism	Conduct disorder in offspring of women who smoked during pregnancy
Cancer of the oesophagus	Cerebrovascular disease	Sudden infant death syndrome
Cancer of the liver	Peripheral vascular disease	Low back pain
Cancer of the cervix	Vascular dementia	Osteoporosis
Cancer of the pancreas	Periodontitis	Tuberculosis
Cancer of the stomach	Macular degeneration	Type II diabetes
Cancer of the urinary tract (kidney, ureter, and bladder)	Cataract	Peptic ulcer disease
Leukemia	Hearing loss	Surgical complications

Smokeless tobacco use

Cancer of the oral cavity	Cancer of the pancreas	

Health Effects: Impact on Nonsmokers

The health costs of smoking also extend to those who do not smoke themselves but who may either inhale secondhand smoke directly or, during pregnancy, are exposed to tobacco constituents in the womb. Nonsmokers living with smokers have an excess risk of 15% to suffer smoking-related diseases (Hill, Blakely, Kawachi, & Woodward, 2004); nonsmoking spouses of smokers are more likely to develop lung cancer, stroke, and ischemic heart disease (United States Department of Health and Human Services [USDHHS] 2004). In the United Kingdom alone, secondhand tobacco smoke may have caused up to 10,000 excess deaths in 2003 (Jamrozik, 2005). Children of mothers who smoke during pregnancy are not only more likely to die from cot death but may also experience other serious and insidious health and social consequences. These effects remain after controlling for putative confounding factors such as low birth weight (DiFranza, Aligne, & Weitzman, 2004)

Financial Effects: Impact on Economy

Tobacco use results in vast health-care costs and is responsible for loss of productivity through absenteeism, fires caused by smoking, diversion of agricultural land and environmental damage. In the United States, smoking-attributable health care costs are thought to exceed $96 billion and lost productivity $97 billion per year (Centers for Disease Control and Prevention, 2007). It is thought that each cigarette pack costs society and individual smokers close to $40 when combining actual price with additionally incurred costs (Sloan, Ostermann, & Picone, 2004). Globally, the health care costs associated with smoking represent around 1% of the gross domestic product (GDP) and the social cost of smoking accounts for a similar proportion. Thus, even when tobacco taxation and the shorter life span of smokers are taken into account in economic models, overall, it is likely that smokers still incur net costs to society (Lightwood, Collins, Lapsley, & Novotny, 2000)

Benefits of Cessation

Arguably, stopping smoking can be considered one of the most important steps a person can take to improve their health and quitting smoking has profound effects on the subsequent risk to develop smoking-related diseases. Smoking cessation has almost immediate benefits by slowing lung function decline, postoperative complications, and halting the occurrence and further progress of heart disease and halves the risk of lung cancer (IARC Working Group, 2007; Peto et al., 2000). Smoking cessation improves reproductive health (Peate, 2005) and quitting smoking may improve mental health (Mino, Shigemi, Otsu, Tsuda, & Babazono, 2000). Around 90% of excess mortality due to smoking can be avoided if smokers stopped before middle age (Peto et al., 2000) but stopping smoking at any age is beneficial (Taylor, Hasselblad, Henley, Thun, & Sloan, 2002). The positive effects of smoking cessation also extend to nonsmokers; partners of ex-smokers are much less likely to develop cancer than nonsmokers living with smokers, and babies born to mothers who stopped smoking during pregnancy are healthier than babies of full-term smoking mothers (National Cancer Institute, 1999). There are also economic advantages, particularly in poorer countries, where money that is needed for vital necessities is spent on tobacco products (WHO, 2004).

Given the enormous benefits of smoking cessation, it is not surprising that of the 45 million or so smokers in the United States, the vast majority (around 70%) would like to quit and about 44% try each year (Rock et al., 2007); however, success rates are very low as only 4%–7% of attempters achieve long-term abstinence (Hughes, 2003). In what follows, we present the main behavioral treatments that have been developed to improve smokers' chances to quit successfully.

FACE-TO-FACE BEHAVIORAL COUNSELING

Consensus Panel Recommendations

Face-to-face behavioral counseling encompasses a range of approaches to smoking from the briefest form of contact in terms of simple advice from a health-care provider about quitting smoking, through to complex behavioral counseling programs run over several weeks. It provides "discussion, advice, encouragement and activities designed to: maximize motivation to maintain abstinence, minimize motivation to smoke, enhance self-regulatory skills and capacity, and improve medication adherence" (West, 2008, p. 3). This may include a variety of components and approaches including anticipated reward and punishment; promoting appropriate identity change; advising on stress reduction, how to avoid high-risk situations, and coping strategies; promoting alternative behaviors; initiating action planning; explaining how medication works; and tackling concerns regarding medication use. Key aspects of program structure often include a specified quit date and recording of expired-air carbon monoxide to confirm self-reported abstinence (West & Shiffman, 2007). Such sessions can be either for an individual or a group.

Behavioral counseling for smoking cessation has been reviewed in a number of consensus panel reviews including the USDHHS (2008) clinical practice guidelines on treating tobacco use and dependence, the UK smoking cessation guidelines for Health Professionals (West, McNeill, & Raw, 2000), and the UK National Institute for Health and Clinical Excellence (NICE) guidelines (NICE, 2008). These documents use a combination of systematic reviews and expert opinion to provide recommendations of the best way to treat tobacco dependence.

The guidelines conclude that behavioral counseling for smoking cessation is an effective treatment. In its briefest form, advice and minimal intervention (up to 5-minute contact) from a physician has been shown to be effective, although there is less evidence for other health professionals. The U.S., UK, and NICE guidelines recommend that all patients should be asked if they use tobacco, unless inappropriate due to presenting condition or personal circumstances, be advised to quit smoking, and effective interventions should be provided if willing. This sort of brief advice likely triggers quit attempts and increases motivation to quit, and will largely affect lighter smokers (USDHHS, 2008; West et al., 2000). As might be expected, increased contact has been shown to be more effective than this type of minimal intervention (USDHHS, 2008), therefore, the focus here will be on more intensive forms of face-to-face support and counseling.

The UK guidelines cite a 7% difference in the 6 month abstinence rates of moderate to heavy smokers seeking intensive behavioral support compared with control groups (West et al., 2000), while the USDHHS guidelines report abstinence rates 2.3 times higher among smokers attending high intensity counseling compared with those receiving no contact (USDHHS, 2008). The NICE guidelines consequently recommend that smokers who want to stop should be referred to an intensive support service, with National Health Service (NHS) Stop Smoking Services being offered throughout the United Kingdom (NICE, 2008). The cost effectiveness of such treatment for smokers is high compared to other health care interventions (Royal College of Physicians, 2000). It is difficult to conclude which components are especially effective as meta-analyses incorporate studies describing varied components of therapy, however, the USDHHS (2008) guidelines propose that practical counseling, such as problem solving and coping skills training, and intratreatment social support are important aspects of treatment that are associated with increased abstinence rates. The

strength of evidence for this is limited for a number of reasons: Studies seldom examine a particular type of counseling in isolation and particular types of therapy tend to correlate with other characteristics of treatment, such as the number of sessions; however, there are some common elements that are typically included in this type of approach including identifying situations that increase risk of relapse and how to anticipate these triggers; learning how to cope with urges; reducing stress and negative mood; providing information about the addictive nature of smoking and withdrawal symptoms; receiving encouragement and concern; and discussion of the quitting process (USDHHS, 2008). There is also some suggestion that more intensive programs result in higher quit rates than briefer treatments. Consequently, the guidelines recommend four or more sessions of more than 10 minutes (USDHHS, 2008; West et al., 2000).

Behavioral support for smoking cessation is available in a variety of different settings and administered by a range of providers. The UK guidelines (West et al., 2000) concluded that there is sufficient evidence to recommend behavioral treatment given by specifically trained smoking cessation specialists and nurses; NICE guidelines echo this conclusion. Interventions delivered by pharmacists can be effective, although the strength of evidence is weaker; however, there is no evidence to support the delivery of programs by other health care providers. There may be a case for recommending treatment by a number of different clinicians, though the increased effectiveness observed in these cases may be due to increased contact time as a result of multiple visits (USDHHS, 2008). Sufficient evidence exists to recommend the use of behavioral support for smokers in the general population who are seeking help with quitting, pregnant women, and smokers in an inpatient setting (USDHHS, 2008; West et al., 2000). There has been little evidence regarding the success of counseling for smoking cessation among adolescent smokers (West et al., 2000), although the most recent guideline report gives a slightly tentative recommendation for counseling in this age group based on a limited number of heterogeneous studies (USDHHS, 2008).

Although not the focus of this chapter, it is important to highlight that all guidelines also strongly support the use of pharmacotherapy for tobacco dependence according to the withdrawal-orientated treatment model. Several effective medications are now available, including NRT, in any one of a number of forms including transdermal patch, chewing gum, nasal spray, inhalator, sublingual tablet, and lozenge. Buproprion or Varenicline may also be effective (USDHHS, 2008; West et al., 2000). The evidence suggests that the effect of behavioral counseling plus some form of medication is greater than either medication or counseling alone and should therefore be offered to all presenting smokers (USDHHS, 2008; West et al., 2000).

Meta-Analyses and Systematic Reviews

There are a number of meta-analyses and systematic reviews including a series of Cochrane Reviews that distinguish between mode of delivery, type of provider, and target population. The most recent Cochrane Review on one-to-one behavioral counseling is based on 21 randomized or quasi-randomized control trial (RCT) studies, with over 7,000 participants (Lancaster & Stead, 2005a). All trials reported the results of an unconfounded intervention of a face-to-face encounter between a smoker and a trained counselor compared to a minimal level intervention, with at least 6 months' follow-up. Counseling was more effective compared to control, although no conclusion could be made as to the comparative effectiveness of one approach over another as the interventions included consisted of a diverse mix of Cognitive Behavior Therapy (CBT), relapse prevention, information regarding the benefits of quitting, advice, nicotine fading, contingency contracts, and counseling based on the stages of

change model (J. O. Prochaska & Norcross, 2001), which proposes that individuals pass through a series of stages of smoking cessation, and consequently that interventions should be tailored to stage. Three studies compared different levels of treatment intensity. A separate meta-analysis of these three studies initially concluded that there was no difference in outcome based on number of sessions provided; however, once two higher intensity interventions in one of the studies were combined to match the other studies there was a significant effect of treatment intensity. A systematic review including some research published since the Cochrane Review described earlier also concluded that counseling, either alone or with pharmacotherapy, increases quit rate success. There was no clear conclusion regarding the intensity of treatment, therefore the authors conclude that more intensive counseling cannot be recommended over briefer treatments (Ranney, Melvin, Lux, McClain, & Lohr, 2006).

Group behavioral counseling, led by professional facilitators, offers the same types of component as individual therapy; however, the intragroup social support offered and opportunities for generating emotional experiences available might suggest that group treatment offers additional benefit. A Cochrane Review of group behavioral counseling included 55 studies, most between six and eight sessions, and, as previously stated, incorporating a wide variety of specific components (Stead & Lancaster, 2005). Like individual therapy, group treatment was effective compared to self-help or no treatment; however, the five studies that compared individual and group counseling found no evidence to suggest that group behavior therapy was any more, or less, effective than individual treatment. Of course, some smokers may not feel that a group setting is appropriate for them, while others may value the support and motivation a group context provides, and group counseling obviously provides the most economic option. Some attempt was made to identify effective components of programs and there was weak evidence that complex interventions including skills-based training may have added benefit.

A number of meta-analyses have examined the effect of smoking cessation counseling when given by specific health-care providers. Rice and Stead (2008), in a Cochrane Review of nursing interventions for smoking cessation, concluded that smoking cessation interventions delivered by nurses were effective. Interventions delivered by nurses who had other roles were not as successful as those delivered by a nurse specifically employed to give smoking cessation provision. A meta-analysis of 41 studies, including over 20,000 participants, examinined physician advice for smoking cessation. Although a less intense form of behavioral counseling than being considered here, a significant effect of physician advice compared to no advice control was found (Stead, Bergson, & Lancaster, 2008). Carr and Ebbert (2006) considered six trials of smoking cessation interventions delivered by oral health professionals in their Cochrane Review and concluded that dental interventions were concluded to be more effective compared to usual care, or no contact. Most studies focused on smokeless tobacco use. Only two studies were included in a Cochrane Review of community pharmacy personnel interventions for smoking cessation, with a total of 976 smokers, although only one showed a significant intervention effect (Sinclair, Bond, & Stead, 2004). Finally, a systematic review of counseling by various health-care providers concluded that physicians were the most effective, followed by multidisciplinary teams, dentists, and nurses (Gorin & Heck, 2004).

Several Cochrane Reviews have assessed the impact of behavioral support for smoking cessation on a variety of different special populations. There are robust results for both hospitalized and cardiac patients, but only if the treatment is prolonged (Barth, Critchley, & Benpel, 2008; Ripotti, Munafo, & Stead, 2007); however, Luker, Chalmers, Caress, and Salmon (2007) and Wapena, van der Meer, Ostelo, Jacobs, and van Schayck (2004) concluded from their recent systematic reviews of smoking cessation treatments for patients with COPD that there was no strong evidence to suggest that behavioral counseling in this patient group is effective. Although findings in a review of preoperative smoking cessation treatment were generally positive, there was little evidence to suggest that treatment is especially important at this time (Moller & Villebro, 2008). A high level of smoking is typically observed among those with other substance use dependence (Richter, Ahluwalia, Mosier, Nazir, & Ahluwalia, 2002). J. J. Prochaska, Delucchi, and Hall (2004) carried out a meta-analysis of smoking cessation interventions among those in substance abuse treatment and concluded that interventions were effective in the short, but not longer, term and that a combination of behavioral intervention plus NRT may be particularly important for this group. High smoking prevalence and a high intensity of smoking is also common in people with psychiatric conditions; however, Ranney et al. (2006) concluded there is little evidence to support the use of specialist programs for this population over those used in the general population.

A large Cochrane Review of 48 trials of smoking cessation treatment during pregnancy found a significant reduction in smoking in the intervention groups compared to control (Lumley, Oliver, Chamberlain, & Oakley, 2004). These programs typically included information on the risks of smoking to the fetus and feedback about the fetus, but also a range of other components. Cognitive behavior therapy was commonly included and found to be most effective, while programs based on the stages of change model were ineffective. A systematic review of smoking cessation interventions in postpartum women identified three studies and concluded that there was no effect on either cessation or later relapse, although readiness to stop and confidence were increased (Levitt, Shaw, Wong, & Kaczorowski, 2007).

Smoking cessation interventions among young people under the age of 20 years have been addressed in a Cochrane Review by

Grimshaw and Stanton (2006). They concluded that, although some approaches are successful, there is currently not enough evidence to routinely recommend behavioral intervention in this age group. Finally, a review of interventions in workplace settings comprised of a very heterogeneous selection of studies (Moher, Hey, & Lancaster, 2005). As smoking interventions are not specific to workplace settings it was concluded that main Cochrane Reviews should be used to judge effectiveness of behavioral support; however, the success of some of these studies does confirm that smoking cessation interventions that occur in the workplace can be effective.

There has been some focus on the use of behavioral interventions to decrease the risk of relapse back to smoking once cessation has occurred. Relapse prevention techniques form part of the overall intervention program of many of the studies included in the earlier reviews and typically involve the provision of cognitive and behavioral strategies to cope with situations where relapse may occur, as well as imaginary cue exposure, aversive smoking, social support, and exercise (Lancaster, Hajek, Stead, West, & Jarvis, 2006). This recently updated Cochrane Review including 42 studies failed to find any benefit of specific relapse prevention programs. The majority of these studies were based on interventions that taught skills in identifying and resolving tempting situations; however, there were methodological limitations with a large number of the included studies and many suffered from lack of power. There is therefore currently little evidence for the success of these specific techniques.

Conclusions

Face-to-face behavioral support encompasses a wide range of different techniques designed to support the smoking cessation process. Behavioral support has been shown to be effective, both in individual and group contexts, and is recommended by a number of guidelines for smoking cessation. Research cannot confidently support particular approaches as effective, although practical support and intratreatment social support are considered important elements. Further research is therefore needed to identify constituents of programs that will confer the most benefit. Higher quality research on relapse prevention would also substantially add to the area. Despite this there are a large number of studies addressing the role of behavioral support in different contexts, by a number of different providers, and to a range of different populations, allowing some evaluation of who such support is appropriate for and who is most appropriate to deliver it. The provision of high-quality behavioral support, drawing on the research that is currently available, and coupled with appropriate pharmacotherapy consequently offers an effective route toward long-term smoking abstinence.

TELEPHONE COUNSELING

Consensus Panel Recommendations

While the individual and intensive approach of face-to-face counseling has good efficacy, it is only used by a relatively small proportion of smokers. Even in the United Kingdom, which has a very developed, publicly funded network of smoking cessation services (McNeill, Raw, Whybrow, & Bailey, 2005), only 5.6% of smokers access such services (Department of Health, 2008). A strategy to improve smoking cessation interventions is therefore to increase both their efficacy and reach (Abrams et al., 1996). Telephone counseling offers the opportunity to substitute face-to-face contact and increase accessibility, but can also be provided as an adjunct to face-to-face counseling or self-help interventions.

Telephone counseling is either proactive or reactive (Lichtenstein, Glasgow, Lando, Ossip-Klein, & Boles, 1996). Proactive telephone counseling refers to the initiation of the phone call by a counselor and reactive telephone counseling refers to smokers initiating contact with a quitline. Consensus panels concur on the efficacy of proactive telephone counseling, recommending their use for smoking cessation (Royal College of Physicians, 2000; USDHHS, 2008; West et al., 2000). The picture is less clear regarding the use of reactive phone counseling as it is difficult to evaluate through RCTs and so most studies rely on follow-up data of smokers who have been in contact with quitlines. Given this lack of appropriate data, the UK consensus panels tentatively suggest that reactive telephone counseling may be effective, especially since it can be seen as a point-of-entry to other, more intensive forms of counseling through referral to smoking cessation services (Royal College of Physicians, 2000; West et al., 2000). In addition, the U.S. guidelines recommend the use of phone counseling in combination with both intensive therapy and medication (USDHHS, 2008).

Meta-Analyses and Systematic Reviews

Several systematic reviews and meta-analyses have evaluated the efficacy of telephone counseling for smoking cessation. A Cochrane Review concluded that proactive telephone counseling is effective, outperforming minimal interventions, and suggests a dose response effect as interventions providing more calls have a greater impact on smoking cessation rates (Stead, Perera, & Lancaster, 2006). A meta-analysis of proactive telephone counseling added to minimal smoking cessation interventions reports a significant adjunct effect (Pan, 2006). A last review, which represents a subanalysis of the Cochrane Review, assessed adjunctive support for reactive telephone counseling and concludes that multiple call back counseling increases abstinence rates for smokers contacting quitlines (Stead, Perera, & Lancaster, 2007). The reviews included 54 RCTs with a total of nearly 38,000 participants. The quality of studies was largely adequate; however, most trials did not provide sufficient information about the randomization method

used or the quality of concealment, and a number of studies used suboptimal randomization based on residency or workplace. Nearly half of trials did not biochemically validate abstinence rates and there was inconsistency in the reporting of point-prevalence and long-term abstinence rates. Most studies evaluated proactive telephone counseling and only four evaluated reactive counseling. There was considerable variation in the number, frequency, and duration of telephone calls, ranging from one to 12 calls carried out over a period of weeks or months and each usually lasting between 10 and 20 minutes. Calls were mainly conducted by professional counselors or trained personnel, followed either a tailored or standard script based on behavior therapy, and involved the provision of emotional and functional support, such as answering queries, giving basic information, and carrying out motivational counseling. Studies recruited participants from a variety of settings, largely from the community or clinics, and targeted the general population, hospitalized patients, pregnant women, and ethnic minority groups, as well as adolescents. Last, comparison groups differed as interventions were compared with behavioral treatment, self-help interventions, brief advice, and participants were given varying access to pharmacological therapy.

Evidence is inconclusive for the efficacy of reactive telephone counseling; some reviews find an effect (Ossip-Klein, Carosella, & Krusch, 1997) while others do not (McFall, et al., 1993). The pooled results of two studies (Orleans et al., 1998; Thompson, Kinne, Lewis, & Woolridge, 1993), where callers to quitlines were either assigned to tailored telephone counseling or standard counseling at the initial call, also revealed no impact of the intervention; however, providing further proactive phone calls following an initial call from smokers increases quit rates from 7.5% to 10.5%. This was a consistent finding despite relatively large heterogeneity in methodology. There was evidence for a dose-response effect as increasing additional proactive counseling calls resulted in greater abstinence rates; however, there was no differential effect as a function of offering either different types of telephone counseling or standard self-help material.

Most studies in the meta-analyses compared proactive counseling initiated by counselors with various control conditions. In trials that provided minimal support to smokers randomized to either receive telephone calls or not, pooled results indicated a positive effect of telephone counseling. The same was true for studies where smokers were provided with pharmacotherapy before being allocated to telephone counseling; however, pooled results indicated no benefit of telephone counseling as an adjunct to brief behavioral interventions. The meta-analyses also find a dose-response effect. Interventions providing less than three proactive phone calls were ineffective; studies with three or more calls increased abstinence rates compared with controls, and studies providing seven or more phone calls were most effective in pooled analysis. Interestingly, both trials that only recruited motivated smokers and trials that did not select by motivation level detected clinically significant effects; however, the effect size was larger in studies specifically recruiting smokers who wanted to quit. There is also evidence that hospital-based smoking cessation interventions may be enhanced by a single proactive telephone call (Miller, Smith, DeBusk, Sobel, & Taylor, 1997) and that changes in practice guidelines to recommend offering proactive telephone and/or NRT to patients may increase abstinence rates (D. A. Katz, Muehlenbruch, Brown, Fiore, & Baker, 2004); however, Roski and colleagues (2003) did not detect an increase in smoking cessation rates following a simlar intervention. Moreover, telephone counseling does not appear to be effective for relapse prevention (Hajek, Stead, West, & Jarvis, 2005).

Randomized Controlled Trials

A recent trial investigated the relative effectiveness of different telephone protocols with or without provision of concurrent NRT and confirmed previous results (Hollis et al., 2007). Only moderate or intensive telephone interventions (more than one call) increased smoking cessation rates and this effect was enhanced by the provision of pharmacotherapy. Another recent study reported a beneficial effect of telephone counseling compared with self-help material but found no evidence for a dose-response effect (Rabius, Pike, Hunter, Wiatrek, & McAlister, 2007). A final trial showed that proactive telephone calls are better than mailed material for reenrolling smokers who had previously called quitlines (Carlini et al., 2008).

Conclusions

Proactive telephone counseling for smoking cessation is effective when it comprises at least three phone calls and has the potential to reach a relatively large proportion of the smoking population. There is currently no evidence that reactive telephone counseling on its own increases abstinence. Therefore, it should be followed by proactive phone calls from counselors; however, in the absence of sufficiently conclusive trial data further studies in this area is required. In agreement with consensus panel recommendations, meta-analyses find that telephone helplines can enhance the effectiveness of pharmacotherapy. While telephone counseling also produces a clinically meaningful impact when added to minimal smoking cessation interventions (e.g., self-help), the evidence is less clear-cut regarding the efficacy of proactive counseling as an addendum to face-to-face behavioral interventions.

SELF-HELP

Consensus Panel Recommendations

Self-help interventions encompass a wide range of treatments ranging from written materials such as leaflets and manuals to electronically delivered material using videos or the Internet.

The rationale for such interventions is similar to that for telephone counseling as such treatments potentially have a much wider reach than individual behavioral counseling, allowing smokers to access support who would not usually be able to attend face-to-face counseling (Griffiths, Lindenmeyer, Powell, Lowe, & Thorogood, 2006). Thus, they attempt to bridge the clinic approach that is aimed at individuals with the public health approach that targets the population (Curry, 1993). Written self-help material usually involves the provision of educational information combined with a quit plan involving a step-by-step guide toward cessation and tips and advice on how to avoid relapse. It may be tailored to the characteristics of smokers and be supplemented with videos to enhance social and cognitive antecedents of behavior change such as self-efficacy. Computerized and Internet-based interventions have the additional advantage of being interactive. Such material allows for greater computational capacity to iteratively and ipsatively integrate user information and provide different media, such as chat rooms, to mimic the interactive nature of face-to-face contact (Cassell, Jackson, & Cheuvront, 1998).

As Internet and interactive media smoking cessation interventions are a relatively new phenomenon, consensus panel guidelines mostly review written self-help material for smoking cessation. Both UK and U.S. guidelines support the use of written material (Royal College of Physicians, 2000; USDHHS, 2008; West et al., 2000). The guidelines specify several caveats for written self-help material. First, interventions have a very marginal effect on abstinence rates as only one additional smoker per 100 smokers will quit when given written self-help material. Second, the evidence for self-help interventions is strongest when these have been tailored, and tailored material should therefore be given preference. Third, consensus panel recommendations do not extend to self-help books as these have not been adequately tested. Fourth, it is not clear

whether adding self-help material to other interventions, such as brief advice or increasing the number of self-help types, is beneficial. Last, the updated U.S. guidelines tentatively recommend the use of e-health and Internet interventions given their potential reach and low cost.

Meta-Analyses and Systematic Reviews

Several meta-analyses and reviews were identified: A Cochrane Review of self-help interventions for smoking cessation (Lancaster & Stead, 2005b), two reviews investigating the use of computerized interventions for health behaviors (Portnoy, Scott-Sheldon, Johnson, & Carey, 2008; Walters, Wright, & Shegog, 2006), and a review evaluating the impact of tailored written self-help material (Noar, Benac, & Harris, 2007). These reviews concluded that standard self-help materials improve quit rates compared with no intervention, but that the effect size is likely to be small. Tailored material was more effective than nontailored material. Computerized health behavior interventions appear to increase smoking cessation rates but reviews highlight the need of further research to confirm these results.

The reviews evaluated 85 studies of self-help interventions that targeted smoking cessation and included nearly 85,000 participants. The quality of studies was judged to be variable. Adequate allocation and randomization procedures were often not described. A large proportion of studies did not validate smoking cessation, arguably due to the wide reach of interventions that made biochemical assessment of smoking status unfeasible. The methodology and content of interventions was eclectic but most studies used behavioral and sociocognitive theories such as the Theory of Planned Behavior (Ajzen, 1991), the Health Belief Model (Becker, 1974), Social Cognitive Theory (Bandura, 1986), or the Stages of Change Model (J. O. Prochaska & DiClemente, 1983) to inform interventions. Written self-help material was compared with either no intervention or written control material. Self-help interventions were also added to brief advice or NRT and several trials evaluated the impact of enhancing self-help interventions by tailoring material or adding video. Computer-based interventions were compared with either no intervention, education-only material, or brief or altered forms of the intervention.

Written standard, nontailored self-help material fared marginally better than no interventions, but self-help material did not enhance telephone counseling, face-to-face advice from health-care providers, the efficacy of NRT, or was effective for pregnant smokers or relapse prevention. Tailored self-help material consistently improved abstinence compared with nontailored, standard material, but the effect depreciated over time. There was no clear trend favoring one type of self-help material over another and neither additional written material nor video improved quit rates. One review (Noar et al., 2007) found that pamphlets and leaflets tended to do better than newsletters, magazines, letters, manuals, or booklets in self-help interventions targeting health behaviors other than just smoking. Moreover, interventions that had more than one contact and used more theoretical concepts to tailor the intervention fared better. In addition, studies that tailored on theoretical concepts and demographic and behavior characteristics showed a greater effect than studies that tailored only on behavior or theoretical concepts.

Some recent meta-analyses and systematic reviews have focused on the use of computer- or Internet-based smoking cessation interventions (Myung, McDonnell, Kazinets, Seo, & Moskowitz, 2009; Shahab & McEwen, 2009; Webb, Joseph, Yardley, & Michie, 2010). These included some 25 studies with over 32,000 participants. The outcomes reported were largely positive; as for printed material, tailored Internet interventions produced better outcomes than nontailored interventions and intensive interventions (more contact time with participants) did better than less intensive computer- or Internet-based interventions. The

treatment effect of these interventions lessened with time but appeared to be superior to standard self-help material, producing abstinence rates comparable to more intensive face-to-face counseling interventions.

Randomized Controlled Trials

As the field of Internet-based interventions for health behavior is rapidly expanding, seven RCTs have recently been published that were not included in reviews. These compared interactive, tailored online interventions with various control conditions and provide evidence that the Internet can be used to deliver wide-reaching and efficacious treatment for smoking cessation. While three trials did not find a significant increase in quit rates, the lack of impact of the intervention appeared to be mediated by participants not making sufficient use of the online service (Japuntich et al., 2006; McKay, Danaher, Seeley, Lichtenstein, & Gau, 2008; Pike, Rabius, McAlister, & Geiger, 2007). The remaining four trials (An et al., 2008; Brendryen, Drozd, & Kraft, 2008; Brendryen & Kraft, 2008; Severson, Gordon, Danaher, & Akers, 2008) observed an increase in abstinence rates of between 5% and 17% compared with controls and confirmed the efficacy of tailoring such interventions. Moreover, in contrast to earlier computerized interventions, all effective Internet interventions made use of the interactive nature of the medium using tunneling (when users are individually guided through the program based on their previous responses), chat forums, and so forth to improve abstinence rates.

Conclusions

Self-help interventions are effective but they do not increase cessation rates to the same extent as face-to-face psychological interventions. In agreement with recommendations of consensus panels, the wider reach and low cost of this approach supports their application as a smoking cessation treatment. Tailored self-help interventions are more effective than non-tailored intervention and Internet-based interventions in particular should be investigated further to establish whether they can emulate the efficacy of face-to-face behavioral interventions by providing an interactive, tailored experience for smokers seeking treatment.

SOCIAL SUPPORT

Consensus Panel Recommendations

Social support can be incorporated into treatment (intratreatment social support) when smokers are provided with encouragement through direct contact with empathetic clinicians (USDHHS, 2008). Social support can also occur outside of the direct treatment setting (extra-treatment social support), when smokers are given assistance to seek support elsewhere or when friends and family are encouraged to aid a smoker's quit attempt. Social support is generally thought to increase a smoker's chance to stop smoking (e.g., Morgan, Ashenberg, & Fisher, 1988). Consensus panel guidelines (Raw, McNeill, & West, 1998; USDHHS, 2008) consider intratreatment social support an important and effective component of intensive behavioral interventions (see previous sections on this topic). Recommendations for extra-treatment social support are less clear. The U.S. guidelines did not find sufficient evidence to advocate the use of extra-treatment social support, and the UK guidelines stated that there is currently only preliminary evidence to suggest that extra-treatment social support components such as *buddying up* smokers should be included in interventions (West et al., 2000).

Meta-Analyses and Systematic Reviews

Relatively few studies have explicitly investigated the impact of social support on abstinence rates. Three systematic reviews have examined the extant literature. A Cochrane Review that evaluated whether enhancement of partner support improves smoking cessation found no

effect of interventions on either increasing partner support or abstinence rates (Park, Schultz, Tudiver, Campbell, & Becker, 2004). Another review, focusing on the use of family-based smoking cessation interventions for COPD patients, was also unable to draw conclusions about the efficacy of extra-treatment social support (Luker et al., 2007); however, as this review mainly included nonrandomized trials that simply reported associations between various social support variables and smoking cessation, these studies are not considered further here. The last review reported tentative evidence that buddy systems may be effective in the context of smoking clinics but not in community interventions (May & West, 2000).

The two relevant reviews included 13 studies with nearly 4,500 participants. The quality of studies was rather low as eight studies had samples below 100 participants thus increasing the likelihood of failure to detect a treatment effect when it is present due to low power. Several studies used smoking reduction rather than cessation as outcome and most studies failed to validate abstinence, biochemically assessing point prevalence rather than continuous abstinence. Two studies did not use an intention to treat schedule to analyze results. Social support was not controlled for at baseline and measured inconsistently. Studies mainly used the Partner Interaction Questionnaire (Mermelstein, Lichtenstein, & McIntyre, 1983) but administered different versions thus making between study comparisons difficult. Interventions were often not described in sufficient detail and were multifactorial, thereby obscuring the effect of social support components. As most studies were carried out in the context of clinics, existing intratreatment social support may have concealed the effect of the supportive intervention. Last, as studies could not be double blinded, therapist effects cannot be ruled out.

Most studies combined standard cessation treatments, such as group meetings, with support interventions that comprised empathy exercises, social support guides, videotapes, behavioral technique sessions, and support calls from counselors. Many studies offered guidance to smokers and a support person, but few gave group training to partners. Only two studies reported a significant treatment effect. In one (Gruder et al., 1993) group meetings were an adjunct to a self-help program and in the other (West, Edwards, & Hajek, 1998) smokers either received individual treatment or buddy support in a smokers' clinic; pooled study results showed no increase in quit rates in treatment compared with control conditions. Out of eight studies only two (Ginsberg, Hall, & Rosinski, 1992; Gruder et al., 1993) found that social support had actually increased in the treatment condition while the remaining studies found no effect or a general decline in partner support across conditions.

Conclusions

Data on the impact of social support on smoking cessation are very limited. Intra-treatment social support is likely to be an important component of most intensive behavioral interventions for smoking cessation but this has not been systematically studied controlling for nonspecific or placebo effects. The best evidence to suggest that such intra-treatment social support has an active effect comes from indirect comparisons of group and individual treatments showing that effect sizes obtained by group treatments are somewhat higher (Lancaster & Stead, 2005a, Stead & Lancaster, 2005). In agreement with consensus panel guidelines, given the paucity and quality of research, there is little evidence that extra-treatment social support improves smoking cessation rates or that such interventions actually affect social support levels.

AVERSIVE SMOKING AND INCENTIVES

Consensus Panel Recommendations

Aversive smoking uses principles from classical and operant conditioning to aid smoking cessation. There are many different forms of aversive smoking but they all pair smoking with an unpleasant stimulus. Incentive-based interventions reinforce the absence of smoking. Since the focus of this chapter is on individual psychological interventions and most studies on competitions and incentives, including quit-and-win contests and contingency contracting, have been conducted at the population level, these will not be discussed in detail. Briefly, competitions and incentives have either a very limited or no impact on smoking cessation, and are therefore not recommended by current guidelines (Raw et al., 1998; USDHHS, 2008); however, they can improve recruitment rates to smoking cessation interventions thereby increasing the overall number of people who stop smoking (Cahill & Perera, 2008a, 2008b).

The main method used in aversive smoking is rapid smoking. Smokers are asked to puff on a cigarette every 6 to 10 seconds and continue to do so for 3 minutes or until they have either smoked three cigarettes or cannot continue. The procedure is then repeated a number of times. During this period, smokers are instructed to concentrate on the unpleasant sensory effects caused by rapid smoking. There are a number of other methods that differ to some degree from rapid smoking by reducing the level of aversive effects experienced by smokers. In paced smoking, the interpuff interval is increased to 30 seconds and is often used as an active control to rapid smoking. By contrast, rapid puffing is analogous to rapid smoking but does not involve inhalation of smoke. Self-paced/focused smoking allows smokers to smoke at their own pace while again focusing on aversive sensations. In covert sensitization or symbolic aversion, smokers imagine aversive smoking and its negative consequences, such as vomiting, as well as relief when discontinuing to smoke. Smoke holding involves participants holding drawn-in smoke in their mouth for 30 seconds while breathing through the nose and focusing on unpleasant sensations from the smoke. Finally, in excessive or satiation or oversmoking, smokers increase their daily cigarette consumption following a particular schedule (e.g., doubling number of cigarettes every other day). Obviously, it is also possible to use aversive stimuli unrelated to smoking such as electric shock or pharmacological methods but these are beyond the remit of this chapter.

The views of consensus panels have fluctuated with regard to aversive smoking interventions. While earlier guidelines endorse aversive smoking as effective (USDHHS, 2000), current guidelines either do not mention or do not recommend the use of aversive smoking given ambivalent evidence and the side effects, such as headaches and nausea, associated with this approach (Raw et al., 1998; USDHHS, 2008; West et al., 2000).

Meta-Analyses and Systematic Reviews

A recent Cochrane Review (Hajek & Stead, 2001) evaluated the state-of-the-art in aversive smoking interventions. It concluded that there is insufficient evidence to support the efficacy of aversive smoking for smoking cessation or to determine whether a dose-response relationship exists between the intensity of the intervention and a successful outcome.

The meta-analysis included 25 RCTs with at least 6 month follow-up and over 1,000 participants. The quality of studies was relatively poor as smoking cessation was not validated biochemically, outcome assessors were not blinded to group allocation, group size was often very low ($N = 20$) and little information was provided about missing drop-outs. Some studies were confounded by different therapists providing treatments. Moreover, good control conditions do not exist for this type of intervention as neither participant nor therapist can be blinded to the treatment condition. This is reflected in the heterogeneity of control conditions in the assessed trials. Given these limitations, results are likely to be biased and need to be interpreted cautiously.

Rapid smoking was assessed by 12 trials and other forms of aversive treatment (rapid puffing,

excessive smoking, focused smoking, smoke-holding, covert sensitization, and electric shock) by 10 studies; nine trials evaluated differences in efficacy of less and more aversive conditions. The meta-analysis of studies suggested that rapid smoking increased smoking cessation rates compared with control treatments; however, studies that found a positive effect tended to be of lower quality and studies adhering most stringently to standard methodological criteria produced nonsignificant results. Other forms of aversive smoking were unsuccessful in increasing abstinence but a borderline dose-response effect was detected; more intensive aversive stimulation produced better outcomes than less aversive ones.

Randomized Controlled Trials

A recent trial of a rapid smoking intervention for attendees of a smoking cessation clinic did not detect an increase in smoking cessation rates but the intervention appeared to decrease short-term craving levels (McRobbie & Hajek, 2007). This suggests that rapid smoking may work through its impact on withdrawal symptoms; however, the effect was short-lived as rapid smoking occurred only once. Another study evaluating the utility of rapid smoking for relapse prevention found that smokers who initiated smoking cessation treatment but had lapsed were not more likely to remain abstinent if they were randomly allocated to rapid smoking than smokers given standard support (Juliano, Houtsmuller, & Stitzer, 2006).

Conclusions

The literature on aversive smoking is relatively old as most studies were conducted over 20 years ago. This is reflected in the methodological inadequacy of the reviewed studies. In concordance with current guidelines, results do not offer incontrovertible evidence that aversive smoking or the use of competitions and incentives is an effective treatment for smoking cessation. Yet, the fact that positive results were observed, especially for rapid smoking, and that a dose-response effect may operate would suggest that aversive smoking may be a useful addition to existing smoking cessation interventions. However, better methodological approaches are needed to provide evidence of sufficient quality to adequately address this hypothesis.

BIOLOGICAL MARKER FEEDBACK

Consensus Panel Recommendations

Biomarkers provide biological indices of smoking-related exposure (e.g., cotinine), harm (e.g., arterial plaque), or susceptibility to increased disease risk (e.g., genetic markers), as merely telling people they are at risk of developing a disease is rarely sufficient to change behavior. Providing people with actual evidence of exposure, susceptibility, or harm may initiate and help maintain changes in smoking behavior by altering cognitive antecedents of behavior change (McClure, 2004). Such interventions personalize risk, increase attention, and stimulate smokers to participate in cessation programs. By raising fear levels, feedback may add to the list of reasons to take health-protective action (Petty, Cacioppo, Sedikides, & Strathman, 1988). Biomarker feedback should therefore motivate and reinforce quit attempts by getting smokers to engage with their fear and do something about it (Lerman, Orleans, & Engstrom, 1993).

The field of biomedical risk assessment is still evolving (Perera & Weinstein, 2000) and there is consequently little in the way of recommendations from consensus panel reviews for the treatment of tobacco dependence. Earlier UK smoking cessation guidelines found no scientific evidence for effectiveness of carbon monoxide monitors used alone (Raw et al., 1998); however, the U.S. guidelines (USDHHS, 2008) stated that modest evidence exists to suggest that biomarker feedback can motivate quit attempts but that too little

information was available to make strong recommendations regarding its effectiveness for smoking cessation. The panel also cautioned that it is currently unclear how biomarker feedback affects those smokers with few signs of exposure, risk, or harm of smoking-related diseases. For instance, genetic risk feedback may make smokers feel secure if no genetic vulnerability is detected. If it is detected common perceptions of immutability of genetic risk may reduce motivation to change behavior thus both a positive or negative outcome may potentially reinforce smoking (Marteau & Lerman, 2001).

Meta-Analyses and Systematic Reviews

Two reviews (Bize, Burnand, Mueller, & Cornuz, 2005; McClure, 2001) have evaluated the use of biomarkers in smoking cessation. The former concluded that due to a lack of good quality evidence no definite statements can be made about the use of biomarker feedback for smoking cessation and that existing evidence of lower quality does not support the view that biological risk assessment increases smoking cessation rates compared with standard treatment. By contrast, the latter review found that preliminary evidence is promising and that biomarker feedback may enhance the likelihood of cessation based on a number of RCTs evidencing a trend toward increased abstinence when feedback is provided.

The reviews included a total of 12 RCTs that used a variety of biomarkers and different methodologies and had more than 5,000 participants. Study methodology was judged to be fairly poor as many trials provided little detail, used suboptimal randomization procedures, failed to appropriately match the intensity of treatment and control conditions, did not use blinded outcome assessment, and relied on self-report to determine smoking cessation. The range of biomarkers about which feedback was given included expired-air carbon monoxide, genetic risk markers, carotid ultrasound scans, and lung function using spirometry.

Trials were carried out in multiple settings and populations varying from inpatients on hospital wards, outpatients in primary care, to the general public in screening centers. Some studies provided single biomarker feedback while others combined several biomarkers.

All studies found evidence that biological feedback was significantly or near-significantly associated with either smoke reduction and/or increased attempts to quit and remain abstinent, suggesting that motivation to quit was improved across studies as, indeed, was the case where this was explicitly measured. Significant continuous abstinence could not be sustained in the majority of trials, and only one study (Bovet, Perret, Cornuz, Quilindo, & Paccaud, 2002), which provided feedback about the existence of carotid plaque, produced an unambiguous positive result. Two studies (Jamrozik et al., 1984; Sanders et al., 1989) reported increased cessation for carbon monoxide feedback but only when compared with a low not a high intensity control condition. Neither spirometry nor genetic risk feedback appeared to increase quit rates. There was no clear association between the number of biomarkers used to provide feedback and smoking cessation.

Randomized Controlled Trials

Since the reviews were published several RCTs have further investigated the use of biomarkers in smoking cessation interventions. While these still suffer from methodological limitations, they provide some evidence for the potential efficacy of biomarker feedback. An RCT providing feedback on expired air carbon monoxide reported an effect intention to stop smoking and on smoking cessation at 6 months; however, this increase in cessation was only observed among those with higher self-efficacy (Shahab, West, & McNeill, 2011). Two studies (Barnfather, Cope, & Chapple, 2005; Cope, Nayyar, & Holder, 2003) used a point of care test of a nicotine metabolite given to pregnant smokers or the general population; feedback increased

smoking cessation rates. A trial in which spirometry was used to compare smokers' chronological age with their lung age reported that smokers given feedback about their increased lung age were more likely to stop smoking (Parkes, Greenhalgh, Griffin, & Dent, 2008). In a small pilot study, cardiovascular patients were shown images of their carotid artery evidencing plaque that resulted in an increase in smoking cessation behaviors and intention to stop smoking but not cessation (Shahab, Hall, & Marteau, 2007). Last, in agreement with previous findings, a study that gave feedback on genetic cancer susceptibility showed no effect on smoking cessation rates in hospital patients (Ito et al., 2006).

Conclusions

In concordance with expert panels, there is currently insufficient evidence to support the use of feedback of biological markers, especially of genetic risk, to increase smoking cessation rates. Biomarker feedback may increase cognitive antecedents of behavior change and quit attempts compared with standard interventions. Moreover, evidence is accumulating to suggest that feedback of arterial plaque, nicotine metabolites, spirometry results framed in terms of lung age and, less so, expired air carbon monoxide may increase smoking abstinence. Yet, a number of these studies have been criticized for methodological weaknesses (Coleman, 2005; Stapleton, 2005) and, thus, positive results need to be considered with caution. Future research therefore needs to improve methodological quality to clarify results and elucidate potential underlying psychological mechanisms that facilitate behavior change instigated by biomarker feedback.

HYPNOTHERAPY

Consensus Panel Recommendations

Hypnotherapy involves the use of exercises to induce deep relaxation and perhaps an *altered state of consciousness* that has been successfully used in combination with other therapies to change behavior patterns (Kirsch & Lynn, 1995). Hypnotherapy for smoking cessation is commonly based on modifications of the one session, three-point method when smokers in trance or deep relaxation are instructed that smoking is a poison that their body should be allowed to protect itself from and that life as a nonsmoker is better (H. Spiegel, 1964). Smokers may also be trained in self-hypnosis to apply as and when needed to strengthen the impact of a single session (N. W. Katz, 1980). It is claimed that the ability of hypnosis to influence underlying, subconscious impulses should reduce desire to smoke, focus smokers on cessation treatments, and increase their motivation to stop (D. Spiegel, Frischholz, Fleiss, & Spiegel, 1993).

There is little evidence to support its application as an adjunct to smoking cessation interventions. United Kingdom (Raw et al., 1998) and U.S. expert panels (USDHHS, 2008) have stated that there is insufficient evidence to recommend the use of hypnotherapy for smoking cessation as too few hypnotherapy trials exist that are sufficiently scientifically rigorous to justify their inclusion in the guidelines. Yet, hypnotherapy remains a very popular method for smoking cessation (Royal College of Physicians, 2000) and, although not proven to be efficacious, may still produce positive outcomes through nonspecific and placebo effects.

Meta-Analyses and Systematic Reviews

Two reviews (Abbot, Stead, White, Barnes, & Ernst, 2000; Green & Lynn, 2000) evaluated the application of hypnotherapy for smoking cessation. The first concluded that hypnotherapy does not increase abstinence rates at 6 months compared with control conditions but the second review finds that hypnotherapy is superior to no treatment or waiting-list control conditions; however, the latter review argues that since similar, nonhypnosis-based techniques such as relaxation produce equivalent results, the effect of hypnosis is nonspecific

and can therefore only be considered possibly efficacious.

Both reviews included a total of 18 RCTs with nearly 1,500 participants. A large number of studies had very small sample sizes ($N < 25$ per group) undermining the reliability of results. In addition, the majority of studies did not specify whether allocation concealment was achieved, whether outcome assessment was blinded, and few trials biochemically verified smoking status. Studies varied substantially in terms of follow-up from 1 week to 10 months and the type and length of hypnotic induction and control conditions. The total duration of hypnosis provided ranged from 30 minutes to 7 hours. Control conditions included waiting lists, health education, nonspecific psychological treatment, relaxation, rapid smoking, and counseling. In several studies, experimenters were confounded with condition as different people carried out treatment and control interventions. As there was scarce description of the exact hypnotic techniques used, it was impossible to compare the effectiveness of different types of hypnosis.

Since no suitable placebo for hypnotherapy exists to control for nonspecific effects, the interpretation of results is difficult. There was significant heterogeneity regarding the impact of hypnosis compared with specific control conditions. Trials comparing hypnosis with no treatment generally found a positive effect, though not all have (Lambe, Osier, & Franks 1986), while studies contrasting hypnosis with an attention-matched or health-education control produced conflicting results with significant effects restricted to trials with very small samples. Two studies (Pederson, Scrimgeour, & Lefcoe, 1975, 1979) found that adding hypnotherapy to counseling increased quit rates compared with counseling alone but both trials had fewer than 20 participants per group and smoking cessation rates in the control condition were very low. There was no empirical support for the effectiveness of hypnosis compared with relaxation techniques, nonspecific psychological treatment, or rapid smoking. Neither could a duration effect be observed where this was compared. In terms of individual differences, few consistent results emerged; however, a meta-analysis (Green, Lynn, & Montgomery, 2006) reported that men may be more likely to benefit from hypnotherapy for smoking cessation than women.

Randomized Controlled Trials

A recent study, not included in the reviews, randomized hospitalized patients to a *cold turkey* control condition and to hypnotherapy, to NRT, or to both (Hasan, Pischke, Saiyed, Macys, & McCleary, 2007). Hypnotherapy was more effective than NRT or the control condition but the study sample was small (N 67) and point prevalence rates were not objectively verified.

Conclusions

Hypnotherapy does not confer a treatment-specific effect in smoking cessation interventions. Studies evidencing a positive effect tend to have poor methodological quality and many studies make it hard to delineate the explicit effects of hypnosis from relaxation, CBT, and other types of interventions. It is therefore impossible to say that it is hypnosis *per se* that is responsible for the observed treatment gains. Future research should attempt to appropriately separate the specific impact of hypnosis through comparison with an adequate placebo; however, given that hypnosis appears to be more effective than waiting list controls, the current limited evidence would suggest that if smokers display a preference for hypnotherapy, they may benefit from hypnotherapy compared with no treatment.

EVIDENCE-BASED PRACTICES

Dependence on tobacco, as any form of drug dependence, represents a complex and multifaceted problem. There are many environmental, biological, and psychological factors that influence why a person starts and continues to smoke. Comprehensive research exists to inform evidence-based practice for clinicians that treat smokers on a regular basis to aid smoking cessation (see Table 8.3).

There is good evidence that face-to-face behavioral counseling is effective for increasing smoking cessation rates, and this finding has been replicated across a large number of studies including different populations of smokers and using varying counseling techniques. Proactive, but not reactive, telephone counseling has been found to reliably increase smoking abstinence. Again, this effect was observed in large study samples comprising different groups of smokers and employing diverse methodological approaches. Although self-help materials typically do not increase smoking cessation rates to a large degree, the small effect they do have is apparent in a wide range of settings and in large population samples. Individually tailored material is more effective and Internet-based self-help interventions, in particular, are likely to become increasingly important as they may produce greater abstinence rates.

The evidence for social support is mixed. While intratreatment social support is believed to aid smoking cessation, there is little or no systematic evaluation available. In contrast, extra treatment social support does not appear to confer a benefit. Aversive smoking, especially rapid smoking, has been shown to be effective for smoking cessation, but poor study quality limits the generalizability of these findings. Last, the use of hypnotherapy and biomarker feedback in smoking cessation interventions has not been unequivocally shown to increase abstinence partly due to limited data and partly due to poor study quality and heterogeneous methodology.

In general, these recommendations come with a number of caveats. It is often difficult to know which aspects of treatment are important, or if there are components that are not particularly effective as programs are typically evaluated in their entirety. For

TABLE 8.3 Evidence Summary

Treatment	Evidence	Estimated Increase of 6-Months Abstinence Rates (95% CI)[#]	Issues
Behavioral counseling	++	7% (3%–10%)	No clear intensity effect or difference for types of counseling
Telephone counseling	++	3% (2%–4%)	Mostly lacking biochemical validation; only clear evidence for proactive counseling
Self-help	+	1% (0%–2%)	Small overall effect; mixed findings; greater effects likely in interactive Internet-based interventions
Social support	–/+	3% (1%–5%)*	Limited data on extra-treatment social support/ Confounding in studies of intratreatment social support studies
Aversive smoking	+	6% (0%–13%)	Poor quality studies
Biomarker feedback	?	Not estimated	Limited data; mixed findings
Hypnotherapy	?	Not estimated	No evidence for specific effect; poor quality studies; mixed findings

++ Good evidence for clinically significant effect;
+Evidence suggestive of clinically significant effect;
?Insufficient evidence to draw general conclusions; –Evidence suggestive of no clinically significant effect
[#] Data derived from USDHHS (2000); West et al. (2000); and Stead et al. (2006)
* Intratreatment social support only

instance, even though the USDHHS guidelines recommend practical counseling and intratreatment support, it is accepted that the evidence for this is not at the strongest level. Additionally, the use of particular intervention strategies is a function of many factors including patient choice, availability, and cost. Finally, in general, the recommendations are only for cigarette smoking as there are few studies on counseling treatments for other forms of tobacco use.

It is important to note that while the focus of this chapter is on psychological approaches to the treatment of tobacco dependence, all guidelines recommend that, unless contraindicated, pharmacotherapy should be used to assist quit attempts. There exists overwhelming evidence that pharmacotherapy is effective and that it works complementary to psychological treatment as it can address different aspects of tobacco dependence, especially withdrawal symptoms such as craving (Hughes, 1995). Moreover, the relative efficacy of pharmacotherapy may be enhanced when combined with more intensive behavioral interventions

than when it is provided on its own or with behavioral interventions of lower intensity (Sutherland, 2003). For this reason, evidence-based practice should incorporate both intensive behavioral treatment and adjunctive pharmacotherapy to achieve the best results for smoking cessation.

In conclusion, there are several evidence-based treatment options for tobacco-related disorders. Research in clinical psychology and other specialties is ongoing in this area and continually improving our understanding of the processes that determine uptake, maintenance, and cessation of smoking. Developments in treatment are consequently expected to occur as new findings accumulate and will be incorporated into future recommendations and guidelines.

REFERENCES

Abbot, N. C., Stead, L. F., White, A. R., Barnes, J., & Ernst, E. (2000). Hypnotherapy for smoking cessation. *Cochrane Database of Systematic Reviews (Online)*, 2, Art. No. CD001008.

Abrams, D. B., Orleans, C. T., Niaura, R. S., Goldstein, M. G., Prochaska, J. O., & Velicer, W. (1996). Integrating individual and public health perspectives for treatment of tobacco dependence under managed health care: A combined stepped-care and matching model. *Annals of Behavioral Medicine, 18,* 290–304.

Ajzen, I. (1991). The theory of planned behavior. *Organizational Behavior and Human Decision Processes, 50,* 179–211.

American Psychiatric Association. (1995). *Diagnostic and statistical manual of mental disorders.* (4th ed., International Version ed.). Washington, DC: Author.

An, L. C., Klatt, C., Perry, C. L., Lein, E. B., Hennrikus, D. J., Pallonen, U. E., . . . Ehlinger, E. P. (2008). The RealU online cessation intervention for college smokers: A randomized controlled trial. *Preventive Medicine, 47,* 194–199.

Armour, B., Malarcher, A., Pechacek, T., & Husten, C. (2005). Annual smoking attributable mortality, years of potential life lost, and productivity losses—United States, 1997–2001. *Morbidity and Mortality Weekly Report, 54,* 625–628.

Bandura, A. (1986). *Social foundations of thought and action: A social cognitive theory.* New York, NY: Academic Press.

Barnfather, K. D., Cope, G. F., & Chapple, I. L. (2005). Effect of incorporating a 10 minute point of care test for salivary nicotine metabolites into a general practice based smoking cessation programme: Randomised controlled trial. *British Medical Journal, 331,* 999.

Barth, J., Critchley, J., & Bengel, J. (2008). Psychosocial interventions for smoking cessation in patients with coronary heart disease. *Cochrane Database of Systematic Reviews (Online), 1,* Art. No. CD006886.

Becker, M. (1974). The health belief model and personal health behavior. *Health Education Monographs, 2,* 324–508.

Benowitz, N. L. (2001). Compensatory smoking of low yield cigarettes. In National Cancer Institute (Ed.), *Risks associated with smoking cigarettes with low machine-measured yields of tar and nicotine* (pp. 39–63). Bethesda, MD: U.S. Department of Health and Human Services, National Institutes of Health, National Cancer Institute.

Benowitz, N. L., Jacob, P. III, Ahijevych, K., Jarvis, M. J., Hall, S., LeHouezec, J., . . . Velicer, W. (2002). Biochemical verification of tobacco use and cessation. *Nicotine and Tobacco Research, 4,* 149–159.

Benowitz, N. L., Kuyt, F., Jacob, P. III, Jones, R. T., & Osman, A. L. (1983). Cotinine disposition and effects. *Clinical Pharmacology and Therapeutics, 34,* 604–611.

Bize, R., Burnand, B., Mueller, Y., & Cornuz, J. (2005). Biomedical risk assessment as an aid for smoking cessation. *Cochrane Database of Systematic Reviews (Online), 4,* Art. No. CD004705.

Bovet, P., Perret, F., Cornuz, J., Quilindo, J., & Paccaud, F. (2002). Improved smoking cessation in smokers given ultrasound photographs of their own atherosclerotic plaques. *Preventive Medicine, 34,* 215–220.

Brendryen, H., Drozd, F., & Kraft, P. (2008). A digital smoking cessation program delivered through internet and cell phone without nicotine replacement (happy ending): Randomized controlled trial. *Journal of Medical Internet Research, 10,* e51.

Brendryen, H., & Kraft, P. (2008). Happy ending: A randomized controlled trial of a digital multi-media smoking cessation intervention. *Addiction, 103,* 478–484.

Breslau, N., & Johnson, E. O. (2000). Predicting smoking cessation and major depression in nicotine-dependent smokers. *American Journal of Public Health, 90,* 1122–1127.

Breslau, N., Kilbey, M. M., & Andreski, P. (1994). DSM-III-R nicotine dependence in young adults: Prevalence, correlates and associated psychiatric disorders. *Addiction, 89,* 743–754.

Cahill, K., & Perera, R. (2008a). Competitions and incentives for smoking cessation. *Cochrane Database of Systematic Reviews (Online),* Art. No. CD004307.

Cahill, K., & Perera, R. (2008b). Quit and Win contests for smoking cessation. *Cochrane Database of Systematic Reviews (Online), 4,* Art. No. CD004986.

Carlini, B. H., Zbikowski, S. M., Javitz, H. S., Deprey, T. M., Cummins, S. E., & Zhu, S. H. (2008). Telephone-based tobacco-cessation treatment: Re-enrollment among diverse groups. *American Journal of Preventive Medicine, 35,* 73–76.

Carr, A. B., & Ebbert, J. O. (2006). Interventions for tobacco cessation in the dental setting. *Cochrane Database of Systematic Reviews (Online), 1,* Art. No. CD005084.

Cassell, M. M., Jackson, C., & Cheuvront, B. (1998). Health communication on the internet: An effective channel for health behavior change? *Journal of Health Communication, 3,* 71–79.

Centers for Disease Control and Prevention. (2007). *Best practices for comprehensive tobacco control programs—2007.* Atlanta, GA: Department of Health and Human Services, Centers for Disease Control and Prevention, and Health Promotion, Office on Smoking and Health.

Choi, W. S., Patten, C. A., Gillin, J. C., Kaplan, R. M., & Pierce, J. P. (1997). Cigarette smoking predicts development of depressive symptoms among U.S. adolescents. *Annals of Behavioral Medicine, 19,* 42–50.

Coburn, R. F., Forster, R. E., & Kane, P. B. (1965). Considerations of the physiological variables that determine the blood carboxyhemoglobin concentration in man. *Journal of Clinical Investigation, 44,* 1899–1910.

Coleman, T. (2005). Near-patient tests for smoking cessation. *British Medical Journal, 331,* 979–980.

Cope, G. F., Nayyar, P., & Holder, R. (2003). Feedback from a point of care test for nicotine intake to reduce smoking during pregnancy. *Annals of Clinical Bio-chemistry, 40,* 674–679.

Curry, S. J. (1993). Self-help interventions for smoking cessation. *Journal of Consulting and Clinical Psychology, 61,* 790–803.

Davis, R., & Curvall, M. (1999). Determination of nicotine and its metabolites in biological fluids: In vivo studies. In J. Gorrod & P. Jacob, III (Eds.), *Analytical determination of nicotine and related compounds and their metabolites* (pp. 583–644). Amsterdam, The Netherlands: Elsevier Science.

De, L. J. (1996). Smoking and vulnerability for schizophrenia. *Schizophrenia Bulletin, 22,* 405–409.

Department of Health. (2008). *NHS Stop smoking services: Service and monitoring guidance—2007/8.* London, England: Author.

DiFranza, J. R., Aligne, C. A., & Weitzman, M. (2004). Prenatal and postnatal environmental tobacco smoke exposure and children's health. *Pediatrics, 113,* 1007–1015.

Doll, R., Peto, R., Boreham, J., & Sutherland, I. (2004). Mortality in relation to smoking: 50 years' observations on male British doctors. *British Medical Journal, 328,* 1519.

Doll, R., Peto, R., Wheatley, K., Gray, R., & Sutherland, I. (1994). Mortality in relation to smoking: 40 years' observations on male British doctors. *British Medical Journal, 309,* 901–911.

Ezzati, M., & Lopez, A. D. (2003). Estimates of global mortality attributable to smoking in 2000. *Lancet, 362,* 847–852.

Ezzati, M., & Lopez, A. D. (2004). Regional, disease specific patterns of smoking-attributable mortality in 2000. *Tobacco Control, 13,* 388–395.

Ezzati, M., Lopez, A. D., Rodgers, A., Vander, H. S., & Murray, C. J. (2002). Selected major risk factors and global and regional burden of disease. *Lancet, 360,* 1347–1360.

Farrell, M., Howes, S., Bebbington, P., Brugha, T., Jenkins, R., Lewis, G., . . . Meltzer, H. (2001). Nicotine, alcohol and drug dependence and psychiatric comorbidity. Results of a national household survey. *British Journal of Psychiatry, 179,* 432–437.

Ginsberg, D., Hall, S. M., & Rosinski, M. (1992). Partner support, psychological treatment, and nicotine gum in smoking treatment: An incremental study. *International Journal of Addictions, 27,* 503–514.

Global Youth Tobacco Survey Collaborative Group. (2002). Tobacco use among youth: A cross country comparison. *Tobacco Control, 11,* 252–270.

Gorin, S. S., & Heck, J. E. (2004). Meta-analysis of the efficacy of tobacco counseling by health care providers. *Cancer Epidemiology, Biomarkers & Prevention, 13,* 2012–2022.

Green, J. P., & Lynn, S. J. (2000). Hypnosis and suggestion-based approaches to smoking cessation:

An examination of the evidence. *International Journal of Clinical and Experimental Hypnosis, 48,* 195–224.

Green, J. P., Lynn, S. J., & Montgomery, G. H. (2006). A meta-analysis of gender, smoking cessation, and hypnosis: A brief communication. *International Journal of Clinical and Experimental Hypnosis, 54,* 224–233.

Griffiths, F., Lindenmeyer, A., Powell, J., Lowe, P., & Thorogood, M. (2006). Why are health care interventions delivered over the internet? A systematic review of the published literature. *Journal of Medical Internet Research, 8,* e10.

Grimshaw, G. M., & Stanton, A. (2006). Tobacco cessation interventions for young people. *Cochrane Database of Systematic Reviews (Online), 4,* Art. No. CD003289.

Gruder, C. L., Mermelstein, R. J., Kirkendol, S., Hedeker, D., Wong, S. C., Schreckengost, J., . . . Miller, T. Q. (1993). Effects of social support and relapse prevention training as adjuncts to a televised smoking-cessation intervention. *Journal of Consulting and Clinical Psychology, 61,* 113–120.

Guindon, G., & Boisclair, D. (2003). *Past, current and future trends in tobacco use.* Washington, DC: The International Bank for Reconstruction and Development/The World Bank.

Hajek, P., & Stead, L. F. (2001). Aversive smoking for smoking cessation. *Cochrane Database of Systematic Reviews (Online), 3,* Art. No. CD000546.

Hajek, P., Stead, L. F., West, R., & Jarvis, M. (2005). Relapse prevention interventions for smoking cessation. *Cochrane Database of Systematic Reviews (Online), 1,* Art. No. CD003999.

Hasan, F., Pischke, K., Saiyed, S., Macys, D., & McCleary, N. (2007). Hypnosis as an aid to smoking cessation of hospitalized patients: Preliminary results. *Chest, 4,* 527a.

Heatherton, T. F., Kozlowski, L. T., Frecker, R. C., & Fagerstrom, K. O. (1991). The Fagerstrom test for nicotine dependence: A revision of the Fagerstrom Tolerance Questionnaire. *British Journal of Addiction, 86,* 1119–1127.

Henningfield, J. E., Stapleton, J. M., Benowitz, N. L., Grayson, R. F., & London, E. D. (1993). Higher levels of nicotine in arterial than in venous blood after cigarette smoking. *Drug and Alcohol Dependence, 33,* 23–29.

Hill, S., Blakely, T., Kawachi, I., & Woodward, A. (2004). Mortality among "never smokers" living with smokers: Two cohort studies, 1981–4 and 1996–9. *British Medical Journal, 328,* 988–989.

Hollis, J. F., McAfee, T. A., Fellows, J. L., Zbikowski, S. M., Stark, M., & Riedlinger, K. (2007). The effectiveness and cost effectiveness of telephone counselling and the nicotine patch in a state tobacco quitline. *Tobacco Control, 16 Supplement 1,* i53–i59.

Hughes, J. R. (1995). Combining behavioral therapy and pharmacotherapy for smoking cessation: An update. *NIDA Research Monographs, 150,* 109.

Hughes, J. R. (2003). Motivating and helping smokers to stop smoking. *Journal of General Internal Medicine, 18*, 1053–1057.

Hyland, A., Vena, C., Bauer, J., Li, Q., Giovino, G., Yang, J., . . . Pederson, L. (2003). Cigarette smoking-attributable morbidity—United States 2000. *Morbidity and Mortality Weekly Report, 52*, 842–844.

International Agency for Research on Cancer Working Group. (2007). *IARC handbooks of cancer prevention. (Vol. II): Reversal of risk after quitting smoking.* Lyon, France: Author.

Ito, H., Matsuo, K., Wakai, K., Saito, T., Kumimoto, H., Okuma, K., . . . Hamajima, N. (2006). An intervention study of smoking cessation with feedback on genetic cancer susceptibility in Japan. *Preventive Medicine, 42*, 102–108.

Jamrozik, K. (2005). Estimate of deaths attributable to passive smoking among UK adults: Database analysis. *British Medical Journal, 330*, 812.

Jamrozik, K., Vessey, M., Fowler, G., Wald, N., Parker, G., & Van, V. H. (1984). Controlled trial of three different antismoking interventions in general practice. *British Medical Journal, 288*, 1499–1503.

Japuntich, S. J., Zehner, M. E., Smith, S. S., Jorenby, D. E., Valdez, J. A., Fiore, M. C., . . . Gustafson, D. H. (2006). Smoking cessation via the Internet: A randomized clinical trial of an internet intervention as adjuvant treatment in a smoking cessation intervention. *Nicotine and Tobacco Research, 8 Supplement 1*, S59–S67.

Jarvis, M. J. (2003). Epidemiology of cigarette smoking and cessation. *Journal of Clinical Psychiatry Monograph, 18*, 6–11.

Jarvis, M. J. (2004). Why people smoke. *British Medical Journal, 328*, 277–279.

Jarvis, M. J., & Sutherland, G. (1998). Tobacco smoking. In A. Bellack & M. Hersen (Eds.), *Health psychology volume 8. Comprehensive clinical psychology* (pp. 645–674). New York, NY: Pergamon.

Jarvis, M. J., Tunstall-Pedoe, H., Feyerabend, C., Vesey, C., & Saloojee, Y. (1987). Comparison of tests used to distinguish smokers from nonsmokers. *American Journal of Public Health, 77*, 1435–1438.

Jha, P., & Chaloupka, F. J. (1999). *Curbing the epidemic: Governments and the economics of tobacco control.* Washington, DC: World Bank.

Juliano, L. M., Houtsmuller, E. J., & Stitzer, M. L. (2006). A preliminary investigation of rapid smoking as a lapse-responsive treatment for tobacco dependence. *Experimental and Clinical Psychopharmacology, 14*, 429–438.

Kabende, L., Teplinskaya, A., Malarcher, A., Husten, C., & Maurice, E. (2007). State-specific prevalence of cigarette smoking among adults and quitting among persons aged 18–35—United States, 2006. *Morbidity and Mortality Weekly Report, 56*, 993–996.

Katz, D. A., Muehlenbruch, D. R., Brown, R. L., Fiore, M. C., & Baker, T. B. (2004). Effectiveness of implementing the agency for healthcare research and quality smoking cessation clinical practice guideline: A randomized, controlled trial. *Journal of the National Cancer Institute, 96*, 594–603.

Katz, N. W. (1980). Hypnosis and the addictions—A critical review. *Addictive Behaviors, 5*, 41–47.

Kenkel, D., & Chen, L. (2000). Consumer information and tobacco use. In P. Jha & F. J. Chaloupka (Eds.), *Tobacco control in developing countries* (pp. 177–214). Oxford, England: Oxford University Press.

Kirsch, I., & Lynn, S. J. (1995). The altered state of hypnosis—Changes in the theoretical landscape. *American Psychologist, 50*, 846–858.

Kotz, D., & West, R. (2008). Explaining the social gradient in smoking cessation: It's not in the trying, but in the succeeding. *Tobacco Control.* doi:10.1136/tc.2008.025981

Kozlowski, L. T., Porter, C. Q., Orleans, C. T., Pope, M. A., & Heatherton, T. (1994). Predicting smoking cessation with self-reported measures of nicotine dependence: FTQ, FTND, and HSI. *Drug and Alcohol Dependence, 34*, 211–216.

Lambe, R., Osier, C., & Franks, P. (1986). A randomized controlled trial of hypnotherapy for smoking cessation. *Journal of Family Practice, 22*, 61–65.

Lancaster, T., Hajek, P., Stead, L. F., West, R., & Jarvis, M. J. (2006). Prevention of relapse after quitting smoking: A systematic review of trials. *Archives of Internal Medicine, 166*, 828–835.

Lancaster, T., & Stead, L. F. (2005a). Individual behavioural counselling for smoking cessation. *Cochrane Database of Systematic Reviews (Online), 2*, Art No CD001292.

Lancaster, T., & Stead, L. F. (2005b). Self-help interventions for smoking cessation. *Cochrane Database of Systematic Reviews (Online), 3*, Art No CD001118.

Lerman, C., Orleans, C. T., & Engstrom, P. F. (1993). Biological markers in smoking cessation treatment. *Seminars in Oncology, 20*, 359–367.

Levitt, C., Shaw, E., Wong, S., & Kaczorowski, J. (2007). Systematic review of the literature on postpartum care: Effectiveness of interventions for smoking relapse prevention, cessation, and reduction in postpartum women. *Birth, 34*, 341–347.

Lichtenstein, E., Glasgow, R. E., Lando, H. A., Ossip-Klein, D. J., & Boles, S. M. (1996). Telephone counseling for smoking cessation: Rationales and meta-analytic review of evidence. *Health Education and Research, 11*, 243–257.

Lightwood, J., Collins, D., Lapsley, H., & Novotny, T. (2000). Estimating the cost of tobacco use. In P. Jha & F. J. Chaloupka (Eds.), *Tobacco control in developing countries* (pp. 63–104). Oxford, England: Oxford University Press.

Lopez, A., Collishaw, N., & Piha, T. (1994). A descriptive model of the cigarette epidemic in developed countries. *Tobacco Control, 3*, 242–247.

Luker, K. A., Chalmers, K. I., Caress, A. L., & Salmon, M. P. (2007). Smoking cessation interventions in chronic obstructive pulmonary disease and the role of the family: A systematic literature review. *Journal of Advanced Nursing, 59*, 559–568.

Lumley, J., Oliver, S. S., Chamberlain, C., & Oakley, L. (2004). Interventions for promoting smoking cessation during pregnancy. *Cochrane Database of Systematic Reviews (Online), 4*, Art. No. CD001055.

Mackay, J., Eriksen, M., & Shafey, O. (2006). *The tobacco atlas.* (2nd ed.). Atlanta, GA: American Cancer Society.

Marteau, T. M., & Lerman, C. (2001). Genetic risk and behavioural change. *British Medical Journal, 322*, 1056–1059.

May, S., & West, R. (2000). Do social support interventions ("buddy systems") aid smoking cessation? A review. *Tobacco Control, 9*, 415–422.

McClure, J. B. (2001). Are biomarkers a useful aid in smoking cessation? A review and analysis of the literature. *Behavioral Medicine, 27*, 37–47.

McClure, J. B. (2004). Motivating prepartum smoking cessation: A consideration of biomarker feedback. *Nicotine and Tobacco Research, 6*, S153–S161.

McFall, S. L., Michener, A., Rubin, D., Flay, B. R., Mermelstein, R. J., Burton, D., . . . Warnecke, R. B. (1993). The effects and use of maintenance newsletters in a smoking cessation intervention. *Addictive Behaviors, 18*, 151–158.

McKay, H. G., Danaher, B. G., Seeley, J. R., Lichtenstein, E., & Gau, J. (2008). Comparing two web-based smoking cessation programs: Randomized controlled trial. *Journal of Medical Internet Research, 10*, e40.

McNeill, A., Raw, M., Whybrow, J., & Bailey, P. (2005). A national strategy for smoking cessation treatment in England. *Addiction, 100*, 1–11.

McRobbie, H., & Hajek, P. (2007). Effects of rapid smoking on post-cessation urges to smoke. *Addiction, 102*, 483–489.

Mermelstein, R., Lichtenstein, E., & McIntyre, K. (1983). Partner support and relapse in smoking-cessation programs. *Journal of Consulting and Clinical Psychology, 51*, 465–466.

Miller, N. H., Smith, P. M., DeBusk, R. F., Sobel, D. S., & Taylor, C. B. (1997). Smoking cessation in hospitalized patients. Results of a randomized trial. *Archives of Internal Medicine, 157*, 409–415.

Mino, Y., Shigemi, J., Otsu, T., Tsuda, T., & Babazono, A. (2000). Does smoking cessation improve mental health? *Psychiatry and Clinical Neurosciences, 54*, 169–172.

Moher, M., Hey, K., & Lancaster, T. (2005). Workplace interventions for smoking cessation. *Cochrane Database of Systematic Reviews (Online), 2*, Art. No. CD003440.

Moller, A., & Villebro, N. (2008). Interventions for preoperative smoking cessation. *Cochrane Database of Systematic Reviews (Online), 3*, Art. No. CD002294.

Morgan, G. D., Ashenberg, Z. S., & Fisher, E. B., Jr. (1988). Abstinence from smoking and the social environment. *Journal of Consulting and Clinical Psychology, 56*, 298–301.

Myung, S. K., McDonnell, D. D., Kazinets, G., Seo, H. G., & Moskowitz, J. M. (2009). Effects of Web- and computer-based smoking cessation programs: meta-analysis of randomized controlled trials. *Archives of Interna Medicine, 169*, 929–937.

National Cancer Institute. (1999). *Health effects of exposure to environmental tobacco smoke: The report of the California Environmental Protection Agency* [Smoking and tobacco monograph no.10] (99-4645 ed.). Bethesda, MD: National Institutes of Health.

National Institute for Health & Clinical Excellence (NICE). (2008). *Smoking cessation services in primary care, pharmacies, local authorities and workplaces, particularly for manual working groups, pregnant women and hard to reach communities.* (Rep. No. NICE public health guidance 10). London, England: Author.

Noar, S. M., Benac, C. N., & Harris, M. S. (2007). Does tailoring matter? Meta-analytic review of tailored print health behavior change interventions. *Psychological Bulletin, 133*, 673–693.

Orleans, C. T., Boyd, N. R., Bingler, R., Sutton, C., Fairclough, D., Heller, D., . . . Baum, S. (1998). A self-help intervention for African American smokers: Tailoring cancer information service counseling for a special population. *Preventive Medicine, 27*, S61–S70.

Ossip-Klein, D. J., Carosella, A. M., & Krusch, D. A. (1997). Self-help interventions for older smokers. *Tobacco Control, 6*, 188–193.

Pan, W. (2006). Proactive telephone counseling as an adjunct to minimal intervention for smoking cessation: A meta-analysis. *Health Education and Research, 21*, 416–427.

Park, E. W., Schultz, J. K., Tudiver, F., Campbell, T., & Becker, L. (2004). Enhancing partner support to improve smoking cessation. *Cochrane Database of Systematic Reviews (Online), 3*, Art. No. CD002928.

Parkes, G., Greenhalgh, T., Griffin, M., & Dent, R. (2008). Effect on smoking quit rate of telling patients their lung age: The Step2quit randomised controlled trial. *British Medical Journal, 336*, 598–600.

Peate, I. (2005). The effects of smoking on the reproductive health of men. *British Journal of Nursing, 14*, 362–366.

Pederson, L. L., Scrimgeour, W. G., & Lefcoe, N. M. (1975). Comparison of hypnosis plus counseling, counseling alone, and hypnosis alone in a community-service smoking withdrawal program. *Journal of Consulting and Clinical Psychology, 43*, 920.

Pederson, L. L., Scrimgeour, W. G., & Lefcoe, N. M. (1979). Variables of hypnosis which are related to success in a smoking withdrawal program. *International Journal of Clinical and Experimental Hypnosis, 27*, 14–20.

Perera, F. P., & Weinstein, I. B. (2000). Molecular epidemiology: Recent advances and future directions. *Carcinogenesis, 21*, 517–524.

Perkins, K. A., Donny, E., & Caggiula, A. R. (1999). Sex differences in nicotine effects and self-administration: Review of human and animal evidence. *Nicotine and Tobacco Research, 1*, 301–315.

Peto, R., Darby, S., Deo, H., Silcocks, P., Whitley, E., & Doll, R. (2000). Smoking, smoking cessation, and lung cancer in the UK since 1950: Combination of national statistics with two case-control studies. *British Medical Journal, 321*, 323–329.

Petty, R. E., Cacioppo, J. T., Sedikides, C., & Strathman, A. J. (1988). Affect and persuasion—A contemporary perspective. *American Behavioral Scientist, 31*, 355–371.

Pike, K. J., Rabius, V., McAlister, A., & Geiger, A. (2007). American Cancer Society's QuitLink: Randomized trial of internet assistance. *Nicotine and Tobacco Research, 9*, 415–420.

Portnoy, D. B., Scott Sheldon, L. A., Johnson, B. T., & Carey, M. P. (2008). Computer delivered interventions for health promotion and behavioral risk reduction: A meta-analysis of 75 randomized controlled trials, 1988–2007. *Preventive Medicine, 47*, 3–16.

Prochaska, J. J., Delucchi, K., & Hall, S. M. (2004). A meta-analysis of smoking cessation interventions with individuals in substance abuse treatment or recovery. *Journal of Consulting and Clinical Psychology, 72*, 1144–1156.

Prochaska, J. O., & DiClemente, C. C. (1983). Stages and processes of self change of smoking: Toward an integrative model of change. *Journal of Consulting and Clinical Psychology, 51*, 390–395.

Prochaska, J. O., & Norcross, J. C. (2001). Stages of change. *Psychotherapy, 38*, 443–448.

Rabius, V., Pike, K. J., Hunter, J., Wiatrek, D., & McAlister, A. L. (2007). Effects of frequency and duration in telephone counselling for smoking cessation. *Tobacco Control, 16 Suppl 1*, i71–i74.

Ranney, L., Melvin, C., Lux, L., McClain, E., & Lohr, K. N. (2006). Systematic review: Smoking cessation intervention strategies for adults and adults in special populations. *Annals of Internal Medicine, 145*, 845–856.

Raw, M., McNeill, A., & West, R. (1998). Smoking cessation guidelines for health professionals: A guide to effective smoking cessation interventions for the health care system. *Thorax, 53, S1–*19.

Rice, V. H., & Stead, L. F. (2008). Nursing interventions for smoking cessation. *Cochrane Database of Systematic Reviews (Online) 1*, Art. No. CD001188.

Richter, K. P., Ahluwalia, H. K., Mosier, M. C., Nazir, N., & Ahluwalia, J. S. (2002). A population-based study of cigarette smoking among illicit drug users in the United States. *Addiction, 97*, 861–869.

Rigotti, N. A., Munafo, M. R., & Stead, L. F. (2007). Interventions for smoking cessation in hospitalised patients. *Cochrane Database of Systematic Reviews (Online) 3*, Art. No. CD001837. (3).

Rock, V., Malarcher, A., Kahende, J., Asman, K., Husten, C., & Caraballo, R. (2007). Cigarette smoking among adults—United States, 2006. *Morbidity and Mortality Weekly Report, 56*, 1157–1161.

Roski, J., Jeddeloh, R., An, L., Lando, H., Hannan, P., Hall, C., & Zhu, S. H. (2003). The impact of financial incentives and a patient registry on preventive care quality: Increasing provider adherence to evidence-based smoking cessation practice guidelines. *Preventive Medicine, 36*, 291–299.

Royal College of Physicians (2000). *Nicotine addiction in Britain. A report of the Tobacco Advisory Group of the Royal College of Physicians.* London, England: Author.

Russell, M. A. H., & Feyerabend, C. (1978). Cigarette smoking: dependence on high nicotine boli. *Drug Metabolism Reviews, 8*, 29–57.

Sanders, D., Fowler, G., Mant, D., Fuller, A., Jones, L., & Marzillier, J. (1989). Randomized controlled trial of anti-smoking advice by nurses in general practice. *Journal of the Royal College of General Practitioners, 39*, 273–276.

Severson, H. H., Gordon, J. S., Danaher, B. G., & Akers, L. (2008). ChewFree.com: Evaluation of a web based cessation program for smokeless tobacco users. *Nicotine and Tobacco Research, 10*, 381–391.

Shafey, O., Dolwick, S., & Guindon, G. (2003). *Tobacco control country profile 2003.* Atlanta, GA: American Cancer Society.

Shahab, L., Hall, S., & Marteau, T. (2007). Showing smokers with vascular disease images of their arteries to motivate cessation: A pilot study. *British Journal of Health Psychology, 12*, 275–283.

Shahab, L., & McEwen, A. (2009). Online support for smoking cessation: A systematic review of the literature. *Addiction, 104*, 1792–1804.

Shahab, L., West, R., & McNeill, A. (2011). A randomized, controlled trial of adding expired carbon monoxide feedback to brief stop smoking advice: Evaluation of cognitive and behavioral effects. *Health Psychology, 30*, 49–57.

Shiffman, S., Waters, A., & Hickcox, M. (2004). The nicotine dependence syndrome scale: A multidimensional measure of nicotine dependence. *Nicotine and Tobacco Research, 6*, 327–348.

Sinclair, H. K., Bond, C. M., & Stead, L. F. (2004). Community pharmacy personnel interventions for smoking cessation. *Cochrane Database of Systematic Reviews (Online) 1*, Art. No. CD003698. (1).

Sloan, F. A., Ostermann, J., & Picone, G. (2004). *The price of smoking*. Cambridge: Massachusetts Institute of Technology.

Sonnenworth, A., & Jarrett, L. (1980). *Gradwohl's clinical laboratory methods and diagnosis* (8th ed.). St. Louis, MO: Mosby.

Spiegel, H. (1964). A single treatment method to stop smoking using ancillary self-hypnosis. *International Journal of Clinical and Experimental Hypnosis, 12*, 230–238.

Spiegel, D., Frischholz, E. J., Fleiss, J. L., & Spiegel, H. (1993). Predictors of smoking abstinence following a single-session restructuring intervention with self-hypnosis. *American Journal of Psychiatry, 150*, 1090–1097.

Stapleton, J. (2005). Don't give up the CO monitor just yet. *British Medical Journal [Online]*. Retrieved from www.bmj.com/cgi/eletters/331/7523/999#120475

Stapleton, J. A., Russell, M. A., Feyerabend, C., Wiseman, S. M., Gustavsson, G., Sawe, U., & Wiseman, D. (1995). Dose effects and predictors of outcome in a randomized trial of transdermal nicotine patches in general practice. *Addiction, 90*, 31–42.

Stead, L. F., Bergson, G., & Lancaster, T. (2008). Physician advice for smoking cessation. *Cochrane Database of Systematic Reviews (Online), 2*, Art. No. CD000165.

Stead, L. F., & Lancaster, T. (2005). Group behaviour therapy programmes for smoking cessation. *Cochrane Database of Systematic Reviews (Online), 2*, Art. No. CD001007 (2).

Stead, L. F., Perera, R., & Lancaster, T. (2006). Telephone counselling for smoking cessation. *Cochrane Database of Systematic Reviews (Online), 3*, Art. No. CD002850.

Stead, L. F., Perera, R., & Lancaster, T. (2007). A systematic review of interventions for smokers who contact quitlines. *Tobacco Control, 16 Suppl 1*, i3–i8.

Sutherland, G. (2003). Evidence for counseling effectiveness for smoking cessation. *Journal of Clinical Psychiatry Monograph, 18*, 22–34.

Taylor, D. H., Jr., Hasselblad, V., Henley, S. J., Thun, M. J., & Sloan, F. A. (2002). Benefits of smoking cessation for longevity. *American Journal of Public Health, 92*, 990–996.

Thompson, B., Kinne, S., Lewis, F. M., & Woolridge, J. A. (1993). Randomized telephone smoking-intervention trial initially directed at blue-collar workers. *Journal of the National Cancer Institute [Monographs]*, 105–112.

Tyas, S. L., & Pederson, L. L. (1998). Psychosocial factors related to adolescent smoking: A critical review of the literature. *Tobacco Control, 7*, 409–420.

U.S. Department of Health and Human Services (USDHHS). (2000). *Treating tobacco use and dependence. Clinical practice guideline* (00-0032

ed.). Rockville, MD: U.S. Dept of Health and Human Services, Public Health Service.

U.S. Department of Health and Human Services (USDHHS). (2004). *The health consequences of smoking: A report of the Surgeon General*. Atlanta, GA: U.S. Department of Health and Human Services, Centers for Disease Control and Prevention, National Center Chronic Disease Prevention and Health Promotion, Office on Smoking and Health.

U.S. Department of Health and Human Services (USDHHS). (2008). *Clinical practical guidelines. Treating tobacco use and dependence—2008 update*. Rockville, MD: U.S. Department of Health and Human Services, Public Health Service.

Wagena, E. J., van der Meer, R. M., Ostelo, R. J., Jacobs, J. E., & van Schayck, C. P. (2004). The efficacy of smoking cessation strategies in people with chronic obstructive pulmonary disease: Results from a systematic review. *Respiratory Medicine, 98*, 805–815.

Walters, S. T., Wright, J. A., & Shegog, R. (2006). A review of computer and Internet-based interventions for smoking behavior. *Addictive Behaviors, 31*, 264–277.

Watkins, S. S., Koob, G. F., & Markou, A. (2000). Neural mechanisms underlying nicotine addiction: Acute positive reinforcement and withdrawal. *Nicotine and Tobacco Research, 2*, 19–37.

Webb, T. L., Joseph, J., Yardley, L., & Michie, S. (2010). Using the Internet to promote health behavior change: A systematic review and meta-analysis of the impact of theoretical basis, use of behavior change techniques, and mode of delivery on efficacy. *Journal of Medical Internet Research, 12*, e4.

Welch, S. L., & Fairburn, C. G. (1998). Smoking and bulimia nervosa. *International Journal of Eating Disorders, 23*, 433–437.

West, R. (2006a). *Theory of addiction*. Oxford, England: Blackwell Publishing Ltd.

West, R. (2006b). Tobacco control: Present and future. *British Medical Bulletin, 77*, 123–136.

West, R. (2008, September). *Evidence from reviews of behavioural interventions*. Presentation given at the annual conference of the Society for Research on Nicotine and Tobacco, Rome, Italy.

West, R., Edwards, M., & Hajek, P. (1998). A randomized controlled trial of a "buddy" systems to improve success at giving up smoking in general practice. *Addiction, 93*, 1007–1011.

West, R., & Jarvis, M. J. (2005). Tobacco smoking and mental disorder. *International Journal of Psychiatry and Behavioral Sciences, 15*, 10–17.

West, R., McNeill, A., & Raw, M. (2000). Smoking cessation guidelines for health professionals: An update. Health education authority. *Thorax, 55*, 987–999.

West, R., & Shiffman, S. (2007). *Fast facts: Smoking cessation* (2nd ed.). Oxford, England: Health Press.

Woody, G. E., Cottler, L. B., & Cacciola, J. (1993). Severity of dependence: Data from the DSM-IV field trials. *Addiction, 88,* 1573–1579.

World Health Organization (WHO). (1992). *International statistical classification of diseases and related health problems* (10th Rev.). Geneva, Switzerland: Author.

World Health Organization (WHO). (1997). *Tobacco or health: A global status report.* Geneva, Switzerland: Author.

World Health Organization (WHO). (2004). Tobacco increases the poverty of individuals and families. www.who.int/tobacco/communications/events/wntd/2004/tobaccofacts_families/en/print.html

9

Illicit Substance-Related Disorders

ELLEN VEDEL AND PAUL M. G. EMMELKAMP

OVERVIEW OF DISORDER

Diagnostic Criteria

The *Diagnostic and Statistical Manual of the American Psychiatric Association (DSM IV-TR)* (American Psychiatric Association [APA], 2000) distinguishes substance abuse from substance dependence and focuses on the maladaptive patterns of use leading to clinical significant impairment, and not on actual quantities and frequencies of use. According to the *DSM IV-TR*, an essential characteristic of substance depen dence is a cluster of cognitive, behavioral, and physiological symptoms indicating that the individual continues to use a particular substance despite significant substance related problems. The formal criteria for substance dependence are listed in Tables 9.1 and 9.2. Since only three endorsements are required, it is possible for a person to meet the current diagnostic criteria for substance dependence without having any physiological symptoms of dependence (e.g., tolerance and/or withdrawal). The *DSM IV-TR* distinguishes 12 classes of substances other than alcohol: amphetamine, caffeine, cannabis, cocaine, hallucinogen, inhalant, nicotine, opioid, phencyclidine, sedative hypnotic anxiolytic, polysubstance use, and other substances. In this chapter the most frequently abused (illicit) substances will be addressed.

SPECIFIC SUBSTANCES

Amphetamines and Methamphetamine

Methamphetamine is a powerful stimulant that can be smoked, snorted, orally ingested, or injected. An intense rush is felt at varying times depending on how taken: immediately if smoked or injected, after 5 minutes if snorted, and after 20 minutes if taken orally. The effects of methamphetamine can last up to 12 hours. Chronic methamphetamine use can result in cardiovascular problems including increased blood pressure and increased risk of stroke. An overdose can lead to convulsions and hyper thermia that are fatal if not treated immediately.

Cannabis

Cannabis refers to marijuana as well as hash ish. Marijuana is a combination of chopped up dried flowering tops, leaves, and stems of the Henna plant or *Cannabis sativa*. Hashish is the brown or black resin from the flowering tops of the same plant, shaped into small rocks. Cannabis is usually smoked, and inhalation produces a state of relaxation and mild euphoria often accompanied by heightened perceptual acuity and intensified sensory inputs. Although *DSM IV-TR* does not men tion cannabis withdrawal, there is increasing

TABLE 9.1 *DSM-IV-TR* **Criteria for Substance Abuse**

A. A maladaptive pattern of substance use leading to clinically significant impairment or distress, as manifested by one (or more) of the following, occurring within a 12-month period:
  1. Recurrent substance use resulting in a failure to fulfill major role obligations at work, school, or home.
  2. Recurrent substance use in situations in which this is physically hazardous.
  3. Recurrent substance-related legal problems.
  4. Continued substance use despite having persistent or recurrent social or interpersonal problems caused or exacerbated by the effects of the substance.
B. The symptoms have never met the criteria for substance dependence for this type of substance.

According to the *DSM-IV-TR*, an essential characteristic of substance dependence is a cluster of cognitive, behavioral, and physiological symptoms indicating that the individual continues to use a particular substance despite significant substance-related problems. The formal criteria for substance dependence are listed in Table 9.2.

Source: Reprinted with permission from the *Diagnostic and Statistical Manual of Mental Disorders, Fourth Edition, Text Revision* (Copyright © 2000). American Psychiatric Association.

evidence that it is associated with restlessness, irritability, anger, and sleep problems (Budney, Hughes, Moore, & Vandrey, 2004). Ten percent of people who start using cannabis will develop dependence and frequent use is associated with a higher risk of dependence.

Opioids

Opiates are a subclass of opioids that are alkaloids extracted from opium. Besides heroin, commonly abused opiates include morphine and codeine. Heroin use leads to immediate feelings of euphoria referred to as a rush, accompanied by a warm flushing of the skin, dry mouth, and a heavy feeling in the user's arms and legs. Effects appear within 10 seconds when injected, but 10 to 15 minutes to be felt when smoked or snorted. Chronic heroin use produces tolerance and withdrawal symptoms.

Cocaine

Cocaine is usually taken by inhalation though the nose but can also be dissolved in water and injected intravenously. Cocaine produces euphoric effects after a few minutes and this lasts from 15 to 30 minutes. Small amounts of cocaine make people energetic and talkative, which explains why it sometimes is described as an antidepressant drug. Larger amounts of cocaine intensify euphoria but can also induce anxiety, restlessness, bizarre aggressive behavior, and paranoia. The smokable form of cocaine is called crack cocaine, and got its name from the crackling sound it makes when smoked. Crack cocaine produces a more rapid and intensely euphoric high lasting from 5 to 10 minutes, sometimes described as orgasmic. Following a period of intense euphoria, an unpleasant period of restlessness, hyper-arousal, and insomnia is accompanied with a craving for more cocaine and often leads to use of sedating agents such as alcohol, heroin, sedatives, or hypnotics to counteract these effects. Cocaine dependence takes longer to develop if taken nasally whereas if smoked or injected the drug can lead to dependence within months or even weeks.

Ecstasy (Methylenedioxy-N-methylamphetamine)

Methylenedioxy-N-methylamphetamine, also known as MDMA and Ecstasy, is a stimulant with psychedelic effects. It is taken orally, and its effects last up to 6 hours. Ecstasy is often used at all-night dance events called raves, so that the user is able to dance longer. The psychological side effects include anxiety, depression, confusion, and paranoia. Potentially dangerous physical effects include increased heart rate and blood pressure, heart and kidney failure, hyperthermia and dehydration, all of which can be fatal under certain circumstances; however, only a small proportion of drug-related emergency admissions are ecstasy-related.

Hallucinogens

Most common forms of hallucinogens are lysergic diethyl amide (LSD), psilocybin, and

TABLE 9.2 *DSM-IV-TR* Criteria for Substance Dependence

A. A maladaptive pattern of substance use, leading to clinically significant impairment or distress, as manifested by three (or more) of the following, occurring at any time within a 12-month period:
1. Tolerance, as defined by either of the following:
    a. A need for markedly increased amounts of the substance to achieve intoxication or desired effect.
    b. Markedly diminished effect with continued use of the same amount of the substance.
2. Withdrawal, as manifested by either of the following:
    a. The characteristic withdrawal syndrome for the substance (criteria sets for withdrawal are listed separately for specific substances).
    b. The same (or a closely related) substance is taken to relive or avoid withdrawal symptoms.
3. The substance is often taken in larger amounts or over a longer period than was intended.
4. There is a persistent desire or unsuccessful effort to cut down or control substance use.
5. A great deal of time is spent in activities necessary to obtain the substance (for example, visiting multiple doctors or driving long distances), use the substance (for example, chain-smoking), or recover from its effects.
6. Important social, occupational, or recreational activities are given up or reduced because of substance use.
7. The substance use is continued despite knowledge of having a persistent or recurrent physical or psychological problem that is likely to have been caused or exacerbated by the substance (for example, current cocaine use despite recognition of cocaine-induced depression, or continued drinking despite recognition that a ulcer was made worse by alcohol consumption).

Source: Reprinted with permission from the *Diagnostic and Statistical Manual of Mental Disorders, Fourth Edition, Text Revision* (Copyright © 2000). American Psychiatric Association.

mescaline. Other substances with hallucinogen effects are magic mushrooms, which refers to a variety of *Psychocybin* fungi that contain various psychedelic substances. The most common effects are feelings of euphoria and altered auditory and visual perceptions, which usually, but not always, are experienced as pleasant.

Polydrug Use

Drug abusers often use a combination of alcohol and/or drugs, rather than one single drug, to counter the unpleasant side effects or withdrawal symptoms of one drug by using another. For example, crack cocaine is frequently used in combination with heroin. Crack is used in order to get a rapid kick, and subsequently heroin is used to alleviate the low and depressed feelings associated with crack use. In alcohol abuse, snorting cocaine counters the sedative effect of alcohol and enables continued alcohol use.

DEMOGRAPHIC VARIABLES AND EPIDEMIOLOGY

The National Epidemiologic Survey on Alcohol and Related Conditions (Grant et al

2004) found 12-month prevalence rates of 2.0% for drug use disorders and 8.5% for alcohol use disorders. In 2002, 9.4% of the United States population were substance abusers or substance dependent, of which 1.4% involved drug and alcohol dependence/abuse, 1.7% drug dependence/abuse, and 6.4% alcohol dependence/abuse (Substance Abuse and Mental Health Services Administration, 2002). Cannabis is the most commonly used illicit drug. In the United States, cannabis accounts for approximately three quarters of all illicit drug use, but this is not reflected in the number of admissions to addiction treatment centers. In 2002, 40% of Americans over 12 years of age had used cannabis at some time in their life and 11% of Americans had used it in the past year. Based on the National House Survey on Drug Abuse, cocaine addiction continues to be an important health problem with an estimated 1.7 million cocaine users in the United States (Substance Abuse and Mental Health Services Administration, 2001). In Europe, the prevalence of cocaine use and dependence is much lower than in the United States, the United Kingdom having the highest rate (Haasen et al., 2004). The widespread availability of amphetamines has made this a popular drug in the United States. In 2002, over 5% of people over 12 years of age reported that they had used methamphetamine at least once. It is estimated that 1.4% of people in the United States over 12 years of age have used heroin at least once in their lifetime (National Household Survey on Drug Abuse, 2001); however, heroin use is mainly restricted to small groups of habitual drug abusers. Epidemiological and clinical studies have revealed that many individuals use multiple substances. In samples of users from the community, a combination of alcohol and cannabis is the most common. In clinical samples, the use of multiple substances is even more common. In opioid dependent individuals, cocaine dependence is the most prevalent current and lifetime substance use disorder followed by alcohol and cannabis dependence (Emmelkamp & Vedel, 2006).

IMPACT OF THE DISORDER

Health

A number of medical complications may occur in individuals who use drugs. In opioid users overdose is common and needs immediate medical attention. Approximately half of all illicit drug users report at least one nonfatal overdose during their lifetime. Many injection-drug users have been infected with hepatitis B and C, which may result in chronic liver disease and risk of death from hepatitis B. Large doses of amphetamines and cocaine, and especially crack cocaine, can result in serious medical complications including ischemia or myocardial infarction. When stimulants are smoked, pulmonary complications are common. Cocaine can induce transient psychotic symptoms, such as paranoia, that typically resolve with abstinence. The term *cocaine-induced psychosis* has been used to describe this syndrome and is quite common among cocaine-dependent individuals. In addition, chronic cocaine use is often associated with *cocaine-induced delirium*. In methamphetamine users,

delusional states including paranoia and hallucinations may occur as well. Over the past decade, research has shown that a substantial number of drug abusers suffer from impairments across cognitive domains (Emmelkamp & Vedel, 2006). In chronic cocaine abusers, cognitive domains, such as attention, memory, decision making, and problem solving are often impaired. Long-term daily consumption of cannabis results in persistent cognitive impairment, even after cessation of use. The negative impact of chronic excessive drug use on brain structure and function is supported by neuro-imaging data (Volkow, Fowler, & Wang, 2003). Although some drug-induced damage is reduced after detoxification for as long as the drug use stops, the extent and the rate of cognitive recovery are highly variable and improvement may be minor (Bates, Voelbel, Buckman, Labouvie, & Barry, 2005). Substance users are more susceptible to various physical problems because of poor diet. Illicit drug users are even more likely to become ill as they have the added risk of HIV infection and AIDS through the use of unsterilized needles and unprotected sex. Moreover, unsterile needles can also lead to infection with hepatitis C. It is estimated that injection-drug use is a factor in one-third of all HIV and more than half of all hepatitis C cases in the United States. Drug consumption increases the likelihood of injury and/or death. Opiate addiction is associated with high morbidity and increased risk of premature death. The mortality rate for regular heroin users is 13 times greater than for the general population. Among those who continually use opiates, estimates are that 42.5% will die within 7.5 years (Galai, Safaeian, Vishov, Bolotin, & Celentano, 2003). The risk of premature death is somewhat lower in addicts who succeed in remaining stable and drug free than in those who continue to use opioids intermittently.

Comorbidity

Substance abusers usually have other psychiatric problems besides the need for drugs. Dual diagnosis of mental health and drug use disorders are common in clinical and community samples, but is highly prevalent among specific populations such as prisoners and the homeless (Emmelkamp & Vedel, 2006). In clinical cases comorbidity is the rule rather than the exception and is a pervasive clinical problem.

Social Problems

The social problems experienced by drug users are great. The lives of most heroin and combination drug users are increasingly centered on obtaining drugs. As an addict becomes more desperate for drugs, they resort to lying and criminal behavior to obtain the drug, including those individuals without premorbid antisocial personality traits. Some will become dealers in order to finance their addiction. A substantial number of female heroin and crack cocaine addicts turn to prostitution. Moreover, problems with housing, employment, and the law are common among cocaine users, especially among crack cocaine users. Furthermore, crack cocaine is often associated with promiscuous sexual behavior, often with unknown partners and sometimes in exchange for money or drugs.

A number of studies suggest that alcohol or drug use is associated with domestic violence, particularly violence in relationships. Notably, using drugs is also associated with a greater chance of being the victim of violence. Women may particularly initiate or increase their substance use to cope with the distress of experiencing violence by their partner. This holds for heroin, cannabis, cocaine, and crack, but not for alcohol. Couples who are both substance abusers are at a higher risk of violence in their relationship. Conflicts about money and sharing drugs often lead to arguments that escalate to partner violence. Some substance abusers become homeless. Many of them have children who live elsewhere, usually with relatives and less often in foster care (Emmelkamp & Vedel, 2006).

MOTIVATIONAL INTERVENTIONS

Lack of motivation and ambivalence about change is widely regarded as a primary obstacle in treating substance use disorders and is related to the high rate of early treatment drop out. Until the 1980s the usual therapeutic way of dealing with unmotivated patients was a confrontational approach, which was thought to be necessary to overcome the resistance of the patient, the pathological denial of substance abuse, and the perceived inherent lack of motivation about changing Substance Abuse. These characteristics were often seen as inherent qualities of the patients themselves. Around 1980, a new style of interviewing substance-abusing people who were ambivalent about change emerged (Miller, 1983). Motivational interviewing aims to elicit concerns about the problems associated with substance abuse and reasons for change from the patient, rather than directly confronting the patient as having to change. Motivational interviewing combines a supportive and empathic counseling style with a directive method for resolving ambivalence in the direction of change.

Consensus Panel Recommendations

The British National Clinical Practice Guidelines (NICE) on psychosocial interventions for drug abuse (2008) addressed the effectiveness of motivational interviewing in the context of brief interventions. Brief interventions are defined by the NICE as interventions with a maximum duration of two sessions. Common elements of brief interventions are expressing empathy, not opposing resistance, offering feedback, and focusing on reducing ambivalence about drug use and possible treatment. A number of brief interventions are based on the principles of motivational interviewing. Stand-alone brief interventions for people who misuse cannabis or stimulants and who are not in formal drug treatment decrease in drug use. There is some evidence that this is also the case for people who misuse opioids, however, in patients who already are in formal drug treatment, an additional brief intervention does not appear to have much additional effect on abstinence, with an exception for those patients that have low baseline motivation.

Randomized Controlled Trials

In the last decade, a number of studies have involved drug users. Motivational interviewing was found to be a useful adjunct to methadone treatment in drug abusers (Saunders, Wilkinson, & Phillips, 1995). Drug abusers ($N = 122$) received either motivational interviewing or psychoeducation. At 6-month follow-up, patients who had received motivational interviewing showed less relapse than the patients in the control condition. Since then, more than 15 randomized controlled trials (RCTs) demonstrated that motivational interviewing had some effects in terms of enhanced motivation in drug-dependent populations, including cannabis-dependent adolescents, opiate-dependent adults, cocaine-dependent adults, amphetamine users, and polydrug users (Dennis et al, 2004; Miller, Yahne, & Tonigan, 2003; Rohsenow et al., 2004; Secades-Villa, Fernande-Hermida, & Arnaez-Montaraz, 2004; Stephens, Roffman, & Curtin, 2000). Most studies found that motivational interviewing led to a better adherence and increased motivation, but only few studies found that motivational interviewing led to decreased drug use or abstinence. Carey et al. (1997) found that four group sessions of motivational interviewing significantly reduced HIV risk behavior in women, including substance use before sex, and decreased rates of unprotected intercourse, the mean effect size of a motivational interviewing approach being $d = 0.56$. In a following study (Carey et al., 2000), 102 women (88% African American) were assigned to either the HIV-motivational interviewing intervention or a health-promotion control group. Post-intervention and follow-up data indicated that women in the HIV-motivational intervention strengthened their risk reduction intentions

relative to controls, increased their condom use, talked more with partners about condom use and HIV testing, and were more likely to have refused unprotected sex.

Not all studies supported the effectiveness of motivational interviewing. For example, four studies found that the addition of motivational interviewing did not enhance treatment effectiveness in polydrug users (Booth, Kwiatkowski, Iguchi, Pinto, & John, 1998; Miller et al., 2003; Schneider, Casey, & Kohn, 2000) and in cocaine-dependent patients (Donovan, Rosengren, Downey, Cox, & Sloan, 2001). Further, *negative* effects were reported for motivational interviewing in mixed psychiatric inpatients with substance use disorders. Motivational interviewing did not enhance engagement in a Specialist Substance Misuse Service (SSMS) after discharge. Of those patients receiving treatment as usual, 17.3% engaged in SSMS; however, similar results were observed in those patients who received one session of motivational interviewing (16.5%) (Baker et al., 2002). These negative results of motivational interviews warrant a different approach. Alternatives for this severe dual diagnoses group might be starting the substance abuse treatment during their stay in the hospital rather than referring these patients after discharge, and increasing the intensity of the motivational interviewing intervention.

There is some evidence that motivational interviewing is more effective for those who are ambivalent or not yet motivated to change substance use than for those already motivated. In a pilot study (Stotts, Schmitz, Rhoades, & Grabowski, 2001), patients in cocaine detoxification with low motivation were more likely to complete detoxification if given motivational interviewing than no motivational interviewing, but the *reverse* was true for patients with high initial motivation. Similarly, motivational interviewing before an intensive treatment program led to less relapse in cocaine and alcohol use at 1-year follow-up, but only in less motivated patients (Rohsenow et al., 2004). In patients with higher pretreatment motivation to change, results were rather negative. Patients who at the start of treatment were highly motivated and received motivational interviewing reported a higher frequency of cocaine use and more severe alcohol problems during the following year than higher motivated individuals who did not receive motivational Interviewing. As noted by the authors: "It might be that the more permissive message used in Motivational Enhancement Therapy is maladaptive for the more motivated who may be impatient for a more directive approach" (p. 872).

Meta-Analyses

Two meta-analyses (Burke, Arkowitz, & Menchola, 2003; Hettema, Steele, & Miller, 2005) analyzed data from clinical trials on the effects of motivational interviewing on substance abuse and health behavior. Motivational interviewing was equivalent to other active treatments and superior to no treatment and placebo controls for problems involving drug abuse. Motivational interviewing resulted in a medium effect size in studies with illicit drug use. Surprisingly, Hettema et al. (2005) found that manual guided motivational interviewing was associated with smaller effect sizes compared to nonmanual guided interviewing. Further, Burke et al. (2003) found an investigator allegiance effect: Studies by the founder of motivational interviewing (W. R. Miller) resulted in better outcome than other studies. Whether this effect is due to differences in training and supervision is unclear, but it shows that results of motivational interviewing by Miller's group may not generalize to other settings. In a study conducted in the Netherlands (De Wildt et al., 2002), in which a large number of treatment centers were involved, a significant effect for treatment center was found, indicating that motivational interviewing was differentially effective in different treatment centers. Taken together, these results suggest that not all clinicians are equally effective in motivational interviewing

and that training and supervision is needed. Studies by Miller, Yahne, Moyers, Martinez, and Pirritano (2004) and Schoener, Madeja, Henderson, Ondersma, and Janisse (2006), underscore the value of training and supervision to achieve skill proficiency in motivational interviewing.

Conclusions

Results with respect to the value of motivational interviewing in drug-using patients are varied and inconclusive. In less motivated patients motivational interviewing led to a better adherence and increased motivation in some, but not all, studies but generally did not decrease drug use. Results were negative for well-motivated patients and in some centers, perhaps because of variations in clinician performance.

BEHAVIORAL INTERVENTIONS

Cue Exposure

Cravings in response to drug-related cues are presumed to play a central role in the continuation of substance use disorders, particularly in relation to lapses during treatment and relapses after treatment. In cue exposure treatment, patients are repeatedly exposed to the sights or smells of substances, such as the sight of white powder on a mirror, until the cravings elicited by these cues substantially weaken. In actual practice, cue exposure is difficult to apply, since generalization needs to be facilitated by identifying and sampling many conditioned stimuli (CS) from the start. After successful reductions in the strength of experienced craving, substance abusing patients are assumed to be more able to resist drug use when confronted with these cues in daily life. In most treatment protocols, cue exposure is not used as a stand-alone treatment, but rather as an adjunct to a broader cognitive behavioral treatment package.

Consensus Panel Recommendations

The National Clinical Practice Guidelines (NICE) on psychosocial interventions for drug abuse (2008) do not address the feasibility of cue exposure in the treatment of drug use disorders since no trials met their eligibility criteria.

Randomized Controlled Trials

Treatments using cue exposure have yielded promising results in illicit drug users (Childress et al., 1993; O'Brien, Childress, McLellan, & Ehrman, 1990; Powell, Bradley, & Gray 1993). Unfortunately, effect sizes are not reported. Others have reported negative results. For example, Dawe et al. (1993) found no difference in cue reactivity and prevention of relapse in opiate addicts treated with either cue exposure therapy or routine treatment ($d = 0.08$). In a controlled study (Marissen, Franken, Blanken, Van den Brink, & Hendriks, 2005) with 127 abstinent opiate-dependent inpatients, results were also rather negative. Although cue exposure led to reduced physiological reactivity, neither subjective craving nor mood improved after cue exposure therapy more than after a credible placebo psychotherapy. In addition, cue exposure therapy led to more dropouts and more relapses than the control condition; however, cue exposure was only conducted within the hospital setting during nine 1-hour sessions in toto. Perhaps the sessions were not frequent enough or long enough for respondent extinction to occur. Merely exposing opiate-dependent patients until craving is reduced may be insufficient, exposure should continue until no craving occurs at all. Further, therapists must correctly identify the relevant CSs: In this case, one can hardly expect that relevant cues from the scene can be reproduced within a hospital setting.

Meta-Analyses

No meta-analysis has been conducted.

Conclusions

Cue exposure therapy is probably efficacious in selected patients with illicit drug use disorders, but only as part of a more comprehensive treatment program. Cue exposure has not been shown to be effective in opiate addicts so far. It should be noted that procedures derived from the animal learning literature that should maximize the potential of respondent extinction training are rarely used in cue exposure treatments. Cue exposure therapy is based on the notion that respondent extinction results in a weakening of the initially conditioned CS–US association; however, in current conceptualizations the CS does not break original CS–US learning, that is, during extinction training CS–US learning remains intact, but new associations develop to the original CS (Conklin, & Tiffany, 2002).

CONTINGENCY MANAGEMENT AND COMMUNITY REINFORCEMENT

Based on operant conditioning, contingency management reinforces behavior other than and incompatible with drug use and related behavior, such as medication compliance, attendance of treatment sessions, and development of interests, skills, and a lifestyle incompatible with drug use. This is typically done with vouchers exchangeable for specific reinforcers. For example, biochemically verified abstinence from recent drug use is reinforced with vouchers exchangeable for retail items meeting a predetermined therapeutic goal. These vouchers are redeemable for goods and services, the value of the vouchers escalating with each successive drug-free specimen. Some studies have used take-home methadone doses as reinforcers in polydrug-abusing methadone patients (Stitzer, Iguchi, & Felch, 1992), but methadone licensing laws in various countries vary and some strictly regulate the use of take-home methadone doses. The main advantage of vouchers is that they can be handed out immediately following the desired behavior. Undesired behaviors do not generate vouchers, which causes these behaviors to become less attractive compared to behaviors that do generate vouchers. Thus, healthy and drug-related behavior can be considered concurrent operants. A number of programs also use punishment following positive drug tests including suspension of employment with subsequent loss of income, removal from house facilities, and transportation to a shelter.

In some treatment protocols, voucher-based incentive is combined with an intensive behavioral treatment known as the Community Reinforcement Approach (CRA) (Hunt & Azrin, 1973). The CRA encourages involvement in rewarding, non-drug-related alternatives to illicit drug use and is directed to change a lifestyle of substance abuse into a lifestyle that is more rewarding than substance abuse. Thus, the emphasis is not only on promoting abstinence of substance abuse, but also on social activities that are incompatible with substance use as well. Community reinforcement may contribute to persistence of abstinence after discontinuation of vouchers.

Consensus Panel Recommendations

The NICE Guidelines on psychosocial interventions for drug abuse (2008) stated that there is strong evidence that contingency management (CM) is associated with longer continuous periods of abstinence for cocaine compared to control conditions. The efficacy of CM has also been demonstrated in the treatment of other substance dependence disorders, including methamphetamine and cannabis dependence. Contingency management is also more effective than control conditions and cognitive behavioral interventions, however, these differences are not sustained at follow-up. Based on a 12-week treatment program, CM demonstrated cost-effectiveness compared to routine care over a 52-week period.

In treatment modalities where CM is combined with methadone maintenance programs, illicit drug use decreases are clinically significant compared to treatment as usual. The evidence for CM in combination with buprenorphine is weak, whether this is a result of specific trial characteristics or more fundamental, a differential effect of methadone and buprenorphine on the reward system underpinning CM is unclear. Finally, the NICE clinical practice guidelines stated that drug services should introduce contingency management for people receiving methadone maintenance treatment or naltrexone maintenance treatment.

Randomized Controlled Trials

Contingency management procedures have been found to be effective in cocaine dependent patients (Higgins & Wong, 1998; Kirby, Marlowe, Festinger, Lamb, & Platt, 1998; Silverman et al., 1998, 2002), opioid dependent patients (Bickel, Amass, Higgins, Badger, & Esch, 1997; Gruber, Chutuape, & Stitzer, 2000; Iguchi et al., 1996; Jones, Haug, Silverman, Stitzer, & Svikis, 2001; Petry & Martin, 2002; Stitzer et al., 1992), metamphetamine dependence (Peck, Reback, Yang, Rotheram-Fuller, & Shoptaw, 2005; Peirce, Petry, & Stitzer, 2006; Petry et al., 2005; Rawson et al., 2006; Roll et al., 2006; Shoptaw et al., 2006), and have also led to a reduced use of marijuana (Carroll et al. 2006; Kadden, Litt, Kabela-Cormier, & Petry, 2007; Petry, 2000). There is also some evidence that CM is effective for cocaine dependent methadone patients (Preston, Umbricht, Wong, & Epstein, 2001; Rawson et al., 2002; Silverman et al., 1996). Positive results of CM procedures have also been reported in adolescent substance users (Azrin et al., 1994; Corby, Roll, Ledgerwood, & Schuster, 2000; Kamon, Budney, & Stanger, 2005).

In contrast to most other treatments in cocaine and opioid dependence, generally high rates of retention and slightly higher rates of abstinence are reported compared to other treatment interventions. There is also some evidence that in a number of patients treatment effects continue after cessation of the contingencies (Higgins, Alessi, & Dantona, 2000). The CM interventions appear to affect the behaviors they target, and they do not readily extend to other areas. For example, Petry, Martin, and Simcic (2005) found that in cocaine-dependent methadone patients no changes in other psychosocial problems or other drug use were noted. Similarly, although the targeted cocaine use was reduced, concurrent opioid use remained fairly constant.

It is important to note that it is not the delivery of the reinforcer per se, but the *contingent* reinforcement that is effective. Stitzer et al. (1992) evaluated methadone take-home privileges as a reward for decreased illicit drug use and found take-home privileges that were contingent on drug-free urine screens more beneficial than noncontingent take-home privileges. Similarly, Silverman et al. (1996) found in cocaine-abusing patients, that contingent reinforcement based on drug-free urine screens resulted in a 42% reduction in abstinence rate for at least 10 weeks, whereas that was only the case for 17% of the yoked control patients, who received noncontingent reinforcers.

Reinforcement is usually contingent upon abstinence; however, CM reinforces completion of a wide range of non-drug-related activities, including those that are physically incompatible with drug use and those that are not (Iguchi et al., 1996, Petry, Tedford, & Martin, 2001). For example, according to Petry et al. (2001) working toward improving family relationships is an important goal for some substance abusers. Engagement in family activities may improve outcomes because family members may provide social reinforcement for both abstinence and a wide range of other healthy behavior, thus preventing relapse. Lewis and Petry (2005) investigated whether participants who selected to engage in family-related activities during CM treatment would have better outcomes than participants who did not select family activities. Family activities

included accompanying a relative to an activity such as a movie, attending a child's school play, visiting a relative in a hospital, or writing letters to a relative. Engaging in only three family activities was associated with some benefits in family functioning and drug abuse treatment outcomes. Cocaine-abusing adults who engaged in family activities remained in treatment longer, and were abstinent for more weeks. Moreover, engaging in family activities was associated with reductions in days of family conflict compared to participants who did not engage in family activities. Sindelar, Elbel, & Petry (2007) tested the cost-effectiveness of contingency management in cocaine abuse comparing lower versus higher prices as reinforcement for abstinence. The higher payout prices were found to be cost-effective across all three outcome measures: average consecutive weeks abstaining, percentage completing 12-week program, and percentage samples of drug-free urine screens.

Meta-Analyses

Several meta-analyses have been conducted regarding the effectiveness of CM. In a meta-analysis by Lussier, Heil, Mongeon, Badger, and Higgins (2006) voucher-based reinforcement therapy generated significantly better outcomes than control conditions. The average effect size was 0.32 (small). More immediate voucher delivery resulted in an effect size that was approximately twice as high (0.37) as delayed delivery (0.19). Further, greater monetary value of the voucher (> $16) resulted in a higher effect size (0.43) as compared to smaller monetary value < $5 (0.23). This meta-analysis also offers support for the efficacy of voucher-based contingency management for facilitating other therapeutic changes such as medication compliance. In a meta-analysis by Schumacher et al. (2007), a series of four RCTs evaluating CM in Birmingham, Alabama, were reanalyzed. Subjects were homeless cocaine users. The CM was more effective than day treatment. At follow-up 6 months after treatment, 55% of the CM group was abstinent as compared to 25% of the day treatment group. In a meta-analysis by Prendergast, Podus, Finney, Greenwell, and Roll (2006) on the effectiveness of community reinforcement approaches in alcohol, tobacco, or illicit drugs, the mean weighted effect size was $d = 0.42$; however, most studies did not involve illicit drug users. The CM was more effective in the treatment of opiate use ($d = 0.65$) and cocaine use ($d = 0.66$) compared to multiple drugs ($d = 0.42$).

In a recent meta-analysis by Dutra et al. (2008), the efficacy of behavioral treatments was compared to control conditions including treatment as usual or inactive treatment for cannabis, cocaine, opiate, and polysubstance abuse and dependence. Thirty-four studies were included ($N = 2340$), 16 studies on CM, of which two combined CM with cognitive behavior therapy (CBT), 13 CBT studies, and five studies on relapse prevention. The CM demonstrated the lowest dropout rates (29.4%) compared to CBT (35.3%), and CBT plus CM (44.5%). The CM produced a moderate-high effect size ($d = 0.58$), compared to CBT ($d = 0.28$) and relapse prevention ($d = 0.32$), which effect sizes are in the low to moderate range. (For description of the treatment procedures, see the Cognitive Behavior Therapy section that follows.) Two studies, combining CBT and CM, demonstrated the highest effects size ($d = 1.02$); however, regarding posttreatment abstinence, CBT plus CM demonstrated more or less similar abstinence rates (26.5%) compared to CBT (27.1%) and CM (31%). Relapse prevention (39%) resulted in the highest levels of abstinence.

Conclusions

Community reinforcement approaches are probably the most effective interventions for illicit drug use disorders. Although there is some evidence that the combination of community reinforcement and CBT is slightly more effective than community reinforcement

as stand-alone treatment, this is based on only a few studies.

COGNITIVE BEHAVIOR THERAPY

Cognitive behavior therapy is a pragmatic mix of traditional behavior therapy, behavior analytic approaches—although this is rarely acknowledged—and cognitive interventions. In the treatment of substance use disorders, CBT emphasizes overcoming skill deficits. Different techniques are used to increase the person's ability to detect and cope with high-risk situations that commonly precipitate relapse. These include interpersonal difficulties as well as intrapersonal discomfort, such as anger, social and other anxiety, and depression. The CBT approaches focus on teaching new strategies and skills for dealing with drug craving and reducing problem behaviors and problematic cognitions through modeling, behavioral practice, homework assignments, and cognitive therapy. The CBT helps patients identify the patterns associated with the perpetuation and maintenance of substance use (functional assessment), and implement new strategies for more effectively coping with antecedents of substance use. Although earlier studies distinguished treatments based on the relapse prevention model of Marlatt and Gordon (1985) from coping skills training (e.g., Monti, Rohsenow, Michalec, Martin, & Abrams, 1997), more recently these approaches are integrated into CBT programs. There is no evidence for the effectiveness of purely cognitive interventions (e.g., Beck, Wright, Newman, & Liese, 1993).

Consensus Panel Recommendations

The NICE Guidelines on psychosocial interventions for drug abuse (2008) concluded that CBT might be effective with cannabis dependence, but is ineffective for cocaine. The conclusion with respect to cocaine was based on the outcomes of eight RCTs only.

including a study on telephone-based continuing care (McKay, Lynch, Shepard, & Pettinati, 2005) and a study on maintenance treatment with substance abusers including alcoholics and cannabis- and/or cocaine-dependent patients (T. G. Brown, Seraganian, Tremblay, & Annis, 2002).

Randomized Controlled Trials

In contrast to the conclusions of the NICE guidelines, there are a number of studies with primarily cocaine-dependent patients that show favorable effects for CBT. Several coping skills-based treatments designed specifically for patients with cocaine abuse or dependence have resulted in significant improvements in cocaine use outcomes. In cocaine-dependent patients, relapse prevention based on CBT principles was more effective than interpersonal psychotherapy and clinical management (Carroll, Rounsaville, & Gawin, 1991; Carroll et al., 1994, 2004). For depressed cocaine abusers, CBT relapse prevention produced better drug use outcomes and retention as compared to supportive clinical management (Carroll, Nich, & Rounsaville, 1995). Brief, individual, cocaine-specific coping skills training based on functional assessment of high risk situations was added to full treatment programs and found to result in significantly less frequent cocaine use compared to a control procedure during the first 3 to 6 months following discharge (Monti et al. 1997; Rohsenow et al. 2004).

A number of studies compared coping skills training with the twelve-step approach based on the principles of Alcoholics Anonymous and Narcotics Anonymous (see later), but results are inconclusive. In the study by Maude-Griffin et al. (1998), CBT was more effective than the 12-step approach. Carroll, Nich, Ball, McCance, and Rounsaville (1998) reported that CBT was as effective as the 12-step approach in terms of reduced cocaine use over time and both treatments were more effective than supportive psychotherapy. In a study of cocaine abusers by Wells, Peterson, Gainey, Hawkins, and Catalano (1994), relapse prevention-based CBT was as equally effective as a 12-step recovery support group: Both treatments led to a considerable reduction in cocaine use at 6-month follow-up; however, the 12-step patients showed significantly greater increases than the relapse prevention patients in alcohol use from 12 weeks to the 6-month follow-up. Further, in a study by McKay et al. (1997), group counseling based on the 12-step enhancement was superior in terms of total abstinence. Given that this is the explicit goal in the 12-step approach, this does not come as a surprise. Relapse prevention-based CBT resulted in less relapse than the 12-step facilitating counseling group. Further, relapse prevention fared better in limiting the extent of cocaine use in the patients still using. In contrast, Crits-Christoph et al. (1999) found that the 12-step approach was more effective than CBT in terms of drug use at the 1-year follow-up. Of note, the CBT condition in the Crits-Christoph et al. study consisted of solely cognitive interventions based on Beck et al. 1993. In sum, there is considerable evidence that relapse prevention-based CBT is effective in the treatment of cocaine use disorders; there is no evidence, however, that cognitive therapy is effective with these disorders.

Results in drug disorders other than cocaine are inconclusive. In amphetamine users, Hawkins, Catalano, Gillmore, and Wells (1989) found coping skills training slightly more effective than a therapeutic community 1 year after treatment, but the difference failed to reach significance. Baker et al. (2005) found that there was a significant increase in the likelihood of abstinence from amphetamines among those receiving two or more treatment sessions of motivational interviewing and coping skills training (between group effect size: 0.20); however, apart from abstinence rate, the group who did not receive motivational interviewing and coping skills training improved equally well. Reduction in amphetamine use was accompanied by significant improvements in stage of change, polydrug use, injecting risk-taking behavior, criminal activity level, and psychiatric distress and depression level. In a study on heroin and metaphetamine users (Yen, Wu, Yen, & Ko, 2004) five sessions of coping skills training resulted in enhanced confidence in managing risk situations, but reductions in drug use were not reported. Rawson et al. (2004) compared treatment as usual with a multicomponent treatment for methamphetamine dependence that included group CBT, group family education, group social support, and individual counseling over 4 months. Both groups improved significantly. The multicomponent treatment was slightly superior during treatment in terms of increased attendance, more drug-free urine samples and longer periods of abstinence, but the superiority of the multicomponent treatment was lost at follow-up. Peck et al. (2005) compared CBT and CM and with a combination of both approaches and found all three treatments to be equally effective; however, the combined approach led to better treatment attendance.

In marijuana users, early studies into relapse prevention based CBT led to mixed results. In a study by Stephens, Roffman, and Curtin (2000), a relapse prevention support group resulted in 37% abstinence rate at 16 month follow-up, which did not differ from the percentage abstinence in patients receiving a brief motivational intervention. In an earlier study, only 15% of the patients were abstinent at 1 year follow-up (Stephens, Roffman, & Simpson, 1994). More recently, a multisite randomized controlled trial compared three conditions: (1) two sessions of motivational interviewing, (2) nine sessions of both motivational interviewing and CBT, and (3) waitlist control. The nine-session treatment reduced marijuana use more than the two-session motivational interviewing. Both treatments were more effective than the waitlist control condition. Most differences between treatments were maintained over the follow-up period (Marijuana Treatment Project Research Group, 2004). There is considerable evidence that opioid dependence

methadone maintenance treatment is effective in decreasing heroin use (Emmelkamp & Vedel, 2006). There is relatively little evidence available that CBT might enhance methadone maintenance treatment. Scherbaum et al. (2005) found that a 20-week group CBT program as an add-on to methadone maintenance led to a small but insignificant difference in drug use at the end of the intervention period compared with methadone maintenance alone. During the follow-up period, however, this difference increased and was significant after the 6-month follow-up. In a study by Hayes et al. (2004), there was also some evidence that adding a particular variant of CBT, Acceptance and Commitment Therapy, to methadone maintenance treatment resulted in better outcome than methadone maintenance treatment on its own.

Meta-Analyses

In a meta-analysis by Irvin, Bowers, Dunn, and Wang (1999), relapse prevention based CBT in substance abuse disorders resulted in a rather modest effect size ($d = 0.25$) that tended to decrease over time. Relapse prevention was most effective in alcohol use disorders in contrast to drug use and smoking. Further, relapse prevention was found to have more effect on psychosocial functioning than on alcohol use. In the meta-analysis of Dutra et al. (2008), the efficacy of CBT was compared to treatment as usual or inactive treatment. The CBT and relapse prevention effect sizes were in the low to moderate range: CBT ($d = 0.28$) and relapse prevention ($d = 0.32$). In contrast, CM produced a moderate to high effect size ($d = 0.58$). Finally, a Cochrane Review (2007) on the treatment of stimulant drugs is of some interest. Knapp, Soares, Farrell, and Silva de Lima (2007) identified 27 RCTs involving 3,663 participants who were dependent on crack or intravenous cocaine or oral amphetamine (one study only). Overall, CBT reduced dropouts from treatment and reduced the use of drugs when compared with drug counseling

The CBT also clearly performed better than clinical management or as usual care.

Conclusions

There is consistent evidence that CBT and relapse prevention are more effective than inactive control conditions, but effect sizes are slightly smaller than those of CR approaches. Results of CBT and relapse prevention with illicit drug users are generally comparable to those achieved with 12-step approaches.

BEHAVIORAL COUPLE THERAPY

In general, behavioral couple therapy (BCT) for substance use disorders focuses on: (a) self-control and coping skills to facilitate and maintain abstinence, (b) improving spouse's ability to cope with substance use-related situations, (c) improving relationship functioning in general, and (d) improving functioning within other social systems the couple is currently involved in. The degree of emphasis on each of these four domains and the techniques used to target these domains varies across different treatment protocols.

Consensus Panel Recommendations

The NICE guideline concluded that BCT was associated with reductions in illicit drug use. This conclusion was based on only three RCTs.

Randomized Controlled Trials

Fals-Stewart, Birchler, and O'Farrell (1996) investigated the value of adding BCT to individual CBT in male polysubstance abusers. Couples who received additional BCT had more positive dyadic adjustment and less time separated compared to couples in which the patient received individual-based treatment only. Further, patients in the combined BCT condition used less drugs and had longer periods of abstinence through the 12-month follow-up period ($d = 0.75$; see Powers, Vedel, & Emmelkamp, 2008); however, some differences in drug use and relationship adjustment between treatment conditions dissolved over the course of 12-month follow-up (Fals-Stewart, Birchler, & O'Farrell, 1996; Fals-Stewart et al., 2000). Similar results were also found in the treatment of female polydrug-abusing patients (Winters, Fals-Stewart, O'Farrell, Birchler, & Kelly, 2002). Comparing the BCT condition consisting of group, individual, and BCT sessions, with an equally intensive individual-based CBT condition, those couples receiving behavioral couple therapy reported fewer substance uses, longer periods of abstinence, and higher relationship satisfaction; however, differences disappeared during follow-up and were no longer significant by the end of 1-year posttreatment. Kelly (2003) compared CBT alone or in combination with either BCT or psychoeducation control among 64 polysubstance-abusing men. At posttreatment, CBT plus BCT was equivalent to comparison conditions in frequency of use and superior on relationship satisfaction; however, at follow-up CBT plus BCT outperformed CBT alone and CBT plus psychoeducation on drug abuse and relationship satisfaction.

In the treatment of substance-abusing patients entering methadone maintenance treatment, patients either received individual-based methadone maintenance or an equally intensive BCT treatment condition, including couples therapy as well as individual counseling. Patients in the BCT condition had fewer opiate- and cocaine-positive urine samples during treatment compared to patients in the standard treatment condition, and at posttreatment reported higher levels of dyadic adjustment and a greater reduction in drug use severity (Fals-Stewart, O'Farrell, & Birchler, 2001).

Meta-Analyses

In a meta-analysis, Powers, Vedel, and Emmelkamp (2008) tested the effectiveness of

BCT compared to individually focused treatment formats, treatment as usual, and CBT for substance use disorders. A comprehensive literature search produced 12 RCT ($N = 754$) that were included in the final analyses, including four studies with illicit drug users. There was a clear overall advantage of BCT compared to individual-based treatments ($d = 0.54$). This was true across outcome domains (frequency of use $d = 0.36$, consequences of use $d = 0.52$, and relationship satisfaction $d = 0.57$). BCT was superior to control conditions only in relationship satisfaction at posttreatment ($d = 0.64$); however, from 3-month to 2-year follow-up, BCT outperformed individual treatment, both with respect to relationship function and substance use. Although the results were not analyzed separately for alcohol abuse and drug abuse, the effect sizes for the drug studies were more or less comparable to the effect sizes for alcohol studies.

Conclusions

BCT is as least as effective as individual CBT and may be more effective in the long run (Powers et al., 2008).

12-STEP ORIENTED TREATMENT PROGRAMS

Treatment and recovery for substance abuse often involves multifaceted approaches, not only in including treatment of the addiction by a professional, but in a number of cases participation in Alcoholics Anonymous (AA) and Narcotics Anonymous (NA) as well. Alcoholics Anonymous was founded in the United States in 1935 and since the mid 1940s has spread around the world. The basic philosophy is summarized in 12 steps, which "are a group of principles, spiritual in their nature, which is practiced as a way of life, can expel the obsession to drink and enable the sufferer to become happily and usefully whole" (p. 15). Narcotics Anonymous (NA) and Cocaine

Anonymous (CA) are the primary self-help group available in many countries offering assistance for recovery from illicit drug use problems. These self-support groups are international fellowships based on the program and organizational traditions first espoused by AA (Kelly, 2003). Self-help groups based on the NA and CA framework offer a 12-step program, regular group meetings, and other assistance for people recovering from substance abuse problems. Enthusiasm for the 12-step approach is high among clinicians in the United States (Forman, Bovasso, & Woody, 2001). In 1988, 95% of U.S. inpatient alcohol treatment programs incorporated AA and NA into their programs (H. P. Brown, Peterson, & Cunningham, 1988). Further, approximately 30% of patients meeting the criteria for substance abuse or dependence in general hospitals attend AA or NA meetings (Johnson, Phelps, & McCuen, 1990). In societies outside the United States, there appears to be much less interest in this approach by substance abuse workers (Day, Lopez Gaston, Furlong, Murali, & Copello, 2005; Luty, 2004). There are nearly twice as many AA and NA fellowships in the United States as in all other countries combined.

Consensus Panel Recommendations

The NICE (2008) guidelines on psychosocial interventions for drug abuse stated that staff working in addiction treatment should routinely provide information to patients about self-help groups and consider facilitating the initial contact.

Randomized Controlled Trials

Twelve-step self-help groups are typically recommended for drug-dependent patients as well, but few studies separate individuals dependent on alcohol alone from those with drug dependence as their primary problem. Benefits of 12-step affiliation have been reported among samples of alcohol and/or drug abusers combined (Christo & Franey, 1995; Miller & Hoffman, 1995; Ouimette, Moos, & Finney, 1998; Toumbourou, Hamilton, U'Ren, Stevens-Jones, & Storey, 2002) and drug abusers (Fiorentine & Hillhouse, 2000; Hayes et al., 2004). In the Collaborative Cocaine Treatment Study (Crits-Christoph et al., 1999) nearly 500 patients were randomized to 12-step-oriented individual therapy, individual CBT, individual emotional supportive therapy, or group drug counseling. In terms of drug use at 1-year follow-up, the 12-step individual therapy was the most effective. In a large study the effectiveness of CBT and 12-step approaches was compared in over 2,000 male veterans treated as inpatients for their substance abuse disorders (36% alcohol, 13% drugs, 51% both alcohol and drugs). Both treatments were equally effective at 1-year follow-up after discharge (Moos, Finney, Ouimette, & Suchinsky, 1999). The only notable exception being percentage of abstinence: At 1-year follow-up, 45% of the 12-step patients reported being abstinent from alcohol and drugs as compared to 36% of the patients in the CBT program. A number of studies compared CBT with the 12-step approach in cocaine abuse: CBT is generally equally effective as the 12-Stepapproach (Carroll et al., 1998; McKay et al., 1997; Wells et al., 1994).

Meta-Analyses

No meta-analyses were published that investigated the effectiveness of AA and NA approaches in illicit drug users.

Conclusions

Given the fact that very few studies have specifically focused on illicit drugs other than cocaine, conclusions with respect to the 12-step approaches are inconclusive; however, results of CBT and relapse prevention with cocaine abuse are generally comparable to those achieved with 12-step approaches.

TREATMENT OF PATIENTS WITH DUAL DIAGNOSIS

Many patients with substance use disorder have other psychiatric problems and in patients with mental illness abuse of substances is common. The term dual diagnosis is used to refer to this population. In recent reviews (Emmelkamp & Vedel, 2006; Tiet & Mausbach, 2007), a number of RCTs were identified testing the efficacy of both psychosocial and pharmacotherapy in people with dual diagnosis, but few focused exclusively on illicit drug users. For depression, no RCT evaluated a psychosocial intervention that was identified for patients abusing substances other than alcohol. Within anxiety disorders, only one RCT evaluated an integrated psychosocial intervention that was for PTSD and drug dependence (Hien, Cohen, Miele, Litt, & Capstick, 2004). For schizophrenia, two RCTs investigated the efficacy of CBT and motivational interviewing (Barrowclough et al., 2001) and an integrated treatment format (Hellerstein, Rosenthal, & Miner, 1995) in patients with any substance-related disorder. For bipolar disorder, only one RCT evaluated a combination of CBT and medication monitoring in patients with any substance-related disorder (Schmitz et al., 2002). For nonspecific severe mental illness, including schizophrenia, schizoaffective, bipolar, or major depressive disorder, there were three RCTs, two on integrated treatment modalities (Lehman, Herron, Schwartz, & Myers, 1993; Burnam et al., 1995) and one on assertive community treatment (Drake, McHugo, & Clark, 1998). Overall, no treatment has been replicated and consistently shown a clear advantage over any comparison condition for dual diagnosis (Tiet & Mausbach, 2007); however, existing efficacious treatments for psychiatric disorders also seem to be effective in dual diagnosis patients, and existing efficacious treatments for substance use disorders seem to be effective in reducing substance use in dual diagnosis patients (Emmelkamp & Vedel, 2006). As formulated in the clinical practice recommendation of the NICE guideline: "Evidence-based psychological treatments (in particular, cognitive behavioural therapy) should be considered for the treatment of co-morbid depression and anxiety disorders. . . ." (p. 117).

DOES PSYCHOTROPIC MEDICATION ENHANCE PSYCHOLOGICAL TREATMENT?

Few studies have investigated combined psychotropic medication and psychotherapy in drug use disorders. Carroll et al. (2004) investigated whether disulfiram enhanced the effects of coping skills training in cocaine-dependent patients. Combining the two provided little additional incremental benefit. In opioid-dependent patients, pharmacological maintenance has been combined with CM. These studies have shown that maintenance treatment with naltrexone (Carroll et al., 2001; Carroll, Sinha, Nich, Babuscio, & Rounsaville, 2002), methadone (Preston et al., 2001), or bupropion (Poling et al., 2006) may be combined with CM.

EVIDENCE-BASED PRACTICES

A treatment is given the title *possibly efficacious* if it is found more effective than no treatment in a single RCT (bronze medal). If this finding is replicated in a second RCT conducted by an independent research team, the treatment method is referred to as *probably efficacious* (silver medal). Treatments found to be superior to conditions that control for nonspecific processes or to another bona fide treatment are efficacious, specific, and are considered to be *well established* (gold medal) (Chambless & Hollon, 1998). In contrast to most other contributions in this handbook, it is nearly impossible to give medals for treatments in the field of illicit drug use for a variety of reasons.

First, to establish the overall effectiveness of a treatment for illicit drug use would mean that a series of RCTs are needed for each separate illicit drug; that is, amphetamine, cannabis, cocaine, hallucinogen, inhalant, opioid, phencyclidine, sedative-hypnotic-anxiolytic, and polysubstance use. As reviewed in this chapter, none of the available treatments has established efficacy across all the illicit drugs encountered in clinical practice. One simply cannot assume that treatment effective with cannabis users will be equally effective with polysubstance users. Even in the case of cocaine, treatment effective with high functioning patients who snort cocaine on a regular basis is not necessarily equally effective with homeless crack cocaine users or vice versa. In the case of metamphetamine, for example, treatment was found to be differentially effective for injectors, smokers, and intranasal users respectively (Rawson, Gonzales, Marinelli-Casey, & Ang, 2007).

Further, the requirements of Chambless and Hollon do not take into account studies with negative results. If there are three RCTs conducted by independent research groups demonstrating the effectiveness of a particular treatment, such a treatment would receive the qualification well established, even if many more studies would fail to demonstrate superiority of this treatment over other treatments. For example, although motivational interviewing fulfills the requirements for a probably efficacious treatment for nearly all substances studied, there are also a number of studies that failed to show its effectiveness in drug abusing populations.

Finally, illicit drug use should be considered a chronic condition. Patients with illicit drug use disorders frequently go through periods of abstinence or nonproblematic use after receiving treatment, however, a substantial number of these patients will eventually engage in problematic drug use again. A large subgroup of illicit drug users will cycle through periods of relapse, treatment reentry, and recovery. In a substantial number of illicit drug users continued interventions or booster sessions are required as is often the case in many medical problems, like diabetes, obesity, and hypertension, but also in psychiatric disorders like schizophrenia and mood disorders. For example, at our present state of knowledge, everybody expects that severe hypertension will reacur when medication is discontinued; although blood pressure will increase with termination of drug treatment, the patient will not be considered a treatment failure. Yet, despite often weak interventions in the area of substance use disorders, many individuals, clinicians, patients managed care agencies, insurance companies, and the general public expect treatment of substance use disorders to produce durable changes within a relatively short period of time. If illicit drug use is a chronic condition, this means that the effectiveness of (a series of) treatment(s) can be established after, for example, 5 years. Such studies, however, have not yet been conducted. Finally, in clinical practice, often a series of individual or combined interventions is used over a prolonged period of time rather than a focused 10-session treatment protocol as is typically done in RCTs. Nevertheless we provide in Table 9.3 a summary of the available evidence in terms of the Chambless

and Hollon criteria. The reader should, however, keep our reservations discussed earlier in mind.

In the research discussed in this chapter, most studies made use of manualized treatment protocols. Manual-based treatments of substance use disorders are empirically supported, but some have questioned the use of them in clinical practice. Critics of manual-based treatments have suggested that the use of manuals preclude idiographic case formulation and undermine therapists' clinical creativity; however, treatment manuals should not be used rigidly without any adjustment to the needs of the individual patient. Most current manuals for substance use disorders provide the necessary flexibility in applying the techniques prescribed.

The prelude to good treatment is a thorough case formulation and problem analysis. It is imperative to conduct a thorough analysis of the different problem areas of the patient (Emmelkamp & Vedel, 2006). This is critical in arriving at a clear definition of the problem behavior and in evaluating the effects of treatment. Thus, before embarking on a specific treatment technique, the therapist utilizes the collected information from the intake sessions and assessment to conduct an analysis of the problem behavior and associated problems.

TABLE 9.3   Chambless and Hollon Criteria for the Various Interventions

	Cocaine	Amphetamine	Opioid	Cannabis	Polysubstance
Cognitive Behavior Therapy/Relapse Prevention	***	**	?[1]	**	
Contingency management	***	*	***	***	***
Cue exposure	**	–	–	–	–
Behavioral couple therapy	–	–	*	–	**[2]
Motivational interviewing[3]	**	*	**	**	**
12-step facilitation	**				*

[1] CBT possibly efficacious as add on to methadone maintenance treatment

[2] Behavioral couple therapy was found more effective than no treatment and treatment was found to be superior to other well-established treatment. However, these findings were not replicated by an independent research team.

[3] Although formally, motivational interviewing fulfills the requirements for a silver medal for all substances studied except amphetamines, it should be noted that (a) effects of motivational interviewing as stand-alone treatment are generally small and (b) there are also a number of studies that failed to show its effectiveness in drug-abusing populations.

* = possibly efficacious (bronze medal)

** = probably efficacious (silver medal)

*** = well-established (gold medal)

This is not identical to arriving at a formal diagnosis. Problem analysis is indispensable for constructing a treatment plan. Patients often present more than one complaint, and in most cases there are functional relationships between these problem areas. Common problems in substance-abusing patients in addition to the substance abuse are anxiety, posttraumatic stress, depressed mood, relationship difficulties, personality disorders, financial problems, and work problems. In a macroanalysis, these relationships are delineated in order to establish where treatment should commence in the first place (for details, see Emmelkamp & Vedel, 2006).

Generally, in the case of illicit drug use in combination with other problems, a rule of thumb is to target the substance abuse first. At the same time, treating substance abuse first does not mean that other problem areas should be neglected or that treatment of co-occurring problems must be postponed until substance abuse treatment has finished. Rather, the co-occurring problem must be monitored during substance abuse treatment and if still prevalent after a period of abstinence or controlled use, must be addressed in treatment, and in some cases referral to specialized treatment centers may be called for.

REFERENCES

Alcoholics Anonymous World Services. (1986). *Alcoholics Anonymous* (3rd ed.). New York, NY: Author.

American Psychiatric Association. (2000). *DSM-IV-TR Diagnostic statistical manual of mental disorder* (4th ed., text rev.). Washington, DC: Author.

Azrin, N. H., McMahon, P. T., Donahue, B., Besalel, V. A., Lapinski, K. J., Kogan, E. S., . . . Galloway, E. (1994). Behavior therapy for drug abuse: A controlled treatment outcome study. *Behaviour Research and Therapy, 32*, 857–866.

Baker, A., Lee, N. K., Claire, M., Lewin, T. J., Grant, T., Pohlman, S., . . . Carr, V. J. (2005). Brief cognitive behavioural interventions for regular amphetamine users: A step in the right direction. *Addiction, 100*, 367–378.

Baker, A., Lewin, T., Reichler, H., Clancy, R., Carr, V., Garrett, R., . . . Terry, M. (2002). Motivational interviewing among psychiatric in-patients with substance use disorders. *Acta Psychiatria Scandinavia, 106*, 233–240.

Barrowclough, C., Haddock, G., Tarrier, N., Lewis, S. W., Moring, J., O'Brien, R., . . . McGovern, J. (2001). Randomized controlled trial of motivational interviewing, cognitive behavior therapy, and family intervention for patients with comorbid schizophrenia and substance use disorders. *American Journal of Psychiatry, 158*, 1706–1713.

Bates, M. E., Voelbel, G. T., Buckman, J. F., Labouvie, E. W., & Barry, D. (2005). Short-term neuropsychological recovery in clients with substance use disorders. *Alcoholism: Clinical and Experimental Research, 29*, 367–377.

Beck, A. T., Wright, F. D., Newman, C. S., & Liese, B. S. (1993). *Cognitive therapy of substance abuse*. New York, NY: Guilford Press.

Bickel, W. K., Amass, L., Higgins, S. T., Badger, G. J., & Esch, R. A. (1997). Effects of adding behavioral treatment to opioid detoxification with buprenorphine. *Journal of Consulting and Clinical Psychology, 65*, 803–810.

Booth, R. E., Kwiatkowski, C., Iguchi, M. Y., Pinto, F., & John, D. (1998). Facilitating treatment entry among out of treatment injection drug users. *Public Health Reports, 113*(Suppl. 1), 116–128.

Brown, H. P., Peterson, J. H., & Cunningham, O. (1988). Rationale and theoretical basis of a behavioral/cognitive approach to spirituality. *Alcoholism Treatment Quarterly, 5*, 47–59.

Brown, T. G., Serapiamen, P., Tremblay, J., & Annis, H. (2002). Matching substance abuse aftercare treatments to client characteristics. *Addictive Behaviors, 27*, 585–604.

Budney, A. J., Hughes, J. R., Moore, B. A., & Vandrey, R. (2004). Review of the validity and significance of cannabis withdrawal syndrome. *American Journal of Psychiatry, 161*, 1967–1977.

Burke, B. L., Arkowitz, H., & Menchola, M. (2003). The efficacy of motivational interviewing: A meta-analysis of controlled clinical trials. *Journal of Consulting and Clinical Psychology, 71*, 843–861.

Burnam, M. A., Morton, S. C., McGlynn, E. A., Petersen, L. P., Stecher, B. M., Hayes, C., & Vaccaro, V. J. (1995). An experimental evaluation of residential and nonresidential treatment for dually diagnosed homeless adults. *Journal of Addiction Disorders, 14*, 111–134.

Carey, M. P., Braaten, L. S., Maisto, S. A., Gleason, J. R., Forsyth, A. D., Durant, L. E., & Jaworski, B. C. (2000). Using information, motivational enhancement, and skills training to reduce the risk of HIV infection for low-income urban women: A second randomized clinical trial. *Health Psychology, 19*, 3–11.

Carey, K. B., Maisto, S. A., Kalichman, S. C., Forsyth, A. D., Wright, E. M., & Johnson, B. T. (1997). Enhancing motivation to reduce the risk of HIV infection for economically disadvantaged urban women. *Journal of Consulting and Clinical Psychology, 65*, 531–541.

Carroll, K. M., Ball, S. A., Nich, C., O'Connor, P. G., Eagen, D. A., Frankforter, . . . Rounsaville, B. J. (2001). Targeting behavioral therapies to enhance naltrexone treatment of opioid dependence. *Archives of General Psychiatry, 58*, 755–761.

Carroll, K. M., Easton, C. J., Nich, C., Hunkele, K. A., Neavins, T. M., Sinha, R., . . . Rounsaville, B. J. (2006). The use of contingency management and motivational/skills-building therapy to treat young adults with marijuana dependence. *Journal of Consulting and Clinical Psychology, 74*, 955–966.

Carroll, K. M., Fenton, L. R., Ball, S. A., Nich, C., Frankforter, T. L., Shi, J., & Rounsaville, B. J. (2004). Efficacy of disulfiram and cognitive behavior therapy in cocaine-dependent outpatients: A randomized placebo-controlled trial. *Archives of General Psychiatry, 61*, 264–272.

Carroll, K. M., Nich, C., Ball, S. A., McCance, E., & Rounsaville, B. J. (1998). Treatment of cocaine and alcohol dependence with psychotherapy and disulfiram. *Addiction, 93*, 713–727.

Carroll, K. M., Nich, C., & Rounsaville, B. J. (1995). Differential symptom reduction in depressed cocaine abusers treated with psychotherapy and pharmacotherapy. *Journal of Nervous and Mental Disease, 181*, 71–79.

Carroll, K. M., Rounsaville, B. J., & Gawin, F. H. (1991). A comparative trial of psychotherapies for ambulatory cocaine abusers: Relapse prevention and interpersonal psychotherapy. *American Journal of Drug and Alcohol Abuse, 17*, 229–247.

Carroll, K. M., Rounsaville, B. J., Gordon, L. T., Nich, C., Jatlow, P., Bisinghini, R. M., & Gawin, F. H. (1994). Psychotherapy and pharmacotherapy for ambulatory cocaine abusers. *Archives of General Psychiatry, 51*, 177–187.

Carroll, K. M., Sinha, R., Nich, C., Babuscio, B., & Rounsaville, B. J. (2002). Contingency management to enhance naltrexone treatment of opioid dependence: A randomized clinical trial of reinforcement magnitude. *Experimental and Clinical Psychopharmacology, 10*, 54–63.

Chambless, D. L., & Hollon, S. D. (1998). Defining empirically supported therapies. *Journal of Consulting and Clinical Psychology, 66*, 7–18.

Childress, A. R., Hole, A. V., Ehrman, R. N., Robbins, S. J., McLellan, A. T., & O'Brien, C. P. (1993). Cue reactivity and cue reactivity interventions in drug dependence. In L. S. Onken, J. D. Blaine, & J. J. Boren (Eds.), *Behavioral treatment for drug abuse and dependence* (pp. 73–95). Rockville, MD: National Institute on Drug Abuse.

Christo, G., & Franey, C. (1995). Drug users' spiritual beliefs, locus of control and the disease concept in relation to Narcotics Anonymous attendance and six-month outcomes. *Drug and Alcohol Dependence, 38*, 51–56.

Conklin, C. A., & Tiffany, S. (2002). Applying extinction research and theory to cue-exposure addiction treatments. *Addiction, 97*, 155–167.

Corby, E. A., Roll, J. M., Ledgerwood, D. M., & Schuster, C. R. (2000). Contingency management interventions for treating the substance abuse of adolescents: A feasibility study. *Experimental and Clinical Psychopharmacology, 8*, 371–376.

Crits-Christoph, P., Liqueland, L., Blaine, J., Frank, A., Luborsky, L., Onken, L. S., . . . Beck, A. T. (1999). Psychosocial treatments for cocaine dependence: National Institute on Drug Abuse Collaborative Cocaine Treatment Study. *Archives of General Psychiatry, 56*, 493–502.

Dawe, S., Powell, J. H., Richards, D., Gossop, M., Marks, I., Strang, J., Gray, J. (1993). Does post-withdrawal cue exposure improve outcome in opiate addiction? A controlled trial. *Addiction, 88*, 1233–1245.

Day, B. M., Lopez Gaston, C., Furlong, E., Murali, V., & Copello, A. (2005). United Kingdom substance misuse treatment workers' attitudes toward 12-step self-help groups. *Journal of Substance Abuse Treatment, 29*, 321–327.

Dennis, M., Godley, S. A., Diamond, G., Tims, F. M., Babor, T., Donaldson, J., . . . Funck, R. (2004). The Cannabis Youth Treatment (CYT) Study: Main findings from two randomized trials. *Journal of Substance Abuse Treatment, 27*, 197–213.

De Wildt, W. A. J. M., Schippers, G. M., Van den Brink, A. S., Potgieter, A. S., Deckers, F., & Bets, D. (2002). Does psychosocial treatment enhance the efficacy acamprosate in patients with alcohol problems? *Alcohol and Alcoholism, 37*, 375–382.

Donovan, D. M., Rosengren, D. B., Downey, L., Cox, G. C., & Sloan, K. L. (2001). Attrition prevention with individuals awaiting publicly funded drug treatment. *Addiction, 96*, 1149–1160.

Drake, R. E., McHugo, G. J., & Clark, R. E. (1998). Assertive community treatment for patients with co-occurring severe mental illness and substance use disorders. *American Journal of Orthopsychiatry, 68*, 201–215.

Dutra, L., Stathopoulou, G., Basden, S. L., Leyro, T. M., Powers, M. B., & Otto, M. W. (2008). A meta-analytic review of psychosocial interventions for substance use disorders. *American Journal of Psychiatry, 165*, 179–187.

Emmelkamp, P. M. G., & Vedel, E. (2006). *Evidence-based treatment for alcohol and drug abuse.* New York, NY: Routledge/Taylor & Francis.

Fals-Stewart, W., Birchler, G. R., & O'Farrell, T. J. (1996). Behavioral couples therapy for male substance-abusing patients: Effects on relationship adjustment and drug-using behavior. *Journal of Consulting and Clinical Psychology, 64*, 959–972.

Fals-Stewart, W., O'Farrell, T. J., & Birchler, G. R. (2001). Behavioral couples therapy for male methadone maintenance patients: Effects on drug-using behavior and relationship adjustment. *Behavior Therapy, 32*, 391–411.

Fals-Stewart, W., O'Farrell, T. J., Feehan, M., Birchler, G. R., Tiller, S., & McFarlin, S. K. (2000). Behavioral couples therapy versus individual-based treatment for male substance-abusing patients: An evaluation of significant individual change and comparison of improvement rates. *Journal of Substance Abuse Treatment, 18*, 249–254.

Fiorentine, R., & Hillhouse, M. P. (2000). Drug treatment and 12-step program participation: The addictive effects of integrated recovery activities. *Journal of Substance Abuse Treatment, 18*, 65–74.

Forman, R. F., Bovasso, G., & Woody, G. (2001). Staff beliefs about addiction treatment. *Journal of Substance Abuse Treatment, 21*, 1–9.

Galai, N., Safaeian, M., Vishov, D., Bolotin, A., & Celentano, D. D. (2003). Longitudinal patterns of drug injection behavior in the ALIVE study cohort, 1988–2000. *American Journal of Epidemiology, 158*, 695–704.

Grant, B. F., Stinson, F. S., Dawson, D. A., Chou, S. P., Dufour, M. C., Compton, W., . . . Kaplan, K. (2004). Prevalence and co-occurrence of substance use disorders and independent mood and anxiety disorders. *Archives of General Psychiatry, 61*, 807–816.

Gruber, K., Chutuape, M. A., & Stitzer, M. L. (2000). Reinforcement-based intensive outpatient treatment for inner-city opiate abusers: A short-term evaluation. *Drug and Alcohol Dependence, 57*, 211–223.

Haasen, C., Prinzleve, M., Zurhold, H., Rehm, J., Guttinger, F., & Fischer, G. (2004). Cocaine use in Europe: A multi-centre study. Methodology and prevalence estimates. *European Addiction Research, 10*, 139–146.

Hawkins, J., Catalano, R., Gillmore, M., & Wells, E. (1989). Skills training for drug abusers: Generalization, maintenance and effects on drug use. *Journal of Consulting and Clinical Psychology, 57*, 559–563.

Hayes, S. C., Wilson, K. G., Gifford, E. V., Bissett, R., Piasecki, M., Batten, S. V., . . . Gregg, J. (2004). A preliminary report of twelve-step facilitation and acceptance and commitment therapy with polysubstance-abusing methadone-maintained opiate addicts. *Behavior Therapy, 35*, 667–88.

Hellerstein, D. J., Rosenthal, R. N., & Miner, C. R. (1995). A prospective study of integrated outpatient treatment for substance-abusing schizophrenic patients. *American Journal of Addiction, 4*, 33–42.

Hettema, J., Steele, J., & Miller, W. R. (2005). Motivational interviewing. *Annual Review of Clinical Psychology, 1*, 91–111.

Hien, D. A., Cohen, L. R., Miele, G. M., Litt, L. C., & Capstick, C. (2004). Promising empirically supported

treatments for women with comorbid PTSD and substance use disorders. *American Journal of Psychiatry, 161*, 1426–1432.

Higgins, S. T., Alessi, S., & Dantona, R. L. (2000). Voucher-based incentives: A substance abuse treatment innovation. *Addictive Behaviors, 27*, 887–910.

Higgins, S. T., & Wong, C. J. (1998). Treating cocaine abuse: What does research tell us? In S. T. Higgins & J. L. Katz (Eds.), *Cocaine abuse: Behavior, pharmacology, and clinical applications* (pp. 343–361). New York, NY: Academic.

Hunt, G. M., & Azrin, N. H. (1973). A community-reinforcement approach to alcoholism. *Behaviour Research and Therapy, 11*, 91–104.

Iguchi, M. Y., Lamb, R. J., Belding, M. A., Platt, J. J., Husband, S. D., & Morral, A. R. (1996). Contingent reinforcement of group participation versus abstinence in a methadone maintenance program. *Experimental and Clinical Psychopharmacology, 4*, 1–7.

Irvin, J. E., Bowers, C. A., Dunn, M. E., & Wang, M. C. (1999). Efficacy of relapse prevention: A meta-analytic review. *Journal of Consulting and Clinical Psychology, 67*, 563–570.

Johnson, N. P., Phelps, G. L., & McCuen, S. K. (1990). Never try to carry a drunk by yourself: Effective use of self-help groups. *Journal of the South Carolina Medical Association, 86*, 7–31.

Jones, H. E., Haug, N. A., Silverman, K., Stitzer, M. L., & Svikis, D. S. (2001). The effectiveness of incentives in enhancing treatment attendance and drug abstinence in methadone-maintained pregnant women. *Drug and Alcohol Dependence, 61*, 297–306.

Kadden, R. M., Litt, M. D., Kabela-Cormier, E., & Petry, N. M. (2007). Abstinence rates following behavioral treatments for marijuana dependence. *Addictive Behaviors, 32*, 1220–1236.

Kamon, J., Budney, A., & Stanger, C. (2005). A contingency management intervention for adolescent marijuana abuse and conduct problems. *American Academy of Child and Adolescent Psychiatry, 44*, 513–521.

Kelly, J. F. (2003). Self-help for substance-use disorders: History, effectiveness, knowledge gaps, and research opportunities. *Clinical Psychology Review, 23*, 639–663.

Kirby, K. C., Marlowe, D. B., Festinger, D. S., Lamb R. J., & Platt, J. J. (1998). Schedule of voucher delivery influences initiation of cocaine abstinence. *Journal of Consulting and Clinical Psychology, 66*, 761–767.

Knapp, W. P., Soares, B., Farrell, M., & Silva de Lima, M. (2007). Psychosocial interventions for cocaine and psychostimulant amphetamines related disorders. *Cochrane Database of Systematic Reviews (Online), 3*, Art. No. CD003023, doi: 10.1002/14651858.CD003023.pub2.

Lehman, A. F., Herron, J. D., Schwartz, R. P., & Myers, C. P. (1993). Rehabilitation for adults with severe mental illness and substance use disorders. *Journal of Nervous and Mental disease, 181*, 86–90.

Lewis, M. W., & Petry, N. M. (2005). Contingency management treatments that reinforce completion of goal-related activities: Participation in family activities and its association with outcomes. *Drug and Alcohol Dependence, 79*, 267–271.

Lussier, J. P., Heil, S. H., Mongeon, J. A., Badger, G. J., & Higgins, S. T. (2006). A meta-analysis of voucher-based reinforcement therapy for substance use disorders. *Addiction, 101*, 192–203.

Luty, J. (2004). Treatment preferences of opiate-dependent patients. *Psychiatric Bulletin, 28*, 47–50.

Marijuana Treatment Project Research Group. (2004). Brief treatments for cannabis dependence: Findings from a randomized multisite trial. *Journal of Consulting and Clinical Psychology, 72*, 455–466.

Marissen, M. A. E., Franken, I. H. A., Blanken, P., Van den Brink, W., & Hendriks, V. M. (2005). Cue exposure therapy for opiate dependent clients. *Journal of Substance Use, 10*, 97–105.

Marlatt, G. A., & Gordon, J. R. (1985). *Relapse prevention: Maintenance strategies in the treatment of addictive behaviors.* New York, NY: Guilford Press.

Maude-Griffin, P. M., Hohenstein, J. M., Humfleet, G. L., Reilly, P. M., Tusel, D. J., & Hall, S. M. (1998). Superior efficacy of cognitive-behavioral therapy for crack cocaine abusers: Main and matching effects. *Journal of Consulting and Clinical Psychology, 66*, 832–837.

McKay, J. R., Alterman, A. I., Cacciola, J. S., Rutherford, M. J., O'Brien, C. P., & Koppenhaver, J. (1997). Group counseling versus individualized relapse prevention aftercare following intensive outpatient treatment for cocaine dependence: Initial results. *Journal of Consulting and Clinical Psychology, 65*, 778–788.

McKay, J. R., Lynch, K. G., Shepard, D. S., & Pettinati, H. M. (2005). The effectiveness of telephone-based continuing care for alcohol and cocaine dependence. *Archives of General Psychiatry, 62*, 199–207.

Miller, N. S., & Hoffman, N. G. (1995). Addictions treatment outcomes. *Alcoholism Treatment Quarterly, 12*, 41–55.

Miller, W. R. (1983). Motivational interviewing with problem drinkers. *Behavioural Psychotherapy, 11*, 441–448.

Miller, W. R., Yahne, C. E., Moyers, T. B., Martinez, J., & Pirritano, M. (2004). A randomized trial of methods to help clinicians learn motivational interviewing. *Journal of Consulting and Clinical Psychology, 72*, 1050–1062.

Miller, W. R., Yahne, C. E., & Tonigan, J. S. (2003). Motivational interviewing in drug abuse services: A randomized trial. *Journal of Consulting and Clinical Psychology, 71*, 754–763.

Monti, P. M., Rohsenow, D. J., Michalec, E., Martin, R. A., & Abrams, D. B. (1997). Brief coping skills treatment for cocaine abuse: Substance use outcomes at 3 months. *Addiction, 92*, 1717–1728.

Moos, R. H., Finney, J. W., Ouimette, P. C., & Suchinsky, R. T. A. (1999). A comparative evaluation of substance abuse treatment: 1. Treatment orientation, amount of care, and 1 year outcomes. *Alcoholism: Clinical and Experimental Research, 25*, 529–536.

National Institute for Health & Clinical Excellence (2008). *The national clinical practice guidelines on psychosocial interventions for drug misuse.* Leicester, United Kingdom: The British Psychological Society.

National Survey on Drug Use and Health. (2001). Retrieved from http://oas.samhsa.gov/nhsda2k2.htm#2k1NHSDA

O'Brien, C., Childress, A. R., McLellan, A. T., & Ehrman, R. (1990). Integrating systematic cue exposure with standard treatment in recovering drug dependent patients. *Addictive Behavior, 15*, 355–365.

Ouimette, P. C., Moos, H., & Finney, J. W. (1998). Influence of outpatient treatment and 12-step group involvement on one-year substance abuse treatment outcomes. *Journal of Studies on Alcohol, 59*, 513–522.

Peck, J. A., Reback, C. J., Yang, X., Rotheram-Fuller, E., & Shoptaw, S. (2005). Sustained reductions in drug use and depression symptoms from treatment for drug abuse in methamphetamine-dependent gay and bisexual men. *Journal of Urban Health, 82* (Suppl. 1), 100–108.

Peirce, J. M., Petry, N. M., & Stitzer, M. L. (2006). Effects of lower-cost incentives on stimulant abstinence in methadone maintenance treatment: A National Drug Abuse Treatment Clinical Trials Network study. *Archives of General Psychiatry, 63*, 201–208.

Petry, N. M. (2000). A comprehensive guide to the application of contingency management procedures in clinical settings. *Drug and Alcohol Dependence, 58*, 9–25.

Petry, N. M., & Martin, B. (2002). Low-cost contingency management for treating cocaine- and opioid abusing methadone patients. *Journal of Consulting and Clinical Psychology, 70*, 398–405.

Petry, N. M., Martin, B., & Simcic, F. (2005). Prize reinforcement contingency management for cocaine dependence. *Journal of Consulting and Clinical Psychology, 73*, 354–359.

Petry, N. M., Peirce, J. M., Stitzer, M. L., Blaine, J., Roll, J. M., Cohen, A., . . . Li, R. (2005). Effect of prize based incentives on outcomes in stimulant abusers in outpatient psychosocial treatment programs: A national drug abuse treatment clinical trials network study. *Archives of General Psychiatry, 62*, 1148–1156.

Petry, N. M., Tedford, J., & Martin, B. (2001). Reinforcing compliance with non-drug-related activities. *Journal of Substance Abuse Treatment, 20*, 33–44.

Poling, J., Oliveto, A., Petry, N., Sofuoglu, M., Gonsai, K., Gonzalez, G., . . . Kosten, T. R. (2006). Six-month trial of bupropion with contingency management for cocaine dependence in a methadone-maintained population. *Archives of General Psychiatry, 63*, 219–228.

Prendergast, M., Podus, D., Finney, J., Greenwell, L., & Roll, J. (2006). Contingency management for treatment of substance use disorders: A meta-analysis. *Addiction, 101*, 1546–1560.

Preston, K. L., Umbricht, A., Wong, C. J., & Epstein, D. H. (2001). Shaping cocaine abstinence by successive approximation. *Journal of Consulting and Clinical Psychology, 69*, 643–654.

Powell, T., Bradley, B., & Gray, J. (1993). Subjective craving for opiates: Evaluation of a cue-exposure protocol for use with detoxified opiate addicts. *British Journal of Clinical Psychology, 32*, 39–53.

Powers, M. B., Vedel, E., & Emmelkamp, P. M. G. (2008). Behavioral couples therapy (BCT) for alcohol and drug use disorders: A meta-analysis. *Clinical Psychology Review, 28*, 952–962.

Rawson, R. A., Gonzales, R., Marinelli Casey, P., & Ang, A. (2007). Methamphetamine dependence: A closer look at treatment response and clinical characteristics associated with route of administration in outpatient treatment. *American Journal of Addiction, 16*, 291–299.

Rawson, R. A., Huber, A., McCann, M., Shoptaw, S., Farabee, D., Reiber, C. & Ling, W. (2002). A comparison of contingency management and cognitive behavioral approaches during methadone maintenance treatment for cocaine dependence. *Archives of General Psychiatry, 59*, 817–824.

Rawson, R. A., Marinelli Casey, P., Anglin, M. D., Dickow, A., Frazier, Y., Gallagher, C., . . . Zweben, J. (2004). A multisite comparison of psychosocial approaches for the treatment of methamphetamine dependence. *Addiction, 99*, 708–717.

Rawson, R. A., McCann, M. J., Flammino, F., Shoptaw, S., Motto, K., Reiber, C. & Ling, W. (2006). A comparison of contingency management and cognitive behavioral approaches for stimulant dependent individuals. *Addiction, 101*, 267–274.

Rohsenow, D. J., Monti, P. M., Martin, R. A., Colby, S. M., Myers, M. G., Gulliver, S. B., . . . Abrams, D. B. (2004). Motivational enhancement and coping skills training for cocaine abusers: Effects on substance use outcomes. *Addiction, 99*, 862–874.

Roll, J. M., Petry, N. M., Stitzer, M. L., Brecht, M. L., Peirce, J. M., McCann, M. J., . . . Kellogg, S. (2006). Contingency management for the treatment of methamphetamine use disorders. *American Journal of Psychiatry, 163*, 1993–1999.

Saunders, J. B., Wilkinson, C. & Phillips, M. (1995). The impact of a brief motivational intervention with opiate users attending a methadone program. *Addiction, 90*, 415–424.

Scherbaum, N., Kluwig, J., Specka, M., Krause, D., Merget, B., Finkbeiner, T., & Gaspar, M. (2005).

Group psychotherpy for opiate addicts in methadone maintenance treatment—A controlled trial. *European Addiction Research, 11*, 163–171.

Schmitz, J. M., Averill, P., Sayre, S., McCleary, P., Moeller, F. G., & Swann, A. (2002). Cognitive-behavioral treatment of bipolar disorder and substance abuse. *Addictive Disorders and Their Treatment, 1*, 17–24.

Schneider, R. J., Casey, J., & Kohn, R. (2000). Motivational versus confrontational interviewing: A comparison of substance abuse assessment practices at employee assistance programs. *Journal of Behavioral Health Services and Research, 27*, 60–74.

Schoener, E. P., Madeja, C. L., Henderson, M. J., Ondersma, S. J., & Janisse, J. J. (2006). Effects of motivational interviewing training on mental health therapist behavior. *Drug and Alcohol Dependence, 82*, 265–275.

Schumacher, J. E., Milby, J. B., Wallace, D., Meehan, D., Kertesz, S., Vuchinich, R., . . . Usdan, S. (2007). Meta analysis of day treatment and contingency-management dismantling research: Birmingham Homeless Cocaine Studies (1990–2006). *Journal of Consulting and Clinical Psychology, 75*, 823–828.

Secades Villa, R., Fernande Hermida, J. R., & Arnaez Montaraz, C. (2004). Motivational interviewing and treatment retention among drug user patients: A pilot study. *Substance Use and Misuse, 39*, 1369–1378.

Shoptaw, S., Huber, A., Peck, J., Yang, X., Liu, J., Dang, J., . . . Ling, W. (2006). Randomized, placebo controlled trial of sertraline and contingency management for the treatment of methamphetamine dependence. *Drug and Alcohol Dependence, 85*, 12–18.

Silverman, K., Higgins, S. T., Brooner, R. K., Montoya, I. D., Cone, E. J., Schuster, C. R., & Preston, K. L. (1996). Sustained cocaine abstinence in methadone maintenance patients through voucher based reinforcement therapy. *Archives of General Psychiatry, 53*, 409–415.

Silverman, K., Svikis, D. S., Wong, C. J., Hampton, J., Stitzer, M. L., & Bigelow, G. E. (2002). A reinforcement based therapeutic workplace for the treatment of drug abuse: Three year abstinence outcomes. *Experimental and Clinical Psychopharmacology, 10*, 228–240.

Silverman, K., Wong, C. J., Umbricht Schneiter, A., Montoya, I. D., Schuster, C. R., & Preston, K. L. (1998). Broad beneficial effects of cocaine abstinence reinforcement among methadone patients. *Journal of Consulting and Clinical Psychology, 66*, 811–824.

Sindelar, J., Elbel, B., & Petry, N. M. (2007). What do we get for our money? Cost effectiveness of adding contingency management. *Addiction, 102*, 309–316.

Stephens, R. S., Roffman, R. A., & Curtin, L. (2000). Comparison of extended versus brief treatments for marijuana use. *Journal of Consulting and Clinical Psychology, 68*, 898–908.

Stephens, R. S., Roffman, R. A., & Simpson, E. E. (1994). Treating adult marijuana dependence: A test of the relapse prevention model. *Journal of Consulting and Clinical Psychology, 62,* 92–99.

Stitzer, M. L., Iguchi, M. Y., & Felch, L. J. (1992). Contingency take-home incentive: Effects on drug use of methadone maintenance patients. *Journal of Consulting and Clinical Psychology, 60,* 972–934.

Stotts, A. L., Schmitz, J. M., Rhoades, H. M., & Grabowski, J. (2001). Motivational interviewing with cocaine-dependent patients: A pilot study. *Journal of Consulting and Clinical Psychology, 69,* 858–862.

Substance Abuse and Mental Health Services Administration. (2001). *National house survey on drug abuse.* Rockville, MD: U.S. Department of Health and Human Services, Public Health Services.

Substance Abuse and Mental Health Services Administration. (2002). *National survey on drug use and health.* Online at www.dhhs.gov/news/press/2003pres/20030905.html

Tiet, Q. Q., & Mausbach, B. (2007). Treatment for patients with dual diagnosis: A review. *Alcoholism: Clinical and Experimental Research, 31,* 513–536.

Toumbourou, J. W., Hamilton, M., U'Ren, A., Stevens-Jones, P., & Storey, G. (2002). Narcotics Anonymous participation and changes in substance use and social support. *Journal of Substance Abuse Treatment, 23,* 61–66.

Volkow, N. D., Fowler, J. S., & Wang, G. J. (2003). Positron emission tomography and single-photon emission computed tomography in substance abuse research. *Seminars in Nuclear Medicine, 33,* 114–128.

Wells, E. A., Peterson, P. L., Gainey, R. R., Hawkins, J. D., & Catalano, R. F. (1994). Outpatient treatment for cocaine abuse: A controlled comparison of relapse prevention and twelve-step approaches. *American Journal of Drug and Alcohol Abuse, 20,* 1–17.

Winters, J., Fals-Stewart, W., O'Farrell, T. J., Birchler, G. R., & Kelly, M. L. (2002). Behavioral couples therapy for female substance abusing patients: Effects on substance use and relationship adjustment. *Journal of Consulting and Clinical Psychology, 70,* 344–355.

Yen, C. F., Wu, H. Y., Yen, J. Y., & Ko, C. H. (2004). Effects of brief cognitive-behavioral interventions on confidence to resist the urges to use heroin and methamphetamine in relapse-related situations. *Journal of Nervous and Mental Disease, 192,* 788–791.

10

Schizophrenia

CHRISTOPHER JONES AND ALAN MEADEN

OVERVIEW OF SCHIZOPHRENIA

The diagnosis of schizophrenia covers a wide range of individuals, whose course varies enormously. Presentation of the core symptoms also varies considerably; individuals present in many different ways and require a range of interventions. Subgroups have been identified, representing clusters of symptoms (e.g., paranoid, catatonic, and hebephrenic). Up to 20% of individuals affected make a full recovery, and 20% have relapses with no intervening deterioration. Schizophrenia continues to court controversy, not just because of its stigmatizing and often disabling effects, but also because of the validity of the syndrome itself and problems in reliably agreeing on its presence (Bentall, 2003).

Diagnostic Criteria

A combination of specific symptoms occurring over a period of usually 1 month is required for a diagnosis of schizophrenia to be made. The American Psychiatric Association's *Diagnostic and Statistical Manual of Mental Disorders (DSM-IV-TR)* (American Psychiatric Association, 2000), requires two of five symptoms. Symptoms may be positive or negative and include hallucinations (somatic, auditory, and visual), delusions (of persecution, thought

withdrawal, insertion, or broadcast); disorganization of thought or behavior; catatonia; flat affect; alogia (poverty of speech); and avolition (inability to initiate or persist in goal-directed activities).

Demographics

Onset most commonly occurs in late adolescence. Approximately 1% of the general population develops schizophrenia over the life span with 10-20 cases per 100,000 of these occurring each year. Those living in urban areas are at greater risk. There is no difference in prevalence between men and women; though women tend to have a later onset and better clinical outcomes. Recovery rates appear better in developing countries (Warner, 1994).

Impact of the Disorder

Schizophrenia is arguably the most serious and disabling of all psychiatric disorders. The World Health Organization (Murray & Lopez, 1996) ranked it as having the second highest burden of care after cardiovascular disease. Chronic disability may result and persist throughout the life span. Those with predominantly positive symptoms may continue to experience acute relapses. Individuals with schizophrenia are at excess risk for suicide and deaths by suicide. The prevalence of suicide ranges from 147–750 deaths per 100,000 and the estimated lifetime risk is between 9% and 13% with rates of self-harm ranging from 20% to 40% (Heisel, 2008).

The social and occupational impact of the disorder is often significant, profoundly effecting daily functioning over the lifetime. The disorder brings with it stigma, social exclusion, and discrimination (Corrigan & Larson, 2008). Consequently, people with schizophrenia may have problems maintaining independent living, enjoying meaningful relationships, and lack rewarding social and leisure activities (American Psychiatric Association, 2000).

TOKEN ECONOMIES

Token economies use learning principles to alter the behavior of a person with schizophrenia by providing tokens that may later be exchanged for other reinforcers contingent on specified target behaviors. Tokens, therefore, bridge the delay between target behavior and delayed reinforcers. Tokens have been used to reinforce a wide range of adaptive behavior including self-help skills, language, and behaviors that result in reductions of symptomatic behavior.

SINGLE CASE EXPERIMENTAL DESIGNS

Commensurate with the origins of the token economy in behavioral analysis, several ABA experimental designs have been reported. Ayllon and Azrin (1965) provided a series of six ABA experimental designs that demonstrated that target behaviors were increased when reinforcement was provided and decreased when reinforcement was discontinued. Similarly, Elliot, Barlow,

Hooper, and Kingerlee (1979) reported 18 ABA experimental designs. It was noted that hygiene and social interaction increased during token reinforcement. Finally, Nelson and Cone (1979) report a case series of 13 patients with psychosis. In a sequential multiple baseline design, target behaviors (i.e., hygiene, "ward work," and social skills) showed substantial improvement during token reinforcement.

Randomized Controlled Trials

A randomized controlled trial (RCT) with 45 female inpatients with chronic psychosis compared token economy with standard care (Maley, Feldman, & Ruskin, 1973). Patients receiving the token economy showed advantages over matched standard care patients with respect to measures of orientation and general functioning. Li and Wang (1994) also reported a RCT of 52 inpatients with schizophrenia receiving either token economy or standard care. The token economy group attended a life skills group and received reinforcement if their daily Brief Psychiatric Rating Scale score exceeded the mean daily score for the token economy cohort for the previous week. The control participants, who were on the same ward and receiving the same interventions, did not receive contingent reinforcement. A significant advantage was observed in favor of the token economy patients for change on the Scale for the Assessment of Negative Symptoms (Weighted Mean Difference [WMD] −12.7, CI −21.44 to −3.96).

Conclusions

Token economies have been successfully employed in the promotion of overt positive behavioral skills and have been successfully applied with respect to the remediation of negative symptoms of schizophrenia. Overall, the balance of the existent evidence would meet Chambless and Hollon's (1998) criteria for an evidence-based therapy.

OPERANT BEHAVIORAL INTERVENTIONS FOR PSYCHOTIC SYMPTOMS

Intervention strategies based on the manipulation of operant reinforcement contingencies have been used to treat a range of overt behaviors consequent upon psychotic illness. Perhaps most notably, behavioral interventions have been used to decrease the rate of delusional speech and to reduce subvocalization during auditory hallucinations.

Single Case Experimental Designs

In a multiple baseline design, the delusional speech of an inpatient man with chronic schizophrenia was significantly reduced by the selective reinforcement of stimulus appropriate responses (Foxx, McMorrow, Davis, & Bittle, 1988). Furthermore, this reduction in delusional speech generalized across settings and was maintained at 15-month follow-up. Similarly, in a case series of four schizophrenic patients with chronic schizophrenia (Liberman, Teigen, Patterson, & Baker, 1973), social reinforcement was contingent upon the amount of time that the participant engaged in *rational talk* during a daily 10 minute interview. Compared to the baseline rate, improvements of between 200% and 600% in the amount of time engaged in rational talk were observed during the contingent reinforcement condition; however, delusional speech returned to baseline levels when the patient was confronted directly with their delusional ideas. This might suggest that there was an increase in rational talk but no alteration in delusion preoccupation and/or conviction.

In a series reversal design with 10 schizophrenic patients (Wincze, Leitenberg, & Agras, 1972), the efficacy of token reinforcement was compared with the effects of feedback with respect to delusional speech. Verbal feedback was effective in reducing delusional speech in approximately 50% of participants but produced adverse reactions in approximately one third of participants. In contrast, the token

reinforcement reduced delusional speech in 70% of participants and was not associated with adverse reactions. The reduction in delusional speech consequent on both token reinforcement and verbal feedback did not generalize to novel situations.

Jimenez, Todman, Perez, Godoy, and Landon-Jimenez (1996) reported on a behaviorally based treatment package to decrease the frequency of verbal responding to auditory hallucinations, and to increase attention to important external stimuli rather than to the hallucinations. Social and token reinforcement was contingent on the absence of overt behavior consistent with the experience of auditory hallucinations. Compared with baseline conditions, there was a significant reduction in auditory hallucinations and an increase in the subject's ability to attend to external tasks. Similarly, Belcher (1988) reported a single case experimental design of the treatment of verbally aggressive hallucinatory outbursts by contingent reinforcement of other behavior. This intervention resulted in a 92% decrease in the number of outbursts at the end of the 20-week program.

More recently, Wilder, Masuda, O'Connor, and Baham (2001) used a reversal design to examine the effects of differential social reinforcement of alternative vocalizations upon bizarre and/or delusional speech. Bizarre speech was reduced and appropriate vocalizations were increased with the provision of contingent attention. Similarly, Lancaster, LeBlanc, Carr, Brenske, Peet, and Culver (2004) reported the differential social reinforcement of alternate vocalizations of two participants with psychosis presenting with bizarre speech. For one participant there was a 69% reduction in bizarre speech and a 191% increase in appropriate vocalizations. The second participant experienced a 62% reduction in bizarre vocalizations but no change in levels of appropriate speech.

Conclusions

The current balance of evidence indicates that operant behavioral interventions would meet

Chambless and Hollon's (1998) criteria for an evidence-based therapy. This literature uses small *N* experimental designs and to date no RCTs have been reported. These methods should incorporate appropriate strategies to promote generalization to novel situations and the maintenance of the therapeutic effect after the cessation of the reinforcing contingency.

SOCIAL SKILLS TRAINING

Deficits in social functioning are a common feature of schizophrenia, which may arise from positive or negative symptoms, social anxiety and avoidance, cognitive deficits, stigma, social isolation, and the erosion of social skills from understimulating environments (Kopelowicz, Liberman, & Zarate, 2006; Tsang, 2001). Anxiety related to social skills deficits may significantly contribute toward first and subsequent episodes of psychosis (Nuechterlein et al., 1994). Accordingly, remediation of social skills deficits may confer benefits beyond the specific social skills targets (Prince, 2006; N. R. Schooler, 2006).

Social Skills Training is a structured psychosocial intervention to enhance social performance and reduce the distress experienced in social situations. Kopelowicz and colleagues (2006) describe social skills training as addressing seven types of social skills: (1) *social perception skills*, such as recognition of others' social and emotional expressions; (2) *processing social information*, including the evaluation of others' social and emotional expressions; (3) *responding or sending skills*, such as effective use of verbal and nonverbal communication; (4) *affiliative skills*, to express affection and appropriate disclosure; (5) *instrumental role skills*, for example, engaging in everyday social activities, such as purchasing food; (6) *interaction skills*, such as starting, maintaining, and terminating conversation; and (7) *behavior governed by social norms*, for example, scripted social activities, such as ordering food at a restaurant. Group social

skills training is often preferred. Programs employ multiple learning-based procedures including problem identification, goal setting, role play, behavioral rehearsal and feedback, social modeling, and homework assignments.

Meta-Analysis of Group Designs

Social skills training has received considerable empirical investigation over 30 years. A large body of clinical evidence has accumulated with mixed methodological quality, employing both RCTs and within-subject experiments, and measuring a variety of clinical outcomes. An early meta-analysis (Benton & Schroeder, 1990) of 27 studies reported that self-rated social skills showed a significant advantage for social skills training (WMD = 0.76; 95% CI 0.59 to 0.93), as did self-rated assertiveness (WMD = 0.69; 95% CI 0.43 to 0.95) and self-rated symptomatology (WMD = 0.32; 95% CI 0.06 to 0.58). Rating by significant others also showed an advantage for social skills training (WMD = 0.34; 95% CI 0.06 to 0.62). Four studies that compared relapse rates following social skills training showed a significant reduction in relapse rates following social skills training (WMD = 0.47; 95% CI 0.18 to 0.76); however, 59% of these studies included participants with mixed or nonpsychotic diagnoses, approximately one third were unpublished, and this meta-analysis did not impose any methodological inclusion criteria.

A second meta-analysis (Corrigan, 1991) was conducted on a larger sample of 73 social skills training studies with developmentally disabled, psychotic, nonpsychotic, and forensic populations. Only 11 studies reported data exclusively on people with schizophrenia and six studies reported outcomes on participants with mixed psychotic diagnoses. Significant advantages for participants experiencing social skills training was observed for self-rated, naturally observed, and role play measures of skilled social behavior. Social skills generalized to nontraining situations and were maintained after completion of the training programs.

Significant advantages were also observed for social skills training on measures of general psychopathology, social anxiety, hostility, and self-esteem. Corrigan (1991) also provides a sensitive analysis for a diagnostic group. Both psychotic and nonpsychotic participants acquired, maintained, and generalized social skills; however, these effects were muted in the psychotic group.

Pilling et al. (2002b) focused specifically on efficacy evidence from high-quality RCTs on participants with schizophrenic spectrum disorders. Nine social skills training studies reporting outcomes on 471 participants met methodological and other quality criteria. No beneficial effects for social skills training were observed in reducing relapse rates, treatment compliance, and global adjustment and quality of life. Social functioning evidenced a heterogeneous outcome with one study (Hayes, Halford, & Varghese, 1995), which showed a nonsignificant trend favoring social skills training on the simulated social interaction task (Curran, 1982) and the conversation with a stranger task (Wallace & Liberman, 1985), while Marder et al. (1996) presented with a significant advantage for social skills training on the Social Adjustment Scale (N. Schooler, Hogarty, & Weissman, 1979). Thus, this meta-

analysis failed to confirm the optimism of the early reviews. Mueser criticized the conclusion in this meta-analysis "regarding the effects of social skills training on social functioning, quality of life, and general functioning [that] were based on an insufficient number of studies" and a "failing to reconcile the conclusions of this meta-analysis with the numerous other reviews of the skills-training literature that have reached very different conclusions" (K. T. Mueser & Penn, 2004, p. 1366).

Most recently, Kurtz and Mueser (2008) reviewed 22 RCTs with 1,521 participants with a diagnosis of schizophrenia or schizophrenia spectrum disorders. Outcomes were grouped into four categories representing the degree of generalization of social skills beyond the training materials (see Table 10.1). A large effect was observed for content-based exams or role plays taken directly from skills training materials. Thus, social skills training programs were effective in teaching content material. A moderate effect was observed for the generalization to other performance-based measures of independent or daily living skills indirectly relating to the content of the training programs. Similarly, there was a moderate effect on general measures of psychosocial functioning and a small effect relating to the

TABLE 10.1   Effect Sizes for Proximal, Immediate, and Distal Outcomes of Social Skills Training

		RCTs	N	Effect Size	95% Confidence Interval
Proximal measures: content-based exams or role plays taken directly from skills training materials.		7	330	1.20	0.96 to 1.43
Proximal mediational measures: performance-based measures of independent or daily living skills.		7	181	0.52	0.34 to 0.71
Immediate measures: measures of general psychosocial functioning and negative symptoms.	Psychosocial functioning	7	171	0.52	0.34 to 0.71
	Negative symptoms	6	363	0.40	0.19 to 0.61
Distal measures: measures are other psychiatric symptoms and relapse.	Other psychiatric symptoms	10	604	0.15	0.01 to 0.31
	Relapse/Rehospitalization	9	485	0.23	0.01 to 0.31

Effect size: small = 0.2, moderate = 0.5, and large = 0.8.
Source: Kurtz and Mueser (2008).

reduction of negative symptoms. No significant effect was observed with regard to the reduction of general psychiatric symptomatology; however, a small advantage for the social skills group was observed with regard to relapse and readmission rates.

Conclusions

Social skills training meets Chambless and Hollon's (1998) criteria for evidence-based psychotherapy: In the literature containing high-quality RCTs and meta-analyses, social skills generalize to other areas of social function and there is evidence of general improvement in independent and daily living activities. In addition, negative symptoms of schizophrenia show some remediation following social skills training and there is evidence of a reduction in relapse and readmission rates. The social performance of both psychotic and non-psychotic patients appears to benefit equally, but there is a smaller reduction of psychiatric symptomatology in patients with psychosis (Corrigan, 1991).

COGNITIVE BEHAVIOR THERAPY

Cognitive behavior therapy (CBT) is a discrete psychological intervention to help people make connections between events, their thoughts, feelings, and behavior with regard to their perceptions or experiences and to re-evaluate them in order to lessen their distress and unhelpful behaviors. The CBT may also involve the promotion of alternative ways of coping with the target symptom. P. D. J. Chadwick, Lowe, Horne, and Higson (1994) and P. D. Chadwick and Lowe (1990) showed how CBT principles, developed for other emotional disorders, could be applied successfully to specific delusional symptoms to reduce belief conviction and distress. Subsequently, P. Chadwick and Birchwood (1994) demonstrated that distress and behavior in relation to hearing voices was mediated by the meaning attributed to them rather than being merely a product of voice activity or content per se. Cognitive behavior therapy now has many variations in practice often including other psychosocial interventions such as Coping Strategies Enhancement (CSE; see later), psychoeducation, and relapse prevention work (Garety et al., 2008; Tarrier et al., 1993, 1998). The label *CBT* has been applied to a variety of interventions with different target symptoms and methods; therefore, it is difficult to provide a single, unambiguous definition. Jones, Cormac, Silvera da Mota Neto, and Campbell (2004) constructed criteria that were both workable and captured the elements of good practice. These included:

> (a) the intervention involves the recipient establishing links between their thoughts, feelings and actions with respect to the target symptom; (b) the intervention involves the correction of the person's misperceptions, irrational beliefs and reasoning biases related to the target symptom; (c) the intervention should involve either the recipient monitoring his or her own thoughts, feelings and behaviors with respect to the target symptom; and/or the promotion of alternative ways of coping with the target symptom. (Jones et al., 2004, p. 3)

Meta-Analysis of Group Designs

Cognitive behavior therapy has received considerable empirical investigation over the last two decades and some 34 RCTs have been conducted mainly focusing on positive and negative symptoms (Rector, Seeman, & Segal, 2003), relapse prevention (Garety et al., 2008), social functioning (Startup, Jackson, & Bendix, 2004; Startup, Jackson, Evans, & Bendix, 2005), and insight (Turkington, Kingdon, & Turner, 2002). The majority compared CBT with standard care, although a substantial number compared CBT with other treatments. Trials have been conducted across first episode and chronic stable psychosis, but not systematically with assertive outreach populations. Given the extent of this literature, we shall focus attention on the meta-analytic evidence regarding efficacy.

Pilling et al., (2002a) reported a meta-analysis of 8 trials with 528 patients. Of the 29 trials, 14 were excluded due to either inadequate randomization, the intervention did not meet the criteria for CBT, or unusable data. CBT did not have beneficial effects on relapse/readmission rates compared with standard care (3 RCT; OR = 0.73; 95% CI 0.37 to 1.47) or other active treatments (4 RCT; OR = 0.74; 95% CI 0.43 to 1.28). Important improvement in mental state was reported in four trials with 273 patients both when compared with standard care (2 RCTs; OR = 0.25; 95% CI 0.1 to 0.64) and other active treatments (4 RCTs; OR = 0.27; 95% CI 0.15 to 0.49). The beneficial effects of CBT were maintained at up to 18 months after end of treatment. Treatment noncompliance did not show advantage for CBT versus standard care in 3 RCTs with 220 patients (OR = 0.9; 95% CI 0.14 to 5.81). Two RCTs reported Global Assessment of Functioning Scale end point data. The CBT did not show an advantage over other active therapies (i.e., supportive counseling, and a problem solving group) (WMD = 0.84; 95% CI 0.69 to 2.38). Pilling et al. (2002a) suggests that CBT shows advantages with regard to important improvement in mental state; but this was defined differently in different studies (Drury, Birchwood, Cochrane, & Macmillan, 1996; Kuipers et al., 1997; Sensky et al., 2000; Tarrier et al., 1998).

Jones et al. (2004) conducted a meta-analysis of reported data from 30 papers containing 19 RCTS. CBT did not reduce relapse and readmission compared with standard care (4 RCTs; N = 357; RR = 0.8; 95% CI 0.5 to 1.5), but did decrease the risk of staying in the hospital (1 RCT; N = 62; RR = 0.5; 95% CI 0.3 to 0.9; NNT 4). CBT was related to important improvement in mental state (2 RCTs; N = 123; RR = 0.7; 95% CI 0.6 to 0.9; NNT 4) but after 1 year the difference was not significant (3 RCTs; N = 211; RR = 0.95; 95%

CI 0.6 to 1.5). This was not observed when CBT was compared with supportive psychotherapy (2 RCT; N = 100; RR = 0.9; 95% CI 0.8 to 1.1). There was no consistent affect on psychometric measures of mental state.

Zimmermann, Favrod, Trieu, and Pomini (2005) conducted a meta-analysis of the effect of CBT on positive symptoms on 15 studies with 1,484 patients. Measures of positive symptoms (e.g., Brief Psychiatric Rating Scale, Psychotic Symptom Rating Scales, Positive and Negative Syndrome Scale, Maudsley Assessment of Delusions Scale) were combined into a single effect (using Hedges' g; small effect = 0.2, medium effect = 0.5, large effect = 0.8) and compared with standard care and nonspecific treatment. There was a significant advantage of CBT (15 RCTs; N = 1484; g = 0.35; 95% CI 0.23 to 0.47), implying that the typical patient would improve more than 64% of the control patients. The advantage of CBT was observed in studies conducted with chronic outpatients with persistent residual symptoms (10 RCTs; N = 798; g = 0.27; 95% CI 0.11 to 0.42) and for inpatients with an acute psychotic episode (3 RCTs; N = 203; g = 0.57; 95% CI 0.31 to 0.83), suggesting that patients with acute episodes receive larger benefits from CBT than patients with a chronic condition, although CBT may still be beneficial for this group.

Most recently, Wykes, Steel, Everitt, and Tarrier (2008) analyzed data from 34 RCTs. Significant advantages were observed for mental status for CBT patients with respect to positive symptoms (32 RCTs; N = 1,918; WMD = 0.37; 95% CI 0.23 to 0.52), negative symptoms (23 RCTs; N = 1,268; WMD 0.437; 95% CI 0.17 to 0.70), social functioning (15 RCTs; N = 867; WMD = 0.38; 95% CI 0.15 to 0.60), and mood ratings (15 RCTs; N = 953; WMD = 0.36; 95% CI 0.08 to 0.65). There were significant correlations between improvement in positive symptoms and worsening hopelessness (r = 0.98; p = 0.02), improvements in negative symptoms and improved social functioning (r = 0.66; p = 0.02), and social functioning and improvements in mood (r = 0.95, p = 0.01)

Individually administered CBT was associated with an effect size of 0.42 and group-based CBT was associated with an effect size of 0.39 (CI = −0.38 to 0.44), thus, there is no evidence of a significant difference between these modes of administration.

Conclusions

Cognitive behavior therapy is associated with meaningful improvement in mental state (Jones et al., 2004; Pilling et al., 2002a; Wykes et al., 2008; Zimmermann et al., 2005). Patients in acute episode benefit from more positive symptom reduction than patients with a chronic condition (Zimmermann et al., 2005). Both positive and negative symptoms of schizophrenia show meaningful remediation with CBT (Wykes et al., 2008). CBT is associated with reduction of stay in the hospital (Jones et al., 2004) but not reduction in relapse rates (Jones et al., 2004; Pilling et al., 2002a) or treatment compliance (Pilling et al., 2002a). CBT may be associated with improved social functioning (Wykes et al., 2008), which in turn may be associated with improved mood (Wykes et al., 2008). Thus, CBT meets Chambless and Hollon's (1998) criteria of an evidence-based therapy for schizophrenia. More recently, researchers have placed greater focus upon the psychological distress and problematic behaviors proceeding from psychiatric symptomatology rather than psychiatric symptomatology in itself (Trower et al., 2004).

COPING STRATEGY ENHANCEMENT

Coping strategy enhancement (CSE) is frequently employed as a component of CBT interventions to promote engagement (improving a sense of control and optimism for change) and lessen the impact of residual symptoms. It may also be used as a discrete intervention or used as part of a larger relapse prevention program. The CSE systematically reviews the person's coping repertoire and triggers antecedents for individual symptoms. Effective coping strategies can then be identified and enhanced and unhelpful ones discarded. New strategies, such as relaxation or distraction, may then be taught to extend the person's coping repertoire.

Randomized Controlled Trials

The SOCRATES trial (Tarrier et al., 1993) included CSE as a prominent element in their CBT package. The number and frequency with which coping strategies were subsequently used increased and patients receiving CSE showed significant reductions in psychotic symptoms compared with no-treatment controls; however, there are no RCTs evaluating CSE as a stand-alone treatment.

Conclusions

CSE alone does not meet Chambless and Hollon's (1998) criteria for an evidence-based therapy.

FAMILY INTERVENTION

Family environment mediates the course and outcome of schizophrenia (Vaughn & Leff, 1976). Patients living in households with high expressed emotion (EE) have significantly poorer social functioning than those living with low EE relatives (Barrowclough & Tarrier, 1990), and family environment predicts relapse (Butzlaff & Hooley, 1998; Marom, Munitz, Jones, Weizman, & Hermesh, 2005). Thus, therapies that reduce high EE may be effective. Family intervention applies behavioral, cognitive, and systemic theories and methods to assist the family to effectively cope with distress and behavioral disturbance, to provide family support and education to improve the way in which the family communicates and solves problems, and to be aware of the early signs of relapse and take preventative action.

Pharoah, Mari, Rathbone, and Streiner (2006) described seven major aims for family intervention programs: (1) construction of an alliance with relatives who care for the person with schizophrenia; (2) reduction of adverse family atmosphere, that is, lowering the emotional climate in the family by reducing stress and burden on relatives; (3) enhancement of the capacity of relatives to anticipate and solve problems; (4) reduction of expressions of anger and guilt by the family; (5) maintenance of reasonable expectations for patient performance; (6) encouragement of relatives to set and keep to appropriate limits while maintaining some degree of separation when needed; and (7) attainment of desirable change in relatives' behavior and belief systems. In order to achieve these aims, family therapy might involve training in communication skills, problem solving, crisis management, relapse prevention, and psychoeducation. Individual programs may also target specific circumstances and difficulties of the family in question. Accordingly, family intervention is often lengthy (more than 10 sessions) and complex, possibly requiring multidisciplinary coordination. Several treatment guidelines exist for the implementation of family intervention (Goldstein, 1994; K. T. Mueser, Gingerich, & Rosenthal, 1994; Sin, Moone, & Newell, 2007) and measures of EE have been developed to identify families at risk (Rutter & Brown, 1966).

Meta-Analysis of Group Designs

Pilling et al. (2002a) presented a meta analysis of 18 methodologically rigorous trials with 1,467 participants. Eleven studies compared relapse rates in persons receiving family intervention with persons receiving other treatments, including standard care. The risk of relapse within a 4-year period was 0.38 for family intervention and 0.54 for other treatments. There was a significant odds ratio of 0.37 (95% CI 0.23 to 0.59; NNT 6) favoring family intervention in the first 12 month

postintervention and compared to other active therapies such as supportive therapy, nursing support, and relatives groups with a focus on education. There was a nonsignificant odds ratio of 0.89 (95% CI 0.71 to 1.38; NNT 23). When hospital readmission rates were also examined for single-family interventions, rather than multifamily groups, a significant odds ratio was observed in the first 12 months (OR = 0.21; 95% CI 0.09 to 0.51; NNT 3) and up to 2 years posttreatment (OR = 0.23; 95% CI 0.11 to 0.46; NNT 1.18). Family function data from measures of burden and expressed emotion showed a small to medium treatment effect size for family burden (2 RCT; WMD −0.43; 95% CI −0.82 to −0.05), but no significant advantage for family intervention with respect to overall EE was observed (4 RCT; OR 0.9; 95% CI 0.48 to 1.72; NNT 27). Thus, family intervention reduces relapse and readmission rates, reduced readmissions and reduced family burden, although no reliable treatment effect was observed for expressed emotion.

Pharoah et al. (2006) present a meta analysis of 43 RCTs of high methodological quality, with 4,124 participants diagnosed with schizophrenia or schizoaffective disorder, comparing family intervention with standard care (see Table 10.2). Family intervention was associated with a reduced number of hospital admissions and the total number of days spent in the hospital up to 2 years after intervention and improvement in clinician's ratings of global functioning. There was no significant difference in attrition rates between family intervention and standard care, suggesting that family intervention is as tolerable as other routine psychiatric interventions. Family intervention was associated with a small, but reliable reduction in Brief Psychiatric Rating Scale scores. In the long term, there was an advantage for family intervention with respect to negative but not positive symptoms. Family intervention was associated with improved understanding of the family member with schizophrenia and increased compliance

TABLE 10.2 Summary of Family Intervention Versus Standard Care and Group Versus Individual Implementation of the Therapy

Dependent Variable	Any Family Intervention Versus Standard Care			Group Family-Based Intervention Versus Individual Family-Based Intervention		
	0 to 6 Months	7 to 12 Months	13 to 24 Months	0 to 6 Months	7 to 12 Months	13 to 24 Months
Suicide and all causes of mortality			7 RCT; $n=377$; RR = 0.79 (0.4 to 1.8)			
Service utilization						
Hospital admission		8 RCT; $n=481$; RR = 0.78 (0.6 to 0.98) NNT 8	3 RCT; $n=228$; RR = 0.46 (0.3 to 0.7); NNT 4			
Days in hospital	1 RCT; $n=48$; WMD = −6.67 (−11.6 to −1.8)					
Clinical global response						
Relapse	3 RCT; $n=213$; RR = 0.71 (0.5 to 1.1)	16 RCT; $n=857$; RR = 0.71 (0.6 to 0.8); NNT 8	6 RCT; $n=348$; RR = 0.82 (0.7 to 0.98)			1 RCT, $n=172$; RR = 0.71 (0.3 to 1.5)
Not improved	2 RCT; $n=112$; RR = 0.4 (0.2 to 0.7); NNT 2				2 RCT; $n=195$, RR = 0.70 (0.4 to 1.2)	3 RCT; $n=197$; RR = 0.71 (0.5 to 1.1)
Global assessment of functioning (GAF)		1 RCT; $n=32$; WMD 10.28 (0.2 to 20.3)	2 RCT; $n=90$; WMD 8.66 (2.9 to 14.4)			
Leaving the study early	6 RCT; $n=481$; RR = 0.86 (0.5 to 1.4)	8 RCT; $n=474$; RR = 0.81 (0.6 to 1.2)	8 RCT; $n=615$; RR = 0.79 (0.6 to 1.2)			
Compliance with medication	7 RCT; $n=369$; RR = 0.74 (0.6 to 0.9); NNT 7					1 RCT; $n=172$; RR = 1.0 (0.5 to 1.9)
Mental state and behavior						
Brief Psychiatric Rating Scale	1 RCT; $n=35$; WMD = −7.10 (−12.5 to −1.8)					
Positive symptoms (delusions, hallucinations, disordered thinking)			1 RCT; $n=32$; WMD = 6.52 (−17.9 to 4.8)			
Negative symptoms (avolition, poor self-care, blunted affect)			1 RCT; $n=32$; WMD = −5.23 (−8.4 to −2.0)			

Note: RR = Relative Risk; WMD = Weighted mean difference; NNT = numbers need to treat with medication and reductions in family burden, EE, and the family's ratings of quality of life. Family intervention resulted in improved social functioning, a small but reliable improvement on the Social Functioning Scale, and a relatively large effect upon the caregiver's ratings of social competence, although there was no significant effect on naturalistic indices of social functioning, such as employment status, ability to live independently, and imprisonment. Pharoah et al. (2006) also compared individual and multiple family group family intervention. There was an advantage for individual family therapy on the ability to live independently, but no significant advantage for relapse rates, global clinical improvement, compliance with medication, or EE; however, many of the salient clinical outcomes were not reported. Accordingly, it is premature to reach conclusions regarding any economic benefits of these different methods of delivery.

Conclusions

Family intervention meets the criteria of an evidence-based therapy (Chambless & Hollon, 1998). The existent literature contains high-quality RCTs and there is considerable consistency in the conclusions of the meta-analyses. Family intervention reduces service utilization, most notably relapse rates and hospital admissions, improves family communication and social functioning, and there may be some benefits to mental status and global functioning; however, it is unclear the degree to which increased compliance with medication may mediate such improvements.

RELAPSE PREVENTION

Early developments focused on establishing reliable methodologies for identifying early warning signs of relapse (M. J. Birchwood et al., 1989) and translated them into practicable methodologies for working with individuals to construct a *relapse signature*, capturing the unique early signs and symptoms of relapse for a given individual and developing a set of coping strategies, often termed a relapse drill, to manage them (M. Birchwood, Spencer, & McGovern, 2000). Relapse prevention work requires individuals to: (a) accept that they have a relapsing condition that needs long-term monitoring, (b) recognize early warning signs, and (c) change their behavior accordingly and/or initiate care and support from others. It may prove difficult to use relapse prevention to less well-engaged populations; for these groups caregivers or health-care professionals may conduct relapse prevention. This model includes psychoeducation, self-monitoring, and implicitly cognitive therapy to reduce hopelessness and perceptions of entrapment that may aid recovery and prevent often traumatic repeated admissions.

Noncontrolled Group Designs

Increases in early warning signs reliably predict relapse (M. J. Birchwood et al.1989) and, although there are a number of individual case studies (M. Birchwood et al. 2000; Bywood, Gresswell, Robertson, & Ellwood, 2006), there are no RCTs of relapse prevention alone. Systematic evaluations have mostly been in the context of broader CBT trials or as part of other illness self-management programs (K. Mueser & Gingerich, 2008).

Conclusions

The existent literature is promising and provides an indirect suggestion of a useful therapeutic program; however, early signs relapse prevention does not currently meet Chambless and Hollon's (1998) criteria of evidence-based psychotherapy due to the paucity of well-controlled studies.

COMPLIANCE THERAPY

Medication compliance is influenced by cognitive impairment (R. Kemp & David, 1996), therapeutic alliance, health beliefs (Llorca, 2008), and treatment tolerability (Perkins, 2002).

It is associated with risk of relapse, symptom exacerbation and rehospitalization (Law, Soumerai, Ross-Degnan, & Adams, 2008; Llorca, 2008), and suicide (Llorca, 2008). Compliance therapy is a brief intervention, typically fewer than 10 sessions, which uses CBT-derived techniques, including motivational interviewing and psychoeducation, and reviews the patient's history, their understanding of the illness, and exploration of their "ambivalence to treatment, maintenance medication, and stigma" (O'Donnell et al., 2003, p. 2).

Randomized Controlled Trials

Tay (2007) reported on a consecutive cohort of 69 participants with relapsed schizophrenia or major depression. Individual or group compliance therapy was implemented by nursing staff. Attitudes toward medication and treatment adherence improved. Patients with a chronic relapsing history of six or more admissions showed a significant but reduced treatment effect, while those with additional personality disorder and/or comorbid substance misuse did not evidence significant improvement.

R. Kemp and colleagues (R. Kemp & David, 1996; R. Kemp, Hayward, Applewhaite, Everitt, & David, 1996; R. Kemp, Kirov, Everitt, Hayward, & David, 1998) reported two RCTs. R. Kemp et al. (1996) randomized 47 participants with psychosis to either compliance therapy (N = 25) or nonspecific counseling (N = 22). The compliance therapy intervention consisted of four to six 20- to 60-minute twice weekly sessions matched against a comparable number of sessions of supportive counseling in which the same therapists listened to the patients' concerns but did not discuss treatment. The compliance therapy group showed approximately 23% greater improvement in medication compliance, sustained at 3- and 6-month follow-up and a 14% increase in mean insight up to 6 months later relative to the control group. The compliance therapy group did not show advantages on the Global Assessment of Function scores immediately after the

intervention; however, the intervention group continued to improve at 3- and 6-month follow-up. Both groups improved on psychiatric symptomatology, as measured by the Brief Psychiatric Rating Scale. R. Kemp et al. (1998) reported outcomes at 18 months in 74 participants, inclusive of 47 participants reported in R. Kemp et al. (1996). At follow-up, the compliance therapy group maintained greater insight and medication compliance. Global social functioning was comparable between groups at the end of the intervention but favored the compliance therapy group over time. The compliance therapy group spent less time in the hospital than the control group during follow-up (compliance therapy = 41.7 days [SD = 75.5]; nonspecific counseling = 61.6 days [SD = 90.8]). Both of these studies employed participants with mixed psychotic diagnoses. As participants with a primary diagnosis of schizophrenia constituted only 70% and 58% of the respective samples, the direct relevance of these data specifically to persons with a diagnosis of schizophrenia is tentative.

O'Donnell et al. (2003) reported a RCT involving 56 participants with a primary diagnosis of schizophrenia, assigned to either compliance therapy (N = 28) or nonspecific counseling (N = 28). Both interventions followed R. Kemp et al.'s (1996, 1998) protocols. Blind raters assessed outcomes at 12 months postintervention. Compliance therapy offered no significant advantage over nonspecific counseling with respect to improving medication compliance at 1 year (OR = 0.65, CI 0.20 to .2.12) and there was no advantage in terms of insight, psychiatric symptomatology, attitudes to treatment, global level of functioning, or quality of life.

Meta-Analysis of Group Designs

McIntosh, Conlon, Lawrie, and Stanfield (2006) conducted a meta-analysis of three RCTs (R. A. Kemp & David, 1995; R. Kemp et al., 1998; O'Donnell et al., 2003). They excluded two trials (R. A. Kemp & David, 1995; R. Kemp et al., 1998) due to heterogeneous patient groups. Based on only one trial (O'Donnell et al., 2003), they concluded that compliance therapy did not substantially affect attitudes to treatment ($N = 50$, WMD DAI score –2.10 CI –6.11 to 1.91) and no advantage was observed for measures of mental state ($N = 50$, WMD PANSS score 6.1 CI –4.54 to 16.74), insight ($N = 50$, WMD SAI –0.5 CI –2.43 to 1.43), global functioning ($N = 50$, WMD GAF –4.20 CI –16.42 to 8.02), and quality of life ($N = 50$, WMD QLS –3.40 CI –16.25 to 9.45).

Conclusions

Compliance therapy is effective in increasing medication compliance in mixed diagnostic groups in which there is a preponderance of participants with schizophrenia or schizophrenia spectrum disorders (R. Kemp et al., 1996, 1998); however, the existent evidence base for compliance therapy would not fulfill the Chambless and Hollon (1998) criteria of an evidence-based therapy as the existent evidence base of efficacy is sensitively dependent on two studies (R. A. Kemp & David, 1995; R. Kemp et al., 1998) that employed heterogeneous patient groups. Further empirical studies of homogeneous patient groups are required before confident conclusions regarding efficacy can be drawn for persons affected by schizophrenia.

PSYCHODYNAMIC AND PSYCHOANALYTIC PSYCHOTHERAPIES

Psychoanalytically informed psychotherapies have long been associated with the treatment of schizophrenia. They came to prominence following Sullivan and Fromm-Riechman in the 1930s and 1950s respectively. These therapies focus on the relationship, unconscious process, and defenses.

Meta-Analysis of Group Designs

Malmberg and Fenton (2001) reported a meta-analysis of 4 RCTs of individual psychodynamic psychotherapy and/or psychoanalysis for people with schizophrenia or severe mental illness. No advantage was observed for psychodynamic psychotherapy when compared with standard care with regard to eligibility for discharge (1 RCT; $N = 92$; RR = 1.1; 95% CI 0.2 to 7.4), reduction in suicide rate (1 RCT; $N = 92$; RR = 0.16; 95% CI 0.01 to 2.93), reduction in medication at 12 months (1 RCT; $N = 92$; RR = 0.95; 95% CI 0.85 to 1.06), and scores on the Menninger Health Sickness Scale (Luborsky, 1962) (1 RCT; $N = 92$; MD = –0.8; 95% CI –5.35 to 3.75). Much debate has focused around the interpretation of the RCTs included in this meta-analysis because diagnostic criteria were broad, each study had its own approach to psychotherapy theory, investigator allegiance might have been a biasing factor, and therapists may have been inexperienced (Tarrier, Haddock, Barrowclough, & Wykes, 2002).

Gottdiener (2004) reported positive outcomes for psychodynamic psychotherapy, with moderate advantages for psychodynamic psychotherapy ($d = 0.65$; 95% CI 0.45 to 1.00) when compared with standard care. Unfortunately, reports aggregated outcomes, and details of specific outcomes (e.g., mental status) were not reported. Therefore, Gottdiener's conclusions should be treated with extreme caution.

Randomized Controlled Trials

Rosenbaum et al. (2005) reported outcomes on 562 patients with first episode psychosis allocated to either T1, psychodynamic psychotherapy and medication, T2, an integrated treatment program including medication, assertive outreach, family therapy, and social skills training, or T3, a treatment as usual group that included medication and social support. Patients receiving T1 or T2 showed greater improvement in Global Assessment of Functioning scores compared to treatment as usual. Patients in both T2 and T3 showed reduced hospital admissions over the first 12 months of treatment; however, no effect was observed for the patients receiving psychodynamic psychotherapy and medication.

Conclusions

Evidence from more methodologically rigorous studies does not support the efficacy of psychodynamic psychotherapy, although the most recent RCTs (Rosenbaum et al., 2005) allude to positive outcomes; however, if the Chambless and Hollon (1998) criteria of an evidence-based therapy is to be met then more methodological robust clinical trials are required.

COGNITIVE REMEDIATION THERAPY

As many as 70% of patients with schizophrenia exhibit cognitive impairment (Palmer et al., 1997) such as deficits in processing speed, controlled attention, working memory, new learning, and executive/reasoning functions (Goldberg & Gold, 1995). Resistant cognitive deficits represent a formidable impediment to occupational and social functioning (Bellack, Dickinson, Morris, & Tenhula, 2005; McGurk & Mueser, 2004), independent living (McGurk & Mueser, 2004), and have been associated with poor response to psychiatric rehabilitation (McGurk & Mueser, 2004).

Cognitive remediation promotes recovery of cognitive and behavioral functioning through teaching and practicing information processing strategies on repeated graded tasks. Cognitive remediation therapy may be administered individually or in groups or as computer-based training (Bellack et al., 2005; Kurtz, Seltzer, Shagan, Thime, & Wexler, 2007; Sartory, Zorn, Groetzinger, & Windgassen, 2005). Two neurobehavioral retraining strategies are commonly employed *drill and practice* and *drill and strategy coaching* reflecting different models of recovery from neurocognitive impairment (Rothi & Horner, 1983). Drill and practice attempts to increase integrity of the injured functional system and is predicated on experience-dependent plasticity

(Robertson & Murre, 1999). Drill and strategy coaching assumes that improvement results from functional reorganization or compensation and is influenced by compensatory reorganization during neurobehavioral recovery (Luria, 1948/1963). Assessment protocols for identifying neurocognitive impairment in persons with schizophrenia are described by Harvey, Keefe, Patterson, Heaton, and Bowie (2008). Global neuropsychological deficit was very well predicted by two measures of processing speed (Trail Making Part B [Reitan, 1958] and the Digit Symbol Subtest of the Wechsler Adult Intelligence Scale, Third Edition [Wechsler, 1997]), and these two measures may be usefully employed as screening tasks prior to administration of a more extensive neuropsychological assessment battery.

Meta-Analysis of Group Designs

There have been several meta-analytic reviews of cognitive remediation with patients with schizophrenia (Krabbendam & Aleman, 2003; Kurtz, Moberg, Gur, & Gur, 2001; McGurk, Twamley, Sitzer, McHugo, & Mueser, 2007; Pilling et al., 2002b; Twamley, Jeste, & Bellack, 2003). Kurtz et al. (2001) reviewed 11 RCTs and reported that cognitive remediation was associated with improved performance on the Wisconsin Card Sorting Task (categories completed: $d = 1.08$, 95% CI 0.8 to 1.37; perseverative errors: $d = 0.93$, 95% CI 0.64 to 1.21; conceptual learning: $d = 0.9$, 95% CI 0.52 to 1.28). Krabbendam and Aleman (2003) reviewed 12 RCTs and found a moderate effect favoring cognitive remediation therapy ($d = 0.45$, 95% CI 0.26 to 0.64). An advantage for drill and strategy coaching (9 RCT, $d = 0.52$, 95% CI 0.25 to 0.78) was observed over drill and practice strategies (6 RCT, $d = 0.34$, 95% CI 0.03 to 0.70), but this difference did not reach statistical significance. Pilling et al. (2002b) examined the efficacy of cognitive remediation therapy in five high-quality RCTs with 170 participants, three domains of cognitive functioning (attention, verbal memory, and visual memory), and total Brief Psychiatric Rating Scale scores. Neither attention (2 RCT; $N = 87$; $d = 0.11$; 95% CI –0.31 to 0.53), verbal memory (4 RCT; $N = 117$; $d = 0.14$; 95% CI –0.23 to 0.50), visual memory (2 RCT; $N = 48$; $d = 0.34$; 95% CI –0.23 to 0.92), or mental state (2 RCT; $N = 84$; $d = -0.23$; 95% CI –0.66 to 0.20) showed any advantage for cognitive remediation therapy.

These three meta-analyses suggest that cognitive remediation therapy is associated with moderate improvements on tests of neurocognitive functioning, but there is insufficient evidence of generalization to other functional outcomes; however, Pilling et al. (2002b) meta-analyzed only a small subset of the available studies and its pessimistic conclusions are inconsistent with the conclusions of the other studies. For example, McGurk et al. (2007) presented a more extensive meta-analysis of 26 RCTs, with 1,151 participants. Seven domains of cognitive function were reported: attention, speed of processing, verbal working memory, verbal learning and memory, visual learning and memory, and reasoning and problem solving. In addition, McGurk et al. (2007) reported three functional outcomes: social cognition,

psychiatric symptomatology, and psychosocial functioning. Effect sizes, confidence intervals, and number of participants for these domains of function are presented in Table 10.3. Small to moderate effects on cognitive abilities was observed in all domains of functioning, except visual learning and memory, evidencing significant advantages for cognitive remediation therapy. Benefits of cognitive remediation therapy were also generalized to social cognition, psychiatric symptomatology, and psychosocial functioning.

Two further RCTs have been published. Lindenmayer et al. (2008) evaluated the feasibility and efficacy of a computer-based cognitive remediation program to improve cognitive and work functioning for 85 intermediate- to long-stay psychiatric inpatients. Patients in the cognitive remediation group demonstrated significantly greater improvements over 3 months than the control group with respect to overall cognitive functioning. In addition, patients who received cognitive remediation worked more weeks than the control group over the 12-month follow-up period. Hodge et al. (2010) examined the efficacy of cognitive remediation in 40 persons with schizophrenia. Significant advantages for cognitive remediation therapy were observed with regard to verbal and visual

TABLE 10.3 Effect Sizes and Confidence Intervals for Cognitive, Social, and Psychiatric Outcomes

Outcome Domain	Effect Size	Lower 95% CI	Upper 95% CI	Participants N
Global cognition	0.41	0.29	0.52	1214
Attention/vigilance	0.41	0.25	0.57	659
Speed of processing	0.48	0.28	0.69	655
Verbal working memory	0.52	0.33	0.72	428
Verbal learning and memory	0.39	0.2	0.58	858
Visual learning and memory	0.09	–0.26	0.43	424
Reasoning/problem solving	0.47	0.3	0.64	564
Social cognition	0.54	0.22	0.88	228
Psychiatric symptoms	0.28	0.13	0.43	709
Psychosocial functioning	0.35	0.07	0.62	615

Note: Effect size: small > = 0.2; moderate > = 0.5; and large > = 0.8

Source: McGurk (2007)

memory, sustained attention and executive functioning, and with a mild to moderate average effect size. Once again, social and occupational outcomes also evidenced improvement as a result of cognitive remediation therapy.

Conclusions

Cognitive remediation therapy fulfills Chambless and Hollon's (1998) criteria of an evidence-based therapy. It is effective with regard to remediating the impairment of cognitive function, with effect sizes generally suggesting moderate improvement. The effects of cognitive remediation therapy can generalize to other domains of functioning, especially social functioning and psychiatric symptomatology. At present there is no evidence of differences between drill and practice and drill and strategy coaching.

SUPPORTIVE COUNSELING

These approaches have their origins in the work of Carl Rogers and other humanistic psychologists and aim to be person centered and, as in the case of some supportive psychotherapies (Van Marle & Holmes, 2002), are integrative, drawing on a broad range of psychotherapeutic approaches. Consequently, these interventions are not well defined and are difficult to manualize and systematically evaluate. They often appear as comparison treatments in CBT trials and have received little independent systematic evaluation. Commonly these therapies are nondirective and involve empathic listening and unconditional positive regard for the client.

Meta-Analyses of Group Designs

A recent meta-analysis (Buckley, Pettit, & Adams, 2007) comprising 1,683 participants compared supportive counseling to standard care and other psychological therapies in the short (< 13 weeks), medium (13 to 26 weeks),

or long term (> 26 weeks). There was no significant difference in relapse rates in either the medium (1 RCT; $N = 54$; RR = 0.12; 95% CI 0.01 to 2.1) or the long term (1 RCT; $N = 54$; RR = 0.96; 95% CI 0.4 to 2.1), and no evidence of a significant advantage for supportive counseling with respect to hospitalization rates (1 RCT; $N = 48$; RR = 1.00; 95% CI 0.1 to 15.1), reduction in antipsychotic medication (1 RCT; $N = 44$; RR = 0.81; 95% CI 0.6 to 1.2), clinically important improvement (medium term, 1 RCT; $N = 63$; RR = 0.95; 95% CI 0.8 to 1.2; long term, 2 RCT; $N = 98$; RR = 0.98; 95% CI 0.8 to 1.1), the Positive and Negative Symptom Scale (1 RCT; $N = 131$; WMD 1.09; 95% CI −2.8 to 0.7) and the Global Assessment Scale (1 RCT; $N = 29$; WMD 1.4; 95% CI −5.1 to 7.9). When compared with other psychological interventions, supportive counseling was found to be significantly *less* effective than rehabilitation programs at reducing hospitalization rates (1 RCT; $N = 132$; RR 2.71; 95% CI 1.2 to 6.0), *less* effective than family therapy with respect to relapse rates (2 RCT; $N = 87$; RR 1.58; 95% CI 1.1 to 2.3) and *less* effective than CBT with respect to improvements on the General Assessment Scale (short term, 1 RCT; $N = 70$; WMD −9.50; 95% CI −16.1 to −2.9; medium term, 1 RCT; $N = 67$; WMD −12.60; 95% CI −19.4 to −5.8). In a small scale study, Haddock et al. (1999) found that compared to CBT, supportive counseling was equally effective. Younger patients who were harder to engage showed the most benefit from supportive counseling (Lewis, Tarrier, & Haddock, 2002; Tarrier et al., 2004).

Conclusions

Supportive counseling does not fulfill the Chambless and Hollon (1998) criteria for an evidence-based therapy. Indeed, there is replicable evidence that supportive counseling is reliably inferior to other evidence-based treatments of schizophrenia. Supportive counseling may be a useful adjunct to existing approaches, particularly where longer term work that emphasizes the importance of the therapeutic relationship is indicated and where the individual may not yet be able to engage in more structured interventions, although there is currently no evidence supporting this assertion.

OVERALL CONCLUSIONS

Psychological and psychosocial interventions have developed rapidly over the past two decades and become widely accepted as part of a comprehensive set of routine interventions in the treatment and management of schizophrenia. These approaches have developed alongside traditional treatments, such as antipsychotic medication, to enable better management and treatment of schizophrenia. Token economies and other operant interventions for overt psychotic behaviors have been demonstrated as effective in remediating both positive and negative symptoms but more empirical evaluation, preferably using randomized between subjects designs, is needed to demonstrate the longevity of these therapeutic effects after the termination of contingent reinforcement.

The CBT initially evolved to address residual positive symptoms (Tarrier et al., 1993; Tarrier et al., 1998), and has now been adapted to work with a range of psychotic symptoms and important comorbidities (Rathod & Turkington, 2005) as well as helping affected individuals adjust to and cope with the life changing consequences of developing the disorder. Although there is insufficient evidence to support its efficacy as a distinct therapy, CSE is often employed as part of a range of treatment programs with demonstrable efficacy to better manage ongoing positive symptoms, as well as emerging symptoms that may herald a relapse. Psychoeducation, both for patients and caregivers, has become a standard intervention to promote insight and implicitly address unhelpful patient and family assumptions. It thereby reduces the risk of relapse and enhances compliance with treatment. Family work is perhaps one of the best known approaches to aid in the prevention of relapse through addressing unhelpful family dynamics and attitudes. This approach is perhaps best exemplified in behavioral family therapy. Social skills training has been demonstrated to be efficacious in improving independent and daily living activities. More recently, cognitive remediation therapy (Wykes & Reader, 2005) has been developed to address the disabling effects of negative symptoms and residual cognitive deficits.

Compliance therapy (R. Kemp et al., 1998) is explicitly intended to promote adherence to medication and foster insight. As the current efficacy literature for compliance therapy is greatly influenced by studies that have used heterogeneous patient groups, the balance of the existent evidence has yet to establish compliance therapy as an effective program of treatment for persons with a primary diagnosis of schizophrenia.

Psychoanalytic interventions have yet to provide sufficient evidence of their efficacy with persons with psychosis; however, the potential of insight-oriented therapies with specific subgroups of persons with psychosis, such as those lacking in insight or who are demoralized, has yet to be fully explored. Similarly, supportive counseling has not yet demonstrated its efficacy with respect to either symptom reduction or service utilization; indeed, supportive counseling has been demonstrated to be less effective than other psychological interventions with respect to a range of different therapeutic outcomes.

The past 30 years have seen considerable efforts to develop psychological interventions for persons with schizophrenia and there is now a considerable cannon of effective therapies available to supplement other modalities of treatment. Psychological interventions have demonstrably beneficial effects with respect to a range of pertinent clinical outcomes, including psychological and psychiatric symptomatology, service utilization, relapse rates, cognitive impairment, and quality of life.

REFERENCES

American Psychiatric Association. (2000). *Diagnostic and statistical manual of mental disorders: DSM-IV-TR*. Washington, DC: Author.

Ayllon, J. M., & Azrin, N. H. (1965). The measurement and reinforcement of behavior of psychotics. *Journal of Experimental Analysis of Behavior, 8*, 357–383.

Barrowclough, C., & Tarrier, N. (1990). Social functioning in schizophrenic patients. I. The effects of expressed emotion and family intervention. *Social Psychiatry and Psychiatric Epidemiology, 25*, 125–129.

Belcher, T. L. (1988). Behavioral reduction of overt hallucinatory behavior in a chronic schizophrenic. *Journal of Behavioral Therapy and Experimental Psychiatry, 19*, 69–71.

Bellack, A. S., Dickinson, D., Morris, S. E., & Tenhula, W. N. (2005). The development of a computer-assisted cognitive remediation program for patients with schizophrenia. *Israel Journal of Psychiatry and Related Sciences, 42*, 5–14.

Bentall, R. P. (2003). *Madness explained: Psychosis and human nature*. London, England: Penguin Press.

Benton, M. K., & Schroeder, H. E. (1990). Social skills training with schizophrenics: A meta-analytic evaluation. *Journal of Consulting and Clinical Psychology, 58*, 741–747.

Birchwood, M., Spencer, E., and McGovern, D. (2000). Schizophrenia: Early warning signs. *Advances in Psychiatric Treatment, 6*, 93–101.

Birchwood, M. J., Smith, J., MacMillan, F., Hogg, B., Prasad, R., Harvey, C., & Bering, S. (1989). Predicting relapse in schizophrenia: The development and implementation of an early signs monitoring system using patients and families as observers. *Psychological Medicine, 19*, 649–656.

Buckley, L. A., Pettit, T., & Adams, C. E. (2007). Supportive therapy for schizophrenia. *Cochrane Database of Systematic Reviews (Online), 4*, Art No CD004716.

Butzlaff, R. L., & Hooley, J. M. (1998). Expressed emotion and psychiatric relapse. *Archives of General Psychiatry, 55*, 547–552.

Bywood, L., Cresswell, D. M., Robertson, C., & Elwood, P. (2006). A behavioural versus a cognitive analysis of the relapse prodrome in psychosis. In J. O. Johannessen, B. Martindale, & J. Cullberg (Eds.), *Evolving psychosis: different stages, different treatments* (pp. 81–105). New York, NY: Routledge.

Chadwick, P., & Birchwood, M. (1994). The omnipotence of voices: A cognitive approach to auditory hallucinations. *British Journal of Psychiatry, 164*, 190–201.

Chadwick, P. D., & Lowe, C. F. (1990). Measurement and modification of delusional beliefs. *Journal of Consulting and Clinical Psychology, 58*, 225–232.

Chadwick, P. D. J., Lowe, C. F., Horne, P. J., & Higson, P. J. (1994). Modifying delusions: The role of empirical testing. *Behaviour Therapy, 25*, 35–49.

Chambless, D. L., & Hollon, S. D. (1998). Defining empirically supported therapies. *Journal of Consulting and Clinical Psychology, 66*, 7–18.

Corrigan, P. W. (1991). Social skills training in adult psychiatric populations: A meta-analysis. *Journal of Behavior Therapy and Experimental Psychiatry, 22*, 203–210.

Corrigan, P. W., & J. E. Larson. (2008). Stigma. In K. T. Mueser & D. V. Jeste (Eds.), *Clinical handbook of schizophrenia* (pp. 533–540). New York, NY: Guilford Press.

Curran, J. P. (1982). A procedure for assessing social skills: The simulated social interaction test. In J. P. Curran & P. M. Monti (Eds.) *Social skills training: A practical handbook for assessment and training* (pp. 348–373). New York, NY: Guilford Press.

Drury, V., Birchwood, M., Cochrane, R., & Macmillan, F. (1996). Cognitive therapy and recovery from acute psychosis: A controlled trial. II. Impact on recovery time. *British Journal of Psychiatry, 169*, 602–607.

Elliot, P. A., Barlow, F., Hooper, A., & Kingerlee, P. E. (1979). Maintaining patients improvements in a token economy. *Behaviour Research and Therapy, 17*, 355–367.

Foxx, R. M., McMorrow, M. J., Davis, L. A., & Bittle, R. G. (1988). Replacing a chronic schizophrenic man's delusional speech with stimulus appropriate responses. *Journal of Behavior Therapy and Experimental Psychiatry, 19*, 43–50.

Garety, P. A., Fowler, D. G., Freeman, D., Bebbington, P., Dunn, G., & Kuipers, E. (2008). Cognitive behavioural therapy and family intervention for relapse prevention and symptom reduction in psychosis: Randomised controlled trial. *British Journal of Psychiatry, 192*, 412–423.

Goldberg, T. E., & Gold, J. M. (1995). Neurocognitive functioning in patients with schizophrenia: an overview. In K. L. Davis, D. Charney, J. T. Coyle, and C. Nemeroff (Eds.), *Psychopharmacology, the fifth generation of progress* (pp. 1245–1257). Philadelphia, PA: Lippincott Williams & Wilkins.

Goldstein, M. J. (1994). Psychoeducational and family therapy in relapse prevention. *Acta Psychiatrica Scandinavica Supplementum, 382*, 54–57.

Gottdiener, W. R. (2004). Psychodynamic psychotherapy for schizophrenia: Empirical support. In J. Read, L. R. Mosher, & R. Bentall (Eds.), *Models of madness: Psychological, social and biological approaches to schizophrenia* (pp. 307–318). London, England: Brunner Routledge.

Haddock, G., Tarrier, N., Morrison, A., Hopkins, R., Drake, R., & Lewis, S. (1999). A pilot study evaluating the effectiveness of individual psychosis. *Social Psychiatry and Psychiatric Epidemiology, 34*, 254–258.

Harvey, P. D., Keefe, R. S., Patterson, T. L., Heaton, R. K., & Bowie, C. R. (2008). Abbreviated neuropsychological assessment in schizophrenia: Prediction of different aspects of outcome. *Journal of Clinical and Experimental Neuropsychology, 31*, 1–10.

Hayes, R. L., Halford, W. K., & Varghese, F. T. (1995). Social skills training with chronic schizophrenic patients: Effects on negative symptoms and community functioning. *Behavior Therapy, 26*, 433–449.

Heisel, M. J. (2008). Suicide. In K. T. Meuser, and D. V. Jeste (Eds.), *Clinical handbook of schizophrenia* (pp. 491–505). New York, NY: Guilford Press.

Hodge, M. A. R., Siciliano, D., Withey, P., Moss, B., Moore, G., Judd, G., . . . Harris, A. (2010). A randomized controlled trial of cognitive remediation in schizophrenia. *Schizophrenia Bulletin, 36*(2), 419.

Jimenez, J. M., Todman, M., Perez, M., Godoy, J. F., & Landon-Jimenez, D. V. (1996). The behavioral treatment of auditory hallucinatory responding of a schizophrenic patient. *Journal of Behavior Therapy and Experimental Psychiatry, 27*, 299–310.

Jones, C., Cormac, I., Silveira da Mota Neto, J. I., & Campbell, C. (2004). Cognitive behaviour therapy for schizophrenia. *Cochrane Database of Systematic Reviews (Online), 4*, Art. No. CD000524.

Kemp, R. A., & David, A. S. (1995). Insight and adherence to treatment in psychotic disorders. *British Journal of Hospital Medicine, 54*, 222–227.

Kemp, R., & David, A. (1996). Psychological predictors of insight and compliance in psychotic patients. *British Journal of Psychiatry: The Journal of Mental Science, 169*, 444–450.

Kemp, R., Hayward, P., Applewhaite, G., Everitt, B., & David, A. (1996). Compliance therapy in psychotic patients: Randomised controlled trial. *British Medical Journal, 312*(7027), 345–349.

Kemp, R., Kirov, G., Everitt, B., Hayward, P., & David, A. (1998). Randomised controlled trial of compliance therapy. 18-month follow-up. *British Journal of Psychiatry: The Journal of Mental Science, 172*, 413–419.

Kopelowicz, A., Liberman, R. P., & Zarate, R. (2006). Recent advances in social skills training for schizophrenia. *Schizophrenia Bulletin, 32*(suppl. 1), S12–S23.

Krabbendam, L., & Aleman, A. (2003). Cognitive rehabilitation in schizophrenia: A quantitative analysis of controlled studies. *Psychopharmacology, 169*, 376–382.

Kuipers, E., Garety, P., Fowler, D., Dunn, G., Bebbington, P., Freeman, D., . . . Hadley, C. (1997). London-East Anglia randomised controlled trial of cognitive-behavioural therapy for psychosis. I: Effects of the treatment phase. *British Journal of Psychiatry, 171*, 319–327.

Kurtz, M. M., Moberg, P. J., Gur, R. C., & Gur, R. E. (2001). Approaches to cognitive remediation of neuropsychological deficits in schizophrenia: A review

and meta-analysis. *Neuropsychology Review, 11*, 197–210.

Kurtz, M. M., & Mueser, K. T. (2008). A meta-analysis of controlled research on social skills training for schizophrenia. *Journal of Consulting and Clinical Psychology, 76*, 491–504.

Kurtz, M. M., Seltzer, J. C., Shagan, D. S., Thime, W. R., & Wexler, B. E. (2007). Computer-assisted cognitive remediation in schizophrenia: What is the active ingredient? *Schizophrenia Research, 89*, 251–260.

Lancaster, B. M., LeBlanc, L. A., Carr, J. E., Brenske, S., Peet, M. M., & Culver, S. J. (2004). Functional analysis and treatment of the bizarre speech of dually diagnosed adults. *Journal of Applied Behavior Analysis, 37*, 395–399.

Law, M. R., Soumerai, S. B., Ross-Degnan, D., & Adams, A. S. (2008). A longitudinal study of medication nonadherence and hospitalization risk in schizophrenia. *Journal of Clinical Psychiatry, 69*, 47–53.

Lewis, S., Tarrier, N., & Haddock, G. (2002). Randomised controlled trial of cognitive-behavioural therapy in early schizophrenia: Acute-phase outcomes. *British Journal of Psychiatry, 181* (suppl. 43), 91–97.

Li, F., & Wang, M. A. (1994). A behavioural training programme for chronic schizophrenic patients: A three-month randomised controlled trial in Beijing. *British Journal of Psychiatry, 164*, 32–37.

Liberman, R. P., Teigen, J., Patterson, R., & Baker, V. (1973). Reducing delusional speech in chronic, paranoid schizophrenics. *Journal of Applied Behavior Analysis, 6*, 57–64.

Lindenmayer, J. P., McGurk, S. R., Mueser, K. T., Khan, A., Wance, D., Hoffman, L., . . . Xie, H. (2008). A randomized controlled trial of cognitive remediation among inpatients with persistent mental illness. *Psychiatric Services (Washington, DC), 59*, 241–247.

Llorca, P. M. (2008). Partial compliance in schizophrenia and the impact on patient outcomes. *Psychiatry Research, 161*, 235–247.

Luborsky, L. (1962). Clinicians judgements of mental health: A proposed scale. *Archives of General Psychiatry, 7*, 407–417.

Luria, A. R. (1948/1963). *Restoration of function after brain injury* (B. Haigh, Trans.). London, England: Pergamon.

Maley, R. F., Feldman, G. L., & Ruskin, R. S. (1973). Evaluation of patient improvement in a token economy treatment program. *Journal of Abnormal Psychology, 82*, 141.

Malmberg, L. and Fenton, M. (2001). Individual psychodynamic psychotherapy and psychoanalysis for schizophrenia and severe mental illness (Cochrane Review). *Cochrane Library, 4.* http://onlinelibrary .wiley.com/doi/10.1002/14651858.CD001360/abstract. Oxford, England: Update Software.

Marder, S. R., Wirshing, W. C., Mintz, J., McKenzie, J., Johnston, K., Eckman, T. A., . . . Liberman, R. P.

(1996). Two-year outcome of social skills training and group psychotherapy for outpatients with schizophrenia. *American Journal of Psychiatry, 153,* 1585–1592.

Marom, S., Munitz, H., Jones, P. B., Weizman, A., & Hermesh, H. (2005). Expressed emotion: Relevance to rehospitalization in schizophrenia over 7 years. *Schizophrenia Bulletin, 31,* 751–758.

McGurk, S. R., & Mueser, K. T. (2004). Cognitive functioning, symptoms, and work in supported employment: A review and heuristic model. *Schizophrenia Research, 70,* 147–173.

McGurk, S. R., Twamley, E. W., Sitzer, D. I., McHugo, G. J., & Mueser, K. T. (2007). A meta-analysis of cognitive remediation in schizophrenia. *American Journal of Psychiatry, 164,* 1791–1802.

McIntosh, A. M., Conlon, L., Lawrie, S. M., & Stanfield, A. C. (2006). Compliance therapy for schizophrenia. *Cochrane Database of Systematic Reviews (Online), 3,* Art. No. CD003442.

Mueser, K., & Gingerich, S. (2008). Illness self management training. In K. T. Mueser & D. V. Jeste (Eds.), *Clinical Handbook of Schizophrenia* (pp. 268–278). New York, NY: Guilford Press.

Mueser, K. T., Gingerich, S. L., & Rosenthal, C. K. (1994). Educational family therapy for schizophrenia: A new treatment model for clinical service and research. *Schizophrenia Research, 13,* 99–107.

Mueser, K. T., & Penn, D. L. (2004). Meta-analysis examining the effects of social skills training on schizophrenia. *Psychological Medicine, 34,* 1365–1367.

Murray, C. J. L., and Lopez, A. D. (Eds.) (1996). *The global burden of disease: A comprehensive assessment of mortality and disability from disease, injuries, and risk factors in 1990 and projected to 2020.* Cambridge, MA: Harvard School of Public Health, on behalf of the World Health Organization and the World Bank: Harvard University Press.

Nelson, G. L., & Cone, J. D. (1979). Multiple baseline analysis of a token economy for psychiatric patients. *Journal of Applied Behavioral Analysis, 12,* 255–271.

Nuechterlein, K. H., Dawson, M. E., Ventura, J., Gitlin, M., Subotnik, K. L., Snyder, K. S., . . . Bartzokis, G. (1994). The vulnerability/stress model of schizophrenic relapse: A longitudinal study. *Acta Psychiatrica Scandinavica Supplementum, 382,* 58–64.

O'Donnell, C., Donohoe, G., Sharkey, L., Owens, N., Migone, M., Harries, R., . . . O'Callaghan, E. (2003). Compliance therapy: A randomised controlled trial in schizophrenia. *British Medical Journal (Clinical Research Ed.), 327*(7419), 834.

Palmer, B. W., Heaton, R. K., Paulsen, J. S., Kuck, J., Braff, D., Harris, M. J., . . . Jeste, D. V. (1997). Is it possible to be schizophrenic yet neuropsychologically normal? *Neuropsychology, 11,* 437–446.

Perkins, D. O. (2002). Predictors of noncompliance in patients with schizophrenia. *Journal of Clinical Psychiatry, 63,* 1121–1128.

Pharoah, F. M., Mari, J., Rathbone, J., & Streiner, D. (2006). Family intervention for schizophrenia. *Cochrane Database of Systematic Reviews (Online), 4,* Art. No. CD000088.

Pilling, S., Bebbington, P., Kuipers, E., Garety, P., Geddes, J., Orbach, G., . . . Morgan, C. (2002a). Psychological treatments in schizophrenia: I. Meta-analysis of family intervention and cognitive behaviour therapy. *Psychological Medicine, 32,* 763–782.

Pilling, S., Bebbington, P., Kuipers, E., Garety, P., Geddes, J., Martindale, B., . . . Morgan, C. (2002b). Psychological treatments in schizophrenia: II. Meta-analyses of randomized controlled trials of social skills training and cognitive remediation. *Psychological Medicine, 32,* 783–791.

Prince, J. D. (2006). Practices preventing rehospitalization of individuals with schizophrenia. *Journal of Nervous and Mental Disease, 194,* 397–403.

Rathod, S., & Turkington, D. (2005). Cognitive behaviour therapy for schizophrenia: A review. *Current Opinion in Psychiatry, 18,* 159–163.

Rector, N. A., Seeman, M. V., & Segal, Z. V. (2003). Cognitive therapy for schizophrenia: A preliminary randomized controlled trial. *Schizophrenia Research, 63,* 1–11.

Reitan, R. M. (1958). Validity of the Trail Making Test as an indicator of organic brain damage. *Perceptual and motor skills, 8,* 271–276.

Robertson, I. H., & Murre, J. M. (1999). Rehabilitation of brain damage: Brain plasticity and principles of guided recovery. *Psychological Bulletin, 125,* 544–575.

Rosenbaum, B., Valbak, K., Harder, S., Knudsen, P., Koster, A., Lajer, M., . . . Andreasen, A. H. (2005). The Danish National Schizophrenia Project: Prospective, comparative longitudinal treatment study of first-episode psychosis. *British Journal of Psychiatry: The Journal of Mental Science, 186,* 394–399.

Rothi, L. J., & Horner, J. (1983). Restitution and substitution: Two theories of recovery with application to neurobehavioral treatment. *Journal of Clinical and Experimental Neuropsychology, 5,* 73–81.

Rutter, M., & Brown, G. W. (1966). The reliability and validity of measures of family life and relationships in families containing a psychiatric patient. *Social Psychiatry and Psychiatric Epidemiology, 1,* 38–53.

Sartory, G., Zorn, C., Groetzinger, G., & Windgassen, K. (2005). Computerized cognitive remediation improves verbal learning and processing speed in schizophrenia. *Schizophrenia Research, 75,* 219–223.

Schooler, N. R. (2006). Relapse prevention and recovery in the treatment of schizophrenia. *Journal of Clinical Psychiatry, 67*(suppl. 5), 19–23.

Schooler, N., Hogarty, G., & Weissman, G. (1979). Social Adjustment Scale II (SAS II). In W. A. Hargreaves, C. C. Attkisson, & J. E. Sorensen (Eds.), *Resource materials for community mental health program evaluator* (pp. 290–303). Washington, DC: US Government Printing Office. DHEW Publication 79-328.

Sensky, T., Turkington, D., Kingdon, D., Scott, J. L., Scott, J., Siddle, R., . . . Barnes, T. R. E. (2000). A randomized controlled trial of cognitive-behavioral therapy for persistent symptoms in schizophrenia resistant to medication. *Archives of General Psychiatry, 57*, 165–172.

Sin, J., Moone, N., & Newell, J. (2007). Developing services for the carers of young adults with early-onset psychosis—implementing evidence-based practice on psycho-educational family intervention. *Journal of Psychiatric and Mental Health Nursing, 14*, 282–290.

Startup, M., Jackson, M. C., & Bendix, S. (2004). North Wales randomized controlled trial of cognitive behaviour therapy for acute schizophrenia spectrum disorders: Outcomes at 6 and 12 months. *Psychological Medicine, 34*, 413–422.

Startup, M., Jackson, M. C., Evans, K. E., & Bendix, S. (2005). North Wales randomized controlled trial of cognitive behaviour therapy for acute schizophrenia spectrum disorders: Two-year follow-up and economic evaluation. *Psychological Medicine, 35*, 1307–1316.

Tarrier, N., Beckett, R., Harwood, S., Baker, A., Yusupoff, L., & Ugarteburu, I. (1993). A trial of two cognitive-behavioural methods of treating drug-resistant residual psychotic symptoms in schizophrenic patients: I. Outcome. *British Journal of Psychiatry, 162*, 524–532.

Tarrier, N., Haddock, G., Barrowclough, C., & Wykes, T. (2002). Are all psychological treatments for psychosis equal? The need for CBT in the treatment of psychosis and not for psychodynamic psychotherapy. *Psychology and Psychotherapy, 75*, 365–374.

Tarrier, N., Lewis, S., Haddock, G., Bentall, R., Drake, R., Kinderman, P., Kingdon, D., . . . Leadley, K. (2004). Cognitive-behavioural therapy in first-episode and early schizophrenia: 18-month follow-up of a randomised controlled trial. *The British Journal of Psychiatry, 184*(3), 231.

Tarrier, N., Yusupoff, L., Kinney, C., McCarthy, E., Gledhill, A., Haddock, G., & Morris, J. (1998). Randomised controlled trial of intensive cognitive behaviour therapy for patients with chronic schizophrenia. *BMJ, 317*(7154), 303.

Tay, S. E. (2007). Compliance therapy: An intervention to improve inpatients' attitudes toward treatment. *Journal of Psychosocial Nursing and Mental Health Services, 45*, 29–37.

Trower, P., Birchwood, M., Meaden, A., Byrne, S., Nelson, A., & Ross, K. (2004). Cognitive therapy for command hallucinations: Randomised controlled trial. *British Journal of Psychiatry, 184*, 312–320.

Tsang, H. W. (2001). Applying social skills training in the context of vocational rehabilitation for people with schizophrenia. *Journal of Nervous and Mental Disease, 189*, 90–98.

Turkington, D., Kingdon, D., & Turner, T. (2002). Effectiveness of a brief cognitive-behavioural therapy intervention in the treatment of schizophrenia. *British Journal of Psychiatry, 180*, 523–537.

Twamley, E. W., Jeste, D. V., & Bellack, A. S. (2003). A review of cognitive training in schizophrenia. *Schizophrenia Bulletin, 29*, 359–382.

Van Marle, S., & Holmes, J. (2002). Supportive psychotherapy as an integrative psychotherapy. In J. Holmes & A. Bateman (Eds.), *Integration in psychotherapy: Models and methods* (pp. 175–195). Oxford, England: Oxford University Press.

Vaughn, C. E., & Leff, J. P. (1976). The influence of family and social factors on the course of psychiatric illness. A comparison of schizophrenic and depressed neurotic patients. *British Journal of Psychiatry, 129*, 125–137.

Wallace, C. J., & Liberman, R. P. (1985). Social skills training for patients with schizophrenia: A controlled clinical trial. *Psychiatry Research, 15*, 239–247.

Warner, R. (1994). *Recovery from schizophrenia* (2nd ed.). London, England: Routledge.

Wechsler, D. (1997). *WAIS-III*. San Antonio, TX: Psychological Corporation.

Wilder, D. A., Masuda, A., O'Connor, C., & Baham, M. (2001). Brief functional analysis and treatment of bizarre vocalizations in an adult with schizophrenia. *Journal of Applied Behavior Analysis, 34*, 65–68.

Wincze, J. P., Leitenberg, H., & Agras, W. S. (1972). The effects of token reinforcement and feedback on the delusional verbal behavior of chronic paranoid schizophrenics. *Journal of Applied Behavior Analysis, 5*, 247–262.

Wykes, T., & Reader, C. (2005). *Cognitive remediation therapy for schizophrenia: Theory and practice*. London, England: Routledge.

Wykes, T., Steel, C., Everitt, B., & Tarrier, N. (2008). Cognitive behavior therapy for schizophrenia: Effect sizes, clinical models, and methodological rigor. *Schizophrenia Bulletin, 34*, 523–537.

Zimmermann, G., Favrod, J., Trieu, V. H., & Pomini, V. (2005). The effect of cognitive behavioral treatment on the positive symptoms of schizophrenia spectrum disorders: A meta-analysis. *Schizophrenia Research, 77*, 1–9.

11

Depression and Dysthymic Disorders

PIM CUIJPERS, ANNEMIEKE VAN STRATEN, ELLEN DRIESSEN, PATRICIA VAN OPPEN,
CLAUDI BOCKTING, AND GERHARD ANDERSSON

OVERVIEW

Unipolar depressive disorders are highly prevalent (European Study of the Epidemiology of Mental Disorders [ESEMeD], 2004; Kessler et al., 1994), have a high incidence (Waraich, Goldner, Somers, & Hsu, 2004), are associated with huge loss of quality of life in patients and their relatives (Saarni et al., 2007; Ustun, Ayuso-Mateos, Chatterji, Mathers, & Murray, 2004), with increased mortality rates (Cuijpers & Smit, 2002), with high levels of service use, and with enormous economic costs (Berto, D'Ilario, Ruffo, Di Virgilio, & Rizzo, 2000; Greenberg & Birnbaum, 2005; Smit, Cuijpers, Oostenbrink, Batelaan, de Graaf, & Beekman, 2006). At this moment major depression is the fourth disorder worldwide in terms of disease burden, and it is expected to be the disorder with the highest disease burden in high income countries by the year 2030 (Mathers & Loncar, 2006).

According to the *DSM IV*, an individual has a major depressive disorder when this person has a depressed mood most of the day and nearly every day during a 2 week period, or has a markedly diminished interest or pleasure in all, or almost all, activities most of the day, nearly every day. Apart from these two key symptoms, this person also has to suffer from other symptoms during the 2 week period, including significant weight loss, insomnia or hypersomnia, psychomotor agitation or retardation, fatigue or loss of energy, feelings of worthlessness or excessive or inappropriate guilt, diminished ability to think or concentrate, indecisiveness, or recurrent thoughts of death. In order to meet the criteria for a major depression, at least five symptoms should be present. A dysthymic disorder is a depressive disorder in which the person has a depressed mood for most of the days, for more days than not, for at least 2 years. In addition, at least two of the other symptoms of major depression have to be present.

Apart from major depression and dysthymia, as defined in the *DSM IV*, several other types and operationalizations have been proposed. As we will see later in this chapter, many psychotherapy researchers define depression by a cut off score on a self report scale for depression, such as the Beck Depression Inventory (BDI) (Beck, Ward, Mendelson, Mock, & Erbaugh, 1961), or the Center for Epidemiological Studies Depression Scale (CES-D) (Radloff, 1977). Some studies specifically focus on persons with subthreshold depression. In most of these studies, subthreshold depression is defined as scoring above a cut off score on a self report scale, but not meeting criteria for major depression or dysthymia. In the *DSM IV*, several other depressive disorders are defined, such as minor depression (with the same criteria as major depression, except that the number of symptoms is two to four, instead of five or more), and brief recurrent depression (also with the same criteria as major depression, only the period is shorter than 2 weeks, and there are several short but very intense periods). In this chapter, we will focus on all psychotherapies for all depressive disorders (except bipolar disorders, which will be reviewed in another chapter) that have been studied in research.

Prevalence of a depressive disorder is twice as high in women than in men, and there are indications that the prevalence of major depression is somewhat lower in older adults than in younger adults, but that the prevalence of milder, minor depression is higher (Beekman, Deeg, Braam, Smit, & Van Tilburg, 1997). On average, a major depressive episode lasts for 20 weeks and the average patient will suffer from four episodes. Relapse rates after recovery from a first episode is 20% to 30% in 3 years. When a person has suffered from three or more episodes, the chance of relapse is 70% to 80%.

In this chapter, we will review evidence-based psychotherapies for depression in adults. For each evidence-based type of psychotherapy, we will summarize consensus panel recommendations, review the results of earlier meta-analyses of efficacy studies, and provide a meta-analytic summary of randomized controlled studies examining each type of psychotherapy. Because of the large number of evidence-based treatments and the very large number of studies to be reviewed in this chapter, we will not cover the results of single subject experimental analyses and meta-analyses of single subject experiments.

METHODS

Selection of Evidence-Based Treatments

For selection of evidence-based treatments we used a database of 115 controlled studies of psychotherapy for adult depression. This database, how it was developed, and the methods used, have been described in detail elsewhere (Cuijpers, van Straten, Warmerdam, & Andersson, 2008). Key materials, overviews of the goals and mission, and an overview of all other meta-analyses that have used this database can be downloaded from the Web site for this project (www.evidencebasedpsychotherapies .org). In brief, the database was developed through a comprehensive literature search (of works dating from 1966 to January 2008) in which we examined a total of 8,861 abstracts in: PsycINFO (2,097), PubMed (1,403 abstracts), Embase (2,207), and the Cochrane Central Register of Controlled Trials (2,204). In order to identify unpublished studies, Dissertation Abstracts International (950 abstracts) was searched. We identified these abstracts by combining terms indicative of psychological treatment and depression. For this database, we also collected the primary studies from earlier meta-analyses of psychological treatments for depression (Cuijpers & Dekker, 2005) and checked the references of included studies. We retrieved a total of 857 papers and 33 dissertations for further study. These papers and dissertations were studied, and we selected the ones that met our inclusion criteria.

For the set of 115 controlled studies of psychotherapy, we included studies in which (1) efficacy of a psychological treatment (2) on adults (3) with a depressive disorder or an elevated level of depressive symptomatology (4) were compared to a control condition (waiting list, care-as-usual, pill placebo, psychological placebo), (5) in a randomized controlled trial. Psychological treatments were defined as interventions in which verbal communication between a therapist and a client was the core element, or in which a psychological treatment was written down in book format (guided self-help or bibliotherapy) while the client worked through it more or less independently, but with some kind of personal support from a therapist (by telephone, e-mail, or otherwise). We excluded studies on children and adolescents (below 18 years of age).

Studies in which the psychological intervention could not be discerned from other elements of the intervention were also excluded (managed care interventions and disease management programs), as were studies in which a standardized effect size could not be calculated (mostly because no test was performed in which the difference between experimental and control group was examined), and studies on inpatients. In some studies a combination of psychotherapy and placebo was compared to placebo only. These studies were excluded because a placebo may have an effect on depression in itself or may alter the effects of psychotherapy (Wampold, Minami, Tierney, Baskin, & Bhati, 2005). In the current review, we will not describe the results of these studies.

For the set of 115 studies, we excluded studies aimed at maintenance treatments and relapse prevention, and studies that included participants who were both anxious and depressed. Comorbid general medical or psychiatric disorders were not used as an exclusion criterion. No language restrictions were applied.

We defined evidence-based as those treatments that were examined in at least two randomized trials conducted by independent researchers in which the treatment was compared to an (untreated) control group (Chambless & Hollon, 1998). These treatments had to use the same manual and/or share a clear rationale about the causes of depression and therapeutical techniques of how to treat depressed persons. In this way, we were able to select 10 psychotherapies for adult depression that could be defined as evidence-based.

Selection of Treatment Guidelines, Meta-Analyses, and Primary Studies on the Efficacy of Evidence-Based Treatments

After selecting the 10 evidence-based psychotherapies, we identified previous meta-analyses and primary studies assessing the efficacy of these treatments. In order to assess consensus panels' recommendations on these treatments, we selected five clinical guidelines for the treatment of depression.

Clinical guidelines: We will describe five international practice guidelines that reflect state-of-the-art recommendations for treating depression; that is, the guideline of the American Psychiatric Association (APA, 2000), the English guideline of the National Institute for Health and Clinical Excellence (NICE, 2007), the Australian and New Zealand guidelines developed by the Royal Australian and New Zealand College of Psychiatrists Clinical Guidelines Team for Depression (RANZCP, 2004), the Dutch guidelines (CBO/ Trimbos Institute, 2005, 2009) and the Swedish SBU guidelines developed by the Swedish Counsel on Technology Assessment in Health Care (Åsberg et al., 2004). Most practice guidelines are multidisciplinary, except for the APA guideline and the RANZCP that have been developed primarily by psychiatrists.

Meta-analyses: In order to identify earlier meta-analyses of the selected evidence-based psychotherapies, we conducted a systematic search in three bibliographical databases: PubMed, PsycINFO and Embase. We combined words indicative of psychotherapy and depression, and limited the resulting hits to meta-analyses. The deadline for the searches was May 1, 2008. Our searches resulted in a total of 1,092 abstracts (85 in PubMed, 658 in PsycINFO, and 349 in Embase).

Inclusion criteria were: (a) statistical meta-analyses (statistical integration of the results of primary studies), (b) of one of the selected evidence-based psychotherapies, (c) published in the English language, (d) published in 1995 or later. Meta-regression analyses, which were specifically aimed at examining the association between the efficacy of treatments and characteristics of the included studies, were excluded from this review, as were meta-analytic studies that did not specify the results for one of the evidence-based treatments. A total of 25 meta-analyses met our inclusion criteria. Basic characteristics and the main results of these studies are reported in Table 11.1.

TABLE 11.1 Selected Characteristics and Results of Meta-Analyses of Psychotherapy for Depression in Adults

1st Author, Year	Target Group	Treatment	Main Comparisons	N_{comp}	Main Outcomes
Barbato and D'Avanzo (2008)	Adults in general	MAR	MAR versus individual therapy	8	$d = 0.06$; 95% CI $-0.29 \sim 0.41$
Barbato and D'Avanzo (2006)	Adults in general	MAR	MAR versus individual therapy	6	$d = -0.12$; 95% CI $-0.56 \sim 0.32$
Bohlmeijer et al. (2003)	Older adults	LRT	LRT versus control	7	$d = 1.23$; 95% CI: $0.92 \sim 1.53$
Chan (2006)	Adults in general	CBT	CBT versus control	21	$d = -1.09$; 95% CI: $-1.41 \sim -0.78$
			Pharmacotherapy versus CBT	7	$d = -0.13$; 95% CI: $-0.28 \sim 0.01$
			Pharmacotherapy versus combined	5	$d = -0.52$; 95% CI: $-0.80 \sim -0.24$
			Psychotherapy versus combined	5	$d = -0.42$; 95% CI: $-0.69 \sim -0.14$
Churchill (2001)	Adults in general	All psychotherapies	Psychotherapy versus control	22	$d = -0.90$; 95% CI: $-1.21 \sim -0.60$
			CBT versus IPT, DYN or NDST	13	$d = -0.27$; 95% CI: $-0.59 \sim 0.06$
			Individual CBT versus group CBT	8	$d = -0.33$; 95% CI: $-0.58 \sim -0.08$
			CBT versus control	20	$d = -1.00$; 95% CI: $-1.35 \sim -0.64$
			CBT versus psychodynamic therapy	6	$OR = 2.11$; 95% CI: $1.17 \sim 3.81$
			CBT versus supportive therapy	9	$d = -0.45$; 95% CI: $-0.89 \sim -0.01$
Cuijpers et al. (2007b)	Adults in general	BAT	BAT versus control	10	$d = 0.87$; 95% CI: $0.60 \sim 1.15$
			BAT versus other psychotherapy	18	$d = 0.12$; 95% CI: $-0.05 \sim 0.29$
Cuijpers et al. (2007b)	Adults in general	PST	PST versus control	13	$d = 0.83$; 95% CI: $0.45 \sim 1.21$
Cuijpers (1998)	Adults in general	Psychoeducational CBT	Psychoeducational CBT versus control	14	$d = -0.65$; 95% CI: $-0.44 \sim 0.85$
De Maat et al. (2007)	Psychiatric outpatients	Psychotherapy versus combined	Psychotherapy versus combined	7	$RR = 1.32$; 95% CI: $1.12 \sim 1.56$
De Maat et al. (2006)	Psychiatric outpatients	Psychotherapy versus pharmacotherapy	Psychotherapy versus pharmacotherapy	10	No significant difference
De Mello et al. (2005)	Adults in general	IPT	IPT versus placebo	9	$WMD = -3.57$; 95% CI: $-5.9 \sim -1.16$
Ekers et al. (2008)	Adults in general	Behavioral treatments	Behavior therapy versus control	12	$SMD = 0.70$; 95% CI: $-1.00 \sim -0.39$
			Behavior therapy versus CBT	12	$SMD = 0.08$; 95% CI: $-0.14 \sim 0.30$
Engels and Vermey (1997)	Older adults	All psychotherapies	Psychotherapy versus control	28	$d = -0.63$ (95% CI nr)
			CBT versus control	7	$d = -0.78$ (95% CI nr)

		Treatment	Comparison	N	Effect size
	Adults in general	All psychotherapies	Psychotherapy in MDD versus control	10	$d = -0.86$ (95% CI nr)
	Adults in general		Psychotherapy versus placebo	6	$d = -0.28$ (95% CI nr)
	Adults in general	All psychotherapies	Pharmacotherapy versus combined	5	$d = -0.34$ (BDI); $d = -0.18$ (HDRS); 95% CI nr
	Adults in general	CBT	CBT versus waiting list	11	$d = -0.89$ (95% CI nr)
	Adults in general		CBT versus other psychotherapy	12	$d = -0.34$ (95% CI nr)
	Adults in general		CBT versus variant CBT	11	$d = 0.03$ (95% CI nr)
	Adults in general	CBT	CBT versus control	20	$d = -0.82$; 95% CI: -0.83; -0.81
	Adults in general		CBT versus pharmacotherapy	17	$d = -0.38$; 95% CI: -0.39; -0.37
	Adults in general		CBT versus behavior therapy	13	$d = -0.05$; 95% CI: -0.08; -0.02
	Adults in general		CBT versus other psychotherapy	22	$d = -0.24$; 95% CI: -0.25; -0.23
	Adults in general	Cognitive bibliotherapy	Cognitive bibliotherapy versus control	17	$d = 0.77$; 95% CI: 0.61 to 0.94
	Older adults	CBT	CBT versus control	7	Too few studies in reported comparisons
	Adults in general	DYN	DYN versus CBT	6	No significant difference
	Older adults	PST	PST	9	$d = 0.50$; 95% CI: 0.14, 0.87
	Older adults	All psychotherapies	CBT versus control	5	$d = -1.14$; 95% CI: $-1.67 \sim -0.60$
			CBT versus DYN	5	$d = -0.27$; 95% CI: $-0.80 \sim 0.25$
	Adults in general	Pharmacotherapy versus combined	Pharmacotherapy versus combined	16	OR $= 1.86$; 95% CI: $1.38 \sim 2.52$
	Adults in general	Internet-based CBT	Internet-CBT versus control	5	$d = 0.32$; 95% CI: $0.08 \sim 0.57$
	Adults in general	CBT versus other psychotherapy	CBT versus other psychotherapy	9	$d = 0.03$; 95% CI: $-0.15 \sim 0.20$
			CBT versus placebo-therapy	11	$d = 0.49$; 95% CI: $0.28 \sim 0.69$
			Psychotherapy versus control (clinician-rated)	26	$d = -1.16$; 95% CI: $-1.00 \sim -1.32$
	Older adults	All psychotherapies	CBT versus waiting list control	5	WMD $= -9.85$, 95% CI -11.97 to -7.73
			Psychotherapy versus control (self-rated)	52	$d = -0.83$; 95% CI: $-0.98 \sim -0.69$

BAT behavioral activation treatment. CBT cognitive behavior therapy. IPT interpersonal psychotherapy. MDD: major depressive disorder. Nr not further specified or not reported. OR odds ratio. RR relative risk. SMD: standardized mean difference. w/wo: with or without. WMD: weighted mean difference.

Primary studies: We distinguished several different categories of primary studies.

Comparisons of psychotherapies to control groups: For each of the evidence-based psychotherapies, we selected the studies examining this psychotherapy from the database of 115 controlled studies of psychotherapy we described earlier (Cuijpers et al., 2008b; www.psychotherapyrcts.org). For each psychotherapy we conducted a separate meta-analysis of the randomized controlled studies examining its efficacy. The methods of these meta-analyses will be described later.

Comparisons of psychotherapies to pharmacotherapies: We have reviewed these studies in an earlier meta-analytic study (Cuijpers, van Straten, van Oppen, & Andersson, 2008). In this, we will summarize the results of this meta-analysis for each specific type of psychotherapy.

Comparisons of psychotherapies to other psychotherapies: We have reviewed these studies also in a separate publication (Cuijpers, van Straten, Andersson, et al., 2008). In the current chapter, we will also report in sum the results of this meta-analysis for each specific type of psychotherapy.

Comparisons of psychotherapies to combined treatments of that same psychotherapy and pharmacotherapy: These studies have also been summarized in an earlier meta-analysis (Cuijpers, van Straten, Warmerdam, & Andersson, 2008), and again we will summarize the results for each psychotherapy.

Comparisons of pharmacotherapy to combined treatments of psychotherapy and pharmacotherapy: These results have also been summarized in an earlier meta-analysis (Cuijpers, Dekker, Hollon, & Andersson, 2009), and we will summarize the results here.

Studies on long-term effects of psychotherapies: In order to examine the long-term efficacy of each of the psychotherapies, we used two different strategies. First, we summarized the results of a recent meta-analysis of studies examining the effects of CBT on relapse and recurrence (Vittengl, Clark, Dunn, & Jarrett, 2007). This is an excellent meta-analysis summarizing all available research in this area. However, this meta-analysis included only studies on CBT, and did not include other psychotherapies. There are some studies that have examined the efficacy of continued interpersonal therapy aimed at relapse prevention. We will review these studies in the paragraph on interpersonal psychotherapy (without conducting a meta-analysis, because there are only a limited number of studies available, and these studies use different designs and follow-up periods). For the other evidence-based psychotherapies we describe in this chapter, we will select the randomized controlled studies from our database that compared the efficacy of an evidence-based psychotherapy to a control condition at least three months after the end of the psychotherapy. Then we will compute effect sizes and conduct meta-analyses according to the methods described later for each psychotherapy (provided that there were sufficient effect sizes).

Analytic Strategies

Recommendations of clinical guidelines, results of earlier meta-analyses, and the results of long-term effects of psychotherapy, are briefly summarized and reviewed, without specific analytic strategies.

In order to integrate results of the post-test efficacy found in primary studies, we conducted a meta-analysis for each of the evidence-based psychotherapies. For these meta-analyses, we first calculated effect sizes (Cohen's d) for each study by subtracting (at post-test) the average score of the control group (M_c) from the average score of the experimental group (M_e) and dividing the result by the pooled standard deviations of the experimental and control group (SD_{ec}). For comparisons of two active treatments (such as psychotherapy versus pharmacotherapy or combined treatment), we calculated the effect sizes in the same way, except that the mean of the control condition is replaced by the mean of the alternative treatment. An effect size of 0.5 thus indicates that the mean of the experimental group is half a standard deviation larger than the mean of the control group (or comparison treatment). Effect sizes of 0.56 and higher can be assumed to be large, while effect sizes of 0.33 to 0.55 are moderate, and lower effect sizes are small (Lipsey, 1990).

In the calculations of effect sizes, only those instruments were used that explicitly measured depression. If more than one depression measure was used, the mean of the effect sizes was calculated, so that each study (or contrast group) contributed with only one effect size. When means and standard deviations were not reported, we used other statistics (*t*-value, *p*-value) to calculate effect sizes.

To calculate pooled mean effect sizes, we used the computer program Comprehensive Meta-Analysis (version 2.2.021), developed for support in meta-analysis. Because we expected considerable heterogeneity, we conducted all analyses using the random effects model (J. P. T. Higgins & Green, 2005).

In order to assess heterogeneity we calculated the I^2 statistic, which is an indicator of heterogeneity in percentages (J. P. Higgins, Thompson, & Deeks, 2003). A value of 0% indicates no observed heterogeneity, and larger values show increasing heterogeneity, with 25% as low, 50% as moderate, and 75% as high heterogeneity. We also calculated the Q statistic, but only report whether this was significant or not.

Because the effect size is difficult to interpret from a clinical perspective we also calculated the numbers needed to be treated (NNT). The NNT is the number of persons that have to be treated in order to generate one more positive outcome than in the control group (Kraemer & Kupfer, 2006). The NNT is easy to interpret from a clinical perspective, but has the disadvantage that it tends to become very large when the effect size is small. Therefore, we only report the NNTs for comparisons between psychotherapies and control groups, not for comparisons between different types of treatment (because these are usually very small and results in very high NNTs, which will probably

only result in confusing figures). We used the formula provided by Kraemer and Kupfer (2006) to calculate the NNT.

For each evidence-based psychotherapy, publication bias was tested by inspecting the funnel plots of the meta-analyses, and by using Duval and Tweedie's (2000) trim and fill procedure, which yields an estimate of the effect size after the publication bias has been taken into account.

In order to examine whether basic characteristics of the studies were associated with the effect sizes, we conducted a series of subgroup analyses for each treatment. In these subgroup analyses, we divided the studies according to major characteristics of the studies. In order to assess these characteristics, we scored each study on the following characteristics: (a) recruitment method: open community recruitment, recruitment from clinical samples, and other; (b) target group: the study was conducted among adults or more specific target populations (such as older adults, student populations, patients with general medical disorders, women with postpartum depression, and other); (c) definition of depression: depressive disorder diagnosed with a formal diagnostic interview (such as the Composite International Diagnostic Interview, [CIDI; Robins et al., 1988; or the Structured Clinical Interview for *DSM* Disorders, [SCID; First, Spitzer, Gibbon, & Williams, 1995], other definition (usually depression defined as scoring above a cut off score on a self report scale, such as the Beck Depression Inventory), (d) format of the therapy: individual, group, or guided self help, (e) type of control group: waiting list, care as usual, and other, and (f) the subgroup analyses were conducted according to the procedures implemented in Comprehensive Meta Analysis version 2.2.021. In the subgroup analyses, we used mixed effects analyses that pooled studies within subgroups with the random effects model but tested for significant differences between subgroups with the fixed effects model.

We assessed quality of the included controlled studies using eight criteria. These criteria were based on an authoritative review of empirically supported psychotherapies (Chambless & Hollon, 1998), and on the criteria proposed by the Cochrane Collaboration to assess the methodological validity of the study (J. P. T. Higgins & Green, 2005). The criteria were: (a) Participants met diagnostic criteria for a depressive disorder (as assessed with a personal diagnostic interview, such as the CIDI, SCID, or SADS, and using a diagnostic system such as the *DSM* or the Research Diagnostic Criteria); (b) The study referred to the use of a treatment manual (either a published manual, or a manual specifically designed for the study); (c) The therapists who conducted the therapy were trained for the specific therapy, either specifically for this study or as a general training; (d) Treatment integrity was checked during the study (by supervision of the therapists during treatment, by recording of treatment sessions, and/or by systematic screening of protocol adherence by a standardized measurement instrument); (e) Data were analyzed with intention-to-treat analyses, in which all persons who were randomized to the treatment and control conditions initially were included in the analyses; (f) The study has a minimal level of statistical power to find significant effects of the treatment, and included 50 or more persons in the comparison between treatment and control group (this allows the study to find standardized effect sizes of 0.80 and larger, assuming a statistical power of 0.80 and alpha of 0.05; calculations in STATA); (g) The study reported that randomization was conducted by an independent (third) party (this variable is positive if an independent person did the randomization, when a computer program was used to assign patients to conditions, or when sealed envelopes were used); and (h) Assessors of outcome were blinded and did not know to which condition the respondents were assigned to (this was only coded when the effect sizes were based on interviewer-based depression ratings; when only self-reports were used, this was not coded).

For each evidence-based treatment, we assessed how many studies met all eight quality criteria, and we examined with a subgroup analysis whether these high-quality studies differed significantly from other studies. Study quality was considered to be especially important because in an earlier meta-analysis we found that the effect sizes found in high-quality studies was lower than in other studies.

COGNITIVE BEHAVIOR THERAPY

There are several different types of CBT. All of these therapies share a focus on the impact a patient's present dysfunctional thoughts have on current behavior and future functioning. CBT is aimed at teaching patients to evaluate, challenge, and modify their dysfunctional beliefs (cognitive restructuring), with the further aim being to change behavior. In this form of treatment the therapist mostly emphasizes homework assignments and outside-of-session activities. Therapists exert an active influence over therapeutic interactions and topics of discussion, use a psychoeducational approach, and teach patients new ways of coping with stressful situations. The CBT is by far the best-studied psychotherapy for depression. As we will see later, of the 115 studies that have compared psychotherapy to untreated control groups, 61% (70) have examined CBT.

When we look in more detail in what way CBT is conducted and to the efficacy research in this area, we can distinguish four major subtypes of CBT. These include CBT according to the manual from Beck and colleagues (Beck, Rush, Shaw, & Emery, 1979); the psychoeducational "Coping with Depression" course; cognitive bibliotherapy; and a broader, less specific rest category of CBT. In this last category, other forms of CBT are described that meet our earlier definition of CBT, but differ in their exact treatment format.

The first and most important type of CBT for depression was developed and manualized by Beck and colleagues (1979). There is no other type of CBT that has been examined in as many randomized controlled trials. It combines a behavioral activation approach with an approach aimed at cognitive restructuring. The behavioral activation approach (also called "activity scheduling") consists of a systematic registration of pleasant activities and the increase of positive interactions between a person and his or her environment. As we will see later, behavioral activation has also been examined as a separate treatment for adult depression, and has been compared in several studies with the cognitive restructuring part of Beck's CBT and with the full CBT package.

The second type of CBT is the "Coping with Depression" course (Lewinsohn, Antonucci, Breckenridge, & Teri, 1984). This intervention is a psychoeducational intervention based on social learning theory and is highly structured. It teaches several mood management skills to its participants, including cognitive restructuring, activity scheduling, and social skills. Participants are more students than patients, and the intervention is led by course leaders instead of therapists. Although originally developed for use in a group format, it can also be applied individually or as guided self-help intervention.

The third type of CBT we distinguish here is cognitive bibliotherapy. In the studies on cognitive bibliotherapy, participants receive a copy of the book *Feeling Good* by David Burns (1980). This book is based on Beck's cognitive therapy and is a true self-help book in the sense that it explains the principles of cognitive therapy very carefully to the reader and teaches how to apply these principles. In the studies on this type of therapy, the participant receives a copy of this book and is called every week by a researcher or therapist very briefly (10 to 20 minutes per call) in order to answer any questions about the book. Most of the studies examining cognitive bibliotherapy we found were conducted by the same research group (Dr. Scogin and colleagues). However, we also found one study that was conducted by an independent group of

researchers (Landreville & Bissonnette, 1997). Because our definition of evidence-based psychotherapy required research from at least two independent research groups, cognitive bibliotherapy met this criterion.

The fourth category of CBT is a rest category. In these interventions cognitive restructuring is an important component, but it may include other components such as behavioral activation, social skills training, relaxation, or coping skills.

In this chapter, we will first discuss earlier meta-analyses examining the efficacy of CBT and the advices given in clinical practice guidelines on the use of CBT. Then we will discuss the effect studies that have examined CBT and have compared it to nontreated control groups, pharmacotherapy, and combined treatments. Finally, we will discuss research on the long-term effects of CBT.

Earlier Meta-Analyses on CBT

In our systematic search for earlier meta-analyses of psychotherapies for adult depression, we found 17 meta-analyses that examined the efficacy of CBT (Table 11.1). These meta-analyses have shown very clearly that CBT is effective compared to untreated controls (Chan, 2006; Churchill et al., 2001; Gaffan, Tsaousis, & Kemp-Wheeler, 1995; Gloaguen, Cottraux, Cucherat, & Blackburn, 1998; Wampold, Minami, Baskin, & Tierney, 2002). Most of these meta-analyses are not limited to one of the subtypes of CBT, but typically include studies on CBT in general. One exception is the meta-analysis of the "Coping with Depression" course, which found that this intervention is indeed effective in reducing depression (Cuijpers, 1998). Another more recent meta-analysis examined the efficacy of cognitive bibliotherapy (Gregory, Canning, Lee, & Wise, 2004), but used a somewhat broader definition of cognitive bibliotherapy as we did. For example, they also included studies on psychoeducational treatments, such as the "Coping with Depression" course

But they did find that this group of cognitive behavioral interventions had large effects on depression, compared to control groups. One other recent meta-analysis examined whether CBT interventions conducted through the Internet are effective in the treatment of depression and anxiety disorders (Spek et al., 2007). This study found that CBT interventions conducted through the Internet have large effects, provided that some sort of professional support was given. Unsupported interventions were also found to be effective, but with much smaller effect sizes.

Another group of meta-analyses has examined the effects of CBT in older adults (Engels & Vermey, 1997; Koder, Brodaty, & Anstey, 1996; McCusker, Cole, Keller, Bellavance, & Berard, 1998; K. C. Wilson, Mottram, & Vassilas, 2008). Although some of these meta-analyses have included only a small part of the available research in this area, they all find that CBT has large effects on depression in older adults.

Several other meta-analyses have compared the efficacy of CBT with that of other psychotherapies. In an older meta-analysis, some indications were found that cognitive behavior therapy was more efficacious than other therapies (Gloaguen et al., 1998). However, this was not confirmed in a meta-analysis of the same set of studies in which cognitive behavior therapy was compared to other high-quality bona fide therapies, which were not explicitly designed as a control condition (Wampold et al., 2002). Another early meta-analysis found indications that the superiority of cognitive behavior therapies over other therapies could be explained by the effects of researcher allegiance (Gaffan et al., 1995). A meta-analysis by De Mello and colleagues (De Mello, de Jesus Mari, Bacaltchuk, Verdeli, & Neugebauer, 2005) examined the comparative effects of interpersonal psychotherapy and cognitive behavior therapy, and concluded that interpersonal psychotherapy was somewhat more efficacious than cognitive behavior therapy. A further meta-analysis examined whether

psychodynamic psychotherapies and cognitive behavior therapy differ significantly from each other (Leichsenring, 2001). No indications were found that they do indeed differ from each other. However, another meta-analysis comparing cognitive behavior therapies to psychodynamic therapies (Churchill et al., 2001), did find that cognitive behavior therapies were more efficacious, although the number of included studies was relatively small. In the same study, it was found that cognitive and behavioral treatments were more efficacious than nondirective supportive therapies. Two earlier meta-analyses (Cuijpers, van Straten, & Warmerdam, 2007b; Ekers, Richards, & Gilbody, 2008) compared the efficacy of behavioral activation therapy and cognitive behavior therapy, and neither study detected significant differences. One meta-analysis grouped psychotherapies for older adults into two broad categories, cognitive behavior therapies on the one hand and psychodynamic and nondirective supportive therapies on the other hand (McCusker et al., 1998). However, they found no significant difference between the two groups. This may be caused by the fact that they included only five studies.

The relative efficacy of CBT, pharmacotherapy, and combined treatments of CBT and pharmacotherapy has been examined in several other meta-analyses. One meta-analysis examining the relative efficacy of CBT and pharmacotherapy did not find significant differences between the two treatments (Chan, 2006), although this meta-analysis has included only a limited selection of currently available studies and may not have sufficient power to detect small differences (see next paragraph). However, one earlier meta-analysis found evidence that CBT is more efficacious than pharmacotherapy (Gloaguen et al., 1998), but this meta-analysis also included only a limited number of the currently available studies. The meta-analyses examining the relative efficacy of psychotherapies and combined treatments have not differentiated between CBT and other psychotherapies and do not give specific information on CBT (De Maat, Dekker, Scho-evers, & De Jonghe, 2006, 2007; Friedman et al., 2004; Pampanolla, Bollini, Tibaldi, Kupelnick, & Munizza, 2004).

Cognitive Behavior Therapy in Clinical Guidelines

Overall, practice guidelines emphasize shared features of effective therapy (e.g., therapeutic alliance, motivation, hopeful expectancy). Most guidelines differentiate between treatment strategies, depending on the severity of depression; that is, mild, moderate, and severe depression with and without psychotic features. All guidelines recommend considering the combination of psychotherapy with antidepressants for the more severe cases of depression. No guideline recommends psychotherapy for depressed patients with psychotic features, since no studies have been conducted yet on the effects of psychotherapy as a single treatment for this subgroup of depressed patients. In addition, some guidelines differentiate in recommendations according to the type of care; that is, primary and secondary care. Overall, in all current practice guidelines CBT has been recommended as the psychotherapeutic treatment of choice.

For mild depression in primary care most guidelines recommend six to eight sessions of brief CBT, but all guidelines address considering alternative first step strategies as well, that is, psychoeducation, exercise, guided self-help computerized CBT (CBO/Trimbos Institute, 2009; NICE, 2004), supportive clinical care (RANZCP, 2004), and Internet treatment (SBU). In contrast, RANZCP states for mild depression that no treatment, including CBT, is more effective than supportive clinical care supported by psychoeducation and supplemented by teaching problem-solving skills. Although the APA concludes that there is no evidence that for mild to moderate depressed patients the combination of psychotherapy and antidepressants is superior to either treatment alone, they recommend a combined

treatment with CBT and antidepressants for this group, especially in patients with psychosocial problems, interpersonal conflicts, pregnancy/lactation or wish to become pregnant, and patients with comorbid personality disorders.

For moderate to severe depressed patients in primary care, NICE recommends antidepressants as first treatment of choice. Antidepressant treatment as first treatment of choice is not completely shared by the RANZCP. They state that CBT is equally effective compared to antidepressant medication. However, all guidelines recommend CBT in case a psychotherapy will be started.

In severely depressed patients, all guidelines recommend combining antidepressants with CBT. In secondary care, NICE and APA (regardless of type of care) give special recommendations for patients who do not respond to antidepressants (often indicated as treatment resistant) and other complex cases. All guidelines recommend considering CBT for patients who do not respond or do not fully respond to antidepressants. In addition, NICE advises to start CBT in patients that relapsed either during use of antidepressants or after finishing antidepressants. For severe depression all guidelines recommend initial treatment with antidepressants. Although, some guidelines (i.e., Dutch guideline) underscore that recent studies indicate that CBT and antidepressants are equally effective. In addition, they address that the combination of CBT (and IPT to a lesser extent) with antidepressants are more effective in cases with severe depression.

The NICE, APA, and Dutch guidelines differentiate in recommendations on course of depression as well by recommending specific treatment along with recurrence of depression. All guidelines stress the importance of reducing relapse in depression by providing psychotherapy. They recommend that acute phase treatment with antidepressants might subsequently be followed by CBT for reducing residual symptoms or to decrease risk of relapse. This sequential approach, that is, augmenting psychotherapy in the continuation and maintenance phase after remission on antidepressants, has been mentioned in most guidelines (for example, specific CBT programs, i.e., Preventive Cognitive Therapy and Mindfulness Based Cognitive Therapy). In addition, CBT in the acute phase is in most guidelines mentioned as first choice of treatment especially in recurrently depressed patients. For recurrently depressed patients, continuation or maintenance CBT after remission is advised by NICE, APA, and the Dutch guidelines.

For chronic depression all guidelines recommend combining antidepressants with CBT. Some guidelines point at considering a specific psychotherapeutic intervention for this group, that is, Cognitive Behavioral Analysis System of Psychotherapy (CBASP). For dysthymic patients the Swedish guideline recommends antidepressant treatment as first choice instead of psychotherapy.

EFFICACY OF CBT

CBT Versus Control Conditions

Cognitive behavior therapy could be compared to a control group in 70 studies, in which 91 comparisons were made between a CBT condition and a control group (in 16 studies two or more types of CBT were compared to a control group). The total number of study participants in these comparisons was 4,257 (2,233 in the CBT groups and 2,024 in the control groups).

The mean effect size of the 91 comparisons, in which the difference between CBT and control groups at post-test was contrasted, was 0.67 (95% CI: 0.57 ∼ 0.78). This indicates a large effect of CBT, corresponding with a NNT of 2.75. Heterogeneity was moderate to high ($I^2 = 59.88$). Results of the analyses are summarized in Table 11.2.

Several effect sizes were very large (> 2.0) and one was very low (–0.77, the only negative effect size, indicating that participants in the control group improved more than those receiving CBT). After removal of these possible

outliers, we found that the effect size was a little smaller ($d = 0.64$; 95% CI: 0.54 ∼ 0.74), heterogeneity dropped somewhat ($I^2 = 52.51$) and the associated NNT was 2.86.

Our analyses included studies in which more than one CBT was compared to a control group, which means that multiple comparisons from one study were included in the same analysis. These multiple comparisons are not independent of each other, however, possibly resulting in an artificial reduction of heterogeneity and a bias in the overall mean effect size. We conducted additional analyses as a consequence, in which we included only one comparison per study (Table 11.2). Only the comparison with the largest effect size was included first, followed by another analysis including only the smallest effect size. As can be seen from Table 11.2, results did not differ very much from those in which all comparisons were included.

Effect sizes were calculated using different measurement instruments. When we limited the effect sizes to those found for the BDI, we found a somewhat higher effect size ($d = 0.79$; 95% CI: 0.65 ∼ 0.93), with moderate to high heterogeneity ($I^2 = 64.73$) and an NNT of 2.36. The mean effect size based on the Hamilton Depression Rating Scale resulted in a comparable effect size ($d = 0.77$; 95% CI: 0.59 ∼ 0.94; Table 11.2).

Both the funnel plot and Duval and Tweedie's trim and fill procedure suggested that there was considerable publication bias. After adjustment for possible publication bias, the mean effect size decreased from 0.67 to 0.41 (95% CI: 0.29 ∼ 0.52; number of trimmed studies: 30).

We conducted a series of subgroup analyses using the characteristics of the studies as described in the Methods section (recruitment method, target group, definition of depression, treatment format, type of control group). We also conducted a subgroup analysis in which we examined whether the efficacy of the four different subtypes of CBT differed significantly from each other. Results of these analyses are presented in Table 11.2.

TABLE 11.2   Efficacy of CBT for Adult Depression Compared to Control Groups: Overall Analyses and Subgroup Analyses

	N_{comp}	D	95% CI	Z	I^{2a}	NNT	P^b
Main analyses							
▪ CBT versus (untreated) controls	91	0.67	0.57 ~ 0.78	12.52****	59.88****	2.75	
▪ 4 outliers removed[c]	87	0.64	0.54 ~ 0.74	12.86****	52.51****	2.86	
▪ One effect size per study (lowest)	70	0.57	0.46 ~ 0.68	10.21****	58.69****	3.18	
▪ One effect size per study (highest)	70	0.66	0.55 ~ 0.78	11.10****	62.82****	2.78	
▪ BDI only	69	0.79	0.65 ~ 0.93	11.13****	64.73****	2.36	
▪ HAM-D only	36	0.77	0.59 ~ 0.94	8.52****	59.36****	2.42	
Publication bias							
▪ After correction for publication bias	91	0.41	0.29 ~ 0.52			4.39	
Subgroup analyses							
Subtypes							0.000
▪ CBT according to Beck et al. (1979)	23	0.82	0.59 ~ 1.05	7.04****	58.90****	2.28	
▪ Cognitive bibliotherapy	8	1.05	0.71 ~ 1.39	6.00****	33.74 ns	1.85	
▪ Coping with depression course	13	0.27	0.16 ~ 0.39	4.61****	0	6.58	
▪ Other CBT	47	0.69	0.54 ~ 0.84	8.85****	59.12****	2.67	
Recruitment							0.000
▪ Community	58	0.86	0.70 ~ 1.01	10.79****	60.37****	2.19	
▪ Clinical samples	18	0.56	0.38 ~ 0.74	6.06****	49.52**	3.25	
▪ Other recruitment	15	0.30	0.18 ~ 0.41	4.96****	12.19 ns	5.95	
Target group							0.309
▪ Adults in general	55	0.63	0.51 ~ 0.76	9.69****	55.93****	2.91	
▪ Specific target group	36	0.75	0.57 ~ 0.94	7.94****	65.41****	2.48	
Specific types of depressive disorders							0.032
▪ Diagnosed mood disorder	48	0.57	0.42 ~ 0.71	7.45****	64.27****	3.18	
▪ Other definition	43	0.79	0.65 ~ 0.94	10.75****	49.88****	2.36	
Format[d]							0.006
▪ Individual	39	0.66	0.51 ~ 0.82	8.44****	51.80****	2.78	
▪ Group	34	0.64	0.45 ~ 0.82	6.78****	65.96****	2.86	
▪ Guided self-help	17	0.83	0.57 ~ 1.08	6.39****	58.22****	2.26	
Control group							0.000
▪ Waiting list	61	0.88	0.74 ~ 1.03	11.95****	53.06****	2.15	
▪ Care as usual	19	0.38	0.22 ~ 0.53	4.86****	46.52**	4.72	
▪ Other	11	0.38	0.21 ~ 0.55	4.43****	29.28 ns	4.72	
Study quality							0.000
▪ High quality	8	0.22	0.09 ~ 0.34	3.41***	1.98 ns	8.06	
▪ Other studies	83	0.74	0.63 ~ 0.85	12.71****	55.65****	2.50	

Notes: * $p < 0.1$, ** $p < 0.05$, *** $p < 0.01$, **** $p < 0.001$, ns = not significant

Abbreviations: CI = confidence intervals, N_{comp} = number of comparisons, NNT = numbers needed to treat

[a] The p values in this column indicate whether the Q statistic is significant (the I^2 statistics do not include a test of significance)

[b] The p values in this column indicate whether the difference between the effect sizes in the subgroups is significant

[c] Three with very large effect sizes (> 2.0, Ayen & Hautzinger, 2004; Pecheur, 1980; Taylor & Marshall, 1977), and one with a large negative effect size (Klein et al., 1985)

[d] In one study (Miranda et al., 2003), participants could choose between an individual or group treatment. This study was removed from these analyses.

As can be seen from this Table, Beck's CBT, cognitive bibliotherapy, and the rest category of CBT did not differ very much from each other in terms of effect sizes. However, the "Coping with Depression" course seemed to be somewhat less effective than the other three subtypes. This may be related to the fact that several of the larger studies examining the "Coping with Depression" course were conducted with complex populations, such as low-income women from minority groups (Miranda et al., 2003), older American Indians with chronic diseases (Manson & Brenneman, 1995), and populations who did not seek treatment for any problems (Dowrick et al., 2000). The fact that the "Coping with Depression" course is a flexible treatment that can easily be adapted for different populations may have led researchers to use this intervention for complex target groups, which in turn resulted in a lower mean effect size.

We also found that effect sizes found in depressed populations recruited from the community resulted in larger effect sizes than in clinical populations, and studies using other recruitment methods (such as systematic screening). Studies in which participants had to meet diagnostic criteria for a mood disorder has significantly lower effect sizes than studies in which other criteria for depression were used (usually scoring above a cut-off on a self-report scale). Unexpectedly, we found that studies using a guided self-help format had larger effect sizes than studies in which an individual or a group format was used. Waiting list control groups resulted in the largest effect size, followed by care-as-usual control groups. Other control groups (usually pill placebo or psychological placebo) resulted in even smaller effect sizes. The other subgroup analysis (examining the difference between adults in general as a target group versus more specific target groups) did not indicate that these groups of studies differed significantly from each other.

CBT Versus Other Treatments and as Part of Combination Treatments

The CBT could be compared to other psychotherapies in 38 studies (with 56 comparisons between CBT and another psychotherapy). The mean effect size indicating the difference between CBT and other psychotherapies at post-test was a nonsignificant 0.03 (95% CI: −0.04 ∼ 0.11), with zero heterogeneity (Table 11.3). This suggests that there is no significant difference between the efficacy of CBT and other psychotherapies. We have explored this result in an earlier paper (Cuijpers, van Straten, Andersson, et al., 2008) and refer the interested reader to this paper for further information. In this chapter, we also report subgroup analyses in which we examined whether major characteristics of the studies were related to the effect sizes. None of these analyses resulted in a significant difference between subgroups (Cuijpers, van Straten, Andersson, et al., 2008).

We examined whether we found a significant difference between the effect sizes found for different subtypes of CBT. As can be seen in Table 11.3, however, we found no indication that this was the case. We also examined whether CBT was more or less effective than other evidence-based therapies for depression. In these analyses, we compared the full category of CBT to each of the other evidence-based therapies for depression. We found no indication that this was the case (Table 11.3).

We could directly compare efficacy of CBT with pharmacotherapy in 15 studies. The effect size indicating the difference between these two treatment modalities at post-test was 0.03 (95% CI: −0.11 ∼ 0.17), which was not significant. Heterogeneity was nonsignificant and low ($I^2 = 26.91$). This suggests that there is no significant difference between the efficacies of CBT and pharmacotherapy. In a more elaborate meta-analysis examining the comparate efficacy of psychotherapy and pharmacotherapy for adult depression (Cuijpers, van Straten, van Oppen, et al., 2008), we found that psychotherapies

TABLE 11.3 Efficacy of Cognitive Behavior Therapy Compared to Other Psychotherapies, Pharmacotherapy, and Combined Therapies

	N_{comp}	D	95% CI	Z	I^{2a}	P
All CBT versus all other psychotherapies	56	0.03	−0.04 ~ 0.11	0.86 ns	0	
Subtypes of CBT vs all other psychotherapies						0.511
– Beck's CBT versus all other psychotherapies	34	−0.02	−0.13 ~ 0.09	−0.41 ns	0 ns	
– CWD versus all other psychotherapies	3	0.10	−0.09 ~ 0.29	1.01 ns	0 ns	
– Cognitive bibliotherapy versus all other psychotherapies	1	0.17	−0.71 ~ 1.05	0.38 ns	0 ns	
– Other CBT versus all other psychotherapies	18	0.11	−0.06 ~ 0.28	1.26 ns	24.71 ns	
CBT versus specific other psychotherapies						0.432
– CBT versus behavioral activation therapy	11	−0.08	−0.29 ~ 0.13	−0.78 ns	0	
– CBT versus psychodynamic treatment	7	0.15	−0.08 ~ 0.38	1.31 ns	0	
– CBT versus interpersonal psychotherapy	5	0.12	−0.33 ~ 0.09	1.13 ns	0	
– CBT versus supportive therapies	18	0.06	−0.10 ~ 0.22	0.76 ns	29.35 ns	
CBT versus problem-solving therapy	2	0.18	0.07 ~ 0.43	1.43 ns	0	
CBT versus social skills training	3	0.06	0.45 ~ 0.57	0.23 ns	0	
CBT versus other psychotherapies	10	0.07	0.17 ~ 0.31	0.60 ns	0	
CBT versus pharmacotherapy	15	0.03	0.11 ~ 0.17	0.43	26.91 ns	
CBT versus different types of pharmacotherapy						0.070
CBT versus SSRI	5	0.12	0.30 ~ 0.06	1.29 ns	0	
CBT versus TCA	7	0.19	0.01 ~ 0.40	1.84*	22.96 ns	
CBT versus other medications	3	0.08	0.38 ~ 0.22	0.53 ns	0.75	
CBT versus combined therapy	8	0.15	0.06 ~ 0.37	1.39 ns	0	
Pharmacotherapy versus combined therapy	6	0.27	0.04 ~ 0.49	2.34**	0	

Notes: * p < 0.1, ** p < 0.05, ns: not significant

[a] A positive *d* indicates that CBT is more effective than the alternative treatment, but when CBT is compared to combined treatments, a positive *d* indicates that the combined treatment is more effective

were less efficacious than pharmacotherapy in people with dysthymia (*d* = 0.28, 95% CI: 0.47 ~ 0.10). However, only one of the studies involved examined CBT.

In that more elaborate meta-analysis, we also found that in patients with major depression, treatments with SSRIs were significantly more effective than psychological treatments, while treatment with other antidepressants did not differ significantly. We examined this in the studies in which CBT was used as psychological treatment. As can be seen in Table 11.3, there was a trend (p < 0.1) indicating that the differences between CBT and psychotherapy differed depending on the type of pharmacotherapy. There was no significant difference

between SSRIs and CBT, but there was a trend (p < 0.1) indicating that CBT was more effective than TCAs.

In our earlier meta-analysis examining the difference between psychotherapies and pharmacotherapy, we found no other significant difference between subgroups of studies. However, we did find that dropout rates were smaller in psychological treatments, compared to pharmacological treatments (OR = 0.66, 95% CI 0.47 ~ 0.92).

We could compare CBT to a combined treatment of CBT and pharmacotherapy directly in eight studies. A meta-analysis of these studies indicated that the effect size of the combined treatment was somewhat higher than that of CBT alone, but this was not significant, possibly due to a lack of statistical power. Heterogeneity was zero in these analyses.

We compared pharmacotherapy to the combination of CBT and pharmacotherapy in six studies and found that the combined treatment was significantly more efficacious than pharmacotherapy alone ($d = 0.27$; 95% CI: $0.04 \sim 0.49$), with zero heterogeneity. The NNT associated with this effect size is 6.58.

Long-Term Effects of CBT

The long-term efficacy of CBT has been described in a meta-analysis of 28 studies including 1,880 adult depressed persons (Vittengl et al., 2007). In this meta-analysis, the authors distinguished between acute-phase CBT (which is aimed at reducing depressive symptoms and producing initial remission in persons with a depressive disorder), and continuation-phase CBT (which is aimed at sustaining remission and reducing the probability of relapse and recurrence). The authors found that a considerable number of responders to acute-phase CBT relapse after discontinuation (29% within 1 year and 54% within 2 years). These rates are comparable to those of other psychotherapies but lower than those associated with relapse rates in pharmacotherapy (Vittengl et al., 2007). This meta-analysis also found evidence that among acute-phase responders, continuation-phase CBT reduced relapse rates compared with assessment only at the end of the continuation treatment (21% reduction) and at follow-up (29% reduction). This meta-analysis had several important limitations, however, limiting the strength of the evidence found. One important limitation was that only a handful of studies was available for each comparison. Furthermore, in the studies in which no continuation-phase treatment was given, it is not clear whether respondents had any type of help for their depression. Because of these limitations the results should be interpreted with caution.

Conclusion

With more than 100 randomized controlled and comparative trials examining its efficacy and 17 meta-analyses, CBT is by far the best studied psychotherapy for adult depression. This large body of research has shown that CBT is an efficacious treatment for depressed adults. It was found to be efficacious in adults in general, but also in more specific target groups, such as older adults, women with postpartum depression, and depressed patients with general medical disorders. It can be effectively delivered in individual, group, and guided self-help formats, and can also be effectively applied through computers and the Internet. Furthermore, there is increasing evidence that in the long-term, CBT can result in reduced relapse rates. It should not come as a surprise, therefore, that CBT has found its way to all treatment guidelines for adult depression and is considered to be a first-line therapy for depression by virtually all clinicians.

There is, however, some reason to be cautious about these results of CBT. The best studies in the field, which meet all quality criteria we defined for these studies, find considerably smaller effect sizes than other studies (such as the NIMH trial; Elkin et al., 1989). In a separate paper, we explored this finding for all psychotherapies and found that it cannot be explained, for example, by the use of waiting list control groups, which typically result in higher effect sizes than care-as-usual or placebo control groups. Probably this difference between high-quality and other studies does indeed represent a true difference. Another concern is that we found strong indications for publication bias, which may have resulted in an overestimation of the effect sizes.

We distinguished different subtypes of CBT, with the CBT using Beck's manual being the best studied, with good effect sizes; however, cognitive bibliotherapy was also found to be efficacious. The psychoeducational "Coping with Depression" course, however, was somewhat less efficacious than other subtypes of CBT. As indicated earlier, this should be considered cautiously, because an advantage of this course is that it can be adapted very well for complex populations. Many of the studies examining it have focused on these complex populations, and it should not come as a surprise that the efficacy is somewhat smaller than that of other subtypes of CBT.

BEHAVIORAL ACTIVATION TREATMENT

A psychological treatment of depression that is closely related with CBT and can be seen as a member of a broader cognitive behavioral family of psychotherapies for depression is behavioral activation treatment (BAT). Behavioral activation treatment is one of the components of many CBT treatments, including Beck's CBT, cognitive bibliotherapy, and the "Coping with Depression" course. But it was originally developed as a separate treatment, and is still used as an independent form of treatment of depression. Based on the strong association between pleasant interactions between a person and his or her environment, this treatment was developed in the 1970s (Lewinsohn, Biglan, & Zeiss, 1976). In this treatment, patients learn techniques to monitor their mood and daily activities, and to see the connection between these. Then the patients learn how to develop a plan to increase the number of pleasant activities and to increase positive interactions with their environment. In this approach, specific attention is paid to social skills and interactions with other people. More recently, this approach has been further developed and examined by Jacobson et al. (1996) and by Dimidjian and colleagues (Dimidjian et al., 2006; Dobson et al., 2008). A manual has also been published (Martell, Addis, & Jacobson, 2001).

Clinical Guidelines and Earlier Meta-Analyses

The BAT has been examined in two earlier meta-analyses (Cuijpers et al., 2007a; Ekers et al., 2008). The first one (Cuijpers et al.,

2007a) was conducted by our group and contains many of the studies that will be analyzed later. The other meta-analysis is also based on almost the same group of studies (although they also included some studies that are based on the "Coping with Depression" course; Ekers et al., 2008). Both meta-analyses concluded that BAT is effective in the treatment of depression and has large effects compared to untreated controls. Both of them also find no significant difference between BAT and CBT, and one of them evidence that BAT is more efficacious than supportive therapies and brief therapies (Ekers et al., 2008). No evidence was found that the effects had decreased at 12-month follow-up or that there were differences between BAT and CBT at follow-up.

The APA regards BAT as effective as CBT and antidepressants, but points out that there are a small amount of BAT trials with random assignment and adequate control arms. The Swedish guideline and the update of the Dutch guidelines recommend behavioral activation as one of the treatments of choice, based on recent evidence.

Efficacy

We could compare BAT to a control group in 11 studies. The total number of respondents in these comparisons was 279 (136 in the BAT groups and 143 in the control groups). The mean effect size was 0.88 (95% CI: 0.48 – 1.28), which corresponds with a NNT of 2.15, indicating a large effect of BAT (Table 11-4). Heterogeneity was moderate (I^2 55.25). One study (P. H. Wilson, Goldin, & Charbonneau, 1983) had a very large effect size and was possibly an outlier. After removal of this study, the resulting effect size was somewhat lower, and heterogeneity dropped to a low to moderate level (Table 11-4). When we limited the effect sizes to those found for the BDI we also found a somewhat lower effect size (d 0.66, 95% CI 0.24 – 1.08, NNT 2.78), with low to moderate heterogeneity. The mean effect size based on the Hamilton

TABLE 11.4   Efficacy of Behavioral Activation Therapy Compared to Control Groups, Other Psychotherapies, Pharmacotherapy, and Combined Therapies

	N_{comp}	D	95% CI	Z	I^{2a}	NNT	P
Behavioral activation versus control groups							
– All studies	11	0.88	0.48 ~ 1.28	4.31****	55.25**	2.15	
– One possible outlier removed	10	0.75	0.39 ~ 1.10	4.11****	41.72*	2.48	
– BDI only	7	0.66	0.24 ~ 1.08	3.09***	45.62*	2.78	
– HAM-D only	4	0.72	0.14 ~ 1.31	2.42**	60.87*	2.56	
Publication bias							
■ After correction for publication bias	11	0.50	0.05 ~ 0.94			3.62	
Subgroup analyses[b, c]							
Target group							0.585
■ Adults in general	7	0.81	0.26 ~ 1.36	2.89***	63.25**	2.30	
■ Specific target group	4	1.02	0.51 ~ 1.53	3.91****	19.31 ns	1.89	
Specific types of depressive disorders							0.826
■ Diagnosed mood disorder	3	0.82	0.05 ~ 1.60	2.08**	72.50**	2.28	
■ Other definition	8	0.93	0.43 ~ 1.42	3.67****	48.45*	2.04	
Format							0.673
■ Individual	8	0.95	0.49 ~ 1.40	4.05****	55.75**	2.01	
■ Group	3	0.71	–0.31 ~ 1.72	1.36 ns	68.72**	2.60	
Control group							0.045
■ Waiting list	8	1.08	0.54 ~ 1.61	3.96****	55.48**	1.81	
■ Other	3	0.42	0.06 ~ 0.78	2.29**	0	4.27	
Behavioral activation versus other psychotherapies							
■ All studies	21	0.14	–0.02 ~ 0.30	1.71*	0		
■ BAT versus CBT	11	0.08	0.13 ~ –0.29	0.78 ns	0		
■ BAT versus supportive psychotherapy	4	0.38	–0.07 ~ 0.83	1.66*	10.09		
■ BAT versus psychodynamic psychotherapy	3	0.21	–0.19 ~ 0.62	1.03	0		

Notes: *: $p < 0.1$; **: $p < 0.05$; ***: $p < 0.01$; ****: $p < 0.001$; ns: not significant
[a] A positive *d* indicates that BAT is more effective than the alternative treatment; but when BAT is compared to combined treatments, a positive *d* indicates that the combined treatment is more effective.
[b] All studies, except two (Comas-Diaz, 1981; Teri et al., 1997) recruited participants through community recruitment; therefore, we did not conduct subgroup analyses with different recruitment methods.
[c] Only one study met all quality criteria; therefore, we did not conduct subgroup analyses examining differences between high-quality and other studies.

Depression Rating scale resulted in a comparable effect size (Table 11.4).

Both the funnel plot and Duval and Tweedie's trim and fill procedure suggested that there was considerable publication bias. After adjustment for possible publication bias, the mean effect size decreased from 0.88 to 0.50 (95% CI: 0.05 ~ 0.94; number of trimmed studies: 4; NNT = 3.62).

We conducted a series of subgroup analyses using characteristics of the studies as described in the Methods section (target group, definition of depression, treatment format, type of control group). We did not conduct subgroup analyses examining different recruitment methods, because most studies recruited participants through community recruitment (only two studies used another recruitment method).

Only one of the studies met all quality criteria, therefore we did not examine differences between high-quality and other studies. Results of the subgroup analyses are presented in Table 11.4. As can be seen from this Table, we found a significant difference between studies using a waiting list control group and studies using another type of control group. The other analyses did not result in significant differences between subgroups.

There was only one study that compared the efficacy of BAT and pharmacotherapy (Dimidjian et al., 2006). This study did not result in evidence pointing at large differences between BAT and pharmacotherapy (effect size 0.06, n.s.). We found no study in which the combination of BAT and pharmacotherapy was compared to pharmacotherapy alone, nor did we find any study in which a combined treatment was compared to BAT alone. Furthermore, we found no study in which the efficacy of BAT could be compared to an untreated control group at follow-up.

Conclusion

BAT has been examined in a considerable number of randomized trials, although most of these were small and only one of them met all the quality criteria we used in this chapter. Results of these studies indicate that BAT has large effects on depression, and the comparative studies show that there is no important difference between BAT and CBT. However, these results should be considered with some caution because of the small number of high quality studies, and because there were some indications for significant publication bias. Furthermore, there are hardly any studies comparing BAT with pharmacotherapy and with combined treatments, and no research is available on the longer term efficacy of BAT.

The BAT is, however, an interesting treatment modality because the high quality study that has examined its efficacy found indications that BAT may be more effective than cognitive restructuring in more severely

depressed participants (Dimidjian et al., 2006). Furthermore, it has been found to be effective in depressed populations for whom other psychotherapies are not feasibe, such as depressed dementia patients and their caregivers (Teri, Logsdon, Uomoto, & McCurry, 1997), and psychiatric inpatients (Hopko, Lejuez, Lepage, Hopko, & McNeill, 2003).

SELF-CONTROL THERAPY

Another psychotherapy that could be considered as belonging to a broader family of cognitive behavior therapies of depression is self-control therapy (SCT). Based on Kanfer's behavioral model of self-control (Kanfer, 1971; Kanfer & Karoly, 1972), Rehm developed SCT in the 1970s (Fuchs & Rehm, 1977). SCT consists of three components: self-monitoring (aimed at changing the selective attention of depressed persons on negative events following their behavior), self-evaluation (aimed at changing the inclination of depressed persons to set unrealistic, perfectionistic, global standards for themselves, making attainment improbable), and self-reinforcement (aimed at increasing self-rewarding and decreasing self-punishment).

The developer of this therapy was involved in most of the studies examining SCT. However, we found two studies in which he was not involved (Rude, 1986; Barlow, 1986), and decided that this treatment met the criteria for being an evidence based psychotherapy. We found no earlier meta analytic study of SCT and this treatment strategy has not been explicitly mentioned in the clinical guidelines.

Efficacy

The eight studies examining the efficacy of SCT included 353 participants (148 in the experimental groups, 170 in the control groups, and 35 in the comparative treatments). We found six studies in which SCT was compared to a control group. One of these studies met all quality criteria (Dunn et al.,

2007). This was also the only study in which a clinical sample was used (the other studies recruited participants from the general population), and in which a diagnostic interview was used to establish the presence of a depressive disorder. In all studies SCT was administered in a group format, while the number of sessions ranged from 6 to 14.

The mean effect size of SCT compared to control groups was 0.45 (95% CI: 0.11 ~ 0.79; NNT = 4.00), with moderate heterogeneity ($I^2 = 47.95$).

One study was a possible outlier (Barlow, 1986). After removal of this study, the effect size was somewhat larger ($d = 0.53$; 95% CI: 0.28 ~ 0.77), but heterogeneity was reduced to zero ($I^2 = 0$). Because of the small number of studies, we did not conduct subgroup analyses.

We found some indications for publication bias. Duval and Tweedie's trim and fill procedure resulted in a considerable reduction of the effect size (adjusted effect size: 0.29; 95% CI: –0.07 ~ 0.64; number of studies trimmed: 2), which was not significantly different from zero anymore.

We could compare SCT directly to other psychotherapies in two studies (with three comparisons; Fleming & Thornton, 1980; Fuchs & Rehm, 1977). Because of this small number of studies, we did not conduct a meta-analysis. However, in one study (Fleming & Thornton, 1980) no significant difference was found between SCT, CBT, and supportive psychotherapy. The other study, however, found that SCT was more effective than supportive psychotherapy (Fleming & Thornton, 1980).

We detected only one study (Roth, Bielski, Jones, Parker, & Osborn, 1982) in which SCT was directly compared to a combined treatment of SCT and pharmacotherapy. This study did not find indications of a difference between the two, although the power was probably too low to find significant differences ($N = 26$). We found no studies in which SCT was directly compared to pharmacotherapy, or studies in which pharmacotherapy was compared to a combined treatment of SCT and pharmacotherapy.

In one of the studies on SCT, data on 3-month follow-up were presented (apart from the comparison at post-test; Robinsohn-Whelen, Hughes, Taylor, Hall, & Rehm, 2007). In this study, SCT for depressed rural women with disabilities was compared to a control group (which had only access to regular care from centers for independent living) 3 months after the end of the treatment. Unfortunately, insufficient data were reported for the calculation of the effect size at follow-up. No other data on the longer-term efficacy of SCT was found.

Conclusion

We found some evidence that SCT is efficacious as a treatment for depression. However, the quality of these studies was not optimal, and we found hardly any research in which SCT was compared to other psychotherapies, pharmacotherapy, combined treatments, or research on longer-term efficacy of SCT. More research is needed to establish the efficacy of SCT.

PROBLEM-SOLVING THERAPY

Problem-solving therapy (PST) is another psychological treatment that could be seen as belonging to a broader family of cognitive behavior therapies. In PST, the patient systematically identifies his or her problems, generates alternative solutions for each problem, selects the best solution, develops and conducts a plan, and evaluates whether this has solved the problem. There are several types of PST for depression. The first type, social problem-solving therapy (SPST), was developed in the 1980s (D'Zurilla & Nezu, 1982; A. M. Nezu & Perri, 1989) and is typically conducted in a group format of 10 to 12 sessions. This treatment focuses not only on the problem-solving skills themselves, but also on changing those attitudes or beliefs that may inhibit or interfere with attempts to engage in the remaining problem-solving tasks. The second type, PST for primary care (PST-PC), was developed in the 1990s (Mynors-Wallis, Gath, Lloyd-Thomas, & Tomlinson, 1995) and is applied individually in six sessions. It focuses on the core elements of problem solving and can be used by trained nurses. A third type of problem solving, self-examination therapy (SET) (Bowman, Scogin, & Lyrene, 1995), is aimed at determining the major goals in their lives, investing energy only in those problems that are related to the goals in their lives, and learning to accept those situations that cannot be changed. Problem-solving skills are the core element of this approach. The SET is typically used in a guided self-help format, but can also be applied in group and individual settings.

Clinical Guidelines and Earlier Meta-Analyses

Problem-solving therapy has been examined in two earlier meta-analyses (Cuijpers, van Straten, & Warmerdam, 2007b; Malouff, Thorsteinsson, & Schutte, 2007). One of these was aimed at reviewing PST for depression (Cuijpers et al., 2007b), while the other was aimed at the efficacy of PST in reducing mental and physical health problems (although it included 10 studies on depression, Malouff et al., 2007). The first meta-analysis (Cuijpers et al., 2007b) used the same data set as the one we will use in here. Both meta-analyses concluded that PST is efficacious in the treatment of depression, with moderate to large effect sizes when compared with control groups.

Most clinical practice guidelines recommend PST especially for mild depression in primary care. For instance, NICE (2004) recommends six to eight brief CBT or PST sessions for mild depression in primary care, but all guidelines address considering alternative first-step strategies as well, that is, psychoeducation, exercise, guided self-help, computerized CBT (NICE, CBO/Trimbos Institute), and supportive clinical care (RANZCP, 2004).

Efficacy

We found 13 studies (14 comparisons) comparing PST to a control group. The mean effect size of these studies was 0.87 (95% CI: 0.49 ~ 1.24), which corresponds with an NNT of 2.16. Heterogeneity was very high ($I^2 = 82.24$, $p < 0.001$).

Visual inspection of the funnel suggested two possible outliers with extremely high effect sizes (A. Nezu, 1986; A. M. Nezu & Perri, 1989). Removal of these studies resulted in a somewhat lower effect size ($d = 0.61$; 95% CI: 0.30 ~ 0.92; corresponding NNT = 2.99), but heterogeneity remained high ($I^2 = 73.80$, $p < 0.001$). When we examined the effect sizes based on the BDI only, somewhat higher effect sizes were found ($d = 1.11$; 95% CI: 0.67 ~ 1.56; NNT = 1.76), with high heterogeneity ($I^2 = 77.65$, $p < 0.001$). The effect sizes based on the Hamilton Depression Rating Scale (HAM-D) were also high ($d = 1.17$; 95% CI: 0.75 ~ 1.59; NNT = 1.69), but heterogeneity was moderate in these analyses ($I^2 = 48.76$, $p < 0.1$).

Both the funnel plot and Duval and Tweedie's trim and fill procedure suggested that there was considerable publication bias. After adjustment for possible publication bias, the mean effect size decreased from 0.87 to 0.28 (95% CI: 0.11 ~ 0.67; number of trimmed studies: 6; NNT = 6.41). This was not significantly different from zero.

In the subgroup analyses, we found a trend indicating that studies in which participants were recruited from the community have higher effect sizes than studies in which participants were recruited from clinical or other samples (Table 11.5). We also found that studies in which a group format was used resulted in significantly higher effect sizes than studies in which an individual or guided self-help format was used. However, the two possible outliers we identified (A. Nezu, 1986; A. M. Nezu & Perri, 1989) both used the group format. After removal of these studies, the difference was still significant ($p = 0.01$).

TABLE 11.5   Efficacy of Problem-Solving Therapy Compared to Control Groups, Other Psychotherapies, and Pharmacotherapy

	N_{comp}	D	95% CI	Z	I^2	NNT	P
Problem-solving versus control groups							
– All studies	14	0.87	0.49 ~ 1.24	4.56****	82.24****	2.16	
– Two possible outliers removed[a]	12	0.61	0.30 ~ 0.92	3.86****	73.80****	2.99	
– BDI only	12	1.11	0.67 ~ 1.56	4.92****	77.65****	1.76	
– HAM-D only	8	1.17	0.75 ~ 1.59	5.51****	48.76*	1.69	
Publication bias							
■ After correction for publication bias	14	0.28	–0.11 ~ 0.67			6.41	
Subgroup analyses							
Recruitment							0.067
■ General population	8	1.43	0.62 ~ 2.25	3.45***	87.07****	1.45	
■ Clinical	4	0.31	–0.16 ~ 0.79	1.30 ns	63.01**	5.75	
■ Other	2	0.65	–0.24 ~ 1.53	1.43 ns	83.93**	2.82	
Target group							0.921
■ Adults in general	10	0.90	0.44 ~ 1.37	3.78****	82.11****	2.10	
■ Specific target group	4	0.85	0.01 ~ 1.70	1.98**	86.89****	2.21	
Specific types of depressive disorders							0.533
■ Diagnosed mood disorder	10	0.94	0.48 ~ 1.39	4.04****	86.39****	2.02	
■ Other definition	4	0.73	0.24 ~ 1.21	2.92***	23.49 ns	2.54	
Format							0.001
■ Individual	5	0.31	–0.04 ~ 0.65	1.75*	77.80***	5.75	
■ Group	6	1.76	1.08 ~ 2.44	5.09****	60.73**	1.27	
■ Guided self-help	3	0.54	0.04 ~ 1.04	2.12**	0	3.36	
Control group							0.000
■ Waiting list	8	1.53	1.03 ~ 2.02	6.02****	53.12**	6.58	
■ Care-as-usual	3	0.27	0.06 ~ 0.48	2.47**	0	6.58	
■ Other	3	0.14	–0.28 ~ 0.57	0.67 ns	74.82	12.82	
Study quality							0.001
■ High quality	2	0.10	–0.22 ~ 0.42	0.63 ns	65.04*	17.86	
■ Other studies	12	1.11	0.61 ~ 1.61	4.33****	81.03****	1.76	
Problem-solving versus other psychotherapies							
■ All studies	7	0.40	–0.07 ~ 0.87	1.68*	72.78***	4.50	
■ One possible outlier removed[b]	6	0.20	–0.17 ~ 0.57	1.05	54.21*	8.93	
Problem-solving versus pharmacotherapy	5	–0.11[b]	–0.27 ~ 0.04	–1.40 ns	0	16.13	

Notes: *: $p < 0.1$; **: $p < 0.05$; ***: $p < 0.01$; ****: $p < 0.001$; ns: not significant
A positive *d* indicates that PST is more effective than the alternative treatment; but when PST is compared to combined treatments, a positive *d* indicates that the combined treatment is more effective.
[a] A. Nezu (1986); A. M. Nezu and Perri (1989)
[b] A. Nezu (1986)

Our subgroup analyses also indicated that the studies in which a waiting list control group was used had significantly higher effect sizes than studies in which care-as-usual or other control groups were used. Two of the studies comparing PST to control conditions met all our quality criteria. These two studies had significantly lower effect sizes than the other studies.

PST could be compared to other psychotherapies in seven studies (Table 11.5). There was a trend ($p < 0.1$) indicating that PST was more effective than other psychotherapies for depression ($d = 0.40$; 95% CI: $-0.07 \sim 0.87$). Heterogeneity, however, was high ($I^2 = 72.78$). Removal of one possible outlier with an extremely high effect size (A. M. Nezu et al., 1989) resulted in a small, nonsignificant effect size ($d = 0.20$; 95% CI: $-0.17 \sim 0.57$) with moderate heterogeneity ($I^2 = 54.21$).

PST could be compared to pharmacotherapy in four studies (five comparisons). The mean effect size indicating the difference between the two types of treatment was -0.11 in favor of pharmacotherapy (95% CI: $-0.27 \sim 0.04$; $p > 0.1$), with zero heterogeneity. We found only one study in which pharmacotherapy was compared to the combination of PST and pharmacotherapy (Mynors-Wallis, Gath, Day, & Baker, 2000). In this study a small, not significant effect size ($d = 0.21$) was found in favor of the combined therapy. This study was also the only study in which PST was compared to the combination of PST and pharmacotherapy (two comparisons, one in which PST provided by a nurse was compared to the combined treatment, and one in which PST by a general practitioner was compared to the combined treatment). Both comparisons resulted in small and nonsignificant effect sizes (0.21 and 0.24) in favor of the combined treatment.

In only one of the controlled studies, PST could be compared to a control condition at 6 and 12 month follow-up (Dowrick et al., 2000). At both follow-up measurements, small, non-significant effect sizes were found ($d = 0.25$ at 6 and $d = 0.13$ at 12 month follow-up).

Conclusion

We found considerable evidence that PST is efficacious in the treatment of depression, compared to control groups. However, heterogeneity was high in most analyses, and our subgroup analyses could only partially explain this heterogeneity. This implies that there are significant differences between study outcomes that cannot be explained by the moderating variables we examined in our subgroup analyses. We also found indications for publication bias. Furthermore, only two studies met all quality criteria, and these two studies resulted in a small, non-significant effect size, which did differ significantly from the other studies. In the studies in which PST was compared directly to other psychotherapies, we found a trend indicating that PST may be more efficacious than other psychotherapies. However, heterogeneity was high in these analyses. We found no significant difference between PST and pharmacotherapy. Because of the mixed results of our meta-analyses of PST, we have to be cautious with the interpretation of these results.

SOCIAL SKILLS TRAINING

The last evidence-based psychotherapy that could be considered as belonging to the broader family of cognitive-behavioral treatments for adult depression is social skills training (SST). Social skills training is a form of behavior therapy in which clients are taught skills that help in the building and retainment of social and interpersonal relationships. In most versions of SST, patients are trained in assertiveness. This means that the client is taught to stand up for his or her rights, through expressing feelings in an honest and respectful way that does not insult people.

SST has been examined as a treatment of depression in the 1970s and 1980s. Despite positive findings, however, not much research has been conducted since then, resulting in a small group of studies, most of which do not meet current standards of randomized controlled trials.

We found no earlier meta-analysis of SST, and none of the clinical guidelines we examined mentioned SST as a possible treatment of adult depression. We did find, however, three studies in which SST was compared to a control condition.

The mean effect size of these studies was 0.63 (95% CI: 0.09 ~ 1.16; NNT = 2.91), with zero heterogeneity. We found no indication for publication bias (adjusted effect size was the same as the unadjusted effect size).

We also found five studies (seven comparisons) in which SST could be compared to other psychotherapies (Cuijpers, van Straten, Andersson, et al., 2008). The mean effect size indicated a small, nonsignificant effect size in favor of SST compared to other psychotherapies for depression ($d = 0.05$; $-0.26 \sim 0.36$; n.s.), with zero heterogeneity ($I^2 = 0$).

We detected no study in which SST was directly compared to pharmacotherapy or a combined treatment of SST and pharmacotherapy. We did find one study in which pharmacotherapy was compared with a combined treatment of SST and pharmacotherapy (Bellack, Hersen, & Himmelhoch, 1981). In this study, no indication was found that the combined treatment was significantly more efficacious than pharmacotherapy alone ($d = -0.10$), but this should be considered with caution because there was not sufficient statistical power to find smaller significant effect sizes.

We found no study in which the effects of SST could be compared to a control group at follow-up.

Despite some early studies showing that SST may be efficacious in the treatment of depression, there is not much strong evidence supporting this claim. The number of studies is small, the quality of these studies is limited, only waiting list control groups are used, no long-term effects are known, and hardly any comparisons with pharmacotherapy or combined treatments are made. On the other hand, the evidence that is available is promising, and more research is certainly warranted.

INTERPERSONAL PSYCHOTHERAPY

Interpersonal psychotherapy (IPT) is a brief and highly structured manual-based form of psychotherapy that addresses interpersonal issues in depression, to the exclusion of all other foci of clinical attention. In the initial phase of IPT, the depressive symptoms are explored and psychoeducation about depression is given. The interpersonal context of the patient is explored and depressive symptoms are linked to recent interpersonal events. There are four possible treatment focuses: complicated grief, interpersonal conflict, role transition, and interpersonal deficits (Van Schaik et al., 2003). Interpersonal psychotherapy has no specific theoretical origin although its theoretical basis can be seen as coming from the work of Sullivan, Meyer, and Bowlby. The current form of the treatment was developed by the late Gerald Klerman and Myrna Weissman in the 1980s (Klerman, Weissman, Rounsaville, & Chevron, 1984).

Clinical Guidelines and Earlier Meta-Analyses

Although IPT has been examined in a considerable number of randomized controlled trials, only one earlier meta-analysis has focused on IPT for depression (De Mello et al., 2005). This meta-analysis found significant and large effects for IPT compared to placebo, and superior effects of IPT compared to cognitive behavior therapy. However, this meta-analysis was based on only half of the currently available studies. Furthermore, in this meta-analysis no analyses of heterogeneity were conducted and there were no subgroup analyses conducted to explore possible causes of heterogeneity. Finally, the possibility of publication bias was not examined.

In all practice guidelines, IPT has been recommended as psychotherapeutic treatment of choice, apart from CBT. For moderate depression the RANZCP (2004) states that IPT is equally effective compared to antidepressant medication. NICE (2004) recommends IPT for moderately to severely depressed patients in primary care, and CBT as first treatment of choice after trying antidepressants. However, in case of a preference of the patient for IPT or if a clinician thinks the patient will benefit from IPT, this treatment strategy should be chosen. The Swedish guidelines (Åsberg et al., 2004) recommend IPT in case of relationship issues, but also overall for mild to moderate depression. The combination of IPT with antidepressants may result in lower risk of relapse after remission (APA, 2000). In addition, some guidelines (APA, 2000; CBO/Trimbos Institute, 2005) underscore the potential value of IPT in the maintenance phase for reducing risk of relapse.

Efficacy

We could compare efficacy of IPT to a control condition in 12 studies. The mean effect size for these studies was 0.68 (95% CI: 0.29 ~ 1.07; p < 0.01), with high heterogeneity (I^2 88.31). This effect size corresponds with an NNT of 2.70 (Table 11.6).

After removal of two possible outliers (Bolton et al., 2003; Forsyth, 2000), the effect size was somewhat reduced (d 0.45; NNT 4.00), and heterogeneity was also reduced to a moderate level (I^2 47.63). The effect sizes based on the BDI and HAM-D resulted in comparable outcomes (Table 11.6). The funnel plot nor Duval & Tweedie's trim and fill method resulted in indications for publication bias (the adjusted and unadjusted effect sizes were exactly the same).

We conducted a series of subgroup analyses in which we divided studies according to major characteristics. Results are presented in Table 11.6. As can be seen, no indications were found that there were significant differences between studies aimed at adults in general compared to studies for more specific target groups, studies aimed at patients with major depression versus studies in which other inclusion criteria were used, and studies aimed at

treatment versus those aimed at prevention. We found a trend (p < 0.1) indicating that studies using clinical samples had smaller effect sizes than studies in which patients were recruited through other methods. We also found that studies in which IPT was used in group format resulted in higher effect sizes than studies in which IPT was used as individual therapy, but this result must be considered with caution because only two studies examined IPT in group format. We also found that type of control group was significantly related to effect size (p < 0.001), with waiting list control groups resulting in the largest effect size, care-as-usual control groups in smaller effect sizes, and other control groups (including pill placebo) in the smallest effect sizes. Only two studies met all quality criteria and these studies resulted in significantly smaller effect sizes than other studies (p < 0.05).

IPT could be directly compared to other psychotherapies in eight studies. In these studies patients were assigned to IPT or another psychotherapy. Such studies have the advantage in that they are well equipped to examine the relative efficacy of different types of treatment because they rule out the possible influence of study characteristics, and they therefore provide reliable evidence about a possible superiority of one type of therapy over the other (Cuijpers, van Straten, Andersson, et al., 2008; Spielmans, Pasek, & McFall, 2007). Effect sizes in these studies do not indicate the strength of the effects of one treatment over a control group, but they represent the strength of the effects of one type of psychotherapy over another. The effect size indicating the difference between IPT and other psychotherapies was 0.21 (in favor of IPT), which indicates that IPT is somewhat more effective than other psychotherapies (p 0.05, Table 11.6). The five studies in which IPT was compared to cognitive behavior therapy resulted in a nonsignificant effect size of 0.12 (in favor of IPT). Heterogeneity was zero to low in these analyses, suggesting that there were few systematic differences between the studies.

TABLE 11.6　Efficacy of Interpersonal Psychotherapy Compared to Control Groups, Other Psychotherapies, and Pharmacotherapy

	N_{comp}	D	95% CI	Z	I^{2a}	NNT	P^b
IPT versus (untreated) controls							
■ All studies	12	0.68	0.29 ~ 1.07	3.39***	88.31****	2.70	
■ Two possible outliers removed[c]	10	0.45	0.23 ~ 0.66	4.09****	47.63**	4.00	
■ BDI only	5	0.74	0.13 ~ 1.35	2.37**	85.60****	2.50	
■ HAM-D only	8	0.50	0.23 ~ 0.77	3.69****	50.68**	3.62	
Publication bias							
■ After correction for publication bias	12	0.68	0.29 ~ 1.07			2.70	
Recruitment							
■ Clinical samples	5	0.34	0.17 ~ 0.52	3.87****	0	5.26	0.076
■ Other recruitment	7	0.89	0.31 ~ 1.46	3.02***	87.69****	2.13	
Target group							
■ Adults in general	5	0.70	−0.02 ~ 1.41	1.92*	93.44****	2.63	0.928
■ Specific target group	7	0.66	0.20 ~ 1.19	2.82***	80.46****	2.78	
Specific types of depressive disorders							
■ Major depressive disorder	7	0.46	0.18 ~ 0.74	3.20***	64.14**	3.91	0.183
■ Other definition	5	0.99	0.26 ~ 1.73	2.64***	88.85****	1.94	
Format							
■ Individual	10	0.45	0.23 ~ 0.66	4.09****	47.63**	4.00	0.000
■ Group	2	1.83	1.56 ~ 2.11	12.93****	0	1.24	
Control group							
■ Waiting list	2	1.41	0.83 ~ 1.98	4.81****	59.57	1.47	0.003
■ Care-as-usual	6	0.63	−0.01 ~ 1.26	1.95*	92.56****	2.91	
■ Other	4	0.32	0.05 ~ 0.58	2.36**	0	5.56	
Study quality							
■ High quality	2	0.21	−0.04 ~ 0.45	1.67*	ns	0	0.026
■ Other studies	10	0.78	0.34 ~ 1.23	3.46***	87.07****	2.39	
Prevention/treatment							
■ Indicated prevention	4	0.75	0.05 ~ 1.45	2.10**	77.95***	2.48	0.814
■ Treatment	8	0.65	0.15 ~ 1.14	2.56**	91.29****	2.82	
IPT versus other therapies							
IPT versus all other psychotherapies	8	0.21	0.01 ~ 0.42	2.02**	21.98 ns		
IPT versus cognitive behavior therapy	5	0.12	−0.33 ~ 0.09	−1.13	0 ns		
IPT versus pharmacotherapy	8	−0.17	−0.32 ~ −0.02	−2.20**	0 ns		
IPT versus combined therapy	4	0.18	−0.03 ~ 0.39	1.67*	0 ns		
Pharmacotherapy vs. combined therapy	8	0.22	0.02 ~ 0.43	2.11**	29.84 ns		

Notes: *: $p < 0.1$; **: $p < 0.05$; ***: $p < 0.01$; ****: $p < 0.001$; ns: not significant

Abbreviations: CI: confidence intervals; N_{comp}: number of comparisons; NNT: numbers-needed-to-treat.

[a] The *p*-values in this column indicate whether the Q-statistic is significant (the I^2 statistics do not include a test of significance).

[b] The *p*-values in this column indicate whether the difference between the effect sizes in the subgroups is significant.

[c] Bolton et al. (2003); Forsyth (2000)

IPT could be compared directly to pharmacotherapy in eight studies. This resulted in an effect size of 0.17 in favor of pharmacotherapy ($p < 0.05$). When IPT was compared to a combination of IPT and pharmacotherapy, an effect size of 0.18 in favor of the combined treatment was found ($p < 0.1$). A comparison of pharmacotherapy with the combination of IPT and pharmacotherapy resulted in an effect size of 0.22 in favor of the combined treatment ($p < 0.05$). Heterogeneity was zero to low in the analyses.

We collected five trials that examined the long-term effects of IPT as a maintenance treatment. Because designs of these studies and the follow-up periods differed considerably, we did not conduct a meta-analysis of the outcomes of these studies. However, we will briefly describe the results of these studies. In the earliest study of IPT, 150 depressed women who had responded to pharmacotherapy were randomized to continuation IPT, placebo, or several other treatment arms (Klerman, DiMascio, Weissman, Prusoff, & Paykel, 1974). Although the relapse rate at 8 month follow-up in the IPT condition was lower (17%) than in the placebo condition (31%), this difference was not significant. In another study, 128 patients who had had at least three episodes of major depression were examined (Frank et al., 1990). Those who responded to a combined acute treatment of pharmacotherapy and IPT were randomized to maintenance IPT, placebo, or combined maintenance IPT plus pharmacotherapy treatments. After 3 years no significant effects of IPT on relapse rates were found, although the effects were in the expected direction (relapse in IPT 46%, in placebo 65%). In the third study (Schulberg et al., 1996), 276 patients were randomized to acute plus maintenance IPT, acute plus maintenance pharmacotherapy, or usual care. At 8 month follow-up, 70% of the patients in the two active treatment arms had recovered, compared to 20% in the usual care group. No significant difference between the two active treatments was found. In the remaining two

trials examining the efficacy of maintenance IPT (Reynolds et al., 1999; Reynolds et al., 2006), IPT was not examined as a single intervention. It was only examined in combination with placebo. However, a placebo may have an effect on depression in itself or may alter the effects of psychotherapy alone (Wampold et al., 2005). In one of the trials (Reynolds et al., 1999) it was found that maintenance IPT plus placebo did reduce relapse significantly compared to placebo alone, but this finding was not supported in the second trial (Reynolds et al., 2006).

Conclusion

We found convincing evidence that IPT is efficacious as an acute treatment of depression. In a meta-analysis of comparative trials, we also found that IPT is significantly more efficacious than other psychotherapies. Furthermore, adding IPT to pharmacotherapy results in significantly higher effect sizes and we found a trend that combined therapy is more effective than IPT alone. However, we also found that high quality studies had significantly lower effect sizes than other studies, pharmacotherapy is significantly more efficacious than IPT, and the research on IPT as a maintenance treatment does not result in very clear outcomes. More research is needed to examine these issues.

NONDIRECTIVE SUPPORTIVE THERAPY

We found a broad category of unstructured therapies that are aimed at supporting depressed patients, without specific psychological techniques other than those common to all approaches, such as helping people to ventilate their experiences and emotions and offering empathy (Cuijpers, van Straten, Andersson, et al., 2008). This nondirective supportive therapy (NDST) is not aimed at solutions, or acquiring new skills. It is based on the assumption that relief from personal problems may be achieved through discussion with others. These nondirective therapies are commonly described in the literature as either counseling or supportive therapy. We distinguished two main types of NDST: (1) NDST explicitly referring to the work of Rogers (1967), which is a specific form of nondirective therapy in which reflection is an important therapeutic technique to elicit feelings; and (2) NDST that did not explicitly refer to the work of Rogers, but met the earlier definition of NDST.

Clinical Guidelines and Earlier Meta-Analyses

We found only one earlier meta-analysis in which efficacy of supportive therapies was examined (Churchill et al., 2001). In this study, supportive therapies were defined as "client-centered, gestalt, process-experiential, non-specific and attention-placebo therapies." In this meta-analysis it was found that cognitive behavior therapies were significantly more effective than supportive therapies, although the number of comparisons was small ($N = 5$).

None of the guidelines, except RANZCP (2004), recommend supportive therapy for depression. The APA (2000) points out that based on very limited controlled studies, supportive group therapy has been suggested to be useful for depression, but future studies are required. However, RANZCP states that for mild depression, supportive clinical care supported by psychoeducation and supplemented by teaching problem-solving skills is the treatment of choice and other treatments are not effective. It has to be mentioned that the recommended supportive clinical care has potentially a broader definition since it also includes PST techniques.

Efficacy

NDST Versus Control Conditions

We could compare efficacy of NDST to a control condition in 13 studies (14 comparisons).

The resulting effect size was 0.57 (95% CI: $0.37 \sim 0.77$), which corresponds to an NNT of 3.18. Heterogeneity was low to moderate ($I^2 = 36.81$). One of the included studies (Ayen & Hautzinger, 2004) had a very high effect size ($d = 2.06$) and was a possible outlier. After removal of this study the effect size was somewhat lower ($d = 0.48$; 95% CI: $0.34 \sim 0.63$; NNT $= 3.76$), and heterogeneity was reduced to zero.

When we limited the effect sizes to the BDI, the resulting effect size was 0.51 (95% CI: $0.22 \sim 0.80$; NNT $= 3.55$), with moderate heterogeneity. But after removal of the possible outlier, heterogeneity again was reduced to zero (Table 11.7). When we limited effect sizes to the HAM-D, we found comparable results (Table 11.7). Duvall and Tweedie's trim and fill procedure did not result in strong indications for publication bias (adjusted effect after correction for publication bias: 0.49; 95% CI: $0.26 \sim 0.73$; number of trimmed studies: 2).

We examined in a subgroup analysis whether the two subtypes of NDST we distinguished (NDST that explicitly referred to the works and methods of Rogers and other NDSTs) differed significantly from each other. Although the NDST that referred to Rogers (1967) had somewhat lower effect sizes than other NDSTs, this difference was not significant. In other subgroup analyses we also found no indication that effect sizes were significantly related to recruitment method, target group, diagnosis of depression, format, or control group. Because only one study met all quality criteria (Cooper, Murray, Wilson, & Romaniuk, 2003; $d = 0.26$; 95% CI: $-0.13 \sim 0.65$), we did not examine differences between high-quality and other studies.

NDST Versus Other Treatments and as Part of Combination Treatments

We found 20 studies (30 comparisons) in which NDST was compared to another psychotherapy. The mean effect size indicating the difference

TABLE 11.7   Efficacy of Non-Directive Supportive Therapy Compared to Control Groups, Other Psychotherapies, and Pharmacotherapy

	N_{comp}	D	95% CI	Z	I^2	NNT	P
Supportive therapy versus control groups							
– All studies	14	0.57	0.37 ~ 0.77	5.71****	36.81	3.18	
– One possible outlier removed[a]	13	0.48	0.34 ~ 0.63	6.38****	0	3.76	
– BDI only	8	0.51	0.22 ~ 0.80	3.47***	46.96	3.55	
– BDI only, one possible outlier removed[a]	7	0.39	0.20 ~ 0.59	3.93****	0	4.59	
– HAM-D only	3	0.64	0.23 ~ 1.06	3.03***	0	2.86	
Publication bias							
▪ After correction for publication bias	14	0.49	0.26 ~ 0.73			3.68	
Subgroup analyses[b]							
Subtype							0.235
▪ NDST according to Rogers	4	0.44	0.21 ~ 0.67	3.76****	0	4.10	
▪ Other NDST	10	0.66	0.38 ~ 0.95	4.56****	49.92**	2.78	
Recruitment							0.662
▪ General population	4	0.83	0.01 ~ 1.66	1.95*	66.98**	2.26	
▪ Clinical	3	0.56	0.29 ~ 0.84	3.99****	0	3.25	
▪ Other	7	0.47	0.27 ~ 0.68	4.49****	16.75	3.85	
Target group							0.709
▪ Adults in general	5	0.54	0.28 ~ 0.79	4.11****	0	3.36	
▪ Specific target group	9	0.61	0.32 ~ 0.89	4.18****	56.57*	2.99	
Specific types of depressive disorders							0.808
▪ Diagnosed mood disorder	9	0.61	0.31 ~ 0.90	4.02****	56.51**	2.99	
▪ Other definition	5	0.56	0.32 ~ 0.80	4.52****	0	3.25	
Format							0.390
▪ Individual	7	0.48	0.30 ~ 0.67	5.14****	3.79	3.76	
▪ Group	7	0.68	0.27 ~ 1.09	3.26***	56.29**	2.70	
Control group							0.119
▪ Waiting list	5	0.91	0.25 ~ 1.57	2.69***	57.87*	2.08	
▪ Care as usual	8	0.44	0.28 ~ 0.60	5.30****	0	4.10	
▪ Other	1	0.97	0.35 ~ 1.59	3.07***	0	1.97	
Supportive therapy versus other psychotherapies							
▪ All studies	30	0.17	0.32 ~ 0.03	2.29**	40.80**	10.42	
▪ Two possible outliers (d = 1.5) removed[c]	28	0.09	0.21 ~ 0.02	1.64 ns	1.95 ns	20.00	
Supportive therapy versus pharmacotherapy	4	0.15	0.62 ~ 0.32	0.62 ns	65.91**	11.90	

Notes: * p < 0.1, ** p < 0.05, *** p < 0.01, **** p < 0.001, ns = not significant

A positive *d* indicates that PST is more effective than the alternative treatment, but when PST is compared to combined treatments, a positive *d* indicates that the combined treatment is more effective.

[a] Ayen & Hautzinger (2004).

[b] Only one study (Cooper et al., 2003) met all quality criteria; therefore, we did not conduct subgroup analyses examining differences between high quality and other studies.

[c] Ayen & Hautzinger (2004), Fuchs and Rehm (1977).

between NDST and other psychotherapies was –0.17 (95% CI: –0.32 ~ –0.03; $I^2 = 40.80$), which indicated a small but significant effect in favor of other psychotherapies. Two of these studies found very large differences between NDST and other psychotherapies ($d > 1.5$; Ayen & Hautzinger, 2004; and Fuchs & Rehm, 1977). After removal of these two possible outliers, the resulting effect size was not significant anymore and heterogeneity was very low ($I^2 = 1.95$).

The difference between NDST and other psychotherapies was explored in depth in a separate publication (Cuijpers, van Straten, Warmerdam, & Andersson, 2008b). In this separate study, subgroup analyses were conducted to explore possible differences between groups of studies. In these analyses, no significant differences were found between the studies that examined NSDT according to Rogers and the studies that examined other forms of NSDT. In some studies, the authors explicitly indicate that NDST was used as a control condition for another type of psychotherapy (such as CBT or IPT). In subgroup analyses we found no indications that studies in which NDST was used as a control condition differed significantly from other studies examining NDST.

We could compare efficacy of NDST with pharmacotherapy in four studies. The mean effect size indicating the difference between NDST and pharmacotherapy was –0.15 (95% CI: –0.62 ~ 0.32), a small, nonsignificant difference in favor of pharmacotherapy. We found only one study in which NDST was compared to the combination of NDST and pharmacotherapy (Markowitz et al., 1998). This study detected a large and significant effect ($d = 0.65$) in favor of the combined treatment. No study was found in which pharmacotherapy was compared to the combination of NDST and pharmacotherapy.

Long-Term Effects of NDST

We found three studies in which efficacy of NDST could be compared to care-as-usual at follow-up (in a fourth study follow-up data were also reported, but the dropout rate was higher than 50% and will therefore not be described here).

In the first study, among primiparous women with postpartum depression, acute treatment effects of NDST were found (Cooper et al., 2003). However, at 4.5-, 9-, 18-, and 60-month follow-up, no significant difference was found between those receiving NDST and those in the care-as-usual control group. In the second study (King et al., 2000), significant effects for NDST were found at 4 months after baseline compared to care-as-usual among depressed primary care patients. But again, 12 months after baseline, no significant difference was found. The third study we found compared NDST in cancer patients ($N = 21$) to care-as-usual ($N = 24$; Evans & Connis, 1995). This study demonstrated a moderate effect ($d = 0.50$) of the intervention compared to the care-as-usual control group at 6-month follow-up.

Conclusion

We found convincing evidence that NDST is effective in the treatment of depression. Although NDST is a broad category of therapies, ranging from Rogerian therapy to support groups for depressed general medical patients and women with postpartum depression, heterogeneity was remarkably low. The number of studies in which NDST was directly compared to other psychotherapies was high (30 comparisons). Although there was a small but significant difference in favor of the other therapies, this difference could be attributed to two possible outliers with extremely high differential effect sizes. After removal of these outliers, the difference between NDST and other therapies was not significant anymore. In several studies, NDST has been used as a control condition for other psychotherapies for adult depression. However, these studies did not indicate that NDST was indeed less effective than the other therapies, suggesting that NDST is an effective treatment for adult depression.

SHORT-TERM PSYCHODYNAMIC PSYCHOTHERAPY

Short-term psychodynamic psychotherapies (STPP) are rooted in psychoanalytical theories and can be distinguished from other psychotherapy methods by their emphasis on the investigation of unconscious feelings, motivations, desires, and fantasies in order to treat the depressive symptoms. The STPP aims at gaining more insight in the depressive symptoms by gradually linking them to the patient's unconscious dynamics, thereby reducing their severity (Busch, Rudden, & Shapiro, 2004). Different types of STPP have been developed by Malan (1963), Mann (1973), Sifneos (1979), Davanloo (1980), Strupp and Binder (1984), Pollack and Horner (1985), and de Jonghe (1994).

Clinical Guidelines and Earlier Meta-Analyses

STPP has been examined in three earlier meta-analyses (Churchill et al., 2001; Leichsenring, 2001; McCusker et al., 1998). McCusker and colleagues (1998) found no significant differences between *rational treatments* (CBT, BT, or CT) and *emotive treatments* (STPP) in the treatment of depression in older ambulatory patients, analyzing four studies. Leichsenring (2001), including six studies comparing STPP with CBT, also demonstrated that both were equally effective in the treatment of depression, a result the author suggested should be regarded as preliminary, due to the small number of included studies. Churchill et al. (2001) compared STPP to CBT and to nondirective supportive therapy (NDST) and found that patients receiving CBT were more likely to recover than those receiving STPP, but found no differences in posttreatment symptoms, symptom reduction, or dropout. Due to a lack of data, no conclusions could be drawn regarding the efficacy of STPP versus NDST.

RANZCP (2004) states that there is no evidence for the effectiveness of STPP, whereas in the Dutch (CBO/Trimbos Institute, 2005, 2009)

and Swedish guidelines (Åsberg et al., 2004) STPP is described as an effective treatment strategy for mild to moderate depression. The APA (2000) mentions STPP for treatment of depression, but underscores that this was based on clinical consensus rather than evidence.

Efficacy

We have explored efficacy of STPP in more depth in an earlier meta-analysis (Driessen et al., 2010) and refer the interested reader to this study for more detailed information. This paragraph contains a summary of this study, reporting on the main results only.

STPP could be compared to control groups at posttreatment in four studies (Table 11.8), including five comparisons and totaling 164 subjects (82 in the STPP conditions and 82 in the control conditions).

The control conditions consisted of waitlist control groups ($N = 4$) and care as usual ($N = 1$). None of these studies met all eight quality criteria. The pooled effect size indicating the difference between STPP and the control conditions at posttreatment was 0.76 (95% CI: 0.34 ~ 1.17), significantly in favor of STPP and corresponding with a NNT of 2.44. Heterogeneity was low ($I^2 = 22.90\%$). After adjusting for possible publication bias, the mean effect size decreased from 0.76 to 0.62 (95% CI: 0.12 ~ 1.11; number of trimmed studies: 1). Because of the small number of comparisons, we did not conduct subgroup analyses.

The STPP was compared with antidepressants in only one study (Salminen et al., 2008), reporting equal efficacy. Two studies compared antidepressants with combined antidepressants and STPP (Burnand, Andreoli, Kolatte, Venturini, & Rosset, 2002; de Jonghe, Kool, van Aalst, Dekker, & Peen, 2001), both finding the addition of STPP to antidepressants more effective than antidepressants alone. One study compared combined STPP and antidepressants with STPP alone (de Jonghe et al., 2004). This study reported equivocal results, client self-report measures suggested the superiority of combined

TABLE 11.8   Efficacy of Short-Term Psychodynamic Psychotherapy (STPP) Compared to Control Groups, Other Psychotherapies, and Pharmacotherapy

	N_{comp}	D	95% CI	Z	I^2	NNT
STPP versus control groups						
– All studies	5	0.76	0.34 ~ 1.17	3.60**	22.90	2.44
Publication bias						
▪ After correction for publication bias		0.62	0.12 ~ 1.11			2.96
STPP versus other psychotherapies						
– All studies	17	–0.42	–0.71 ~ –0.14	–2.93**	58.04**	4.27
– One possible outlier removed[a]	10	–0.37	–0.70 ~ –0.05	–2.24*	57.95*	4.85
– BDI only	12	–0.37	–0.65 ~ –0.09	–2.55*	*40.41*	4.85
– HAM-D only	3	–0.14	–0.53 ~ 0.26	–0.68	0.00	12.82

Notes: *$p < .05$; **$p < .01$; italic numbers indicate a nonsignificant trend ($p < .10$). A positive d indicates that STPP is more effective than the alternative treatment; but when STPP is compared to combined treatments, a positive d indicates that the combined treatment is more effective.
[a] Shapiro et al. (1994)

treatment, while therapist self-reports and independent measures did not confirm these findings. Because these numbers of studies were too small to calculate separate analyses, we compared STPP with other psychotherapies only.

We could compare STPP with other psychotherapies at posttreatment in 10 studies, totaling 17 comparisons over 628 subjects (266 in the STPP conditions and 362 in the other psychotherapy conditions). The other psychotherapies consisted of cognitive behavior therapy ($N = 11$), behavior therapy ($N = 3$), cognitive therapy ($N = 2$), supportive therapy ($N = 1$), nondirective counseling ($N = 1$), and art therapy ($N = 1$). Table 11.8 shows the results of this comparison. The pooled mean effect size for the difference at posttreatment was –0.42 (95% CI: –0.71 ~ –0.14), indicating a moderate and significant superiority of the other psychotherapies. Heterogeneity was moderate ($I^2 = 58.04\%$). Repeating this analyses, excluding one study that included multiple comparisons (Shapiro et al., 1994), resulted in a somewhat lower effect size ($d = –0.37$; 95% CI: –0.70 ~ –0.05). Using only the BDI as outcome measure resulted in a somewhat lower effect size as well ($N = 12$; $d = –0.37$; 95% CI: –0.65 ~ –0.09), while using only the HAM-D as outcome measure no significant differences were found between STPP

and other psychotherapies ($d = –0.14$; 95% CI: –0.53 ~ 0.26). However, this analysis included three comparisons only.

Only one study compared STPP with a control condition at follow-up (Cooper et al., 2003). This study (among women with postpartum depression) found no differences between STPP and the care-as-usual control group at 4.5-, 9-, 18-, and 60-month follow-up.

Conclusion

We found indications that STPP is effective in the treatment of depression in adults when compared to waiting list or care-as-usual conditions. These results are in line with earlier reviews on efficacy of STPP for general psychiatric disorders, which generally found STPP superior to minimal or no treatment (Abbass et al., 2006; Anderson & Lambert, 1995; Crits-Christoph, 1992; Leichsenring et al., 2004; Svartberg & Stiles, 1991). Comparing STPP to other treatments, we found that other psychotherapies might be more efficacious at posttreatment. For studies addressing the efficacy of STPP versus antidepressants, STPP versus combined treatments, and combined treatment versus antidepressants, as well as STPP follow-up, research is scarce.

These results should be interpreted with caution, however, because of the suboptimal quality of the included studies and the possibility of publication bias. Furthermore, different STPP types were used in the studies, and it remains unclear whether these results hold up for one specific STPP type.

REMINISCENCE AND LIFE REVIEW THERAPY FOR OLDER ADULTS

Reminiscence has been defined as "the vocal or silent recall of events in a person's life, either alone or with another person or group of people" (Woods, Portnoy, Head, & Jones, 1992). In life review therapy (LRT), reminiscence is used in a structured and evaluative format to resolve past and current conflicts or for lending meaning and coherence to past or current experiences (Bohlmeijer, Roemer, Cuijpers, & Smit, 2007). In the last few decades, LRT has been used in several target populations with differing goals, including the stimulation of cognitive functioning in the demented elderly, an increase in life satisfaction and quality of life in older adults in general, and as a treatment method for older adults with depressive symptoms or major depression. LRT is based on the work by Butler (1963) who postulated life review as a naturally occurring process, mainly in late life, that is characterized by the progressive return to consciousness of past experiences, and, particularly, the resurgence of unresolved conflicts that is caused by the realization of approaching death. Basic characteristics of LRT are: structure (systematic focus on whole life span), integration (focus on both positive and negative events), and evaluation

Clinical Guidelines and Earlier Meta-Analyses

We found two earlier meta-analyses examining the efficacy of LRT in depressed older adults (Bohlmeijer, Smit, & Cuijpers, 2003;

Pinquart, Duberstein, & Lyness, 2007). Both found large and significant effect of LRT in depressed older adults compared to control groups ($d = 1.23$ and $d = 1.00$ respectively), although they also included nonrandomized controlled studies. None the reviewed treatment guidelines mention the use of LRT in depression.

Efficacy

We found four studies (six comparisons) between LRT and a control condition, with a total of 268 participants (173 in the LRT conditions and 95 in the control conditions).

None of these studies met all quality criteria. The mean effect sizes of these comparisons was 1.33 (95% CI: 0.53 ~ 2.13; NNT 1.53), with high heterogeneity (I^2 85.17, p 0.001). However, the two effect sizes from one study had very high effect sizes (3.01 and 1.61 respectively; Fry, 1983). After removal of these possible outliers, the mean effect size dropped to 0.76 (95% CI: 0.34 ~ 1.18; NNT 2.44), and heterogeneity dropped to zero. There was no indication for publication bias (the adjusted effect size was exactly the same as the unadjusted effect size). Because of the small number of effect sizes, we did not conduct subgroup analyses.

We found no study in which LRT was directly compared to another psychological treatment, to pharmacotherapy, or a combined treatment of pharmacotherapy and LRT, nor did we find a study in which pharmacotherapy was compared to a combined treatment of LRT and pharmacotherapy.

None of the studies reported data on follow-up measurements at which LRT could be compared to control groups.

Conclusion

Although the number of studies examining the efficacy of LRT is relatively small, we did find significant indications that LRT may be an efficacious treatment of depression in older adults. However, no studies have compared LRT therapy to other types of treatments or combinations of treatments, and none of the studies on LRT met all our quality criteria. Although LRT is a promising treatment, especially because it is acceptable and feasible among older adults, more research is needed to establish its relative efficacy better.

COUPLE THERAPY

Couple therapy (COT) is a form of psychological intervention in which the presence of both partners in sessions is required (Snyder, Castellani, & Whishman, 2006). There are several models to treat couples, including cognitive, behavioral, systemic or insight-oriented approaches. While they differ in theory and in how the therapy is conducted, they share the aim of modifying negative interactional patterns and promoting supportive aspects of dyadic relationships, with the aim to change the interpersonal aspect linked to depression. Within CBT there are a diversity of approaches, from more behavioral to ones that integrate acceptance (Jacobson, Christensen, Prince, Cordova, & Eldridge, 2000). Couple therapy has been advocated for depressed patients who have a regular partner and is motivated by the fact that there is a high prevalence of couple distress that can lead to emotional problems (Wheeler, Christensen, & Jacobson, 2001). Hence, treating both partners in a relationship can result in improved mental health for one or both partners in the couple.

Clinical Guidelines and Earlier Meta-Analyses

We found one earlier meta-analysis examining the efficacy of COT in depressed adults (Barbato & D'Avanzo, 2006, 2008). This meta-analysis identified only two studies in which COT was compared with a control condition, and several more in which COT was compared with other psychotherapies. This study

demonstrated that COT had a large effect on depression compared to the untreated controls, but no significant difference was found between COT and other psychotherapies, although there were indications that COT resulted in lower levels of couple distress.

Relationship problems in couples may be both a cause and a consequence of depression. The NICE (2004) recommends considering couple therapy (marital therapy) for patients who have a regular partner if individual therapy was not successful (15 to 20 sessions). The APA (2000), Swedish (Åsberg et al., 2004), and Dutch guidelines (CBT/Trimbos Institute, 2004, 2009) recommend COT, especially COT based on CBT techniques, if there is an indication of marital distress.

Efficacy

We found two studies in which COT was compared to a control condition (Beach & O'Leary, 1992; Teichmann, Bar-El, Shor, Sirota, & Elizur, 1995), with a total of 60 participants (30 in the COT conditions and 30 in the control groups). None of the two studies met all quality criteria. The mean effect size of these studies was 0.66 (95% CI: $0.03 \sim 1.29$; NNT = 1.54), with low heterogeneity ($I^2 = 30.41$). Because of the small number of effect sizes, we did not examine publication bias (at least three studies are needed to examine this), nor did we conduct subgroup analyses.

Two more studies compared efficacy of COT with pharmacotherapy (Dessaulles, Johnson, & Denton, 2003; Leff et al., 2000). Both found no significant difference between the two treatments ($d = 0.00$; 95% CI: $-0.42 \sim 0.42$; $I^2 = 0$). Three other studies compared COT with individual therapies (Emanuels-Zuurveen & Emmelkamp, 1996, 1997; Jacobson, Dobson, Fruzzetti, Schmaling, & Salusky, 1991). A meta-analysis of these three studies resulted in a small, nonsignificant effect size in favor of the comparison therapy (COT was less effective; $d = -0.24$; 95% CI: $-0.63 \sim 0.15$;

TABLE 11.9   Overview of the Results of Meta-Analyses of Evidence-Based Psychotherapies for Adult Depression

	Psychotherapy Versus Control				Versus Other Psychotherapies		Versus Pharmacotherapy		Versus Combined Treatment		PHA Versus Combined Treatment	
	N	D	NNT	ADJ	N	D	N	D	N	D	N	D
Cognitive behavior therapy	91	0.67	2.75	0.41	56	0.03	15	0.03	8	0.15	6	0.27**
Behavioral activation therapy	11	0.88	2.15	0.50	21	0.14*	1	–	0	–	0	–
Self-control therapy	6	0.45	4.00	0.29	2	–	–	–	1	–	0	–
Problem-solving therapy	14	0.87	2.16	0.41	7	0.40*	5	–0.11	1	–	1	–
Social skills training	3	0.63	2.91	0.63	7	0.05	0	–	0	–	1	–
Interpersonal psychotherapy	12	0.68	2.70	0.68	8	0.21**	8	–0.17**	4	0.18*	8	0.22
Nondirective supportive therapy	14	0.57	3.18	0.49	30	0.17**	4	–0.15	1	–	0	–
Short-term psychodynamic psychotherapy	5	0.76	2.44	0.62	17	0.42***	1	–	1	–	2	–
Life review therapy	6	1.33	1.53	1.33	0		0		0		0	
Couple therapy	2	0.66	2.78		3	0.24	2	0.00	0		0	

Notes: *: *p* > 0.1; **: *p* > 0.05; ***: *p* > 0.01

Abbreviations: Adj: adjusted effect size after correction for publication bias; NNT: numbers needed to be treated

F 17.44, n.s.). None of the studies reported data on follow-up measurements at which COT could be compared to control groups.

Conclusion

The number of studies examining COT is too small to draw definite conclusions about its efficacy. The available evidence suggests that COT may be effective in the treatment of depression compared to control groups, but there is no convincing evidence that it is better than other psychotherapies. More research is needed to establish its relative efficacy.

OVERALL CONCLUSIONS

In this chapter we reviewed meta-analyses, clinical guidelines, and primary studies of 10 evidence-based psychotherapies for adult depression. The primary studies of these 10 psychotherapies were analyzed in a series of meta-analyses. In Table 11.9 we have summarized the results of these meta-analyses. As can be seen, by far the majority of studies have examined the efficacy of CBT. However,

a considerable number of studies have examined BAT, PST, IPT, and NDST (with more than 10 controlled studies examining each of them). SCT, SST, STPP, and COT were each examined in a handful of studies and have a much smaller research base. However, all psychotherapies were found to have a significant effect on depression in adults compared to control groups, and when comparing the different types of psychotherapy directly, we found only few indications that some therapies were more efficacious than others (Cuijpers, van Straten, Andersson, et al., 2008). Furthermore, the detected differences between studies were small and could very well be caused by outliers. A considerable number of studies also compared efficacy of psychotherapy to pharmacotherapy and combined treatments. However, by far the majority of these studies examined CBT, and to a lesser extent IPT. Several of the other therapies were not compared to these treatments at all or only in one or two studies. Most evidence indicates that CBT is as effective as pharmacotherapy and that a combined treatment is more efficacious than pharmacotherapy alone, but not than CBT alone. IPT seems to be somewhat less efficacious than pharmacotherapy and there was a trend indicating that a combined treatment of IPT and pharmacotherapy is more efficacious than IPT alone. At the long term, there is evidence that CBT may prevent relapse rates.

A major concern found in the current chapter is that so few studies met all our quality criteria. For most of the included psychotherapies no studies were found that met all quality criteria. And for the psychotherapies that were examined with high-quality studies (cognitive behavior therapy, problem-solving therapy, and interpersonal psychotherapy), we found indications that these studies resulted in significantly lower effect sizes than the other studies. This suggests that the efficacy of psychotherapies may have been overestimated.

Another major concern is that we found strong indications for significant publication bias for several psychotherapies (Table 11.9). After correcting for publication bias, the effect sizes for most psychotherapies were considerably smaller than the original effect sizes. This is another indication that the currently published research may have overestimated the efficacy of several psychotherapies.

Limitations

Our study has several limitations. One important limitation is that we only examined studies that met our definition of evidence-based psychotherapies. This implies that psychotherapies that have been examined in only one study are not included, even if this study is very large and has a high quality. One important example of a psychotherapy that was excluded for this reason is the Cognitive Behavioral Analysis System of Psychotherapy (CBASP), which has been studied in only one study (Keller et al., 2000), even though this study included 681 depressed patients, which is by far the largest psychotherapy study described in this chapter. We also did not include any third-generation cognitive therapies. Another limitation is that the number of

studies examining several of the psychotherapies was small and that the quality of these studies was not optimal.

We found only few studies that were specifically aimed at dysthymia. Many of the included studies were aimed at patients with either major depression or dysthymia (or both), but very few examined patients with dysthymia only. Furthermore, most of these studies examined combined treatments of psychotherapy and pharmacotherapy and very few compared psychotherapies to untreated controls. This implies that we cannot draw any definite conclusions about psychotherapies for dysthymia.

We also found that very few studies examined the long-term efficacy of psychotherapies, with the exception of cognitive behavior therapy and to a lesser extent interpersonal psychotherapy. This research has shown that cognitive behavior therapy probably has a significant effect on relapse rates, and interpersonal psychotherapy may be beneficial at the longer term. From other psychotherapies we do not know very much about their efficacy at the longer term.

Despite the limitations of this study, we can conclude that there is a large body of research showing that psychotherapies are efficacious in the treatment of depression.

REFERENCES

Abbass, A. A., Hancock, J. T., Henderson, J., & Kisely, S. (2006). Short-term psychodynamic psychotherapies for common mental disorders. *Cochrane Database Systematic Reviews, 4*, Art. No. CD004687.

American Psychiatric Association (APA). (2000). *Practice guideline for the treatment of patients with Major Depressive Disorder, second edition*. Washington, DC: Author.

Anderson, E. M., & Lambert, M. J. (1995). Short-term dynamically oriented psychotherapy: A review and meta-analysis. *Clinical Psychology Review, 15,* 503–514.

Åsberg, M., Bengtsson, F., Hagberg, B., Henriksson, F., Jonsson, B., Karlsson, I., . . . Thelander, S. (2004). Treatment of depression. *Swedish Council on Technology Assessment in Health Care (SBU), Report no. 166*: 38.

Ayen, I., & Hautzinger, M. (2004). Kognitive Verhaltenstherapie Bei Depressionen Im Klimakterium: Eine Kontrollierte, Randomisierte Interventionsstudie. [Cognitive behavior therapy for depression in menopausal women. A controlled, randomized treatment study]. *Zeitschrift fur Klinische Psychologie und Psychotherapie, 33,* 290–299.

Barbato, A., & D'Avanzo, B. (2006). Marital therapy for depression. *Cochrane Database of Systematic Reviews, 2,* Art. No. CD004188.

Barbato, A., & D'Avanzo, B. (2008). Efficacy of couple therapy as a treatment for depression: A meta-analysis. *Psychiatric Quarterly, 79,* 121–132.

Barlow, J. P. (1986). *A group treatment for depression in the elderly* (Unpublished doctoral dissertation). University of Houston, Houston, TX.

Barrett, J. E., Williams J. W. Jr., Oxman, T. E., Frank, E., Katon, W., Sullivan, M., . . . Sengupta, A. S. (2001). Treatment of dysthymia and minor depression in primary care: A randomized trial in patients aged 18 to 59 years. *Journal of Family Practice, 50,* 405–412.

Beach, S. R., & O'Leary, K. D. (1992). Treating depression in the context of marital discord: Outcome and predictors of response of marital therapy versus cognitive therapy. *Behavior Therapy, 23,* 507–528.

Beck, A. T., Rush, J., Shaw, B., & Emery, G. (1979). *Cognitive therapy of depression.* New York, NY: Guilford Press.

Beck, A. T., Ward, C. H., Mendelson, M., Mock, J., & Erbaugh, J. (1961). An inventory for measuring depression. *Archives of General Psychiatry, 4,* 561–571.

Beekman, A. T., Deeg, D. J., Braam, A. W., Smit, J. H., & Van Tilburg, W. (1997). Consequences of major and minor depression in later life: A study of disability, well-being and service utilization. *Psychological Medicine, 27,* 1397–1409.

Bellack, A. S., Hersen, M., & Himmelhoch, J. (1981). Social skills training compared with pharmacotherapy and psychotherapy in the treatment of unipolar depression. *American Journal of Psychiatry, 148,* 1562–1567.

Berto, P., D'Ilario, D., Ruffo, P., Di Virgilio, R. E., & Rizzo, F. (2000). Depression: Cost of illness studies in the international literature, a review. *Journal of Mental Health Policy and Economy, 3,* 3–10.

Bohlmeijer, E., Roemer, M., Cuijpers, P., & Smit, F. (2007). The effects of reminiscence on psychological well-being in older adults: A meta-analysis. *Aging & Mental Health, 11,* 291–300.

Bohlmeijer, E., Smit, F., & Cuijpers, P. (2003). Effects of reminiscence and life review on late-life depression: A meta-analysis. *International Journal of Geriatric Psychiatry, 18,* 1088–1094.

Bolton, P., Bass, J., Neugebauer, R., Verdeli, H., Clougherty, K. F., Wickramaratne, P., . . . Weissman, M. (2003). Group interpersonal psychotherapy for depression in rural Uganda: A randomized controlled trial. *Journal of the American Medical Association, 289,* 3117–3124.

Bowman, D., Scogin, F., & Lyrene B. (1995). The efficacy of self-examination therapy and cognitive bibliotherapy in the treatment of mild to moderate depression. *Psychotherapy Research, 5,* 131–140.

Burnand, Y., Andreoli, A., Kolatte, E., Venturini, A., & Rosset, N. (2002). Psychodynamic psychotherapy and clomipramine in the treatment of major depression. *Psychiatric Services, 53,* 585–590.

Burns, D. (1980). *Feeling good.* New York, NY: Signet.

Busch, F. N., Rudden, M., & Shapiro, T. (2004). *Psychodynamic treatment of depression.* Washington, DC: American Psychiatric Publishing, Inc.

Butler, R. N. (1963). The life-review: An interpretation of reminiscence in the aged. *Psychiatry, 26,* 65–76.

CBO/Trimbos Institute. (2005). *Multidisciplinary Dutch guideline for depression.* Utrecht, the Netherlands: Author.

CBO/Trimbos Institute. (2009). *Multidisciplinary Dutch guideline for depression, an update.* Utrecht, the Netherlands: Author.

Chambless, D. L., & Hollon, S. D. (1998). Defining empirically supported therapies. *Journal of Consulting and Clinical Psychology, 66,* 7–18.

Chan, E. K. H. (2006). *Efficacy of cognitive behavioral, pharmacological, and combined treatments of depression: A meta analysis* (unpublished doctoral dissertation). University of Calgary, Alberta, Canada.

Churchill, R., Hunot, V., Corney, R., Knapp, M., McGuire, H., Tylee, A., & Wessely, S. (2001). A systematic review of controlled trials of the effectiveness and cost effectiveness of brief psychological treatments for depression. *Health Technology Assessment, 5,* 35.

Comas-Diaz, L. (1981). Effects of cognitive and behavioral group treatment on the depressive symptomatology of Puerto Rican women. *Journal of Consulting and Clinical Psychology, 49,* 627–632.

Cooper, P., Murray, L., Wilson, A., & Romaniuk, H. (2003). Controlled trial of the short- and long-term effect of psychological treatment of post partum depression. 1. Impact on maternal mood. *British Journal of Psychiatry, 182,* 412–419.

Crits-Christoph, P. (1992). The efficacy of brief dynamic psychotherapy: A meta-analysis. *American Journal of Psychiatry, 149,* 151–157.

Cuijpers, P. (1998). A psycho-educational approach to the treatment of depression: A meta-analysis of Lewinsohn's "Coping with Depression" course. *Behavior Therapy, 29,* 521–533.

Cuijpers, P., & Dekker, J. (2005). Psychologische behandeling van depressie; een systematisch overzicht van meta-analyses. *Nederlands Tijdschrift voor Geneeskunde, 149,* 1892–1897.

Cuijpers, P., Dekker, J., Hollon, S. D., & Andersson, G. (2009). *Adding psychotherapy to pharmacotherapy in the treatment of depressive disorders in adults: A meta-analysis.* Manuscript submitted for publication.

Cuijpers, P., & Smit, F. (2002). Excess mortality in depression: A meta-analysis of community studies. *Journal of Affective Disorders, 72*, 227–236.

Cuijpers, P., van Straten, A., Andersson, G., & van Oppen, P. (2008). Psychotherapy for depression in adults: A meta-analysis of comparative outcome studies. *Journal of Consulting and Clinical Psychology, 76*, 909–922.

Cuijpers, P., van Straten, A., van Oppen, P., & Andersson, G. (2008). Are psychological and pharmacological interventions equally effective in the treatment of adult depressive disorders? A meta-analysis of comparative studies. *Journal of Clinical Psychiatry, 69*, 1675–1685.

Cuijpers, P., van Straten, A., & Warmerdam, L. (2007a). Behavioral treatment of depression: A meta-analysis of activity scheduling. *Clinical Psychology Review, 27*, 318–326.

Cuijpers, P., van Straten, A., & Warmerdam, L. (2007b). Problem solving therapies for depression: A meta-analysis. *European Psychiatry, 22*, 9–15.

Cuijpers, P., van Straten, A., Warmerdam, L., & Andersson, G. (2008a). Psychological treatment versus combined treatment of depression: A meta-analysis. *Depression & Anxiety.*

Cuijpers, P., van Straten, A., Warmerdam, L., & Andersson, G. (2008b). Psychological treatment of depression: A meta-analytic database of randomized studies. *BMC Psychiatry, 8*, 36.

Davanloo, H. (1980). *Short-term dynamic psychotherapy.* New York, NY: J. Aronson.

De Jonghe, F. (1994). Psychoanalytic supportive psychotherapy. *Journal of the American Psychoanalytic Association, 42*, 421–446.

De Jonghe, F., Hendriksen, M., van Aalst, G., Kool, S., Peen, V., Van, R., . . . Dekker, J. (2004). Psychotherapy alone and combined with pharmacotherapy in the treatment of depression. *British Journal of Psychiatry, 185*, 37–45.

De Jonghe, F., Kool, S., van Aalst, G., Dekker, J., & Peen, J. (2001). Combining psychotherapy and antidepressants in the treatment of depression. *Journal of Affective Disorders, 64*, 217–229.

De Maat, S., Dekker, J., Schoevers, R., & de Jonghe, F. (2006). Relative efficacy of psychotherapy and pharmacotherapy in the treatment of depression: A meta-analysis. *Psychotherapy Research, 16*, 566–578.

De Maat, S. M., Dekker, J., Schoevers, R. A., & de Jonghe, F. (2007). Relative efficacy of psychotherapy and combined therapy in the treatment of depression: A meta-analysis. *European Psychiatry, 22*, 1–8.

De Mello, M. F., de Jesus Mari, J., Bacaltchuk, J., Verdeli, H., & Neugebauer, R. (2005). A systematic review of research findings on the efficacy of interpersonal therapy for depressive disorders. *European Archives of Psychiatry and Clinical Neuroscience, 255*, 75–82.

Dessaulles, A., Johnson, S. M., & Denton, W. H. (2003). Emotion-focused therapy for couples in the treatment of depression: A pilot study. *American Journal of Family Therapy, 31*, 345–353.

Dimidjian, S., Hollon, S. D., Dobson, K. S., Schmaling, K. B., Kohlenberg, R. J., Addis, M. E., . . . Jacobson, N. S. (2006). Randomized trial of behavioral activation, cognitive therapy, and antidepressant medication in the acute treatment of adults with major depression. *Journal of Consulting and Clinical Psychology, 74*, 658–670.

Dobson, K. S., Hollon, S. D., Dimidjian, S., Schmaling, K. B., Kohlenberg, R. J., Gallop, R. J., . . . Jacobson, N. S. (2008). Randomized trial of behavioral activation, cognitive therapy, and antidepressant medication in the prevention of relapse and recurrence in major depression. *Journal of Consulting and Clinical Psychology, 76*, 468–477.

Dowrick, C., Dunn, G., Ayuso-Mateos, J. L., Dalgard, O. S., Page, H., Lehtinen, V., . . . Wilkinson, G. (2000). Problem solving treatment and group psychoeducation for depression: Multicentre randomised controlled trial. Outcomes of Depression International Network (ODIN) Group. *British Medical Journal, 321*, 1450–1454.

Driessen, E., Cuijpers, P., de Maat, S. C. M., Abbass, A. A., de Jonghe, F., & Dekker, J. J. M. (2010). The efficacy of short-term psychodynamic psychotherapy for depression: A meta-analysis. *Clinical Psychology Review, 30*, 25–36.

Dunn, N. J., Rehm, L. P., Schillaci, J., Soucheck, J., Mehta, P., Ashton, C. M., . . . Hamilton, J. D. (2007). A randomized trial of self-management and psychoeducational group therapies for comorbid chronic posttraumatic stress disorder and depressive disorder. *Journal of Traumatic Stress, 20*, 221–237.

Duval, S., & Tweedie, R. (2000). Trim and fill: A simple funnel-plot-based method of testing and adjusting for publication bias in meta-analysis. *Biometrics, 56*, 455–463.

D'Zurilla, T. J., & Nezu, A. (1982). Social problem solving in adults. In P. C. Kendall (Ed.), *Advances in cognitive-behavioral research and therapy* (Vol. 1, pp. 202–274). New York, NY: Academic Press.

Ekers, D., Richards, D., & Gilbody, S. (2008). A meta-analysis of randomized trials of behavioural treatment of depression. *Psychological Medicine, 38*, 611–623.

Elkin, I., Shea, M. T., Watkins, J. T., Imber, S. D., Sotsky S. M., Collins, J. F., . . . Parloff, M. B. (1989). Treatment of depression collaborative research program. *Archives of General Psychiatry, 46*, 971–982.

Emanuels-Zuurveen, L., & Emmelkamp, P. M. (1997). Spouse-aided therapy with depressed patients. *Behavior Modification, 21*, 62–77.

Emanuels-Zuurveen, L., & Emmelkamp, P. M. G. (1996). Individual behavioural-cognitive therapy v. marital therapy for depression in maritally distressed couples. *British Journal of Psychiatry, 169*, 181–188.

Engels, G. I., & Vermey, M. (1997). Efficacy of non-medical treatments of depression in elders: A quantitative analysis. *Journal of Clinical Geropsychology, 3*, 17–35.

European Study of the Epidemiology of Mental Disorders (ESEMeD). (2004). Prevalence of mental disorders in Europe: Results from the European Study of the Epidemiology of Mental Disorders (ESEMeD) project. *Acta Psychiatrica Scandinavica, 109*, S21–S27.

Evans, R. L., & Connis, R. T. (1995). Comparison of brief group therapies for depressed cancer patients receiving radiation treatment. *Public Health Reports, 110*, 306–311.

First, M. B., Spitzer, R. L., Gibbon, M., & Williams, J. B. W. (1995). The structured clinical interview for DSM-III-R personality disorders (SCID-II, Version 2.0): Part I: Description. *Journal of Personality Disorders, 9*, 83–91.

Fleming, B. M., & Thornton, D. W. (1980). Coping skills training as a component in the short-term treatment of depression. *Journal of Consulting and Clinical Psychology, 48*, 652–654.

Forsyth, K. M. (2000). *The design and implementation of a depression prevention program* (Unpublished doctoral dissertation). University of Rhode Island, Kingston, RI.

Frank, E., Kupfer, D. J., Perel, J. M., Cornes, C., Jarrett, D. B., Mallinger, A. G., . . . Grochocinski, V. J. (1990). Three-year outcomes for maintenance therapies in recurrent depression. *Archives of General Psychiatry, 47*, 1093–1099.

Friedman, M. A., Detweiler-Bedell, J. B., Leventhal, H. E., Horne, R., Keitner, G. I., & Miller, I. W. (2004). Combined psychotherapy and pharmacotherapy for the treatment of major depressive disorder. *Clinical Psychology: Science and Practice, 11*, 47–68.

Fry, P. S. (1983). Structured and unstructured reminiscence training and depression among the elderly. *Clinical Gerontologist, 1*, 15–37.

Fuchs, C. Z., & Rehm, L. P. (1977). A self-control behavior therapy program for depression. *Journal of Consulting and Clinical Psychology, 45*, 206–215.

Gaffan, E. A., Tsaousis, I., & Kemp-Wheeler, S. M. (1995). Researcher allegiance and meta-analysis: The case of cognitive therapy for depression. *Journal of Consulting and Clinical Psychology, 63*, 966–980.

Gloaguen, V., Cottraux, J., Cucherat, M., & Blackburn, I. M. (1998). A meta-analysis of the effects of cognitive therapy in depressed patients. *Journal of Affective Disorders, 49*, 59–72.

Greenberg, P. E., & Birnbaum, H. G. (2005). The economic burden of depression in the US: Societal and patient perspectives. *Expert Opinions in Pharmacotherapy, 6*, 369–376.

Gregory, R., Canning, S., Lee, T., & Wise, J. (2004). Cognitive bibliotherapy for depression: A meta-analysis. *Professional Psychology Research and Practice, 35*, 275–280.

Higgins, J. P. T., & Green, S. (Eds.). (2005). Cochrane handbook for systematic reviews of interventions 4.2.5 [updated May 2005]. In *The Cochrane Library, 2005; Issue 3*. Chichester, England: Wiley.

Higgins, J. P., Thompson, S. G., & Deeks, J. J. (2003). Measuring inconsistency in meta-analyses. *British Medical Journal, 327*, 557–560.

Hopko, D. R., Lejuez, C. W., Lepage, J. P., Hopko, S. D., & McNeill, D. W. (2003). A brief behavioral activation treatment for depression: A randomized pilot trial within an inpatient psychiatric hospital. *Behavior Modification, 27*, 458–469.

Jacobson, N. S., Christensen, A., Prince, S. E., Cordova, J., & Eldridge, K. (2000). Integrative behavioral couple therapy: An acceptance-based, promising new treatment for couple discord. *Journal of Consulting and Clinical Psychology, 68*, 351–355.

Jacobson, N. S., Dobson, K., Fruzzetti, A. E., Schmaling, K. B., & Salusky, S. (1991). Marital therapy as a treatment for depression. *Journal of Consulting and Clinical Psychology, 59*, 547–557.

Jacobson, N. S., Dobson, K. S., Truax, P. A., Addis, M. E., Koerner, K., Gollan, J. K., . . . Prince, S.E., (1996). A component analysis of cognitive behavioral treatment for depression. *Journal of Consulting and Clinical Psychology, 64*, 295–304.

Kanfer, F. H. (1971). The maintenance of behavior by self-generated stimuli and reinforcement. In A. Jacobs, & L. B. Sachs (Eds.), *The psychology of private events: Perspective on covert response systems*. New York, NY: Academic Press.

Kanfer, F. H., & Karoly, P. (1972). Self-control: A behavioristic excursion into the lion's den. *Behavior Therapy, 3*, 398–416.

Keller, M. B., McCullough, J. P., Klein, D. N., Arnow, B., Dunner, D. L., Gelenberg, A. J., . . . Zajecka, J. (2000). A comparison of nefazodone, the cognitive behavioral analysis system of psychotherapy, and their combination for the treatment of chronic depression. *New England Journal of Medicine, 342*, 1462–1470.

Kessler, R. C., McGonagle, K. A., Zhao, S., Nelson, C. B., Hughes, M., Eshleman, S., . . . Kendler, K. S. (1994). Lifetime and 12-months prevalence of DSM-III-R psychiatric disorders in the United States: Results from the National Comorbidity Survey. *Archives of General Psychiatry, 51*, 8–19.

King, M., Sibbald, B., Ward, E., Bower, P., Lloyd, M., Gabbay, M., & Byford, S. (2000). Randomised controlled trial of non-directive counselling, cognitive behaviour therapy and usual general practitioner care in the management of depression as well as mixed anxiety and depression in primary care. *Health Technology Assessment, 4*, 1–83.

Klein, M. H., Greist, J. H., Gurman, A. S., Neimeyer, R. A., Lesser, D. P., Bushnell, N. J., & Smith, R. E. (1985). A comparative outcome study of group psychotherapy vs. exercise treatments for depression. *International Journal of Mental Health, 13*, 148–177.

Klerman, G. L., DiMascio, A., Weissman, M. M., Prusoff, B., & Paykel, E. S. (1974). Treatment of depression by drugs and psychotherapy. *American Journal of Psychiatry, 131*, 186–191.

Klerman, G. L., Weissman, M. M., Rounsaville, B. J., & Chevron, E. S. (1984). *Interpersonal psychotherapy of depression*. New York, NY: Basic Books.

Koder, D. A., Brodaty, H., & Anstey, K. J. (1996). Cognitive therapy for depression in the elderly. *International Journal Of Geriatric Psychiatry, 11*, 97–107.

Kraemer, H. C., & Kupfer, D. J. (2006). Size of treatment effects and their importance to clinical research and practice. *Biological Psychiatry, 59*, 990–996.

Landreville, P., & Bissonnette, L. (1997). Effects of cognitive bibliotherapy for depressed older adults with a disability. *Clinical Gerontologist, 17*, 35–55.

Leff, J., Vearnals, S., Brewin, C. R., Wolff, G., Alexander, B., Asen, E., . . . Everitt, B. (2000). The London Depression Intervention Trial Randomised controlled trial of antidepressants v. couple therapy in the treatment and maintenance of people with depression living with a partner: Clinical outcome and costs. *British Journal of Psychiatry, 177*, 95–100.

Leichsenring, F. (2001). Comparative effects of short-term psychodynamic psychotherapy and cognitive-behavioral therapy in depression: A meta-analytic approach. *Clinical Psychology Review, 21*, 401–419.

Leichsenring, F., Rabung, S., & Leibing, E. (2004). The efficacy of short-term psychodynamic psychotherapy in specific psychiatric disorders: A meta-analysis. *Archives of General Psychiatry, 61*, 1208–1216.

Lewinsohn, P. M., Antonucci, D. O., Breckenridge, J. S., & Teri, L. (1984). The *"Coping with Depression" course*. Eugene, OR: Castalia Publishing Company.

Lewinsohn, P. M., Biglan, A., & Zeiss, A. M. (1976). Behavioral treatment of depression. In P. O. Davidson (Ed.), *The behavioral management of anxiety, depression and pain* (pp. 91–146). New York, NY: Brunner/Mazel.

Lipsey, M. W. (1990). *Design sensitivity: Statistical power for experimental research*. Newbury Park, CA: Sage.

Malan, D. H. (1963). *A study of brief psychotherapy*. London, England: Tavistock Publications.

Malouff, J. M., Thorsteinsson, E. B., & Schutte N. S. (2007). The efficacy of problem solving therapy in reducing mental and physical health problems: A meta-analysis. *Clinical Psychology Review, 27*, 46–57.

Mann, J. (1973). *The limited psychotherapy*. Cambridge, MA: Harvard University Press.

Manson, S. M., & Brenneman, D. L. (1995). Chronic disease among older American Indians: Preventing depressive symptoms and related problems of coping. In D. K. Pagett (Ed.), *Handbook on ethnicity, aging, and mental health* (pp. 284–303). Westport, CT: Greenwood Press.

Markowitz, J. C., Kokcis, J. H., Fishman, B., Spielman, L. A., Jacobsberg, L. B., Frances, A. J., . . . Perry, S. W. (1998). Treatment of depressive symptoms in human immunodeficiency virus–positive patients. *Archives of General Psychiatry, 55*, 452–457.

Martell, C. R., Addis, M. E., & Jacobson, N. S. (2001). *Depression in context. Strategies for guided action*. New York, NY: W. W. Norton.

Mathers, C. D., & Loncar, D. (2006). Projections of global mortality and burden of disease from 2002 to 2030. *PLoS Medicine, 3*, e442.

McCusker, J., Cole, M., Keller, E., Bellavance, F., & Berard, A. (1998). Effectiveness of treatments of depression in older ambulatory patients. *Archives of Internal Medicine, 158*, 705–712.

Miranda, J., Chung, J. Y., Green, B. L., Krupnick, J., Siddique, J., Revicki, D. A., & Belin, T. (2003). Treating depression in predominantly low-income young minority women: A randomized controlled trial. *Journal of the American Medical Association, 290*, 57–65.

Mynors-Wallis, L. M., Gath, D. H., Day, A., & Baker, F. (2000). Randomised controlled trial of problem solving treatment, antidepressant medication, and combined treatment for major depression in primary care. *British Medical Journal, 320*, 26–30.

Mynors-Wallis, L. M., Gath, D. H., Lloyd-Thomas, A. R., & Tomlinson, D. (1995). Randomised controlled trial comparing problem solving treatment with amitriptyline and placebo for major depression in primary care. *British Medical Journal, 310*, 441–445.

National Institute for Health and Clinical Excellence (NICE). (2004). Depression: Management of depression in primary and secondary care [amendments 2007], www.nice.org.uk/nicemedia/pdf/cg023fullguideline.pdf

Nezu, A. (1986). Efficacy of social problem-solving therapy approach for unipolar depression. *Journal of Consulting and Clinical Psychology, 54*, 196–202.

Nezu, A. M., & Perri, M. G. (1989). Social problem-solving therapy for unipolar depression: An initial dismantling investigation. *Journal of Consulting and Clinical Psychology, 57*, 408–413.

Pampanolla, S., Bollini, P., Tibaldi, G., Kupelnick, B., & Munizza, C. (2004). Combined pharmacotherapy and psychological treatment for depression: A systematic review. *Archives of General Psychiatry, 61*, 714–719.

Pecheur, D. R. (1980). *A comparison of the efficacy of secular and religious cognitive behavior modification in the treatment of depressed christian college students*. (Unpublished doctoral dissertation). Rosemead

Graduate School of Professional Psychology, La Mirada, CA.

Pinquart, M., Duberstein, P. R., & Lyness, J. M. (2007). Effects of psychotherapy and other behavioral interventions on clinically depressed older adults: A meta-analysis. *Aging & Mental Health, 11*, 645–657.

Pollack, J., & Horner, A. (1985). Brief adaptation-oriented psychotherapy. In A. Winston (Ed.), *Clinical and research issues in short-time dynamic psychotherapy.* Washington, DC: American Psychiatric Press.

Radloff, L. (1977). The CES-D scale: A self-report depression scale for research in the general population. *Applied Psychological Measurement, 1*, 385–401.

Reynolds, C. F. III, Dew, M. A., Pollock, B. G., Mulsant, B. H., Frank, E., Miller, M. D., . . . Kupfer, D. J. (2006). Maintenance treatment of major depression in old age. *New England Journal of Medicine, 354*, 1130–1138.

Reynolds, C. F., III, Miller, M. D., Pasternak, R. E., Frank, E., Perel, J. M., Cornes, C., . . . Kupfer, D. J. (1999). Treatment of bereavement-related major depressive episodes in later life: A controlled study of acute and continuation treatment with nortriptyline and interpersonal psychotherapy. *American Journal of Psychiatry, 156*, 202–208.

Robins, L. N., Wing, J., Wittchen, H.-U., Helzer, J. E., Babor, T. F., Burke, J., . . . Towle, L. H. (1988). The Composite International Diagnostic Interview: An epidemiologic instrument suitable for use in conjunction with different diagnostic systems and in different cultures. *Archives of General Psychiatry, 45*, 1069–1077.

Robinsohn Whelen, S., Hughes, R. B., Taylor, H. B., Hall, J. W., & Rehm, L. P. (2007). Depression self-management program for rural women with physical disabilities. *Rehabilitation Psychology, 52*, 254–262.

Rogers, C. (1967). *On becoming a person: A therapist's view of psychotherapy.* London, England: Constable.

Roth, D., Bielski, R., Jones, M., Parker, W., & Osborn G. (1982). A comparison of self-control therapy and combined self-control therapy and anti-depressant medication in the treatment of depression. *Behavior Therapy, 13*, 133–144.

Royal Australian and New Zealand College of Psychiatrists Clinical Practice Guidelines (RANZCP) (2004). Australian and New Zealand clinical practice guidelines for the treatment of depression. Team for depression. *Australian and New Zealand Journal of Psychiatry, 38*, 389–407.

Rude, S. S. (1986). Relative benefits of assertion or cognitive self-control treatment for depression as a function of proficiency in each domain. *Journal of Consulting and Clinical Psychology, 54*, 390–394.

Saarni, S. I., Suvisaari, J., Sintonen, H., Pirkola, S., Koskinen, S., Aromaa, A., & Lönnqvist, J. (2007). Impact of psychiatric disorders on health-related quality of life: general population survey. *British Journal of Psychiatry, 190*, 326–333.

Salminen, J. K., Karlsson, H., Hietala, J., Kajander, J., Aalto, S., Markkula, J., . . . Toikka, T. (2008). Short-term psychodynamic psychotherapy and fluoxetine in major depressive disorder: A randomized comparative study. *Psychotherapy and Psychosomatics, 77*, 351–357.

Schulberg, H. C., Block, M. R., Madonia, M. J., Scott, C. P., Rodriguez, E., Imber, S. D., . . . Coulehan, J. L. (1996). Treating major depression in primary care practice. Eight-month clinical outcomes. *Archives of General Psychiatry, 53*, 913–919.

Shapiro, D. A., Barkham, M., Rees, A., Hardy, G. E., Reynolds, S., & Startup, M. (1994). Effects of treatment duration and severity of depression on the effectiveness of cognitive-behavioral and psychodynamic-interpersonal psychotherapy. *Journal of Consulting and Clinical Psychology, 62*, 522–534.

Sifneos, P. E. (1979). *Short-term dynamic psychotherapy: Evaluation and technique.* New York, NY: Plenum Medical.

Smit, F., Cuijpers, P., Oostenbrink, J., Batelaan, N., de Graaf, R., & Beekman, A. (2006). Excess costs of common mental disorders: Population-based cohort study. *Journal of Mental Health Policy and Economy, 9*, 193–200.

Snyder, D. K., Castellani, A. M., & Whisman, M. A. (2006). Current status and future directions in couple therapy. *Annual Review of Clinical Psychology, 57*, 317–344.

Spek, V., Cuijpers, P., Nyklícek, I., Riper, H., Keyzer, J., & Pop, V. (2007). Internet-based cognitive behavior therapy for mood and anxiety disorders: A meta-analysis. *Psychological Medicine, 37*, 319–328.

Spielmans, G. I., Pasek, L. F., & McFall, J. P. (2007). What are the active ingredients in cognitive and behavioral psychotherapy for anxious and depressed children? A meta-analytic review. *Clinical Psychology Review, 27*, 642–654.

Strupp, H., & Binder, J. L. (1984). *Psychotherapy in a new key.* New York, NY: Basic Books.

Svartberg, M., & Stiles, T. C. (1991). Comparative effects of short-term psychodynamic psychotherapy: A meta-analysis. *Journal of Consulting and Clinical Psychology, 59*, 704–714.

Taylor, F. G., & Marshall, W. L. (1977). Experimental analysis of a cognitive-behavioral therapy for depression. *Cognitive Therapy and Research, 1*, 59–72.

Teichmann, Y., Bar-El, Z., Shor, H., Sirota, P., & Elizur, A. (1995). A comparison of two modalities of cognitive therapy (individual and marital) in treating depression. *Psychiatry, 58*, 136–148.

Teri, L., Logsdon, R. G., Uomoto, J., & McCurry, S. M. (1997). Behavioral treatment of depression in dementia patients: A controlled clinical trial. *Journals of Gerontology. Series B, Psychological sciences and social sciences, 52*, P159–P166.

Ustun, T. B., Ayuso-Mateos, J. L., Chatterji, S., Mathers, C., & Murray, C. J. L. (2004). Global burden of depressive disorders in the year 2000. *British Journal of Psychiatry, 184,* 386–392.

Van Schaik, A., van Marwijk, H., Ader, H., van Dyck, R., de Haan, M., Penninx, B., . . . Beekman, A. (2003). Interpersonal psychotherapy for elderly patients in primary care. *American Journal of Geriatric Psychiatry, 14,* 777–786.

Vittengl, J. R., Clark, L. A., Dunn, T. W., & Jarrett, R. B. (2007). Reducing relapse and recurrence in unipolar depression: A comparative meta-analysis of cognitive-behavioral therapy's effects. *Journal of Consulting and Clinical Psychology, 75,* 475–488.

Wampold, B. E., Minami, T., Baskin, T. W., & Tierney, S. C. (2002). A meta-(re)analysis of the effects of cognitive therapy versus 'other therapies' for depression. *Journal of Affective Disorders, 68,* 159–165.

Wampold, B. E., Minami, T., Tierney, S. C., Baskin, T. W., & Bhatki, K. S. (2005). The placebo is powerful: Estimating placebo effects in medicine and psychotherapy from randomized clinical trials. *Journal of Clinical Psychology, 61,* 835–854.

Waraich, P., Goldner, E. M., Somers, J. M., & Hsu, L. (2004). Prevalence and incidence studies of mood disorders: A systematic review of the literature. *Canadian Journal of Psychiatry, 49,* 124–138.

Wheeler, J. G., Christensen, A., & Jacobson, N. S. (2001). Couple distress. In D. H. Barlow (Ed.), *Clinical handbook of psychological disorders* (pp. 609–630). New York, NY: Guilford Press.

Wilson, P. H., Goldin, J. C., & Charbonneau, P. M. (1983). Comparative efficacy of behavioral and cognitive treatments of depression. *Cognitive Therapy and Research, 7,* 111–124.

Wilson, K. C., Mottram, P. G., & Vassilas, C. A. (2008). Psychotherapeutic treatments for older depressed people. *Cochrane Database of Systematic Reviews, 23*(1), Art. No. CD004853.

Woods, B., Portnoy, S., Head, D., & Jones, G. (1992). Reminiscence and life-review with persons with dementia: Which way forward? In G. M. Jones & B. M. L. Miesen (Eds.), *Care giving in dementia* (pp. 137–161). London, England: Routledge.

12

Panic Disorder

NAOMI KOERNER, VALERIE VORSTENBOSCH, AND MARTIN M. ANTONY

OVERVIEW OF THE DISORDER

This chapter begins with an overview of panic disorder, including its diagnostic features, epidemiology, and course, as well as its direct and indirect costs. Next, we provide an overview of guidelines for evidence-based treatment of panic disorder. This is followed by a description of conceptual models of panic disorder. In the last portion of the chapter, we summarize data on the efficacy and effectiveness of treatments for panic disorder, with a focus on cognitive behavioral treatment, the current gold standard for panic disorder. This is followed by a description of cognitive behavioral treatment strategies. The chapter concludes with an overview of research on other treatments for panic disorder.

Diagnostic Features

According to the current *Diagnostic and Statistical Manual of Mental Disorders* (*DSM-IV-TR*, American Psychiatric Association, 2000) the defining feature of panic disorder is "the presence of recurrent, unexpected panic attacks followed by at least one month of persistent concern about having another panic attack, worry about the possible implications or consequences of the panic attack, or a significant behavioral change related to the attacks" (p. 433). Panic attacks are defined in the *DSM-IV-TR* as a discrete period in which

there is a sudden onset of intense fear or discomfort that peaks within 10 minutes and is accompanied by at least four of 13 somatic or cognitive symptoms (e.g., palpitations, shortness of breath, fear of losing control or going crazy, fear of dying). Three types of panic attacks are described in the *DSM-IV-TR*: (1) unexpected (uncued) panic attacks, which refer to attacks that are not associated with a situational trigger; (2) situationally bound (cued) panic attacks, which refer to attacks that occur immediately upon exposure to, or in anticipation of, an anxiety producing stimulus; and (3) situationally predisposed panic attacks, which refer to attacks that are likely to occur upon exposure to an anxiety producing stimulus, but do not necessarily occur immediately upon exposure (American Psychiatric Association, 2000).

Panic disorder may also be associated with the presence or absence of agoraphobia, anxiety about having panic attacks or panic-like symptoms in places or situations in which escape might be difficult or in which help may not be available. Examples of common agoraphobic situations include travelling alone in a car, bus, or plane or being in a crowded place. Individuals with agoraphobia often avoid these types of situations or endure them with marked distress and, in the most severe cases, some individuals may even be unable to leave their home.

Last, in order to receive a diagnosis of panic disorder, an individual's panic attacks cannot be due to the direct physiological effects of a substance (e.g., caffeine) or a general medical condition (e.g., hyperthyroidism) and cannot be better accounted for by another Axis I disorder.

Epidemiology

The estimated lifetime prevalence of panic disorder is approximately 4.7% (Kessler et al., 2006). The age of onset for panic disorder is typically during late adolescence or early adulthood. In the National Comorbidity Survey Replication (NCS-R; Kessler et al., 2006), the average age of onset was 24 years of age, with half the sample reporting an onset between 16 and 40 years of age (Kessler, Berglund, Demler, Jin, & Walters, 2005). Some studies have suggested that prevalence rates decrease later in life and that late onsets (i.e., onsets later than 55 years of age) may be associated with less symptomatology and less distress, particularly in relation to body sensations and panic-related cognitions and emotions (Sheikh, Swales, Carlson, & Lindley, 2004). Specifically, compared to younger individuals with panic disorder, older individuals tend to experience fewer panic symptoms, less frequent panic attacks, less distress in response to cognitions and feelings during panic attacks, higher global functioning, and less severe panic disorder overall (Sheikh et al., 2004).

Panic disorder has consistently been found to be more common among women than among men (Goodwin et al., 2005; Kessler et al., 2006). The overall ratio of women to men for panic disorder has been reported to be about 2:1 (Kessler et al., 2006). Panic disorder has also been found to be more severe among women than among men. Specifically, women with panic disorder are more likely to experience more severe agoraphobic avoidance, more catastrophic thoughts associated with panic attacks, more body sensations and are more likely to fear their body sensations, than are men with panic disorder (Turgeon, Marchand, & Dupuis, 1998). Women tend to report more respiration-related symptoms than do men (e.g., difficulty breathing, feeling faint, and feeling smothered; Sheikh, Leskin, & Klein, 2002). Previous research has suggested that fluctuations in ovarian hormones (e.g., progesterone) may influence respiratory rates (Klein, 1993) and decreases in progesterone levels may be associated with worsening panic (Le Mellédo et al., 2001).

Comorbidity

Comorbidity rates for panic disorder differ depending on whether current or lifetime comorbidity rates are identified. For example, Brown, Campbell, Lehman, Grisham, and Mancill (2001) found that when current diagnoses were considered, 42% of individuals with panic disorder reported at least one additional Axis I anxiety disorder or mood disorder; however, when lifetime diagnoses were considered, comorbidity rates for additional Axis I anxiety disorders and mood disorders were much higher, such that 75% of individuals with a diagnosis of panic disorder had at least one or more comorbid diagnosis (Brown et al., 2001). This lifetime comorbidity rate is comparable to what was found in the aforementioned NCS-R (Kessler et al., 2006). Other studies have found that specific phobia, social phobia, generalized anxiety disorder, major depressive disorder, dysthymic disorder, bipolar disorder, and substance abuse are common co-occurring diagnoses (Brown et al., 2001; Goisman, Goldenberg, Vasile, & Keller, 1995; Goodwin & Hoven, 2002).

The presence of agoraphobia has been found to be associated with a greater likelihood of comorbid Axis I disorders for individuals with panic disorder (Brown et al., 2001; Kessler et al., 2006; Kikuchi et al., 2005). In the case of comorbidity with other anxiety disorders (e.g., social phobia and generalized anxiety disorder) and major depressive disorder, it has been suggested that the presence of agoraphobia may be a more important determinant of comorbidity than the panic disorder in itself (Kessler et al., 2006; Kikuchi et al., 2005). For example, in the NCS-R, the odds of having an additional anxiety disorder or major depressive disorder were consistently higher for those with agoraphobia than for those without agoraphobia (Kessler et al., 2006). Similarly, Brown et al. (2001) found that individuals with a principal diagnosis of panic disorder with agoraphobia had a greater rate of Axis I comorbidity than did individuals with a principal diagnosis of panic disorder without agoraphobia (42% and 62%, respectively); however, when lifetime diagnoses were considered, there was a negligible difference between Axis I comorbidities, suggesting that the relationship between agoraphobia and Axis I comorbidity may not generalize to lifetime psychological patterns of individuals with panic disorder and panic disorder with agoraphobia (Brown et al., 2001).

Course of the Disorder

Although the onset of panic disorder usually occurs in late adolescence or early adulthood, individuals tend to wait many years before seeking treatment (Katschnig & Amering, 1998). Generally, the course of panic disorder is chronic, with some waxing and waning symptomatology. For example, in a 1-year follow-up study, 92% of individuals with panic disorder and 41% of individuals who were initially in remission reported experiencing panic attacks during the year following their initial assessment (Ehlers, 1995). Similar results were observed in a 4-year follow-up study, such that 45% of individuals reported experiencing persistent panic attacks during the follow-up period, 24% reported experiencing episodic panic attacks with some panic free periods, and 31% reported that they were in remission and doing well during the follow-up period (Katschnig et al., 1995).

Impact of the Disorder

Panic disorder is associated with a high degree of functional impairment and a marked reduction

in quality of life (Antony, Roth, Swinson, Huta, & Devins, 1998; Stein et al., 2005). A recent study of primary care outpatients found that panic disorder significantly contributed to the prediction of poor functioning, reduced health-related quality of life and a greater number of missed work days (Stein et al., 2005). In terms of quality of life, a review by Mogotsi, Kaminer, and Stein (2000) indicated that individuals with panic disorder are more likely to report decreases in life satisfaction and general well-being and are more likely to receive welfare or disability payments than are individuals with other psychiatric disorders. For individuals with panic disorder, previous research has suggested that poorer quality of life may be predicted by comorbid depression, worry, severity of chest pain, and decreased quality of social support (Mogotsi et al., 2000).

In addition, individuals with panic disorder are also more likely to overutilize the health care system, as compared to the general population and individuals with other psychiatric disorders (Roy Byrne et al., 1999). In a study conducted by Barsky, Delamater, and Orav (1999), patients with panic disorder made significantly more physician visits, emergency room visits and mental health visits in 1 year than did other general medical outpatients. Further, a recent study found that the presence of panic disorder was not only associated with higher overall medical utilization but also with more frequent visits to cardiology, emergency medicine and family medicine than was generalized anxiety disorder, obsessive-compulsive disorder, social phobia, and specific phobia (Deacon, Lickel, & Abramowitz, 2008). Given that distressing and spontaneously occurring somatic symptoms are often associated with panic attacks, it is not unexpected that individuals with panic disorder would seek both emergency and general medical services more than individuals with other anxiety disorders (Deacon et al., 2008). In addition, previous research has also shown that physicians often misidentify panic disorder in emergency medicine (Fleet et al.,

1996) and primary care settings (Spitzer et al., 1994). This is probably a factor that leads individuals with panic disorder to seek out extensive and often unnecessary medical services (Deacon et al., 2008).

As a result of the high degree of functional impairment and elevated medical utilization, the economic burden of panic disorder is considerable. There is a paucity of data on the direct and indirect costs of panic disorder and most psychological disorders; however, one large study indicated that the economic burden of anxiety disorders, in general, for 1998 was estimated to be $63.1 billion in the United States (Greenberg et al., 1999). The largest components of the costs were nonpsychiatric direct medical costs, direct psychiatric treatment costs and total workplace costs (absenteeism and cutback days), which accounted for 54%, 31%, and 10% of the total cost estimate, respectively. Data from Greenberg et al. (1999) indicated that panic disorder was associated with one of the highest rates of psychiatric service use as well as substantial impairment in workplace performance (Greenberg et al., 1999). Further, in 1999, the average lifetime medical cost, including inpatient, outpatient and prescription drug charges, for an individual with panic disorder was estimated to be about $8,708 (Marciniak et al., 2005).

Given the exorbitant costs of panic disorder, efforts should be directed toward improving capacity for early identification and treatment of this disorder, particularly as there are a number of empirically validated assessment tools and evidence-based treatments available. In the following section, current guidelines for evidence-based practice will be reviewed.

GUIDELINES FOR EVIDENCE-BASED TREATMENTS FOR PANIC DISORDER

A number of treatment guidelines have been developed to inform mental health professionals of evidence-based treatments that are available for panic disorder. The specific guidelines that are referred to in Table 12.1 include those by the Royal Australian and New Zealand College of Psychiatrists (2003), the National Institute for Health and Clinical Excellence (United Kingdom) (McIntosh et al., 2004), the Canadian Psychiatric Association (Swinson et al., 2006), and the American Psychiatric Association (Stein et al., 2009). The reader is encouraged to refer directly to these guidelines for more detail. Overall, these treatment guidelines suggest that either cognitive behavior therapy (CBT) or medication may be offered as a first line treatment for individuals with panic disorder. With regards to medication, there appears to be a consensus across guidelines, such that selective serotonin reuptake inhibitors (SSRIs) and tricyclic antidepressants (TCAs) appear to be the most useful medications for the treatment of panic disorder. Although there may be some advantages to combining medication and CBT, it should be noted that there is still controversy regarding the usefulness of combining the two treatments, particularly over the long term (Furukawa, Watanabe, & Churchill, 2006).

PSYCHOLOGICAL MODELS OF PANIC ATTACKS AND PANIC DISORDER

In the 1960s and 1970s, biological theories of panic attacks and panic disorder were predominant. Such theories emerged from the early work of Donald Klein (e.g., Klein & Fink, 1962), in which imipramine was found to reduce panic episodes, but not overall levels of anxiety, speaking to possible fundamental physiological differences between panic attacks and anxiety. In addition, a number of studies demonstrated that certain pharmacological and biological agents, such as yohimbine (Charney, Beninger, & Breier, 1984) and carbon dioxide inhalation (van den Hout & Griez, 1984), were capable of inducing panic attacks in individuals with panic disorder but not in nonanxious

TABLE 12.1 Overview of Evidence-Based Clinical Practice Guidelines for Panic Disorder

	Recommended Psychological Treatments	Recommended Pharmacological Treatments	Recommendations Regarding Combination Treatments
Australian and New Zealand Clinical Practice Guidelines 2003	Cognitive behavioral treatment	TCAs	If using a combined approach, initiate CBT before medication and maintain medication during medication discontinuation
National Institute for Health and Clinical Excellence 2004	Cognitive behavioral treatment; to specific; CBT-based bibliotherapy; combined with brief contact may be needed	SSRIs; SSRIs; TCAs 2nd line	No explicit guidelines for combination treatments
Canadian Psychiatric Association Standards et al.	Cognitive behavioral treatment	SSRIs, SNRIs; TCAs, benzodiazepines 2nd line; MAOIs, certain anticonvulsants, adjunctive atypical antipsychotics 3rd line	Provision of CBT sessions around the time of benzodiazepine or antidepressant discontinuation may attenuate relapse
American Psychiatric Association Stein et al.	Cognitive behavioral treatment; psychodynamic psychotherapy; psychotherapy 2nd line limited evidence	SSRIs, SNRIs, TCAs; Add benzodiazepine to an antidepressant to treat residual anxiety symptoms (augmentation strategy); MAOIs 2nd line	There is not sufficient evidence at this time to recommend combined psychological and pharmacological treatment; more research is needed

Note: CBT = cognitive behavior therapy; SSRI = selective serotonin reuptake inhibitor; SNRI = serotonin and norepinephrine reuptake inhibitor; MAOI = monoamine oxidase inhibitor individuals. This work eventually led Klein to hypothesize that neurobiological disturbances, specifically heightened sensitivity to increasing levels of carbon dioxide, trigger respiratory dysregulation, which in turn causes panic attacks (Klein, 1993).

In the mid 1980s, psychological models of panic disorder began to emerge. A number of conceptual models of cognitive and behavioral factors in panic attacks and panic disorder were developed and tested during this period. Three models that have been well researched include Clark's cognitive theory of panic (1986), Reiss's expectancy model of fear (Reiss, 1991; Reiss & McNally, 1985) and Barlow's (1988, 2002) integrated model based on emotion theory. Each of these models contributed significantly to the development of efficacious cognitive behavioral treatments for panic disorder. In the following paragraphs, we will provide an overview of each of these theories. We will also provide an overview of conditioning theories of panic disorder. Conditioning theories were among the first explanatory theories of panic disorder (e.g., Wolpe & Rowan, 1989; for a review, see Bouton, Mineka, & Barlow, 2001); however, these theories fell by the wayside because they were overly complex. Recently, Bouton et al. (2001) proposed a contemporary learning theory that accounts for the limitations of the earlier models.

Clark's Cognitive Model of Panic Disorder

In a seminal paper, Clark (1986) described a cognitive approach to understanding panic disorder. As mentioned earlier, biological theories of panic disorder posited that certain individuals are physiologically predisposed to experience panic attacks, particularly in response to agents that induce respiratory dysregulation. Clark (1986) noted that a small number of studies conducted with individuals *without* a history of an anxiety disorder had shown that there was actually considerably more variation in responses to induced panic sensations than would be expected given their non-clinical status. He proposed that whether or not carbon dioxide inhalation, hyperventilation, or noradrenergic agents, such as yohimbine, induce panic sensations depends, in part, on the *interpretation* that an individual imposes on the bodily sensations that he or she experiences following delivery of a panic inducing agent or procedure. Clark suggested that panic attacks may result from "the catastrophic misinterpretation of certain bodily sensations" (p. 462), whereby a healthy individual mistakenly interprets momentary bodily sensations, such as heart palpitations and dizziness, as signs that he or she is dying or is losing his or her sanity. In other words, threat appraisals and interpretations are imposed on the experience of nonharmful sensations. According to Clark's model, panic attacks result from excessive focus on unpleasant bodily sensations that are precipitated by relatively innocuous external or internal triggers. According to Clark's theory, external events, such as standing in a supermarket line, may trigger anxious symptoms. Similarly, running up a flight of stairs may trigger sensations that mimic anxiety symptoms (e.g., chest tightness). The model proposes that individuals who are prone to panic attacks pay excessive attention to benign sensations, which increases their intensity, making it more likely that an individual will experience their feared outcome—a panic attack. Clark suggested that the cognitive processes that give rise to panic attacks may, to a certain extent, operate at an automatic level, which would explain why panic attacks are often experienced as coming out of the blue. Clark proposed: (a) that individuals with panic disorder are more likely to interpret innocuous bodily sensations as threatening relative to individuals without an anxiety disorder, (b) that interpretations mediate the panic-inducing effects of noradrenergic agents and procedures such as carbon dioxide inhalation, and (c) that treatment success is contingent upon modification of interpretation biases. Tests of Clark's model have provided support for all of these predictions.

First, a number of studies have shown that individuals with panic disorder have a greater tendency to impose threatening interpretations on their experience of certain bodily sensations compared with individuals who do not have an anxiety disorder. The experience of a panic attack, however, is not necessarily a clinical phenomenon, since many individuals will experience a panic attack at some point during their lifetime. Thus, a more stringent test of Clark's hypothesis that catastrophic misinterpretations may be a causal factor in panic disorder consists of a comparison between individuals with panic disorder and individuals who have had panic attacks, but who do not have symptoms that are consistent with panic disorder. Individuals with and without panic disorder experience similar physical sensations during panic attacks (sweating, nausea); however, fear of dying, fear of having a heart attack, and fear of losing control distinguish individuals with panic disorder from individuals without panic disorder (McNally, Hornig, & Donnell, 1995).

Second, a number of studies have confirmed that fear of panic sensations is influenced by the interpretations that are imposed on them. For example, Salkovskis and Clark (1990) experimentally manipulated interpretations of sensations associated with voluntary hyperventilation. Participants were then asked to hyperventilate. Participants generally experienced changes in heart rate and respiration that were comparable to those experienced and reported by individuals with panic disorder; however, individuals in the positive interpretation condition reported the highest levels of positive affect, whereas individuals in the negative interpretation condition reported the highest levels of negative affect.

Regarding Clark's third prediction, there is evidence to suggest that changes in momentary interpretations of somatic symptoms are a predictor of treatment outcome. In two investigations of the efficacy of cognitive treatment for panic disorder, Clark and colleagues (1994, 1999) showed that a tendency to impose catastrophic interpretations on the experience of bodily sensations at posttreatment was a significant predictor of poorer outcome during a follow-up period of up to 1 year. More recent findings are discussed in further detail later in this chapter in the section on predictors of treatment outcome.

Reiss's Expectancy Theory

Reiss, among others (e.g., Rachman, 1976) noted that conditioning accounts of fear acquisition and maintenance were limited in their ability to explain fear responses. Reiss's *expectancy theory*, like Clark's model, attempted to account for appraisal processes that may contribute to individuals' motivation to avoid feared situations. Reiss and colleagues (1985; 1991) proposed that three core fears contribute to the development and maintenance of fear-based anxiety disorders, such as panic attacks and panic disorder, as well as phobias: fear of danger/illness/injury, fear of anxiety, and fear of negative social evaluation (Reiss, 1991). Expectancy theory proposes that two appraisal processes contribute to each of these fears: *expectation* of a negative outcome and *sensitivity* to (i.e., fear of) a negative outcome, if such an outcome were to occur. The component of the model that has been the most well researched (Schmidt & Woolaway-Bickel, 2006) is *anxiety sensitivity*, a dispositional characteristic that arises from "beliefs about the personal consequences of experiencing anxiety" (Reiss, 1991, p. 145). Individuals characterized by high levels of anxiety sensitivity report believing that anxiety can lead to bodily damage, mental incapacitation, and negative social consequences. As a result, individuals who are high in anxiety sensitivity tend to fear their anxious arousal (Reiss, Peterson, Gursky, & McNally, 1986; Zvolensky & Schmidt, 2007). Research on the construct of anxiety sensitivity has been extensive. The findings to date indicate that anxiety sensitivity is implicated in various forms of anxiety, including panic disorder and posttraumatic stress disorder (Taylor, 1999). Anxiety sensitivity is considered to be a well-established cognitive risk factor for panic disorder (Smits, Powers, Cho, & Telch, 2004; Taylor, Koch, & McNally, 1992; Wen & Zinbarg, 2007).

Two important distinctions have been drawn between Reiss's expectancy theory and Clark's theory of castastrophic misinterpretations, given that faulty appraisal processes are at the center of both theories (Schmidt & Woolaway-Bickel, 2006). The first difference concerns the event that the anxious individual is interpreting. Clark's theory suggests that individuals with panic disorder misinterpret their actual physical symptoms, such that pounding heart and sweating, for example, are interpreted as signs of an impending heart attack. Reiss's theory, on the other hand, suggests that individuals who experience panic attacks may not necessarily conclude that they are having a heart attack or dying when they are experiencing uncomfortable physical sensations. Rather, they hold inflated beliefs about the possible *long-range effects or implications* of having panic attacks, for example, "having panic attacks could have long-term implications for my health" (Schmidt & Woolaway-Bickel, 2006).

The second distinction pertains to the relationship between the faulty or inflated appraisals and the experience of anxious arousal. Clark suggests that an individual's misinterpretation of an initial panic attack leads to fear of the possibility of subsequent panic attacks. Reiss's model suggests that an individual can hold negative beliefs about the experience of anxiety without ever having had the experience of a panic attack (Schmidt & Woolaway-Bickel, 2006). That is, individuals' beliefs about the possible consequences of panic episodes may precede the onset of actual panic attacks.

Barlow's Integrated Model of Panic Disorder

Barlow (1988, 2002) proposed a diathesis-stress model of panic disorder that consists of biological and psychological components. His model posits that certain individuals are *biologically* predisposed to experience episodes of heightened physiological arousal and fear or *false alarms*, as Barlow calls them, following periods of stress. Some individuals subsequently develop anxious apprehension over the possible occurrence of these false alarms, which leads to what Barlow calls *learned alarms* (i.e., classically conditioned episodes of panic triggered by arousal cues that were previously associated with false alarms). The model further proposes that biologically vulnerable individuals who have a psychological vulnerability to experience external and internal (e.g., emotional, bodily) events as *unpredictable and uncontrollable* are at increased risk for developing panic disorder. According to the model, biological and psychological vulnerabilities interact to promote enhanced attentional focus on bodily sensations, thereby increasing the likelihood that these sensations will become cues for possible learned alarms in the future. Classically conditioned fear of potentially threatening sensations is central in Barlow's model, in contrast with Clark's model, which emphasizes catastrophic misinterpretations of sensations. In addition, whereas Barlow views anxiety and fear (i.e., panic) as distinct emotions, Clark does not distinguish between these states.

A number of studies have provided support for low perceived control of internal events as a factor in panic disorder. Sanderson, Rapee, and Barlow (1989) examined the influence of beliefs about the controllability of panic symptoms on the actual experience of panic sensations induced via a carbon dioxide challenge. All participants were informed in advance that the inhalation of carbon dioxide could induce a panic attack. Half of the participants were told that they could not control the amount of carbon dioxide that was being delivered whereas the other participants were led to believe that they could, by turning a dial. In actuality, the amount of carbon dioxide being delivered was equivalent for both groups. The results showed that individuals who believed that they could not control the amount of carbon dioxide were more likely to experience a panic attack and to report catastrophic panic-related thoughts than individuals who were led to believe that they could control the flow of carbon dioxide. It is noted that other research suggests that individuals with panic disorder also have reduced perceptions of their ability to control *external*, uncertain events (Zvolensky et al., 2001).

Bouton, Mineka, and Barlow's Modern Learning Theory

Early conditioning theories proposed that panic attacks and agoraphobia are caused in large part by associations formed between the initial panic attack (UCS) and exogenous situations and stimuli that were present at the time the initial panic attack was experienced (CS). In a classic paper, Goldstein and Chambless (1978) proposed that exogenous cues are not the only cues that have the potential to elicit panic attacks. They suggested that low level anxious arousal may become associated with panic attacks via *interoceptive conditioning*. First described by Razran (1961), interoceptive conditioning refers to a process whereby relatively benign physical sensations come to signal the onset of more intense physiological symptoms and full blown panic. The notion of interoceptive conditioning made a significant contribution to behavioral theories of panic disorder as it provided an explanation for so called uncued panic attacks (i.e., attacks that occur in the absence of an exogenous cue).

Conditioning theories, including those centering on interoceptive conditioning, eventually came under fire for a number of reasons (see Bouton et al., 2001; Mineka & Oehlberg, 2008). First, they did not distinguish between

panic and *anxiety*. Second, what constituted the conditioned and unconditioned stimulus (CS and UCS) and the conditioned and unconditioned response (CR and UR) in the experience of a panic attack, was unclear. Third, conditioning theories did not make predictions regarding the circumstances under which an individual with a panic history would *not* have a panic attack. Bouton et al. (2001) noted that conditioning theories have been criticized for overpredicting the experience of panic attacks. This is a particularly important point, as individuals with panic disorder do not invariably have a panic attack every time they are exposed to learned cues.

Bouton, Mineka, and Barlow's (2001) *modern learning theory* is a conditioning theory that attempts to circumvent the limitations described earlier. Consistent with older theories, modern learning theory hypothesizes that exteroceptive and interoceptive conditioning play important roles in the etiology of panic disorder. Situations and stimuli that coincide with the experience of an initial attack become conditioned cues for subsequent attacks. These initially neutral cues take on a negative valence by way of its pairing with the panic attack. Modern learning theory makes additional predictions to account for the complex nature of associative learning in panic disorder. The theory outlines the factors that make it more likely that panic will be conditioned, such as the presence of predisposing biological factors and/or exposure to stress. In addition, the theory emphasizes the importance of distinguishing between panic and anxiety and proposes ways in which anxiety and panic may interact to facilitate the development of panic disorder. One possibility is that anxiety develops as a conditioned response to an initial panic attack but also potentiates panic via subcortical processes that operate outside of awareness. In this case, the boundary between CR and CS is blurred, modern learning theory proposes that the same stimulus can in fact have different roles. The theory also suggests that aside from low level somatic sensations, other subtle cues, such as thoughts, can become signals for a panic attack. Modern learning theory explains (a) how safety behaviors (e.g., carrying a bottle of anxiolytic medication) can prevent the panic response from extinguishing, (b) why extinguishing multiple conditioned stimuli (i.e., cues) at the same time is more effective for reducing panic than extinguishing cues one at a time, and (c) why it is crucial for individuals to induce panic symptoms during in vivo exposure.

Bouton et al. (2001) also underscore the impact of contextual control on panic symptoms. To optimize extinction of panic cues, it is important to vary the contexts in which exposure is carried out. Context refers to an individual's external environment (e.g., therapist's office, home) as well as his or her internal environment (e.g., the emotional and physiological state of an individual at the time of extinction). Contemporary learning theory predicts that return of fear is more likely if the context in which exposure has occurred differs markedly from contexts encountered post-exposure. For example, if individuals with panic disorder systematically expose themselves to their feared sensations in the therapist's office but not at home, a relapse following seemingly successful treatment may be more likely. The same reasoning applies to internal contexts. For example, psychoactive agents, such as medication or caffeine, create a particular internal environment—if these agents are taken consistently during exposure but cease to be taken post exposure, an individual may experience a return of fear (Mystkowski, Mineka, Vernon, & Zinbarg, 2003).

In a test of the interoceptive conditioning hypothesis of panic disorder, Acheson, Forsyth, Prenoveau, and Bouton (2007) used 5-second exposures to 20% carbon dioxide enriched air as an interoceptive conditioned stimulus (CS) and longer exposures to air enriched with the same proportion of carbon dioxide as an aversive UCS to assess whether pairing a CS and UCS in this manner leads to a conditioned fear of physiological sensations. Participants who received consistent pairings

of the CS and UCS during the fear acquisition phase reported a greater level of fear and distress in response to a probe presentation of the CS-only than did individuals who were exposed to repeated presentations of the CS-only during fear acquisition. This finding suggests that interoceptive fear can be conditioned in a lab context.

COGNITIVE BEHAVIORAL TREATMENT OF PANIC DISORDER

Research on cognitive factors in panic disorder has led to the development of a number of cognitive treatments, two of which have received considerable empirical support: the panic control treatment devised by Barlow and Craske (2007) and the cognitive treatment developed by Clark, Salkovskis, and colleagues (Clark, 1989; Clark et al., 1994; Gelder, Clark, & Salkovskis, 1993). Both treatments have in common strategies aimed at changing appraisals and interpretations of bodily sensations. The cognitive behavioral treatment of panic disorder typically consists of 12 to 15 weekly sessions. Treatment is delivered either in individual or group format and booster sessions may be offered depending on the clinical setting. Cognitive behavioral treatments often share the following strategies: psychoeducation, cognitive reevaluation, interoceptive exposure, and in vivo exposure. A fifth component is breathing retraining, a treatment strategy that is included in the panic control treatment developed by Barlow and Craske (1994, 2007) and that has come under some scrutiny in recent years.

Psychoeducation

The initial sessions of treatment focus on providing information to the client about the nature of anxiety and panic attacks. The main objective of psychoeducation is to identify and address erroneous notions that the client may have about anxiety and to socialize the client to cognitive conceptualizations of panic attacks and panic disorder.

Cognitive Reevaluation

Most cognitive behavioral treatments include strategies that are designed to help clients identify and challenge cognitions that are likely to be triggering or maintaining their symptoms. In the case of panic disorder, such strategies help clients identify and challenge faulty appraisals of their panic experiences. Reiss's expectancy theory proposes that *expectations* or predictions that a feared outcome will occur are characteristic of disorders such as specific phobias and panic disorder. For individuals with panic disorder, the panic attack in itself is one feared outcome; however, identification and modification of clients' subjective estimates of the probability that they will (or will not) have panic attacks in particular situations is not the focus of cognitive strategies, as this is likely to be an unproductive endeavor that could ultimately lead to an impasse in treatment. By definition, individuals with panic disorder *do* experience recurrent panic attacks in a variety of situations; as such, it would be difficult for clients to challenge their predictions about whether they will experience a panic attack in a given situation. Therefore, cognitive strategies tend to focus on clients' estimations of the *costs* (i.e., assuming that one *will* experience a panic attack, what would be so bad about that?). Individuals with panic disorder make a number of predictions or appraisals that are amenable to change via cognitive strategies: (a) Catastrophic misinterpretations of bodily sensations (e.g., "I am feeling chest pain, that must mean there is something wrong with my heart"), (b) predictions about the immediate consequences if one were to experience panic sensations (e.g., "If I start to panic, I will faint"), and (c) predictions about one's ability to cope (e.g., "If I were to lose control of my anxiety in front of my boss and colleagues, I would not be able to cope with the embarrassment").

Cognitive reevaluation involves *identifying erroneous beliefs and examining the evidence that supports and does not support these beliefs*. For example, if a client reports that he or she is concerned about fainting during a panic attack (Clark & Ehlers, 1993), the clinician may ask the client to think about the number of times he or she has felt faint and has not actually fainted, and to think of explanations for why fainting has not occurred. One explanation that the client is likely to offer is that he or she has managed to prevent himself or herself from fainting, which is why it has not yet occurred. The clinician would then offer the alternative explanation: That fainting is precipitated by a drop in blood pressure and that during a panic attack, blood pressure typically rises, making it unlikely that one would faint (Clark & Ehlers, 1993).

Behavioral experiments are a critical component of cognitive reevaluation in that they provide clients with the opportunity to test their predictions and to collect corrective information. Returning to the previous example, an individual who holds the belief that he or she could faint during a panic attack would be encouraged to test this prediction by intentionally inducing, via hyperventilation, sensations that are associated with faintness, such as dizziness, blurry vision, and to withhold any attempts at preventing fainting. Clients invariably discover that panic sensations do not cause fainting (Clark & Ehlers, 1993).

Exposure

Exposure is the *repeated* and *systematic* confrontation of feared and avoided stimuli. In *interoceptive* exposure (Goldstein & Chambless, 1978), an individual is encouraged to intentionally induce unpleasant panic-like sensations and to withhold attempts at preventing or dampening these sensations. Examples of interoceptive exposure exercises include spinning (to induce dizziness and nausea), running in place (to increase heart rate), breathing through a narrow straw (to induce feelings of suffocation), and hyperventilating (Antony, Roth Ledley, Liss & Swinson, 2006). Studies have shown that interoceptive exposure is effective as part of a comprehensive cognitive behavioral treatment package (Barlow, Gorman, Shear, & Woods, 2000) and in isolation (Craske, Rowe, Lewin, & Noriega-Dimitri, 1997). In a recent investigation, Antony and colleagues (2006) conducted a detailed investigation of the immediate effects of interoceptive exercises that are commonly used in clinical practice. Participants with panic disorder and nonclinical control participants were asked to complete 13 common symptom induction exercises and three control exercises that were not expected to induce unpleasant sensations (breathing slowly for one minute, counting backward to oneself for 30 seconds, and closing one's eyes and imagining being in a peaceful place). After each exercise, participants rated the intensity of 13 *DSM-IV* panic symptoms. Relative to nonclinical participants, individuals with panic disorder responded more strongly to the exercises, including one of the control exercises. Breathing through a straw, hyperventilation, and running in place produced the greatest number of symptoms. In addition breathing through a straw, hyperventilating, spinning, and using a tongue depressor induced moderate and higher levels of fear. Breathing through a straw, spinning, and hyperventilating were also evaluated as being highest in intensity in another study (Schmidt & Trakowski, 2004), which suggests that these may have the greatest clinical utility.

The use of in vivo exposure in the treatment of panic disorder is similar to how it is used in the treatment of other forms of anxiety, including specific phobia, and social anxiety disorder. Individuals are asked to enter situations and places in which panic attacks have occurred or that are perceived by the individual as having the potential to trigger panic attacks. Clients are asked to develop a hierarchy of feared and avoided situations and then confront situations one at a time, beginning with those that induce a manageable level of fear.

The principal objective of interoceptive and in vivo exposure procedures is for the individual to fully engage in the experience of panic sensations. One mechanism by which exposure is hypothesized to reduce panic attacks and fear of anxiety is cognitive change. That is, individuals learn that most of their feared outcomes, such as fainting or "going crazy" are not going to occur as a result of a panic attack and that they are capable of coping with experiences that are unpleasant or even aversive (Arntz, 2002). In this way, there may be considerable overlap in the mechanisms underlying the effectiveness of exposure and behavioral experiments. In fact, some would argue that there is little distinction between these two strategies.

Breathing Retraining

Some cognitive behavioral treatment protocols (e.g., Barlow & Craske, 2007) include breathing retraining—diaphragmatic breathing strategies aimed at helping individuals to regulate their breathing and preempt hyperventilation. The inclusion of breathing retraining stems back to early theories that proposed a link between panic attacks and hypocapnia (Meuret, Wilhelm, Ritz, & Roth, 2003). Breathing retraining as a treatment strategy for panic disorder has come under a great deal of scrutiny (and criticism) in recent years (e.g., Meuret et al., 2003; Meuret, Ritz, Wilhelm, & Roth, 2005; Schmidt et al., 2000). Its use appears to contravene a core tenet of cognitive and behavioral conceptualizations of panic disorder and other forms of anxiety, namely, that efforts to avoid or reduce panic symptoms alleviate symptoms in the short term but only maintain fear in the long term (Salkovkis, Clark, & Gelder, 1996). Schmidt and colleagues (2000) argued that teaching individuals how to control their breathing has the potential to be counter-therapeutic because it may prevent them from learning that their feared sensations are not dangerous (Meuret et al., 2003; Schmidt et al., 2000). Proponents of breathing training maintain that it is intended for use as a coping skill; however, others have argued that the line between coping and safety seeking can be blurred and its use may lessen the effectiveness of exposure. Another perspective has been that breathing retraining may be useful for bolstering one's belief that one is capable of managing anxiety symptoms; however, it can similarly be argued that this may instill only an *illusion* of control, as breathing retraining is not a failsafe strategy. In fact, it can be argued that exposure is perhaps the most powerful means of instilling a sense of control in an individual with panic disorder, as individuals observe first hand that they are capable of readily inducing symptoms of panic in themselves and of tolerating the symptoms without having to resort to avoidant coping.

Schmidt and colleagues (2000) conducted a controlled outcome study comparing the efficacy of CBT with a breathing retraining component to CBT without it, to assess the incremental utility of breathing retraining. They found that treatment outcomes were similar regardless of whether breathing retraining was included in the treatment package. Although CBT plus breathing retraining was not associated with worse outcomes than CBT alone, it also did not augment the efficacy of CBT. In other words, omitting the breathing retraining component from CBT streamlines treatment considerably, which may in itself be a sufficient reason to exclude it.

Taken together, there is ongoing debate regarding the utility of breathing retraining in the treatment of panic disorder. To our knowledge, no consensus has been reached. Clinicians are advised to use clinical judgment in deciding whether to incorporate it into treatment. If there is a risk that a client may use it as a safety behavior to prevent panic attacks, clinicians should consider not using it in treatment and having a discussion with the client about the disadvantages of using breathing strategies to manage panic attacks. In their most recent revision of their treatment protocol, Barlow and Craske (2007) highlight that research on the incremental utility of

breathing retraining remains inconclusive at this time and suggest that it be presented as a tool to "facilitate movement forward" in exposure, not as a panic control strategy. They recommend that breathing retraining not be used with clients who may use breathing skills to "control" their panic symptoms.

REVIEW OF RESEARCH ON THE EFFICACY OF COGNITIVE BEHAVIORAL TREATMENTS FOR PANIC DISORDER

Cognitive Behavioral Treatment Versus Placebo or No Treatment

The superiority of cognitive behavioral treatment to wait-list and placebo controls has been established in numerous studies. Clum, Clum, and Surls (1993) compared the effect sizes of 29 controlled studies of treatments for panic disorder with or without agoraphobia. Psychological coping treatments consisting of cognitive restructuring, relaxation, and/or exposure were included in the analysis and were evaluated against a drug or psychological placebo or a no treatment condition ($N = 10$ studies). Psychological coping treatments were more effective than control interventions; however, these findings are to be interpreted with caution since treatments labeled as *psychological placebos* consisted of panic education, a treatment strategy that is included in most treatment packages for panic disorder.

In a subsequent meta-analysis, Gould, Otto, and Pollack (1995) reviewed the findings of 43 controlled studies of cognitive behavioral and pharmacological treatments. Cognitive behavioral treatments included in the analysis consisted of cognitive reevaluation, interoceptive exposure, in vivo exposure, flooding, and relaxation strategies. Seven studies comparing combined interoceptive exposure and cognitive restructuring to a wait list or supportive treatment control condition were identified and yielded an average effect size of 0.88. An updated meta-analysis by Mitte (2005) similarly showed that cognitive behavioral treatment was more efficacious than placebo treatment and no treatment in reducing symptoms of anxiety and depression.

Efficacy of Individual Cognitive Behavioral Treatment Strategies

A small number of studies have assessed the utility of individual components of cognitive-behavioral treatment packages for panic disorder. The findings of these studies are summarized in the following paragraphs.

Psychoeducation. To our knowledge, only two studies have examined the efficacy of psychoeducation alone for panic disorder (Rees, Richards, & Smith, 1999; Shear, Pilkois, Cloitre, & Leon, 1994). In a study by Shear et al. (1994), clients were randomly assigned to one of two 15-session treatments. In the CBT condition, treatment consisted of three sessions of psychoeducation about the nature and causes of anxiety and panic. The remaining sessions focused on cognitive restructuring, breathing retraining, progressive muscle relaxation, and exposure. In the non-prescriptive treatment condition, clients also received three sessions of psychoeducation and in the remaining sessions, the therapist engaged in reflective listening and discussed the importance of reducing stress. Both conditions resulted in significant panic disorder symptom reduction in the majority of participants. The extent of symptom improvement was similar for both treatments, which suggests that delivery of the complete CBT package was no more effective than provision of psychoeducation. In a study by Rees et al. (1999), individuals were randomly assigned to either self-monitoring (i.e., daily monitoring of panic attacks and other anxiety and mood symptoms) or psychoeducation. Psychoeducation, but not self-monitoring, led to decreases in general mood and anxiety symptoms; however, neither intervention led to a change in panic attack frequency. These findings stand in contrast with those of Shear et al.

in that they suggest that reduction of panic attacks requires more than psychoeducation.

Taken together, it is unclear whether psychoeducation in isolation is effective as a panic disorder treatment; however, there are newer data that suggest that it may have utility as a *preventative* intervention. Findings from a longitudinal investigation (Schmidt et al., 2007) indicate that the delivery of a 30-minute psychoeducation intervention to individuals at high cognitive risk for panic disorder by virtue of high scores on the *Anxiety Sensitivity Index* led to significant reductions in anxiety sensitivity.

Cognitive restructuring. To our knowledge, only one study has examined the utility of cognitive restructuring as a treatment for panic disorder. Salkovskis, Clark, and Hackmann (1991) assigned clients to focal cognitive therapy or non-focal treatment. In focal cognitive therapy, clients received two sessions of cognitive restructuring in which they learned how to identify and challenge misappraisals and misattributions of their bodily sensations. In the nonfocal treatment condition, clients were encouraged to learn strategies for minimizing stress in their environment. The majority of individuals who received focal treatment reported an immediate decrease in panic frequency; nonfocal treatment did not lead to reductions in panic frequency. Although the findings suggest that cognitive restructuring may be useful for panic, other interventions, such as behavioral experiments, are also effective for bringing about cognitive change. To our knowledge, no study has compared the differential effects of cognitive restructuring and behavioral experiments on panic disorder.

Exposure. At least two studies (Barlow et al., 2000; Craske et al., 1997) have provided support for the efficacy of interoceptive exposure delivered as a part of a cognitive behavioral treatment package. In a study by Ito et al. (2001), interoceptive exposure, in vivo exposure, and their combination were compared. Clients in each of the treatment conditions received seven 1-hour sessions and were asked to carry out 1-hour between-session exercises on a daily basis. Clients were reassessed between 6 and 12 months post-treatment. Relative to a wait-list control, interoceptive exposure alone, in vivo exposure alone, and the combination of both forms of exposure all led to significant reductions in symptoms of panic disorder and agoraphobia as well as decreases in catastrophic misinterpretations of panic attacks. The combined approach did not confer any additional benefits.

Breathing retraining. To our knowledge, with the exception of early case studies (e.g., Rapee, 1985), there have been no investigations of the singular effects of breathing retraining on panic disorder; however, as mentioned earlier, findings from a study by Schmidt and colleagues (2000) suggest that breathing retraining does not augment the efficacy of CBT.

Pharmacological Treatment Versus Placebo or No Treatment

A number of meta-analyses have demonstrated the superiority of pharmacological treatments (SSRI and non-SSRI antidepressants and benzodiazepines) to placebo treatments (Boyer, 1995; Clum et al., 1993; Otto, Tuby, Gould, McLean, & Pollack, 2001; Wilkinson, Balestrieri, Ruggieri, & Bellantuono, 1991; see McCabe & Gifford, 2009 and Pollack & Simon, 2009, for reviews).

Comparisons of Pharmacological Treatments

The relative efficacy of antidepressants and benzodiazepines has been compared in a number of meta-analyses. Wilkinson et al. (1991) found that antidepressants and benzodiazepines were both more efficacious than placebo but were not significantly different from one another when their effect sizes were compared. In a meta-analysis by Clum et al. (1993) antidepressants, benzodiazepines, and other medications, which included minor tranquilizers and beta-blockers, all led to better outcomes than did placebo treatments. Effect size comparisons indicated that antidepressants were more efficacious than the other medications. In a subsequent analysis by Boyer (1995), SSRIs, impiramine (a TCA) and alprazolam (a benzodiazepine) were all more efficacious than placebo in the treatment of panic disorder; selective serotonin reuptake inhibitors were superior to the other treatments. In a meta-analysis by Gould et al. (1995), non-SSRI antidepressants and benzodiazepines resulted in better treatment outcomes than did placebo treatments; however, outcome did not differ as a function of medication type.

Otto et al. (2001) conducted a meta-analysis of the efficacy and acceptability of selective serotonin reuptake inhibitors (SSRIs) for panic disorder to determine whether SSRIs are associated with a better treatment outcome than older, non-SSRI antidepressants. The effect sizes associated with older antidepressants and SSRIs were found to be comparable. Bakker, van Balkom, and Spinhoven (2002) reviewed the results of 43 studies of the efficacy of pharmacological treatment for panic disorder and did not find any significant differences between SSRIs and tricyclic antidepressants in terms of short-term efficacy; however, SSRIs were associated with a lower rate of drop-out relative to tricyclic antidepressants. The authors reasoned that differences in side-effect profile may have accounted for these differences.

Taken together, research has provided support for SSRIs, serotonin norepinephrine reuptake inhibitors (SNRIs) and benzodiazepines in the treatment of panic disorder (Pollack & Simon, 2009); however, an important limitation of these treatments is that side effects may lead individuals to terminate treatment prematurely. In addition, benzodiazepines are difficult to taper and their discontinuation can bring about unpleasant withdrawal symptoms (Smits, O'Cleirgh, & Otto, 2006).

Comparisons of Cognitive Behavioral, Pharmacological, and Combination Treatments

Given that cognitive behavioral treatment and pharmacological treatment are both more efficacious than placebo treatments and no treatment, the relative efficacy of cognitive behavioral treatment, pharmacological treatment, and their combination has generated considerable interest. A number of randomized controlled trials (RCTs) have involved direct comparisons between CBT and antidepressant medication (Bakker, van Dyck, Spinhoven, & van Balkom, 1999; Barlow et al., 2000; Black, Wesner, Bowers, & Gabel, 1993; Clark et al., 1994). Studies have also directly compared CBT and pharmacological treatment as monotreatments, to combination treatment (Barlow et al., 2000; Sharp et al., 1996; van Apeldoorn et al., 2008).

Cognitive behavioral treatment versus antidepressant medication. In studies by Black et al. (1993) and Bakker et al. (1999), treatment with an SSRI led to significantly better outcomes than did CBT. In a study by Sharp et al. (1996), CBT alone led to better outcomes than did fluvoxamine alone. In studies by Clark et al. (1994) and Barlow et al. (2000), there were no significant differences between CBT alone and imipramine alone over the short term.

Comparisons of CBT, antidepressant medication, and their combination. In a study by Sharp et al. (1996), 190 clients with panic disorder with or without agoraphobia were randomly assigned to one of five conditions: fluvoxamine alone, placebo, fluvoxamine plus CBT, placebo plus CBT, or CBT alone. Participants were assessed at pretest, posttest, and at 6-month follow-up. All active treatments resulted in better outcomes than did the placebo conditions; however, CBT alone or in combination with fluvoxamine were associated with the greatest treatment gains.

Barlow et al. (2000) conducted a RCT comparing the efficacy of cognitive behavior therapy (CBT), imipramine, and their combination in the treatment of panic disorder. Pill placebo and CBT plus placebo were included as control conditions. CBT alone and imipramine alone were superior to pill placebo. In intent to treat and completer analyses, CBT was found to be equivalent to imipramine; however, the rate of attrition was lower among individuals who received CBT. Although individuals who responded to imipramine showed a higher quality of response in the acute phase than did individuals who received CBT, the gains associated with imipramine, both in isolation or in combination with CBT, declined over the course of the follow-up period relative to CBT or CBT plus placebo. Further, acceptability was higher for CBT than for imipramine. Combined CBT and imipramine was associated with minimal benefit and, unexpectedly, was associated with higher rates of relapse than CBT alone and imipramine alone.

In a study by van Apeldoorn et al. (2008), clients were randomly assigned to CBT, SSRI, or CBT plus SSRI in parallel. Relative to CBT alone, CBT plus SSRI treatment led to better outcomes; however, the combined approach was not significantly more efficacious than SSRI alone.

Taken together, the findings with regard to combination approaches are equivocal. A review by Otto, Behar, Smits, and Hofmann (2009) suggested that the combination approach might be most efficacious when CBT is introduced into the treatment plan during discontinuation of benzodiazepines or antidepressants.

Summary

A considerable number of RCTs have been conducted to test the efficacy of treatments for panic disorder. Meta-analyses have provided consistent support for the efficacy of cognitive behavioral treatment and pharmacological treatment for panic disorder relative to inactive control interventions (see McCabe & Gifford, 2009 and Pollack & Simon, 2009, for reviews). Multicomponent cognitive behavioral treatment is currently the gold standard psychological treatment for panic disorder. Among pharmacological treatments, SSRIs, SNRIs, and benzodiazepines appear to be efficacious; however, as noted earlier, these medications can lead to side effects that may cause clients to discontinue treatment. Further, use of benzodiazepines can lead to dependence. There are data that suggest that the gains acquired with CBT are maintained for a longer period of time than are the gains attained with pharmacological treatment. With regard to the combination of CBT and pharmacological treatment, findings suggest that this approach might be most effective when CBT is delivered during medication taper.

Findings from naturalistic studies of the effectiveness of CBT for panic disorder have also been published in recent years. Stuart, Treat, and Wade (2000) examined the effectiveness of CBT (panic control treatment; Barlow & Craske, 1994) delivered in a community mental health center. The results showed that 89% of treatment completers reported symptoms that no longer met criteria for panic disorder. Furthermore, the magnitude of reduction in symptoms from pretreatment to posttreatment and through the 1-year follow-up period was comparable to reductions observed in published controlled trials. Addis and colleagues (2004) conducted an effectiveness study comparing CBT (panic control treatment; Barlow & Craske, 1994) to treatment as usual in a managed care setting. Given that this was an uncontrolled study, clients with comorbid conditions were included in the study and medication use was monitored, but not controlled in either of the treatment conditions. At posttreatment, 42% of clients in the CBT condition reported symptom reductions that met criteria for clinically significant change, compared with 19% of participants in the treatment as usual condition. The same authors published 1- and 2-year follow-up data (Addis et al., 2006) showing that among treatment completers, those who received CBT reported fewer symptoms of panic and agoraphobia than did individuals who received

treatment as usual. In addition, a greater proportion of individuals in the CBT condition maintained the gains they achieved during treatment through the follow-up period.

Predictors of Treatment Outcome

A number of studies have examined predictors of short-term and longer-term outcome following CBT for panic disorder (for reviews, see Dow et al., 2007; McCabe & Gifford, 2009). In terms of clinical variables, *severity of panic disorder at pretreatment* (i.e., frequency of panic attacks, overall level of anxiety, presence and severity of agoraphobia) has been shown to be a significant predictor of outcome at posttreatment and at follow-up (Brown & Barlow, 1995; Dow et al., 2007). The presence of *comorbid depression* has also been cited as a predictor of worse outcome in some studies (Fava et al., 2001; Ronalds, Creed, Stone, Webb, & Tomenson, 1997; Sharp & Power, 1999) but has not been shown, in other studies, to be a factor that affects treatment outcome (e.g., McLean, Woody, Taylor, & Koch, 1998). Comorbid depression appears to be an unreliable predictor of treatment outcome (McCabe & Gifford, 2009).

McCabe and Gifford (2009) pointed out that one of the difficulties in assessing the impact of comorbidity on treatment outcome is that certain types of psychiatric and medical comorbidity are usually an exclusion criterion in clinical trials; as such, published data on their impact on outcome for panic disorder are minimal. A growing body of literature suggests that the co-occurrence of *substance use* with panic disorder may be an important factor for clinicians to attend to. Daily cigarette smoking, in particular, has been linked to greater severity of panic disorder and has also emerged as a putative risk factor for this condition (for a review, see Feldner, Zvolensky, Babson, Leen-Feldner, & Schmidt, 2008). Research suggests that smoking may interact with premorbid anxiety sensitivity to enhance vulnerability to panic attacks (Feldner et al.,

2008). Alcohol abuse and dependence has also been linked to panic disorder. Individuals who experience recurrent panic attacks may use alcohol to self-medicate (McEvoy & Shand, 2008). Before clients start treatment for panic disorder, a thorough assessment is conducted to determine the presence of problematic substance use, in particular alcohol and drugs. Clients are typically advised to seek treatment for substance use disorders before participating in CBT for panic disorder. The concern is that clients may increase their use of substances to cope with the heightened anxiety during treatment, particularly exposure. Concurrent substance use may undermine the effectiveness of interoceptive and in vivo exposure in that clients may turn to substances as a safety aid; however, we are not aware of any research that has explicitly tested this hypothesis.

In a large scale study, Marshall, Zvolensky, Sachs-Ericsson, Schmidt, and Bernstein (2008) examined the association between *physical illness* and panic attacks and found that individuals with concurrent medical problems and panic attacks, although not necessarily panic disorder, reported a greater degree of disability than did individuals with either in isolation. In a recent review, Sala, Cox, and Sareen (2008) noted that there has been interest in the association between cardiovascular disease and panic disorder given that a number of panic symptoms can be mistaken as signs of a cardiovascular problem. Their review suggests that a small number of studies have found that the presence of a cardiovascular problem, such as myocardial infarction, is related to increased reports of panic attacks. The review by Sala et al. also suggested that respiratory problems (e.g., asthma and COPD), vestibular dysfunction, unexplained gastrointestinal symptoms, and thyroid disease are also associated with increased likelihood of panic disorder. Although there appears to be an association between panic disorder and certain medical conditions, it is not known whether these medical conditions are risk factors for panic disorder. A possibility is that the experience of medical symptoms may interact with

preexisting high levels of anxiety sensitivity to increase the likelihood of panic attacks; research is needed to test this hypothesis. Furthermore, the aforementioned medical conditions may be prevalent among individuals with other forms of anxiety; the associations outlined in the review by Sala et al. may not be specific to panic disorder.

An early study by Clark and colleagues (1994) suggested that reductions in catastrophic misinterpretations of bodily sensations were a better predictor of positive treatment outcome at 15-month follow-up than were reductions in panic-related automatic thoughts. A number of studies have since assessed whether panic-related cognitions predict treatment outcome. Hicks and colleagues (2005) assessed changes in momentary catastrophic interpretations in individuals who received either CBT, imipramine, or a combined treatment as part of their participation in a large RCT (Barlow et al., 2000). Participants completed a self-report measure of catastrophic cognitions that individuals with panic disorder commonly have when experiencing innocuous or unexplained somatic symptoms. Cognitions were classified as physical (e.g., "I will have a stroke"), mental ("I will become hysterical"), and social ("people will stare at me"). CBT, imipramine, and the combination treatment led to reductions in all three types of catastrophic cognitions; however, only social cognitions emerged as predictors of treatment outcome. Regardless of treatment condition, individuals who reported high levels of social fears at pretreatment and posttreatment reported more panic symptoms at posttreatment relative to individuals who did not endorse cognitions centering on social catastrophes. In a follow-up investigation, Hofmann and colleagues (2007) used a different analytic strategy to examine changes in cognitive appraisals as a predictor of treatment outcome in the same data set and found that changes in physical, mental, and social appraisals partially mediated treatment changes only for participants who received CBT, in isolation or in combination with imipramine, and that mediation was most robust for cognitive appraisals regarding the immediate physical consequences of panic symptoms. In a subsequent investigation, Cho, Smits, Powers, and Telch (2007) examined changes in momentary interpretations of panic symptoms over the course of CBT. They found that treatment led to significant decreases in catastrophic interpretations and that changes in these cognitions emerged as a significant long-term predictor of agoraphobia, anxiety, and impairment. Taken together, these findings support Clark's hypothesis regarding the importance of catastrophic misinterpretations in panic disorder; however, it remains unclear whether changes in specific types of interpretations are differentially predictive of outcome.

Enduring beliefs about the long-term physical, mental, and social consequences of experiencing high levels of anxiety have also been examined as a predictor of treatment outcome. Findings by Smits et al. (2004) suggested that changes in anxiety sensitivity are an important predictor of outcome in cognitive behavioral treatment, which indicates that CBT may be effective not only in modifying momentary appraisals of panic symptoms, but also in changing beliefs that are hypothesized to be of a longstanding nature and to confer vulnerability to the development of panic disorder.

OTHER TREATMENTS

There are a number of alternative treatments, aside from CBT and pharmacotherapy that may also be useful for the treatment of panic disorder; however, the data for many of these treatments are currently insufficient to support their routine use. Treatments that will be discussed in this section include psychodynamic psychotherapy, exercise, and alternative and complementary therapies.

Psychodynamic Psychotherapy

Panic-focused psychodynamic psychotherapy (PFPP, Milrod, Busch, Cooper, & Shapiro,

1997) is a type of brief psychodynamic psychotherapy that focuses specifically on the treatment of panic disorder. PFPP is a 24-session manualized treatment that consists of the following three phases: (1) acute panic, (2) panic vulnerability, and (3) termination. The total number of sessions that are allotted for each treatment phase varies depending on the individual (Milrod et al., 1997).

During the first phase, the therapist tries to uncover the unconscious meaning of the individual's panic symptoms by exploring the circumstances and feelings that were associated with the onset of the panic, the personal meaning of the panic symptoms, and the feelings and content of the panic episodes. The goals for this first phase of treatment include relieving panic symptoms and reducing agoraphobia symptoms. During the second phase of PFPP, vulnerability to panic is lessened through the understanding and altering of individuals' core unconscious conflicts. The expected responses for this second phase of treatment include improved relationships, less conflict, and reduced panic recurrence. Finally, during the third phase of PFPP, the individual re-experiences separation and/or anger themes with the therapist so that all of their underlying feelings can be communicated and understood. The objectives for this third phase of treatment include being able to manage separations, anger, and independence (Busch, Milrod, & Singer, 1999).

In terms of outcome research, PFPP has shown promising preliminary results in an open-trial study conducted by Milrod et al. (2001). Specifically, participants experienced reductions in panic attacks, preoccupation with panic attacks, and cognitions that frequently affect individuals with panic disorder, such as concerns regarding their bodies, fears, and arousability (Milrod et al., 2001). In addition, individuals reported improvements in quality of life. Further support for PFPP was provided through a RCT conducted by the same group of researchers (Milrod et al., 2007). Their findings showed that, compared to the individuals who received applied relaxation training, individuals who received PFPP showed greater reductions in severity of panic symptoms, functional impairment, and a tendency toward greater reductions in depressive symptoms. Although these findings seem promising, more systematic studies are needed before PFPP can be considered an efficacious treatment for panic disorder.

Exercise

There is also some evidence supporting exercise as a treatment for panic disorder. Generally, individuals with panic disorder refrain from exercise because they fear that exercise will trigger physiological sensations that are often associated with panic attacks, such as heart palpitations and sweating (Broocks et al., 1998); however, research shows that individuals often do not experience a panic attack while exercising (Antony et al., 2006). Furthermore, a recent study by Esquivel et al. (2008) showed that individuals who engaged in moderate or hard exercise before participating in a 35% carbon dioxide challenge reported *fewer* panic symptoms than did individuals who engaged in light exercise before the challenge. From a behavioral perspective, exercise may be useful because it could help individuals reevaluate their physiological sensations and reduce their level of fear (Broocks et al., 1998).

When selecting exercise as a treatment strategy, clinicians should take the following into consideration (Smits, Powers, Berry, & Otto, 2007). First, an initial medical evaluation should be conducted to ensure that individuals do not have any type of cardiovascular disease or acute infectious disease that may make exercise contraindicated. Second, the intensity and frequency of the program should be such that workout sessions of moderate to high intensity should last for up to 30 minutes and should be completed approximately two to four times a week. Overall, the exercise program should last at least four weeks so that individuals have a chance to develop an appropriate exercise training habit (Smits et al., 2007).

In terms of outcome research, Broocks et al. (1998) compared the therapeutic effects of a 10-week aerobic exercise (i.e., running) program to clomipramine or placebo for individuals with panic disorder. Overall, the exercise condition and clomipramine condition were associated with greater improvements, compared to the placebo condition. When compared to the exercise condition, the clomipramine condition not only improved symptoms earlier and had a lower dropout rate, it also was associated with less severe panic disorder, overall. Thus, although the results of the exercise program were somewhat promising, it was generally less effective than clomipramine. In addition, Broman-Fulks, Berman, Rabian, and Webster (2004) investigated the impact of an aerobic exercise program on anxiety sensitivity. A high-intensity aerobic exercise condition was compared to a low-intensity walking condition. Overall, the high- and low-intensity groups were both associated with reductions in anxiety sensitivity; however, the high-intensity condition produced more rapid reductions in anxiety sensitivity, yielded almost twice as many treatment responders (i.e., individuals whose anxiety sensitivity scores decreased by one or more standard deviations) and was associated with a greater reduction in fear of physiological sensations, as compared to the low-intensity condition (Broman-Fulks et al., 2004). Thus, although exercise seems like a promising alternative treatment for panic disorder, further research is required before it can be considered for routine use.

Complementary and Alternative Treatments

Complementary and alternative medicine (CAM) is frequently used by individuals to prevent and/or treat health problems. Specifically, 62% of respondents in a 2002 U.S. survey revealed using some type of

CAM in the last year to treat health problems (Barnes, Powell-Griner, McFann, & Nahin, 2004). In addition, individuals with self-defined anxiety attacks and/or depression have reported using CAM more than conventional therapies (Kessler et al., 2001). Similarly, individuals with panic disorder have also reported using alternative medicines more than individuals who do not have the disorder (Unutzer et al., 2000).

Despite its high frequency of use, there has been little systematic research conducted on the effectiveness of CAM (for a review, see Connor & Vaishnavi, 2009). Given that many different types of CAM treatments are available and may be used without supervision from a conventional health-care provider, it is important that individuals be informed about the effectiveness of these treatments. In terms of panic disorder, there is limited research regarding the effectiveness of different CAM treatments. Although Mantani et al. (2002) found that two Japanese herbal medicines, Kami-shoyo-san and Hange-koboku-to were helpful in relieving panic attacks for four individuals with panic disorder, there has been a lack of recent evidence supporting CAM treatments as possible treatments for panic disorder. Thus, given the increasing popularity of CAM treatments, it is imperative that future research assess the effectiveness of these treatments so that individuals are able to make better educated decisions.

EMPIRICALLY VALIDATED PSYCHOLOGICAL TREATMENTS FOR PANIC DISORDER

In 1995, the Task Force on the Promotion and Dissemination of Psychological Procedures (Society of Clinical Psychology, Division 12, American Psychological Association), from here on referred to as *Task Force*, published criteria for evaluation of the efficacy of psychological treatments (Chambless et al., 1996, 1998; Task Force, 1995). Empirically validated treatments for a range of psychological disorders, including panic disorder, were listed in publications by the Task Force (1995), Chambless et al. (1996) and Chambless et al. (1998). Treatments were assigned to one of two categories: *well-established treatments* and *probably efficacious treatments*. Cognitive behavioral treatment consisting of psychoeducation, cognitive reevaluation, exposure, and (in some protocols) breathing retraining was classified as a well-established treatment for panic disorder with and without agoraphobia and is a first-line treatment in the practice guidelines reviewed earlier. The list of empirically supported treatments was recently updated by the American Psychological Association Society of Clinical Psychology (2009) and is now maintained online. In the online list, cognitive behavioral treatment for panic disorder is classified as having strong research support (equivalent to the well-established designation). In the original list, applied relaxation was included as a probably efficacious treatment for panic disorder on the basis of one investigation by Öst (1988). In the online list, applied relaxation is listed as having modest research support. In addition, psychoanalytic treatment appears in the online list as having modest research support and is also classified as controversial. Taken together, the weight of the evidence suggests that cognitive behavioral treatment as a package is the psychological treatment that has the most evidence supporting it at this time.

Our understanding of the mechanisms involved in panic disorder has developed considerably over the past two decades due to the growth of research on this disorder. As a result, it has become important to not only demonstrate that a particular treatment reduces the symptoms of panic disorder, but that it is in fact changing the processes underlying the disorder. If the list of empirically supported treatments undergoes further revision, information about the mechanisms of action of well-established treatments would be useful. Given that cognitive behavioral treatment as a multicomponent package has received strong empirical support, it is also anticipated that there will be an increased focus on evaluating the efficacy of the individual strategies that comprise CBT for panic disorder. Individual treatment strategies were not included in the original list of empirically validated psychological treatments; however, a better understanding of the effects of these components is warranted. It may lead to the development of treatments that are more cost effective. As noted earlier, initial research has shown that breathing retraining does not augment the effects of cognitive behavioral treatment for panic disorder, therefore omitting it may streamline treatment and reduce costs. In addition, knowing more about the effectiveness of individual components is important from a practical perspective. As Herbert (2003) noted, clinicians may not adhere to manualized treatment as stringently in practice as is required in randomized controlled trials. Clinicians may use certain treatment strategies and not others for various reasons (for example, complexity of clinical presentation, limited number of treatment sessions). Data on the efficacy of individual treatment strategies would enable clinicians to make well-informed choices when developing individualized treatment plans for their clients.

CURRENT DIRECTIONS IN PANIC DISORDER TREATMENT RESEARCH

During the last three decades, tremendous progress has been made in conceptualizations and treatments for panic disorder. Cognitive-behavioral treatments for panic disorder are firmly grounded in empirical research on the cognitive and behavioral processes that maintain and give rise to panic attacks. Results from numerous clinical trials indicate that CBT is as effective as pharmacological treatments in the short term, but that gains are more likely to be maintained over a longer period of time with CBT. Given the success of treatments for panic

disorder, the focus has recently turned toward the adaptation of cognitive behavioral treatments for use in *prevention* (Feldner et al., 2008; Schmidt et al., 2007). Prevention interventions are delivered to individuals who are considered to be at high risk for the development of panic-spectrum problems, but whose symptoms do not yet meet diagnostic criteria for a disorder. Preventative programs are aimed at modifying anxiety sensitivity, which is an established cognitive risk factor for panic disorder. A recent study (Feldner et al., 2008) reported findings from a pilot prevention intervention targeting anxiety sensitivity and daily cigarette smoking. Initial findings from studies by Schmidt et al. (2007) and Feldner et al. (2008) are promising and indicate that the reduction of cognitive risk for panic may in fact be attainable. Large-scale longitudinal studies are required to determine whether prevention programs can actually reduce the incidence of panic disorder.

REFERENCES

Acheson, D. T., Forsyth, J. P., Prenoveau, J. M., & Bouton, M. E. (2007). Interoceptive fear conditioning as a learning model of panic disorder: An experimental evaluation using 20% CO_2-enriched air in a non-clinical sample. *Behaviour Research and Therapy, 45*, 2280–2294.

Addis, M. E., Hatgis, C., Cardemil, E., Jacob, K., Krasnow, A. D., & Mansfield, A. (2006). Effectiveness of cognitive-behavioral treatment for panic disorder versus treatment as usual in a managed care setting: 2-year follow-up. *Journal of Consulting and Clinical Psychology, 74*, 377–385.

Addis, M. E., Hatgis, C., Krasnow, A. D., Jacob, K., Bourne, L., & Mansfield, A. (2004). Effectiveness of cognitive-behavioral treatment for panic disorder versus treatment as usual in a managed care setting. *Journal of Consulting and Clinical Psychology, 72*, 425–635.

American Psychiatric Association. (2000). *Diagnostic and statistical manual of mental disorders* (4th ed., text rev.). Washington, DC: Author.

American Psychological Association Division 12—Society of Clinical Psychology. (2009). Research-supported psychological treatments. Retrieved from www.PsychologicalTreatments.org

Antony, M. M., Roth Ledley, D., Liss, A., & Swinson, R. P. (2006). Responses to symptom induction exercises in panic disorder. *Behaviour Research and Therapy, 44,* 85–98.

Antony, M. M., Roth, D., Swinson, R. P., Huta, V., & Devins, G. M. (1998). Illness intrusiveness in individuals with panic disorder, obsessive compulsive disorder, or social phobia. *Journal of Nervous and Mental Disease, 186,* 311–315.

Arntz, A. (2002). Cognitive therapy versus interoceptive exposure as treatment of panic disorder without agoraphobia. *Behaviour Research and Therapy, 40,* 325–341.

Bakker, A., van Balkom, A. J., & Spinhoven, P. (2002). SSRIs vs. TCAs in the treatment of panic disorder: A meta-analysis. *Acta Psychiatrica Scandinavica, 106,* 163–167.

Bakker, A., van Dyck, R., Spinhoven, P., & van Balkom, A. J. (1999). Paroxetine, clomipramine, and cognitive therapy in the treatment of panic disorder. *Journal of Clinical Psychiatry, 60,* 831–838.

Barlow, D. H. (1988). *Anxiety and its disorders: The nature and treatment of anxiety and panic.* New York, NY: Guilford Press.

Barlow, D. H. (2002). *Anxiety and its disorders: The nature and treatment of anxiety and panic* (2nd ed.) New York, NY: Guilford Press.

Barlow, D. H., & Craske, M. G. (1994). *Mastery of your anxiety and panic II.* Albany, NY: Graywind.

Barlow, D. H., & Craske, M. G. (2007). *Mastery of your anxiety and panic, 4th ed. workbook.* New York, NY: Oxford.

Barlow, D. H., Gorman, J. M., Shear, M. K., & Woods, S. W. (2000). Cognitive behavioral therapy, imipramine, or their combination for panic disorder: A randomized controlled study. *Journal of the American Medical Association, 283,* 2529–2536.

Barnes, P. M., Powell-Griner, E., McFann, K., & Nahin, R. L. (2004). Complementary and alternative medicine use among adults: United States, 2002. *Advance Data, 27,* 1–19.

Barsky, A. J., Delamater, B. A., & Orav, J. E. (1999). Panic disorder patients and their medical care. *Psychosomatics, 40,* 50–56.

Black, D. W., Wesner, R., Bowers, W., & Gabel, J. (1993). A comparison of fluvoxamine, cognitive therapy, and placebo in the treatment of panic disorder. *Archives of General Psychiatry, 50,* 44–50.

Bouton, M. E., Mineka, S., & Barlow, D. H. (2001). A modern learning theory perspective on the etiology of panic disorder. *Psychological Review, 108,* 4–32.

Boyer, W. (1995). Serotonin reuptake inhibitors are superior to imipramine and alprazolam in alleviating panic attacks: A meta-analysis. *International Clinical Psychopharmacology, 10,* 45–49.

Broman-Fulks, J. J., Berman, M. E., Rabian, B. A., & Webster, M. J. (2004). Effects of aerobic exercise on anxiety sensitivity. *Behaviour Research and Therapy, 42,* 125–136.

Broocks, A., Bandelow, B., Pekrun, G., George, A., Meyer, T., Bartmann, U., . . . Rüther, E. (1998). Comparison of aerobic exercise, clomipramine and placebo in the treatment of panic disorder. *American Journal of Psychiatry, 155,* 603–609.

Brown, T. A., & Barlow, D. H. (1995). Long-term outcome in cognitive-behavioral treatment of panic disorder: Clinical predictors and alternative strategies for assessment. *Journal of Consulting and Clinical Psychology, 63,* 754–765.

Brown, T. A., Campbell, L. A., Lehman, C. L., Grisham, J. R., & Mancill, R. B. (2001). Current and lifetime comorbidity of the DSM-IV anxiety and mood disorders in a large clinical sample. *Journal of Abnormal Psychology, 110,* 585–599.

Busch, F. N., Milrod, B. L., & Singer, M. B. (1999). Theory and technique in psychodynamic treatment of panic disorder. *Journal of Psychotherapy Practice and Research, 8,* 234–242.

Chambless, D. L., Baker, M. J., Baucom, D. H., Beutler, L. E., Calhoun, K. S., Crits-Christoph, P., & Daiuto, A. (1998). Update on empirically validated therapies, II. *The Clinical Psychologist, 51,* 3–16.

Chambless, D. L., Sanderson, W. C., Shoham, V., Bennett Johnson, S., Pope, K. S., Crits-Christoph, P., Baker, M., . . . Woody, S. R. (1996). An update on empirically validated therapies. *The Clinical Psychologist, 49,* 5–18.

Charney, D. S., Heninger, G. R., & Breier, A. (1984). Noradrenergic function in panic anxiety: Effects of yohimbine in healthy subjects and patients with agoraphobia and panic disorder. *Archives of General Psychiatry, 41,* 751–763.

Cho, Y., Smits, J. A. J., Powers, M. B., & Telch, M. J. (2007). Do changes in panic appraisal predict improvement in clinical status following cognitive behavioral treatment for panic disorder? *Cognitive Therapy and Research, 31,* 695–707.

Clark, D. M. (1986). A cognitive approach to panic. *Behaviour Research and Therapy, 24,* 461–470.

Clark, D. M. (1989). Anxiety states: Panic and generalized anxiety. In K. Hawton, P. M. Salkovskis, J. Kirk, & D. M. Clark (Eds.), *Cognitive behaviour therapy for psychiatric problems: A practical guide* (pp. 52–96). New York, NY: Oxford University Press.

Clark, D. M., & Ehlers, A. (1993). An overview of the cognitive theory and treatment of panic disorder. *Applied and Preventive Psychology, 2,* 131–139.

Clark, D. M., Salkovskis, P. M., Hackmann, A., Middleton, H., Anastasiades, P., & Gelder, M. G. (1994). A comparison of cognitive therapy, applied relaxation and imipramine in the treatment of panic disorder. *British Journal of Psychiatry, 164,* 759–769.

Clark, D. M., Salkovskis, P. M., Hackmann, A., Wells, A., Ludgate, J., & Gelder, M. (1999). Brief cognitive therapy for panic disorder: A randomized controlled trial. *Journal of Consulting and Clinical Psychology, 67,* 583–589.

Clum, G. A., Clum, G. A., & Surls, R. (1993). A meta-analysis of treatments for panic disorder. *Journal of Consulting and Clinical Psychology, 61,* 317–326.

Connor, K. M., & Vaishnavi, S. (2009). Complementary and alternative approaches to treating anxiety disorders. In M. M. Antony & M. B. Stein (Eds.), *Oxford handbook of anxiety and related disorders* (pp. 451–460). New York, NY: Oxford.

Craske, M. G., Rowe, M., Lewin, M., & Noriega-Dimitri, R. (1997). Interoceptive exposure versus breathing retraining within cognitive-behavioural therapy for panic disorder with agoraphobia. *British Journal of Clinical Psychology, 36,* 85–99.

Deacon, B., Lickel, J., & Abramowitz, J. S. (2008). Medical utilization across the anxiety disorders. *Journal of Anxiety Disorders, 22,* 344–350.

Dow, M. G. T., Kenardy, J. A., Johnston, D. W., Newman, M. G., Taylor, C. B., & Thomson, A. (2007). Prognostic indices with brief and standard CBT for panic disorder: I. Predictors of outcome. *Psychological Medicine, 37,* 1493–1502.

Ehlers, A. (1995). A 1-year prospective study of panic attacks: Clinical course and factors associated with maintenance. *Journal of Abnormal Psychology, 104,* 164–172.

Esquivel, G., Diaz-Galvis, J., Schruers, K., Berlanga, C., Lara-Muñoz, C., & Griez, E. (2008). Acute exercise reduces the effects of a 35% CO_2 challenge in patients with panic disorder. *Journal of Affective Disorders, 107,* 217–220.

Fava, G. A., Rafanelli, C., Grandi, S., Conti, S., Ruini, C., Mangelli, L., & Belluardo, P. (2001). Long-term outcome of panic disorder with agoraphobia treated by exposure. *Psychological Medicine, 31,* 891–898.

Feldner, M. T., Zvolensky, M. J., Babson, K., Leen-Feldner, E. W., & Schmidt, N. B. (2008). An integrated approach to panic prevention targeting the empirically supported risk factors of smoking and anxiety sensitivity: Theoretical basis and evidence from a pilot project evaluating feasibility and short-term efficacy. *Journal of Anxiety Disorders, 22,* 1227–1243.

Fleet, R. P., Dupuis, G., Marchand, A., Burelle, D., Arsenault, A., & Beitman, B. D. (1996). Panic disorder in emergency department chest pain patients: Prevalence, comorbidity, suicidal ideation, and physical recognition. *American Journal of Medicine, 101,* 371–380.

Furukawa, T. A., Watanabe, N., & Churchill, R. (2006). Psychotherapy plus antidepressant for panic disorder with or without agoraphobia. *British Journal of Psychiatry, 188,* 305–312.

Gelder, M. G., Clark, D. M., & Salkovskis, P. (1993). Cognitive treatment for panic disorder. *Journal of Psychiatry Research, 27,* 171–178.

Goisman, R. M., Goldenberg, I., Vasile, R. G., & Keller, M. B. (1995). Comorbidity of anxiety disorders in a multicenter anxiety study. *Comprehensive Psychiatry, 36,* 303–311.

Goldstein, A. J., & Chambless, D. L. (1978). A reanalysis of agoraphobia. *Behavior Therapy, 9,* 47–59.

Goodwin, R. D., Faravelli, C., Rosi, S., Cosci, F., Truglia, E., de Graaf, R., . . . Wittchen, H.-U. (2005). The epidemiology of panic disorder and agoraphobia in Europe. *European Neuropsychopharmacology, 15,* 435–443.

Goodwin, R. D., & Hoven, C. W. (2002). Bipolar-panic comorbidity in the general population: Prevalence and associated comorbidity. *Journal of Affective Disorders, 70,* 27–33.

Gould, R. A., Otto, M. W., & Pollack, M. H. (1995). A meta-analysis of treatment outcome for panic disorder. *Clinical Psychology Review, 15,* 819–844.

Greenberg, P. E., Sisitsky, T., Kessler, R. C., Finkelstein, S. N., Berndt, E. R., Davidson, J. R. T., . . . Fyer, A. J. (1999). The economic burden of the anxiety disorders in the 1990s. *Journal of Clinical Psychiatry, 60,* 427–435.

Herbert, J. D. (2003). The science and practice of empirically supported treatments. *Behavior Modification, 27,* 412–430.

Hicks, T. V., Leitenberg, H., Gorman, J. M., Barlow, D. H., Shear, M. K., & Woods, S. W. (2005). Physical, mental, and social catastrophic cognitions as prognostic factors in cognitive-behavioral and pharmacological treatments for panic disorder. *Journal of Consulting and Clinical Psychology, 73,* 506–514.

Hofmann, S. G., Suvak, M. K., Barlow, D. H., Shear, K. M., Meuret, A. E., Rosenfield, D., . . . Woods, S. W. (2007). Preliminary evidence for cognitive mediation during cognitive-behavioral therapy of panic disorder. *Journal of Consulting and Clinical Psychology, 75,* 374–379.

Ito, L. M., De Araujo, L. A., Tess, V. L. C., De Barros-Neto, T. P., Asbahr, F. R., & Marks, I. (2001). Self-exposure therapy for panic disorder with agoraphobia. *British Journal of Psychiatry, 178,* 331–336.

Katschnig, H., & Amering, M. (1998). The long-term course of panic disorder and its predictors. *Journal of Clinical Psychopharmacology, 18* (suppl. 1), 6S–11S.

Katschnig, H., Amering, M., Stolk, J. M., Klerman, G. L., Ballenger, J. C., Briggs, A., . . . Roth, M. (1995). Long term follow-up after a drug trial for panic disorder. *British Journal of Psychiatry, 167,* 487–494.

Kessler, R. C., Berglund, P., Demler, O., Jin, R., & Walters, E. E. (2005). Lifetime prevalence and age-of-onset distributions of DSM-IV disorders in the National Comorbidity Survey Replication. *Archives of General Psychiatry, 62,* 593–602.

Kessler, R. C., Chiu, W. T., Jin, R., Ruscio, A. M., Shear, K., & Walters, E. E. (2006). The epidemiology of panic attacks, panic disorder, and agoraphobia in the National Comorbidity Survey Replication. *Archives of General Psychiatry, 63,* 415–424.

Kessler, R. C., Soukup, J., Davis, R. B., Foster, D. F., Wilkey, S. A., van Rompay, M. I., & Eisenberg, D. M. (2001). The use of complementary and alternative therapies to treat anxiety and depression in the United States. *American Journal of Psychiatry, 158,* 289–294.

Kikuchi, M., Komuro, R., Oka, H., Kidani, T., Hanaoka, A., & Koshino, Y. (2005). Panic disorder with and without agoraphobia: Comorbidity within a half-year of the onset of panic disorder. *Psychiatry and Clinical Neurosciences, 59,* 639–643.

Klein, D. F. (1993). False suffocation alarms and spontaneous panic: Subsuming the CO_2 hypersensitivity theory. *Archives of General Psychiatry, 50,* 8–19.

Klein, D. F., & Fink, M. (1962). Psychiatric reaction patterns to imipramine. *American Journal of Psychiatry, 119,* 432–438.

Le Mellédo, J. M., Jhangri, G. S., Lott, P., Tait, G. R., McManus, K., Geddes, M., . . . Lara, N. (2001). Effect of medroxyprogesterone pretreatment on pentagastrin-induced panic symptoms in females with panic disorder. *Psychiatry Research, 101,* 237–242.

Mantani, N., Hisanaga, A., Kogure, T., Kita, T., Shimada, Y., & Terasawa, K. (2002). Four cases of panic disorder successfully treated with Kampo (Japanese herbal) medicines: Kami-shoyo-san and Hange-koboku-to. *Psychiatry and Clinical Neurosciences, 56,* 617–620.

Marciniak, M. D., Lage, M. J., Dunayevich, E., Russell, J. M., Bowman, L., Landbloom, R. P., . . . Levine, L. R. (2005). The cost of treating anxiety: The medical and demographic correlates that impact total medical costs. *Depression and Anxiety, 21,* 178–184.

Marshall, E. C., Zvolensky, M. J., Sachs-Ericsson, N., Schmidt, N. B., & Bernstein, A. (2008). Panic attacks and physical health problems in a representative sample: Singular and interactive associations with psychological problems, and interpersonal and physical disability. *Journal of Anxiety Disorders, 22,* 78–87.

McCabe, R. E., & Gifford, S. (2009). Psychological treatment of panic disorder and agoraphobia. In M. M. Antony & M. B. Stein (Eds.), *Oxford handbook of anxiety and related disorders* (pp. 308–320). New York, NY: Oxford University Press.

McEvoy, P. M., & Shand, F. (2008). The effect of comorbid substance use disorders on treatment outcome for anxiety disorders. *Journal of Anxiety Disorders, 22,* 1087–1098.

McIntosh, A., Cohen, A., Turnbull, N., Esmonde, L., Dennis, P., Eatock, J., . . . Salkovskis, P. (2004). *Clinical guidelines and evidence review for panic disorder and generalised anxiety disorder.* Sheffield, London: National Collaborating Centre for Primary Care.

McLean, P. D., Woody, S., Taylor, S., & Koch, W. J. (1998). Comorbid panic disorder and major depression: Implications for cognitive-behavioral therapy. *Journal of Consulting and Clinical Psychology, 66,* 240–247.

McNally, R. J., Hornig, C. D., & Donnell, C. D. (1995). Clinical versus nonclinical panic: A test of suffocation

false alarm theory. *Behaviour Research and Therapy, 33,* 127–131.

Meuret, A. E., Ritz, T., Wilhelm, F. H., & Roth, W. T. (2005). Voluntary hyperventilation in the treatment of panic disorder—functions of hyperventilation, their implications for breathing training, and recommendations for standardization. *Clinical Psychology Review, 25,* 285–306.

Meuret, A. E., Wilhelm, F. H., Ritz, T., & Roth, W. T. (2003). Breathing training for treating panic disorder. *Behavior Modification, 27,* 731–754.

Milrod, B., Busch, F., Cooper, A., & Shapiro, T. (1997). *A manual for panic-focused psychodynamic psychotherapy.* Washington, DC: American Psychiatric Press.

Milrod, B., Busch, F., Leon, A. C., Aronson, A., Roiphe, J., Rudden, M., . . . Shear, M. K. (2001). A pilot open trial of brief psychodynamic psychotherapy for panic disorder. *Journal of Psychotherapy Practice & Research, 10,* 239–245.

Milrod, B., Leon, A. C., Busch, F., Rudden, M., Schwalberg, M., Clarkin, J., . . . Shear, M. K. (2007). A randomized controlled clinical trial of psychoanalytic psychotherapy for panic disorder. *American Journal of Psychiatry, 164,* 265–272.

Mineka, S., & Oehlberg, K. (2008). The relevance of recent developments in classical conditioning to understanding the etiology and maintenance of anxiety disorders. *Acta Psychologica, 127,* 567–580.

Mitte, K. (2005). A meta-analysis of the efficacy of psycho- and pharmacotherapy in panic disorder with and without agoraphobia. *Journal of Affective Disorders, 88,* 27–45.

Mogotsi, M., Kaminer, D., & Stein, D. J. (2000). Quality of life in the anxiety disorders. *Harvard Review of Psychiatry, 8,* 273–282.

Mystkowski, J. L., Mineka, S., Vernon, L. L., & Zinbarg, R. E. (2003). Changes in caffeine states enhance return of fear in spider phobia. *Journal of Consulting and Clinical Psychology, 71,* 243–250.

Öst, L. (1988). Applied relaxation vs. progressive relaxation in the treatment of panic disorder. *Behaviour Research and Therapy, 26,* 13–22.

Otto, M. W., Behar, E., Smits, J. A. J., & Hofmann, S. G. (2009). Combining pharmacological and cognitive behavioral therapy in the treatment of anxiety disorders. In M. M. Antony & M. B. Stein (Eds.), *Oxford handbook of anxiety and related disorders* (pp. 429–440). New York, NY: Oxford.

Otto, M. W., Tuby, K. S., Gould, R. A., McLean, R. Y. S., & Pollack, M. H. (2001). An effect-size analysis of the relative efficacy and tolerability of serotonin selective reuptake inhibitors for panic disorder. *American Journal of Psychiatry, 158,* 1989–1992.

Pollack, M. H., & Simon, N. M. (2009). Pharmacotherapy for panic disorder and agoraphobia. In M. M. Antony & M. B. Stein (Eds.), *Oxford handbook of anxiety and related* disorders (pp. 295–307). New York, NY: Oxford University Press.

Rachman, S. (1976). The passing of the two-stage theory of fear and avoidance: Fresh possibilities. *Behaviour Research and Therapy, 14*, 125–131.

Rapee, R. M. (1985). A case of panic disorder treated with breathing retraining. *Journal of Behavior Therapy and Experimental Psychiatry, 16*, 63–65.

Razran. G. (1961). The observable unconscious and the inferable conscious in current Soviet psychophysiology. *Psychological Review*, 68, 81–147.

Rees, C. S., Richards, J. C., & Smith, L. M. (1999). The efficacy of information-giving in cognitive-behavioural treatment for panic disorder. *Behaviour Change, 16*, 175–181.

Reiss, S. (1991). Expectancy model of fear, anxiety, and panic. *Clinical Psychology Review, 11*, 141–153.

Reiss, S., & McNally, R. J. (1985). The expectancy model of fear. In S. Reiss & R. R. Bootzin (Eds.), *Theoretical issues in behavior therapy* (pp. 107–122). New York, NY: Academic Press.

Reiss, S., Peterson, R. A., Gursky, D. M., & McNally, R. J. (1986). Anxiety sensitivity, anxiety frequency and the predictions of fearfulness. *Behaviour Research and Therapy, 24*, 1–8.

Ronalds, C., Creed, F., Stone, K., Webb, S., & Tomenson, B. (1997). Outcome of anxiety and depressive disorders in primary care. *British Journal of Psychiatry, 171*, 427–433.

Royal Australian and New Zealand College of Psychiatrists Clinical Practice Guidelines Team for Panic Disorder and Agoraphobia. (2003). Australian and New Zealand clinical practice guidelines for the treatment of panic disorder and agoraphobia. *Australian and New Zealand Journal of Psychiatry, 37*, 641–656.

Roy-Byrne, P. P., Stein, M. B., Russo, J., Mercier, E., Thomas, R., McQuaid, J., . . . Sherbourne, C. D. (1999). Panic disorder in the primary care setting: Comorbidity, disability, service utilization, and treatment. *Journal of Clinical Psychiatry, 60*, 492–499.

Sala, T., Cox, B. J., & Sareen, J. (2008). Anxiety disorders and physical illness comorbidity: An overview. In M. J. Zvolensky & J. A. J. Smits (Eds.), *Anxiety in health behaviors and physical illness* (pp. 131–154). New York, NY: Springer.

Salkovskis, P. M., & Clark, D. M. (1990). Affective responses to hyperventilation: A test of the cognitive model of panic. *Behaviour Research and Therapy, 28*, 51–61.

Salkovskis, P. M., Clark, D. M., & Gelder, M. G. (1996). Cognition-behaviour links in the persistence of panic. *Behaviour Research and Therapy, 34*, 453–458.

Salkovskis, P. M., Clark, D. M., & Hackmann, A. (1991). Treatment of panic attacks using cognitive therapy without exposure or breathing retraining. *Behaviour Research and Therapy, 29*, 161–166.

Sanderson, W. C., Rapee, R. M., & Barlow, D. H. (1989). The influence of an illusion of control on panic attacks induced via inhalation of 5.5% carbon dioxide-enriched air. *Archives of General Psychiatry, 46*, 157–162.

Schmidt, N. B., Eggleston, A. M., Woolaway-Bickel, K., Fitzpatrick, K. K., Vasey, M. W., & Richey, A. (2007). Anxiety Sensitivity Amelioration Training (ASAT): A longitudinal primary prevention program targeting cognitive vulnerability. *Journal of Anxiety Disorders, 21*, 302–319.

Schmidt, N. B., & Trakowski, J. (2004). Interoceptive assessment and exposure in panic disorder: A descriptive study. *Cognitive and Behavioral Practice, 11*, 81–92.

Schmidt, N. B., & Woolaway-Bickel, K. (2006). Cognitive vulnerability to panic disorder. In L. B. Alloy & J. H. Riskind (Eds.), *Cognitive vulnerability to emotion disorders* (pp. 207–234). Mahwah, NJ: Erlbaum.

Schmidt, N. B., Woolaway-Bickel, K., Trakowski, J., Santiago, H., Storey, J., Koselka, M., . . . Cook, J. (2000). Dismantling cognitive-behavioral treatment for panic disorder: Questioning the utility of breathing retraining. *Journal of Consulting and Clinical Psychology, 68*, 417–424.

Sharp, D. M., & Power, K. G. (1999). Predicting treatment outcome for panic disorder and agoraphobia in primary care. *Clinical Psychology and Psychotherapy, 6*, 336–348.

Sharp, D. M., Power, K. G., Simpson, R. J., Swanson, V., Moodie, E., Anstee, J. A., & Ashford, J. J. (1996). Fluvoxamine, placebo, and cognitive behaviour therapy used alone and in combination in the treatment of panic disorder and agoraphobia. *Journal of Anxiety Disorders, 10*, 219–242.

Shear, M. K., Pilkonis, P. A., Cloitre, M., & Leon, A. C. (1994). Cognitive behavioral treatment compared with nonprescriptive treatment of panic disorder. *Archives of General Psychiatry, 51*, 395–401.

Sheikh, J. I., Leskin, G. A., & Klein, D. F. (2002). Gender differences in panic disorder: Findings from the National Comorbidity Survey. *American Journal of Psychiatry, 159*, 55–58.

Sheikh, J. I., Swales, P. J., Carlson, E. B., & Lindley, S. E. (2004). Aging and panic disorder: Phenomenology, comorbidity, and risk factors. *American Journal of Geriatric Psychiatry, 12*, 102–109.

Smits, J. A J., O'Cleirigh, C. M., & Otto, M. W. (2006). Combining cognitive-behavioral therapy and pharmacotherapy for the treatment of panic disorder. *Journal of Cognitive Psychotherapy: An International Quarterly*, 20, 75–84.

Smits, J. A. J., Powers, M. B., Berry, A. C., & Otto, M. W. (2007). Translating empirically supported strategies into accessible interventions: The potential utility of exercise for the treatment of panic disorder. *Cognitive and Behavioral Practice, 14*, 364–374.

Smits, J. A. J., Powers, M. B., Cho, Y., & Telch, M. J (2004). Mechanism of change in cognitive-behavioral treatment of panic disorder: Evidence for the fear of fear mediational hypothesis. *Journal of Consulting and Clinical Psychology, 72,* 646–652.

Spitzer, R. L., Williams, J. B., Kroenke, K., Linzer, M., deGruy, F. V. III, Hahn, S. R., . . . Johnson, J. G. (1994). Utility of a new procedure for diagnosing mental disorders in primary care: The PRIME-MD 1000 study. *Journal of American Medical Association, 272,* 1749–1756.

Stein, M. B., Goin, M. K., Pollack, M. H., Roy-Byrne, P., Sareen, J., Simon, N. M., & Campbell-Sills, L. (2009). *Practice guideline for the treatment of patients with panic disorder* (2nd ed.). Retrieved from http://www.psychiatryonline.com/pracGuide/pracGuideChapToc 9.aspx

Stein, M. B., Roy-Byrne, P. P., Craske, M. G., Bystritsky, A., Sullivan, G., Pyne, J. M., . . . Sherbourne, C. D. (2005). Functional impact and health utility of anxiety disorders in primary care outpatients. *Medical Care, 43,* 1164–1170.

Stuart, G. L., Treat, T. A., & Wade, W. A. (2000). Effectiveness of an empirically based treatment for panic disorder delivered in a service clinic setting: 1 year follow up. *Journal of Consulting and Clinical Psychology, 68,* 506–512.

Swinson, R. P., Antony, M. M., Bleau, P., Chokka, P., Craven, M., Fallu, A., . . . Walker, J. R. (2006). Clinical practice guidelines: Management of anxiety disorders. *Canadian Journal of Psychiatry, 51* (suppl. 2), 1S–92S.

Task Force on Promotion and Dissemination of Psychological Procedures. (1995). Training in and dissemination of empirically validated psychological treatments: Report and recommendations. *Clinical Psychologist, 48,* 3–23.

Taylor, S. (1999). *Anxiety sensitivity: Theory, research, and treatment of the fear of anxiety.* Mahwah, NJ: Erlbaum.

Taylor, S., Koch, W. J., & McNally, R. J. (1992). How does anxiety sensitivity vary across the anxiety disorders? *Journal of Anxiety Disorders, 6,* 249–259.

Turgeon, L., Marchand, A., & Dupuis, G. (1998). Clinical features in panic disorder with agoraphobia: A comparison of men and women. *Journal of Anxiety Disorders, 12,* 539–553.

Unutzer, J., Klap, R., Sturm, R., Young, A. S., Marmon, T., Shatkin, J., . . . Wells, K. B. (2000). Mental disorders and the use of alternative medicine: Results from a national survey. *American Journal of Psychiatry, 157,* 1851–1857.

van Apeldoorn, F. J., van Hout, W. J. P. J., Mersch, P. P. A., Huisman, M., Slaap, B. R., Hale, W. W., . . . Den Boer, J. A. (2008). Is a combined therapy more effective than either CBT or SSRI alone? Results of a multicenter trial on panic disorder with or without agoraphobia. *Acta Psychiatrica Scandinavica, 117,* 260–270.

van den Hout, M. A., & Griez, E. (1984). Panic symptoms after inhalation of carbon dioxide. *British Journal of Psychiatry, 144,* 503–507.

Wen, L., & Zinbarg, R. E. (2007). Anxiety sensitivity and panic attacks: A 1 year longitudinal study. *Behavior Modification, 31,* 145–161.

Wilkinson, G., Balestrieri, M., Ruggeri, M., & Bellantuono, C. (1991). Meta-analysis of double blind placebo controlled trials of antidepressants and benzodiazepines for patients with panic disorders. *Psychological Medicine, 21,* 991–998.

Wolpe, J., & Rowan, V. C. (1989). Panic disorder: A product of classical conditioning. *Behaviour Research and Therapy, 26,* 441–450.

Zvolensky, M. J., Heffner, M., Eifert, G. H., Spira, A. P., Feldner, M. T., & Brown, R. A. (2001). Incremental validity of perceived control dimensions in the differential prediction of interpretative biases for threat. *Journal of Psychopathology and Behavioral Assessment, 23,* 75–83.

Zvolensky, M. J., & Schmidt, N. B. (2007). Introduction to anxiety sensitivity: Recent findings and new directions. *Behavior Modification, 31,* 139–144.

13

Obsessive-Compulsive Disorder

MONNICA WILLIAMS, MARK B. POWERS, AND EDNA B. FOA

OVERVIEW OF DISORDER

Diagnostic Criteria

According to the text revision of the fourth edition of the *Diagnostic and Statistical Manual of Mental Disorders DSM-IV-TR* (American Psychiatric Association, 2000), obsessive-compulsive disorder (OCD) is characterized by recurrent obsessions and/or compulsions that interfere substantially with daily functioning. Obsessions are "persistent ideas, thoughts, impulses, or images that are experienced as intrusive and inappropriate and cause marked anxiety or distress" (p. 457). Obsessional content is sometimes categorized into six areas including: aggression (fears of harming others), contamination, sex, hoarding/saving, religion, and symmetry/exactness. For example, in one sample of OCD patients, 69% had aggressive obsessions, 57% had contamination obsessions, 53% symmetry/exactness obsessions, 34% somatic obsessions, 30% hoarding obsessions, and 24% religious obsessions (Antony, Downie, & Swinson, 1998). However, having obsessions with this content alone is not sufficient for a diagnosis of OCD. In fact, nearly 90% of the general population report thoughts with similar content (Ladouceur et al., 2000; Rachman & De Silva, 1978). What distinguishes OCD obsessions from nonclinical obsessions are the

greater frequency, intensity, and discomfort. People with OCD attach much greater meaning and threat to these thoughts than the general population. Individuals with OCD vary widely in how strongly they believe that their obsession concerns are realistic; only 4% believe with absolute certainty that their feared consequences will actually occur (E. B. Foa et al., 1995), while most acknowledge to varied degrees that their reactions to the thoughts are excessive or unreasonable. The OCD thoughts, impulses, or images are not simply excessive worries about real life problems as in generalized anxiety disorder (GAD) and are not consistent with the individual's self-perception (ego dystonic or inappropriate).

In addition to frequent obsessions, most individuals with OCD (98%) engage in actions (compulsions) to reduce discomfort from obsessions (E. B. Foa et al., 1995). Compulsions are "repetitive behaviors or mental acts of which the goal is to prevent or reduce anxiety or distress" (p. 457). As in the case of obsessions, compulsions are also often grouped into categories including: cleaning, checking, repeating, counting, ordering/arranging, and hoarding/collecting. The most common compulsion reported by patients with OCD is checking (Ruscio, Stein, Chiu, & Kessler, 2010). See Table 13.1 for other common obsessions/compulsions (Ruscio et al., 2010).

TABLE 13.1   Distribution of OCD Symptoms

	% of OCD Cases Reporting Each O/C
Checking	79.3
Hoarding	62.3
Ordering	57.0
Moral	43.0
Sexual/religious	30.2
Contamination	25.7
Harming	24.2
Illness	14.3
Other	19.0

For most patients with OCD, compulsions are functionally linked to the obsession/s. For example, a person with a fear of contamination may resort to washing their hands to prevent harm or to reduce discomfort. As noted earlier, many patients report excessive checking. Interestingly, these patients often report memory impairment driving them to recheck tasks. However, studies suggest that this low confidence in memory is not associated with general memory impairment (MacDonald, Antony, Macleod, & Richter, 1997; McNally & Kohlbeck, 1993). The *DSM-IV-TR* criteria for OCD include obsessions or compulsions that are recognized as unreasonable or excessive; cause significant interference or distress; and are not better accounted for by another Axis I, substance, or general medical condition.

Demographic Variables

It is estimated that between 2 and 3 million people are suffering from OCD in the United States. The National Comorbidity Survey Replication (NCS-R) showed that approximately 1.6% of the United States population reported OCD at some point in their lives (Kessler, Berglund, et al., 2005), with 1% of the sample experiencing obsessive-compulsive disorder within the last year (Kessler, Chiu, Demler, Merikangas, & Walters, 2005).

Prevalence of OCD is similar across ethnic and national groups. For example, a recent sample of 3,417 African Americans showed an OCD lifetime prevalence of 1.6% (Himle et al., 2008). Interestingly, while prevalence rates of OCD among African Americans were identical to the overall prevalence in the NCS-R, age of onset was later (mean = 31.8 years old) and use of mental health services was much lower, resulting in greater disability. Studies using different diagnostic systems (e.g., *ICD-10*) in various countries find roughly similar rates (see Figure 13.1).

Unlike many other anxiety disorders, males and females are equally represented in OCD populations (Rasmussen & Tsuang, 1986). However, onset is often earlier in males (13–15) than females (20–24) (Rasmussen & Eisen, 1990). Age of onset can be as young as 2 years old but most often occurs in early adolescence to young adulthood (Rasmussen & Eisen, 1990). As in the case of several mental disorders, OCD often appears to coincide with major stressors. In approximately 60% of cases, OCD follows a stressful experience (Kolada, Bland, & Newman, 1994; Rachman, 1997), traumatic life experience (De Silva & Marks, 1999; Rheaume, Freeston, Léger, & Ladouceur, 1998), or pregnancy and childbirth (Wisner, Peindl, Gigliotti, & Hanusa, 1999). Unfortunately, research suggests that without treatment the natural course of OCD is chronic (Antony et al., 1998; Eisen & Steketee, 1998). Indeed, most patients continue to meet full criteria for OCD or still show residual symptoms over time (Steketee, Eisen, Dyck, Warshaw, & Rasmussen, 1999).

Impact of Disorder

Obsessive-compulsive disorder results in severe personal distress and interferes with employment, relationships, and the daily activities of living (Ruscio et al., 2010). Individuals with severe OCD report significant impairment in home (100%), work (80%),

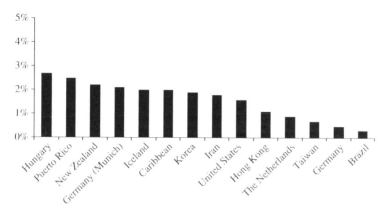

Figure 13.1   Prevalence of OCD Worldwide

relationships (87%), and social life (87%) (Ruscio et al., 2010). One study showed that 22% of treatment-seeking participants with OCD were unemployed compared to the 6% unemployment rate for the U.S. general population at the time (Koran, Thienemann, & Davenport, 1996). Another study showed an even higher unemployment rate (40%) among patients with OCD (Steketee, Grayson, & Foa, 1987). OCD patients are also overrepresented in health care populations. One survey showed that OCD patients saw dermatologists and cardiologists more often than the general public and even more than individuals with panic disorder or GAD (Friedman, Hatch, Paradis, Popkin, & Shalita, 1993; Kennedy & Schwab, 1997). Such high medical utilization, unemployment, and lost productivity due to OCD cost the U.S. economy billions of dollars each year (Koran, 2000; Leon, Portera, & Weissman, 1995). It is estimated that in 1990 the direct and indirect cost of OCD to the U.S. economy was $8.4 billion (DuPont, Rice, Shiraki, & Rowland, 1995). OCD is considered one of the top 10 causes of disability worldwide (Lopez & Murray, 1998).

Individuals with OCD may struggle with obsessions and compulsions for up to 17 hours a day or more (Gallup, 1990). Not surprisingly, this time commitment and distress often interferes with interpersonal relationships,

Half of OCD sufferers report losing friends and a quarter say that OCD caused the end of an intimate relationship (Gallup, 1990). This is consistent with other findings that approximately 60% of OCD patients report difficulty maintaining relationships (Calvocoressi et al., 1995). Celibacy rates are also elevated in OCD populations even relative to other anxiety disorders (Steketee et al., 1987), and approximately half of married patients with OCD report significant marital distress (Emmelkamp, De Haan, & Hoogduin, 1990; Riggs, Hiss, & Foa, 1992).

Comorbidity among patients with OCD is more the rule than the exception. The most recent finding is that a full 90% of respondents with OCD meet criteria for at least one additional *DSM-IV* disorder (Ruscio et al., 2010). See Table 13.2 for lifetime comorbidity of OCD with other *DSM-IV* disorders (data from Ruscio et al., 2010).

Anxiety disorders were the most common additional diagnosis, followed by mood disorders, impulse control disorders, and substance use disorders. Previous studies show similarly high rates of comorbidity, with about half of all patients with OCD meeting criteria for at least one other Axis I disorder (Lucey, Butcher, Clare, & Dinan, 1994; Rasmussen & Eisen, 1990). For example, one study showed that 57% of patients with OCD had another

TABLE 13.2   Comorbidity of OCD

	% OCD Cases With Comorbid Disorder
Any anxiety disorder	**75.8**
Panic disorder	20.0
Specific phobia	42.7
Social phobia	43.5
Generalized anxiety disorder	8.3
Posttraumatic stress disorder	19.1
Any mood disorder	**63.3**
Major depressive disorder	40.7
Dysthymic disorder	13.1
Bipolar disorder	23.4
Any substance use disorder	**38.6**
Alcohol abuse/dependence	38.6
Alcohol dependence	23.7
Drug abuse/dependence	21.7
Drug dependence	13.9
Any disorder	**90.0**

current Axis I diagnosis (Brown, Campbell, Lehman, Grisham, & Mancill, 2001) and 86% had lifetime comorbidity. Weissman et al. (1994) found that half of individuals with OCD also meet criteria for another anxiety disorder and approximately 30% also meet criteria for major depression (Crino & Andrews, 1996; Weissman et al., 1994). Eating disorders are also common among women with OCD. Ten percent of women with OCD have a history of anorexia (Kasvikis, Tsakiris, & Marks, 1986) and a third had a history of bulimia (Hudson & Pope, 1987).

Although effective treatment significantly improves quality of life among individuals with OCD (Bystritsky et al., 1999), only a minority of patients (29%) receive treatment specifically for OCD (Ruscio et al., 2010), and many suffer for years with OCD before receiving adequate treatment. People with OCD may feel excessive shame and hide their symptoms from others, attributing their struggles to personal weakness or failure (Pallanti, 2008). On average, OCD patient suffer 8 to

10 years before seeking treatment for the disorder (Marques et al., 2010; Rasmussen & Tsuang, 1986).

Assessment

Assessment of OCD is usually accomplished through a series of clinical interviews and self-report measures. Here we only cover the most common assessment tools. For a comprehensive list of other measures, please see the *Practitioner's Guide to Empirically Based Measures of Anxiety* (Antony, Orsillo, & Roemer, 2001).

Yale-Brown Obsessive-Compulsive Scale

The most widely used OCD outcome measure is the Yale-Brown Obsessive-Compulsive Scale (Y-BOCS) (Goodman, Price, Rasmussen, Mazure, Delgado, et al., 1989; Goodman, Price, Rasmussen, Mazure, Fleischmann, et al., 1989). It is a semistructured interview that takes approximately 30 minutes to complete. The Y-BOCS consists of a checklist of obsessions and compulsions and a 10-item severity scale. The checklist is most often administered pretreatment and helps in treatment planning. The obsessions are listed in the categories mentioned previously, including: aggressive (fear of harming others), contamination, sexual, hoarding/saving, religious, symmetry or exactness, somatic, and miscellaneous. The compulsions list is organized into categories including: cleaning/washing, checking, repeating, counting, ordering/arranging, hoarding/collecting, and miscellaneous. The severity scale rates the time occupied by obsessions and compulsions, how much they interfere with functioning, how much distress they cause, attempts to resist, and level of control. Items are rated on a 5-point scale ranging from 0 (no symptoms) to 4 (severe symptoms). The severity scale is usually administered pretreatment and often periodically throughout treatment. The total score is calculated by adding items 1 through 10, yielding scores between 0 and 40.

The Y-BOCS shows good reliability ($\alpha = 0.88$ to 0.91) and validity (Goodman, Price, Rasmussen, Mazure, Delgado, et al., 1989; Goodman, Price, Rasmussen, Mazure, Fleischmann, et al., 1989; McKay, Danyko, Neziroglu, & Yaryura-Tobias, 1995), including across multiracial/ethnic groups in the United States (Washington, Norton, & Temple, 2008). Scores above 16 may be considered in the clinical range and the mean for OCD patients is 21.9 ($SD = 8$). Scores for healthy people without OCD are quite low (Mean = 0.31, $SD = 1.21$) (Simpson et al., 2006). Alternative forms of the Y-BOCS include a self-report version (Baer, 2000), a computerized version (Rosenfeld, Dar, Anderson, Kobak, & Greist, 1992), a child version (Scahill et al., 1997), a body dysmorphic disorder version (Phillips et al., 1997), a version for heavy drinkers (Modell, Glaser, Cyr, & Mountz, 1992), a version for individuals who shop compulsively (Monahan, Black, & Gabel, 1996), and a version for individuals with trichotillomania (Stanley, Prather, Wagner, Davis, & Swann, 1993). In addition, the Y-BOCS has been translated into approximately 25 languages (R. W. Lam, Michalak, & Swinson, 2005). A new version of the Y-BOCS (Y-BOCS II; Storch et al., 2010) is under development.

Obsessive-Compulsive Inventory-Revised (OCI-R)

The Obsessive Compulsive Inventory Revised (OCI-R) is an 18-item self-report measure of distress from obsessions and compulsions (E. B. Foa et al., 2002). The total score ranges between 0 and 72. The questionnaire also includes six subscales, including washing, checking, ordering, obsessing, hoarding, and neutralizing. Subscale scores range between 0 and 12. The OCI-R has shown good internal consistency ($\alpha = 0.81$ to 0.93), test retest reliability ($r = 0.82$ to 0.84), and discriminant validity (E. B. Foa et al., 2002). A clinical cutoff score of 21 differentiates OCD patients from nonpatients (E. B. Foa et al., 2002). The OCI-R has been translated into Spanish (Fullana et al., 2005), Italian (Sica et al., 2009), Korean (Lim et al., 2008),

German (Gönner, Leonhart, & Ecker, 2007, 2008), Icelandic (Smári, Ólason, Eypórsdóttir, & Frölunde, 2007), and French (Zermatten, Van der Linden, Jermann, & Ceschi, 2006).

Maudsley Obsessional Compulsive Inventory (MOC or MOCI)

The Maudsley Obsessional Compulsive Inventory (MOC or MOCI) contains 30 dichotomously scored (true/false) items that assess obsessive-compulsive symptoms in the areas of contamination fears and washing behaviors, checking, and worries (Hodgson & Rachman, 1977). The MOCI takes 5 minutes to complete and scores can range from 0 to 30. The means for OCD patients (Richter, Cox, & Direnfeld, 1994) and student samples (Dent & Salkovskis, 1986) are 13.67 ($SD = 6.01$) and 6.32 ($SD = 3.92$), respectively. Reliability (Richter et al., 1994) and validity (Hodgson & Rachman, 1977) are acceptable, although this measure has been shown to have questionable validity when used with African Americans (Thomas, Turkheimer, & Oltmanns, 2000).

Padua Inventory–Washington State University Revision (PI-WSUR)

The original Padua Inventory contained 60 items about obsessions and compulsions on a 5-point rating scale in four main areas: contamination fears, checking, impaired control over mental activities, and worries about losing control over one's behaviors (Sanavio, 1988). Two revised versions of the scale have been published including the 41-item PI-R (Van Oppen, Hoekstra, & Emmelkamp, 1995) and the 39-item PI-WSUR (Burns, Keortge, Formea, & Sternberger, 1996). The mean total score for individuals with OCD is 54.93 ($SD = 16.72$). The scale takes approximately 10 minutes to complete. Reliability and validity for the scale are good to excellent (Burns et al., 1996). This measure has some problematic items and subscales when used with African Americans (M. T. Williams & Turkheimer, 2007; M. T. Williams, Turkheimer, Schmidt, & Oltmanns, 2005).

The PI-WSUR has been translated into Spanish and German, and the original inventory is available in English, Italian, Dutch, French, German, Greek, Hurdu, Japanese, and Spanish.

PSYCHOLOGICAL TREATMENTS FOR OCD

Early Treatments for OCD

Obsessive-compulsive disorder used to be viewed as extremely difficult, if not impossible, to treat. Psychoanalytic thought, based on Freud's theories of unconscious drives and wishes, produced many theories and interesting case studies, but no systematic treatment approaches that could be reliably replicated. Nonetheless, due to lack of alternatives, psychodynamic approaches continued to be advanced as the treatment of choice for OCD despite limited clinical benefit (Greist & Jefferson, 2007).

Salzman and Thaler (1981) conducted a review of the literature and concluded that the traditional approaches to the treatment of OCD "require drastic revision because they have added nothing to the comprehension or resolution of these disorders." (p. 291). The authors noted that studies of the day were calling for an approach that included more of a focus on the here-and-now, restraint from the tendency to make psychodynamic interpretations of past experiences, and a commitment to action in the present.

In his 1983 psychiatric review of OCD, Jenike lamented that psychology had little to offer people suffering from the disorder. He stated that "OCD is generally easy to diagnose but extremely difficult to treat successfully. . . . The abundance of therapeutic approaches available suggests that none is clearly effective in the majority of cases. Psychotherapy and ECT are ineffective treatments for pure OCD" (Jenike, 1983, p. 110).

At present it is widely recognized that, for OCD, psychodynamic approaches have little evidence base to justify their use. Concerning psychodynamic therapy and psychoanalysis, the most current expert guidelines note that "there is doubt as to whether it has a place in mental health services for OCD" at all (National Institute for Health and Clinical Excellence, 2006, p. 104). Therefore the remainder of this chapter will focus on cognitive behavioral approaches to treatment.

Cognitive Behavior Therapy (CBT)

Numerous behavioral approaches, based on learning theory, were developed to alleviate OCD-related distress, with varying degrees of success. The goal was to reduce fear by exposing the patient to the very thing that was feared or avoided until the patient adapted, or habituated, to the situation. Systematic desensitization, developed by Wolpe (1969), was useful for several types of phobias and was also applied in the treatment of OCD. This approach involved applied relaxation during gradual exposure (primarily imaginal exposure) to feared items and situations.

The goal of desensitization is to eliminate the patient's anxiety, which in turn eliminates the need for compulsions or rituals. The important components of treatment are to first create a hierarchy of anxiety-provoking stimuli; second, to train the patient in physical relaxation techniques; and third, to present items from the hierarchy to the patient while in the relaxed state. The theory is that anxiety and relaxation are incompatible, therefore in the face of the treatment the anxiety will dissipate. Compulsions are not addressed directly because in theory the rituals will no longer be necessary once the anxiety is gone (Wolpe, 1969). Systematic desensitization produced only limited success with OCD.

Aversive therapy consists of punishment for an undesirable response. The theory behind this therapy is that an activity that is repeatedly paired with an unpleasant experience will be extinguished. Aversive experiences that have been used to change behaviors include drugs that induce nausea (i.e., disulfiram for alcohol dependence), electrical shocks (i.e., for paraphilias or addictions), or any other stimuli aversive to the patient. This technique has been used in treating a variety of disorders. The most common application in OCD has been the rubber band snapping technique, whereby the patient wears a rubber band on the wrist and is instructed to snap it every time he or she has an obsessive thought, resulting in a sharp pain; thus the pain and obsession become connected (Mastellone, 1974). This method was not shown to be very effective (J. N. Lam & Steketee, 2001), resulting in many discouraged OCD patients with inflamed wrists. Thought-stopping, by having the therapist or patient shout "stop" every time the there is an obsessional rumination has also not been shown to be effective (James & Blackburn, 1995; Stern, 1978).

Perhaps the reason for the limited utility of thought-stopping can be best explained by the theories of social psychologist Daniel Wegner, who demonstrated that thought suppression exerts a paradoxical effect, whereby the person attempting to suppress a thought actually becomes preoccupied with it (Wegner, Schneider, Carter, & White, 1987). Wegner determined that the very task of suppressing a thought is difficult, leading people to grasp the thought in consciousness even as they simultaneously try to release it. When a person is no longer required to suppress a thought, and is then asked to express that thought, they do so more vigorously, mentioning it more often than if they had simply been asked to express the thought from the beginning. Thus, there are both immediate and deferred urges to become preoccupied with the very thought that is being suppressed, which is exactly what occurs in OCD.

Viktor Frankl (1975) advanced a theory called paradoxical intention, which bypasses the tendency to become obsessed with an unwanted thought by deliberately bringing it to the forefront of consciousness. This theory is based on the idea that the important part is not the obsession per se, rather the patient's attitude toward it. With paradoxical intention, the patient is encouraged to wish for the thing that is most feared, even to the point of exaggerating it until it seems humorous. The element of humor is a deliberate and key element of Frankl's approach. He believed, rightly, that the tendency to fight against the obsession only made it stronger, so the trick to breaking the cycle is to pursue the obsession rather than resisting it. By exaggerating and confronting the obsession, the idea eventually becomes absurd to the patient. Frankl claimed a 46% recovery rate with this technique.

The first breakthrough occurred in the 1960s, when Meyer (1966) described two patients successfully treated with a behavioral therapy program that included prolonged exposure to distressing objects and situations, coupled with strict prevention of rituals. This account was followed by several reports of a series of patients that supported Meyer's findings (e.g., E. B. Foa & Goldstein, 1978; Meyer, Levy, & Schnurer, 1974), and additional studies were then conducted to dismantle the effects of the treatment components.

Rachman, Hodgson, and Marks (1971) reported positive results in a controlled study of 10 patients with chronic OCD that compared two types of exposure — modeling versus flooding. Participants were inpatients for 7 weeks, all of whom received relaxation as a control treatment prior to exposure. Flooding involved exposing the patient to the most feared item at the top of the hierarchy. Modeling, as described in this study, was closer to the technique used by Meyer (1966). It involved starting by confronting patients with situations that evoked relatively low levels of distress and moving gradually to situations that evoked increasingly higher distress. The patients engaged in exposure to each situation after observing the therapist doing the exposure first. Both flooding and modeling significantly reduced obsessions, but the modeling group reported less general anxiety after treatment.

I. Marks, Hodgson, and Rachman (1975) reported results of a series of studies in which patients with OCD were treated with in vivo exposures in a partially controlled design. Treatment included 23 sessions administered over 4–12 weeks to a total of 20 inpatients. The OCD symptoms improved significantly after 3 weeks of treatment with in vivo exposure, and improvement was sustained through the follow-up period. After 2 years, three quarters of the patients were improved or much improved and five were unchanged. Relaxation exercises did not contribute to the success of the treatment, and in this study, modeling-based treatment was not better than exposure alone.

E. B. Foa and Goldstein (1978) reported successful results with a 2-week intensive outpatient treatment program for 21 OCD patients, using exposure and response prevention. Patients were treated by ongoing exposure to distressing stimuli and then prevented from engaging in rituals. In most instances, ritual prevention was monitored by relatives to ensure compliance with treatment protocols. Therapists conducted imaginal exposure of possible disasters that might result if rituals were not performed until patients reported a reduction in anxiety. Sixty-six percent of participants were symptom-free after treatment, and 20% improved partially. Only three did not benefit from the treatment program, which was attributed to overvalued ideation, or a strong belief that their fears were realistic.

The positive outcome of emerging OCD treatments was an early milestone for the promotion of CBT. The CBT researchers experimented with a number of techniques that have been refined into what is now called exposure and ritual prevention (EX/RP)—an effective psychological strategy for the treatment of OCD. The word *response* in EX/RP is often replaced by *ritual* as the word response is too broad—not all responses are compulsions. Though behaviorally based, EX/RP includes both behavioral and cognitive techniques. A more cognitive approach, that is cognitive therapy (CT), is advocated by some and may be appropriate for patients who are not responsive to behavioral strategies. However, EX/RP and CT both typically include behavioral and cognitive elements. EX/RP has been used in a variety of formats, including individual and group treatment, family-based treatment, computer-based treatment, self-help techniques, and intensive programs (NICE, 2006). The remainder of this section will describe the important components of EX/RP and CT for OCD.

In vivo exposure. Exposure is the cornerstone of EX/RP treatment. In vivo exposure has been shown to reduce obsessions and related distress (Kozak & Foa, 1996). This technique involves repeated and prolonged confrontation with situations that cause anxiety. Exposure sessions may last anywhere from 45 minutes to 2 hours. The immediate goal is for the patient to remain in the situation long enough to experience some reduction in anxiety and to realize that the feared disastrous consequences do not occur. With repeated exposures, the peak of the distress, as well as the overall distress, decreases over sessions (Kozak & Foa, 1996, p. 72–73). Thus, the patient habituates to the stimuli in two ways, within the session and between sessions.

Typically, exposure is gradual and the patient begins by facing objects and situations that result in only moderate levels of anxiety. Constructed in collaboration with the patient, the list of distress-evoking stimuli are placed in a hierarchical manner, beginning with the least distressing stimuli and gradually proceeding to more distressing ones. A rating scale of 0–100 (often called a SUDS scale for Subjective Units of Distress/Discomfort Scale) is used to rate the expected amount of distress associated with each item. After an item from the hierarchy is confronted in session with a therapist, the patient then practices self-exposure to the same item as daily homework. Once mastered, the patient faces the next progressively more distressing object or situation. The patient learns (a) that the feared consequence will not occur, (b) to better tolerate anxiety, and (c) that anxiety diminishes over time even without performing the rituals.

Imaginal exposure. In some cases it is not possible to construct an in vivo exposure to a patient's fear, and in these instances an exposure can be done in the imagination. Situations especially appropriate for an imaginal exposure are those in which the patient fears he may change in a fundamental way (i.e., shifting in sexual orientation or becoming a serial killer), cause a distal catastrophe (i.e., starting a chain of events that results in harm coming to unknown people), or that the outcome of failing to do a ritual is far in the future (i.e., going to hell or dying from cancer).

Imaginal exposure was used by E. B. Foa and Goldstein (1978) for the treatment of OCD. To conduct an imaginal exposure, the therapist and patient develop a detailed scene together based on the patient's worst fear. The story will describe a catastrophe befalling the patient and/or loved ones as a direct result of the patient's failure to perform rituals. The therapist might first recount the story aloud and then have the patient do the same, ideally in the present tense to make the events seem more real. The SUDS levels are taken at various points throughout the narrative to assure that the story is evoking enough anxiety to be productive. The exposure is typically recorded to facilitate repeated listening as homework.

Imaginal exposure is effective when it evokes the same distress in a person as the actual obsession. A person with OCD typically fights the obsession because they believe that if they entertain the ideas, the feared outcome will be more likely to occur. However, fighting the obsession only strengthens it. By repeating the distressing ideas in the form of a narrative, the person with OCD habituates to the fears and also learns that dwelling on the thoughts does not make them occur. The person gains a new perspective on the fear and is able to attend to it more objectively (E. Foa & Wilson, 2001).

Response/ritual prevention. The ritual or response prevention component involves instructions for the patient not to engage in compulsions or rituals of any sort. This is important because patients perceive that the

rituals prevent the occurrence of a feared outcome. Only by stopping the rituals do patients learn that rituals do not protect them from their obsessional concerns. E. B. Foa et al. (1995) found that in the vast majority of cases rituals have a functional relationship with the obsessional thought (i.e., "washing will prevent me from becoming ill," or "if I don't wash I will be distressed forever and will fall apart"); many times this functional relationship is logical (e.g., "checking will prevent me from making mistakes") but sometimes it has a magical flavor (i.e., "If I tie my shoes four times the right way, my children will not be killed in a traffic accident"). Sometimes patients cannot articulate any negative outcome that is prevented by performing the rituals. Rather, the performance of the ritual "just feels right"; in this case the function of the ritual is to reduce anxiety or discomfort, and the disastrous consequence is psychological, such as falling apart.

Implementation of ritual prevention involves a detailed analysis of all compulsions or rituals performed by the patient. Typically patients are asked to keep daily logs of all rituals performed. The therapist uses these logs initially to identify the rituals that need to be stopped, and, as treatment progresses, it is used to identify areas of difficulty that need more therapeutic attention.

Cognitive therapy. The OCD patients feel anxious or distress when engaging with their obsessional thoughts or images, because they interpret them as warnings of events that are dangerous and likely to occur. Cognitive therapy is designed to help patients identify these automatic unrealistic thoughts and change their interpretations of the thoughts, resulting in decreased obsessions and distressing compulsions.

In the first stage of CT, patients are taught to identify their worries as obsessions and their rituals as compulsions. The patient keeps a daily diary of obsessions, called a thought record. In the thought record, patients write down their obsessions and the interpretations associated with the obsessions. Important details to record may include what the patient was doing when the obsession began, the content of the obsession, the meaning attributed to the obsession, and what the patient did in response to the obsession (usually a compulsion).

The therapist reviews the thought records with the patient with an emphasis on how the obsession was interpreted. Using reasoning and Socratic questioning, the therapist helps the patient challenge their unrealistic beliefs. This helps the patient to identify the cognitive distortion, typically a faulty assessment of danger, an exaggerated sense of responsibility, or fears that thinking something negative will make it come true (thought–action fusion).

Once patients are able to identify their obsessions and compulsions as symptoms of OCD, the therapist initiates a few behavioral experiments to disprove errors in thinking about cause and effect. For example, if a patient believes that smoking four cigarettes will prevent her family from being harmed in an auto accident, the therapist may instruct the patient to smoke only three cigarettes and then wait to see if family members are actually harmed that day in an auto accident. The therapist may then use the results of this experiment as material for discussion about other types of magical thinking. Over time, patients learn to identify and reevaluate beliefs about the potential consequences of engaging in or refraining from compulsive behaviors and subsequently begin to eliminate compulsions.

Treatment by symptom subtype. Although CBT treatments are highly effective, it is important to keep in mind that not all symptom presentations are well-represented in the treatment-outcome literature. OCD is a highly heterogeneous disorder, and there is ample evidence to suggest that some OCD subtypes respond better to contemporary CBT methods than others. For example, compulsive hoarding seems to be more resistant to treatment, and sexual obsessions may require a longer course of therapy (Abramowitz, Schwartz, Franklin, & Furr, 2003; Grant et al., 2006). Treatment of cleaning/washing and checking is best represented in the literature, whereas mental compulsions (sometimes called *pure obsessional* types) are underrepresented (NICE, 2006; M. T. Williams et al., 2011). It is difficult to know how well other less recognized forms of OCD respond to treatment, as people with these types of OCD are generally less likely to be identified by mental health professionals and are subsequently less likely to be included in treatment studies. There is an urgent need for more research into how to best tailor treatment to target specific OCD subtypes.

Cultural variations in treatment. Most randomized trials of OCD patients have been conducted in the United States and Europe (i.e., Cottraux et al., 2001; De Araujo, Ito, Marks, & Deale, 1995; Emmelkamp, Vissner, & Hoekstra, 1988; E. B. Foa et al., 2005), with scattered reports from a handful of other areas, most notably Japan (Nakatani et al., 2005), India (Mehta, 1990), and Brazil (Cordioli et al., 2003). When treatments are conducted with non-Western patients, cultural adaptations may be necessary. For example Mehta (1990) found that outcomes for Indian patients were improved when CBT was administered according to a family-based model, taking into consideration the centrality of the patients' family in this particular cultural group.

In North America, the United States is 68% non-Hispanic European Americans, but all North American RCTs have consisted of predominately European Americans. African Americans and Hispanic groups remain underrepresented in treatment studies, and OCD in minority populations is not well understood (Nydegger & Paludi, 2006; M. Williams, Yun, Powers, & Foa, 2010). This fact compromises what we know about the generalizability of OCD treatments to other ethnic groups.

Consensus Panel Recommendations

A number of expert consensus guidelines were published over the past 30 years for the psychological treatment of OCD. These guidelines have evolved over time with increasing evidence from emergent literature. The first guideline entered into widespread use was developed by the Quality Assurance Project (QAP) of Australia and was published in 1985 (QAP, 1985). At this time, the success of the drug clomipramine (Anafranil) had been established but there was still considerable uncertainty about the primacy of CBT as a psychotherapeutic treatment for OCD. The guidelines state, "for those patients who have no significant personality disorder, either short-term dynamic psychotherapy or cognitive behaviour therapy is indicated if the illness has lasted less than a year or if obsessions are the predominant symptoms. When compulsions predominate, particularly when they have been present for more than a year, response prevention is the treatment of choice. Tricyclic antidepressants and cingulotractomy are also worthy of consideration in patients with persisting symptoms" (QAP, 1985, p. 240). The recommendation for psychosurgery demonstrates the traditional perception among professionals that OCD is a treatment resistant condition.

Over the next 10 years, the role of SSRIs and CBT had become well established. In a 1996 treatment manual for OCD, Kozak and Foa wrote, "Neither psychodynamic psychotherapy nor a wide variety of pharmacotherapies has been successful with [OCD]. . . . There are two treatments with established efficacy: behavior therapy by prolonged exposure and pharmacotherapy with SRIs" (Kozak & Foa, 1996, p. 71).

In the next year, the landmark expert consensus guidelines for OCD were published in the *Journal of Clinical Psychiatry* (Frances, Docherty, & Kahn, 1997). These guidelines were the product of survey feedback from 69 expert OCD clinicians who were sent a questionnaire about the best treatment for OCD. The survey enjoyed an exceptional response rate of 87%. Potential treatments presented to experts were rated as being a "treatment of choice," followed by first line, second line, and third line approaches. The study found that the expert clinicians usually

preferred to begin treating OCD patients with either CBT alone or a combination of CBT and SRI medication, where the inclusion of medication depended on the severity of symptoms and age of the patient. With milder OCD, experts preferred to use CBT alone, and as severity increased, the experts were more likely to recommend the addition of medication or medication alone. Combined treatment consisting of CBT and SRI medication was the favored approach for OCD. Cognitive therapy was recommended for targeting dysfunctional beliefs and improving compliance with behavioral assignments. Thirteen to 20 sessions of individual therapy with between session homework assignments was the most recommended format for CBT, but with severe OCD or when treatment must be done quickly, intensive CBT (daily CBT for 3 weeks) was recommended (Frances, Docherty, & Kahn, 1997).

In 2003, Greist et al. (2003) published expert guidelines for the long-term treatment of OCD in adults based on proceedings from the World Council of Anxiety meeting held in 2000 and a review of the literature. Both psychotherapy and pharmacotherapy were recommended for OCD, either alone or in combination, with cognitive behavior therapy (exposure and response prevention) indicated as the psychotherapy of choice.

Perhaps the most complete examination was undertaken by the British National Institute for Health and Clinical Excellence (NICE, 2006). In their 442 page *Core Interventions in the Treatment of OCD & BDD*, they lament "the limited number of RCTs that compare active treatments with controls." However, the guidelines do concede that among the existing adequate studies, clinician administered EX/RP appears to be "an effective treatment for OCD" (NICE, 2006, p. 101). After a thorough examination of all treatments, the authors wrote, "There is insufficient evidence to support the use of other psychological therapies, hypnosis, or homeopathy therapies as routine treatments for the core features of OCD. This lack of evidence is in contrast with a much larger evidence base for cognitive and/or behavioural therapies, although there are important limitations to the latter. Based on current evidence, ensuring access to adequate cognitive and/or behavioural therapies would currently appear to provide people with OCD with the best chance of improvement through psychological therapies" (NICE, 2006, p. 108).

Randomized Controlled Trials of CBT for OCD

The earliest RCTs for OCD are described previously and include seminal studies by Rachman et al. (1971), I. Marks et al. (1975), and E. B. Foa and Goldstein (1978), which established exposure and ritual prevention as effective treatment for OCD. These studies are sometimes difficult to compare to more contemporary studies because *DSM-III* criteria for OCD and well-known outcome measures, such as the Y-BOCS, were not yet available. Nonetheless, these studies formed the foundation of future work by establishing effective CBT treatment approaches.

By the 1980s, CBT gained wide acceptance as an effective treatment for OCD. However, it was not clear which components of CBT were the most effective. Research clinicians differed in how to best approach treatment, and so subsequent trials tended to compare one form of CBT with another. Here we describe some of the major RCTs that were conducted. This does not describe every study that has been published, and only randomized, controlled psychotherapy studies, with nine or more subjects per cell are included. Studies are reviewed by topical area.

Exposure Versus Ritual Prevention

Although EX/RP was shown to be an effective treatment for OCD, it was not clear if the exposures, ritual prevention, or both were the essential ingredients of the treatment. E. B. Foa, Steketee, and Grayson (1984) conducted a randomized trial with OCD patients ($N = 32$) who had contamination fears and cleaning rituals severe enough to interfere with daily functioning. Participants were assigned to one of three treatment groups, in vivo exposures only, ritual prevention only, or a combination of the two techniques. Each person received daily treatment for 2 hours per day, over 3 weeks, for a total of 15 sessions. Each patient also received two home visits by the therapist of 4 hours each. All groups experienced significant improvement posttreatment, with the combined EX/RP group showing the greatest improvement with the best maintenance of gains at follow-up. Thus it was concluded that both exposure and ritual prevention were important components of OCD treatment.

Cognitive Therapy Compared to *In Vivo* Exposure

The first randomized control study comparing cognitive therapy to in vivo exposure was conducted by Emmelkamp et al. (1988). The form of cognitive therapy used in his study was Rational Emotive Therapy (RET), which focused on helping patients analyze irrational thoughts, followed by work to confront and modify the thoughts to reduce distress. Patients were 20 OCD patients with no prior CBT. Both treatments consisted of 10 1-hour sessions of treatment over 8 weeks, followed by a posttest and a follow-up assessment one month later. Treatment resulted in moderate improvements in both groups that were maintained at 1-month follow-up. Improvement was measured by the MOCI and other scales of cognitions and anxiety. No significant differences were found between treatments. One notable weakness in the study is that treatment groups were not well matched on age (12-year group age difference), homework assigned was less than typical for CBT, and the small sample size (nine per cell). After the 1-month follow-up, two thirds of the patients received more sessions, according to their clinical need, so longer-term maintenance of gains could not be determined.

Emmelkamp and Beens (1991) conducted a second study of RET and in vivo exposure. Participants were randomized to either (a)

4 weeks of CT followed by 4 weeks of CT plus in vivo exposure or (b) 4 weeks of in vivo exposure followed by 4 more weeks of in vivo exposure. Patients were 21 OCD patients with no prior CBT. Six 1-hour sessions of treatment were given over 4 weeks, followed by a waiting period of 4 weeks before the crossover treatment was administered for an additional 4 weeks. Improvement was measured by the MOCI and other scales of cognitions and anxiety. Again, both treatments were equally effective with no significant differences at the midpoint or posttreatment. Although the treatment groups were better matched in this study, there were still some issues such as a high dropout rate, homework assigned was less than typical for CBT, and a small sample size (10–11 per cell). Moreover, the CT condition included some exposure (to test unrealistic fears), whereas the in vivo condition included neither CT nor imaginal exposure.

Van Oppen et al. (1995) conducted a treatment study comparing CT to EX/RP. Seventy-one OCD patients were randomly assigned to either CT or in vivo exposure. Sixteen 45-minute sessions were administered. In the CT condition, treatment focused on "overestimation of danger and inflated personal responsibility," and after session 6, behavioral experiments were included to test the basis of unrealistic beliefs. The exposure condition consisted of EX/RP working up a hierarchy of feared and avoided situations, with no discussion of feared consequences until after session 6. Outcome measures included the Y-BOCS and Padua Inventory. Patients in both groups improved significantly, and CT patients did better on all measures of improvement with significant change on the Y-BOCS and Padua Inventory. Weaknesses of the study include lack of follow-up and the duration of the sessions were shorter than is typical for CBT.

Cottraux et al. (2001) conducted a study involving 62 OCD patients who received 20 sessions of CT or EX/RP for OCD. Treatment included 4 weeks of intensive treatment (16 hours) and 12 weeks of maintenance (4 hours). The EX/RP and CT produced equal improvements in OCD symptoms after 4 weeks, based on the Y-BOCS, although EX/RP patients showed greater improvement on a measure of intrusive thoughts and CT patients were more improved in anxiety and depression. By week 52, most of the differences had vanished, but the EX/RP group had lower Y-BOCS scores and the CT group had less depression as measured by the BDI. The cognitive treatment included some behavioral techniques, such as behavioral experiments to test unrealistic fears and cognitive schemas, but no cognitive techniques were described as part of the EX/RP treatment.

In another dismantling study of CT and exposure for OCD (Vogel, Stiles, & Gotestam, 2004), 35 outpatients with OCD were randomly assigned to receive exposure plus relaxation, exposure plus cognitive therapy, or wait-list. The CBT portion of the treatment consisted of 2-hour sessions held twice a week for 6 weeks using EX/RP along with either CT or relaxation; this was followed by 10 more sessions of in vivo and/or imaginal exposure. Outcome measures included the Y-BOCS and BDI. The two CBT treatments were equally effective, and patients showed significant improvement posttreatment and through 12-month follow-up. It should be noted, however, that this study suffered from a high attrition rate among treated patients, particularly in the EX/RP plus relaxation group.

Imaginal Exposure Compared to *In Vivo* Exposure

E. B. Foa, Steketee, Turner, and Fischer (1980) examined the effects of imaginal exposure added to in vivo exposure. The study included 15 OCD patients with checking rituals. The first group received 90 minutes of uninterrupted imaginal exposure, which focused on disastrous consequences, followed by 30 minutes of exposure to in vivo situations that would normally result in compulsive rituals. The second group was given 2 hours of in vivo exposure only. Both groups were prohibited from performing rituals. At the end of treatment, both groups showed equal improvement.

but at follow-up, those who received only the in vivo exposure showed some deterioration. Thus, imaginal exposure seemed to contribute to the maintenance of treatment gains.

Subsequently, Foa, Steketee, and Grayson (1985) compared imaginal exposure versus in vivo exposure. Nineteen OCD patients were randomly assigned to one of two treatment conditions, imaginal or in vivo exposure. No response prevention was instituted. Participants received 15 2-hour sessions over a 3-week period, and in the fourth week received two home visits. Patients made moderate improvements and continued to improve at follow-up, an average of 10 months after treatment. Improvement was based on several assessor ratings and the MOCI, which indicated no significant differences between treatments at posttest or follow-up. It was concluded that both techniques offered important and lasting benefits to patients with OCD. De Araujo et al. (1995) examined the use of imaginal exposure in 46 British patients with OCD. Participants were given 9 weekly sessions of EX/RP, each session lasting 1.5 hours. Half were given 1 hour of in vivo exposure and 30 minutes of imaginal, and half received 1.5 hours of strictly in vivo exposures. All participants were provided psychoeducation and assigned 90 minutes of homework daily, based on the exposure that was done in session. Outcome measures included the Y-BOCS. Follow-up was reported at 20 and 32 weeks. There were no significant group differences at any time-point, and no significant differences in relapse. For the most part, participants maintained their gains. There was no control group in this study.

EX/RP Compared to Wait-List or Placebo

One small study of EX/RP for OCD study compared exposure and response prevention with a general anxiety management treatment program as a credible control condition for OCD among 18 outpatients (Lindsay, Crino, & Andrews, 1997). The anxiety management condition consisted of relaxation techniques, breathing exercises, and problem-solving about non-OCD life stressors. Participants were given 15 hours of treatment over a 3-week period, each with 1 hour per day of homework. The EX/RP group showed significant improvements based on the Y-BOCS, MOCI, and Padua Inventories. No long-term follow-up results were reported.

Freeston et al. (1997) conducted a study to test the effectiveness of EX/RP on mental rituals. Twenty-nine OCD patients with only mental rituals were randomly assigned to treatment or wait-list conditions. Patients in the treatment condition received cognitive behavior therapy consisting of psychoeducation about the occurrence and maintenance of obsessive thoughts, exposure (in vivo and imaginal), response prevention of all compulsions (including mental neutralizing strategies), cognitive restructuring, and relapse prevention. Based on Y-BOCS and Padua Inventory scores, treated patients improved significantly over pretest and wait-list, and treatment gains were maintained at 6-month follow-up. Thus EX/RP was shown to be effective with a group of patients that were often considered resistant to treatment.

Individual EX/RP Compared to Family EX/RP

Because the family can play such an important role in the functioning of an OCD patient, Mehta (1990) conducted a study to test whether training family members as co-therapists would be a helpful intervention. Thirty patients with a prior unsuccessful trial of medication for OCD were randomized to either individual or family-based treatment. Treatment consisted of 24 sessions of EX/RP, twice per week. In the family-based condition, family members were provided with psychoeducation, given specific instructions on how to best support the patient, instructed not to participate in rituals, and one family member was taught to be the co-therapist.

Both groups improved significantly on the MOCI from baseline, but the family-based treatment resulted in a superior outcome with more durable gains.

Group Treatments for OCD

McLean et al. (2001) examined the effects of cognitive therapy compared with EX/RP in the group treatment of 76 patients and a wait-list control. Treatments were conducted in groups of six to eight participants with two therapists, for 12 consecutive weeks, and sessions were 2.5 hours each. The CT treatment included some behavioral experiments, but no mention was made as to whether cognitive elements were included in the EX/RP condition. Outcome measures included the clinician version of the Y-BOCS as well as a self-report version. Both treatments resulted in improvement over baseline, but EX/RP was found be superior to CT, and this remained true at the 3-month follow-up.

Cordioli et al. (2003) conducted a study of group treatment for OCD with 47 patients who were randomly assigned to 12 weekly sessions of group EX/RP or wait list. Group EX/RP involved eight people per group with two therapists. Improvement was assessed based on Y-BOCS scores and other measures. The group EX/RP condition outperformed the wait list at posttreatment and at the 3-month follow-up period.

Self-Administered CBT for OCD

Greist et al. (2002) conducted a study comparing several types of self-directed therapies, including one administered by a computerized voice response system. One purpose of this investigation was to determine if the treatment of OCD could be done in a more cost-effective manner that would make it more accessible to patients. In this large study, 218 patients from eight different sites were randomly assigned to one of three conditions: clinician-guided treatment, computer-based treatment, or non-OCD-related self-study relaxation exercises.

The clinician-guided treatment consisted of 11 1-hour weekly sessions to negotiate self-exposure homework to be performed for 1 hour each day and recorded in diaries. The self-paced computer-based treatment consisted of a workbook and interactive telephone system that guided patients in self-exposure homework and relapse prevention in nine steps. The relaxation condition involved a written manual and audiotapes, with homework to be practiced for 1 hour per day and recorded daily in a diary over 10 weeks; no exposure or ritual prevention instructions were included. According to the Y-BOCS and other measures, both the computer-based and clinician-guided treatment resulted in moderate improvements but the relaxation treatment was ineffective.

EX/RP and Medication

There have been a number of studies done comparing medication to CBT. For the purposes of this chapter, we are only discussing studies where the effects of CBT can also be clearly compared to a nonmedication condition.

The first such study was done by I. M. Marks, Stern, Mawson, Cobb, and McDonald (1980), examining clomipramine or pill placebo with EX/RP or relaxation for OCD. This was followed by another study by I. M. Marks et al. (1988), involving clomipramine, placebo, self-controlled exposure, and/or therapist-aided exposure. Results suggested that the addition of EX/RP had a positive effect.

As OCD tends to be highly comorbid with depression, depressed patients show fewer long-term benefits from OCD treatment. E. B. Foa, Kozak, Steketee, and McCarthy (1992) hypothesized that reducing depressive symptoms prior to therapy would enhance the effects of EX/RP. To test this, 39 patients were divided into highly and mildly depressed groups, then randomized to receive imipramine or placebo for 6 weeks. This was followed by 3 weeks of intensive daily EX/RP, then 12 weeks of weekly supportive psychotherapy. The EX/RP was successful in reducing OC symptoms, but imipramine did not make the EX/RP more effective. Both depressed and nondepressed patients responded equally well to the EX/RP for OCD. Both imipramine and EX/RP decreased depressive symptoms in patients.

To separate the effects of CT from EX/RP and to evaluate the added effect of medication, van Balkom et al. (1998) designed a study in which 117 OCD patients were randomly assigned to CT, EX/RP, fluvoxamine plus CT, fluvoxamine plus EX/RP, or wait-list control. The CT and EX/RP were conducted in 16 45-minute sessions. In the medication conditions, CBT was not started until after stabilization on fluvoxamine for 8 weeks. Results indicated that patients made moderate improvements, and all four active treatments were superior to wait-list, with no significant differences between them. Notably, until halfway through treatment, the EX/RP condition did not address the participant's faulty assessment of risk nor did the CT condition include behavioral experiments; thus both CBT treatments were somewhat weaker than typical, which may have weakened the results of the study.

Nakatani et al. (2005) conducted a randomized study of 28 patients with OCD. Subjects were randomly assigned to one of three treatment conditions: CBT (EX/RP with pill placebo), fluvoxamine (with autogenic training, a placebo for CBT), or a control group (autogenic training + pill placebo). The CBT treatment consisted of EX/RP delivered in 12 weekly 45-minute sessions by two psychiatrists. Outcome measures included the Y-BOCS. Patients in the EX/RP and fluvoxamine groups showed significantly more improvement than those in the control group in the total Y-BOCS. Moreover, the EX/RP group showed significantly more reduction in total Y-BOCS score at the end of treatment than the medication group.

E. B. Foa et al. (2005) compared EX/RP to clomipramine in a randomized, placebo-controlled trial of 122 participants with OCD. Patients were randomized to receive either EX/RP, clomipramine, pill placebo, or a combination of both EX/RP plus clomipramine. Treatment consisted of 15 2-hour sessions given over a 3-week period. Outcome measures included the Y-BOCS. At 12 weeks, both groups receiving EX/RP showed a good response to treatment, the clompiramine-alone condition resulted in moderate improvement, and the placebo group was unimproved. The effect of EX/RP did not significantly differ from that of EX/RP plus clomipramine.

Collectively, results of these studies suggest that medication does not add to the effectiveness of CBT for OCD, which is a change from earlier thought that the combination of medication and CBT was most effective.

Augmentation of Medication Treatment

Most OCD patients are already taking an SRI when they seek psychological intervention. Therefore, Simpson et al. (2008) conducted a study to determine if EX/RP could result in additional gains. The study compared stress management training (SMT) to EX/RP in 108 patients with OCD symptoms who were already taking a stable dose of an SRI. Treatment consisted of 17 sessions of CBT twice per week, where each session was 90–120 minutes in length. EX/RP included both in vivo and imaginal exposures. SMT included deep breathing, progressive muscle relaxation, positive imagery, assertiveness training, and problem-solving techniques. SMT was intended as a credible control condition to account for the effects of patient expectancy, the therapeutic relationship, and other nonspecific factors. Patients in both groups were asked to monitor symptoms and complete 1 hour of homework daily. EX/RP was found to be significantly better than SMT at reducing OC symptoms. Based on the Y-BOCS, EX/RP patients showed good improvement at the end of treatment, whereas SMT patients had only improved slightly. No follow-up scores were reported.

Meta-Analyses of CBT for OCD

Given the many often conflicting research findings, variations in treatment procedures, and differing outcome measures, it can be difficult to identify a clear best choice for CBT treatment of OCD. In such cases, a meta-analysis of studies can be useful to distill the results of several studies into a clearer picture. Here we review meta-analyses of CBT for OCD in adults. Meta-analyses of child and adolescent studies are cited earlier in the chapter.

Abramowitz (1996) conducted a meta-analysis to determine the degree of symptom improvement associated with four different variations of EX/RP. The study examined a total of 38 trials from 24 controlled and uncontrolled studies. Results suggested that therapist-supervised exposure was more effective than self-exposure. Complete response prevention during exposure therapy was better than partial or no response prevention. The combination of in vivo and imaginal exposure was better than in vivo exposure alone in reducing anxiety. There was no significant difference between treatments that included gradual exposure and those that included flooding.

A meta-analysis by Eddy, Dutra, Bradley, and Westen, (2004) examined data from 15 different clinical trials. Treatments examined included EX/RP, CT, and active and inactive control conditions. Approximately two thirds of the patients who completed treatment improved, but only a third met recovery criteria. Among the intent to treat sample, which included dropouts, about one half of patients improved and only a quarter recovered. Findings were strongest for EX/RP over CT and individual over group therapy. The authors also commented that most studies excluded patients with several common conditions, including thought disorders, concurrent medications, and substance use disorders. A smaller number also excluded common conditions, such as comorbid depression. Given that comorbidity is quite high among OCD patients, it can be difficult to determine if some treatments are

more effective with certain comorbidities versus others. As mentioned earlier in this chapter, up to 90% of OCD patients have a history of at least one additional disorder. Accordingly, the authors urge future studies to include more patients with comorbid conditions, and to examine its association with outcome within studies (Eddy et al., 2004).

Rosa-Alcázar, Sánchez-Meca, Gómez-Conesa, and Marín-Martínez (2008) conducted a meta-analysis examining data from 19 controlled psychotherapy treatment studies for OCD. Both EX/RP and CT were found to be highly effective, as well as their combination, with no significant differences between treatments. The authors found no differences between in vivo versus in vivo plus imaginal exposure in EX/RP for OCD; however interestingly, the combination of in vivo and imaginal exposure resulted in a greater reduction of depressive symptoms than in vivo exposure alone. There was evidence that therapist-supervised exposure was more effective than assisted self-exposure. The effect size of the improvement was greater for studies conducted by psychologists rather than psychiatrists, and more recent studies had larger effect sizes that older ones.

The authors note the similarity of the findings for EX/RP and CT, and point out that both techniques incorporate similar treatment strategies. For example, CT most often involves behavioral experiments that include exposure to anxiety evoking situations to challenge irrational thoughts, thereby incorporating behavioral components. On the other hand, the application of EX/RP involves challenging the patient about unrealistic beliefs and irrational thoughts surrounding decision making under uncertainty, so the recommended application of EX/RP contains important elements of cognitive therapy. It could be that EX/RP is more effective than CT, but the studies that compare EX/RP with CT have taken special care to avoid the use of cognitive elements in EX/RP resulting in an incomplete application of the technique, whereas the application of CT in research studies usually includes elements of exposure (Rosa-Alcázar et al., 2008).

Evidence-Based Practices

Over 40 years of published research has led to the wide consensus among researchers and clinicians that cognitive behavior therapy is an effective treatment for OCD (Frances et al. 1997; Greist et al., 2003; NICE, 2006). Exposure-based treatments have the largest evidence base to support their use for OCD. EX/RP, which includes elements of CT, appears to be most effective, whereas exposure without cognitive elements appears to be equally as effective as CT. Based on the existing literature EX/RP is recommended as the first-line treatment for OCD, with CT as a second choice alternative.

EX/RP has the strongest support, but some patients drop out prematurely (25–30%), and although about 80% of treatment completers respond well, 20% do not; therefore, about 50% of patients with OCD who are referred for treatment are not helped (Abramowitz, 2006). It will be important for clinical researchers to continue to refine CBT techniques to maximize improvement and make treatment more palatable to those in need of help. Usefulness of other psychological interventions and alternative therapies is difficult to determine, as there is very little published literature. The lack of evidence to support the use of psychodynamic therapies was discussed previously in this chapter, but continues to be commonly administered. There has been one published RCT on an alternative therapy, yogic meditation (Shannahoff-Khalsa et al., 1999) in the treatment of OCD, but no RCTs have been published on any other psychological interventions, such as hypnosis, virtual reality therapy, homeopathy, or an integrated psychological approach. Furthermore, no well-designed single case studies have been published on either other psychological interventions or alternative/complementary therapies (NICE, 2006). Patients interested in alternative approaches should be informed that there is no evidence base to support these practices. Further work is needed to validate alternative treatments for OCD.

More work also needs to be done to determine how to best tailor treatment to individual needs. Most studies do not have sufficient power to break down treatment response by OCD subtype. Some subtypes have been studied more than others, and some subtypes are typically excluded from RCTs. Most people with OCD have comorbid disorders, but studies typically exclude participants with substance abuse, psychosis, or bipolar disorder, thus we do not know how effective treatments are for comorbid populations. In terms of ethnic and racial differences, North American RCTs have consisted of predominately European Americans, and OCD in minority populations is not well understood (M. T. Williams et al., 2011). There are also many cultures worldwide for which CBT treatment of OCD has not been tested. These remaining gaps in our knowledge represent an important challenge for future investigation.

REFERENCES

Abramowitz, J. S. (1996). Variants of exposure and response prevention in the treatment of obsessive-compulsive disorder: A meta-analysis. *Behavior Therapy, 27,* 583–600.

Abramowitz, J. S. (2006). The psychological treatment of obsessive-compulsive disorder. *Canadian Journal of Psychiatry, 51,* 407–416.

Abramowitz, J. S., Schwartz, S. A., Franklin, M. E., & Furr, J. M. (2003). Symptom presentation and outcome of cognitive-behavioral therapy for obsessive-compulsive disorder. *Journal of Consulting and Clinical Psychology, 71,* 1049–1057.

American Psychiatric Association (APA). (2000). *Diagnostic and statistical manual for mental disorders* (4th ed., text rev.). Washington, DC: Author.

Antony, M. M., Downie, F., & Swinson, R. P. (1998). Diagnostic issues and epidemiology in obsessive-compulsive disorder. In R. P. Swinson (Ed.), *Obsessive-compulsive disorder: Theory, research, and treatment.* (pp. 30–32). New York, NY: Guilford Press

Antony, M. M., Orsillo, S. M., & Roemer, L. (Eds.). (2001). *Practitioner's guide to empirically based measures of anxiety.* New York, NY: Kluwer.

Baer, L. (2000). *Getting control: Overcoming your obsessions and compulsions (rev. ed.).* New York, NY: Plume.

Brown, T. A., Campbell, L. A., Lehman, C. L., Grisham, J. R., & Mancill, R. B. (2001). Current and lifetime comorbidity of the DSM-IV anxiety and mood disorders in a large clinical sample. *Journal of Abnormal Psychology, 110,* 585–599.

Burns, G. L., Keortge, S. G., Formea, G. M., & Sternberger, L. G. (1996). Revision of the Padua Inventory of obsessive compulsive disorder symptoms: Distinctions between worry, obsessions, and compulsions. *Behaviour Research and Therapy, 34,* 163–173.

Bystritsky, A., Saxena, S., Maidment, K., Vapnik, T., Tarlow, G., & Rosen, R. (1999). Quality-of-life changes among patients with obsessive-compulsive disorder in a partial hospitalization program. *Psychiatric Services, 50,* 412–414.

Calvocoressi, L., Lewis, B., Harris, M., Trufan, S. J., Goodman, W. K., McDougle, C. J., & Price, L. H. (1995). Family accommodation in obsessive compulsive disorder. *American Journal of Psychiatry, 152,* 441–443.

Cordioli, A. V., Heldt, E., Bochi, D. B., Margis, R., De Sousa, M. B., Tonello, J. F., . . . Kapczinski, F. (2003). Cognitive behavioral group therapy in obsessive compulsive disorder: A randomized clinical trial. *Psychotherapy and Psychosomatics, 72,* 211–216.

Cottraux, J., Note, I., Yao, S. N., Lafont, S., Note, B., Mollard, E., . . . Dartigues, J. F. (2001). A randomized controlled trial of cognitive therapy versus intensive behavior therapy in obsessive compulsive disorder. *Psychotherapy and Psychosomatics, 70,* 288–297.

Crino, R. D., & Andrews, G. (1996). Obsessive compulsive disorder and axis I comorbidity. *Journal of Anxiety Disorders, 10,* 37–46.

De Araujo, L. A., Ito, L. M., Marks, I. M., & Deale, A. (1995). Does imagined exposure to the consequences of not ritualising enhance live exposure for OCD? A controlled study I. Main outcome. *British Journal of Psychiatry, 167* (July), 65–70.

Dent, H. R., & Salkovskis, P. M. (1986). Clinical measures of depression, anxiety and obsessionality in non-clinical populations. *Behaviour Research and Therapy, 24,* 689–691.

De Silva, P., & Marks, M. (1999). The role of traumatic experiences in the genesis of obsessive-compulsive disorder. *Behaviour Research and Therapy, 37,* 941–951.

DuPont, R. L., Rice, D. P., Shiraki, S., & Rowland, C. R. (1995). Economic costs of obsessive-compulsive disorder. *Medical interface, 8,* 102–109.

Eddy, K. T., Dutra, L., Bradley, R., & Westen, D. (2004). A multidimensional meta-analysis of psychotherapy and pharmacotherapy for obsessive-

compulsive disorder. *Clinical Psychology Review, 24,* 1011–1030.

Eisen, J. L., & Steketee, G. (1998). Course of illness in obsessive-compulsive disorder. In L. J. Dickstein, M. B. Riba, & J. M. Oldham (Eds.), *Review of psychiatry* (Vol. 16, pp. III/73–III/95). Washington, DC: American Psychiatric Press.

Emmelkamp, P. M. G., & Beens, H. (1991). Cognitive therapy with obsessive-compulsive disorder: A comparative evaluation. *Behaviour Research and Therapy, 29,* 293–300.

Emmelkamp, P. M. G., De Haan, E., & Hoogduin, C. A. L. (1990). Marital adjustment and obsessive-compulsive disorder. *British Journal of Psychiatry, 156,* 55–60.

Emmelkamp, P. M. G., Visser, S., & Hoekstra, R. J. (1988). Cognitive therapy vs exposure in vivo in the treatment of obsessive-compulsives. *Cognitive Therapy and Research, 12,* 103–114.

Foa, E. B., & Goldstein, A. (1978). Continuous exposure and complete response prevention in the treatment of obsessive-compulsive neurosis. *Behavior Therapy, 9,* 821–829.

Foa, E. B., Huppert, J. D., Leiberg, S., Langner, R., Kichic, R., Hajcak, G., & Salkovskis, P. M. (2002). The Obsessive Compulsive Inventory: Development and validation of a short version. *Psychological Assessment, 14,* 485–496.

Foa, E. B., Kozak, M. J., Goodman, W. K., Hollander, E., Jenike, M. A., & Rasmussen, S. A. (1995). DSM-IV field trial: Obsessive compulsive disorder. *American Journal of Psychiatry, 152,* 90–96.

Foa, E. B., Kozak, M. J., Steketee, G. S., & McCarthy, P. R. (1992). Treatment of depressive and obsessive compulsive symptoms in OCD by imipramine and behaviour therapy. *British Journal of Clinical Psychology, 31,* 279–292.

Foa, E. B., Liebowitz, M. R., Kozak, M. J., Davies, S., Campeas, R., Franklin, M. E., . . . Tu, X. (2005). Randomized, placebo-controlled trial of exposure and ritual prevention, clomipramine, and their combination in the treatment of obsessive-compulsive disorder. *American Journal of Psychiatry, 162,* 151–161.

Foa, E. B., Steketee, G., & Grayson, J. B. (1984). Deliberate exposure and blocking of obsessive compulsive rituals: Immediate and long-term effects. *Behavior Therapy, 15,* 450–472.

Foa, E. B., Steketee, G., & Grayson, J. B. (1985). Imaginal and in vivo exposure: A comparison with obsessive compulsive checkers. *Behavior Therapy, 16,* 292–302.

Foa, E. B., Steketee, G., Turner, R. M., & Fischer, S. C. (1980). Effects of imaginal exposure to feared disasters in obsessive-compulsive checkers. *Behaviour Research and Therapy, 18,* 449–455.

Foa, E., & Wilson, R. (2001). *Stop obsessing!* New York, NY: Bantam Books.

Frances, A., Docherty, J. P., & Kahn, D. A. (1997). Treatment of obsessive-compulsive disorder. *Journal of Clinical Psychiatry, 58*(Suppl. 4), 5–72.

Frankl, V. E. (1975). Paradoxical intention and dereflection. *Psychotherapy, 12,* 226–237.

Freeston, M. H., Ladouceur, R., Gagnon, F., Thibodeau, N., Rheaume, J., Letarte, H., & Bujold, A. (1997). Cognitive-behavioral treatment of obsessive thoughts: A controlled study. *Journal of Consulting and Clinical Psychology, 65,* 405–413.

Friedman, S., Hatch, M., Paradis, C. M., Popkin, M., & Shalita, A. R. (1993). Obsessive compulsive disorder in two black ethnic groups: Incidence in an urban dermatology clinic. *Journal of Anxiety Disorders, 7,* 343–348.

Fullana, M. A., Tortella-Feliu, M., Caseras, X., Andión, O., Torrubia, R., & Mataix-Cols, D. (2005). Psychometric properties of the Spanish version of the Obsessive-Compulsive Inventory—Revised in a non-clinical sample. *Journal of Anxiety Disorders, 19,* 893–903.

Gallup. (1990). *A Gallup study of obsessive-compulsive sufferers.* Princeton, NJ: Author.

Gönner, S., Leonhart, R., & Ecker, W. (2007). The German version of the Obsessive-Compulsive Inventory-Revised: A brief self-report measure for the multidimensional assessment of obsessive-compulsive symptoms [*Das zwangsinventar OCI-R—die Deutsche version des Obsessive-Compulsive Inventory-Revised: Ein kurzes selbstbeurteilungsinstrument zur mehrdimensionalen messung von zwanqssymptomen], 57,* 395–404.

Gönner, S., Leonhart, R., & Ecker, W. (2008). The Obsessive-Compulsive Inventory-Revised (OCI-R): Validation of the German version in a sample of patients with OCD, anxiety disorders, and depressive disorders. *Journal of Anxiety Disorders, 22,* 734–749.

Goodman, W. K., Price, L. H., Rasmussen, S. A., Mazure, C., Delgado, P., Heninger, G. R. & Charney, D. S. (1989). The Yale-Brown Obsessive Compulsive Scale. II. Validity. *Archives of General Psychiatry, 46,* 1012–1016.

Goodman, W. K., Price, L. H., Rasmussen, S. A., Mazure, C., Fleischmann, R. L., Hill, C. L., . . . Charney, D. S. (1989). The Yale-Brown Obsessive Compulsive Scale. I. Development, use and reliability. *Archives of General Psychiatry, 46,* 1006–1011.

Grant, J. E., Pinto, A., Gunnip, M., Mancebo, M. C., Eisen, J. L., & Rasmussen, S. A. (2006). Sexual obsessions and clinical correlates in adults with obsessive-compulsive disorder. *Comprehensive Psychiatry, 47,* 325–329.

Greist, J. H., Bandelow, B., Hollander, E., Marazziti, D., Montgomery, S. A., Nutt, D. J., et al. (2002). WCA Recommendations for the long-term treatment of obsessive-compulsive disorder in adults. *CNS Spectrums, 8*(8 Suppl. 1), 7–16.

Greist, J. H., & Jefferson, J. W. (2007). OCD. In G. O. Gabbard (Ed.), *Gabbard's treatments of psychiatric disorders* (4th ed.), (chap. 31). Arlington, VA: American Psychiatric Publishing.

Greist, J. H., Marks, I. M., Baer, L., Kobak, K. A., Wenzel, K. W., Hirsch, M. J., . . . Clary, C. M. (2002). Behavior therapy for obsessive-compulsive disorder guided by a computer or by a clinician compared with relaxation as a control. *Journal of Clinical Psychiatry, 63,* 138–145.

Himle, J. A., Muroff, J. R., Taylor, R. J., Baser, R. E., Abelson, J. M., Hanna, G. L., . . . Jackson, J. S. (2008). Obsessive-compulsive disorder among African Americans and blacks of Caribbean descent: Results from the national survey of American life. *Depression and Anxiety, 25,* 993–1005.

Hodgson, R. J., & Rachman, S. (1977). Obsessional-compulsive complaints. *Behaviour Research and Therapy, 15,* 389–395.

Hudson, J. I., & Pope, H. G. (1987). Depression and eating disorders. In O. G. Cameron (Ed.), *Presentations of depression: Depressive symptoms in medical and other psychiatric disorders* (pp. 33–66). Oxford, England: Wiley.

James, I. A., & Blackburn, I. M. (1995). Cognitive therapy with obsessive-compulsive disorder. *British Journal of Psychiatry, 166,* 444–450.

Jenike, M. A. (1983). Obsessive compulsive disorder. *Comprehensive Psychiatry, 24,* 99–115.

Kasvikis, Y. G., Tsakiris, F., & Marks, I. M. (1986). Past history of anorexia nervosa in women with obsessive-compulsive disorder. *International Journal of Eating Disorders, 5,* 1069–1075.

Kennedy, B. L., & Schwab, J. J. (1997). Utilization of medical specialists by anxiety disorder patients. *Psychosomatics, 38,* 109–112.

Kessler, R. C., Berglund, P., Demler, O., Jin, R., Merikangas, K. R., & Walters, E. E. (2005). Lifetime prevalence and age-of-onset distributions of DSM-IV disorders in the National Comorbidity Survey Replication. *Archives of General Psychiatry, 62,* 593–602.

Kessler, R. C., Chiu, W. T., Demler, O., Merikangas, K. R., & Walters, E. E. (2005). Prevalence, severity, and comorbidity of 12-month DSM-IV disorders in the National Comorbidity Survey Replication. *Archives of General Psychiatry, 62,* 617–627.

Kolada, J. L., Bland, R. C., & Newman, S. C. (1994). Epidemiology of psychiatric disorders in Edmonton. Obsessive-compulsive disorder. *Acta Psychiatrica Scandinavica Supplement, 376,* 24–35.

Koran, L. M. (2000). Quality of life in obsessive-compulsive disorder. *Psychiatric Clinics of North America, 23,* 509–517.

Koran, L. M., Thienemann, M. L., & Davenport, R. (1996). Quality of life for patients with obsessive-compulsive disorder. *American Journal of Psychiatry*, *153*, 783–788.

Kozak, M. J., & Foa, E. B. (1996). Obsessive compulsive disorder. In V. B. V. Hasselt & M. Hersen (Eds.), *Sourcebook of psychological treatment manuals for adult disorders* (pp. 65–122). New York, NY: Plenum Press.

Ladouceur, R., Freeston, M. H., Rhéaume, J., Dugas, M. J., Gagnon, F., Thibodeau, N., & Fournier, S. (2000). Strategies used with intrusive thoughts: A comparison of OCD patients with anxious and community controls. *Journal of Abnormal Psychology*, *109*, 179–187.

Lam, R. W., Michalak, E. E., & Swinson, R. P. (2005). *Assessment scales in depression, mania, and anxiety*. London, England: Taylor & Francis.

Lam, J. N., & Steketee, G. S. (2001). Reducing obsessions and compulsions through behaviour therapy. *Psychoanalytic Inquiry*, *21*, 157–182.

Leon, A. C., Portera, L., & Weissman, M. M. (1995). The social costs of anxiety disorders. *British Journal of Psychiatry, Supplement, April* (27), 19–22.

Lim, J. S., Kim, S. J., Jeon, W. T., Cha, K. R., Park, J. H., & Kim, C. H. (2008). Reliability and validity of the Korean version of Obsessive-Compulsive Inventory-Revised in a non-clinical sample. *Yonsei Medical Journal*, *49*, 909–916.

Lindsay, M., Crino, R., & Andrews, G. (1997). Controlled trial of exposure and response prevention in obsessive-compulsive disorder. *British Journal of Psychiatry*, *171*, 135–139.

Lopez, A. D., & Murray, C. C. J. L. (1998). The global burden of disease, 1990–2020. *Nature Medicine*, *4*, 1241–1243.

Lucey, J. V., Butcher, G., Clare, A. W., & Dinan, T. G. (1994). The clinical characteristics of patients with obsessive-compulsive disorder: A descriptive study of an Irish sample. *Irish Journal of Psychological Medicine*, *11*, 11–14.

MacDonald, P. A., Antony, M. M., Macleod, C. M., & Richter, M. A. (1997). Memory and confidence in memory judgements among individuals with obsessive-compulsive disorder and non-clinical controls. *Behaviour Research and Therapy*, *35*, 497–505.

Marks, I., Hodgson, R., & Rachman, S. (1975). Treatment of chronic obsessive-compulsive neurosis by in-vivo exposure. *British Journal of Psychiatry*, *127*, 349–364.

Marks, I. M., Lelliott, P., Basoglu, M., Noshirvani, H., Monteiro, W., Cohen, D., & Kasvikis, Y. (1988). Clomipramine, self-exposure and therapist-aided exposure for obsessive-compulsive rituals. *British Journal of Psychiatry*, *152*, 522–534.

Marks, I. M., Stern, R. S., Mawson, D., Cobb, J., & McDonald, R. (1980). Clomipramine and exposure for obsessive-compulsive rituals. *British Journal of Psychiatry*, *136*, 1–25.

Marques, L., LeBlanc, N. J., Weingarden, H. M., Timpano, K. R., Jenike, M., & Wilhelm, S. (2010). Barriers to treatment and service utilization in an Internet sample of individuals with obsessive-compulsive symptoms. *Depression and Anxiety*, *27*, 470–475. doi: 10.1002/da.20694

Mastellone, M. (1974). Aversion therapy: A new use for the old rubber band. *Journal of Behavior Therapy and Experimental Psychiatry*, *5*, 311–312.

McKay, D., Danyko, S., Neziroglu, F., & Yaryura-Tobias, J. A. (1995). Factor structure of the Yale-Brown obsessive-compulsive scale: A two dimensional measure. *Behaviour Research and Therapy*, *33*, 865–869.

McLean, P. D., Whittal, M. L., Thordarson, D. S., Taylor, S., Sochting, I., Koch, W. J., . . . Anderson, K. W. (2001). Cognitive versus behavior therapy in the group treatment of obsessive-compulsive disorder. *Journal of Consulting and Clinical Psychology*, *69*, 205–214.

McNally, R. J., & Kohlbeck, P. A. (1993). Reality monitoring in obsessive-compulsive disorder. *Behaviour Research and Therapy*, *31*, 249–253.

Mehta, M. (1990). A comparative study of family-based and patient-based behavioural management in obsessive-compulsive disorder. *British Journal of Psychiatry*, *157*, 133–135.

Meyer, V. (1966). Modification of expectations in cases with obsessional rituals. *Behaviour Research and Therapy*, *4*, 273–280.

Meyer, V., Levy, R., & Schnurer, A. (1974). A behavioral treatment of obsessive-compulsive disorders. In H. R. Beech (Ed.), *Obsessional states* (pp. 233–258). London, England: Methuen.

Modell, J. G., Glaser, F. B., Cyr, L., & Mountz, J. M. (1992). Obsessive and compulsive characteristics of craving for alcohol in alcohol abuse and dependence. *Alcoholism: Clinical and Experimental Research*, *16*, 272–274.

Monahan, P., Black, D. W., & Gabel, J. (1996). Reliability and validity of a scale to measure change in persons with compulsive buying. *Psychiatry Research*, *64*, 59–67.

Nakatani, E., Nakagawa, A., Nakao, T., Yoshizato, C., Nabeyama, M., Kudo, A., . . . Kawamoto, M. (2005). A randomized controlled trial of Japanese patients with obsessive-compulsive disorder: Effectiveness of behavior therapy and fluvoxamine. *Psychotherapy and Psychosomatics*, *74*, 269–276.

National Institute for Health and Clinical Excellence (NICE). (2006). *Obsessive-compulsive disorder: Core interventions in the treatment of obsessive-compulsive disorder and body dysmorphic disorder*. The British Psychological Society & The Royal College of Psychiatrists. Retrieved www.nice.org.uk

Nydegger, R. V., & Paludi, M. (2006). Obsessive-compulsive disorder. In T. Plante (Ed.), *Mental disorders of the new millennium* (pp. 101–135). New York, NY: Praeger.

Pallanti, S. (2008). Transcultural observations of obsessive-compulsive disorder. *American Journal of Psychiatry 165*, 169–170.

Phillips, K. A., Hollander, E., Rasmussen, S. A., Aronowitz, B. R., DeCaria, C., & Goodman, W. K. (1997). A severity rating scale for body dysmorphic disorder: Development, reliability, and validity of a modified version of the Yale-Brown obsessive compulsive scale. *Psychopharmacology Bulletin, 33*, 17–22.

Quality Assurance Project of Australia (QAP). (1985). Treatment outlines for the management of obsessive-compulsive disorders. The quality assurance project. *Australian and New Zealand Journal of Psychiatry, 19*, 240–253.

Rachman, S. (1997). A cognitive theory of obsessions. *Behaviour Research and Therapy, 35*, 793–802.

Rachman, S., & De Silva, P. (1978). Abnomral and normal obsessions. *Behaviour Research and Therapy, 16*, 233–248.

Rachman, S., Hodgson, R., & Marks, I. M. (1971). The treatment of chronic obsessive-compulsive neurosis. *Behaviour Research and Therapy, 9*, 237–247.

Rasmussen, S. A., & Eisen, J. L. (1990). Epidemiology of obsessive compulsive disorder. *Journal of Clinical Psychiatry, 51*(Suppl.), 10–13.

Rasmussen, S. A., & Tsuang, M. T. (1986). Clinical characteristics and family history in DSM-III obsessive-compulsive disorder. *American Journal of Psychiatry, 143*, 317–322.

Rheaume, J., Freeston, M. H., Léger, E., & Ladouceur, R. (1998). Bad luck: An underestimated factor in the development of obsessive-compulsive disorder. *Clinical Psychology and Psychotherapy, 5*, 1–12.

Richter, M. A., Cox, B. J., & Direnfeld, D. M. (1994). A comparison of three assessment instruments for obsessive-compulsive symptoms. *Journal of Behavior Therapy and Experimental Psychiatry, 25*, 143–147.

Riggs, D. S., Hiss, H., & Foa, E. B. (1992). Marital distress and the treatment of obsessive compulsive disorder. *Behavior Therapy, 23*, 585–597.

Rosa-Alcázar, A. I., Sánchez-Meca, J., Gómez-Conesa, A., & Marín-Martínez, F. (2008). Psychological treatment of obsessive-compulsive disorder: A meta-analysis. *Clinical Psychology Review, 28*, 1310–1325.

Rosenfeld, R., Dar, R., Anderson, D., Kobak, K. A., & Greist, J. H. (1992). A computer-administered version of the Yale-Brown obsessive-compulsive scale. *Psychological Assessment, 4*, 329–332.

Ruscio, A. M., Stein, D. J., Chiu, W. T., & Kessler, R. C. (2010). The epidemiology of obsessive-compulsive disorder in the national comorbidity survey replication. *Molecular Psychiatry, 15*, 53–63.

Salkovskis, P. M., & Harrison, J. (1984). Abnormal and normal obsessions—A replication. *Behaviour Research and Therapy, 22*, 549–552.

Salzman, L., & Thaler, F. H. (1981). Obsessive-compulsive disorders: A review of the literature. *American Journal of Psychiatry, 138*, 286–296.

Sanavio, E. (1988). Obsessions and compulsions: The Padua inventory. *Behaviour Research and Therapy, 26*, 169–177.

Scahill, L., Riddle, M. A., McSwiggin-Hardin, M., Ort, S. I., King, R. A., Goodman, W. K., . . . Leckman, J. F. (1997). Children's Yale-Brown Obsessive Compulsive Scale: Reliability and validity. *Journal of the American Academy of Child & Adolescent Psychiatry, 36*, 844–852.

Shannahoff-Khalsa, D. S., Ray, L. E., Levine, S., Gallen, C. C., Schwartz, B. J., & Sidorowich, J. J. (1999). Randomized controlled trial of yogic meditation techniques for patients with obsessive-compulsive disorder. *CNS Spectrums, 4*, 34–47.

Sica, C., Ghisi, M., Altoè, G., Chiri, L. R., Franceschini, S., Coradeschi, D., & Melli, G. (2009). The Italian version of the obsessive compulsive inventory: Its psychometric properties on community and clinical samples. *Journal of Anxiety Disorders, 23*, 204–211.

Simpson, H. B., Foa, E. B., Liebowitz, M. R., Ledley, D. R., Huppert, J. D., Cahill, S., . . . Petkova, E. (2008). A randomized, controlled trial of cognitive-behavioral therapy for augmenting pharmacotherapy in obsessive-compulsive disorder. *American Journal of Psychiatry, 165*, 621–630.

Simpson, H. B., Rosen, W., Huppert, J. D., Lin, S. H., Foa, E. B., & Liebowitz, M. R. (2006). Are there reliable neuropsychological deficits in obsessive-compulsive disorder? *Journal of Psychiatric Research, 40*, 247–257.

Smárt, J., Ólason, D. T., Eypórsdóttir, Á., & Frölunde, M. B. (2007). Psychometric properties of the obsessive compulsive inventory-revised among Icelandic college students. *Scandinavian Journal of Psychology, 48*, 127–133.

Stanley, M. A., Prather, R. C., Wagner, A. L., Davis, M. L., & Swann, A. C. (1993). Can the Yale-Brown obsessive compulsive scale be used to assess trichotillomania? A preliminary report. *Behaviour Research and Therapy, 31*, 171–177.

Steketee, G., Eisen, J., Dyck, I., Warshaw, M., & Rasmussen, S. (1999). Predictors of course in obsessive compulsive disorder. *Psychiatry Research, 89*, 229–238.

Steketee, G., Grayson, J. B., & Foa, E. B. (1987). A comparison of characteristics of obsessive-compulsive disorder and other anxiety disorders. *Journal of Anxiety Disorders, 1*, 325–335.

Stern, R. S. (1978). Obsessive thoughts: The problem of therapy. *British Journal of Psychiatry, 133*, 200–205.

Storch, E. A., Rasmussen, S. A., Price, L. H., Larson, M. J., Murphy, T. K., & Goodman, W. K. (2010). Development and psychometric evaluation of the

Yale-Brown Obsessive-Compulsive Scale—Second Edition. *Psychological Assessment, 22*, 223–232.

Thomas, J., Turkheimer, E., & Oltmanns, T. F. (2000). Psychometric analysis of racial differences on the Maudsley obsessional compulsive inventory. *Assessment, 7*, 247–258.

Van Balkom, A. J., de Haan, E., van Oppen, P., Spinhoven, P., Hoogduin, K. A., & van Dyck, R. (1998). Cognitive and behavioral therapies alone versus in combination with fluvoxamine in the treatment of obsessive compulsive disorder. *Journal of Nervous & Mental Disease, 186*, 492–499.

Van Oppen, P., Hoekstra, R. J., & Emmelkamp, P. M. G. (1995). The structure of obsessive-compulsive symptoms. *Behaviour Research and Therapy, 33*, 15–23.

Vogel, P. A., Stiles, T. C., & Gotestam, K. G. (2004). Adding cognitive therapy elements to exposure therapy for obsessive compulsive disorder: A controlled study. *Behavioural and Cognitive Psychotherapy, 32*, 275–290.

Washington, C. S., Norton, P. J., & Temple, S. (2008). Obsessive-compulsive symptoms and obsessive-compulsive disorder: A multiracial/ethnic analysis of a student population. *Journal of Nervous and Mental Disease, 196*, 456–461.

Wegner, D. M., Schneider, D. J., Carter, S., & White, T. (1987). Paradoxical effects of thought suppression. *Journal of Personality and Social Psychology, 53*, 5–13.

Weissman, M. M., Bland, R. C., Canino, G. J., Greenwald, S., Hwu, H. G., Chung Kyoon, L., . . . Yeh, E. K. (1994). The cross national epidemiology of obsessive compulsive disorder: The Cross National Collaborative Group. *Journal of Clinical Psychiatry, 55*(3 Suppl.), 5–10.

Williams, M. T., Farris, S. G., Turkheimer, E., Pinto, A., Ozanick, K., Franklin, M. E., . . . Foa, E. B. (2011). The myth of the pure obsessional type in obsessive-compulsive disorder. *Depression & Anxiety, 28*, 495–500.

Williams, M. T., & Turkheimer, E. (2007). Identification and explanation of racial differences in measures of contamination anxiety. *Behaviour Research and Therapy, 45*, 3041–3050.

Williams, M. T., Turkheimer, E., Schmidt, K., & Oltmanns, T. (2005). Ethnic identification biases responses to the Padua Inventory for obsessive-compulsive disorder. *Assessment, 12*, 174–185.

Williams, M., Yun, Y. G., Powers, M. B., & Foa, E. B. (2010). Minority representation in clinical trials for obsessive-compulsive disorder. *Journal of Anxiety Disorders, 24*, 171–177.

Wisner, K. L., Peindl, K. S., Gigliotti, T., & Hanusa, B. H. (1999). Obsessions and compulsions in women with postpartum depression. *Journal of Clinical Psychiatry, 60*, 176–180.

Wolpe, J. (1969). *The practice of behavior therapy* (1st ed.). New York, NY: Pergamon Press.

Zermatten, A., Van der Linden, M., Jermann, F., & Ceschi, G. (2006). Validation of a French version of the obsessive compulsive inventory revised in a non clinical sample. *Revue Europeene de Psychologie Appliquee, 56*, 151–155.

14

Posttraumatic Stress and Acute Stress Disorders

MARK B. POWERS, NISHA NAYAK, SHAWN P. CAHILL, AND EDNA B. FOA

POSTTRAUMATIC STRESS AND ACUTE STRESS DISORDERS

In this chapter, we discuss the nature, causes, and treatment of posttraumatic stress and acute stress disorders. For each disorder, we will discuss the following: a brief description of the disorder, a brief description of each treatment, treatment guidelines and consensus panel recommendations, randomized controlled trials (RCTs), meta analyses, and then summarize evidence based practice associated with the available data. We only cover those treatments with a significant literature.

POSTTRAUMATIC STRESS DISORDER

Diagnostic Criteria

Posttraumatic stress disorder (PTSD) was included for the first time in the third edition of the *Diagnostic and Statistical Manual of Mental Disorders (DSM III)* (American Psychiatric Association [APA], 1980). Posttraumatic stress disorder consists of symptom clusters with affective, cognitive, and behavioral components that some individuals develop in reaction to a traumatic event and that are associated with distress and impairment in functioning. According to the *DSM IV*

(APA, 1994), the traumatic experience must meet the following criteria: first, the person "experienced, witnessed, or was confronted with an event or events that involved actual or threatened death or serious injury, or a threat to the physical integrity of self or others" (Criterion A1); and, second, the person responded with "intense fear, helplessness, or horror" (Criterion A2) (APA, 1994, pp. 427 428). This definition contrasts with the previous conceptualization of a trauma in *DSM III R* as a rare event "outside the range of usual human experience" (APA, 1987). Another notable feature of this definition of trauma is that psychological harm alone does not satisfy Criterion A1. Rather, actual or threatened harm to one's physical being must have been present at the time of the trauma. Examples of events that would meet Criterion A1 include, but are not limited to, a serious accident, a natural disaster, a sexual or physical assault, being threatened with a weapon or violence, childhood physical or sexual abuse, military combat, exposure to a war zone, imprisonment, torture, or diagnosis with a life threatening illness. Although verbal, emotional, or psychological abuse often produces negative psychological effects, the abuse may or may not meet the Criterion A1 definition of trauma depending on the case. For example, if such abuse conveyed physical threat because of explicit statements or behavior or the victim's perception, then the abuse could meet the *DSM-IV* definition of a traumatic experience. In contrast, childhood sexual abuse is judged as a traumatic experience, even if Criteria A1 and A2 technically are not met.

The *DSM-IV* groups PTSD symptoms into three clusters: reexperiencing, avoidance/numbing, and hyperarousal. To receive a PTSD diagnosis, individuals must show symptoms in each category. First, he or she must have at least one symptom of reexperiencing, such as distressing memories of the trauma, nightmares, flashbacks, or emotional or physical reactivity to trauma reminders. Second, three or more symptoms of avoidance or numbing are necessary, as indicated by attempts to avoid trauma-related thoughts or feelings, attempts to avoid trauma-related activities and situations, inability to recall important parts of the trauma, diminished interest in activities, feelings of detachment from others, restricted range of affect, or sense of a foreshortened future. Finally, a PTSD diagnosis requires the presence of two or more hyperarousal symptoms, such as difficulty falling or staying asleep, irritability, difficulty concentrating, hypervigilance, and exaggerated startle response.

Factor analytic studies have raised questions about the validity of the three-cluster symptom structure for PTSD that is codified in the *DSM*. While early exploratory factor analysis (EFA) studies of PTSD measures differed in the number and order of factors, a consistent finding was that numbing symptoms clustered with hyperarousal symptoms rather than with avoidance symptoms (Foa, Riggs, & Gershuny, 1995; Taylor, Koch, Kuch, Crockett, & Passey, 1998). This factor structure contrasts with that presented in the *DSM*. Several subsequent confirmatory factor analysis (CFA) studies provided strong support for a four-factor model, with numbing emerging as a separate factor from both avoidance and hyperarousal (Asmundson et al., 2000; Cox, Mota, Clara, & Asmundson, 2008; King,

Leskin, King, & Weathers, 1998; Naifeh, Elhai, Kashdan, & Grubaugh, 2008). A different four-factor model that includes a dysphoria factor (i.e., numbing symptoms clustered with nonspecific symptoms, such as insomnia and concentration difficulties) and a PTSD-specific arousal factor (e.g., hypervigilance, exaggerated startle) has also received some support (Krause, Kaltman, Goodman, & Dutton, 2007; Simms, Watson, & Doebbeling, 2002.). Although questions still remain regarding the precise factor structure of PTSD symptoms, a fairly robust finding is that avoidance and numbing fall into separate clusters rather than a single one as represented by the *DSM-IV* model (Asmundson, Stapleton, & Taylor, 2004).

Duration is another element of the PTSD diagnosis, which requires that the disturbance is present for greater than one month. PTSD is specified as chronic if the symptoms persist longer than three months. Although most individuals who develop significant posttraumatic stress symptoms will initially develop them shortly after the trauma, *DSM* does permit specification of PTSD with delayed onset in cases where symptom onset occurs six months or more after the traumatic event. As in the case of all mental disorders, PTSD symptoms must cause significant distress or impairment in social, occupational, or other areas of functioning.

Exposure to a traumatic event is a necessary but not sufficient condition for this diagnosis, as the majority of persons exposed to trauma will not go on to develop clinical traumatic stress reaction. Whereas the estimated prevalence of lifetime trauma is as high as 81.7% (Sledjeski, Speisman, & Dierker, 2008), the lifetime prevalence of PTSD is much lower at 6.7% (Kessler, Berglund, et al., 2005). Nevertheless, significant distress following a trauma is very common. One study of rape victims showed that 94% of the sample met symptom criteria for PTSD immediately after the trauma (Mean = 12.64 days postassault) (data from Rothbaum, Foa, Riggs, Murdock, &

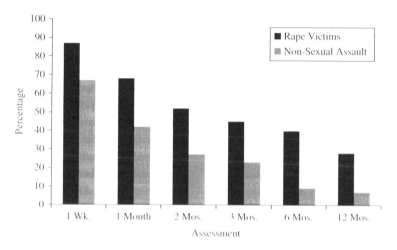

Figure 14.1   Percent of Participants With PTSD Symptoms as a Function of Time Since Attempted or Completed Rape

Source: "A Prospective Examination of Post Traumatic Stress Disorder in Rape Victims," by B. Rothbaum, E. Foa, D. Riggs, T. Murdock, and W. Walsh, 1992, *Journal of Traumatic Stress,* 5, pp. 455–475.

Walsh, 1992). This rate fell to 65%, 47%, 42%, and 30% at 1 month, 3 months, 9 months, and 12 months postassault respectively. The interpretation of these results is limited by participant attrition and use of a convenience sample. Other studies have yielded consistent findings of lower rates of persistent PTSD, ranging from 11% to 23%, at one or more years posttrauma (Duggan & Gunn, 1995; Mayou, Ehlers, & Bryant, 2002). These results point to the natural recovery process that often occurs after a trauma.

The findings described earlier and illustrated in Figure 14.1 highlight two key points. First, it is the rule rather than the exception to experience PTSD symptoms following sexual assault. Second, cases of natural recovery largely occur in the first 3 months posttrauma. The 1 month duration criterion precludes diagnosing an individual with PTSD within the first month after a trauma. A primary reason for this requirement is to avoid pathologizing normal and temporary responses to traumatic experiences.

Demographic Variables

Next, we examine demographic variables associated with PTSD. Because past experience of a criterion trauma is a requisite feature of PTSD, demographic variables associated with both trauma exposure and persistent PTSD symptoms are considered below.

Sex. Reliable sex differences have been observed for both PTSD and trauma exposure. Women and girls are nearly twice as likely to meet criteria for PTSD (Kessler, Sonnega, Bromet, Hughes, & Nelson, 1995; Olff, Langeland, Draijer, & Gersons, 2007; Tolin & Foa, 2006.) This difference cannot be accounted for by overall rates of trauma exposure as studies have shown that exposure to trauma is more commonly reported by males (Kessler et al., 1995; Norris, 1992). Women endorse higher rates of lifetime sexual assault and childhood sexual molestation (Breslau, 2002; Hatch & Dohrenwend, 2007), suggesting trauma type could account for the difference; however, women are still more likely to meet criteria for PTSD even after event type is controlled (Breslau, 2002; Tolin & Foa, 2006). Women appear to have a significantly greater conditional risk of developing PTSD after trauma exposure (13.0% vs. 6.2%) (Breslau, Chilcoat, Kessler, Peterson, & Lucia, 1999; Breslau et al., 1998). In particular, the sex difference appears due to women's greater risk of developing PTSD following assaultive violence, which may sensitize women to the impact of subsequent trauma (Breslau & Anthony, 2007; Breslau et al., 1999).

Race/ethnicity. Racial/ethnic minority status has been cited as a risk factor for both trauma exposure and PTSD. Studies in the United States and other Western countries have indicated that members of minority groups are more likely to experience trauma (Breslau, 2002; Flett, Kazantzis, Long, MacDonald, & Millar, 2004). Whereas some earlier results found lifetime prevalence of trauma to be lower among African Americans (Breslau, Davis, Andreski, & Peterson, 1991), later work, including both prospective and cross-sectional studies, found that the likelihood of trauma exposure was higher among non-Whites (Breslau, Davis, & Andreski, 1995; Breslau et al., 1998). With respect to PTSD, higher rates of PTSD have been observed among ethnic minorities, but these differences did not persist after controlling for socio-demographic variables such as SES and residential area (Breslau et al., 1998; Kessler et al., 1995). Moreover, results from the more recent National Comorbidity Study Replication (NCS-R) revealed no significant differences in lifetime prevalence of PTSD across different race-ethnic groups (J. Breslau et al., 2006). It is noteworthy that results from the National Vietnam Veterans Readjustment Study found higher rates of combat-related PTSD in theater veterans among Hispanic soldiers, and this heightened risk persisted even after controlling for premilitary and military risk factors (Kulka et al., 1990; Ortega & Rosenheck, 2000). A similar difference was observed among a sample of urban police officers, with Hispanic officers reporting significantly more PTSD symptoms (Pole et al., 2001).

Age. Another reliable finding is that risk of trauma exposure changes across the life span (Hatch & Dohrenwend, 2007). Traumatic experiences increase over the course of childhood, reaching a peak during late adolescence to early adulthood for many trauma types and then decrease with further age (Breslau et al., 1998; Norris, 1992). After age 20, the risk of

most classes of trauma, including assaultive violence, declines substantially, except for sudden unexpected death of a loved one, which has a sustained chance of occurrence through one's forties (Breslau et al., 1998). The relation between PTSD and age is less clear. Based on results from the NCS-R, those who meet criteria for PTSD tend to be significantly younger than those with trauma but no PTSD or those without trauma history (Kessler, Berglund, et al., 2005). In military personnel, age is confounded with cohort effects related to the war zone or theater experience, thus results must be interpreted with caution. Still, the oldest cohort of veterans in a VA sample (i.e., age 65 and older) showed significantly lower rates of PTSD, despite greater likelihood of combat exposure and even after adjusting for race and sex (Frueh et al., 2007). Another interesting age-related finding is that, at least for sexual assault among women, one study found that younger age of assault was associated with greater risk of PTSD in a dose-response fashion (Masho & Ahmed, 2007).

Impact of Disorder

As previously noted, traumatic experiences are common, putting many individuals at risk for developing a traumatic stress reaction. Earlier studies, based on *DSM-III-R* criteria, reported rates of trauma exposure of 40%–70%, and lifetime prevalence of PTSD of 5%–6% in men and 10%–14% in women (Breslau, 2002). For example, the first National Comorbidity Survey (NCS) found trauma exposure rates of 60 to 70% and lifetime rates of PTSD for women and men of 10.4% and 5%, respectively (Breslau, 1998; Kessler et al., 1995). More recent research using the *DSM-IV* and its expanded trauma definition has yielded higher lifetime PTSD prevalence estimates of 18.3% in women and 10.2% in men (Breslau et al., 1998; Olff et al., 2007); however, the NCS-R study also used the *DSM-IV* and yielded a somewhat lower overall lifetime prevalence figure of 6.8%, perhaps because its large nationally representative sample included older respondents and was more geographically diverse than the original NCS (Kessler, Berglund, et al., 2005).

Compared to individuals without PTSD, even those with another psychiatric diagnosis, individuals with PTSD are more likely to have other current or past psychiatric diagnoses, with lifetime psychiatric comorbidity rates on the order of 80% (Fairbank, Ebert, & Caddell, 2001). The disorder shows significant comorbidity with various mood and anxiety disorders, and lower but still significant overlap with alcohol abuse and dependence (Alonso et al., 2004a; Kessler, Chiu, et al., 2005). In the initial NCS, nearly 50% of participants who reported lifetime PTSD also reported a history of depression (Kessler et al., 1995). In a separate study, 32% of women with current PTSD met criteria for major depression compared to only 4% of women without PTSD (Kilpatrick, Resnick, Saunders, & Best, 1998).

Other major burdens of PTSD are economic effects and associated functional impairment. The economic burden takes the form of both increased cost of care, unemployment, and lost wages. Analyses of large databases indicate that, after controlling for other factors, PTSD was associated with a nearly $4,000 increase in total lifetime medical costs per patient (Marciniak et al., 2005). Studies in veterans have shown that both PTSD diagnosis and symptom severity are negatively related to employment, with PTSD associated with over 3 times greater chance of unemployment in some samples (Smith, Schnurr, & Rosenheck, 2005; Zatzick et al., 1997). Even when working, veterans with a lifetime diagnosis of PTSD had a significantly reduced hourly wage (Savoca & Rosenheck, 2000). Similarly, in a large scale population study, PTSD diagnosis predicted greater work days lost and poorer mental and physical quality of life, even after controlling for age, sex, and comorbidity (Alonso et al., 2004b). PTSD can also have a profound effect on interpersonal functioning, with a recent review by Galovski and Lyons (2004)

demonstrating the negative impact of combat-related PTSD on relationship distress and dissolution and parenting abilities (Galovski & Lyons, 2004).

Finally, the deleterious effects of PTSD on physical health and negative health behaviors are being increasingly recognized. A recent study reported that nontraumatized, traumatized, and PTSD groups each had incrementally greater risk for a number of chronic medical diseases, including chronic pain conditions and heart disease (Sledjeski et al., 2008). Consistent with this evidence, a wide literature indicates that PTSD is associated with disturbances in cardiovascular, gastrointestinal, neuroendocrine, and immune function (Stam, 2007). PTSD is associated with greater odds of lifetime and current smoking, which may partly account for its negative impact on health (Feldner, Babson, & Zvolensky, 2007; Fu et al., 2007). Biological studies suggest that the dysregulation of the hypothalamic-pituitary-adrenal axis (HPA axis) in PTSD, including hypersecretion of cortisol, may be associated with age related memory impairments (Yehuda et al., 2005).

Posttraumatic Stress Disorder Treatment

Currently, cognitive behavior therapy (CBT) is the treatment of choice for chronic PTSD. Cognitive behavior therapy is not a simple technique but rather a broad approach that includes a range of techniques, the goals of which are to reduce the intensity and frequency of distressing negative emotional reactions, modify erroneous cognitions, and promote functioning. The CBT programs for PTSD include variants of exposure therapy, stress inoculation training (SIT), and cognitive therapy (CT). Each of these programs has been administered by itself or in combination with one another. A fourth treatment for PTSD that has received empirical support is eye movement desensitization and reprocessing (EMDR) (Shapiro, 1995), a treatment that utilizes elements of exposure and cognitive restructuring but with the addition of therapist-directed rapid eye movements or other bilateral stimuli. Two recent innovations in the treatment of PTSD are the application of imagery rehearsal therapy to PTSD-related nightmares (Krakow & Zadra, 2006) and the use of technology, such as virtual reality technology (Powers & Emmelkamp, 2008) and delivery of therapy via the Internet. As the research on these more recent treatments is relatively limited they will not be further discussed in this chapter.

Exposure therapy. As described previously, PTSD is characterized by the reexperiencing of the traumatic event and attempts to ward off the intrusive symptoms or avoid the trauma-reminders, even when such trigger stimuli are not inherently dangerous. Given these two broad categories of feared stimuli (the traumatic memories and triggers that are reminders of the trauma), the core components of exposure programs for the disorder are (1) imaginal exposure, which involves revisiting the traumatic memory, repeated recounting it aloud, and processing the revisiting experience; and (2) in vivo exposure, which involves the repeated confrontation of trauma-related situations and objects that evoke excessive anxiety but are not inherently dangerous. The goal of this treatment is to promote processing of the trauma memory (Foa, Huppert, & Cahill, 2006) and to reduce distress and avoidance elicited by the trauma reminders. Additionally, individuals with pronounced symptoms of emotional numbing and depression are encouraged to engage in pleasurable activities even if these activities do not elicit fear or anxiety but instead have dropped out of the person's repertoire due to loss of interest (Foa, Hembree, & Rothbaum, 2007). The rationale for this latter component is similar to the use of behavioral activation strategies in treatment of depression (Martell, Addis, & Jacobson, 2001).

Exposure therapy programs that have been evaluated in RCT differ in the type of exposure techniques used, how they are implemented,

and what other nonexposure techniques are utilized. For example, some researchers have relied exclusively on imaginal exposure (Bryant, Moulds, Guthrie, Dang, & Nixon, 2003; Keane, Fairbank, Caddell, & Zimering, 1989; Tarrier et al., 1999), whereas others have relied exclusively on in vivo exposure (Basoglu, Salcioglu, Livanou, Kalender, & Acar, 2005). By contrast, the prolonged exposure (PE) program developed by Foa and colleagues (Foa et al., 1999; Foa et al., 2005; Foa et al., 2007; Foa, Rothbaum, Riggs, & Murdock, 1991; Resick, Nishith, Weaver, Astin, & Feuer, 2002; Rothbaum, Astin, & Marsteller, 2005; Rothbaum et al., 2006; Schnurr et al., 2007) and a similar program developed by Marks and colleagues (Marks, Lovell, Noshirvani, Livanou, & Thrasher, 1998; Richards, Lovell, & Marks, 1994; Taylor et al., 2003) utilized both imaginal and in vivo techniques. Exposure therapy programs also differ in the extent to which exposure techniques are the primary focus in therapy, such as the programs developed by Foa and colleagues and Marks and colleagues, or are substantially supplemented with other CBT techniques such as stress inoculation and CT procedures, such as the CBT program developed by Blanchard, Hickling, and colleagues (Blanchard et al., 2003; Hickling & Blanchard, 1997; Maercker, Zollner, Menning, Rabe, & Karl, 2006). In some CBT programs, such as Resick's cognitive processing therapy program (discussed in greater detail later) and the Blanchard and Hickling program just mentioned, exposure to the trauma memory is implemented through narrative writing exercises.

Stress inoculation training. Veronen and Kilpatrick (1983) adopted Meichenbaum's (1974) SIT approach for the treatment of PTSD symptoms in female rape victims (Meichenbaum, 1974; Veronen & Kilpatrick, 1983). As applied to PTSD, SIT includes education about trauma-related symptoms plus anxiety management techniques such as controlled breathing and relaxation training, cognitive restructuring, guided (task enhancing) self-dialogue, assertiveness training, role-playing, covert modeling, and thought-stopping. Once the various techniques have been introduced, the therapist and patient work together to select and implement the techniques in a flexible manner to address the patient's current concerns or specific symptoms. As with exposure therapy, SIT programs vary from one another, with the most notable difference being that some programs include an exposure component (Veronen & Kilpatrick, 1983) whereas others do not (Foa et al., 1999; Foa et al., 1991). Although interest in the study of SIT for PTSD has diminished in recent years, one innovative use of SIT has been to target anger among veterans with chronic PTSD and significant anger problems (Chemtob, Hamada, Novaco, & Gross, 1997).

Cognitive therapy. CT for PTSD is derived from Beck's model of treatment for depression (A. T. Beck, Rush, Shaw, & Emery, 1979) and its extension to anxiety (A. T. Beck, Emery, & Greenberg, 1985), wherein the goal of therapy is help patients identify trauma related dysfunctional beliefs that influence emotional and behavioral responses to a situation (Marks et al., 1998; Tarrier et al., 1999). Once identified, patients are taught to evaluate the thoughts in a logical, evidence based manner. Information that supports or refutes the belief is examined as are alternative ways of interpreting the problematic situation. The therapist helps patients to weigh the evidence and consider alternative interpretations before deciding whether the belief accurately reflects reality, and if not, to replace or modify it. The CT programs differ in the length and number of sessions. Moreover, some CT programs include an exposure component, such as Resick's cognitive processing therapy (CPT) (Resick et al., 2002; Resick & Schnicke, 1992) and the CT program based on Ehlers and Clark's cognitive theory of PTSD (Ehlers & Clark, 2000; Ehlers, Clark, Hackmann, McManus, & Fennell, 2005; Ehlers, et al., 2003), whereas other CT programs do not (Marks et al., 1998; Tarrier et al., 1999).

Eye movement desensitization and reprogramming. In EMDR (Shapiro, 1989, 1991, 1995, 2001), the therapist asks the patient to generate images, thoughts, and feelings about the trauma, to evaluate their aversive qualities, and to make alternative cognitive appraisals of the trauma or their behavior during it. As the patient initially focuses on the distressing images and thoughts, and later focuses on the alternative cognition, the therapist elicits rapid, lateral alternating eye movements by instructing the patient to visually track the therapist's finger as it is moved back and forth across the patient's visual field. Originally, Shapiro (1991) regarded these eye movements as essential to the processing of the traumatic memory, but the importance of the eye movements has not gained empirical support (Spates, Koch, Pagoto, Cusack, & Waller, 2009). Some EMDR programs have replaced the eye movement components with other procedures (e.g., patient alternating finger tapping from right to left hand, claiming equivalent mechanisms underlying these various procedures) (Shapiro, 2001); however, dismantling studies have not demonstrated that these movements affect symptom reduction (Cahill, Carrigan, & Frueh, 1999), and well designed treatment outcome research studies have found no advantage of EMDR over exposure therapy alone (Rothbaum et al., 2005; Taylor et al., 2003).

Consensus Panel Recommendations

According to consensus panels such as the Institute of Medicine (IOM), the National Institute of Clinical Excellence (NICE), APA, and ISTSS the treatment of choice for chronic PTSD is exposure therapy or some other form of CBT. The IOM of the National Academies (2008) reviewed 53 psychotherapy and 37 pharmacotherapy RCTs in the treatment of PTSD and concluded that:

> Based on its assessment of the psychotherapy approaches for which randomized controlled trials were available: exposure, EMDR, cognitive restructuring, coping skills training,

other therapies, and psychotherapies administered in a group format—the committee found the evidence for all but one psychotherapeutic approach inadequate to reach a conclusion regarding efficacy. The evidence was sufficient to conclude the efficacy of exposure therapies in treating patients with PTSD. (pp. 127–128)

The IOM committee also concluded that the evidence was inadequate to determine the efficacy of pharmacotherapy for PTSD. Similarly, the ISTSS guidelines stated that, "CBT that comprises exposure therapy (imaginal and in vivo exposure), CT, SIT, or one of the many combination programs that incorporate some form of exposure with formal CT (e.g., CPT) or SIT is recommended as first-line treatment for chronic PTSD" (p. 556). The NICE (2005) guidelines were similar stating that, "Drug treatments for PTSD should not be used as routine first-line treatment for adults (in general use or by specialist mental health professionals) in preference to trauma-focused psychological therapy" (p. 19).

Controlled Trials

Although the IOM recommendations single out exposure-based treatment, different CBT programs appear to yield relatively similar levels of improvement. Similarly, studies that have compared combined CBT programs with the constituent components (e.g., exposure therapy plus SIT vs. exposure therapy alone vs. SIT alone) have generally failed to find significant benefit for the combined treatment compared to the individual treatments. This may in part be attributed to low statistical power to detect small differences due to low sample size, although two relevant studies utilized samples comprising 50 or more participants in each condition. Foa and colleagues (2005) compared exposure therapy alone ($N = 79$) with exposure therapy plus cognitive restructuring ($N = 74$). Both treatments were clearly superior to wait-list, and the degree of improvement from pre- to posttreatment, expressed in terms of standard deviation

units (i.e., within-group effect sizes), was similar for the two treatments but numerically larger for the exposure therapy condition ($d = 1.45$) than the combined condition ($d = 1.30$). Resick and colleagues (2008) compared standard CPT ($N = 53$), which includes some exposure through writing and reading a trauma narrative, with a version of CPT in which writing and reading the trauma narrative was removed ($N = 50$). A third comparison condition in this study was one in which participants engaged in repeated writing about the trauma and reading the narrative without any formal CT. All three conditions were associated with significant improvement; however, group comparisons conducted at posttreatment indicated the CPT condition without writing was superior to the writing condition, whereas standard CPT was not different from either the writing condition or CPT variation without the writing component. It should be noted, however, that the writing only condition included six sessions delivered every other week, whereas the other two conditions included 12 sessions each delivered weekly. This procedural difference might have reduced the efficacy of the writing-only treatment. Thus, Foa et al. (2005) found adding CT did not enhance the combination of imaginal plus in vivo exposure, and Resick et al. (2008) found that removing exposure via writing and reading the trauma narrative did not reduce the efficacy of CPT. Dismantling studies of EMDR in which participants were individuals with PTSD or trauma-related symptoms indicate that variations of EMDR in which eye movements are replaced by other laterally alternating stimuli (Pitman et al., 1996) or simply removed (Boudewyns & Hyer, 1996; Renfrey & Spates, 1994), and in which the formal cognitive restructuring (i.e., reprocessing) procedures are replaced with more desensitization trials (Cusack & Spates, 1999) produce similar improvement. As with most studies comparing different CBT programs, the EMDR dismantling studies are limited by small samples with adequate power to detect only large differences between treatment conditions; however, the pattern of means in these studies suggest that, even if there are differences between EMDR and the dismantled variations, the differences are quite small. For a summary of controlled trials of CBT for PTSD, see Table 14.4 (pp. 352–353).

Meta-Analyses of Group Designs

The efficacy of CBT in the treatment of PTSD among adults has been the focus of considerable research in the past 20 years that has been summarized in several recent narrative and meta-analytic reviews. In the second edition of ISTSS treatment guidelines (Foa, Keane, Friedman, & Cohen, 2009), Cahill, Rothbaum, Resick, and Follette (2009) identified 64 studies in which participants were randomly assigned to some form of CBT and at least one other study condition. The single most common comparison condition was wait-list (39 studies), although several (19) studies utilized some form of nonspecific control treatment, such as relaxation, supportive counseling, psychoeducation, or treatment as usual. In addition, 12 studies directly compared two or more CBT programs (excluding EMDR), such as some form of exposure therapy compared with SIT (Foa et al., 1999; Foa et al., 1991) or CT (Marks et al., 1998; Resick et al., 2002; Tarrier et al., 1999), or comparing individual CBT programs with combined programs such as exposure therapy plus SIT or CT compared to exposure therapy alone (Foa et al., 1999; Foa et al., 2005; Marks et al., 1998; Paunovic & Ost, 2001), SIT alone (Foa et al., 1999), or CT alone (Marks et al., 1998; Resick et al., 2008). Another seven studies directly compared EMDR with some other CBT program (Devilly & Spence, 1999; Ironson et al., 2002; Lee et al., 2002; Power et al., 2002; Rothbaum et al., 2005; Taylor et al., 2003; Vaughan et al., 1994), although concerns have been raised about the randomization procedures used in the Devilly and Spence study (1999). Separate chapters on EMDR in the earlier (Chemtob, Tolin, Van der Kolk, & Pitman, 2000) and revised edition (Spates et al., 2009) of

the ISTSS guidelines together identify a total of 18 studies including the aforementioned seven studies that either assessed the efficacy of EMDR or attempted to dismantle the components of EMDR, such as eye movements and other laterally alternating stimuli (e.g., tapping; Pitman et al., 1996), and its cognitive restructuring component (Cusack & Spates, 1999).

In broad summary of the 75 studies reviewed in the ISTSS guideline chapters, the vast majority found that treatment with CBT was associated with significant improvement on measures of PTSD symptoms and frequently other associated emotional reactions, such as depression and anxiety. Moreover, CBT is routinely found to be significantly more efficacious than wait-list controls, and as or more efficacious than nonspecific control treatment; however, studies directly comparing different CBT treatments have found only small differences between treatment conditions that generally fail to achieve statistical significance, possibly due in part to sample sizes that are not large enough to detect small differences. In addition, the direction of the difference between conditions does not reliably replicate. For example, the first study to directly compare exposure therapy with SIT (Foa et al., 1991) found some evidence of a slight advantage for SIT, particularly immediately posttreatment, whereas a subsequent study (Foa et al., 1999) found some evidence for a slight advantage for exposure therapy. Similarly, among the seven studies comparing EMDR with some other CBT program, three provided some evidence of a slight advantage to CBT (Devilly & Spence, 1999; Rothbaum et al., 2005; Taylor et al., 2003) and three found some evidence of a slight advantage for EMDR (Lee et al., 2002; Power et al., 2002; Vaughan et al., 1994). In the seventh study (Ironson et al., 2002), there was not even a hint of superiority for one treatment over the other. In general, then, the differences between CBT and wait-list are substantially larger than the differences among the various CBT programs, and when differences do occur among active treatments, the direction of the difference is not consistent across studies, which suggests that different CBT programs yield similar degrees of improvement. It is important to note that exposure therapy has gained much more empirical evidence for its efficacy than other forms of CBT and EMDR.

Similar conclusions about the general efficacy of different CBT programs were drawn from a meta-analysis of psychotherapy for PTSD by R. Bradley, Greene, Russ, Dutra, and Westen (2005). These authors reviewed 26 studies that yielded a total of 44 active treatment conditions, 15 wait-list control conditions, and 8 non-specific control treatment conditions (e.g., supportive counseling). The mean within-group effect size for active treatments was 1.43 (95% $CI = 1.23–1.64$), which was superior to that of wait-list ($d = 0.35$, $CI = 0.19–0.51$) and non-specific control ($d = 0.59$, $CI = 0.30–0.88$). The various specific CBT approaches yielded similar effect sizes with overlapping confidence intervals: exposure therapy ($d = 1.57$, $CI = 1.11–2.04$), SIT or CT ($d = 1.65$, $CI = 0.96–2.35$), exposure therapy plus SIT or CT ($d = 1.66$, $CI = 1.18–2.14$), and EMDR ($d = 1.43$, $CI = 1.02–1.83$).

Somewhat more guarded conclusions were drawn from a recent meta-analysis conducted under the auspices of the IOM (2008). This meta-analysis focused only on the highest quality studies and included in their evaluation consideration of lost data due to dropout and the statistical methods used to deal with such missing data. Based on the study selection criteria used by the Institute, the review committee considered 24 RCT of some form of exposure therapy (alone, or in combination with SIT or CT; notably, CPT was designated as an exposure therapy for the purposes of the IOM review); 10 studies of EMDR; three studies of CT; and four studies of coping skills training, which included SIT treatment and relaxation control conditions. Consistent with the previous reviews, the IOM concluded regarding exposure therapy that, "the evidence is sufficient to conclude the efficacy of exposure therapies in the treatment of PTSD" (p. 8). By contrast, the Institute concluded regarding EMDR, CT, and coping skills training that the evidence is "inadequate to determine the efficacy" (p. 9) of these other treatments.

Conclusions

Overall, the data suggest that the various forms of CBT are effective in treating chronic PTSD with no major differences in outcome between treatments; however, exposure-based treatments have the largest amount of support to date.

ACUTE STRESS DISORDER

Diagnostic Criteria

Acute stress disorder (ASD) was added as a diagnostic disorder in *DSM-IV* (APA, 1994). Like PTSD, the diagnosis requires the traumatic experience and reexperiencing symptom criteria. It also includes avoidance and hyperarousal symptoms, but requires only marked levels of symptoms. A distinguishing feature of ASD is that three of five dissociative symptoms must have been present during or after the trauma (APA, 1994), such as numbing, detachment, or absence of emotion; reduced awareness of surroundings; derealization; depersonalization; or dissociative amnesia. It is notable that numbing is separated into a dissociation symptom cluster under the ASD diagnosis, rather than grouped with effortful avoidance as in the PTSD diagnosis. Confirmatory factor analysis indicates that this four-factor structure provides a good fit to the diagnostic items, although this finding does not provide support for ASD as a diagnosis or predictor per se (Brooks et al. 2008).

A limitation of the 1-month duration criterion for PTSD is that it excludes those victims of trauma who immediately exhibit significant symptoms that may demand clinical attention. Acute stress disorder was introduced to fill a diagnostic gap for those individuals experiencing high distress in this acute phase after a trauma (Bryant & Harvey, 1997). In this case, the diagnosis of ASD can be applied if symptoms emerge within the month after the trauma and last for at least 2 days. A second goal of the ASD diagnosis was to predict who would eventually develop PTSD after a trauma (Harvey & Bryant, 2002).

Dissociative symptoms were included as a criterion for acute stress disorder based on the view that they were a risk factor for development of PTSD (R. D. Marshall, Spitzer, & Liebowitz, 1999). Dissociative symptoms had been found to correlate with PTSD symptoms and to predict PTSD diagnosis (Marmar et al., 1994). Furthermore, patients with PTSD had been reported to have higher hypnotizability, an indicator of the ability to experience dissociation, than patients with other psychiatric diagnoses (Spiegel, Hunt, & Dondershine, 1988); however, the value of the ASD diagnosis and, in particular of the dissociative symptom criterion, has been questioned, at least in part due to predictive validity (Bryant, 2003; Harvey & Bryant, 2002; G. N. Marshall & Schell, 2002; R. D. Marshall et al., 1999). For example, results from a recent clinical trial of admitted hospital patients revealed that the majority of those who developed PTSD did not previously meet ASD criteria and that dissociative symptoms had low sensitivity in predicting later PTSD (Bryant, Creamer, O'Donnell, Silove, & McFarlane, 2008). Although many of those diagnosed with ASD go on to develop PTSD, the majority of people who develop PTSD did not initially meet ASD criteria (Bryant, 2007). Because peritraumatic dissociation and ASD are not consistent predictors of PTSD and the mechanisms of dissociation are not adequately understood, it has been suggested that *DSM-5* definitions of ASD and PTSD should not stress the role of peritraumatic dissociation (Bryant, 2007).

Impact of Disorder

Although incidence rates based on epidemiological studies are not available for ASD, empirical studies indicate that 13%-19% of trauma victims meet criteria for this diagnosis (Brewin, Andrews, Rose, & Kirk, 1999; Harvey & Bryant, 1999). These rates are lower than the

rate of acute PTSD (i.e., when duration criterion is ignored, as in the Rothbaum et al., 1992, study), perhaps due to the more restrictive criteria of ASD (Harvey & Bryant, 2002) or differences in sample (e.g. assault survivors compared with motor vehicle crash survivors). The likelihood of developing ASD after a trauma seems to be similar across children and adults (Brewin et al., 1999; Meiser-Stedman, Dalgleish, Smith, Yule, & Glucksman, 2007).

Acute Stress Disorder Treatment

The two primary treatments for acute stress reactions that have been investigated are psychological debriefing and brief cognitive behavior therapy (B-CBT). Both treatments focus on the prevention of extended symptoms (chronic PTSD). Psychological debriefing (Dyregrov, 1989; Raphael, 1986; Rose, 1997) evolved from critical incident stress debriefing (Mitchell, 1983). The 1-3 hour (individual or group) debriefing most often occurs within 1 week of the trauma. The session includes seven primary stages: (1) the introduction, (2) expectations and facts, (3) thoughts and impressions, (4) emotional reactions, (5) normalization, (6) future planning/coping, and (7) disengagement. Psychological debriefing was intended to be implemented as a group rather than individual intervention and as one component of a more comprehensive approach to critical incident stress management (Bisson, McFarlane, Rose, Ruzek, & Watson, 2009). By contrast, the randomized controlled trials of psychological debriefing have focused primarily on individually administered psychological debriefing implemented as a stand-alone intervention; some studies have utilized groups, but these were not randomized. The B-CBT (4-5 sessions) typically includes psychoeducation, stress management skills, CT, and exposure therapy (Keane & Barlow, 2002; Litz & Bryant, 2009). Treatment is initiated 2-4 weeks post trauma and is based on the same treatment components developed for the treatment of chronic PTSD.

Consensus Panel Recommendations

Psychological debriefing (individual or group) is not recommended in published guidelines prepared under the auspices of the International Society for Traumatic Stress Studies (ISTSS) (Foa et al., 2009), the United Kingdom's NICE (2005), or the APA (Ursano et al., 2004). For example, the ISTSS guidelines state that

> . . . there is no evidence to suggest that single-session individual psychological debriefing is effective in the prevention of posttraumatic stress disorder (PTSD) symptoms shortly after a traumatic event or in the prevention of longer-term psychological sequelae . . . The current evidence suggests that individual psychological debriefing should not be used following traumatic events, and that there is unlikely to be a significant beneficial effect of group psychological debriefing; therefore, its use is not advocated. (Foa et al., 2009, p. 540)

Likewise the APA guidelines state, "there is no evidence at present that establishes psychological debriefing as effective in preventing PTSD or improving social and occupational functioning. In some settings, it has been shown to increase symptoms" (Ursano et al., 2004, p. 34); however, the recommendations for early CBT are more complex. Overall, ISTSS, NICE, and APA guidelines conclude there is evidence in support of early CBT in the prevention of PTSD; however, ISTSS further qualified the recommendations by type of trauma. The ISTSS guidelines state there is strong evidence for the efficacy of CBT in preventing chronic PTSD among patients with most traumas, but the evidence is not as strong for traumas with interpersonal violence (rape or nonsexual assault). They recommended that in the case of physical and sexual assault CBT should only be applied after a period of monitoring and support.

Controlled Trials

The results of RCT of individual psychological debriefing are somewhat mixed, but a potentially important pattern appears to be emerging.

Although patients receiving psychological debriefing in general report high levels of satisfaction with the intervention and studies utilizing valid and reliable measures of PTSD symptoms find improvement over time, studies that included an untreated control condition have not found any benefit on specific PTSD measures (Conlon, Fahy, & Conroy, 1999; Rose, Brewin, Andrews, & Kirk, 1999). Thus, symptom reduction following psychological debriefing in these studies is better attributed to natural recovery. Even more concerning, however, is the possibility of an iatrogenic effect of psychological debriefing, such that the intervention may impede natural recovery among some individuals (Bisson, Jenkins, Alexander, & Bannister, 1997; Carlier, Lamberts, Van Uchelen, & Gersons, 1998; Carlier, Voerman, & Gersons, 2000; Mayou, Ehlers, & Hobbs, 2000). For a summary of controlled trials of psychological debriefing, see Table 14.1 for RCTs and Table 14.2 for non-RCTs.

Overall, B-CBT appears to speed recovery from early PTSD symptoms (Foa, Hearst-Ikeda, & Perry, 1995; Foa, Zoellner, & Feeny, 2006) and ASD and may reduce the incidence of PTSD 6 months later (Bryant, Harvey, Dang, Sackville, & Basten, 1998; Bryant, Moulds, & Nixon, 2003; Bryant, Sackville, Dang, Moulds, & Guthrie, 1999), although long-term (1 year or greater) follow-up studies of intent-to-treat samples have found similar rates of PTSD for B-CBT and supportive counseling (Bryant et al., 2003). The only study to directly compare the combination of exposure therapy plus anxiety management training to exposure therapy alone, Bryant et al. (1999), found no significant differences between the two treatments. In a more recent study (Bryant et al., 2008), participants who received exposure therapy improved much more than those receiving cognitive restructuring, which did not differ from wait-list. It seems that the specific active component in B-CBT is exposure. See Table 14.3 for a summary of controlled trials of B-CBT to date.

TABLE 14.1 Psychological Debriefing—Randomized Controlled Trials

Study	Problem	Time Posttrauma	Treatment	Main Outcome Measure	Major Findings
[illegible]	[illegible]	Not reported	CISD (N = 312, SMC (N = 359, SO (N = 281)	PCL	NS
[illegible]	[illegible]	2–4 days	Debriefing (N = 57, Standard care (N = 46)	IES	Standard care > Debriefing
[illegible]	[illegible]	< 1 week	Immediate debriefing (N = 10, Immediate debriefing –3-month social worker input (N = 30, Standard care (N = 30)	Traumatic neurosis symptoms	Immediate debriefing+social worker > Immediate debriefing
[illegible]	[illegible]	< 8 hours	Debriefing (N = 15, Standard care (N = 15)	Composite of anxiety scores	Debriefing > Standard care
[illegible]	[illegible]	< 10 hours & > 48 hours	Individual or small group debriefing (N = 36, Delayed debriefing (N = 41)	PTSD Symptom Scale—Self Report	Under 10 hour group > over 48 hours group
[illegible]	[illegible]	< 1 day	Debriefing (N = 18, Advice Leaflet (N = 22)	IES	NS
[illegible]	[illegible]	< 1 day	Debriefing (N = 54, Standard care (N = 46)	IES	NS
[illegible]	[illegible]	2–3 hours	Debriefing (N = 59, Standard care (N = 55)	IES	Standard care > Debriefing
[illegible]	[illegible]	1 day	Debriefing (N = 21, Standard care (N = 18)	IES	NS
[illegible]	[illegible]	Not reported	CISD (N = 338, Stress education class (N = 316, No intervention (N = 325)	PCL	NS
[illegible]	[illegible]	< 1 month	Debriefing (N = 45, Education (N = 46, Standard care N = 47)	PSS	NS
[illegible]	[illegible]	11–19 days	Emotional debriefing (N = 63, Psychoeducational debriefing (N = 63, No intervention (N = 63)	SI-PTSD	NS. Some evidence of worsening in emotional debriefing
[illegible]	[illegible]	< 24 hours	Individual counseling	IES	NS

CISD = Critical Incident Stress Debriefing; IES = Impact of Events Scale; NS = Nonsignificant; PCL = PTSD Checklist; PSS = PTSD Symptom Scale; SI-PTSD = Structured Interview for PTSD; SMC = Stress Management Class; SO = Survey Only (No active intervention)

TABLE 14.2 Psychological Debriefing—Nonrandomized Controlled Trials

Paper	Population	Time Posttrauma	Treatment	Main Outcome Measure	Major Findings
Carlier et al. (1998)	Airplane crash ($N = 105$)	As soon as possible	Group debriefing ($N = 46$), Standard care ($N = 59$)	*DSM-III-R*, PTSD	8 months: no effect, 18 months: Standard care > Debriefing
Carlier et al. (2000)	Police officers ($N = 243$)	24 hours	Debriefing ($N = 86$), Refused group debriefing ($N = 82$), Group before group debriefing introduced ($N = 75$)	DTS, IES	Reexperiencing at 1 week: Debriefing > Refusal, Pregroup 6 months: no differences
M. P. Deahl, Gillham, Thomas, Searle, and Srinivasan (1994)	Gulf War dead body handling ($N = 29$)	Variable	Standard care ($N = 14$), Dyregrov GPD ($N = 15$)	IES	No overall effect
M. Deahl et al. (2000)	Male military peacekeepers ($N = 106$)	End of 6-month tour of duty	Group CISD ($N = 54$), Assessment-only control ($N = 52$)	IES, HADS	Posttreatment: NS. 1-year follow-up: Assessment-only control > Group CISD
Eid, Johnsen, and Weisaeth (2001)	Military personnel and firefighters exposed to car accident ($N = 27$)	1 day	Group with debriefing, Group without debriefing	PTSS-10, IES, GHQ-30	Group with Debriefing > Group without debriefing on PTSS–10 score
Hytten and Hasle (1989)	Firefighters ($N = 58$)	Soon after	PD ($N = 39$), Standard care ($N = 19$)	IES	No effect
Jenkins (1996)	Emergency service personnel ($N = 29$)	< 24 hours	Standard care ($N = 14$), Group CISD ($N = 15$)	SCL-90	Lower depression and anxiety: Group CISD > Standard care
Kenardy et al. (1996)	Emergency workers ($N = 195$)	Not reported	PD ($N = 62$), Standard care ($N = 133$)	GHQ-12, IES	No effect
Matthews (1998)	Assaulted direct care mental health workers ($N = 63$)	Within 1 week	PD ($N = 14$), Rejected PD ($N = 18$), Not offered PD ($N = 31$)	9-item IES satisfaction	No significant differences overall Decrease in IES score: Rejected PD > PD, not offered PD
Wee, Mills, and Koehler (1999)	Emergency medical service workers during Los Angeles civil disturbances ($N = 65$)	1–3 days	PD, Selected not to have PD	FRI-A	PD > Selected not to have PD

Note: The major findings only present statistically significant differences. CISD = Critical Incident Stress Debriefing; DTS = Davidson Trauma Scale; FRI-A = Frederick Reaction Index-Adult; GHQ = General Health Questionnaire; GPD = Group Psychological Debriefing; HADS = Hospital Anxiety and Depression Scale; IES = Impact of Events Scale; NS = Nonsignificant; PD = Psychological Debriefing; PTSS-10 = Posttraumatic Stress Syndrome 10-Questions Inventory; SCL–90 = Symptom Checklist 90

TABLE 14.3 CBT Early Intervention—Randomized Controlled Trials

Study	Diagnosis	Treatment	Length of Treatment	Main Outcome Measure	Major Findings
		B-CBT N=65, Standard care N=6?	1–6 weeks	IES	B-CBT > standard care
		B-CBT N=76, Standard care N=76	4 weeks	IES	NS
		B-CBT N=12, SC N=12	5 weeks	IES Intrusion, IES Avoidance	B-CBT > SC
		PE N=14, PE+AM N=15, SC N=16	5 weeks	IES Intrusion, IES Avoidance	PE, PE+AM > SC
		B-CBT N=41, SC N=28	5 weeks	CAPS	Symptom intensity: B-CBT > SC Symptom frequency: NS
		B-CBT N=33, B-CBT-hypnosis N=30, SC N=24	6 weeks	IES Intrusion, IES Avoidance	B-CBT+hypnosis > B-CBT, SC; B-CBT > SC
		B-CBT N=19, B-CBT-hypnosis N=18, SC N=16	6 weeks	CAPS	B-CBT, B-CBT+hypnosis > SC
		PE N=30, CR N=30, WL N=30	5 weeks, 90-minute sessions	CAPS-2, IES-Intrusions, IES-Avoidance	PE > CR, WL
		CT+coping skills training N=20, PMR N=2?	5 weeks	SSPSDS	NS
		B-CBT N=31, SC N=29, RA N=30	4 weeks	PSS-I	NS
		MSI N=8, Supportive listening N=9	2 sessions via telephone	PDS	MSI > supportive listening
		SH N=75, WL N=67	Not applicable (self-directed)	PDS	NS
		B-CBT N=41 SWT N=42, WL N=40	Five 1.5 hour sessions for ASD, Ten 1.5 hour sessions for PTSD	IES	B-CBT, SWT > WL

AM = anxiety management; B-CBT = cognitive behavior therapy; CAPS = Clinician Administered PTSD; MSI = Memory Structuring Intervention; NS = Nonsignificant; PDS = PostTraumatic Diagnostic Scale; PE = Prolonged ...; PSS-I = PTSD Symptom Scale-Interview; RA = repeated assessment; SC = supportive counseling; SH = self-help booklet; SWT = Structured Writing Therapy; WL = wait-list.

TABLE 14.4 Summary of Randomized Controlled Trials of CBT for PTSD

Study	Population	Major Findings
Basoglu, Salcioglu, and Livanou (2007)	31 male and female earthquake survivors with PTSD in Turkey	EX > WL
Basoglu et al. (2005)	59 male and female earthquake survivors in Turkey	EX > WL
J. G. Beck, Coffey, Foy, Keane, and Blanchard (2009)	44 male and female survivors of motor vehicle accidents (MVA) with chronic PTSD	COMB > WL
Bichescu, Neuner, Schauer, and Elbert (2007)	18 male and female Romanian political detainees randomly selected from a larger sample from a previous study (Bichescu et al., 2005)	EX > EDU
Blanchard et al. (2003)	98 male and female survivors of motor vehicle accidents (MVA) with chronic PTSD (81) or subthreshold PTSD (17)	COMB > SC > WL
Boudewyns and Hyer (1990)	51 male Vietnam War inpatient veterans	EX > TAU
R. G. Bradley and Follingstad (2003)	49 incarcerated women with histories of childhood sexual (CSA) and/or physical abuse	EX/DBT > WL
Bryant et al. (2003)	58 male and female survivors of physical assault (31) and MVAs (27)	EX = COMB > SC
Chard (2005)	71 women with PTSD from at least one episode of childhood sexual abuse	CPT > WL
Chemtob et al. (1997)	28 male Vietnam War veterans with PTSD and clinically elevated anger scores	SIT > TAU
Cloitre, Koenen, Cohen, and Han (2002)	58 women with PTSD related to childhood sexual abuse, physical abuse, or both	EX/DBT > WL
Cooper and Clum (1989)	22 male Vietnam War combat veterans	EX > TAU
Davis and Wright (2007)	43 men and women who experienced a traumatic event and were having nightmares at least once a week for the previous 3 months; 27 (63%) met full criteria for PTSD	COMB > WL
Difede, Cukor, et al. (2007)	21 men and women with PTSD related the September 11, 2001, terrorist attacks on the World Trade Center	EX > WL
Difede, Malta, et al. (2007)	31 male and female disaster workers exposed to the September 11, 2001, terrorist attack on the World Trade Center or its aftermath meeting criteria for PTSD (21) or subthreshold (10) PTSD	COMB > TAU
Duffy, Gillespie, and Clark (2007)	58 men and women with PTSD related to terrorism and civil conflict in Northern Ireland	CT > WL
Echeburúa, DeCorral, Sarasua, and Zubizarreta (1996)	20 women with PTSD from either rape in adulthood (11) or CSA (9)	COMB > RLX
Ehlers et al. (2003)	97 male and female MVA survivors entered a 3-week self-monitoring phase; 85 participants still meeting PTSD randomized to study conditions	CT > SELF = WL
Ehlers et al. (2005)	28 men and women with PTSD following civilian traumas, primarily MVAs (15)	CT > WL
Falsetti, Resnick, Davis, and Gallagher (2001)	22 women with comorbid PTSD and panic attacks	COMB > WL
Fecteau and Nicki (1999)	23 men and women with PTSD following MVAs	COMB > WL
Foa et al. (1999)	96 female sexual and nonsexual assault survivors with PTSD	EX = EX/ SIT = SIT > WL
Foa et al. (2005)	179 female sexual and nonassault or CSA survivors	EX = EX/CT > WL
Foa et al. (1991)	55 female rape survivors	EX = SIT > SC > WL

TABLE 14.4   Summary of Randomized Controlled Trials of CBT for PTSD (*Continued*)

Study	Population	Major Findings
Frank et al. (1988)	167 women, 138 survivors of sexual assault and 29 nonvictimized controls; 99 sought immediate treatment, 39 sought delayed treatment; treatment participants were also compared with a repeated assessment condition from a separate sample (see Kilpatrick & Calhoun, 1988)	CT = SD > WL
Frommberger et al. (2004)	21 men and women with chronic PTSD following civilian traumas	COMB = PAR
Gersons, Carlier, Lamberts, and Van Der Kolk (2000)	42 male and female Dutch police officers with a primary diagnosis of PTSD	COMB > WL
Glynn et al. (1999)	42 male Vietnam War veterans with combat-related PTSD	COMB = COMB/BFT > WL
Hinton et al. (2005)	40 male and female Cambodian refugees meeting criteria for PTSD and current neck-focused or orthostasis-triggered panic attacks; all participants had PTSD despite a minimum of one year of treatment with an adequate dose of an SSRI medication plus supportive counseling	COMB > WL
Hinton et al. (2004)	12 male and female Cambodian and Vietnamese refugees with PTSD, most having panic episodes related to headaches and/or orthostatic cues; all participants had PTSD despite a minimum of one year of treatment with an adequate dose of an SSRI medication plus supportive counseling	COMB > WL
Hirai and Clum (2005)	36 men and women, mixture of college students seeking class credit and individuals from the larger community, who experienced civilian trauma with at least subclinical trauma symptoms (meeting reexperiencing and avoidance criteria)	COMB > WL
Hollifield, Sinclair-Lian, Warner, and Hammerschlag (2007)	84 men and women with PTSD	COMB = ACU > WL
Ironson, Freund, Strauss, and Williams (2002)	22 men and women with primary PTSD following civilian trauma, primarily interpersonal assault	EX = EMDR
Keane et al. (1989)	24 male Vietnam War veterans with PTSD	EX > WL
Krakow, Hollifield, et al. (2001)	168 female sexual assault survivors with self-reported trauma symptoms, 83% had pretreatment Clinician-Administered PTSD Scale (CAPS) scores > 65	COMB > WL
Kubany, Hill, and Owens (2003)	37 female survivors of domestic violence	COMB > WL
Kubany et al. (2004)	125 women survivors of domestic violence	COMB > WL
Lange et al. (2003)	184 men and women meeting criteria for mild to relatively severe PTSD following a range of civilian traumas; nearly twice as many participants were randomized to treatment (122) as to control (62)	COMB > WL
Lange, Van de Ven, Schrieken, and Emmelkamp (2001)	50 male and female students suffering from trauma-related symptoms following a range of civilian traumas participating for course credit	COMB > WL
Lee, Gavriel, Drummond, Richards, and Greenwald (2002)	22 men and women with PTSD after 6-week run-in phase; 24 randomly assigned to each treatment condition; the final person was incarcerated	COMB = EMDR
Lindauer, Gersons, et al. (2005)	24 men and women with primary PTSD from interpersonal violence, accidents, or disaster	COMB > WL

(*Continued*)

TABLE 14.4 Summary of Randomized Controlled Trials of CBT for PTSD (*Continued*)

Study	Population	Major Findings
Lindauer, Vlieger, et al. (2005)	24 men and women with PTSD following civilian traumas	COMB > WL
Litz, Engel, Bryant, and Papa (2007)	45 Department of Defense service members with PTSD as a result either of the Pentagon attack on September 11, 2001, or combat in Iraq/Afghanistan	COMB > SC
Maercker et al. (2006)	48 male and female survivors of MVAs with PTSD (22) or subsyndromal PTSD (20)	CBT > WL
Marks et al. (1998)	87 men and women with chronic PTSD from a range of civilian traumas	EX = CT = EX/CT > RLX
McDonagh et al. (2005)	74 women with PTSD and histories of CSA	COMB > SC > WL
Monson et al. (2006)	60 male and female veterans with chronic military-related PTSD	CPT > WL
Mueser et al. (2008)	108 patients with comorbid severe mental illness (major depressive disorder, bipolar disorder, schizoaffective disorder and schizophrenia) and PTSD following a range of civilian traumas, most commonly sexual (34%) or physical abuse in childhood (17%), the sudden death of a loved one (15%), and adult sexual (13%) or physical assault (11%)	COMB > TAU
Neuner, Schauer, Klaschik, Karunakara, and Elbert (2004)	43 male and female Sudanese refuges living in a Uganda refugee settlement diagnosed with PTSD	EX > SC = EDU
Otto et al. (2003)	10 female Cambodian refugees with PTSD despite treatment with clonazepam in combination with an SSRI other than sertraline	COMB+SERT > SERT
Paunovic and Öst (2001)	20 male and female refugees with PTSD	EX+COMB
Power et al. (2002)	105 men and women with PTSD from a range of civilian traumas	COMB = EMDR > WL
Resick et al. (2008)	150 female assault survivors, sexual or nonassault occurring in childhood or adulthood	CPT-C = CPT > WA
Resick et al. (2002)	171 female sexual assault survivors with PTSD	EX = CPT > WL
Richards et al. (1994)	14 men and women with chronic PTSD following a range of civilian traumas	Imaginal EX = In vivo EX
Rothbaum et al. (2005)	74 female rape survivors with chronic PTSD	EX = EMDR > WL
Rothbaum et al. (2006)	Two-phase study, 88 men and women with chronic PTSD began Phase I of treatment; 65 participants randomized in Phase II	EX/SERT > SERT
Schauer et al. (2006)	32 survivors of organized violence, physical and sexual torture	EX > TAU
Schnurr et al. (2007)	284 female veterans with chronic PTSD	EX > SC
Schnurr et al. (2003)	360 male Vietnam War veterans with combat-related PTSD	EX > SC
Tarrier et al. (1999)	72 men and women with chronic PTSD after completing a 4-week monitoring phase were allocated to treatment	Imaginal EX = CT
Taylor et al. (2003)	60 men and women, most (97%) with chronic PTSD	EX > EMDR = RLX
Vaughan et al. (1994)	36 men and women with PTSD	EX = EMDR > RLX
Zlotnick et al. (1997)	48 female CSA with PTSD	DBT > WL

Note: The major findings only present statistically significant differences. ACU = acupuncture; BFT = behavioral family therapy; CT = cognitive therapy; COMB = combination CBT; CPT = cognitive processing therapy; DBT = dialectical behavior therapy; EDU = education; EMDR = eye movement desensitization and reprocessing; EX = exposure therapy; NS = Nonsignificant; RLX = relaxation therapy; SC = supportive counseling; SELF = self-help reading; SIT = stress inoculation therapy; TAU = treatment as usual; WA = written accounts; WL = wait-list

Meta-Analyses Of Group Designs

A meta-analysis of seven studies of psychological debriefing showed that debriefing did not significantly reduce symptoms of PTSD (van Emmerik, Kamphuis, Hulsbosch, & Emmelkamp, 2002). In contrast, a meta-analysis of 25 studies of early trauma interventions suggested that trauma-focused CBT was more effective than wait-list or supportive counseling for individuals with significant traumatic stress symptoms, particularly for those who met criteria for a diagnosis of ASD and acute PTSD (Bisson, Roberts, Kitchiner, & Kenardy, 2009). Other meta-analyses with mixed samples (e.g., ASD and PTSD) are not discussed here (Kornor et al., 2008).

Conclusions

Treatment guidelines, individual trials, and meta-analyses all suggest that the debriefing of all trauma victims is not warranted. There is evidence in support of early CBT in the prevention of PTSD, but further research is needed. One of the major factors limiting progress in the development of highly efficacious prevention programs is the phenomenon of natural recovery. As longitudinal studies of trauma survivors have shown, most individuals exposed to a traumatic event experience a decline in PTSD symptoms in the weeks and months following the traumatic event (Blanchard et al., 1996; Riggs, Rothbaum, & Foa, 1995; Rothbaum et al., 1992). Thus, efficacious preventative programs must either promote more rapid or complete recovery than would occur naturally or researchers need to be able to reliably identify subpopulations least likely to recover in the absence of intervention, as has been generally true of the diagnostic criteria for ASD (Harvey & Bryant, 2002). With these considerations in mind, the extant research suggests that brief versions (i.e., four to five sessions compared to nine or more sessions) of the same CBT programs that are effective in the treatment of chronic PTSD, when administered starting within a few

weeks of the trauma, can speed recovery for some individuals displaying PTSD symptoms and/or prevent the development of chronic PTSD.

EVIDENCE-BASED PRACTICES

The evidence to date from all sources (consensus panel recommendations, meta-analyses, and RCTs) suggests that cognitive behavioral interventions should be considered the treatments of choice for PTSD. Specific recommendations vary depending on the amount of time between the index trauma and the point of intervention. Immediately following a traumatic event psychological debriefing of all exposed individuals is contraindicated. Rather, a watch and wait strategy is preferred. Most trauma survivors experience PTSD symptoms that improve with the passage of time. For those individuals where intervention is indicated prior to meeting criteria for chronic PTSD, B-CBT should be considered. CBT should be considered the standard of care for patients with chronic PTSD. The CBT programs with the largest evidence base to date are the exposure-based treatments. Thus, the major thrust of evidence-based practice should be focused on connecting trauma survivors with CBT practitioners if they continue to experience PTSD symptoms after a period of 3 months.

REFERENCES

Adler, A. B., Litz, B. T., Castro, C. A., Suvak, M., Thomas, J. L., Burrell, L., . . . Bliese, P. D. (2008). A group randomized trial of critical incident stress debriefing provided to U.S. peacekeepers. *Journal of Traumatic Stress, 21,* 253–263.

Alonso, J., Angermeyer, M. C., Bernert, S., Bruffaerts, R., Brugha, T. S., Bryson, H., . . . ESEMeD/MHEDEA 2000 Investigators, European Study of the Epidemiology of Mental Disorders (ESEMeD) Project (2004a). Prevalence of mental disorders in Europe: Results from the European Study of the Epidemiology of Mental Disorders (ESEMeD) project. *Acta Psychiatrica Scandinavica, 420,* 21–27.

Alonso, J., Angermeyer, M. C., Bernert, S., Bruffaerts, R., Brugha, T. S., Bryson, H., . . . ESEMeD/MHEDEA

2000 Investigators, European Study of the Epidemiology of Mental Disorders (ESEMeD) Project. (2004b). 12-month comorbidity patterns and associated factors in Europe: Results from the European Study of the Epidemiology of Mental Disorders (ESEMeD) project. *Acta Psychiatrica Scandinavica, 420,* 28–37.

Alonso, J., Angermeyer, M. C., Bernert, S., Bruffaerts, R., Brugha, T. S., Bryson, H., . . . ESEMeD/MHEDEA 2000 Investigators, European Study of the Epidemiology of Mental Disorders (ESEMeD) Project. (2004c) Disability and quality of life impact of mental disorders in Europe: Results from the European Study of the Epidemiology of Mental Disorders (ESEMeD) project. *Acta Psychiatrica Scandinavica Supplement, 420,* 38–46.

American Psychiatric Association. (1980). *Diagnostic and statistical manual for mental disorders (3rd ed., DSM-III).* Washington, DC: Author.

American Psychiatric Association. (1987). *Diagnostic and statistical manual for mental disorders (3rd ed., revised.) (DSM-III-R).* Washington, DC: Author.

American Psychiatric Association. (1994). *Diagnostic and statistical manual for mental disorders (4th ed.) (DSM-IV).* Washington, DC: Author.

Andre, C., Lelord, F., Legeron, P., Reignier, A., & Delattre, A. (1997). Effectiveness of early intervention on 132 bus drivers who have been victims of aggression: A controlled study. *Encephale, 23,* 65–71.

Asmundson, G. J. G., Frombach, I., McQuaid, J., Pedrelli, P., Lenox, R., & Stein, M. B. (2000). Dimensionality of posttraumatic stress symptoms: A confirmatory factor analysis of *DSM-IV* symptom clusters and other symptom models. *Behaviour Research and Therapy, 38,* 203–214.

Asmundson, G. J. G., Stapleton, J. A., & Taylor, S. (2004). Are avoidance and numbing distinct PTSD symptom clusters? *Journal of Traumatic Stress, 17,* 467–475.

Basoglu, M., Salcioglu, E., & Livanou, M. (2007). A randomized controlled study of single-session behavioural treatment of earthquake-related posttraumatic stress disorder using an earthquake simulator. *Psychological Medicine, 37,* 203–213.

Basoglu, M., Salcioglu, E., Livanou, M., Kalender, D., & Acar, G. (2005). Single-session behavioral treatment of earthquake-related posttraumatic stress disorder: A randomized waiting list controlled trial. *Journal of Traumatic Stress, 18,* 1–11.

Beck, J. G., Coffey, S. F., Foy, D. W., Keane, T. M., & Blanchard, E. B. (2009). Group cognitive behavior therapy for chronic posttraumatic stress disorder: An initial randomized pilot study. *Behavior Therapy, 40,* 82–92.

Beck, A. T., Emery, G., & Greenberg, R. L. (1985). *Anxiety disorders and phobias: A cognitive perspective.* New York, NY: Basic Books.

Beck, A. T., Rush, A. J., Shaw, B. F., & Emery, G. (1979). *Cognitive therapy of depression.* New York, NY: Guilford Press.

Bichescu, D., Neuner, F., Schauer, M., & Elbert, T. (2007). Narrative exposure therapy for political imprisonment-related chronic posttraumatic stress disorder and depression. *Behaviour Research and Therapy, 45,* 2212–2220.

Bisson, J. I., Jenkins, P. L., Alexander, J., & Bannister, C. (1997). Randomised controlled trial of psychological debriefing for victims of acute burn trauma. *British Journal of Psychiatry, 171,* 78–81.

Bisson, J. I., McFarlane, A. C., Rose, S., Ruzek, J. I., & Watson, P. J. (2009). Psychological debriefing. In E. B. Foa, T. M. Keane, M. J. Friedman, & J. A. Cohen (Eds.), *Effective treatments for PTSD: Practice guidelines from the International Society for Traumatic Stress Studies* (pp. 83–116). New York, NY: Guilford Press.

Bisson, J. I., Roberts, N. P., Kitchiner, N. J., & Kenardy, J. (2009). Systematic review and meta-analysis of multiple-session early interventions following traumatic events. *American Journal of Psychiatry, 166,* 293–301.

Bisson, J. I., Shepherd, J. P., Joy, D., Probert, R., & Newcombe, R. G. (2004). Early cognitive-behavioural therapy for post-traumatic stress symptoms after physical injury: Randomised controlled trial. *British Journal of Psychiatry, 184,* 63–69.

Blanchard, E. B., Hickling, E. J., Barton, K. A., Tayeor, A. E., Loos, W. R., & Jones-Alexander, J. (1996). One-year prospective follow-up of motor vehicle accident victims. *Behaviour Research and Therapy, 34,* 775–786.

Blanchard, E. B., Hickling, E. J., Devineni, T., Veazey, C. H., Galovski, T. E., Mundy, E., . . . Buckley, T. C. (2003). A controlled evaluation of cognitive behaviorial therapy for posttraumatic stress in motor vehicle accident survivors. *Behaviour Research and Therapy, 41,* 79–96.

Bordow, S., & Porritt, D. (1979). An experimental evaluation of crisis intervention. *Social Science and Medicine, 13 A*(3), 251–256.

Boudewyns, P. A., & Hyer, L. (1990). Physiological response to combat memories and preliminary treatment outcome in Vietnam veteran PTSD patients treated with direct therapeutic exposure. *Behavior Therapy, 21,* 63–87.

Boudewyns, P. A., & Hyer, L. A. (1996). Eye movement desensitization and reprocessing (EMDR) as treatment for post-traumatic stress disorder (PTSD). *Clinical Psychology and Psychotherapy, 3,* 185–195.

Bradley, R. G., & Follingstad, D. R. (2003). Group therapy for incarcerated women who experienced interpersonal violence: A pilot study. *Journal of Traumatic Stress, 16,* 337–340.

Bradley, R., Greene, J., Russ, E., Dutra, L., & Westen, D. (2005). A multidimensional meta-analysis of psychotherapy for PTSD. *American Journal of Psychiatry, 162,* 214–227.

Breslau, J., Aguilar-Gaxiola, S., Kendler, K. S., Su, M., Williams, D., & Kessler, R. C. (2006). Specifying race-ethnic differences in risk for psychiatric disorder in a USA national sample. *Psychological Medicine, 36,* 57–68.

Breslau, N. (1998). Epidemiology of trauma and post-traumatic stress disorder. In R. Yehuda (Ed.), *Psychological trauma* (pp. 1–29). Washington, DC: American Psychiatric Association.

Breslau, N. (2002). Epidemiologic studies of trauma, post-traumatic stress disorder, and other psychiatric disorders. *Canadian Journal of Psychiatry, 47,* 923–929.

Breslau, N., & Anthony, J. C. (2007). Gender differences in the sensitivity to posttraumatic stress disorder: An epidemiological study of urban young adults. *Journal of Abnormal Psychology, 116,* 607–611.

Breslau, N., Chilcoat, H. D., Kessler, R. C., Peterson, E. L., & Lucia, V. C. (1999). Vulnerability to assaultive violence: Further specification of the sex difference in post-traumatic stress disorder. *Psychological Medicine, 29,* 813–821.

Breslau, N., Davis, G. C., & Andreski, P. (1995). Risk factors for PTSD-related traumatic events: A prospective analysis. *American Journal of Psychiatry, 152,* 529–535.

Breslau, N., Davis, G. C., Andreski, P., & Peterson, E. (1991). Traumatic events and posttraumatic stress disorder in an urban population of young adults. *Archives of General Psychiatry, 48,* 216–222.

Breslau, N., Kessler, R. C., Chilcoat, H. D., Schultz, L. R., Davis, G. C., & Andreski, P. (1998). Trauma and posttraumatic stress disorder in the community: The 1996 Detroit area survey of trauma. *Archives of General Psychiatry, 55,* 626–632.

Brewin, C. R., Andrews, B., Rose, S., & Kirk, M. (1999). ASD and posttraumatic stress disorder in victims of violent crime. *American Journal of Psychiatry, 156,* 360–366.

Brooks, R., Silove, D., Bryant, R., O'Donnell, M., Creamer, M., & McFarlane, A. (2008). A confirmatory factor analysis of the acute stress disorder interview. *Journal of Traumatic Stress, 21,* 353–355.

Bryant, R. A. (2003). Early predictors of posttraumatic stress disorder. *Biological Psychiatry, 53,* 789–795.

Bryant, R. A. (2007). Does dissociation further our understanding of PTSD? *Journal of Anxiety Disorders, 21,* 183–191.

Bryant, R. A., Creamer, M., O'Donnell, M. L., Silove, D., & McFarlane, A. C. (2008). A multisite study of the capacity of acute stress disorder diagnosis to predict posttraumatic stress disorder. *Journal of Clinical Psychiatry, 69,* 923–929.

Bryant, R. A., & Harvey, A. G. (1997). Acute stress disorder: A critical review of diagnostic issues. *Clinical Psychology Review, 17,* 757–773.

Bryant, R. A., Harvey, A. G., Dang, S. T., Sackville, T., & Basten, C. (1998). Treatment of ASD: A comparison of cognitive-behavioral therapy and supportive

counseling. *Journal of Consulting and Clinical Psychology, 66,* 862–866.

Bryant, R. A., Mastrodomenico, J., Felmingham, K. L., Hopwood, S., Kenny, L., Kandris, E., . . . Creamer, M. (2008). Treatment of ASD: A randomized controlled trial. *Archives of General Psychiatry, 65,* 659–667.

Bryant, R. A., Moulds, M. L., Guthrie, R. M., Dang, S. T., & Nixon, R. D. V. (2003). Imaginal exposure alone and imaginal exposure with cognitive restructuring in treatment of posttraumatic stress disorder. *Journal of Consulting and Clinical Psychology, 71,* 706–712.

Bryant, R. A., Moulds, M. L., Guthrie, R. M., & Nixon, R. D. V. (2005). The additive benefit of hypnosis and cognitive-behavioral therapy in treating acute stress disorder. *Journal of Consulting and Clinical Psychology, 73,* 334–340.

Bryant, R. A., Moulds, M. L., & Nixon, R. V. D. (2003). Cognitive behaviour therapy of ASD: A four-year follow-up. *Behaviour Research and Therapy, 41,* 489–494.

Bryant, R. A., Moulds, M. L., Nixon, R. D. V., Mastrodomenico, J., Felmingham, K., & Hopwood, S. (2006). Hypnotherapy and cognitive behaviour therapy of acute stress disorder: A 3-year follow-up. *Behaviour Research and Therapy, 44,* 1331–1335.

Bryant, R. A., Sackville, T., Dang, S. T., Moulds, M., & Guthrie, R. (1999). Treating ASD: An evaluation of cognitive behavior therapy and supportive counseling techniques. *American Journal of Psychiatry, 156,* 1780–1786.

Bunn, T. A., & Clarke, A. M. (1979). Crisis intervention: An experimental study of the effects of a brief period of counselling on the anxiety of relatives of seriously injured or ill hospital patients. *British Journal of Medical Psychology, 52,* 191–195.

Cahill, S. P., Carrigan, M. H., & Frueh, B. C. (1999). Does EMDR work? And if so, why? A critical review of controlled outcome and dismantling research. *Journal of Anxiety Disorders, 13,* 5–33.

Cahill, S. P., Rothbaum, B. O., Resick, P., & Follette, V. M. (2009). Cognitive-behavioral therapy for adults. In E. B. Foa, T. M. Keane, M. J. Friedman, & J. A. Cohen (Eds.), *Effective treatments for PTSD: Practice guidelines from the International Society for Traumatic Stress Studies* (2nd ed., pp. 139–222). New York, NY: Guilford Press.

Campfield, K. M., & Hills, A. M. (2001). Effect of timing of critical incident stress debriefing (CISD) on posttraumatic symptoms. *Journal of Traumatic Stress, 14,* 327–340.

Carlier, I. V. E., Lamberts, R. D., Van Uchelen, A. J., & Gersons, B. P. R. (1998). Disaster-related post-traumatic stress in police officers: A field study of the impact of debriefing. *Stress Medicine, 14,* 143–148.

Carlier, I. V. E., Voerman, A. E., & Gersons, B. P. R. (2000). The influence of occupational debriefing on post-traumatic stress symptomatology in traumatized police officers. *British Journal of Medical Psychology, 73,* 87–98.

Chard, K. M. (2005). An evaluation of cognitive processing therapy for the treatment of posttraumatic stress disorder related to childhood sexual abuse. *Journal of Consulting and Clinical Psychology, 73,* 965–971.

Chemtob, C. M., Hamada, R. S., Novaco, R. W., & Gross, D. M. (1997). Cognitive-behavioral treatment for severe anger in posttraumatic stress disorder. *Journal of Consulting and Clinical Psychology, 65,* 184–189.

Chemtob, C. M., Tolin, D. F., Van der Kolk, B. A., & Pitman, R. K. (2000). Eye movement desensitization and reprocessing. In E. B. Foa, T. M. Keane, & M. Friedman (Eds.), *Effective treatments for PTSD: Practice guidelines from the International Society for Traumatic Stress Studies* (pp. 139–154). New York, NY: Guilford Press.

Cloitre, M., Koenen, K. C., Cohen, L. R., & Han, H. (2002). Skills training in affective and interpersonal regulation followed by exposure: A phase-based treatment for PTSD related to childhood abuse. *Journal of Consulting and Clinical Psychology, 70,* 1067–1074.

Conlon, L., Fahy, T. J., & Conroy, R. (1999). PTSD in ambulant RTA victims: A randomized controlled trial of debriefing. *Journal of Psychosomatic Research, 46,* 37–44.

Cooper, N. A., & Clum, G. A. (1989). Imaginal flooding as a supplementary treatment for PTSD in combat veterans: A controlled study. *Behavior Therapy, 20,* 381–391.

Cox, B. J., Mota, N., Clara, I., & Asmundson, G. J. G. (2008). The symptom structure of posttraumatic stress disorder in the National Comorbidity Study Replication Survey. *Journal of Anxiety Disorders, 22,* 1523–1528.

Cusack, K., & Spates, C. R. (1999). The cognitive dismantling of Eye Movement Desensitization and Reprocessing (EMDR) treatment of posttraumatic stress disorder (PTSD). *Journal of Anxiety Disorders, 13,* 87–99.

Davis, J. L., & Wright, D. C. (2007). Randomized clinical trial for treatment of chronic nightmares in trauma-exposed adults. *Journal of Traumatic Stress, 20,* 123–133.

Deahl, M. P., Gillham, A. B., Thomas, J., Searle, M. M., & Srinivasan, M. (1994). Psychological sequelae following the gulf war. Factors associated with subsequent morbidity and the effectiveness of psychological debriefing. *British Journal of Psychiatry, 164,* 60–65.

Deahl, M., Srinivasan, M., Jones, N., Thomas, J., Neblett, C., & Jolly, A. (2000). Preventing psychological trauma in soldiers: The role of operational stress training and psychological debriefing. *Psychology and Psychotherapy: Theory, Research and Practice, 73,* 77–85.

Devilly, G. J., & Spence, S. H. (1999). The relative efficacy and treatment distress of EMDR and a cognitive-behavior trauma treatment protocol in the amelioration of posttraumatic stress disorder. *Journal of Anxiety Disorders, 13,* 131–157.

Difede, J., Cukor, J., Jayasinghe, N., Patt, I., Jedel, S., & Spielman, L. (2007). Virtual reality therapy for the treatment of posttraumatic stress disorder following September 11, 2001. *Journal of Clinical Psychiatry, 68,* 1639–1647.

Difede, J., Malta, L. S., Best, S., Henn-Haase, C., Metzler, T., Bryant, R., & Marmar, C. (2007). A randomized controlled clinical treatment trial for World Trade Center attack-related PTSD in disaster workers. *Journal of Nervous and Mental Disease, 195,* 861–865.

Dolan, L., Bowyer, D., Freeman, C., & Little, K. (1999). Critical incident stress debriefing after trauma: Is it effective? Unpublished raw data.

Duffy, M., Gillespie, K., & Clark, D. M. (2007). Posttraumatic stress disorder in the context of terrorism and other civil conflict in Northern Ireland: Randomised controlled trial. *British Medical Journal, 334* (7604), 1147–1150.

Duggan, C., & Gunn, J. (1995). Medium-term course of disaster victims: A naturalistic follow-up. *British Journal of Psychiatry, 167,* 228–232.

Dyregrov, A. (1989). Caring for helpers in disaster situations: Psychological debriefing. *Disaster Management, 2,* 25–30.

Echeburúa, E., De Corral, P., Sarasua, B., & Zubizarreta, I. (1996). Treatment of acute posttraumatic stress disorder in rape victims: An experimental study. *Journal of Anxiety Disorders, 10,* 185–199.

Ehlers, A., & Clark, D. M. (2000). A cognitive model of posttraumatic stress disorder. *Behaviour Research and Therapy, 38,* 319–345.

Ehlers, A., Clark, D. M., Hackmann, A., McManus, F., & Fennell, M. (2005). Cognitive therapy for post-traumatic stress disorder: Development and evaluation. *Behaviour Research and Therapy, 43,* 413–431.

Ehlers, A., Clark, D. M., Hackmann, A., McManus, F., Fennell, M., Herbert, C., & Mayou, R. (2003). A randomized controlled trial of cognitive therapy, a self-help booklet, and repeated assessments as early interventions for posttraumatic stress disorder. *Archives of General Psychiatry, 60,* 1024–1032.

Eid, J., Johnsen, B. H., & Weisaeth, L. (2001). The effects of group psychological debriefing on acute stress reactions following a traffic accident: A quasi-experimental approach. *International Journal of Emergency Mental Health, 3,* 145–154.

Fairbank, J. A., Ebert, L., & Caddell, J. M. (2001). Posttraumatic stress disorder. In P. B. Sutker & H. E. Adams (Eds.), *Comprehensive handbook of psychopathology (3rd ed.)* (pp. 183–209). New York, NY: Kluwer.

Falsetti, S. A., Resnick, H. S., Davis, J., & Gallagher, N. G. (2001). Treatment of posttraumatic stress disorder with comorbid panic attacks: Combining cognitive processing therapy with panic control treatment techniques. *Group Dynamics, 5*, 252–260.

Fecteau, G., & Nicki, R. (1999). Cognitive behavioural treatment of post traumatic stress disorder after motor vehicle accident. *Behavioural and Cognitive Psychotherapy, 27*, 201–214.

Feldner, M. T., Babson, K. A., & Zvolensky, M. J. (2007). Smoking, traumatic event exposure, and post-traumatic stress: A critical review of the empirical literature. *Clinical Psychology Review, 27*, 14–45.

Flett, R. A., Kazantzis, N., Long, N. R., MacDonald, C., & Millar, M. (2004). Gender and ethnicity differences in the prevalence of traumatic events: Evidence from a New Zealand community sample. *Stress and Health, 20*, 149–157.

Foa, E. B., Dancu, C. V., Hembree, E. A., Jaycox, L. H., Meadows, E. A., & Street, G. P. (1999). A comparison of exposure therapy, stress inoculation training, and their combination for reducing posttraumatic stress disorder in female assault victims. *Journal of Consulting and Clinical Psychology, 67*, 194–200.

Foa, E. B., Hearst-Ikeda, D., & Perry, K. J. (1995). Evaluation of a brief cognitive behavioral program for the prevention of chronic PTSD in recent assault victims. *Journal of Consulting and Clinical Psychology, 63*, 948–955.

Foa, E. B., Hembree, E. A., Cahill, S. P., Rauch, S. A., Riggs, D. S., Feeny, N. C., & Yadin, E. (2005). Randomized trial of prolonged exposure for post traumatic stress disorder with and without cognitive restructuring: Outcome at academic and community clinics. *Journal of Consulting & Clinical Psychology, 73*, 953–964.

Foa, E. B., Hembree, E. A., & Rothbaum, B. O. (2007). *Prolonged exposure therapy for PTSD: Emotional processing of traumatic experiences.* New York, NY: Oxford University Press.

Foa, E. B., Huppert, J., & Cahill, C. (2006). Emotional processing theory: An update. In B. O. Rothbaum (Ed.), *Pathological anxiety: Emotional processing in etiology and treatment* (pp. 3–24). New York, NY: Guilford Press.

Foa, E. B., Keane, T. M., Friedman, M. J., & Cohen, J. A. (2009). *Effective treatments for PTSD: Practice guidelines from the International Society for Traumatic Stress Studies.* New York, NY: Guilford Press.

Foa, E. B., Riggs, D. S., & Gershuny, B. A. (1995). Arousal, numbing, and intrusion: Symptom structure of PTSD following assault. *American Journal of Psychiatry, 152*, 116–120.

Foa, E. B., Rothbaum, B. O., Riggs, D. S., & Murdock, T. B. (1991). Treatment of posttraumatic stress disorder in rape victims: A comparison between cognitive behavioral procedures and counseling. *Journal of Consulting and Clinical Psychology, 59*, 715–723.

Foa, E. B., Zoellner, L. A., & Feeny, N. C. (2006). An evaluation of three brief programs for facilitating recovery after assault. *Journal of Trauma Stress, 19*, 29–43.

Frank, E., Anderson, B., Duffy Stewart, B., Dancu, C., Hughes, C., & West, D. (1988). Efficacy of cognitive behavior therapy and systematic desensitization in the treatment of rape trauma. *Behavior Therapy, 19*, 403–420.

Frommberger, U., Stieglitz, R. D., Nyberg, E., Richter, H., Novelli-Fischer, U., Angenendt, J., . . . Berger, M. (2004). Comparison between paroxetine and behaviour therapy in patients with posttraumatic stress disorder (PTSD): A pilot study. *International Journal of Psychiatry in Clinical Practice, 8*, 19–23.

Frueh, B. C., Grubaugh, A. L., Acierno, R., Elhai, J. D., Cain, G., & Magruder, K. M. (2007). Age differences in posttraumatic stress disorder, psychiatric disorders, and healthcare service use among veterans in Veterans Affairs primary care clinics. *American Journal of Geriatric Psychiatry: Official Journal of the American Association for Geriatric Psychiatry, 15*, 660–672.

Fu, S. S., McFall, M., Saxon, A. J., Beckham, J. C., Carmody, T. P., Baker, D. G., & Joseph, A. M. (2007). Post traumatic stress disorder and smoking: A systematic review. *Nicotine and Tobacco Research, 9*, 1071–1084.

Galovski, T., & Lyons, J. A. (2004). Psychological sequelae of combat violence: A review of the impact of PTSD on the veteran's family and possible interventions. *Aggression and Violent Behavior, 9*, 477–501.

Gersons, B. P. R., Carlier, I. V. E., Lamberts, R. D., & Van Der Kolk, B. A. (2000). Randomized clinical trial of brief eclectic psychotherapy for police officers with posttraumatic stress disorder. *Journal of Traumatic Stress, 13*, 333–347.

Gidron, Y., Gal, R., Freedman, S., Twiser, I., Lauden, A., Snir, Y., & Benjamin, J. (2001). Translating research findings to PTSD prevention: Results of a randomized controlled pilot study. *Journal of Traumatic Stress, 14*, 773–780.

Glynn, S. M., Eth, S., Randolph, E. T., Foy, D. W., Urbaitis, M., Boxer, L., . . . Crothers, J. (1999). A test of behavioral family therapy to augment exposure for combat-related posttraumatic stress disorder. *Journal of Consulting and Clinical Psychology, 67*, 243–251.

Harvey, A. G., & Bryant, R. A. (1999). The relationship between acute stress disorder and posttraumatic stress disorder: A 2-year prospective investigation. *Journal of Consulting and Clinical Psychology, 67*, 985–988.

Harvey, A. G., & Bryant, R. A. (2002). Acute stress disorder: A synthesis and critique. *Psychological Bulletin, 128*, 892–906.

Hatch, S. L., & Dohrenwend, B. P. (2007). Distribution of traumatic and other stressful life events by race/ethnicity, gender, SES, and age: A review of the research. *American Journal of Community Psychology, 40*, 313–332.

Hickling, E. J., & Blanchard, E. B. (1997). The private practice psychologist and manual-based treatments: Post-traumatic stress disorder secondary to motor vehicle accidents. *Behaviour Research and Therapy, 35,* 191–203.

Hinton, D. E., Chhean, D., Pich, V., Safren, S. A., Hofmann, S. G., & Pollack, M. H. (2005). A randomized controlled trial of cognitive-behavior therapy for Cambodian refugees with treatment-resistant PTSD and panic attacks: A cross-over design. *Journal of Traumatic Stress, 18,* 617–629.

Hinton, D. E., Pham, T., Tran, M., Safren, S. A., Otto, M. W., & Pollack, M. H. (2004). CBT for Vietnamese refugees with treatment-resistant PTSD and panic attacks: A pilot study. *Journal of Traumatic Stress, 17,* 429–433.

Hirai, M., & Clum, G. A. (2005). An internet-based self-change program for traumatic event related fear, distress, and maladaptive coping. *Journal of Traumatic Stress, 18,* 631–636.

Hobbs, M., & Adshead, G. (1996). Preventive psychological intervention for road crash survivors. In M. Mitchell (Ed.), *The aftermath of road accidents: Psychological, social and legal perspectives* (pp. 159–171). London, England: Routledge.

Hobbs, M., Mayou, R., Harrison, B., & Worlock, P. (1996). A randomised controlled trial of psychological debriefing for victims of road traffic accidents. *British Medical Journal, 313*(7070), 1438–1439.

Hollifield, M., Sinclair-Lian, N., Warner, T. D., & Hammerschlag, R. (2007). Acupuncture for posttraumatic stress disorder: A randomized controlled pilot trial. *Journal of Nervous and Mental Disease, 195,* 504–513.

Hytten, K., & Hasle, A. (1989). Fire fighters: A study of stress and coping. *Acta Psychiatrica Scandinavica Supplement, 80*(355), 50–55.

Institute of Medicine. (2008). *Treatment of posttraumatic stress disorder: An assessment of the evidence.* Washington, DC: National Academic Press.

Ironson, G., Freund, B., Strauss, J. L., & Williams, J. (2002). Comparison of two treatments for traumatic stress: a community-based study of EMDR and prolonged exposure. *Journal of Clinical Psychology, 58,* 113–128.

Jenkins, S. R. (1996). Social support and debriefing efficacy among emergency medical workers after a mass shooting incident. *Journal of Social Behavior and Personality, 11,* 477–492.

Keane, T. M., & Barlow, D. H. (2002). Posttraumatic stress disorder. In D. H. Barlow (Ed.), *Anxiety and its disorders: The nature and treatment of anxiety and pani* (2nd ed., pp. 418–453). New York, NY: Guilford Press.

Keane, T. M., Fairbank, J. A., Caddell, J. M., & Zimering, R. T. (1989). Implosive (flooding) therapy reduces symptoms of PTSD in Vietnam combat veterans. *Behavior Therapy, 20,* 245–260.

Kenardy, J. A., Webster, R. A., Lewin, T. J., Carr, V. J., Hazell, P. L., & Carter, G. L. (1996). Stress debriefing and patterns of recovery following a natural disaster. *Journal of Traumatic Stress, 9,* 37–49.

Kessler, R. C., Berglund, P., Demler, O., Jin, R., Merikangas, K. R., & Walters, E. E. (2005). Lifetime prevalence and age-of-onset distributions of *DSM-IV* disorders in the National Comorbidity Survey Replication. *Archives of General Psychiatry, 62,* 593–602.

Kessler, R. C., Chiu, W. T., Demler, O., Merikangas, K. R., & Walters, E. E. (2005). Prevalence, severity, and comorbidity of 12-month *DSM-IV* disorders in the National Comorbidity Survey Replication. *Archives of General Psychiatry, 62,* 617–627.

Kessler, R. C., Sonnega, A., Bromet, E., Hughes, M., & Nelson, C. B. (1995). Posttraumatic stress disorder in the National Comorbidity Survey. *Archives of General Psychiatry, 52,* 1048–1060.

Kilpatrick, D. G., Resnick, H. S., Saunders, B. E., & Best, C. L. (1998). Rape, other violence against women, and post-traumatic stress disorder: Critical issues in assessing the adversity-stress-psychopathology relationship. In B. P. Dohrenwend (Ed.), *Adversity, stress, and psychopathology* (pp. 161–176). New York, NY: Oxford University Press.

King, D. W., Leskin, G. A., King, L. A., & Weathers, F. W. (1998). Confirmatory factor analysis of the clinician-administered PTSD scale: Evidence for the dimensionality of posttraumatic stress disorder. *Psychological Assessment, 10,* 90–96.

Kornor, H., Winje, D., Ekeberg, Ø., Weisaeth, L., Kirkehei, I., Johansen, K., & Steiro, A. (2008). Early trauma-focused cognitive-behavioural therapy to prevent chronic post-traumatic stress disorder and related symptoms: A systematic review and meta-analysis. *Bio Med Central (BMC) Psychiatry, 8,* 81.

Krakow, B., Hollifield, M., Johnston, L., Koss, M., Schrader, R., Warner, T. D., . . . Prince, H. (2001). Imagery rehearsal therapy for chronic nightmares in sexual assault survivors with posttraumatic stress disorder: A randomized controlled trial. *Journal of the American Medical Association, 286,* 537–545.

Krakow, B., & Zadra, A. (2006). Clinical management of chronic nightmares: Imagery rehearsal therapy. *Behavioral Sleep Medicine, 4,* 45–70.

Krause, E. D., Kaltman, S., Goodman, L. A., & Dutton, M. A. (2007). Longitudinal factor structure of posttraumatic stress symptoms related to intimate partner violence. *Psychological Assessment, 19,* 165–175.

Kubany, E. S., Hill, E. E., & Owens, J. A. (2003). Cognitive trauma therapy for battered women with PTSD: Preliminary findings. *Journal of Traumatic Stress, 16,* 81–91.

Kulka, R. A., Schlenger, W. E., Fairbank, J. A., Hough, R. L., Jordan, B. K., Marmar, C. R., & Weiss, D. S. (1990). *Trauma and the Vietnam war generation: Report of findings from the National Vietnam*

Veterans Readjustment Study. New York, NY: Bunner/Mazel.

Lange, A., Rietdijk, D., Hudcovicova, M., van de Ven, J. P., Schrieken, B., & Emmelkamp, P. M. G. (2003). Interapy: A controlled randomized trial of the standardized treatment of posttraumatic stress through the internet. *Journal of Consulting & Clinical Psychology,71*, 901-909.

Lange, A., Van de Ven, J. P., Schrieken, B., & Emmelkamp, P. M. G. (2001). Interapy. Treatment of posttraumatic stress through the Internet: A controlled trial. *Journal of Behavior Therapy and Experimental Psychiatry, 32*, 73-90.

Lee, C., Gavriel, H., Drummond, P., Richards, J., & Greenwald, R. (2002). Treatment of PTSD: Stress inoculation training with prolonged exposure compared to EMDR. *Journal of Clinical Psychology, 58*, 1071-1089.

Lee, C., Slade, P., & Lygo, V. (1996). The influence of psychological debriefing on emotional adaptation in women following early miscarriage: A preliminary study. *British Journal of Medical Psychology, 69*, 47-58.

Lindauer, R. J. L., Gersons, B. P. R., Van Meijel, E. P. M., Blom, K., Carlier, I. V. E., Vrijlandt, I., & Olff, M. (2005). Effects of brief eclectic psychotherapy in patients with posttraumatic stress disorder: Randomized clinical trial. *Journal of Traumatic Stress, 18*, 205-212.

Lindauer, R. J. L., Vlieger, E. J., Jalink, M., Olff, M., Carlier, I. V. E., Majoie, C. B. L. M., ... Gersons, B. P. R. (2005). Effects of psychotherapy on hippocampal volume in out-patients with post-traumatic stress disorder: A MRI investigation. *Psychological Medicine, 35*, 1421-1431.

Litz, B. T., & Adler, A. (2005). A controlled trial of group debriefing. Unpublished raw data.

Litz, B. T., Engel, C. C., Bryant, R. A., & Papa, A. (2007). A randomized, controlled proof of concept trial of an internet-based, therapist-assisted self-management treatment for posttraumatic stress disorder. *American Journal of Psychiatry, 164*, 1676-1683.

Litz, B. T., & Bryant, R. A. (2009). Early cognitive-behavioral interventions for adults. In E. B. Foa, T. M. Keane, M. J. Friedman, & J. A. Cohen (Eds.), *Effective treatments for PTSD: Practice guidelines from the International Society for Traumatic Stress Studies* (pp. 117-135). New York, NY: Guilford Press.

Maercker, A., Zollner, T., Menning, H., Rabe, S., & Karl, A. (2006). Dresden PTSD treatment study: Randomized controlled trial of motor vehicle accident survivors. *BioMed Central Psychiatry, 6*, 29.

Marciniak, M. D., Lage, M. J., Dunayevich, E., Russell, J. M., Bowman, L., Landbloom, R. P., & Levine, L. (2005). The cost of treating anxiety: The medical and demographic correlates that impact total medical costs. *Depression and Anxiety, 21*, 178-184.

Marks, I., Lovell, K., Noshirvani, H., Livanou, M., & Thrasher, S. (1998). Treatment of posttraumatic stress disorder by exposure and/or cognitive restructuring: A Controlled Study. *Archives of General Psychiatry, 55*, 317-325.

Marmar, C. R., Weiss, D. S., Schlenger, W. E., Fairbank, W. A., Jordan, K., Kulka, R. A., & Hough, R. L. (1994). Peritraumatic dissociation and posttraumatic stress in male Vietnam theater veterans. *American Journal of Psychiatry, 151*, 902-907.

Marshall, G. N., & Schell, T. L. (2002). Reappraising the link between peritraumatic dissociation and PTSD symptom severity: Evidence from a longitudinal study of community violence survivors. *Journal of Abnormal Psychology, 111*, 626-636.

Marshall, R. D., Spitzer, R., & Liebowitz, M. R. (1999). Review and critique of the new *DSM-IV* diagnosis of ASD. *American Journal of Psychiatry, 156*, 1677-1685.

Martell, C., Addis, M. E., & Jacobson, N. S. (2001). *Depression in context: Strategies for guided action*. New York, NY: W. W. Norton.

Masho, S. W., & Ahmed, G. (2007). Age at sexual assault and posttraumatic stress disorder among women: Prevalence, correlates, and implications for prevention. *Journal of Women's Health, 16*, 262-271.

Matthews, L. R. (1998). Effect of staff debriefing on posttraumatic stress symptoms after assaults by community housing residents. *Psychiatric Services, 49*, 207-212.

Mayou, R. A., Ehlers, A., & Bryant, B. (2002). Posttraumatic stress disorder after motor vehicle accidents. Three-year follow-up of a prospective longitudinal study. *Behaviour Research and Therapy, 40*, 665-675.

Mayou, R. A., Ehlers, A., & Hobbs, M. (2000). Psychological debriefing for road traffic accident victims. Three-year follow-up of a randomised controlled trial. *British Journal of Psychiatry, 176*, 589-593.

McDonagh, A., McHugo, G., Sengupta, A., Demment, C. C., Schnurr, P. P., Friedman, M., ... Descamps, M. (2005). Randomized trial of cognitive-behavioral therapy for chronic posttraumatic stress disorder in adult female survivors of childhood sexual abuse. *Journal of Consulting and Clinical Psychology, 73*, 515-524.

Meichenbaum, D. (1975). Self-instructional methods. In F. H. Kanfer & A. P. Goldstein (Eds.), *Helping people change* (pp. 357-391). New York, NY: Pergamon Press.

Meiser-Stedman, R., Dalgleish, T., Smith, P., Yule, W., & Glucksman, E. (2007). Diagnostic, demographic, memory quality, and cognitive variables associated with ASD in children and adolescents. *Journal of Abnormal Psychology, 116*, 65-79.

Mitchell, J. T. (1983). When disaster strikes... the critical incident stress debriefing process. *Journal of Emergency Medical Services, 8*, 36-39.

Monson, C. M., Schnurr, P. P., Resick, P. A., Friedman, M. J., Young-Xu, Y., & Stevens, S. P. (2006). Cognitive processing therapy for veterans with military-related posttraumatic stress disorder. *Journal of Consulting and Clinical Psychology, 74*, 898–907.

Mueser, K. T., Rosenberg, S. D., Xie, H., Jankowski, M. K., Bolton, E. E., Lu, W., . . . Wolfe, R. (2008). A randomized controlled trial of cognitive-behavioral treatment for Posttraumatic Stress Disorder in severe mental illness. *Journal of Consulting and Clinical Psychology, 76*, 259–271.

Naifeh, J. A., Elhai, J. D., Kashdan, T. B., & Grubaugh, A. L. (2008). The PTSD Symptom Scale's latent structure: An examination of trauma exposed medical patients. *Journal of Anxiety Disorders, 22*, 1355–1368.

National Institute for Clinical Excellence (NICE). (2005). *Post-traumatic stress disorder (PTSD): The management of PTSD in adults and children in primary and secondary care.* London, England: Author.

Neuner, F., Schauer, M., Klaschik, C., Karunakara, U., & Elbert, T. (2004). A comparison of narrative exposure therapy, supportive counseling, and psychoeducation for treating posttraumatic stress disorder in an African refugee settlement. *Journal of Consulting and Clinical Psychology, 72*, 579–587.

Norris, F. H. (1992). Epidemiology of trauma: Frequency and impact of different potentially traumatic events on different demographic groups. *Journal of Consulting and Clinical Psychology, 60*, 409–418.

Olff, M., Langeland, W., Draijer, N., & Gersons, B. P. R. (2007). Gender differences in posttraumatic stress disorder. *Psychological Bulletin, 133*, 183–204.

Ortega, A. N., & Rosenheck, R. (2000). Posttraumatic stress disorder among Hispanic Vietnam veterans. *American Journal of Psychiatry, 157*, 615–619.

Otto, M. W., Hinton, D., Korbly, N. B., Chea, A., Ba, P., Gershuny, B. S., & Pollack, M. H. (2003). Treatment of pharmacotherapy-refractory posttraumatic stress disorder among Cambodian refugees: A pilot study of combination treatment with cognitive-behavior therapy vs sertraline alone. *Behaviour Research and Therapy, 41*, 1271–1276.

Paunovic, N., & Öst, L. G. (2001). Cognitive-behavior therapy vs exposure therapy in the treatment of PTSD in refugees. *Behaviour Research and Therapy, 39*, 1183–1197.

Pitman, R. K., Orr, S. P., Altman, B., Longpre, R. E., Poiré, R. E., & Macklin, M. L. (1996). Emotional processing during eye movement desensitization and reprocessing therapy of Vietnam veterans with chronic posttraumatic stress disorder. *Comprehensive Psychiatry, 37*, 419–429.

Pole, N., Best, S. R., Weiss, D. S., Metzler, T., Liberman, A. M., Fagan, J., & Marmar, C. R. (2001). Effects of gender and ethnicity on duty-related posttraumatic stress symptoms among urban police officers. *Journal of Nervous and Mental Disease, 189*, 442–448.

Power, K., McGoldrick, T., Brown, K., Buchanan, R., Sharp, D., Swanson, V., & Karatzias, A. (2002). A controlled comparison of eye movement desensitization and reprocessing versus exposure plus cognitive restructuring versus waiting list in the treatment of post-traumatic stress disorder. *Clinical Psychology and Psychotherapy, 9*, 299–318.

Powers, M. B., & Emmelkamp, P. M. G. (2008). Virtual reality exposure therapy for anxiety disorders: A meta-analysis. *Journal of Anxiety Disorders, 22*, 561–569.

Raphael, B. (1986). *When disaster strikes: A handbook for caring professions.* London, England: Hutchinson.

Renfrey, G., & Spates, C. R. (1994). Eye movement desensitization: A partial dismantling study. *Journal of Behavior Therapy and Experimental Psychiatry, 25*, 231–239.

Resick, P. A., Galovski, T. E., Uhlmansiek, M. O., Scher, C. D., Clum, G. A., & Young-Xu, Y. (2008). A randomized clinical trial to dismantle components of cognitive processing therapy for posttraumatic stress disorder in female victims of interpersonal violence. *Journal of Consulting and Clinical Psychology, 76*, 243–258.

Resick, P. A., Nishith, P., Weaver, T. L., Astin, M. C., & Feuer, C. A. (2002). A comparison of cognitive-processing therapy with prolonged exposure and a waiting condition for the treatment of chronic posttraumatic stress disorder in female rape victims. *Journal of Consulting and Clinical Psychology, 70*, 867–879.

Resick, P. A., & Schnicke, M. K. (1992). Cognitive processing therapy for sexual assault victims. *Journal of Consulting and Clinical Psychology, 60*, 748–756.

Richards, D. A., Lovell, K., & Marks, I. M. (1994). Posttraumatic stress disorder: Evaluation of a behavioral treatment program. *Journal of Traumatic Stress, 7*, 669–680.

Riggs, D. S., Rothbaum, B. O., & Foa, E. B. (1995). A prospective examination of symptoms of posttraumatic stress disorder in victims of nonsexual assault. *Journal of Interpersonal Violence, 10*, 201–214.

Rose, S. (1997). Psychological debriefing: History and methods counseling. *Journal of the British Association of Counseling, 8*, 48–51.

Rose, S., Brewin, C. R., Andrews, B., & Kirk, M. (1999). A randomized controlled trial of individual psychological debriefing for victims of violent crime. *Psychological Medicine, 29*, 793–799.

Rothbaum, B. O., Astin, M. C., & Marsteller, F. (2005). Prolonged exposure versus eye movement desensitization and reprocessing (EMDR) for PTSD rape victims. *Journal of Traumatic Stress, 18*, 607–616.

Rothbaum, B. O., Cahill, S. P., Foa, E. B., Davidson, J. R. T., Compton, J., Connor, K. M., . . . Hahn, C. (2006). Augmentation of sertraline with prolonged exposure in the treatment of posttraumatic stress disorder. *Journal of Traumatic Stress, 19*, 625–638.

Rothbaum, B. O., Foa, E. B., Riggs, D. S., Murdock, T., & Walsh, W. (1992). A prospective examination of post-traumatic stress disorder in rape victims. *Journal of Traumatic Stress, 5,* 455–475.

Savoca, E., & Rosenheck, R. (2000). The civilian labor market experiences of Vietnam-era veterans: The influence of psychiatric disorders. *Journal of Mental Health Policy and Economics, 3,* 199–207.

Schauer, M., Elbert, T., Gotthardt, S., Rockstroh, B., Odenwald, M., & Neuner, F. (2006). Imaginary reliving in psychotherapy modifies mind and brain. *Wiedererfahrung durch psychotherapie modifiziert geist und gehirn, 16,* 96–103.

Schnurr, P. P., Friedman, M. J., Engel, C. C., Foa, E. B., Shea, M. T., Chow, B. K., . . . Bernardy, N. (2007). Cognitive behavioral therapy for posttraumatic stress disorder in women: a randomized controlled trial. *Journal of the American Medical Association, 297,* 820–830.

Schnurr, P. P., Friedman, M. J., Foy, D. W., Shea, M. T., Hsieh, F. Y., Lavori, P. W., . . . Bernardy, N. C. (2003). Randomized trial of trauma-focused group therapy for posttraumatic stress disorder: Results from a Department of Veterans Affairs Cooperative Study. *Archives of General Psychiatry, 60,* 481–489.

Shapiro, F. (1989). Eye movement desensitization: A new treatment for post traumatic stress disorder. *Journal of Behavior Therapy and Experimental Psychiatry, 20,* 211–217.

Shapiro, F. (1991). Eye movement desensitization and reprocessing procedure: From EMD to EMDR: A new treatment model for anxiety and related trauma. *Behavior Therapist, 14,* 133–135.

Shapiro, F. (1995). *Eye movement desensitization and reprocessing.* New York, NY: Guilford Press.

Shapiro, F. (2001). *Eye movement desensitization and reprocessing: Basic principles, protocols, and procedures* (2nd ed.). New York, NY: Guilford Press.

Sijbrandij, M., Olff, M., Reitsma, J. B., Carlier, I. V. E., & Gersons, B. P. R. (2006). Emotional or educational debriefing after psychological trauma. Randomised controlled trial. *British Journal of Psychiatry, 189,* 150–155.

Simms, L. J., Watson, D., & Doebbeling, B. N. (2002). Confirmatory factor analyses of posttraumatic stress symptoms in deployed and nondeployed veterans of the Gulf War. *Journal of Abnormal Psychology, 111,* 637–647.

Sledjeski, E. M., Speisman, B., & Dierker, L. C. (2008). Does number of lifetime traumas explain the relationship between PTSD and chronic medical conditions? Answers from the National Comorbidity Survey Replication (NCS-R). *Journal of Behavioral Medicine, 31,* 341–349.

Smith, M. W., Schnurr, P. P., & Rosenheck, R. A. (2005). Employment outcomes and PTSD symptom severity. *Mental Health Services Research, 7,* 89–101.

Spates, C. R., Koch, E., Pagoto, S., Cusack, K., & Waller, S. (2009). Eye movement desensitization and reprocessing. In E. B. Foa, T. M. Keane, M. Friedman, & J. Cohen (Eds.), *Effective treatments for PTSD (2nd ed.)* (pp. 279–305). New York, NY: Guilford Press.

Spiegel, D., Hunt, T., & Dondershine, H. E. (1988). Dissociation and hypnotizability in posttraumatic stress disorder. *American Journal of Psychiatry, 141,* 301–305.

Stam, R. (2007). PTSD and stress sensitisation: A tale of brain and body: Part 1: Human studies. *Neuroscience & Biobehavioral Reviews, 31,* 530–557.

Tarrier, N., Pilgrim, H., Sommerfield, C., Faragher, B., Reynolds, M., Graham, E., & Barrowclough, C. (1999). A randomized trial of cognitive therapy and imaginal exposure in the treatment of chronic posttraumatic stress disorder. *Journal of Consulting and Clinical Psychology, 67,* 13–18.

Taylor, S., Koch, K., Kuch, W. J., Crockett, D. J., & Passey, G. (1998). The structure of posttraumatic stress symptoms. *Journal of Abnormal Psychology, 107,* 154–160.

Taylor, S., Thordarson, D. S., Federoff, I. C., Maxfield, L., Lovell, K., & Ogrodniczuk, J. (2003). Comparative efficacy, speed, and adverse effects of three PTSD treatments: Exposure therapy, EMDR, and relaxation training. *Journal of Consulting and Clinical Psychology, 71,* 330–338.

Tolin, D. F., & Foa, E. B. (2006). Sex differences in trauma and posttraumatic stress disorder: A quantitative review of 25 years of research. *Psychological Bulletin, 132,* 959–992.

Turpin, G., Downs, M., & Mason, S. (2005). Effectiveness of providing self-help information following acute traumatic injury: Randomised controlled trial. *British Journal of Psychiatry, 187,* 76–82.

Ursano, R. J., Bell, C., Eth, S., Friedman, M., Norwood, A., Pfefferbaum, B., . . . Steering Committee on Practice Guidelines. Practice guideline for the treatment of patients with ASD and posttraumatic stress disorder. *American Journal of Psychiatry, 161*(11 Suppl.), 1–31.

Van Emmerik, A. A. P., Kamphuis, J. H., & Emmelkamp, P. M. G. (2008). Treating acute stress disorder and posttraumatic stress disorder with cognitive behavioral therapy or structured writing therapy: A randomized controlled trial. *Psychotherapy and Psychosomatics, 77,* 93–100.

Van Emmerik, A. A. P., Kamphuis, J. H., Hulsbosch, A. M., & Emmelkamp, P. M. G. (2002). Single session debriefing after psychological trauma: A metaanalysis. *Lancet, 360*(9335), 766–771.

Vaughan, K., Armstrong, M. S., Gold, R., O'Connor, N., Jenneke, W., & Tarrier, N. (1994). A trial of eye movement desensitization compared to image habituation training and applied muscle relaxation in posttraumatic stress disorder. *Journal of Behavior Therapy and Experimental Psychiatry, 25,* 283–291.

Veronen, L. J., & Kilpatrick, D. G. (1983). Stress management for rape victims. In D. Meichenbaum &

M. E. Jaremko (Eds.), *Stress reduction and prevention* (pp. 341–374). New York, NY: Plenum Press.

Wee, D. F., Mills, D. M., & Koehler, G. (1999). The effects of critical incident stress debriefing (CISD) on emergency medical services personnel following the Los Angeles civil disturbance. *International Journal of Emergency Mental Health, 1,* 33–37.

Yehuda, R., Golier, J. A., Harvey, P. D., Stavitsky, K., Kaufman, S., Grossman, R. A., & Tischler, L. (2005). Relationship between cortisol and age-related memory impairments in Holocaust survivors with PTSD. *Psychoneuroendocrinology, 30,* 678–687.

Zatzick, D. F., Marmar, C. R., Weiss, D. S., Browner, W. S., Metzler, T. J., Golding, J. M., . . . Wells, K. B. (1997). Posttraumatic stress disorder and functioning and quality of life outcomes in a nationally representative sample of male Vietnam veterans. *American Journal of Psychiatry, 154,* 1690–1695.

Zlotnick, C., Shea, T. M., Rosen, K., Simpson, E., Mulrenin, K., Begin, A., & Pearlstein, T. (1997). An affect-management group for women with posttraumatic stress disorder and histories of childhood sexual abuse. *Journal of Traumatic Stress, 10,* 425–436.

15

Somatoform and Factitious Disorders

LESLEY A. ALLEN AND ROBERT L. WOOLFOLK

OVERVIEW OF DISORDERS

Physical symptoms with uncertain medical explanations are some of the most common presentations in primary care. As many as 25% of visits to primary care physicians are prompted by physical symptoms that lack any clear organic pathology (Gureje, Simon, Ustun, & Goldberg, 1997). Patients presenting with medically unexplained physical symptoms (MUPS) provide significant challenges to health care providers. These patients tend to overuse health care services, derive little benefit from treatment, and experience protracted impairment, often lasting many years (G. R. Smith, Monson, & Ray, 1986a). Often, MUPS patients are dissatisfied with the medical services they receive and repeatedly change physicians (Lin et al., 1991). These treatment-resistant patients frustrate physicians with their frequent complaints and dissatisfaction with treatment (Hahn, 2001; Lin et al., 1991). Because standard medical care has been relatively unsuccessful in treating somatoform and factitious disorders, alternative treatments have been developed.

The chapter will summarize the treatment of various somatoform and factitious disorders. All the somatoform and factitious disorders are characterized by the presence of physical symptom(s) that suggest a general medical

condition but are not fully explained by a general medical condition. Somatoform disorders differ from factitious disorders in the extent to which the symptoms are intentionally produced or feigned. Symptoms related to a factitious disorder are intentionally produced or feigned in order to assume the sick role. Symptoms related to a somatoform disorder are not under voluntary control.

SOMATIZATION DISORDER AND SUBTHRESHOLD SOMATIZATION: OVERVIEW OF DISORDER

Diagnostic Criteria and Prevalence

Somatization disorder is the contemporary conceptualization of a syndrome that was once labeled hysteria and, more recently, Briquet's syndrome. The criteria for Briquet's syndrome were symptoms associated with a diagnosis of hysteria and were incorporated into the Feighner diagnostic criteria (Feighner et al., 1972) that were the precursor to *DSM-III*. According to the current *Diagnostic and Statistical Manual of Mental Disorders* (*DSM-IV*) (American Psychiatric Association [APA], 1994), somatization disorder is characterized by a lifetime history of at least four unexplained pain complaints (e.g., in the back, chest, joints), two unexplained nonpain gastrointestinal complaints (e.g., nausea, bloating), one unexplained sexual symptom (e.g., sexual dysfunction, irregular menstruation), and one pseudoneurological symptom (e.g., seizures, paralysis, numbness). For a symptom to be counted toward the diagnosis of somatization disorder, its presence must be medically unexplained or its degree of severity be substantially in excess of the associated medical pathology. Also, each symptom must either prompt the seeking of medical care or interfere with the patient's functioning. In addition, at least some of the somatization symptoms must have occurred prior to the patient's 30th birthday (APA, 1994). The course of somatization disorder tends to be characterized by symptoms that wax and wane, remitting only to return later and/or be replaced by new unexplained physical symptoms. Thus, somatization disorder is a chronic, polysymptomatic disorder whose requisite symptoms need not be manifested concurrently.

Epidemiological research suggests that somatization disorder is relatively rare. The prevalence of somatization disorder in the general population has been estimated to be 0.1% to 0.7% (Faravelli et al., 1997; Robins & Reiger, 1991; Weissman, Myers, & Harding, 1978). When patients in primary care, specialty medical, and psychiatric settings are assessed, the rate of somatization is higher than in the general population, with estimates ranging from 1.0% to 5.0% (Altamura et al., 1998; Fabrega, Mezzich, Jacob, & Ulrich, 1988; Fink, Steen Hansen, & Søndergaard, 2005; Gureje, Simon, et al., 1997; Kirmayer & Robbins, 1991; Peveler, Kilkenny, & Kinmonth, 1997).

Although somatization disorder is classified as a distinct disorder in *DSM-IV*, it has been argued that somatization disorder represents the extreme end of a somatization continuum (Escobar, Burnam, Karno, Forsythe, & Golding, 1987; Kroenke et al., 1997). The number of unexplained physical symptoms reported correlates positively with the patient's degree of

emotional distress and functional impairment (Katon et al., 1991). A broadening of the somatization construct has been advocated by those wishing to underscore the many patients encumbered by unexplained symptoms that are not numerous enough to meet criteria for full somatization disorder (Escobar et al., 1987; Katon et al., 1991; Kroenke et al., 1997).

DSM-IV includes a residual diagnostic category for subthreshold somatization cases. *Undifferentiated somatoform disorder* is a diagnosis characterized by one or more medically unexplained physical symptom(s) lasting for at least six months (APA, 1994). Long considered a category that is too broad because it includes patients with only one unexplained symptom as well as those with many unexplained symptoms, undifferentiated somatoform disorder never has been well-validated or widely applied (Kroenke, Sharpe, & Sykes, 2007).

Two research teams have suggested categories for subthreshold somatization using criteria less restrictive and requiring less extensive symptomatology than the standards for *DSM-IV*'s full somatization disorder. Escobar and colleagues proposed the label *abridged somatization* to be applied to men experiencing four or more unexplained physical symptoms or to women experiencing six or more unexplained physical symptoms (Escobar et al., 1987). Kroenke et al. suggested the category of *multisomatoform disorder* to describe men or women currently experiencing at least three unexplained physical symptoms and reporting a 2-year history of somatization (Kroenke et al., 1997).

Both of these subthreshold somatization categories appear to be significantly more prevalent than is *somatization disorder* as defined by *DSM-IV*. Abridged somatization has been observed in 4% of community samples (Escobar et al., 1987) and 16% to 22% of primary care samples (Escobar, Waitzkin, Silver, Gara, & Holman, 1998; Gureje, Simon, et al., 1997; Kirmayer & Robbins, 1991). The occurrence of multisomatoform disorder has been estimated at 8% of primary care patients (Jackson & Kroenke, 2008; Kroenke et al., 1997).

Demographic and Clinical Characteristics

The demographic characteristic most often associated with somatization is gender. In the Epidemiological Catchment Area (ECA) study, women were 10 times more likely to meet criteria for somatization disorder than were men (Swartz, Landerman, George, Blazer, & Escobar, 1991). Higher rates of occurrence in women, though not as extreme, also have been found in most studies employing subthreshold somatization categories, such as Escobar's abridged somatization or Kroenke's multisomatoform disorder (Escobar, Rubio-Stipec, Canino, & Karno, 1989; Kroenke et al., 1997). A more complex picture of the association between gender and somatization was suggested by the WHO's Cross-National study in which female primary care patients were more likely to meet criteria for full somatization disorder, but no more likely to meet Escobar's abridged somatization criteria than were their male counterparts (Gureje, Simon, et al., 1997). On the severe end of the continuum, somatization disorder is uncommon in men. Gender differences are less obvious in the various subthreshold syndromes.

Ethnicity, race, and education have been associated with somatization disorder and subthreshold somatization. Epidemiological research has shown somatization patients more likely to be nonwhite and less educated than nonsomatizers (Gureje, Simon, et al., 1997; Robins & Regier, 1991). Findings on ethnicity have been less consistent across studies. In the ECA study, Hispanics were no more likely to meet criteria for somatization disorder than were non-Hispanics (Robins & Regier, 1991). The WHO study, conducted in 14 different countries, revealed a higher incidence of somatization, as defined by either ICD-10 or Escobar's abridged criteria, in Latin American

countries than in the United States (Gureje, Simon, et al., 1997).

Much attention has focused on somatization patients' illness behavior and the resulting impact of that behavior on the health-care system. These patients disproportionately use and misuse health-care services. When standard diagnostic evaluations fail to uncover organic pathology, somatization patients tend to seek additional medical procedures, often from several different physicians. Patients may even subject themselves to unnecessary hospitalizations and surgeries, which introduce the risk of iatrogenic illness (Fink, 1992). One study found that somatization disorder patients, on average, incurred 9 times the U.S. per capita health-care cost (G. R. Smith et al., 1986a). Abridged somatization and multisomatoform disorder also have been associated with significant health-care utilization (Escobar, Golding, et al. 1987; Kroenke et al., 1997).

The abnormal illness behavior of somatizing patients extends beyond medical offices and hospitals to patients' workplaces and households. Somatizers withdraw from both productive and pleasurable activities because of discomfort, fatigue, and/or fears of exacerbating their symptoms. In a study assessing the efficacy of cognitive behavior therapy for somatization disorder, we found 19% of patients meeting DSM-IV criteria for somatization disorder to be receiving disability payments from either their employers or the government (Allen, Woolfolk, Escobar, Gara, & Hamer, 2006). Estimates of unemployment among somatization disorder patients range from 36% to 83% (Allen et al., 2006; G. R. Smith et al., 1986a; Yutzy et al., 1995). Whether working outside their homes or not, these patients report substantial functional impairment. Some investigators have found that somatization disorder patients report being bedridden for 2 to 7 days per month (Katon et al., 1991; G. R. Smith et al., 1986a). Likewise, high levels of functional impairment have been associated with subthreshold somatization (Allen, Gara, Escobar, Waitzkin, &

Cohen-Silver, 2001; Escobar, Golding, et al., 1987; Gureje, Simon, et al., 1997; Jackson & Kroenke, 2008; Kroenke et al., 1997).

In addition to their physical complaints, many somatization patients complain of psychiatric distress. As many as 80% of patients meeting criteria for somatization disorder or subthreshold somatization meet *DSM* criteria for another lifetime Axis I disorder, usually an anxiety or mood disorder (G. R. Smith et al., 1986a; Swartz, Blazer, George, & Landerman, 1986). When investigators consider only current psychiatric diagnoses, rates of psychiatric comorbidity associated with somatization are closer to 50% (Allen et al., 2001; Simon & Von Korff, 1991). Also, overall severity of psychological distress, defined as the number of psychological symptoms reported, correlates positively with the number of functional somatic symptoms reported (Katon et al., 1991; Simon & Von Korff, 1991).

Randomized Controlled Trials

Several different psychosocial interventions have been used to treat somatization, some administered by mental health providers and others administered by nonmental health providers. All approaches seem to have been theoretically grounded in social learning theory. The studies are reviewed as follows.

Cognitive Behavior Therapy

Three studies have compared the efficacy of individually administered cognitive behavior therapy (CBT) with standard medical care for patients manifesting a diverse set of unexplained physical symptoms. Only one study has been published treating patients meeting *DSM-IV* criteria for full somatization disorder (Allen et al., 2006). Two studies were conducted in primary care settings with patients who were diagnosed with subthreshold somatization, defined as abridged somatization in one study (Escobar et al., 2007), and defined as five or more unexplained physical symptoms

in the other (Sumathipala, Hewege, Hanwella, & Mann, 2000). All three studies showed that individual CBT coincided with greater reductions in somatic complaints than did standard medical care (Allen et al., 2006; Escobar et al., 2007; Sumathipala et al., 2000). Allen et al. (2006) found that 40% of their CBT-treated participants, versus 7% of the control group, were judged to have achieved clinically significant improvement, defined as being *very much improved* or *much improved* on a clinician-rated scale of somatization severity. Also, CBT was associated with enhanced physical functioning in Allen et al., (2006) and reduced health-care utilization in two studies (Allen et al., 2006; Sumathipala et al., 2000). Long-term maintenance of symptom relief was demonstrated in two studies; one showed significant differences in somatization symptomatology 6 months after treatment completion (Escobar et al., 2007), and the other showed symptom improvement lasted for 12 months after the treatment phase of the study (Allen et al., 2006). Table 15.1 summarizes treatment effect sizes for the studies that reported sufficient data for such calculations.

Two groups of investigators have conducted controlled treatment trials assessing the efficacy of CBT with a less severely disturbed group of patients, those complaining of at least one psychosomatic symptom. In one study patients treated with individual CBT showed greater improvement in their psychosomatic complaints than did patients treated with standard medical care (Speckens, van Hemert, et al., 1995). The other study found group CBT, lead by a trained physician, superior to a waiting-list control condition in reducing physical symptoms and hypochondriacal beliefs (Lidbeck, 1997). In both studies improvements were observed after treatment as well as 6 months later (Lidbeck, 1997; Speckens, van Hemert, et al., 1995) (see Table 15.1 for effect sizes). Lidbeck's CBT participants seemed to maintain reductions in somatization and hypochondriacal beliefs 18 months after treatment (Lidbeck, 2003).

TABLE 15.1   Treatment Effect Sizes for CBT for Somatization

Author	N	Control	Measures	Posttx	6-Mo. Posttx	12-Mo. Posttx
Allen et al., 2006	84	WL	CGI-S	0.51	0.68	0.66
			Sx Diary	0.53	0.74	0.55
			MOS-PF	−0.24	−0.29	−0.34
Escobar et al., 2007	172	WL	PHQ-15	0.41	0.43	
			MOS-PF	−0.11	0.17	
Speckens et al., 1995	77	WL	Sx Intensity	0.58	0.43	
			Whitely	0.12	0.24	
Lidbeck, 1997	50	SMC	IBQ	0.67	0.81	
			Whitely	0.51	0.60	
			Medication Use	0.65	0.55	

Note: Effect sizes calculated as $d = (m1 - m2)/sd_{pooled}$

Posttx = Posttreatment

WL = Waiting list

SMC = Standard medical care

CGI-S = Clinical Global Impression Severity scale (Allen et al., 2006)

Sx Diary = 7 day mean of daily ratings of the maximum severity of somatic symptoms.

MOS-PF = Physical functioning scale of the Medical Outcomes Study scale (Ware & Sherbourne, 1992)

PHQ-15 = 15 item self-report scale of somatic symptoms from the PRIME-MD (Kroenke, Spitzer, & Williams, 2002)

Sx Intensity = Self-report of mean intensity of symptoms over the past month

IBQ = Illness Behaviour Questionnaire (Pilowsky, 1993)

Whitely = Whitely Index, a measure of hypochondriacal beliefs (Pilowsky, 1993)

Modifying Primary Care Physicians' Behavior

Other approaches to the treatment of somatization have been focused on primary care physicians' behavior. G. R. Smith and colleagues sent a psychiatric consultation letter to patients' primary care physicians, describing somatization disorder and providing recommendations to guide primary care (G. R. Smith, Monson, & Ray, 1986b). The recommendations to physicians were straightforward: (a) to schedule somatizers' appointments every 4 to 6 weeks instead of as needed appointments, (b) to conduct a physical examination in the organ system or body part relevant to the presenting complaint, (c) to avoid diagnostic procedures and surgeries unless clearly indicated by underlying somatic pathology, and (d) to avoid making disparaging statements, such as "your symptoms are all in your head." Patients whose primary physicians had received the consultation letter experienced better health outcomes, such as physical functioning and cost of medical care, than those whose physicians had not received the letter. The results were replicated in three additional studies, one study using patients meeting criteria for full somatization disorder (Rost, Kashner, & Smith, 1994) and two studies using patients with subthreshold somatization (Dickinson et al., 2003; G. R. Smith, Rost, & Kashner, 1995).

One other study examined the effect of group psychotherapy conducted in the primary care setting on the physical and emotional functioning of patients meeting *DSM* criteria for full somatization disorder. Group treatment was developed to provide peer support, psychoeducation, and coping skills and to encourage emotional expression. This group intervention, in combination with standard medical care augmented by the psychiatric consultation letter described earlier, was associated with significantly greater improvements in physical functioning and mental health than was the control condition, that is, standard medical treatment augmented by the psychiatric consultation letter (Kashner, Rost, Cohen, Anderson, & Smith, 1995).

Given the success of the previously described consultation letter, the success of CBT, and the difficulties involved in distinguishing between medically explained and medically unexplained symptoms, some investigators have attempted to train primary care physicians to better detect somatization and to incorporate CBT techniques into their treatment of these patients. Three groups have reported controlled clinical trials on the effects of such physician training (Larisch, Schweickhardt, Wirsching, & Fritzsche, 2004; Rief, Martin, Rauh, Zech, & Bender, 2006; Rosendal et al., 2007). The one study providing the most extensive physician training (25 hours) resulted in no association between physician training and patients' symptomatology, functioning, or quality of life (Rosendal et al., 2007). Two other studies found less intensive physician training programs, 12 hours (Larisch et al., 2004) or 1 day (Rief et al., 2006), to coincide with no clear improvement in somatization symptomatology; however, Rief and colleagues did find their training to result in fewer health-care visits for the 6 months subsequent to training (Rief et al., 2006).

One additional study examined the effect of training primary care clinicians to identify and treat somatization using a biopsychosocial model (R. C. Smith et al., 2006). Nurse practitioners were trained to provide a multidimensional intervention in primary care. The treatment incorporated biopsychosocial conceptualizations, behavioral recommendations, and medication management of somatization. The nurses' training program was intensive, entailing 84 hours over 10 weeks. Patients who received treatment from these trained nurses reported modest improvements on self-report scales of mental health such as mood and energy and physical functioning. A post hoc analysis was interpreted by the study's investigators as suggesting improvements were attributable to more frequent and appropriate use of antidepressant medication among patients of nurses who received the training (R. C. Smith et al., 2006).

Summary

The extraordinary financial costs of somatization, along with the associated suffering and disability, make it a public health concern. Initial findings on the characteristics of somatizing patients support a cognitive behavioral rationale for treatment. However, we cannot yet label CBT as an empirically supported treatment for somatization disorder (Chambless & Hollon, 1998) since only one randomized controlled trial has been published on CBT for full somatization disorder (Allen et al., 2006). Although its findings were positive, a majority of the treated patients continued to suffer with significant symptomatology after treatment ended. Additional randomized controlled trials are required to replicate these findings. Four other controlled clinical trials suggest CBT reduces physical discomfort, functional limitations, and physician visits in patients with one or more unexplained physical symptom. Thus, we can say that CBT for subthreshold somatization has been empirically supported (Chambless & Hollon, 1998).

Studies designed to alter primary care treatment of somatization have had mixed results. G. R. Smith et al.'s psychiatric consultation letter, providing treatment recommendations for specific patients and labeling their symptoms as somatization, has repeatedly been shown to produce reductions in medical utilization. However, extensive training of physicians aimed at broadly affecting their approaches to working with somatization patients in their practices has had minimal effects on patient symptomatology and behavior.

CONVERSION DISORDER: OVERVIEW OF DISORDER

Diagnostic Criteria and Prevalence

Conversion symptoms, also described as pseudoneurological symptoms, are abnormalities or deficits in voluntary motor or sensory function that are medically unexplained. Some of the most common pseudoneurological symptoms are pseudoseizures, pseudoparalysis, and psychogenic movement disorders. According to *DSM-IV*, conversion disorder is characterized by the presence of one or more pseudoneurological symptoms that are associated with psychological stressor(s) or conflict(s) (APA, 1994). The diagnosis of conversion disorder requires a thorough psychiatric evaluation as well as a physical examination in order to rule out organic neurological illness. Patients presenting with conversion symptoms typically have normal reflexes and normal muscle tone.

The course of conversion disorder appears to be different from that of somatization disorder, which tends to be chronic (Kent, Tomasson, & Coryell, 1995). The onset and course of conversion disorder often take the form of an acute episode. Symptoms may remit within a few weeks of an initial episode and they may recur in the future. Some research indicates that a brief duration of symptoms prior to treatment is associated a better prognosis (Crimlisk et al., 1998; Hafeiz, 1980; Ron, 2001).

Estimates of the prevalence of conversion disorder have varied widely, ranging from 0.01% to 0.3% in the community (Faravelli et al., 1997; Stefansson, Messina, & Meyerowitz, 1979). As is the case with the other somatoform disorders, conversion disorder is much more common in medical and psychiatric practices than in community samples. As many as 25% of neurology clinic patients may present for treatment of a medically unexplained neurological symptom (Creed, Firth, Timol, Metcalfe, & Pollock, 1990; Perkin, 1989).

Demographic and Clinical Characteristics

The demographic characteristics of conversion disorder have not been investigated extensively. Nevertheless, there is some evidence that conversion disorder is more common among women (Deveci et al., 2007; Faravelli et al., 1997), nonWhites (Stefansson et al., 1979), and individuals from lower socioeconomic classes (Folks, Ford, & Regan,

1984; Stefansson et al., 1979). Comorbid psychiatric distress in patients with pseudoneurological symptoms is high; it has been estimated that 30% to 90% of patients seeking treatment for pseudoneurological symptoms also meet criteria for at least one other psychiatric disorder, typically somatoform disorders, affective disorders, anxiety disorders, or personality disorders (Binzer, Andersen, & Kullgren, 1997; Crimlisk et al., 1998; Mokleby, Blomhoff, et al., 2002; Sar, Akyuz, Kundakci, Kiziltan, & Dogan, 2004). A comorbid personality disorder diagnosis has been found to indicate poor prognosis of conversion disorder (Mace & Trimble, 1996).

Like somatization disorder, conversion disorder is costly to the health-care system, especially when symptoms are chronic (Mace & Trimble, 1996). Patients with long-standing conversion symptoms are likely to submit themselves to unnecessary diagnostic and medical procedures. R. Martin and colleagues reported an average of $100,000 being spent per year per conversion disorder patient (R. Martin, Bell, Hermann, & Mennemeyer, 2003).

Randomized Controlled Trials

Conversion disorders have been treated with various approaches, including hypnosis, CBT, biofeedback, family therapy, spa treatment, pharmacotherapy, surgery, electroconvulsive therapy (ECT), physiotherapy, and inpatient psychiatric care. Only three randomized controlled trials on the treatment of conversion disorder have been published. Two assessed the efficacy of hypnosis (Moene, Spinhoven, Hoogduin, & van Dyck, 2002, 2003) and one assessed the efficacy of paradoxical intention therapy (Ataoglu, Ozcetin, Icmeli, & Ozbulut, 2003).

In their first study on hypnosis, Moene et al. (2002) compared the efficacy of adding hypnotherapy to an inpatient treatment for patients with motor-type conversion symptoms. All study participants were inpatients receiving a multidisciplinary treatment including group therapy, problem solving, social skills training, exercise, physiotherapy, and bed rest. Twenty-four patients were randomly assigned to receive one hypnotherapy preparatory session and eight weekly 1-hour hypnotherapy sessions. The hypnotherapy strategies were aimed at: (a) direct symptom alleviation using suggestions designed to alter conditioned cues to motor symptoms, and (b) emotional expression/insight involving age regression to explore factors implicated in the development of the symptoms. Also, hypnotherapy-treated participants were instructed to practice self-hypnosis for 30 minutes each day. The control comparison condition consisted of one preparatory session and eight weekly 1-hour therapy sessions "aimed at optimizing non-specific or common therapy factors." (p. 69). Participants were encouraged to think and write about therapy sessions for homework. Assessments conducted 8 months after enrollment suggested that the motor symptoms of both groups had improved following baseline; however, there were no between-group differences (Moene et al., 2002).

In a second study, the same group of investigators treated outpatients diagnosed with motor-type conversion disorder. In this study, a slightly longer hypnotherapy intervention, including one preparatory session and 10 weekly 1-hour sessions, was associated with better outcomes than was a waiting-list control condition (Moene, Spinhoven, Hoogduin, & van Dyck, 2003). The content of the hypnotherapy strategies and homework were the same as in their previous study (Moene et al., 2002). Experimental patients received significantly lower scores on the Video Rating Scale for Motor Symptoms and on an interviewer-based measure of physical limitations (International Classification of Impairments, Disabilities, and Handicaps [ICIDH] subscale for physical activities) than did those randomized to the control waiting-list condition (Moene et al., 2003). The treatment effect sizes were $d = 1.55$ for the Video Rating Scale for Motor Symptoms, and $d = 0.30$ for the ICIDH. Because these findings are based on

treatment completers (i.e., 44 of the 49 randomized participants), not the intent-to-treat sample, they probably overestimate true differences between the treatment and control sample.

A third study compared paradoxical intention therapy provided as a part of a 3-week inpatient program with a 7-week outpatient pharmacotherapy intervention using diazepam (5 to 15mg daily) combined with four outpatient medication management sessions. The paradoxical intention therapy was administered twice per day and involved asking patients to imagine anxiety-provoking situations and/or experiences. The aim was to trigger conversion attacks by helping patients reexperience putative underlying trauma (Ataoglu et al., 2003). At the end of treatment there were no differences in the number of conversion symptoms between the groups, though the paradoxical intention group did report greater reductions in anxiety than did the diazepam group. Nevertheless, the study's findings have little validity because the differences between groups may have been attributable to other differences in treatment (i.e., inpatient versus outpatient, medication vs. talk therapy) rather than to the paradoxical intention therapy itself (Ataoglu et al., 2003).

Summary

At present no treatment for conversion disorder has been demonstrated to be empirically supported, as defined by Chambless and Hollon (1998). The only three published randomized controlled trials contain significant methodological flaws. Before any guidelines for treatment can be formulated, there is a need for well-designed randomized controlled trials to assess the efficacy of interventions with this population.

PAIN DISORDER

Pain disorder is characterized by clinically significant pain that is judged to be affected by psychological factors (APA, 1994). Very little research has been conducted that addresses pain disorder as defined by *DSM-IV* (or its *DSM-III-R* counterpart, somatoform pain disorder) as a discrete diagnostic category. Instead, researchers have tended to formulate research based on the anatomical site and the chronicity of the pain. Thus, there is a voluminous literature on distinct pain conditions, for example, back pain, chest pain, pelvic pain, and headaches. In none of these studies have investigators attempted to distinguish between pain that was apparently affected by psychological factors and pain that was apparently not, presumably because such a distinction is too difficult to make and perhaps unreliable. Many experts have suggested the elimination of the pain disorder category from future versions of *DSM* (Birket-Smith & Mortenson, 2002; Kroenke et al., 2007; Sullivan, 2000). Given the paucity of research on pain disorder and the uncertainty of its future as a diagnostic category, we will not address the topic any further. We have, however, addressed related conditions in the functional somatic syndrome section of this chapter.

HYPOCHONDRIASIS: OVERVIEW OF DISORDER

Diagnostic Criteria and Prevalence

According to *DSM-IV*, hypochondriasis is defined as a "preoccupation with fears of having, or the idea that one has, a serious disease based on the person's misinterpretation of bodily symptoms" (APA, 1994, p. 462). This preoccupation must persist despite medical evaluation and physician reassurance and cause significant distress or impairment in one's functioning (APA, 1994). Thus, unlike in somatization where the distress and dysfunction experienced is due to the physical symptoms themselves, in hypochondriasis the distress and dysfunction is due to the patient's interpretation of the meaning of his or her symptoms. The

course of hypochondriasis is often chronic: As many as 50% of patients meeting *DSM* criteria for hypochondriasis have excessive health concerns for many years (Barsky, Fama, Bailey, & Ahern, 1998; Barsky, Wyshak, Klerman, & Latham, 1990).

There are only a few epidemiological studies that have examined the prevalence of hypochondriasis. Studies that have utilized a clinical interview to assess prevalence have suggested that hypochondriasis occurs rarely in the general population. Such estimates range from 0.02% to 1.6% (Faravelli et al., 1997; Looper & Kirmayer, 2001; A. Martin & Jacobi, 2006). In primary care, estimates range from 0.8% to 6.3% (Barsky et al., 1990; Gureje, Ustun, & Simon, 1997; Escobar et al., 1998).

Demographic and Clinical Characteristics

Unlike somatization disorder, hypochondriasis does not appear to be related to gender (Barsky et al., 1990; Gureje Ustun, et al., 1997; Looper & Kirmayer, 2001). Men are as likely to meet *DSM* criteria for hypochondriasis as are women. Findings have been inconsistent on whether hypochondriasis is related to education, socioeconomic status, and ethnicity (Barsky et al., 1990; Gureje Ustun, et al., 1997).

Like patients with somatization disorder and milder versions of somatization, those with hypochondriasis exhibit abnormal illness behavior. They overutilize health care (Gureje Ustun, et al., 1997; Looper & Kirmayer, 2001), subjecting themselves to multiple physician visits and multiple diagnostic procedures. They report great dissatisfaction with their medical care (Barsky, 1996; Noyes et al., 1993). In addition, patients diagnosed with hypochondriasis report substantial physical impairment and functional limitations related to employment (Escobar et al., 1998; Gureje Ustun, et al., 1997; Looper & Kirmayer, 2001; Noyes et al., 1993). Also, hypochondriasis frequently co-occurs with other Axis I disorders, such as mood, anxiety, or other somatoform disorders (Gureje Ustun, et al., 1997; Noyes et al., 1994).

Randomized Controlled Trials

Psychosocial treatments for hypochondriasis have been examined in six randomized controlled trials. The interventions in all six studies were theoretically grounded in social learning theory and were administered on an individual basis.

The interventions labeled as cognitive therapy (CT) for hypochondriasis (Clark et al., 1998; Visser & Bouman, 2001) are procedurally similar to the point of being indistinguishable from those labeled CBT for hypochondriasis (Barsky & Ahern, 2004; Greeven et al., 2007; Warwick, Clark, Cobb, & Salkovskis, 1996). All of these interventions focused on identifying and challenging patients' misinterpretations of physical symptoms as well as constructing more realistic interpretations of them. Barsky and Ahern (2004) stated that in addition to restructuring cognitions they attempted to reduce patients' tendency to amplify physical symptoms and to alter patients' illness behaviors. Warwick et al.'s CBT (1996) and Clark et al.'s CT (1998) combined cognitive restructuring with exposure to interoceptive and/or external stimuli along with response prevention after exposure. What differed most among these interventions was their duration. Barsky and Ahern's (2004) treatment entailed six 90-minute sessions. Visser and Bouman's (2001) intervention consisted of 12 weekly sessions, each presumably lasting 1 hour, though session duration was not indicated. The duration of Greeven et al.'s (2007) CBT which was "based on the treatment protocol used by Visser and Bouman," (p. 93) ranged from 6 to 16 sessions. Both Clark et al.'s (1998) and Warwick et al.'s (1996) treatments involved 16 1-hour sessions.

All CT and CBT interventions were associated with significantly greater reductions in hypochondriacal symptoms than was the comparable waiting-list control condition (Barsky & Ahern, 2004; Clark et al., 1998; Greeven et al., 2007; Visser & Bouman, 2001; Warwick et al., 1996). Treatment effect sizes are presented in Table 15.2. Barsky and Ahern's study was the only one that examined long-term differences between the waiting-list group and the treated group: Ten months after treatment completion patients enrolled in CBT reported a greater decline in hypochondriacal cognitions than did controls. Also, Barsky and Ahren's CBT-treated patients reported a significantly greater increase in daily activities than did controls, even 10 months after treatment (Barsky & Ahern, 2004).

Visser and Bouman (2001) also assessed the efficacy of a largely behavioral intervention, exposure plus response prevention. Patients receiving this treatment constructed hierarchies of their own hypochondriacal fears and avoidance behavior patterns, such as checking, reassurance seeking, and avoidance of interoceptive and/or external stimuli. Afterward, they were given assignments of in vivo exposure and response prevention. Patients treated with exposure reported significantly greater reductions in their hypochondriacal symptoms than did wait-list control participants. Although Visser and Bouman also compared exposure plus response prevention to their CT intervention described earlier, the study was not sufficiently powerful to distinguish between the two treatments. Treatment effects sizes for both interventions relative to the waiting-list control condition are presented in Table 15.2.

Clark et al. (1998) created a psychosocial alternative to CT, behavioral stress management (BSM), that did not directly address hypochondriacal concerns. It was intended to address anxiety related to hypochondriasis by training patients in relaxation, problem solving, assertiveness training, and time management. Clark et al. found behavioral stress management significantly more effective in alleviating hypochondriacal concerns than was a waiting list. Clark et al. also compared this treatment to their CT described earlier. At

TABLE 15.2   Treatment Effect Sizes for the Psychosocial Treatments for Hypochondriasis

Author	Treatment	Control	Measures	Posttx	3/4-Mo. Posttx	7-Mo. Posttx	10/12-Mo. Posttx
Barsky and Ahern, 2004	CBT	SMC	Whitely Index	0.51			0.64
			Daily activities	0.56			0.55
Warwick et al., 1996	CBT	WL	Global problem	1.71			
			Time worrying	1.42			
			Disease convict	2.02			
Clark et al., 1998	CT	WL	Time worrying	1.53			
			Disease convict	2.64			
Clark et al., 1998	BSM	WL	Time worrying	1.12			
			Disease convict	1.21			
Clark et al., 1998	CT	BSM	Time worrying	0.51	0.28		0.06
			Disease convict	1.21			
Visser and Bouman, 2001	CT	WL	Health anxiety	1.27			
			Illness behavior	0.62			
Visser and Bouman, 2001	Exposure	WL	Health anxiety	0.74			
			Illness behavior	0.23			
Visser and Bouman, 2001	CT	Exposure	Health anxiety	0.39		0.25	
			Illness behavior	0.37	0.28		
Greeven et al., 2007	CBT	Placebo	Whitely Index	0.45			
			Health anxiety	0.33			
			Illness behavior	0.13			
Greeven et al., 2007	Paxil	Placebo	Whitely Index	0.40			
			Health anxiety	0.14			
			Illness behavior	0.27			
Fava et al., 2000	Explan	WL	Illness worry	1.48			
			Hypochondriasis	0.34			
			# Physician visits	0.92			

Note: Effect sizes calculated as $d = (m1 - m2)/sd_{pooled}$
SMC = Standard medical care
WL = Waiting list
BSM = Behavioral stress management
Placebo = pill placebo
Explan = Explanatory therapy
Whitely Index is a measure of hypochondriacal beliefs (Pilowsky, 1993)
Daily activities were assessed with the Functional Status Questionnaire (Jette et al., 1986)
Global problem was assessed by an independent rater on a one-item visual analog scale (0–8)
Time worrying (about health) is a self-report one-item visual analog scale (0–8)
Disease convict = Disease conviction, a self-report one-item visual analog scale (0–8)
Illness Attitude Scale = Health Anxiety subscale (R + I, Kellner, 1987; Speckens et al., 1995b)
Illness Attitude Scale = Illness Behavior subscale (R + I, Kellner, 1987; Speckens et al., 1995b)
Illness Attitude Scale = Worry about Illness subscale (R + I, Kellner, 1987)
Illness Attitude Scale = Hypochondriasis (R + I, Kellner, 1987)

posttreatment, CT-treated participants experienced greater reductions in their hypochondrical cognitions than did BSM-treated participants. Nevertheless, 12 months after the posttreatment assessment, these differences were not observed (Clark et al., 1998). Table 15.2 shows the treatment effect sizes for these interventions.

Finally, Fava et al. examined the efficacy of explanatory therapy (R. Kellner, 1983) for hypochondriasis in hopes of identifying a beneficial treatment that is less complex and easier to administer than CBT (Fava, Grandi, Rafanelli, Fabbri, & Cazzaro, 2000). Explanatory therapy is a physician-administered individual therapy consisting of patient education, reassurance, and training in selective attention (i.e., reducing somatic attention). Like the cognitive and behavioral treatments described earlier, explanatory therapy resulted in greater reductions in worry about illness than was the waiting list control condition (Fava et al., 2000). Although explanatory therapy was also associated with greater reductions in physician visits than was the control group, the mean reduction in visits was minimal (three visits) considering the treatment group received eight additional visits as part of their explanatory therapy (Fava et al., 2000) (see Table 15.2).

The one study comparing a psychosocial intervention with a pharmacological intervention demonstrated that CBT was more effective than a placebo pill, but no more effective than paroxetine, in reducing hypochondriacal beliefs (Greeven et al., 2007) (see Table 15.2). Despite the statistical significance of these findings, the clinical significance of changes observed in this study suggests that patients experienced only modest improvement. Instead of using Jacobson's recommendation of a change of 1.96 standard deviations from the pretreatment mean as an index of clinically significant change, the investigators judged as clinically significant a change of 1.0 standard deviation. Using this more lenient criterion, only 45% of CBT recipients and 30% of paroxetine recipients versus 14% of waiting-list controls responded to treatment at clinically significant levels (Greeven et al. 2007).

Summary

The findings from controlled trials on CBT for hypochondriasis suggest these interventions are effective in reducing hypochondrical concerns. Sufficient data have been presented to label these types of interventions for hypochondriasis as empirically supported (Chambless & Hollon, 1998). However, additional research is needed to address some of the deficits in this literature. Long-term benefits have only been assessed relative to a control condition in one study. None of the studies demonstrated that treatment has meaningful affects on measures of health-care utilization. Also inadequately examined is the impact of treatment on the functional impairment so often observed in hypochondriasis. Clinically meaningful change has not been observed. In addition, it has yet to be demonstrated that one intervention appears more potent than the others.

Meta-Analysis

A recent meta-analysis of the psychosocial intervention literature on hypochondriasis is consistent with our assessment of the research (Thomson & Page, 2007). In their analysis assessing the efficacy of all forms of psychotherapy studied in randomized controlled trials (i.e., combining the results of the studies described before except Barsky and Ahern's, which did not include a posttreatment assessment point), Thomson and Page found the psychotherapy conditions to outperform the waiting-list conditions (SMD (random) [95% CI] = −0.86 [−1.25 to −0.46]). An internal analysis of the data from this meta-analysis revealed that the total amount of time with a therapist was highly correlated with the effect size as measured by standardized mean difference ($r^2 = 0.93$, $r = 0.090$ (95% CI

0.056–0.124) $p = 0.002$) (Thomson & Page, 2007). The authors suggested that despite the methodological problems with some of the literature (e.g., some investigators failed to use adequate sample sizes, intention-to-treat statistical analyses, and validated hypochondriasis scales), "psychotherapy using cognitive therapy, exposure plus response prevention, cognitive behaviour therapy or behavioural stress management approaches are effective in reducing symptoms of hypochondriasis" (p. 12).

Also noteworthy is the setting where studies on the treatment of hypochondriasis have been conducted. In each study, except that of Barsky and Ahern, patients were referred to mental health clinics by their general practitioner or mental health professional. Thus, not one of these treatments was specifically designed to be conducted in a primary care medical setting where hypochondriasis is frequently first observed and where psychological interventions might be most advantageously applied. Because the participants in the studies described earlier were willing to participate in treatment in a mental health facility, they may not be representative of the majority of hypochondrical patients who are seeking treatment for physical, not psychological symptomatology.

BODY DYSMORPHIC DISORDER: OVERVIEW OF DISORDER

Diagnostic Criteria and Prevalence

Body dysmorphic disorder (BDD) is characterized by a preoccupation with an imagined defect in appearance. If a slight physical irregularity is present, the person's concern must be excessive to meet criteria for BDD. Also required for a diagnosis of BDD is significant distress or impairment caused by this preoccupation (APA, 1994). Typically, patients are concerned about their skin or complexion, the size of the nose or head, or the attractiveness of the hair; however, the preoccupation may concern any body part

Body dysmorphic disorder tends to be chronic; in one study Phillips et al. found only a .09 probability of full remission and .21 probability of partial remission over the course of a year (Phillips, Pagano, Menard, & Stout, 2006).

The prevalence of BDD is uncertain. Research conducted in community settings has produced varying estimates: a prevalence of 0.7% in a community setting in Italy (Faravelli et al., 1997), 1.7% in a national survey of German adolescents and adults (Rief, Buhlmann, Wilhelm, Borkenhagen, & Brähler, 2006), and 2.4% in a telephone survey of U.S. adults (Koran, Abujaoude, Large, & Serpe, 2008). The prevalence of BDD in medical practices has been found to be substantially higher than that found in the general population: 4% of general medicine patients (Phillips, 1996), 3% to 16% of cosmetic surgery patients (Sarwer & Crerand, 2008), and 8% to 15% of dermatology patients (Sarwer & Crerand, 2008).

Demographic and Clinical Characteristics

Very little research has been conducted on sex and cultural differences in BDD. Phillips and Diaz found that women and men were equally likely to meet criteria for BDD (Phillips & Diaz, 1997). We are aware of no systematic investigation of race and culture in BDD, though the condition has been described in various cultures around the world (Phillips, 1996).

Patients meeting criteria for BDD have been shown to have substantial functional impairment (Phillips, 2000). Negative thoughts about one's appearance interfere with concentration at work and the social lives of patients. In addition, individuals with BDD are so afraid of exposing their flaw to others that they go to great lengths to hide it. They may spend substantial amounts of time camouflaging their perceived defect or avoiding activities in which they will be conspicuous (Phillips, McElroy, Keck, Pope, & Hudson, 1993). Avoidance of social activities and work is common (Phillips et al., 1993).

Health-care use associated with BDD tends to be directed toward seeking various appearance enhancing medical treatments, especially cosmetic surgery and dermatological procedures. For patients with BDD, these treatments typically fail to alleviate distress (Crerand, Phillips, Menard, & Fay, 2005; Phillips, Grant, Siniscalchi, & Albertini, 2001). Investigators have found that 48% to 76% of patients with BDD sought cosmetic surgery, dermatological treatment, or dental procedures (Crerand et al., 2005; Phillips et al., 2001; Veale, Boocock, et al., 1996) and 26% received multiple procedures (Veale, Boocock, et al., 1996).

Patients meeting criteria for BDD experience an enormous amount of emotional distress and psychiatric comorbidity (Phillips, Menard, Fay, & Weisberg, 2005; Veale, Boocock, et al., 1996). Depression and suicidal thoughts are frequent (Gunstad & Phillips, 2003; Phillips & Menard, 2006). Also common is social phobia and obsessive-compulsive disorder (Gunstad & Phillips, 2003). Often, compulsions are related to the perceived physical defect, such as checking mirrors or brushing one's hair. Many of these patients also admit to substance, particularly alcohol, use and dependence disorders (Grant, Menard, Pagano, Fay, & Phillips, 2005; Gunstad & Phillips, 2003).

Many patients preoccupied with an imagined defect in their physical appearance have such inaccurate perceptions of their appearance that they meet *DSM-IV* criteria for delusional disorder, somatic type. About 50% of clinical samples meeting criteria for BDD also meet criteria for delusional disorder, somatic type (Phillips, McElroy, & Keck, 1994); however, instead of considering this somatic type of delusional disorder a comorbid condition with BDD, a growing body of research suggests psychotic variants of BDD are simply a more severe form of nonpsychotic BDD and are, therefore, best conceived as on the same continuum. It seems that nonpsychotic and psychotic BDD share the same demographic characteristics, clinical characteristics, and response to treatment (Phillips, 2004). Further evidence suggests that the cognitions of BDD patients involving such matters as the degree of conviction with which these patients hold their beliefs are more indicative of a dimensional rather than a categorical structure (Phillips, 2004). Thus, the research data suggest a dimensional model of BDD with varying levels of insight indicating severity of the condition.

Randomized Controlled Trials

Only two randomized controlled trials have been published on the efficacy of psychosocial treatment for BDD (Rosen, Reiter, & Orosan, 1995; Veale, Gournay, et al., 1996). Both assessed the efficacy of CBT involving the restructuring of dysfunctional beliefs about one's body and exposure to avoided situations plus response prevention; for example, preventing checking behavior and reassurance seeking. Whereas Rosen et al.'s treatment was administered in eight 2-hour group sessions, Veale et al. administered treatment in 12 weekly individual sessions. Both groups of investigators compared the effects of CBT with those of a waiting list control condition.

Both studies provided strong evidence for the short-term efficacy of CBT for BDD. Rosen et al. found that 81.5% of treated participants but only 7.4% of control participants experienced clinically significant improvement, in that their scores on the Body Dysmorphic Disorder Examination (BDDE) dropped more than two standard deviations *and* they no longer met criteria for BDD. The effect size on the BDDE was substantial ($d = 2.81$) (Rosen et al., 1995). Follow-up assessment, occurring 4.5 months after posttreatment, was conducted with only CBT participants, 74% of whom continued to have achieved clinically meaningful gains (Rosen et al., 1995). Veale et al. reported that at posttreatment 77.8% of the treatment group either had absent or subclinical BDD symptomatology whereas all waiting list participants still met criteria for BDD.

Furthermore, Veale's effect sizes on the BDDE and on a BDD-modified Yale-Brown Obsessive Compulsive Scale were also noteworthy ($d = 2.65$ and 1.81, respectively) (Veale, Gournay, et al., 1996). Follow-up was not investigated in this study.

In all, CBT for BDD must be considered an evidence-based treatment. Although the potency of the treatments described in these two well-designed controlled trials is noteworthy, a number of questions remain about the efficacy of CBT for BDD. No additional RTCs have been published. CBT has not been compared with alternative treatments, nor with an attention control. It is unclear whether treatment gains reported earlier could be attributable to nonspecific aspects of therapy. Also, long-term follow-up has not been adequately studied. Other important outcomes, such as physical and social functioning and health-care use, have not been assessed. Finally, the generalizability of these findings is unclear. Between the two studies only 36 patients have been treated. Rosen et al.'s sample consisted of women, 83% of whom had body weight and shape concerns. Veale et al.'s sample specifically excluded potential participants with body weight and shape concerns.

RELATED CONDITIONS— FUNCTIONAL SOMATIC SYNDROMES: OVERVIEW OF DISORDER

Diagnostic Criteria and Prevalence

The term *functional somatic syndrome* is used to describe groups of co-occurring symptoms that are medically unexplained. Each area of medicine identifies at least one functional somatic syndrome for patients who present with symptoms that are common in that area of medicine, but have uncertain pathology and a poor prognosis. Three polysymptomatic functional somatic syndromes frequently encountered by both mental health and primary care practitioners are irritable bowel syndrome

(IBS), chronic fatigue syndrome (CFS), and fibromyalgia. As will be discussed later, they all share many of the characteristics of the somatoform disorders.

Irritable bowel syndrome is characterized by persistent abdominal pain along with altered bowel habits and abdominal distension that cannot be explained by organic pathology (Thompson, Dotevall, Drossman, Heaton, & Kruis, 1989). It has been estimated that 8% to 20% of the U.S. population, 12% of primary care patients (Drossman, Whitehead, & Camilleri, 1997), and 22% to 28% of gastroenterologists' patients are afflicted with IBS (Harvey, Salih, & Read, 1983; Thompson & Heaton, 1980).

Chronic fatigue syndrome is characterized by unexplained fatigue, lasting at least 6 months, that causes substantial reductions in activities. At least four of the following symptoms must have co-occurred with the fatigue: Significant memory impairment or concentration difficulties, sore throat, tender lymph nodes, muscle pain, joint pain, headache, nonrestorative sleep, and postexertional fatigue (Fukuda et al., 1994). CFS's prevalence has been estimated to be 0.002% to 0.6% in the general population and 2.6% in primary care settings (Jason et al., 1999; Reyes et al., 2003; Wessely, Chalder, Hirsch, Wallace, & Wright, 1997).

A diagnosis of *fibromyalgia* is given for chronic widespread pain and multiple tender points that have no known biological basis and are accompanied by nonrestorative sleep, fatigue, and malaise (Wolfe et al., 1990). Fibromyalgia has been estimated to occur in about 2% of the U.S. population and in 6% to 20% of general medical outpatients (Wolfe, Ross, Anderson, Russell, & Hebert, 1995).

Demographic and Clinical Characteristics

Women are more likely than men to suffer from IBS (Drossman et al., 1993), CFS (Jason et al., 1999; Reyes et al., 2003), and fibromyalgia (Wolfe et al., 1995). Although the incidence of CFS and fibromyalgia have been shown to be elevated in minority groups in the United States, larger epidemiological studies are required to confirm these findings (Gansky & Plesh, 2007; Jason et al., 1999).

Our decision to include the research on IBS, CFS, and fibromyalgia in this chapter on somatoform disorders may invite controversy. Some medical specialists, focusing upon the bodily organ or somatic system of their specialization, assume these disorders have distinct pathophysiological causes and draw sharp distinctions among these syndromes. Other authorities suggest these syndromes should be viewed as one disorder. After all, many patients diagnosed with one functional somatic syndrome meet diagnostic criteria for one or more of the other functional somatic syndromes, resulting in multisystem comorbid functional syndromes (Buchwald & Garrity, 1994; Goldenberg, Simms, Geiger, & Komaroff, 1990; Veale, Kavanagh, Fielding, & Fitzgerald, 1991; Yunus, Masi, & Aldag, 1989). Also, investigators have noted similarities in the illness behaviors, illness beliefs, and psychological functioning of patients diagnosed with one of these functional

somatic syndromes and those diagnosed with somatization syndromes (Barsky & Borus, 1999; Wessely, Nimnuan, & Sharpe, 1999). As discussed earlier regarding patients with somatoform disorders, patients with functional somatic syndromes tend to adopt a sick role (Parsons, 1951), overutilizing medical services, and withdrawing from their normal activities. They tend to assume their symptoms are signs of a serious, disabling illness that is likely to worsen; they think catastrophically about their health. They frequently suffer from concurrent emotional disorders (see Woolfolk & Allen, 2007, for further review).

Randomized Controlled Trials

Various psychosocial interventions have been used to treat the functional somatic syndromes. Short-term dynamic therapy, relaxation training, hypnotherapy, exercise regimens, operant behavior therapy, cognitive therapy, and CBT have been tested in controlled studies with one or more of the patient groups described earlier. The studies are reviewed later. Tables 15.3, 15.4, and 15.5 provide treatment effect sizes

TABLE 15.3   Treatment Effect Sizes for Psychosocial Treatments of Irritable Bowel Syndrome

Author	Treatment	Control Measures	Posttx	12-Mo. Posttx
Short-term dynamic therapy trials				
Creed et al., 2003	Dynamic therapy	SMC	Pain severity 0.170.02	MOS-PF0.390.58
Svetdlund et al., 1983	Dynamic therapy	SMCIBS	Severity 0.200.52	
Relaxation trials				
Blanchard et al., 1993	PMRWLIBS severity 1.09			
Whorwell et al., 1984	Hypnotherapy Placebo IBS severity 1.10			
Cognitive/Cognitive Behavior therapy trials				
Greene and Blanchard, 1994	CTWLIBS severity 0.46			
Neff and Blanchard, 1987	CBTWLIBS severity 0.70			
VanDulmen et al., 1996	Group CBTWLIBS severity 0.39			

Note: Effect sizes calculated as $d = (m1 - m2)/sd_{pooled}$
SMC = Standard Medical Care

TABLE 15.4 Treatment Effect Sizes for Psychosocial Treatments of Chronic Fatigue Syndrome

Author	Treatment	Control Measures	Posttx	6-Mo. Posttx
Fulcher & White, 1997	Graded exercise	Flexibility/relaxation	Fatigue severity 0.73	MOS-PF 0.69
Deale et al., 2001	CBT	Relaxation training	Fatigue severity 0.46 0.90	MOS-PF 0.69 1.13

Note: Effect sizes calculated as $d = (m1 - m2)/sd_{pooled}$
MOS-PF = Physical functioning scale of the Medical Outcomes Study scale (Ware & Sherbourne, 1992)

TABLE 15.5 Treatment Effect Sizes for Psychosocial Treatments of Fibromyalgia

Author	Treatment	Control Measures	Posttx	4-Mo. Posttx
Ferraccioli et al., 1987	EMG biofeedback	False biofeedback	Self-report pain 3.03	Tender points 4.99
L. Martin et al., 1996	Exercise group	Relaxation	Tender points 0.97	FIQ 0.34
Keel et al., 1998	CBT + exercise	Autogenic training	Self-report pain 0.22 0.35	

Note: Effect sizes calculated as $d = (m1 - m2)/sd_{pooled}$
Self-reported pain = using a visual analogue scale
FIQ = Fibromyalgia Impact Questionnaire

for IBS, CFS, and fibromyalgia, respectively, for published studies that reported sufficient data to make such calculations. A more detailed examination of this literature can be found elsewhere (Allen, Escobar, Lehrer, Gara, & Woolfolk, 2002).

Short-Term Dynamic Therapy

Psychodynamic theory has proposed that unexplained physical symptoms are produced to protect the patient from traumatic, frightening, and/or depressing emotional experiences. If an individual fails to process a trauma adequately, it is hypothesized, the original affect later may be converted into physical symptoms (Engel, 1959). Short-term dynamically oriented treatments that explore the stress and emotional distress associated with physical symptoms have been studied systematically with IBS patients. In one study, a short-term dynamic therapy aimed at "modifying maladaptive behaviour and finding new solutions to problems" (p. 589) resulted in significantly greater improvement in IBS symptoms than did a standard medical care condition. Differences between groups were observed after treatment as well as 1 year later

(Svedlund, Sjodin, Ottosson, & Dotevall, 1983) (see Table 15.3).

Another trial examined the efficacy of a combined short-term dynamic therapy and relaxation training aimed at helping participants explore the links between IBS symptoms and emotional factors. The treatment was supplemented by audiotape administered relaxation methods that participants were instructed to use at home. Immediately after the 3-month intervention phase, participants receiving psychotherapy and relaxation training reported significantly greater improvements in IBS symptoms than did participants receiving standard medical care (Guthrie, Creed, Dawson, & Tomenson, 1991). Psychodynamic therapy plus relaxation training was also more recently compared with pharmacotherapy with paroxetine and to standard medical care for IBS. Although there were no differences among the three treatment conditions in patient reported abdominal pain, both dynamic plus relaxation therapy and paroxetine coincided with greater improvement in physical functioning than did standard medical care a year after treatment (see Table 15.3). Furthermore, psychotherapy plus relaxation, but not paroxetine, was associated with greater reductions in health-care costs during the year after treatment (Creed et al., 2003).

Relaxation Training

Psychophysiologists have described several mechanisms that produce somatic symptoms in the absence of organic pathology (Clauw, 1995; Gardner & Bass, 1989). These mechanisms include overactivity or dysregulation of the autonomic nervous system, smooth muscle contractions, endocrine overactivity, and hyperventilation. Miscellaneous techniques, directed at reducing physiological arousal and physical discomfort associated with unexplained physical symptoms, have been studied within controlled experimental designs. Small studies have shown that relaxation techniques, such as EMG-biofeedback and guided imagery, reduce pain associated with fibromyalgia more effectively than do sham relaxation treatments (Ferraccioli et al., 1987; Fors, Sexton, & Gotestam, 2002). In another small trial, patients treated with progressive muscle relaxation reported greater relief in their irritable bowel symptoms than did patients in a control comparison treatment condition (Blanchard, Greene, Scharff, & Schwarz-McMorris, 1993) (see Table 15.3).

Hypnotherapy

Hypnotherapy, designed to produce generalized relaxation and control of intestinal mobility, has been successfully applied to IBS as well as to fibromyalgia. In three different studies, hypnotherapy was associated with less abdominal pain and fewer abnormal bowel habits than was either of two comparison conditions, supportive psychotherapy combined with a placebo pill (Whorwell, Prior, & Farragher, 1984) or a symptom-monitoring condition (Galovski & Blanchard, 1998; Palsson, Turner, Johnson, Burnett, & Whitehead, 2002). The one study assessing the efficacy of hypnotherapy for fibromyalgia found it to be associated with greater pain

relief than was physical therapy (Haanen et al., 1991). In an attempt to examine the mechanism of improvement, Palsson et al. showed that improvements seen in IBS symptoms after hypnotherapy were related to improvements in somatization and in anxiety, but not related to physiological measures of rectal pain threshold, rectal smooth muscle tone, or autonomic functioning (Palsson et al., 2002).

Exercise

Exercise interventions have been developed for CFS and fibromyalgia in accordance with evidence suggesting that exercise improves mood, pain thresholds, and sleep (Minor, 1991; Weyerer & Kupfer, 1994). One theory explaining the benefits of exercise proposes that exercise produces increases in serum levels of beta-endorphin-like immunoreactivity, adrenocorticotropic hormone, prolactin, and growth hormone (Harber & Sutton, 1984). In most studies, graded exercise treatments have coincided with improvements in physical functioning, fatigue, and global perceived well-being in patients diagnosed with CFS or fibromyalgia (Fulcher & White, 1997; L. Martin et al., 1996; McCain, Bell, Mai, & Halliday, 1988; Powell, Bentall, Nye, & Edwards, 2001; Richards & Scott, 2002). Some trials have even shown exercise to outperform relaxation and/or stretching comparison interventions (Fulcher & White, 1997; L. Martin et al., 1996; McCain et al., 1988; Richards & Scott, 2002). Although both statistically and clinically significant gains have been reported, the findings reported previously probably are not generalizable to all CFS and fibromyalgia patients. First, some investigators have not found an association between exercise treatments and symptom relief (King, Wessel, Bhambhani, Sholter, & Maksymowych, 2002; Mengshoel, Komnaes, & Forre, 1992). Second, many patients are disinclined to exercise and, thus, are unlikely to enroll in exercise studies. Finally, some studies have produced high attrition rates (L. Martin et al., 1996; Wearden et al., 1998) indicating that even those patients who agree to undergo an exercise regimen may not adhere to it.

Operant Behavior Therapy

Operant behavior therapy manipulates the consequences of patients' illness behavior with the aim of alleviating the associated pain and impairment. In operant behavior therapy, healthy behaviors and increased activity levels are reinforced; additional activities are expected to result in positive interactions with the outside world, experiences of joy, and a sense of productivity. Pain behaviors, such as taking medication, wincing, complaining, and seeking treatment, are identified, labeled, and consequated. A recent study compared the efficacy of an inpatient, operant behavioral treatment to that of an inpatient physical therapy for fibromyalgia (Thieme, Gromnica-Ihle, & Flor, 2003). Operant behavior therapy was conducted in groups of five to seven patients for 5 weeks. Immediately after treatment, as well as 6 and 15 months after treatment, operant behavior therapy was associated with substantial reductions in pain intensity, use of medication, and physician visits (Thieme et al., 2003). The only other randomized controlled study of behavior therapy for a functional somatic syndrome was conducted with outpatients diagnosed with IBS. In this study, patients who received 6 to 15 sessions of individual behavior therapy reported no more improvement than did control participants (Corney, Stanton, Newell, Clare, & Fairclough, 1991). Discrepancies in findings from these two studies may be related to differences in patient populations (fibromyalgia vs. IBS, inpatient vs. outpatient) or the mode of administration of the intervention (group vs. individual). At present, operant behavior therapy for functional somatic syndromes does not yet meet Chambless and Hollon's criteria for empirically supported treatment (1998).

Cognitive Therapy

One group of investigators has assessed the efficacy of a purely cognitive intervention for IBS. Cognitive therapy focuses on and attempts to alter faulty thinking patterns associated with functional somatic symptoms. Three trials with IBS patients have shown individual cognitive therapy to be associated with greater reductions in IBS symptoms than was either a waiting list control condition or a support group (Greene & Blanchard, 1994; Payne & Blanchard, 1994; Vollmer & Blanchard, 1998) (see Table 15.3).

Cognitive Behavior Therapy

Cognitive behavior therapy aims to alter dysfunctional thoughts and behaviors associated with somatic symptoms. With IBS patients, CBT usually has included a relaxation component. Controlled trials of CBT interventions for IBS have produced inconsistent results. Five trials showed CBT, administered individually, relieved bowel symptoms more effectively than did standard medical care (Heymann-Monnikes et al., 2000; Shaw et al., 1991), an educational attention control condition (Drossman et al., 2003), or a waiting list (Lynch & Zamble, 1989; Neff & Blanchard, 1987). In a sixth study, CBT administered as a group treatment resulted in greater improvements in IBS symptoms than did a waiting list control condition (Van Dulmen, Fennis, & Blejenberg, 1996). Four other investigations found no difference between individual CBT and a control condition (Bennett & Wilkinson, 1985; Blanchard et al. 1992a; Blanchard et al., 1992b; Boyce, Talley, Balaam, Koloski, & Truman, 2003).

Studies of CBT for IBS have not yielded a consistent pattern of results. Discrepancies in the findings of the earliest studies were to be expected, given their lack of methodological rigor. Findings that have emerged from the two most recently published and methodologically sound studies on CBT for IBS also are not congruent (Boyce et al., 2003; Drossman et al.,

2003). Identifiable differences between the more recent studies' designs and outcome measures potentially provide some insight into the discrepancies in findings. Whereas Drossman et al. found CBT more effective than an educational intervention, Boyce et al. found CBT no more effective than an 8-week relaxation treatment (Boyce et al., 2003; Drossman et al., 2003). Because Boyce et al.'s comparison treatment condition, a relaxation intervention, has been demonstrated in past studies to reduce IBS symptoms (Blanchard et al., 1993), it was likely to have been more active than was Drossman et al.'s control condition. Drossman et al.'s primary outcome measure was a composite of the following variables: satisfaction with treatment, global well-being, diary abdominal pain scores, and health-related quality of life (Drossman et al., 2003). Boyce et al., on the other hand, measured outcome with the Bowel Symptom Severity Scale, a measure of frequency, disability, and distress caused by each of eight gastrointestinal symptoms. Treatment satisfaction and global well-being were not assessed in the Boyce et al. study (2003). These two studies suggest CBT may help patients with IBS cope with their symptoms and with their lives better than would educational sessions, but may not relieve specific IBS symptoms any better than would relaxation alone.

When CBT has been administered to CFS patients, it has not included relaxation training. Instead, encouragement to increase activities, including exercise, has been a key component of these interventions. In one study CBT was no more effective than the control treatment (Lloyd et al., 1993), whereas in three other studies CBT reduced fatigue significantly more than did relaxation (Deale, Chalder, Marks, & Wessely, 1997), support groups (Prins et al., 2001), or standard medical care (Sharpe et al., 1996). One study found the superiority of CBT over relaxation to be maintained 5 years after treatment (Deale, Kaneez, Chalder, & Wessely, 2001). The trials

that found CBT to be efficacious employed more intensive treatments than did the one unsuccessful trial. The clinical impact achieved in the successful trials, coupled with the methodological quality of the trials, lends further support to the use of CBT with CFS patients (see Tables 15.4 and 15.5).

For fibromyalgia, the efficacy of group CBT, but not of individually administered CBT, has been studied in controlled trials with fibromyalgia patients. Patients treated with a six-session group CBT reported significantly greater reductions in physical functioning, but not in pain, 12 months after baseline when compared with patients who had received standard medical care (Williams et al., 2002). Another trial, comparing the efficacy of a group CBT to that of group relaxation training (autogenic training), showed no differences between the conditions at posttreatment; however, 4 months later CBT participants reported a greater reduction in pain intensity than did the autogenic training participants (Keel, Bodoky, Gerhard, & Muller, 1998). Two trials comparing a CBT/education group with a discussion/education group found no differences in pain complaints or functioning between the two treatment conditions (Nicassio et al., 1997; Vlaeyen et al., 1996). The findings of a less than powerful impact of CBT on fibromyalgia may reflect the ineffectiveness of group-administered treatment for this population. The benefits of individual CBT have yet to be explored with fibromyalgia patients.

Summary

As a whole, psychosocial interventions have been moderately effective in reducing the physical symptoms associated with functional somatic syndromes. Investigators who reported long-term outcome data suggest that benefits persist as much as a year after treatment. Although detailed descriptions of most interventions are not provided in research articles, close scrutiny of the studies' methods sections suggests a great deal of overlap among the interventions. For example, one of the dynamically oriented therapies included a relaxation component. The other dynamic treatment involved directive interventions: encouraging patients to change maladaptive behavior and to engage in problem-solving exercises. The CBT often incorporated relaxation training or homework assignments directing patients to engage in physical exercise. With so much overlap among treatments, perhaps it is not surprising that none of the interventions appears to be more potent than any of the others.

Despite the extensive literature on various treatments for the functional somatic syndromes, it seems that only CBT for IBS and CBT for CFS meet Chambless and Hollon criteria for empirically supported treatments (Chambless & Hollon, 1998). Although short-term dynamic therapy, relaxation training, hypnosis, and exercise have been shown to be effective for one or more of the functional somatic syndromes in multiple randomized controlled trials, additional methodologically sound studies are required before any one of these interventions can be labeled as empirically supported.

Psychosocial Versus Pharmacological Treatments

A few studies have compared the efficacy of a psychosocial intervention with a pharmacological treatment for functional somatic syndromes. CFS patients who participated in an exercise treatment reported greater improvements in fatigue and functional capacity than did CFS patients treated with fluoxetine (Wearden et al., 1998). Guided imagery produced superior results in fibromyalgia pain than did amitriptyline (Fors et al., 2002), and Svedlund et al.'s (1983) psychodynamic treatment outperformed the control treatment, which included physician-prescribed bulking agents, anticholinergic drugs, antacids, and minor tranquilizers. Fors et al. and Svedlund et al.'s studies suggest a psychosocial intervention might be more effective than the

medications most frequently prescribed for fibromyalgia and IBS, respectively. Nevertheless, too few studies have made the kinds of comparisons that would allow this conclusion to be asserted with certitude. Additional research is needed to examine the relative efficacy, and also the combined efficacy, of pharmacological and behavioral interventions with functional somatic syndromes and with somatoform disorders.

FACTITIOUS DISORDER: OVERVIEW OF DISORDER

Diagnostic Criteria and Prevalence

A diagnosis of factitious disorder is made when a patient intentionally produces, feigns, or exaggerates physical or psychological symptoms in order to assume the sick role. Identifiable external incentives, as would be the case when a person malingers for a specific purpose, are not present in factitious disorder (APA, 1994). Patients meeting *DSM-IV* criteria for factitious disorder with predominantly physical signs and symptoms are represented in most fields of medicine. Symptoms may be fabricated (e.g., claiming blindness when vision is unimpaired), intentionally produced (e.g., hematuria when patient intentionally pricks a finger to add blood to his/her urine), or exaggerated (e.g., exaggerations of pain). In factitious disorder with predominantly psychological signs or symptoms, patients may feign, exaggerate, or intentionally produce (e.g., such as with psychoactive substances) psychiatric symptoms, often psychosis.

The prevalence of factitious disorder has not been systematically investigated. Verification of the diagnosis is particularly difficult. Not only do organic explanations have to be excluded, but also the patient's role in and motivation for creating the symptom has to be determined. Physicians may be reluctant to consider factitious disorder as a potential differential diagnosis (Krahn, L., & O'Connor, 2003). One study surveying physicians in internal medicine, neurology, dermatology, and surgery for their estimates of the prevalence of factitious disorder with predominantly physical symptoms in their practices found a range from 0.0001% to 15%, with an average of 1.3% (Fliege et al., 2007).

Demographic and Clinical Characteristics

The scientific literature on factitious disorder consists of only case studies and clinical record reviews. At present, the demographic and clinical characteristics of factitious disorder are unknown.

Randomized Controlled Trials

Treatment approaches for factitious disorder also have not been investigated systematically. Some clinicians have suggested that treatment should include confrontation of the patient (van der Feltz-Cornelis, 2002), while others recommend supportive, nonconfrontational treatment (Eisendrath, Rand, & Feldman, 1996). Many patients discontinue treatment when confronted directly with the diagnosis (Krahn et al., 2003). At present, we have no evidence to guide our treatment of factitious disorders.

EVIDENCE-BASED PRACTICE AND SOMATOFORM AND FACTITIOUS DISORDERS

An evaluation of the empirical research on psychosocial treatments for somatoform and related disorders suggests that in some respects it mirrors the literature on evaluating the efficacy of psychotherapy with generic mental disorders. A number of different focused psychosocial treatments have been shown to be superior to various control conditions, especially waiting lists or standard medical treatment. Effect sizes are respectable, relative to other medical or quasimedical interventions. There is little evidence that one form of treatment is superior to any other. Treatments that are appropriately conceived as forms of CBT

are the most frequently studied, have a creditable record of success, and, by the sheer volume of data, would appear to be the best candidates for a designation of empirically supported treatments.

Although the literature on the specific somatoform and factitious disorders is relatively small, a few global conclusions can be posited. CBT for somatization, hypochondriasis, BDD, IBS, and CFS has been empirically supported, probably with some lasting effects; however, there is little data on the impact of treatment on health-care utilization, especially when the cost of a psychosocial intervention such as those described earlier is factored into the equation. There is inadequate data on the treatment of conversion disorder, of pain disorder, or of factitious disorder to make any conclusion. The data on CBT's efficacy on BDD is the most powerful. Effect sizes are large and the vast majority of patients appear to have made clinically meaningful gains from treatment; however, the two groups of investigators who have systematically studied CBT's efficacy in BDD acknowledge residual symptoms persist and argue for a longer, more intensive treatment before these patients are likely to resolve their difficulties. Longer term treatments for other somatoform disorders have been recommended by others as well (Woolfolk & Allen, 2007).

We have very little data on the mechanisms by which efficacious psychosocial treatments may have their impact upon somatoform disorders. There are multiple reasons for this. First, the mediators and moderators style of research has not been extensively applied to research on somatization. Second, the treatments studied have not been disassembled into discrete components and those constituents systematically assessed. Evidence that might shed some light on this issue, that pertaining to differential efficacy of treatment, is also scant. This absence of evidence, to some extent, is the result of much overlap among treatments. Even treatments with very different labels, for example, brief psychodynamic therapy and

CBT, turn out to be similar procedurally, with both identifying stressors and providing training in relaxation. When reading the somatoform treatment literature, careful attention must be paid to methods sections, as the labeling of treatments can often be somewhat misleading.

Somatoform researchers as a whole recommend treatment for these conditions be administered in primary care settings. It has been estimated that 50% to 80% of patients with somatoform disorders, who are referred for mental health services, fail to seek mental health treatment (Escobar et al., 1998; Regier et al., 1988). Barriers to following through with psychiatric referrals occur at both the systemic level (e.g., lack of collaboration between and proximity of primary care physicians and mental health practitioners, lack of mental health training for primary care physicians, inadequate mental health insurance) and individual level (e.g., concerns about the stigma of having a psychiatric disorder, resistance to psychiatric diagnosis, health beliefs that lead to somatic presentations, pessimism, and fatigue) (Pincus, 2003). The efficacy of CBT conducted in primary care has not been studied adequately for hypochondriasis or BDD.

The treatment of somatoform and factitious disorders via psychosocial methods is very much in its infancy. The methodological quality of the early research has been uneven. Nevertheless, there is sufficient evidence to believe that psychosocial interventions have therapeutic value for a number of the disorders. For somatization, hypochondriasis, BDD, and many of the functional somatic syndromes, CBT is likely the treatment of choice by default in that no other intervention has demonstrated efficacy.

REFERENCES

Allen, L. A., Escobar, J. I., Lehrer, P. M., Gara, M. A., & Woolfolk, R. L. (2002). Psychosocial treatments for multiple unexplained physical symptoms: A review of the literature. *Psychosomatic Medicine, 64*, 939–950.

Allen, L. A., Gara, M. A., Escobar, J. I., Waitzkin, H., & Cohen-Silver, R. (2001). Somatization: A debilitating syndrome in primary care. *Psychosomatics, 42*, 63–67.

Allen, L. A., Woolfolk, R. L., Escobar, J. I., Gara, M. A., & Hamer, R. M. (2006). Cognitive-behavioral therapy for somatization disorder: A randomized controlled trial. *Archives of Internal Medicine, 166*, 1512–1518.

Altamura, A. C., Carta, M. G., Tacchini, G., Musazzi, A., Pioli, M. R., & the Italian Collaborative Group on Somatoform Disorders. (1998). Prevalence of somatoform disorders in a psychiatric population: An Italian nationwide survey. *European Archives of Psychiatry and Clinical Neuroscience, 248*, 267–271.

American Psychiatric Association. (1994). *Diagnostic and statistical manual of mental disorders* (4th ed.). Washington, DC: Author.

Ataoglu, A., Ozcetin, A., Icmeli, C., & Ozbulut, O. (2003). Paradoxical therapy in conversion reaction. *Journal of Korean Medicine, 18*, 581–584.

Barsky, A. J. (1996). Hypochondriasis: Medical management and psychiatric treatment. *Psychosomatics, 37*, 48–56.

Barsky, A. J., & Ahern, D. K. (2004). Cognitive behavior therapy for hypochondriasis: A randomized controlled trial. *Journal of the American Medical Association, 291*, 1464–1470.

Barsky, A. J., & Borus, J. F. (1999). Functional somatic syndromes. *Annals of Internal Medicine, 130*, 910–921.

Barsky, A. J., Fama, J. M., Bailey, E. D., & Ahern, D. K. (1998). A prospective 4- to 5-year study of DSM-III-R hypochondriasis. *Archives of General Psychiatry, 55*, 737–744.

Barsky, A. J., Wyshak, G., Klerman, G. L., & Latham, K. S. (1990). The prevalence of hypochondriasis in medical outpatients. *Social Psychiatry and Psychiatric Epidemiology, 25*, 89–94.

Bennett, P., & Wilkinson, S. (1985). A comparison of psychological and medical treatment of the irritable bowel syndrome. *British Journal of Clinical Psychology, 24*, 215–216.

Binzer, M., Andersen, P. M., & Kullgren, G. (1997). Clinical characteristics of patients with motor disability due to conversion disorder: A prospective control group study. *Journal of Neurology, Neurosurgery, and Psychiatry, 63*, 83–88.

Birket-Smith, M., & Mortensen, E. L. (2002). Pain in somatoform disorders: Is somatoform pain disorder a valid diagnosis? *Acta Psychiatrica Scandinavica, 106*, 103–108.

Blanchard, E. B., Greene, B., Scharff, L., & Schwarz-McMorris, S. P. (1993). Relaxation training as a treatment for irritable bowel syndrome. *Biofeedback and Self-Regulation, 18*, 125–132.

Blanchard, E. B., Schwarz, S. P., Suls, J. M., Gerardi, M. A., Scharff, L., Greene, B., . . . Malamood, H. S. (1992a). Two controlled evaluations of multicomponent psychological treatment of irritable bowel syndrome (study 1). *Behaviour Research and Therapy, 30,* 175–189.

Blanchard, E. B., Schwarz, S. P., Suls, J. M., Gerardi, M. A., Scharff, L., Greene, B., . . . Malamood, H. S. (1992b). Two controlled evaluations of multicomponent psychological treatment of irritable bowel syndrome (study 2). *Behaviour Research and Therapy, 30,* 175–189.

Boyce, P. M., Talley, N. J., Balaam, B., Koloski, N. A., & Truman, G. (2003). A randomized controlled trial of cognitive behavioral therapy, relaxation training, and routine clinical care for the irritable bowel syndrome. *American Journal of Gastroenterology, 98,* 2209–2218.

Buchwald, D., & Garrity, D. (1994). Comparison of patients with chronic fatigue syndrome, fibromyalgia, and multiple chemical sensitivities. *Archives of Internal Medicine, 154,* 2049–2053.

Chambless, D. L., & Hollon, S. D. (1998). Defining empirically supported therapies. *Journal of Consulting and Clinical Psychology, 66,* 7–18.

Clark, D. M., Salkovskis, P. M., Hackmann, A., Wells, A., Fennell, M., Ludgate, J., . . . Gelder, M. (1998). Two psychological treatments for hypochondriasis: A randomised controlled trial. *British Journal of Psychiatry, 173,* 218–225.

Clauw, D. J. (1995). The pathogenesis of chronic pain and fatigue syndromes, with special reference to fibromyalgia. *Medical Hypotheses, 44,* 369–378.

Corney, R. H., Stanton, R., Newell, R., Clare, A., & Fairclough, P. (1991). Behavioural psychotherapy in the treatment of irritable bowel syndrome. *Journal of Psychosomatic Research, 35,* 461–469.

Creed, F., Fernandes, L., Guthrie, E., Palmer, S., Ratcliffe, J., Read, N., . . . Tomenson, B. (2003). The cost-effectiveness of psychotherapy and paroxetine for severe irritable bowel syndrome. *Gastroenterology, 124,* 303–317.

Creed, F., Firth, D., Timol, M., Metcalfe, R., & Pollock, S. (1990). Somatization and illness behaviour in a neurology ward. *Journal of Psychosomatic Research, 34,* 427–437.

Crerand, C. E., Phillips, K. A., Menard, W., & Fay, C. (2005). Nonpsychiatric medical treatment of body dysmorphic disorder. *Psychosomatics, 46,* 549–555.

Crimlisk, H. L., Bhatia, K., Cope, H., David, A., Marsden, C. D., & Ron, M. A. (1998). Slater revisited: 6-year follow-up study of patients with medically unexplained motor symptoms. *British Medical Journal, 316,* 582–586.

Deale, A., Chalder, T., Marks, I., & Wessely, S. (1997). Cognitive behavior therapy for chronic fatigue syndrome: A randomized controlled trial. *American Journal of Psychiatry, 154,* 408–414.

Deale, A., Kaneez, A., Chalder, T., & Wessely S. (2001). Long-term outcome of cognitive behavior therapy

versus relaxation therapy for chronic fatigue syndrome: A 5-year follow-up study. *American Journal of Psychiatry, 158,* 2038–2041.

Deveci, A., Taskin, O., Dinc, G., Yilmaz, H., Demet, M. M., Erbay-Dundar, P., . . . Ozmen, E. (2007). Prevalence of pseudoneurological conversion disorder in an urban community in Manisa, Turkey. *Social Psychiatry and Psychiatric Epidemiology, 42,* 857–864.

Dickinson, W. P., Dickinson, L. M., deGruy, F. V., Main, D. S., Candib, L. M., & Rost, K.(2003). A randomized clinical trial of a care recommendation letter intervention for somatization in primary care. *Annals of Family Medicine, 1,* 228–235.

Drossman, D. A., Li, Z., Andruzzi, E., Temple, R. D., Talley, N. J., Thompson, W. G., . . . Corazziari, E. (1993). U.S. householder survey of functional gastrointestinal disorders: Prevalence, sociodemography and health impact. *Digestive Disease Science, 38,* 1569–1580.

Drossman, D. A., Toner, B. B., Whitehead, W. E., Diamant, N. E., Dalton, C. B., Duncan, S., . . . Bangdiwala, S. I. (2003). Cognitive-behavioral therapy versus education and desipramine versus placebo for moderate to severe functional bowel disorders. *Gastroenterology, 125,* 19–31.

Drossman, D. A., Whitehead, W. E., & Camilleri, M. (1997). Medical position statement: Irritable bowel syndrome. *Gastroenterology, 112,* 2118–2119.

Eisendrath, S. J., Rand, D. C., & Feldman, M. D. (1996). Factitious disorders and litigation. In M. D. Feldman & S. J. Eisendrath (Eds.), *The spectrum of factitious disorders* (pp. 65–81). Washington, DC: American Psychiatric Publishing.

Engel, G. L. (1959). Psychogenic pain and the pain-prone patient. *American Journal of Medicine, 26,* 899–918.

Escobar, J. I., Burnam, A., Karno, M., Forsythe, A., & Golding J. M. (1987). Somatization in the community. *Archives of General Psychiatry, 44,* 713–718.

Escobar, J. I., Gara, M. I., Diaz-Martinez, A. M., Interian, A., Warman, M., Allen, L. A., . . . Rodgers, D. (2007). Effectiveness of a time-limited cognitive behavior therapy–type intervention among primary care patients with medically unexplained symptoms. *Annals of Family Medicine, 5,* 328–335.

Escobar, J. I., Gara, M., Waitzkin, H., Silver, R. C., Holman, A., & Compton, W. (1998). *DSM-IV* hypochondriasis in primary care. *General Hospital Psychiatry, 20,* 155–159.

Escobar, J. I., Golding, J. M., Hough, R. L., Karno, M., Burnam, M. A., & Wells, K. B. (1987). Somatization in the community: Relationship to disability and use of services. *American Journal of Public Health, 77,* 837–840.

Escobar, J. I., Rubio-Stipec, M., Canino, G., & Karno, M. (1989). Somatic symptom index (SSI): A new and abridged somatization construct. Prevalence and epidemiological correlates in two large community samples. *Journal of Nervous & Mental Disease, 177,* 140–146.

Escobar, J. I., Waitzkin, H., Silver, R. C., Gara, M., & Holman, A. (1998). Abridged somatization: A study in primary care. *Psychosomatic Medicine, 60,* 466–472.

Fabrega, H., Mezzich, J., Jacob, R., & Ulrich, R. (1988). Somatoform disorder in a psychiatric setting: Systematic comparisons with depression and anxiety disorders. *Journal of Nervous and Mental Disease, 176,* 431–439.

Faravelli, C., Salvatori, S., Galassi, F., Aiazzi, L., Drei, C., & Cabras, P. (1997). Epidemiology of somatoform disorders: A community survey in Florence. *Social Psychiatry and Psychiatric Epidemiology, 32,* 24–29.

Fava, G. A., Grandi, S., Rafanelli, C., Fabbri, S., & Cazzaro, M. (2000). Explanatory therapy in hypochondriasis. *Journal of Clinical Psychiatry, 61,* 317–322.

Feighner, J. P., Robins, E., Guze, S. B., Woodruff, R. A., Jr., Winokur, G., & Munoz, R. (1972). Diagnostic criteria for use in psychiatric research. *Archives of General Psychiatry, 26,* 57–63.

Ferraccioli, G., Ghirelli, L., Scita, F., Nolli, M., Mozzani, M., Fontana, S., . . . De Risio, C. (1987). EMG biofeedback training in fibromyalgia syndrome. *Journal of Rheumatology, 14,* 820–825.

Fink, P. (1992). Surgery and medical treatment in persistent somatizing patients. *Journal of Psychosomatic Research, 36,* 439–447.

Fink, P., Steen Hansen, M., & Søndergaard, L. (2005). Somatoform disorders among first time referrals to a neurology service. *Psychosomatics, 46,* 540–548.

Fliege, H., Grimm, A., Eckhardt-Henn, A., Gieler, U., Martin, K., & Klapp, B. F. (2007). Frequency of ICD-10 factitious disorder: Survey of senior hospital consultants and physicians in private practice. *Psychosomatics, 48,* 60–64.

Folks, D. G., Ford, C. V., & Regan, W. M. (1984). Conversion symptoms in a general hospital. *Psychosomatics, 25,* 285–295.

Fors, E. A., Sexton, H., & Gotestam, K. G. (2002). The effect of guided imagery and amitriptyline on daily fibromyalgia pain: A prospective, randomized, controlled trial. *Journal of Psychiatric Research, 36,* 179–187.

Fukuda, K., Straus, S. E., Hickie, I., Sharpe, M. C., Dobbins, J. G., & Komaroff, A. (1994). The chronic fatigue syndrome: A comprehensive approach to its definition and study. *Annals of Internal Medicine, 121,* 953–959.

Fulcher, K. Y., & White, P. D. (1997). Randomised controlled trial of graded exercise in patients with the chronic fatigue syndrome. *British Medical Journal, 314,* 1647–1652.

Galovski, T. E., & Blanchard, E. B. (1998). The treatment of irritable bowel syndrome with hypnotherapy. *Applied Psychophysiology and Biofeedback, 23,* 219–232.

Gansky, S. A., & Plesh, O. (2007). Widespread pain and fibromyalgia in a biracial cohort of young women. *Journal of Rheumatology, 34,* 810–817.

Gardner, W. N., & Bass, C. (1989). Hyperventilation in clinical practice. *British Journal of Hospital Medicine, 41,* 73–81.

Goldenberg, D. L., Simms, R. W., Geiger, A., & Komaroff, A. K. (1990). High frequency of fibromyalgia in patients with chronic fatigue seen in a primary care practice. *Arthritis and Rheumatism, 33,* 381–387.

Grant, J. E., Menard, W., Pagano, M. E., Fay, C. & Phillips, K. A. (2005). Substance use disorders in individuals with body dysmorphic disorder. *Journal of Clinical Psychiatry, 66,* 309–316.

Greene, B., & Blanchard, E. B. (1994). Cognitive therapy for irritable bowel syndrome. *Journal of Consulting and Clinical Psychology, 62,* 576–582.

Greeven A., van Balkom, A. J., Visser, S., Merkelbach, J. W., van Rood, Y. R., van Dyck, R., . . . Spinhoven, P. (2007). Cognitive behavior therapy and paroxetine in the treatment of hypochondriasis: A randomized controlled trial. *American Journal of Psychiatry, 164,* 91–9.

Gunstad, J. & Phillips, K. A. (2003). Axis I comorbidity in body dysmorphic disorder. *Comprehensive Psychiatry, 44,* 270–276.

Gureje, O., Simon, G. E., Ustun, T., Goldberg, D. P. (1997). Somatization in cross-cultural perspective: A World Health Organization study in primary care. *American Journal of Psychiatry, 154,* 989–995.

Gureje, O., Ustun, T. G., & Simon, G. E. (1997). The syndrome of hypochondriasis: A cross-national study in primary care. *Psychological Medicine, 27,* 1001–1010.

Guthrie, E., Creed, F., Dawson, D., & Tomenson, B. (1991). A controlled trial of psychological treatment for the irritable bowel syndrome. *Gastroenterology, 100,* 450–457.

Haanen, H. C. M., Hoenderdos, H. T. W., van Romunde, L. K. J., Hop, W. C. J., Mallee, C., Terwiel, J. P., & Hekster, G. B. (1991). Controlled trial of hypnotherapy in the treatment of refractory fibromyalgia. *Journal of Rheumatology, 18,* 72–75.

Hafeiz, H. B. (1980). Hysterical conversion: A prognostic study. *British Journal of Psychiatry, 136,* 548–551.

Hahn, S. R. (2001). Physical symptoms and physicians' experienced difficulty in the physician-patient relationship. *Annals of Internal Medicine, 134,* 897–904.

Harber, V. J., & Sutton, J. R. (1984). Endorphins and exercise. *Sports Medicine, 1,* 154–171.

Harvey, R. F., Salih, S. Y., & Read, A. E. (1983). Organic and functional disorders in 2000 gastroenterology outpatients. *Lancet, 1,* 632–634.

Heymann-Monnikes, I., Arnold, R., Florin, I., Herda, C., Melfsen, S., & Monnikes, H. (2000). The combination of medical treatment plus multicomponent behavioral therapy is superior to medical treatment alone in the therapy of irritable bowel syndrome. *American Journal of Gastroenterology, 95,* 981–994.

Jackson, J. L., & Kroenke, K. (2008). Prevalence, impact, and prognosis of multisomatoform disorder in primary care: A 5-year follow-up study. *Psychosomatic Medicine, 70,* 430–434.

Jason, L. A., Richman, J. A., Rademaker, A. W., Jordan, K. M., Plioplys, A. V., Taylor, R. R., . . . Plioplys, S. (1999). A community-based study of chronic fatigue syndrome. *Archives of Internal Medicine, 159,* 2129–2137.

Jette, A. M., Davies, A. R., Cleary, P. D., Calkins, D. R., Rubenstein, L. V., Fink, A., . . . Delbanco, T. L. (1986). The functional status questionnaire: Reliability and validity when used in primary care. *Journal of General Internal Medicine, 1,* 143–149.

Kashner, T. M., Rost, K., Cohen, B., Anderson, M., & Smith, G. R. (1995). Enhancing the health of somatization disorder patients: Effectiveness of short-term group therapy. *Psychosomatics, 36,* 462–470.

Katon, W., Lin, E., Von Korff, M., Russo, J., Lipscomb, P., & Bush, T. (1991). Somatization: A spectrum of severity. *American Journal of Psychiatry, 148,* 34–40.

Keel, P. J., Bodoky, C., Gerhard, U., & Muller, W. (1998). Comparison of integrated group therapy and group relaxation training for fibromyalgia. *Clinical Journal of Pain, 14,* 232–238.

Kellner, R. (1983). Prognosis of treated hypochondriasis. *Acta Psychiatrica Scandanavica, 67,* 69–76.

Kellner, R. J. (1987). *Abridged manual of the illness attitude scales (mimeograph).* Albuquerque, NM: Department of Psychiatry, University of New Mexico School of Medicine.

Kent, D. A., Tomasson, K., Coryell, W. (1995). Course and outcome of conversion and somatization disorder. A four-year follow-up. *Psychosomatics, 36,* 138–144.

King, S. J., Wessel, J., Bhambhani, Y., Sholter, D., & Maksymowych, W. (2002). The effects of exercise and education, individually or combined, in women with fibromyalgia. *Journal of Rheumatology, 29,* 2620–2627.

Kirmayer, L. J., & Robbins, J. M. (1991). Three forms of somatization in primary care: Prevalence, co-occurrence, and sociodemographic characteristics. *Journal of Nervous and Mental Disease, 179,* 647–655.

Koran, L. M., Abujaoude, E., Large, M. D., & Serpe, R. T. (2008). The prevalence of body dysmorphic disorder in the United States adult population. *CNS Spectrums, 13,* 316–322.

Krahn, L. E., Li, H., & O'Connor, M. K. (2003). Patients who strive to be ill: Factitious disorder with physical symptoms. *American Journal of Psychiatry, 160,* 1163–1168.

Kroenke, K., Sharpe, M., & Sykes, R. (2007). Revising the classification of somatoform disorders: Key

questions and preliminary recommendations. *Psychosomatics, 48,* 277–285.

Kroenke, K., Spitzer, R. L., deGruy, F. V., Hahn, S. R., Linzer, M., Williams, J. B., . . . Davies, M. (1997). Multisomatoform disorder: An alternative to undifferentiated somatoform disorder for the somatizing patient in primary care. *Archives of General Psychiatry, 54,* 352–358.

Kroenke, K., Spitzer, R. L., & Williams, J. B. (2002). The PHQ-15: Validity of a new measure for evaluating the severity of somatic symptoms. *Psychosomatic Medicine, 64,* 258–266.

Larisch, A., Schweickhardt, A., Wirsching, M., & Fritzsche, K. (2004). Psychosocial interventions for somatizing patients by the general practitioner: A randomized controlled trial. *Journal of Psychosomatic Research, 57,* 507–514.

Lidbeck, J. (1997). Group therapy for somatization disorders in general practice: Effectiveness of a short cognitive-behavioural treatment model. *Acta Psychiatrica Scandinavica, 96,* 14–24.

Lidbeck, J. (2003). Group therapy for somatization disorders in primary care: Maintenance of treatment goals of short cognitive-behavioural treatment one-and-a-half-year follow-up. *Acta Psychiatrica Scandinavica, 107,* 449–456.

Lin, E. H., Katon, W., Von Korff, M., Bush, T., Lipscomb, R., Russo, J., & Wagner, E. (1991). Frustrating patients: Physician and patient perspectives among distressed high users of medical services. *Journal of General Internal Medicine, 6,* 241–246.

Lloyd, A. R., Hickie, I., Brockman, A., Hickie, C., Wilson, A., Dwyer, J., & Wakefield, D. (1993). Immunologic and psychologic therapy for patients with chronic fatigue syndrome: A double-blind, placebo-controlled trial. *American Journal of Medicine, 94,* 197–203.

Looper, K. J., & Kirmayer, L. J. (2001). Hypochondriacal concerns in a community population. *Psychological Medicine, 31,* 577–584.

Lynch, P. M., & Zamble, E. (1989). A controlled behavioral treatment study of irritable bowel syndrome. *Behavior Therapy, 20,* 509–523.

Mace, C. J., & Trimble, M. R. (1996). Ten-year prognosis of conversion disorder. *British Journal of Psychiatry, 169,* 282–288.

Martin, A., & Jacobi, F. (2006). Features of hypochondriasis and illness worry in the general population in Germany. *Psychosomatic Medicine, 68,* 770–777.

Martin, L., Nutting, A., Macintosh, B. R., Edworthy, S. M., Butterwick, D., & Cook, J. (1996). An exercise program in the treatment of fibromyalgia. *Journal of Rheumatology, 23,* 1050–1053.

Martin, R., Bell, B., Hermann, B., & Mennemeyer, S. (2003). Non epileptic seizures and their costs: The role of neuropsychology. In G. P. Pritigano & N. H. Pliskin (Eds.), *Clinical neuropsychology and cost outcome research: A beginning* (pp. 235–258). New York, NY: Psychology Press.

McCain, G. A., Bell, D. A., Mai, F. M., & Halliday, P. D. (1988). A controlled study of the effects of a supervised cardiovascular fitness training program on the manifestations of primary fibromyalgia. *Arthritis and Rheumatism, 31*, 1135–1141.

Mengshoel, A. M., Komnaes, H. B., & Forre, O. (1992). The effects of 20 weeks of physical fitness training in female patients with fibromyalgia. *Clinical and Experimental Rheumatology, 10*, 345–349.

Minor, M. A. (1991). Physical activity and management of arthritis. *Annals of Behavioral Medicine, 13*, 117–124.

Moene, F. C., Spinhoven, P., Hoogduin, K. A., & van Dyck, R. (2002). A randomized controlled clinical trial on the additional effect of hypnosis in a comprehensive treatment programme for in-patients with conversion disorder of the motor type. *Psychotherapy and Psychosomatics, 71*, 66–76.

Moene, F. C., Spinhoven, P., Hoogduin, K. A., & van Dyck, R. (2003). A randomized controlled clinical trial of a hypnosis based treatment for patients with conversion disorder, motor type. *International Journal of Clinical and Experimental Hypnosis, 51*, 29–50.

Mokleby, K., Blomhoff, S., Malt, U. F., Dahlstrom, A., Tauboll, E., & Gjerstad, L. (2002). Psychiatric comorbidity and hostility in patients with psychogenic nonepileptic seizures compared with somatoform disorders and healthy controls. *Epilepsia, 43*, 193–198.

Neff, D. F., & Blanchard, E. B. (1987). A multi-component treatment for irritable bowel syndrome. *Behavior Therapy, 18*, 70–83.

Nicassio, P. M., Radojevic, V., Weisman, M. H., Schuman, C., Kim, J., Schoenfeld-Smith, K., & Krall, T. (1997). A comparison of behavioral and educational interventions for fibromyalgia. *Journal of Rheumatology, 24*, 2000–2007.

Noyes, R., Kathol, R. G., Fisher, M. M., Phillips, B. M., Suelzer, M. T., & Holt, C. S. (1993). The validity of DSM-III-R hypochondriasis. *Archives of General Psychiatry, 50*, 961–970.

Noyes, R., Kathol, R. G., Fisher, M. M., Phillips, B. M., Suelzer, M. T., & Woodman, C. L. (1994). Psychiatric comorbidity among patients with hypochondriasis. *General Hospital Psychiatry, 16*, 78–87.

Palsson, O. S., Turner, M. J., Johnson, D. A., Burnett, C. K., & Whitehead, W. E. (2002). Hypnosis treatment for severe irritable bowel syndrome: Investigation of mechanism and effects on symptoms. *Digestive Diseases and Sciences, 47*, 2605–2614.

Parsons, T. (1951). Illness and the role of the physician: A sociological perspective. *American Journal of Orthopsychiatry, 21*, 452–460.

Payne, A., & Blanchard, E. B. (1995). A controlled comparison of cognitive therapy and self-help support

groups in the treatment of irritable bowel syndrome. *Journal of Consulting and Clinical Psychology, 63*, 779–786.

Perkin, G. D. (1989). An analysis of 7,836 successive new outpatient referrals. *Journal of Neurology, Neurosurgery, and Psychiatry, 52*, 447–448.

Peveler, R., Kilkenny, L., & Kinmonth A. L. (1997). Medically unexplained physical symptoms in primary care: A comparison of self-report screening questionnaires and clinical opinion. *Journal of Psychosomatic Research, 42*, 245–252.

Phillips, K. A. (1996). *The broken mirror: Understanding and treating body dysmorphic disorder*. New York, NY: Oxford University Press.

Phillips, K. A. (2000). Quality of life for patients with body dysmorphic disorder. *Journal of Nervous & Mental Disease, 188*, 170–175.

Phillips, K. A. (2004). Psychosis in body dysmorphic disorder. *Journal of Psychiatriatric Research, 38*, 63–72.

Phillips, K. A., & Diaz, S. (1997). Gender differences in body dysmorphic disorder. *Journal of Nervous & Mental Disease, 185*, 570–577.

Phillips, K. A., Grant, J., Siniscalchi, J., & Albertini, R. S. (2001). Surgical and nonpsychiatric medical treatment of patients with body dysmorphic disorder. *Psychosomatics, 42*, 504–510.

Phillips, K. A., McElroy, S. L., & Keck, P. E. Jr. (1994). A comparison of delusional and nondelusional body dysmorphic disorder in 100 cases. *Psychopharmacological Bulletin, 30*, 179–186.

Phillips, K. A., McElroy, S. L., Keck, P. E. Jr., Pope, H. G. Jr., & Hudson, J. I. (1993). Body dysmorphic disorder: 30 cases of imagined ugliness. *American Journal of Psychiatry, 150*, 302–308.

Phillips, K. A., & Menard, W. (2006). Suicidality in body dysmorphic disorder: A prospective study. *American Journal of Psychiatry, 163*, 1280–1282.

Phillips, K. A., Menard, W., Fay, C., & Weisberg, R. (2005). Demographic characteristics, phenomenology, comorbidity, and family history in 200 individuals with body dysmorphic disorder. *Psychosomatics, 46*, 317–325.

Phillips, K. A., Pagano, M. E., Menard, W., & Stout, R. L. (2006). A 12-month follow-up study of the course of body dysmorphic disorder. *American Journal of Psychiatry, 163*, 907–912.

Pilowsky, I. (1993). Dimensions of illness behaviour as measured by the Illness Behaviour Questionnaire: A replication study. *Journal of Psychosomatic Research, 37*, 53–62.

Pincus, H. A. (2003). The future of behavioral health and primary care: Drowning in the mainstream or left on the bank? *Psychosomatics, 44*, 1–11.

Powell, P., Bentall, R. P., Nye, F. J., & Edwards, R. H. T. (2001). Randomised controlled trial of patient education to encourage graded exercise in chronic fatigue syndrome. *British Medical Journal, 322,* 387–390.

Prins, J. B., Bleijenberg, G., Bazelmans, E., Elving, L. D., de Boo, T. M., Severens, J. L., . . . van der Meer, J. W. M. (2001). Cognitive behaviour therapy for chronic fatigue syndrome: A multicentre randomized controlled trial. *Lancet, 357,* 841–847.

Regier, D., Boyd, J., Burke, J., Rae, D. S., Myers, J. K., Kramer, M., . . . Locke, B. Z. (1988). One-month prevalence of mental disorders in the United States: Based on five epidemiological catchment area sites. *Archives of General Psychiatry, 45,* 977–986.

Reyes, M., Nisenbaum, R., Hoaglin, D. C., Unger, E. R., Emmons, C., Randall, B., . . . Reeves, W. C. (2003). Prevalence and incidence of chronic fatigue syndrome in Wichita, Kansas. *Archives of Internal Medicine, 163,* 1530–1536.

Richards, S. C. M., & Scott, D. L. (2002). Prescribed exercise in people with fibromyalgia: Parallel group randomised controlled trial. *British Medical Journal, 325,* 185–189.

Rief, W., Buhlmann, U., Wilhelm, S., Borkenhagen, A., & Brähler, E. (2006). The prevalence of body dysmorphic disorder: A population-based survey. *Psychological Medicine, 36,* 877–885.

Rief, W., Martin, A., Rauh, E., Zech, T., & Bender, A. (2006). Evaluation of general practitioners' training: How to manage patients with unexplained physical symptoms. *Psychosomatics, 47,* 304–311.

Robins, L. N., & Reiger, D. (1991). *Psychiatric disorders in America: The epidemiological catchment area study.* New York, NY: Free Press.

Ron, M. (2001). The prognosis of hysteria/somatization disorder. In P. W. Halligan, C. Bass, and J. C. Marshall (Eds.), *Contemporary approaches to the study of hysteria* (pp. 271–282). Oxford: Oxford University Press.

Rosen, J. C., Reiter, J., & Orosan, P. (1995). Cognitive-behavioral body image therapy for body dysmorphic disorder. *Journal of Consulting and Clinical Psychology, 63,* 263–269.

Rosendal, M., Olesen, F., Fink, P., Toft, T., Sokolowski, I., & Bro, F. (2007). A randomized controlled trial of brief training in the assessment and treatment of somatization in primary care: Effects on patient outcome. *General Hospital Psychiatry, 29,* 364–373.

Rost, K., Kashner, T. M., & Smith, G. R. (1994). Effectiveness of psychiatric intervention with somatization disorder patients: Improved outcomes at reduced costs. *General Hospital Psychiatry, 16,* 381–387.

Sar, V., Akyuz, G., Kundakci, T., Kiziltan, E., & Dogan, O. (2004). Childhood trauma, dissociation, and psychiatric comorbidity in patients with conversion disorder. *American Journal of Psychiatry, 161,* 2271–2276.

Sarwer, D. B., & Crerand, C. E. (2008). Body dysmorphic disorder and appearance enhancing medical treatments. *Body Image, 5,* 50–58.

Sharpe, M., Hawton, K., Simkin, S., Surawy, C., Hackmann, A., Klimes, I., . . . Seagroatt, V. (1996). Cognitive behaviour therapy for the chronic fatigue syndrome: A randomised controlled trial. *British Medical Journal, 312,* 22–26.

Shaw, G., Srivastava, E. D., Sadlier, M., Swann, P., James, J. Y., & Rhodes, J. (1991). Stress management for irritable bowel syndrome: A controlled trial. *Digestion, 50,* 36–42.

Simon, G. E., & Von Korff, M. (1991). Somatization and psychiatric disorder in the NIMH Epidemiologic Catchment Area Study. *American Journal of Psychiatry, 148,* 1494–1500.

Smith, G. R., Monson, R. A., & Ray, D. C. (1986a). Patients with multiple unexplained symptoms: Their characteristics, functional health, and health care utilization. *Archives of Internal Medicine, 146,* 69–72.

Smith, G. R., Monson, R. A., & Ray, D. C. (1986b). Psychiatric consultation letter in somatization disorder. *New England Journal of Medicine, 314,* 1407–1413.

Smith, G. R., Rost, K., & Kashner, M. (1995). A trial of the effect of a standardized psychiatric consultation on health outcomes and costs in somatizing patients. *Archives of General Psychiatry, 52,* 238–243.

Smith, R. C., Lyles, J. S., Gardiner, J. C., Sirbu, C., Hodges, A., Collins, C., . . . Goddeeris, J. (2006). Primary care clinicians treat patients with medically unexplained symptoms: A randomized controlled trial. *Journal of General Internal Medicine, 21,* 671–677.

Speckens, A. E. M., van Hemert, A. M., Spinhoven, P., Hawton, K. E., Bolk, J. H., & Rooijmans, G. M. (1995). Cognitive behavioural therapy for medically unexplained physical symptoms: A randomised controlled trial. *British Medical Journal, 311,* 1328–1332.

Speckens, A. E. M., Spinhoven, P., Sloekers, P. P. A., Bolk, J. H., & Van Hemert, A. M. (1995). A validation study of the Whitely index, the illness attitude scales and the somatosensory amplification scale in general medical and general practice patients. *Journal of Psychosomatic Research, 40,* 95–104.

Stefansson, J. G., Messina, J. A., & Meyerowitz, S. (1979). Hysterical neurosis, conversion type: Clinical and epidemiological considerations. *Acta Psychiatrica Scandanavica, 53,* 119–138.

Sullivan, M. D. (2000). *DSM-IV* pain disorder: A case against the diagnosis. *International Review of Psychiatry, 12,* 91–98.

Sumathipala, A., Hewege, S., Hanwella, R., & Mann, A. H. (2000). Randomized controlled trial of cognitive behaviour therapy for repeated consultations for medically unexplained complaints: a feasibility study in Sri Lanka. *Psychological Medicine, 30,* 747–757.

Svedlund, J., Sjodin, I., Ottosson, J. O., & Dotevall, G. (1983). Controlled study of psychotherapy in irritable bowel syndrome. *Lancet, 2,* 589–592.

Swartz, M., Blazer, D., George, L., & Landerman, R. (1986). Somatization disorder in a community population. *American Journal of Psychiatry, 143,* 1403–1408.

Swartz, M., Landerman, R., George, L., Blazer, D., & Escobar, J. (1991). Somatization. In L. N. Robins & D. Reiger (Eds.), *Psychiatric disorders in America* (pp. 220–257). New York, NY: Free Press.

Thieme, K., Gromnica-Ihle, E., & Flor, H. (2003). Operant behavioral treatment of fibromyalgia: A controlled study. *Arthritis Care and Research, 49,* 314–320.

Thompson, W. G., Dotevall, G., Drossman, D. A., Heaton, K. W., & Kruis, W. (1989). Irritable bowel syndrome: Guidelines for the diagnosis. *Gastro enterology International, 2,* 92–95.

Thompson, W. G., & Heaton, K. W. (1980). Functional bowel disorders in apparently healthy people. *Gastroenterology, 79,* 283–288.

Thomson, A. B., & Page, L. A. (2007). Psychotherapies for hypochondriasis. *Cochrane Database of Systematic Reviews, 4,* Art. No: CD006520.

Van der Feltz Cornelis, C. (2002). The impact of factitious disorder on the physician-patient relationship. An epistemological model. *Medicine, Health Care, & Philosophy, 5,* 253–261.

Van Dulmen, A. M., Fennis, J. F. M., & Bleijenberg, G. (1996). Cognitive behavioral group therapy for irritable bowel syndrome. Effects and long term follow up. *Psychosomatic Medicine, 58,* 508–514.

Veale, D., Boocock, A., Gournay, K., Dryden, W., Shah, R., Wilson, R., & Walburn, J. (1996). Body dysmorphic disorder. A survey of fifty cases. *British Journal of Psychiatry, 169,* 196–201.

Veale, D., Gournay, K., Dryden, W., Boocock, A., Shah, F., Wilson, R., & Walburn, J. (1996). Body dysmorphic disorder. A cognitive behavioural model and pilot randomised controlled trial. *Behaviour Research and Therapy, 34,* 717–729.

Veale, D., Kavanagh, G., Fielding, J. F., & Fitzgerald, O. (1991). Primary fibromyalgia and the irritable bowel syndrome. Different expressions of a common pathogenetic process. *British Journal of Rheumatology, 40,* 220–222.

Visser, S., & Bouman, T. K. (2001). The treatment of hypochondriasis. Exposure plus response prevention vs cognitive therapy. *Behaviour Research and Therapy, 39,* 423–442.

Vlaeyen, J. W. S., Teeken-Gruben, N. J. G., Goossens, M. E. J. B., Rutten-van Molken, M. P. M. H., Pelt, R. A. G. B., van Eek, H., & Heuts, P. H. T. G. (1996). Cognitive-educational treatment of fibromyalgia: A randomized clinical trial. I. Clinical effects. *Journal of Rheumatology, 23,* 1237–1245.

Vollmer, A., & Blanchard, E. B. (1998). Controlled comparison of individual versus group cognitive therapy for irritable bowel syndrome. *Behavior Therapy, 29,* 19–33.

Ware, J. E., & Sherbourne, C. D. (1992). The MOS 36-item short-form health survey (SF-36). *Medical Care, 30,* 473–483.

Warwick, H. M. C., Clark, D. M., Cobb, A. M., & Salkovskis, P. M. (1996). A controlled trial of cognitive-behavioural treatment of hypochondriasis. *British Journal of Psychiatry, 169,* 189–195.

Wearden, A. J., Morris, R. K., Mullis, R., Strickland, P. L., Pearson, D. J., Appleby, L., . . . Morris, J. A. (1998). Randomized, double blind, placebo controlled treatment trial of fluoxetine and graded exercise for chronic fatigue syndrome. *British Journal of Psychiatry, 172,* 485–490.

Weissman, M. M., Myers, J. K., & Harding, P. S. (1978). Psychiatric disorders in a U.S. urban community: 1975 1976. *American Journal of Psychiatry, 135,* 459–462.

Wessely, S., Chadler, T., Hirsch, S., Wallace, P., & Wright, D. (1997). The epidemiology of chronic fatigue and chronic fatigue syndrome: A prospective primary care study. *American Journal of Public Health, 87,* 1449–1455.

Wessely, S., Nimnuan, C., & Sharpe, M. (1999). Functional somatic syndromes. One or many? *Lancet, 354,* 936–939.

Weyerer, S., & Kupfer, B. (1994). Physical exercise and psychological health. *Sports Medicine, 17,* 108–116.

Whorwell, P. J., Prior, A., & Farragher, E. B. (1984). Controlled trial of hypnotherapy in the treatment of severe refractory irritable bowel syndrome. *Lancet, 2,* 1232–1234.

Williams, D. A., Cary, M. A., Groner, K. H., Chaplin, W., Glazer, L. J., Rodriguez, A. M., & Clauw, D. J. (2002). Improving physical functional status in patients with fibromyalgia. A brief cognitive behavioral intervention. *Journal of Rheumatology, 29,* 1280–1286.

Wolfe, F., Ross, K., Anderson, J., Russell, I. J., & Hebert, L. (1995). The prevalence and characteristics of fibromyalgia in the general population. *Arthritis and Rheumatism, 38,* 19–28.

Wolfe, F., Smythe, H. A., Yunus, M. B., Bennett, R. M., Bombardier, C., Goldenberg, D. . . . Sheon, R. P. (1990). The American College of Rheumatology 1990 criteria for the classification of fibromyalgia: Report of the Multicenter Criteria Committee. *Arthritis and Rheumatism, 33,* 160–172.

Woolfolk, R. L. & Allen, L. A. (2007). *Treating somatization: A cognitive-behavioral approach.* New York, NY: Guilford Press.

Yunus, M. B., Masi, A. T., & Aldag, J. C. (1989). A controlled study of primary fibromyalgia syndrome:

Clinical features and association with other functional syndromes. *Journal of Rheumatology, 16* (Suppl. 19), 62–71.

Yutzy, S. H., Cloninger, R., Guze, S. B., Pribor, E. F., Martin, R. L., Kathol, R. G., . . . Strain J. J. (1995). *DSM-IV* field trial: Testing a new proposal for somatization disorder. *American Journal of Psychiatry, 152,* 97–101.

16

Erectile Dysfunction (ED)

TAMARA MELNIK, SIDNEY GLINA, AND ÁLVARO N. ATALLAH

OVERVIEW OF DISORDER

Diagnostic Criteria

Erectile dysfunction is defined as the persistent inability to achieve or to maintain an erection sufficient for sexual intercourse (American Psychiatric Association, 1994). Erectile dysfunction is a prevalent, aging-related disorder in men that has been associated with multiple medical and psychosocial risk factors (Bacon et al., 2003; Feldman, Goldstein, Hatzichristou, Krane, & McKinlay, 1994; Laumann, Paik, & Rosen, 1999). The importance of understanding and treating ED cannot be ignored, as sexual interaction leads not only to procreation, but also functions to promote intimacy and connectedness between partners and allows for the experience of pleasure through touch. Therefore, experiencing ED may have profound effects on the quality of an individual's or couple's life (Lue et al., 2004). Furthermore, ED can be a silent marker of other comorbidities such as diabetes, coronary artery disease, and metabolic syndrome (Lue et al., 2004).

Demographic Variables

The proportion of men that reports ED varies from country to country and according to methodological issues. In a systematic review of population-based studies across the world, the prevalence of ED ranged from 2% in men younger than 40 years, to 86% in men 80 years and older (Prins, Blanker, Bohnen, Thomas, & Bosch, 2002). Several studies demonstrated an increasing prevalence of ED beginning at approximately age 40 years and continuing throughout life (Bacon et al., 2003; Feldman et al., 1994; Laumann, Paik, & Rosen, 1999). Prevalence of complete ED increases with age and approximately 70% of men in their seventies have ED. The MALES study (Fisher et al., 2004) showed no difference among ethnic groups in the prevalence of erectile dysfunction, but did reveal a prevalence of ejaculatory dysfunction among Hispanic men. Black men likewise had a greater chance of ejaculatory dysfunction than white men (Sand, Fisher, Rosen, Heiman, & Eardley, 2008). Erectile dysfunction was estimated to affect 52 million men in the United States. The Krimpen Study revealed that the annual incidence rate for ED increased from 7.7 per 100 men aged 50-59 years to 20.5 per 100 men aged 70-78 years.

Erectile dysfunction severely compromises not only sexual satisfaction, which is well known to be closely linked to overall life satisfaction, but is also associated with lower

TABLE 16.1   Drugs That May Cause ED

Type of Drug	Generic Names
Diuretics and Antihypertensives	Hydrochlorothiazide; Chlorthalidone; Triamterene; Furosemide; Bumetanide; Guanfacine; Methyldopa; Clonidine; Verapamil; Nifedipine; Hydralazine; Captopril; Enalapril; Metoprolol; Propranolol; Labetalol; Atenolol; Phenoxybenzamine; Spironolactone
Antidepressants, anti-anxiety drugs, and antiepileptic drugs	Fluoxetine; Tranylcypromine; Sertraline; Isocarboxazid Amitriptyline; Amoxipine; Clomipramine Desipramine; Nortriptyline; Phenelzine; Buspirone; Chlordiazepoxide; Clorazepate; Diazepam; Doxepin; Imipramine; Lorazepam; Oxazepam; Phenytoin
Antihistamines	Dimehydrinate; Diphenhydramine; Hydroxyzine; Meclizine; Promethazine
Non-steroidal anti-inflammatory drugs	Naproxen; Indomethacin
Parkinson's disease medications	Biperiden; Benztropie; Trihexyphenidyl; Procyclidine; Bromocriptine; Levodopa
Antiarrythmics	Disopyramide
Histamine H_2-receptor antagonists	Cimetidine; Nizatidine; Ranitidine
Muscle relaxants	Cyclobenzaprine; Orphenadrine
Prostate cancer medications	Flutamide; Leuprolide
Chemotherapy medications	Busulfan; Cyclophosphamide

Note: A summary of the psychological causes involved in psychogenic ED and the topics to be covered in a psychosexual interview were outlined and reviewed by Tiefer and Schuetz-Mueller (1995).

quality of life, lower self-esteem, depression, anxiety, and adverse effects on interpersonal relationships. Moreover, ED can have a negative impact on the well-being of partners of those affected (Schouten et al., 2005).

On the basis of epidemiological data, we know that psychological and interpersonal factors affect prevalence and severity of ED, both independently and in conjunction with organic factors. Specifically, dysthymia and depression, anxiety disorders, stress and abuse, sedentary lifestyle, alcohol consumption, and loss of household income in recent years all have been associated in various studies with increased rates of ED (Araujo, Durante, Feldman, Goldstein, & McKinlay, 1998; Bacon et al., 2003; Feldman et al., 1994; Laumann et al., 1999).

The etiology in individual cases has been typically ascribed to organic, psychogenic, and mixed factors (Rosen, 2001). Etiology of organic ED can be classified in four great arms: vascular, neurogenic, hormonal, and drug-induced (Araujo, Durante, Feldman, Goldstein, & McKinlay, 1998; Bacon et al., 2003; Feldman et al., 1994; Laumann et al., 1999). Table 16.1

lists drugs that may cause ED and Table 16.2 lists potential psychological causes of ED.

Impact of the Disorder

The launch of oral therapy based mainly on the phosphodiesterase type 5 inhibitors has brought a very effective, noninvasive and safe way to treat ED and is considered, together with psychotherapy and the use of vacuum devices, as one of the first-line therapies for this clinical condition (Lue et al., 2004). In patients with organic ED, nonresponders to oral treatment or with contraindications to their use, the next step is the use of intracavernous autoinjection of vasoactive drugs or penile prothesis implants (Mulcahy & Wilson, 2006); however, despite efficacy and overall safety of these drugs (Padma-Nathan, 2000; Rosen & McKenna, 2002), increasing evidence suggests that a substantial proportion of men with ED discontinue treatment or fail to seek help. A recent large-scale, multinational study of more than 25,000 men in eight countries (The Multinational Men's Attitudes

TABLE 16.2 Psychological Causes of Erectile Dysfunction

Predisposing Factors

Restrictive upbringing

Disturbed family relationships

Inadequate sexual information

Traumatic early sexual experiences

Early insecurity in psychosexual role

Precipitants

Childbirth

Unreasonable expectations

Dysfunction in the partner

Discord in the general relationship

Reaction to organic factors

Depression and anxiety

Traumatic sexual experience

Aging, infidelity

Maintaining Factors

Performance anxiety

Guilt

Inadequate sexual information

Psychiatric disorder

Discord in the general relationship

Loss of attraction between partners

Fear of intimacy

Impaired self-image

Restricted foreplay

Sexual myths

Poor communication

to Life Events and Sexuality [MALES] Study, Sand et al., 2008), found that 58% of men with erection problems had discussed their problem with a health professional, although fewer than half of these men received a prescription for sildenafil or other medication and only 16% were continuing to use the drug at the time of the study. Multiple reasons were cited for the high rate of discontinuation, including psychological disorders associated, lack of education or counseling from physicians, fear of side effects, partner concerns, cost, distrust of medications, and because it is not a curative therapy.

According to Althof (2002), although physicians had a simple, efficacious, and safe treatment for ED after the introduction of sildenafil in 1998, psychosocial barriers may interfere with patients making effective use of these interventions. Considerations in forming and maintaining an effective psychotherapeutic treatment relationship should include an investigation of: (a) variations in presenting sexual disorders, etiologies, concurrent symptoms, and behavior; (b) chronological age, developmental history, sexual development, risk factors, and life stage; (c) sociocultural and familial factors (e.g., gender identity, ethnicity, race, social class, religion, disability status, family structure, and sexual orientation); (d) environmental context (e.g., health-care disparities) and stressors (e.g., unemployment, major life events); and (e) personal sexual preferences, values, and preferences related to treatment (e.g., goals, beliefs, world-views, and treatment expectations). In some cases, treatment with pharmacological agents alone does not address complexities of the causative or resulting psychological issues. A full understanding and treatment must include a complete and constant review of the medical, psychological, relational, and cultural factors that are affecting the person(s) with sexual problem(s) (Althof, 2000). The role of psychotherapy is clearer than ever before in optimizing therapeutic outcome. Althof (2000) suggested four goals for psychotherapy for ED: reduce or eliminate performance anxiety, understand the context in which men make love, implement psychoeducation and modification of sexual scripts, and identify and work through the resistances to medical intervention that lead to premature discontinuation.

The good prognostic indicators for successful outcome of psychotherapy have been reviewed by LoPiccolo (1985), LoPiccolo and Stock (1986), and Hawton, Catalan, Martin, and Fagg (1986). The positive factors include (a) presence of lack of adequate sexual stimulation of the man by his partner, (b) unrealistic expectations of the male's sexual capability, (c) relationship issues that give positive reinforcement to the man and physical attraction between the partners, and (d) absence of serious psychiatric disorder in either. LoPiccolo (1985) listed some negative prognostic factors that include: (a) an unwillingness on the part of either the man or his wife to reconsider male sex-role demands; (b) presence of pedophilia or transvestism; (c) extreme, deep-seated religious beliefs; and (d) clinical depression. Hawton et al. (1986) has also noted that a good general relationship of the couple, a motivation for therapy, the quality of the sexual relationship despite the presence of the sexual problem and early engagement in homework assignments led to a better outcome. Hawton et al. (1986) emphasized that one of the most important outcomes of couple's sex therapy is the teaching of the couple how to cope with relapse.

While there is a consensus in literature that psychosocial and relationship variables impede or facilitate compliance, treatment outcome, and long-term satisfaction, there is insufficient evidence to support psychotherapy approaches for the treatment of ED. The objective of this chapter is to systematically review scientific evidences for the efficacy of psychological interventions in the treatment of erectile dysfunction. Five fundamental clinical issues are addressed: (1) Which is the first line choice of psychological interventions for the treatment of ED? (2) Which demographic patient characteristics are predictors to response to psychotherapy? (3) the effectiveness of psychological interventions compared to oral drugs, (4) the effectiveness of psychological interventions compared to local injection, and (5) the effectiveness of psychological interventions compared to vacuum devices.

METHODS

We conducted a systematic review and meta-analysis based on the Cochrane Collaboration Methods Guidelines of randomized controlled trials (RCTs) and quasi-randomized controlled trials (QRCTs) evaluating efficacy of psychological interventions for ED. To be included, studies should have subjects with the following characteristics: men with diagnosis of ED based on *DSM-III, DSM-III-R, DSM-IV,* or *ICD-10* criteria, or any other described criteria; older than 18 years; of any ethnic group and nationality; and regardless of comorbidities or use of concomitant medication, with the exception to prior use of phosphodiesterase-5 inhibitors. By psychological interventions, authors considered psychoeducative methods and/or psychotherapy of any kind used for treating ED of at least 4 weeks of duration. The primary outcome is a change in the ED status, as measured by validated questionnaires (e.g., *International Index of Erectile Function,* and number of patients per treatment group who did not show successful sexual intercourse (i.e., persistence of ED). Treatment compliance was measured by the number of dropouts during the trial.

The wide search for clinical trials had no restrictions on language and date of the study, and included the following sources: (a) electronic databases: MEDLINE (1966 to 2008), Embase (1980 to 2008), PsycINFO (1974 to 2008), LILACS (1980 to 2008), Cochrane Register of Controlled Trials (2008-1) Dissertation Abstracts (2008). The optimal MEDLINE, Embase, and LILACS sensitive search strategies for identification of RCTs and systematic reviews were combined with the phrases presented in Table 16.1; (b) cross checking the references of all identified trials; (c) the first authors of all included trials will contact for further information or information regarding unpublished trials; (d) hand searching of the *International Journal of Impotence Research and Journal of Sex and Marital Therapy* since its first issue; (e) contact with scientific societies for ED. Table 16.3 contains the search strategies used.

For the selection of studies identified with the search strategy, two authors independently evaluated references, extracted the data, assessed trial quality, and analyzed the results. Disagreement was resolved by consensus with

TABLE 16.3   Search Strategy

1# (ED*) OR (impotency*) OR (erection failure) OR (male sexual dysfunction)
2# psychotherapy* OR (psychological intervention) OR (psychoeducation) OR (coping skills) OR (brief motivational counseling) OR (sexual therapy) OR (anxiety management training) OR (marital therapy) OR (group therapy) OR (cognitive therapy) OR (behavior* therapy) OR (focal therapy*) OR (general counseling) OR (psychodynamic therapy) OR (supportive therapy) OR (psychoanalyses) OR (interpersonal therapy) OR (cognitive therapy) OR (individual therapy) OR (couples therapy) OR (waiting list)
3# #1 AND #2

*Keyword (Truncation Searching allows retrieving documents containing variations on a search term.)

a third author. For the methodological quality assessment, the quality of each trial was based on the criteria of quality established in the Cochrane Handbook (Higgins & Green, 2005), which measures selection bias (considering mainly randomization procedure), attrition bias (withdrawals and dropouts), and detection bias (evaluators blinded).

The program Review Manager 4.2.10 was used for meta-analysis. For dichotomous data (remission, clinical improvement, and dropouts), relative risks (RR) with 95% confidence intervals (CI) were estimated based on a fixed effects model and on the random effects model when heterogeneity was present and according to an intention to treat analysis. The number needed to treat (NNT) was also presented for statistically significant results ($p < 0.10$). Continuous outcomes were analysed if the mean and standard deviation of endpoint measures were presented in original articles. For the meta-analysis of continuous outcomes, weighted mean differences (WMD) between groups were estimated. Only nonskewed data were presented in this review. Heterogeneity was assessed by a chi-square test, and it is assumed to be present when significance level is lower than 0.10 ($p < 0.10$). When significant heterogeneity is present, attempts were made to explain the differences based on clinical characteristics of the included studies.

RESULTS

The search strategy generated 3,007 references. MEDLINE ($N = 1,845$), Cochrane Library ($N = 78$), Embase ($N = 454$), LILACS

($N = 124$), PsycINFO ($N = 501$), Dissertation Abstracts ($N = 5$). Two papers were identified by cross-checking references. Twenty-two full papers were evaluated for inclusion in this study (see Table 16.3). Nine randomized controlled trials and two quasi-randomized trials (Ansari, 1976; van der Windt, Dohle, van der Tak, & Slob, 2002) fulfilled the inclusion criteria. Although no restrictions were made in terms of languages of original reports, all studies included were published in English, included outpatients, and were done in the United States of America (Banner, 2007; Baum, Randrup, Junot, & Hass, 2000; Goldman & Carroll, 1990; Kilmann et al., 1987; Munjack et al., 1984; Price, Reynolds, Cohen, Anderson, & Schochet, 1981), England (Ansari, 1976; Wylie, Jones, & Walters, 2003;), The Netherlands (van der Windt et al., 2002), Germany (Kockott, Dittmar, & Nusselt, 1975), and Brazil (Melnik & Abdo, 2005). Duration of included trials ranged from 4 weeks to 12 months.

Table 16.4 summarizes the papers. The 11 trials evaluated 398 men. Each trial included between 16 and 70 participants. Their mean age was 47.4 years old. Baseline ED severity was estimated in all trials. Diagnoses were stated as primary ED ($N = 2$) and secondary ED ($N = 9$). The most common duration of ED was at least 3 to 6 months of duration. Exclusion criteria applied in most trials included penital anatomic deformity, primary nonerectile sexual disorder (e.g., hypoactive sexual disorder), hyperprolactinaemia, hypogonadism, major psychiatric disorders not well controlled with therapy (including schizophrenia and major depression), alcohol, or substance abuse

TABLE 16.4 Randomized (RCTs) and Quasi-Randomized (QRCTs) Controlled Trials Evaluating Psychological Interventions for ED

Study	Methods	Participants	Interventions	Outcomes
Ansari (1976)	1. Allocation: quasi-randomized 2. Three groups: oxazepam, Modified Masters techinique, and no treatment	$N = 61$ (55) Age = group I—mean 29 years, group II—mean 46.4, group III—45.0 Diagnosis: psychogenic and mixed ED	1. Oxazepam 30–90 mg/day ($N = 16$) 2. Modified Masters technique ($N = 21$) 3. No treatment ($N = 18$)	• Dropout • Persistence of erectile dysfunction
Banner (2007)	1. Allocation: randomized 2. Two groups: sildenafil versus sildenafil plus cognitive behavioral sex therapy	$N = 57$ couples (50) Age = group I—55.3 years, group II—57.2 years Diagnosis: psychogenic ED	1. sildenafil 50 mg ($N = 27$) 2. sildenafil 50 mg plus cognitive behavioral sex therapy ($N = 30$)	• Dropout • Persistence of erectile dysfunction • IIFE
Baum et al. (2000)	1. Allocation: randomized 2. Two groups Sex therapy versus PGE1 low dose	$N = 50$ Age: PGE1 group mean age = 49.6 ST mean age = 50.1 Diagnosis: psychogenic ED	1. Sex therapy-weekly sessions during 12 weeks ($N = 25$) 2. PGE1 low dose (2.5–5.0) ($N = 25$)	• Dropout • Sex situations producing erections • Satisfaction with the treatment • Confidence in performance after 6 months
Goldman and Carroll (1990)	1. Allocation: randomized 2. Two groups Workshop versus Control	$N = 20$ couples Age = mean 61 years Diagnosis: secondary ED	1. Workshop ($N = 10$) 2. Control ($N = 10$)	Sexual Interaction Inventory (SII) Frequency of Sexual Behavior Form (SSBF) Aging Sexual Knowledge and Attitude (ASKAS)
Kilmann et al. (1987)	1. Allocation: randomized 2. Four groups: Communication techniques training, Sexual techniques training, Combination, Attention-placebo, No treatment	$N = 20$ couples age = mean 51 years (31–67)	1. Communication techniques training (CTT) ($N = 4$ couples) 2. Sexual techniques training (STT) ($N = 4$) 3. Combination (CTT+STT) ($N = 4$) 4. Attention-placebo (control group) ($N = 4$) 5. No treatment ($N = 4$)	• MAT* • SII* • Coital Success* • SAI* • SPR*

	Design	Sample/Diagnosis	Interventions	Outcomes
[illegible]	Authors randomized. Three groups: Behavior therapy group, Routine therapy seen by Psychiatrists, and Waiting list	N = 24 men with a partnership; age = mean 31; Diagnosis = ED	1. Behavior therapy group (14 sessions of systematic desensitization) (N = 8) 2. Routine therapy seen by psychiatrists 4 times at intervals of 3–5 weeks (N = 8) 3. Waiting list (N = 8)	• Drop out • Persistence of erectile dysfunction
[illegible]	Authors randomized. Three groups: group therapy plus 50 mg sildenafil citrate, 50 mg sildenafil citrate, Group therapy	N = 30; mean age = 39 ±; Diagnosis = Psychogenic ED	1. Group therapy (weekly sessions for 6 months) plus 50 mg sildenafil citrate orally on demand for 6 months 2. 50 mg sildenafil citrate orally on demand for 6 months 3. Group therapy (weekly sessions for 6 months)	• Drop out • Persistence of erectile dysfunction • IIFE*
[illegible]	Authors randomized. Two groups: rational-emotive therapy versus waiting list	N = 16 married or living with their sexual partner; Age = 19–63 mean 47.5 years	1. 12 bi-weekly, rational-emotive therapy sessions (6 weeks) versus 2. 6 weeks waiting list	• Persistence of erectile dysfunction • Sex attempts
[illegible]	Authors randomized. Two groups: group therapy versus waiting list	N = 21 men who had no steady sexual partner; age = 28–61 (mean 45 ±); Diagnosis = Secondary ED; Center: Los Angeles	1. Eight weekly 2-hour sessions of group therapy (conducted by dual sex therapists) 2. Waiting list	• Persistence of erectile dysfunction
[illegible]	Authors quasi-randomized. Two groups: ICI androskat 0.25 mL with SC versus ICI androskat 0.25 mL without SC	N = 70 (57 analyzed); Age = 32–75, mean 56 years; Excluded = major organic cases for ED (all etiologies)	1. ICI (androskat 0.25 mL) with SC (N = 28) 2. ICI (androskat 0.25 mL) without SC (N = 29)	• Drop out • Persistence of erectile dysfunction • Partners reporting the treatment to be disturbing
[illegible]	Authors randomized. Two groups: Relationship therapy and Masters Sex therapy versus Therapy plus VCD	N = 45 couples; Age = 40; Diagnosis = Psychogenic and mixed ED	1. Relationship therapy and Masters Sex therapy (each session lasted 40–50 minutes every 2 weeks) 2. Therapy plus VCD at the session	Response to treatment as assessed by therapist

Note: ED = Erectile Dysfunction; IIEF = International Index of Erectile Function; ICI = Intracavernosal injection; ITT = Intention to Treat; MAT = Marital Adjustment Test; SC = Sex therapy; SII = Sexual Interaction Inventory; SPR = Sexual Pleasure Rating; VCD = Vacuum device

Considering the diversity of psychological interventions, psychotherapy models were categorized according to their theoretical base into five groups. First was Rational-Emotive Therapy (RET), which incorporates core elements of both behavioral and cognitive models. The RET challenges negative automatic thoughts and dysfunctional underlying beliefs maintaining ED through collaborative hypothesis testing, behavioral tasks, and skills training. A number of cognitive behavior therapies guided by manuals have been designed, including problem-solving therapy and self-control therapy, which are conducted over 12–16 sessions. Key elements of the model include psychoeducational and cognitive intervention, sexual and performance anxiety reduction, script assessment and modification, conflict resolution and relationship enhancement, and relapse prevention training (Ellis, 1992). Second, Sex Group Therapy (GT), which was developed specifically as a time-limited (8–16 sessions) therapy for ED, uses the connection between ED and current interpersonal experiences and includes social skills training and homework assignments concerning anxiety in sexual situations, education, and information about male sexuality generally; communication training; myths about male sexuality; nondemand pleasuring; and permission to engage in self-pleasuring (Rosen, 2001). The third therapy was Modified Masters and Johnson therapy. Masters and Johnson therapy is based on the notion that sexual dysfunction can have many causes, and that these can be tackled effectively with treatment programs that combine education, homework assignments, and counseling (Masters & Johnson, 1970). Modified Masters and Johnson therapy set a high bar for sex therapy outcome research: Never before or since has such a large scale study ($N = 792$) reported such a highly successful posttreatment and 5-year follow-up with an overall failure rate of only 15%. Educational Interventions are the fourth therapy. This approach uses workshops focused on disseminating information about psychological and physiological changes that occur in the sexual response (Goldman & Carroll, 1990).

Finally, systematic desensitization is a behavior therapy technique often used for the treatment of sexual dysfunctions in which deep muscle relaxation is used to reduce the anxiety associated with certain situations (Rimm & Masters, 1987).

The 11 studies included in this review examined eight comparisons. Some results could be pooled or summarized, as they were homogeneous. Intention to treat analysis was performed if all applicable data were available. The following scales were used in included studies: International Index of Erectile Function (IIFE), Sexual Interaction Inventory (SII), Aging Sexual Knowledge and Attitudes (ASKAS) Knowledge Scale (AKLS), ASKAS Attitude Scale (AKAS), Fear of Negative Evaluation (FNE), and the Success/Experience Patient Weekly Report Form. For most of these scales, data were skewed and could not be presented in graphical form or subjected to meta-analysis. Many continuous outcomes were described in terms of means without corresponding standard deviations.

Which Should Be the First-Line Psychological Intervention?

Randomized Controlled Trials: Rational Emotive Therapy

Munjack et al. (1984) conducted a study involving 16 self-referred men aged 19–63 years (mean 47.5 years) presenting with secondary ED. Subjects studied were randomly assigned to either a treatment group or a control group (waiting list, no treatment). Treatment consisted of 6 weeks of biweekly RET.

Data from the intercourse success/attempts ratio indicated that during the 6-week course of the study, all intervention subjects achieved successful intercourse, and only one in the control group had successful intercourse attempts during the study period. An increase in the number of successful attempts from onset of treatment to treatment completion was significant (RR 0.07; 95% CI; 0.00, 1.00; $N = 16$; $p = 0.05$). Follow-up data for success/attempt ratios were collected for subjects in the

RET group at 6 to 9 months posttreatment and revealed that treatment gains were partially maintained. Specifically, three subjects of the treatment group had ratio scores of 0%.

Randomized Controlled Trials: Sex Group Therapy

Price et al. (1981) conducted a study involving 21 men without partners who presented erectile difficulties. Treatment consisted of weekly 2-hour group sessions administered by two dual-sex therapy teams. With regard to clinical significance, 14 of the 14 treatment condition subjects reported improvement with their erectile functioning. All seven waiting list, no treatment members reported no change. Data collected at 6 months following treatment for the subjects in the treatment conditions revealed that 10 of the 14 subjects in the treatment condition reported improvement in satisfaction with changes in erectile functioning compared with pretreatment functioning.

Kilmann et al. (1987) studied the effects of three group treatment formats on 20 men with secondary ED. After comprehensive medical and psychological screening, each couple was assigned to one of three treatment groups (Communication Technique Training, Sexual Technique Training, and Combination Treatment) or to one of two control groups (Attention Placebo, No Treatment). In the three treatment groups and the attention placebo group, each subject participated in their respective formats in twice weekly sessions for a total of 20 hours. The no treatment control group received sex education and treatment after a 5 week waiting list period. Although these two studies when individually analyzed failed to show significant differences favoring the sex group therapy over waiting list for the outcome "persistence of ED." The meta-analysis of these trials favored the active intervention group (see Figure 16.1) (RR 0.13, 95% CI 0.04 to 0.43, N = 37) (Kilmann et al., 1987; Price et al., 1981), with 95% of response for sex therapy, and 0% for the waiting list group NNT 1.07 (95% CI 0.86 to 1.44).

The mean percentage per participant of intercourse attempts that were successful appeared greater for sex group therapy compared to other types of group interventions (RET, systematic desensitization, Masters and Johnson modified therapy). Three treatment groups (Masters and Johnson modified therapy, systematic desensitization, rational-emotive therapy) demonstrated substantial gains in success/experience intercourse rates but were not statistically significant ($p = 0.14$, $p = 0.27$, $p = 0.05$ respectively).

Randomized Controlled Trials: Psychoeducational Intervention Versus No Treatment

Goldman and Carroll (1990) studied the effect of a psychoeducational intervention as an adjunct to treatment of ED in older couples. Twenty couples who presented to a multidisciplinary center for ED were recruited for participation. Inclusion criteria were as follows (a) between the ages of 55 and 75 years, (b) heterosexual, (c) in an ongoing relationship of at least six months duration, (d) had experienced secondary ED, and (e) exhibited no major psychiatric disorder or severe marital distress at initial evaluation. Assessments were conducted at intake and immediately following treatment. Although the workshop group improved in the levels of ASKA Knowledge Scale, data analysis revealed that the workshop participants reported no significant increases (WMD −5.65; 95% CI −14.74 3.44; N = 20). Scores on the ASKAS Attitude Scale (WMD 0.70, 95% CI −23.28, 24.68; N = 20) and Sexual Interaction Inventory mean pleasure (WMD 0.20, 95% CI −0.32 0.72; N = 20) revealed no statistically significant changes in scores from pre- to posttreatment compared to the control condition.

Systematic Desensitization Versus Standard Medical Treatment

Kockott et al. (1975) conducted a study to assess the therapeutic effectiveness of systematic desensitization of ED. Three groups of eight patients each were formed. They were

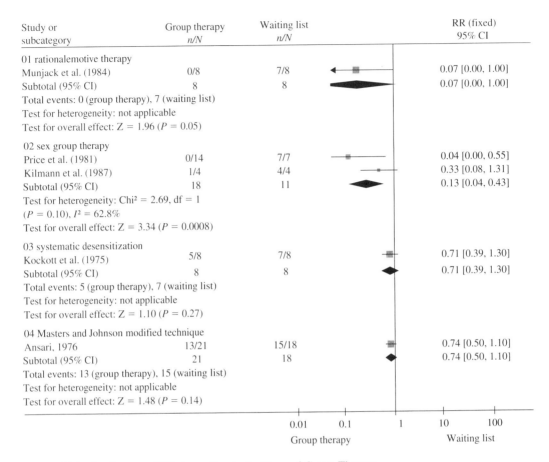

Study or subcategory	Group therapy n/N	Waiting list n/N		RR (fixed) 95% CI
01 rationalemotive therapy				
Munjack et al. (1984)	0/8	7/8		0.07 [0.00, 1.00]
Subtotal (95% CI)	8	8		0.07 [0.00, 1.00]
Total events: 0 (group therapy), 7 (waiting list)				
Test for heterogeneity: not applicable				
Test for overall effect: Z = 1.96 (P = 0.05)				
02 sex group therapy				
Price et al. (1981)	0/14	7/7		0.04 [0.00, 0.55]
Kilmann et al. (1987)	1/4	4/4		0.33 [0.08, 1.31]
Subtotal (95% CI)	18	11		0.13 [0.04, 0.43]
Test for heterogeneity: Chi² = 2.69, df = 1 (P = 0.10), I² = 62.8%				
Test for overall effect: Z = 3.34 (P = 0.0008)				
03 systematic desensitization				
Kockott et al. (1975)	5/8	7/8		0.71 [0.39, 1.30]
Subtotal (95% CI)	8	8		0.71 [0.39, 1.30]
Total events: 5 (group therapy), 7 (waiting list)				
Test for heterogeneity: not applicable				
Test for overall effect: Z = 1.10 (P = 0.27)				
04 Masters and Johnson modified technique				
Ansari, 1976	13/21	15/18		0.74 [0.50, 1.10]
Subtotal (95% CI)	21	18		0.74 [0.50, 1.10]
Total events: 13 (group therapy), 15 (waiting list)				
Test for heterogeneity: not applicable				
Test for overall effect: Z = 1.48 (P = 0.14)				

0.01   0.1   1   10   100
Group therapy   Waiting list

Figure 16.1   Persistence of ED According to the Type of Group Therapy

treated with systematic desensitization or conventional medication and general advice (standard medical treatment) or put in the control group (waiting list, no treatment). Therapeutic effects were investigated on the behavioral, subjective, and physiological levels. There were no significant differences among the systematic desensitization group and standard medical treatment in outcome persistence of ED (RR 1.00; 95% CI 0.47–2.14, N = 16; p = 1.00).

Meta-Analysis: Group Psychotherapy Versus Wait-List or No Treatment Control

A meta-analysis of five trials comparing group therapy to the control group (waiting list, no treatment) to evaluate the outcome persistence of ED found significant differences between group therapy and the control group (RR 0.40, 95%

CI 0.17 to 0.98, N = 100; NNT 1.61, 95% CI 0.97 to 4.76) (Figure 16.2) (Ansari, 1976; Kilmann et al., 1987; Kockott et al., 1975; Munjack et al., 1984; Price et al., 1981). After a 6-month follow-up, there was a continued maintenance of reduction of men with persistence of ED in favor of psychotherapy (RR 0.43, 95% CI 0.26 to 0.72, N = 37; NNT 1.58, 95% CI 1.17 to 2.43) (Munjack et al., 1984; Price et al., 1981).

Which Demographic Patient Characteristics Predict Reponse to Psychotherapy?

According to the literature there are some patients' demographic characteristics that are implicated in better response to psychotherapy: severity, age, and marital status. Therefore, we performed a subgroup analysis.

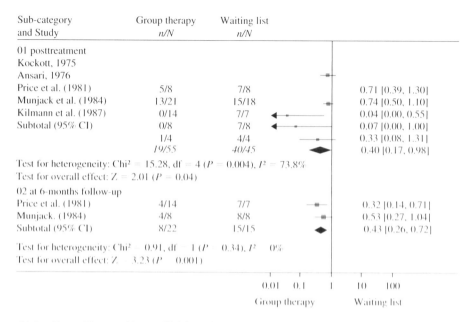

Sub-category and Study	Group therapy n/N	Waiting list n/N		
01 posttreatment				
Kockott, 1975				
Ansari, 1976				
Price et al. (1981)	5/8	7/8		0.71 [0.39, 1.30]
Munjack et al. (1984)	13/21	15/18		0.74 [0.50, 1.10]
Kilmann et al. (1987)	0/14	7/7		0.04 [0.00, 0.55]
Subtotal (95% CI)	0/8	7/8		0.07 [0.00, 1.00]
	1/4	4/4		0.33 [0.08, 1.31]
	19/55	40/45		0.40 [0.17, 0.98]

Test for heterogeneity: Chi² = 15.28, df = 4 (P = 0.004), I² = 73.8%
Test for overall effect: Z = 2.01 (P = 0.04)

02 at 6-months follow-up				
Price et al. (1981)	4/14	7/7		0.32 [0.14, 0.71]
Munjack. (1984)	4/8	8/8		0.53 [0.27, 1.04]
Subtotal (95% CI)	8/22	15/15		0.43 [0.26, 0.72]

Test for heterogeneity: Chi² = 0.91, df = 1 (P = 0.34), I² = 0%
Test for overall effect: Z = 3.23 (P = 0.001)

0.01 0.1 1 10 100
Group therapy   Waiting list

Figure 16.2   Group Therapy Versus Waiting List: Persistence of Erectile Dysfunction

Erectile Dysfunction Severity

Men categorized at baseline as having primary ED appeared less likely than those with secondary ED to experience improved erections and successful sexual intercourse; however, for men in both categories of ED severity, primary (RR 0.57; 95% CI, 0.40–0.82, N = 71; 3 studies) (Ansari, 1976; Kockott et al., 1975; Munjack et al., 1984) and secondary (RR 0.10, 95% CI 0.02, 0.40, N = 29; 2 studies) (Kilmann et al., 1987; Price et al., 1981) group therapy produced significantly better results than waiting list treatment for the outcome persistence of ED.

Patient Age

In a subgroup analysis comparing one study with men between 30 and 39 years old (Kockott et al., 1975) to four studies with men 45 years old and older (Ansari, 1976; Kilmann et al., 1987; Munjack et al., 1984; Price et al., 1981), no statistical differences were identified.

Partnership Status

In a subgroup analyses, dividing studies with men with fixed partnerships (Ansari, 1976; Kilmann et al., 1987; Kockott et al., 1975;

Munjack et al., 1984) (p = 0.0006) and men without fixed partnerships (Price et al., 1981), only men without fixed partnership had a statistically significant difference (p = 0.02).

Psychological Interventions Versus Oral Drugs

Randomized Controlled Trials: Group Therapy Versus Sildenafil Citrate

One study, Melnik and Abdo (2005), directly compared group therapy versus sildenafil citrate in the treatment of ED (Figure 16.3). This study found significant difference between group therapy and the sildenafil group for mean score of International Index of Erectile Function (IIEF) (WMD = 12.40, 95% CI 20.81, 3.99 N = 20, p = 0.004). The rate of IIEF was superior in the group therapy group. There was also a significant difference at the 3 month follow-up (WMD = 9.67, 95% CI 17.03, 2.31, N = 20) as well as for the number of dropouts between the two groups (WMD 0.38, 95% CI 0.05, 2.77, N = 20). The dropout rate was higher in the sildenafil group. Four of six dropouts were in this group

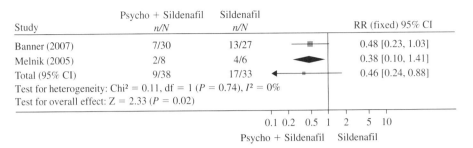

Study	Psycho + Sildenafil n/N	Sildenafil n/N	RR (fixed) 95% CI
Banner (2007)	7/30	13/27	0.48 [0.23, 1.03]
Melnik (2005)	2/8	4/6	0.38 [0.10, 1.41]
Total (95% CI)	9/38	17/33	0.46 [0.24, 0.88]

Test for heterogeneity: Chi² = 0.11, df = 1 (P = 0.74), I² = 0%
Test for overall effect: Z = 2.33 (P = 0.02)

0.1 0.2 0.5 1   2   5   10
Psycho + Sildenafil   Sildenafil

Figure 16.3   Group Therapy Plus Sildenafil Citrate Versus Sildenafil Citrate: Persistence of Erectile Dysfunction

Randomized Controlled Trials: Group Therapy Versus Oxazepam

Few data are available as to efficacy of benzodiazepines for ED. Results from one trial with oxazepam, Ansari (1976), revealed no difference between group therapy and oxazepam (RR 0.76, 95% CI 0.30, 1.92, $N = 37$).

Meta-Analysis: Group Therapy Plus Sildenafil Citrate Versus Sildenafil Citrate Alone

Two studies, Melnik and Abdo (2005) and Banner (2007), compared group therapy plus sildenafil citrate versus sildenafil citrate in the treatment of ED (see Figure 16.3). The meta-analysis found a significant difference between group therapy plus sildenafil citrate, and the sildenafil group for posttreatment verified successful intercourse attempts (RR 0.46, 95% CI 0.24, 0.88, NNT = 3.57 CI 2– 16.7, $N = 71$). There was also a significant difference for the number of dropouts between the two groups (RR 0.29, 95% CI 0.09, 0.93, $N = 77$), also favoring the combined intervention.

Psychological Interventions Versus Local Injections

Randomized Controlled Trials: Intracavenosal Injection Plus Sex Therapy Versus Intracavenosal Injection

Van der Windt et al. (2002) compared intracavernosal injection (ICI) therapy with and without sexological counseling (SC) in men with ED. In this randomized study, men were alternately assigned to ICI with or without sexological counseling (–SC). In all, 70 patients were included, that is, 35 in each group; 57 (28 –SC, 29 +SC) were interviewed by telephone after a mean follow-up of 11.3 months to determine their use of ICI and reasons for discontinuing.

There were no differences between the groups discontinuing ICI (overall 30%), ($p = 0.35$) and in reasons for discontinuing ICI (24% did so because of the return of spontaneous erections) or in sexual functioning. For the outcome persistence of ED no significant results were found ($p = 0.24$). Van der Windt et al. (2002) presented data related to partner reporting treatment to be disturbing, and there were no differences in favor of ICI therapy with sexological counseling men with ED (RR = 1.29 IC = 95%, 0.39, 4.33).

Randomized Controlled Trials: Intracavenosal Injection Versus Intracavenosal Injection

Baum et al. (2000) compared standard sex therapy and self-injection therapy using low-dose prostaglandin E1 (PGE1). Fifty men with psychogenic ED were divided into two groups: standard sex therapy for 12 weeks or treatment using low-dose (2.5–5.0 micrograms) PGE1.

For the outcomes *persistence ED* and *dropout rates* no significant results were found between groups ($p = 0.25$, and $p = 0.40$, respectively). The outcome *satisfaction with the treatment* revealed that 69% of patients in the PGE1 group were satisfied with their treatment compared to 75% receiving sex therapy (RR = 0.81 IC = 95%, 0.25, 2.64), with no statistical difference. Frequency of intercourse reported in patient diaries for the two groups was similar: 20.5 per month for PGE1 versus 20.0 per month for sex therapy. The reported duration of erection by patients receiving PGE1 therapy was longer than that reported by those receiving sex therapy (35 minutes versus 10 minutes). One relevant aspect described in this study is a comparison of costs of treatment. Sex therapy is approximately 25% more expensive than the PGE1 treatment.

Meta-Analysis: Sex Therapy Versus Prostoglandin E1

A meta-analysis of two trials comparing sex therapy to PGE1 (Baum et al., 2000; Van der Windt et al., 2002) did not find the significant result *persistence of ED* (RR 1.11 IC 95%, 0.62, 1.97; N 86, two studies); however, a trend was observed favoring sex therapy in the study.

Psychological Interventions Versus Vacuum Devices

Randomized Controlled Trials: Sex Therapy Versus Vacuum Devices

Wylie et al. (2003) studied 45 patients diagnosed with predominant psychogenic ED. Twenty-five couples were allocated to also receive a vacuum constriction device (VCD), also known as a vacuum erectile device, at the second session (group 1), whereas 20 couples had psychotherapy without a VCD. Twenty-one couples (84%) in group 1 reported improvement after the initial psychotherapy and VCD sessions compared with 12 of the 20 couples (60%) who reported improvement after couple psychotherapy in group 2. Subsequently, three of the four couples in group 1 reported no improvement and that they had not used the pump provided. Results revealed no difference between psychotherapy with a VCD

and psychotherapy without a VCD after 3 weeks of treatment (RR 0.40, 95% CI 0.14–1.1.14, N = 45) and after 6 weeks of treatment (RR 0.27, 95% CI 0.01–6.27 N = 45).

DISCUSSION

Evidence-based practice in psychology is the integration of the best available research with clinical expertise in the context of patient characteristics, culture, and preferences (Sackett, Straus, Richardson, Rosenberg, & Haynes, 2000). According to the consensus panel recommendations for sexual dysfunction, the current model of splitting psychological and medical treatments is outdated and lessens the long-term effectiveness of, and satisfaction with, either treatment. Sexual behaviors in this perspective can be viewed as interactions of the following aspects: biological, psychological, interpersonal, and cultural (Lue et al., 2004). As far as we know, this review is the first attempt of a meta-analysis of randomized controlled trials relevant to psychosocial interventions for erectile dysfunction.

This review confirmed that there is, in fact, a dearth of well designed research on psychotherapy for erectile dysfunction. Our literature search identified around 3,000 references on the topic, but only 11 studies could be reanalyzed and presented by the criteria of random assignment and a controlled condition. Of the 22 studies eligible for inclusion, seven had methodological flaws or contained insufficient information to allow inclusion (Golden, Price, Heinrich, & Lobitz, 1978; Hartmann & Langer, 1993; Hawton et al., 1986; Lobitz & Baker, 1979; Reynolds, Cohen, Schochet, Price, & Anderson, 1981; Stravynski et al., 1997; Zilbergeld, 1975).

General results of this systematic review found that group psychotherapies were effective in treating erectile dysfunction (Ansari, 1976; Kilmann et al., 1987; Kockott et al., 1975; Munjack et al., 1984; Price et al., 1981). Related to the type of psychotherapy, two trials

(Kilmann et al., 1987; Price et al., 1981) showed superiority of group therapy focused on sexuality. Sex therapy is a well-established form of treatment (Masters & Johnson, 1970). Since then the treatment program has been modified in various ways and other treatment approaches introduced (LoPiccolo & Stock, 1986; Rosen, 2001).

Regarding subgroup analysis, no differences were found related to the severity of ED, type of partnership, and mean group age. Although the potential roles of these differences in characteristics in the literature are negatively related to good prognosis (Rosen, 2001), the variation in efficacy outcomes cannot be evaluated in the included studies. A range of factors makes it difficult to draw conclusions from the subgroup analysis, and include small samples sizes, differences in study design, definitions of outcome variables, and varying amounts of psychotherapy provided.

Only one study (Melnik & Abdo, 2005) found a significant difference favoring group therapy versus sildenafil in mean score of IIEF. The rate of dropout was higher in the sildenafil group (4 vs. 2). This result suggests that despite the overall efficacy of sildenafil and its worth in treating ED, oral drug therapy is not always effective when used alone (Althof, 2002; Rosen, 2001). Sometimes the single use can reveal or reinforce other sexual problems, such as lack of sexual desire and premature ejaculation. In some cases, other issues may come to light following unsuccessful or successful use of sildenafil (LoPiccolo & Stock, 1986). For some couples, sexual problems represent a neurotic reaction of deep relational conflicts, lack of communication or power struggles, and drug therapy may not be a solution to these conflicts (Rosen, 2001).

Significant differences also were found in the rate of persistence of erectile dysfunction between group therapy plus sildenafil citrate and the sildenafil only for posttreatment (Banner, 2007; Melnik & Abdo, 2005). Strengths of these studies included pretreatment assessments, such as careful clinical history and psychiatric evaluation, focused urological evaluation and selected laboratory tests, and use of blind raters. One study by Ansari (1976) compares benzodiazepines, specifically oxazepam versus psychotherapy, and found no difference between the two treatments. Overall, no significant differences were found for any of the efficacy measures in comparing sex therapy and ICI (Baum et al., 2000; Van der Windt et al., 2002); however, satisfaction with treatment revealed that 69% of patients in the PGE1 group were satisfied with their treatment compared to 75% receiving sex therapy (Baum et al., 2000).

Early combination treatment of psychotherapy plus a physical treatment, such as VCD, may lead to a beneficial response in men with ED compared to therapy alone. Eighty-four percent of couples reported some improvement after the initial psychotherapy and VCD sessions compared with 60% who reported some improvement in group 2 (Wylie et al., 2003); however, no significant differences were found for any of the efficacy measures between psychotherapy with VCD and psychotherapy without a VCD after 3 and 6 weeks of treatment.

Although we limited our analysis to randomized and quasi-randomized controlled trials, the majority of the studies had potential methodological flaws. Just three studies described a clearly adequate method of allocation concealment with the use of sealed envelopes. Other limitations were related to small samples, limited length of follow-up, validated outcomes, not reporting of intention-to-treat analyses, and variability in study design. Consequently, we were often unable to pool data, limiting our analyses to erectile dysfunction remission and dropout rates. We could not access important issues like improvement in quality of life and impact of the interventions in relationship satisfaction. Meta-analyses are less robust with small trials and thus the results should be interpreted with caution (Task Force on Promotion and Dissemination of Psychological Procedures, 1995).

The availability of oral therapy has significantly altered the way in which erectile dysfunction is treated. While this medication is effective in restoring erectile function, it is often necessary to include the psychological and behavioral aspects of patients' diagnosis and management, as well as considering organic causes and risk factors. Integrating sex therapy and other psychological techniques into office practice will improve effectiveness in treating ED.

CONCLUSIONS

There was evidence that group psychotherapy may improve ED. Treatment response varied between patient subgroups, but focused sex group therapy showed greater efficacy than control group (no treatment). In a meta-analysis that compared group therapy plus sildenafil citrate versus sildenafil, men randomized to receive group therapy plus sildenafil showed significant improvement of successful intercourse, and were less likely than those receiving only sildenafil to drop out. Group psychotherapy also significantly improved ED compared to sildenafil citrate alone. Regarding the effectiveness of psychosocial interventions for the treatment of ED compared to local injection, vacuum devices, and other psychosocial techniques, no differences were found.

Evidence-Based Practices

Which should be the first line choice of psychological intervention for the treatment of ED? In conclusion, there is evidence that group psychotherapy improved ED. Focused sex group therapy showed greater efficacy than the control group (no treatment). Which demographic patient characteristics are predictors to response to psychotherapy? Until now, no differences were found related to the severity of ED, type of partnership, and mean group age. What is the effectiveness of psychological interventions compared to oral drugs? In a

meta-analysis that compares sildenafil versus group therapy plus sildenafil citrate, men randomized to receive group therapy showed significant improvement of successful intercourse rate and were less likely than those receiving only sildenafil to drop out. One study revealed that group psychotherapy had significantly higher scores compared with patients that were exclusively treated with sildenafil citrate. What is the effectiveness of psychological interventions compared to local injection and the effectiveness of psychological interventions compared to vacuum devices? As to the effectiveness of psychological interventions for the treatment of ED compared to local injection and vacuum devices, no difference was found.

Future Research

In the future, combined treatments may be the rule rather than the exception. There also is a need to develop scientifically proven algorithms and methods for combined treatments. There is need for collaboration between health care practitioners from different disciplines in evaluation, treatment, and education issues surrounding sexual dysfunction. In many cases, neither psychotherapy alone nor medical intervention alone is sufficient for the lasting resolution of sexual problems. Assessment of male, female, and couples' sexual dysfunction should ideally include inquiry about predisposing, precipitating, maintaining, and contextual factors. Treatment of lifelong and/or chronic dysfunction will be different from acquired or recent dysfunction. Research is needed to identify efficacious combined and/or integrated treatments for sexual dysfunction.

There is also a need for well conducted and reported randomized controlled trials, which are essential to establish effectiveness of psychological interventions for ED. Large randomized clinical trials with longer follow-up, to examine whether psychological interventions help patients with ED, are needed. These studies would need to consider the study setting as this may have a confounding effect on the results. The questions that should be raised include the following: Does the effectiveness depend upon personality factors, psychiatric comorbid diagnosis, length of therapy time, severity of ED use, or any other factors? Inherent problems in the field of psychological interventions for sexual disorders are recruitment difficulties, motivation of patients, study adherence, blinding, follow-up difficulties, questionable results, high attrition rates, low study completion rates, and comparable, unintended selection for highly motivated patients.

Those researchers conducting clinical trials should clearly state the method of randomization, allocation concealment, blinding where possible, perform intention to treat analysis, with power calculations performed prior to the trial. More pragmatic studies can be designed and delivered that provide usable data for better understanding of this important intervention in the field of sexuality.

REFERENCES

American Psychiatric Association. 1994. *Diagnostic and statistical manual of mental disorders* (4th ed.). Washington, DC: Author.

Althof, S. I. (2000). The patient with erectile dysfunction: Psychological issues. *Nurse Practitioner, June* (Suppl.), 11–3.

Althof, S. I. (2002). When an erection alone is not enough: Biopsychosocial obstacles to lovemaking. *International Journal of Impotence Research, 14* (Suppl.) 1, 99–104.

Ansari, J. M. A. (1976). Impotence: Prognosis (a controlled study). *British Journal of Psychiatry, 128*, 194–198.

Araújo, A. B., Durante, R., Feldman, H. A., Goldstein, I., & McKinlay, J. B. (1998). The relationship between depressive symptoms and male erectile dysfunction: Cross-sectional results from The Massachusetts Male Aging Study. *Psychosomatic Medicine, 60*, 458–465.

Bacon, C. G., Mittleman, M. A., Kawachi, I., Giovannucci, E., Glasser, D. B., & Rimm, E. B. (2003). Sexual function in men older than 50 years of age: Results from the health professionals follow-up study. *Annals of Internal Medicine, 139*, 161–168.

Banner, L. L., & Anderson, R. U. (2007). Integrated sildenafil and cognitive behavior sex therapy for psychogenic erectile dysfunction: A pilot study. *Journal of Sexual Medicine, 4*, 1117–1125.

Baum, N., Randrup, E., Junot, D., & Hass, S. (2000). Prostragandin E1 versus sex therapy in the management of psychogenic erectile dysfunction. *International Journal of Impotence Research, 12*, 191–194.

Ellis, A. (1992). Group rational-emotive and cognitive-behavioral therapy. *International Journal of Group Psychotherapy, 42*, 63–80.

Feldman, H. A., Goldstein, I., Hatzichristou, D. G., Krane, R. J., & McKinlay, J. B. I. (1994). Impotence and its medical and psychosocial correlates: Results of the Massachusetts male aging study. *Journal of Urology, 151*, 54–61.

Fisher, W. A., Rosen, R. C., Eardley, I., Niederberger, C., Nadel, A., Kaufman, J., & Sand, M. (2004). The multinational men's attitudes to life events and sexuality (MALES) study Phase II: Understanding PDE5 inhibitor treatment seeking patterns, among men with erectile dysfunction. *Journal of Sexual Medicine, 1*, 150–160.

Golden, J. S., Price, S., Heinrich, A. G., & Lobitz, W. C. (1978). Group vs. couple treatment of sexual dysfunctions. *Archives of Sexual Behavior, 7*, 593–602.

Goldman, J., & Carroll, J. L. (1990). Educational intervention as an adjunct treatment of erectile dysfunction in older couples. *Journal of Sex and Marital Therapy, 16*, 127–141.

Hartmann, U., & Langer, D. (1993). Combination of psychosocial therapy and intrapenile injections in the treatment of erectile dysfunctions: Rationale and predictors of outcome. *Journal of Sex Education and Therapy, 19*, 1–12.

Hawton, K., Catalan, J., Martin, P., & Fagg, J. (1986). Long term outcome of sex therapy. *Behaviour Research and Therapy, 24*, 665–675.

Higgins, J. P. T., & Green, S., (Eds.). (2005). Cochrane handbook for systematic reviews of interventions 4.2.5 (updated May 2005). *Cochrane Library, 3*. Chichester, England: John Wiley & Sons.

Kilmann, R. P., Milan, J. R., Boland, P. J., Nankin, R. H., Davidson, E., West, O. M., . . . Devine, J. M. (1987). Group treatment of secondary erectile dysfunction. *Journal of Sex and Marital Therapy, 13*, 168–182.

Kockott, G., Dittmar, F., & Nusselt, L. (1975). Systematic desensitization of erectile impotence: A controlled study. *Archives of Sexual Behavior, 4*, 493–500.

Laumann, E. O., Paik, A., & Rosen, R. C. (1999). The epidemiology of erectile dysfunction: Results from the National Health and Social Life Survey. *International Journal of Impotence Research, September 11*(Suppl. 1), S60–64.

Lobitz, W. C., & Baker, E. L., Jr. (1979). Group treatment of single males with erectile dysfunction. *Archives of Sexual Behavior, 8*, 127–123.

LoPiccolo, J. (1985). Diagnosis and treatment of male sexual dysfunction. *Journal of Sex and Marital Therapy, 11*, 215–232.

LoPiccolo, J., & Stock, W. E. (1986). Treatment of sexual dysfunction. *Journal of Consulting and Clinical Psychology, 54,* 158–167.

Lue, T. F., Giuliano, F., Montorsi, F., Rosen, R. C., Andersson, K. E., & Althof, S. . . . Wagner, G. (2004). Summary of the recommendations on sexual dysfunctions in men. *Journal of Sexual Medicine, 1,* 6–23.

Masters, W. H., & Johnson, V. E. (1970/1981). *Human sexual inadequacy* (reissue ed.). New York, NY: Little, Brown.

Melnik, T., & Abdo, C. H. N. (2005). Psychogenic erectile dysfunction: Comparative study of three therapeutic approaches. *Journal of Sex and Marital Therapy, 31,* 243–255.

Mulcahy, J. J., & Wilson, S. K. (2006) Current use of penile implants in erectile dysfunction. *Current Urology Reports, 7,* 485–489.

Munjack, D. J., Schlaks, A., Sanchez, V. C., Usigli, R., Zulueta, A., & Leonard, M. (1984). Rationale emotive therapy in the treatment of erectile failure: An initial study. *Journal of Sex and Marital Therapy, 10,* 170–175.

Padma-Nathan, H. (2000). Diagnostic and treatment strategies for erectile dysfunction: The "process of care" model. *International Journal of Impotence Research, 12*(Suppl. 4), S119–S121.

Price, C. S., Reynolds, R. S., Cohen, B. D., Anderson, A. J., & Schochet, B. V. (1981) Group treatment of erectile dysfunction for men without partners: A controlled evaluation. *Archives of Sexual Behavior, 10,* 253–268.

Prins, J., Blanker, M. H., Bohnen, A. M., Thomas, S., & Bosch, J. L. (2002). Prevalence of erectile dysfunction: A systematic review of population based studies. *International Journal of Impotence Research, 14,* 422–432.

Reynolds, B. S., Cohen, B. D., Schochet, B. V., Price, S. C., & Anderson, A. J. (1981) Dating skills training in the group treatment of erectile dysfunction men without partners. *Journal of Sex and Marital Therapy, 7,* 184–194.

Rimm, D. C., & Masters, J. C. (1987) *Behavior therapy: Techniques and empirical findings.* New York, NY: Academic Press.

Rosen, R. C. (2001) Psychogenic erectile dysfunction: Classification and management. *Urologic Clinics of North America, 28,* 269–278.

Rosen, R. C., & McKenna, K. E. (2002) PDE-5 inhibition and sexual response: Pharmacological mechanisms and clinical outcomes. *Annual Review of Sex Research, 13,* 36–88.

Sackett, D. L., Straus, S. E., Richardson, W. S., Rosenberg, W., & Haynes, R. B. (2000). *Evidence-based medicine: How to practice and teach EBM* (2nd ed.). London, England: Churchill Livingstone.

Sand, M. S., Fisher, W., Rosen, R., Heiman, J., & Eardley, I. (2008). Erectile dysfunction and constructs of masculinity and quality of life in the multinational Men's Attitudes to Life Events and Sexuality (MALES) study. *Journal of Sexual Medicine, 5,* 583–594.

Schouten, B. W., Bosch, J. L., Bernsen, R. M., Blanker, M. H., Thomas, S., & Bohnen, A. M. (2005). Incidence rates of erectile dysfunction in the Dutch general population. Effects of definition, clinical relevance and duration of follow-up in the Krimpen Study. *International Journal of Impotence Research, 17,* 58–62.

Stravynski, A., Gaudette, G., Lesage, A., Petit, N., Pascale, C., Fabian, J., & Lamontagne, Y. (1997). The treatment of sexually dysfunctional men without partners: A controlled study of three behavioural group approaches. *British Journal of Psychiatry, 170,* 338–344.

Task Force on Promotion and Dissemination of Psychological Procedures. (1995). Training in and dissemination of empirically validated psychological treatments: Report and recommendations. *Clinical Psychologist, 48,* 3–23.

Tiefer, L., & Schuetz-Mueller, D. (1995). Psychological issues in diagnosis and treatment of erectile disorders. *Urologic Clinics of North America, 22,* 161–173.

Van der Windt, F., Dohle, G. R., van der Tak, J., & Slob, A. K. (2002) Intracavernosal injections therapy with or without sexological counseling in men with erectile dysfunction. *BJU International, 89,* 901–904.

Wylie, K. R., Jones, R. H., & Walters, S. (2003) The potential benefit of vacuum devices augmenting psychosexual therapy for erectile dysfunction. *Journal of Sex and Marital Therapy, 29,* 227–236.

Zilbergeld, B. (1975) Group treatment of sexual dysfunction in men without partners. *Journal of Sex and Marital Therapy, 1,* 204–214.

17

Sexual Dysfunctions
in Women

MONIEK M. TER KUILE, STEPHANIE BOTH, AND JACQUES J. D. M. VAN LANKVELD

OVERVIEW OF DISORDER

The *Diagnostic and Statistical Manual of
Mental Disorders*, 4th ed. *(DSM-IV-TR)*
(American Psychiatric Association [APA],
2000) classifies sexual dysfunctions into disorders of desire, arousal, orgasm, and pain
(including genital pain and vaginismus). As
the psychological treatment procedures differ
between these sexual disorders, we will review
the treatments for each disorder separately. To
state if a treatment is evidence based we follow
the criteria of Chambless and Hollon (1998). In
light of new empirical data there is a growing
consensus about female sexual (dys)function
ing and shortcomings in the traditional
nosology of women's sexual disorders. An
international consensus conference concluded
that the *DSM-IV-TR* definitions of female
sexual dysfunction are unsatisfactory, stemming in part from the problematic conceptualization of the female sexual response cycle
(Basson et al., 2003). That is, the *DSM-IV-TR*
definition of women's sexual dysfunction is
based on a model that is more characteristic of
men than of women (Kaplan, 1979; Masters &
Johnson, 1966) with the assumed sequential
stages of desire, arousal, and orgasm. The
panel developed a revised classification
system (Basson et al., 2003), which will be
discussed in this chapter for each disorder

separately. Although the *DSM-IV* classifies
women's sexual disorders separately, comorbidity of these dysfunctions is high (Segraves &
Segraves, 1991; Talakoub et al., 2002) and
the impact of the disorders is for most of the
dysfunctions very similar. Therefore, we will
discuss the impact of the sexual disorder
across dysfunctions first.

Impact of Sexual Disorder

In women, the experience of sexual dysfunction is strongly associated with feelings of
physical and emotional dissatisfaction in
the relationship and general unhappiness
(Laumann, Park, & Rosen, 1999). Bancroft,
Loftus, and Long (2003) found that neither
relative frequency of sexual thoughts, frequency of orgasms, nor lubrication or pain
problems predicted sexual distress, whereas
emotional and relational well being were the
best predictors of sexual distress. In an English
study, all female sexual problems were significantly related to anxiety and depression,
and arousal, orgasmic, and desire problems
were strongly related to marital difficulties
(Dunn, Croft, & Hackett, 1999). Although it
must be emphasized that the results of these
studies do not imply causality, they do show a
close link between sexual dysfunction and
general personal well being and relationship

satisfaction. In a Swedish population study, 1,335 women indicated the amount of personal distress caused by the sexual dysfunction. Of those women reporting sexual disabilities (47%), about half of these women (26% of the total sample) reported that the sexual disability was also distressing her. Manifestly distressing sexual dysfunction in women was associated with low levels of satisfaction with the partner relationship and with male sexual dysfunctions, especially erectile dysfunction (K. Fugl-Meyer & Fugl-Meyer, 2002; Oberg & Fugl-Meyer, 2005). Thus, the impact of sexual disorder in women is very closely related to emotional and relational well-being.

PROBLEMS WITH LOW SEXUAL DESIRE

Overview of Disorder

Diagnostic criteria. In *DSM-IV-TR*, the condition of low or reduced sexual desire is referred to as hypoactive sexual desire disorder (HSDD) and is described as: "Persistent or recurrent deficiency (or absence) of sexual fantasies and desire for sexual activity. This disturbance causes marked distress or interpersonal difficulty" (APA, 2000, p. 541). Sexual desire and interest deal with the individual experience of wanting to become or to continue being sexual. Sexual desire may include erotic fantasies and thoughts and may be expressed as the initiative to engage in self- or other-directed sexual behavior. For a discussion of operational definitions of sexual desire, see Heiman (2001). Absent or low sexual interest is not intrinsically pathological, but may become problematic in the context of interpartner sexual desire discrepancy (Bancroft et al., 2003).

Sexual desire is governed by both biological and psychological factors. Here we address psychological factors. The term *hypoactive sexual desire* appears to imply that sexual desire possesses an intrinsically activating or

motivating quality, independent of other aspects of sexual functioning. This notion is supported by linear models of the sexual response (Kaplan, 1979; Lief, 1977; Masters & Johnson, 1966) in which desire is considered a prerequisite for normal arousal and orgasm; however, recently, it has been stated that to understand women's sexual desire, one should move from a focus on spontaneous desire to a response cycle model in which the seeking of, or receptivity to, sexual stimuli leads to feelings of arousal and desire. Basson presented a circular model (Basson, 2000, 2005; Basson et al., 2004) that differentiates between newly formed and long-term relationships. In this view, the sexual response of women in new relationships can well be described by a linear sequence, and the woman can experience her sexual motivation as a need stemming from within; however, sexual motivation of women in older relationships could be more accurately described as a state of sexual neutrality and receptivity. Women may decide to engage in sexual behavior as a result of a large array of sexual and nonsexual motives (Meston & Buss, 2007), including the wish to experience physical pleasure, to show affection, to please or pacify a partner, to feel strong or desirable, to dispel boredom, to distract from negative preoccupations, to continue a long-standing habit, or to meet a felt obligation. When engaging in sexual behavior, processing of sexual stimuli may result in responsive sexual arousal and desire. The rewarding quality of the sexual experience will facilitate future receptivity.

Consequently, cognitive processes that interfere with obtaining reward from sexual activity will also impair sexual desire, including ruminative, worrisome ideation (Barlow, 1986; van den Hout & Barlow, 2000), low outcome expectancy (Bach, Brown, & Barlow, 1999), displaced focus of attention (Meston, 2006), general insufficient attentional capacity (Elliott & O'Donohue, 1997; Salemink & van Lankveld, 2006), and level of propensity to experience sexual excitation versus sexual inhibition (Bancroft & Janssen, 2000; Carpenter, 2002).

Demographic variables. Depending on the diagnostic criteria, survey method, and samples across different countries and ethnic groups, 5% to 46% of women report low sexual desire (Laumann et al., 2005; Mercer et al., 2003; Simons & Carey, 2001). Studies reporting higher prevalence rates were based on post-menopausal women. When both low sexual desire and distress were used as criteria, thus matching diagnostic requirements for *DSM* classification, lower percentages were found. To give an example, prevalence of sexual dys-function was assessed by postal questionnaire in 356 Australian women between 20 and 70 years old (Hayes, Dennerstein, Bennett, & Fairley, 2008). When assessed with instruments that strictly adhere to *DSM-IV-TR* criteria, including presence of sexual dysfunction and sexual distress, HSDD was found in 16% (95% confidence intervals: 12% to 20%), whereas 32% to 58% of these participants would have shown HSDD according to the criteria used by Laumann et al. (2005). Psychosocial risk factors for low sexual desire in women are longer relationship duration (Basson, 2000; Klusmann, 2002), whereas not being married and starting a new relationship are positively related to feelings of sexual desire (Avis et al., 2005). Marital satisfaction (Dennerstein, Koochaki, Barton, & Graziottin, 2006; Trudel, Boulos, & Matte, 1993; Trudel, Landry, & Larose, 1997), marital happiness (Donnelly, 1993), intimacy between partners (McCabe, 1997), and partner communication (Brezsnyak & Whisman, 2004; Stulhofer, Gregurovic, Pikic, & Galic, 2005) are associated with more frequent sexual desire. Other sexual dysfunc-tions in either the woman or the partner also interfere with sexual desire (Segraves & Segraves, 1991).

Prevalence of depressive disorders and pre-menstrual syndrome are higher in women with low sexual desire (Moreira, Jr., Glasser, Santos, & Gingell, 2005; Schreiner-Engel & Schiavi, 1986) and most antidepressants interfere with female sexual functioning, with the possible exceptions of bupropion and nefazodone (Ferguson, 2001). Low sexual desire is highly prevalent in women with psychotic disorders (Kockott & Pfeiffer, 1996). The largest inhibitory effect on sexual desire was found in patients on neuroleptic medication. Low sexual desire seems not to be associated with drug or alcohol use (Johnson, Phelps, & Cottler, 2004). Childhood sexual abuse disrupts adult sexual functioning (see Leonard & Follette, 2002; Rumstein-McKean & Hunsley, 2001), but the effects of sexual trau-matization on sexual desire are not consistent (McHichi Alami & Kadri, 2004).

Treatment

Compared with other sexual problems, sexual desire problems have traditionally been con-sidered to be more difficult to treat (Beck, 1995; Heiman, 2001). The circular model of sexual desire implies that low sexual desire is a consequence of problematic functioning in other domains of sexuality, the partner rela-tionship, or the physical and psychological condition of the female client or her partner. It also implies that treatment should focus on helping the client to increase the rewards necessary to experience stronger motivation to engage in sexual activity including other aspects of the woman's sexual functioning, such as her sexual arousal response and lubri-cation during sexual stimulation, ability to experience orgasm, or reduction of pain during sex. Treatment might also help to improve her partner's or her own skills of erotic stimulation and to relieve her partner's sexual dysfunction. Treatment might also aim to increase the rewards and reduce punishment that the woman experiences within nonsexual domains of her relationship. In the following paragraphs, we review the treatment programs that have been empirically tested and found beneficial: sex therapy and cognitive behavior therapy.

Sex therapy or sensate focus was first described by Masters and Johnson (1970)

When starting treatment, the rationale of treatment is explained, sexual education is given, and a temporary ban on intercourse is suggested. The partners then follow a program of exercises, including mutual nongenital and genital pleasuring, communication exercises, and exercises aimed at reducing performance demand and the resulting anxiety. In some formats, cognitive interventions have been added to the treatment (Hurlbert, 1993; Hurlbert, White, Powell, & Apt, 1993).

Consensus panels. In 2004, a consensus panel emphasized a general lack of controlled outcome studies, but asserted that cognitive behavioral techniques, including sensate focus therapy, show efficacy in women with low desire (Basson et al., 2004, pp. 889–890). These conclusions were based on four controlled studies discussed later.

Randomized controlled trials. Table 17.1 provides a summary of controlled psychological outcome studies for HSDD. The interpretation of the results of some studies is complicated by the use of heterogeneous samples, including patients with HSDD as well as with other sexual dysfunction types (van Lankveld, Everaerd, & Grotjohann, 2001), or the reporting of lumped analyses of outcome in which the results for various diagnostic groups were indistinguishable.

Hurlbert (1993) investigated 55 women with HSDD and compared group therapy alone with group therapy combined with orgasm consistency training. Group therapy included sensate focus exercises and techniques to increase the male partner's ejaculatory self-control. Orgasm consistency training included: (a) an introduction to directed masturbation, (b) instructing the couple to allow the woman to reach orgasm during sexual interaction before the male partner climaxes and before intercourse is initiated (the "ladies come first" rule), and (c) the coital alignment technique to ensure direct clitoral stimulation by the penis during intercourse. Women who received both group therapy and orgasm consistency training reported more improvement with respect to

sexual arousal and sexual assertiveness at posttreatment and at follow-up evaluations after 3 and 6 months. This group also reported more sexual satisfaction at the 6-month follow-up. These results must be treated with caution as one of the 29 (3%) couples of the standard therapy and 15 of the 26 (58%) couples in the orgasm consistency training group were excluded from analyses because their husbands could not make all the treatment appointments.

Because the first study did not examine the effect of treatment on perceived level of sexual desire, a second study of 57 women with HSDD was conducted (Hurlbert et al., 1993). Participants were randomly allocated to a women-only group, a couples group, or a waiting list control group. Both active treatments included the orgasm consistency training. Compared with waiting list, women in both treatment groups reported improved sexual desire at posttreatment. Women in the couples group reported higher frequency of sexual fantasy following treatment, and at follow-up the couples group was superior to the women-only group on measures of sexual compatibility between partners, sexual self-esteem, sexual desire, fantasy, and sexual satisfaction.

MacPhee, Johnson, and Van der Veer (1995) compared couples with female HSDD who received emotionally focused couples therapy (EFT) with waiting list couples and couples without female HSDD. Differences between waiting list and treatment were small, treated women showed only improvement on one measure of sexual desire as well as a decrease in depressive symptoms. After treatment 24% of the treated women was improved on sexual desire compared to 8% of the women in the control group. Only 12% of the women could be considered as recovered (Jacobson & Truax, 1991). In general, recovery and improvement rates were also higher for treated males compared to nontreated males. However, no data for the males are presented on the main outcome measures.

TABLE 17.1 Randomized Controlled Trials for Sexual Dysfunctions in Women

Reference	N	Treatment	Participant Characteristics	Outcome
			Hypoactive sexual desire disorder (HSDD)	
	55	T: OCT: DM – CAT – women some first – standard sex therapy; G vs standard sex therapy; G: eight weekly 2-hour sessions	M age = 31; HSDD = 100%	OCT – standard sex therapy > Standard sex therapy; gains maintained at 6-month FU
	57	OCT – standard sex therapy; G-C vs OCT – standard sex therapy; G-women vs WL: eight weekly 2-hour sessions	M age = 30; HSDD = 100%	OCT – standard sex therapy (G-C) > OCT + standard sex therapy (G-women) > WL: gains maintained at 6-month FU
	44	EFT: marital therapy; C vs WL 10 weekly sessions	M age = 41; HSDD = 100% Partner specific = 56%	EFT > WL; EFT: 24%; WL = 4% improved/recovered frequency sexual contact gains maintained at 3-month FU
	74	CBT: G-C vs WL: 12 weekly 2-hour sessions	M age = 37; HSDD = 100% Partner specific = 65%	CBT > WL: gain maintained at 3-month + 1-year FU
	31	CBT: Bibliotherapy vs WL 10 weeks	M age = 36; HSDD = 49%	CBT > WCL at posttreatment CBT = WLC at 10-week FU
			Sexual Arousal Disorder	
			No studies located	
			Orgasm Disorder (OD)	
	11	T: DM – SD – AT – relaxation; IC vs WL: 16 weekly sessions	M age = 29; primary, OD = 55% secondary, OD = 45%	T > WL: Post: secondary 40% = primary 22% orgasmic; 9-month FU: secondary 60% > primary 0% orgasmic in at least 50% of the occasions
	83	DM – SF: C vs SF: C vs WL weekly – 3 first eight sessions	M age = 26; primary, OD = 100%	DM – SF > SF DM – SF: 90% orgasmic by any means; 85% coital orgasmic; SF: 53% orgasmic. 47% coital orgasmic: gains maintained at 1-year FU
	7	DM bibliotherapy: I vs DM video instruction: I vs WL six weekly sessions	M age = 29; Primary, OD = 100%	DM bibliotherapy = DM video instruction > WL DM: 60% orgasmic (masturbation), 33% coital orgasmic vs. WL: 0% orgasmic: gains maintained/improved at 1-year FU

(Continued)

TABLE 17.1 Randomized Controlled Trials for Sexual Dysfunctions in Women (*Continued*)

Reference	N	Treatment	Participant Characteristics	Outcome
Andersen (1981)	30	DM (G) vs. SD (G) vs. WL; sessions twice weekly for 5 weeks	Age: 19–42; Primary OD = 100%	DM = SD = WL; DM: 20%; SD: 10%; WL: 10% orgasmic[1] post; DM = SD at 6 week FU; DM = 40%; SD = 10% orgasmic
Delehanty (1982)	28	DM + AT (G) vs. WL; 10 weekly sessions	M age = 30; Primary OD or secondary OD > 5 years	DM + AT > WL; DM + AT: 82% orgasmic[1] at 4-month FU
Fichten, Libman, and Brender (1983)	23	T: DM, SF, Education, relaxation (C) vs. T (G) vs. Bibliotherapy; 14 weeks	M age = 33; Secondary OD = 100%	No change in orgasm[1]
Heiman and LoPiccolo (1983)	41	T: DM, SF, CBT, communication training, system approach (C) weekly vs. T: (C) daily: 15 sessions	M age = 30; Primary OD = 61%; Secondary OD = 39%	T daily = T weekly; Primary: 63% increased freq orgasm (masturbation); 25% increase in freq coital orgasm; Secondary: 0% increase of freq orgasm (masturbation); 18% increase in coital orgasm; Gains maintained at 3-month FU
Kilmann et al. (1986)	55	DM + SF vs. 2(DM + SF + communication skills) vs. communication skills vs. attention placebo vs. WL; All: two 2-hour sex education (C) and then randomization 10 weekly sessions (G)	M age = 33; Secondary OD = 100%	T (4 conditions) > control (WL + attention placebo) in > 50% of coitus an orgasmic response; Posttreatment: T = 26% vs. control = 0%; 6-month FU T = 31% vs. control = 9%
Hurlbert and Apt (1995)	36	DM versus CAT: four 30-minute sessions (C) and eight 90-minute sessions (G)	M age = 28; Secondary OD = 100%	CAT > DM; CAT: 56% increase in frequency of coital orgasm; DM: 27% increase
Other interventions				
Mathews et al. (1976)	18	SD + counseling (C) vs. SF + counseling (C) vs. SF bibliotherapy (C); 10 weeks	M age = 28; Primary OD = 72%; HSDD = 94%	11% improved orgasmic response (on scale); no difference between groups posttreatment and 4-month FU
Sotile and Kilmann (1978)	22	SD (G): 15 sessions, twice weekly vs. WL (within design)	M age = 28; Primary OD = 36%; Secundary OD = 64%	SD (G) > WL period; Secondary OD > primary OD: noncoital orgasmic frequency with partner at post- and 6-month FU

	N	Treatment	Sample	Results
Riggen and Kuriansky	4	Kegel exercises (G) vs relaxation exercises (G) vs control group (12 weeks)	M age = 32. Primary, OD or anorgasmia during previous 2 years	Kegel = relaxation = control Orgasmic ability by any means: 25%
Fitger et al.	3	T SD + bibliotherapy techniques (I) three weeks, +2 weeks (A) SF + counseling (C) (8 weeks) vs WL	Age 18–36. Primary, OD = 100%	Post: T (I) > SF + counseling = WL T = 88%; SF + counseling = 25%; WL = 0% orgasmic ability over 60% of the time 4-year FU: T (I) = SF + counseling (C) > WL T = 75%; SF + counseling = 38%; WL = 10%

Dyspareunia

Bergeron et al.; Bergeron, Khalifé, Glazer and Binik	78	Vestibulectomy vs EMG-bio (eight weekly) 45-min sessions vs CBT (G) (eight weekly) 2-hour sessions	M age = 27. Dyspareunia = 100% Provoked	Vestibulectomy = EMG bio = CBT (G) for pain during intercourse at 3 and 6 months Results remain at 2½-year FU
Danielson, Torstensson, Brodda-Jansen and Bohm-Starke	46	EMG-bio vs medical treatment (topical) lidocaine	M age = 24. Dyspareunia = 100%	EMG bio = medical treatment for pain during intercourse at 6- and 12-month FU

Vaginismus

Schnyder, Schnyder-Luthi, Ballinari and Blaser	44	SD in vivo vs SD in vitro, every 2 weeks. Session M = 65	M age = 28. Primary, VAG = 43%	SD in vivo = SD in vitro: 97% intercourse (possible)
van Lankveld et al.	117	CBT (G) Ten 2-hour sessions vs biblioth six (weekly), 15-min telephone contact vs WL	M age = 29. Primary, VAG = 100%	CBT (G) = biblio > WL 14% intercourse (possible) at 3 months
ter Kuile et al.	1	Therapist-aided exposure vs WL. Max three 2-hour sessions in one week within N = 1 design	M age = 29. Primary, VAG = 100%	Exposure > WL. 90% intercourse (possible) at 3 months; Results remain at a 1-year FU

Trudel et al. (2001) conducted an RCT of cognitive behavior therapy for female HSDD compared with a waiting list control group. Treatment was administered in 2-hour, weekly group sessions of couple sex therapy over 12 weeks. Group interventions included sex education; couple sexual intimacy enhancing exercises; sensate focus; communication skills training; emotional communication skills training; sexual fantasy training; cognitive restructuring; and various homework assignments, including reading a manual. Assessments were collected in 74 couples with female HSDD. Couples with concurrent depressive disorder in either partner were excluded. At posttreatment, improvement in the treated group was greater than improvement in the waiting list with regard to HSD complaints. At pretreatment all women in both groups met criteria for HSDD. After the data were combined from the initial treatment group and the waiting list group only, 26% of the participating women still met criteria for HSDD at posttreatment. This percentage increased to 36% at the 3-month follow-up and then remained stable until 12-month follow-up. There were also positive changes on measures of sexual functioning, including pleasure with sexual activities and decreased frequency of negative thoughts during sex.

Van Lankveld et al. (2001) conducted an RCT of cognitive behavioral bibliotherapy in a sample of couples with various sexual dysfunctions. Of the female participants, 49% met *DSM* criteria for HSDD. Compared with waiting list control group, treatment resulted in increased frequency of sexual interaction at posttreatment assessment. However, at follow-up after 3 months, these treatment gains were not maintained.

No meta-analyses of either group designs or single subject experimental designs were identified for this review.

Conclusions

Sex therapy and cognitive behavioral treatments have demonstrated gains in sexual functioning of women with HSDD, including increased sexual interest and desire. More effective treatments appear to include a combination of sex therapy and cognitive behavioral strategies, deal with couples rather than women alone, and typically involve techniques that address more elements of sexual functioning than sexual desire alone. The scarcity of data prevents strong conclusions regarding the effectiveness of some procedures, techniques, or formats over others. Approaches including a broad focus appear to be most efficacious; however, several of these studies were methodologically weak and their results should be treated with caution. Orgasm consistency training (Hurlbert, 1993; Hurlbert et al., 1993) and cognitive behavioral treatment (Trudel et al., 2001) are promising approaches that need replication to establish their robustness.

Currently, no published studies investigated the effect on female sexual desire of either psychological, pharmacological, or combined treatments for depression, although there is some evidence with regard to pharmacological treatment of antidepressant-induced sexual dysfunction, including female low sexual desire. For example, Taylor, Rudkin, and Hawton (2005) reviewed 15 RCTs, including 393 women, comparing management strategies for antidepressant-induced sexual dysfunction. There was a trend favoring treatment with bupropion. Lowering the dose, change of medication, or the use of temporary drug holidays are possible approaches to antidepressant-induced decreases of sexual desire in clinically depressed women.

FEMALE SEXUAL AROUSAL DISORDER

Overview of Disorder

Diagnostic criteria. Female sexual arousal disorder (FSAD) is defined in the *DSM-IV-TR* as "a persistent or recurrent inability to attain or to maintain until completion of sexual activity an adequate genital lubrication-swelling response of sexual excitement that causes marked distress or interpersonal difficulty" (APA, 2000, p. 502). The *DSM-IV-TR* definition of FSAD has been criticized as it focuses exclusively on the genital response, whereas the absence of or markedly diminished feelings of subjective sexual arousal, sexual excitement, and sexual pleasure are not mentioned (Basson et al., 2003).

In the few studies that measured genital responding in women with sexual arousal problems, medically healthy women diagnosed with FSAD respond with an increase of vaginal vasocongestion that is comparable with the response of women without sexual problems under laboratory conditions while viewing erotic videos (Basson et al., 2004); however, women with FSAD report less positive affect and often more negative affect in response to these sexual stimuli than women without sexual problems (Laan, van Driel, & van Lunsen, 2008). These studies indicate that medically healthy women with FSAD are equally capable of genital responding as women without sexual problems to explicit erotic stimuli, suggesting that these sexual arousal problems may be related to inadequate erotic stimulation in daily life or negative evaluation of the sexual situation (Laan, Everaerd, & Both, 2005).

Demographic variables. Depending on the diagnostic criteria, survey method, sampling strategies, country and ethnic groups, 8% to 15% of all women and 21% to 28% of sexual active women experience lubrication difficulties (Lewis et al., 2004). About two thirds of the women who reported lubrication difficulties reported this as a problem and the vast majority of them were unsatisfied with their sexual life (A. R. Fugl-Meyer & Fugl-Meyer, 1999). Some studies found that FSAD was more prevalent with increasing age, especially in women over 50 years, while others have not found this (Lewis et al., 2004). Age-related decline in sexual arousal may be partially attributable to physical factors related to menopause, such as reduced estrogen (Meston, Seal, & Hamilton, 2008). Medical factors that interfere with arousal include endocrine and cardiovascular problems, and use of

antidepressants and antipsychotics; however, other than using antidepressants, women with FSAD report low levels of medical problems (Meston et al., 2008). Psychosocial risk factors for sexual arousal disorders include marital difficulties (Dunn et al., 1999; Osborn, Hawton, & Gath, 1988), negative attitudes regarding sexuality, aging, higher levels of perceived stress or emotional problems (Laumann et al., 1999), depression and anxiety (Dunn et al., 1999), and being in an abusive relationship (Avis et al., 2005; Laumann et al., 1999), whereas not being married, starting a new relationship, and using contraception are positively related to sexual arousal.

Treatment

Psychological treatment of sexual arousal problems consists of sensate focus exercises and masturbation training, with the emphasis on becoming more self-focused and assertive (Laan et al., 2005). Cognitive behavioral techniques are often added for cognitive restructuring of beliefs and myths related to sexual dysfunction. Couple therapy is also a common component of sex therapy to enhance communication in the relationship. In 2004, a consensus panel emphasized a general lack of controlled outcome studies and it recommended that the focus on loss of subjective sexual arousal is made in future studies (Basson et al., 2004, p. 890). No randomized controlled trials, simple subject designs, meta-analyses of group or single-subject experimental designs were found for this problem. Thus, there are no evidence-based psychological interventions for FSAD, although directed masturbation training or comparable treatments may be effective for FSAD as they are for female orgasmic disorder (FOD) (Laan et al., 2005).

FEMALE ORGASMIC DISORDER

Overview of Disorder

Diagnostic criteria. In the *DSM-IV-TR*, FOD is described as a persistent or recurrent delay in, or absence of, orgasm following a normal sexual excitement phase (APA, 2000) and the disturbance must cause marked distress or interpersonal difficulty. The *DSM-IV-TR* describes subtypes of FOD as: (a) lifelong (primary) versus acquired (secondary), and (b) generalized (never experiencing orgasm) versus situational (reaching orgasm only with specific stimulation). The *DSM* acknowledges that women exhibit wide variability in the type and intensity of stimulation that triggers orgasm. The diagnosis of the disorder is based on the clinician's judgment that the women's capacity to orgasm is less than would be reasonable for her age, sexual experience, and adequacy of sexual stimulation; however, a definition of orgasm or indications of what is a reasonable capacity are not provided. Recently, an international expert committee (Meston, Hull, Levin, & Sipski, 2004) defined orgasm as

> a variable, transient peak sensation of intense pleasure, creating an altered state of consciousness, usually accompanied by involuntary, rhythmic contractions of the pelvic striated circumvaginal musculature, often with concomitant uterine and anal contractions and myotonia that resolves the sexually-induced vasocongestion (sometimes only partially), usually with an induction of well-being and contentment. (p. 785)

Regarding capacity to orgasm, the expert committee stated that a woman who can obtain orgasm through intercourse with manual stimulation but not through intercourse alone would not meet criteria for clinical diagnosis (Meston et al., 2004).

Given the variability in type and intensity of stimulation needed to reach orgasm, and the physiological and subjective components of orgasm, it is not surprising that there is substantial variety in the orgasmic problems women report. Women may seek help because they never have experienced orgasm; because they are capable of reaching orgasm by masturbation, but not during sexual contact

with a partner; because they can reach orgasm with a partner, but not or seldom through intercourse; because they cannot reach orgasm except with a vibrator or through other specific types of sexual stimulation; or because they orgasm physically, but do not, or only weakly, experience feelings of pleasure or satisfaction.

Following the definition of *DSM-IV-TR*, FOD is only diagnosed when there is a normal sexual excitement phase that is not followed by orgasm; however, many women with lifelong, generalized anorgasmia experience little sexual excitement or report problems maintaining sexual excitement. Thus, the diagnosis of orgasmic disorder may be made when, according to *DSM-IV-TR* criteria, FSAD would be more accurate. Some women with HSDD have a history of sexual excitement problems and anorgasmia, resulting in a lack of sexually rewarding experiences. Thus, orgasmic problems often involve sexual arousal problems, and desire problems can be caused by arousal and orgasmic problems. Unsurprisingly, there is often comorbidity of anorgasmia, FSAD, and HSDD (Segraves & Segraves, 1991). Several theorists have suggested that the majority of female sexual difficulties reflect disruptions in sexual arousal (Laan et al., 2005; Meston & Bradford, 2007).

Demographic variables. The National Health and Social Life Survey (Laumann et al., 1999) indicated that inability to reach orgasm is the second most frequently reported sexual problem in women. In this random sample of 1,749 women aged 18 to 59 years, 24% reported presence of inability to reach orgasm for several months during the past 12 months; however, in a review of 10 years of research on the prevalence of sexual dysfunction, Simons and Carey (2001) reported a pooled current and 1-year prevalence estimate of 7% to 10% for FOD. Thus, a precise estimate of the prevalence of the disorder is difficult to determine since few well-designed studies have been conducted and definitions of orgasmic disorder differ between studies (Meston et al., 2004). Sociodemographic factors like age, race or ethnicity, or a history of being sexually abused appear not to be associated with orgasmic problems in women; however, education level seems to be related, with women who have graduated from college being half as likely to experience problems achieving orgasm as women who have not graduated from high school (Laumann et al., 1999). Perhaps more educated women have more liberal views on sexuality and are more inclined to seek pleasure as a goal of sexual activity (Meston & Bradford, 2007). Medical conditions including damage to the central nervous system, the spinal cord, or the peripheral nerves caused by trauma or multiple sclerosis can result in orgasmic difficulties (Sipski, 1998). Drugs that increase serotonergic activity (e.g., antidepressants, paroxitine, fluoxetine, sertraline) or decrease dopaminergic activity (e.g., antipsychotics) are reported to delay or inhibit orgasm in women (Meston & Bradford, 2007).

Treatment

Cognitive behavioral approaches for FOD focus on promoting changes in attitudes and thoughts, decreasing anxiety, and increasing orgasmic ability and sexual satisfaction. The approaches generally include behavioral exercises like systemic desensitization, sensate focus, and directed masturbation (DM). DM has been developed specifically for orgasmic disorder in women (LoPiccolo & Lobitz, 1972) and is based on the sex therapy format introduced by Masters and Johnson (1970). Masters and Johnson already included specific interventions in their treatment method for making possible orgasms for women who never or seldom experienced them. LoPiccolo and Lobitz (1972) elaborated on the work of Masters and Johnson, and designed a 9-step DM program for anorgasmic women that consisted of education, self-exploration and body awareness, masturbation exercises, and sensate focus. Initially the program involved both partners but later, Barbach (1974b)

transformed the masturbation program of LoPiccolo and Lobitz to a group treatment format for women without their partners—the so-called preorgasmic women's groups. The use of the word *preorgasmic* stressed the view that anorgasmia was thought to be mainly the result of an inadequate learning process. In this view, women who never experienced orgasm missed a history of discovery of their own sexuality that was supposed to be repaired through learning of adequate masturbation skills that resulted in sexual arousal and orgasm. Eventually, these skills could be applied in interaction with a partner. The masturbation program became available for a larger audience through self-help books (Barbach, 1974a; Heiman, LoPiccolo, & LoPiccolo, 1976).

DM is characterized by the prescription of behavioral exercises that are performed privately at home and focus initially on body awareness and body acceptance, and on visual and tactile exploration of the body. Women are encouraged to discover the areas of the body that produce pleasure when touched. Women are then instructed in masturbation techniques, to use fantasy and imagery to increase sexual excitement and to use topical lubricants, vibrators, and the use of erotic literature or film is often recommended. Frequently, Kegel (1952) exercises involving contraction and relaxation of the pelvic floor muscles are prescribed since they may increase women's awareness of sensations in the genitals and sexual arousal. For women who are inhibited in achieving orgasm due to fear of losing control, role play orgasm is recommended (Heiman & LoPiccolo, 1988).

In this chapter, only evidence from controlled clinical trials for efficacy of cognitive behavioral approaches will be discussed. For an extensive review of controlled and uncontrolled outcome studies, we refer to Meston et al. (2004).

Consensus panel. Treatment of FOD has been approached from psychoanalytic, cognitive behavioral, system theory, and pharmacological perspectives. In 2004 an international expert committee (Meston et al., 2004) concluded that substantial empirical outcome research is available only for cognitive behavioral approaches and, to a lesser degree, for pharmacological approaches. They reviewed more than 50 uncontrolled and controlled cognitive behavioral studies, and 23 uncontrolled and controlled pharmacological treatment studies that included 16 studies of women with antidepressant-induced orgasmic dysfunction. Based on the controlled studies, the expert committee concluded that DM is an empirically valid and efficacious treatment for lifelong FOD, but that there are no empirically validated treatments for acquired FOD. Regarding pharmacological treatments, they concluded that controlled studies did not show agents to be more effective than placebo.

Randomized controlled trials. Table 17.1 described the RCTs of DM and other cognitive behavioral approaches for orgasmic disorder. DM has been applied in different settings, including group, individual, couple, and bibliotherapy. Generally, the treatment is brief, between 10 and 20 sessions. Many outcome studies report DM is successful for treatment of primary orgasmic disorder. In a number of studies high success rates are reported, with 60% to 90% of women being able to experience orgasm by masturbation, and a lower percentage (33% to 85%) being able to experience orgasm with coitus (McMullen & Rosen, 1979; Riley & Riley, 1978). Although in primary orgasmic disorder being able to experience orgasm clearly is a clinically significant result, data on satisfaction with orgasmic capability or ease in reaching orgasm compared to a nonclinical population are not available. Generally, treatment effects are maintained or even improved at follow-up. The treatment is successful in different settings like group, individual, and couple therapy. One study reported success of written or videotaped masturbation assignments with minimal therapist contact, indicating that self-directed masturbation may be a valuable and cost-effective treatment format (McMullen & Rosen, 1979).

Learning how to become orgasmic during masturbation does not necessarily generalize to being orgasmic during sexual activity with a partner. In cases of situational anorgasmia, when a woman is able to attain orgasm through masturbation but not with her partner, couple treatment with a focus on communication, adequate clitoral stimulation, and engaging in intercourse using positions that maximize clitoral stimulation, seem to be more effective than DM. Hurlbert and Apt (1995) compared the effectiveness of DM with coital alignment technique in women with secondary orgasmic disorder. Coital alignment is a technique in which the woman assumes the female supine posture, and the man positions himself up forward on the women, higher than in the conventional missionary position. Hurlbert and Apt (1995) found that coital alignment resulted in a 56% increase in frequency of coital orgasm, compared to 27% with DM.

Most outcome studies applied a combination of education, systematic desensitization, sensate focus, communication training, and DM. There are very few studies that investigated the independent contribution of different treatment components. Comparison of DM alone with systemic desensitization alone shows equal success rates for DM and systemic desensitization in women with primary orgasmic disorder (Andersen, 1981). Comparison of sensate focus with or without DM in a couple format showed better results for the combination treatment (Riley & Riley, 1978). Thus, for the treatment of primary orgasmic disorder, sensate focus alone seems less appropriate; masturbation exercises are an important component. Regarding the frequently prescribed Kegel exercises, Roughan and Kunst (1981) found no difference in orgasmic ability between women who received treatment including Kegel exercises and women who received relaxation therapy or no treatment, which suggests that Kegel exercises alone are not sufficient to treat anorgasmia.

This review found no meta-analyses of group designs, no single subject experiments and no meta-analyses of single subject experiments.

Conclusions

For women with primary orgasmic disorder, DM is an empirically validated, and efficacious treatment (Heiman & Meston, 1997; Meston et al., 2004; O'Donohue, Dopke, & Swingen, 1997). For women with secondary orgasmic disorder, DM may be helpful; however, for women who can reach orgasm alone through masturbation but not with coitus, a couples approach, including communication training and adequate clitoral stimulation techniques like coital alignment technique, may be more beneficial.

SEXUAL PAIN DISORDERS

Dyspareunia: Overview of Disorder

Diagnostic criteria. Dyspareunia is defined in *DSM-IV-TR* as recurrent genital pain associated with sexual intercourse that causes distress and interpersonal problems. Dyspareunia should not be diagnosed if it is caused exclusively by vaginismus, lack of lubrication or a medical condition (APA, 2000). In practice, the latter criterion may be limiting and difficult to establish, as sexual pain is frequently associated with lack of sexual arousal and the persistent difficulty in allowing vaginal entry of a penis, it is difficult to judge the causes of the different complaints. Accordingly, an international consensus committee recommended the following more inclusive revision of the definition of dyspareunia: "Persistent or recurrent pain with attempted or completed vaginal entry and/or penile-vaginal intercourse" (Basson et al., 2003, p. 226). Although not a formal aspect of the definition, dyspareunia is typically described as either superficial (e.g., associated with the vulva

and/of vaginal entrance) or deep (perceived as located in the abdominal or internal organs, often associated with penile thrusting) (Meston & Bradford, 2007). As the etiology of deep dyspareunia is nearly always somatic (e.g. endometriosis) and since most of the cases are superficial, we will focus on that category. Provoked vestibulodynia (PV), formerly referred to as vulvar vestibulitis syndrome, and is thought to be the most frequent type of superficial dyspareunia in premenopausal women. PV is defined as burning or pain that is localized strictly to the vestibule of the vulva and is provoked by pressure or friction in the vestibule (Friedrich, 1987). Its etiology is unknown and the presence or absence of inflammation in the vestibular tissue is debated. Generalized vulvodynia is diagnosed when pain is located on the whole vulva, not only on the vestibulum. It can be triggered by physical contact (provoked) or the discomfort occurs spontaneously, without a specific physical trigger (Moyal-Barracco & Lynch, 2004). Generalized vulvodynia is rare, compared to provoked vestibulodynia, and is diagnosed as a chronic pain problem rather than a sexual problem (Harlow, Wise, & Stewart, 2001). Women who have provoked vestibulodynia are mostly premenopausal and generalized vulvodynia is more commonly observed in older women (Harlow et al., 2001).

Demographic variables. The prevalence rates of dyspareunia in the general population vary between 3%-18% depending on geographic location and setting. Lower prevalence rates are found in Northern European countries, whereas the higher prevalence rates are from the United States (Weijmar Schultz et al., 2005). For example, Laumann et al. (1999) found that about 16% of the American women reported persistent or recurrent sexual pain in the past year, with older age associated with a lower likelihood of sexual pain. Women with dyspareunia also report higher levels of anxiety and depression, but sexual traumatisation appears not to play a significant role. Women with dyspareunia are more erotophobic, reflecting negative and conservative attitudes toward sex (Weijmar Schultz et al., 2005).

Treatment

In attempts to relieve pain, a variety of medical and nonmedical interventions have been used. Medical interventions include local temporary use of inert or corticosteroid ointments, surgical excision of the painful vestibular tissue (vestibulectomy), and psychological interventions include electromyographic biofeedback training and cognitive behavior therapy (CBT). For an extensive review of controlled and uncontrolled outcome studies, we refer to Landry, Bergeron, Dupuis and Desrochers (2008).

Consensus panel recommendations. There are only a handful RCTs for dyspareunia, mostly for vestibulodynia, thus current guidelines and recommendations are largely based on clinical observations and uncontrolled data (Landry et al., 2008) A consensus meeting on sexual pain and its management concluded that "sexual pain disorders are heterogeneous, multisystemic, and multifactorial disorders that should be treated in a multimodal way according to etiologic, risk factors and context . . . there is no 'one size fits all' all approach and no 'or-or' approach but an 'and-and' approach . . . . For vestibulodynia, the options include surgery, cognitive behavior therapy, biofeedback, or a combination of any of these methods. Shifts in preference for a certain approach will depend on the country in question, women's attitude regarding psychosexual therapy versus surgery, individual health care system" (Weijmar Schultz et al., 2005, pp. 310–311).

Randomized controlled trials. Until now there have been only five RCTs evaluating the effect of medical and nonmedical interventions for dyspareunia (Bergeron et al., 2001; Bornstein & Abramovici, 1997; Bornstein, Livnat, Stolar, & Abramovici, 2000; Danielson et al., 2006; Nyirjesy et al., 2001) and they have included only women with provoked vestibulodynia. Treatment of dysparenia (non-provoked

vestibulodynia) has thus far not been evaluated in controlled studies. Only two of the five studies examined the effect of psychological intervention (Bergeron, et al., 2001; Danielson et al., 2006) and these are discussed below.

Bergeron et al. (2001) conducted the only RCT that examined the effect of CBT. CBT for dyspareunia focuses on reducing catastrophising fear of pain and re-establishing satisfying sexual functioning (e.g., non-penetrative sex), with the final purpose of reduction of coital pain. CBT was delivered in eight 2-hour group sessions with seven to eight women per group over a 12-week period. The treatment package included: (a) education and information about vestibulodynia and how dyspareunia impacts on desire and arousal; (b) education concerning a multifactorial view of pain; (c) education about sexual anatomy, progressive muscle relaxation; (d) abdominal breathing; (e) Kegel exercises; (f) vaginal dilatation; (g) distraction techniques focusing on sexual imagery; (h) rehearsal of coping self-statements; (i) communication skills training; and (j) cognitive restructuring. Seventy-eight women were randomized either to group CBT, EMG-biofeedback or vestibulectomy (surgery). All three treatment groups reported significant improvements in pain during intercourse and psychosexual functioning on the short- and long-term (Bergeron et al., 2008). The average coital pain reduction was for vestibulectomy 53%, for EMG-biofeedback 35%, and for group CBT 38%. No differences were found between the three treatments. The effect sizes for improvement in psychosexual function varied between 0.21 and 0.32, and can be considered as modest (Cohen, 1977).

Electromyography (EMG) with visual feedback for dyspareunia was introduced by Glazer, Rodke, Swencionis, Hertz and Young (1995). The rationale for using EMG biofeedback is explained by the fact that women with vulvar pain often demonstrate pelvic muscle hyper-irritability and that the EMG biofeedback training could re-establish normal functioning (Glazer et al., 1995). Women are trained to use a vaginal EMG sensor and a biofeedback device in the clinic and are then asked to complete a standard pelvic floor training program at home twice a day consisting of pelvic floor contraction exercises of various durations, separated by prescribed rest periods. Participants received eight 45-minute sessions over 12 weeks. Two controlled studies investigated the effect of EMG biofeedback for women with dyspareunia (Bergeron et al. 2001; Danielson et al., 2006). Both studies used an adapted version the EMG-visual feedback procedures of Glazer et al. (1995). Bergeron et al. (2001) compared EMG biofeedback training with CBT group treatment and vestibulectomy, as described above. The average coital pain reduction for EMG biofeedback was 35% and the improvement in sexual function was modest (d 0.32) The results of EMG biofeedback were comparable to CBT and vestibulectomy.

In Sweden, Danielson et al. (2006) compared the efficacy of EMG biofeedback with topical lidocaine treatment in a sample of 46 women. Both treatments were continued for 4 months. Biofeedback treatment was mainly carried out according to Glazer et al. (1995). Both treatments resulted in significantly improved values for vestibular pressure pain thresholds, coital pain and sexual functioning at the 12 month follow-up. No differences in effectiveness were found between the two treatment groups. At the 12 month follow up, within the EMG biofeedback completers sample, 2 of 18 (11%) considered themselves as completed cured, 12 of 18 (67%) had improved, 3 of 18 (17%) reported no change, and one person did not answer. The treatment outcome was similar for the women in the lidocaine group, with 2 of 19 (11%) completed cured, 10 of 19 (53%) improved, 3 of 19 (16%) no change, and four with missing values. The treatments were well tolerated but the compliance with the EMG biofeedback training program was low.

No meta-analyses of group designs, no single subject experiments or meta-analyses of single subject experiments were found for this chapter.

Conclusions

CBT and EMG biofeedback are promising psychological treatment procedures for dyspareunia in women. Both have effects comparable to surgery and pharmacological treatment. Although patients reported significantly less pain during intercourse and improved sexual functioning, the effect sizes were modest (Cohen, 1977). It is notable that in two medication RCTs, large placebo effects were found and no differences were observed between the placebo and treatment (Bornstein et al., 2000; Nyirjesy et al., 2001). As treatment and placebo results are very similar, this may indicate a nonspecific treatment effect possible due to expectancies for improvement, enrolling in a study about sexuality and/or talking to a professional about sexual concerns (Meston & Bradford, 2007); however, as all the participants improved irrespective of treatment procedure and a no-treatment condition was included in one of the RCT studies, it also may be possible that the results found in these five studies are just an effect of the passage of time. Future research using RCTs with a wait-list control group are need. In clinical practice the treatment of dyspareunia is often individual or with the partner rather than in a group. The treatment package of an individual therapy or partner therapy often resembles a combination of the elements of group CBT (Bergeron et al., 2001). With the modest treatment effects found, it is important to realize that painless intercourse may not be a realistic therapeutic goal for many women.

Vaginismus: Overview of Disorder

Diagnostic criteria Vaginismus is defined in *DSM-IV-TR* as an involuntary contraction of the musculature of the outer third of the vagina interfering with intercourse, causing distress and interpersonal difficulty (APA, 2000). This definition has received considerable criticism. For example the only unique diagnostic criterion for vaginismus is a vaginal spasm that interferes with intercourse that has never been validated. Recently, Reissing, Binik, Kahlife, Cohen, and Amsel (2004) investigated the roles of vaginal spasm in vaginismus and the ability of psychologists, gynecologists, and physical therapists to agree on a diagnosis of vaginismus. Diagnostic agreement was poor for vaginismus; vaginal spasm measures did not differentiate between women in the vaginismus and dyspareunia groups. These data suggest that the spasm-based definition of vaginismus is not adequate as a diagnostic marker for vaginismus. An international consensus committee has suggested revised criteria, recommending that vaginismus be defined as "persistent difficulties to allow vaginal entry of a penis, a finger, and/or any object, despite the woman's expressed wish to do so. There is variable involuntary pelvic muscle contraction, (phobic) avoidance and anticipation/fear/experience of pain. Structural or other physical abnormalities must be ruled out/addressed" (Basson et al., 2003, p. 266). Vaginismus can be classified as either lifelong (primary) or acquired (secondary). Lifelong vaginismus occurs when the woman has never been able to have intercourse. In acquired vaginismus, a woman loses the ability to have intercourse after a nonsymptomatic period of time. Acquired vaginismus can develop as a sequel to dyspareunia. The following criteria may be useful to account for and summarize the key symptoms experienced by women with vaginal penetration problems: (a) Vaginal penetration is impossible in all or the majority of attempts because of vaginal and/or pelvic muscle hypertonicity and/or muscle guarding at the entrance to the vagina; (b) vaginal penetration is avoided for all or the majority of opportunities because of recurrent or chronic vulvar, vaginal, or pelvic pain; or (c) vaginal penetration is avoided for all or the majority of opportunities because of associated significant anxiety and/or panic, and may be accompanied by feelings of disgust, dread, and/or fear (Reissing, 2009).

Demographic variables. Because many epidemiological studies excluded questions about vaginismus, the prevalence of vaginismus is not well established (Meston & Bradford, 2007), though it is estimated to vary between 1% and 6% (Lewis et al., 2004). Women with vaginismus were found to have increased comorbid anxiety disorders, while depression rates were increased. A history of sexual traumata has been linked with vaginismus, although the data are inconsistent. Vaginismus is unrelated to marital distress (Weijmar Schultz et al., 2005).

Treatment

Since Masters and Johnson (1970), most therapies for vaginismus have used vaginal dilatation in which initially the woman becomes accustomed to self-touch to the introitus and insertion of her own finger or dilators through the introitus and part way into her vagina and then places the first of a series of inserts of gradually increasing diameter into her vagina. In reality, of course, there is no actual dilation but rather a gradual reduction of reflex protection of involuntary tightening (Weijmar Schultz et al., 2005). Gradual exposure is nearly always combined with relaxation, which in the literature is described as systematic desensitization. These core elements are often included within the context of a broader approach involving cognitive restructuring, education, sex therapy, and homework assignments (Reissing, Binik, & Khalife, 1999).

Consensus panels. A consensus meeting on sexual pain and its management concluded that "the traditional treatment of vaginismus with vaginal 'dilation' plus psycho-education, desentization, and so forth is not evidence based" (Weijmar Schultz, et al. 2005, pp. 301). They recommend a multidimensional, multidisciplinary approach. No specific recommendations are formulated for the treatment of vaginismus. A specific guidelines committee for the management of vaginismus recommend an eclectic approach for vaginismus that includes: (a) Diagnosis of vaginismus should be made only after a clinical examination and full history; (b) the use of vaginal trainers should de discussed with all patients; (c) vaginal penetration by a penis should not be assumed to be the desired outcome of women with vaginismus; and (d) information regarding sexual function and pelvic anatomy should be made available to all patients (Crowley, Richardson, & Goldmeier, 2006, pp. 17). Both committees do give a detailed review of the literature but the clinical recommendations for the treatment of vaginismus are not very specific and seem largely dependent on the opinion of persons in guidelines commissions.

Randomized controlled trials. There are only two RCTs investigating the effect of behavior therapy and CBT in the treatment of vaginismus (Schnyder et al., 1998; van Lankveld et al., 2006) (see Table 17.1). Schnyder et al. (1998) investigated the effect of two types of systematic dezensitisation in 44 women with vaginismus of whom 19 had lifelong vaginismus. Both groups received information and relaxation exercises. In the first group, the physician introduced the dilator. In the second group, the physician provided verbal instruction for introducing the dilator. Four sizes of vaginal dilators made of silicon were used with a lubricant. The program included a desensitization exercise. The participants were told to perform the exercise for 10 to 15 minutes, 5 times per week. Therapy sessions were conducted every 2 weeks to support progress made in treatment, reduce resistance, and to use larger dilators. There were no differences between the groups at the end of the study. Forty three of 44 participants reported successful penetrative sexual intercourse suggesting that common elements of the therapies used were successful. At the follow up, 18 of 36 participants (50%, 8 missing) reported that the vaginismus had altogether disappeared, while 17 (48%) reported that it had improved. Success tended to occur faster in the absence

of sexual desire disorders. Sexual desire had improved in 14 of 39 women (36%, 5 missing), remained the same in 20 (51%), and diminished in 5 (13%). These data were only collected at the follow-up. The mean number of treatment sessions was six. There is a degree of uncertainty over the randomization procedures as participants were free to change treatments after initial assignment that may equate with a high risk of selection bias and seriously weakens confidence in the results (McGuire & Hawton, 2001).

In the second study, 117 women with lifelong vaginismus were randomly assigned to cognitive behavior therapy either in group therapy or in a bibliotherapy format, or to a wait-list control group. Treatment included sexual education, relaxation exercises, gradual exposure, cognitive therapy, and sensate focus exercises. All participants received the same self-help manual on the treatment of vaginismus and a CD with spoken instructions for relaxation and sexual fantasy exercises. Group therapy comprised ten 2 hour group sessions over 12 weeks consisting of six to nine participants. Partners did not attend the group sessions. For the participants in the minimal contact, bibliotherapy format, six twice weekly 15 minute telephone contacts with professionals who offered assistance were scheduled. The group therapy required, on average, 5.5 hours of direct therapist contact per participant, compared with an average of 1.5 hours of telephone contact during bibliotherapy. After receiving CBT for 3 months, 18% of the treated participants successfully attempted penile vaginal intercourse, compared with none of the participants in the control group. CBT did not produce changes in subjective aspects of sexual functioning of the participants or their partners. Similarly, CBT did not produce changes regarding nonsexual marital and general life dissatisfaction in female participants or partners when the treated groups and the control condition were compared. There were no differences between the two treatments formats at 3 months and at

1-year follow-up (Van Lankveld et al., 2006). Given the equal results, it appears justified from a cost-effectiveness perspective to advise women with lifelong vaginismus to start with bibliotherapy. In a stepped-care approach, group therapy can be advised as the next step when bibliotherapy proves ineffective. The authors concluded that CBT for lifelong vaginismus is effective on the main outcome measure (intercourse), but the small effect size of CBT leaves much room for improvement.

Meta-analyses of group designs. A Cochrane Review investigated the clinical effectiveness of treatments for vaginismus (McGuire & Hawton, 2001, last updated 2005). The selection criteria for this review were: (a) controlled trials comparing treatments for vaginismus with another treatment; and (b) a placebo treatment, treatment as usual, or waiting list control. The reviewers extracted data that were verified with the trial investigator where possible. Three potential trials were identified, but data were only available from two of these. One trial comparing two forms of systematic desensitization with hypnotherapy was excluded because it was not randomized. The included trial compared two forms of systematic desensitization and reported no discernible differences between them (Schnyder et al., 1998; see earlier for more detail). The conclusion of the authors was: "in spite of encouraging results reported from uncontrolled case series there is very limited evidence from controlled trials concerning the effectiveness of treatments for vaginismus. Further trials are needed to compare therapies with waiting list control and with other therapies" (McGuire & Hawton, 2001, p. 1).

Single-subject experiments. Because in the CBT study of van Lankveld et al. (2006) it was found that intercourse was partly mediated by changes in fear of coitus and changes in avoidance behavior (ter Kuile et al., 2007), it was hypothesized that the effectiveness of treatment for vaginismus may be enhanced by focusing more explicitly and systematically on exposure to stimuli feared during penetration.

To address this ter Kuile et al. (2009) developed a prolonged and therapist-aided exposure therapy that took place both in a hospital setting and at home. Exposure at the hospital was self-controlled; that is, the participant performed the vaginal penetration exercises by herself, while a female therapist gave her directions on how to do the exercises and motivated her to expose herself to the anxiety-provoking penetration stimuli. Exposure at the hospital constituted of a maximum of three 2-hour sessions during one week. After each session, the participant and her partner were given a number of specific exposure homework assignments in which penetration exercises with the partner were also involved. To investigate the effectiveness of therapist-aided exposure for lifelong vaginismus, a replicated randomized single subject experimental AB-phase design was used. Using this design, repeated measurements were first taken during baseline (A-phase), where no treatment was provided, for each individual participant. After treatment (B-phase) commences, repeated measures continue to be taken. This way, a comparison could be made between behavior at baseline and in the intervention phase. The baseline phase served the same purpose as a control group receiving no treatment in a group comparison study. If behavior changes from baseline to treatment, it can be assumed that the intervention was responsible for this change. Replication of the AB design over several participants increases the strength of these findings (Barlow & Hersen, 1984). Randomization is also used in single case experiments as to clinical trials to control for confounding variables related to time, such as history and maturation. Within this context, randomization refers to randomly determining the moment of phase change (i.e., randomly deciding how many measurement occasions there will be in the A and in the B-phase). Ten consecutive women with lifelong vaginismus participated. Nine of the 10 participants reported having intercourse after treatment and in 5 of the 9, intercourse was possible within the first week of treatment. The results maintained at 1-year follow-up. Further, exposure was successful in decreasing fear and negative penetration beliefs at post-treatment and 1-year follow-up. Although 90% reported intercourse, for more than half of the participants, the scores for vaginismus were still not within the normal range of sexual functioning for women, indicating that these participants still reported some discomfort during intercourse.

Conclusions

The success rates found in the controlled studies of Schnyder et al. (1998) (97%) and ter Kuile et al. (2009) (90%), are comparable with effects sizes reported in earlier, uncontrolled outcome studies (McGuire & Hawton, 2001; Reissing et al., 1999) and much larger than the success rates found in a randomized control trial of CBT (van Lankveld et al., 2006), where only 18% of the women were able to have intercourse after 3 months of CBT treatment. We may conclude that focusing explicitly and systematically on exposure to stimuli feared during penetration appears to be an effective treatment for lifelong vaginismus. Replication studies in the form of randomized single case multielement designs or RCTs using larger samples are warranted to be certain that the results found in these two studies can be generalized to daily clinical practice.

EVIDENCE-BASED PRACTICE

We only identified 23 controlled studies that investigated the effect of a psychological treatment for women with sexual dysfunction, 16 of which were conducted between the mid 1980s and 1995. Heiman and Meston's (1997) review concluded that only DM for primary anorgasmia fulfilled the criteria of well established, and that DM for secondary anorgasmia fall within the probably efficacious

group. This conclusion is still valid today. Orgasm consistency training, coital alignment (Hurlbert, 1993; Hurlbert et al., 1993), and CBT, including sensate focus exercises, are promising approaches in the treatment of HSDD. There are no evidence-based psychological treatments for FSAD, but directed masturbation or comparable approaches may be as effective for FSAD as they are for OD, although we await the evidence on this possibility (Laan et al., 2005). There are no well-established psychological treatment for dyspareunia and vaginismus; however, CBT and EMG biofeedback are promising psychological treatment procedures for dyspareunia. Focusing explicitly and systematically on exposure to stimuli feared during penetration appears to be an effective treatment for women with vaginismus. Little is known about which treatment components are most effective (Meston & Bradford, 2007). Thus, despite their widespread clinical acceptance, few psychological treatments for women's sexual dysfunction are empirically supported.

REFERENCES

American Psychiatric Association (2000). *Diagnostic and statistical manual of mental disorders* (4th ed., text rev.). Washington, DC: Author.

Andersen, B. L. (1981). A comparison of systematic desensitization and directed masturbation in the treatment of primary orgasmic dysfunction in females. *Journal of Consulting and Clinical Psychology, 49,* 568–570.

Avis, N. E., Zhao, X., Johannes, C. B., Ory, M., Brockwell, S., & Greendale, G. A. (2005). Correlates of sexual function among multi-ethnic middle-aged women: Results from the Study of Women's Health Across the Nation (SWAN). *Menopause 12,* 385–398.

Bach, A. K., Brown, T. A., & Barlow, D. H. (1999). The effects of false negative feedback on efficacy expectancies and sexual arousal in sexually functional males. *Behavior Therapy, 30,* 79–95.

Bancroft, J., & Janssen, E. (2000). The dual control model of male sexual response: A theoretical approach to centrally mediated erectile dysfunction. *Neuroscience and Biobehavioral Reviews, 24,* 571–579.

Bancroft, J., Loftus, J., & Long, J. S. (2003). Distress about sex: A national survey of women in heterosexual relationships. *Archives of Sexual Behavior, 32*, 193–208.

Barbach, L. G. (1974a). *For yourself.* New York, NY: Doubleday.

Barbach, L. G. (1974b). Group treatment of preorgasmic women. *Journal of Sex and Marital Therapy, 1*, 139–145.

Barlow, D. H. (1986). Causes of sexual dysfunction: The role of anxiety and cognitive interference. *Journal of Consulting and Clinical Psychology, 54*, 140–148.

Barlow, D. H., & Hersen, M. (1984). *Single-case experimental designs: Strategies for studying behaviour change* (2nd ed.). Oxford, England: Pergamon Press.

Basson, R. (2000). The female sexual response: A different model. *Journal of Sex & Marital Therapy, 26*, 51–65.

Basson, R. (2005). Female hypoactive sexual desire disorder. In R. Balon & R. T. Segraves (Eds.), *Handbook of sexual dysfunction.* (pp. 43–66) Boca Raton, FL: Taylor & Francis.

Basson, R., Leiblum, S., Brotto, L., Derogatis, L., Fourcroy, J., Fugl-Meyer, K., . . . Weijmar Schultz, W. W. (2003). Definitions of women's sexual dysfunction reconsidered: Advocating expansion and revision. *Journal of Psychosomatic Obstetrics and Gynecology, 24*, 221–229.

Basson, R., Weijmar Schultz, W. C. M., Binik, Y. M., Brotto, L. A., Eschenbach, D. A., Laan, E., . . . Redmond, G. (2004). Women's sexual desire and arousal disorders and sexual pain. In T. F. Lue, R. Basson, R. Rosen, F. Giuliano, S. Khoury & F. Montorsi (Eds.), *Sexual medicine: Sexual dysfunctions in men and women* (pp. 851–974). Paris, France: Health Publications.

Beck, J. G. (1995). Hypoactive sexual desire disorder: An overview. *Journal of Consulting and Clinical Psychology, 63*, 919–927.

Bergeron, S., Binik, Y. M., Khalife, S., Pagidas, K., Glazer, H. I., Meana, M., & Amsel, R. (2001). A randomized comparison of group cognitive-behavioral therapy, surface electromyographic biofeedback, and vestibulectomy in the treatment of dyspareunia resulting from vulvar vestibulitis. *Pain, 91*, 297–306.

Bergeron, S., Khalife, S., Glazer, H. I., & Binik, Y. M. (2008). Surgical and behavioral treatments for vestibulodynia—Two-and-one-half-year follow-up and predictors of outcome. *Obstetrics and Gynecology, 111*, 159–166.

Bornstein, J., & Abramovici, H. (1997). Combination of subtotal perineoplasty and interferon for the treatment of vulvar vestibulitis. *Gynecologic and Obstetric Investigation, 44*, 53–56.

Bornstein, J., Livnat, G., Stolar, Z., & Abramovici, H. (2000). Pure versus complicated vulvar vestibulitis: A randomized trial of fluconazole treatment. *Gynecologic and Obstetric Investigation, 50*, 194–197.

Brezsnyak, M., & Whisman, M. A. (2004). Sexual desire and relationship functioning: The effects of marital satisfaction and power. *Journal of Sex and Marital Therapy, 30*, 199–217.

Carpenter, D. L. (2002). The dual control model: Gender, sexual problems, and the prevalence of sexual excitation and inhibition profiles. *Dissertation Abstracts International: Section B: The Sciences and Engineering, 63*(5-B), 2575.

Chambless, D. L., & Hollon, S. D. (1998). Defining empirically supported treatments. *Journal of Consulting and Clinical Psychology, 66*, 7–18.

Cohen, J. (1977). *Statistical power analysis for the behavioral sciences.* (rev. ed.). New York, NY: Academic press.

Crowley, T., Richardson, D., & Goldmeier, D. (2006). Recommendations for the management of vaginismus: BASHH special interest group for sexual dysfunction. *International Journal of STD & AIDS, 17*, 14–18.

Danielson, I., Torstensson, T., Brodda-Jansen, G., & Bohm-Starke, N. (2006). EMG biofeedback versus topical lidocaine gel: A randomized study for the treatment of women with vulvar vestibulitis. *Acta Obstetricia et Gynecologica Scandinavica, 85*, 1360–1367.

Delehanty, R. (1982). Changes in assertiveness and changes in orgasmic response occurring with sexual therapy for preorgasmic women. *Journal of Sex and Marital Therapy, 8*, 198–208.

Dennerstein, L., Koochaki, P., Barton, I., & Graziottin, A. (2006). Hypoactive sexual desire disorder in menopausal women: A survey of Western European women. *Journal of Sexual Medicine, 3*, 212–222.

Donnelly, D. A. (1993). Sexually inactive marriages. *The Journal of Sex Research, 30*, 171–179.

Dunn, K. M., Croft, P. R., & Hackett, G. I. (1999). Association of sexual problems with social, psychological, and physical problems in men and women: A cross sectional population survey. *Journal of Epidemiology and Community Health, 53*, 144–148.

Elliott, A. N., & O'Donohue, W. T. (1997). The effects of anxiety and distraction on sexual arousal in a nonclinical sample of heterosexual women. *Archives of Sexual Behavior, 26*, 607–624.

Ferguson, J. M. (2001). The effects of antidepressants on sexual functioning in depressed patients: A review. *Journal of Clinical Psychiatry, 62* (Suppl. 3), 22–34.

Fichten, C. S., Libman, E., & Brender, W. (1983). Methodological issues in the study of sex therapy: Effective components in the treatment of secondary orgasmic dysfunction. *Journal of Sex and Marital Therapy, 9*, 191–202.

Friedrich, E. G. (1987). Vulvar vestibulitis syndrome. *Journal of Reproductive Medicine, 32*, 110–114.

Fugl-Meyer, A. R., & Fugl-Meyer, K. S. (1999). Sexual disabilities, problems and satisfaction in 18–74 year old Swedes. *Scandinavian Journal of Sexology, 2,* 79–105.

Fugl-Meyer, K., & Fugl-Meyer, A. R. (2002). Sexual disabilities are not singularities. *International Journal of Impotence Research, 14,* 487–493.

Glazer, H. I., Rodke, G., Swencionis, C., Hertz, R., & Young, A. W. (1995). Treatment of vulvar vestibulitis syndrome with electromyographic biofeedback of pelvic floor musculature. *Journal of Reproductive Medicine, 40,* 283–290.

Harlow, B. L., Wise, L. A., & Stewart, E. G. (2001). Prevalence and predictors of chronic lower genital tract discomfort. *American Journal of Obstetrics and Gynecology, 185,* 545–550.

Hayes, R. D., Dennerstein, L., Bennett, C. M., & Fairley, C. K. (2008). What is the "true" prevalence of female sexual dysfunctions and does the way we assess these conditions have an impact? *Journal of Sexual Medicine, 5,* 777–787.

Heiman, J. R. (2001). Sexual desire in human relationships. In W. Everaerd, E. Laan, & S. Both (Eds.), *Sexual appetite, desire and motivation: Energetics of the sexual system* (pp. 117–135). Amsterdam, The Netherlands: Royal Dutch Academy of Science.

Heiman, J. R., & LoPiccolo, J. (1983). Clinical outcome of sex therapy. *Archives of General Psychiatry, 40,* 443–449.

Heiman, J. R., & LoPiccolo, J. (1988). *Becoming orgasmic: A sexual and personal growth program for women* (rev. and expanded ed.). New York, NY: Simon & Schuster.

Heiman, J. R., LoPiccolo, L., & LoPiccolo, J. (1976). *Becoming orgasmic: A sexual growth program for women.* Englewood Cliffs, NJ: Prentice-Hall.

Heiman, J. R., & Meston, C. M. (1997). Evaluating sexual dysfunction in women. *Clinical Obstetrics and Gynecology, 40,* 616–629.

Hurlbert, D. F. (1993). A comparative study using orgasm consistency training in the treatment of women reporting hypoactive sexual desire. *Journal of Sex and Marital Therapy, 19,* 41–55.

Hurlbert, D. F., & Apt, C. (1995). The coital alignment technique and directed masturbation: A comparative study on female orgasm. *Journal of Sex and Marital Therapy, 21,* 21–29.

Hurlbert, D. F., White, L. C., Powell, R. D., & Apt, C. (1993). Orgasm consistency training in the treatment of women reporting hypoactive sexual desire: An outcome comparison of women-only groups and couples-only groups. *Journal of Behavior Therapy and Experimental Psychiatry, 24,* 3–13.

Jacobson, N. S., & Truax, P. (1991). Clinical significance: A statistical approach to defining meaningful change in psychotherapy research. *Journal of Consulting and Clinical Psychology, 59,* 12–19.

Johnson, S. D., Phelps, D. L., & Cottler, L. B. (2004). The association of sexual dysfunction and substance use among a community epidemiological sample. *Archives of Sexual Behavior, 33,* 55–63.

Kaplan, H. S. (1979). *Disorders of sexual desire.* New York, NY: Brunner/Mazel.

Kegel, A. H. (1952). Sexual functions of the pubococcygeus muscle. *Western Journal of Surgery and Obstetric Gynecology, 60,* 521–524.

Kilmann, P. R., Mills, K. H., Caid, C., Davidson, E., Bella, B., Milan, R., . . . Montgomery, B. (1986). Treatment of secondary orgasmic dysfunction: An outcome study. *Archives of Sexual Behavior, 15,* 211–229.

Klusmann, D. (2002). Sexual motivation and the duration of partnership. *Archives of Sexual Behavior, 31,* 275–287.

Kockott, G., & Pfeiffer, W. (1996). Sexual disorders in nonacute psychiatric outpatients. *Comprehensive Psychiatry, 37,* 56–61.

Laan, E., Everaerd, W., & Both, S. (2005). Female sexual arousal disorders. In R. Balon & R. T. Segraves (Eds.), *Handbook of sexual dysfunctions* (pp. 123–154). New York, NY: Marcel Dekker.

Laan, E., van Driel, E. M., & van Lunsen, R. H. W. (2008). Genital responsiveness in healthy women with and without sexual arousal disorder. *Journal of Sexual Medicine, 5,* 1424–1435.

Landry, T., Bergeron, S., Dupuis, M. J., & Desrochers, G. (2008). The treatment of provoked vestibulodynia: A critical review. *Clinical Journal of Pain, 24,* 155–171.

Laumann, E. O., Nicolosi, A., Glasser, D. B., Paik, A., Gingell, C., Moreira, E., . . . GSSAB Investigators' Group (2005). Sexual problems among women and men aged 40–80 y: Prevalence and correlates identified in the Global Study of Sexual Attitudes and Behaviors. *International Journal of Impotence Research, 17,* 39–57.

Laumann, E. O., Paik, A., & Rosen, R. C. (1999). Sexual dysfunction in the United States: Prevalence and predictors. *Journal of the American Medical Association, 281,* 537–544.

Leonard, L. M., & Follette, V. M. (2002). Sexual functioning in women reporting a history of child sexual abuse: Review of the empirical literature and clinical implications. *Annual Review of Sex Research, 13,* 346–388.

Lewis, R. W., Fugl-Meyer, K. S., Bosch, R., Fugl-Meyer, A. R., Laumann, E. O., Lizza, E., & Martin-Morales, A. (2004). Definition, classification, and epidemiology of sexual dysfunction. In T. F. Lue, R. Basson, R. Rosen, F. Guiliano, S. Khoury, & F. Montorsi (Eds.), *Sexual medicine: Sexual dysfunctions in men and women* (pp. 37–72). Paris, France: Health Publications.

Lief, H. I. (1977). Inhibited sexual desire. *Medical Aspects of Human Sexuality, 7,* 94–95.

LoPiccolo, J., & Lobitz, W. C. (1972). The role of masturbation in the treatment of orgasmic dysfunction. *Archives of Sexual Behavior, 2,* 163–171.

MacPhee, D. C., Johnson, S. M., & Van der Veer, M. M. (1995). Low sexual desire in women: The effects of marital therapy. *Journal of Sex and Marital Therapy, 21,* 159–182.

Masters, W. H., & Johnson, V. E. (1966). *Human sexual response.* Oxford, England: Little, Brown.

Masters, W. H., & Johnson, V. E. (1970). *Human Sexual Inadequacy.* Boston, MA: Little, Brown.

Mathews, A., Bancroft, J., Whitehead, A., Hackmann, A., Julier, D., Bancroft, J . . . . Shaw, P. (1976). The behavioural treatment of sexual inadequacy: A comparative study. *Behaviour Research and Therapy, 14,* 427–436.

McCabe, M. P. (1997). Intimacy and quality of life among sexually dysfunctional men and women. *Journal of Sex & Marital Therapy, 23,* 276–290.

McGuire, H., & Hawton, K. (2001). Interventions for vaginismus. In Cochrane Database of Systematic Reviews 2001, Issue 2. (Art. No.: CD001760). Retrieved from www.mrw.interscience.wiley.com .ezproxy.leidenuniv.nl:2048/cochrane/clsysrev/articles/ CD001760/frame.html

McHichi Alami, K., & Kadri, N. (2004). Moroccan women with a history of child sexual abuse and its long-term repercussions: A population-based epidemiological study. *Archives of Womens Mental Health, 7,* 237–242.

McMullen, S. & Rosen, R.C. (1979). Self-administered masturbation training in the treatment of primary orgasmic dysfunction. *Journal of Consulting and Clinical Psychology, 47,* 912–918.

Mercer, C. H., Fenton, K. A., Johnson, A. M., Wellings, K., Macdowall, W., McManus, S., . . . Erens, B. (2003). Sexual function problems and help seeking behaviour in Britain: National probability sample survey. *British Medical Journal, 327,* 426–427.

Meston, C. M. (2006). The effects of state and trait self-focused attention on sexual arousal in sexually functional and dysfunctional women. *Behaviour Research and Therapy, 44,* 515–532.

Meston, C. M., & Bradford, A. (2007). Sexual dysfunctions in women. *Annual Review of Clinical Psychology, 3,* 233–256.

Meston, C. M., & Buss, D. M. (2007). Why humans have sex. *Archives of Sexual Behavior, 36,* 477–507.

Meston, C. M., Hull, E., Levin, R. J., & Sipski, M. (2004). Disorders of orgasm in women. In T. F. Lue, R. Basson, R. Rosen, F. Giuliano, F. Khoury, & F. Monorsi (Eds.), *Sexual medicine: Sexual dysfunctions in men and women* (pp. 783–850). Paris, France: Health Publications.

Meston, C. M., Seal, B. N., & Hamilton, L. D. (2008). Problems with arousal and orgasm in women. In D. L.

Rowland & L. Incrocci (Eds.), *Handbook of sexual and gender identity disorders* (pp. 188–219). Hoboken, NJ: Wiley.

Moreira, E. D., Jr., Glasser, D., Santos, D. B., & Gingell, C. (2005). Prevalence of sexual problems and related help-seeking behaviors among mature adults in Brazil: Data from the global study of sexual attitudes and behaviors. *Sao Paulo Medical Journal, 123,* 234–241.

Moyal-Barracco, M. & Lynch, P. J. (2004). 2003 ISSVD terminology and classification vulvodynia—A historical perspective. *Journal of Reproductive Medicine, 49,* 772–777.

Munjack, D., Cristol, A., Goldstein, A., Phillips, D., Goldberg, A., Whipple, K., . . . Kanno, P. (1976). Behavioural treatment of orgasmic dysfunction: A controlled study. *British Journal of Psychiatry, 129,* 497–502.

Nyirjesy, P., Sobel, J. D., Weitz, M. V., Leaman, D. J., Small, M. J., & Gelone, S. P. (2001). Cromolyn cream for recalcitrant idiopathic vulvar vestibulitis: Results of a placebo controlled study. *Sexually Transmitted Infections, 77,* 53–57.

Oberg, K., & Fugl-Meyer, K. S. (2005). On Swedish women's distressing sexual dysfunctions: Some concomitant conditions and life satisfaction. *Journal of Sexual Medicine, 2,* 169–180.

Obler, M. (1982). A comparison of a hypnoanalytic/ behavior modification technique and a cotherapist-type treatment with primary orgasmic dysfunctional females: Some preliminary results. *Journal of Sex Research, 18,* 331–345.

O'Donohue, W., Dopke, C. A., & Swingen, D. N. (1997). Psychotherapy for female sexual dysfunction: A review. *Clinical Psychology Review, 17,* 537–566.

Osborn, M., Hawton, K., & Gath, D. (1988). Sexual dysfunction among middle aged women in the community. *British Medical Journal, 296,* 959–962.

Reissing, E. D. (2009). Vaginismus. In A. T. Goldstein, C. F. Pukall, & I. Goldstein (Eds.), *Female sexual pain disorders: Evaluation and management* (pp. 229–234). Oxford, England: Blackwell.

Reissing, E. D., Binik, Y. M., & Khalife, S. (1999). Does vaginismus exist? A critical review of the literature. *Journal of Nervous and Mental Disease, 187,* 261–274.

Reissing, E. D., Binik, Y. M., Khalife, S., Cohen, D., & Amsel, R. (2004). Vaginal spasm, pain, and behavior: An empirical investigation of the diagnosis of vaginismus. *Archives of Sexual Behavior, 33,* 5–17.

Riley, A. J., & Riley, E. J. (1978). A controlled study to evaluate directed masturbation in the management of primary orgasmic failure in women. *British Journal of Psychiatry, 133,* 404–409.

Roughan, P. A., & Kunst, L. (1981). Do pelvic floor exercises really improve orgasmic potential? *Journal of Sex and Marital Therapy, 7,* 223–229.

Rumstein-McKean, O., & Hunsley, J. (2001). Interpersonal and family functioning of female survivors of childhood sexual abuse. *Clinical Psychology Review, 21*, 471–490.

Salemink, E., & van Lankveld, J. J. (2006). The effects of increasing neutral distraction on sexual responding in women with and without sexual problems. *Archives of Sexual Behavior, 35*, 179–190.

Schnyder, U., Schnyder-Luthi, C., Ballinari, P., & Blaser, A. (1998). Therapy for vaginismus: In vivo versus in vitro desensitization. *Canadian Journal of Psychiatry-Revue Canadienne de Psychiatrie, 43*, 941–944.

Schreiner-Engel, P., & Schiavi, R. C. (1986). Lifetime psychopathology in individuals with low sexual desire. *Journal of Nervous and Mental Disease, 174*, 646–651.

Segraves, K. B., & Segraves, R. T. (1991). Hypoactive sexual desire disorder: Prevalence and comorbidity in 906 subjects. *Journal of Sex & Marital Therapy, 17*, 55–58.

Simons, J. S., & Carey, M. P. (2001). Prevalence of sexual dysfunctions: Results from a decade of research. *Archives of Sexual Behavior, 30*, 177–219.

Sipski, M. L. (1998). Sexual functioning in the spinal cord injured. *International Journal of Impotence Research, 10*, S128–S130.

Sotile, W. M., & Kilmann, P. R. (1978). Effects of group systematic desensitization on female orgasmic dysfunction. *Archives of Sexual Behavior, 7*, 477–491.

Stulhofer, A., Gregurovic, M., Pikic, A., & Galic, I. (2005). Sexual problems of urban women in Croatia: Prevalence and correlates in a community sample. *Croatian Medical Journal, 46*, 45–51.

Talakoub, L., Munarriz, R., Hoag, L., Gioia, M., Flaherty, E., & Goldstein, I. (2002). Epidemiological characteristics of 250 women with sexual dysfunction who presented for initial evaluation. *Journal of Sex and Marital Therapy, 28*(Suppl 1), 217–224.

Taylor, M. J., Rudkin, L., & Hawton, K. (2005). Strategies for managing antidepressant-induced sexual dysfunction: Systematic review of randomised

controlled trials. *Journal of Affective Disorders, 88*, 241–254.

ter Kuile, M. M., Bulte, I., Beekman, A., Weijenborg, P. T. M., Melles, R., & Onghena, P. (2009). Therapist-aided exposure in the treatment of lifelong vaginismus: A Replicated single-case design. *Journal of Consulting and Clinical Psychology, 77*, 149–159.

ter Kuile, M. M., Van Lankveld, J. J. D. M., De Groot, H. E., Melles, R., Nefs, J., & Zandbergen, M. (2007). Cognitive behavioural therapy for women with lifelong vaginismus: Process and prognostic factors. *Behaviour Research and Therapy, 45*, 359–373.

Trudel, G., Boulos, L., & Matte, B. (1993). Dyadic adjustment in couples with hypoactive sexual desire. *Journal of Sex Education and Therapy, 19*, 31–36.

Trudel, G., Landry, L., & Larose, Y. (1997). Low sexual desire: The role of anxiety, depression and marital adjustment. *Sexual and Marital Therapy, 12*, 95–99.

Trudel, G., Marchand, A., Ravart, M., Aubin, S., Turgeon, L., & Fortier, P. (2001). The effect of a cognitive behavioral group treatment program on hypoactive sexual desire in women. *Sexual and Relationship Therapy, 16*, 145–164.

Van den Hout, M. A., & Barlow, D. (2000). Attention, arousal and expectancies in anxiety and sexual disorders. *Journal of Affective Disorders, 61*, 241–256.

Van Lankveld, J. J. D. M., Everaerd, W., & Grotjohann, Y. (2001). Cognitive behavioral bibliotherapy for sexual dysfunctions in heterosexual couples: A randomized waiting list controlled clinical trial in the Netherlands. *Journal of Sex Research, 38*, 51–67.

Van Lankveld, J. J. D. M., ter Kuile, M. M., De Groot, H. E., Melles, R., Nefs, J., & Zandbergen, M. (2006). Cognitive behavioral therapy for women with lifelong vaginismus: A randomized waiting list controlled trial of efficacy. *Journal of Consulting and Clinical Psychology, 74*, 168–178.

Weijmar Schultz, W. W., Basson, R., Binik, Y., Eschenbach, D., Wesselmann, U., & Van Lankveld, J. (2005). Women's sexual pain and its management. *Journal of Sexual Medicine, 2*, 301–316.

18

Paraphilias and Sexual Offending

LEIGH HARKINS AND ANTHONY R. BEECH

OVERVIEW OF DISORDER

Paraphilias are defined in the *Diagnostic and Statistic Manual for Mental Disorders*, 4th edition, text revision *(DSM-IV-TR)* (American Psychological Association [APA], 2000), as sexual disorders in which the individuals have recurrent, intense, sexually arousing thoughts, fantasies, urges, or behaviors involving atypical activities or targets. The paraphilias defined in *DSM-IV-TR* are: exhibitionism, fetishism, frotteurism, paraphilia not otherwise specified, pedophilia, sexual masochism, sexual sadism, transvestic fetishism, and voyeurism (see later in the chapter for definitions of each of these). Although some of these paraphilias are legally defined as sexual offenses (i.e., exhibitionism, frotteurism, pedophilia and voyeurism), others clearly are not (i.e., transvestism), while the rest inhabit a gray area where some aspects of the paraphilic activity may be legal or illegal, dependent upon issues of consent (i.e., fetishism, paraphilia not otherwise specified, masochism, sadism).

As for legal, as opposed to psychiatric, definitions of sexual offenses, these occur when an individual forces another to engage in sexual activity, or if the sexual partner does not have the ability to consent. This includes exposing sexual material to minors, production of material depicting minors engaged in sexual activity, and possession of such images. Thus, sexual offending covers a wider range of illegal sexual activities than current *DSM* diagnostic criteria.

The chapter is in two main sections. The first gives a brief overview of each of the *DSM* criteria plus an overview of offenses not well defined or covered in *DSM* (i.e., child molestation, rape, and Internet sexual offending). This is followed by material covering demographic criteria and the impact of these problems on the individual and their victims. The second examines the effectiveness of current treatments (behavioral, pharmacological, cognitive behavioral treatment, systemic) for (illegal) *DSM* paraphilias, and sexual offending more generally, taking account of whether these criteria meet the Chambless and Hollon (1998) criteria for evidence-based practice (i.e., evidence is provided from two or more, well conducted studies by at least two independent researchers, or from three small experiments reporting data from at least nine participants).

DIAGNOSTIC CRITERIA

DSM Paraphilias

The diagnostic criteria contained in the latest *DSM-IV-TR* (APA, 2000) are reported here. Note all of these indicate that the problem must have affected the individual for at least six months, and have caused clinically significant distress or impairment, in social, occupational, or other areas of functioning.

Exhibitionism is defined by the following criteria: recurrent, intense, sexually arousing fantasies or behaviors, involving exposing one's genitals to others without their consent. Fetishism involves a sexual interest in non-living objects. The most common targets of this paraphilia are female underwear, feet, and shoes. It is common for sexual dysfunction to occur in the absence of the fetish target. Frotteurism involves recurrent, intense, sexually arousing fantasies, sexual urges or behaviors involving touching and rubbing against a nonconsenting person. Such behavior(s) commonly occur in crowded public places (e.g., buses or trains). Paraphilia not otherwise specified is included for paraphilias that are not covered by other categories including necrophilia, bestiality (zoophilia), coprophilia, klismaphilia (enemas), and urophilia. Pedophilia is defined by an individual experiencing recurrent and intense sexually arousing fantasies, sexual urges or behaviors involving sexual activity with children less than 14 years old. Additionally, the perpetrator should be at least age 16 years, and the perpetrator at least five years older than their victim(s). Sexual masochism involves sexual arousal to the act of being humiliated, beaten, bound, or made to suffer in some other manner. In some cases, these fantasies are evoked during masturbation or intercourse. Some masochistic acts are engaged in alone. In sexual sadism, the individual derives sexual excitement from the physical, or psychological, suffering (including humiliation) of another person. Transvestic fetishism describes men cross-dressing in womens' clothing. In a number of cases sexual arousal is produced by the person imagining themselves as female. Voyeurism describes the act of observing nonconsenting individuals naked or undressing, or engaged in sexual activity. Masturbation can occur while engaged in the activity, or later to what has been seen.

The *DSM-IV* paraphilia criteria have been questioned in terms of definitions, usefulness, and reliability. Lussier and Piché (2008), for example, noted that *DSM* definitions "have done little to clarify the vexing definitional problems in the clinical and scientific literature" (p. 132). Others have suggested that paraphilic definitions are not practically useful. Wilson, Abracen, Picheca, Malcolm, and Prinzo (2003), for example, found that a diagnosis of pedophilia was not related to long-term recidivism, and has little to say in terms of assessment and indications of treatment need. Indeed, *DSM* diagnosis of pedophilia is commonly ignored in research and practice (Marshall, 1997). A number of problems have also been raised in terms of diagnosing sadism (Marshall & Kennedy, 2003). Research has illustrated that idiosyncratic diagnostic methods are used, and there is a lack of consensus in applying this diagnosis (Levenson, 2004; Marshall, Kennedy, Yates, & Serran, 2002).

As for reliability of *DSM* diagnoses, Levenson (2004), in 295 cases that were assessed as part of civil commitment procedures in Florida, found that the reliability between diagnosticians was unacceptably low for pedophilia (Cohen's $\kappa = 0.65$), sexual sadism ($\kappa = 0.30$), exhibitionism ($\kappa = 0.47$), and paraphilia not otherwise specified ($\kappa = 0.36$).

Sexual Offending

We will now examine illegal sexual behaviors (i.e., child abuse, rape, and Internet offending) not well defined by *DSM* classifications.

Child abuse. It is problematic to use the term *pedophilia* to describe *all* offenses against child victims, as this classification only applies to about 25%–40% of those who commit contact offenses against children (Marshall, 1997). Individuals who sexually abuse children are a wide-ranging group, from those who are primarily sexually aroused by children, those who are aroused to both children and adults, and to those who are aroused to adults but who abuse children for a variety of reasons to do with power, control, or sense of entitlement. Therefore, it is common practice to use the term *child molester* or *child abuser*, and to classify these offenders by their relationship to their victim (i.e., intra/extrafamilial), victim gender, and age group (pre/postpubescent) (Bourget & Bradford, 2008; Feelgood & Hoyer, 2008; R. D. Laws & O'Donohue, 2008).

Rape. No *DSM* category specifically relates to diagnosing individuals who have committed this type of offense. In some instances sexual sadism may be employed, where the offense fits this category. The category paraphilia not otherwise specified is sometimes used where a *DSM* diagnosis must be assigned in order for someone to receive treatment (Marshall, 2006); however, given its lack of specificity, the term has little utility in assessment or treatment. More usefully, rapist typologies exist that highlight the underlying motivations for rape, and which are useful in assessment and treatment (Beech, Oliver, Fisher, & Beckett, 2005). Generally, such typologies focus on whether the rape was motivated by sexual, or nonsexual, needs (Robertiello & Terry, 2007). Knight and Prentky (1990), for example, developed a system that distinguishes between *angry* (pervasively angry toward all or vindictive toward women), *sexual* (opportunistic/planned), or *sadistic* rape.

Internet sexual offending. It is only recently that attention has been drawn to the use of the Internet to download illegal sexual material, commonly child pornography. Evidence suggests that Internet offenders are a heterogeneous group (Elliott, Beech, Mandeville-Norden, & Hayes, 2009). Researchers (Krone, 2004; Lanning, 2001; Sullivan & Beech, 2004) have suggested a four-group typology of such individuals that can be summed up as follows: (1) *prurient interest*, those who access the Internet impulsively or out of a general curiosity; (2) *fantasy only*, those who access/trade images to fuel a sexual interest in children (Webb, Craissati, & Keen, 2007); (3) *Cross-over offenders*, those who utilize the Internet as

part of a larger pattern of contact sexual offending (Hernandez, 2000); (4) and *commercial exploitation*, those who produce or trade images for money.

DEMOGRAPHIC VARIABLES

We will now examine the demographic features of *DSM* paraphilias and the types of offenses not well described by *DSM* criteria.

DSM Paraphilias

It is difficult to establish demographic characteristics for all of those diagnosed with *DSM* paraphilias. A review of pedophilia and fetishism reported that these paraphilias are more common in males, all races and socioeconomic groups are represented, and that the interest usually begins by adolescence (Wiederman, 2003); however, studies tend to report relatively small samples (e.g., Chalkley & Powell, 1983), or are selected from one geographical area (e.g., Craissati & Beech, 2004), making findings difficult to generalize. However, one large scale study (*N* = 561) by Abel and Rouleau (1990) found that the majority were relatively young, moderately well educated, came from all socioeconomic levels, and ethnicity was representative of the general population. This study also demonstrated that those involved in one paraphilic activity commonly also engaged in others. We will now discuss specific demographic characteristics for paraphilias, where available.

Exhibitionism. Legally defined in the United Kingdom as indecent exposure, onset generally begins in the mid-teens (Abel & Rouleau, 1990; Smukler & Schiebel, 1975). Although primarily a male disorder, Langstrom and Seto (2006), in a Swedish sample, found that 3.2% of self-reported acts were committed by females. Blair and Lanyon (1981), reviewing data from 1950–1980 found that educational level and vocational interest did not appear to differ from that found in the general population, while two thirds had been in a relationship. Many exhibitionists have been found to be involved in other forms of paraphilic behavior (Abel, Becker, Cunningham-Rathner, & Rouleau, 1987).

Fetishism. Fetishism usually begins by adolescence; however, the fetish object may have been endowed with special significance since early childhood (APA, 2000). The course of fetishism tends to persist once established. Fetishists are most commonly male (Chalkley & Powell, 1983; Darcangelo, 2008). All races and socioeconomic groups are typically well represented (Wiederman, 2003).

Frotteurism. Approximately 30% of the general population has committed an act that would qualify as frotteuristic (Freund, Seto, & Kuban, 1997; Templeman & Stinnett, 1991). Frotteurism usually starts in adolescence, with most acts occurring between the ages of 15 to 25, at which point there is a decline in frequency (Abel & Rouleau, 1990; APA, 2000). Freund and Seto (1998) report that nearly a fifth of rapists also reported activities of frotteurism.

Pedophilia. Pedophiles are most commonly male, although it is seen in a small number of females (Cohen & Galynker, 2002; McConaghy, 1998; Seto, 2008). There is a large degree of heterogeneity of pedophiles in terms of education, socioeconomic status, and ethnicity (Seto, 2008). Pedophilia typically first appears in adolescence (Cohen & Galynker, 2002; Weiderman, 2003). Abel and Rouleau (1990) reported in their sample of 561 sexual offenders, 50% of pedophiles with male victims had developed their sexual interest by age 15 years, while 40% of those with unrelated female victims had developed their sexual interest by age 18 years. Similar findings are reported by others (Freund & Kuban, 1993; Marshall, Barbaree, & Eccles, 1991). Pedophilic interest is stable across the life span, as pedophiles report that their sexual interest in children has been present since from an early age (Hanson, Steffy, & Gauthier, 1993). For example, Freund and Kuban (1993) report in

their sample that curiosity in nude children was reported to begin between ages 7 and 11 years.

Sexual masochism. Engaging in sexual masochism characteristically does not result in criminal charges, although in rare cases this may happen. Masochists typically do not necessarily seek professional help (Hucker, 2008), making it difficult to identify the demographic characteristics associated with this paraphilia. Studies have demonstrated that higher education levels, income, and occupational status are found in this group, compared to the general population (Moser & Levitt, 1987; Sandnabba, Santilla, & Nordling, 1999; Spengler, 1977). Masochistic practices include needles insertion, applying electrical currents to the body, and self-asphyxia (hypoxyphilia) (Hucker, 2008); however, it is difficult in many instances to disentangle masochistic and sadist practices. On average, individuals start engaging in sadomasochistic practices in their early 20s (Moser & Levitt, 1987).

Sexual sadism. Limited information suggests that this paraphilia is most often found in males (Kingston & Yates, 2008). Dietz, Hazelwood, and Warren (1990), for example, in a descriptive analysis of personal and offense characteristics of 30 *DSM* diagnosed sadists, reported that all subjects were White males.

Voyeurism. Abel and Rouleau (1990) reported that 50% of voyeurs in their sample reported that their paraphilia had developed by the age of 15 years (Abel & Rouleau, 1990). Offenses are typically committed by men (Lavin, 2008; Mann, Ainsworth, Al-Attar, & Davies, 2008); however, there are some rare cases of females who meet the diagnostic criteria for voyeurism (Hurlbert, 1992).

Sexual Offending

We will now examine demographic details of sexual offenses not well defined by *DSM* criteria.

Child Abuse. In 2006 in the United States, 8.8% of child maltreatment referrals made to child protective services were for children who suffered sexual abuse (U.S. Department of Health and Human Services, 2008). As for the perpetrators, 26.2% were parents, while 29.1% were another relative, 6.1% were an unmarried partner of a parent, 4.4% were a friend or neighbor, 0.3% were a foster parent, 0.9% were a residential facility staff member, another professional, or legal guardian. These figures highlight that the majority of perpetrators are known to the victim. Abusers are commonly men (Hilton & Mezey, 1996), but women also represent a significant proportion. For example, ChildLine, a telephone helpline in the United Kingdom, reported that between April 2002 and March 2003, 12% of children calling reported that they had been abused by a female. Extrafamilial abusers (i.e., the more pedophilic) were significantly more likely than intrafamilial abusers to be unmarried (e.g., Smallbone & Wortley, 2001).

Rape. These offenders tend to be blue-collar workers of low socioeconomic status, and to have left school early (Beech et al., 2005). There are no clear characteristics of a typical rapist, in that they have been found to be similar to nonsexual offenders in terms of sociodemographic variables (Dreznick, 2003; Gannon & Ward, 2008). Rapists are typically younger than child molesters (Craissati & Beech, 2004; Dickey, Nussbaum, Chevolleau, & Davidson, 2002). Rapists typically report that their deviant interest had developed by age 21 years (Abel & Rouleau, 1990).

Internet sexual offending. The statistics on the number of people who use the Internet for sexual offending is limited because they only come to attention in countries where both possession and distribution of child pornography are illegal and where detection is acted upon by the authorities (Quayle, 2008). The extent of both the amount of child pornography currently available on the Internet, and the number of users accessing it, is difficult to estimate due to the inherently dynamic nature of the system (Taylor & Quayle, 2003), however, in the United Kingdom, the online regulatory body, the Internet Watch Foundation

(IWF), recently reported that they had positively identified 2,755 worldwide Internet domains containing images of child sexual abuse, 80% of which were found to be commercial in nature. Analysis of the content of these sites indicated that 80% of the images recovered were of children less than 10 years of age. As for gender of image, 79% of images were of female victims, 7% were male, and 14% depicted both male and female victims.

The age of onset of Internet offending is nearly impossible to quantify, because it has only been recently that the Internet has been widely available for such use (Quayle, 2008); however, in a UK study examining nearly 500 men convicted of Internet offenses, men were typically in their 40s, with a quarter being in a current relationship (Elliott et al., 2009). The images that were most often viewed were female (53%) or both male and female (37%).

IMPACT OF DISORDER

DSM Paraphilias

Paraphilias and sexual offending have a potential impact on the individual, their victims, the general population, the individual and their families. For the victim, there are a number of physical and psychological effects of sexual victimization, including posttraumatic stress disorder (PTSD) (APA, 2000). For the general population, it may produce a possible fear of crime related to sex offending (Thomas, 2005). For families, the public stigma of having a family member arrested for their sexual behavior is difficult (Murphy & Page, 2008). We will now examine this in terms of paraphilias, and wider definitions of sexual offenses.

Exhibitionists. Exhibitionists report more psychological problems, lower satisfaction with life, and greater drug and alcohol use than those in the general population (Langstrom & Seto, 2006). Due to the time exhibitionists commit to setting up or engaging in these behaviors, time available for more prosocial pursuits is limited (Murphy & Page, 2008). For example, Bader, Schoeneman-Morris, Scalora, and Casady (2008) report that 30% of exhibitionists in their sample were charged with more than one exposure event. Hendrix and Meyer (1976) report anecdotal evidence of one exhibitionist who reported exposing himself to females between 600 and 700 times without ever being apprehended. Around a third of offenders escalated in the seriousness of their sexual offending to a contact sexual offense following an initial conviction for Exhibitionism (Rabinowitz Greenberg, Firestone, Bradford, & Greenberg, 2002). In fact, noncontact sexual offenses, such as exhibitionism, are commonly regarded as risk factors for more serious contact offenses (Harris, Phenix, Hanson, & Thornton, 2003; Thornton, et al., 2003). The functions of the behavior reveal differing motives that affect the risk presented by the individual. Similarly, Sugarman, Dumughn, Saad, Hinder, and Bluglass (1994) examined the psychiatric records of 210 exhibitionists in the United Kingdom and found that 26% had a conviction for at least one contact sexual offense, including two rapes, three attempted rapes, and 60 child offenses.

Problems arise in trying to determine victim impact, because only a small number of victims report these offenses to the police (e.g., 28% reported by Riordan, 1999); however, nearly half of a nonclinical sample of women reported by Riordan (1999) had been victims of indecent exposure, and for 57% the exposure occurred prior to the age of 16. Exposure to adolescents and even children is common (10% of cases; Bader et al., 2008).

Fetishism. Some individuals experience feelings of guilt, shame, and depression regarding their paraphilic behavior, whereas others report little distress except for possibly considering the reactions of others, and hence may make attempts to conceal their activities (Wiederman, 2003), although many individuals see their fetishes as sources of pleasure (Darcangelo, Hollings, & Paladino, 2008) and

may only seek treatment because of legal or interpersonal pressure to do so (Wiederman, 2003). Although it is rare for this paraphilia to come to the attention of the authorities, fetishism can occasionally create victims in cases involving burglary to steal fetishistic items (Schlesinger & Revitch, 1999).

Frotteurism. This is often treated as something of a nuisance crime by criminal justice systems (Krueger & Kaplan, 2008), as victims typically do not usually suffer physical injuries (Beller, Garelik, & Cooper, 1980), and are commonly unaware of the act itself (Lussier & Piché, 2008). Further, due to the circumstances where this paraphilia occurs, it is difficult to identify the perpetrator (Krueger & Kaplan, 2008). A study examining acts of frotteurism on the New York subway system found that victims were mostly female, and sexual contact was most likely to occur from the rear (Beller et al., 1980).

Pedophilia. There is little distinction to be made in terms of the impact on society or the victim, dependent on whether or not a perpetrator of child sexual abuse meets the criteria for pedophilia. Therefore, the impact of this paraphilia will be discussed under the broader heading of *child molestation* following.

Sexual masochism. The impact of this paraphilia does not receive a great deal of attention because the only people potentially harmed are those who consent to it. Therefore, masochistic practices rarely result in criminal charges, although some exceptions are noted (Hucker, 2008); however, even though the individual may be consenting, there is the potential for serious physical harm. In fact, in cases involving hypoxyphilia (near asphyxiation), fatalities can occur. In some cases masochists have been coerced into more extreme behaviors than those that they enjoy, hence becoming victims themselves. Approximately 30% also engage in sadistic behavior. In cases of consensual sadomasochism, the sadistic and masochistic partners both derive pleasure for either inflicting, having pain inflicted on them, or both. A sample of men who engage in these consensual practices are generally found to be socially well adjusted (Sandnabba et al., 1999), with only 6% reporting that they were emotionally disturbed by their behavior (Moser & Levitt, 1987). Some individuals (16%) reported that they had sought help from a therapist regarding their sado-masochism desires. Just under a third reported that they felt there was a reasonable danger that their behavior could escalate to a dangerous extent (see later).

Sexual sadism. This paraphilia will inevitably have a negative impact on victims as the intended outcome of sadistic behavior is their suffering (Marshall & Hucker, 2006). Sadistic acts, carried out in victims, may range from restraint through whipping, beating, stabbing, strangulation, torture, to mutilation, hence causing extreme psychological and physical harm. The severity of sadistic acts can increase over time, especially when it is associated with antisocial personality disorder (APA, 2000), where individuals may seriously injure or even kill their victims. Such practices can clearly lead to psychological harm, including PTSD and dissociative disorders (APA, 2000).

Voyeurism. This paraphilia typically receives little attention, because it is a noncontact offense; however, for unsuspecting victims, voyeurism has a great deal of impact. Victims are horrified, humiliated, mortified, and extremely fearful when they discover they have been watched or recorded (Simon, 1997). Preexisting psychological problems can exacerbate the trauma the person experiences (Simon, 1997).

Sexual Offending

We will now examine the impact of sexual offenses not well defined by *DSM* criteria.

Child abuse. The World Health Organization (2006) estimates that 150 million female children and 73 million male children have experienced forced sexual intercourse or other forms of sexual violence. Physical injuries occur, but are not as common as in other types of abuse (McConaghy, 1998). In 2006, 0.3% of child sexual abuse cases resulted in a fatality

for the child (U.S. Department of Health and Human Services, 2008).

Sexual abuse has been related to a number of negative behavioral outcomes in children, such as fear, nightmares, withdrawn behavior, cruelty, delinquency, regressive behavior, running away, poor self-esteem, general behavior problems, and sexually inappropriate behavior (Kendall-Tackett, Williams, & Finkelhor, 1993). Other studies have also noted that inappropriate sexualized behaviors in children and adolescents are more likely to develop in victims of child sexual abuse, compared to nonabused children (Beitchman, Zucker, Hood, daCosta, & Akman, 1991). Children reporting sexual abuse involving intercourse, compared with nonabused children, had an increased odds incidence of major depression and suicide attempts (Fergusson, Horwood, & Lynskey, 1996; Fergusson, Lynskey, & Horwood, 1996).

A variety of adult psychiatric conditions arising from child sexual abuse have also been reported including anxiety and acute stress disorders, bulimia nervosa, depression, dissociative identity disorder, personality disorders (such as borderline personality disorder), PTSD, and substance abuse (Fergusson, Horwood, et al., 1996; Putnam, 2003; Spataro, Mullen, Burgess, Wells, & Moss, 2004). The lifetime prevalence for major depression is 3 to 5 times more common in women who have experienced child sexual abuse, than women who have not (Putnam, 2003).

Rape. Myhill and Allen (2002), reporting on the British Crime Survey of sexual victimization, in a sample of 6,944 women aged 16 to 59, found that 4.9% of women reported being raped since the age of 16 years. Women aged 16 to 24 years were most at risk. Women were most likely to be attacked by men they knew, current partners accounting for 45% of the rapes, strangers accounting for 8%. Only 20% of the rapes were reported to the police. There was also a bias in reporting according to the relationship with the offender. Stranger rapes were far more likely to be reported (36%) than date rape (8%).

As for victim impact, physical injuries can include nongenital physical injuries, vaginal and/or anal lacerations, bleeding, and pain (Hampton, 1995). Postassault medical necessities, such as injury detection, forensic medical examination and evidence collection, and screening and treatment for sexually transmitted infections and pregnancy, can also be extremely difficult for victims (Campbell, 2008). Secondary victimization can occur through contact with the legal system, such as law enforcement officers discouraging the victims from reporting the crime, and medical staff, due to insensitivity in their examinations (Campbell, 2008).

As for psychological symptoms, rape has been shown to be related to an increased risk of PTSD (Kilpatrick & Acierno, 2003). Other psychological symptoms include depression, substance abuse, suicidality, and panic attacks (Kilpatrick & Acierno, 2003). Male victims of rape experience many of the same symptoms that are observed in women, although heterosexual men also experience additional problems with reconciling their heterosexual, masculine identity with their victim experience (Rentoul & Appleboom, 1997). Indeed, it has been noted that there are differences observed in how men and women react to being the victim of rape according to different forms of social conditioning they experience (Crome & McCabe, 2001).

Internet sexual offending. One of the key questions in relation to Internet sexual offenses is if such offending individuals will ever commit a contact sexual offense. Schneider (2000) found that access to online sexual material can escalate, with some material initially accessed out of curiosity, then becoming the primary focus of interest; however, Calder (2004) noted that the move from viewing abusive images of children on the Internet to contact offending is a massive one. Sullivan and Beech (2004) similarly suggested that not every offender who masturbates to indecent images of children will inevitably progress to contact sexual offenses; however, the subjective risk of them doing so would increase as their engagement in subsequent conditional pairing of online fantasy with masturbation and orgasm may lower their inhibitions for doing so. Certainly, making the distinction between different types of Internet offenders as noted earlier is important in understanding the impact of such behaviors on the individual in question. As for impact upon victims of Internet sexual offending, these are victims of child sexual abuse and hence have suffered the same consequences (as outlined earlier) as other victims of child sexual abuse.

EVIDENCE-BASED PRACTICE

Existing evidence for the effectiveness of treatment for the paraphilias and different types of sexual offenses will be reviewed here where it exists, using the criteria outlined by Chambless and Hollon (1998).

DSM Paraphilias

Although cognitive behavioral treatment (CBT) is the most common approach with sexual offenders (Hanson et al., 2002; Kingston & Yates, 2008; Mann et al., 2008), there is little to no research examining its effectiveness for most paraphilias. Studies reporting behavioral treatment, many conducted from the 1950s to the 1980s, are much more common. These tend to show positive results, but often have limited follow-up periods leading to questions as to whether the positive outcomes are maintained. The empirical evidence for their efficacy of these behavioral procedures on their own has been questioned (D. R. Laws & Marshall, 1990; Marshall, Anderson, & Fernandez, 1999). For instance, questions arise as to whether observed changes can be maintained out of the environment in which they were engendered such as the therapist's office. Pharmacological treatment will not be examined, as useful reviews of such treatment exist elsewhere (Bourget & Bradford, 2008; Rösler & Witztum, 2000).

Exhibitionism

There is relatively more information examining treatment outcome with exhibitionists. Examining overall treatment for exhibitionism in a meta-analysis, Lösel and Schmucker (2005) found a significant effect for sex offender treatment in general across 24 comparisons. The treatment approach used in these studies was not specified but for the entire sample, including studies of individuals with child and adult victims. The CBT approaches revealed the most robust treatment effect aside from castration and hormonal medication. Alexander (1999) also found positive treatment effects for exhibitionists ($N = 331$) in her meta-analysis in that none of those who attended a CBT/Relapse Prevention (RP) program reoffended, compared to 21% of those who attended a *group/behavioral/other* treatment program, and 57% of untreated.

A narrative review by Marshall, Jones, Ward, Johnston, and Barbaree (1991) concluded that CBT was the most effective form of therapy for exhibitionists. An older narrative review by Kilmann, Sabalis, Gearing, Bukstel, and Scovern (1982) reported seven group outcome studies (samples ranging from 10 to 45 participants), and 15 mostly narrative single case studies examining treatment efficacy with exhibitionists. Some of these studies included follow-up periods ranging from six months to four years. The specific design of these case studies (e.g., reversal, multiple baseline, or multielements designs) is unclear. One exception to this was a study by Wardlaw and Miller (1978) that used an ABA design for three individuals. There was no self-reported return to exhibitionistic urges or behavior at three- to four-year follow-up and no further convictions for exhibitionism for the two cases this information was available for. Kilmann et al. concluded that, although none of the studies reviewed had comparison groups, "the behavioral procedures appeared more effective in the shorter time frame than traditional verbal, insight-oriented psychotherapy" (p. 208).

Conclusions. The strongest evidence available from meta-analyses suggests that sex offender treatment in general (Lösel & Schmucker, 2005), and more specifically Cognitive Behavior Therapy/Relapse Prevention programs, are effective in treating exhibitionism (Alexander, 1999). Some evidence suggests that behavioral approaches are useful, although these findings are preliminary in the absence of studies with comparison or control groups. According to the Chambless and Hollon (1998) criteria, there is no support for evidence-based practice with exhibitionists.

Fetishism

Most of the information available examining treatment of fetishism is based on single case studies (Darcangelo et al., 2008). In a review of treatment for paraphilias, 11 single case narrative studies were identified, all using behavioral approaches (Kilmann et al., 1982). The reported outcomes examined in these studies were positive, although based mainly on self-report. As well, the authors noted that these results are only suggestive due to the uncontrolled nature of the studies examined. Lowenstein (1997) examined 76 individuals with a range of fetishes; however, transvestic fetishism, sadomasochism, and aggressive rape were included as fetishes in this study. Treatment was a combined approach using "combined directive guidance and behavior modification with cognitive rational emotive approaches" (p. 61). Seventy of the 76 participants had favorable results. Most reduced their fetishistic behavior and the related harmful effects of their fetishes.

As for the details of single case studies, in an example of a man with a fetish related to feet, treatment consisted of pairing the fetish item with aversive consequences (Kumpukrishnan, Pawlak, & Varan, 1988). Arousal to the stimuli was reported to be eliminated by the 15th session and maintained after 4 months without any booster sessions. Another study reported on the treatment of a man with a fetish for women's tights (Marshall & Lippens, 1977).

His treatment involved masturbatory satiation (i.e., continuing to masturbate to fetishistic stimuli following orgasm). The results from this study revealed that the individual lost interest in his fetish item measured by penile response, self-report, and verbal content of his fantasies after nine sessions.

Conclusions. There is currently not enough evidence to establish that treatment for fetishism has met Chambless and Hollon's (1998) criteria for effective treatment, as in existing fetishes are examined in combination with other types of paraphilias, and only single case nonexperimental studies are reported; however, anecdotally, it appears that the use of behavioral modification is useful.

Frotteurism

There are not any publications that describe treatment outcome for those with frotteurism (Krueger & Kaplan, 2008). Instead, they are included among larger samples of individuals with paraphilias. Existing case studies appear to only focus on medical treatment approaches (Cannas et al., 2006). No conclusions can be drawn about the treatment of frotteurism based on Chambless and Hollon's (1998) criteria for effective treatment.

Pedophilia

Many studies that examine treatment outcome with men diagnosed with pedophilia generally include them among a more encompassing sample of individuals who have child victims (i.e., child abusers). For this reason, treatment for individuals who meet the criteria for pedophilia are included in larger samples of child abusers discussed in the section on *Child Abuse* that follows; however, several studies have looked specifically at treatment for those diagnosed as pedophiles. For example, eight narrative single case studies were reviewed by Kilmann et al. (1982). Positive results were found for each study, although no follow-up periods were specified for any study. Another

study reviewed by Killmann et al. used an ABA reversal design (Barlow, Leitenberg, & Agras, 1969). They found that a reversal effect was demonstrated, with no urges reported at the end of the treatment. Killmann et al. concluded that the most support was provided for the effectiveness of behaviorally oriented approaches to treatment; however, these findings are subject to the same criticisms of behavioral approaches discussed previously (i.e., lack of evidence that the positive treatment gains are sustained).

In a narrative review of medical reports on treatment of pedophilia, Hughes (2007) concluded that behavior therapy is effective in combination with some antiandrogenic medications. Schober and colleagues (2005) found CBT combined with leuprolide acetate, as compared to CBT alone, significantly reduced pedophilic fantasies, urges, and masturbation. Although this study was well designed, the results are limited by the sample size of five.

The treatment of pedophilia has also been examined from a cost-benefit perspective (Shanahan & Donato, 2001). The authors were conservative in overestimating treatment costs, assuming only one to two new victims for each individual, and allowing for a reduction in recidivism of 2% to 14% following treatment. They also conducted a number of calculations to determine cost per offense based on the effects of a sexual offense using several different methods of deriving their estimates. They concluded if the reduction in recidivism rates was anything greater than 6%, assuming some sort of intangible effects of sexual abuse on the victims such as pain and suffering, overall net benefits are observed if one reoffense victim is assumed, and even greater benefits are observed if two victims of reoffense are assumed. They concluded that prison-based CBT programs for pedophiles are likely to be of net benefit to society.

Conclusions. There is not enough evidence to support any particular treatment for pedophilia based on Chambless and Hollon's (1998) criteria for effective treatment, although there is some preliminary support for the use of pharmacotherapy in conjunction with CBT using single case, small *N* studies.

Sexual Masochism

There is a paucity of research examining treatment of those diagnosed with masochism. Some positive results have been reported for behavior therapies in single case studies (Hucker, 2008). In particular, aversion therapy resulted in reduced arousal to masochistic fantasy in a number of narrative case studies (Marks, Gelder, & Bancroft, 1970; Marks, Rachman, & Gelder, 1965; Pinard & Lamontagne, 1976); however, these studies relied on the use of electric shocks, which have been suggested could cause arousal as opposed to inhibiting it (Hucker, 2008). Thus, no conclusions can be drawn about the effectiveness of treatment based on Chambless and Hollon (1998) criteria.

Sexual Sadism

Research examining treatment outcome for sexual sadists is sparse. There is some evidence from narrative case studies in the 1970s supporting the use of behavioral methods for treating sadism (Hayes, Brownell, & Barlow, 1978; D. R. Laws, Meyer, & Holmen, 1978); however, while CBT is the most common treatment approach with sexual offenders, there is little current research examining its effectiveness specifically with sadists (Kingston & Yates, 2008). One example comes from Beech et al. (2005) who reported pre- to post-CBT treatment gains using clinical significant change analysis in 44 sadistically motivated sexual murderers, although none were diagnosed with *DSM* sexual sadism. As a group they took more responsibility for their offending, and were less likely to ascribe their offenses to poor mental health, such as depression. Attitudes toward other people in general and to victims were less hostile, while generalized angry thinking had also been reduced.

Horley (2005) reported positive results using fixed-role therapy, a dramaturgical approach to psychotherapy in which a client is asked to adopt a new personality in the form of a character whose characteristics are inconsistent with the current troubled self, in an incarcerated male client who displayed symptoms of sadomasochism and hebephilia (attraction to adolescents). At 18-months follow-up, this client no longer reported violent fantasies and official reports did not show any criminal convictions.

Conclusions. Additional research is needed before any conclusions can be drawn based on Chambless and Hollon's (1998) criteria for effective treatment, due to the paucity of research findings.

Voyeurism

There is only a very limited amount of published literature on the treatment of sexual voyeurism (Mann et al., 2008), with previous reviews suggesting little evidence supporting any particular treatment approach (Hanson & Harris, 1997). Several psychoanalytic case studies have been reported but treatment has varied considerably precluding any conclusions being drawn (Mann et al., 2008). Some behavioral case studies have also been reported. For example, Gaupp, Stern, and Ratliff (1971), in a single narrative case study, reported a reduction in interest in voyeurism and a more satisfying relationship with his partner after treatment using electric shock aversive therapy. Killman et al. (1982) reported positive results based on the subject's self report in a review of four narrative case studies of voyeurism that used behavioral approaches. The recent literature that exists tends to examine single case studies using pharmacological treatment approaches (Mann et al., 2008). Little research exists examining the impact of CBT despite this being one of the most commonly used approaches for the treatment of sexual offenders (Mann et al., 2008).

Conclusions. Given the current status of the research there does not appear to be enough evidence in support of any particular treatment approach for voyeurism, based on Chambless and Hollon's (1998) criteria for effective treatment, at the present time.

SEXUAL OFFENDING

This section will review the evidence for the effectiveness of treatment for sexual offender types (i.e., child abusers, rapists, and exhibitionists). Randomized control trials (RCTs) are suggested as the gold standard in the evaluation of treatment and this type of design is somewhat more prevalent in assessment of treatment for different types of sex offending, in contrast to paraphilias, where, as noted previously, case studies or cases series are the norm. In RCT designs, sexual offenders are randomly placed in either a group that will receive treatment, or a no treatment control group. This approach potentially controls for any preexisting known and unknown differences between the groups. Therefore, it is argued by proponents of this approach that any observed differences can be attributed to treatment.

Similarly, systematic review methodologies used to identify relevant studies are more prevalent in the evaluation of sex offender treatment. Greenhalgh (1997) noted the following about systematic reviews: (a) They provide an overview of primary studies examining a particular question using explicit and reproducible methods; (b) the use of the explicit methods ensures that the amount of bias in terms of identifying and rejecting studies that can occur in other types of reviews is limited; (c) conclusions can be regarded as accurate and reliable. We will now examine studies using these approaches in more detail.

Randomized Controlled Trials

Romero and Williams (1983) examined treatment outcome among sex offenders on probation in 1966, who were randomly assigned to either a group psychotherapy program ($N = 148$) or to group who received intensive probation supervision, but with no therapeutic intervention ($N = 83$). These groups were followed for 10 years. In this study, a greater number of the treated group reoffended (13.6%) than those who did not attend treatment (7.2%), but this difference was not significant; however, treatment offered in 1966 bears little resemblance to contemporary treatment.

Borduin, Henggeler, Blaske, and Stein (1990) compared the treatment outcome of groups of male adolescents arrested for sexual offenses who were randomly assigned to either multisystemic therapy (MST) ($N = 8$), which assumes that behavior problems are multidetermined and multidimensional, or to individual therapy ($N = 8$), which was a blend of psychodynamic, humanistic, and behavioral approaches, between 1983 and 1985. These adolescents were followed for approximately 3 years. Those who attended the MST sexually reoffended at a significantly lower rate (12.5%) than those who attended the individual therapy (75%).

Robinson (1995) examined sex offenders ($N = 505$) among a larger group of other types of offenders ($N = 3026$) who attended a cognitive skills training program, which was implemented between 1990 and 1994. This program was designed to address offenders' deficits in self-control, interpersonal problem solving, social perspective taking, and critical reasoning skills, which has led to criminal behavior in their past. Those who attended treatment were compared to a group of men who were randomly allocated to a waiting list control group ($N = 84$ sexual offenders among 541 total waiting list controls). The groups were followed for an average of 22.7 months. They found a 57.8% reduction in convictions among the sex offenders. Those who completed treatment reoffended at a rate of 8.2% compared to 19.6% in the control group. Only six individuals out of the total sample of treatment completers ($N = 1,444$) committed a new offense. This constituted a 69% reduction in sexual offenses for the entire sample if the waiting list controls are considered to represent the expected rate of recidivism without treatment. The dropout rate was also significantly lower for sexual offenders (9.9%) compared to the non-sex offenders (15.1%).

J. Marques, Day, Nelson, and West (1994) conducted a longitudinal outcome study using random assignment to treatment ($N = 259$) and control groups. They included comparison groups of those offenders who volunteered to attend treatment but were not randomly assigned to the treatment group (volunteer controls; $N = 225$), and a group of offenders who did not volunteer for treatment (nonvolunteer controls; $N = 220$). The treatment program was a CBT model focusing on RP. The treatment program ran for 2 years. Treated participants were treated in the community for 1 year postrelease. The majority of the participants were followed up for at least five years. The latest report of the recidivism data for this study (J. K. Marques, Wiederanders, Day, Nelson, & van Ommeren, 2005) does not demonstrate any significant differences in the sexual recidivism rates of those assigned to any of the three groups: treated (22.0%), volunteer controls (20.0%), and nonvolunteer controls (19.1%). Marques and colleagues also created the *Got it* scale to indicate the degree to which those who attended treatment derived benefit from the program, in addition to recidivism rates. They based their scores on posttreatment psychometric measures relevant to the goals of the program, and phallometric scores indicating deviant arousal. Here they found an effect of treatment, in that high risk offenders who *Got it* reoffended at a significantly lower rate (10%) than those who had not *Got it* (50%).

Systematic Reviews of RCTs

There have been two comparatively recent systematic reviews examining RCTs (Bilby, Brooks-Gordon, & Wells, 2006; Kenworthy, Adams, Bilby, Brooks-Gordon, & Fenton,

2004). Both examined the same nine RCT studies ($N = 567$), which included studies of participants aged 18 years or older, treated in prison, community, or psychiatric settings. Interventions were classified as behavioral, CBT, psychodynamic, or other (cognitive, social, educational therapy, transtheoretical counseling group therapy). Acceptable comparison groups were comprised of drug treatment (i.e., medroxyprogesterone) and/or standard care. Although the authors suggested that CBT appeared superior to standard care (Kenworthy et al., 2004), this was based on just J. Marques et al. (1994); however, as discussed before, J. K. Marques et al. (2005) reported no significant differences in recidivism rates between treatment and control groups.

Conclusions. It is evident that the RCTs that have been conducted do not provide conclusive evidence for the effectiveness of treatment or indeed which treatment approaches are superior. The findings of Romero and Williams (1983) are based on a treatment program that would not likely be consistent with current approaches. Although Borduin et al.'s study clearly produced effective results in adolescents, it must be noted that it is only based on 16 individuals. Furthermore, it is unknown as to whether this MST would be effective with adults. For treatment of adults, the Robinson et al. study clearly shows benefits, but the results reported are not for a sex offender specific treatment program, however, the more carefully controlled Marques et al. study did not find any evidence of effective treatment. It does provide some promising results in terms of reduced recidivism for those individuals who derived benefit from treatment measured by the *Got it* scale.

Although latter studies can be said to broadly fit Chambless and Hollon's (1998) criteria (i.e., evidence is provided from two or more well conducted studies by at least two independent researchers), there was failure to find clear evidence of treatment effects. There are various possible explanations for the lack of overall treatment effects. It could be due to the fact that the men included were low-to-moderate risk to begin with in the control groups, so they would not be expected to reoffend at a very high rate anyway (Abracen & Looman, 2004), or that the intensity of the treatment was too high given the risk level of the offenders (Marshall & Anderson, 2000). This would be in contrast to the Risk Principle of effective correctional treatment, which indicates that the highest risk offender should receive the highest intensity treatment and that too much treatment can be detrimental if it is not proportional to risk level (Andrews & Bonta, 2003).

There are ethical concerns with the use of the RCT method in sex offender treatment as this approach entails withholding treatment from a randomly selected control group of men to ascertain whether they reoffend at a higher rate than those who were randomly assigned to treatment. (See Marshall & Marshall [2007] for an extensive discussion of this and Seto et al., [2008] for a rebuttal). Unlike other types of RCT designs, for example, in studies examining treatment for depression, those who are assigned to no treatment are not actually the ones who suffer the consequences of not getting treatment. Here, there is the possibility of producing more victims by withholding the most efficacious treatment for offenders who clearly need it. Despite these concerns, some researchers suggest that RCT designs are the only method that can provide conclusive evidence for treatment efficacy in the sex offender field (Rice & Harris, 2003).

Meta-Analyses of Group Designs

Due to an inability to draw firm conclusions from the RCTs at the present time, it is important to consider a number of other treatment evaluation methods. For a review of the various methods of measuring sex offender treatment effectiveness, see Harkins and Beech (2007). One of the main approaches to evaluating various treatment approaches has been through the use of meta-analysis. This approach combines the results from a number of studies to determine if there is an overall effect. Meta-analysis is useful because it allows for small effect sizes to be detected in the large sample sizes that typically result from amalgamating studies.

The starting point of any meta-analysis involves the selection of a summary statistic or effect measure, typically an odds ratio (OR), the ratio of the odds of an event occurring in two groups. Egger, Smith, and Altman (2005) recommended that all measures of effect should also be accompanied by confidence intervals (CI). Interpretation of the OR is as follows: A value of 1.0 would indicate no difference between the groups being compared; typically values below 1.0 indicate treatment having a positive effect; values above 1.0 indicate treatment having a negative effect. (Some studies report the values of ORs the other way around, so that larger values indicate a positive effect of treatment, e.g., Lösel & Schmucker, 2005). If CIs cross 1.0, the results are not significant. We will now briefly report on three recent meta-analyses of sex offender treatment studies.

Hanson et al. (2002) conducted a meta-analysis examining treatment evaluation studies with the aim of including all credible studies of psychological treatment for sexual offenders using different treatment designs identified prior to May 2000. In order to be included, studies had to have included a comparison group. This could have included the use of those who had received no treatment, as well as those who attended programs that were determined to be inadequate or inappropriate. This search yielded 43 studies ($N = 9,534$) from 23 published and 20 unpublished community and institutional treatment programs, with an average length of follow-up time being 46 months. Hanson et al. reported a significant effect of treatment (12.3% for treated vs. 16.8% for untreated samples). Averaged across all types of treatment there was a significant effect of treatment (OR = 0.81, CI 0.71 to 0.94). Breaking down treatment, by type of approach, Hanson et al. found that older treatment options (i.e., nonbehavioral/non-CBT) appeared to have little effect in reducing recidivism (OR = 1.19, CI 0.77–1.86), and CBT had a positive treatment effect (OR = 0.60, CI 0.48–0.75).

Lösel and Schmucker (2005) reported results that were generally consistent with those of Hanson et al. (2002). They analyzed 69 studies (N = 22,181) that were completed prior to June 2003. This meta-analysis also identified a positive effect of treatment with treated sexual offenders (OR = 1.70, CI 1.35–2.13). (Note in this study a higher OR indicated a larger treatment effect). They found that physical treatments (i.e., surgical castration and hormone treatments) had larger effects (OR = 7.37, CI 4.14–13.11) than psychosocial approaches (OR = 1.32, CI 1.07–1.62). Both CBT (OR = 1.45, CI 1.12–1.86) and classical behavior therapy (OR = 2.19, CI 1.22–3.92) were also shown to have a significant impact on sexual recidivism. In contrast, more psychotherapeutic approaches (i.e., insight oriented, therapeutic community, and other unclear psychosocial approaches) did not significantly influence recidivism.

In the most recent meta-analysis, Robertson, Beech, and (in preparation) examined 54 treatment studies (N = 14,694), which included a range of different designs all using a control group. Results indicated a positive effect of treatment for both sexual (OR = 0.56, CI 0.45–0.71) and general recidivism (OR = 0.50, CI 0.39–0.65). Results indicated an advantage of systemic and CBT approaches in reducing both sexual (OR = 0.24, CI 0.06–0.92 and OR = .47, CI 0.37–0.61, respectively) and general recidivism (OR = 0.24, CI 0.10–0.65 and OR = 0.51, CI 0.06–0.92, respectively). Robertson et al. suggest that these results lend support for the efficacy of sexual offender treatment, particularly when the strongest treatment designs (i.e., when RCT and incident cohort designs are combined) are used, with systemic therapy and CBT appearing to hold the most promise for effective interventions.

Conclusions. Taken together, these results provide support for the general effectiveness

of sex offender treatment at reducing recidivism. In particular, support is provided for CBT approaches in each of the meta-analyses, fulfilling Chambless and Hollon's (1998) criteria. Additional support is provided for the use of physical treatment approaches (e.g., surgical castration) and systemic treatment. This evidence has come from evaluation methods other than RCT studies, which has not provided conclusive evidence in addressing the question of effectiveness of sex offender treatment.

Child Abuse

Some studies and reviews have reported treatment outcome specifically with child abusers among their overall examination of treatment effectiveness with sex offenders. Alexander (1999) found that child abusers reoffended at a lower rate than untreated offenders in her meta-analysis (14.4% and 25.8%, respectively). In fact, those who attended a CBT/RP program reoffended at a lower rate (8.1%) than those who attended a group/behavioral/other (18.3%), or unspecified (13.6%) program, and all recidivated at a lower rate than the untreated group (25.8%). Lösel and Schmucker (2005), in their meta-analysis, reported positive effect for treatment for extrafamilial child abusers in nine studies (OR = 2.15, CI 1.11–4.16), but not for incestuous child abusers in 10 studies (OR = 1.02, CI 0.58–1.80).

Conclusions. Evidence from Alexander (1999) supports the use of CBT with sex offenders with child victims. Treatment in general is supported by Lösel and Schmucker (2005) for extrafamilial offenders, but not intrafamilial (i.e., incest) offenders. These studies can be said to broadly meet Chambless and Hollon's (1998) criteria.

Rape

Maletzky and Steinhauser (2002), in a study looking at treatment outcome over 25 years follow-up for a CBT program for sex offenders (N = 7275), reported that rapists (21.2%) had a comparatively worse response to treatment than child abusers (6.3% for those with female child victims; 9.4% for those with male child victims) and exhibitionists (13.5%). Similarly, Alexander (1999) reported on 528 rapists and did not find a significant difference between the recidivism rates of the treated (20.1%) and untreated rapists (23.7%). J. K. Marques and colleagues (2005) did not find a positive treatment effect for the rapists in their RCT study with the rapists reoffending at a rate of 20.4% compared to 29.4% for the volunteer controls, and 14.0% for the nonvolunteers. There was also no significant relationship found between the *Got it* scale and recidivism for the rapists.

In contrast, Lösel and Schmucker (2005) reported a positive effect for treatment for rapists (OR = 4.91, CI 1.64–14.68), but this analysis was based on only five studies. Similarly, Nicholaichuk, Gordon, Gu, and Wong (2000), found that the recidivism rate for treated rapists ($N = 168$) was significantly lower than for the untreated comparison group ($N = 50$)—14% and 42%, respectively; however, the authors were unable to determine whether the men in the comparison group may have been treatment dropouts, which would indicate an increased risk of recidivism.

Conclusions. The strongest available evidence suggests that treatment is not effective for rapists given that three studies report no effect of treatment while two do.

Internet Sexual Offending

No evaluations of the impact of treatment for Internet offenders have so far been conducted. Thus, no conclusions can be drawn about the effectiveness of treatment for this group.

EVIDENCE-BASED PRACTICE FOR PARAPHILIAS AND SEXUAL OFFENSES

There are currently far too few well-designed studies to provide support for evidence-based

practice with any of the paraphilias, assessed using the Chambless and Hollon (1998) criteria. There is, however, a growing body of evidence for the effectiveness of sex offender treatment from meta-analyses. In particular, support is provided for CBT approaches in each of the meta-analyses examining treatment outcome studies with mixed groups of sex offenders, and for child abusers alone, fulfilling Chambless and Hollon's (1998) criteria; however, if CBT is more carefully targeted to rapists with different types of motivations (i.e., violent, sexual, sadistic), then treatment may be more successful with this type of offender (Beech et al., 2005; Eccleston & Owen, 2007). The effectiveness of treatment for Internet offenders has yet to be examined.

REFERENCES

Abel, G., Becker, J., Cunningham-Rathner, J., & Rouleau, J. (1987). Self reported sex crimes of 561 non-incarcerated paraphiliacs. *Journal of Interpersonal Violence, 2,* 3–25.

Abel, G., & Rouleau, J. (1990). The nature and extent of sexual assault. In W. L. Marshall, D. R. Laws, & H. E. Barbaree (Eds.), *Handbook of sexual assault: Issues, theories and treatment of the offender* (pp. 9–12). New York, NY: Plenum Press.

Abracen, J., & Looman, J. (2004). Issues in the treatment of sexual offenders: Recent developments and directions for future research. *Aggression and Violent Behavior, 9,* 229–246.

Alexander, M. (1999). Sexual offender treatment efficacy revisited. *Sexual Abuse: A Journal of Research and Treatment, 11,* 101–116.

American Psychological Association. (2000). *Diagnostic and statistical manual for mental disorders* (4th ed., text rev.). Washington, DC: Author.

Andrews, D. A., & Bonta, J. (2003). *The psychology of criminal conduct* (3rd ed.). Cincinnati, OH: Anderson.

Bader, S. M., Schoeneman-Morris, S. A., Scalora, M. J., & Casady, T. K. (2008). Exhibitionism: Findings from a midwestern police contact sample. *International Journal of Offender Therapy and Comparative Criminology, 52,* 270–279.

Barlow, D. H., Leitenberg, H., & Agras, W. S. (1969). Experimental control of sexual deviation through manipulation of the noxious scene in covert sensitization. *Journal of Abnormal Psychology, 74,* 596–601.

Beech, A., Oliver, C., Fisher, D., & Beckett, R. C. (2005). STEP 4: The Sex Offender Treatment Programme in prison: Addressing the needs of rapists and sexual murderers. Retrieved from www.hmprisonservice.gov.uk/assets/documents/100013DBStep_4_SOTP_report_2005.pdf

Beitchman, J. H., Zucker, K. J., Hood, J. E., daCosta, G. A., & Akman, D. (1991). A review of the short-term effects of child sexual abuse. Child Abuse and Neglect, 15, 537–556.

Beller, A., Garelik, S., & Cooper, S. (1980). Sex crimes in the subway. Criminology, 18, 35–52.

Bilby, C., Brooks-Gordon, B., & Wells, H. (2006). A systematic review of psychological interventions for sexual offenders II: Quasi-experimental and qualitative data. Journal of Forensic Psychiatry and Psychology, 17, 467–484.

Blair, C. D., & Lanyon, R. I. (1981). Exhibitionism: Etiology and treatment. Psychological Bulletin, 89, 439–463.

Borduin, C. M., Henggeler, S. W., Blaske, D. M., & Stein, R. J. (1990). Multisystemic treatment of adolescent sexual offenders. International Journal of Offender Therapy and Comparative Criminology, 34, 105–113.

Bourget, D., & Bradford, J. M. W. (2008). Evidential basis for the assessment and treatment of sex offenders. Brief Treatment and Crisis Intervention, 8, 130–146.

Calder, M. C. (2004). The Internet: Potential, problems and pathways to hands on sexual offending. In M. C. Calder (Ed.), Child sexual abuse and the Internet: Tackling the new frontier (pp. 1–24). Lyme Regis, England: Russell House.

Campbell, R. (2008). The psychological impact of rape victims' experiences with the legal, medical, and mental health systems. American Psychologist, November, 702–717.

Cannas, A., Solla, P., Floris, G., Tacconi, P., Loi, D., Marcia, E., & Marrosu, M. G. (2006). Hypersexual behaviour, frotteurism, and delusional jealousy in a young parkinsonian patient during dopaminergic therapy with pergolide: A rare case of iatrogenic paraphilia. Progress in the Neuro-Psychopharmacology and Biological Psychiatry, 30, 1539–1541.

Chalkley, A. J., & Powell, G. E. (1983). The clinical description of 48 cases of sexual fetishism. British Journal of Psychiatry, 142, 292–295.

Chambless, D. L., & Hollon, S. D. (1998). Defining empirically supported therapies. Journal of Consulting and Clinical Psychology, 66, 7–18.

Cohen, L. J., & Galynker, I. I. (2002). Clinical features of pedophilia and implication for treatment. Journal of Psychiatric Practice, 8, 276–289.

Craissati, J., & Beech, A. R. (2004). The characteristics of convicted rapists: Sexual victimization and compliance in comparison to child molesters. Journal of Interpersonal Violence, 19, 225–240.

Crome, S. A., & McCabe, M. P. (2001). Adult rape scripting within a victimological perspective. Aggression and Violent Behavior, 6, 395–413.

Darcangelo, S. (2008). Fetishism: Psychopathology and theory. In D. R. Laws & W. O'Donohue (Eds.), Sexual deviance: Theory, assessment and treatment (2nd ed., pp. 108–118). New York, NY: Guilford Press.

Darcangelo, S., Hollings, A., & Paladino, G. (2008). Fetishism: Assessment and treatment. In D. R. Laws & W. O'Donohue (Eds.), Sexual deviance: Theory, assessment and treatment (2nd ed., pp. 119–130). New York, NY: Guilford Press.

Dickey, R., Nussbaum, D., Chevolleau, K., & Davidson, H. (2002). Age as a differential characteristic of rapists, pedophiles, and sexual sadists. Journal of Sex and Marital Therapy, 28, 211–218.

Dietz, P. E., Hazelwood, M. S., & Warren, D. S. W. (1990). The sexually sadistic criminal and his offenses. Bulletin of the American Academy of Psychiatry and the Law, 16, 163–178.

Dreznick, M. T. (2003). Heterosocial competence of rapists and child molesters: A meta-analysis. Journal of Sex Research, 40, 170–178.

Eccleston, L., & Owen, K. (2007). Cognitive treatment "just for rapists": Recent developments. In T. A. Gannon, T. Ward, A. R. Beech, & D. Fisher (Eds.), Aggressive offenders' cognition: Research, theory, and practice (pp. 135–153). Chichester, England: Wiley.

Egger, M., Smith, G. D., & Altman, D. G. (2005). Systematic reviews in health care: Meta-analysis in context (5th ed.). London, England: BMJ Publishing Group.

Elliott, I. A., Beech, A. R., Mandeville-Norden, R., & Hayes, E. (2009). Psychological profiles of Internet sexual offenders: Comparisons with contact sexual offenders. Sexual Abuse: A Journal of Research and Treatment, 21, 76–92.

Feelgood, S., & Hoyer, J. (2008). Child molester or paedophile? Sociolegal versus psychological classification of sexual offenders against children. Journal of Sexual Aggression, 14, 33–43.

Fergusson, D., Horwood, L., & Lynskey, M. (1996). Childhood sexual abuse and psychiatric disorder in young adulthood: II. Psychiatric outcomes of childhood sexual abuse. Journal of the American Academy of Child Adolescent Psychiatry, 35, 1365–1374.

Fergusson, D., Lynskey, M., & Horwood, L. (1996). Childhood sexual abuse and psychiatric disorder in young adulthood: I. Prevalence of sexual abuse and factors associated with sexual abuse. Journal of the American Academy of Child Adolescent Psychiatry, 35, 1355–1364.

Freund, K., & Kuban, M. (1993). Toward a testable developmental model of pedophilia: The development of erotic age preference. Child Abuse and Neglect, 17, 315–324.

Freund, K., & Seto, M. C. (1998). Preferential rape in the theory of courtship disorder. *Archives of Sexual Behavior, 27*, 433–443.

Freund, K., Seto, M. C., & Kuban, M. (1997). Frotteurism: The theory and of courtship disorder. In D. R. Laws & W. O'Donohue (Eds.), *Sexual Deviance: Theory, assessment, and treatment.* (pp. 111–130). London, England: Guilford Press.

Gannon, T. A., & Ward, T. (2008). Rape: Psychopathology and theory. In D. R. Laws & W. O'Donohue (Eds.), *Sexual deviance: Theory, assessment and treatment* (2nd ed., pp. 336–355). New York, NY: Guilford Press.

Gaupp, L. A., Stern, R. M., & Ratliff, R. G. (1971). The use of aversion-relief procedures in the treatment of a case of voyeurism. *Behavior Therapy, 2*, 585–588.

Greenhalgh, T. (1997). How to read a paper: Papers that summarise other papers (systematic reviews and meta-analyses). *British Medical Journal, 315*, 672–675.

Hampton, H. L. (1995). Care of the woman who has been raped. *New England Journal of Medicine, 332*, 234–237.

Hanson, R. K., Gordon, A., Harris, A. J. R., Marques, J. K., Murphy, W., Quinsey, V., & Seto, M. C. (2002). First report of the collaborative outcome data project on the effectiveness of psychological treatment for sex offenders. *Sexual Abuse: A Journal of Research and Treatment, 14*, 169–194.

Hanson, R. K., & Harris, A. J. R. (1997). Voyeurism: Assessment and treatment. In D. R. Laws & W. O'Donohue (Eds.), *Sexual deviance: Theory, assessment, and treatment* (pp. 311–331). New York, NY: Guilford Press.

Hanson, R. K., Steffy, R. A., & Gauthier, R. (1993). Long-term recidivism of child molesters. *Journal of Consulting and Clinical Psychology, 51*, 646–652.

Harkins, L., & Beech, A. R. (2007). Measurement of the effectiveness of sex offender treatment. *Aggression and Violent Behavior, 12*, 36–44.

Harris, A., Phenix, A., Hanson, R. K., & Thornton, D. (2003). *Static-99 coding rules revised—2003.* Ottawa: Department of the Solicitor General of Canada.

Hayes, S. C., Brownell, K. D., & Barlow, D. H. (1978). The use of self-administered covert sensitization in the treatment of exhibitionism and sadism. *Behavior Therapy, 9*, 283–289.

Hendrix, E., & Meyer, R. (1976). Toward more comprehensible and durable client changes: A case report. *Psychotherapy: Theory, Research, and Practice, 13*, 263.

Hernandez, A. E. (2000, November). *Self-reported contact sexual offenses by participants in the Federal Bureau of Prisons' sex offender treatment program: Implications for Internet sex offenders.* Paper presented at the 19th Research and treatment conference of the association for the treatment of sexual abusers, San Diego, CA.

Hilton, M. R., & Mezey, G. C. (1996). Victims and perpetrators of child sexual abuse. *British Journal of Psychiatry, 169*, 408–415.

Horley, J. (2005). Fixed-role therapy with multiple paraphilias. *Clinical Case Studies, 4*, 72–80.

Hucker, S. J. (2008). Sexual masochism: Assessment and treatment. In D. R. Laws & W. O'Donohue (Eds.), *Sexual deviance: Theory, assessment and treatment* (2nd ed., pp. 264–271). New York, NY: Guilford Press.

Hurlbert, D. F. (1992). Voyeurism in an adult female with schizoid personality: A case report. *Sex Education and Therapy, 18*, 17–21.

Hughes, J. R. (2007). Review of medical reports on pedophilia. *Clinical Pediatrics, 46*, 667–682.

Kendall-Tackett, K. A., Williams, L. M., & Finkelhor, D. (1993). Impact of sexual abuse of children: Review and synthesis of recent empirical studies. *Psychological Bulletin, 119*, 164–180.

Kenworthy, T., Adams, C. E., Bilby, C., Brooks-Gordon, B., & Fenton, M. (2004). Psychological interventions for those who have sexually offended or are at risk of offending. *Cochrane Database of Systematic Reviews.* Issue 4. Art. No.: CD004858. doi:10.1002/14651858 .CD004858.

Kilmann, P. R., Sabalis, R. F., Gearing, M. L., Bukstel, L. H., & Scovern, A. W. (1982). The treatment of sexual paraphilias: A review of the outcome research. *Journal of Sex Research, 18*, 193–252.

Kilpatrick, D. G., & Acierno, R. (2003). Mental health needs of crime victims: Epidemiology and outcomes. *Journal of Traumatic Stress, 16*, 119–32.

Kingston, D. A., & Yates, P. M. (2008). Sexual sadism: Assessment and treatment. In D. R. Laws & W. O'Donohue (Eds.), *Sexual deviance: Theory, assessment and treatment* (2nd ed., pp. 231–249). London, England: Guilford Press.

Knight, R. A., & Prentky, R. A. (1990). Classifying sexual offenders: The development and corroboration of taxonomic models. In W. L. Marshall, D. R. Laws, & H. E. Barbaree (Eds.), *Handbook of sexual assault: Issues, theories, and treatment of the offender* (pp. 23–52). New York, NY: Plenum Press.

Krone, T. (2004). A typology of online child pornography offending. *Trends and Issues in Crime and Criminal Justice, 279*, 1–6.

Krueger, R. B., & Kaplan, M. S. (2008). Frotteurism: Assessment and treatment. In D. R. Laws & W. O'Donohue (Eds.), *Sexual deviance: Theory, assessment and treatment* (2nd ed., pp. 150–163). New York, NY: Guilford Press.

Kunjukrishnan, R., Pawlak, A., & Varan, L. R. (1988). The clinical and forensic psychiatric issues of retifism. *Canadian Journal of Psychiatry, 33*, 819–825.

Långström, N., & Seto, M. C. (2006). Exhibitionist and voyeuristic behavior in a Swedish national population survey. *Archives of Sexual Behavior, 35*, 427–435.

Lanning, K. V. (2001). *Child molesters: A behavioral analysis.* Retrieved from www.ncmec.org/en_US/publications/NC70.pdf

Lavin, M. (2008). Voyeurism: Psychopathology and theory. In D. R. Laws & W. O'Donohue (Eds.), *Sexual deviance: Theory, assessment and treatment* (2nd ed., pp. 305–319). New York, NY: Guilford Press.

Laws D. R., & Marshall, W. L. (1990). A conditioning theory of the etiology and maintenance of deviant sexual preference and behavior. In W. L. Marshall, D. R. Laws, & H. E. Barbaree (Eds.), *Handbook of sexual assault: Issues, theories, and treatment of the offender* (pp. 209–230). New York, NY: Plenum Press.

Laws, D. R., Meyer, J., & Holman, M. L. (1978). Reduction of sadistic sexual arousal by olfactory aversion: A case study. *Behaviour Research and Therapy, 16*, 281–283.

Laws, R. D., & O'Donohue, W. T. (Eds.). (2008). *Sexual deviance: Theory, assessment, and treatment.* London, England: Guilford Press.

Levenson, J. S. (2004). Reliability of sexually violent predator civil commitment criteria in Florida. *Law and Human Behavior, 28*, 357–368.

Losel, F., & Schmucker, M. (2005). The effectiveness of treatment for sexual offenders: A comprehensive meta-analysis. *Journal of Experimental Criminology, 1*, 117–146.

Lowenstein, L. F. (1997). Fetishes: General and specific. *Psychopathology in Private Practice, 16*, 53–65.

Lussier, P., & Piche, L. (2008). Frotteurism: Psychopathology and theory. In D. R. Laws & W. O'Donohue (Eds.), *Sexual deviance: Theory, assessment and treatment* (2nd ed., pp. 305–319). New York, NY: Guilford Press.

Maletzky, B. M., & Steinhauser, C. (2002). A 25-year follow-up of cognitive/behavioural therapy with 7,275 sexual offenders. *Behavior Modification, 26*, 123–147.

Mann, R. E., Ainsworth, F., Al Attar, Z., & Davies, M. (2008). Voyeurism: Assessment and treatment. In D. R. Laws & W. O'Donohue (Eds.), *Sexual deviance: Theory, assessment and treatment* (2nd ed., pp. 305–319). New York, NY: Guilford Press.

Marks, I. M., Gelder, M. G., & Bancroft, J. H. J. (1970). Sexual deviants two years after electric aversion. *British Journal of Psychiatry, 117*, 173–185.

Marks, I. M., Rachman, S., & Gelder, M. G. (1965). Methods for assessment of aversion treatment in fetishism with masochism. *Behaviour Research and Therapy, 3*, 253–258.

Marques, J., Day, D. M., Nelson, C., & West, M. A. (1994). Effects of cognitive-behavioral treatment on sex offender recidivism: Preliminary results of a longitudinal study. *Criminal Justice and Behavior, 21*, 28–54.

Marques, J. K., Wiederanders, M., Day, D. M., Nelson, C., & van Ommeren, A. (2005). Effects of a relapse prevention program on sexual recidivism: Final results from California's Sex Offender Treatment and Evaluation Program (SOTEP). *Sexual Abuse: A Journal of Research and Treatment, 17*, 79–107.

Marshall, W. L. (1997). Pedophilia: Psychopatholgy and theory. In D. R. Laws & W. O'Donohue (Eds.). *Sexual Deviance: Theory, assessment, and treatment.* (pp. 152–174). London, England: Guilford Press.

Marshall, W. L. (2006). Diagnostic problems with sexual offenders. In W. L. Marshall, Y. M. Fernandez, L. E. Marshall, & G. A. Serran (Eds.), *Sexual offender treatment: Controversial issues* (pp. 33–43). Chichester, England: Wiley.

Marshall, W.L. & Anderson, D (2000). Do relapse prevention components enhance treatment effectiveness? In D. M. Laws, S. M. Hudson, & T. Ward (Eds.) *Remaking relapse prevention with sex offenders: A sourcebook* (pp. 39–55). London, England: Sage.

Marshall, W. L., Anderson, D., & Fernandez, Y. (1999). *Cognitive behavioural treatment of sexual offenders.* Chichester, England: Wiley.

Marshall, W. L., Barbaree, H. E., & Eccles, A. (1991). Early onset and deviant sexuality in child molesters. *Journal of Interpersonal Violence, 6*, 323–336.

Marshall, W. L., & Hucker, S. J. (2006). Issues in the diagnosis of sexual sadism. *Sexual Offender Treatment, 1*, 1–5. Available from www.sexual-offender-treatment.org

Marshall, W. L., Jones, R., Ward, T., Johnston, P., & Barbaree, H. E. (1991). Treatment outcome with sex offenders. *Clinical Psychology Review, 11*, 4654–4685.

Marshall, W. L., & Kennedy, P. (2003). Sexual sadism in sexual offenders: An elusive diagnosis. *Aggression and Violent Behavior, 8*, 1–22.

Marshall, W. L., Kennedy, P., Yates, P., & Serran, G. (2002). Diagnosing sexual sadism in sexual offenders: Reliability across diagnosticians. *International Journal of Offender Therapy and Comparative Criminology, 46*, 668–677.

Marshall, W. L., & Lippens, K. (1977). The clinical value of boredom: A procedure for reducing inappropriate sexual interests. *Journal of Nervous and Mental Disease, 165*, 283–287.

Marshall, W. L., & Marshall, L. E. (2007). The utility of the random controlled trial for evaluating sexual offender treatment: The gold standard or an inappropriate strategy? *Sexual Abuse: A Journal of Research and Treatment, 19*, 175–191.

McConaghy, N. (1998). Pedophilia: A review of the evidence. *Australian and New Zealand Journal of Psychiatry, 32*, 252–265.

Moser, C., & Levitt, E. E. (1987). An exploratory descriptive study of sadomasochistically oriented sample. *Journal of Sex Research, 23*, 322–337.

Murphy, W. D., & Page, I. J. (2008). Exhibitionism: Psychopathology and theory. In D. R. Laws & W. O'Donohue (Eds.), *Sexual deviance: Theory, assessment and treatment* (2nd ed., pp. 61–75). New York, NY: Guilford Press.

Myhill, A., & Allen, J. (2002) *Rape and sexual assault of women: The extent and nature of the problem. Home Office Research Study 237.* London, England: Home Office Research, Development and Statistics Directorate.

Nicholaichuk, T., Gordon, A., Gu., D., & Wong, S. (2000). Outcome of an institutional sexual offender treatment program: A comparison between treated and matched untreated offenders. *Sexual Abuse: A Journal of Research and Treatment, 12,* 139–153.

Pinard, G., & Lamontagne, Y. (1976). Electrical aversion, aversion relief, and sexual retraining in treatment of fetishism and masochism. *Journal of Behavior Therapy and Experimental Psychiatry, 7,* 71–74.

Putnam, F. W. (2003). Ten-year research update review: Child sexual abuse. *Journal of the American Academy of Child and Adolescent Psychiatry, 42,* 269–278.

Quayle, E. (2008). Online sex offending: Psychopathology and theory. In D. R. Laws & W. O'Donohue (Eds.), *Sexual deviance: Theory, assessment and treatment* (2nd ed., pp. 439–458). New York, NY: Guilford Press.

Rabinowitz Greenberg, S. R., Firestone, P., Bradford, J. M., & Greenberg, D. M. (2002). Prediction of recidivisim in exhibitionists: Psychological, phallometric, and offense factors. *Sexual Abuse: A Journal of Research and Treatment, 14,* 329–347.

Rentoul, L., & Appleboom, N. (1997). Understanding the psychological impact of rape and serious sexual assault of men: A literature review. *Journal of Psychiatric and Mental Health Nursing, 4,* 267–274.

Rice, M. E., & Harris, G. T. (2003). The size and sign of treatment effects in sex offender therapy. In R. A. Prentky, E. S. Janus, & M. C. Seto (Eds.), *Sexually coercive behavior: Understanding and management. Annals of the New York Academy of Sciences, 989,* 428–440.

Riordan, S. (1999). Indecent exposure: The impact upon the victim's fear of sexual crime. *Journal of Forensic Psychiatry, 10,* 309–316.

Robertiello, G., & Terry, K. J. (2007). Can we profile sex offenders? A review of sex offender typologies. *Aggression and Violent Behavior, 12,* 508–518.

Robertson, C., Beech, A. R., & Freemantle, N. (in preparation). A meta-analysis of treatment outcome studies: Comparisons of treatment designs and treatment deliver. *Sexual Abuse: A Journal of Research and Treatment.*

Robinson, D. (1995). *The impact of cognitive skills training on post-release recidivism among Canadian federal offenders* (No. R-41). Ottawa, ON: Correctional Service Canada, Correctional Research and Development.

Romero, J. J., & Williams, L. M. (1983). Group psychotherapy and intensive probation supervision with sex offenders. *Federal Probation, 47,* 36–42.

Rösler, A., & Witzum, E. (2000). Pharmacotherapy of paraphilias in the next millennium. *Behavioral Sciences and the Law, 18,* 43–56.

Sandnabba, K., Santilla, P., & Nordling, N. (1999). Sexual behavior and social adaptation among sadomasochistically-oriented males. *Journal of Sex Research, 36,* 273–282.

Schlesinger, L. B., & Revitch, E. (1999). Sexual burglaries and sexual homicide: Clinical, forensic, and investigative considerations. *Journal of the American Academy of Psychiatry and the Law, 27,* 227–238.

Schneider, J. P. (2000). Effects of cybersex addiction on the family: Results of a survey. *Sexual Addiction and Compulsivity, 7,* 31–58.

Schober, J. M., Kuhm, P. J., Kovacs, P. G., Earle, J. H., Byrne, P. M., & Fries, A. M. (2005). Leuprolide acetate suppresses pedophilic urges and arousability. *Archives of Sexual Behavior, 34,* 691–705.

Seto, M. C. (2008). Pedophilia: Psychopathology and theory. In D. R. Laws & W. O'Donohue (Eds.), *Sexual deviance: Theory, assessment and treatment* (2nd ed., pp. 164–182). New York, NY: Guilford Press.

Seto, M. C., Marques, J., Harris, G. T., Chaffin, M., Lalumière, M. L., Miner, M. H., . . . Quinsey, V. L. (2008). Good science and progress in sex offender treatment are intertwined: A response to Marshall and Marshall (2007). *Sexual Abuse: A Journal of Research and Treatment, 20,* 247–255.

Shanahan, M., & Donato, R. (2001). Counting the cost: Estimating the economic benefit of pedophile treatment programs. *Child Abuse and Neglect, 25,* 541–555.

Simon, R. I. (1997). Video voyeurs and the covert taping of unsuspecting victims: Psychological and Legal consequences. *Journal of Forensic Science, 42,* 884–889.

Smallbone, S. W., & Wortley, R. K. (2001). Child sexual abuse: Offender characteristics and modus operandi. *Australian Institute of Criminology, Trends and Issues in Crime and Criminal Justice, 193,* 1–6.

Smukler, A. J., & Schiebel, D. (1975). Personality characteristics of exhibitionists. *Diseases of the Nervous System, 36,* 600–603.

Spataro, J., Mullen, P. E., Burgess, P. M., Wells, D. M., & Moss, S. A. (2004). Impact of child sexual abuse on mental health: Prospective study in males and females. *British Journal of Psychiatry, 184,* 416–421.

Spengler, A. (1977). Manifest sadomasochism of males: Results of an empirical study. *Archives of Sexual Behavior, 6,* 441–456.

Sugarman, P., Dumughn, C., Saad, K., Hinder, S. & Bluglass, R. (1994). Dangerousness in exhibitionists. *Journal of Forensic Psychiatry, 5,* 287–296.

Sullivan, J., & Beech, A. R. (2004). Are collectors of pornography a risk to children? In M. Calder (Ed.), *Policing paedophiles on the Internet* (pp. 69–84). Sussex, England: Pavilion.

Taylor, M., & Quayle, E. (2003). *Child pornography: An Internet crime.* Hove, England: Brunner-Routledge.

Templeman, T. L., & Stinnett, R. D. (1991). Patterns of sexual arousal and history in a "normal" sample of young men. *Archives of Sexual Behavior, 20,* 137–150.

Thomas, T. (2005). *Sex crime: Sex offending and society* (2nd ed.). Cullompton, Devon, England: Willan.

Thornton, D., Mann, R., Webster, S., Blud, L., Travers, R., Friendship, C., & Erickson, M. (2003). Distinguishing between and combining risks for sexual and violent recidivism. In R. A. Prentky, E. S. Janus, & M. C. Seto (Eds.), *Sexually coercive behavior: Understanding and management. Annals of the New York Academy of Sciences, 989,* 223–235.

U.S. Department of Health and Human Services, Administration on Children, Youth and Families. (2008). *Child Maltreatment 2006.* Washington, DC: U.S. Government Printing Office.

Wardlaw, G. R., & Miller, P. J. (1978). A controlled exposure technique in the elimination of exhibitionism.

Journal of Behavior Therapy and Experimental Psychiatry, 9, 27–32.

Webb, L., Craissati, J., & Keen, S. (2007). Characteristics of Internet child pornography offenders: A comparison with child molesters. *Sexual Abuse: A Journal of Research and Treatment, 199,* 449–465.

Wiederman, M. W. (2003). Paraphilia and fetishism. *Sex Therapy, 11,* 315–321.

Wilson, R. J., Abracen, J., Picheca, J. E., Malcolm, P. B., & Prinzo, M. (2003, October). *Pedophilia: An evaluation of the diagnostic and risk management methods.* Paper presented at the 23rd Annual Research and Treatment Conference of the Association for the Treatment of Sexual Offenders, St. Louis, MO.

World Health Organization. (2006). *Global estimates of health consequences due to violence against children.* Background paper to the UN Secretary General's study on violence against children. Geneva, Switzerland: Author.

19

Sleep Disorders in Adults

ALLISON G. HARVEY AND NATASHA DAGYS

OVERVIEW OF DISORDER

Diagnostic Criteria

Insomnia is characterized by an ongoing difficulty getting to sleep, staying asleep, waking up too early, or waking up and feeling that the sleep obtained was not restorative. In addition to the sleep complaint, the individual with insomnia must report daytime impairment (Edinger et al., 2004). Four classification systems offer specific diagnostic criteria for insomnia. The *Diagnostic and Statistical Manual* (4th ed., text rev.) *(DSM-IV-TR)* (American Psychiatric Association, 2000) and the *International Classification of Diseases* (10th rev.) *(ICD-10)* (World Health Organization, 1992) offer a small number of broad categories based on current symptoms and functioning. In contrast, the Research Diagnostic Criteria (RDC) (Edinger et al., 2004) and the *International Classification of Sleep Disorders* (2nd ver.) *(ICSD-2)* (American Academy of Sleep Medicine, 2005) offer a larger number of subtypes that require the assessor to make judgments about the causes of the insomnia. Research is needed to resolve the differences between the four nomenclatures and to determine the validity and reproducibility of both the broad categories and the subtypes.

It is important to note that in the past insomnia that is comorbid with another psychiatric disorder was referred to as secondary insomnia. Given the accruing evidence indicating that insomnia is an important but underrecognized mechanism in the multifactorial cause and maintenance of psychiatric disorders (A. G. Harvey, 2008; National Institutes of Health, 2005; Smith, Huang, & Manber, 2005), current standards recommend that insomnia be considered a *comorbid* rather than secondary diagnosis (Morin et al., 2006; National Institutes of Health, 2005).

Demographic Variables

Insomnia is among the most frequent complaints brought to the attention of health care practitioners and the most prevalent of all sleep disorders in the general population. Epidemiological surveys indicate that 6% of the adult population meet diagnostic criteria for insomnia, 12% report insomnia symptoms with daytime consequences, and an additional 15% are dissatisfied with their sleep (Ohayon, 2002). Other estimates indicate that between 9% and 12% of the adult population complain of chronic insomnia, with an additional 15% to 20% reporting occasional trouble sleeping (Ancoli-Israel & Roth, 1999; Gallup Organization, 1991; Mellinger, Balter, & Uhlenhuth, 1985). Insomnia is more prevalent among women, older adults, and patients with medical or psychiatric disorders (Ford & Kamerow, 1989; Simon & Von Korff, 1997). There is evidence, although preliminary given the cross-sectional method employed, that increased risk for insomnia is associated with being divorced, separated, or widowed, having a stressful lifestyle, physical inactivity, irregular bedtimes, alcohol dependence, heavy caffeine use, and cigarette smoking (Edinger & Means, 2005).

Impact of the Disorder

Chronic insomnia carries an important burden for the individual and for society, as evidenced by its negative psychosocial, occupational, health, and economic repercussions. For example, individuals with chronic sleep disturbances report more psychological distress and impairments of daytime functioning relative to good sleepers; they take more frequent sick leaves and utilize health-care resources more often than good sleepers. Persistent insomnia significantly heightens the risk of accidents (Ohayon, Caulet, Philip, Guilleminault, & Priest, 1997), is associated with prolonged use of hypnotic medications, and longitudinal studies indicate that insomnia heightens the risk of depression, anxiety, and substance-related problems (Becker, Brown, & Jamieson, 1991; Breslau, Roth, Rosenthal, & Andreski, 1996; Chang, Ford, Mead, Cooper-Patrick, & Klag, 1997; Ford & Kamerow, 1989; Mellinger et al., 1985; Simon & Von Korff, 1997; Vollrath, Wicki, & Angst, 1989; Weissman, Greenwald, Nino-Murcia, & Dement, 1997).

COGNITIVE BEHAVIOR THERAPY FOR INSOMNIA

Cognitive behavior therapy for chronic insomnia, which we will refer to as CBT-I, has been a topic of interest to researchers and clinicians for over 40 years. It is usually administered as a multicomponent treatment over 2 to 10 sessions in either individual (e.g., Edinger, Wohlgemuth, Radtke, Marsh, & Quillian, 2001) or group format (e.g., Espie, Inglis, Tessier, &

Harvey, 2001; Morin, Colecchi, Stone, Sood, & Brink, 1999). However, many RCTs have compared the efficacy of one component to another with more recent studies examining the efficacy of a combination of the components. The components that can be included under the umbrella of CBT-I are briefly described next. These components have been described in full elsewhere (e.g., Morin & Espie, 2003; Perlis, Jungquist, Smith, & Posner, 2005).

Stimulus control, developed by Bootzin (1972), involves the person with insomnia being asked to go to bed only when they are tired, to limit their activities in bed to sleep and sex, to get out of bed at the same time every morning, to not nap, and, when sleep onset does not occur within 10–15 minutes, patients are asked to get up and go to another room. The rationale underlying this treatment is that insomnia is the result of maladaptive conditioning between the environment (bed/bedroom) and sleep-incompatible behaviors (e.g., worry/frustration at not being able to sleep). The stimulus control intervention aims to reverse this association by limiting the sleep incompatible behaviors engaged in within the bedroom environment (Bootzin, 1972).

The *sleep restriction* component was developed by Spielman, Saskin, and Thorpy (1987). The aim of this intervention is to maximize sleep efficiency and the association between the bed and sleep. The treatment begins by restricting the time spent in bed to the person's estimated average amount of nighttime sleep. The aim is to bring the total amount of time in bed as close as possible to the total sleep time. As such, subsequent instructions may involve the time spent in bed being either increased (as the sleep becomes consolidated) or decreased (to further maximize sleep efficiency).

Sleep hygiene training involves providing education about behaviors known to interfere with sleep such as intake of caffeine, alcohol, and nicotine, daytime napping, variable sleep scheduling, exercise within 4 hours of bed, and reading while in bed. After the initial education session, monitoring these sleep-unfriendly behaviors on a daily basis is conducted to ensure patients improve the compatibility of their lifestyle with sleep.

Relaxation training can include progressive muscle relaxation, diaphragmatic breathing, autogenic training, biofeedback, meditation, yoga, and hypnosis. These interventions are designed to reduce psychophysiological arousal.

Paradoxical intention involves explicitly instructing patients to try to stay awake when they get into bed. The rationale underpinning this intervention is that the paradoxical instruction reduces the anxiety associated with trying to fall asleep causing the patient to relax and fall asleep faster (Ascher & Efran, 1978).

Cognitive restructuring, introduced by Morin (1993), aims to alter irrational beliefs about sleep and typically involves "providing accurate information and having the patient identify and rehearse alternative belief statements" (Bootzin & Rider, 1997, p. 327).

Taken together, the goal of CBT-I is to target those factors that are presumed to perpetuate or even exacerbate sleep disturbances, including maladaptive sleep habits and irregular sleep-wake schedules, dysfunctional beliefs, and hyperarousal.

Consensus Panel Recommendations

In 1999 a task force commissioned by the American Academy of Sleep Medicine published a review of studies that have evaluated the efficacy of psychological treatments published up to 1998 for chronic insomnia (Chesson et al., 1999; Morin et al., 1999). This has been updated to include the evidence published up to 2004 (Morgenthaler et al., 2006; Morin et al., 2006). Table 19.1 summarizes this evidence across both reviews. American Psychological Association criteria for a well-established treatment and a probably efficacious treatment were used (Chambless & Hollon, 1998). As evident in Table 19.1, empirically supported treatments for chronic insomnia include stimulus control, sleep restriction, paradoxical intention and relaxation, as well as the multicomponent CBT-I intervention. Moreover, these reviews establish CBT-I as an evidence-based treatment for (a) primary or psychophysiological insomnia, (b) insomnia associated with a medical or psychological condition or a mix of both, (c) insomnia among older adults and insomnia among chronic hypnotic uses, and (d) use in conjunction with hypnotic medication taper. The task force also concluded that CBT-I can be effectively implemented on a one-to-one basis, in groups, or in a self-help format. The gains made are well maintained in the short (1-3 months), intermediate (6 months) and long-term (>12 months) (Morin et al., 2006).

Systematic Reviews and Meta-Analyses

Evidence regarding the efficacy of CBT-I for insomnia has been summarized in several

TABLE 19.1 Summary of Practice Parameters for Psychological Treatments for Insomnia

Treatment	Up to 1998 (drawn from Morin et al., 1999)	1998-2004 (drawn from Morin et al., 2006)
Stimulus control	Well established	Well established
Relaxation	Well established	Well established
Paradoxical intention	Well established	Well established
Sleep restriction	Probably efficacious	Well established
CBT-I	Probably efficacious	Well established
Cognitive therapy	Not supported	Not supported
Sleep hygiene	Not supported	Not supported

meta-analyses and systematic reviews. Morin, Culbert, and Schwartz (1994) reviewed 59 studies (involving 2,102 patients) published from 1974 to 1993. Murtagh and Greenwood (1995) reviewed 66 studies published from 1973 to 1993. Smith et al. (2002) reviewed studies published from 1966 to 2000. They focused on 21 studies (total of 470 patients) that evaluated the acute treatment response of CBT-I and benzodiazepines or benzodiazepine receptor agonists for chronic insomnia. Irwin, Cole, and Nicassio (2006) compared the effect of CBT-I for individuals under versus over 55 years of age. The review covered publication dates of 1966 to 2004, involving 51 studies. Pallesen, Nordhus, and Kvale (1998) and Montgomery and Dennis (2008) also reviewed the efficacy of CBT-I for adults who are older than 60 years of age. Pallesen et al. (1998) reviewed 13 RCTs (published up to 1998 and involving 388 patients) and Montgomery and Dennis (2008) reviewed six RCTs involving 224 patients (published up to 2002).

Evidence from these meta-analyses indicate that CBT-I produces reliable changes in several sleep parameters, including sleep-onset latency (range of effect sizes: 0.88–1.05), number of awakenings (0.53–0.83), duration of awakenings (0.65–1.03), total sleep time (0.42–0.49) and sleep quality ratings (0.94–1.44). When transformed into a percentile rank, these data indicate that approximately 70% to 80% of insomnia patients benefit from psychological treatment. In terms of absolute changes, sleep-onset latency is reduced from 54–65 minutes at baseline to about 30–37 minutes at posttreatment. The number of awakenings decreases from 1.63–2.44 per night to 0.44–1.67 after treatment and duration of awakenings is decreased from 68–70 minutes at baseline to 30–38 minutes following treatment. Total sleep time is typically increased by a modest 30 minutes, from 5.5–6 hours to 5.8–6.5 hours after treatment.

CBT-I is clearly effective for adults regardless of age, although efficacy is slightly lower in older adults (Montgomery & Dennis, 2008;

Pallesen et al., 1998); however, the authors of these meta-analyses consistently note that while the majority of patients benefit from treatment, only a small proportion (20%–30%) achieve full remission and the overall average improvement is only about 50%–60%, a degree of change that is likely to be clinically significant but not enough to convincingly move the average patient in to the good sleeper range. Many patients continue experiencing residual sleep disturbances after treatment.

Randomized Controlled Trials

The reader is referred to Table 19.1 (Morin et al., 1999) and Table 19.2 (Morin et al., 2006) for a detailed review of the randomized controlled trials (RCTs) that have been completed prior to 2004. The overall picture that emerges from these reviews has already been summarized. Table 19.2 in this chapter provides an overview of the RCTs that have been completed since 2004. Clearly, evidence continues to accrue for CBT-I and several of its subcomponents. In the past few years there has been a particularly encouraging development; trials have been focusing on testing CBT-I for insomnia that is comorbid with a psychiatric or medical disorder. The results are very encouraging for patients with insomnia that is comorbid with: (a) fibromyalgia (Edinger, Wohlgemuth, Krystal, & Rice, 2005); (b) a range of medical conditions including osteoarthritis, coronary artery disease, or pulmonary disease (Rybarczyk et al., 2005); cancer (Espie et al., 2008; Savard, Simard, Ivers, & Morin, 2005); and (c) depression (Manber et al., 2008).

Single Subject Experimental Analyses

Several studies utilizing a multiple baseline design have been published. Baillargeon, Demers, and Ladouceur's (1998) study of 24 insomnia patients demonstrated that family physicians can administer stimulus control treatments effectively. Eighty percent of the participants reported improved sleep-onset

TABLE 19.2 Summary of RCTs of CBT-I From 2005 to 2008

Study	Sample Size (number, %female, mean age) Diagnosis	Treatment and Control Conditions	Treatment Duration and Longest FU	Outcome Measures	Main Findings
		Self-monitoring, audiotaped relaxation and self-monitoring	4 weeks, 20 months	Sleep diary; Structured Sleep History Interview, Sleep Questionnaire, SSS, SES, BSI	Significant improvement across treatment groups in WASO, TST, SE, SQ, insomnia frequency, and sleep self-efficacy expectations. No significant difference between the three groups. At FU, significant improvement in WASO, perceived insomnia frequency, and insomnia-related distress compared to controls.
		CBT, SH, UC	6 weeks, 6 months	PSG, sleep diary, actigraphy, ISQ, SF-36, MPQ, Brief Pain Inventory, POMS	CBT group showed 48% reduction in TWT. SE and SOL, TWT reduced by 20% in SH group and UC reduced by 3%. Fifty-seven percent of participants in the CBT group met subjective sleep improvement criteria (compared to 17% in SH and 0 in UC), and 43% met objective improvement criteria compared to 7% in SH and 0 in UC.
		CBT-group, self-help, information control	6 weeks, 12 months	Sleep diary, DBAS-10, Hospital Anxiety and Depression Scale	SOL and WASO were reduced by 41% and 50%, respectively. TST, SQ, and SE increased by 21%, 87%, and 21%, respectively. These changes were greater in CBT patients compared to the control group.
		Self-help by-treatment control	6 weeks, 6 months	Sleep diary, ISI, PSQI, BDI-II, STAI	The treatment group improved in WASO, decreased TWT by 20 minutes and increased TST by 21 minutes and SE by 4%. ISI and PSQI scores were reduced. No significant change occurred in the control group.
		Classroom CBT, home-based video CBT, delayed-treatment control	8 weeks, 4 months	Sleep log, PSQI, DBAS, Geriatric Depression Scale, BAI, Short-Form MPQ, Life Satisfaction Index-Short Form, SF-36	The video CBT group had significant changes comparable to the classroom CBT group in SOL, WASO, TIB, and PSQI and DBAS scores. Both groups obtained significantly better results than the delayed-treatment control.

(Continued)

464

TABLE 19.2 Summary of RCTs of CBT-I From 2005 to 2008 (*Continued*)

Study	Sample Size (enrolled/completed; % female; mean age); Diagnosis	Treatment and Control Conditions	Treatment Duration and Longest FU	Outcome Measures	Main Findings
Rybarczyk, Stepanski, et al. (2005)	92/88; 67.4%; 68.9; insomnia associated with a medical condition (osteoarthritis, coronary artery disease, or pulmonary disease)	CBT; SMW placebo control	8 weeks; no FU	Sleep diary; PSQI, Sleep Impairment Index, DBAS, POMS, Geriatric Depression Scale, SF-36, Sickness Impact Profile: Somatic Autonomy and Social Behavior subscales, Short-form MPQ	CBT group showed greater improvements in SE, SOL, WASO, TIB, and number of naps, as well as in PSQI, SII, and DBAS scores. Overall treatment efficacy rate was for 78% for CBT compared to 24% for SMW.
Savard et al. (2005)	57/53; 100%; 54; insomnia associated with a medical condition (breast cancer)	CBT; wait-list control	8 weeks; 12 months	Sleep diary; PSG; Insomnia Interview Schedule, SCID, ISI, HADS, MFI, European Organization for Research and Treatment of Cancer Quality of Life Questionnaire	Sleep diary: SE increased significantly by 15%, significant improvements in TWT, SOL, WASO, and PSG. Marginally significant improvements on SOL and TST. CBT participants also scored lower on the ISI and on depression and anxiety.
Germain et al. (2006)	35/35; 71.4%; 70.2; primary insomnia but without the medical or psychiatric exclusion criteria	Brief behavioral treatment of insomnia; information-only control	4 weeks; no FU	Pittsburgh Sleep Diary; PSQI, Hamilton Rating Scale for Depression, Hamilton Rating Scale for Anxiety	Significant reduction in SOL and WASO by 21.5 and 33.5 minutes, respectively, in the BBTI group. Trend toward increased SE but no statistical significance. TST did not increase significantly.
Sivertsen et al. (2006)	46/45; 47.8%; 60.8; primary insomnia	CBT; med (zopiclone); placebo medication control	6 weeks; 6 months	Sleep diary; PSG	PSG: CBT participants showed a significant reduction in TWT (52%) and increase in SE (9%), compared to a SE decrease in the zopiclone group. No changes in TST at posttreatment but the CBT group showed a significant increase at FU. The CBT group spent less time in slow-wave sleep. Sleep diary: TWT, TST, and SE improved in all groups with no significant group differences. At FU, CBT participants showed a significant increase in TST and decrease in TWT.

Study	Intervention	Duration, FU	Measures	Results
[illegible]	CBT, med, CBT and med (lorazepam/placebo ...)	5 weeks, 8 months	Sleep diary; PSG; Pre-Sleep Arousal Scale, DBAS, PSQI	At posttreatment. Med group showed shorter SOL, greater SE, and longer TST than the CBT group. At FU, the CBT group showed the greatest improvement with shorter SOL and higher SE, while the Med group returned to baseline levels. Combined group showed the greatest results at posttreatment but these changes were not maintained at FU.
[illegible]	Taper only, taper and self-help CBT	8 weeks, 6 months	Sleep diary, ISI, Clinical Institute Withdrawal Assessment-Benzodiazepines, BDI, STAI, SF-36	Taper and Self-help CBT group increased SE by 8% and decreased TWT by 55 minutes between pre- and posttreatment, while taper only group showed no improvement in SE and an increase in TWT of 13 minutes. 68.1% were drug free at posttreatment (no difference between groups). At FU, there was no significance difference in ISI scores between the groups.
[illegible]	1, 2, 4 or 8 CBT sessions, ... control	8 weeks, 6 months	PSG, sleep diary, actigraphy, ISQ, BDI, STAI, POMS, SES	Sleep diary: One- and four-session groups increased in SE (12% and 10%, respectively) and decreased in WASO (53.6 minutes and 52.4 minutes) and TWT (64.3 minutes and 58.5 minutes); four-session group decreased WASO (42.5 minutes). Actigraphy: One- and four-session groups decreased in TWT (21.3 minutes and 29.9 minutes); four-session group increased SE (4.7%). No other significant changes comparing CBT groups to WL, though eight-session group significantly decreased TST from baseline to FU. The four-session group was the only condition that had a significant improvement in SE and TWT at FU and thus proved most efficacious.
[illegible]	CBT in primary care, TAU	5 weeks, 6 months	Sleep diary, actigraphy, PSQI, HADS, Epworth Sleepiness Scale	CBT group showed reductions in SOL (39%) and WASO (35%) and an increase in SE (13%), with some loss of effect at FU. The

(Continued)

TABLE 19.2 Summary of RCTs of CBT-I From 2005 to 2008 (Continued)

Study	Sample Size (enrolled/completed; % female; mean age); Diagnosis	Treatment and Control Conditions	Treatment Duration and Longest FU	Outcome Measures	Main Findings
					TAU patients increased in WASO (10%) and had a no significant increase in SE (9.1%). Treatment response to CBT was favorable but effect sizes were lower than efficacy studies.
Espie et al. (2008)	150/128; 68.7%; 61; insomnia associated with a medical condition (cancer)	CBT; TAU	5 weeks: 6 months	Sleep diary; actigraphy; PSQI, Epworth Sleepiness Scale, HADS, Fatigue Symptom Inventory, Functional Assessment of Cancer Therapy	CBT was associated with a significantly higher reduction of 16 minutes in SOL and 38 minutes in WASO and increase of 10% in SE. TST increased in the CBT group but this was not significant. CBT participants also reported a higher quality of life posttreatment compared to TAU participants. Significance of results was maintained at FU.
Manber et al. (2008)	30/22; 61%; 35; insomnia comorbid with major depressive disorder	Med (escitalopram) and CBT; Med and Quasi-desensitization control therapy	12 weeks	Sleep diary; actigraphy; Hamilton Rating Scale for Depression, SCID, ISI	Med + CBT participants showed significantly greater improvement in TWT, SE, and SQ and ISI scores. The rates of remission of MDD and insomnia were higher in Med + CBT participants than in Med + control participants (62% vs. 33% and 50% vs. 8%). No significant changes were observed on TST.
Soeffing et al. (2008)	47/47; 63.8%; 64.3; primary insomnia	Multicomponent (Rel+SC+SH); placebo control	8 weeks: no FU	Sleep diary; Epworth Sleepiness Scale, Insomnia Impact Scale, Fatigue severity Scale, Geriatric Depression scale, STAI, SF-36	Significant improvement in the treatment group in SOL, WASO, and SE. No significant improvements in daytime function.

Abbreviations: BAI: Beck Anxiety Inventory; BDI: Beck Depression Inventory; BSI: Brief Symptom Inventory; CBT: Cognitive behavior therapy; FU: Follow-up; HADS: Hospital Anxiety and Depression Scale; ISI: Insomnia Severity Index; ISQ: Insomnia Symptom Questionnaire; MDD: major depressive disorder; Med: Mediation; SC: Stimulus control; MFI: Multidimensional Fatigue Inventory; Dysfunctional Beliefs and Attitudes about Sleep; MPQ: McGill Pain Questionnaire; POMS: Profile of Mood States; PSG: Polysomnography; PSQI: Pittsburgh Sleep Quality Index; Rel: Relaxation; SCID: Structured Clinical Interview for the *DSM-IV-TR*; SE: Sleep efficiency; SES: Self-Efficacy Scale; SF-36: 36-Item Short Form Health Survey; SH: Sleep hygiene; SMW: Stress management and wellness; SOL: Sleep-onset latency; SQ: Sleep quality; SSS: Stanford Sleepiness Scale; STAI: State-Trait Anxiety Inventory; TAU: Treatment as usual; TIB: Time in bed; TST: Total sleep time; TWT: Total wake time; UC: Usual care; WASO: Wake after sleep onset latency, and six of the seven patients using hypnotics at pretreatment had either reduced or stopped use by the end of treatment. Others have reported clinically significant improvements to sleep. This has been demonstrated in older adults who were given stimulus control and sleep education (Hoelscher & Edinger, 1988), individuals with insomnia and chronic pain who were given stimulus control and sleep restriction (Morin, Kowatch, & Wade, 1989), individuals with insomnia associated with traumatic brain injury who were given CBT-I (Ouellet & Morin, 2007), to facilitate benzodiazepine discontinuation (Morin, Colecchi, Ling, & Sood, 1995; CBT-I and supervised medication taper), and for women treated for nonmetastatic breast cancer (Quesnel, Savard, Simard, Ivers, & Morin, 2003; CBT-I). A multiple baseline design was also utilized by Relinger and Bornstein (1979) to evaluate 5 weeks of paradoxical intention with four patients. Improvements to sleep were observed and maintained at the 12-week follow up. Two other studies utilized a multiple baseline design to evaluate the utility of sequential treatment involving medication and CBT-I; these will be reviewed under the heading Sequential CBT-I and Pharmacological Therapies later.

To the best of our knowledge, the only study to use a reversal design (A-B-A-B) was reported by Haynes, Price, and Simons (1975). Following a two-week baseline, participants received 30-minute weekly sessions in which stimulus control instructions were delivered and compliance was monitored. When 5 consecutive days of stability in sleep were reached, participants were instructed to go back to using their pre-intervention patterns of behavior; care was taken not to suggest that this would reverse improvement to sleep. When there was a trend toward baseline levels of insomnia or 4 weeks had elapsed, stimulus control procedures were reinstated. Sleep improved in all of the four participants, but two did not demonstrate clear reversal trends. Several explanations were offered for the latter including that

improvements to sleep as a result of stimulus control may be resistant to reversing.

Meta-Analyses of Single Subject Experiments

The authors found no meta-analyses of single subject research.

COMPARISON BETWEEN CBT-I AND PHARMACOLOGICAL THERAPIES

As already reviewed, a meta-analysis of 21 studies ($N = 470$ patients) concluded that there were no differences in the short-term benefits of CBT-I and pharmacotherapy, except that CBT-I resulted in greater improvement on sleep-onset latency (Smith et al., 2002). It must be emphasized that this meta-analysis focused only on the *acute* effects of treatment (i.e., the effects prior to the cessation of treatment). This is important because the few studies that have compared longer term outcomes have indicated that the improvements observed following CBT-I are sustained, whereas the improvements observed via medications are lost once treatment has ceased (e.g., Morin et al., 1999).

Combined CBT-I and Pharmacological Therapies

Combined psychological and pharmacological interventions should theoretically optimize outcome by capitalizing on the more immediate effects of medication and the more sustained effects of psychological therapy. Again, few studies have addressed this issue. Those that have observed that long-term outcomes are more variable among patients receiving a combined intervention, relative to those treated with CBT-I alone, in that some patients remain well over time but others are at greater risk for relapse after discontinuation of medication (Hauri, 1997; Jacobs, Pace-Schott, Stickgold, & Otto, 2004; Morin et al., 1999). Thus, despite the intuitive appeal in combining treatment approaches, there is currently no evidence that adding medication to CBT-I produces an additive effect on long-term outcome, relative to CBT-I alone.

Sequential CBT-I and Pharmacological Therapies

Two studies using a multiple baseline design have addressed this issue. The first, reported by Vallieres, Morin, Guay, Bastien, and LeBlanc (2004), involved six participants who received one of the following treatment sequences across 10 weeks of treatment: A combined approach in which participants received both CBT-I and medication, an overlapping approach in which participants received medication for 5 weeks with CBT-I being introduced in the fourth week, and a sequential approach in which participants received medication for 5 weeks followed by CBT-I alone for 5 weeks. All approaches resulted in improvement to sleep, with a slight advantage to the overlapping sequence; however, in the sequential approach improvements to sleep were observed only after the introduction of CBT-I.

Vallieres, Morin, and Guay (2005) reported the results of 17 patients who received one of a slightly different set of treatments: medication for 5 weeks followed by combined CBT-I and medication for 5 weeks, combined treatment for 5 weeks followed by CBT-I alone, or CBT-I alone. Again, all treatments resulted in improved sleep, with an advantage to combined treatment followed by CBT-I alone. However, most of the sleep improvement was obtained after the introduction of CBT-I.

Before leaving this discussion comparing CBT-I with pharmacological treatments for insomnia, we note that two studies compared the acceptability of pharmacological and psychological interventions (Morin, Gaulier, Barry, & Kowatch, 1992; Vincent & Lionberg, 2001). In both studies, individuals were presented with descriptions of psychological and pharmacological treatments for insomnia and asked to make various ratings. In both studies, the psychological treatments were rated as a more acceptable form of treatment relative to pharmacological treatments. Also, dropout rates from studies of CBT-I are typically low (between 10% and 20%).

Open Trials and Case Series of CBT-I

Open trials and case series can be helpful for providing preliminary data on a newly developed or extended treatment. We found two studies published since the Morin et al. (2006) review that used this method to provide a preliminary test of extensions to CBT-I.

Taylor, Lichstein, Weinstock, Sanford, and Temple (2007) recruited 10 patients with insomnia and mild depression. Six sessions of CBT-I were administered. At posttreatment all patients showed significant improvement in sleep-onset latency, wake time after sleep onset, total sleep time, sleep efficiency, and sleep quality. Moreover, depression scores improved throughout treatment and were significantly lower at 3-month follow-up. Among the patients who completed CBT-I none met criteria for insomnia and 87.5% had normal depression scores. These improvements were maintained at 3-month follow-up. These findings are consistent with the RCT published by Manber et al. (2008) and summarized in Table 19.1.

Biancosino et al. (2006) examined the effect of two sessions of group psychoeducation involving stimulus control instructions, sleep restriction, and sleep hygiene for 36 severely mentally ill inpatients with comorbid insomnia. A reduction in the administration of hypnotic medications was observed, along with improvements in sleep-onset latency and time awake after sleep onset. These improvements in sleep were maintained at 3-month follow-up, indicating this brief psychoeducation intervention had significant effects on insomnia symptoms in patients with severe mental illness.

Open Trials and Case Series of Newer Psychological Treatments

Sleep retraining. Harris, Lack, Wright, Gradisar, & Brooks (2007) tested the effectiveness of Intensive Sleep Retraining in 17 patients with insomnia. The treatment involved *a single night* in which the participants stayed in the sleep lab. A minimum of 50 sleep onset retraining trials were delivered. Each involved the participant being asked to simply let themselves fall asleep. They were allowed to sleep for 3.1 minutes. Thirty minutes later the next trial was administered. This intervention is conceptualized as a method "to decondition the insomnia arousal response to the sleep onset attempt" (p. 282). The improvements to sleep were impressive, particularly given the time investment. Improvements were also noted in daytime functioning and psychological measures of fatigue and anxiety. These outcomes were maintained at the 2-month follow-up assessment.

Cognitive therapy. An open trial of 19 patients with chronic insomnia adapted the cognitive theory/therapy approach of Aaron T. Beck to insomnia (A. G. Harvey, Sharpley, Ree, Stinson, & Clark, 2007). A novel feature of this treatment is that half of the sessions target nighttime sleeplessness and half of the sessions targets daytime functioning. Significant improvement in both nighttime and daytime impairment was retained up to the 12-month follow-up. As evident in Table 19.1, no previous study has evaluated a purely cognitive therapy approach to the treatment of insomnia. However, these preliminary findings await replication in a RCT.

Mindfulness and acceptance-based approaches. Mindfulness-Based Stress Reduction (MBSR) (Britton, Shapiro, Penn, & Bootzin, 2003; Carlson & Garland, 2005), Mindfulness-Based Cognitive Therapy for Insomnia (Heidenreich, Tuin, Pflug, Michal, & Michalak, 2006), Acceptance and Commitment Therapy (ACT) for Insomnia (Akerlund, Bolanowski, & Lundh, 2005) and Mindfulness Meditation with CBT-I (Bootzin & Stevens, 2005; Ong, Shapiro, & Manber, 2008) are being developed as treatments for insomnia. These approaches have in common that they conceptualize insomnia as an inability to cognitively, emotionally, and physiologically deactivate or disengage (Lundh,

2005). Acceptance, rather than control and suppression of the thoughts, has been argued to facilitate deactivation and, in turn, promote sleep. Several open trials have reported promising results for providing training in meditation with CBT-I for chronic insomnia (30 patients, 6 weeks of treatment; Ong et al., 2008), administering mindfulness-based cognitive therapy for chronic insomnia (16 patients; Heidenreich et al., 2006) and for insomnia that is comorbid with an anxiety disorder (19 patients, 8 weeks of treatment; Yook et al., 2008). In addition, Akerlund et al. (2005) carried out a small pilot study of a five-session acceptance- and mindfulness-based treatment of insomnia with 10 participants. The results showed a significant decrease from to pre- to posttest for insomnia severity and a large and significant decrease on presleep cognitive arousal. On sleep diary measures, however, there were no significant differences from pre- to posttreatment.

EVIDENCE-BASED PRACTICES

The results for CBT-I and several of its subcomponents are very encouraging. Specifically, CBT-I (with or without relaxation), stimulus control, sleep restriction, relaxation, and paradoxical intention all meet the American Psychological Association criteria for a well-established treatment (Chambless & Hollon, 1998); however, there is clearly considerable scope for improvement. A proportion of patients fail to respond and even for those who do improve, the majority do not move into a category of *high end state functioning* nor do they meet criteria for a *good sleeper*. Hence, there is a critical need for treatment development research. More potent interventions need to be developed so that patients can be offered an optimal treatment (A. G. Harvey & Tang, 2003). Specific domains in which this work should focus include:

- We have reviewed preliminary evidence for a number of promising novel treatment approaches that await replication in RCTs that include appropriate controls for therapist attention, patient expectation, and passage of time. These novel approaches should be further developed and/or, if ready, tested in RCTs. The field would benefit from greater discussion of and openness to, new treatment approaches.

- While there is clear improvement in insomnia symptoms following CBT-I, there is currently limited evidence of further clinically meaningful changes. Hence, there is a need to examine the impact of CBT-I on daytime functioning, psychological well-being, and quality of life (Buysse, Ancoli-Israel, Edinger, Lichstein, & Morin, 2006).

- There is currently minimal evidence as to the mediators and moderators of change associated with CBT-I outcomes, although there are three studies that have reported correlates or predictors of improvement following CBT-I. In a follow-up study of patients who had completed CBT-I, Harvey and Payne (L. Harvey, Inglis, & Espie, 2002) identified self-reported use of stimulus control and sleep restriction to be the best predictor of improvement in sleep, and cognitive restructuring was the next best predictor. Two other studies have reported reduction in dysfunctional beliefs to be associated with the maintenance of improvement in sleep (Edinger et al., 2001; Morin, Blais, & Savard, 2002). Moreover, Verbeek, Schreuder, and Declerck (1999) found that there were more treatment responders among those who received the cognitive therapy component (83%) than among those who did not receive it (56%).

- Montgomery and Dennis (2008) raised concerns about the durability of CBT-I for older adults. They called for research on the utility of booster sessions as a method for enhancing the durability of CBT-I.

- Tailoring treatments to specific perpetuating factors has been tried in the past (e.g.,

Sanavio, 1988). In the ensuing years much continues to be learned about the measurement of specific perpetuating factors and the reversal of them in therapy. Hence, it may be profitable to revisit this issue.

- The cost effectiveness of CBT-I has not, to the best of our knowledge, been formally evaluated. This is an important domain for future research. It seems likely that CBT-I will be highly cost-effective given the evidence that it can be delivered in just four sessions (Edinger, Wohlgemuth, Radtke, Coffman, & Carney, 2007) and the improvements to sleep typically endure even up to 24 months posttreatment (Morin et al., 1999).

- Most outcome evidence available is derived from studies of primary insomnia, with sufficient attention to treatment efficacy for insomnia comorbid with psychiatric disorders. Studies published so far indicate that treating comorbid depression and insomnia not only improves the sleep but also improves the depression (Manber et al., 2008; Taylor et al., 2007).

Despite its high prevalence and negative psychosocial and economic impact, insomnia often goes unrecognized and remains untreated. In the NIMH survey of medication use, 7% of the respondents and only 15% of those reporting serious insomnia had used either a prescribed or over-the-counter sleeping aid within the previous year (Mellinger et al., 1985). Barriers to treatment seeking exist from both the perspective of the patient as well as the clinician (Stinson, Tang, & Harvey, 2006). From the patient's perspective, the most common barriers to treatment include: (a) perception of insomnia as benign, trivial, or as a problem one should be able to cope with alone (Ancoli-Israel & Roth, 1999; Stinson et al., 2006); (b) lack of awareness of available treatment options (Morin et al., 1992); (c) perception of available treatment options as ineffective (Israel & Lieberman, 2004); (d) perception of available treatment options as unattractive (Morin et al., 1992); (e) personal constraints on treatment seeking (Shochat, Umphress, Israel, & Ancoli-Israel, 1999); and, although not yet examined in the insomnia literature, (f) stigma surrounding psychological difficulties may also be a barrier to treatment seeking (Hinshaw & Cicchetti, 2000). From the clinician's perspective, the most common barriers to treatment have been identified as: (a) primary care physicians having poor knowledge of sleep disorders (Benca, 2005; Léger, 2000; Papp, Penrod, & Strohl, 2002; Rosen, Rosekind, Rosevear, Cole, & Dement, 1993), (b) a lack of clear consensus on diagnostic criteria for insomnia (Israel & Lieberman, 2004; Léger, 2000), (c) primary care physicians considering insomnia to be secondary to other diagnoses (Léger, 2000), and (d) time in a primary care consultation being too short and primary care physician workload being too high (Benca, 2005; Freeborn, Hooker, & Pope, 2002).

Issues of the effective dissemination of CBT-I need to be addressed. Most individuals with insomnia who initiate treatment do so without professional consultation and often resort to a host of self-help remedies of limited benefit and questionable safety (e.g., alcohol, over-the-counter drugs, herbal/dietary supplements). When insomnia is brought to professional attention, typically to a primary care physician (Stinson et al., 2006), treatment is usually limited to pharmacotherapy. More than 50% of patients who consult their physician are prescribed a medication intended to improve sleep (hypnotics, sedating anti-depressants) (Hohagen et al., 1993; Ohayon & Caulet, 1996). Although health care professionals are receptive to non-drug therapies for insomnia, nonpharmacological interventions are not well known and are infrequently used in clinical practice (Rothenberg, 1992). The exception is the general sleep hygiene recommendations, but these are not empirically supported when delivered alone (see Table 19.1). Hence, disseminating the skills involved in delivering CBT-I is an important public

health issue. Traditionally CBT-I has been delivered by clinical psychologists. We have reviewed evidence that CBT-I can be effectively delivered by nurses (Espie et al., 2001; Espie et al., 2007) and physicians (Baillargeon et al., 1998). While these are positive steps in increasing the availability of CBT-I, there has been controversy about training methods and standards to ensure an adequate dose of CBT-I is delivered.

REFERENCES

Akerlund, R., Bolanowski, L., & Lundh, L. G. (2005). [A pilot study of an ACT-inspired approach to the treatment of insomnia]. Unpublished raw data.

American Academy of Sleep Medicine. (2005). *International classification of sleep disorders:Diagnostic and coding manual* (2nd ed.).Westchester, IL: Author.

American Psychiatric Association. (2000). *Diagnostic and statistical manual of mental disorders* (4th ed., text rev.). Washington, DC: Author.

Ancoli-Israel, S., & Roth, T. (1999). Characteristics of insomnia in the United States: Results of the 1991 National Sleep Foundation Survey. *Sleep, 22* (Suppl. 2), S347–S353.

Ascher, L. M., & Efran, J. (1978). The use of paradoxical intention in cases of delayed sleep onset insomnia. *Journal of Consulting and Clinical Psychology, 46,* 547–550.

Baillargeon, L., Demers, M., & Ladouceur, R. (1998). Stimulus-control: Nonpharmacologic treatment for insomnia. *Canadian Family Physician, 44,* 73–79.

Becker, P., Brown, W., & Jamieson, A. (1991). Impact of insomnia: Assessment with the sickness impact profile. *Sleep Research, 20,* 206.

Belleville, G., Guay, C., Guay, B., & Morin, C. M. (2007). Hypnotic taper with or without self-help treatment of insomnia: A randomized clinical trial. *Journal of Consulting Clinical Psychology, 75,* 425–438.

Benca, R. M. (2005). Diagnoses and treatment of chronic insomnia: A review. *Psychiatric Services, 56,* 332–343.

Biancosino, B., Rocchi, D., Dona, S., Kotrotsiou, V., Marmai, L., & Grassi, L. (2006). Efficacy of a short-term psychoeducational intervention for persistent non-organic insomnia in severely mentally ill patients: A pilot study. *European Psychiatry, 21,* 460–462.

Bootzin, R. R. (1972). Stimulus-control treatment for insomnia. *Proceedings of the American Psychological Association, 7,* 395–396.

Bootzin, R. R., & Rider, S. P. (1997). Behavioral techniques and biofeedback for insomnia. In M. R. Pressman & W. C. Orr (Eds.), *Understanding sleep*

The evaluation and treatment of sleep disorders (pp. 315–338). Washington, DC: American Psychological Association.

Bootzin, R. R., & Stevens, S. J. (2005). Adolescents, substance abuse, and the treatment of insomnia and daytime sleepiness. *Clinical Psychology Review, 25,* 629–644.

Breslau, N., Roth, T., Rosenthal, L., & Andreski, P. (1996). Sleep disturbance and psychiatric disorders: a longitudinal epidemiological study of young adults. *Biological Psychiatry, 39,* 411–418. doi:10.1016/0006-3223(95)00188-3

Britton, W. B., Shapiro, S. L., Penn, P. E., & Bootzin, R. R. (2003). Treating insomnia with mindfulness-based stress reduction. *Sleep, 26,* A309.

Buysse, D. J., Ancoli-Israel, S., Edinger, J. D., Lichstein, K. L., & Morin, C. M. (2006). Recommendations for a standard research assessment of insomnia. *Sleep, 29,* 1155–1173.

Carlson, L. E., & Garland, S. N. (2005). Impact of mindfulness-based stress reduction (MBSR) on sleep, mood, stress and fatigue symptoms in cancer outpatients. *International Journal of Behavioral Medicine, 12,* 278–285.

Chambless, D. L., & Hollon, S. D. (1998). Defining empirically supported therapies. *Journal of Consulting Clinical Psychology, 66,* 7–18.

Chang, P. P., Ford, D. E., Mead, L. A., Cooper-Patrick, L., & Klag, M. J. (1997). Insomnia in young men and subsequent depression. The Johns Hopkins Precursors Study. *American Journal of Epidemiology, 146,* 105–114.

Chesson, A. L., Jr., Anderson, W. M., Littner, M., Davila, D., Hartse, K., Johnson, S., . . . Rafecas, J. (1999). Practice parameters for the nonpharmacologic treatment of chronic insomnia. An American Academy of Sleep Medicine report. Standards of Practice Committee of the American Academy of Sleep Medicine. *Sleep, 22,* 1128–1133.

Creti, L., Libman, E., Bailes, S., & Fichten, C. S. (2005). Effectiveness of cognitive-behavioral insomnia treatment in a community sample of older individuals: More questions than conclusions. *Journal of Clinical Psychology in Medical Settings, 12,* 153–164.

Edinger, J. D., Bonnet, M. H., Bootzin, R. R., Doghramji, K., Dorsey, C. M., Espie, C. A., . . . American Academy of Sleep Medicine Work Group (2004). Derivation of research diagnostic criteria for insomnia: Report of an American Academy of Sleep Medicine Work Group. *Sleep, 27,* 1567–1596.

Edinger, J. D., & Means, M. K. (2005). Overview of insomnia: Definitions, epidemiology, differential diagnosis, and assessment. In M. H. Kryger, T. Roth, & W. C. Dement (Eds.), *Principles and practice of sleep medicine* (4th ed., pp. 702–713). Philadelphia, PA: Saunders.

Edinger, J. D., Wohlgemuth, W. K., Krystal, A. D., & Rice, J. R. (2005). Behavioral insomnia therapy for fibromyalgia patients: A randomized clinical trial. *Archives of Internal Medicine, 165,* 2527–2535.

Edinger, J. D., Wohlgemuth, W. K., Radtke, R. A., Coffman, C. J., & Carney, C. E. (2007). Dose-response effects of cognitive-behavioral insomnia therapy: A randomized clinical trial. *Sleep, 30,* 203–212.

Edinger, J. D., Wohlgemuth, W. K., Radtke, R. A., Marsh, G. R., & Quillian, R. E. (2001). Does cognitive-behavioral insomnia therapy alter dysfunctional beliefs about sleep? *Sleep, 24,* 591–599.

Espie, C. A., Fleming, L., Cassidy, J., Samuel, L., Taylor, L. M., White, C. A., . . . Paul, J. (2008). Randomized controlled clinical effectiveness trial of cognitive behavior therapy compared with treatment as usual for persistent insomnia in patients with cancer. *Journal of Clinical Oncology, 26,* 4651–4658.

Espie, C. A., Inglis, S. J., Tessier, S., & Harvey, L. (2001). The clinical effectiveness of cognitive behaviour therapy for chronic insomnia: Implementation and evaluation of a sleep clinic in general medical practice. *Behaviour Research and Therapy, 39,* 45–60.

Espie, C. A., MacMahon, K. M., Kelly, H. L., Broomfield, N. M., Douglas, N. J., Engleman, H. M., . . . Wilson, P. (2007). Randomized clinical effectiveness trial of nurse-administered small-group cognitive behavior therapy for persistent insomnia in general practice. *Sleep, 30,* 574–584.

Ford, D. E., & Kamerow, D. B. (1989). Epidemiologic study of sleep disturbances and psychiatric disorders. An opportunity for prevention? *Journal of the American Medical Association, 262,* 1479–1484. doi:10.1001/jama.262.11.1479

Freeborn, D. K., Hooker, R. S., & Pope, C. R. (2002). Satisfaction and well-being of primary care providers in managed care. *Evaluation and the Health Professions, 25,* 239–254.

Gallup Organization. (1991). *Sleep in America.* Princeton, NJ: Author.

Germain, A., Moul, D. E., Franzen, P. L., Miewald, J. M., Reynolds, C. F. III, Monk, T. H., & Buysse, D. J. (2006). Effects of a brief behavioral treatment for late-life insomnia: Preliminary findings. *Journal of Clinical Sleep Medicine, 2,* 403–406.

Harris, J., Lack, L., Wright, H., Gradisar, M., & Brooks, A. (2007). Intensive sleep retraining treatment for chronic primary insomnia: A preliminary investigation. *Journal of Sleep Research, 16,* 276–284.

Harvey, A. G. (2008). Sleep disturbance as a transdiagnostic process across psychiatric disorders. *Current Directions in Psychological Science, 17,* 299–303.

Harvey, A. G., Sharpley, A. L., Ree, M. J., Stinson, K., & Clark, D. M. (2007). An open trial of cognitive therapy for chronic insomnia. *Behaviour Research and Therapy, 45,* 2491–2501.

Harvey, A. G., & Tang, N. K. (2003). Cognitive behaviour therapy for primary insomnia: Can we rest yet? *Sleep Medicine Reviews, 7,* 237–262.

Harvey, L., Inglis, S., & Espie, C. A. (2002). Insomniacs' reported use of CBT components and relationship to long-term clinical outcome. *Behaviour Research and Therapy, 40,* 75–83.

Hauri, P. J. (1997). Cognitive deficits in insomnia patients. *Acta Neurologica Belgica, 97,* 113–117.

Haynes, S. N., Price, M. G., & Simons, J. B. (1975). Stimulus control treatment of insomnia. *Journal of Behavior Therapy and Experimental Psychiatry, 6,* 279–282.

Heidenreich, T., Tuin, I., Pflug, B., Michal, M., & Michalak, J. (2006). Mindfulness-based cognitive therapy for persistent insomnia: A pilot study. *Psychotherapy and Psychosomatics, 75,* 188–189.

Hinshaw, S. P., & Cicchetti, D. (2000). Stigma and mental disorder: Conceptions of illness, public attitudes, personal disclosure, and social policy. *Developmental Psychopathology, 12,* 555–598.

Hoelscher, T. J., & Edinger, J. D. (1988). Treatment of sleep-maintenance insomnia in older adults: Sleep period reduction, sleep education, and modified stimulus control. *Psychology and Aging, 3,* 258–263.

Hohagen, F., Rink, K., Kappler, C., Schramm, E., Riemann, D., Weyerer, S., & Berger, M. (1993). Prevalence and treatment of insomnia in general practice. A longitudinal study. *European Archives of Psychiatry and Clinical Neuroscience, 242,* 329–336.

Irwin, M. R., Cole, J. C., & Nicassio, P. M. (2006). Comparative meta-analysis of behavioral interventions for insomnia and their efficacy in middle-aged adults and in older adults 55+ years of age. *Health Psychology, 25,* 3–14.

Israel, A. G., & Lieberman, J. A. (2004). *Tackling insomnia: Diagnostic and treatment issues in primary care. Insomnia in primary care: A postgraduate medicine special report.* Minneapolis, MN: McGraw-Hill Healthcare Information Group.

Jacobs, G. D., Pace-Schott, E. F., Stickgold, R., & Otto, M. W. (2004). Cognitive behavior therapy and pharmacotherapy for insomnia: A randomized controlled trial and direct comparison. *Archives of Internal Medicine, 164,* 1888–1896.

Jansson, M., & Linton, S. J. (2005). Cognitive-behavioral group therapy as an early intervention for insomnia: A randomized controlled trial. *Journal of Occupational Rehabilitation, 15,* 177–190.

Leger, D. (2000). Public health and insomnia: Economic impact. *Sleep, 23*(Suppl. 3), S69–S76.

Lundh, L.-G. (2005). The role of acceptance and mindfulness in the treatment of insomnia. *Journal of Cognitive Psychotherapy, 19,* 29–39.

Manber, R., Edinger, J. D., Gress, J. L., San Pedro-Salcedo, M. G., Kuo, T. F., & Kalista, T. (2008). Cognitive behavioral therapy for insomnia enhances depression outcome in patients with comorbid major depressive disorder and insomnia. *Sleep, 31,* 489–495.

Mellinger, G. D., Balter, M. B., & Uhlenhuth, E. H. (1985). Insomnia and its treatment: Prevalence and correlates. *Archives of General Psychiatry, 42,* 225–232.

Montgomery, P., & Dennis, J. (2008). Cognitive behavioural interventions for sleep problems in adults aged 60+. *Cochrane Database of Systematic Reviews, 3,* CD003161.

Morgenthaler, T., Kramer, M., Alessi, C., Friedman, L., Boehlecke, B., Brown, T., . . . American Academy of Sleep Medicine. (2006). Practice parameters for the psychological and behavioral treatment of insomnia: An update. An American Academy of Sleep Medicine report. *Sleep, 29,* 1415–1419.

Morin, C. M. (1993). *Insomnia: Psychological assessment and management.* New York, NY: Guilford Press.

Morin, C. M., Beaulieu-Bonneau, S., LeBlanc, M., & Savard, J. (2005). Self-help treatment for insomnia: A randomized controlled trial. *Sleep, 28,* 1319–1327.

Morin, C. M., Blais, F., & Savard, J. (2002). Are changes in beliefs and attitudes about sleep related to sleep improvements in the treatment of insomnia? *Behaviour Research and Therapy, 40,* 741–752.

Morin, C. M., Bootzin, R. R., Buysse, D. J., Edinger, J. D., Espie, C. A., & Lichstein, K. L. (2006). Psychological and behavioral treatment of insomnia: An update of recent evidence (1998–2004). *Sleep, 29,* 1396–1406.

Morin, C. M., Colecchi, C. A., Ling, W. D., & Sood, R. K. (1995). Cognitive behavior therapy to facilitate benzodiazepine discontinuation among hypnotic-dependent patients with insomnia. *Behavior Therapy, 26,* 733–745.

Morin, C. M., Colecchi, C., Stone, J., Sood, R., & Brink, D. (1999). Behavioral and pharmacological therapies for late-life insomnia: A randomized controlled trial. *Journal of the American Medical Association, 281,* 991–999.

Morin, C. M., Culbert, J. P., & Schwartz, S. M. (1994). Nonpharmacological interventions for insomnia: A meta-analysis of treatment efficacy. *American Journal of Psychiatry, 151,* 1172–1180.

Morin, C. M., & Espie, C. A. (2003). *Insomnia: A Clinician's Guide to Assessment and Treatment.* New York, NY: Kluwer Academic/Plenum.

Morin, C. M., Gaulier, B., Barry, T., & Kowatch, R. A. (1992). Patients' acceptance of psychological and pharmacological therapies for insomnia. *Sleep, 15,* 302–305.

Morin, C. M., Hauri, P. J., Espie, C. A., Spielman, A. J., Buysse, D. J., & Bootzin, R. R. (1999). Nonpharmacologic treatment of chronic insomnia. An American Academy of Sleep Medicine review. *Sleep, 22,* 1134–1156.

Morin, C. M., Kowatch, R. A., & Wade, J. B. (1989). Behavioral management of sleep disturbances secondary to chronic pain. *Journal of Behavior Therapy and Experimental Psychiatry, 20,* 295–302.

Murtagh, D. R., & Greenwood, K. M. (1995). Identifying effective psychological treatments for insomnia: A meta-analysis. *Journal of Consulting Clinical Psychology, 63,* 79–89.

National Institutes of Health. (2005). NIH state-of-the-science conference statement on manifestations and management of chronic insomnia in adults. *NIH Consensus and State-of-the-Science Statements, 22,* 1–30.

Ohayon, M. M. (2002). Epidemiology of insomnia: What we know and what we still need to learn. *Sleep Medicine Reviews, 6,* 97–111.

Ohayon, M. M., & Caulet, M. (1996). Psychotropic medication and insomnia complaints in two epidemiological studies. *Canadian Journal of Psychiatry, 41,* 457–464.

Ohayon, M. M., Caulet, M., Philip, P., Guilleminault, C., & Priest, R. G. (1997). How sleep and mental disorders are related to complaints of daytime sleepiness. *Archives of Internal Medicine, 157,* 2645–2652.

Ong, J. C., Shapiro, S. L., & Manber, R. (2008). Combining mindfulness meditation with cognitive-behavior therapy for insomnia: A treatment-development study. *Behavior Therapy, 39,* 171–182.

Ouellet, M. C., & Morin, C. M. (2007). Efficacy of cognitive-behavioral therapy for insomnia associated with traumatic brain injury: A single-case experimental design. *Archives of Physical Medicine and Rehabilitation, 88,* 1581–1592.

Pallesen, S., Nordhus, I. H., & Kvale, G. (1998). Non-pharmacologial interventions for insomnia in older adults: A meta-analysis of treatment efficacy. *Psychotherapy: Theory, Research and Practice, 35,* 472–482.

Papp, K. K., Penrod, C. E., & Strohl, K. P. (2002). Knowledge and attitudes of primary care physicians toward sleep and sleep disorders. *Sleep & Breathing, 6,* 103–109.

Perlis, M. L., Jungquist, C., Smith, M. T., & Posner, D. (2005). *Cognitive Behavioral Treatment of Insomnia: A Session-by-Session Guide.* New York, NY: Springer-Verlag.

Quesnel, C., Savard, J., Simard, S., Ivers, H., & Morin, C. M. (2003). Efficacy of cognitive-behavioral therapy for insomnia in women treated for nonmetastatic breast cancer. *Journal of Consulting and Clinical Psychology, 71,* 189–200.

Relinger, H., & Bornstein, P. H. (1979). Treatment of sleep-onset insomnia by paradoxical instruction. *Behavior Modification, 3,* 203–222.

Rosen, R. C., Rosekind, M., Rosevear, C., Cole, W. E., & Dement, W. C. (1993). Physician education in sleep and sleep disorders: A national survey of U.S. medical schools. *Sleep, 16,* 249–254.

Rothenberg, S. (1992). A pilot survey in the medical community on the use of behavioral treatments for insomnia. *Sleep Research, 21,* 355.

Rybarczyk, B., Lopez, M., Schelble, K., & Stepanski, E. (2005). Home-based video CBT for comorbid geriatric insomnia: A pilot study using secondary data analyses. *Behavioral Sleep Medicine, 3,* 158–175.

Rybarczyk, B., Stepanski, E., Fogg, L., Lopez, M., Barry, P., & Davis, A. (2005). A placebo-controlled test of cognitive-behavioral therapy for comorbid insomnia in older adults. *Journal of Consulting Clinical Psychology, 73,* 1164–1174.

Sanavio, E. (1988). Pre-sleep cognitive intrusions and treatment of onset-insomnia. *Behaviour Research and Therapy, 26,* 451–459.

Savard, J., Simard, S., Ivers, H., & Morin, C. M. (2005). Randomized study on the efficacy of cognitive-behavioral therapy for insomnia secondary to breast cancer, part I: Sleep and psychological effects. *Journal of Clinical Oncology, 23,* 6083–6096.

Shochat, T., Umphress, J., Israel, A. G., & Ancoli-Israel, S. (1999). Insomnia in primary care patients. *Sleep, 22* (Suppl. 2), S259–S265.

Simon, G. E., & Von Korff, M. (1997). Prevalence, burden, and treatment of insomnia in primary care. *American Journal of Psychiatry, 154,* 1417–1423.

Sivertsen, B., Omvik, S., Pallesen, S., Bjorvatn, B., Havik, O. E., Kvale, G., . . . Nordhus, I. H. (2006). Cognitive behavioral therapy vs zopiclone for treatment of chronic primary insomnia in older adults: A randomized controlled trial. *Journal of the American Medical Association, 295,* 2851–2858.

Smith, M. T., Huang, M. I., & Manber, R. (2005). Cognitive behavior therapy for chronic insomnia occurring within the context of medical and psychiatric disorders. *Clinical Psychology Review, 25,* 559–592.

Smith, M. T., Perlis, M. L., Park, A., Smith, M. S., Pennington, J., Giles, D. E., & Buysse, D. J. (2002). Comparative meta-analysis of pharmacotherapy and behavior therapy for persistent insomnia. *American Journal of Psychiatry, 159,* 5–11.

Soeffing, J. P., Lichstein, K. L., Nau, S. D., McCrae, C. S., Wilson, N. M., Aguillard, R. N., . . . Bush, A. J. (2008). Psychological treatment of insomnia in hypnotic-dependant older adults. *Sleep Medicine, 9,* 165–171.

Spielman, A. J., Saskin, P., & Thorpy, M. J. (1987). Treatment of chronic insomnia by restriction of time in bed. *Sleep, 10,* 45–56.

Stinson, K., Tang, N. K., & Harvey, A. G. (2006). Barriers to treatment seeking in primary insomnia in the United Kingdom: A cross-sectional perspective. *Sleep, 29,* 1643–1646.

Taylor, D. J., Lichstein, K. L., Weinstock, J., Sanford, S., & Temple, J. R. (2007). A pilot study of cognitive-behavioral therapy of insomnia in people with mild depression. *Behavior Therapy, 38,* 49–57.

Vallieres, A., Morin, C. M., & Guay, B. (2005). Sequential combinations of drug and cognitive behavioral therapy for chronic insomnia: An exploratory study. *Behaviour Research and Therapy, 43,* 1611–1630.

Vallieres, A., Morin, C. M., Guay, B., Bastien, C. H., & LeBlanc, M. (2004). Sequential treatment for chronic insomnia: A pilot study. *Behavioral Sleep Medicine, 2,* 94–112.

Verbeek, I., Schreuder, K., & Declerck, G. (1999). Evaluation of short-term nonpharmacological treatment of insomnia in a clinical setting. *Journal of Psychosomatic Research, 47,* 369–383.

Vincent, N., & Lionberg, C. (2001). Treatment preference and patient satisfaction in chronic insomnia. *Sleep, 24,* 411–417.

Vollrath, M., Wicki, W., & Angst, J. (1989). The Zurich study. VIII. Insomnia: Association with depression, anxiety, somatic syndromes, and course of insomnia. *European Archives of Psychiatry and Neurology Science, 239,* 113–124.

Weissman, M. M., Greenwald, S., Nino-Murcia, G., & Dement, W. C. (1997). The morbidity of insomnia uncomplicated by psychiatric disorders. *General Hospital Psychiatry, 19,* 245–250.

World Health Organization. (1992). *International classification of diseases* (10th rev.) (ICD-10). Geneva, Switzerland: Author.

Wu, R., Bao, J., Zhang, C., Deng, J., & Long, C. (2006). Comparison of sleep condition and sleep-related psychological activity after cognitive-behavior and pharmacological therapy for chronic insomnia. *Psychotherapy and Psychosomatics, 75,* 220–228.

Yook, K., Lee, S. H., Ryu, M., Kim, K. H., Choi, T. K., Suh, S. Y., . . . Kim, M. J. (2008). Usefulness of mindfulness-based cognitive therapy for treating insomnia in patients with anxiety disorders: A pilot study. *Journal of Nervous and Mental Disorders, 196,* 501–503.

20

Pathological Gambling

BECKY L. NASTALLY AND MARK R. DIXON

Many people take risks of one sort or another each and every day of their lives. Often times these risks involve driving faster than the speed limit, making poor diet choices, or betting a few dollars on the night's lottery. When seemingly irrelevant and benign choices begin to accumulate into patterns of behavior that alter an individual's quality of life, it may be possible a problem or pathology has developed. Gambling, an activity that most individuals have engaged in during their lifetime, is a growing cultural issue. Once thought of as a taboo activity that drew images of mobsters and the Las Vegas strip, gambling is now available almost everywhere across the United States. Thirty years ago only two states in the country allowed any legalized form of gambling. Today that statistic has reversed. Gambling is now legal in 48 out of 50 states (Black & Moyer, 1998), all except for Utah and Hawaii, and Internet access allows residents anywhere an opportunity to wager. With such a rise in accessibility to gambling, a drastic increase in revenue has occurred. From 1999 to 2007, the amount of total gross gaming revenue in the United States nearly doubled from $58 billion to $92 billion (American Gaming Association, 2009).

Americans now spend more money on gambling than many other forms of entertainment (Ghezzi, Lyons, & Dixon, 2000). Casino expansion to places like the Midwest and the east coast of the United States is a multibillion dollar industry that not only showcases gambling but boasts fine dining restaurants, Las Vegas-quality live shows, world class shopping, and other adult recreational opportunities. In an economic downturn, proponents of casino expansion are quick to highlight the role of casinos in reinforcing the travel and tourism industry of any region. According to the 2009 State of the States Survey of Casino Entertainment conducted by the American Gaming Association, the majority of travel tourism professionals agrees that casinos contribute substantially to the amount of visitors states receive each year and 90% of those from non casino states assert that introducing legal gambling would attract much needed business from out of state tourists. It is in this way that increasing pro-gambling legislation is painted as a win-win situation.

Unfortunately, statistics on the costs of gambling are not reported as often. With the increased access to and greater legal, as well as social, approval of gambling, there has been a rise in rates of disordered gambling. For instance, in the United States, problem gambling is estimated to occur in 2.3% of the population (Kessler et al., 2008), while worldwide the rates of problem gambling are higher, ranging from 2% to 5% (Petry, 2005).

Additionally, economists estimated in 2004 that the social costs of gambling equaled close to $54 billion each year, which is half the annual cost of drug abuse in the United States. These figures include costs of gambling-related crime, opportunity costs in the form of lost work time, and bankruptcies and other financial hardships experienced by gambling addicts (Grinols, 2004).

In addition to societal costs, there are inherent costs to the individual who gambles pathologically. Studies show that gambling disorders can have detrimental effects on an individual as well as close friends and family members. For example, it has been found that individuals with gambling problems may have a higher rate of family-related dysfunction, including child or spousal abuse (Jacobs, 1989). Other potential side effects or consequences of gambling may include alcohol and other drug addictions (Hall et al., 2000), significant financial problems (Petry, 2005), and suicide or suicidal ideation (Phillips, Welty, & Smith, 1997). Yet another individual cost may include treatment for gamblers deemed as pathological.

Research has shown that specific demographics are associated with pathological gambling. For example, there has been evidence of a relationship between age and pathological gambling in that an early age of onset was associated with a higher likelihood of disordered gambling (Volberg, 1994). As for ethnicity, large-scale surveys have shown that nonwhite minorities gamble at higher rates than Caucasians (Welte, Barnes, Wieczorek, Tidwell, & Parker, 2001). Lower socioeconomic status (National Research Council, 1999) and divorce (Cunningham-Williams, Cottler, Compton, & Spitznagel, 1998) are also demographics consistent with increased levels of problem gambling. The bottom line of these findings is that poor minorities gamble; rich people do not. In essence, the gambling industry has created a tax on the uneducated without them knowing it.

ATTEMPTING AN EVIDENCE-BASED PRACTICE

From a psychological perspective, there are still many unanswered questions about pathological or problematic gambling. Its etiology and treatment continue to be a topic of theoretical discourse among researchers from all psychosocial paradigms; however, in recent years researchers in this area have made tremendous progress in assessing, manipulating, and treating the psychological processes involved in maintaining this behavioral pathology. Evidence-based practice requires the precursory steps of drawing from a well-documented and well-conducted literature base on the topic at hand. In the realm of pathological gambling, practitioners that need to carry out effective treatments should turn to the literature on gambling research. This research is comprised of three domains: assessment, psychological processes, and treatment.

The first step to an effective application of an evidence-based practice relies on accurate assessment of the disorder. Within the domain of pathological gambling, several assessment instruments have been developed that can aid the practitioner. After reliable and valid assessment has been completed, one must draw from the body of literature that has documented the various psychological, behavioral, and cognitive processes that impact an individual's potential for pathological gambling. This division of literature is vast and eclectic; however, common, overarching processes exist that, while discussed in differing vernaculars, are globally documented within the gambling research community. Finally, treatment models need to be considered. Ideally, treatment models will rest upon the former two components necessary for optimal evidence-based practice. Yet, this is not often the case. Treatment promotions are sometimes lacking in any linkage to assessment or process discoveries, and endorsement of such treatments should be tentative. In the pages that follow, we outline evidence-based assessment methods, process demonstrations and experimentations, as well as treatment model efficacy. Together, this information will allow the treatment provider to make sound scientific choices when providing care for persons with pathological gambling disorders.

EVIDENCE-BASED ASSESSMENT

Gambling is a principle inherent in nature.
—Edmund Burke,
House of Commons speech (1780)

The *Diagnostic and Statistical Manual for Mental Disorders* (4th ed., text rev.) (*DSM-IV-TR*) (American Psychiatric Association, 2000) has recognized pathological gambling as a disorder in its own right. This level of gambling is characterized by excessive talking, planning, and thinking about gambling, needing to gamble with increasing amounts of money to achieve the same effect, being repeatedly unsuccessful at attempting to reduce frequency of gambling, gambling as an escape-maintained behavior, experiencing significant financial hardship or loss of opportunity as a result of gambling, and lying to or jeopardizing relationships with close members of one's personal life regarding gambling. Despite the vast body of literature that exists on the comorbidity of pathological gambling and other mental disorders (Black & Moyer, 1998; Ibanez et al., 2001; Welte et al., 2001), surprisingly the aforementioned conditions must occur without being accounted for by a manic episode. Since the *DSM* describes mania as related to impulsivity, it seems it would be difficult in certain situations to reliably distinguish between the two.

The gravity of problematic gambling may also be determined through other avenues. For example, researchers Shaffer, Hall, and Van der Bilt, who conducted a study on the prevalence of disordered gambling in the United States and Canada in 1999, helped to conceptualize gambling behavior on a continuum or level system. Level 0 Gambling represents

individuals who have never gambled in their lifetime, Level 1 Gambling is considered social or recreational gambling that does not result in problematic behavior, Level 2 Gambling refers to behavior that could be problematic although specific descriptions vary; and lastly, Level 3 Gambling is characterized by significant problems and is associated with the terms *compulsive* and *disordered*.

Assessment instruments commonly used to evaluate gambling behavior are standardized questionnaires, such as the South Oaks Gambling Screen (SOGS) (Lesieur & Blume, 1987). The SOGS is a 20-item questionnaire that screens for gambling pathology. This assessment is the most widely used in the field (Shaffer, Hall, Vander Bilt, 1999), perhaps due to its ease of administration and a series of documented psychometric properties that appear to validate its use (see Gambino & Lesieur, 2006, for a complete review). For example, it has been shown to have high internal, criterion, and convergent validity when compared with the *DSM-IV* definition of pathological gambling. Scores on the SOGS range from 0 to 20 with at least a 5 characterized as a potential pathological gambler.

Like the SOGS, the Canadian Problem Gambling Index, or CPGI (Ferris & Wynne, 2001), is a standardized questionnaire but is unique in that it is characterized as a problem gambling indicator among populations that are not necessarily pathological. The CPGI is a 31-item questionnaire with a score between 8 and 27 being indicative of problem gambling. The psychometrics of the CPGI have been evaluated and it has been shown to have high internal consistency and good face, criterion-related, and predictive validity (Ferris & Wynn, 2001).

The Gambling Symptom Assessment Scale (G-SAS) (Stinchfield, Govoni, & Frisch, 2004) is an instrument that tracks self-reported urges and thoughts about gambling and was designed for individuals undergoing treatment. The questionnaire consists of 12 items that assess the frequency and strength of the urges as well as the individual's ability to control them. Response options range from 0 (none) to 4 (extreme) with the maximum score being 48 and scores above 31 being indicative of severe symptoms of gambling pathology. Psychometric assessment of the instrument has yielded positive results including good test-retest reliability and internal consistency (Stinchfield et al., 2004) as well as concurrent validity (Kim, Grant, Potenza, Blanco, & Hollander, 2009).

The aforementioned instruments seek to measure severity of gambling and/or urge to gamble; however, they do not allow for an identification of the causes or sustaining variables that produced and maintain the gambling activity. The GFA, or Gambling Functional Assessment (Dixon & Johnson, 2007), does in fact allow practitioners to identify potential environmental variables that maintain gambling behavior. This instrument is a 20-item survey that contains questions representing four separate hypothesized maintaining functions of gambling (attention, escape, sensory, and tangible). The person completing the assessment is asked to respond to each question as it applies to their own gambling behavior given the scale of 0 (Never) to 6 (Always). The highest score an individual may obtain on any one functional category is 30 and typically the highest scoring category is thought to indicate evidence of a particular maintaining function. Studies on the psychometrics of the GFA have yielded good internal consistency, test-retest reliability, and construct validity (Miller, Meier, Muehlenkamp, & Weatherly, 2009; Miller, Meier, & Weatherly, 2009).

While there is a series of assessments to evaluate gambling behavior directly, the practitioner may in fact find clients not willing to accurately report the severity of their problem. Furthermore, there are significant demand characteristics embedded in assessments that clearly require respondents to acknowledge that they have a problem with gambling. Recently, some researchers in the gambling community have suggested the utility of

evaluating correlations between gambling severity and results of assessments that do not directly measure gambling per se, but general impulsivity or risk taking. The literature on delay discounting, for example, is often associated with other impulse control disorders, such as alcoholism (Petry, 2001) and drug addiction (Madden, Bickel, & Jacobs, 1999). It is logical that a pathological gambling problem, one that not only could be conceptualized similarly but occurs very often comorbidly with the previous afflictions, also correlates with differences in the way an individual discounts larger, later rewards over sooner, smaller ones (see Madden, Ewan, & Lagorio, 2007). Whether this relationship is predictive in either direction remains to be verified; however, there is increasing evidence toward this assumption (e.g., Weatherly, Marino, Ferraro, & Slagle, 2008).

Another assessment that may correlate with rates of pathological gambling is the Iowa Gambling Task (IGT) (Bechara, Damasio, Damasio, & Anderson, 1994). This task assesses impulsivity as well; however, it uses a unique procedure to do so. While engaged in the task an individual must discriminate between monetary choices that consist of large, short-term gains that also include large losses, and consistent, small short-term gains with no losses. It is hypothesized that the non-impulsive person would be able to discriminate the more advantageous choice as the latter of the two. As one may predict, individuals who have substance abuse disorders, such as alcohol dependence and heroin addiction, tend to perform poorly on the task (Bechara et al., 2001; Petry, Bickel, & Arnett, 1998). Because pathological gambling highly correlates with these problems, it is logical to believe that problem gamblers may exhibit similar performances.

Recent data obtained using functional magnetic neuroimaging suggests that severity of gambling, as measured using the SOGS (Lesieur & Blume, 1987), also appears to be correlated with various brain activation levels when gamblers are engaging in actual gambling activity (Habib & Dixon, 2010). In summary, there is a series of simple-to-use validated questionnaires that directly measures gambling severity, perceived control over gambling, and the causes for gambling. When coupled with availability of supplemental indirect assessments of impulsivity and neurological make-up, the practitioner is well equipped to accurately identify if a given individual has a significant problem with excessive gambling behavior.

EVIDENCE-BASED PRACTICE ON GAMBLING PROCESSES

Even as I approach the gambling hall, as soon as I hear, two rooms away, the jingle of money poured out on the table, I almost go into convulsions.

Fyodor Dostoevsky,
The Gambler (1867)

Theoretical explanations of the processes that cause a person to become a pathological gambler vary widely. Ranging from personality to neurochemical levels, many disciplines of science have proposed underlying mechanisms that contribute to problem gambling. Perhaps the most well documented accounts come from the field of psychology. Psychology is undoubtedly a fractioned social science, yet a few fundamental gambling processes have been agreed upon. The vernacular changes across authors, and origination of the process as either being in the environment or within the gambler himself vacillates by subdiscipline, but what remains constant is empirical evidence that certain psychological variables affect the observed behavior of a person that ends up a pathological gambler.

Among a wide variety of processes hypothesized to play a role in the development of pathological gambling, perhaps one of the most pervasive is the illusion of control (Langer, 1975; Langer & Roth, 1975). The illusion of control is the idea that outcomes of pure chance can be dictated by the actions of an individual. So, an example of this within a

gambling context may be rolling the dice hard for a high number and soft for a lower number or choosing to push a button in order to stop the reels of a slot machine on command. Its pervasiveness lies in the fact that the gambling industry tends to foster this and other cognitive distortions, for example, by designing slot machines with stopping devices or making choice such a prominent aspect of many forms of gambling like the lottery or roulette. Some theorists posit this type of widely held illogical belief is a major determinant, and thus a cause of excessive gambling (P. H. Delfabbro & Winefield, 2000; Ladouceur & Walker, 1996). The data behind the theory of the illusion of control occurring in pathological gamblers to a greater extent than nonpathological gamblers has been mixed, however.

The gambler's fallacy, which is another example of illogical beliefs about the nature of how gambling outcomes are distributed, is the notion that following a string of losses, a gambler is bound or due to win eventually. This is, of course, contrary to the actuality that outcomes on any gambling device are randomly determined and each instance of play is entirely independent from the next. Still, many gamblers insist that a recent history of losses on a slot machine, for example, makes them more susceptible to winning. This notion is also perpetuated in the gaming industry. An example at many casinos is a posting of recent prior win locations on a roulette table insinuating that this has some effect on future outcomes, however, like the illusion of control, demonstrating this belief objectively in a laboratory using problem gamblers has proven to be rather complex.

One of the earliest behavior analytic studies to demonstrate the illusion of control was one done by Dixon, Hayes, and Ebbs (1998) using roulette players. During conditions the participants had a choice of selecting their own number bets or having the experimenter do so for them. Results indicated that all participants chose to engage in self-selected choice making despite the fact that the location of the wheel in which the ball lands is completely random in the game of roulette. Other studies have empirically demonstrated the illusion of control as well. For example, Wong and Austin (2008) sought out to replicate this finding and extend external validity by incorporating a casino-style roulette table and real Las Vegas dealer. The findings of this study determined that within a group of experienced roulette players, the two participants with the highest SOGS (Lesieur & Blume, 1987) scores chose to engage in illusory control options on almost every single trial. Such preference for self-determined gambling has also been demonstrated in pathological gamblers playing slot machines through the use of stopping devices among other gaming options (Johnson & Dixon, 2009).

Despite clear demonstrations of the illusion of control in gamblers in the aforementioned studies, there have been studies that have provided evidence against the theory as it relates only to gambling pathology. In a study on the role of experience in video poker players, both experienced and novice participants made statements regarding the luck of certain betting strategies as well as some consistent with the gambler's fallacy, but there was no significant difference between the groups according to how regularly they played (Weatherly, Austin, & Farwell, 2007). In a subsequent study on the role of illusory beliefs and mental illness (depression) in maintaining gambling, poker players were exposed to a series of conditions that consisted of: (1) being able to make all choices on their own with no information as to optimal play, (2) receiving information about optimal play by the experimenter but the ability to play how they wished, and (3) directions they must comply with the information given about optimal play (Dannewitz & Weatherly, 2007). Results of this study indicated that all participants actually gambled longer and made larger bets as their control over the game decreased. Thus, the data seemed to show that the loss of control, at least with the game of poker, actually reinforced gambling rather than the opposite.

Elusiveness of the illusion of control and the gambler's fallacy has also been observed within the cognitive literature. While some researchers have been successful in replicating seminal studies on the illusion of control occurring more often when players are more experienced or familiar with the task (Joukhador, Blaszczynski, & Maccallum, 2004), other studies have had great difficulty in doing so (Ladouceur, Mayrand, Dussault, Letarte, & Tremblay, 1984). Some researchers and theorists have suggested that these fallacies may be hard to capture because of the constraints of the laboratory. For example, P. Delfabbro (2004) points out that gambling experiments often take place in artificial or analog settings, novice gamblers are frequently selected as participants, and the function of gambling as a research participant differs substantially from the function of gambling under non-experimental conditions. These contextual variables may influence a behavior that is different from the one of interest.

Notwithstanding, illogical rule formation of pathological gamblers has been demonstrated in artificial contexts (Dixon et al., 1998; Johnson & Dixon, 2009; Wong & Austin, 2008). What is interesting is that in some of these studies, when behavior consistent with the illusion of control or gambler's fallacy occurred, often the experimenters were able to manipulate it. For example, response cost contingencies for engaging in these behavior patterns (i.e., having to forfeit chips in order to choose their own bets) were effective in reducing behaviors like choosing to roll the dice or pick the numbers instead of letting the experimenter make these decisions (Johnson & Dixon, 2009).

Additionally, research has been done on the effect of accurate versus inaccurate rules on gambling behavior prior to the occurrence of illusory control behavior (Dixon, 2000; Dixon, Hayes, & Aban, 2000; Weatherly & Meier, 2008). Dixon (2000) investigated the effect of rules on betting variations in the game of roulette. After participants had the opportunity to play the game without rules, only contacting the programmed contingencies of the game itself, accurate and inaccurate rules about the probabilities of winning given by the experimenter were introduced. Three main findings regarding rules came from the study. It was found that the number of trials played decreased following accurate as opposed to inaccurate rules, and both the number of chips each participant wagered and the self-reports of participants' winning varied with the rule condition.

In a similar study by Dixon, Hayes, and Aban (2000), the role of rules on roulette players' behavior was again evaluated only this time the game was computer simulated. In this study, programmed contingencies were experimentally compared with the introduction of self-rules in that across conditions, rules, as well as magnitude of payout value, varied. Results of this study (like those of Dixon, 2000) provided evidence that participants in a gambling context will follow rules (accurate or not) even after a prolonged exposure to programmed contingencies of the game itself. One more example of rule following in gamblers is one by Weatherly and Meier (2008). In a between groups design, this experiment evaluated the effect of differing types of accurate rules about slot machine play (independence of turns vs. diminishing returns vs. both) on participants' gambling persistence and risk taking. Results indicated that the introduction of accurate information about the game was successful in decreasing subsequent play, however, no significant differences were found between the types of information.

The findings from these studies on the manipulation of gambling behavior have implications that are both conceptual and clinical in nature. Of conceptual importance is that the ability to manipulate these illusory behaviors, or gambling behavior in general, through environmental contingencies provides evidence against conceptualizations of gambling that lie in the individual traits or personality of the gambler (e.g., Gupta, Derevensky, & Ellenbogen, 2006;

Loxton, Nguyen, Casey, & Dawe, 2008). It seems that illogical beliefs or affinities for gambling are not static characteristics of the organism, but rather dynamic behavior emitted according to the environmental contingencies or context.

Of clinical importance, especially toward evidence-based models of treatment for pathological gambling, is simply the demonstration of changes or reductions in behavior that can be made. Having said this, while research on basic gambling processes can inform treatments designed to address excessive gambling, there is still much work to do. For example, a significant portion of this research is conducted using non-problem gamblers. External validity of these studies is barred by ethical dilemmas that involve asking participants with a known pathology to engage in a behavior that has proven extremely detrimental to them; however, it is maintained that the literature provided here, which has not demonstrated that these findings should not generalize to pathological gamblers, has great potential for guiding a successful treatment regimen for problem gamblers.

When developing treatment components based on the documented processes described previously, clinicians should seek out ways to teach the client the dangers of beliefs in illusory control, how the gamblers fallacy is precisely that, and how despite contacting negative consequences of losing, they may still be driven to gamble. This determination to continue gambling appears to be based on irrational rules or beliefs about the game. Regardless if we call it an *illusion* or a *fallacy*, evidence tends to suggest that losses alone are not enough to keep people from gambling. Instead, the psychological processes of verbal behavior, self-rules, or conceptualizations about how they are doing while playing the game are what overrides the actual experience of the loss. It appears that only after sustaining considerable financial hardship that one may begin to question his/her own irrational beliefs, and begin the process of seeking treatment

EVIDENCE-BASED TREATMENTS FOR PATHOLOGICAL GAMBLING

> He was so sure he would lose that he had not played everything—as if to prolong the sensation of losing.
>
> —Andre Malraux,
> Man's Fate (1934)

Currently, practitioners use a number of different treatments for pathological gambling and there are two primary modalities: psychological and pharmacological. While both modalities seek to produce the same result, in the most basic terms a reduction in frequency of gambling, each does so differently. Psychological treatments work by manipulating an individual's environment and/or cognitions and pharmacological treatments work by changing the biology of the individual. The different treatment modalities pose some interesting questions about what it means to treat an individual who gambles excessively. For example, using pharmacological interventions implies that the cause or root of a gambling problem lies in abnormal levels of neurochemicals like serotonin. Focusing on interventions that deal with triggers in the environment, however, relies on the position that gambling is at least partly shaped by external contingencies. Another interesting issue is the appropriate goal of treatment and whether abstinence is a viable objective across individuals (see Ladouceur, Lachance, & Fournier, 2009).

In the description that follows, early and current trends in the treatment of pathological gambling are presented with examples of each that demonstrate effectiveness. The psychological treatments consist of early behavioral modification techniques, purely cognitive models, cognitive behavior therapy, and finally the 12-step model that was developed for use in alcohol and narcotic addiction. On the pharmacological side, studies are presented that have shown promise of treating excessive gambling using the medical model.

A meta-analysis of theory driven, psychological treatments of Pathological Gambling conducted by Pallesen, Mitsem, Kvale, Johnsen, and Molde, (2005) revealed an overall effect size of 2.01 (using 22 different studies that utilized some variation of cognitive, behavioral, or eclectic therapy, or a 12-step model). Based on these results, the authors concluded that psychological treatments seemed to be effective in the short and long term for addressing gambling problems; however, questions arise as to these claims. First, whether one of these psychological treatments is more effective than the other is an important question. Since the field of gambling treatment outcome research is relatively young, few studies have been conducted that directly compare different strategies. Second, these authors report a variety of different outcome measures utilized in the listed studies. These include meeting *DSM* criteria for pathological gambling, urges to gamble, and subjective ratings of improvement among many others. The difficulty is that studies utilizing different variables of change are difficult to compare.

Behavior Therapy

Behavior therapies were among some of the first treatments used by practitioners in the history of treatment for gambling. These included systematic desensitization, with and without exposure, and sometimes aversive conditioning of unwanted behaviors and thoughts. The goal of imaginal desensitization therapy (McConaghy, Armstrong, Blaszczynski, & Allcock, 1983) was to pair stimuli associated with addictive behavior with relaxation training in order to decrease anxiety. This technique relied on principles of classical conditioning. In a study evaluating desensitization therapy, McConaghy et al. (1983) first asked patients to imagine a scene that may occasion gambling behavior. Then, the experimenter presented segments of this scene and using 20-second intervals introduced relaxation techniques. One year following treatment, 70% of desensitization patients maintained gambling frequency reductions.

Although today the widespread use of aversion therapy has gone out of fashion, this technique was used for a variety of addictions in the early days of behaviorism. It too relies on the principles of respondent conditioning in that an aversive stimulus (such as electric shock or a noxious substance) is paired with stimuli associated with the addictive substance or behavior. One such study describes delivering shocks to a patient who reported compulsive gambling and problematic thoughts while he observed himself engaging in the behavior by way of video recording and simultaneously listened to auditory stimuli associated with gambling (Barker & Miller, 1966). After receiving a 10-day treatment with more than 450 shocks, the authors asserted the participant reported zero levels of gambling at 2-month follow-up.

Cognitive Therapy

Rather than environmental stimuli at the forefront of a conceptualization of gambling behavior, purely cognitive treatment for pathological gambling was developed with the gambler's illogical, and consequently maladaptive, cognitive belief system as the root of the problem (Hodgins & Petry, 2004). This basis for treatment was fortuitous in four randomized controlled trials conducted from 1996 to 2003 (Petry, 2005).

The first study by Echeburua, Baez, and Fernandez Montalvo (1996) examined the effects of stimulus control training with in vivo exposure, cognitive restructuring only, and a combination of these methods on gambling frequency in a wait-list control design. At 6-month follow-up, 75% of participants in the first condition abstained from or greatly reduced their gambling frequency while 63% and 38% of participants in the second and third groups, respectively, obtained the same results. Using a similar methodology, a study by Sylvain, Ladouceur, and Boisvert (1997) directly compared the effects of a treatment package consisting of cognitive restructuring, problem solving techniques, social skills training, and

relapse prevention against a wait-list control. Results of this trial indicated that nearly 40% of those participants in the experimental group reported a 50% improvement in five dependent variables related to gambling while only 6% of the control group made such gains.

More recently, Ladouceur and colleagues conducted two randomized studies that evaluated the effect of cognitive restructuring and relapse prevention on multiple measures of gambling as compared with a wait-list control both in an individual (Ladouceur et al., 2001) and group session format (Ladouceur et al., 2003). The findings of Ladouceur et al. (2001) determined that those in the treatment group made 25% greater gains than those in the control group and this effect was increased to 37% when the same format was delivered in a group format (Ladouceur, 2003). These studies outline the effectiveness of cognitive therapy and showcase different modes of treatment delivery.

Cognitive Behavior Therapy

While solely cognitive models have shown promise in treating gambling, current research is showing that when combined with behavioral therapeutic approaches the outcomes can be even more favorable. The principles of behavior analysis are not only undoubtedly involved in some of the studies conducted from a cognitive perspective cited earlier, but they also play a primary role in today's most widely accepted treatment for pathological gambling, cognitive behavior therapy, or CBT. Like many treatments for addiction, CBT as it is used with gambling mainly capitalizes on stimulus control and reinforcement. Since this therapy is now the most widely used intervention for psychiatric conditions, including addiction disorders (DeRubeis & Crits-Christoph, 1998), it is surprising that its use in gambling treatment has only recently come under widespread investigation.

CBT targets psychological problems from both a cognitive and behavioral theoretical framework. Specifically, gambling behavior is treated through awareness and manipulation of intermittent reinforcement, and illogical thought patterns and erroneous beliefs are restructured (Hodgins & Petry, 2004). To highlight, one technique that is utilized is trigger awareness. In behavioral terms, a *trigger* is no more than a simple antecedent condition in which gambling takes place in the presence of, and by rearranging one's environment it is hoped that these stimuli are removed or at least become less salient. Differential reinforcement of behaviors incompatible (DRI) and alternative to gambling (DRA) also represent aspects of treatment (Petry, 2005). From a cognitive perspective, a trigger is an increase in the level of arousal as gambling thoughts and urges increase, and the goal is to target this (Tavares, Zilberman, & el-Guebaly, 2003). CBT has been shown to be effective at reducing gambling in many controlled studies and what follows is a brief discussion of one recent and powerful demonstration of this strategy.

In 2006, Petry and her colleagues compared the effects of CBT versus Gamblers Anonymous (GA) in over 200 gamblers. Participants were assigned to one of three experimental conditions: GA referral, GA referral plus CBT workbook, or GA referral plus eight sessions of individual CBT. The primary dependent measures in the study included frequency of days as well as amount of money gambled. The groups of participants gambled on average 14 days a month with $1,200 at baseline. Data were also collected midtreatment (after 1 month), posttreatment, and at 6 months and 1 year following treatment. Results indicated that following treatment all groups showed some improvement; however, gambling in the groups exposed to one of the CBT components was reduced to a greater degree than those exposed to GA referral alone. Some of these effects were maintained at the 6-month and 1-year follow-ups (Petry et al., 2006) and other studies have observed similar results of CBT for the treatment of Pathological Gambling

(Milton, Crino, Hunt, & Prosser, 2002; Wulfert, Blanchard, & Martell, 2003).

Gamblers Anonymous

With the rise of applications of traditional 12-step models in the treatment of pathological gambling, it would be ill advised to omit it from the present discussion; however, because the present chapter is on evidence-based practice of treating gambling and no randomized controlled trials have been conducted evaluating its effect in isolation (Viets & Miller, 1997), it is presented last among other forms of psychological modes of treatment.

Gamblers Anonymous follows the model of Alcoholics Anonymous and reinforces meeting the requirements of each step in order to completely abstain from gambling (Petry, 2005). One study on the efficacy of GA that stands out is one by Stewart and Brown (1988) in which the attendance of three meetings over the course of 16 years was reported. Unfortunately, only 7% of the 232 attendees abstained from gambling at 1 year.

Gamblers Anonymous may be more effective as a supplemental treatment, perhaps as part of a package instead of in isolation (Petry, 2005). For example, Russo, Taber, McCormick, and Ramirez, (1984) conducted a study on the effectiveness of group and individual therapy combined with GA in 100 treatment-seeking gamblers and found that nearly 30% of the sample reported abstinence from gambling at the 1-year follow-up, and that GA attendance was correlated highly with the reported abstinence. Gamblers who attend GA have also been found to be more likely to seek professional treatment (Petry, 2003).

Pharmacological Treatment

No medication has been documented by the Food and Drug Administration (Hollander, Kaplan, & Pallanti, 2004) and no clinical trials have been conducted on the use of antipsychotics (Hollander, Sood, Pallatini, Baldini-Rossi, & Baker, 2005) for the treatment of pathological gambling. However, some small group and single case designs have noted self-reported behavior changes. Pharmacological treatments that are used for pathological gambling generally fit into the categories of various selective serotonin reuptake inhibitors (SSRIs), mood stabilizers, and opioid antagonists (Hollander et al., 2005). Such medical interventions may work to normalize levels of brain chemistry or to address co-occurring psychiatric conditions and reduce symptoms of gambling disorders.

Examples of the use of pharmacological treatments for excessive gambling include Grant and colleagues (2006) who experimented with use of the opioid antagonist, nalmefene, as an outpatient treatment for gambling symptoms. Within a 16-week, randomized double blind, placebo-controlled trial using 207 pathological gamblers, their results indicated a statistically significant difference in gambling severity among the groups and few side effects were reported using low doses of the drug (Grant et al., 2006). Another example (Hollander et al., 2000) documented a significant interaction effect between the order of administration of the drug and placebo. While there are exceptions (e.g., Grant et al., 2006), findings of many studies on the use of medical interventions for pathological gambling are weakened by methodological limitations (Hollander et al., 2005). In fact, the many criticisms include not using double blinds, vague descriptions of the characteristics of participants, inconsistence among treatment efficacy measures, and small N sizes (Grant, Kim, & Potenza, 2003). As a result, it appears that the understanding of medical drug-based treatment for pathological gamblers is in its infantile stage and a substantial amount of research still needs to be conducted.

A Possible Extension of Acceptance and Commitment Therapy

While the aforementioned treatment strategies are beneficial to a practitioner faced with

reducing gambling cognitions and behavior, it is possible that the best way to treat pathological gambling has not yet been determined. Thus, it is important to research other models of therapy in hopes of providing the best treatment for every individual. For example, to date there is increasing research on the efficacy of a treatment approach called Acceptance and Commitment Therapy (ACT) (Hayes, Strosahl, & Wilson, 1999) on many psychological problems, including substance abuse (Hayes et al., 2004), smoking (Gifford et al., 2004), and obsessive-compulsive disorder (Twohig, Hayes, & Masuda, 2006). In fact, ACT has been shown to be more effective on some measures than cognitive behavior therapy or 12-step models of treatment for a variety of outpatient problems (Hayes et al., 2004; Lappalainen et al., 2007) including pain tolerance (Masedo & Esteve, 2007). Therefore, in the paragraphs that follow we describe the ACT approach to psychological suffering and argue that this model may have utility in the treatment of pathological gambling.

ACT is a therapeutic approach to psychological problems that has been described as part of a third wave of behavioral and cognitive therapies, with philosophical roots in functional contextualism (Hayes, 2004). This therapy is practiced within an empirical foundation of Relational Frame Theory (see Hayes, Barnes-Holmes, & Roche, 2001), which is a post-Skinnerian, although behavioral, account of language and cognition. At the core of ACT are six basic psychological processes that include acceptance, defusion, self as context, contact with the present moment, values, and committed action (Hayes, Luoma, Bond, Masuda, & Lillis, 2006).

The first process, *acceptance*, is perhaps its most distinct feature separating it from a pure, cognitive therapeutic approach. Instead of the goal being to stop, control, or restructure unwanted thoughts, emotions, or urges, this process involves accepting these cognitions and actually experiencing them more fully. The second process of *defusion* targets harmful literal language (thoughts and other verbal behavior) serving as causal entities to behavior. For example, just because a person has the thought "they will die if they do not have a cigarette" does not mean that they will actually die and that because they had this thought, they must in fact smoke the cigarette. Work on the third process, *self as context*, focuses on identifying a transcendent sense of self, consciousness, or knowing rather than arriving at these things by way of surface level thoughts or other cognitions. Fourth, *contact with the present moment*, is the idea that much of psychological suffering can be defined as maladaptive perspective taking from either the past (as is often the case with depression) or the future (often the case with anxiety). Thinking in terms of one's situation in the present and letting direct contact with contingencies rather than thoughts dictate behavior is offered as a more adaptive alternative. The fifth and sixth processes, *values* and *committed action* are processes that promote committing to living a life that is important and having that, among other things, be a major predictor of the outcome of therapy. The order in which these processes occur here is for use of simple description and by no means dictates the order in which they should attempt to be moved in therapeutic contexts.

Given this description, it seems logical that ACT may be beneficial in the area of gambling for many reasons. Perhaps the most glaring is the focus on thoughts as determinants of behavior. Common cognitive distortions of some pathological gamblers, such as the illusion of control and the gambler's fallacy, have been discussed here and breaking down the causal relationship between thought processes and behavior would no doubt be advantageous. While some may argue that traditional CBT models could accomplish this just as well, there is evidence to suggest that avoiding or averting an individual's attention from urges or cravings can actually be counterproductive (see Masedo & Esteve, 2007). For this reason, an acceptance-based therapy may be preferable.

Additionally, contact with the present moment is not traditionally a process that is moved in CBT and may be of value in this context. For example, the behavior of *chasing wins* or adhering to the gambler's fallacy could be conceptualized as discounting the present in order to obtain probable outcomes in the future. By becoming more aware of the present moment, perhaps the negative consequences that have occurred as a result of excessive gambling can become more salient. And lastly, emphasizing the importance of living a valued life and contacting reinforcers other than those involved in gambling could also be used as an effective strategy in discouraging gambling.

A Proposed Model of ACT for Pathological Gambling

Accompanying in-session treatment according to the ACT model, one may use the self-monitoring of gambling behavior as well as gambling-related urges and acceptance strategies, homework that involves the use of experiential exercises, and the possibility of attending GA meetings to supplement the work being done in session. Use of an ACT protocol in the treatment of problem gambling has yet to be evaluated empirically in an experimentally controlled manner. It is our hope that the model will spark interest in practitioners who address gambling problems in private practice, as well as inspire gambling researchers to investigate alternative methods of treatment.

During the initial stages of this proposed gambling treatment, the therapist will spend time acclimating the client to the therapy by reviewing the history and scope of the gambling problem. This is done through awareness and ranking of the painful and difficult issues the client experiences as a result of gambling. This time should also be spent emphasizing the values in the client's life that may be currently neglected as a result of gambling. Over the next few sessions, the therapist works to establish the often detrimental relationship of gambling and language, and introduces the idea of experiential avoidance. The latter is a core assumption in the ACT model that trying to control or avoid one's own experience leads to more harm in the long run. Acceptance and willingness as alternatives to experiential avoidance as it relates to gambling urges and thoughts are offered to the client. This is done by undermining the practice of taking thoughts and urges as literal truths and this work is extended into later sessions. Treatment then progresses to the process of self as context as an alternative to defining oneself merely by a label. For example, in a gambling context such labels may be *gambling addict* or *too stupid to not realize I need to stop gambling*. During later sessions or final stages of treatment, the therapist and client begin to investigate and increase awareness of the client's personal values and work on committed action and maintenance of the ACT core processes.

EVIDENCE-BASED TREATMENTS FOR PATHOLOGICAL GAMBLING

In conclusion, assessment of and treatment for the pathological gambler is promising. The practitioner has many tools that can effectively identify the severity of and causes for problem gambling. After an evidence-based assessment, a treatment that is geared toward understanding by the client of the various psychological and biological processes at work will allow for a better chance of recovery from this disorder. Given the increase in access to legalized gambling, our society has an obligation to identify the most effective treatment for the many pathological gamblers who are unable to help themselves. This can only be possible through efforts on behalf of both researchers and clinicians dedicated to a goal of evidence-based treatment. On the clinician side, practicing therapy without an eye toward the current published literature that documents the most effective methods of care is risky. And, that is a gamble that no therapist should consider making.

REFERENCES

American Gaming Association. (2009). *2008 State of the states: The AGA survey of casino entertainment.* Retrieved from www.americangaming.org/assets/files/aga_2008_sos.pdf

American Psychiatric Association. (2000). *Diagnostic and statistical manual of mental disorders* (4th ed., text rev.). Washington, DC: Author.

Barker, J. C., & Miller, M. (1966). Aversion therapy for compulsive gambling. *British Medical Journal, 9,* 115.

Bechara, A., Damasio, A. R., Damasio, H., & Anderson, S. W. (1994). Insensitivity to future consequences following damage to the human prefrontal cortex. *Cognition, 50,* 7–15.

Bechara, A., Dolan, S., Denburg, N., Hindes, A., Anderson, S. W., & Nathan, P. E. (2001). Decision-making deficits, linked to a dysfunctional ventromedial prefrontal cortex, revealed in alcohol and stimulant abusers. *Neuropsychologia, 39,* 376–389.

Black, D. M., & Moyer, T. (1998). Clinical features and psychiatric comorbidity of participants with pathological gambling behavior. *Psychiatric Services, 49,* 1434–1439.

Cunningham-Williams, R. M., Cottler, L. B., Compton, W. M. III, & Spitznagel, E. L. (1998). Taking chances: Problem gamblers and mental health disorders results from the St. Louis Epidemiologic Catchment Area Study. *American Journal of Public Health, 88,* 1093–1096.

Dannewitz, H., & Weatherly, J. N. (2007). Investigating the illusion of control in mildly depressed and non-depressed individuals during video-poker play. *The Journal of Psychology: Interdisciplinary and Applied, 141,* 307–319.

Delfabbro, P. (2004). The stubborn logic of regular gamblers: Obstacles and dilemmas in cognitive gambling research. *Journal of Gambling Studies, 20,* 1–21.

Delfabbro, P. H., & Winefield, A. H. (2000). Predictors of irrational thinking in slot machine gambling. *Journal of Psychology, 134,* 17–28.

DeRubeis, R. J., & Crits-Christoph, P. (1998). Empirically supported individual and group psychological treatments for adult mental disorders. *Journal of Consulting and Clinical Psychology, 66,* 37–52.

Dixon, M. R. (2000). Manipulating the illusion of control: Variations in gambling as a function of perceived control over chance outcomes. *Psychological Record, 50,* 705–719.

Dixon, M. R., Hayes, L. J., & Aban, I. B. (2000). Examining the roles of rule following, reinforcement and pre-experimental histories on risk-taking behavior. *Psychological Record, 50,* 687–704.

Dixon, M. R., Hayes, L. J., & Ebbs, R. E. (1998). Engaging in "illusory control" during repeated risk-taking. *Psychological Reports, 83,* 959–962.

Dixon, M. R., & Johnson, T. E. (2007). The gambling functional assessment (GFA): An assessment device for identification of the maintaining variables of pathological gambling. *Analysis of Gambling Behavior, 1*, 44–49.

Echeburua, E., Baez, C., & Fernandez-Montalvo, J. (1996). Comparative effectiveness of three therapeutic modalities in the psychological treatment of pathological gambling: Long-term outcome. *Behavioural and Cognitive Psychotherapy, 24*, 51–72.

Ferris, J., & Wynne, H. (2001, February). *The Canadian Problem Gambling Index final report.* Phase II final report to the Canadian Inter-Provincial Task Force on Problem Gambling. Retrieved from www.ccsa.ca/2003%20and%20earlier%20CCSA%20Documents/ccsa-008805-2001.pdf

Gambino, B., & Lesieur, H. (2006). The south oaks gambling screen (SOGS): A rebuttal to critics. *Journal of Gambling Issues, 17*, 1–16.

Ghezzi, P., Lyons, C. M., & Dixon, M. R. (2000). Gambling from a socioeconomic perspective. In W. K. Bickel & R. E. Vuchinich (Eds.), *Reframing health behavior change with behavioral economics* (pp. 315–340). New York, NY: Erlbaum.

Gifford, E. V., Kohlenberg, B. S., Hayes, S. C., Antonuccio, D. O., Piasecki, M. M., Rasmussen-Hall, M. L., & Palm, K. M. (2004). Acceptance-based treatment for smoking cessation. *Behavior Therapy, 35*, 689–705.

Grant, J. E., Kim, S. W., & Potenza, M. N. (2003). Advances in the pharmacological treatment of pathological gambling. *Journal of Gambling Studies, 19*, 85–109.

Grant, J. E., Potenza, M. N., Hollander, E., Cunningham-Williams, R., Nurminen, T., Smits, G., & Kallio, A. (2006). A multicenter investigation of the opioid antagonist nalmefene in the treatment of pathological gambling. *American Journal of Psychiatry, 163*, 303–312.

Grinols, E. L. (2004). *Gambling in America: Costs and benefits.* Cambridge, England: Cambridge University Press.

Gupta, R., Derevensky, J. L., & Ellenbogen, S. (2006). Personality characteristics and risk-taking tendencies among adolescent gamblers. *Canadian Journal of Behavioural Science, 38*, 201–213.

Habib, R., & Dixon, M. R. (2010). Neurobehavioral evidence for the "near-miss" effect in pathological gamblers. *Journal of the Experimental Analysis of Behavior, 93*, 313–328.

Hall, G. W., Carriero, N. J., Takushi, R. Y., Montoya, I. D., Preston, K. L., & Gorelick, D. A. (2000). Pathological gambling among cocaine-dependent outpatients. *American Journal of Psychiatry, 157*, 1127–1133.

Hayes, S. C. (2004). Acceptance and commitment therapy, relational frame theory, and the third wave of behavioral and cognitive therapies. *Behavior Therapy, 35*, 639–665.

Hayes, S. C., Barnes-Holmes, D., & Roche, B. (2001). *Relational frame theory: A post-Skinnerian account of human language and cognition.* New York, NY: Kluwer Academic.

Hayes, S. C., Luoma, J. B., Bond, F. W., Masuda, A., & Lillis, J. (2006). Acceptance and commitment therapy: Model, processes, and outcomes. *Behaviour Research and Therapy, 44*, 1–25.

Hayes, S. C., Strosahl, K., & Wilson, K. G. (1999). *Acceptance and commitment therapy: An experiential approach to behavior change.* New York, NY: Guilford Press.

Hayes, S. C., Wilson, K. G., Gifford, E. V., Bissett, R., Piasecki, M., Batten, S. V., . . . Gregg, J. (2004). A preliminary trial of twelve-step facilitation and acceptance and commitment therapy with poly-substance-abusing methadone-maintained opiate addicts. *Behavior Therapy, 35*, 667–688.

Hodgins, D. C., & Petry, N. M. (2004). Cognitive and behavioral treatments. In J. E. Grant & M. N. Potenza (Eds.), *Pathological gambling: A clinical guide to treatment* (pp. 169–189). Arlington, VA: American Psychiatric Publishing.

Hollander, E., DeCaria, C. M., Finkell, J. N., Begaz, T., Wong, C. M., & Cartwright, C. (2000). A randomized double-blind fluvoxamine/placebo crossover trial in pathological gambling. *Biological Psychiatry, 47*, 813–817.

Hollander, E., Kaplan, A., & Pallanti, S. (2004). Pharmacological treatments. In J. E. Grant & M. N. Potenza (Eds.), *Pathological gambling: A clinical guide to treatment* (pp. 189–206). Washington, DC: American Psychiatric Publishing.

Hollander, E., Sood, E., Pallanti, S., Baldini-Rossi, N., & Baker, B. (2005). Pharmacological treatments of pathological gambling. *Journal of Gambling Studies, 21*, 101–110.

Ibanez, A., Blanco, C., Donahue, E., Lesieur, H. R., Perez de Castro, I., Fernandez-Piqueras, J., & Saiz-Ruiz, J. (2001). Psychiatric comorbidity in pathological gamblers seeking treatment. *American Journal of Psychiatry, 158*, 1733–1735.

Jacobs, D. F. (1989). Illegal and undocumented: A review of teenage gambling and the plight of children of problem gamblers in America. In H. J. Shaffer, S. A. Stein, B. Gambino, & T. N. Cummings (Eds.), *Compulsive gambling: Theory, research, and practice* (pp. 249–293). Lanham, MD: Lexington Books.

Johnson, T. E., & Dixon, M. R. (2009). Altering response chains in pathological gamblers using a response cost procedures. *Journal of Applied Behavior Analysis, 42*, 735–740.

Joukhador, J., Blaszczynski, A., & Maccallum, F. (2004). Superstitious beliefs in gambling among problem and non-problem gamblers: Preliminary data. *Journal of Gambling Studies 20*, 171–179.

Kessler, R. C., Hwang, I., LaBrie, R., Petukhova, M., Sampson, N. A., Winters, K. C., & Shaffer, H. J. (2008). The prevalence and correlates of DSM-IV pathological gambling in the national comorbidity survey replication. Psychological Medicine, 38, 1351–1360.

Kim, S. W., Grant, J. E., Potenza, M. N., Blanco, C., & Hollander, E. (2009). The gambling symptom assessment scale (G-SAS): A reliability and validity study. Psychiatry Research, 166, 76–84.

Ladouceur, R., Lachance, S., & Fournier, P. M. (2009). Is control a viable goal in the treatment of pathological gambling? Behaviour Research and Therapy, 47, 189–197.

Ladouceur, R., Mayrand, M., Dussault, R., Letarte, A., & Tremblay, J. (1984). Illusion of control: Effects of participation and involvement. Journal of Psychology, 117, 47–52.

Ladouceur, R., Sylvain, C., Boutin, C., Lachance, S., Doucet, C., & Leblond, J. (2003). Group therapy for pathological gamblers: A cognitive approach. Behaviour Research and Therapy, 41, 587–596.

Ladouceur, R., Sylvain, C., Boutin, C., Lachance, S., Doucet, C., Leblond, J., & Jacques, C. (2001). Cognitive treatment of pathological gambling. Journal of Nervous and Mental Disease, 189, 774–780.

Ladouceur, R., & Walker, M. B. (1996). A cognitive perspective on gambling. In P. M. Salkovkis (Ed.), Trends in cognitive and behavioural therapies (pp. 89–120). London, England: Wiley.

Langer, E. J. (1975). The illusion of control. Journal of Personality and Social Psychology, 32, 311–328.

Langer, E. J., & Roth, J. (1975). Heads you win, tails it's chance: The illusion of control as a function of the sequence of outcomes in a purely chance task. Journal of Personality and Social Psychology, 32, 951–955.

Lappalainen, R., Lehtonen, T., Skarp, E., Taubert, E., Ojanen, M., & Hayes, S. C. (2007). The impact of CBT and ACT models using psychology trainee therapists: A preliminary controlled effectiveness trial. Behavior Modification, 31, 488–511.

Lesieur, H. R., & Blume, S. B. (1987). The South Oaks Gambling Screen (SOGS): A new instrument for the identification of pathological gamblers. American Journal of Psychiatry, 144, 1184–1188.

Loxton, N. J., Nguyen, D., Casey, L., & Dawe, S. (2008). Reward drive, rash impulsivity and punishment sensitivity in problem gamblers. Personality and Individual Differences, 45, 167–173.

Madden, G. J., Bickel, G. J., & Jacobs, E. A. (1999). Discounting of delayed rewards in opioid-dependent outpatients: Exponential or hyperbolic discounting functions? Experimental Clinical Psychopharmacology, 7, 284–293.

Madden, G. J., Ewan, E. E., & Lagorio, C. H. (2007). Toward an animal model of gambling: Delay

discounting and the allure of unpredictable outcomes. Journal of Gambling Studies, 23, 63–83.

Masedo, A. I., & Esteve, M. R. (2007). Effects of suppression, acceptance and spontaneous coping on pain tolerance, pain intensity, and distress. Behaviour Research and Therapy, 45, 199–209.

McConaghy, N., Armstrong, M. S., Blaszczynski, A., & Allcock, C. (1983). Controlled comparison of aversive therapy and imaginal desensitization in compulsive gambling. British Journal of Psychiatry, 142, 366–372.

Miller, J. C., Meier, E., Muehlenkamp, J., & Weatherly, J. N. (2009). Testing the construct validity of Dixon and Johnson's (2007) gambling functional assessment. Behavior Modification, 33, 156–174.

Miller, J. C., Meier, E., & Weatherly, J. N. (2009). Assessing the reliability of the gambling functional assessment. Journal of Gambling Studies, 25, 121–129.

Milton, S., Crino, R., Hunt, C., & Prosser, E. (2002). The effect of compliance improving interventions on the cognitive behavioural treatment of pathological gambling. Journal of Gambling Studies, 18, 207–229.

National Research Council. (1999). Pathological gambling: A critical review. Washington, DC: American Psychological Association.

Pallesen, S., Mitsem, M., Kvale, G., Johnsen, B. H., & Molde, H. (2005). Outcome of psychological treatments of pathological gambling: A review and meta-analysis. Addiction, 100, 1412–1422.

Petry, N. M. (2001). Pathological gamblers, with and without substance use disorders, discount delayed rewards at high rates. Journal of Abnormal Psychology, 110, 482–487.

Petry, N. M. (2003). Patterns and correlates of gamblers anonymous attendance in pathological gamblers seeking professional treatment. Addictive Behaviors, 28, 1049–1062.

Petry, N. M. (2005). Pathological gambling: Etiology, comorbidity, and treatment. Washington, DC: American Psychological Association.

Petry, N. M., Ammerman, Y., Bohl, J., Doersch, A., Gay, H., Kadden, R., Steinberg, K. (2006). Cognitive behavioral therapy for pathological gamblers. Journal of Consulting and Clinical Psychology, 74, 555–567.

Petry, N. M., Bickel, W. K., & Arnett, M. (1998). Shortened time horizons and insensitivity to future consequences in heroin addicts. Addiction, 93, 729–738.

Phillips, D. P., Welty, W. R., & Smith, M. M. (1997). Elevated suicide levels associated with legalized gambling. Suicide & Life Threatening Behavior, 27, 373–378.

Russo, A. M., Taber, J. I., McCormick, R. A., & Ramirez, L. F. (1984). An outcome study of an outpatient treatment program for pathological gamblers. *Hospital and Community Psychiatry, 141,* 318–319.

Shaffer, H. J., Hall, M. N., & Vander Bilt, J. (1999). Estimating the prevalence of disordered gambling behavior in the United States and Canada: A research synthesis. *American Journal of Public Health, 89,* 1369–1376.

Stewart, R. M., & Brown, R. I. (1988). An outcome study of Gamblers Anonymous. *British Journal of Psychiatry, 152,* 284–288.

Stinchfield, R., Govoni, R., & Frisch, G. R. (2004). Screening and assessment instruments. In J. E. Grant & M. N. Potenza (Eds.), *Pathological gambling: A clinical guide to treatment* (pp. 169–189). Arlington, VA: American Psychiatric Publishing.

Sylvain, C., Ladouceur, R., & Boisvert, J.-M. (1997). Cognitive and behavioral treatment of pathological gambling: A controlled study. *Journal of Consulting and Clinical Psychology, 65,* 727–732.

Tavares, H., Zilberman, M. L., & el-Guebaly, N. (2003). Are there cognitive and behavioral approaches specific to the treatment of pathological gambling? *Canadian Journal of Psychiatry, 48,* 22–27.

Twohig, M. P., Hayes, S. C., & Masuda, A. (2006). Increasing willingness to experience obsessions: Acceptance and commitment therapy as a treatment for obsessive compulsive disorder. *Behavior Therapy, 37,* 3–13.

Viets, L., & Miller, W. R. (1997). Treatment approaches for pathological gamblers. *Clinical Psychology Review, 17,* 689–702.

Volberg, R. A. (1994). The prevalence and demographics of pathological gamblers: Implications for public health. *American Journal of Public Health, 84,* 237–241.

Weatherly, J. N., Austin, D. P., & Farwell, K. (2007). The role of "experience" when people gamble on three different video-poker games. *Analysis of Gambling Behavior 1,* 34–43.

Weatherly, J. N., Marino, J. M., Ferraro, F. R., & Slagle, B. (2008). Temporal discounting predicts how people gamble on a slot machine. *Analysis of Gambling Behavior, 2,* 135–142.

Weatherly, J. N., & Meier, E. (2008). Does providing accurate information about slot machines alter how participants play them? *Analysis of Gambling Behavior, 2,* 2–11.

Welte, J., Barnes, G., Wieczorek, W., Tidwell, M. C., & Parker, J. (2001). Alcohol and gambling pathology among U.S. adults: Prevalence, demographic patterns and comorbidity. *Journal of Studies on Alcohol, 62,* 706–712.

Wong, L., & Austin, J. L. (2008). Investigating illusion of control in experienced and non-experienced gamblers: Replication and extension. *Analysis of Gambling Behavior, 1,* 12–24.

Wulfert, E., Blanchard, E. B., & Martell, R. (2003). Conceptualizing and treating pathological gambling: A motivational enhanced cognitive behavioural approach. *Cognitive and Behavioral Practice, 10,* 61–72.

21

Adjustment Disorder

BRIAN P. O'CONNOR AND HILARY CARTWRIGHT

OVERVIEW OF DISORDER

Adjustment disorder (AD) is a severe emotional reaction to an identifiable stressor or stressors. Persons with AD experience distress but their stress-related symptoms do not meet the criteria for other, more specific disorders. Adjustment disorder differs from generalized anxiety disorder because it involves specific stressors. Adjustment disorder differs from posttraumatic stress disorder and acute stress disorder because stressors in AD are less intense. Challenging life events generate distress in perhaps most people. In persons with AD, distress is more persistent and impairing than is normatively the case.

Stressors in AD can be objectively traumatic but they can also appear relatively minor. Examples of stressors include romantic relationship breakups, failures in school, relocation to a new living or working environment, work problems, physical illness, marriage, divorce, becoming a parent, parental divorce, retirement, and military service. Clinicians and other observers should realize that how stressors are perceived and experienced by individuals matters more than the apparent objective features of the stressors. Chronic stressors are considered more likely to cause AD, but the effects are almost certainly moderated by social support.

The symptoms of AD can vary widely among persons with the AD diagnosis. Examples of emotional and cognitive symptoms include sadness, hopelessness, lack of enjoyment, crying episodes, irritability, anxiety, suicidal thoughts, worry, concentration difficulties, and feeling overwhelmed. Examples of behavioral symptoms of AD include sleep problems, fighting, reckless driving, mismanagement of finances, avoidance of family or friends, diminished school or work performance, truancy, and vandalism.

AD has been described as the *linchpin* between normalcy and major psychiatric disturbance. It straddles the border between significant morbidity and normal experiences of distress associated with acute and chronic stressors (Strain & Diefenbacher, 2008). It has also been described as a *cryptic* and *waste basket diagnosis* (Fard, Hudgens, & Weiner, 1979; Greenberg, Rosenfeld, & Ortega, 1995). Consequently, there has been much less research focusing specifically on AD than on other *DSM* disorders. The huge research literature in health psychology on coping with stressful life events is undoubtedly relevant. But relatively few of the published investigations in health psychology have focused on the unique features of AD as it is defined in the *DSM*.

DIAGNOSTIC CRITERIA

Adjustment disorder was introduced into American psychiatric nomenclature in the

Diagnostic and Statistical Manual (3rd ed.) (American Psychiatric Association, 1980), and it appears in the current *DSM-IV-TR* with only minor changes. The diagnostic criteria for AD in the *DSM-IV-TR* are:[1]

1. The development of emotional or behavioral symptoms in response to an identifiable stressor(s) occurring within 3 months of the onset of the stressor(s).
2. These symptoms or behaviors are clinically significant as evidenced by either of the following: (a) marked distress that is in excess of what would be expected from exposure to the stressor, or (b) significant impairment in social or occupational (academic) functioning.
3. The stress-related disturbance does not meet the criteria for another specific Axis I disorder and is not merely an exacerbation of a preexisting Axis I or Axis II disorder.
4. The symptoms do not represent bereavement.
5. Once the stressor (or its consequences) has terminated, the symptoms do not persist for more than an additional six months.

AD may be acute, and it is considered chronic when it lasts more than six months. There are six subtypes: (1) AD with depressed mood is when the predominant manifestations are symptoms such as depressed mood, tearfulness, or feelings of hopelessness; (2) AD with anxiety is when the predominant manifestations are symptoms such as nervousness, worry, or jitteriness, or, in children, fears of separation from major attachment figures; (3) AD with mixed anxiety and depressed mood is when the predominant manifestation is a combination of depression and anxiety; (4) AD with disturbance of conduct is when the predominant manifestation is a disturbance in conduct in which there is violation of the rights of others or of major age-appropriate societal norms and rules (e.g., truancy, vandalism, reckless driving, fighting, defaulting on legal responsibilities); (5) AD with mixed disturbance of emotions and conduct is when the predominant manifestations are both emotional symptoms (e.g., depression, anxiety) and a disturbance of conduct; and (6) unspecified AD, which is a category that is used for maladaptive reactions (e.g., physical complaints, social withdrawal, or work or academic inhibition) to stressors that are not classifiable as one of the other specific subtypes.

The *DSM* criteria for AD are considered by many to be too vague (Casey, Dowrick, & Wilkinson, 2001; Gur, Hermesh, Laufer, Gogol, & Gross-Isseroff, 2005; Jones, Yates, Williams, Zhou, & Hardman, 1999; Strain et al., 1998). Vagueness has both limited the volume of research on the topic and raised questions about the validity of AD as a psychiatric phenomenon. Our understanding of AD has also been limited by its frequent exclusion from psychometrically valid structured rating scales and clinical interviews. Development of reliable and valid assessment tools is necessary for more careful delineations of the AD construct. Clinicians and researchers need better diagnostic tools if they are to differentiate AD from major psychiatric disturbances and from normative adjustment reactions. Better diagnostic tools are necessary for differentiating between distress that will resolve on its own and distress that requires some level of intervention (Casey et al., 2001). Better diagnostic tools are required to more fully understand the impact that Adjustment Disorders have on individuals and society. Finally, better diagnostic tools are required for proper evaluations of the effectiveness of treatments for AD.

---

[1] The following list is reprinted with permission from the *Diagnostic and Statistical Manual of Mental Disorders, Fourth Edition, Text Revision* (Copyright © 2000). American Psychiatric Association.

DEMOGRAPHIC VARIABLES

There has been little epidemiological research on AD. The disorder has not been assessed in

TABLE 21.1   Prevalence Estimates for Adjustment Disorder

Authors	Client Population/ Setting	Methodology	N	Adjustment Disorder Diagnosis
APA (2000)	Children, adolescents, elderly	Not available	Not available	2%–8%
APA (2000)	General hospital inpatients	Not available	Not available	12%
APA (2000)	Mental health consultants	Not available	Not available	10%–30%
APA (2000)	Special medical groups	Not available	Not available	~50%
Almqvist, Puura, and Kumpulainen (1999)	8–9-year-olds in Finland	Parent interview	4,389	6.8%–7.7%
Bird, Canino, and Rubio-Stipec (1988)	Children and adolescents	Clinical assessment measures	2,036 households	4.2%–7.6%
Casey et al. (2006)	Epidemiological survey	Telephone and mail-out screening		< 1%
Doan and Petti (1989)	Clinical	Chart review	796	7%
Greenberg et al. (1995)	Psychiatric emergency service	Retrospective chart review	Not available	7.1% (adults) 34.4% (adolescents)
Hillard, Slomowitz, and Levi (1987)	Psychiatric emergency room	Chart review	100	13% (adults) 42% (adolescents)
Jacobson et al. (1980)	Pediatric patients	Clinical diagnosis	20,000	25%–65% of cases with a psychiatric diagnosis
McCauley, Russell, Bedford, Khan, and Kelly (2001)	General hospital, deliberate self-harm	Chart review	70	35.7%
Mezzich, Fabrega, Coffman, and Haley (1989)	Psychiatric outpatients	Semi-structured assessment form	11,282	10% (all ages) 16% (under 18 years)
Pelkonen, Marttunen, Henriksson, and Lonnqvist (2007)	Psychiatric outpatient clinic	Chart review	290	30.7%
Rait, Jacobsen, Lederberg, and Holland (1988)	Pediatric cancer patients	Chart review of psychiatry consultation/liaison referrals	58	5.2%
Rothenhausler et al. (2005)	Cardiac surgery patients	Prospective follow-up study	34	12.4%
Strain et al. (1998)	Consultation liaison psychiatry	Retrospective chart/ data base review	1,039	12%

the major epidemiological investigations, such as the Epidemiological Catchment Assessment and the National Comorbidity Survey. The demographic and risk factors for AD are consequently based on patterns derived from a variety of studies that have typically used specialized samples, which makes broad generalizations quite tentative.

Some trends have nevertheless emerged in the literature. Table 21.1 provides a summary of the prevalence estimates of AD that have been reported for community, psychiatric, and medical samples.

AD is a common diagnosis. The disorder can occur at any point in the life span, but it is more common in children and adolescents. Young people are vulnerable because they have less well-developed coping skills and resources. Among adults, AD is 2 times more common among women than among men and the reason for this difference remains unclear. AD is also more common among disadvantaged persons (Vanin, 2008) and among persons who have experienced previous traumas.

Casey et al. (2006) surveyed 14, 387 persons between the ages 18 and 64 in urban and rural regions of Britain, Ireland, Finland, Spain, and Norway. They found that adjustment disorder was evident in less than 1% of the survey respondents, and that it was not distinguishable from depressive disorders on a gold standard assessment measure of depressive symptoms. The authors suggested that the low prevalence of AD was possibly due to absence of specific criteria for AD diagnoses in both the *ICD-10* and *DSM-IV*. Casey et al.'s (2006) findings are in contrast with the more commonly mentioned 2%–8% range prevalence estimates of AD in the general population (see Table 21.1).

Estimates of prevalence of AD in child and adolescent community samples vary between 2% and 8% (APA, 2000; Strain & Newcorn, 2003). Perhaps the most elaborate investigation was conducted by Almqvist et al. (1999), who assessed the prevalence of psychiatric disorders in two birth cohorts of children in Finland. They found that AD was the third most common psychiatric diagnosis, with between 6.8% and 7.7% of children meeting the criteria for AD. Bird et al. (1988) used both structured and unstructured clinical assessment measures in a probability sample of 2,036 households in Puerto Rico. They found that between 4.2% and 7.6% of children met the diagnostic criteria for AD, with the variation in the estimates being due to the stringency of the scoring criteria for AD.

AD prevalence estimates are much higher in clinical samples than in community samples. Mezzich et al. (1989) surveyed the files on all patients at a university hospital clinic using a semistructured assessment form. Almost 10% of the sample of over 11,000 patients met the criteria for AD, which was the second most common diagnosis. Nine percent of the primary diagnoses were for AD. Only depression was more common than AD. AD was the sole Axis I disorder in 30% of the cases that met the criteria for AD. Strain et al. (1998) assessed the frequency of AD in psychiatric inpatient consultation-liaison settings at seven university teaching hospitals. They collected prospective data on 1,039 referrals and reported that 12% of their sample were confirmed cases of AD.

AD is typically reported to occur in 16% to 34% of child and adolescent psychiatric patients. In the Mezzich et al. (1989) study, 16% of the patients who were under 18 years of age met the criteria for AD. Pelkonen et al. (2007) collected prospective data on nonpsychotic adolescents referred for outpatient psychiatric interventions over a 5-year period in urban Finland. AD was the second most common diagnosis in their group of 290 adolescent outpatients, with 30.7% of adolescents receiving the diagnosis. Males with AD tended to have experienced occupational or school stressors, whereas females with AD more often experienced parental illness. A retrospective review of psychiatric emergency room hospital records by Hillard, Slomowitz, and Levi (1987) revealed that 42% of adolescents were diagnosed with AD, which was the most common diagnosis in the sample.

AD estimates sometimes reach the 50% range among patients coping with cancer, HIV, cardiac surgery, burns, or strokes (APA, 2000; Strain & Newcorn, 2003). Rothenhausler et al. (2005) conducted a prospective 12-month study on the psychiatric morbidity associated with cardiac and cardiopulmonary bypass surgery. Prior to surgical intervention, none of the patients met criteria for adjustment disorder. However, at discharge, 32.4% of participants met *DSM-IV* criteria for adjustment disorder with depressed features.

IMPACT OF DISORDER

Although persons with AD do not meet the criteria for other Axis I disorders, consequences of AD should not be considered mild, negligible, or signs of normal distress. AD can have adverse effects on close relationships, parenting, and academic and occupational performance. AD can involve an assortment of negative emotions including, as mentioned earlier, sadness, hopelessness, lack of enjoyment, crying episodes, irritability, anxiety, suicidal thoughts, worry, concentration difficulties, and feeling overwhelmed. AD can also involve an assortment of behavioral problems including sleep problems, fighting, reckless driving, mismanagement of finances, avoidance of family or friends, diminished school or work performance, truancy, and vandalism. It is also estimated that approximately 70% of persons with AD meet the criteria for at least one other Axis I disorder (Kryzhanovskaya & Canterbury, 2001). Most of the research has focused on suicide and on differences between AD and other disorders with regard to long-term outcomes. The primary studies will now be described.

Andreasen and Hoenk (1982) conducted a 5-year retrospective follow-up study of adults and adolescents with initial diagnoses of AD. They found that 71% of their adult sample was well in follow-up assessment, supporting the notion of time limited, situation dependent maladaptive reactions to stressors. Kovacs, Gatsonis, Pollock, and Parrone (1994) found that over 96% of patients recovered from a specific episode of AD. Bronisch (1991) followed persons with AD diagnoses for 5 years and found that 83% had favorable outcomes and did not go on to develop chronic mental health problems after they were discharged from a crisis stabilization unit. Only 17% developed chronic or severe problems, 2% committed suicide, and utilization of out-patient services was low. Similarly, Jones, Yates, and Zhou (2002) examined readmission

rates of adult inpatients with affective disorders and found that persons diagnosed with AD were less likely to be readmitted following discharge compared with individuals who were diagnosed with affective and anxiety disorders.

However, in the Andreasen and Hoenk (1982) study, 50% of adolescents with initial diagnoses of AD subsequently developed psychotic disorders, mood disorders, and/or antisocial personality disorder, and 29% were later diagnosed with significant substance abuse disorders. These findings suggest that a diagnosis of AD during adolescence should be considered a red flag for future, more serious mental illness.

Greenberg et al. (1995) reported corroborating findings. They found that adults diagnosed with AD had shorter index hospitalizations, and fewer hospital psychiatric readmissions and rehospitalizations than individuals with other psychiatric diagnoses. In contrast, adolescents with AD did not differ from comparison subjects with more serious diagnoses on readmissions or rehospitalization. Greenberg et al. (1995) also found evidence of diagnostic variability across time. Forty percent of patients admitted to a psychiatric emergency facility with diagnoses of AD were given different diagnoses by the time of their discharge. Additionally, of those diagnosed with AD on the initial hospitalization, only 18% were given this same diagnosis at readmission.

The findings for suicidal ideation and attempted suicide among persons with AD will likely surprise some readers. Although AD is often considered a milder diagnosis than other Axis I disorders, persons with AD nevertheless sometimes experience overwhelming despondency, agitation, and negative affect in response to stressors. Approximately 30% of patients with AD have suicidal ideation (Snyder, Strain, & Wolf, 1990). Among persons who attempt suicide, 58% meet the criteria for AD. Between 9% and 19% of persons who commit suicide have AD (Goldston, Daniel, Reboussin, Reboussin, Kelley, & Frazier, 1998). Psychological autopsies on persons with AD who commit suicide sometimes reveal a rapidly developed suicide progress with few prior indications of psychiatric problems (Portzky, Audenaert, & van Heeringen, 2005).

Kryzhanovskaya and Canterbury (2001) conducted a 1-year retrospective chart review of individuals admitted to a general hospital's psychiatric inpatient unit and compared persons with AD to persons with other psychiatric diagnoses. Persons with AD had significantly more suicidal ideation, a longer history of suicidal ideation, and a longer history of suicide attempts than individuals with alternate *DSM* Axis I diagnoses. McCauley, Russell, Bedford, Khan, and Kelly (2001) reviewed the files of patients admitted to a rural general hospital following incidents of deliberate self-harm. AD was the most common diagnosis, occurring in 35.7% of the sample. In a study of 140 patients hospitalized for deliberate self-poisoning, Mitrev (1996) found that his entire sample met the criteria for AD and that 18% had chronic AD. Most of the suicides were impulsive. A 5-year follow-up study found that hospital admissions for persons with AD were shorter and that 2% committed suicide, which was lower than the rate for major depression (Greenberg et al., 1995; see also Simons, Rohde, Kennard, & Robins, 2005).

Notable levels of suicidality have also been reported for adolescent referrals, inpatients, and outpatients (Greenberg et al., 1995; Pelkonen, Marttunen, Henrikson, & Lonnqvist, 2005, 2007). McGrath (1989) conducted a retrospective chart review of 325 consecutive hospital admissions for deliberate self-poisoning and found that 58% of the adolescents met the diagnostic criteria for AD. Runeson (1989) found that 14% of 58 consecutive adolescents and young adults who committed suicide met the criteria for AD. In fact, AD with depressed mood is the most common diagnosis in adolescents who attempt suicide (Bhatia, Aggarwal, & Aggarwal, 2000; Skopek & Perkins, 1998).

TREATMENT

By definition, AD begins within 3 months of the onset of an identifiable stressor and lasts no longer than 6 months after the stressor has ceased. Most people recover from AD without lingering symptoms if they have no previous history of mental illness and if they have stable social support. These facts have led some reviewers to claim that interventions for AD are not required unless the individual is acutely suicidal (Casey, 2001). However, a more widely shared view is that interventions are needed to alleviate distress and to reduce the risk of suicide and future psychopathology, especially among younger people.

Surveys of the attitudes of psychiatrists indicate that 65% recommend a combination of medication and psychotherapy (Horowitz, 1986; Uhlenhuth, Balter, Ban, & Yang, 1995). The remaining 35% recommend either no treatment at all or psychotherapy alone. The degree of functional impairment and the severity of the stressors are the determining factors in treatment recommendations. There has also been an increase in prescriptions of antidepressants for AD between 1985 and 1993–1994 (Olfson et al., 1998), with clinicians prescribing antidepressants for AD as they prescribe them for depression (Strain et al., 1998). Casey (2001) claims that this reflects a failure to appreciate AD as time-limited disorder and a failure to distinguish between mere symptoms of depression and true depressive illness.

There are very few treatment outcome studies for AD in the research literature, especially when compared with the large literatures that exist for the many other disorders that are covered in this handbook. At least four factors account for the paucity of research. First, AD is, by definition, a brief disorder that often disappears on its own. Second, AD is a reaction to stressors and is not a regular illness. Third, a very wide range of stressors can be involved in AD, making the population of AD sufferers quite heterogeneous. Treatment outcome studies would have to be designed for persons facing the same kind of stressors (e.g., divorce, cancer) and with roughly the same levels of impairment. Finally, persons with AD are sometimes included in treatment outcome studies for related disorders when they have relevant symptoms, such as anxiety or depression. These factors together have probably led many potential researchers to believe that treatment outcome studies for AD are either unwarranted, difficult, or unnecessary because the treatments that are effective for other *DSM* conditions should also be effective in treating milder versions of the same symptoms that emerge in cases of AD.

Paucity of treatment outcome research is a real problem for clinicians who need empirically validated methods for dealing with the distressed AD patients that they regularly see in their practices. Clinicians need to be able to do something other than simply say, "Go home, relax, you'll be fine in a few months" to patients in the midst of a *nervous breakdown*. The material that is presented in the following sections of this chapter is the best of the very small set of studies that have been published to date.

CONSENSUS PANEL RECOMMENDATIONS

Only one consensus paper on the treatment of AD has been published to date: the "Dutch practice guidelines for managing ADs in occupational and primary health care" (Van der Klink & van Dijk, 2003). These recommendations and guidelines were developed by a team of 21 occupational health physicians and one psychologist, with feedback from other physicians, psychologists, and psychiatrists. They were designed for occupational physicians and for general practitioners dealing with mental health problems. Evidence for the recommendations were based on just one randomized controlled trial (Van der Klink,

Blonk, Schene, & van Dijk 2003) and apparently on the recommendations that are commonly made in the psychiatric literature, which are discussed next. The Dutch panel recommendations center on a three-phase model, which was based on cognitive behavioral principles, stress inoculation training, and graded activity designed to enhance patient problem solving in their work environments.

The first phase is generally dominated by crisis, burnout, acute distress, or nervous breakdown. Patients are tired, disorganized, and the task for treating professionals is to move the client toward understanding and acceptance of the stressors that have led them to this point. The second phase of the intervention involves facilitating clients' insight into the stressors that have caused them distress, exploration of solutions, and the acquisition of skills to cope with the stressors in future. Clients are encouraged to make an inventory of stressors in any domain of their lives and to devise solutions that involve either manipulating or accepting the stressor. The third phase, rehabilitation, involves putting into practice solutions and skills that were developed in the second phase. Patients are actively engaged in their own interventions. The model is based on patients who have successfully recovered from ADs that have negatively impacted work functioning.

These Dutch panel recommendations are for managing ADs in occupational and primary health care settings. Formal panel recommendations are currently not available for general counseling and psychiatric contexts. We, therefore, now present a summary of the general recommendations that have been provided by diverse AD experts, including Casey (2001), Gur et al. (2005), Levitas and Hurley (2005), Schatzberg (1990), Stram and Newcorn (2007), Stram and Diefenbacher (2008), and Vann (2008). This panel has never met, but there are recurring themes that run through their recommendations and conclusions.

Primary goals of AD interventions are symptom relief, restoration of functioning, and prevention of the development of more serious disorders. The primary form of treatment is talking. Recommended treatments include individual psychotherapy (e.g., cognitive behavior therapy, relaxation techniques, dynamic supportive therapy), family therapy, and self-help/support groups. Medical crisis counseling and psychoeducation may benefit patients dealing with medical stressors. Approaches to AD-specific issues that are recommended in the literature were nicely summarized by Strain and Diefenbacher (2008):

> The treatment of AD rests primarily on psychotherapeutic measures that enable reduction of the stressor, enhanced coping with the stressor that cannot be reduced or removed, and establishment of a support system to maximize adaptation. The first goal is to note significant dysfunction secondary to a stressor and help the patient to moderate this imbalance. Many stressors may be avoided or minimized (e.g., taking on more responsibility than can be managed by the individual or putting oneself at risk by having unprotected sex with an unknown partner). Other stressors may elicit an overreaction on the part of the patient (e.g., abandonment by a lover). The patient may attempt suicide or become reclusive, damaging his or her source of income. In this situation, the therapist would attempt to help the patient put his or her rage and other feelings into words rather than into destructive actions and assist more optimal adaptation and mastery of the trauma-stressor. The role of verbalization cannot be overestimated in an attempt to reduce the pressure of the stressor and enhance coping. The therapist also needs to clarify and interpret the meaning of the stressor for the patient . . . . Otherwise, the patient's pernicious fantasies—"all is lost"—may take over in response to the stressor (i.e., the mastectomy) and make her dysfunctional in work and/or sex and precipitate a painful disturbance of mood that is incapacitating. (p. 124)

Interventions must be tailored for individuals depending on their current and historical difficulties. Brief, time-limited interventions are required that support the patient's efforts to identify and understand stressors, develop skills for managing and coping with challenges, and build supportive relationships to buffer against stressors. Other treatment goals include helping patients understand their roles in generating the stressful life events, reviewing and reinforcing the positive steps the patient has taken to deal with the stress, learning how to cope with and avoid stressors, and helping patients view their experiences as opportunities for development. Longer lasting interventions are recommended for clients experiencing chronic stressors or comorbid mental health challenges. Pharmacological interventions are often recommended as possible important adjuncts to psychotherapeutic interventions for patients experiencing high levels of distress. Family therapy is recommended for child and adolescent patients.

RANDOMIZED CONTROLLED TRIALS

Extensive searches of electronic databases in psychology and medicine revealed only four randomized controlled trial studies of psychotherapies for AD. The nature of the therapies and of the AD patients varied across these four studies. None of the studies was conducted on children with AD.

Van der Klink et al. (2003) evaluated the Dutch three-phase model of intervention for AD in the workplace (described earlier) using a prospective cluster randomized controlled trial design. The 192 participants were individuals who met the *DSM-IV* criteria for AD, who had missed at least two weeks of work because of their AD, who did not meet the criteria for other disorders, and who did not have a comorbid physical condition. Occupational physicians were randomly assigned to either a care-as-usual condition or to the model intervention condition. (The physicians were randomly assigned because the employers of the participants did not permit the assignment of their workers to other physicians.) There was not a no treatment control group in this study. The care-as-usual condition involved empathic counseling, instruction about stress, lifestyle advice, and discussions of work problems. Physicians in the model treatment condition received 3 days of training on the model intervention techniques. At 3 months, significantly more patients in the model treatment group than in the care-as-usual group had returned to work. At 52 weeks, all of the patients had returned to work, but there were fewer sickness leaves in the model treatment group than in the care-as-usual group. The AD recurrence rate was also lower in the model treatment group. However, there were no differences between the two conditions on patient self-report measures of symptoms. Symptom levels in both groups at the outset of the study were higher than the reference population norms, and the symptom levels in both groups decreased to normative levels over time.

The van der Klink et al. (2003) study was both an incomplete and a severe test of the treatment model. It was incomplete because there was no true control group. The test was severe because outcomes for the model treatment participants were compared with the outcomes for participants who experienced a care as usual intervention that was already known to be effective. The use of occupational physicians as the therapists for the intervention may have also attenuated the effects. It is possible that experienced psychologists may have learned and implemented the intervention model better than physicians.

De Leo (1989) randomly assigned 70 AD outpatients to five possible conditions: (1) psychoanalytically oriented supportive therapy, in which patients were seen twice per week over 4 weeks, (2) antidepressant medication, (3) benzodiazepine, (4) a methyl donor drug with antidepressant properties, or (5) a placebo pill condition. There was a range of AD stressors among the patients (who were apparently Italian), including marital and relationship problems, school problems, and financial difficulties. Self-report measures

of depression were obtained before and after a 4-week observation period. There were significant decreases in depression scores in all four treatment groups and in the placebo group. No one treatment was better than another treatment. Patients in the placebo improved as much as the patients in the treatment groups. Limitations with this study include the small and heterogeneous AD sample, the short intervention period, the use of just one self-report outcome measure, and a paucity of statistical analyses of the data. Psychoanalytically oriented supportive therapy is also not the kind of intervention that is recommended by most experts on AD.

Maina, Forner, and Bogetto (2005) examined the effectiveness of brief dynamic therapy (BDT) and of brief supportive therapy (BST) among 30 Italian patients with minor depressive disorders, which included AD, dysthymia, and minor depressive disorder. Patients were randomly assigned to one of the two treatment conditions or to a waiting list control condition. Self reports and clinician ratings of symptoms were obtained at baseline, at the end of treatment, and after 6 months. Patients in both the BST and BDT evinced better outcomes than those in the waiting list control group. At 6 month follow up, BST participants maintained their gains, while the BDT participants showed further reductions in depressive symptomatology. Unfortunately, the authors reported findings for their entire sample and the effects for just the AD patients are not available. The findings from this small sample investigation are nevertheless consistent with those on De Leo (1989) in suggesting the effectiveness of brief dynamic and supportive therapy.

There is only one published trial of treatments for AD in medical patients. Gonzalez-James and Turnbull Plaza (2003) examined the effectiveness of treatments for AD among 144 acute myocardial infarction patients. They randomly assigned the patients to one of four conditions: (1) a novel *mirror therapy*, (2) gestalt psychotherapy, (3) a discussion with a cardiologist regarding lifestyle changes, cardiovascular health, and rehabilitation; or (4) a wait-list control group. The mirror therapy involved efforts to "balance psychocorporal energy and create awareness of causes of physical symptoms" (p. 299), cognitive methods for enhancing disease acceptance and self-esteem, treatments to program new patient habits, increase medical treatment adherence and patient understanding of mental processes in depressive emotions, and use of a mirror to facilitate patient acceptance of the physical reality of their conditions. While patients in all three treatment groups improved over time, patients in the mirror therapy group displayed the greatest reductions in depressive symptoms and health concerns.

META-ANALYSES OF GROUP DESIGNS

There are no published meta-analyses of group design studies on AD.

SINGLE-SUBJECT EXPERIMENTAL ANALYSES

There are no single subject experimental studies of AD in the published literature. Descriptive case studies are nevertheless available. For example, Stricklin-Parker and Schneider (2005) used a cognitive behavioral intervention for a young woman with a primary diagnosis of AD with mixed anxiety and depressed mood, a history of unstable relationships and impulsivity, but no personality disorder. Twenty-four sessions were completed over 9 months that involved rapport building and several cognitive restructuring techniques. The therapist challenged automatic thoughts and corresponding negative emotional experiences that were associated with stressors involving financial difficulties, educational/occupational difficulties, and living arrangements. Using *collaborative empiricism*, the

therapist worked with the client to explore and challenge core beliefs, challenge automatic thoughts and a range of cognitive distortions that emerged from these core beliefs, and explored and engaged in planning for behavioral change that would reduce symptoms. Role playing was also used in preparation for the implementation of the planned behavioral changes. At the end of therapy, the client recognized the links between her thoughts, emotions, and behaviors. Her anxiety and depressive symptoms were dramatically reduced, and she had developed a rewarding romantic partnership. Powell and McCone (2004) presented a case study of cognitive behavior therapy with a 20-year-old male who developed AD with anxiety after the September 11, 2001, terrorist attacks. Allen (2000) published a case study of a brief cognitive behavioral intervention for a 10-year-old girl with AD that was triggered by family and interpersonal stressors.

META-ANALYSES OF SINGLE SUBJECT EXPERIMENTS

There are no published meta-analyses of single subject experiments on AD.

CONCLUSIONS

Almost every review of the literature in every discipline ends with a call for more research. These calls are typically made by conservative scientists who want more replications and more efforts to resolve conflicting findings. In this context, the need for treatment outcome studies on AD can truly be considered exceptionally strong and even dire. There are almost no AD treatment outcome studies to review and consequently no conflicting findings to resolve. The paucity of research is striking given the seriousness of AD. The disorder occurs in 2% to 8% of the general population and it is one of the most common, if not the most common, diagnosis among child and adult psychiatric patients. Adjustment disorder may involve serious personal distress, an assortment of cognitive and behavioral problems, nervous breakdowns, hospitalization, marital problems, job absenteeism, and more suicidal thoughts and suicide attempts than most other *DSM* disorders. Yet there have been only four randomized controlled trials of treatments for AD and only a handful of descriptive case studies!

A variety of factors is likely responsible for the limited number of studies on the topic. Adjustment disorder is a brief disorder that often disappears on its own, is a reaction to stressors, and is not a regular illness. A very wide range of stressors can be involved in AD, making the population of AD sufferers quite heterogeneous. Assessment and diagnostic tools for AD are not as well developed as the tools for other *DSM* disorders. Adjustment disorder patients are sometimes included in treatment outcome studies for related disorders, leading potential researchers to believe that the treatments that are effective for other *DSM* conditions should also be effective in treating milder versions of the same symptoms that emerge in cases of AD. These factors have together resulted in clinicians not having empirically validated treatment options for the many distressed AD clients that they regularly encounter in their practices.

Psychotherapy outcome studies are needed for the kinds of general treatments that are recommended for AD in the literature. Outcome studies should involve samples of AD patients that are homogeneous with regard to the nature of their stressors. The effects of AD treatments will presumably vary depending on whether the persons with AD are stressed by serious medical conditions versus psychosocial issues. Research is needed to identify the effective and noneffective components in treatment packages. We need more comparisons of psychotherapeutic interventions with pharmacological interventions. Only one small sample and flawed study of this kind has been published to date. Perhaps most important is the need for studies on the treatment of AD in children and adolescents. Younger people are most vulnerable to AD and are at greater risk for developing serious psychological problems once they have AD. Yet not a single psychotherapy outcome study on young people with AD could be found in the literature.

When the existing AD randomized controlled trial studies and descriptive case studies are considered in relation to the criteria for empirically validated treatments (Task Force on Promotion and Dissemination of Psychological Procedures, 1995; Chambless et al., 1996), the conclusion is obvious and grim. No treatment for AD can be considered empirically validated at the present time. At least two good between-group design experiments demonstrating efficacy are required, or a series of single case design experiments. No single case experiments exist, and no between-groups design experiment has been replicated. A further criterion for empirically validated treatments is that experiments must be conducted with treatment manuals. The creation of treatment manuals for AD would itself be a significant development in this field.

EVIDENCE-BASED PRACTICES

The following list of practices for AD cannot be considered evidence based because of the paucity of treatment outcome research on the disorder. Instead, the list is a summary of the most common recommendations that appear in the literature.

1. The primary goals of AD interventions are symptom relief, restoration of functioning, enhanced coping with the stressor that cannot be reduced or removed, establishment of a support system to maximize adaptation, and prevention of the development of more serious disorders.
2. The primary form of treatment is talking. Recommended treatments include individual psychotherapy (e.g., cognitive

behavior therapy, relaxation techniques, dynamic supportive therapy), family therapy, and self-help/support groups. Medical crisis counseling and psychoeducation may benefit patients dealing with medical stressors.

3. Other treatment goals include helping patients understand their roles in the stressful life events, reviewing and reinforcing the positive steps the patient has taken to deal with the stress, learning how to cope with and avoid stressors, and helping the patient view their experiences as opportunities for development.

4. Pharmacological interventions are often recommended as possible important adjuncts to psychotherapeutic interventions for patients experiencing high levels of distress.

REFERENCES

Allen, K. (2000). A brief cognitive-behavioral intervention for a 10-year-old child with an adjustment disorder: A case study. *Behavior Change, 17,* 84–89.

Almqvist, F., Puura, K., & Kumpulainen, K. (1999). Psychiatric disorders in 8–9-year-old children based on a diagnostic interview with the parents. *European Child and Adolescent Psychiatry, 8,* 17–28.

American Psychiatric Association. (1980). *Diagnostic and statistical manual of mental disorders* (3rd ed.). Washington, DC: Author.

American Psychiatric Association. (2000). *Diagnostic and statistical manual of mental disorders* (4th ed., text rev.). Washington, DC: Author.

Andreasen, N. C., & Hoenk, P. R. (1982). The predictive value of adjustment disorders. A follow-up study. *American Journal of Psychiatry, 139,* 584–590.

Bhatia, M. S., Aggarwal, N. K., & Aggarwal, B. B. L. (2000). Psychosocial profile of suicide ideators, attempters and completers in India. *International Journal of Social Psychiatry, 46,* 155–163.

Bird, H. R., Canino, G., & Rubio-Stipec, M. (1988). Estimates of the prevalence of childhood maladjustment in a community survey in Puerto Rico: The use of combined measures. *Archives of General Psychiatry, 45,* 1120–1126.

Bronsich, T. (1991). Adjustment reactions: A long-term prospective and retrospective follow-up of former patients in a crisis intervention ward. *Acta Psychiatrica Scandinavia, 84,* 86–93.

Casey, P. (2001). Adult adjustment disorder: A review of its current diagnostic status. *Journal of Psychiatric Practice, 7,* 32–40.

Casey, P., Dowrick, C., & Wilkinson, G. (2001). Adjustment disorders. Fault line in the psychiatric glossary. *British Journal of Psychiatry, 179,* 479–481.

Casey, P., Marcay, M., Kelly, B. D., Lehtinen, V., Ayuso-Mateos, J. L., Dalgard, O. S., & Dowrick, C. (2006). Can adjustment disorder and depressive disorder be distinguished? Results from ODIN. *Journal of Affective Disorders, 92,* 291–297.

Chambless, D. L., Sanderson, W. C., Shoham, V., Johnson, S. B., Pope, K. S., Crits-Christoph, P., . . . McCurry, S. (1996). An update on empirically validated therapies. *Clinical Psychologist, 49,* 5–18.

De Leo, D. (1989). Treatment of adjustment disorder. A comparative evaluation. *Psychological Reports, 64,* 51–54.

Doan, R., & Petti, P. (1989). Clinical and demographic characteristics of child and adolescent partial hospital patients. *Journal of the American Academy of Child & Adolescent Psychiatry, 28,* 66–69.

Fard, F., Hudgens, R.W., & Weiner, A. (1979). Undiagnosed psychiatric illness in adolescents: A prospective study. *Archives of General Psychiatry, 35,* 279–281.

Goldston, D. B., Daniel, S. S., Reboussin, B., Reboussin, D. M., Kelley, A. E., & Frazier, P. H. (1998). Psychiatric diagnoses of previous suicide attempters, first-time attempters, and repeat attempters on an adolescent inpatient psychiatry unit. *Journal of the American Academy of Child and Adolescent Psychiatry, 37,* 924–932.

Gonzalez-Jaimes, E. I., & Turnbull-Plaza, B. (2003). Selection of psychotherapeutic treatment for adjustment disorder with depressive mood due to acute myocardial infarction. *Archives of Medical Research, 34,* 298–304.

Greenberg, W. M., Rosenfeld, D. N., & Ortega, E. A. (1995). Adjustment disorder as an admission diagnosis. *American Journal of Psychiatry, 152,* 459–461.

Gur, S., Hermesh, H., Laufer, N., Gogol, M., & Gross-Isseroff, R. (2005). Adjustment disorder: A review of diagnostic pitfalls. *Israel Medical Association Journal, 7,* 726–731.

Hillard, J. R., Slomowitz, M., & Levi, L. S. (1987). A retrospective study of adolescents' visits to a general hospital psychiatric emergency service. *American Journal of Psychiatry, 144,* 432–436.

Horowitz, M. J. (1986). Stress response syndromes: A review of posttraumatic and adjustment disorders. *Hospital and Community Psychiatry, 37,* 241–249.

Jacobson, A. M., Goldberg, I. D., Burns, B. J., Hoeper, E. W., Hankin, J. R., & Hewitt, K. (1980). Diagnosed mental disorder in children and use of health services in four organized health care settings. *American Journal of Psychiatry, 137*, 559–565.

Jones, R., Yates, W. R., Williams, S., Zhou, M., & Hardman, L. (1999). Outcome for adjustment disorder with depressed mood: Comparison with other mood disorders. *Journal of Affective Disorders, 55*, 55–61.

Jones, R., Yates, W. R., & Zhou, M. (2002). Readmission rates for adjustment disorders: Comparison with other mood disorders. *Journal of Affective Disorders, 71*, 199–203.

Kovacs, M., Gatsonis, C., Pollock, M., & Parrone, P. L. (1994). A controlled prospective study of *DSM-III* adjustment disorder in childhood: Short-term prognosis and long-term predictive validity. *Archives of General Psychiatry, 51*, 535–541.

Kryzhanovskaya, L., & Canterbury, R. (2001). Suicidal behavior in patients with adjustment disorders. *Crisis, 22*, 125–131.

Levitas, A., & Hurley, A. (2005). Diagnosis and treatment of adjustment disorders in people with intellectual disability. *Mental Health Aspects of Developmental Disabilities, 8*, 52–60.

Maina, G., Forner, F., & Bogetto, F. (2005). Randomized controlled trial comparing brief dynamic and supportive therapy with waiting list condition in minor depressive disorders. *Psychotherapy and Psychosomatics, 74*, 43–50.

McCauley, M., Russell, V., Bedford, D., Khan, A., & Kelly, R. (2001). Assessment following deliberate self-harm: Who are we seeing and are we following the guidelines? *Irish Journal of Psychiatric Medicine, 18*, 116–119.

McGrath, J. (1989). A survey of deliberate self-poisoning. *Medical Journal of Australia, 150*, 317–322.

Mezzich, J., Fabrega, H., Coffman, G., & Haley, R. (1989). *DSM-III* disorders in a large sample of psychiatric patients: Frequency and specificity of diagnoses. *American Journal of Psychiatry, 146*, 212–219.

Mitrev, I. (1996). A study of deliberate self-poisoning in patients with adjustment disorders. *Folia Med (Plovdiv), 38*(3–4), 11–16.

Olfson, M., Marcus, S., Pincus, H., Zito, J., Thompson, J., & Zarin, D. (1998). Antidepressant prescribing practices of outpatient psychiatrists. *Archives of General Psychiatry, 55*, 310–316.

Pelkonen, M., Marttunen, M., Henriksson, M., & Lonnqvist, J. (2005). Suicidality in adjustment disorder: Clinical characteristics of adolescent outpatients. *European Child and Adolescent Psychiatry, 14*, 174–180.

Pelkonen, M., Marttunen, M., Henriksson, M., & Lonnqvist, J. (2007). Adolescent adjustment disorder: Precipitant stressors and distress symptoms of 89 outpatients. *European Psychiatry, 22*, 288–295.

Portzky, G., Audenaert, K., & van Heeringen, K. (2005). Adjustment disorder and the course of the suicidal process in adolescents. *Journal of Affective Disorders, 87*, 265–270.

Powell, S., & McCone, D. (2004). Treatment of adjustment disorder with anxiety: A September 11, 2001, case study with a 1-year follow up. *Cognitive and Behavioral Practice, 11*, 331–336.

Rait, D. S., Jacobsen, P. B., Lederberg, M. S., & Holland, J. C. (1988). Characteristics of psychiatric consultations in a pediatric cancer center. *American Journal of Psychiatry, 145*, 363–364.

Rothenhausler, H. B., Griesser, B., Nollert, G., Reichart, B., Schelling, G., & Kapfhammer, H. P. (2005). Psychiatric and psychosocial outcome of cardiac surgery with cardiopulmonary bypass: A prospective 12-month follow-up study. *General Hospital Psychiatry, 27*, 18–28.

Runeson, B. (1989). Mental disorder in youth suicide. *DSM-III-R* Axes I and II. *Acta Psychiatrica Scandinavia, 79*, 490–497.

Schatzberg, A. F. (1990). Anxiety and adjustment disorder: A treatment approach. *Journal of Clinical Psychiatry, 51*, 20–24.

Simons, A. D., Rohde, P., Kennard, B. D., & Robins, M. (2005). Relapse and recurrence prevention in the treatment for adolescents with depression study. *Cognitive and Behavioral Practice, 12*, 240–251.

Skopek, M. A., & Perkins, R. (1998). Deliberate exposure to motor vehicle exhaust gas: The psychosocial profile of attempted suicide. *Australian and New Zealand Journal of Psychiatry, 32*, 830–848.

Snyder, S., Strain, J. J., & Wolf, D. (1990). Differentiating major depression from adjustment disorder with depressed mood in the medical setting. *General Hospital Psychiatry, 12*, 159–165.

Strain, J. J., & Diefenbacher, A. (2008). The adjustment disorders: The conundrums of the diagnoses. *Comprehensive Psychiatry, 48*, 121–130.

Strain, J. J., & Newcorn, J. (2003). Adjustment disorders. In R. E. Hales & S. C. Yudofsky (Eds.), *Textbook of clinical psychiatry* (4th ed., pp. 765–780). Washington, DC: American Psychiatric Publishing.

Strain, J. J., & Newcorn, J. (2007). Adjustment disorder. In J. A. Bourgeois, R. E. Hales, & S. C. Yudofsky (Eds.), *The American Psychiatric Publishing board prep and review guide for psychiatry* (pp. 291–295). Washington, DC: American Psychiatric Publishing.

Strain, J. J., Smith, G. C., Hammer, J. S., McKenzie, D. P., Blumenfield, M., & Muskin, P. (1998). Adjustment disorder: A multisite study of its utilization and interventions in the consultation-liaison psychiatry setting. *General Hospital Psychiatry, 20*, 139–149.

Stricklin-Parker, E., & Schneider, B. A. (2005). Ann: A case study. *Clinical Case Studies, 4*, 415–428.

Task Force on Promotion and Dissemination of Psychological Procedures. (1995). Training in and dissemination of empirically-validated psychological treatments. *Clinical Psychologist, 48*, 323.

Uhlenhuth, E. H., Balter, M. B., Ban, T. A., & Yang, K. (1995). International study of expert judgment on therapeutic use of benzodiazepines and other psychotherapeutic medications: III. Clinical features affecting experts' therapeutic recommendations in anxiety disorders. *Psychopharmacology Bulletin, 31*, 289–96.

Van der Klink, J. J. L, Blonk, R. W. B., Schene, A. H., & van Dijk, F. J. H. (2003). Reducing long term sickness absence by an activating intervention in adjustment

disorders: A cluster randomised controlled design. *Occupational and Environmental Medicine, 60*, 429–437.

Van der Klink, J. J. L., & van Dijk, F. J. H. (2003). Dutch practice guidelines for managing adjustment disorders in occupational and primary health care. *Scandinavian Journal of Work and Environmental Health, 29*, 278–287.

Vanin, J. R. (2008). Adjustment disorder with anxiety. In J. R. Vanin & J. D. Helsley (Eds.), *Anxiety disorders: A pocket guide for primary care* (pp. 129–134). New York, NY: Humana Press.

22

Borderline Personality Disorder

JOEL R. SNEED, ERIC A. FERTUCK, DORA KANELLOPOULOS, AND MICHELLE E. CULANG-REINLIEB

OVERVIEW OF DISORDER

The origin of borderline personality disorder (BPD) dates back to the original use of the term *borderline* as delineating a group of patients who were neither neurotic nor psychotic (Stern, 1938). While early descriptions clarified similarities and differences between the phenomenology of BPD and other disorders, it was the advent of *DSM III* criteria that allowed for reliable diagnosis and the facilitation of research into the disorder (Fertuck, Lenzenweger, Clarkin, Hoermann, & Stanley, 2006). BPD is currently defined by frantic efforts to avoid abandonment, unstable interpersonal relationships, emotional lability, intense and inappropriate anger, impulsivity that is self destructive (including drug use, indiscriminant sexual relations, and suicidal and parasuicidal behavior), stress related dissociation and paranoia, and chronic feelings of emptiness (American Psychiatric Association, 2000). Recurrent suicidal behaviors, along with self mutilation (i.e., cutting, burning, etc.), are often referred to as parasuicidal and are defined as nonfatal, intentional self injurious behaviors with intent to cause bodily harm or risk death (Linehan, 1993a).

The burden and suffering caused by BPD is profound. BPD is associated with an up to

10% rate of completed suicide (Black, Blum, Pfohl, & Hale, 2004), which is similar to the rate for major depression and schizophrenia, and 400 times greater than the suicide rate of the general population. Nonsuicidal self-injury (Simeon et al., 1992), intense and chronic emotional pain (Stiglmayr et al., 2005), and chronic physical illnesses (Frankenburg & Zanarini, 2004) are also prevalent.

The symptoms characteristic of BPD have been categorized in several ways. For example, Linehan (1993a) argued that the *DSM IV* criteria can be reorganized according to five domains of dysregulation: emotional (the primary disturbance), interpersonal, cognitive, behavioral, and self. Others have suggested that the symptoms fall along three primary dimensions: interpersonal and identity disturbance, emotional instability, and impulsive and aggressive behaviors (Sanislow, Grilo, & McGlashan, 2000). While individuals with BPD may vary in the severity of these features, they are highly intercorrelated in BPD, and cohere into a unitary syndrome (Clifton & Pilkonis, 2007).

In clinical settings, nearly three quarters of those diagnosed with BPD are female (Swartz et al., 1989), however, epidemiological studies of representative community samples indicate an equal sex ratio (Lenzenweger, Lane,

Loranger, & Kessler, 2007; Torgerson, Kringlen, & Cramer, 2001). Population prevalence estimates for BPD range from 0.3% to 1.6% (Lenzenweger et al., 2007), which is comparable to other major psychiatric disorders, such as schizophrenia. Given these associations, it is not surprising that BPD is associated with extensive health-care utilization (Bender et al., 2001). It is estimated that approximately 11% of psychiatric outpatients and 19% of psychiatric inpatients meet criteria for BPD (Marshall & Serin, 1997). There is also a substantial co-occurrence between BPD and other Axis I disorders, such as major depression (Joyce et al., 2003; Stanley & Wilson, 2006), substance abuse (Trull, Sher, Minks-Brown, Durbin, & Burr, 2000; Wilson et al., 2006), anxiety disorders (Skodol et al., 2002), posttraumatic stress disorder (Heffernan & Cloitre, 2000; Landecker, 1992), eating disorders (Zanarini, Frankenburg, Hennen, Reich, & Silk, 2004), and—to a lesser degree—bipolar mood disorder (Atre-Vaidya & Hussain, 1999; Deltito et al., 2001; Gunderson et al., 2006; Henry et al., 2001; Paris, Gunderson, & Weinberg, 2007). Suicide attempts increase dramatically in borderline patients with co-occurring major depression and substance abuse (Fertuck, Makhija, & Stanley, 2007; Jacobs, Brewer, & Klein-Benheim, 1999; Tanney, 2000).

Traditionally, clinicians have considered BPD a difficult-to-treat condition with a negative long-term prognosis (Stern, 1938; Stone, Hurt, & Stone, 1987); however, a more recent meta-analysis suggests that psychotherapeutic treatment for BPD is associated with a sevenfold greater rate of recovery compared to the natural history of the disorder (Perry, Banon, & Ianni, 1999). In addition, the long-term prognosis for individuals with BPD appears more positive than previously appreciated (Lenzenweger, 2008; Zanarini, Frankenburg, Hennen, & Silk, 2003). Importantly, in the last two decades, clinicians and researchers have developed and evaluated targeted, BPD-specific psychosocial and

pharmaceutical treatment options that have preliminary support from randomized controlled trials (RCTs). Consequently, many clinicians now express a cautious but founded optimism for the efficacy of psychosocial treatments for BPD (Gabbard, 2007).

The aim of this chapter is to review and summarize empirically supported psychosocial treatments for BPD. In addition, we delineate the emerging trends and challenges for the future of empirically supported treatment including multimodal, integrative treatments, treatment mechanism research, and patient–treatment matching by BPD subtypes and stage of recovery.

EMPIRICALLY SUPPORTED TREATMENTS

We will use the principles established by the American Psychological Association (Levant, 2005) on Evidence-Based Practice in Psychology (EBPP) to evaluate whether a given treatment has been demonstrated to be effective. According to the Policy Statement on Evidence-Based Practice in Psychology (EBPP), "The purpose of EBPP is to promote effective psychological practice and enhance public health by applying empirically supported principles of psychological assessment, case formulation, therapeutic relationship, and intervention" (p. 5). This statement was inspired by the debate and controversy over the original criteria put forth by Division 12 of the APA to rigorously define empirically validated treatments (Chambless & Hollon, 1998). The original definition has two levels: *well established* and *probably efficacious*. To be well established, a treatment must have support from at least two well-conducted randomized clinical trials (RCTs) with active control groups conducted by at least two independent groups of researchers. Probably efficacious treatments require only one RCT with an active control or two RCTs with wait-list controls. Additionally, the original criteria require that the treatment have a well-articulated manual and that the diagnostic characteristics of the patient group samples be clearly specified by *DSM-IV* criteria.

CONSENSUS PANEL RECOMMENDATIONS

The American Psychiatric Association published guidelines in 2001 for the treatment of BPD that advocate for a combined psychotherapy and targeted pharmacotherapy approach with psychotherapy being the primary treatment component and pharmacotherapy the adjunctive component (Oldham, 2005). Although the majority of RCTs involve treatment of BPD with DBT, the updated guidelines noted a number of new manualized psychotherapy approaches being examined in open treatment trials. Since the publication of the update, several RCTs have been published that we have reviewed (see the following). Augmenting psychotropic agents, such as SSRIs, atypical antipsychotics, and mood stabilizers, are also recommended to treat targeted symptoms such as affective dysregulation, cognitive-perceptual disturbances, or impulse dyscontrol in BPD.

There are now several psychosocial treatments for BPD with varying empirical support from RCTs (see Table 22.1). In the following section, we summarize the nature and research support for the most established approaches. The section is divided into treatments that are comprehensive and treatments that are adjunctive.

COMPREHENSIVE TREATMENTS

Dialectical Behavior Therapy

Dialectical behavior therapy (Linehan, 1993a) is a flexible, cognitive-behavioral treatment characterized by weekly individual sessions, weekly skills training groups, and telephone coaching to help generalize newly learned skills beyond therapy sessions. The central focus of DBT is on the dialectical tension between accepting the patient's emotional experience and effecting adaptive change through the use of chain analyses, self-monitoring diaries, and contingency management, particularly with respect to life-threatening and therapy-interfering behaviors. It also emphasizes education, role playing, and problem solving strategies. DBT's focus on mindfulness, dialectics, and the therapeutic relationship distinguish it from standard CBT.

According to the theoretical underpinnings of DBT, the emotional dysregulation that typifies BPD has its etiology in the interaction between biology and environment. The biological underpinnings of emotional dysregulation are high sensitivity and high reactivity to painful affect, as well as a slow return to emotional baseline after arousal. As a result, borderline patients are primed for high emotional reactivity because the biological concomitants of negative affectivity are still active and have not returned to premorbid levels. In conjunction with biological vulnerability, borderline patients are often subjected to invalidating environments. Typical features of the invalidating environment are being exposed to caregivers or significant others who: (a) respond erratically and inappropriately to private emotional experiences, (b) are insensitive to people's emotional states, (c) have a tendency to over- or underreact to emotional experiences, (d) emphasize control over negative emotions, and (e) have a tendency to trivialize painful experiences and/or attribute such experiences to negative traits, such as lack of motivation or discipline. It is theorized that the interaction between emotional vulnerability and invalidating environments results in not being able to label and modulate emotions, tolerate emotional or interpersonal distress, or trust private experiences as valid.

According to DBT, parasuicidal behaviors that have been traditionally thought of as

TABLE 22.1 Summary of RCTs of Psychotherapy for Borderline Personality Disorder (BPD)

Article	Sample	Treatment Groups	Duration	Outcomes
Bateman and Fonagy (1999)	Psychiatric inpatients with BPD ($N = 38$; ages 16 to 65)	MBT in partial hospitalization ($N = 19$) versus TAU ($N = 19$)	18 months	MBT showed greater decreases in self-mutilation, suicide attempts, anxiety, depression, and severity of symptom reports than TAU. Reduction in hospital admissions and length of stay for MBT group in last 6 months of study; in the TAU group, there was an increase in the same time period.
Bateman and Fonagy (2008)	Follow-up of patients with BPD in partial hospitalization setting from 1999 study ($N = 38$; ages 16 to 65)	MBT group received additional 18 months of outpatient treatment versus TAU	5-year postdischarge follow-up	Fewer MBT patients met criteria for BPD compared to TAU. MBT patients had less use of services and medication had longer duration of employment than TAU.
Blum et al. (2008)	BPD patients with no previous participation in STEPPS ($N = 124$; Mean age = 31.5; SD = 9.5)	STEPPS + TAU ($N = 65$) versus TAU ($N = 59$)	20 weeks	Differences in affective, cognitive, impulsive, affective, and interpersonal domains of Zanarini Rating Scale for BPD as well as improvements in global functioning favoring the STEPPS group.
Clarkin, Levy, Lenzenweger, and Kernberg (2007)	Patients with BPD ($N = 90$; ages 18 to 50)	TFP ($N = 23$); DBT ($N = 17$); and ST ($N = 22$)	1 year	TFP and DBT were significantly associated with improvement in suicidality. TFP and ST were associated with improvement in anger. TFP was associated with improvement in Barratt Factor 2 Impulsivity as well as irritability, verbal assault, and direct assault. ST was predictive of improvement in Barratt Factor 3 Impulsivity.
Davidson et al. (2006)	Patients with BPD who had received emergency psychiatric services in past year ($N = 106$; ages 18 to 65)	CBT + TAU ($N = 54$) versus TAU only ($N = 52$)	1 year treatment; 1 year follow-up	No differences between the groups in suicidal acts, inpatient, or emergency hospitalization. There was a statistically significant difference in the mean number of suicide acts (small effect size) as well as lower anxiety and BPRS distress favoring CBT at the end of 2 years.
Giesen-Bloo et al. (2006)	Patients with BPD ($N = 86$; ages 18 to 60)	TFP ($N = 42$) versus SFT ($N = 44$)	3 years	Both treatments related to significant increases in quality of life, reduction in all BPD symptoms, and reduction in general psychopathologic dysfunction. SFT group had greater reduction in BPD symptoms, general psychopathology than TFP. Higher dropout rate for TFP than SFT.
Gregory et al. (2008)	Patients with BPD and active alcohol abuse/dependence ($N = 30$; ages 18 to 45)	DDP ($N = 15$) versus TAU ($N = 15$)	12–18 months	Significant improvement in parasuicide, alcohol misuse, and institutional care over time for DDP but not for TAU.
Koons et al. (2001)	Women with BPD recruited from a VA clinic ($N = 20$; ages 21 to 46)	DBT ($N = 10$) versus TAU ($N = 10$)	6 months	DBT patients had greater reductions in suicidal ideation, depression, hopelessness, and anger compared to TAU at posttreatment.

Study	Population	Treatment comparison	Duration	Findings
	Adults with BPD $N=90$ ages 18 to 50	TFP $N=31$ versus SPT $N=30$ versus DBT $N=29$	1 year	Reflective function, attachment coherence, and security of attachment had a significantly greater increase over the year of treatment for the TFP group versus the other two therapy groups. There were no significant changes across groups for resolution of loss or trauma.
	Chronically parasuicidal women with BPD recruited from outpatient clinic $N=44$ ages 18 to 45	DBT $N=22$ versus TAU $N=22$	1 year	DBT patients had significant reductions in parasuicidal behavior, were significantly more likely to start and to complete treatment, stayed in treatment longer, and had significantly fewer inpatient hospital days compared to TAU. Findings were maintained throughout the posttreatment follow-up year.
	Women with BPD and at least two instances of parasuicidal behavior $N=39$ ages 18 to 45	DBT $N=19$ versus TAU $N=20$	1 year	Parasuicide repeat rate and the likelihood of any psychiatric hospitalization were lower for DBT versus TAU completers; this difference remained during the 12–18 month follow-up period. During the follow-up year, DBT patients reported significantly better Global Assessment Scale scores and employment performance than TAU.
	Women with BPD $N=28$ ages 18 to 45	DBT $N=13$ versus TAU $N=15$	1 year	DBT was more effective than TAU in the community in improving interpersonal and general adjustment in women with BPD. DBT patients rated selves better on trait anger scores and on overall social adjustment posttreatment.
	Women with BPD and substance use disorder $N=28$ ages 18 to 45	DBT $N=12$ modified for substance abuse versus TAU $N=16$	1 year	Significant reduction in substance abuse, improvements in social and global adjustment, and greater retention rates for DBT versus TAU. Improvements in social and global adjustment greater for DBT versus TAU at follow-up. Greater adherence of therapists to DBT treatment manual resulted in better outcomes.
	Heroin-dependent women with BPD $N=23$ ages 18 to 45	DBT $N=11$ modified for substance users versus CVT + 12S $N=12$. Both groups also received opiate agonist therapy	1 year	Both treatments when combined with opiate agonist treatment were effective in reducing opiate use and maintaining the reduction to 4-month posttreatment. CVT + 12S had greater retention rate than DBT. DBT group was more accurate in self-recording opiate use.
	Women with BPD $N=101$ ages 18 to 45	DBT $N=52$ versus CBTE $N=49$	1 year	DBT group had half the rate of suicide attempts, was more effective at reducing emergency room visits, and inpatient psychiatric care for suicide ideation compared to the CTBE group. DBT was more than twice as effective as CTBE in keeping subjects in treatment.

(Continued)

TABLE 22.1 Summary of RCTs of Psychotherapy for Borderline Personality Disorder (BPD) (*Continued*)

Article	Sample	Treatment Groups	Duration	Outcomes
Linehan, McDavid, Brown, Sayrs, and Gallop (2008)	Women with BPD and high levels of irritability and anger (N = 24; ages 18 to 60)	DBT + placebo (N = 12) versus DBT + olanzapine (N = 12)	6 months	Irritability, aggression, and self-injurious behavior improved significantly during treatment for both conditions. Irritability and aggression tended to decrease more rapidly for olanzapine, while self-inflicted injury tended to decrease more placebo group.
Spinhoven, Giesen-Bloo, van Dyck, Kooiman, and Arntz (2007)	Patients with BPD (N = 78; ages 18 to 60)	SFT (N = 44) versus TFP (N = 34)	3 years	The quality of the therapeutic alliance increased for patients for both SFT and TFP but therapist frustration decreased for SFT while it increased for TFP. Compared to SFT significantly more patients in TFP dropped out early.
Turner (2000)	Patients with BPD (N = 24; Mean age = 22)	DBT (N = 12) with no separate skills group versus CCT (N = 12)	1 year	DBT group showed a greater reduction in global mental health functioning, self-harm behaviors, and hospitalization days at both 6 and 12 months. DBT had lower impulsivity than CCT at 12 months.
Van den Bosch, Koeter, Stijnen, Verheul, and van den Brink (2005)	Women with BPD with and without substance abuse (N = 58; ages 18 to 45)	DBT (N = 27) versus TAU (N = 31)	6-month follow-up	DBT had a significantly greater decrease in impulsive and self-mutilating behavior and alcohol consumption than TAU. The treatment effects were sustained for the 6-month period after termination of treatment.
Van Den Bosch, Verheul, Schippers, and van den Brink (2002)	Women with BPD with and without substance abuse (N = 58; ages of 18 to 45)	DBT (N = 27) versus TAU (N = 31)	1 year	Substance abuse was not effectively targeted by either treatment. DBT had greater retention rate and showed greater reductions of self-mutilating behavior and self-damaging impulsive acts than TAU. Beneficial effect of DBT on self-mutilating behaviors was greater for those patients that had higher baseline behaviors.
Verheul et al. (2003)	Women with BPD (N = 64; ages 18 to 70)	DBT (N = 31) versus TAU (N = 33)	1 year	DBT had a decrease in self-mutilating behaviors and a greater retention rate than TAU. Impact of DBT was more pronounced for participants who reported higher baseline frequencies of self-mutilating behaviors.
Weinberg, Gunderson, Hennen, and Cutter (2006)	Women with BPD (N = 30; ages 18 to 40)	MACT + TAU (N = 15) versus TAU (N = 15).	6 to 8 weeks	The MACT group had significantly greater decrease in frequency and severity of deliberate self-harm (DSH) at both 6–8 weeks and at the 6-month follow-up. No significant differences between groups were observed for suicidal ideation and time to repeat DSH.

Note: MBT = Mentalization-Based Therapy; TAU = Treatment As Usual; STEPPS = Systems Training for Emotional Predictability and Problem Solving; TFP = Transference Focused Psychotherapy; DBT = Dialectical Behavioral Therapy; ST = Supportive Therapy; CBT = Cognitive Behavior Therapy; SFT = Schema Focused Therapy; DDP = Dynamic Deconstructive Psychotherapy; MPSP = Modified Psychodynamic Supportive Psychotherapy; CVT = Comprehensive Validation Therapy; CBTE = Community-Based Treatment by Experts; CCT = Client Centered Therapy; MACT = Manual-Assisted Cognitive Therapy manipulative and controlling are reframed as maladaptive attempts at problem solving and emotion regulation. Linehan argued that a dialectical perspective looks for the wisdom or the adaptiveness of the parasuicidal gesture; that is, although the gesture is dysfunctional, it has been shaped by an environment that actively teaches emotional invalidation. As such, this model posits that parasuicidal gestures serve self-regulatory functions and also serve to elicit responses in significant others who have not responded appropriately to the patient's emotional needs. According to Linehan (1993a), what maybe viewed as dysfunctional, distorted, and destructive, may actually be adaptive, accurate, and constructive.

Weekly skills training groups (Linehan, 1993b) aim to replace the maladaptive problem-solving strategies characteristic of BPD patients with more constructive and adaptive strategies that help the patient build a life worth living. The four areas of skills training include core mindfulness, interpersonal effectiveness, emotion regulation, and distress tolerance. Mindfulness strategies integrate Zen meditation practices and epitomize the acceptance versus change dialectic, which lies at the heart of DBT. The core mindfulness module distinguishes between rational mind, emotion mind, and wise mind. The wise mind represents an integration of rational and emotion mind and can be thought of as the individual's intuition. Mindfulness exercises form the core of the module and aim to decrease impulsivity and allow for the implementation of more adaptive strategies learned in the other modules. The interpersonal module provides strategies and techniques for dealing with and negotiating difficult interpersonal interactions based on a clear understanding of the priorities in a given situation. Emotion regulation provides the patient with an organizing framework for understanding emotions, and exercises that aim to enhance the capacity to label and understand the antecedents, consequences, and function of emotional expression.

Finally, distress tolerance aims to provide the patient with various crisis strategies in order to prevent maladaptive coping that historically has hindered the individual from living a meaningful and productive life.

Randomized clinical trials of DBT. We identified 11 RCTs of DBT in patients meeting criteria for BPD. Eight of these studies were with patients meeting BPD criteria alone whereas three examined the efficacy of DBT in BPD patients meeting criteria for comorbid substance abuse or dependence. Following, we summarize their main findings.

Linehan et al. (1991) randomized 44 women aged 18 to 45 years with BPD to either DBT ($N = 22$) or to treatment as usual (TAU) ($N = 22$) for 12 months. The DBT program was comprehensive and included individual psychotherapy, 150-minute group skills training including training in interpersonal skills, distress tolerance/reality acceptance skills, and emotion regulation skills. Patients were exposed to all skills teaching twice within this 12-month trial. The TAU patients were given alternative therapy referrals from which they could choose. The DBT-treated patients showed statistically significant reductions in parasuicidal behavior. They were more likely to start (100% vs. 73%) and remain in treatment (83% vs. 42%) longer than TAU patients. Additionally, DBT participants had significantly fewer inpatient hospital days compared to TAU patients. These findings were maintained throughout the posttreatment follow-up year.

Linehan et al. (1993) randomized 39 women aged 18 to 45 years old with BPD to DBT ($N = 19$) or TAU ($N = 20$) for 1 year. Participants were also assessed 6 and 12 months after treatment termination. Throughout the treatment year, the rate of parasuicidality and the likelihood of any psychiatric hospitalization were lower for DBT than TAU completers. During the 6-month follow-up period, DBT completers continued to have fewer episodes of parasuicidality and fewer medically treated episodes than TAU completers. During the

12-month follow-up period, there was no difference between groups on parasuicide measures, but inpatient psychiatric days were lower in the DBT group than the TAU group. During the posttreatment follow-up, DBT subjects reported significantly better Global Assessment Scale scores and employment performance than TAU subjects.

Linehan and colleagues (1994) randomized 26 women with BPD aged 18 to 45 years to either DBT ($N = 13$) or TAU ($N = 13$). The DBT treatment was compared to TAU in which participants received alternative therapy referrals and participation in any type of treatment available in the community. Results indicated that DBT was more effective than TAU in improving interpersonal and general adjustment and DBT patients reported lower scores on anger and overall social adjustment at 12 months; however, there were no differences between the groups at 1 year with regard to general satisfaction.

Verheul et al. (2003) randomized 64 women with BPD aged 18 to 70 years to either DBT ($N = 31$) or TAU ($N = 33$). Retention was found to be higher for DBT than TAU at 12 months. Although the frequency and course of suicidal behaviors were not significantly different across treatments, the DBT group had a greater decrease in self-mutilation compared to the TAU group. Participants in the DBT group showed greater improvement over time compared to the TAU group in self-damaging impulsive behaviors. Differences between groups could not be explained by use of psychotropic medication because both groups included a similar number of patients on antidepressants. The impact of DBT was more pronounced for participants who reported greater frequency of self-mutilating behaviors at baseline. Additionally there was a non-significant trend toward greater effectiveness of DBT compared to TAU in patients with severe suicidal behavior at baseline.

Koons et al. (2001) randomized 20 women with BPD aged 21 to 46 years from a VA clinic to either DBT ($N = 10$) or TAU ($N = 10$) for 6 months of treatment. All of the components of standard DBT were utilized; however, because of shorter treatment duration compared to the recommended 12-month DBT treatment contract, skills training was conducted only once. Patients in the DBT condition showed greater reductions in suicidal ideation, depression, hopelessness, and anger compared to TAU patients posttreatment.

Turner (2000) randomized 24 patients with modified BPD (mean age $= 22$ years) to DBT ($N = 12$) or Client Centered Therapy (CCT; $N = 12$). Assessments were conducted at pretreatment, and 6- and 12-month time points. The DBT was modified in the two ways: Psychodynamic techniques were incorporated to conceptualize patient behavioral, emotional, and cognitive relationship schemas, and skills training was conducted during individual therapy. Twice weekly CCT emphasized empathy and provided a supportive environment that facilitated individuation. Although parasuicidality decreased for both groups, decreases in parasuicidality were greatest for those randomized to modified DBT. Although both groups showed reductions in impulsivity and depression, there were no differences between the groups at 6 months; however, modified DBT showed greater reduction in impulsivity and depression than the CCT-treated group at 12 months. Anger ratings were also significantly lower for the modified DBT group than for the CCT group at 12 months. The DBT-treated patients showed a greater improvement in global mental health functioning as assessed by decreases in Brief Psychiatric Rating Scale (BPRS) scores at 12 months, as well as by a greater reduction in hospitalization days at both 6 and 12 months.

Linehan et al. (2006) randomized 101 patients with BPD aged 18 to 45 years to either DBT ($N = 52$) or Community Treatment by Experts (CTBE) ($N = 49$). The CTBE therapists were community psychotherapy experts, but did not include CBT experts. The CTBE therapists received equivalent fees for their services but were not required to attend biweekly supervision as did DBT therapists. The DBT-treated patients had half the rate of suicide attempts as the CTBE group (23.1% vs. 46%) at 2-years postrandomization. The DBT was more effective at reducing emergency room visits and inpatient psychiatric care for suicide ideation. The DBT was also more than twice as effective as CTBE in retaining subjects. The dropout rate among DBT-treated patients was 25% compared to 59% among CTBE-treated patients.

Linehan and colleagues (2008) randomized 24 women with BPD aged 18–24 years to either 6 months of individual and group DBT plus daily placebo (N = 12) or 6 months of individual and group DBT plus daily olanzapine (N = 12). Olanzapine, an atypical antipsychotic that may be beneficial in reducing anger, irritability, and assaultive behaviors, was chosen to complement DBT treatment for patients with irritability and anger features of BPD. Self-injurious behavior decreased significantly for both groups, as did irritability and verbal and physical aggression. Patients in the DBT plus olanzapine condition showed a more rapid decrease by week 7 and through the third month compared to the DBT plus placebo condition. There was also a greater decrease in depression scores in the DBT plus olanzapine group than the DBT plus placebo group.

Linehan et al. (1999) randomized 28 women aged 18 to 45 years who met criteria for BPD and substance use disorder to DBT (N = 12) or TAU (N = 16). The DBT treatment lasted for 1 year and was modified for use with people with substance abuse by incorporating a set of organized interventions designed to increase the positive valence of the therapy and therapist, and by adopting a dialectical stance on drug use that focused on skills for preventing relapse after drug use. The TAU consisted of community mental health counselors and programs or individual psychotherapy. Assessments were conducted at 4, 8, and 12 months during treatment, and also 4 months post-treatment at 16 months. Patients treated with DBT showed greater reductions in Substance

Abuse compared to TAU. Additionally, dropout rates were much lower in the DBT group (36%) as compared to the TAU group (73%). There were no differences between the treatment groups on measures of psychopathology at endpoint; however, at the 4-month follow-up assessment, DBT subjects showed better global and social adjustment. Significant reductions in parasuicidal episodes and anger were found for both groups; however, within the DBT condition, treatment adherence by the therapist predicted greater improvement.

Van den Bosch and colleagues (2002) randomized 58 women with BPD aged 18–65 years with or without comorbid substance abuse to DBT (N = 27) or TAU (N = 31). No treatment differences were observed between groups with regard to number of days of alcohol, medication, or cannabis use or overall severity scores for alcohol and drug problems. Dropout rates were lower in the DBT group (37%) compared to the TAU group (77%). The DBT-treated patients also showed greater reductions in self-mutilation and self-damaging impulsive acts compared to the TAU group. The beneficial effect of DBT on self-mutilating behaviors was greater on those that had higher baseline self-mutilating behaviors. In a follow-up study these differences between DBT and TAU were sustained 6 months after DBT treatment was discontinued despite the continuation of TAU (van den Bosch et al., 2005). In addition, the DBT group showed greater reductions in alcohol consumption than the TAU group 6 months after discontinuing.

Linehan et al. (2002) randomized 23 women with BPD and comorbid heroin dependence to either DBT (N = 11) or Comprehensive Validation Therapy plus Narcotics Anonymous (CVT + 12S, N = 12). CVT + 12S consisted of nondirective individual psychotherapy that proscribed CBT problem-solving strategies and included DBT acceptance-based strategies and weekly attendance at Narcotics Anonymous meetings. Both treatments were augmented using opiate agonist therapy (ORLaam). Both treatments were effective in reducing opiate use and maintaining that reduction at the 4-month posttreatment follow-up; however, the DBT group maintained the reduction in opiate use throughout the treatment trial, while the TAU group significantly increased drug use during the final 4 months of treatment. The CVT + 12S group had much higher retention rates compared to the DBT group (100% vs. 36%). Improvements on global adjustment were observed in both treatments although there were no differences between conditions; however, the DBT group was more accurate in self-recording opiate use.

Summary of DBT. In the early studies that established DBT as the first treatment for BPD supported in an RCT, Linehan and colleagues showed that DBT treatment over 1 year significantly reduces parasuicidality and decreases hospitalization and dropout from therapy (Linehan et al., 1991, 1993). Subsequent studies by other independent groups have supported these findings (Koons et al., 2001; Verheul et al., 2003) making DBT the only treatment meeting criteria for a well-established treatment for BPD.

Studies have also extended DBT to BPD with comorbid substance abuse or dependence (Linehan et al., 1999, 2002; van den Bosch et al., 2002). The results of these studies have been mixed. One showed greater improvement in substance abuse compared to TAU (Linehan et al., 1999) whereas two showed no difference between groups in substance abuse (Linehan et al., 2002; van den Bosch et al., 2002); however, since the TAU groups received various active forms of treatment, the failure to detect a difference may reflect the lack of power of studies with relatively small numbers of participants to detect differences between treatments. Dropout rates in two of the studies were lower in the DBT group (Linehan et al., 1999; van den Bosch et al., 2002) whereas in one of the studies dropout rates were higher in DBT (Linehan et al., 2002); however, dropout rates tended to be lower in DBT, which may be attributable to the pretreatment contracting phase.

Two important issues emerge from this review with respect to DBT. First, it is unclear whether the gains made in DBT are sustained over long periods of time. While some studies suggest that treatment gains are sustained (Linehan et al., 2006), other studies have shown that after 2 years, there is no difference between groups with regard to parasuicidal behaviors (Linehan et al., 1993). Of course, the failure to detect a difference between treatments may reflect a lack of power of studies with relatively small numbers of participants. Second, although a large number of RCTs support the effectiveness of DBT in BPD patients, none of these studies compare DBT to another specific mode of psychotherapy. In the one study to date that compared DBT to Transference Focused Psychotherapy (TFP, see later), the two treatments were comparable with respect to suicidality at outcome (Clarkin et al., 2007).

Schema-Focused Therapy

Schema-focused therapy (SFT) (Young, 1994) was developed to treat patients with personality disorder diagnoses that would otherwise not respond well to traditional cognitive therapy. It is an integrative therapy that combines cognitive, behavioral, interpersonal, and experiential techniques to identify and change maladaptive schemas and their associated ineffective coping strategies (McGinn & Young, 1997). SFT predominantly differs from traditional cognitive therapy because of its focus on early childhood experiences in treatment, the use of the therapeutic relationship to facilitate change, and the active confrontation of maladaptive behavioral and belief patterns (McGinn & Young, 1997).

Schemas are psychological constructs that are comprised of memories, bodily sensations, emotions, and cognitions that develop during childhood and are elaborated through one's life. These schemas or core beliefs are expressed in enduring and chronic patterns of thinking, feeling, and behaving. These overdeveloped behavioral patterns are thought to impair adaptive functioning. The SFT defines 18 potential schemas, which can be grouped into five domains: disconnection and rejection, impaired autonomy and performance, impaired limits, other-directedness, and overvigilance and inhibition. The sets of schema modes, groups of schemas that are active at a particular moment, common and specific to BPD include detached protector, punitive parent, abandoned/abused child, and angry/impulsive child. BPD patients are assumed to spontaneously and repeatedly flip from one schema mode to another in an attempt to cope with their difficulties. Moreover, the modes of patients with BPD are dissociated from one another so that when one mode is active, the patient does not have access to other modes, limiting their ability to modulate active modes. The therapeutic goal is to develop and maintain healthy schema modes while changing or eliminating maladaptive ones.

The putative mechanism of change in SFT is to help the patient to become less influenced by these pervasive schemas through the use of the therapy relationship, homework assignments, and the exploration of past traumas. The behavioral, cognitive, experiential, and interpersonal techniques focus on establishing a positive therapeutic alliance, increasing emotional awareness, developing an effective individualized distress management plan, and helping patients modify their maladaptive schemas. In this way, it is believed that patients will develop new, more adaptive beliefs about themselves and other important people in their life. Simultaneously, they will develop those underdeveloped behavioral strategies that facilitate better functioning in life and promote emotional well-being.

The goal of SFT for BPD is to help the patient internalize the Healthy Adult Mode, which is modeled by the therapist, in order to regulate their emotional and behavioral patterns and effectively express their needs and emotions. SFT for BPD patients consists of three main phases that correspond to early

childhood development: the Bonding and Emotional Regulation, Schema Mode Change, and Autonomy stages. The Bonding and Emotional Regulation stage consists of mutual bonding between patient and therapist and educating the patient about effective emotion regulation. In this stage, the therapist actively encourages the patient to express their needs and emotions while providing empathy and validation. The therapist also teaches coping techniques that enable the patient to stabilize their own emotions. In the Schema Mode Change stage, the therapist uses limited reparenting to model the Healthy Adult Mode, which provides patients with the power to fight against their own maladaptive coping modes and perform appropriate and adaptive adult functions. Patients will gradually internalize this model as their own Healthy Adult Mode. In the Autonomy stage, the therapist helps the patient learn to develop healthy relationships outside of therapy and let go of past destructive relationships. The therapist teaches the patient to follow natural inclinations in regard to important life decisions. Finally, the therapist gradually terminates the therapy to promote further individuation.

Giesen-Bloo et al. (2006) compared the effectiveness of SFT compared to TFP, a psychoanalytically based, twice-weekly treatment (see following). This study included patients with BPD, aged 18 to 60 years, randomized to TFP ($N = 42$) or SFT ($N = 44$) for 3 years. Therapy in both conditions was conducted during 50-minute, twice-weekly sessions for 3 years. Dropout rates were higher among TFP patients (54.8%) compared to SFT patients (38.6%). Significant reductions in all BPD symptoms and general dysfunction and increases in quality of life were observed for both treatment groups, however, SFT patients showed significantly greater reductions in BPD symptoms, general psychopathology, and in changes in personality constructs related to the focus of SFT and TFP.

In subsequent analyses examining quality of the therapeutic relationship, the therapeutic alliance was rated higher for SFT than TFP by both therapist and patient (Spinhoven, et al., 2007). The quality of the therapeutic alliance increased for patients for both SFT and TFP, but therapist frustration decreased for SFT while it increased for TFP. The authors postulated that the greater rates of dropout observed in their previous study (Giesen-Bloo et al., 2006) may be due to poor alliance in the TFP condition.

Summary of SFT. One seminal study has demonstrated promising initial support for SFT in the long-term (up to three years) treatment of BPD. To date, this is the longest trial of a psychosocial treatment for BPD, and its duration conforms more closely to what is observed in clinical practice and naturalistic studies in the treatment of BPD (Perry et al., 1999). It is unclear how SFT compares to other established treatments for BPD, particularly since the quality of TFP adherence has been criticized (Yeomans, 2007).

Cognitive Behavior Therapy

Cognitive behavior therapy (CBT) for BPD developed by Davidson and colleagues (Davidson, Tyrer, et al., 2006) is similar to SFT in that it purports to help ". . . patients develop new, more adaptive beliefs about self and others and work on developing underdeveloped behavioral strategies to promote improved levels of social and emotional functioning" (p. 452). The goal of CBT is to help the patient identify maladaptive core beliefs, which are linked to emotions and overdeveloped behavioral patterns, and impair the patient's ability to function in an adaptive manner (Davidson, 2007). In personality disorders, these dysfunctional beliefs inhibit the expression of more adaptive beliefs and are activated across many situations, persistently biasing the interpretation of life experiences. Core beliefs, or conceptions of self and others, are thought to have developed as a result of recurring negative childhood experiences and are associated with behaviors that serve as coping mechanisms. Although these behaviors may have been adaptive in childhood, they become dysfunctional later in life as the patient is exposed to new environments and relationships and serve to maintain maladaptive beliefs, or cognitive schemas. The core beliefs and behaviors that arise from negative childhood experiences are thought to contribute to the formation of characteristics that are common in personality disorders such as poor interpersonal relationships.

In therapy, the patient and therapist should not only work toward changing dysfunctional beliefs, but the patient should also gain an understanding of how these negative beliefs developed (Davidson, 2007). Taking a comprehensive family, developmental, and social history and then using the data to formulate the core problems of the patient accomplish this. Following this step, they can then work to change dysfunctional beliefs and behaviors using various cognitive and behavioral strategies so the patient can more effectively deal with everyday life problems as they arise.

One of the tenets of CBT is that each session of therapy follows a specific pattern so that both patient and therapist can effectively engage in therapy, control crises, keep track of assignments, and focus on the goals of therapy (Davidson, 2007). Five phases of CBT for personality disorders have been outlined. Phase one consists of educating the patient about the structure and process of therapy. The therapist assesses and formulates patient problems within the cognitive model to help the patient understand the connection between maladaptive behavioral patterns and core beliefs. Also in this stage, the specific goals of treatment are developed based on the presenting problems of the patient. In phase two, the therapist and patient work together to prioritize the problems and reduce the occurrence of behaviors that can cause harm to self and others. The goal of phase three is to develop more adaptive and less rigid core beliefs and behaviors and, in phase four, these new beliefs and behaviors are reinforced. In the final stage, the patient and therapist review and reflect on the progress they have made and focus on the gradual termination of therapy and relapse prevention.

Davidson and colleagues (Davidson, Norrie, et al., 2006; Davidson, Tyrer, et al., 2006) conducted a multicenter study that randomized 106 BPD patients aged from 18 to 65 years to either CBT plus TAU ($N = 54$) or TAU only ($N = 52$) for 1 year of active treatment and a subsequent follow-up at 1-year post-treatment. There were no significant differences between groups on the primary outcome measures of suicidal acts, inpatient psychiatric hospitalization, or accident and emergency room attendance at the end of active treatment (1 year) or the 1-year posttreatment follow-up; however, there was a significant difference between the groups at the 1-year posttreatment follow-up in the mean number of suicidal acts.

Summary of CBT. In the only trial of Davidson's CBT approach to BPD, there were no differences between the groups in the primary outcomes but the authors noted differences between the groups at the 1-year posttreatment follow-up in the mean number of suicidal acts; however, the effect size corresponding to this difference was small by conventional standards (Cohen, 1988; Cohen, 1992).

Mentalization-Based Therapy

Mentalization-based therapy (MBT) for BPD is a psychoanalytically oriented treatment delivered in the context of a partial hospital setting. MBT focuses on increasing *mentalization*, which entails making sense of the actions of oneself and others on the basis of intentional mental states, such as desires, feelings, and beliefs. MBT posits that individuals with BPD have a core instability or inhibition of mentalization, particularly in the context of relationships with significant others. The focus of therapy is on the patient's moment-to-moment state of mind. The

therapist and patient identify prementalizing modes of experience and transform them into more adaptive modes. The focus is not on relationship patterns per se, but on the way in which patients think, feel, and understand their interpersonal experiences. Because the treatment takes place as part of a partial hospital program, there are individual and group psychotherapy components, as well as expressive therapy using art and writing groups as well as medication management.

Bateman and Fonagy (1999) randomized 38 participants with BPD to an 18-month trial of MBT ($N = 19$) or TAU ($N = 19$). There was a significant decline in self-mutilation in the MBT group and no decline in self-mutilation in the TAU group. Separation between the two treatment groups with regard to self-mutilation occurred at 12 months and was statistically significant at 18 months. There was also a statistically significant difference between the groups in average length of inpatient hospital stays (3 days vs. 21 days for MBT and TAU, respectively). Self-reported state and trait anxiety scores and Beck Depression Inventory scores significantly decreased for the MBT group but not for TAU. In addition, the MBT group showed a significant reduction relative to the TAU group in the severity but not number of symptoms reported.

In a landmark follow-up study, Bateman and Fonagy (2008) demonstrated that there was a significant difference between the MBT and TAU groups in number of suicide attempts at 5-year follow-up. Consistent with this finding, there were more emergency room visits and greater use of polypharmacy among those in the TAU group. The number of hospital days was also higher among the TAU group as compared to the MBT group. At the end of the follow-up period, only 13% of the MBT group met diagnostic criteria for BPD as compared to 87% in the TAU group. Similarly, 46% of the MBT group and 11% of the TAU group had GAF scores above 60 indicating that the level of overall functioning was significantly higher in the MBT group.

Summary of MBT. MBT is a psychodynamically informed, comprehensive, partial day hospitalization program for the treatment of BPD. Only one RCT has been published that has evaluated the effectiveness of this treatment for BPD, thus MBT is a promising treatment for BPD, which awaits replication. One issue that emerges from this review is the length of time for MBT to take effect as treatment gains did not emerge until 1 year; however, the 5-year follow-up suggested that the gains are sustained over long periods.

Transference-Focused Psychotherapy

Transference-focused psychotherapy (TFP) (Clarkin, Yeomans, & Kernberg, 2006) is the first manualized, psychoanalytic treatment for BPD and other personality disorders. TFP is a twice-weekly outpatient therapy with the option of auxiliary treatments to target specific problems. By combining structure and limit-setting with an approach that focuses on mental and emotional experiences with the therapist (i.e., the transference), TFP aims to improve the underlying psychological structure that drives the symptoms of BPD. TFP is organized into two main phases. Phase I aims to reduce and control suicidal and self-destructive behaviors. Phase II includes the core of the treatment that endeavors to foster the development of a coherent sense of self and others, or, improved quality of object relations, in the individual with BPD. Phase II is accomplished through: (a) fostering reflection on mental states of self and other; and (b) delineating, elaborating, and integrating the individuals with BPD's emotions, motivations, and expectations of self and other in the context of the therapeutic relationship, or, the transference.

TFP is based on object relations theory (Kernberg, 1996), a psychoanalytic model of psychological structure that posits core impairments in the conceptions of self and significant others (i.e., object relations) in BPD and other personality disorders. TFP aims to increase the coherence of these conceptions of self and other to effect stable, long-term reductions in suicidality and aggressive behaviors, emotional turbulence, the capacity to have satisfying and meaningful relationships, and to improve the capacity for work and career.

The mechanisms of therapeutic action of TFP (Levy, Clarkin, et al., 2006) occur in the context of a clear and mutually agreed upon framework for treatment that defines the expectations and roles of the patient and therapist. With this in place, the patient is provided a safe haven to express emotionally charged and disparate conceptions of self and others within the therapeutic relationship. By delineating these conceptions of self and other as they unfold in the therapeutic relationship, the therapist aims to integrate polarized and contradictory emotional experiences of self and significant others in the individual with BPD. This integration is posited to faciliate the patient's experience of themselves into forms that are richer, more coherent, and more realistic. Change in these psychological structures is posited to cause a toning down of emotional turbulence and an improvement in the stability and quality of interpersonal relationships.

Improvement in TFP occurs when the patient attends to the therapist's delineation and elaboration of the patient's understanding of self and other. Ideally, in the course of TFP, the individual with BPD develops their own ability to reflect upon their sense of self and others both independently and in collaboration with the therapist. In TFP, the ability to step outside of one's immediate, emotionally charged experience and observe it without feeling totally immersed facilitates an integration of the contradictory conceptions of self and other that are seen to be at the core of BPD symptoms.

Clarkin et al. (2007) randomized 90 patients with BPD aged 18–50 years to 1 year of treatment of TFP ($N = 23$), DBT ($N = 17$), or supportive psychodynamic psychotherapy (SPT; $N = 22$). SPT is a psychodynamically oriented supportive psychotherapy that is different from TFP in that it does not focus upon the therapeutic relationship itself. Analyses were conducted using data on patients with at least three assessment points. All treatments resulted in broad positive changes in subjects with BPD; however, only TFP and DBT resulted in improvement in suicidality, whereas only TFP and SPT were associated with improvement in anger. Impulsivity was a primary outcome of interest measured in this study, using the Barratt Impulsiveness Scale, which consists of three main factors. Only TFP produced improvement on Barratt Factor 2, a measure of motor impulsivity and perseverance; this factor is composed of indicators of behavioral impulsivity. Additionally, only TFP demonstrated improvement in irritability as well as verbal and direct assault, whereas only SPT produced improvement on Barratt Factor 3, a measure of nonplanning impulsiveness; this factor is composed of indicators of self-control and cognitive complexity. All three treatments resulted in improvements in depression, anxiety, global functioning, and social adjustment.

At 12 months of treatment, Levy, Meehan, et al. (2006) examined differences in attachment organization and reflective function (RF), the capacity to coherently understand the mental states of self and other in the three treatment groups. The study hypothesized that TFP would significantly increase RF and narrative coherence and significantly reduce lack of resolution of loss and trauma in attachment interviews compared to SPT and DBT. The TFP group showed greater improvements in reflective function, attachment coherence, and security of attachment after 1 year compared to the DBT and SPT groups. There were no significant changes across groups for resolution of loss or trauma.

Summary of TFP. TFP is an ambitious treatment that aims to improve the symptoms of BPD by improving the coherence and integration of concepts of self and other. In one trial, TFP performed comparably to DBT at

1 year, and there were some indications of superiority over SPT; however, TFP has yet to be compared to TAU. Further, long-term follow-up and cost-effectiveness studies are necessary to gauge the durability and efficiency of treatment gains. Given the intensity and focus of TFP, the treatment developers have argued that the gains are more durable than other treatments based on clinical experience; however, there are no systematic data to support these claims as of yet. Further, TFP is a sophisticated and intensive treatment, and it is unclear how readily and rapidly psychotherapists can develop competence in the delivery of TFP. It may turn out that TFP is a highly specialized treatment for a subset of BPD patients who are highly motivated, intelligent, and able to demonstrate some initial control over the most self-destructive and impulsive behaviors they display.

Dynamic Deconstructive Psychotherapy

Dynamic deconstructive psychotherapy (DDP) is a time-limited, manualized treatment developed for very challenging BPD cases such as those that have co-occurring substance abuse or additional personality disorders. The DDP involves individual weekly sessions over 12 to 18 months. Adjunctive group therapy is encouraged, but not required. The treatment model of DDP is based on the belief that symptoms of BPD, such as identity disturbance, are related to core neurocognitive deficits in processing of emotional experiences. Specifically, deficits in association (i.e., trouble relating emotions to their verbal labels), attribution (i.e., polarized all or nothing attribution of experiences to self or others), and alterity (having a reference point outside the subjectivity of the self). These neurocognitive processes form the basis for a coherent sense of self, one that is differentiated from others. Further examples of these deficits include difficulties identifying and verbalizing specific emotions, incoherent narrative accounts of interpersonal experience, unstable and polarized attributions that are poorly grounded in reality, and use of compensatory maladaptive behaviors and/or idealized attachments to self-soothe. DDP aims to remediate these deficits by helping patients label their emotions, integrate polarized attributions of self and others, and develop alterity by providing self-other experiences in the context of therapy (Gregory et al., 2008). Treatment is structured into 45- to 50-minute individual weekly sessions for a duration of 12 to 18 months. In addition to individual psychotherapy, DDP encourages but does not require group therapy participation. Overall, DDP aims to activate specific neurocognitive functions that are impaired through a primary focus on current interpersonal interactions while de-emphasizing the exploration of past trauma (Gregory et al., 2008).

Gregory et al. (2008) randomized 30 adults between the ages of 18 and 45 years with BPD and active alcohol abuse or dependence to DDP ($N = 15$) or TAU ($N = 15$) for 1 year. There were no differences between groups in parasuicide, alcohol use, or institutional care during the course of the study but there was a significant improvement in these symptoms over time for DDP but not TAU patients. The proportion of DDP subjects reporting parasuicidal behavior decreased from 73% at baseline to 30% at 12 months, which corresponded to a 21% absolute risk reduction for DDP compared to TAU. Absolute risk reduction is the difference in probability between the two treatment groups in the proportion of participants manifesting a behavioral outcome (e.g., parasuicidal behavior). The proportion of DDP subjects reporting alcohol misuse decreased from 67% at baseline to 30% at the end of treatment. The absolute risk reduction for alcohol misuse for DDP relative to TAU was 15%. The proportion of DDP participants needing institutional care decreased from 67% at baseline to 10% at 12 months, which corresponded to a 12% absolute risk reduction for DDP relative to TAU. Additionally, unlike TAU, DDP improved core symptoms of BPD,

depression and dissociation, compared to pretreatment.

Summary of DDP. DDP is a relatively new treatment that targets a particularly vulnerable BPD population, those with co-occurring substance abuse or dependence. DDP has some preliminary support from a small sample RCT. One potentially important aspect of this treatment is that it can be disseminated relatively easily as relatively inexperienced therapists can be trained to administer DDP competently (Gregory et al., 2008). If the observed reductions in suicidality and alcohol abuse are replicated in a larger sample, it may represent an important treatment for a particularly difficult to treat subgroup of individuals with BPD; however, the absolute risk reductions estimates were small and whether it is worth the allocation of significant resources to train and implement this form of treatment for this modest gain is unclear.

ADJUNCTIVE PSYCHOSOCIAL TREATMENTS FOR SPECIFIC SYMPTOMS

Several treatments for symptoms dimensions of BPD have been developed that are designed to be adjunctive to TAU or other psychotherapeutic or medication treatments. These treatments may be particularly important in geographic areas that do not have access to therapists trained in the comprehensive therapies. These treatments target the most dangerous aspects of BPD and may be able to be taught and disseminated more efficiently. Two adjunctive psychosocial treatments have garnered empirical support from RCTs, Manual-Assisted Cognitive Therapy (MACT) and Systems Training for Emotional Predictability and Problem Solving (STEPPS).

Manual-Assisted Cognitive Therapy

Manual-Assisted Cognitive Therapy is a six-session therapy that incorporates elements of

DBT, CBT, and bibliotherapy, a therapy that focuses on reading self-healing, educational material. Each session is structured around a chapter of a booklet, covering functional or behavioral analysis of episodes of parasuicide, emotion regulation strategies, problem-solving strategies, management of negative thinking, management of substance use, and strategies aimed at preventing relapse.

To evaluate the effectiveness of this short, adjunctive treatment, Weinberg and colleagues (2006) randomized 30 women with BPD between the ages of 18 and 40 years with a history of at least one instance of deliberate self-harm to treatment with either MACT + TAU (N = 15) or TAU (N = 15) for 6 to 8 weeks. Because MACT is an adjunctive therapy to TAU, patients also received additional forms of mental health care such psychotropic medications and individual and group psychotherapy as needed. Level of suicide ideation and deliberate self-harm (DSH) were assessed at baseline, 6–8 weeks, and at 6 months posttreatment. The MACT group had significantly greater decrease in frequency and severity of deliberate self-harm at both 6–8 weeks and 6 months follow-up; however, a greater amount of concurrent treatment was associated with a greater decrease in deliberate self-harm, although concurrent treatment was a smaller contributor to improvement than MACT. No significant differences between groups were observed for suicidal ideation and time to repeat deliberate self-harm.

Systems Training for Emotional Predictability and Problem Solving

STEPPS is a 20-week group therapy treatment for patients with BPD that is meant to supplement TAU. A systems element of this treatment involves educating family members and therapists about BPD and instructing them on constructive ways of interacting with individuals with BPD. STEPPS consists of three components. A psychoeducational component that reframes BPD as an emotional intensity problem, an emotion management component that teaches effective strategies for managing the intense emotions that are characteristic of the disorder, and a behavioral management component that teaches goal setting, healthy eating behaviors, sleep hygiene, regular exercise, leisure activities, health monitoring (e.g., medication adherence), avoidance of self-harm, and interpersonal effectiveness.

Blum et al. (2008) randomized 134 BPD patients to either STEPPS plus TAU (N = 65) or TAU alone (N = 59). Treatment lasted for 20 weeks and subjects were assessed throughout a 1-year follow-up time period after treatment had ended. There were no differences between the groups in suicide attempts and self-harm, although STEPPS was superior to TAU with regard to depression and the cognitive, impulsive, affective, and disturbed relationship domains of the Zanarini Rating Scale for Personality Disorder.

META-ANALYSES OF GROUP DESIGNS

Several meta-analyses have been conducted examining the efficacy of psychotherapy for the treatment of personality disorders. Leichsenring and Leibing (2003) examined the effectiveness of psychodynamic therapy and CBT in the treatment of personality disorders in a meta-analysis of 25 studies, 13 of which included patients with BPD. Improvement in symptom severity and personality measures was observed in BPD patients following both psychodynamic therapy and CBT. McMain and Pos (2007) reviewed psychotherapy studies with a focus on personality disorders. They concluded that psychotherapy was successful in the treatment of BPD. Patients receiving CBT, including specialized skills-based interventions such as MACT and STEPPS, showed an improvement in BPD symptoms and psychopathology and a decrease in frequency of suicide attempts. DBT in particular led to a reduction in suicidal behaviors, hospitalizations, and self-mutilating behaviors and an improvement in treatment retention and general psychopathology. Moreover, BPD patients receiving schema-focused therapy showed improvement in symptom severity and psychopathologies. Finally, Binks et al. (2006) included seven RCTs in a meta-analysis of psychological treatments in patients with BPD and found that DBT led to a decrease in self-harm, suicidal ideation, parasuicidal behavior, and general psychiatric severity. From these reviews, it appears that psychotherapy is an effective intervention in the treatment of BPD. While DBT has received the most support, psychodynamic, cognitive behavioral, and schema-focused psychotherapies were also found to be effective.

WHAT WORKS FOR BORDERLINE PERSONALITY DISORDER?

At this point, DBT has the most consistent support in reducing suicidality and para-suicidality in RCTs for BPD and is the only treatment meeting criteria as a well-established treatment for BPD. DBT consistently demonstrates reductions in parasuicidality, hospitalizations due to suicidal behavior, decreases in anger, impulsivity, and depression, as well as lower rates of drop out, compared to TAU and treatment by experts; however, DBT has not demonstrated superiority over other forms of specialized treatments, such as TFP, and has not been compared to other specialized treatments such as MBT and SFT. DBT has also been modified substantially in different studies and remained effective, which bodes well for its use in different settings and populations. For example, in Turner (2000), treatment was conducted in 6 rather than 12 months, psychodynamic conceptualization was used, and skills training was conducted in individual rather than group sessions. In addition, DBT modified for the treatment of BPD with comorbid substance abuse appears effective, although one study showed no improvement in drug use behavior (van den Bosch et al., 2002). Thus, DBT appears to be an effective and flexible treatment for BPD with and without substance abuse.

Our review also reveals a number of other comprehensive treatments for BPD that show promise and meet criteria for being probably efficacious. With regard to SFT and CBT, Giesen-Bloo et al. (2006) and Spinhoven et al. (2007) suggest that SFT is superior to TFP with regard to reducing certain psychiatric symptoms and retaining patients over time; however, the implementation of the TFP arm in this study has been questioned. Yeomans (2007) argued that the therapists in the TFP arm were not adequately trained, that the treatment was more consistent with a general psychodynamic approach to BPD, and that the BPD-tailored aspects of TFP were missing. The two additional studies comparing SFT and CBT to TAU were somewhat inconsistent. One study did not show any differences between SFT and CBT and TAU in reducing parasuicidality but did show differences in the mean number of suicide attempts, although the effect size was small (Davidson, Norrie, et al., 2006).

With regard to psychoanalytically informed treatments, there is growing evidence that manualized forms of these treatments are also probably efficacious. In one trial, TFP performed comparably to DBT at 1 year, and there were some indications of superiority over supportive psychotherapy. TFP-treated patients in a subsequent paper showed greater improvements in reflective function, attachment coherence, and security of attachment after 1 year compared to the DBT and SPT groups. MBT showed decreases in self-mutilation compared to TAU but these differences did not emerge until after 18 months of treatment (Bateman & Fonagy, 1999); however, long-term follow-up suggested that these gains are maintained and perhaps even improved over a 5-year time span (Bateman & Fonagy, 2008). No other treatment has demonstrated this level of long-term efficacy for BPD.

One possibility that the MBT data support is the notion of an *incubation effect* in which short-term gains are relatively modest, whereas long-term gains are more robust and stable. This appears to be the opposite of what has occurred in DBT trials. For example, DBT treatment was associated with greater reductions in parasuicidality and psychiatric hospitalization at 12 and 18 months compared to TAU, but at 24 months from baseline, there were no longer any differences between the groups in parasuicidality whereas psychiatric hospitalizations remained lower in the DBT group (Linehan et al., 1993). This suggests that DBT may be more beneficial in the short term but for long-term gains more dynamically oriented approaches may be preferred. Of course, it is possible that this particular RCT of DBT lacked the statistical power to detect true differences that were actually present at 24 months due to small sample sizes. Nevertheless, one possibility is to implement a sequential treatment approach to BPD that uses DBT initially for 1 year to develop skills and reduce behavioral dysregulation and then transition to a more dynamically informed treatment for long-term gains. Future research should examine this possibility.

Another theme that emerges from this review is that different treatments may have different effects on different symptom dimensions in BPD. For example, DBT is clearly effective in reducing affective instability and parasuicidality whereas TFP demonstrates greater improvements in areas like aggression, reflective functioning, and attachment organization. Thus, perhaps different treatments are perhaps acting in different ways to improve different sets of systems in quite possibly different subgroups of BPD patients. This possibility is supported by research indicating that there are distinct subgroups of BPD. One study applied finite mixture modeling to a sample of 90 subjects with BPD and found three distinct groups. One group was characterized by low levels of antisocial, paranoid, and aggressive features, another group was characterized by

high levels of paranoid features, and a third group was characterized by high levels of antisocial and aggressive features (Lenzenweger, Clarkin, Yeomans, Kernberg, & Levy, 2008).

An area of potential confusion is the number of CBT treatments that we reviewed. For example, DBT, SFT, and CBT are all identified as CBT treatments. In general, cognitive behavior therapies fall on a continuum ranging from the more behavioral to the more cognitive. In this regard, DBT falls much more on the behavioral than the cognitive end of the spectrum. There is very little if any challenging of automatic thoughts or use of thought records in DBT, which are staples of cognitive behavioral treatments. In fact, from a DBT perspective, identifying and challenging dysfunctional thoughts could easily be considered invalidating. The emphasis in DBT is much more on behavior analysis of skills deficits, skills training, and validation. SFT predominantly differs from traditional cognitive therapy because of its focus on early childhood experiences in treatment, the use of the therapeutic relationship to facilitate change, and the active confrontation of maladaptive behavioral and belief patterns (McArdle, 2001). SFT and CBT are most alike in that both are essentially cognitive behavioral treatments with a focus on identifying maladaptive thoughts and core beliefs. Perhaps one way they differ from each other is that SFT places more emphasis on working with core beliefs as well as incorporating the therapeutic relationship than does CBT.

Demonstrating efficacy in an RCT does not elucidate why or how the change came about. Therefore, it is important that we begin addressing questions such as, "Under what conditions and for which patients is treatment most helpful?" and, "Why and how do effective treatments work?" (Kazdin, 2007; Kraemer, Wilson, Fairburn, & Agras, 2002). Treatment mechanism studies are designed to answer these how and why and for whom treatment works questions (Kraemer et al., 2002). Mechanism studies move beyond efficacy and effectiveness studies by generating knowledge about how a treatment impacts basic cognitive, emotional, and neurobiological processes and symptoms of a given disorder. Mechanism research can support strong, causal inferences about what interventions work for which patients under what conditions. In doing so, mechanism studies can contribute to improvements of existing treatments. For example, are the reductions in parasuicidality observed in several DBT studies mediated by improved emotion regulation as DBT theory suggests? This is a crucial step for an efficacious treatment, as it may be effective, but not through the mechanisms theorized to subserve therapeutic change (Longmore & Worrell, 2007). Moreover, is the sequence of changes in cognitive, emotional, and social processes important in the treatment of BPD? For example, does change in interpersonal behavior precede changes in impulsivity and emotion regulation? Alternately, do all these processes change concurrently in BPD? Do changes in basic processes always precede symptom change? Or, do changes in symptoms and functioning occur in tandem with changes in emotion, cognition, and behavior? Does treating some symptoms, such as severe depression, pave the way for changing other processes such as emotion regulation? Which processes are the most resistant to change? Are there particular treatment strategies that are more effective in changing some basic processes than others? Does knowledge of pretreatment status in basic processes (e.g., low levels of impulse control) inform who responds to what treatments and treatment combinations?

It is interesting, but not too long ago, the prevailing view was that patients with BPD were untreatable (Stern, 1938; Stone et al., 1987). For example, in describing different approaches to handling a patient who walked out in a rage on her therapist in midsession, Basch (1980) writes:

> Had the therapist diagnosed Miss Banks's behavior as clinically borderline, there can

be no doubt of his next steps: He would have to contact her, if necessary take the blame for her leaving and apologize for upsetting her, induce her to return for treatment, give up at least for the moment, any notion of conducting an insight-oriented psychotherapy, do his best to shore up her defenses against her inner turmoil, and help her adapt to the limitations of a psychologically marginal existence. (pp. 60–61)

Today, the outlook is not so grim (Gabbard, 2007; Lenzenweger, 2008; Perry et al., 1999; Zanarini et al., 2003). As our review shows, there are a range of well-established (e.g., DBT) and probably efficacious (e.g., MBT, TFP, SFT) treatments that exist, and patients with BPD no longer need to fear living a psychologically marginal existence.

REFERENCES

American Psychiatric Association. (2000). *Diagnostic and statistical manual of mental disorders* (4th ed.) *(DSM-IV-TR)*. Washington, DC: Author.

Atre-Vaidya, N., & Hussain, S. M. (1999). Borderline personality disorder and bipolar mood disorder: Two distinct disorders or a continuum? *Journal of Nervous and Mental Diseases, 187,* 313–315.

Basch, M. F. (1980). *Doing psychotherapy*. New York, NY: Basic Books.

Bateman, A., & Fonagy, P. (1999). Effectiveness of partial hospitalization in the treatment of borderline personality disorder: A randomized controlled trial. *American Journal of Psychiatry, 156,* 1563–1569.

Bateman, A., & Fonagy, P. (2008). 8-year follow-up of patients treated for borderline personality disorder: Mentalization-based treatment versus treatment as usual. *American Journal of Psychiatry, 165,* 631–638.

Bender, D. S., Dolan, R. T., Skodol, A. E., Sanislow, C. A., Dyck, I. R., McGlashan, T. H., & Gunderson, J. G. (2001). Treatment utilization by patients with personality disorders. *American Journal of Psychiatry, 158,* 295–302.

Binks, C., Fenton, M., McCarthy, L., Lee, T., Adams, C. E., & Duggan, C. (2006). Psychological therapies for people with borderline personality disorder. *Cochrane Database of Systematic Reviews*,(1), Art. No.: CD005652. doi: 005610.001002/14651858.CD14005652

Black, D. W., Blum, N., Pfohl, B., & Hale, N. (2004). Suicidal behavior in borderline personality disorder: Prevalence, risk factors, prediction, and prevention. *Journal of Personal Disorders, 18,* 226–239.

Blum, N., St. John, D., Pfohl, B., Stuart, S., McCormick, B., Allen, J., & Black, D. W. (2008). Systems training for emotional predictability and problem solving (STEPPS) for outpatients with borderline personality disorder: A randomized controlled trial and 1-year follow-up. *American Journal of Psychiatry, 165,* 468–478.

Chambless, D. L., & Hollon, S. D. (1998). Defining empirically supported therapies. *Journal of Consulting and Clinical Psychology, 66,* 7–18.

Clarkin, J. F., Levy, K. N., Lenzenweger, M. F., & Kernberg, O. F. (2007). Evaluating three treatments for borderline personality disorder: A multiwave study. *American Journal of Psychiatry, 164,* 922–928.

Clarkin, J. F., Yeomans, F., & Kernberg, O. F. (2006). *Psychotherapy of borderline personality: Focusing on object relations.* Arlington, VA: American Psychiatric Publishing.

Clifton, A., & Pilkonis, P. A. (2007). Evidence for a single latent class of diagnostic and statistical manual of mental disorders borderline personality pathology. *Comprehensive Psychiatry, 48,* 70–78.

Cohen, J. (1988). *Statistical power analysis for the behavioral sciences* (2nd ed.). Hillsdale, NJ: Erlbaum

Cohen, J. (1992). A power primer. *Psychological Bulletin, 112,* 155–159.

Davidson, K. (2007). *Cognitive therapy for personality disorders: A guide for clinicians.* New York, NY: Routledge.

Davidson, K., Norrie, J., Tyrer, P., Gumley, A., Tata, P., Murray, H., & Palmer, S. (2006). The effectiveness of cognitive behavior therapy for borderline personality disorder: Results from the borderline personality disorder study of cognitive therapy (BOSCOT) trial. *Journal of Personal Disorders, 20,* 450–465

Davidson, K., Tyrer, P., Gumley, A., Tata, P., Norrie, J., Palmer, S., . . . Macaulay, F. (2006). A randomized controlled trial of cognitive behavior therapy for borderline personality disorder: Rationale for trial, method, and description of sample. *Journal of Personal Disorders, 20,* 431–449

Deltito, J., Martin, L., Riefkohl, J., Austria, B., Kissilenko, A., & Corless, C. M. P. (2001). Do patients with borderline personality disorder belong to the bipolar spectrum? *Journal of Affective Disorders, 67,* 221–228

Fertuck, E. A., Lenzenweger, M. F., Clarkin, J. F., Hoermann, S., & Stanley, B. (2006). Executive neurocognition, memory systems, and borderline personality disorder. *Clinical Psychology Review, 26,* 346–375

Fertuck, E. A., Makhija, N., & Stanley, B. (2007). The nature of suicidality in borderline personality disorder. *Primary Psychiatry, 14,* 40–47

Frankenburg, F. R., & Zanarini, M. C. (2004). The association between borderline personality disorder

and chronic medical illnesses, poor health-related lifestyle choices, and costly forms of health care utilization. *Journal of Clinical Psychiatry, 65,* 1660–1665.

Gabbard, G. O. (2007). Do all roads lead to Rome? New findings on borderline personality disorder. *American Journal of Psychiatry, 164,* 853–855.

Giesen-Bloo, J., Van Dyck, R., Spinhoven, P., van Tilburg, W., Dirksen, C., van Asselt, T., . . . Arntz, A.. (2006). Outpatient psychotherapy for borderline personality disorder: Randomized trial of schema-focused therapy vs transference-focused psychotherapy. *Archives of General Psychiatry, 63,* 649–658.

Gregory, R. J., Chlebowski, S., Kang, D., Remen, A. L., Soderberg, M. G., & Virk, S. (2008). A controlled trial of psychodynamic psychotherapy for co-occurring borderline personality disorder and alcohol use disorder. *Psychotherapy: Theory, Research, Practice, Training, 45,* 28–41.

Gunderson, J. G., Daversa, M. T., Grilo, C. M., McGlashan, T. H., Zanarini, M. C., Shea, M. T., & Stout, R. L. (2006). Predictors of 2-year outcome for patients with borderline personality disorder. *American Journal of Psychiatry, 163,* 822–826.

Heffernan, K., & Cloitre, M. (2000). A comparison of posttraumatic stress disorder with and without borderline personality disorder among women with a history of childhood sexual abuse: Etiological and clinical characteristics. *Journal of Nervous and Mental Diseases, 188,* 589–595.

Henry, C., Mitropoulou, V., New, A. S., Koenigsberg, H. W., Silverman, J., & Siever, L. J. (2001). Affective instability and impulsivity in borderline personality and bipolar II disorders: Similarities and differences. *Journal of Psychiatric Research, 35,* 307–312.

Jacobs, D. G., Brewer, M., & Klein-Benheim, M. (1999). Suicide assessment: An overview and recommended protocol. In D. G. Jacobs (Ed.), *The Harvard Medical School guide to suicide assessment and intervention* (pp. 3–39). San Francisco, CA: Jossey-Bass

Joyce, P. R., Mulder, R. T., Luty, S. E., McKenzie, J. M., Sullivan, P. F., & Cloninger, R. C. (2003). Borderline personality disorder in major depression: Symptomatology, temperament, character, differential drug response, and 6-month outcome. *Comprehensive Psychiatry, 44,* 35–43

Kazdin, A. E. (2007). Mediators and mechanisms of change in psychotherapy research. *Annual Review of Clinical Psychology, 3,* 1–27

Kernberg, O. F. (1996). *A psychoanalytic theory of personality disorders.* New York, NY: Guilford Press

Koons, C. R., Robins, C. J., Lindsey-Tweed, L., Lynch, T. R., Gonzalez, A. M., Morse, J. Q., & Bastian, L. A. (2001). Efficacy of dialectical behavior therapy in women veterans with borderline personality disorder. *Behavior Therapy, 32,* 371–390

Kraemer, H. C., Wilson, G. T., Fairburn, C. G., & Agras, W. S. (2002). Mediators and moderators of treatment effects in randomized clinical trials. *Archives of General Psychiatry, 59*, 877–883.

Landecker, H. (1992). The role of childhood sexual trauma in the etiology of borderline personality disorder: Considerations for diagnosis and treatment. *Psychotherapy, 29*, 234–242.

Leichsenring, F., & Leibing, E. (2003). The effectiveness of psychodynamic therapy and cognitive behavior therapy in the treatment of personality disorders: A meta-analysis. *American Journal of Psychiatry, 160*, 1223–1232.

Lenzenweger, M. F. (2008). Epidemiology of personality disorders. *Psychiatric Clinics of North America, 31*, 395–403.

Lenzenweger, M. F., Clarkin, J. F., Yeomans, F. E., Kernberg, O. F., & Levy, K. N. (2008). Refining the borderline personality disorder phenotype through finite mixture modeling: Implications for classification. *Journal of Personality Disorders, 22*, 313–331.

Lenzenweger, M. F., Lane, M. C., Loranger, A. W., & Kessler, R. C. (2007). *DSM-IV* personality disorders in the national comorbidity survey replication. *Biological Psychiatry, 8*, 668–676.

Levant, R. F. (2005). *Report of the 2005 presidential task force on evidence-based practice*: Washington, DC: American Psychological Association.

Levy, K. N., Clarkin, J. F., Yeomans, F. E., Scott, L. N., Wasserman, R. H., & Kernberg, O. F. (2006). The mechanisms of change in the treatment of borderline personality disorder with transference focused psychotherapy. *Journal of Clinical Psychology, 62*, 481–501.

Levy, K. N., Meehan, K. B., Kelly, K. M., Reynoso, J. S., Weber, M., Clarkin, J. F., & Kernberg, O. F. (2006). Change in attachment patterns and reflective function in a randomized control trial of transference-focused psychotherapy for borderline personality disorder. *Journal of Consulting and Clinical Psychology, 74*, 1027–1040.

Linehan, M. M. (1993a). *Cognitive-behavioral treatment of borderline personality disorder*. New York, NY: Guilford Press.

Linehan, M. M. (1993b). *Skills manual for treating borderline personality disorder*. New York, NY: Guilford Press.

Linehan, M. M., Armstrong, H. E., Suarez, A., Allmon, D., & Heard, H. L. (1991). Cognitive-behavioral treatment of chronically parasuicidal borderline patients. *Archives of General Psychiatry, 48*, 1060–1064.

Linehan, M. M., Comtois, K. A., Murray, A. M., Brown, M. Z., Gallop, R. J., Heard, H. L., & Lindenboim, N. (2006). Two-year randomized controlled trial and follow-up of dialectical behavior therapy vs therapy by experts for suicidal behaviors and borderline personality disorder. *Archives of General Psychiatry, 63*, 757–766.

Linehan, M. M., Dimeff, L. A., Reynolds, S. K., Comtois, K. A., Welch, S. S., Heagerty, P., & Kivlahan, D. R. (2002). Dialectical behavior therapy versus comprehensive validation therapy plus 12-step for the treatment of opioid dependent women meeting criteria for borderline personality disorder. *Drug and Alcohol Dependence, 67*, 13–26.

Linehan, M. M., Heard, H. L., & Armstrong, H. E. (1993). Naturalistic follow-up of a behavioral treatment for chronically parasuicidal borderline patients. *Archives of General Psychiatry, 50*, 971–974.

Linehan, M. M., McDavid, J. D., Brown, M. Z., Sayrs, J. H., & Gallop, R. J. (2008). Olanzapine plus dialectical behavior therapy for women with high irritability who meet criteria for borderline personality disorder: A double-blind, placebo-controlled pilot study. *Journal of Clinical Psychiatry, 69*, 999–1005.

Linehan, M. M., Schmidt, H., Dimeff, L. A., Craft, J. C., Kanter, J., & Comtois, K. A. (1999). Dialectical behavior therapy for patients with borderline personality disorder and drug-dependence. *American Journal of Additions, 8*, 279–292.

Linehan, M. M., Tutek, D. A., Heard, H. L., & Armstrong, H. E. (1994). Interpersonal outcome of cognitive behavioral treatment for chronically suicidal borderline patients. *American Journal of Psychiatry, 151*, 1771–1776.

Longmore, R. J., & Worrell, M. (2007). Do we need to challenge thoughts in cognitive behavior therapy? *Clinical Psychology Review, 27*, 173–187.

Marshall, W. L., & Serin, R. (1997). Personality disorders. In S. M. Turner & M. Hersen (Eds.), *Adult psychopathology and diagnosis* (3rd ed., pp. 508–543). New York, NY: Wiley.

McArdle, J. J. (2001). A latent difference score approach to longitudinal dynamic structural analyses. In R. Cudeck, S. d. Toit & D. Sorbom (Eds.), *Structural equation modeling: Present and future* (pp. 342–380). Lincolnwood, IL: Scientific Software International.

McGinn, L. K., & Young, J. E. (1997). Schema-focused therapy. In P. M. Salkovskis & S. Rachman (Eds.), *Frontiers of cognitive therapy* (pp. 182–207). New York, NY: Guilford Press.

McMain, S., & Pos, A. E. (2007). Advances in psychotherapy of Personality Disorders: A research update. *Current Psychiatry Reports, 9*, 46–52.

Oldham, J. M. (2005). *Guideline watch: Practice guideline for the treatment of patients with borderline personality disorder*. Arlington, VA: American Psychiatric Association.

Paris, J., Gunderson, J., & Weinberg, I. (2007). The interface between borderline personality disorder and bipolar spectrum disorders. *Comprehensive Psychiatry, 48*, 145–154.

Perry, J. C., Banon, E., & Ianni, F. (1999). Effectiveness of psychotherapy for personality disorders. *American Journal of Psychiatry, 156*, 1312–1321.

Sanislow, C. A., Grilo, C. M., & McGlashan, T. H. (2000). Factor analysis of the *DSM-III-R* borderline personality disorder criteria in psychiatric inpatients. *American Journal of Psychiatry, 157*, 1629–1633.

Simeon, D., Stanley, B., Frances, A., Mann, J. J., Winchel, R., & Stanley, M. (1992). Self-mutilation in personality disorders: Psychological and biological correlates. *American Journal of Psychiatry, 149*, 221–226.

Skodol, A. E., Gunderson, J. G., Pfohl, B., Widiger, T. A., Livesley, W. J., & Siever, L. J. (2002). The borderline diagnosis I: Psychopathology, comorbidity, and personality structure. *Biological Psychiatry, 51*, 951–963.

Spinhoven, P., Giesen-Bloo, J., van Dyck, R., Kooiman, K., & Arntz, A. (2007). The therapeutic alliance in schema-focused therapy and transference-focused psychotherapy for borderline personality disorder. *Journal of Consulting and Clinical Psychology, 75*, 104–115.

Stanley, B., & Wilson, S. T. (2006). Heightened subjective experience of depression in borderline personality disorder. *Journal of Personal Disorders, 20*, 307–318.

Stern, A. (1938). Psychoanalytic investigation of and therapy in the borderline group of neuroses. *Psychoanalytic Quarterly, 7*, 467–489.

Stiglmayr, C. E., Grathwol, T., Linehan, M. M., Ihorst, G., Fahrenberg, J., & Bohus, M. (2005). Aversive tension in patients with borderline personality disorder. A computer-based controlled field study. *Acta Psychiatrica Scandinavia, 111*, 372–379.

Stone, M. H., Hurt, S. W., & Stone, D. K. (1987). PI 500 Long-term follow-up of borderline inpatients meeting *DSM-III* criteria I: Global outcome. *Journal of Personality Disorders, 1*, 291–298.

Swartz, M. S., Blazer, D. G., George, L. K., Winfield, I., Zakris, J., & Dye, E. (1989). Identification of borderline personality disorder with the NIMH Diagnostic Interview Schedule. *American Journal of Psychiatry, 146*, 200–205.

Tanney, B. L. (2000). Psychiatric diagnoses and suicidal acts. In R. W. Maris, A. L. Berman, & M. M. Silverman (Eds.), *Comprehensive textbook of suicidology* (pp. 311–341). New York, NY: Guilford Press.

Torgersen, S., Kringlen, E., & Cramer, V. (2001). The prevalence of personality disorders in a community sample. *Archives of General Psychiatry, 58*, 590–596.

Trull, T. J., Sher, K. J., Minks-Brown, C., Durbin, J., & Burr, R. (2000). Borderline personality disorder and substance use disorders: A review and integration. *Clinical Psychology Review, 20*, 235–253.

Turner, R. M. (2000). Naturalistic evaluation of dialectical behavior therapy-oriented treatment for borderline personality disorder. *Cognitive and Behavioral Practice, 7*, 413–419.

Van den Bosch, L. M., Koeter, M. W., Stijnen, T., Verheul, R., & van den Brink, W. (2005). Sustained efficacy of dialectical behaviour therapy for borderline personality disorder. *Behaviour Research and Therapy, 43*, 1231–1241.

Van den Bosch, L. M., Verheul, R., Schippers, G. M., & van den Brink, W. (2002). Dialectical behavior therapy of borderline patients with and without substance use problems. Implementation and long-term effects. *Addictive Behavior, 27*, 911–923.

Verheul, R., Van den Bosch, L. M., Koeter, M. W., De Ridder, M. A., Stijnen, T., & Van Den Brink, W. (2003). Dialectical behaviour therapy for women with borderline personality disorder: 12-month, randomised clinical trial in The Netherlands. *British Journal of Psychiatry, 182*, 135–140.

Weinberg, I., Gunderson, J. G., Hennen, J., & Cutter, C. J., Jr. (2006). Manual assisted cognitive treatment for deliberate self-harm in borderline personality disorder patients. *Journal of Personality Disorders, 20*, 482–492.

Wilson, S. T., Fertuck, E. A., Kwitel, A., Stanley, M. C., & Stanley, B. (2006). Impulsivity, suicidality and alcohol use disorders in adolescents and young adults with borderline personality disorder. *International Journal of Adolescent Medicine and Health, 18*, 189–196.

Yeomans, F. (2007). Questions concerning the randomized trial of schema-focused therapy vs. transference-focused psychotherapy. *Archives of General Psychiatry, 64*, 609–610.

Young, J. E. (1994). *Cognitive therapy for personality disorders: A schema-focused approach*. Sarasota, FL: Professional Resource Press.

Zanarini, M. C., Frankenburg, F. R., Hennen, J., Reich, D. B., & Silk, K. R. (2004). Axis I comorbidity in patients with borderline personality disorder: 6-year follow-up and prediction of time to remission. *American Journal of Psychiatry, 161*, 2108–2114.

Zanarini, M. C., Frankenburg, F. R., Hennen, J., & Silk, K. R. (2003). The longitudinal course of borderline psychopathology: 6-year prospective follow-up of the phenomenology of borderline personality disorder. *American Journal of Psychiatry, 160*, 274–283.

23

Other Personality Disorders

MARY MCMURRAN

OVERVIEW OF DISORDERS

Diagnostic Criteria

Personality disorders are psychiatric conditions described in the *Diagnostic and Statistical Manual of Mental Disorders* (4th ed., text rev.) *(DSM-IV-TR)* (American Psychiatric Association, 2000) and the *International Classification of Diseases* (10th rev.) *(ICD-10)* Classification of Mental and Behavioural Disorders (World Health Organization, 1992). The development of these two classification systems has been coordinated to promote congruence and so these criteria are highly similar (Widiger, 2001). Primacy will be given to *DSM-IV* definitions in this chapter.

Personality disorders are usually diagnosed only in adults, since traits evident in childhood may not persist into adult life, although diagnosis of a person under age 18 years is possible if features have been present for at least 1 year. The definition of a personality disorder, provided by *DSM-IV-TR* (American Psychiatric Association, 2000), is "an enduring pattern of inner experience and behavior that deviates markedly from the expectations of the individual's culture, is pervasive and inflexible, has an onset in adolescence or early adulthood, is stable over time, and leads to distress or impairment" (p. 685). The key features of personality disorder are that the person's behavior and experiences are persistent, pervasive, and problematic. Personality disorders are defined on Axis II of the *DSM-IV* to ensure that they are not overlooked through the focus of attention being on Axis I disorders.

The *DSM-IV-TR* general criteria for diagnosing a personality disorder are:

A. An enduring pattern of inner experience and behavior that deviates markedly from the expectations of the individual's culture. This pattern is manifested in two (or more) of the following areas: cognition (i.e., ways of perceiving and interpreting self, other people, and events) (1) affectivity (i.e., the range, intensity, lability, and appropriateness of emotional response); interpersonal functioning, impulse control B. The enduring pattern is inflexible and pervasive across a broad range of personal and social situations. C. The enduring pattern leads to clinically significant distress or impairment in social, occupational, or other important areas of functioning. D. The pattern is stable and of long duration and its onset can be traced back at least to adolescence or early adulthood. E. The enduring pattern is not better accounted for as a manifestation or consequence of another mental disorder. F. The enduring pattern is not due to the direct physiological effects of a substance (e.g., a drug of abuse, a medication) or a general medical condition (e.g., head trauma). (p. 689)[1]

[1] Reprinted with permission from the *Diagnostic and Statistical Manual of Mental Disorders, Fourth Edition, Text Revision* (Copyright © 2000). American Psychiatric Association.

The *DSM-IV* personality disorders are grouped in three clusters: Cluster A: odd or eccentric (paranoid, schizoid, and schizotypal); Cluster B: dramatic or flamboyant (antisocial, borderline, histrionic, and narcissistic); and Cluster C: anxious or fearful (avoidant, dependent, and obsessive-compulsive). These clusters represent a hierarchical model with the individual personality disorders belonging to one of three latent factors or clusters. Empirical support for these clusters is equivocal, with some studies upholding the three-cluster structure (Bagby, Joffe, Parker, & Schuller, 1993), and others not (Blais, McCann, Benedict, & Norman, 1997; Schopp & Trull, 1993).

Cluster A Disorders[2]

Paranoid personality disorder is characterized by distrust and unfounded suspicions, preoccupation with unjustified doubts about others' loyalty or trustworthiness, reluctance to confide in others, reading hidden, demeaning, or threatening meaning into benign remarks, persistent bearing of grudges, readiness to perceive attacks on his or her character, quickness to react angrily, and recurrent unjustified suspiciousness about the faithfulness of his or her spouse or sexual partner.

Schizoid personality disorder is characterized by detachment from relationships. It may include a restricted range of expression of emotions. The person may not desire or enjoy close relationships. He or she may prefer solitary activities, have little interest in sex, take pleasure in few or no activities, lack close friends, appear indifferent to the praise or criticism of others, and show emotional coldness, detachment, or flattened affect.

Schizotypal personality disorder is marked by social and interpersonal deficits. These deficits may include acute discomfort with close relationships, cognitive or perceptual distortions, and eccentricities of behavior. Other characteristics include ideas of reference, odd beliefs or magical thinking, unusual perceptual experiences, odd speech, suspiciousness or paranoid ideas, inappropriate or constricted affect, odd, eccentric, or peculiar behavior, lack of close friends, and persistent and excessive social anxiety associated with paranoid fears.

Cluster B Disorders

Antisocial personality disorder includes conduct disorder beginning before age 15 years in addition to a pervasive pattern of disregard for and violation of the rights of others in adulthood. It may include failure to abide by the law, which may be shown by repeatedly behaving in ways that are grounds for arrest, deceitfulness, impulsivity, irritability and aggressiveness, reckless disregard for safety, consistent irresponsibility, and lack of remorse.

Borderline personality disorder is described in detail in Chapter 22.

Histrionic personality disorder is characterized by excessive emotionality and attention seeking. This may include discomfort in situations in which the individual is not the center of attention. It may include inappropriate sexually seductive or provocative behavior in interactions with others, rapidly shifting and shallow emotional expression, use of physical appearance to draw attention to his or herself, excessively impressionistic speech that may lack detail, self-dramatization, and suggestibility; the person may consider relationships to be more intimate than they are.

Narcissistic personality disorder is characterized by grandiosity, need for admiration, and lack of empathy. This may include a grandiose sense of self-importance, preoccupation with fantasies of unlimited success, and a belief that one is special and unique. A person with narcissistic personality disorder may require excessive admiration, may feel entitled and be interpersonally exploitative, and may lack empathy, be envious, believe others are envious of him or her, and be arrogant.

---

[2]The following text under the headings "Cluster A Disorders," "Cluster B Disorders," "Cluster C Disorders," and "Personality Disorder Not Otherwise Specified" was provided by Peter Sturmey.

Cluster C Disorders

Avoidant personality disorder includes social inhibition, feelings of inadequacy, and hypersensitivity to negative evaluation. Symptoms may include avoidance of occupations that involve significant interpersonal contact for fear of criticism, unwillingness to get involved with others unless certain of being liked, showing restraint in intimate relationships for fear of being shamed or ridiculed, preoccupation with being criticized or rejected, and feeling inhibited in new interpersonal situations because of feelings of inadequacy. The person may view himself or herself as socially inept, personally unappealing, or inferior to others, and be reluctant to take personal risks or engage in new activities because they may prove embarrassing.

Dependent personality disorder includes an excessive need to be taken care of that leads to submissive and clinging behavior. The person fears separation. Symptoms include difficulty making everyday decisions without excessive reassurance. They person may need others to assume responsibility for most major life areas. He or she may have difficulty expressing disagreement due to unrealistic fears of loss of support or approval, and have difficulty initiating projects or doing things independently because of lack of self-confidence. The individual may also go to excessive lengths to obtain nurturance and support, feel uncomfortable or helpless when alone, urgently seek another relationship when a close relationship ends, and be unrealistically preoccupied with fear of being left to take care of himself or herself.

Obsessive-compulsive personality disorder can include preoccupation with orderliness and perfectionism, including mental and interpersonal control, at the expense of flexibility, openness, and efficiency. Symptoms may also include preoccupation with details and rules, perfectionism that interferes with task completion, excessive devotion to work and productivity, over-conscientiousness, and over-scrupulousness. Obsessive-compulsive disorder is also characterized by inflexibility about

matters of morality, ethics, or values. This disorder may include inability to discard worn-out or worthless objects, a reluctance to delegate tasks, miserliness, rigidity, and stubbornness.

Personality Disorder Not Otherwise Specified

Personality disorder not otherwise specified refers to a personality disorder that does not meet the criteria for another other personality disorder sufficiently intense to cause distress or impairment. It may include a mixed personality disorder, which has features of more than one disorder. It may also refer to a personality disorder not included in *DSM-IV-TR*, such as *depressive personality disorder*.

Prevalence

Coid, Yang, Tyrer, Roberts, and Ullrich (2006) interviewed a representative sample of 626 adults from nearly 9,000 screened in a national study in Great Britain using the Structured Clinical Interview for *DSM-IV* Axis II Disorders (SCID-II) (First, Gibbon, Spitzer, Williams, & Benjamin, 1997). Their estimated prevalence of personality disorders is shown in Table 23.1. An estimated 4.4% of the population have at least one personality disorder, with men (5.4%) more likely to have a personality disorder than women (3.4%). In fact, all personality disorders apart from schizotypal were more prevalent in men. The most prevalent personality disorder type was obsessive-compulsive, and no cases of histrionic or narcissistic personality disorders were identified. Other studies have identified higher population prevalence rates, with 13.4% in a Norwegian sample (Torgerson, Kringlen, & Kramer, 2001), 9.0% in one U.S. sample (Samuels et al., 2002), and 14.9% in another U.S. sample (Lenzenweger, Lane, Loranger, & Kessler, 2007). These differences in prevalence may reflect the use of different versions of the *DSM* or variations in the sensitivity of the diagnostic tests used. The SCID-II (First et al., 1997) was used in the British study, the Structured Interview for *DSM-III-R* Personality

TABLE 23.1   Prevalence (%) of *DSM-IV* Personality Disorders in the General Population

Personality Disorder	UK	Norway	United States	United States
	DSM-IV (Coid et al., 2006)	*DSM-III-R* (Torgerson et al., 2001)	*DSM-IV* (Samuels et al., 2002)	*DSM-IV* (Lenzenweger et al., 2007)
Cluster A	1.60	4.10	2.10	6.20
Paranoid	0.70	2.40	0.70	2.30
Schizoid	0.80	1.70	0.90	4.90
Schizotypal	0.06	0.60	0.60	3.30
Cluster B	1.20	3.10	4.50	2.30
Antisocial	0.60	0.70	4.10	1.00
Borderline	0.70	0.70	0.50	.60
Histrionic	0.00	2.00	0.20	0.00
Narcissistic	0.00	0.80	0.03	0.00
Cluster C	2.60	9.40	2.80	6.80
Avoidant	0.80	5.00	1.80	5.20
Dependent	0.10	1.50	0.10	0.60
Obsessive-compulsive	1.90	2.00	0.90	2.40
Personality disorder (NOS)	1.60			
Any personality disorder	4.40	13.40	9.00	11.90

Disorders (SIDP-R) (Pfohl, Blum, Zimmerman, & Stangl, 1989) in the Norwegian study, and the International Personality Disorder Examination (IPDE) (Loranger, 1997) in the U.S. studies. There may also be differences in how data were analyzed. Lastly, there may be genuine differences between cultures in the prevalence of personality disorders.

To put personality disorder prevalence rates into perspective, the lifetime prevalences in the general population for major mental disorders are: 0.87% for schizophrenia, 0.32% for schizoaffective disorder, 0.07% for schizophreniform disorder, 0.18% for delusional disorder, 0.24% for bipolar I disorder, 0.35% for major depressive disorder with psychotic features, 0.42% for substance-induced psychotic disorders, and 0.21% for psychotic disorders due to a general medical condition (Perälä et al., 2007). Thus, personality disorders are highly prevalent. Whether there is a need to offer treatments to people with personality disorders depends upon their impact on the individual, on his or her family and friends, and on society.

Comorbidity

There is considerable comorbidity of personality disorders with other personality disorders and with major mental disorders. Coid et al. (2006) found that of those who were diagnosable with any personality disorder, 53% had one disorder, 22% had two disorders, 11% had three disorders, and 14% had four or more disorders. The average number of personality disorders for any personality disordered person was 1.92. There was also a high level of comorbidity between clusters, indicating that having a disorder in any one cluster is associated with having a disorder in the other two clusters. Tyrer and Johnson (1996) examined a graded system for classifying the severity of personality disorder in 163 psychiatric patients based upon the number of conditions diagnosed and whether or not these were from the same cluster. The four levels of disorder were: (1) no personality disorder; (2) personality difficulty, that is, meets subthreshold criteria for one or more personality disorders; (3) simple personality disorder, that is, one or more personality disorders within one cluster; and (4) complex personality disorder, that is, two or more personality disorders from different clusters. Patients with complex personality disorders had the highest level of symptoms and improved least in treatment over a 2-year follow-up.

Personality disorders frequently co-occur with Axis I disorders, although for the most part the co-occurrence follows base rates (McGlashan et al., 2000). Coid et al. (2006) found that most people with personality disorders sought help for their Axis I disorders rather than their personality disorders, suggesting that many people with personality disorders may be in treatment for other mental disorders. When personality disorders occur in association with an Axis I disorder, this generally has an increased negative impact upon the individual's functioning (Newton-Howes, Tyrer, & Weaver, 2008) and treatment outcome (Mennin & Heimberg, 2000; Newton-Howes, Tyrer, & Johnston, 2006; Reich, 2003). There is, therefore, a need to treat personality disorder in conjunction with the treatment of other mental disorders.

Comorbidity may reflect some connection among co-occurring disorders or there may simply be diagnostic overlap. There is overlap in the criteria for personality disorders, hence boundaries are unclear and classes are not mutually exclusive. For example, impulsivity is diagnostic of both antisocial and borderline personality disorders, and suspiciousness is diagnostic of both paranoid and schizotypal personality disorders. There is also overlap between criteria for personality disorders and other psychiatric conditions. For example, schizotypal personality disorder and Axis I psychotic disorders share diagnostic commonalities, as do avoidant personality disorder and Axis I social phobia. Thus, care must be taken to avoid over-interpreting the co-occurrence of disorders. While there is evidence of comorbidity of different personality disorders with each other and of personality disorders with major mental

disorders, artifactual associations due to diagnostic overlap need to be considered (Dolan-Sewell, Krueger, & Shea, 2001).

Impact of Personality Disorders

Personality disorders are associated with significantly increased rates of premature mortality (Harris & Barraclough, 1998), perhaps because the behavior of people with personality disorder puts them at risk of both natural and unnatural causes of death. One candidate behavior is substance abuse, which is strongly associated with personality disorder. Coid et al. (2006) showed that the odds of alcohol dependence were substantially increased for those in Cluster B (adjusted odds ratio 4.21), and, to a lesser degree, those in Cluster A (adjusted odds ratio 1.61), although those in Cluster C were *less* likely to be alcohol dependent (adjusted odds ratio 0.36). The likelihood of drug dependence was elevated for all personality clusters (adjusted odds ratios of 1.32, 1.87, and 1.93 for Clusters A, B, and C, respectively). Verheul, van den Brink, and Hartgers (1995) reviewed 50 studies of the co-occurrence of personality disorders of people in treatment for substance abuse, finding a median prevalence of co-occurrence of 61%, with illicit drug users showing higher personality disorder prevalence rates than problem drinkers. The association was particularly strong between substance misuse and antisocial and borderline personality disorders.

Compared with people with no disorder, those with personality disorders suffer more general health problems (Noren et al., 2007). Rendu, Moran, Patel, Knapp, and Mann (2002) assessed the costs of treating people with personality disorders in UK primary care at almost twice that of people without personality disorders, with the excess costs attributable to personality disorder in combination with common mental disorders such as anxiety disorders and mild depression.

Interpersonal and social dysfunction are core features of personality disorder (Nur, Tyrer,

Merson, & Johnson, 2004; Seivewright, Tyrer, & Johnson, 2004; Skodol et al., 2005). In general, personality pathology prevents the satisfactory achievement of life tasks, namely survival and reproduction (Livesley & Lang, 2005). These disorders are associated with financial difficulties and problems maintaining jobs (Norén et al., 2007), marital dissatisfaction and intimate partner violence (South, Turkheimer, & Oltmanns, 2008), crime (Johnson et al., 2000), and poor quality of life (Soeteman, Verheul, & Busschbach, 2008). Personality disorder in conjunction with an Axis I disorder, especially depression, is particularly strongly predictive of poor social functioning (Newton-Howes et al., 2008). Dual diagnosis of personality disorder and an Axis I disorder is of clear importance in relation to a person's health and welfare.

TREATMENT OF PERSONALITY DISORDERS

Consensus Panels

Over the past decade, the management and treatment of people with personality disorders has become a major issue in UK non-forensic and forensic mental health services. The catalyst was the double murder of a woman and her 6-year-old daughter by Michael Stone. During his trial it was revealed that he had sought help from a forensic mental health service, but help was not forthcoming because Stone was diagnosed as suffering from an untreatable personality disorder. Recognizing the possibility that had Stone received treatment he may not have committed these attacks, a number of changes were initiated in service provision for people with personality disorders. Importantly, non-forensic mental health services were seen as points of early intervention, potentially preventing risk of harm. Consequently, the National Institute of Mental Health for England (2003) instructed general mental health services not to exclude people with personality disorders from treatment, but rather to develop services for this particular group. The guidance given in this document, which was based on evidence from clinicians, service users, and academics, is summarized in Table 23.2. A range of treatments is endorsed, with the recommendation that all therapies should follow a set of guiding principles. These are

> that therapy should: be well structured, devote effort to achieving adherence, have a clear focus, be theoretically coherent to both therapist and patient, be relatively long term, be well integrated with other services available to the patient, [and] involve a clear treatment alliance between therapist and patient. (National Institute of Mental Health for England, 2003, p. 23)

TABLE 23.2   Guidance on the Development of Services for People With Personality Disorders (from the National Institute of Mental Health for England, 2003)

1. Services should be provided by a specialist multidisciplinary team operating from a psychology or psychotherapy department or, in areas of high concentration of people with personality disorder, in a specialist day patient center.
2. Team members should be collaborative and be able to communicate effectively, get on well with each other, and be clear about the boundaries of treatment.
3. There should be clear protocols for referral and interagency working.
4. The specialist team would undertake a comprehensive assessment of personality disorder, comorbid mental health or addiction problems, and risk of harm to self or others.
5. The specialist team would take on patients who experience significant distress or difficulty.
6. The specialist team would provide consultancy and support for staff working with people with personality disorder in a range of settings.
7. The specialist team would provide case supervision and training for staff working with people with personality disorder in a range of settings.
8. The specialist team would develop close links with forensic services to share and develop expertise and pool resources.
9. The specialist team would support service users to develop a self-help network.
10. An out-of-hours service should be developed to support people with personality disorder when in crisis.

The published guidelines were supported by Department of Health funding of 11 dedicated community-based pilot services for people with personality disorder (Crawford et al., 2007). Among other things, the evaluation of these pilots identified service users' opinions of these dedicated services. Based upon these views, 49 descriptors were drawn up and formed the basis of a systematic survey of expert authors, service providers and service users conducted to establish a consensus on how dedicated community-based services for people with personality disorder should be delivered (Crawford et al., 2008). There was consensus on 21 descriptors (see Table 23.3).

Antisocial Personality Disorder

The UK's National Institute for Health and Clinical Excellence (2009) has produced a comprehensive clinical guideline for the treatment, management, and prevention of antisocial personality disorder (see also Kendall et al., 2009). This guideline addressed the general principles of service provision, including ensuring equitable access, providing multiagency care, and ensuring seamlessness between institutions and community services. Specific recommendations were made for risk assessment and risk management. The guidance was to conduct a comprehensive assessment covering violence and other antisocial behaviors, personality functioning, comorbid mental disorders, and the need for psychological, social, and occupational interventions. This assessment should inform a multiagency management plan. Regarding treatment, the guideline stressed the importance of fostering client motivation to engage, developing a therapeutic relationship, and promoting client

TABLE 23.3   Consensus Views on Delivery of Community-Based Services for People with Personality Disorder (from Crawford et al., 2008)

1. Organization of services
    i.   It is unacceptable for community mental health teams to have a policy of not working with people with personality disorder
    ii. A person from the team referring a person to a dedicated personality disorder service should remain in regular contact with the patient/client
    iii. Most people with personality disorder do not require dedicated services
    iv. Dedicated personality disorder services should be open to self-referrals
    v.   Dedicated personality disorder teams should provide services to people with personality disorder who also hear voices/experience psychotic symptoms
2. Service delivery
    i.   Interventions should be delivered over years, not months
    ii.   Care plans with short- and long-term goals are important
    iii. Limits on staff availability and boundaries need to be clear and consistent throughout treatment
    iv.   Responsibility for the client should be shared by the team
    v.   More intensive support should be available at times of crisis
    vi.   Some clients cannot cope with groups
    vii. Risk management should involve choice and responsibility on the part of the person concerned
    viii. Users and carers should be involved in making decisions about service development
    ix.   Services should try to obtain users' consent to contact caregivers
    x.   Services should be provided under the care program approach.*
3. Staffing issues
    i.   Personal qualities of staff are more relevant than professional qualifications
    ii.   Staff must have a forum in which they can reflect on their practice
    iii. Teams need to consist of people with a range of professional and nonprofessional backgrounds
    iv.   Training should be given to teams rather than individuals
4. User and caregiver involvement
    i.   Teams should have regular input from an expert by experience (i.e., a service user worker)
    ii.   Service users can successfully run groups if they are trained and supported

* The care program approach is a formal system of needs assessment, care planning, and care coordination.

autonomy and choice. Psychosocial interventions were endorsed as the principal means of addressing symptoms and behaviors, including offending, associated with antisocial personality disorder. Pharmacological interventions "should not be routinely used for the treatment of antisocial personality disorder or associated behaviors of aggression, anger, and impulsivity" (p. 9), although pharmacological interventions are supported for the treatment of comorbid disorders, including alcohol and drug misuse.

Randomized Controlled Trials

Meta-analyses of treatment outcomes for personality disorders show a strong positive effect of treatment, with both cognitive behavioral and psychodynamic approaches showing good effects (Leichsenring & Leibing, 2004; Leichsenring & Rabung, 2008; Perry, Banon, & Ianni, 1999). The most commonly used measure of effect size is Cohen's d, calculated by subtracting the post-treatment mean from the pre-treatment mean and dividing by the square root of the pooled standard deviations. An effect size of 0.20 is considered small, 0.50 medium, and 0.80 large. Cohen's d for studies in these meta-analyses vary depending upon the type of measure used (self-report or observer rated) and whether the calculations were adjusted to take sample size into account. Nonetheless, effect sizes were large, ranging from 0.82 to 1.79; however, these meta-analyses suffered from the inclusion of studies that used methods other than randomized controlled trials (RCTs) and, of relevance in relation to this chapter, they included treatments for borderline personality disorder.

A more rigorous systematic review has been conducted by Duggan, Huband, Smailagic, Ferriter, and Adams (2007), who examined evaluations of treatments for people with personality disorder published up to the end of 2006. Their inclusion criteria were that study populations were diagnosed for personality disorder using a standardized procedure and

that the study was a randomized controlled treatment trial of a psychological therapy. Results for those studies that reported data in sufficient detail to permit the computation of effect sizes are presented in Table 23.4, excluding studies of treatment trials for borderline personality disorder. These studies show that most RCTs are not adequately powered; hence, the results may not be reliable. Furthermore, comparing the results of studies is hampered by the wide variety of outcome measures used. This latter point reflects the lack of agreement about exactly what treatments for personality disorders should do—relieve symptoms, improve functioning, or change personality. It is clear that there is no single treatment that prevails and none stands out as the treatment of choice.

Randomized controlled trials for the treatment of specific personality disorders other than borderline are practically nonexistent. Two treatment trials for antisocial personality disorder are represented in Duggan et al.'s (2007) systematic review. Both of these focus not on antisocial personality disorder *per se* but rather on substance misuse, which, as mentioned earlier, is a commonly co-occurring disorder. Two other trials of substance misuse treatments for people with personality disorders have been published since Duggan et al.'s review. Ball (2007) compared Dual Focus Schema Therapy (DFST), a combination of schema therapy and relapse prevention designed for personality-disordered substance misusers, with 12-step therapy. Thirty opioid-dependent personality-disordered outpatients, most of whom had antisocial personality disorder (63%), were randomized and, over the 6-month course of treatment, the DFST group reduced their substance use frequency more rapidly than the 12-step group. Neufeld et al. (2008) randomized 100 opioid-dependent outpatients with antisocial personality disorder to contingency management or counseling. The contingency management group attended more treatment sessions, but urinalysis for drug use did not differ between groups over 6 months.

TABLE 23.4 Randomized Controlled Trials of Psychological Treatments for People With Personality Disorder Other Than Borderline

Personality Disorder	Treatment Groups (number per group)	Treatment Duration	Participants and Setting	Main Outcomes	Effect Size (95% Confidence Interval)	Authors
Antisocial	1. Contingency management CM for opioid dependence $N = 21$ 2. Methadone maintenance for opioid dependence $N = 21$	13 weeks	Men and women in a community methadone treatment program	More in CM group transferred to routine care after 3 months	Relative risk 0.50 (0.26–0.97)	Brooner et al. (1998)
Antisocial	1. CBT plus methadone maintenance for cocaine dependence $N = 31$ 2. Contingency management plus methadone maintenance for cocaine dependence $N = 35$ 3. CBT plus contingency management plus methadone maintenance for cocaine dependence $N = 34$	16 weeks	Men and women in an inpatient narcotic treatment program	No difference in cocaine-free urine samples during treatment		Messina et al. (2003)
Avoidant	1. CBT $N = 21$ 2. Brief dynamic therapy BDT $N = 23$ 3. Waiting list control WLC $N = 18$	6 months	Men and women referred to a community mental health center	CBT group showed greater reduction posttreatment than BDT group on the Personality Disorder Belief Questionnaire (PDBQ) (Arntz, Dreesen, Schouten, & Weertman, 2004) obsessive and avoidance scales. No differences on measures of anxiety, social phobia, or avoidance	PDBQ obsessive scale: Weighted mean difference −18.50 (−33.77–3.23) PDBQ avoidance scale: Weighted mean difference −0.90 (−1.68–0.12)	Emmelkamp et al. (2006)
Avoidant	1. CBT $N = 28$ 2. Pharmacotherapy fluvoxamine $N = 27$ 3. Placebo $N = 27$	15 weeks	Men and women in treatment in outpatient anxiety disorder clinics	No differences in treatment noncompletion or insomnia as a side effect		Oosterbaan et al. (2001)

(Continued)

TABLE 23.4 Randomized Controlled Trials of Psychological Treatments for People With Personality Disorder Other Than Borderline (*Continued*)

Personality Disorder	Treatments Groups (number in group)	Treatment Duration	Participants and Setting	Main Outcomes	Effect Size (95% Confidence Interval)	Authors
Mixed Cluster B	(1) Manual-assisted cognitive therapy (MACT) ($N = 18$) (2) Treatment as Usual (TAU) ($N = 16$)	6 months	Men and women presenting at mental health services after an episode of deliberate self-harm	No difference in suicidal acts during treatment. No differences in anxiety or depression posttreatment. No difference in retention in treatment		Evans et al. (1999)
Mixed Cluster C	(1) Creative coping group ($N = 16$) (2) Wellness and lifestyle group (W&L) ($N = 15$)	Not stated	Men and women psychiatric service inpatients	W&L showed less acting out behaviors at 6 months No differences in depression or hopelessness at 6 months	Relative risk 3.13 (1.06–9.21)	Springer, Lohr, Buchtel, and Silk (1995)
Mixed Cluster C	(1) Cognitive therapy ($N = 25$) (2) Short-term psychodynamic therapy ($N = 25$)	40 weeks	Men and women outpatients referred to a hospital psychiatry department	Both groups improve equally in symptoms, interpersonal problems, or Millon Clinical Multiaxial Inventory scores		Svartberg et al. (2004)
Mixed all PD	(1) Psychoeducation plus medication ($N = 15$) (2) Nonstructured intervention plus medication ($N = 22$)	20 weeks	Men and women outpatients in treatment for bipolar disorder	Fewer in psychoeducation relapsed with a mood disorder at 24 months	Relative risk 0.67 (0.47–0.95)	Colom et al. (2004)
Mixed all PD	(1) Short psychodynamic supportive therapy plus antidepressants ($N = 49$) (2) Antidepressants only ($N = 36$)	6 months	Men and women in treatment for depression in an outpatient mental health clinic	Psychotherapy group showed greater improvement in Symptom Checklist-90 (SCL-90) scores and on Quality of Life in Depression Scale (QLDS) (Tuynman-Qua, de Jonghe, McKenna, & Hunt, 1992) scores	SCL-90: Weighted mean difference −9.62 (−15.01 −4.23) Depression: Weighted mean difference 7.01 (3.32 −10.70)	Kool et al. (2003)
Mixed all PD	(1) Manual-assisted cognitive therapy (MACT) ($N = 101$) (2) Treatment as Usual (TAU) ($N = 101$)	Up to 7 treatment sessions	Men and women who were referred to a mental health service for outpatient treatment after an episode of self-harm	No difference in self-harm at 6 or 12 months		Tyrer et al. (2004)

					Vinnars, Barber, Norén, Gallop, and Weinryb (2005)
Measured SCL-90 Intensive psychotherapy N = ... 2. Nonmanualized community-delivered psychotherapy N = ...		Men and women referred to outpatient mental health centers	40 weeks. Average 51 sessions	Equivalent improvement in global assessment of functioning at end of treatment or at 1-year follow-up	
					Winston et al. (1994)
Measured SCL-90 1. Brief adaptive psychotherapy: BAP N = ... 2. Short-term dynamic psychotherapy: STDP N = ... 3. Waiting list control WLC N = ...	Men and women outpatients accepted for treatment at a medical center	40 weeks treatment, 15 weeks of waiting list	BAP superior to WLC at 6-month and 1-year follow-up on SCL-90, social adjustment, and targeted complaint STDP superior to WLC at 6-month and 1-year follow-up on SCL-90 No differences between BAP and STDP on SCL-90 or social adjustment No differences across groups on treatment retention	BAP>WLC SC L-90: Weighted mean difference −8.32 (−11.84 −4.80) Social adjustment: Weighted mean difference −0.35 (−0.55 −0.15) Target complaint: Weighted mean difference −2.64 (−3.85 −1.43) STDP>WLC SC L-90: Weighted mean difference −5.32 (−9.17 −1.29)	

Source: Degnan et al. 2016

To these studies focusing on substance use may be added a recent exploratory RCT of cognitive behavior therapy (CBT) for violent men with antisocial personality disorder (Davidson et al., 2009). This has shown that men in the community can be recruited to a trial and be assessed at follow-up (of the 52 randomized, 79% were available for follow-up at 12 months). There were no significant differences between groups on substance use, anxiety, depression, anger, self-schemas, or social functioning, although a larger scale study is required to test outcomes properly.

There are more treatments for groups of mixed personality disorders, with groups constituted either from within one cluster or across all clusters. Given high levels of comorbidity among personality disorders, there is some sense in developing generic treatments. To the eight trials with mixed groups identified by Duggan et al. (2007), four additional RCTs published after the systematic review may be added. Huband, McMurran, Evans, and Duggan (2007) conducted a randomized controlled trial comparing community outpatients with any personality disorder treated with, on average, 12 weekly sessions of psychoeducation and problem-solving therapy ($N = 87$) with those on a waiting list ($N = 89$). The treated group showed a greater improvement on a self-report measure of social functioning and on self-reported anger control 24 weeks after recruitment. Abbass, Sheldon, Gyra, and Kalpin (2008) randomized personality disordered community adults to receive intensive short-term dynamic psychotherapy ($N = 14$) or to a minimal-contact delayed-treatment control condition of monthly support sessions ($N = 13$). The psychotherapy group received, on average, 28 weekly sessions, and the control group was in contact, on average, for 15 weeks. The psychotherapy-treated patients improved significantly more than controls on symptoms, interpersonal problems, general functioning, and employment. Lynch et al. (2007) reported data on 35 older adults with personality disorders in treatment for major

depression. Patients were randomized to receive dialectical behavior therapy plus medication or medication alone. After 6 months of treatment, there were no group differences in depression; however, personality disorder features had improved more for the therapy group. Problems with interpersonal sensitivity and interpersonal aggression were lower for the therapy group after treatment and at 3-month posttreatment follow-up. Zorn, Roder, Müller, Tschacher, and Thommen (2007) reported data from 60 personality disordered patients, mostly with narcissistic personality disorder, randomized to schema-focused emotive behavioral therapy or either a wait-list control or placebo treatment (social skills training). The therapy group showed significantly better improvements on measures of interpersonal functioning, emotional coping, somaticisation, paranoid thinking, and aggressiveness.

SINGLE CASE STUDIES AND EXPERIMENTAL DESIGN STUDIES

There are few rigorous single case designs in the evaluation of personality disorder treatments. Of those published, two report a series of single case studies and two report one case only.

Davidson and Tyrer (1996) delivered cognitive therapy to five men with antisocial personality disorder. Participants kept a daily diary of their main problem experiences. After a baseline phase of 16 days, there was a treatment phase of between 2 and 18 sessions (median = 9 sessions). Time series analyses were conducted on three patients with a significant improvement on only one rating in one man's case—an improvement in his relationship with his wife.

Using a crossover design, in which the individual serves as his or her own control, Weertman and Arntz (2007) compared the effectiveness of schema-focused therapy with therapy aimed at rescripting childhood memories with people with personality disorders other than borderline, schizotypal, schizoid, or antisocial. After an alliance-building and assessment phase (12 sessions), there were two 24-session phases—one focused on present schemas and one on childhood memories. The order of these phases was counterbalanced. Analyses of data from 17 patients, using a composite measure of symptoms and schemas, showed that both components of treatment were effective with the focus on current schemas more effective than the focus on childhood memories ($d = 0.70$ and 0.54 respectively).

Using an A-B-A experimental design, Kellett (2007) examined the effectiveness of 24 sessions of cognitive analytic therapy with a patient presenting with histrionic personality disorder. Personality disorder symptoms experienced by the patient were kept in a daily diary. Data collected in the first 3 weeks were used as the baseline, those collected over the next 26 weeks represented the intervention period, and data for a further 22 weeks represented the follow-up period. Statistically significant improvements were evident on self-recorded attention to physical appearance, feelings of emptiness, and feeling like a child. Clinically significant improvement was evident on measures of depression, symptoms, and personality structure.

Porcerelli, Dauphin, Ablon, Leitman, and Bambery (2007) evaluated the effects of 5 years of psychoanalysis (four times weekly reducing to three times weekly) with a man with avoidant personality disorder. Symptoms were measured at intake, and then annually up to 2 years after the end of treatment. Significant improvements were found in symptoms, functioning, avoidant personality disorder, and object relations, with d between 1.00 and 3.50.

These single case studies and experimental designs indicate some support for schema and early memory therapy. Additional support for cognitive analytic therapy and psychoanalysis needs to be amassed before controlled evaluations can be recommended.

Evidence-Based Practices

According to Chambless and Hollon (1998), RCTs are considered the most robust form of evidence of treatment efficacy; however, they caution that "studies must have been conducted with methods that are adequately sound to justify reasonable confidence in the data" (p. 8). Many of the trials on personality disorder treatment reported in the literature are underpowered; that is, the numbers included in the studies are too few to generate reliable results. Chambless and Hollon suggest that a sample size of 25 to 30 per condition allows a reasonably stable estimate of the effects of treatment; others would consider these numbers too few to detect even a medium-sized treatment effect. Furthermore, to be considered efficacious, at least two independent studies need to have been conducted on any one treatment with the same client population. In personality disorder treatment trials, outcome measures vary, thus hampering any comparison between trials. Based on these criteria, only *possibly efficacious* treatments for personality disorders other than borderline can be identified.

Contingency management plus methadone maintenance is probably more efficacious than methadone maintenance alone or counseling for people with antisocial personality disorder in treatment for substance misuse (Brooner, Kidorf, King, & Stoller, 1998; Neufeld et al., 2008). Therapies that focus on changing maladaptive schemas associated with the personality disorder are possibly efficacious for improving personality disorder symptoms and schemas (Weertman & Arntz, 2007; Zorn et al., 2007) and more promising than 12-step treatment for reducing substance misuse (Ball, 2007). Psychoeducation and problem-solving approaches are probably efficacious for improving personality disorder symptoms (Colom et al., 2004; Huband et al., 2007). Dialectical behavior therapy is possibly efficacious for improving personality disorder symptoms in older adults (Lynch et al., 2007).

All of these treatments are specific varieties of cognitive behavioral treatments, yet therapies designated more generally as cognitive therapies gave mixed results, with equivalence to brief psychodynamic therapy (Svartberg, Stiles, & Seltzer, 2004) and offering no advantage in treatment for anxiety in people with avoidant personality disorder (Oosterbaan, van Balkom, Spinhoven, van Oppen, & van Dyck, 2001). Similarly, nonspecified cognitive behavior therapies added nothing to contingency management for substance misusers (Messina, Farabee, & Rawson, 2003) and showed no effect on self-harm or mood (Evans et al., 1999; Tyrer et al., 2004). It may be that cognitive behavioral treatments for personality disorders need to be based upon specific theories of personality disorder in order to be effective. Brief psychodynamic therapies are probably efficacious compared with medication alone or no active treatment for improving psychiatric symptoms and improving quality of life in depression (Abbass et al., 2008; Kool, Dekker, Duijsens, de Jonghe, & Puite, 2003; Winston et al., 1994), although they are not superior to cognitive behavior therapy (Svartberg et al., 2004).

In conclusion, there is some evidence of what is likely to be efficacious in the treatment of people with personality disorders. Importantly, the style of delivering therapies is perceived as important, requiring dedicated teams or services that provide a range of therapies and support, which are delivered in collaboration between the therapist and the service user. No one psychological treatment has been identified as superior, and there is considerable work to be done in identifying what works best with whom and over what time period. At present, a broad range of cognitive behavioral, psychosocial, and psychodynamic therapies should remain on the agenda. If treatment is to be long term, then research also needs to be long term. At present, there is little to be said about what works with specific personality disorder types. Given the high comorbidity of personality disorders, the issue

of what works with which particular personality disorder is particularly challenging; however, the issue of comorbidity is partly a classification problem. Looking to the future, major changes are expected to the classification of personality disorders in the next revision of the *Diagnostic and Statistical Manual* (Widiger, Simonsen, Krueger, Livesley, & Verheul, 2005). This will have major implications for research into personality disorders.

REFERENCES

Abbass, A., Sheldon, A., Gyra, J., & Kalpin, A. (2008). Intensive short-term dynamic psychotherapy for *DSM-IV* personality disorders: A randomized controlled trial. *Journal of Nervous and Mental Disease, 196,* 211–216.

American Psychiatric Association. (2000). *Diagnostic and statistical manual of mental disorders* (4th ed., text rev.). Arlington, VA: Author.

Arntz, A., Dreessen, L., Schouten, E., & Weertman, A. (2004). Beliefs in personality disorders: A test with the personality disorder belief questionnaire. *Behaviour Research and Therapy, 42,* 1215–1225.

Bagby, R. M., Joffe, R. T., Parker, J. D. A., & Schuller, D. R. (1993). Re-examination of the evidence for the *DSM-III* personality disorder clusters. *Journal of Personality Disorders, 7,* 320–328.

Ball, S. A. (2007). Comparing individual therapies for personality disordered opioid dependent patients. *Journal of Personality Disorders, 21,* 305–321.

Blais, M. A., McCann, J. T., Benedict, K. B., & Norman, D. K. (1997). Toward an empirical/theoretical grouping of the *DSM-III-R* personality disorders. *Journal of Personality Disorders, 11,* 191–198.

Brooner, R. K., Kidorf, M., King, V. L., & Stoller, K. (1998). Preliminary evidence of good treatment response in antisocial drug abusers. *Drug and Alcohol Dependence, 49,* 249–260.

Chambless, D. L., & Hollon, S. D. (1998). Defining empirically supported theories. *Journal of Consulting and Clinical Psychology, 66,* 7–18.

Coid, J., Yang, M., Tyrer, P., Roberts, A., & Ullrich, S. (2006). Prevalence and correlates of personality disorder in Great Britain. *British Journal of Psychiatry, 188,* 423–431.

Colom, F., Vieta, E., Sánchez-Moreno, J., Matinez-Arán, A., Torrent, C., Reinares, M., . . . Comes M. (2004). Psychoeducation in bipolar patients with comorbid personality disorders. *Bipolar Disorders, 6,* 294–298.

Crawford, M., Price, K., Rutter, D., Moran, P., Tyrer, P., Bateman, A., . . . Weaver, T. (2008). Dedicated community-based services for adults with personality disorder: Delphi study. *British Journal of Psychiatry, 193*, 342–343.

Crawford, M., Rutter, D., Price, K., Weaver, T., Josson, M., Tyrer, P., . . . Taylor, E. (2007). *Learning the lessons: A multi-method evaluation of dedicated community-based services for people with personality disorder.* London, England: National Co-ordinating Centre for NHS Service Delivery and Organisation. Retrieved from www.sdo.nihr.ac.uk/sdo832004.html.

Davidson, K. M., & Tyrer, P. (1996). Cognitive therapy for antisocial and borderline personality disorders: Single case study series. *British Journal of Clinical Psychology, 35*, 413–429.

Davidson, K. M., Tyrer, P., Tata, P., Cooke, D., Gumley, A., Ford, I., . . . Crawford, M.J. (2009). Cognitive behaviour therapy for violent men with antisocial personality disorder in the community: An exploratory randomized controlled trial. *Psychological Medicine, 39*, 569–577.

Dolan-Sewell, R. T., Krueger, R. F., & Shea, M. T. (2001). Co-occurrence with syndrome disorders. In W. J. Livesley (Ed.), *Handbook of personality disorders: Theory, research and treatment* (pp. 84–104). New York, NY: Guilford Press

Duggan, C., Huband, N., Smailagic, N., Ferriter, M., & Adams, C. (2007). The use of psychological treatments for people with personality disorder: A systematic review of randomized controlled trials. *Personality and Mental Health, 1*, 95–125.

Emmelkamp, P. M. G., Benner, A., Kuipers, A., Feiertag, G. A., Koster, H. C., & van Apeldoorn, F. J. (2006). Comparison of brief dynamic and cognitive behavioural therapies in avoidant personality disorder. *British Journal of Psychiatry, 189*, 60–64.

Evans, K., Tyrer, P., Catalan, J., Schmidt, U., Davidson, K., Dent, J., . . . Thompson, S. (1999). Manual-assisted cognitive-behaviour therapy (MACT): A randomized controlled trial of a brief intervention with bibliotherapy in the treatment of recurrent deliberate self-harm. *Psychological Medicine, 29*, 19–25.

First, M. B., Gibbon, M., Spitzer, R. L., Williams, J. B. W., & Benjamin, L. S. (1997). *Structured clinical interview for DSM-IV axis II personality disorders.* Arlington, VA: American Psychiatric Publishing

Harris, E. C., & Barraclough, B. (1998). Excess mortality of mental disorder. *British Journal of Psychiatry, 173*, 11–53.

Huband, N., McMurran, M., Evans, C., & Duggan, C. (2007). Social problem-solving plus psychoeducation for adults with personality disorder: A pragmatic randomized controlled trial. *British Journal of Psychiatry, 190*, 307–313.

Johnson, J. G., Cohen, P., Smailes, E., Kasen, S., Oldham, J. M., Skodol, A. E., & Brook, J. S. (2000). Adolescent personality disorders associated with violence and criminal behaviour during adolescence and early adulthood. *American Journal of Psychiatry, 157*, 1406–1412.

Kellett, S., (2007). A time series evaluation of the treatment of histrionic personality disorder with cognitive analytic therapy. *Psychology and Psychotherapy: Theory, Research and Practice, 80*, 389–405.

Kendall, T., Pilling, S., Tyrer, P., Duggan, C., Burbeck, R., Meader, N., & Taylor, C. (2009). Borderline and antisocial personality disorders: A summary of NICE guidance. *British Medical Journal, 338*, b93.

Kool, S., Dekker, J., Duijsens, I.J., de Jonghe, F., & Puite, B. (2003). Efficacy of combined therapy and pharmacotherapy for depressed patients with or without personality disorders. *Harvard Review of Psychiatry, 11*, 133–141.

Leichsenring, F., & Leibing, E. (2004). The effectiveness of psychodynamic therapy and cognitive behaviour therapy in the treatment of personality disorders: A meta-analysis. *American Journal of Psychiatry, 160*, 1223–1232.

Leichsenring, F., & Rabung, S. (2008). Effectiveness of long-term psychodynamic psychotherapy: A meta-analysis. *Journal of the American Medical Association, 300*, 1551–1565.

Lenzenweger, M. F., Lane, M. C., Loranger, A. W., & Kessler, R. C. (2007). DSM-IV personality disorders in the national comorbidity survey replication. *Biological Psychiatry, 62*, 553–564.

Livesley, W. J., & Lang, K. L. (2005). Differentiating normal, abnormal, and disordered personality. *European Journal of Personality, 19*, 257–268.

Loranger, A. W. (1997). *The international personality disorder examination.* Odessa, FL: Psychological Assessment Resources.

Lynch, T. R., Cheavens, J. S., Cukrowicz, K. C., Thorp, S. R., Bronner, L. & Beyer, J. (2007). Treatment of older adults with co-morbid personality disorder and depression: A dialectical behaviour therapy approach. *International Journal of Geriatric Psychiatry, 22*, 131–143.

McGlashan, T. H., Grilo, C. M., Skodol, A. E., Gunderson, J. G., Shea, M. T., Morey, L. C., . . . Stout, R. L. (2000). The collaborative longitudinal personality disorders study. Baseline axis I/II and II/II diagnostic co-occurrence. *Acta Psychiatrica Scandinavica, 102*, 256–264.

Mennin, D. S., & Heimberg, R. G. (2000). The impact of comorbid mood and personality disorders in the cognitive behavioral treatment of panic disorder. *Clinical Psychology Review, 20*, 339–357.

Messina, N., Farabee, D., & Rawson, R. (2003). Treatment responsivity of cocaine-dependent patients with antisocial personality disorder to cognitive-behavioral and contingency management interventions. *Journal of Consulting and Clinical Psychology, 71*, 320–329.

National Institute for Health and Clinical Excellence. (2009). *Antisocial personality disorder: Treatment, management and prevention*. London, England: Author. www.nice.org.uk/Guidance/CG77

National Institute of Mental Health for England. (2003). *Personality disorder: No longer a diagnosis of exclusion*. London, England: Department of Health.

Neufeld, K. J., Kidorf, M. S., Kolodner, K., King, V. L., Clark, M., & Brooner, R. K. (2008). A behavioural treatment for opioid-dependent patients with antisocial personality disorder. *Journal of Substance Abuse Treatment, 34*, 101–111.

Newton-Howes, G., Tyrer, P., & Johnston, T. (2006). Personality disorder and the outcome of depression: Meta-analysis of published studies. *British Journal of Psychiatry, 188*, 13–20.

Newton-Howes, G., Tyrer, P., & Weaver, T. (2008). Social function of patients with personality disorder in secondary care. *Psychiatric Services, 59*, 1033–1037.

Norén, K ., Lindgren, A., Haellstom, T., Thormaehlen, B., Vinnars, B., Wennberg, P., . . . Barber, J. P. (2007). Psychological distress and functional impairment in patients with personality disorders. *Nordic Journal of Psychiatry, 61*, 260–270.

Nur, U., Tyrer, P., Merson, S., & Johnson, T. (2004). Relationship between clinical symptoms, personality disturbance, and social function: A statistical enquiry. *Irish Journal of Psychological Medicine, 21*, 19–22.

Oosterbaan, D. B., van Balkom, A. J., Spinhoven, P., van Oppen, P., & van Dyck, R. (2001). Cognitive therapy versus moclobemide in social phobia: A controlled study. *Clinical Psychology and Psychotherapy, 8*, 263–273.

Perälä, J., Suvisaari, J., Saarni, S. I., Kuoppasalmi, K., Isometsä, E., Pirkola, S., . . . Lönnqvist, J. (2007). Lifetime prevalence of psychotic and bipolar I disorders in a general population. *Archives of General Psychiatry, 64*, 19–28.

Perry, J. C., Banon, E., & Ianni, F. (1999). Effectiveness of psychotherapy for personality disorders. *American Journal of Psychiatry, 156*, 1312–1321.

Pfohl, B., Blum, N., Zimmerman, M., & Stangl, D. (1989). *Structured interview for DSM-III-R personality (SIDP-R)*. Iowa City: University of Iowa College of Medicine.

Porcerelli, J. H., Dauphin, V. B., Ablon, J. S., Leitman, S., & Bambery, M. (2007). Psychoanalysis with avoidant personality disorder: A systematic case study. *Psychotherapy: Theory, Research, Practice, and Training, 44*, 1–13.

Reich, J. (2003). The effect of Axis II disorders on the outcome of treatment of anxiety and unipolar depressive disorders: A review. *Journal of Personality Disorders, 17*, 387–405.

Rendu, A., Moran, P., Patel, A., Knapp, M., & Mann, A. (2002). Economic impact of personality disorders in UK primary care attenders. *British Journal of Psychiatry, 181*, 62–66.

Samuels, J., Eaton, W. W., Bienvenu, O. J., Brown, C. H., Costa, P. T., & Nestadt, G. (2002). Prevalence and correlates of personality disorders in a community sample. *British Journal of Psychiatry, 180*, 536–542.

Schopp, L. H., & Trull, T. J. (1993). Validity of the *DSM-III-R* personality disorder clusters. *Journal of Psychopathology and Behavioral Assessment, 15*, 219–237.

Seivewright, H., Tyrer, P., & Johnson, T. (2004). Persistent social dysfunction in anxious anddepressed patients with personality disorder. *Acta Psychiatrica Scandinavica, 109*, 104–109.

Skodol, A. E., Pagano, M. E., Bender, D. S., Shea, M. T., Gunderson, J. G., Yen, S., . . . McGlashan, T. H. (2005). Stability of functional impairment in patients with schizotypal, borderline, avoidant, or obsessive–compulsive personality disorder over two years. *Psychological Medicine, 35*, 443–451.

Soeteman, D. I., Verheul, R., & Busschbach, J. J .V. (2008). The burden of disease in personality disorders: Diagnosis-specific quality of life. *Journal of Personality Disorders, 22*, 259–268.

South, S. C., Turkheimer, E., & Oltmanns, T. F. (2008). Personality disorder symptoms and marital functioning. *Journal of Consulting and Clinical Psychology, 76*, 769–780.

Springer, T., Lohr, N. E., Buchtel, H. A., & Silk, K. R. (1995). A preliminary report of short-term cognitive-behavioural group therapy for inpatients with personality disorders. *Journal of Psychotherapy Practice and Research, 5*, 57–71.

Svartberg, M., Stiles, T. C., & Seltzer, M. H. (2004). Randomized, controlled trial of the effectiveness of short-term dynamic psychotherapy and cognitive therapy for cluster C personality disorders. *American Journal of Psychiatry, 161*, 810–817.

Torgerson, S., Kringlen, E., & Kramer, V. (2001). The prevalence of personality disorders in a community sample. *Archives of General Psychiatry, 58*, 590–596.

Tuynman-Qua, H., de Jonghe, F., McKenna, S., & Hunt, S. (1992). *Quality of life in depression scale*. Houten, The Netherlands: Ibero.

Tyrer, P., & Johnson, T. (1996). Establishing the severity of personality disorder. *American Journal of Psychiatry, 153*, 1593–1597.

Tyrer, P., Tom, B., Byford, S., Schmidt, U., Jones, V., Davidson, K., et al., (2004). Differential effects of manual assisted cognitive behavior therapy in the treatment of recurrent deliberate self-harm and personality disturbance: The POPMACT study. *Journal of Personality Disorders, 18*, 102–116.

Verheul, R., van den Brink, W., & Hartgers, C. (1995). Prevalence of personality disorders among alcoholics and drug addicts: An overview. *European Addiction Research, 1,* 166–177.

Vinnars, B., Barber, J. P., Norén, K., Gallop, R., & Weinryb, R. M. (2005). Manualized supportive-expressive psychotherapy versus nonmanualized community-delivered psychodynamic therapy for patients with personality disorders: Bridging efficacy and effectiveness. *American Journal of Psychiatry, 1620,* 1933–1940.

Weertman, A., & Arntz, A. (2007). Effectiveness of treatment of childhood memories in cognitive therapy for personality disorders: A controlled study contrasting methods focusing on the present and methods focusing on childhood memories. *Behaviour Research and Therapy, 45,* 2133–2143.

Widiger, T. A. (2001). Official classification systems. In W. J. Livesley (Ed.), *Handbook of personality disorders: Theory, research and treatment* (pp. 60–83). New York, NY: Guilford Press.

Widiger, T. A., Simonsen, E., Krueger, R., Livesely, W. J., & Verheul, R. (2005). Personality disorder research agenda for the *DSM-V. Journal of Personality Disorders, 19,* 315–338.

Winston, A., Laikin, M., Pollack, J., Samstag, L. W., McCullough, L., & Muran, J. C. (1994). Short-term psychotherapy of personality disorders. *American Journal of Psychiatry, 151,* 190–194.

World Health Organization. (1992). *The ICD-10 classification of mental and behavioural Disorders.* Geneva, Switzerland: Author.

Zorn, P., Roder, V., Müller, D. R., Tschacher, W., & Thommen, M. (2007). Schema focused emotive behavioural therapy (SET): A randomised controlled trial on patients with Cluster B and C personality disorders. *Verhaltenstherapie, 17,* 233–241.

24

Relational Problems

SHERRY A. M. STEENWYK, MICHELLE A. DOEDEN, JAMES L. FURROW, AND DAVID C. ATKINS

OVERVIEW

Relational problems are one of the most common presenting problems for individuals as well as couples and impacts individual mental health and couple functioning in addition to physical health and economic productivity (reviewed later in Impact of Relational Problems). This chapter provides an overview of relational problems with an emphasis on evidence-based, couple therapy approaches.

Diagnostic Criteria

For most common psychiatric problems there are clearly delineated diagnostic criteria, and clinical diagnosis is a core part of assessment and treatment planning. This is largely not true for relational distress, and most couple therapists do not use diagnoses to frame their treatment planning. Although diagnoses per se have not been a focus of assessment, there are a number of well-validated assessment tools for relationship problems. These are predominantly self-report measures of relationship satisfaction, and common assessment instruments include the dyadic adjustment scale (Spanier, 1976), marital assessment test (Locke & Wallace, 1959), and the multidimensional marital satisfaction inventory revised (Snyder, 1997). For an excellent overview of assessment based on such measures, Snyder, Heyman, and Haynes (2005)

present a multimethod, multilevel protocol for assessing couples.

The lack of diagnostic criteria for relational distress has been strongly influenced by its treatment in the *DSM*, though this may be changing. The *DSM-IV-TR* (American Psychiatric Association, 2000) does not include formal, diagnostic criteria for relational problems. Instead, relational problems are included in the V codes (e.g., relational problem related to a mental disorder or general medical condition, partner relational problem) and under Axis IV as psychosocial problems (e.g., problems with primary support group, problems related to the social environment). Relational functioning is also broadly considered in the global assessment of functioning in Axis V. However, due to inadequate empirical support at the time of its writing (in 1994), the current descriptions of relational problems in the *DSM* are limited (Beach, Wamboldt, Kaslow, Heyman, & Reiss, 2006).

One of the primary motivations for the *DSM* is to have a reliable set of criteria to describe psychiatric syndromes. Reliable diagnostic criteria facilitate communications among and between clinicians and researchers. Clinically, and in research, good diagnosis helps us know that we are discussing and treating the same (or different) problems. Clearly, these same goals and motivations apply to relational problems, and Heyman et al. (2009) summarize recent work on developing and validating diagnostic criteria for 11 relational disorders—spanning areas of abuse (partner and child) and relational problems (partners, parenting, and parent-child). Each set of criteria follows general *DSM* guidelines. For example, the criteria for partner relational problems include criteria A and B, which we briefly paraphrase here. Criteria A pertains to relationship dissatisfaction as seen by: (a) pervasive unhappiness, (b) thoughts of divorce/separation, or (c) perceived need for professional help. Criteria B focuses on the impact of relationship dissatisfaction on at least one of the following areas: behavioral symptoms (e.g., conflict difficulties, pervasive withdrawal), cognitive symptoms (e.g., global negative attributions of partner), and affective symptoms (e.g., anger or contempt).

Field trials of these diagnostic criteria have been completed for the abuse diagnoses, revealing highly reliable agreement, exceeding the inter-rater reliability seen across many common Axis I diagnoses (Heyman et al., 2009). Studies of partner relational problem criteria are just beginning. Even with such criteria and field trials supporting their reliability, it remains to be seen whether relational distress will be recognized as formal diagnostic criteria in the *DSM*. The *DSM* has developed from a primarily biological framework, and thus problems that are outside the person (e.g., between partners or family members) challenge core assumptions about the nature of psychiatric diagnoses as being within a person and fundamentally biological. Regardless of their status vis-à-vis the *DSM*, reliable diagnostic categories and criteria would facilitate clinical work with couples.

Demographic Variables

Prevalence rates for relationship problems are often estimated using divorce rates. As an example, the average young couple in the United States marrying today faces a 40% to 50% likelihood of divorce in their lifetime (Kreider & Fields, 2002). General estimates suggest up to 20% of marital couples report problems in their relationship, and over a third of those not reporting problems have considered divorce from their current partner or were themselves divorced from a previous partner (Weiss & Halford, 1996). An ongoing debate within psychiatry and clinical psychology focuses on whether disorders represent qualitatively different (and disordered) states, or whether they represent the end of a continuum. Recent studies have used taxometric methods as one means of assessing the qualitative versus dimensional distinction (Waller & Meehl, 1998). Recent studies applying taxometric methods suggest that relational problems do appear to be qualitatively different from satisfied relationships and found base rates for marital conflict ranging from 0.21 to 0.31 in the general population (Whisman, Beach, & Snyder, 2008). These findings suggest that, at any given time, approximately 20% to 30% of couples in the United States could be identified as meeting a qualitatively distinct criterion for marital distress.

Individuals experiencing relational distress often delay or do not pursue therapeutic treatment. Experts suggest that as few as 10% of married couples seek counseling in dealing with relationship issues (Johnson et al., 2001). Those who seek help may delay treatment for several years following the onset of interpersonal difficulties (Notarius & Buongiorno, 1992, as cited in Gottman & Gottman, 1999). For couples seeking a divorce, less than 25% have sought help from a couple therapist and note reasons such as reluctance of a partner to seek help or simply lacking awareness of a problem in the relationship (Wolcott, 1986).

Findings on gender differences in seeking couple therapy are mixed. A number of studies suggest that women are more likely to seek couple therapy (B. Doss, Atkins, & Christensen, 2003; Guillebeaux, Storm, & Demaris, 1986; Wolcott, 1986). These findings parallel studies suggesting that women are more positively disposed toward seeking therapy in general, particularly in relationships where couples hold more traditional gender role assumptions (B. Doss et al., 2003). B. D. Doss,

Simpson, and Christensen (2004) found that outside of sexual issues, husbands and wives are often seeking couple therapy for different reasons. The most common problems reported by couple therapists are interpersonal issues, including problems communicating and a loss of affection. Wives tend to report more reasons for seeking therapy, higher rates of negativity, and less positivity in their complaints compared to their husbands. Gender differences related to seeking couple therapy likely emerge from three preexisting influences including a husband's general reluctance to seek psychotherapy, the influence of social networks in support of therapy for wives, and a tendency for wives to monitor the well-being of these relationships (B. Doss et al., 2003).

Overall, few studies have found significant demographic differences in the access of treatment for relational distress. In their review, B. Doss et al. (2003) note that while differences have been identified for age and level of education there is no clear consensus from existing studies on the direction of these effects. Though studies on the relationship of marital functioning to physical health have identified gender differences (Kiecolt-Glaser & Newton, 2001), examination of similar effects of psychopathology have proven largely inconclusive (Whisman, 2007).

IMPACT OF RELATIONAL PROBLEMS

Relational problems have shown reliably negative impacts on couples, families, and individuals. Marital distress and divorce have been found to be associated with several negative consequences for spouses and children, as well as far-reaching economic costs. A review of studies conducted in the 1990s found, compared to married individuals, divorced adults experienced decreased psychological well-being, increased health problems, increased negative life events, greater social isolation, a lower standard of living, and greater parental role strain (Amato, 2000). The same review revealed that children of divorced

parents scored lower on measures of academic success, conduct, psychological adjustment, self-concept, social competence and health, and that parental divorce continues to be a risk factor in adulthood. Other research has shown a strong association between relational distress and psychological problems in general, and particularly with depression (Whisman, 1999). The significance and pervasive effects of parental divorce in childhood upon adult functioning continue to be debated (Amato, 2003).

Relational problems resulting in divorce are not only associated with various costs for the individuals involved in the dissolved marriage, there are also economic costs felt by health insurers and the government, where it has been estimated that an individual divorce will cost the government approximately $30,000 (Caldwell, Woolley, & Caldwell, 2007). Health insurers also pay a heavy burden due to medical service utilization. This utilization has been found to be reduced for couples that complete treatment and decrease their relational distress, which in turn lightens the burden placed on health insurers (Caldwell et al., 2007). The economic cost of divorce can also be felt by individual businesses due to decreased work productivity. One study found a significant association between marital distress and number of lost work days for men married 10 years or less (Forthofer, Markman, Cox, Stanley, & Kessler, 1996).

The preceding list of negative sequelae of divorce and relational problems underscore the critical importance of effective interventions for couples experiencing relationship problems. We now turn to specific couple therapies, reviewing their empirical support and making recommendations for evidence-based practice of relational distress.

TRADITIONAL BEHAVIORAL COUPLE THERAPY

Introduction

Traditional behavioral couple therapy (TBCT), historically referred to as behavioral marital therapy), is a couple therapy approach based on social learning and behavioral principles. Early applications of these theories to couples are seen in Stuart's (1969) token economy programs, and the skills-based approach of Weiss, Hops, and Patterson (1973). The first randomized trial of TBCT was Jacobson (1977), and since then it has been the most widely studied couple therapy.

Traditional behavioral couple therapy takes a directive, prescriptive approach and is focused on positive change in the partners' behavior (Jacobson & Margolin, 1979). The two main components of TBCT are behavior exchange (BE) and communication/problem-solving training (CPT). Behavior exchange utilizes homework assignments to promote positive cognitive, attributional, and behavioral changes to enhance a couple's relationship (Jacobson, 1984). Communication/problem-solving training involves training in communication and conflict resolution skills and is intended to work synergistically with BE (Jacobson & Christensen, 1996). Sessions tend to have a didactic focus with the therapist acting as collaborative coach and instructor. Therapists first train couples in each of the skills and then work with couples to practice the new skills in session, debrief homework assignments, troubleshoot problems in using the skills, and prepare for generalization and maintenance when therapy ends. Traditional behavioral couple therapy is very practical and skills-based and has been used with a wide variety of populations.

Consensus Panel Recommendations

At present, there are no formal panel recommendations for relational distress and couple therapy. However, the criteria for empirically supported treatments, developed by the American Psychological Association Division 12 committee on science and practice, has identified TBCT as a well-established "beneficial treatment for marital distress" (APA Division 12, n.d.).

Similarly, Chambless and Ollendick (2001), in their review of empirically supported therapies,

designated TBCT as a "well-established treatment." Criteria for empirically supported treatments include: efficacy demonstrated by at least two between-group design experiments conducted by different investigators or teams, clear description of treatment utilized in experiments, and sample specifications given in experiments. At the time of both of these recommendations, TBCT was the only couple therapy to meet these criteria.

Randomized Clinical Trials for Relational Problems

Numerous randomized trials have examined efficacy of TBCT for relational problems. Summary information on the 18 published randomized clinical trials (RCTs) of TBCT for relational problems is provided in Table 24.1. We will comment on the following broad categories: efficacy status, follow-up results, and limitations.

Efficacy status. Results from the RCTs clearly establish that TBCT is both beneficial and efficacious for couples experiencing relational distress. The 23 studies represent data gathered from 947 couples with an average of 35 years of age, relationship duration of 10 years, 1.5 children, and 15 years of education. Ethnicity was not reported in several studies, but it can be assumed that the vast majority of participating couples were Caucasian. The mean number of sessions administered ranged from 5 to 23. Across studies, exclusion criteria typically included couples not living together, sexual dysfunction as a primary area of concern, alcoholism or severe psychological problems in either partner, and lack of significant relational distress. The number of therapists involved in each study ranged from one to seven, with varied experience levels (e.g., master's-level social workers, clinical psychology doctoral students, and licensed clinicians).

As seen in Table 24.1, many studies compared TBCT with a wait-list control or attention-placebo condition. The results are fairly consistent, indicating that TBCT improves

TABLE 24.1 TBCT Trials

Study	N of Therapists	Mean N of Sessions	Attrition %	Exclusion Criteria	Treatment Conditions (N of groups)	Major Results	Effect Size	Length of Follow-Up	Effect Size at Follow-Up
				g	1. BMT (28); 2. Attention-placebo (2?)	1 > 2	n/a	2 years	Improvement maintained at fu
				g	1. BMT (18); 2. Communication problem-solving (18); 3. Behavioral contracting (18); 4. Wait-list 18	1 = 2 = 3 > 4	0.87	3 months	0.90
			H:	d, e, g, n	1. BMT (8); 2. BMT – cognitive restructuring (8); 3. Wait-list (8)	1 = 2 > 3	0.79	6 months	0.87
			H:	d, e, n	1. BMT – cognitive restructuring for couples – emotional expressiveness training (12); 2. BMT (12); 3. BMT – cognitive restructuring for couples (12); 4. BMT – emot exp training (12); 5. Wait-list (12)	1 = 2 = 3 = 4 > 5; 1 = 2 = 3 = 4	0.83	6 months	0.98
				d, e, n	1. Conjoint BMT (19); 2. Group BMT (19); 3. Individual BMT (19)	1 = 2 = 3	H: 3.18; W: 2.50 (all 3 txs)	6 months	H: 4.71; W: 3.68 (all 3 txs)
			H:	d, e, g, n	1. Behavioral contracting (8); 2. Systematic therapy (8); 3. Wait-list (5)	1 = 2 > 3	0.83	6 months	0.97
			TBCT H: W: IBCT H: W:		1. IBCT (68); 2. TBCT (68)		0.78	2 years	0.63

(Continued)

TABLE 24.1 TBCT Trials (Continued)

Study	N of Therapists	Mean N of Sessions	Attrition (%)	Exclusion Criteria	Treatment Conditions (N of groups)	Major Results	Effect Size	Length of Follow-Up	Effect Size at Follow-Up
Crowe (1978)	3	10	0	g, j, k, *	1: BMT (14); 2: Group analytic therapy (14); 3: Attention-placebo (14)	1 = 2 = 3	n/a	3, 9, 18 months	n/a
P. Emmelkamp, van der Helm, MacGillavry, and van Zanten (1984)	4	14	26%	d, e, g,	1: Communication problem-solving + behavioral contracting; 2: Behavioral contracting + communication problem solving (17)	1 = 2	n/a	1, 12 months	n/a
P. M. G. Emmelkamp et al. (1988)	7	9	32%	e, k	1: BMT (18); 2: Cognitive restructuring for couples (14)	1 = 2	0.70	1 month	Improvement maintained at fu
Ewart (1978)	n/a	n/a	n/a	n/a	1: BMT (18); 2: Wait-list (6)	W: 1 > 2 H: 1 = 2	n/a	n/a	n/a
Girodo, Stein, and Dotzenroth (1980)	3	5	n/a	b, d, f, *	1: BMT (6); 2: Minnesota Couples' Communication Program (12); 3: Wait-list (6)	1 = 2 = 3	0.09	No fu	No fu
Hahlweg, Revenstorf, and Schindler (1982)	6	15	9%, replaced; 13% at fu	a, e, h, k, *	1: BMT (17); 2: Group BMT (16); 3: Emotional expressiveness training (16); 4: Group em. ex. training (19); 5: Wait-list (17)	1 = 2 = 3 > 4 = 5	2.23	6, 12 months	1.0, 1.0 (BMT & Group BMT combined)
Halford et al. (1993)	5	14	0%	a, i, j, *	1: BMT (13); 2: BMT + cognitive restructuring + affect exploration + generalization training (13)	1 = 2	1.66	3 months	0.74
Jacobson (1977)	1	8	17%	e	1: BMT (5) 2: Wait-list (5)	1 > 2	3.04	1 year	Improvement maintained at fu
Jacobson (1978)	3	8	13% of 1, 2, and 3 at fu	n/a	1: BMT + good faith behavioral contracting (8); 2: BMT + quid pro quo behavioral cont. (9); 3: Attention-placebo (7); 4: Wait-list (6)	1 = 2 > 3, 4	2.21	6 months	Improvement maintained at fu

554

				Treatment groups (N)	Contrast	Effect size	Follow-up	
				1 BMT (9); 2 Communication problem-solving (9); 3 Behavior exchange (9); 4 Wait-list (9)	1 = 2 = 3 > 4	0.40	6 months (1984); 2 years (1987)	0.35 (1987)
				1 EFT (15); 2 Communication problem-solving (15); 3 Wait-list (15)	1 > 2 > 3	2.26	2 months	2.23
				1 BMT (4); 2 Attention-placebo (5)	1 > 2	n/a	6 months	Improvement maintained at fu
			*	1 BMT (29); 2 Insight-oriented marital therapy (30); 3 Wait-list (20)	1 = 2 > 3	0.37	6 months (1989); 4 years (1991)	Improvement maintained at 6-month fu. 38% BMT divorced at 4-year fu
				1 BMT (10); 2 Attention-Placebo/Normal Controls (6); 3 Wait-list (4)	2 = 3, 1 > 2, 3	n/a	n/a	n/a
				1 Communication Therapy (10); 2 BMT (10); 3 Wait-list (10)	1 = 2 = 3	n/a	4 months	n/a
			*	1 Group BMT (5); 2 Conjoint BMT (5); 3 Wait-list (5)	1 = 2 > 3	1: 1.95; 2: 2.00	6 months	1: 1.81; 2: 2.61

Note. ... das = Dyadic adjustment scale. Common exclusionary criteria: a = cohabit or married < 1 year: b = plans for divorce or separated; c = ... treatment ... the last year: d = alcohol or other drug problems; e = sexual dysfunction as primary concern; f = concurrent psychological treatment: g = living apart; h = ...; i = ... significant psychological distress; j = psychological diagnoses that might interfere with treatment. k = either partner exhibiting psychoses; l = domestic violence; m = continuing ...

Our ... additional exclusionary ... (non exclusive) list exclusionary criteria. Studies with an asterisk indicate that there are additional exclusionary criteria, which can be found in the ...

... Effect Size = M post - M pre / SD pre

marital satisfaction more effectively than no treatment. Effect sizes characterize the pre-therapy to posttherapy change in standard deviation units, and across all 18 studies effect sizes ranged from 0.09 to 3.18. Overall, the evidence based on posttest data points to TBCT being "an efficacious and specific intervention for marital distress" (Baucom, Shoham, Mueser, Daiuto, & Stickle, 1998, p. 58).

Follow-up results. Table 24.1 also presents data on posttherapy, follow-up results where available. The majority of studies had relatively brief follow-up periods of 6 months or less. Over this time frame, Hahlweg and Markman (1988) reported on eight studies with an average effect size of 1.17, leading them to conclude, "BMT produces long-lasting stable effects for those couples who remain together" (p. 445). However, the relatively small number of studies with follow-up periods of longer than 1 year paint a more qualified picture of TBCT's long-term efficacy. Jacobson, Schmaling, and Holtzworth-Munroe (1987) found an effect size of 0.35 at 2 years post-therapy, and Snyder, Wills, and Grady-Fletcher (1991) found a divorce rate of 38% for TBCT at 4 years posttherapy. These rather negative effects are moderated somewhat by recent data from the largest trial of TBCT to date (Christensen et al., 2004). At 5 years post-therapy, 28% of couples who received TBCT were divorced (Christensen, Atkins, Baucom, & Yi, 2009). For those still together, there was an effect size of 0.92 for TBCT couples 5 years posttherapy.

Meta-Analyses for Relational Problems

Several meta-analyses of couple therapy (Byrne, Carr, & Clark, 2004; Dunn & Schwebel, 1995; Shadish et al., 1993) and TBCT specifically (Hahlweg & Markman, 1988; Jacobson et al., 1984; Shadish & Baldwin, 2005) support the conclusion that TBCT is more effective in reducing couple distress than a control condition. These studies computed posttreatment effect sizes against control

conditions ranging from 0.59 (Shadish & Baldwin, 2005) to 0.95 (Byrne et al., 2004; Hahlweg & Markman, 1988). The lower effect size found in Shadish and Baldwin (2005) was due, in part, to the inclusion of unpublished dissertations. Jacobson et al. (1984) examined four outcome studies and found a weighted mean improvement rate of 54.7% and deterioration rate of 5.4%. About one-third (35.3%) of couples moved from the distressed to nondistressed range over the course of treatment.

Application of TBCT to Other Conditions

This chapter is primarily focused on couple therapy applied to relational problems, but TBCT also has been applied as a treatment for individual psychopathologies (i.e., using the couple-based interventions of TBCT but focused primarily on one partner's mental health problems), most notably alcohol and drug abuse problems. We briefly mention these findings here and also provide references to additional studies and reviews. A recent meta-analysis of the use of TBCT with an alcohol and drug use population found that TBCT outperformed individual-based treatments across 12 RCTs (Powers, Vedel, & Emmelkamp, 2008). The TBCT was significantly more effective than individual treatments on measures of relationship satisfaction posttreatment ($d = 0.64$), and continued to be more effective at follow-up ($d = 0.51$). Frequency of drug and alcohol use ($d = 0.45$) and consequences of use ($d = 0.50$) were also significantly improved by TBCT relative to individual treatment as early as 3 months following treatment. This is particularly notable in that there are very few instances of superior outcome of one active treatment over another.

Couple therapy interventions have also been applied to depression and anxiety, though with less support than that just reviewed for alcohol and drug abuse. Baucom et al. (1998, p. 67) suggest that TBCT is "a possibly efficacious treatment for depression of women in maritally distressed couples" based on two studies (Jacobson, Dobson, Fruzzetti, Schmaling, & Salusky, 1991; O'Leary & Beach, 1990). Both studies found that TBCT was comparable to individual cognitive therapy in alleviating depression in maritally distressed couples.

Conclusions

As the previous sections highlight, TBCT has numerous studies supporting its basic efficacy. Moreover, the length of follow-up in some studies is unprecedented (e.g., Christensen et al., 2009; Snyder et al., 1991). On the other hand, TBCT has generally not been shown superior to other bona fide treatments, with the exception of its use with alcohol and drug disorders. Moreover, TBCT has spawned a number of related couple therapies, which are garnering further empirical support (reviewed later in Promising Treatments).

EMOTIONALLY FOCUSED COUPLE THERAPY

Introduction

Emotionally focused couple therapy (EFT) was developed by Leslie Greenberg and Susan Johnson (1988) following Greenberg & Safran's (1987) theories of emotional change and Johnson's (1986) interest in adult attachment bonds. Johnson, Hunsley, Greenberg, and Schindler (1999) suggest a number of distinctive treatment assumptions about the role of emotion and adult attachments in promoting relational health. First, intimacy in a couple's relationship is best understood as an attachment bond. Second, ongoing patterns of couple distress prevent partners from forming a secure attachment. Third, engaging each partner's emotional experience is crucial in both defining and redefining a couple's relationship. Fourth, emotional responses must be addressed in therapy to change a couple's negative interactional patterns. Finally, a

couple's ability to express attachment needs and desires is adaptive and facilitates intimacy (Johnson, 2004).

The primary treatment manuals for EFT (Greenberg & Johnson, 1988; Johnson, 2004) describe EFT as a brief, systematic approach (8–20 sessions) that incorporates both an interpersonal focus on negative interaction patterns and an intrapsychic focus on an individual's attachment-related emotional experience. Treatment follows a 9-step change process that unfolds in three stages: de-escalation of problematic interaction patterns, changing interactional positions, and consolidation and integration (Johnson, 2004). The process of change assumes a therapist's ability to foster a safe and collaborative therapeutic alliance, a therapist's active engagement of each partner's attachment-related emotional responses, and the enactment of more adaptive responses to these emotional needs. EFT is not meant for use with violent or separating couples (Johnson, 2004).

Consensus Panel Recommendations

As noted previously in the section on TBCT, there are not formal panel recommendations for couple therapy. Baucom et al. (1998) and Chambless and Ollendick (2001) categorized EFT as "efficacious, and possibly specific." In light of the sampling criteria used in the predominance of EFT outcome studies prior to 1998, Baucom et al. suggested that EFT is an effective treatment for mild to moderately distressed couples who still maintain an emotional attachment, but questioned if there is substantial support for efficacy with severe relational distress.

Randomized Clinical Trials for Relational Problems

Effectiveness of EFT treatment for relational problems is based on seven clinical trials (Table 24.2). A summary of these trials is reviewed as follows, focusing on an assessment

TABLE 24.2 EFT Trials

Study	N of Therapists	N of Sessions	Attrition (%)	Exclusion Criteria	Treatment Conditions (N of groups)	Major Results	Effect Size	Length of Follow-Up	Effect Size at Follow-Up
Dandeneau and Johnson (1994)	10	6	3%, replaced	a, c, d, f; das <95	1: EFT (12); 2: CMT (12); 3: wait-list control (12)	1=2=3	0.79	10 weeks	1.48
Denton, Burleson, Clark, Rodriguez, and Hobbs (2000)	8	8	36%	d, e, g, h; das >97	1: EFT (22); 2: wait-list (14)	1>2	n/a	No fu	No fu
Goldman and Greenberg (1992)	7	10	21% at fu	a, b, c, d; das >95	1: IST (14); 2: EFT (14); 3: wait-list control (14)	1=2>3	1.67	4 months	0.69
James (1991)	14	12	0	a, c, d, e; das >100, <70	1: EFT (14); 2: EFT+CT (14); 3: wait-list (14)	1=2>3	ES1=2.14 ES2=2.19	4 months	ES1=1.63
Johnson and Greenberg (1985a)	6	8	2% at fu	a, b, c, d, e, f; das >100, <70	1: CBT problem solving (15); 2: EFT experiential intervention (15); 3: wait-list control (15)	2>1>3	2.26	2 months	2.23
Johnson and Greenberg (1985b)	7	8	0	a, b, c, d, e, f; das <100	(within subjects repeated measures, 14); 1: 8-week waiting period; 2: after tx; 3: 8-week fu	2>1	0.94	8 weeks	n/a
Johnson and Talitman (1997)	13	12	6%	a, d, c; das >97	EFT, no control (36)	79% clin sig improv; 82% at fu	1.26	3 months	n/a

Note: fu = follow up; n/a = not available/insufficient info; das = dyadic adjustment scale. Common exclusionary criteria: a = cohabit or married < 1 year; b = plans for divorce or separated; c = psychiatric treatment within the last year; d = alcohol or other drug problems.; e = sexual dysfunction as primary concern; f = concurrent psychological treatment; g = living apart; h = unmarried; i = no significant relational distress; j = psychological diagnoses that might interfere with treatment; k = either partner exhibiting psychoses; l = domestic violence; m = continuing extramarital affair

*Due to space constraints, we are not able to exhaustively list exclusionary criteria. Studies with an asterisk indicate that there are additional exclusionary criteria, which can be found in the primary source. Effect Size = (M post – M pre) / SD pre

of the efficacy of the approach, follow-up results, and limitations of the findings.

Efficacy status. Results from five RCTs of EFT for the treatment of couple distress (Dandeneau & Johnson, 1994; Denton, Burleson, Clark, Rodriguez, & Hobbs, 2000; Goldman & Greenberg, 1992; James, 1991; Johnson & Greenberg, 1985a) indicate that EFT is both beneficial and efficacious. These five studies represent data gathered from 205 couples, where the average participant is 38 years of age, in their current relationship/marriage for 11 years, has 1.4 children, and completed 15 years of education. The participant's ethnicity was not reported in three of the studies, but it appears that there is limited evidence of ethnic diversity among these couples. Mean number of sessions received ranged from six to twelve 1-hour to 75-minute sessions, and each study involved 6 to 14 therapists. A number of exclusionary criteria were used in the selection of participating couples. Couple members were excluded if the couple reported sexual dysfunction as a primary concern, reported alcoholism or other substance problems in either partner, participated in ongoing psychological treatment, or had made immediate plans to separate or divorce. Dyadic Adjustment Scale (DAS) scores were used in most studies to categorize couples as distressed. In two studies, DAS scores were used to include distressed couples who fell below a DAS score of 100 and to exclude participants who fell below 70 because of the severity of their relational distress. In Dandeneau and Johnson's (1994) study of happy couples, a cutoff score of 95 or higher was required to be included in the study. Each sample included a range of DAS scores for participants, and of those reported in these studies the range for participants was 84.2–87, comparable to RCTs for IBCT.

The five clinical trials were based on the comparison of EFT to a wait list control and three of the studies also included a comparison with an alternative treatment condition.

Results consistently showed that EFT significantly increased marital satisfaction above scores reported by couples in the wait-list condition. Across all five of the studies, effect sizes ranged from 0.79 to 2.26. Results from two other studies contribute empirical support for the EFT model though neither study included randomization to treatment condition. Johnson and Greenberg (1985b) conducted a within-subjects investigation examining 14 couples that participated in an 8-week waiting period followed by 8 weeks of treatment. These couples showed significant decreases in couple distress between postwait and posttreatment periods. Similarly, Johnson, and Talitman (1997) found a significant reduction in relational distress among the 36 couples participating in their within-subject design.

Follow-up results. Based on four studies with follow-up intervals of 10 weeks to 4 months, effect sizes for treatment follow-up is 0.69 to 2.23. These studies show that couples are able to maintain the gains they made through EFT for 2 to 4 months posttreatment (James, 1991; Johnson & Greenberg, 1985a). However, as seen in the Goldman and Greenberg (1992) study, severely distressed couples receiving EFT did not maintain similar gains at 4 month follow-up. By contrast, nondistressed couples showed no significant decreases in couple distress following six sessions of EFT but showed significantly greater decreases in couple distress than CMT at 10 week follow up (Dandeneau & Johnson, 1994). The implications of these results suggest that EFT leads to decreased couple distress for mildly to moderately distressed couples, but further study is needed to validate similar outcomes for severely distressed couples.

Meta-Analyses for Relational Problems

Various meta analyses of couple therapy have described EFT as an efficacious treatment for couple distress (Byrne et al., 2004; Dunn &

Schwebel, 1995; Johnson et al., 1999; Shadish & Baldwin, 2003; Wood, Crane, Schaalje, & Law, 2005). Findings from the initial clinical trial (Johnson & Greenberg, 1985a) provide preliminary support for a specific and superior treatment (to communication training), yet this finding has not been replicated. In a review of couple and family therapy meta-analyses, EFT has been described as a meta-analytically supported treatment (Shadish & Baldwin, 2003).

Wood et al. (2005) conducted a meta-analysis of couple therapy approaches by examining treatment results and their relation to couple distress levels. The authors conclude that EFT is significantly more effective than specific TBCT interventions for treating moderately distressed couples. The EFT showed the highest mean gain effect sizes compared to controls. These effects were higher than TBCT, TBCT components, mixed treatments, and other treatments. Similarily, in another meta-analysis, Byrne and colleagues (2004) found that EFT was shown to lead to short- and long-term positive results for couples who are mildly to moderately distressed (Byrne et al., 2004). Two studies within this analysis suggested that EFT may be more effective than problem-solving therapy and less effective than integrated systemic therapy. Based on posttreatment outcomes from five EFT studies on average, 73% of the couples receiving EFT improved and 51% of the couples recovered. Dunn and Schwebel (1995) found in their meta-analysis that more insight-informed therapies, including Insight-Oriented Marital Therapy (Snyder & Wills, 1989) and EFT (Greenberg & Johnson, 1988), were significantly more effective than no treatment in creating positive changes in a couple's relationship.

Finally, in Johnson and colleagues' (1999) meta-analysis of the primary RCT studies, the authors found an overall effect size of 1.31, which they contrast with Dunn and Schwebel's (1995) effect size of 0.90 for couple therapy in general. The four studies in this analysis all included measures of treatment integrity with a variety of therapists participating in the treatment. Couples receiving EFT showed significant decreases in marital distress with over half of the couples receiving EFT recovered.

Application of EFT to Other Treatment Conditions

Whereas EFT was designed primarily as a treatment for couple distress, various studies have examined its benefits in support for treatment of other conditions. These studies include the use of EFT with the treatment of depression (Dessaulles, Johnson, & Denton, 2003), of couples with chronically ill children (Cloutier, Manion, Walker, & Johnson, 2002; Walker, Johnson, Manion, & Cloutier, 1996), of females with low sexual desire (MacPhee, Johnson, & Van Der Veer, 1995), and for couples with a partner who has suffered childhood sexual abuse (MacIntosh & Johnson, 2008). These studies provide further support for the efficacy of EFT with various conditions that may lead to couple distress, and while the treatment did prove beneficial, this was not always evident in the reduction of relationship distress among these specific populations.

Conclusions

These studies provide a broad base of empirical support for Emotionally Focused Couple Therapy as a treatment for couple distress. Approximately half of couples are considered recovered following 10–12 sessions of EFT (Byrne et al., 2004). Predictors of the effectiveness of the model suggest that a couple's initial level of distress is less influential on treatment compared to other models (Johnson & Talitman, 1997). Follow-up studies suggest that EFT treatment gains are sustained for the immediate period following therapy and some couples continue to improve following the end of treatment (Johnson, 2003; Cloutier et al. 2002).

PROMISING TREATMENTS

Although not reaching the level of empirical support for TBCT or EFT, several additional treatments have been tested in clinical trials, including Integrative Behavioral Couple Therapy (IBCT) (Christensen et al., 2004; Jacobson & Christensen, 1998), Insight-Oriented Marital Therapy (IOMT) (Snyder & Wills, 1989), and Cognitive or Cognitive Behavioral Couple Therapy (CBCT) (Baucom, Sayers, & Sher, 1990). Because initial examinations of these approaches suggest their helpfulness in decreasing marital distress, they are discussed briefly here.

Integrative Behavioral Couple Therapy

Integrative Behavioral Couple Therapy (IBCT) (Jacobson & Christensen, 1998), an approach developed in the late 1980s and early 1990s, was designed to build on the theory of TBCT by adding a focus on emotional acceptance. The motivation for IBCT arose, in part, from the finding that TBCT was only successful with couples who are willing to compromise and change (Jacobson et al., 1987). Integrative Behavioral Couple Therapy, on the other hand, emphasizes emotional acceptance of the partner's behaviors rather than change (Jones, Christensen, & Jacobson, 2000). Theoretically, change occurs in IBCT through the increased acceptance and intimacy that occurs as a result of couples experiencing their relationships differently (Jones et al., 2000). A significant aspect of IBCT is the therapist's formulation of the couple, which guides the therapist's interventions and helps the couple to understand their relationship dynamics and move toward acceptance; the primary agent of change in IBCT. Clinicians are directed to Jacobson and Christensen's (1998) treatment manual for further description of the model. For couples receiving IBCT, Christensen and Jacobson (2000) developed a beneficial self-help book to follow in conjunction with treatment.

Although support for IBCT is in the beginning stages, two RCTs have demonstrated its efficacy in decreasing relationship distress. A RCT of 21 distressed couples showed that couples receiving IBCT had greater increases in marital satisfaction than couples receiving TBCT, and more of the couples receiving IBCT than those receiving TBCT were either improved or recovered based on clinical significance data (Jacobson, Christensen, Prince, Cordova, & Eldridge, 2000). Additionally, a randomized clinical trial of 134 seriously and chronically distressed couples comparing IBCT with TBCT showed that both approaches produced clinically significant improvement in relationship satisfaction, stability, and communication (Christensen, Atkins, Yi, Baucom, & George, 2006). The 2-year follow-up study on 130 of these same couples showed that both treatments resulted in clinically significant improvement (Christensen et al., 2006). However, for the couples that stayed together 2 years following treatment, those who received IBCT showed greater stability than those who received TBCT. Moreover, results at 5 years posttherapy showed that 25.7% of couples receiving IBCT had divorced, and those couples still together demonstrated an effect size of 1.03 relative to their pretreatment level of relational problems (Christensen et al., 2009). These results suggest that IBCT is at least as effective as TBCT when working with severely and chronically distressed couples.

Insight-Oriented Marital Therapy

Insight-Oriented Marital Therapy (IOMT) is a psychodynamic approach to couple therapy that helps couples identify and resolve unconscious desires and sources of conflict in their relationship through the therapist's use of clarification, interpretation, and instruction in empathy, listening, and communication. One study has examined the efficacy of IOMT in comparison with BMT (Snyder & Wills, 1989). Seventy-nine couples were assigned to TBCT, IOMT, or a wait-list condition

Results showed that couples receiving TBCT and IOMT showed significant decreases in relationship distress following treatment and that they maintained these improvements at 6-month follow-up. Regarding clinical significance, 73.3% of the couples receiving IOMT improved following treatment and 60.7% of the couples were improved at 6-month follow-up. Forty percent of couples receiving IOMT were no longer distressed following treatment and 42.9% were no longer distressed at 6-month follow-up. The effect sizes for IOMT posttherapy and at follow-up ranged from 0.86 to 1.01. In a 4-year follow-up study with 59 of the couples receiving either IOMT or TBCT, Snyder et al. (1991) found that a significantly higher percentage of couples receiving TBCT (38%) had divorced compared to those receiving IOMT (3%). Couples receiving IOMT were significantly less distressed than those receiving BMT. Although more research needs to be conducted on IOMT, this initial research suggests that it may be a beneficial treatment for marital distress. Baucom et al. (1998) and Chambless and Ollendick (2001) both reported IOMT as "possibly efficacious."

Cognitive Behavioral Marital Therapy

Cognitive Behavioral Marital Therapy (CBMT) (Baucom et al., 1990) places an emphasis on the ways partners think about their relationship and helping them understand their relationship in new and healthy ways. Therapists help partners consider alternative explanations for their partners' negative behaviors as well as help them identify and change their unrealistic expectations about being in a relationship. In one instance (Huber & Milstein, 1985) cognitive interventions were tested on their own, though more typically they have been tested as adjunctive interventions included within a TBCT protocol. Several small trials have supported the efficacy of CBMT, including (a) a study of 17 couples comparing CBMT with a wait-list condition

(Huber & Milstein, 1985); (b) an RCT of 24 distressed couples to CBMT, TBCT, or a wait-list condition (Baucom & Lester, 1986); (c) an RCT of 60 couples assigned to one of five treatment conditions (TBCT, cognitive restructuring and TBCT, emotional expressiveness training and TBCT, all interventions in a complete package, or wait-list; Baucom et al., 1990); and (d) an RCT of 26 couples assigned to receive either TBCT or enhanced TBCT, which included TBCT plus cognitive restructuring, affect exploration, and generalization training (Halford, Sanders, & Behrens, 1993). In summary, in all of these studies, CBMT was at least as effective as TBCT in significantly decreasing marital distress. Results also suggest that adding cognitive components to TBCT does not necessarily increase the effectiveness of TBCT. Reviews have concluded that CBMT is "possibly efficacious" (Baucom et al., 1998; Chambless & Ollendick, 2001).

PSYCHOEDUCATION, PREVENTION, AND ENRICHMENT

Psychoeducation, prevention, and enrichment programs are designed to enhance relationship satisfaction and prevent relational problems. We briefly consider their efficacy here, given their relevance to relational problems. Psychoeducational programs offer a range of activities that focus on promoting awareness, providing feedback, informing beliefs, and building skills to enhance relationship adjustment (Halford, Markman, Stanley, & Kline, 2002). Although couples may vary in the ways they value various educational practices, only programs emphasizing skills-based components have been rigorously examined in controlled trial evaluations (Halford et al., 2002); consequently, a number of prevention programs have not been systematically evaluated (Stanley, 2001).

Halford et al. (2002) identified 12 controlled trials evaluating relationship education programs that also included follow-up assessments of six months or more. Among these programs, only Prevention and Relationship Enhancement Program (PREP) (Markman, Stanley, & Blumberg, 1994) had been evaluated using RCTs including long-term follow-up evaluation. The PREP is classified as an efficacious couple enrichment program (Jakubowski, Milne, Brunner, & Miller, 2004). A number of other programs including the Relationship Enhancement Program (RE) (Guerney, 1977, 1987; Guerney & Maxson, 1990) and the Minnesota Couples Communication Project (MCCP) (Miller, Nunnally, & Wackman, 1975) demonstrated improvement in couples' communication and relationship satisfaction, but these results were not based on RCTs.

INTIMATE PARTNER VIOLENCE

In the research and clinical literature on relational problems, a critical consideration is intimate partner violence (IPV), and IPV has often been an exclusion criterion for couple therapy. As such, we briefly consider its treatment here. Treatment for IPV has largely focused on the individual treatment of male perpetrators and female victims. Babcock, Green, and Robie (2004) provide a detailed review of the mixed outcomes for programs designed to treat perpetrators of intimate partner violence. In their review of 17 studies of IPV treatment, Stith, Rosen, McCollum, and Thomsen (2002) found that 50% to 80% of the men who completed a psychoeducational group therapy program were nonviolent at follow-up (6 months–11 years posttreatment.) Yet only one third to two thirds of the participants completed treatment in these studies, suggesting that group treatment may not be the treatment of choice for all batterers or that only those batterers motivated to change will stay with therapy.

Recent attention has been given to the promise of conjoint couple therapy as a treatment for common couple violence. This type of couple aggression is characterized as bidirectional aggression that is of mild to moderate levels of severity and frequency (Holzworth-Munroe, Marshall, Meehan, & Rehman, 2003). These authors note that this type of domestic aggression is common in couple therapy populations with as many as 50% of couples reporting some incidence of aggression within the past year and the majority of the time these acts are reciprocated between males and females. Conjoint treatment of IPV assumes careful assessment of violence risk of both partners (Bograd & Mederos, 1999; Stith, et al., 2002) given the potential consequence of physical aggression. Yet, a review of conjoint treatment of couples with IPV did not show that female partners were at greater risk of harm (Stith, Rosen, McCollum, & Thomsen, 2004).

Stith and colleagues (2002) reviewed six experimental studies that included individual, conjoint, and group treatment for male IPV, and the authors found no significant differences in treatment type for reduction of a male partner's acts of violence. The authors report that IPV conjoint treatment with carefully screened couples is at least as effective as traditional models of psychoeducational group treatment for male perpetrators. Further, Stith et al. (2002) found that all but one of eight additional evaluation studies showed that IPV ceased among couples receiving conjoint treatment. There was no evidence of greater risk of IPV during treatment for female participants compared to the gender specific treatment programs.

In conclusion, though it seems that couple therapy is an appropriate treatment for intimate partner violence according to these results, clinicians need to use caution when screening couples and deciding whether conjoint treatment is the best option. Although couple treatment appears to be helpful in treating intimate partner violence, research in this area is still in the beginning stages in comparison to research on treatment for marital distress.

EVIDENCE-BASED PRACTICES

In making recommendations for evidence-based practice for treating relational problems, let us begin with a few straightforward recommendations: Both TBCT and EFT have demonstrated superiority to control conditions in multiple RCTs, which has been supported in multiple meta-analyses. Thus, we would consider both of these approaches to have established a substantial evidence base that promotes their use in clinical practice. There are also a number of treatments that offer promising evidence as a treatment of relational distress. These approaches represent both broadly compatible (e.g., EFT and IOMT) or innovative developments (e.g., TBCT and IBCT). The evidence base for conjoint treatment of interpersonal violence and prevention and couples enrichment education is preliminary, yet recent efforts to establish empirical support of these practices recognize their potential to establishing a broad scope of empirical practices relevant to relational problems.

In conclusion, we offer three recommendations for future development to advance an empirical base of support for the treatment of relational problems. These include broadening the diversity in couples included in clinical samples, supporting and promoting the continued development and study of promising practices, and developing practice resources to support training and adherence to these treatment models in everyday practice.

The clinical populations represented in a majority of the RCT studies of couples therapy remain limited in representing the diversity of couples receiving clinical treatment. There are few studies that clearly denote the recruitment of minority couples. A secondary analysis of the Christensen et al. (2004) trial suggests that ethnic-minority couples had similar levels of distress and improvement to Caucasian couples (Yi, George, Atkins, & Christensen, 2009). However, this can only be regarded as very preliminary. Moreover, there are no clinical trials with gay and lesbian couples, although some clinicians have suggested ways in which empirical models could be extended (e.g., IBCT; Martell & Prince, 2005).

In a related concern, the clinical trials of EFT for relational problems have, in more than one study, been limited to moderately distressed couples. This has been cited as a potential limitation of the EFT evidence base to date (Baucom et al., 1998). Recent studies and use of the model with couples coping with a partner's depression, a partner's childhood sexual abuse, or a chronically ill child suggest that model is beneficial for couples facing significant stressors. Future studies selecting for more distressed populations will likely need to extend the 10–12 session treatment condition common in most EFT RCT protocols.

Clearly, TBCT has the broadest evidence base and has demonstrated significant utility in application to other treatment populations (e.g., Substance Abuse). Moreover, it has been the basis for several newer treatments (e.g., CBMT, IBCT). Anecdotally, it would appear that TBCT in its RCT protocol format is relatively uncommon in clinical practice, whereas its components are oftentimes used flexibly within a broader CBT framework. It may be that the ongoing developments of CBT and the introduction of IBCT represent innovations in the standard TBCT practice and extend the contribution of the original model. As such, further attention is warranted to the unique contribution of these models and the form of TBCT used in actual practice.

CONCLUSIONS

This review has pointed to a number of clinical models for relational problems that have been shown to be either efficacious or promising practices. Further review of empirical studies point to the contribution of couple therapy to a variety of treatment issues where a couple's relationship may prove directly impacted by that disorder (stressor) or an ancillary treatment to the particular disorder (resource). Training clinicians in the use of these models requires an ongoing assessment of adherence and fidelity to the model. In a majority of the empirical studies reviewed in this chapter, researchers test the adherence of participating clinicians to the treatment model under study. Critical to the training and advancement of empirically based practices is the assurance that similar methods of assessing fidelity to a model's treatment are available to trainers and supervisors overseeing the development of competency in one of these approaches. We do assume that the application and resulting benefits of these clinical practices to the treatment of relational distress is contingent upon the development of methods of training that assure the instruction and resulting practice of the clinicians who adopt these approaches.

REFERENCES

Amato, P. R. (2000). The consequences of divorce for adults and children. *Journal of Marriage and the Family, 62*, 1269–1287.

Amato, P. R. (2003). Reconciling divergent perspectives: Judith Wallerstein, quantitative family research and children of divorce. *Family Relations, 52*, 332–339.

American Psychological Association Division 12. (n.d.). *Marital distress: A guide to beneficial psychotherapy. Empirically supported treatments.* Retrieved from www.apa.org/divisions/div12/rev_est/marital.html

American Psychiatric Association. (2000). *Diagnostic and statistical manual of mental disorders* (4th ed., text rev.). Washington, DC: Author.

Azrin, N. H., Besalel, V. A., Bechtel, R., Michalicek, A., Mancera, M., Carroll, D., . . . Cox, J. (1980). Comparison of reciprocity and discussion-type counseling for marital problems. *American Journal of Family Therapy, 8*(1), 21–28.

Babcock, J. C., Green, C. E., & Robie, C. (2004). Does batterers' treatment work? A meta-analytic review of domestic violence treatment. *Clinical Psychology Review, 23*, 1023–1053.

Baucom, D. H. (1982). A comparison of behavioral contracting and problem-solving/communications training in behavioral marital therapy. *Behavior Therapy, 13*, 162–174.

Baucom, D. H., & Lester, G. W. (1986). The usefulness of cognitive restructuring as an adjunct to behavioral marital therapy. *Behavior Therapy, 17*, 385–403.

Baucom, D. H., Sayers, S. L., & Sher, T. G. (1990). Supplementing behavioral marital therapy with cognitive restructuring and emotional expressiveness training: An outcome investigation. *Journal of Consulting and Clinical Psychology, 58*, 636–645.

Baucom, D. H., Shoham, V., Mueser, K. T., Daiuto, A. D., & Stickle, T. R. (1998). Empirically supported couple and family interventions for marital distress and adult mental health problems. *Journal of Consulting and Clinical Psychology, 66*, 53–88.

Beach, S. R., Wamboldt, M. Z., Kaslow, N. J., Heyman, R. E., & Reiss, E. (2006). Describing relationship problems in *DSM-V*: Toward better guidance for research and clinical practice. *Journal of Family Psychology, 20*, 359–368.

Bennun, I. (1985). Behavioral marital therapy: An outcome evaluation of conjoint, group and one spouse treatment. *Scandinavian Journal of Behaviour Therapy, 14*, 157–168.

Boelens, W., Emmelkamp, E., MacGillavry, D., & Markvoort, M. (1980). A clinical evaluation of marital treatment: Reciprocity counseling vs. system theoretic counseling. *Behavior Analysis and Modification, 4*, 85–96.

Bograd, M., & Mederos F. (1999). Battering and couples therapy: Universal screening and selection of treatment modality. *Journal of Marital and Family Therapy, 25*, 291–312.

Byrne, M., Carr, A., & Clark, M. (2004). The efficacy of behavioral couples therapy and emotionally focused therapy for couple distress. *Contemporary Family Therapy, 26*, 361–387.

Caldwell, B. E., Woolley, S. R., & Caldwell, C. J. (2007). Preliminary estimates of cost-effectiveness for marital therapy. *Journal of Marital and Family Therapy, 33*, 392–405.

Chambless, D. L., & Ollendick, T. H. (2001). Empirically supported psychological interventions: Controversies and evidence. *Annual Review of Psychology, 52*, 685–716.

Christensen, A., Atkins, D. C., Baucom, B. D., & Yi, J. (2009). Marital status and satisfaction five years following a randomized clinical trial comparing traditional and integrative couple therapy. *Journal of Consulting and Clinical Psychology, 78*, 225–235.

Christensen, A., Atkins, D. C., Berns, S., Wheeler, J., Baucom, D. H., & Simpson, L. E. (2004). Traditional versus integrative behavioral couple therapy for significantly and chronically distressed married couples. *Journal of Consulting and Clinical Psychology, 72*, 176–191.

Christensen, A., Atkins, D. C., Yi, J., Baucom, D. H., & George, W. H. (2006). Couple and individual adjustment for 2 years following a randomized clinical trial comparing traditional versus integrative behavioral couple therapy. *Journal of Consulting and Clinical Psychology, 74,* 1180–1191.

Christensen, A., & Jacobson, N. S. (2000). *Reconcilable differences.* New York, NY: Guilford Press.

Cloutier, P. F., Manion, I. G., Walker, J. G., & Johnson, S. M. (2002). Emotionally focused interventions for couples with chronically ill children: A 2-year follow-up. *Journal of Marital and Family Therapy, 28,* 391–398.

Crowe, M. J. (1978). Conjoint marital therapy: A controlled outcome study. *Psychological Medicine, 8,* 623–636.

Dandeneau, M. L., & Johnson, S. M. (1994). Facilitating intimacy: Interventions and effects. *Journal of Marital and Family Therapy, 20,* 17–33.

Denton, W. H., Burleson, B. R., Clark, T. E., Rodriguez, C. P., & Hobbs, B. V. (2000). A randomized trial of emotion-focused therapy for couples in a training clinic. *Journal of Marital and Family Therapy, 26,* 65–78.

Dessaulles, A., Johnson, S. M., & Denton, W. H. (2003). Emotion-focused therapy for couples in the treatment of depression: A pilot study. *American Journal of Family Therapy, 31,* 345–353.

Doss, B., Atkins, D. C., & Christensen, A. (2003). Deciding with their feet? Husbands and wives seeking marital therapy. *Journal of Marital and Family Therapy, 29,* 165–177.

Doss, B. D., Simpson, L. E., & Christensen, A. (2004). Why do couples seek marital therapy? *Professional Psychology: Research and Practice, 35,* 608–614.

Dunn, R. L., & Schwebel, A. I. (1995). Meta-analytic review of marital therapy outcome research. *Journal of Family Psychology, 9,* 58–68.

Emmelkamp, P., van der Helm, M., MacGillavry, D., & van Zanten, B. (1984). Marital therapy with clinically distressed couples: A comparative evaluation of system-theoretic, contingency contracting, and communication skills approaches. In K. Hahlweg & N. S. Jacobson (Eds.), *Marital interaction: Analysis and modification* (pp. 36–52). New York, NY: Guilford Press.

Emmelkamp, P. M. G., van Linden, van den Heuvell, C., Ruphan, M., Sanderman, R., Scholing, A., & Stroink, F. (1988). Cognitive and behavioral interventions: A comparative evaluation with clinically distressed couples. *Journal of Family Psychology, 1,* 365–377.

Ewart, C. K. (1978, August). *Behavior contracts in couple therapy: An experimental evaluation of quid pro quo and good faith models.* Paper presented at the annual meeting of the Association for Advancement of Behavior Therapy, Toronto, Ontario, Canada.

Forthofer, M. S., Markman, H. J., Cox, M., Stanley, S., & Kessler, R. C. (1996). Associations between marital distress and work loss in a national sample. *Journal of Marriage and Family, 58,* 597–605.

Girodo, M., Stein, S. J., & Dotzenroth, S. E. (1980). The effects of communication skills training and contracting on marital relations. *Behavioral Engineering, 6,* 61–76.

Goldman, A., & Greenberg, L. (1992). Comparison of integrated systemic and emotionally focused approaches to couples therapy. *Journal of Consulting and Clinical Psychology, 60,* 962–969.

Gottman, J. M., & Gottman, J. S. (1999). The marriage survival kit. In R. Berger & M. T. Hanna (Eds.), *Preventative approaches in couples therapy* (pp. 304–330). Philadelphia, PA: Brunner/Mazel.

Greenberg, L. S., & Johnson, S. M. (1988). *Emotionally focused therapy for couples.* New York, NY: Guilford Press.

Greenberg, L. S., & Safran, J. D. (1987). *Emotion in psychotherapy: Affect, cognition, and the process of change.* New York, NY: Guilford Press.

Guerney, B. G. (1977). *Relationship enhancement.* San Francicsco, CA: Jossey-Bass.

Guerney, B. G. (Ed.). (1987). *Relationship enhancement manual.* Bethesda, MD: Ideal.

Guerney, B. G., & Maxson, P. (1990). Marital and family enrichment research: A decade review and a look ahead. *Journal of Marriage and the Family, 52,* 1127–1135.

Guillebeaux, F., Storm, C. L., & Demaris, A. (1986). Luring the reluctant male: A study of males participating in marriage and family therapy. *Family Therapy, 13,* 215–225.

Hahlweg, K., Revenstorf, D., & Schindler, L. (1982). Treatment of marital distress: Comparing formats and modalities. *Advances in Behaviour Research and Therapy, 4,* 57–74.

Hahlweg, K., & Markman, H. J. (1988). Effectiveness of behavioral marital therapy: Empirical status of behavioral techniques in preventing and alleviating marital distress. *Journal of Consulting and Clinical Psychology, 56,* 440–447.

Halford, W. K., Markman, H. J., Stanley, S., & Kline, G. H. (2002). Relationship enhancement. In D. H. Sprenkle (Ed.), *Effectiveness research in marriage and family therapy* (pp. 191–222). Alexandria, VA: American Association for Marriage and Family Therapy.

Halford, W. K., Sanders, M. R., & Behrens, B. C. (1993). A comparison of the generalization of behavioral marital therapy and enhanced behavioral marital therapy. *Journal of Consulting and Clinical Psychology, 61,* 51–60.

Heyman, R. E., Smith Slep, A. M., Beach, S. R. H., Wamboldt, M. Z., Kaslow, N. J., & Reiss, D. (2009). Relationship problems and the *DSM*: Needed improvements and suggested solutions. *World Psychiatry, 8,* 7–14.

Holzworth-Munroe, A., Marshall, A. D., Meehan, J. C. & Rehman, U. (2003). Physical aggression. In D. Snyder and M. Whisman (Eds.), *Treating difficult couples* (pp. 201–230). New York, NY: Guilford Press.

Huber, C. H., & Milstein, B. (1985). Cognitive restructuring and a collaborative set in couples' work. *American Journal of Family Therapy, 13*, 17–27.

Jacobson, N. S. (1977). Problem-solving and contingency contracting in the treatment of marital discord. *Journal of Consulting and Clinical Psychology, 45*, 92–100.

Jacobson, N. S. (1978). Specific and nonspecific factors in the effectiveness of a behavioral approach to the treatment of marital discord. *Journal of Consulting and Clinical Psychology, 46*, 442–452.

Jacobson, N. S. (1984). A component analysis of behavioral marital therapy: The relative effectiveness of behavioral exchange and communication/problem-solving training. *Journal of Consulting and Clinical Psychology, 52*, 295–305.

Jacobson, N. S., & Christensen, A. (1996). *Integrative couple therapy: Promoting acceptance and change.* New York, NY: Norton.

Jacobson, N. S., & Christensen, A. (1998). *Acceptance and change in couple therapy: A therapist's guide to transforming relationships.* New York, NY: W. W. Norton & Company.

Jacobson, N. S., Christensen, A., Prince, S. E., Cordova, J., & Eldridge, K. (2000). Integrative behavioral couple therapy: An acceptance based, promising new treatment for couple discord. *Journal of Consulting and Clinical Psychology, 68*, 351–355.

Jacobson, N. S., Dobson, K., Fruzzetti, A. E., Schmaling, D. B., & Salusky, S. (1991). Marital therapy as a treatment for depression. *Journal of Consulting and Clinical Psychology, 59*, 547–557.

Jacobson, N. S., Follette, W. C., Revenstorf, D., Baucom, D. H., Hahlweg, K., & Margolin, G. (1984). Variability in outcome and clinical significance of behavioral marital therapy: A reanalysis of outcome data. *Journal of Consulting and Clinical Psychology, 52*, 497–504.

Jacobson, N. S., & Margolin, G. (1979). *Marital therapy: Strategies based on social learning behavior exchange principles.* New York, NY: Brunner/Mazel.

Jacobson, N. S., Schmaling, K. B., & Holtzworth-Munroe, A. (1987). Component analyses of behavioral marital therapy: 2 year follow-up and prediction of relapse. *Journal of Marital and Family Therapy, 13*, 187–195.

Jakubowski, S. F., Milne, E. P., Brunner, H., & Miller, R. B. (2001). A review of empirically supported marital enrichment programs. *Family Relations, 53*, 528–536.

James, P. S. (1991). Effects of a communication training component added to an emotionally focused couples therapy. *Journal of Marital and Family Therapy, 17*, 263–275.

Johnson, C. A., Stanley, S. M., Glenn, N. D., Amato, P. R., Nock, S. L., Markman, H. J., & Dion, M. R. (2001). *Marriage in Oklahoma: 2001 baseline statewide survey on marriage and divorce.* Stillwater: Oklahoma State University Bureau for Social Research.

Johnson, S. M. (1986). Bonds or bargains: Relationship paradigms and their significance for marital therapy. *Journal of Marital and Family Therapy, 12*, 259–267.

Johnson, S. M. (2003). The revolution in couple therapy: A practitioner-scientist perspective. *Journal of Marital and Family Therapy, 28*, 391–399.

Johnson, S. M. (2004). *The practice of emotionally focused couple therapy* (2nd ed.). New York, NY: Brunner-Routledge.

Johnson, S. M., & Greenberg, L. S. (1985a). Differential effects of experiential and problem-solving interventions in resolving marital conflict. *Journal of Consulting and Clinical Psychology, 53*, 175–184.

Johnson, S. M., & Greenberg, L. S. (1985b). Emotionally focused couples therapy: An outcome study. *Journal of Marital and Family Therapy, 11*, 313–317.

Johnson, S. M., Hunsley, J., Greenberg, L. S., & Schindler, D. (1999). Emotionally focused couples therapy: Status and challenges. *Clinical Psychology Science and Practice, 6*, 67–79.

Johnson, S. M., & Talitman, E. (1997). Predictors of success in emotionally focused marital therapy. *Journal of Marital and Family Therapy, 23*, 135–152.

Jones, J., Christensen, A., & Jacobson, N. (2000). Integrative behavioral couple therapy. In F. M. Dattilio & L. J. Bevilacqua (Eds.), *Comparative treatments for relationship dysfunction* (pp. 186–209). New York, NY: Spring Publishing.

Kiecolt-Glaser, J. K., & Newton, T. L. (2001). Marriage and health: His and hers. *Psychological Bulletin, 127*, 472–503.

Kreider, R. M., & Fields, J. M. (2002). Number, timing, and duration of marriages and divorces: 1996. *Current Pop Rep P70-80*. Washington, DC: U.S. Census Bureau.

Liberman, R., Levine, J., Wheeler, E., Sanders, N., & Wallace, C. J. (1976). Marital therapy in groups: A comparative evaluation of behavioral and interaction formats. *Acta Psychiatrica Scandinavica, 266*, 1–34.

Locke, H. J., and Wallace, K. M. (1959). Short marital adjustment and prediction tests: Their reliability and validity. *Marriage and Family Living, 21*, 251–255.

MacIntosh, H. B., & Johnson, S. (2008). Emotionally focused therapy for couples and childhood sexual abuse survivors. *Journal of Marital and Family Therapy, 34*, 298–315.

MacPhee, D. C., Johnson, S. M., & Van Der Veer, M. C. (1995). Low sexual desire in women: The effects of marital therapy. *Journal of Sex & Marital Therapy, 21*, 159–182.

Markman, H. J., Stanley, S. M., & Blumberg, S. L. (1994). *Fighting for your marriage: Positive steps for a loving and lasting relationship.* San Francisco, CA: Jossey-Bass.

Martell, C. R., & Prince, S. E. (2005). Treating infidelity in same-sex couples. *Journal of Clinical Psychology, 61,* 1429–1438.

Miller, S., Nunnally, E., & Wackman, D. (1975). Minnesota Couples Communication Program (MCCP): Premarital and marital groups. In D. H. Olson (Ed.), *Treating relationships* (pp. 21–40). Lake Mills, IA: Graphic.

O'Leary, K. D., & Beach, S. R. H. (1990). Marital therapy: A viable treatment for depression and marital discord. *American Journal of Psychiatry, 147,* 183–186.

O'Leary, K. D., & Turkewitz, H. (1981). A comparative outcome study of behavioral marital therapy and communication therapy. *Journal of Marital and Family Therapy, 7,* 159–169.

Powers, M. B., Vedel, E., & Emmelkamp, P. M. G. (2008). Behavioral couples therapy (BCT) for alcohol and drug use disorders: A meta-analysis. *Clinical Psychology Review, 28,* 952–962.

Shadish, W. R., & Baldwin, S. A. (2003). Meta-analyses of MFT interventions. *Journal of Marital and Family Therapy, 29,* 547–570.

Shadish, W. R., & Baldwin, S. A. (2005). Effects of behavioral marital therapy: A meta-analysis of randomized controlled trials. *Journal of Consulting and Clinical Psychology, 73,* 6–14.

Shadish, W. R., Montgomery, L. M., Wilson, P., Wilson, M. R., Bright, I., & Okwumabua, T. (1993). Effects of family and marital psychotherapies: A meta-analysis. *Journal of Consulting and Clinical Psychology, 61,* 992–1002.

Snyder, D. K. (1997). *Marital satisfaction inventory, revised.* Los Angeles, CA: Western Psychological Services.

Snyder, D. K., Heyman, R. E., & Haynes, S. N. (2005). Evidence-based approaches to assessing couple distress. *Psychological Assessment, 17,* 288–307.

Snyder, D. K., & Wills, R. M. (1989). Behavioral versus insight-oriented marital therapy: Effects on individual and interspousal functioning. *Journal of Consulting and Clinical Psychology, 57,* 39–46.

Snyder, D. K., Wills, R. M., & Grady-Fletcher, A. (1991). Long-term effectiveness of behavioral versus insight-oriented marital therapy: A 4-year follow-up study. *Journal of Consulting and Clinical Psychology, 59,* 138–141.

Spanier, G. B. (1976). Measuring dyadic adjustment: New scales for assessing the quality of marriage and similar dyads. *Journal of Marriage and the Family, 38,* 15–28.

Stanley, S. (2001). Making the case for premarital training. *Family Relations, 50,* 272–280.

Stith, S. M., Rosen, K. H., McCollum, E. E., & Thomsen, C. J. (2002). Domestic violence. In D. H. Sprenkle (Ed.), *Effectiveness research in marriage and family therapy* (pp. 223–254). Alexandria, VA: American Association for Marriage and Family Therapy.

Stith, S. M., Rosen, K. H., McCollum, E. E., & Thomsen, C. J. (2004). Treating intimate partner violence within

intact couple relationships: Outcomes of multi-couple versus individual couple therapy. *Journal of Marital and Family Therapy, 30,* 305–318.

Stuart, R. B. (1969). An operant interpersonal treatment for marital discord. *Journal of Consulting and Clinical Psychology, 33,* 675–682.

Tsoi-Hoshmand, L. (1976). Marital therapy: An integrated behavioral learning approach. *Journal of Marriage and Family Counseling, 2,* 179–191.

Walker, J. G., Johnson, S., Manion, I., & Cloutier, P. (1996). Emotionally focused marital intervention for couples with chronically ill children. *Journal of Consulting and Clinical Psychology, 64,* 1029–1036.

Waller, N. G., & Meehl, P. E. (1998). *Multivariate taxometric procedures: Distinguishing types from continua.* Newbury Park, CA: Sage.

Weiss, R. L. & Halford, W.K. (1996). Managing marital therapy: Helping partners change. In V. B. Hasselt & M. Hersen (Eds.), *Sourcebook of psychological treatment manuals for adult disorders* (pp. 489–538). New York, NY: Springer.

Weiss, R. L., Hops, H., & Patterson, G. R. (1973). A framework for conceptualizing marital conflict, a technology for altering it, some data for evaluating it. In L. A. Hamerlynck, L. C., Handy, and E. J. Mash (Eds.), *Behavioral change: Methodology, concepts, and practice* (pp. 309–342). Champaign, IL: Research Press.

Whisman, M. A. (1999). Marital dissatisfaction and psychiatric disorders in a community sample: Results from the National Comorbidity Survey. *Journal of Abnormal Psychology, 108,* 701–706.

Whisman, M. A. (2007). Marital distress and *DSM-IV* Psychiatric disorders in a population-base national survey. *Journal of Abnormal Psychology, 116,* 638–643.

Whisman, M. A., Beach, S. R. H. & Snyder, D. K. (2008). Is marital discord taxonic and can taxonic status be assessed reliably? Results from a national, representative sample of married couples. *Journal of Consulting and Clinical Psychology, 76,* 745–755.

Wilson, G. L., Bernstein, P. H., & Wilson, L. J. (1988). Treatment of relationship dysfunction: An empirical evaluation of group and conjoint behavioral marital therapy. *Journal of Consulting and Clinical Psychology, 56,* 929–931.

Wolcott, I. H. (1986). Seeking help for marital problems before separation. *Australian Journal of Sex, Marriage, and Family, 7,* 154–164.

Wood, N. D., Crane, D. R., Schaalje, G. B., & Law, D. D. (2005). What works for whom: A meta-analytic review of marital and couples therapy in reference to marital distress. *American Journal of Family Therapy, 33,* 273–287.

Yi, J., George, W. H., Atkins, D. C., & Christensen, A. (2009). *Ethnic minorities in couple therapy: How do they fare?* Manuscript submitted for publication.

25

Nonpharmacological Interventions for Chronic Pain

JOHN G. ARENA AND REBECCA L. JUMP

OVERVIEW OF DISORDER

The International Association for the Study of Pain, in its classic definition (1986), defined pain as "An unpleasant sensory and emotional experience associated with actual or potential tissue damage, or described in terms of such damage" (p. 216). This definition—indeed no definition—can capture the complex biological, psychological, and social factors that make up the phenomena of pain. Chronic pain—that is, pain of 6 months duration or greater—is one of the most vexing problems remaining in modern medicine.

It is estimated that pain is the principal cause of visits to primary care providers in the United States (Bindman, Forrest, Britt, Crampton, & Majeed, 2007; Schappert, 1999; Sobel, 1993) and that the costs of chronic pain exceeds the cost of HIV/AIDS, cardiovascular disease, and cancer combined (Cousins, 1995). More Americans suffer from chronic pain than diabetes, heart disease, and cancer combined (American Academy of Pain Medicine, 2008). According to the Centers for Disease Control and Prevention, one in four adults in the United States reported that they suffered a day long

bout of pain in the past month, and one in ten adults have pain that has lasted a year or more (Centers for Disease Control, National Center for Health Statistics, 2006). In 1999, the Gallup poll conducted a comprehensive survey on pain (Arthritis Foundation, 1999). They found that 89% of Americans age 18 and older suffer from pain at least once a month, and that 43% of adults (an estimated 89 million Americans at the time) reported that pain frequently affected their participation in some activities. The Gallup survey also found that 15% of Americans (26 million Americans in 1999) who suffered from pain monthly characterized it as severe pain, and that 46% of women report experiencing daily pain, compared to only 37% of men. A recent survey by Krueger and Stone (2008) essentially replicated these results. The presence of chronic pain at least doubles and may increase by fourfold an individual's risk of death by suicide (Tang & Crane, 2006).

Pain is such a significant problem in the United States that since 2001 the Joint Commission on Accreditation of Healthcare Organizations Comprehensive Accreditation Manual for Hospitals Official Handbook has considered pain the *fifth vital sign* in the care of hospitalized patients. The handbook states that pain intensity ratings should be gathered at admissions assessment, along with body temperature, pulse rate, respiration rate, and blood pressure. Just as importantly, it recommends that competency in pain assessment and treatment should be determined in all new clinical staff during the orientation period, and that education in pain be ongoing for all clinical staff.

Despite its prevalence in the United States and throughout the industrialized world, a significant number of pain patients prove refractory to traditional medical approaches to pain, such as pharmacological and surgical interventions. This has necessitated the development of nontraditional approaches to pain management. This chapter is intended to give the reader an overview of the major nonpharmacological, evidenced-based approaches to chronic pain being utilized by pain practitioners at the present time.

Low Back Pain

Chronic low back pain (LBP) is one of the most significant health problems in the United States today. According to the Centers for Disease Control and Prevention, more than one quarter of the adults they interviewed said they experienced LBP in the past 3 months (Centers for Disease Control, National Center for Health Statistics, 2006). In 1999, the Arthritis Foundation enlisted the Gallup Organization to conduct a comprehensive survey on pain in America (Arthritis Foundation, 1999), which revealed that more women than men experience frequent back pain (24% vs. 19%). Others have estimated that from 12% to 45% of the adult population will suffer from LBP at any one time, and that 60% to 80% of the population will at some point in their lives experience LBP (Andersson & McNeill, 1989). Back pain is the most frequent cause of activity limitations in people 45 years old and younger, and is the number one cause of

compensatable disabilities in individuals under 45 years old according to the American Academy of Pain Medicine (2008). About 2% of American workers have compensatable back injuries a year (Wheeler, 2007).

Twelve percent of all sick leave is taken because of LBP, and the average sick leave period is 30 days (Borenstein & Wiesel, 1989). Low back pain also accounts for 25% of all compensatable disabilities in the workplace (Cavanaugh & Weinstein, 1994; Fordyce, 1995). Estimates are that on any given day, 0.5% of the work force has been disabled for more than 6 months as a result of LBP (American Academy of Pain Medicine, 2008; Wood & Bradley, 1980), and that 2% of all workers injure their backs on the job each year (Teasell & White, 1994). Between 1971 and 1981, the number of Americans disabled as a result of LBP grew at a rate 14 times the population growth (Wheeler, 2007).

The vast majority of costs are spent by a small minority of back pain patients, generally believed to be between 2% and 8% (Engel, Von Korff, & Katon, 1996; Maetzel & Li, 2002). Although females may report LBP symptoms more frequently than men, men have twice the surgery rate (Cavanaugh & Weinstein, 1994). Low back pain is responsible for at least $16 billion a year in the United States in *direct medical costs*, such as surgeries, hospital/physician visits, and disability insurance payouts (Borenstein & Wiesel, 1989), with some estimates going up to $100 billion (Frymoyer, Akeson, Brandt, Goldenberg, & Spencer, 1989; Wheeler, 2007). Indirect medical costs, such as sickness, absence, and lost productivity, are much higher. The personal pain and suffering of the chronic LBP sufferer are incalculable—how can one put a price on time missed from family and friends?

Although most LBP is temporary and alleviated within a month or two, a considerably large minority of individuals suffer from chronic LBP. This segment of the LBP population has been increasing greatly in recent years, in spite of the fact that the percentage of Americans who suffer from LBP has remained the same. Unfortunately, our ability to treat these chronic LBP patients successfully, or even to predict who will be a successful treatment candidate, is at best fair. Even more troubling, our understanding of the factors involved in the etiology and maintenance of chronic LBP is remarkably limited. Only 10%–15% of patients with LBP have demonstrated pathology or a clear-cut cause for their symptoms (Frymoyer et al., 1989). Many factors have been associated with an increase in LBP, and an excellent concise reference for these factors is C. E. Dionne's (1999) seminal chapter on epidemiology of LBP. Factors that have been implicated in increasing the likelihood of having LBP are being male, of low socioeconomic status, having low educational levels, having a history of previous back pain or traumatic injury, being obese, being of greater height, mental stress at work, operating vibrating equipment at work, the physical workload of a job, frequent bending and lifting at work, job satisfaction, depression, self-confidence, a propensity to somatization, cigarette smoking, and the greater the number of children one has.

In spite of the fact that we know so little about the etiology of chronic LBP, Arena and his colleagues (Arena & Blanchard, 2002b; Arena, Sherman, Bruno, & Young, 1989, 1991; Sherman & Arena, 1992) have argued that some diagnostic schema needs to be incorporated in both LBP research and clinical work if clinicians are ever to understand LBP and improve on current treatments. They have used the criteria and diagnostic schema set forth by the American Academy of Orthopedic Surgery (1996).

Headache

There are two major types of headaches, migraine and tension. We will focus in on these types of headaches, as the bulk of the headache literature in general, and, especially, the

nonpharmacological intervention literature, is focused on these two kinds of headaches.

Migraine headache is episodic and characterized by a throbbing/pulsating/pounding type of pain that generally starts on one side of the head, although as the headache progresses, it often encompasses both sides. It typically starts over an eye or in the temple region and can last anywhere from 2 hours to 3 days. Frequently it is accompanied by nausea and, sometimes, vomiting, as well as sensitivity to noise (phonophobia) and, especially, light (photophobia). A migraine can occur on a frequency of two a week to only one or two a year; the average migraineur has one to two headaches a month. Approximately 10% of migraine headache patients have a prodrome—that is, preheadache symptoms that can occur up to 30 minutes before a headache, such as seeing flashing lights or squiggly lines, experiencing a disturbance in speech, or a tingling feeling in the arms or hands. Those migraine headache sufferers with a prodrome are described as classic migraineurs; those without a prodrome are termed common migraineurs.

Tension headache is generally less episodic and is characterized by a steady, dull ache or pressure that is generally on both sides of the head. It is sometimes described as a tight band or cap around the head, a soreness, a nagging, or a vice-like pain. It typically begins in the forehead, temple, back of the head and neck, or shoulder regions, and encompasses the entire head. A tension headache can last from 30 minutes to 7 days. If headache occurs less than 15 days a month, they are termed episodic tension type headache; if the headache is experienced 15 or more days a month, they are termed chronic tension type headache. The pain associated with tension headache is considered to be of generally lesser intensity than that of migraine headache.

Up to half of patients with migraine headache also meet the criteria for tension headache. These individuals have been labeled as *Mixed Migraine and Tension Type Headache* or *Combined Migraine and Tension Type*

Headache. Most clinicians and researchers have typically lumped both pure migraine and mixed migraine and tension headaches together under the label of vascular headache and treated them similarly.

Headaches are a true biopsychosocial phenomenon, affecting psychological and social factors of an individual's life as well as the more obvious physiological concerns. Depression, anxiety, and anger are common sequela of headache, as are dysfunctions in occupational areas, such as lowered job productivity and increased days off from work, and interpersonal relations, such as being unable to participate in family outings and social functions (e.g., parties, picnics, etc.). Of course, the reverse is also true, that psychological and social factors affect headache intensity, frequency, and duration. For example, psychological stress has been shown to exacerbate and bring on head pain.

Tension-type headache is believed to be the most prevalent form of headache. It is more common in females than males, with a male to female ratio of approximately 1:1.5 (Rasmussen, 1999). Age of onset is generally in the second decade, and it peaks between the ages of 30 and 39. Rasmussen, Jensen, Schroll, and Olesen (1991), using the diagnostic criteria of the International Headache Society, found that lifetime prevalence for episodic or chronic tension-type headache was 78% for men and women combined, 69% for men and 88% for women. In that study, the prevalence of tension headache in the previous month was 48% overall. Interestingly, among subjects with migraine in the previous month, 62% had coexisting tension headache. This study is extremely important because it is the first investigation to include a representative random population, to use operational diagnostic criteria, and to include a clinical interview as well as a general physical and neurological examination of all participants. It suggests that the incidence and prevalence of chronic tension headache is much higher than previously believed. Silberstein and Lipton (2000)

estimated that 4%–5% of the U.S. population suffers from primary chronic daily headache, of which the majority is tension-like.

Clinicians who work with headache patients should use a standardized set of inclusion and exclusion criteria for diagnosis, such as those of the Ad Hoc Committee on the Classification of Headache (1962) or the Headache Classification Committee of the International Headache Society (1988, 2004).

INTERVENTIONS

Biofeedback

Biofeedback is a term that first arose in the 1960s for a methodology that uses instrumentation to record the physiological responses of organisms and then in real time give information about those physiological responses back to the organism. It is presumed that by getting such timely feedback about physiological responding, the organism will learn how to control the desired physiological response. In 2008, a Task Force convened by the Association for Applied Psychophysiology and Biofeedback, the Biofeedback Certification Institute of America, and the International Society for Neurofeedback and Research defined biofeedback. It concluded that,

> Biofeedback is a process that enables an individual to learn how to change physiological activity for the purposes of improving health and performance. Precise instruments measure physiological activity such as brainwaves, heart function, breathing, muscle activity, and skin temperature. These instruments rapidly and accurately "feedback" information to the user. The presentation of this information—often in conjunction with changes in thinking, emotions, and behavior—supports desired physiological changes. Over time, these changes can endure without continued use of an instrument. (Association for Applied Psychophysiology and Biofeedback, 2011)

In practice, the process of clinical biofeedback training involves the use of a machine—usually a computer-based system in contemporary applications—which allows a therapist to monitor the patient's bodily responses, most common of which are surface muscle tension or surface skin temperature. Information concerning the patient's physiological responses are then relayed back to the patient, generally either through an auditory modality, a tone which goes higher or lower depending on, say, electrical activity of the target muscles increasing or decreasing, and/or a visual modality, now usually a computer screen where, for example, surface skin temperature is sampled and then graphed on a second-by-second basis in real time. Through this physiological feedback, it is anticipated that the patient will learn how to control his or her bodily responses through mental means.

Biofeedback for chronic pain disorders is a biopsychosocial technique that has been in existence since the seminal work in 1970 with tension headache sufferers (Budzynski, Stoyva, & Adler, 1970). There are two major types of biofeedback employed with pain disorders today surface electromyography (EMG) and thermal (or surface temperature).

There are two general theories underlying the use of biofeedback for most chronic benign medical disorders, such as headache and LBP. The first is a direct psychophysiological theory, which attributes the etiology and/or maintenance of the disorder to specific physiological pathology, which biofeedback training modulates in a therapeutic direction. For example, it has traditionally been assumed that tension headache is caused by sustained contraction of skeletal muscles in the forehead, neck, and shoulder regions. Through the use of biofeedback, the patient learns to decrease muscle tension levels, leading to a decrease in headache activity. The second theory is predominantly psychological and postulates that there is a relationship between situational stress and the disorder in question. Through the use of biofeedback, the patient learns to

regulate physiological responses such as muscle tension levels or sympathetic nervous system activity, leading to a decrease in overall stress levels, which brings about symptomatic relief. It is not necessary to view these theories as competing; they may be more appropriately viewed as complementary. Most clinicians subscribe to both theories, depending upon the patient's presenting problem, clinical findings, and medical history.

Relaxation Therapy

Relaxation therapy is a systematic approach to teaching people to gain awareness of their physiological responses and achieve both a cognitive and physiological sense of tranquility without the use of the machinery employed in biofeedback. It is a general term usually used to describe various techniques that are believed to lead to stress reduction (Manzoni, Pagnini, Castelnuovo, & Molinari, 2003). There are various forms of relaxation (Lichstein, 1988; Payne, 2005; Poppen, 1998; Smith, 1990) including progressive muscle relaxation therapy (Jacobson, 1929), meditation (Lichstein, 1988), autogenic training (Linden, 1994; Luthe, 1969 1973; Stetter & Kupper, 2002), and guided imagery (Bellack, 1973). By far, the most widely used relaxation procedures in headache and LBP are variants of Jacobsonian progressive muscle relaxation therapy, and we will be mostly emphasizing those procedures in this chapter.

There are four primary theories underlying the use of relaxation therapy for chronic pain. The first theory is a general stress reduction theory, which is based on the belief that most patients who suffer from chronic pain are under a prodigious amount of stress. If practitioners can teach their patients to learn how to deal with that stress and cope more effectively with stressors in their life by using relaxation procedures, there should be a corresponding decrease in the patient's pain activity. The second theory states that most pain is caused directly by, exacerbated by, or maintained by elevated levels of muscle tension, muscle sprain, strain, or spasm, and if the patient can learn how to reduce muscle tension levels through relaxation therapy, there will be a corresponding reduction in pain levels. The third, and simplest, theory is that of distraction. This is by far the easiest to explain to patients, as they have all had the experience of immersing themselves in a good book or TV show, and not being aware of their pain while doing so. The fourth theory is the decreased sympathetic nervous system arousal theory, and this is the most difficult to explain to pain patients, as it involves education about the sympathetic nervous system (i.e., the sympathetic nervous system being that part of the autonomic nervous system that gets one prepared to fight or flee). Often times pain patients have abnormalities in their sympathetic nervous systems. Some have sympathetic nervous systems that always remain activated, while others experience a failure to effectively modulate the sympathetic system, so it activates or shuts down for no apparent reason. Relaxation therapy appears to decrease sympathetic nervous system arousal and to modulate sympathetic outflow better, thus decreasing pain levels.

Relaxation therapy regimen based on an abbreviated form of Jacobsonian progressive muscle relaxation therapy has been successfully used with pain patients (Arena, Hightower, & Chang, 1988; Blanchard et al., 1982). Progressive muscle relaxation therapy generally involves the tensing and then relaxing of muscle groups throughout the body. Patients are informed that, in essence, when they tense their muscles and relax them they are forcing those muscles to relax, and that this is important, because most headache sufferers have been tense for so long that they have forgotten what it feels like to be relaxed. Patients are instructed to pay special attention to the contrast between a tense and a relaxed state. Between each muscle group, the therapist typically includes 20 seconds or so of *relaxation patter*—statements such as, "Just

let yourself become more and more relaxed;" "The relaxation is flowing into all the areas of your body;" and "Notice the pleasant feelings of warmth and heaviness that are coming into your body as your muscles relax completely."

A muscle discrimination procedure is added in a latter session to help patients distinguish between the different levels of muscle tension in their bodies. First they tense their muscles to full strength, then 50% tension and, finally, 25% tension. Still later, patients are introduced to the concept of portability through a technique known as *relaxation by recall*, and the trainer begins to stress the importance of daily practice in the everyday world. Relaxation by recall is based on the tension-release exercises, with the difference being that patients are taught to become relaxed without actually tensing their muscles. They are instructed to focus their attention on the muscle groups in their body and determine whether their muscles are relaxed or if there is some residual tightness or tension present. If they notice that a particular muscle group is tense, they just let go of the muscle tension that is present and recall what it feels like for that muscle group to relax.

Finally, a strategy called, *cue-controlled relaxation* is taught. This procedure involves: (a) taking a deep breath, (b) holding it for a second or two, (c) consciously breathing out, (d) mentally repeating the word "relax" as one exhales, and (e) doing a quick body scan and using the relaxation by recall procedures to find and eliminate any remaining muscle tension that may be present in the body.

There are three other relaxation techniques that deserve special attention. They are (1) autogenic relaxation training, (2) relaxing imagery, and (3) diaphragmatic breathing.

The initial description of thermal biofeedback training for migraine headache by Sargent, Green, and Walters (1972) included the use of limited autogenic training (Schultz & Luthe, 1969)—in particular, training in relaxation, heaviness, and warmth. Autogenic training is a meditational form of relaxation that focuses on very specific self-instructions. Patients are told that the therapist will be giving them a series of phrases that are in the first person. The patients are to repeat the phrase verbatim (hence the use of the first person) to themselves; as the patients give themselves these self-instructions, they should try to have the experience described and notice the peripheral sensations. Depending on the length of the phrase, generally 30 to 60 seconds are allowed between phrases. It is a useful practice to routinely give each patient a copy of the phrases to use at home as he or she chooses.

Relaxing, or guided, imagery, with the exception of prayer, is perhaps the oldest of all relaxation techniques. It has been used in the various forms of Yoga and Zen meditation to supplement other approaches to relaxation. Feuerstein (1975) points out that 2,000 years ago pleasant nature scenes were common relaxing strategies in Tantra Yoga. Interestingly, Lichstein (1988) notes that pleasant nature scenes are the most commonly used subjects for adults in guided imagery today. The earliest example of imagery being applied in modern times is that of Chappell and Stevenson (1936). Peptic ulcer patients were taught in a group format relaxing imagery scenes to use to counteract anxiety that was assumed to exacerbate their ulcers. At a 3-year follow-up, 26 of 28 subjects were still markedly improved, whereas subjects in an untreated control group continued to suffer from ulcers. Nowadays, however, imagery is nearly always combined with other relaxation strategies.

The theoretical logic behind relaxing or guided imagery in the treatment of chronic headache is straightforward. Through imaging a relaxing scene, one will be able to achieve a state of both mental and physical relaxation that is similar to what patients would feel if they were actually experiencing the relaxing event, which would consequently lead to reduction in headache pain. If one is imagining a scene that has previously been experienced, then relaxing imagery is quite similar to

relaxation by recall procedures (i.e., one is recalling what it was like when your mind and body were calm and relaxed). See Arena and Blanchard (1996) for sample relaxing imagery scripts.

Many relaxation techniques place special emphasis on breathing. Most adults do not breathe diaphragmatically; to do so one needs to take deep, slow, relaxing breaths and push the air down into the chest, expanding the belly, not the thoracic cavity and shoulders. It is pointed out to the pain patient that it is difficult to become very anxious if one is breathing correctly. Frequently the therapist asks if the patient has ever had a panic attack or ever seen someone become very nervous. It is pointed out that one of the first things that occurs during a panic attack is that breathing becomes very rapid and shallow (i.e., one begins to hyperventilate). Patients are told that they can prevent high levels of anxiety by breathing diaphragmatically. Examples of scripts of relaxation training can be found in Arena & Blanchard (1996, pp. 195–196).

Cognitive Behavior Therapy

Cognitive behavior therapy (CBT) is a widely accepted and empirically supported component of comprehensive pain management. The CBT approaches are based on two assumptions. The first assumption is that an individual's thoughts, self-statements, and internal dialogue can affect their emotional state, behaviors, and physiology. The second assumption is that each of these modalities can affect the others. That is, not only can self-talk affect one's emotions, physiology, and behaviors, but one's behaviors can affect self-talk, emotions, and physiology. Therefore, CBT generally involves identifying maladaptive thoughts, emotions, and behaviors that routinely precede or exacerbate pain activity, with the therapist subsequently teaching patients in a systematic manner to modify these thoughts, feelings, and behaviors. In addition, behavioral interventions are used to affect the other modalities by increasing positive health behaviors and modifying activity levels. The goal of CBT is to assist individuals in developing a more adaptive repertoire of pain-coping strategies based on modifying ways of thinking and behaving in response to pain.

A wealth of evidence exists in support of the efficacy of CBT in treating LBP, headache, and other chronic pain disorders (Turk, Swanson, & Tunks, 2008). CBT has been shown to reduce levels of pain and disability, improve mood, and restore function (McCracken & Turk, 2002; Morley, Eccleston, & Williams, 1999; Sullivan, Feuerstein, Gatchel, Linton, & Pransky, 2005). The CBT protocols are often integrated with other treatment modalities in multidisciplinary pain clinics to provide comprehensive care, and the literature (Flor, Flydrich, & Turk, 1992 for meta-analytic review) provides strong support for success in reducing pain reports, restoring function, returning to work, and reduced health-care utilization rates as compared to unimodal and standard medical treatments.

The CBT approach to pain management begins with psychoeducation. Patients are provided with descriptions and explanations of the relationship between pain and mood, as well as a detailed presentation of the connections linking thoughts with affective, behavioral, and physiological responses. The patient is guided in developing an understanding of how these factors interact and help determine the individual's experience of pain. Homework assignments designed to heighten the individual's awareness of how their specific beliefs, appraisals, and expectations relate to mood and pain levels are essential to achieving the goals of treatment. The CBT approach generally includes a combination of stress management, problem solving, activity pacing, and assertiveness (Turk, Swanson, & Tunks, 2008).

In clients with chronic pain, stress and pain are interrelated factors sharing a bidirectional relationship. The pain itself is a stressor and the effects of pain create a cascade of secondary stressors throughout most domains of one's life. Many times, the effects of pain extend beyond the individual to also affect others in the person's social network. Early in treatment, patients are informed that what they think about a situation partly determines the stressfulness of the situation, and that their activity levels can lead to increases in their pain. They are offered hope that they can more effectively control their pain by learning mental strategies for the management of stress and by modifying their activity levels. The role of the therapist is to assist the patient in identifying activities and unreasonable expectations or beliefs, which may explain their bodily responses to a variety of stressful situations. For example, the patient may believe that he or she must be loved by everyone. When experiencing a situation that is interpreted as not supporting this core belief, the patient becomes depressed, which can lead to increased LBP or a migraine headache. The therapist aids the patient to examine the logical validity and behavioral and emotional consequences of continuing to hold these maladaptive expectancies and beliefs. Patients are taught to identify these maladaptive cognitions or beliefs in the real world as soon as possible so as to interrupt the chain of maladaptive thoughts. They are taught coping strategies to implement to counteract the maladaptive thoughts. Typically, these involve reappraisal of the actual risks and consequences of the situation, self-instructions designed at counteracting the specific maladaptive beliefs or thoughts (e.g., "I don't have to be loved by everyone to be a good person"), or a relaxation technique designed to counteract generalized worries and anxiety when there is no immediate or specific performance demands.

Individuals with chronic pain are at risk for developing or employing preexisting maladaptive styles of thinking to their situations, which can result in self-compromising and defeating attitudes and behaviors, as well as contribute to negative mood states, such as depression and anxiety (Gatchel, Peng, Peters, Fuchs, & Turk, 2007). Poor adjustment to chronic pain and mood disturbance are closely related. Turner, Jensen, and Romano (2000) identified the following pain-related beliefs as being most highly associated with depression scores: low perceived ability to control pain, perceiving oneself as disabled, belief that pain signifies damage, belief that emotions influence pain, and belief that pain is permanent.

One type of maladaptive cognition commonly found in chronic pain patients is catastrophizing, which relates to the tendency to dwell on the worst possible negative outcome for a given situation (A. T. Beck, 1976). Pain catastrophizing is related to an overemphasis on the most extreme negative consequences conceivable due to the pain (Turner & Aaron, 2001). A substantial body of literature links catastrophizing with increased pain and illness behavior as well as physical and psychological dysfunction (Gatchel et al., 2007). Catastrophizing, a cognitive component of fear-based anxiety, contributes to the physiological and behavioral activation of the fear network such that pain is interpreted as extremely threatening (Rosenstiel & Keefe, 1983). For example, it is not uncommon for pain patients to express, "I can't stand the pain," "This is never going to get better," or "I can't live like this." Beliefs such as these are capable of influencing decisions regarding activity, rest, self-care, treatment compliance, and return to work.

Cognitive interventions for catastrophizing and other forms of distorted or maladaptive thinking include teaching patients to first identify such thoughts. Thought records, which provide a structured format for monitoring and logging dysfunctional thoughts, can be helpful in these therapeutic interventions. Once patients have learned to identify negative or self-limiting thoughts, the next step is to assist patients in modifying, challenging, and restructuring maladaptive thoughts. This can be achieved by examining the objectivity of certain thoughts, which oftentimes present a

negative slant. Guiding patients in thinking about the evidence for and against a thought, offering alternative perspectives about the belief, and devising behavioral experiments to test the validity of a belief, serve to help the individual achieve a more balanced, reformulated belief (J. S. Beck, 1995).

The following is an example of how this type of intervention can be utilized within the therapeutic context. If a pain patient believes that he (or she) will never have fun again, the therapist might start by having the patient define what fun means to him/her, specify interests and activities that are fun, assess the degree of limitation imposed by the pain condition, and explore possibilities for modifying activities, incorporating new activities, or finding novel ways to participate in the same activities. This type of intervention can be especially helpful for individuals who are withdrawing from or resisting pleasurable activities "until the pain is better." In other words, the restructured belief resulting from the intervention might be, "My pain limits my ability to do all the things I used to do but I can still have fun in different but rewarding ways." The challenge for the therapist is to assist the patient in developing systematic ways of identifying, challenging, and modifying beliefs and thoughts that are self-limiting and promote dysfunction in mood, behavior, and quality of life.

One of the most important tools of the cognitive behavior therapist is the pain diary. Although a pain diary is ubiquitously employed in pain research and treatment, it is frequently used only as an outcome measure with psychophysiological interventions (i.e., patients monitor only their pain activity on, say, a 0–10 scale four times a day). In cognitive behavioral procedures, however, the pain diary is used to monitor more than pain levels — the therapist frequently has the patient monitor emotional, cognitive, and behavioral activity such as thoughts or self-statements, activities, and emotions. These additional factors are either time-sampled and recorded at the same times that pain levels are, or are documented when pain levels or emotional states reach a certain threshold. Greater recognition of patterns and relationships among these variables allows individuals to begin to modify how they are thinking and responding in targeted ways in order to alter the outcome of their pain activity.

Pain diaries are also helpful in tracking the patient's activity levels. In many cases, overactivity and underactivity can be problematic for the chronic pain patient. Overactivity can result from the patient's desire to maintain premorbid levels of activity and productivity, a desire to avoid through distraction, or the tendency to ignore the sensations that indicate increased tension or pain, among other possible explanations. Underactivity may relate to fear avoidance (Vlaeyen & Linton, 2000) in which pain is perceived as threatening, and activity believed to increase pain is thus avoided. Underactivity may also be related to underlying mood disturbance. Risks of inactivity include physical deconditioning and disordered muscle coordination (Leeuw et al., 2007), which can lead to increased pain and disability.

Activity pacing is a strategy used to assist patients in achieving a functional level of activity that strikes a balance between overdoing it and avoidance. For individuals with a pattern of pushing themselves too hard, which can result in several days of inactivity due to a pain flare, they are taught to incorporate regular rest periods so that they can maintain consistent levels of activity and eliminate the long recovery periods necessitated by overactivity. In contrast, for individuals who tend to be sedentary and who avoid activity, strategies to increase activity are employed. Strategies may target fear avoidance through graded exposure exercises (see Vlaeyen, De Jong, Onghena, Kerckhoffs-Hansen, & Kole-Snijders, 2002), cognitive strategies to examine and restructure maladaptive thinking, and beliefs, behavioral activation strategies, goal setting, and problem solving.

Cognitive behavior therapies are generally combined with relaxation or biofeedback procedures and help to facilitate and augment perceptions of self-control (Turk, Swanson, & Tunks, 2008). Indeed, relaxation therapy and biofeedback are considered techniques that cognitive behavior therapists employ to help directly alter physiology, and therefore indirectly affect self-statements, emotions, and behaviors. Achieving a subjective sense of increased relaxation can simultaneously impact physiological tension and reduce emotional distress. Furthermore, in contrast to traditional medical interventions (i.e., medication, injections, etc.), the execution of relaxation practices fosters a greater sense of personal control for the individual through proactive intervention to gain a greater sense of mastery over the effects of the pain, as well as to reduce or prevent the exacerbation of pain. Greater mastery over pain also leads to improvements in mood.

CBT represents an expansive collection of techniques, strategies, and skills from which to choose in designing a CBT intervention. Treatment effects are not uniform across studies, resulting in difficulty discerning the specific predictors of treatment outcomes. Thus, despite the vast literature supporting the efficacy of CBT interventions for the treatment of chronic pain, there remains a lack of empirical evidence as to which components of the approaches are the true agents of change. To date, no standardized set of CBT interventions with demonstrated empirical superiority has emerged in the literature. Moreover, the degree to which efficacious CBT protocols can be generalized across subgroups of chronic pain patients remains speculative and largely undetermined.

Exercise

Exercise therapy is an intervention that is widely used in various musculoskeletal conditions, as well as chronic low back pain. Exercise-based interventions targeting improvement in chronic LBP include a diverse array of activities, such as stretching, muscle strengthening, walking, pool exercises, and aerobic exercise. Exercise can be prescribed and guided by health professionals or conducted individually within the home or nonhospital settings, such as local fitness centers. Exercise regimens can be individually tailored or standardized and can be individually or group-based. Exercise therapy for chronic pain is often integrated with other treatments and is frequently a component of multidisciplinary treatments (Dziedzic, Jordan, & Foster, 2008).

A typical exercise regimen is based on initiating and increasing a routine of physical activity in a graded fashion. It is important to begin with a minimal level of exercise and to gradually build as the individual adjusts and fear related to reinjury or pain exacerbation subsides. For some patients, it is not uncommon to remain seated or lying down for the majority of the day. Over time, these individuals become highly deconditioned and consequently, fatigue easily upon minimal exertion. This cycle tends to reinforce the person's subjective sense of physical compromise and difficulty. Depending on the nature of the chronic pain condition and the associated mobility challenges and functional limitations, most individuals are able to engage in an exercise program designed to increase movement and activity levels.

Walking is often an excellent starting point for exercise therapy, particularly in patients who have become highly inactive and sedentary in response to their pain. Initial goals for walking as an exercise intervention are based on the patient's baseline level of activity and perceived abilities. The exercise prescription could be as simple as walking through the house for a designated period of time and slowly building on the duration over time. For patients who are able to walk outside, distance or time goals are collaboratively established with the therapist and gradual increases are encouraged across time.

Basic tips for developing a walking program include starting slow and gradually building in order to avoid overexertion and pain exacerbation. Appropriate shoes are important for providing support and preventing injury. Many individuals benefit from finding a walking partner. This adds a social aspect to the exercise, which can be beneficial for many. Having a walking buddy also assists with motivation because it is easier to talk oneself out of exercising if no one else will be affected by the decision. It is also essential to consume plenty of water or other liquids to remain hydrated and prevent cramping. Stretching before and after walking also assists with avoiding pulls or strains. For more advanced exercises and participation in sports, it is wise to consult with a physician or physical therapist regarding guidelines and restrictions resulting from the specific pain condition.

It can be helpful to have patients log their exercise sessions for frequency, duration, and pain levels. This strategy serves several purposes, including increasing accountability to self and to the therapist. It helps solidify the patient's commitment to following through with the exercise therapy prescription. In addition, it provides a log of the exercise sessions and the ability to track patterns and improvements over time. Finally, the exercise diary serves as a product of a personal accomplishment for patients who are compliant with the regimen. Amidst the many frustrations and challenges faced when living in chronic pain, successes of any magnitude are important to encourage, recognize, and commend.

Motivation to engage in regular exercise is often the primary barrier to compliance with exercise regimens. Numerous factors may influence motivation, including beliefs that exercise and activity increase pain, that exercise is too hard or impossible, or that exercise does not benefit the person's pain level. The therapist is tasked with addressing and, at times, challenging these beliefs in order to assist the individuals in reducing the barriers to motivation. Education regarding the importance of preventing deconditioning and promoting health is also an important element for providing patients with incentive to comply with exercise regimens. Additional barriers include behavioral initiation despite feeling tired, hurting, and perhaps sedated by medication. It is helpful to schedule exercise at a time when the pain is typically at a manageable level and energy is at its peak.

Motivation levels may also be compromised by coexisting mood disturbance, such as symptoms of depression and anxiety. For example, an individual experiencing comorbid depressive symptoms may dwell on that fact that he or she is no longer able to play tennis or go jogging and thus may resist engaging in exercise altogether. Identifying and addressing such psychological barriers are important tasks of the therapist and can make a significant difference in the success of an exercise intervention. Another very important task of the therapist is to validate the difficulty of exercising for someone disabled by chronic pain. It is essential that the therapist join with the patient by acknowledging how difficult it is to be motivated and committed to exercising.

REVIEW OF THE EVIDENCE-BASED LITERATURE

Template for Determining the Efficacy of Interventions

Although there are many templates that one can employ to evaluate evidence-based interventions, in this chapter we will use the one outlined in the Association for Applied Psychophysiology and Biofeedback's and the Society for Neuronal Regulation's Joint Efficacy Task Force Report (Moss & Gunkelman, 2002) titled, "Template for Developing Guidelines for the Evaluation of the Clinical Efficacy of Psychophysiological Interventions." The Joint Task Force proposed the following criteria for levels of evidence of

efficacy: Level 1 (not empirically supported) refers to treatments supported only by anecdotal reports and/or case studies. Level 2 (possibly efficacious) refers to treatments supported by at least one study of designs that lack random assignment and subject/experimenter blindness and internal control conditions. The study or studies must have sufficient statistical power and clearly defined outcome measures. Level 3 (probably efficacious) includes treatments supported by multiple studies using the following designs: those that employ historical controls, observational studies, wait-list or intent-to-treat control designs, or within-subject and intrasubject replication designs. As in Level 2 studies, the studies must have sufficient statistical power and clearly defined outcome measures. Level 4 (efficacious) are those treatments supported by at least one study utilizing a single-blind, random-assignment control design, a double-blind controlled study, or a treatment equivalence or treatment superiority design. As in Levels 2 and 3, the study or studies must have sufficient statistical power and clearly defined outcome measures. Finally, Level 5 treatments (efficacious and specific) are supported by at least two independent research groups and have shown the investigational treatment to be superior to a well-established treatment and/or a credible placebo or sham therapy.

The more studies from independent research groups, the more studies that produce clinical significance (e.g., the number of subjects who received a meaningful reduction in pain levels; in pain, generally defined as at least a 50% reduction in pain levels) in addition to statistical significance, the more outcome measures employed, and the more details given that allow careful replication of the study, the greater the scientific power of the intervention.

Headache

Nonpharmacological interventions for recurrent headache have been the most widely researched of all the pain disorders. Numerous consensus panels have concluded that the three major nonpharmacological interventions (biofeedback, CBT, and relaxation therapy) should be used alongside pharmacologic interventions for chronic tension and migraine headache. Rains, Penzien, McCrory, and Gray (2005) listed over 10 professional organizations that have formally endorsed behavioral intervention for recurrent headache, including the American Academy of Neurology, the American College of Physicians, the American Medical Association, the National Institute of Health, and the World Health Organization. Indeed, the endorsement of biofeedback by the American Headache Society in 1978 (Board of Directors, American Headache Society, 1978) is one of the earliest formal endorsements of a behavioral treatment by a medical organization for a traditional medical problem. Using the Joint Task Force Criteria outlined earlier, biofeedback, relaxation therapy, and CBT for both migraine and tension headache are all efficacious and specific.

Biofeedback

The initial report on the use of frontal electromyographic (EMG) biofeedback with tension-type headache appeared in 1970 (Budzynski, Stoyva, & Adler). It was followed with a small scale controlled clinical trial in 1973 (Budzynski, Stoyva, Adler, & Mullaney). The earliest report on the use of thermal biofeedback with migraine headache appeared in 1972 (Sargent, Green, & Walters). Since that time, there have been over 100 treatment outcome studies and numerous meta-analyses on biofeedback for both migraine and tension headache. Although other types of biofeedback have been used with both tension and migraine headache, the most widely employed with migraine is thermal or temperature biofeedback, whereas the gold standard for biofeedback with tension headache has been EMG biofeedback. It is important to

note that both thermal and EMG biofeedback for headache are presumed to be prophylactic as opposed to abortive procedures.

Meta-analyses. The most comprehensive efficacy review of biofeedback for headache was recently conducted by Nestoriuc, Martin, Rief, and Andrasik (2008). This paper screened over 150 studies, including RCTs and uncontrolled quasi-experimental designs. Using strict, predefined inclusion criteria, they selected 94 studies to include in their meta-analysis, with over 3,500 subjects. The average headache patient in this study had headaches for over 14 years and the mean number of sessions of treatment was 11. They found medium to large effect sizes for biofeedback in adult migraine and tension-type headache patients. For completers, effect sizes from pretreatment to posttreatment were 0.58 for migraine and 0.70 for tension-type headache. They also computed effect sizes for intent to treat. In these analyses, dropouts were considered treatment failures and replaced with zero effects. Even when using this more stringent intent to treat approach, analyses yielded effect sizes of 0.53 for migraine and 0.59 for tension type headache. These effects were also found to be sustained at follow up. No differences were found between the various types of biofeedback modalities, such as blood volume pulse, hand surface temperature, or frontal EMG. For both migraine and tension headache, the research has generally shown that combining biofeedback with other therapies such as relaxation or CBT leads to enhanced treatment outcomes.

What is so very significant in this and other comprehensive review studies is how results have remained remarkably consistent over nearly 30 years of headache research. For example, Blanchard, Andrasik, Ahles, Teders, and O'Keefe in 1980 found quite similar results in their first meta analyses of the literature, as have others who have examined this research (Lake, 2001; Penzien, Rains, & Andrasik, 2002; Rains, Penzien, McCrory, & Gray, 2005).

Relaxation Therapy

Although progressive muscle relaxation training, as developed by Edmund Jacobson (1938) had been anecdotally reported to have been used with headache patients, the first systematic report of its use with tension-type headache was by Tasto and Hinkle in 1973. One of the earliest controlled clinical trials of the use of relaxation with tension-type headache was published by Chesney and Shelton in 1976. Blanchard, Theobald, Williamson, Silver, and Brown (1978) evaluated abbreviated PMR in a controlled trial involving migraineurs and found it to be effective and equivalent to thermal biofeedback. An alternative form of relaxation, known as Autogenic Training, was described by Schultz and Luthe (1969). It involves a more passive, self-instructive form of relaxation that emphasizes autonomic function. It is frequently used as an adjunct to thermal biofeedback for migraine (Stetter & Kupper, 2002). The rationale for relaxation therapy for both migraine and tension headache are the same as the rationale for relaxation therapy for pain in general described earlier.

Meta-analyses. There have been fewer RCTs and meta-analyses of relaxation therapy than there have biofeedback for headache. In the best meta-review of relaxation therapy for migraine headache to date, that of the U.S. Headache Consortium (Campbell, Penzien, & Wall, 2000), they concluded that relaxation achieved "a statistically significant and moderately large effect size of 0.55" (p. 7). In that study, they reviewed 10 studies that involved relaxation therapy and combined all forms of relaxation together. Overall percent improvement for relaxation alone was 41%.

McCrory, Penzien, Hasselbald, and Gray (2001) conducted a detailed meta-analysis of the relaxation literature for tension-type headache. This analysis employed 19 trials of relaxation therapy (again they comingled the various types of relaxation) and came to similar conclusions of moderate-large effect

sizes. Overall percent improvement for relaxation alone was 37%. As with biofeedback, the research has generally supported the enhanced efficacy of combined treatments, such as relaxation with biofeedback or relaxation with CBT.

A recent meta-analysis concluded that relaxation therapy consisting of autogenic training (AT) as a sole therapy was not supported as a superior treatment over other therapies for tension headache (Kanji, White, & Ernst, 2006). Seven trials met inclusion criteria for the meta-analysis. The authors concluded that only limited evidence was found to support AT as superior to wait-list control. AT was found to be less effective than biofeedback and comparable to hypnosis. They cited numerous factors in the methodological quality of the research literature, thereby limiting the ability to draw conclusions about the effectiveness of autogenic training in the treatment of tension headache.

Again, what is so very significant in this comprehensive review study is how results have been consistent over nearly 30 years of headache research. As with biofeedback, Blanchard, Andrasik, Ahles, Teders, and O'Keefe in 1980 found quite similar results in their first meta-analysis of the literature, and others have also arrived at similar conclusions (Lake, 2001; Penzien, Rains, & Andrasik, 2002; Rains, Penzien, McCrory, & Gray, 2005).

Cognitive Behavior Therapy

In 1981, two of the earliest studies examining cognitive behavioral approaches for chronic headache were published. In one (Kemsdorf, Kochanowicz, & Costell, 1981), which utilized two single subject experimental designs, and incorporated EMG biofeedback and cognitive coping skills training with tension headache, the authors demonstrated that changes in frontal EMG levels were not associated with improvement in headache activity, only changes in coping skills was associated with headache improvement. In the other

(Bakal, Demjen, & Kaganov, 1981), 45 chronic headache sufferers of various diagnoses were given a cognitive treatment based on Meichenbaum's cognitive theory of self-control. Treatments led to reductions in pain and other variables regardless of headache diagnosis.

Meta-analyses. Most reviews and meta-analyses have strongly supported the efficacy of CBT for both migraine and tension headache. In the best meta-review of CBT for migraine and tension headache to date, that of the U.S. Headache Consortium (Campbell et al., 2000; McCrory et al., 2001), the authors evaluated seven trials examining CBT for migraine headache and 13 trials for tension headache. They concluded for migraine that, "an average of 49% improvement in headache activity. Results from a standardized meta-analysis using data from five of the seven trials suggest a significant clinical improvement with a moderately large effect size score of 0.54" (Campbell et al., 2000, pp. 9 10). Similar results were found for tension headache (McCrory et al., 2001). Again, as with biofeedback and relaxation, these results have been quite stable over time since the first meta analytic reviews in 1985 of CBT for migraine (Penzien, Holroyd, Holm, & Hursey, 1985) and 1986 for tension headache (Holroyd & Penzien, 1986) as have other reviews (Lake, 2001; Penzien et al., 2002; Rains et al., 2005) There are a number of problems with the cognitive behavioral literature for headache, primarily, the addition of relaxation therapy or biofeedback as a component of CBT in many of the studies.

Exercise

Exercise is frequently recommended to headache patients and is generally accepted as a reasonable adjunctive treatment, despite the fact that evidence of the effectiveness of exercise continues to be relatively limited. Very few studies have examined the effects of exercise therapy as an independent treatment variable as it is more often blended into a comprehensive or multidisciplinary treatment approach. It also remains unknown as to whether exercise-related changes are acting on physiological variables (e.g., neurotransmitters), psychological variables (e.g., stress reduction), or a combination. It should also be noted that in a small percentage of individuals (< 10%), exercise can be a trigger for migraines (Nadelson, 2006).

Dittrich and colleagues (2008) investigated the effects of a 6-week aerobic exercise treatment program combined with progressive muscle relaxation (N 15) compared to standard medical treatment (N 15) for female migraine patients. Significant reductions in pain levels were found in the intervention group compared to the control group. No differences in psychological variables were found between groups at the end of the study. This study was limited by a small sample size and the combination of relaxation and exercise in one treatment group precluded the possibility of determining the extent to which relaxation and exercise independently accounted for the reduction in pain.

In a comprehensive review of the literature on the effectiveness of exercise therapy as a single treatment option in migraine headache, Busch and Gaul (2008) found that while most studies did not report a reduction of headache frequency or duration, there were reductions in pain intensity associated with regular exercise. A total of eight trials and four case reports were included in the review; however, the authors pointed out that the studies did not meet valid criteria of good clinical practice and presented many methodological limitations. They concluded the effect of aerobic exercise on migraine headache could only be carefully estimated rather than determined due to the numerous methodological shortcomings of the existing studies. Thus, the evidence for exercise therapy as a single treatment for migraine headaches requires additional investigation.

Existing data are insufficient to draw a conclusion as to the effectiveness of exercise therapy in the treatment of headache. More well-designed, randomized controlled trials are needed to determine the true value and underlying mechanisms of the effects of exercise on headaches. Furthermore, no studies investigating exercise therapy as a single treatment option for tension headache were identified. This is an area of the literature in significant need of additional investigation.

Cost-Effectiveness of Nonpharmacological Interventions for Headache

The cost effectiveness of nonpharmacological interventions for chronic headache has long been established, beginning with the seminal article by Blanchard, Jaccard, Andrasik, Guarnieri, and Jurish (1985). In this study, they compared self-reported medical costs from a number of headache patients (tension headache, migraine headache, and combined migraine-tension) who underwent relaxation therapy, EMG biofeedback (tension headache only), thermal biofeedback (migraine and combined headache only), and a combination of relaxation therapy plus biofeedback. Average costs for 2 years prior to the nonpharmacological treatments were $955 per patient, versus $42 for the 2 years following treatment. As Blanchard and his colleagues concluded,

> it does appear that on average, headache patients experience a marked reduction in medical costs after self-regulatory treatment. Based on subsample means, this reduction is on the order of 95%; taking a conservative estimate based on X − 3 SEM for pretreatment and X + 3 SEM for posttreatment, the reduction is still 83%. (p. 67)

Nearly every study that has examined the issue has come to the same conclusion. For example, Smitherman, Penzien, and Rains (2007) reviewed the cost-effectiveness of the major nonpharmacological interventions for headache (relaxation therapy, biofeedback, and CBT) and concluded that the "treatments are the least-expensive preventative intervention for headache in the long run (by year five)" (p. 473).

Nonpharmacological interventions in headache have ubiquitously led to significant decreases in depression and anxiety. Here again, Blanchard and his colleagues provided the seminal studies (Blanchard et al., 1982, 1986): In any form, relaxation therapy, EMG biofeedback, thermal biofeedback, and a combination of relaxation therapy and biofeedback, for any of three types of headache patients, tension headache, migraine headache, and combined migraine-tension, successful treatment led to both clinically and statistically significant decreases in self-reported depression and trait anxiety.

Finally, minimal therapist, nonpharmacological interventions have proven to be the most cost-effective treatments (see future directions, later). As Smitherman et al. (2007) pointed out, "minimal-contact approaches are the least-expensive treatment option after one year, compared with clinic-based behavioral treatments, as well as low-, moderate-, and high-priced prophylactic medications" (p. 473).

Summary of Treatment Outcome for Migraine and Tension Headache

For migraine headache, when comparisons are made between relaxation therapy, CBT, and thermal biofeedback, there are generally no statistically significant differences in outcome for the three treatments. Rains and her colleagues (2005) presented a summary of the meta-analyses of the behavioral treatments for migraine. Average percent improvement for relaxation alone was approximately 35%, thermal biofeedback was also approximately 35%, combined relaxation and thermal biofeedback was approximately 55% (the latter based on much fewer studies), and CBT was approximately 45%. Although the statistical data does not completely support the efficacy of combined treatment, from a clinical perspective, we have argued (Arena & Blanchard, 2002a; Blanchard & Arena, 1999) that combined relaxation and thermal biofeedback or cognitive therapy by itself is most efficacious for the treatment of migraine headache. The addition of a cognitive therapy component does *not* seem to improve overall outcome with migraine headache (Blanchard, Appelbaum, Radnitz, Michultka, et al., 1990), even with sample sizes of 30 per condition. When comparing pharmacological treatments, such as proprananol and flunarizine with relaxation and biofeedback, there is virtually no difference in treatment outcomes (Andrasik, 2007; Penzien et al., 2002). There is simply insufficient data on exercise for migraine headache to make any definitive conclusions.

We have argued (J. G. Beck, Andrasik, & Arena, 1984; Blanchard et al., 1982; Blanchard & Arena, 1999) that clinical significance, which we and others in the headache literature have defined as the percentage of individuals who achieve a 50% or greater reduction in headache activity, is a more important measure than overall (grouped) percent improvement. This allows the clinician to determine the likelihood that their patient will achieve a meaningful reduction in their pain levels. For migraine headache, relaxation studies generally have 30% to 50% of their subjects achieving this goal; for thermal biofeedback, the percentages are typically between 40% and 55%, and for CBT (which usually includes a relaxation or biofeedback component) the percentages are approximately 60%.

When comparisons are made between the three major psychological interventions for tension headache EMG biofeedback, relaxation therapy, and CBT again, no statistically significant differences are found. Rains and her colleagues (2005) presented a summary of the meta-analyses of the behavioral treatments for migraine. Average percent improvement for relaxation alone was approximately 40%, for EMG biofeedback approximately 47%, combined relaxation and thermal biofeedback was approximately 55% (the latter based on much fewer studies), and CBT was again approximately 45%. While the addition of a cognitive therapy component

to either relaxation or biofeedback does not add much to migraine headache outcome, it does seem to make a difference when added to a relaxation regimen with tension headache (Blanchard, Appelbaum, Radnitz, Morrill, et al., 1990). From a clinical significance perspective, approximately 45%–55% of individuals with tension headache achieve clinical significance (50% or greater reduction in headache activity) with relaxation therapy, 50%–60% for EMG biofeedback, and 60%–80% for CBT (again, usually a combination of CBT with relaxation or, in much fewer instances, biofeedback). We would suggest, based on available data, for a CBT component along with relaxation or biofeedback for the nonpharmacological treatment of tension headache.

There have been fewer studies comparing pharmacological approaches for tension headache in general, as compared to migraine, and even fewer that have compared nonpharmacological to pharmacological approaches. In the best study to date, Holroyd and his colleagues (Holroyd et al., 2001) showed superiority to a combination stress management and antidepressant condition (64% clinical improvement) versus stress management (35%) or medication (38%) alone conditions. Based on the previous data, we would suggest a combination treatment of either relaxation therapy or EMG biofeedback with CBT, or a combination of a pharmacological agent (usually an antidepressant) with relaxation, EMG biofeedback, or CBT. As with migraine headache, there is insufficient data to make meaningful recommendations regarding tension headache and exercise.

Future Directions

There are two exciting areas that are likely to be the future direction of nonpharmacological headache research. The first involves cognitive change mechanisms that likely underlie successful improvement in treatment. The second is the use of nontraditional treatment delivery systems.

In our opinion, the most sophisticated and methodologically elegant study to date that has examined change mechanisms underlying improvements in headache was conducted by Holroyd et al. (1984). In that study, 43 college students who suffered from tension headache were randomly assigned to one of four possible biofeedback conditions in a 2×2 factorial design. In the first factor, although all subjects were led to believe that they were decreasing their forehead EMG levels, only half the subjects were given feedback contingent on decreased EMG activity; the other half were given feedback contingent on increasing EMG activity. The second factor consisted of a high success group (bogus video displays demonstrating high success compared to the rest of the subjects in the experiment) or a moderate-success group (bogus video displays indicating moderate success compared to the rest of the group). It made no difference whether subjects learned to increase or decrease their muscle tension levels; the high-success feedback group showed substantially greater improvements in headache activity (53%) than the moderate-success group (26%).

Blanchard, Kim, Hermann, and Steffek (1994) gave progressive muscle relaxation therapy to 14 tension headache sufferers. At the end of each session, they were also given computerized bogus feedback regarding their performance: Six were led to believe that they were highly successful in the relaxation task, whereas eight were informed that they were only moderately successful. Patients who perceived themselves as highly successful at relaxation reported a greater amount of improvement in their headache activity, as measured by the daily headache diary, than those with perceptions of moderate success. These findings extend the results of the Holroyd et al. (1984) study, since they were obtained on a treatment-seeking sample of adults who were in their mid-30s and who had suffered from headaches an average of over 10 years.

Rokicki et al. (1997) replicated to some extent their 1984 work, using a young adult population of 30 tension headache subjects who were given a combination of relaxation therapy and EMG biofeedback. Improvements in headache activity were correlated with increases in self-efficacy induced by biofeedback training.

Preliminary results from the Arena laboratory (Arena & Blanchard, 2002a) also strongly support the work of Holroyd and his colleagues: Although it involved a small sample size of less than 10 per cell, individuals given high success feedback were much likelier to be successful at EMG biofeedback (mean reduction in headache activity pre-post $= 53.2\%$) than those given moderate success feedback (who had a mean *increase* in headache activity of 2.3%). Similarly, as in the Holroyd study, whether tension headache subjects were taught to increase or decrease EMG levels during biofeedback training made no difference in treatment outcome (37.7% decrease in pre-post headache activity for those who were taught to increase their EMG activity, versus 42.9% decrease for those taught to decrease their muscle tension levels). These results were obtained on a treatment-seeking sample of adults who were over age 30 and had headaches for at least 10 years.

These studies demonstrated the importance of cognitive mediating factors such as perceived success and self-efficacy in biofeedback training and relaxation therapy and, taken together, are supportive of a cognitive self-efficacy component being a primary change mechanism involved in successful psychophysiological treatment for tension headache. Further research is needed to extend these results to treatment-seeking adults and to migraine headache. They suggest that clinicians who work with headache patients should attempt to put their patients' results in the best light possible.

As the efficacy of nonpharmacological interventions for chronic headache has been well established, researchers have begun to examine alternative treatment delivery systems. Jurish and colleagues (1983) examined the efficacy of minimal therapist contact (a home-based treatment utilizing manuals, a portable hand thermometer, and two office sessions) versus traditional therapist contact (16 office sessions of relaxation therapy combined with thermal biofeedback) with vascular headache sufferers. Both treatments were effective. Although results indicated that the office-based treatment appeared to be more effective, the trend did not attain statistical significance.

Devineni and Blanchard (2005) conducted a RCT that evaluated an Internet-delivered behavioral regimen composed of progressive relaxation, limited biofeedback with autogenic training, and stress management versus a symptom monitoring wait-list control. Treatment led to a significantly greater decrease in headache activity than symptom monitoring alone, with 39% of treated individuals showed clinically significant improvement on self-report measures of headache symptoms at posttreatment, with 47% of participants maintaining improvement at 2-month follow-up. The Internet program was more time efficient than traditional clinical treatment, although the outcome numbers were generally less positive than usually obtained from office-based treatments.

Arena, Dennis, Devineni, Maclean, and Meador (2004) presented a case series that evaluated the preliminary effectiveness and feasibility of an analogue telemedicine system for delivery of psychophysiological treatment for vascular headache (relaxation therapy and thermal biofeedback). Three of four subjects were improved on measures of headache activity. These findings were encouraging for a follow-up study of the clinical utility and broader viability of headache treatment via distance technology.

Arena, Hannah, and Meador (in press) evaluated the results of a standard office-based (N = 20) psychosocial treatment compared to a telehealth (N = 25) system, in which participants received all treatment through a videoconferencing system at the clinic, having no face-to-face contact with the therapist for the delivery of psychophysical treatment (12 sessions of relaxation therapy and thermal biofeedback). Results indicated no difference between the telehealth and standard groups posttreatment, with both groups having over 50% improvement. More importantly, in terms of clinical improvement (< 50% improvement), there was also no difference between the groups. One-year follow-up on a subset of the subjects demonstrated that treatment results maintained. Thus, telehealth delivered psychophysiological treatment for vascular headache appears to be promising, although there were a number of limitations to the Arena study. That study had subjects interacting with their therapist through a closed circuit videoconferencing system housed at a research lab. Subjects were aware that the therapist was in the same building and could come to their assistance if necessary, although this was never the case. This may have affected treatment in a positive direction. In addition, the study utilized a medium bandwidth resolution. There is no way of knowing whether high-resolution would have led to improved treatment outcome or lower resolution, such as through a videophone using existing hard wired telephone lines, would negatively affect treatment results.

It is clear that future research in the area of alternative ways to deliver nonpharmacological interventions for chronic headache need to be conducted. Overcoming barriers to dissemination of nonpharmacological interventions of which time and distance are two of the major barriers to such dissemination is vitally important. Telehealth-based interventions can assist in surmounting such barriers.

Low Back Pain

Nonpharmacological interventions for low back pain have been less researched than headache disorders. Nonetheless, they have been endorsed both by guidelines and by professional societies. Unlike headache, in which biofeedback, relaxation therapy, and CBT have been endorsed as stand-alone treatments, with LBP these interventions have been recommended to be used after a patient has proved refractory to traditional conservative medical intervention. For example, the influential Joint Clinical Practice Guideline from the American College of Physicians and the American Pain Society (Chou et al., 2007) recommend,

> For patients who do not improve with self-care options, clinicians should consider the addition of nonpharmacologic therapy with proven benefits—for acute LBP, spinal manipulation; for chronic or subacute LBP, intensive interdisciplinary rehabilitation, exercise therapy, acupuncture, massage therapy, spinal manipulation, yoga, cognitive-behavioral therapy, or progressive relaxation (weak recommendation, moderate-quality evidence). (p. 486)

The seminal guidelines of the Department of Veterans Affairs–Department of Defense Evidenced-Based Clinical Practice Guidelines Working Group on Low-Back Pain or Sciatica in the Primary Care Setting (Department of Veterans Affairs/Department of Defense, 1999) also made a similar recommendation. Using the Joint Task Force criteria for efficacy outlined earlier, biofeedback, relaxation therapy, and CBT for LBP would be characterized as efficacious.

Biofeedback

There have been far fewer biofeedback treatment outcome studies of LBP than there have been of chronic headache. The only biofeedback modality employed has been electromyographic biofeedback applied primarily to the paraspinal region (usually L4-L5), although some number of studies have employed forehead placement. There is no difference in the clinical biofeedback outcomes based on which muscle site is used (Arena & Blanchard, 2002a).

We have previously reviewed the biofeedback literature on LBP, and have detailed the methodological limitations of many of the studies (Arena & Blanchard, 2002b; Sherman & Arena, 1992). These include small sample sizes, failure to describe the instrumentation and biofeedback procedures sufficiently to allow replication of the research, the lack of clearly defined LBP diagnostic categories (many studies simply combine all subjects into a single diagnostic group), explicit inclusion and exclusion criteria (many studies combine both chronic and acute subjects), adequate control groups, pain diaries, and multiple outcome measures.

To illustrate, one of the best biofeedback studies is by Flor and Birbaumer (1993). They had 78 subjects who suffered from chronic musculoskeletal pain (57 low back and 21 temporomandibular joint dysfunction) randomly assigned into one of three groups: EMG biofeedback to the site of the pain (back or jaw), CBT, or conservative medical treatment. Results at posttreatment showed reductions in pain levels for all three groups, with only the reduction for the biofeedback group being statistically significant. At both 6- and 24-month follow-up, the EMG biofeedback group was significantly superior to both the CBT and conservative medical treatment groups on such measures as emotional distress and pain-related use of the health-care system. On pain severity, it was superior to the CBT group at 6-month follow-up, and superior at both 6- and 24-month follow-up to the conservative medical treatment group. Unfortunately, no separate results for LBP versus TMJ pain were provided, and even within the LBP subjects there were a mixture of various etiologies and diagnoses; however, this study is important because it demonstrated that biofeedback was superior to, "the best presently available medical interventions" (p. 655).

In our last review (Arena & Blanchard, 2002b) we concluded that biofeedback by itself appears to hold promise as a clinically useful technique in the treatment of individuals with LBP; however, we argued that a more useful approach would be if biofeedback was incorporated into a multimodal treatment program approach, and that clearly has been the case. Multimodal programs involve a rehabilitation approach aimed at functional restoration and usually employ 100 or more hours of intensive psychosocial intervention. The success of biofeedback for LBP has led to it being incorporated routinely into such multidisciplinary pain programs. Guzman and colleagues (2001, 2002) and Nordin, Balague, and Cedraschi (2006) have called for similar incorporation. Consequently, the literature examining biofeedback as a single modality for LBP has all but ceased and there have been no studies of biofeedback as a sole treatment since our last review.

Relaxation Therapy

The modern use of relaxation therapy for LBP began in 1982, with a single study case report of a relaxation procedure by Trent (1982), and a randomized comparison of relaxation therapy versus CBT by Turner (1982). The later study is the first systematic report of its use, although anecdotally its use had been noted as early as Jacobson's seminal work on progressive muscle relaxation therapy in 1929. The rationale for relaxation therapy for LBP is the same as the rationale for relaxation therapy for pain in general described earlier.

Randomized controlled trials. Miller and Arena (2004) reviewed the relaxation therapy literature for LBP. They examined 14 studies and concluded that the relaxation literature for back pain is as methodologically flawed as the biofeedback literature. Only half of the studies reviewed had 10 or more subjects per group, had a control group comparison, or gave enough information to replicate the relaxation procedures. More importantly, 10 out of the 14 studies (71%) did not include the LBP diagnoses, commingling all subjects into a single diagnostic group. Overall averaged percentage of improvement for relaxation alone was 37%, with a wide range from 0% to

100%. Some glaring observations stood out regarding the analyses. First, although the majority of the studies had significant limitations, when taken as a whole they appeared to be reliably in support of the efficacy of relaxation therapy for chronic back pain. Second, deficiencies in the research on relaxation treatment for back pain were similar to those on biofeedback for back pain. Large-scale outcome studies were needed, comparing (a) relaxation with EMG biofeedback, (b) cognitive therapy versus relaxation, (c) relaxation versus traditional medical strategies, and (d) relaxation in conjunction with other treatments versus traditional medical strategies. Last, only two studies have been conducted since 1990 with relaxation as the sole treatment. This latter finding was likely due to the fact that so many multimodal approaches to back pain combine relaxation with other types of behavioral treatments, as has occurred in the biofeedback literature for LBP.

Two recent RCTs have been published looking at relaxation techniques for LBP since the Miller and Arena review. Mehling, Hamel, Acree, Byl, and Hecht (2005) examined breath therapy (N = 16), a form of diaphragmatic breathing, versus standard physical therapy (N = 12) for older adults with chronic LBP. Pain levels decreased both pre- to posttreatment and pretreatment to 6-month follow-up in both groups, with no statistically significant difference between the two interventions. Recently, Morone, Greco, and Weiner (2008) compared mindfulness meditation to a wait-list control group. Participants were 37 older adults (mean age 74.9 years) who were randomized into an 8-week mindfulness-based meditation program or wait-list control. Results indicated no significant difference between the two groups on pain intensity/severity measures posttreatment and on 3-month follow-up. Significant improvement in favor of the meditation group was found on the total score of the Chronic Pain Acceptance Questionnaire and the Activities Engagement subscale, as well as in a scale that measured physical functioning. At 3-month follow-up,

76% of the participants reported that they continued to meditate.

Cognitive Behavior Therapy

One of the major challenges in examining the evidence for CBT interventions for chronic LBP is that no standardized protocol or set of CBT exists. There is tremendous variability in terms of the array of techniques that fall under the CBT heading, leading to difficulty when trying to identify those that have been applied successfully in the LBP population and in which combinations. The CBT techniques are often blended into comprehensive or multidisciplinary treatment approaches, making it very difficult to determine the effective components of multifaceted treatments.

Meta-analyses and systematic reviews. Although numerous reviews preceded, Morley, Eccleston, and Williams (1999) completed the first systematic review and meta-analysis of randomized controlled trials for chronic pain, excluding headache. They conducted a meta-analysis on 25 trials comparing the effectiveness of CBT to wait-list control and alternative treatment control conditions. Pain conditions were mixed and CBT interventions varied. Significant effect sizes (median effect size = 0.5) were found across the measured domains of cognitive behavioral interventions when compared to control groups. The CBT interventions contributed to significant changes in measures of pain experience, mood, cognitive coping and appraisal, pain behavior, and social role function. When compared to other treatments and control groups, the efficacy of CBT was maintained for pain experience, cognitive coping, and social role function; however, the authors pointed out that most trials had inadequate statistical power and did not report the details of the intervention. In addition, the variability in treatment quantity and quality limited the conclusions drawn in their meta-analysis. Finally, they noted that interventions were often brief and administered by inexperienced therapists.

Ostelo and colleagues (2007) systematically reviewed psychological treatments for LBP. The CBT interventions were found to be moderately superior to a wait-list control group for pain intensity but not for functional status; however, CBT was not found to be superior to other noninvasive treatments with positive treatment effects nor did the addition of CBT lead to incremental benefits in outcomes. Results from another recent high-quality systematic review (Hoffman, Papas, Chatkoff, & Kerns, 2007) of 22 randomized controlled trials were consistent with the findings of Ostelo and colleagues.

There is also evidence that CBT interventions can lead to substantial decreases in the rate of acute back pain patients who develop chronic disability. Linton, Boersma, Jansson, Svard, and Botvalde (2005) evaluated the preventive effects of a CBT ($N = 185$; 158 completed follow-up at 1 year) on future sick leave and health-care utilization in nonspecific back and neck pain patients. Treatment groups consisted of minimal care, CBT, and CBT plus physical therapy. The CBT and CBT plus PT groups had fewer health-care visits and sick leave days at the 12-month follow-up. The minimal care group had a fivefold increased risk for developing long-term disability. There were no differences between the CBT and CBT plus PT groups.

Exercise

Physical exercise is believed to reduce pain and improve function in musculoskeletal pain conditions (Bergman, 2007). Specific to LBP, stretching and strengthening have been shown to improve pain and disability levels. The same has not been found for acute LBP (Dziedzic et al., 2008). The degree to which exercise acts on the person's physiology in ways that reduce pain and/or exerts an effect indirectly through increased self-efficacy and decreased distress remains unknown. Additional investigations designed to determine the mechanisms of action are needed.

Meta-analyses and systematic reviews. In a systematic review of 21 trials evaluating the effectiveness of exercise therapy for patients with LBP, Smidt, de Vet, Bouter, & Dekker (2006) reported that exercise therapy is effective compared to no treatment and to standard care provided by a general practitioner. Exercise therapy was found to be equally effective to conventional physiotherapy. The authors noted insufficient evidence to support a particular type of exercise therapy. In addition, according to the authors, the nature of the intervention (group vs. individual, supervised vs. unsupervised, short-term vs. long-term effectiveness of outcomes) remains to be determined. In a meta-regression analysis, Hayden, van Tulder, Malmivaara, and Koes (2005) found that individualized regimens, supervision, stretching, and strengthening were associated with the best outcomes. Likewise, Taylor, Dodd, Shields, and Bruder (2007) found that exercise interventions that were individually tailored, intensive, and were practitioner supported produced better results than independent home exercise.

Hayden and colleagues (2005) published a review based on a quantitative meta-analysis of exercise therapy for nonspecific LBP. They evaluated the effectiveness of exercise therapy across 43 RCTs including 3,907 individuals for reducing pain and disability in adults with nonspecific acute, subacute, and chronic LBP compared to no treatment and other conservative treatments. Results provided strong support that exercise therapy is at least as effective as other conservative treatments in improving functional outcomes and decreasing pain. Improvements were more significant for health care populations compared with general or mixed populations, for which the results were less consistent. In a more recent review, Dziedzic and colleagues (2008) found similar results in support of exercise therapy as an effective management strategy for reducing pain and disability in both subacute (6–12 weeks) and chronic LPB.

As pointed out by Hayden and colleagues (2005), the empirical support for the effectiveness of exercise therapy in chronic LBP patients is fraught with several important limitations. First, the clinical relevance, or significance of *statistically* significant differences, between exercise therapy interventions and other conservative treatments remains unclear. In addition, only a small number of the trials included were considered to be of high quality. One of the primary factors limiting the quality of RCTs for exercise therapy is that exercise is typically poorly defined and specified, resulting in a vague and heterogeneous array of treatments. The existing evidence offers promise for the role of exercise in promoting function and lowering pain; however, more rigorous, high-quality trials are needed to more effectively evaluate the potential of this treatment to benefit the chronic LBP population.

Cost-Effectiveness of Nonpharmacological Interventions for Low Back Pain

Unfortunately, as in the treatment outcome research, the literature on cost-effectiveness of nonpharmacological treatments for LBP often combine the various interventions, making it difficult to attribute cost effectiveness solely to a particular treatment. Johnson and colleagues (Johnson et al., 2007) compared an exercise and education intervention delivered by physical therapists using a cognitive behavioral approach to an information-alone comparison group and concluded that the intervention "produces small non significant improvements over the 15 months following randomization compared to education alone" (p. 1583).

Mirza and Deyo (2007) reviewed randomized clinical trials comparing surgical to nonsurgical treatment of lumbar disk degeneration. They concluded that although there were only three trials that used a structured rehabilitation program incorporating CBT, surgery "may not be more efficacious than structured cognitive behavior therapy" (p. 816). Given the cost of back surgery, if these findings hold true, it is clear that CBT is significantly more cost-effective than surgery. There were a number of methodological limitations to the three studies however, including two of the three studies being underpowered, low compliance with treatment, and a sizable (20%) loss to follow-up.

Recently, there have been two seminal studies that have examined the cost-effectiveness of cognitive behavioral treatments for LBP. In a landmark paper, Linton et al. (2005) compared a minimal treatment group to CBT alone, and CBT plus physical therapy (see earlier). They found that the combined group had significantly less health-care visits than the minimal treatment group; the difference between the two active groups was not significant. Although statistical significance was not given, on 12-month follow-up, the combined group had the least absenteeism, followed by the cognitive behavior therapy group, with the most absenteeism in the minimal treatment group. Of most significance, Linton and his colleagues found that, "the participants in the minimal treatment group had a five-fold higher risk of being on long-term sick leave as compared with the two active groups" (p. 115).

In an influential study, Schweikert and his coauthors (2006) randomly assigned 409 patients with chronic LBP to either a standard 3-week inpatient rehabilitation program or a standard program plus six sessions of CBT. In terms of pain intensity, no difference was found between the two groups. Six months after treatment, however, the cognitive group was absent from work 5.4 days less than the standard group. The authors concluded that, "adding a cognitive behavioral component to standard therapy may reduce work days lost and thus decrease indirect costs" (p. 2519). We find these results extremely promising—saving nearly 11 workdays a year is substantially cost-effective.

Two other studies have examined cost-effectiveness for LBP, but unfortunately have comingled a number of nonpharmacological interventions. Herman, Szczurko, Cooley, and Mills (2008) compared standard treatment to standard treatment plus a mixture of nonpharmacological interventions including acupuncture, relaxation, exercise, dietary advice, and a back care booklet. A number of measures of cost-effectiveness were utilized, including societal costs per participant, absenteeism, participant savings in adjunctive care, and quality adjusted life years. On all measures, the treatment intervention group was superior to the standard group. Moffett et al. (1999) compared a progressive exercise program with usual primary care management. The exercise classes included strengthening exercises for all main muscle groups, relaxation therapy, stretching exercises, and brief education on back care using a cognitive behavioral approach. On a disability questionnaire, a pain scale, and days off work, the experimental group was superior to the standard treatment at both 6-month and 1-year follow-up. Of especial note, "The intervention group . . . reported only 378 days off work compared with 607 in the control group" (p. 279).

Summary of Treatment Outcome for Lower Back Pain

It is clear that there is a strong body of literature supporting the efficacy of exercise as a treatment for chronic lower back pain. Van Tulder, Koes, and Malmivaara (2006) and Hayden and his colleagues (2005) exhaustively reviewed the literature and came to this same conclusion. Surprisingly, there have been few comparisons of exercise with pharmacological interventions. Bronfort, Goldsmith, Nelson, Boline, and Anderson (1996) compared trunk-strengthening exercises by itself or added to spinal manipulative therapy or a course of nonsteroidal antiinflammatory agents, and found no difference between the three groups. The data are not as conclusive for relaxation therapy, CBT, and biofeedback. Although there is enough empirical support for each of these three psychological modalities, it is clear that there is more data supporting the efficacy of CBT approaches than either biofeedback or relaxation therapy. At this point, we would argue for a combination approach of exercise plus CBT for the treatment of lower back pain. There is a paucity of research on combining the more traditional psychological approaches for lower back pain with pharmacological interventions.

Future Directions

Unlike the headache literature, basic methodological deficiencies need to be addressed in the nonpharmacological treatment research of LBP. Studies need to have larger sample sizes, as too many of the studies have 10 or fewer subjects. Investigators need to describe their procedures and, in the case of biofeedback, instrumentation sufficiently to allow replication of the research. Most studies lack clearly defined LBP diagnostic categories and combined all subjects into a single LBP diagnostic group. The majority of studies do not have adequate inclusion and exclusion criteria, some even combine both chronic and acute subjects. Many studies lack adequate control groups, do not employ pain diaries, and have single outcome measures. With a disorder as complex as LBP, measures of functionality as well as pain are essential. Before more complex issues are addressed, these basic ones must be implemented.

Once these issues are addressed, then there are a number of studies that need to be conducted. Direct comparisons of biofeedback to relaxation therapy to cognitive therapy to exercise are clearly needed. Second, although more studies are including follow-ups, longer (at least one year) and larger scale (at least 50 per group) follow-up studies are required. Third, comparisons of various biofeedback treatment procedures, such as paraspinal versus frontal electrode placement, or training while supine versus training while standing, are necessary. Fourth, further evaluations of

patient characteristics predictive of outcome, such as gender, race, chronicity, psychopathology, and psychophysiological reactivity, are needed. Finally, as the nonpharmacological interventions are nowadays incorporated into a multimodal type of treatment, component analysis of such interventions (e.g., what additional improvement does relaxation therapy give to the multimodal treatment?) are vitally needed and overdue.

OTHER CHRONIC PAIN DISORDERS

Behavioral treatments have been used with varying success with other chronic pain syndromes; so many, in fact, that the authors cannot hope to review all of them here. Rather, we will try to summarize what we feel are the most interesting applications for clinicians and researchers, including most areas where a sizeable or growing literature exists, as well as one area where, although promising, there is a paucity of treatment studies.

Arthritis

Arthritis is simply the inflammation of a joint. This inflammation over time will usually lead to stiffness, warmth, swelling, redness, and pain in the afflicted joint. There are over 100 types of arthritis. The most common type is osteoarthritis, which is caused by the breakdown and eventual loss of the cartilage in one or more joints. Rheumatoid arthritis is an autoimmune disease in which the immune system is overactive and causes chronic inflammation of the joints. Nondrug interventions have been used for over 30 years with arthritis.

Exercise has been a mainstay of arthritis treatment and its efficacy has been repeatedly demonstrated, although its effect on joint stiffness has not been conclusively demonstrated (Blackham, Garry, Cummings, Russell, & Dealleaume, 2008). Of the more traditional psychological treatments, most now involve

CBT and relaxation therapy, either alone or in combination (Ottonello, 2007). Reviews of the literature have strongly supported the efficacy of CBT and relaxation for both osteoarthritis and rheumatoid arthritis (Astin, Beckner, Soeken, Hochberg, & Berman, 2002; Bradley & Alberts, 1999). Using the Task Force efficacy outlined earlier, both relaxation therapy and CBT would be deemed efficacious in the treatment of arthritis pain. While biofeedback, particularly temperature biofeedback, was employed in earlier research, now exercise, CBT, and relaxation therapy are the nonpharmacological modalities generally employed for arthritis pain.

While most of the studies involving relaxation therapy and CBT have small sample sizes, and many are only single blind, taken together they are impressive. It is essential that larger scale studies be conducted comparing combination therapies to a single therapy, both among the nonpharmacological interventions, as well as comparisons to pharmacological approaches. One very exciting area of research involves determining whether behavioral interventions are efficacious with minorities. Recently, McIlvane, Baker, Mingo, and Haley (2008) reviewed the behavioral intervention literature for arthritis and found that in only two of 25 RCTs examined indicated whether racial/ethnic group differences were found (in both, minorities were similar to Caucasians), and only six studies examined attrition by race. This area is a quite promising future direction for arthritis researchers and clinicians, especially given the large number of minorities who suffer from rheumatic diseases.

Fibromyalgia

Fibromyalgia is a type of nonarticular, noninflammatory rheumatism that is characterized by diffuse pain, sleep disturbance, tenderness, and functional impairment. Van Koulil et al., (2007) recently reviewed the nonpharmacological literature for the treatment of fibromyalgia. They concluded that, while no treatment has been shown to fully alleviate the symptoms of this significant pain disorder, nonpharmacological interventions, such as CBT and exercise, have generally been shown to be more efficacious than pharmacological treatments. They also concluded that a combination of CBT and exercise training have been shown to be the most effective in relieving the pain of fibromyalgia. While most of the biofeedback literature has employed EMG biofeedback, there have been studies that have employed EEG (Kayiran, Dursun, Ermutlu, Dursun, & Karamürsel, 2007; Mueller, Donaldson, Nelson, & Layman, 2001) and heart rate variability biofeedback (Hassett et al., 2007). Relaxation has generally not been used as a stand-alone technique with fibromyalgia; however, the strongest RCT (Fors, Sexton, & Götestam, 2002) showed relaxation that included guided imagery to be superior to amitriptyline as well relaxation that included focusing in on "the active workings of the internal pain control systems" (p. 179). Additional research is needed to compare: (a) the various types of relaxation with each other, (b) EMG biofeedback versus EEG biofeedback, (c) relaxation versus EMG biofeedback versus CBT versus exercise, and (d) the four nonpharmacological interventions in combination with each other.

Myofascial Pain Dysfunction Syndrome

Myofascial pain dysfunction syndrome, which is also known as temporomandibular joint (TMJ) syndrome, is considered a subtype of craniomandibular dysfunction that is caused by hyperactivity of the masticatory muscles. It is characterized by diffuse pain in the muscles of mastication, mastication muscle tenderness, and joint sounds and limitations. Although disagreement exists as to the cause of the hyperactivity, such as occlusal problems versus psychological stress, several researchers have examined the use of EMG biofeedback and relaxation therapy as a treatment, which can provide relief by teaching patients to relax the muscles of the jaw. Consistent with the logic of this approach, the most common biofeedback electrode placement is on the masseter muscle, although frontal muscle placements have also been used. Various exercise approaches and CBT have also been used, usually in combination with some form of relaxation exercises.

Meta-analyses and reviews of the literature have generally found biofeedback and CBT to be efficacious, using the Task Force criteria delineated earlier, and exercise and relaxation therapy to be probably efficacious (Arena & Blanchard, 2002a; Crider, Glaros, & Gevirtz, 2005; Medlicott & Harris, 2006; Orlando, Manfredeni, Salvetti, & Bosco, 2007). In the best review to date of the biofeedback literature for myofascial pain dysfunction syndrome (Crider et al., 2005), the authors employed the treatment efficacy criteria outlined earlier by the Association for Applied Psychophysiology and Biofeedback. They concluded that surface EMG training as the sole intervention, or combined with some form of relaxation therapy, are probably efficacious treatments. They noted that surface EMG combined with CBT is an efficacious treatment using the treatment efficacy criteria.

Türp et al. (2007) recently conducted a review of the myofascial pain dysfunction syndrome literature, looking at single modality care provided by a dentist—generally occlusal splints—versus a combination treatment. Eleven studies met their criteria for inclusion. They found no superiority of the combination therapy as opposed to simple dental care, with the exception that, "In temporomandibular pain patients with major psychological disturbances, patients benefited more from a combined therapeutic approach compared with simple care" (p. 138). It appears that additional research in this area is called for, examining the effects of psychological factors as well as combination therapy.

Complex Regional Pain Syndrome

Complex regional pain syndrome is a troubling disorder whose cause is unknown and is manifested by severe, excruciating pain that is out of proportion to the severity of the injury and gets progressively worse over time. It was previously known as reflex sympathetic dystrophy or causalgia. Complex regional pain syndrome most often initially affects a section of the arms, legs, hands, or feet, and then frequently radiates outward to encompass the entire appendage. Symptoms typically include dramatic changes in the color and temperature of the skin over the affected limb or body part, accompanied by intense burning pain, skin sensitivity, sweating, and swelling. Sometimes the skin is so sensitive that individuals cannot sleep with even a sheet touching the affected area.

Thermal biofeedback and relaxation therapy have been shown to have some promise in this area. Using the Joint Efficacy Task Force Report (2002) criteria, they would be considered possibly efficacious, given the paucity of studies in the literature. Blanchard (1979) presented the first use of thermal biofeedback for this disorder in a single subject experimental design. At 1-year follow-up, the patient remained pain free. Grunert, Devine, Sanger, Matloub, and Green (1990) found that a combination of thermal biofeedback, relaxation therapy, and supportive psychotherapy significantly reduced reflex sympathetic dystrophy pain by 48%. These results were maintained at 1-year follow-up, with 14 of 20 patients returning to work. For any clinician working with such extremely refractory pain patients, these results are indeed exciting. Once again, large scale, controlled studies need to be conducted.

EVIDENCE-BASED PRACTICE AND PAIN DISORDERS

In this section, to aid the reader, we would like to summarize which nonpharmacological treatments have and have not been found to have established efficacy using the Task Force criteria (see earlier) and the criteria set forth by Chambless and Hollon (1998) of (1) two or more well-conducted randomized controlled

TABLE 25.1   Non-Pharmacological Treatments for Pain: Summary of Treatment Effectiveness

Pain Disorder	Non-Pharmacological Treatment			
	Biofeedback	CBT	Exercise	Relaxation
Migraine headache	Efficacious	Efficacious	Efficacy not demonstrated	Efficacious
Tension headache	Efficacious	Efficacious	Efficacy not demonstrated	Efficacious
Low back pain	Efficacious	Efficacious	Efficacious	Efficacious
Arthritis	Efficacy not demonstrated	Efficacious	Efficacious	Efficacious
Fibromyalgia	Efficacy not demonstrated	Efficacy not demonstrated	Efficacy not demonstrated	Efficacy not demonstrated
Myofascial pain dysfunction syndrome	Efficacious	Efficacious	Efficacy not demonstrated	Efficacy not demonstrated
Complex regional pain syndrome	Efficacy not demonstrated	Efficacy not demonstrated	Efficacy not demonstrated	Efficacy not demonstrated

Note: Please note that "efficacy not demonstrated" does not mean that the intervention has been deemed not to be effective. It denotes that sufficient data is as yet available to conclusively deem the treatment effective or noneffective.

trials by at least two different research groups, or (2) three or more well-conducted small sample sized experiments (with 10 or more subjects in each) conducted by at least two separate research groups. Table 25.1 presents this information.

As the reader can see, relaxation therapy, biofeedback, and CBT have been shown to be efficacious for the two major pain disorders we have focused on in this chapter—both migraine and tension headache, as well as LBP. Exercise has been demonstrated to be efficacious for lower back pain, but for headache its efficacy has yet to be proven. Exercise, relaxation, and CBT are proven evidence-based treatments for arthritis. Biofeedback is probably efficacious for arthritis, but additional studies are needed. The various nonpharmacological interventions for fibromyalgia have not yet been proven efficacious. Biofeedback and CBT have been found to be efficacious for myofascial pain dysfunction syndrome, whereas relaxation therapy and exercise, while probably effective, require additional studies. Data for the efficacy of nonpharmacological interventions for complex regional pain disorder is simply not there, although the biofeedback literature appears to hold the most promise.

It has been our hope in writing this chapter to introduce the reader to the primary evidenced-based nonpharmacological interventions employed at the present time by mental health professionals to deal with the complex problem of chronic pain—namely biofeedback, CBT, exercise, and relaxation therapy. All of these approaches have been employed by psychologists and other mental health professionals for at least three decades, but—with the notable exceptions of biofeedback, relaxation therapy, and CBT for headache and exercise for arthritis—basic research, especially large scale comparisons of the various treatment approaches, needs to be conducted. For many chronic pain disorders, determining the efficacy of the various interventions as a function of patient demographics such as age and race needs to be examined further, as do alternative methods of treatment delivery, such as bibliotherapy or telehealth approaches. As with most areas in the social sciences today, additional research is most definitely needed.

One final note: Most behavioral clinicians, who are the prototypical readers of this chapter, have had some exposure to the use of CBT, exercise, and relaxation procedures through their applications with more traditional psychological problems such as anger, anxiety, and depression. Biofeedback, which requires more specialized training, is based on learning theory—both operant and classical conditioning. All the health psychologist does is take the sound principles of psychology and learning theory and apply these principles to nontraditional areas of psychology such as chronic pain. We hope that we have inspired the readers of this chapter to apply some of these approaches to their patients with chronic pain. It is indeed a great source of comfort when one realizes that psychologists and other mental health practitioners can use their science to alleviate both the psychological as well as physical suffering of their patients.

REFERENCES

Ad Hoc Committee on the Classification of Headache. (1962). Classification of headache. *Journal of the American Medical Association, 179*, 127–128.

American Academy of Orthopedic Surgery. (1996). *Common orthopedic procedures and codes: A reference guide* (2nd Ed.). New York, NY: Authors.

American Academy of Pain Medicine. (2008). *AAPM facts and figures on pain*. Retrieved from www.painmed.org/patient/facts.html

Andersson, G. B. J., & McNeill, T. W. (1989). *Lumbar spine syndromes: Evaluation and treatment*. New York, NY: Springer Verlag.

Andrasik, F. (2007). What does the evidence show? Efficacy of behavioural treatments for recurrent headaches in adults. *Neurological Sciences, 28*, S70–S77.

Arena, J. G., & Blanchard, E. B. (1996). Biofeedback and relaxation therapy for chronic pain disorders. In R. J. Gatchel and D. C. Turk (Eds.), *Chronic pain: Psychological perspectives on treatment* (179–230). New York, NY: Guilford Press.

Arena, J. G., & Blanchard, E. B. (2002a). Biofeedback therapy for chronic pain disorders. In J. D. Loeser, D. Turk, R. C. Chapman, and S. Butler (Eds.), *Bonica's management of pain* (3rd ed., pp. 1755–1763). Baltimore, MD: Williams & Wilkins.

Arena, J. G., & Blanchard, E. B. (2002b). Biofeedback training for chronic pain disorders: A primer. In R. J. Gatchel and D. C. Turk (Eds.), *Chronic pain: Psychological perspectives on treatment* (2nd ed., pp. 159–186). New York, NY: Guilford Press.

Arena, J. G., Dennis, N., Devineni, T., Maclean, R., & Meador, K. (2004). A pilot study of feasibility and efficacy of telemedicine-delivered psychophysiological treatment for vascular headache. *Telemedicine Journal and E-Health, 10*, 449–454.

Arena, J. G., Hannah, S. L., & Meador, K. J. (in press). *A comparison of standard office-based versus telemedicine-delivered biofeedback and relaxation therapy for chronic vascular headache.*

Arena, J. G., Hightower, N. E., & Chang, G. C. (1988). Relaxation therapy for tension headache in the elderly: A prospective study. *Psychology and Aging, 3*, 96–98.

Arena, J. G., Sherman, R. A., Bruno, G. M., & Young, T. R. (1989). Electromyographic recordings of five types of low back pain subjects and non-pain controls in different positions. *Pain, 37*, 57–65.

Arena, J. G., Sherman, R. A., Bruno, G. M., & Young, T. R. (1991). Electromyographic recordings of five types of low back pain subjects and non pain controls in different positions: Effect of pain state. *Pain, 45*, 23–28.

Arthritis Foundation. (1999). Speaking of pain: How to talk with your doctor about pain; pain in America: Highlights from a Gallup survey. Retrieved from www.arthritis.org/conditions/speakingofpain/factsheet.asp

Association for Applied Psychophysiology and Biofeedback. (2011). Retrieved from www.aapb.org/consumers_biofeedback.html

Astin, J., Beckner, W., Soeken, K., Hochberg, M. & Berman, B. (2002). Psychological interventions for rheumatoid arthritis: A meta-analysis of randomized controlled trials. *Arthritis and Rheumatism, 47*, 291–302.

Bakal, D. A., Demjen, S., & Kaganov, J. A. (1981). Cognitive behavioral treatment of chronic headache. *Headache, 21*, 81–86.

Beck, A. T. (1976). *Cognitive therapy and the emotional disorders.* New York, NY: The New American Library.

Beck, J. G., Andrasik, F., & Arena, J. G. (1984). Group comparison designs. In A. S. Bellack & M. Hersen (Eds.), *Research methods in clinical psychology* (pp. 100–138). New York, NY: Pergamon Press.

Beck, J. S. (1995). *Cognitive therapy: Basics and beyond.* New York, NY: Guilford Press.

Bellack, A. (1973). Reciprocal inhibition of a laboratory conditioned fear. *Behaviour Research and Therapy, 11*, 11–18.

Bergman, S. (2007). Management of musculoskeletal pain. *Best Practice and Research in Clinical Rheumatology, 1*, 153–166.

Bindman, A. B., Forrest, C. B., Britt, H., Crampton, P., & Majeed, A. (2007). Diagnostic scope and exposure to primary care physicians in Australia, New Zealand, and the United States: Cross sectional analysis of results from three national surveys. *British Medical Journal, 334,* 1230–1231.

Blackham, J., Garry, J., Cummings, D., Russell, R. & Dealleaume, L. (2008). Does regular exercise reduce the pain and stiffness of osteoarthritis? *Journal of Family Practice, 57,* 476–477.

Blanchard, E. B. (1979). The use of temperature biofeedback in the treatment of chronic pain due to causalgia. *Biofeedback and Self-Regulation, 4,* 183–188.

Blanchard, E. B., Andrasik, F., Ahles, T. A., Teders, S. J., & O'Keefe, D. (1980). Migraine and tension-type headache: A meta-analytic review. *Behavior Therapy, 11,* 613–631.

Blanchard, E. B., Andrasik, F., Appelbaum, K. A., Evans, D. D., Myers, P., & Barron, K. D. (1986). Three studies of the psychologic changes in chronic headache patients associated with biofeedback and relaxation therapies. *Psychosomatic Medicine, 48,* 73–83.

Blanchard, E. B., Andrasik, F., Neff, D. F., Arena, J. G., Ahles, T. A., Jurish, S. E., . . . Rodichok, L. D. (1982). Biofeedback and relaxation training with three kinds of headache: Treatment effects and their prediction. *Journal of Consulting and Clinical Psychology, 50,* 562–575.

Blanchard, E. B., Appelbaum, K. A., Radnitz, C. L., Michultka, D. M., Morrill, B., Kirsch, C., . . . Dentinger, M. P. (1990). A placebo-controlled evaluation of abbreviated progressive muscle relaxation and relaxation combined with cognitive therapy in the treatment of tension headache. *Journal of Consulting and Clinical Psychology, 58,* 210–215.

Blanchard, E. B., Appelbaum, K. A., Radnitz, C. L., Morrill, B., Michultka, D., Kirsch, C., . . . & Barron, K. D. (1990). A controlled evaluation of thermal biofeedback and thermal biofeedback combined with cognitive therapy in the treatment of vascular headache. *Journal of Consulting and Clinical Psychology, 58,* 216–224.

Blanchard, E. B., & Arena, J. G. (1999). Biofeedback, relaxation training and other psychological treatments for chronic benign headache. In M. L. Diamond & G. D. Solomon (Eds.), *The practicing physician's approach to headache* (6th ed., pp. 209–224). New York, NY: W. B. Saunders.

Blanchard, E. B., Jaccard, J., Andrasik, F., Guarnieri, P., & Jurish, S. E. (1985). Reduction in headache patients' medical expenses associated with biofeedback and relaxation treatments. *Biofeedback and Self-Regulation, 10,* 63–68.

Blanchard, E. B., Kim, M., Hermann, C., & Steffek, B. D. (1994). The role of perception of success in the thermal biofeedback treatment of vascular headache. *Headache Quarterly, 5,* 231–236.

Blanchard, E. B., Theobald, D. E., Williamson, D. A., Silver, B. V., & Brown, D. A. (1978). Temperature biofeedback in the treatment of migraine headaches. *Archives of General Psychiatry, 35,* 581–588.

Board of Directors, American Headache Society. (1978). Biofeedback therapy. *Headache, 18,* 107.

Borenstein, D. G., & Wiesel, S. W. (1989). *Low back pain: Medical diagnosis and comprehensive management.* Philadelphia, PA: W. B. Saunders.

Bradley, L., & Alberts, K. (1999). Psychological and behavioral approaches to pain management for patients with rheumatic disease. *Rheumatic Diseases Clinics of North America, 25,* 215–232.

Bronfort, G., Goldsmith, C., Nelson, C., Boline, P. & Anderson, A. (1996). Trunk exercise combined with spinal manipulative or NSAID therapy for chronic low back pain: A randomized, observer-blinded clinical trial. *Journal of Manipulative and Physiological Therapeutics, 19,* 570–582.

Budzynski, T., Stoyva, J., & Adler, C. (1970). Feedback induced muscle relaxation: Application to tension headache. *Journal of Behavior Therapy and Experimental Psychiatry, 1,* 205–211.

Budzynski, T. H., Stoyva, J. M., Adler, C. S., & Mullaney, D. J. (1973). EMG biofeedback and tension headache: A controlled outcome study. *Psychosomatic Medicine, 6,* 509–514.

Busch, V. & Gaul, C. (2008). Exercise in migraine therapy—Is there any evidence for efficacy? A critical review. *Headache, 48,* 890–899.

Campbell, J. K., Penzien, D. B., & Wall, E. M. (2000). Evidenced-based guidelines for migraine headache: Behavioral and physical treatments. Retrieved from www.aan.com/professionals/practice/pdfs/gl0089.pdf

Cavanaugh, J. & Weinstein, J. (1994). Low back pain: Epidemiology, anatomy, and neurophysiology. In P. Wall & R. Melzack (Eds.), *Textbook of pain* (3rd Ed.) (pp. 4414–45). New York, NY: Churchill Livingstone.

Centers for Disease Control, National Center for Health Statistics. (2006). *Chart book on trends in the health of Americans with special features on pain.* Washington, DC: Government Printing Office (GPO stock number 017-022-01602-8).

Chambless, D. L. & Hollon, S. D. (1998). Defining empirically supported therapies. *Journal of Clinical and Consulting Therapy, 66,* 7–18.

Chappell, M. N., & Stevenson, T. I. (1936). Group psychological training in some organic conditions. *Mental Hygiene, 20,* 588–597.

Chesney, M. A., & Shelton, J. L. (1976). A comparison of muscle relaxation and electromyogram biofeedback treatments for muscle contraction headache. *Journal of Behavior Therapy and Experimental Psychiatry, 7,* 221–225.

Chou, R., Qaseem, A., Snow, V., Casey, D., Cross, J. T., Shekelle, P., & Owens, D. (2007). Diagnosis and treatment of low back pain: A Joint Clinical Practice Guideline from the American College of Physicians and the American Pain Society. *Annals of Internal Medicine, 147,* 478–491.

Cousins, M. J. (1995). Foreword. In W. E. Fordyce (Ed.), *Back pain in the workplace: Management of disability in non-specific conditions* (p. ix). Seattle, WA: International Association for the Study of Pain.

Crider, A., Glaros, A., & Gevirtz, R. (2005). Efficacy of biofeedback-based treatments for temporomandibular disorder. *Applied Psychophysiology and Biofeedback, 30*, 433–445.

Department of Veterans Affairs/Department of Defense. (November, 1999). *Low back pain or sciatica in the primary care setting*. Washington, DC: Office of Quality and Performance publication (10Q-CPG/LBP-99).

Deviveni T., & Blanchard E. B. (2005). A randomized controlled trial of an internet-based treatment for chronic headache. *Behaviour Research and Therapy, 43*, 277–292.

Dionne, C. E. (1999). Low back pain. In I. K. Crombie, P. R. Croft, S. J. Linton, L. LeResche, & M. Von Korff (Eds.), *International association for the study of pain task force on epidemiology: Epidemiology of pain* (pp. 283–298). Seattle, WA: International Association for the Study of Pain Press.

Dittrich, S. M., Gunther, V., Franz, G., Burtscher, M., Holzner, B., & Kopp, M. (2008). Aerobic exercise with relaxation: Influence on pain and psychological well being in female migraine patients. *Clinical Journal of Sports Medicine, 18*, 363–365.

Dziedzic, K., Jordan, J. L., & Foster, N. E. (2008). Land and water based exercise therapies for musculoskeletal conditions. *Best Practice & Research Clinical Rheumatology, 22*, 407–418.

Engel, C. C., Von Korff, M., & Katon, W. J. (1996). Back pain in primary care: Predictors of high health care costs. *Pain, 65*, 197–204.

Feuerstein, G. (1975). *Textbook of yoga*. London, England: Rider.

Flor, H., & Birbaumer, N. (1993). Comparison of the efficacy of electromyographic biofeedback, cognitive behavioral therapy, and conservative medical interventions in the treatment of chronic musculoskeletal pain. *Journal of Consulting and Clinical Psychology, 61*, 653–658.

Flor, H., Fydrich, T., & Turk, D. (1992). Efficacy of multidisciplinary pain treatment centers: A meta-analytic review. *Pain, 49*, 221–30.

Fordyce, W. E. (Ed.). (1995). *Back pain in the workplace: Management of disability in nonspecific conditions: A report of the Task Force on Pain in the Workplace of the International Association for the Study of Pain*. Seattle, WA: International Association for the Study of Pain.

Fors, E., Sexton, H., & Gotestam, K. (2002). The effect of guided imagery and amitriptyline on daily fibromyalgia pain: A prospective, randomized, controlled trial. *Journal of Psychiatric Research, 36*, 179–187.

Frymoyer, J. W., Akeson, W., Brandt, K., Goldenberg, D., & Spencer, D. (1989). Postural support structures:

Part A. Clinical perspective. In J. W. Frymoyer & S. L. Gordon (Eds.), *New perspectives in low back pain* (pp. 217–248). Park Ridge, IL: American Academy of Orthopedic Surgeons.

Gatchel, R. J., Peng, Y. B., Peters, M. L., Fuchs, P. N., & Turk, D. C. (2007). The biopsychosocial approach to chronic pain: Scientific advances and future directions. *Psychological Bulletin, 133*, 581–684.

Grunert, B. K., Devine, C. A., Sanger, J. R., Matloub, H. S., & Green, D. (1990). Thermal self-regulation for pain control in reflex sympathetic dystrophy syndrome. *Journal of Hand Surgery, 15*, 615–618.

Guzman, J., Esmail, R., Karjalainen, K., Malmivaara, A., Irvin, E., & Bombardier, C. (2001). Multidisciplinary rehabilitation for chronic low back pain: Systemic review. *British Medical Journal, 322*, 1511–1516.

Guzman, J., Esmail, R., Karjalainen, K., Malmivaara, A., Irvin, E., & Bombardier, C. (2002). Multidisciplinary bio psycho social rehabilitation for chronic low back pain: *Cochrane Database Systemic Review*, Art. No. CD000963. Retrieved from www.ncbi.nlm.nih.gov/pubmed/11869581

Hassett, A., Radvanski, D., Vaschillo, E., Vaschillo, B., Sigal, L., Karavidas, M., . . . Lehrer P. (2007). A pilot study of the efficacy of heart rate variability (HRV) biofeedback in patients with fibromyalgia. *Applied Psychophysiology and Biofeedback, 32*, 1–10.

Hayden, J. A., van Tulder, M. W., Malmivaara, A. V., & Koes, B. W. (2005). Meta analysis: Exercise therapy for nonspecific low back pain. *Annals of Internal Medicine, 142*, 765–775.

Headache Classification Committee of the International Headache Society. (1988). Classification and diagnostic criteria for headache disorders, cranial neuralgias and facial pain. *Cephalgia, 8*(Suppl. 7), 29–34.

Headache Classification Committee of the International Headache Society. (2004). The international classification of headache disorders (2nd Ed.). *Cephalgia, 24* (Suppl. 1), 9–160.

Herman, P. M., Szczurko, O., Cooley, K., & Mills, E. J. (2008). Cost-effectiveness of naturopathic care for chronic low back pain. *Alternative Therapies in Health and Medicine, 14*, 32–39.

Hoffman, B. M., Papas, R. K., Chatkoff, D. K., & Kerns, R. D. (2007). Meta-analysis of psychological interventions for chronic low back pain. *Health Psychology, 26*, 1–9.

Holroyd, K. A., O'Donnell, F. J., Stensland, M., Lipchik, G. L., Cordingley, G. E., & Carlson, B. W. (2001). Management of chronic tension-type headache with tricyclic antidepressant medication, stress management therapy, and their combination: a randomized controlled trial. *Journal of the American Medical Association, 285*, 2208–2215.

Holroyd, K. A., & Penzien, D. B. (1986). Client variables and the behavioral treatment of recurrent tension headache: A meta-analytic review. *Journal of Behavioral Medicine, 9,* 515–536.

Holroyd, K. A., Penzien, D. B., Hursey, K. G., Tobin, D. L., Rogers, L., Holm, J. E., . . . Chila, A. G. (1984). Change mechanisms in EMG biofeedback training: cognitive changes underlying improvements in tension headache. *Journal of Consulting and Clinical Psychology, 52,* 1039–1053.

International Association for the Study of Pain Subcommittee on Taxonomy & Merskey, H. (Eds.). (1986). Classification of chronic pain syndromes and definitions of pain terms. *Pain,* (Suppl. 3), S1–S226.

Jacobson, E. (1929). *Progressive relaxation.* Chicago, IL: University of Chicago Press.

Johnson, R. E., Jones, G. T., Wiles, N. J., Chaddock, C., Potter, R. G., Roberts, C., . . . Macfarlane, G. J. (2007). Active exercise, education, and cognitive behavioral therapy for persistent disabling low back pain. *Spine, 32,* 1578–1585.

Joint Commission on Accreditation of Healthcare Organizations. (2001). *2001 comprehensive accreditation manual for hospitals (CAMH): The official handbook.* Terrance, IL: Author.

Jurish, S. E., Blanchard, E. B., Andrasik, F., Teders, S. J., Neff, D. F., & Arena, J. G. (1983). Home- versus clinic-based treatment of vascular headache. *Journal of Consulting and Clinical Psychology, 51,* 743–751.

Kanji, N., White, A. R., & Ernst, E. (2006). Autogenic training for tension-type headaches: A systematic review of controlled trials. *Complementary Therapies in Medicine, 14,* 144–150.

Kayiran, S., Dursun, E., Ermutlu, N., Dursun, N., & Karamürsel, S. (2007). Neurofeedback in fibromyalgia syndrome. *Journal of the Turkish Society of Algology, 19,* 47–53.

Kemsdorf, R. B., Kochanowicz, N. A., & Costell, S. (1981). Cognitive skills training versus EMG biofeedback in the treatment of tension headaches. *Biofeedback and Self-Regulation, 6,* 93–102.

Krueger, A., & Stone, A. (2008). Assessment of pain: a community-based diary survey in the USA. *Lancet, 371,* 1519–1525.

Lake, A. E. (2001). Behavioral and nonpharmacologic treatments of headaches. *Medical Clinics of North America, 85,* 1055–1075.

Leeuw, M., Goossens, M. E. J. B., Linton, S. J., Crombez, G., Boersma, K., & Vlaeyen, J. W. S. (2007). The fear-avoidance model of musculoskeletal pain: Current state of scientific evidence. *Journal of Behavioral Medicine, 30,* 77–94.

Lichstein, K. L. (1988). *Clinical relaxation strategies.* New York, NY: Wiley.

Linden, W. (1994). Autogenic training: A narrative and quantitative review of clinical outcome. *Biofeedback and Self Regulation, 19,* 227–264.

Linton, S. J., Boersma, K., Jansson, M., Svard, L., & Botvalde, M. (2005). The effects of cognitive-behavioral and physical therapy preventive interventions on pain-related sick leave. *Clinical Journal of Pain, 21,* 109–119.

Luthe, W. (Ed.). (1969–1973). *Autogenic therapy* (Vols. 1–6). New York, NY: Grune & Stratton.

Maetzel, A., & Li, L. (2002). The economic burden of low back pain: A review of studies published between 1996 and 2001. *Best Practices Research in Clinical Rheumatology, 16,* 23–30.

Manzoni, G., Pagnini, F., Castelnuovo, G., & Molinari, E. (2003). Relaxation training for anxiety: A ten-years systematic review with meta-analysis. *Bio Medical Central Psychiatry, 8,* 41–52.

McCracken, L. M., & Turk, D. C. (2002). Behavioral and cognitive-behavioral treatment for chronic pain: Outcome, predictors of outcome and treatment process. *Spine, 27,* 2564–2573.

McCrory, D. C., Penzien, D. B., Hasselblad, V., & Gray, R. N. (2001). *Evidence report: Behavioral and physical treatments for tension-type and cervicogenic headaches.* Des Moines, IA: Foundation for Chiropractic Education and Research. (Product No. 2085).

McIlvane, J., Baker, T., Mingo, C., & Haley, W. (2008). Are behavioral interventions for arthritis effective with minorities? Addressing racial and ethnic diversity in disability and rehabilitation. *Arthritis and Rheumatism, 59,* 1512–1518.

Medlicott, M., & Harris, S. (2006). A systemic review of the effectiveness of exercise, manual therapy, electrotherapy, relaxation training and biofeedback in the management of temporomandibular disorder. *Physical Therapy, 86,* 955–973.

Mehling, W., Hamel, K., Acree, M., Byl, N., & Hecht, F. (2005). Randomized, controlled trial of breath therapy for patients with chronic low-back pain. *Alternative Therapies in Health and Medicine, 11,* 44–52.

Miller, D., & Arena, J. G. (2004). *Relaxation therapy for lower back pain: A review of the literature.* Unpublished manuscript. Augusta, GA: Department of Veterans Affairs Medical Center.

Mirza, S. K., & Deyo, R. A. (2007). Systematic review of randomized trials comparing lumbar fusion surgery to nonoperative care for treatment of chronic back pain. *Spine, 32,* 816–823.

Moffett, J. K., Torgerson, D., Bell-Syer, S. Jackson, D., Llewlyn-Phillips, H., Farrin, A., & Barber, J. (1999). Randomised controlled trial of exercise for low back pain: Clinical outcomes, costs and preferences. *British Medical Journal, 319*(7295), 279–283.

Morley, S., Eccleston, C., & Williams, A. (1999). Systematic review and meta-analysis of randomized control trials of cognitive behavior and behavior therapy for chronic pain in adults, excluding headache. *Pain, 80,* 1–13.

Morone N. E., Greco, C. M., & Weiner, D. K. (2008). Mindfulness meditation for the treatment of chronic low back pain in older adults: a randomized controlled pilot study. *Pain, 134,* 310–319.

Moss, D., & Gunkelman, J. (2002). Task force on methodology and empirically supported treatments: Introduction. *Applied Psychophysiology and Biofeedback, 27,* 271–272.

Mueller, H., Donaldson, C., Nelson, D., & Layman, M. (2001). Treatment of fibromyalgia incorporating EEG-Driven stimulation: A clinical outcomes study. *Journal of Clinical Psychology, 57,* 933–952.

Nadelson, C. (2006). Sports and exercise-induced migraines. *Current Sports Medicine Reports, 5,* 29–33.

Nestoriuc, Y., Martin, A., Rief, W., & Andrasik, F. (2008). Biofeedback treatment for headache disorders: A comprehensive efficacy review. *Applied Psychophysiology and Biofeedback, 33,* 25–40.

Nordin, M., Balague, F., & Cedraschi, C. (2006). Non specific lower back pain: Surgical versus nonsurgical treatment. *Clinical Orthopaedics and Related Research, 443,* 156–167.

Orlando, B., Manfredini, D., Salvetti, G., & Bosco, M. (2007). Evaluation of the effectiveness of biobehavioral therapy in the treatment of temporomandibular disorders: A literature review. *Behavioral Medicine, 33,* 101–118.

Ostelo, R., van Tulder, M., Vlaeyen, J., Linton, S., Morley, S., & Assendelft, W. (2007). Behavioral treatment of chronic low back pain (review). *Cochrane Library, 4,* 1–25.

Ottonello, M. (2007). Cognitive behavioral interventions in rheumatic disease. *Giornale Italiano di Medicina del Lavoro ed Ergonomia, 29,* 19–23.

Payne, R. A. (2005). *Relaxation techniques: A practical handbook for the health care professional.* 3rd edition. London, England: Churchill Livingstone.

Penzien, D. B., Holroyd, K. A., Holm, J. E., & Hursey, K. G. (1985). Psychometric characteristics of the Bakal Headache Assessment Questionnaire. *Headache, 25,* 55–58.

Penzien, D. B., Rains, J. C., & Andrasik, F. (2002). Behavioral management of recurrent headache: Three decades of experience and empiricism. *Applied Psychophysiology and Biofeedback, 27,* 163–181.

Poppen, R. (1988). *Behavioral relaxation training and assessment* (2nd ed.). Thousand Oaks, CA: SAGE Publications, Inc.

Rains, J. C., Penzien, D. B., McCrory, D. C., & Gray, R. N. (2005). Behavioral headache treatment: History, review of the empirical literature, and methodological critique. *Headache, 45*(Suppl 2), S92–S109.

Rasmussen, B. K. (1992). Epidemiology and socioeconomic impact of headache. *Cephalea, 5*(Suppl), 90–94.

Rasmussen, B. K., Jensen, R., Schroll, M., & Olesen, J. (1991). Epidemiology of headache in a general

population—A prevalence study. *Journal of Clinical Epidemiology, 44,* 1147–1157.

Rokicki, L. A., Holroyd, K. A., France, C. R., Lipchik, G. L., France, J. L., Kvaal, S. A. (1997). Change mechanisms associated with combined relaxation/EMG biofeedback training for chronic tension headache. *Applied Psychophysiology and Biofeedback, 22,* 21–41.

Rosenstiel, A. K., & Keefe, F. G. (1983). The use of coping strategies in chronic low back pain patients: Relationship to patient characteristics and current adjustment. *Pain, 17,* 33–44.

Sargent, J. D., Green, E. E., & Walters, E. D. (1972). The use of autogenic feedback training in a pilot study of migraine and tension headaches. *Headache, 12,* 120–124.

Schappert, S. M. (1999). Ambulatory care visits to physicians offices, hospital outpatient departments, and emergency departments, United States, 1997. *Vital Health Statistics, 13,* 1–39.

Schultz, J. H., & Luthe, U. (1969). *Autogenic training* (Vol. I). New York, NY: Grune and Stratton.

Schweikert, B., Jacobi, J., Seitz, R., Cziske, R., Ehlert, A., Knab, J., & Leidl, R. (2006). Effectiveness and cost effectiveness of adding a cognitive behavioral treatment to the rehabilitation of chronic low back pain. *Journal of Rheumatology, 33,* 2519–2526.

Sherman, R. A., & Arena, J. G. (1992). Biofeedback in the assessment and treatment of low back pain. In J. Basmajian & R. Nyberg (Eds.), *Spinal manipulative therapies* (pp. 177–197). New York, NY: Williams & Wilkins.

Silberstein, S. D., & Lipton, R. B. (2000). Chronic daily headache. *Current Opinions in Neurology, 13,* 277–283.

Smidt, N., de Vet, H. C. W., Bouter, L. M., & Dekker, J. (2006). Effectiveness of exercise therapy: A best evidence summary of systematic reviews. *Australian Journal of Physiotherapy, 51,* 71–85.

Smith, J. C. (1990). *Cognitive behavioral relaxation training: A new system of strategies for treatment and assessment.* New York, NY: Springer Publishing Company.

Smitherman, T. A., Penzien, D. B., & Rains, J. C. (2007). Challenges of nonpharmacologic interventions in chronic tension-type headache. *Current Pain and Headache reports, 11,* 471–477.

Sobel, D. S. (1995). Mind matters, money matters: The cost effectiveness of clinical behavioral medicine. *Mental Medicine Update, 2,* 1–8.

Stetter, F., & Kupper, S. (2002). Autogenic training: A meta-analysis of clinical outcome studies. *Applied Psychophysiology and Biofeedback, 27,* 45–98.

Sullivan, M. J., Feuerstein, M., Gatchel, R., Linton, S. J., & Pransky, G. (2005). Integrating psychosocial and behavioral interventions to achieve optimal rehabilitation outcomes. *Journal of Occupational Rehabilitation, 15,* 475–489.

Tang, N. K., & Crane, C. (2006). Suicidality in chronic pain: a review of the prevalence, risk factors and psychological links. *Psychological Medicine, 36,* 575–586.

Tasto, D. L., & Hinkle, J. E. (1973). Muscle relaxation treatment for tension headaches. *Behaviour Research and Therapy, 11,* 347–349.

Taylor, N. F., Dodd, K. J., Shields, N., & Bruder, A. (2007). Therapeutic exercise in physiotherapy practice is beneficial: A summary of systematic reviews. *The Australian Journal of Physiotherapy, 53,* 7–16.

Teasell, R. W., & White, K. (1994). Clinical approaches to low back pain: Part 1. Epidemiology, diagnosis, and prevention. *Canadian Family Physician, 40,* 481–486.

Trent, J. T. (1982). Cognitive relaxation as a treatment of chronic pain: A single case experiment. *American Journal of Clinical Biofeedback, 5,* 59–64.

Turner, J. A. (1982). Comparison of group progressive-relaxation training and cognitive-behavioral group therapy for chronic low back pain. *Journal of Consulting and Clinical Psychology, 50,* 757–765.

Turner, J. A., & Aaron, L. A. (2001). Pain-related catastrophizing: What is it? *Clinical Journal of Pain, 17,* 65–71.

Turner, J. A., Jensen, M. P., & Romano, J. M. (2000). Do beliefs, coping and catastrophizing independently predict functioning in patients with chronic pain? *Pain, 85,* 115–125.

Turk, D. C., Swanson, K. S., & Tunks, E. R. (2008). Psychological approaches in the treatment of chronic pain patients—When pills, scalpels, and needles are not enough. *Canadian Journal of Psychiatry, 35,* 213–223.

Türp, J., Jokstad, A., Motschall, E., Schindler, H., Windecker-Gétaz, I., & Ettlin, D. (2007). Is there superiority of multimodal as opposed to simple therapy in patients with temporomandibular disorders? A quantitative, systematic review of the literature. *Clinical Oral Implants Research, 18*(Suppl. 3), 138–150.

Van Koulil, S., Effting, M., Kraaimaat, F., van Lankveld, W., van Helmond, T., Cats, H., . . . Evers, A. (2007). Cognitive–behavioural therapies and exercise programmes for patients with fibromyalgia: State of the art and future directions. *Annals of the Rheumatic Diseases, 66,* 571–581.

Van Tulder, M., Koes, B., & Malmivaara, A. (2006). Outcome of non-invasive treatment modalities on back pain: An evidenced-based review. *European Spine Journal, 15,* S64–S81.

Vlaeyen, J. W. S., De Jong, J. R., Onghena, P., Kerckhoffs-Hansen, M., & Kole-Snijders, A. M. (2002). Can pain-related fear be reduced? The application of cognitive-behavioural exposure in vivo. *Pain Research Management, 7,* 144–153.

Vlaeyen, J. W. S., and Linton, S. J. (2000). Fear-avoidance and its consequences in chronic musculoskeletal pain: A state of the art. *Pain, 85,* 317–332.

Wheeler, A. H. (2007). Pathophysiology of chronic back pain. Retrieved from www.emedicine.com/neuro/topic516.htm.

Wood, P. H. N., & Bradley, E. M. (1980). Epidemiology of low back pain. In M. I. Jayson (Ed.), *The lumbar spine and back pain* (pp. 13–17). London, England: Pitman.

26

Hypochondriasis and Health-Related Anxiety

STEVEN TAYLOR, DEAN MCKAY, AND JONATHAN S. ABRAMOWITZ

OVERVIEW OF DISORDER

Health anxiety occurs when a person interprets bodily changes, sensations, or other stimuli (e.g., medical test results) as suggesting that his or her health is in jeopardy. Health anxiety can be adaptive, especially if it motivates the person to obtain appropriate medical care. However, health anxiety can also be excessive; that is, disproportionate to the degree of health-related threat. Excessive health anxiety is associated with many different disorders, such as panic disorder, obsessive-compulsive disorder, illness phobia, and hypochondriasis. The focus of the present chapter is on health anxiety as it occurs in both the full and sub-syndromal (abridged) forms of hypochondriasis. We begin with a description of the clinical features of hypochondriasis, followed by a short review of the research on the etiology of the disorder. The major forms of treatment are described, followed by a review of treatment outcome findings. We also examine the limited research on prognostic indicators, and raise a number of considerations for improving treatment outcome. We conclude by offering evidence-based guidelines for treatment selection.

CLINICAL FEATURES OF HYPOCHONDRIASIS

Diagnostic Criteria and Other Key Features

Although hypochondriasis is currently conceptualized as a somatoform disorder in *DSM-IV* (American Psychiatric Association [APA], 2000), anxiety is such a prominent feature that it has been argued that hypochondriasis should be reclassified as an anxiety disorder (Mayou, Kirmayer, Simon, Kroenke, & Sharpe, 2005). Hypochondriasis is characterized by a preoccupation with fears of having, or the idea that one has, a serious disease, based on a misinterpretation of bodily sensations (APA, 2000). The focus of the person's health-related concerns can be highly specific (e.g., shortness of breath), or the concerns may be vague, variable, and generalized (e.g., diffuse bodily aching) (Barsky & Klerman, 1983). Preoccupation persists despite appropriate medical evaluation and reassurance from physicians. To diagnose hypochondriasis, the beliefs that one has a serious disease cannot be delusional or restricted to a specific concern about appearance, and they must be markedly distressing or associated with interference in daily functioning. Symptoms must persist for at least six months and cannot be better accounted for by another disorder. Hypochondriasis with poor insight is specified if, for most of the time, the individual fails to recognize that his or her concerns are excessive or unreasonable (APA, 2000).

Excessive health anxiety is typically accompanied by repetitive reassurance-seeking behavior, whereby the person looks for repeated affirmation from others (e.g., family physicians, family members) that there is nothing wrong with his or her health. Receiving reassurance provides short-term relief from health anxiety. However, the effects are transient, typically lasting no more than 24 hours (Haenen, de Jong, Schmidt, Stevens, & Visser, 2000). In fact, reassurance seeking appears to perpetuate severe health anxiety in the long term (Taylor & Asmundson, 2004; H. M. Warwick & Salkovskis, 1990), as discussed later in this chapter. Other common behavioral reactions include recurrent bodily checking (e.g., frequent breast self-examinations; repeated palpation of internal lumps or external abrasions), checking medical textbooks or the Internet for information about dreaded diseases, using self-administered medical tests (e.g., home kits for measuring blood pressure), and consuming various kinds of mainstream and alternative medicines (e.g., herbal preparations) (Eastin & Guinsler, 2006; Taylor & Asmundson, 2004).

People with excessive health anxiety may perpetually adopt a sick role, living as invalids and avoiding all effortful activities. They may complain persistently about their health, discussing their concerns at great length with anyone who will listen. This can lead to strained relationships with their family, friends, and physicians. Frustration on the part of physician and patient are not uncommon. Doctor shopping—visiting many different physicians in the hope of finding help—is often the result. This puts people with excessive health anxiety at risk of unnecessary or repeated medical and surgical treatments, some of which can produce adverse side effects or treatment complications (e.g., scarring and pain from exploratory surgery). Thus, health anxiety can be worsened by iatrogenic (physician-induced) factors (Taylor & Asmundson, 2004).

Abridged Hypochondriasis

Health anxiety can be clinically important even when the person does not meet full diagnostic criteria for hypochondriasis. This is known as abridged hypochondriasis (Gureje, Üstün, & Simon, 1997), which may be associated with clinically significant distress and impairment (Creed, 2006; Martin & Jacobi, 2006). Examples of abridged hypochondriasis include: (a) recurrent episodes of excessive health anxiety, with each episode lasting less than six months; (b) persistent, excessive health anxiety that undermines the person's quality of life but does not significantly interfere with daily functioning; (c) a period of excessive health anxiety, lasting longer than 6 months, that eventually responds to medical reassurance; and (d) mild health anxiety (i.e., insufficiently severe or debilitating to meet criteria for hypochondriasis) that persists for years (Barsky, Cleary, Sarnie, & Klerman, 1993; Fink et al., 2004; Taylor & Asmundson, 2004). Throughout this chapter, we use the term *excessive health anxiety* to refer to both full and abridged forms of hypochondriasis.

Diagnostic Controversies

Hypochondriasis is part of the somatoform disorders, which includes somatization disorder, conversion disorder, body dysmorphic disorder, and pain disorder. While all four are associated with excessive concerns over health, physical features, or physical experiences, there is limited research on factors that discriminate among them. In fact, there is considerable controversy over diagnostic criteria for all the conditions in the somatoform disorder cluster (Kroenke, 2007b). Controversy over the classification of somatoform disorders emerged shortly after the publication of the *DSM-IV*. According to Kroenke, Sharpe, and Sykes (2007), there are several important areas that require clarification for somatoform disorders as the next edition of the *DSM* is prepared. One of the central arguments involves use of the terms hypochondriasis, somatoform, and somatization, as these diagnostic labels are typically rejected by patients, leading to treatment resistance.

Another problematic aspect of the somatoform disorders involves heterogeneity of the class of disorders it covers. For example, some medical conditions (e.g., fibromyalgia) have frequently co-occurring somatoform diagnoses (e.g., pain disorder). Revisions to the *DSM* should include acknowledgement of this overlap, and reclassify several of the existing somatoform disorders into other categories that account for a prominent real medical etiology that is associated with significant somatic complaints (Kroenke et al., 2007). It has been suggested that such heterogeneity, and the problem of comorbid medical conditions of varying etiology, has lead to moderate treatment effects when studies of therapy are aggregated (Schweickhardt, Larisch, & Fritzsche, 2005).

At this point, there does not appear to be an emerging consensus of how to best reorganize the classification system for somatoform disorders. However, there are some encouraging signs that, although categories within somatoform disorders are problematic (Riel & Rojas, 2007), cognitive behavior therapies for all somatoform disorders have a benefit on anxiety and depression, and reduce medical costs (Kroenke, 2007a).

Prevalence, Course, and Costs

The research generally indicates that excessive health anxiety is equally common among women and men (Creed & Barsky, 2004). Full hypochondriasis has a lifetime prevalence in the general population of 1%–5%, and is found in 2%–7% of primary care outpatients (APA, 2000). It is thought that abridged hypochondriasis is more common than the full-blown disorder (Kirmayer & Robbins, 1991; Looper & Kirmayer, 2001), although lifetime prevalence of abridged hypochondriasis is unknown.

Excessive health anxiety typically develops in early adulthood (APA, 2000), often when the person is under stress, seriously ill or recovering from serious illness, or has suffered the loss of a family member (Barsky & Klerman, 1983). Excessive health anxiety can occur or be exacerbated when a person is exposed to disease-related media information via the popular media or medical information resources (Taylor & Asmundson, 2004). Excessive health anxiety is often chronic and frequently comorbid with anxiety and mood disorders as well as somatization disorder (APA, 2000).

It is unclear whether prevalence of excessive health anxiety varies with age. Research conducted to date has been based largely on cross sectional (cohort) studies, the results of which have been mixed. Some studies suggest that health anxiety is greater in older than younger people (Altamura, Carta, Tacchini, Musazzi, & Pioli, 1998; Gureje et al., 1997; Verhaak, Meijer, Visser, & Wolters, 2006), whereas other research has found no difference between age groups (Barsky, Frank, Cleary, Wyshak, & Klerman, 1991). Longitudinal studies are needed to further examine if and how health anxiety changes with age.

People with excessive health anxiety typically present to their physicians with medically unexplained symptoms. That is, these are complaints of bodily sensations or alterations for which no disease process can be found, despite adequate medical investigation. People with excessive health anxiety, compared to people without this problem, are more likely to visit to primary care physicians and specialists, to have medical laboratory tests and investigative surgical procedures, to have greater physical limitations, to take more days of bed rest, and to be subsisting on disability benefits (Barsky, Ettner, Horsky, & Bates, 2001; Escobar et al., 1998; Hollifield, Paine, Tuttle, & Kellner, 1999). Consequently, excessive health anxiety is a considerable economic burden on the health-care system. According to one estimate, the total health-care costs in the United States attributable to medically unexplained symptoms, after adjusting for the presence of comorbid psychiatric disorders, is $256 billion annually (Barsky, Orav, & Bates, 2006).

ETIOLOGY OF EXCESSIVE HEALTH ANXIETY

The cognitive model of excessive health anxiety (Salkovskis, Warwick, & Deale, 2003; H. M. C. Warwick & Salkovskis, 2001) is currently considered to be the most promising way of understanding the disorder (Marcus, Gurley, Marchi, & Bauer, 2007; Taylor & Asmundson, 2004). The model proposes excessive health anxiety arises from dysfunctional beliefs about sickness, health, and health care, including beliefs that lead the person to misinterpret the significance and dangerousness of benign bodily changes and sensations. Benign bodily changes and sensations arise from any number of sources, including harmless perturbations in physiological processes, minor diseases, and autonomic arousal associated with anxiety or other emotional states. The human body is noisy; bodily sensations are daily or weekly occurrences even for healthy people (Pennebaker, 1982). For the most part, these sensations are mild or transient, and not associated with disease. However, dangerousness of these sensations tends to be overestimated by people with excessive health anxiety.

According to the cognitive model, dysfunctional beliefs persist because of the way the person interprets health-related behavior. People with excessive health anxiety typically experience many health-related false alarms, where their frightening bodily sensations turn out to be innocuous. Instead of disconfirming beliefs that one's health is at risk, the experience is interpreted in a manner that is consistent with the dysfunctional belief. For example, the person may reason that just because a bodily sensation turned out to be benign today does not preclude the possibility that at some point in the future the same sensation could be due to a serious disease ("I was lucky this time, next time it could be serious"). Dysfunctional beliefs also persist because the person engages in maladaptive coping behaviors in a misguided attempt to allay their fears. Among the most important of the maladaptive coping behaviors are persistent reassurance seeking and repetitive health-related checking. Such behaviors appear to persist because they are associated with short-term reduction in anxiety (Lucock, White, Peake, & Morley, 1998). In the longer term, they can perpetuate health anxiety because they prevent the dysfunctional beliefs from being disconfirmed and, in fact, can provide spurious confirmatory evidence for the beliefs. For example, repeatedly palpating a lymph node to check for swelling presumed to be indicative of cancer will actually lead to swelling and tenderness which, in turn, may be misinterpreted as evidence of cancer. Repeatedly seeking and receiving reassurance can also prolong preoccupation with illness by extending the amount of time individuals spend discussing their health, and by exposing them to alarming information about rare but lethal medical conditions.

Consistent with the cognitive model, research generally suggests that people with excessive health anxiety, compared to controls, are more likely to (a) report experiencing a lot of bodily sensations, but are no better at detecting their occurrence; (b) interpret bodily sensations as indicators of poor health or serious disease; (c) believe that good health is associated with few or no bodily sensations; (d) believe that they are weak and unable to tolerate stress; (e) overestimate the probability of contracting diseases; (f) overestimate the dangerousness of diseases; and (g) selectively attend to, dwell on, and recall health-related information (Marcus et al., 2007; Taylor & Asmundson, 2004). Also consistent with the cognitive model is behavioral-genetic research indicating the environmental factors that account for most (63%–90%) of the variance in scores on measures of health anxiety (Taylor, Thordarson, Jang, & Asmundson, 2006). Important environmental factors include early learning experiences (e.g., episodes of actual illness, receiving treats or other reinforcements only when sick, observing how significant others cope with illness) that lead one to acquire dysfunctional beliefs about health and disease (Taylor & Asmundson, 2004).

DESCRIPTION OF TREATMENTS

Early treatments for excessive health anxiety, such as psychodynamic psychotherapy, were considered to be largely ineffective (Knight, 1941; Ladee, 1966). During the 1960s and 1970s, however, there were promising developments in behavioral treatments, which were refined in the 1980s and 1990s into empirically supported cognitive behavioral interventions. During the 1980s and 1990s, there were also some encouraging developments in pharmacotherapy for excessive health anxiety.

General Features of Treatment

Treatment of excessive health anxiety, whether psychosocial or pharmacologic in nature, is conducted in the context of good medical management. Primary care physicians play an important role in encouraging patients to try a course of cognitive behavior therapy (CBT) or pharmacotherapy. All treatments include nonspecific factors (e.g., therapist warmth and empathy) along with some form of psychoeducation. A typical course of cognitive behavioral treatment or pharmacotherapy

lasts 12–16 weeks in treatment studies, and typically longer in routine clinical practice, depending on the nature and severity of the patient's problems. Booster sessions are also offered, as needed.

CBT and Related Treatments

There are several interventions that are similar to, or overlap with, one another: Psychoeducation, explanatory therapy, cognitive therapy, exposure and response prevention, CBT, and behavioral stress management. Table 26.1 summarizes the components of these interventions.

Psychoeducation. This involves provision of information about the nature of health anxiety and its treatment. Specific content depends on the type of treatment that the patient receives. If treatment is based on the cognitive model, for example, then psychoeducation involves the following: (a) information about the role of thoughts in producing health anxiety; (b) information on the role of selective attention in health anxiety; (c) education on the role of checking, reassurance seeking, avoidance, and other maladaptive behaviors in perpetuating health anxiety; (d) information on the role of stress in producing bodily sensations; and (e) cognitive restructuring exercises (Bouman, 2002). The *noisy body* analogy is often used as part of psychoeducation. Here, patients are educated about how people, even healthy people, have noisy bodies and that harmless bodily sensations are common even among healthy people. Thus, troubling bodily sensations are relabeled as harmless bodily noise rather than indications of disease. Psychoeducation differs from the provision of reassurance in that the patient is presented with new information. By comparison, provision of reassurance involves the repeated presentation of old information (e.g., reminding the patient each week that they are healthy, or repeatedly performing medical tests to placate the patient).

Explanatory therapy. This treatment includes a number of interventions intended to

TABLE 26.1   Cognitive Behavioral and Related Treatments for Hypochondriasis

Components	Psycho Education	Explanatory Therapy	Cognitive Therapy	Exposure and Response Prevention	Cognitive Behavior Therapy	Behavioral Stress Management
Thorough medical and psychiatric evaluation	+	+	+	+	+	+
Nonspecific treatment factors (e.g., therapist attention, warmth, and empathy)	+	+	+	+	+	+
Detailed education about the causes of bodily sensations and health anxiety	+	+	+	+	+	+
Monitoring of bodily sensations, emotions, and thoughts	+	+	+	+	+	+
Extensive use of cognitive restructuring exercises	−	−	+	−	+	+
Systematic exposure exercises	−	−	−	+	+	+
Relaxation training	+	−	−	−	+/−	+
Assertiveness training	−	−	−	−	−	+
Stimulus control exercises for reducing worry	−	−	−	−	−	+
Time management training	−	−	−	−	−	+
Provision of repeated assurance that patient does not have a serious disease	−	+	−	−	−	−

+ Intervention used
− not used
+/− sometimes used

Source: From "Current Directions in the Treatment of Hypochondriasis," by S. Taylor, G. J. G. Asmundson, and M. J. Coons, 2005, *Journal of Cognitive Psychotherapy, 19*, pp. 291–310. Reprinted by permission of Springer Publishing.

persuade patients that there is nothing wrong with their physical health (Kellner, 1979, 1992). Treatment involves repeated physical examinations, performed whenever the patient requests one, or when the patient reports new bodily concerns. Patients are also repeatedly told that there is nothing physically wrong with them, and are sometimes given anxiolytic medication if they are anxious. Explanatory therapy is, therefore, based primarily on reassurance and psychoeducation.

A major concern with explanatory therapy concerns the use of reassurance. Many clinical investigators consider it counterproductive to repeatedly tell the patient that there is nothing wrong with them (e.g., Barsky, 1996; Taylor & Asmundson, 2004; H. M. Warwick & Salkovskis,

1985). Patients with excessive health anxiety typically fail to benefit from reassurance (APA, 2000). Persistently offering reassurance may encourage the patient to be dependent on the advice of the therapist. It would be preferable to teach patients to assure themselves about the meaning and significance of their bodily concerns. Research using single case designs has shown that excessive health anxiety persists when patients receive reassurance and abates when reassurance seeking is discouraged (Salkovskis & Warwick, 1986). Given these concerns, explanatory therapy is not widely used today as a treatment for excessive health anxiety.

Exposure and response prevention. Common features of excessive health anxiety include fear and avoidance of stimuli that the person associates with disease. Accordingly, clinicians have combined various forms of exposure therapy to reduce excessive health anxiety: in vivo exposure (e.g., exposure to hospitals, doctors for patients who fear these disease-related stimuli), interoceptive exposure (e.g., physical exercises to induce feared bodily sensations such as rapid heartbeat), and imaginal exposure (e.g., imagining fearful scenarios, such as the development of cancer). Exposure is conducted within treatment sessions and as homework assignments. Response prevention is combined with exposure in order to encourage the patient to delay or refrain from checking and reassurance seeking.

CBT and behavioral stress management. These interventions begin with psychoeducation. CBT also involves cognitive restructuring and behavioral exercises. Cognitive restructuring is used, for example, to examine beliefs about the meaning of bodily sensations. Behavioral exercises are used to further test beliefs and to highlight the unhelpful effects of maladaptive coping behaviors. For example, to test the effects of reassurance seeking or bodily checking, the patient could be encouraged to refrain from these behaviors for a period of time. Once patients refrain from reassurance seeking, they often find that they are less preoccupied with their health, and feel less vulnerable, because they are not exposed to daily reminders of morbidity and mortality. Alternatively, the patient could be instructed to increase checking or reassurance seeking. Typically, this leads to an increase in health-related preoccupation and distress, and thereby helps teach the person about the counterproductive nature of persistent checking and reassurance seeking (Taylor & Asmundson, 2004).

Behavioral stress management emphasizes the role of stress in producing harmless but unpleasant bodily sensations. The patient is encouraged to practice various stress management exercises (e.g., relaxation training, time management, problem solving) as a means of managing stress. This reduces the bodily sensations that fuel hypochondriacal concerns. Behavioral stress management was originally developed as a control condition (controlling, for example, nonspecific treatment factors) in a randomized controlled study comparing CBT, behavioral stress management, and a wait-list control (Clark et al., 1998). Although planned as a control condition, behavioral stress management proved to be useful in reducing health anxiety, as discussed later in this chapter.

Pharmacotherapies

The two most widely used classes of medication in the treatment of excessive health anxiety are tricyclic antidepressants and selective serotonin reuptake inhibitors. The doses of these and other agents, as used in clinical studies of excessive health anxiety, are as follows: Clomipramine (25–225 mg/day), imipramine (125–150 mg/day), fluoxetine (20–80 mg/day), fluvoxamine (300 mg/day), paroxetine (up to 60 mg/day), duloxetine (120 mg/day), and nefazodone (200–500 mg/day) (Greeven et al., 2007; Politi & Emanuele, 2007; Taylor & Asmundson, 2004). Nefazodone was withdrawn from the market in 2003 due to its hepatotoxic effects.

CASE STUDIES AND UNCONTROLLED TRIALS

CBT and Related Treatments

An open trial of group psychoeducation suggested that this intervention is associated with a reduction in health anxiety (Bouman, 2002). For treatment completers, the intervention was associated with reductions in health anxiety along with a mean reduction of 40% in the frequency of medical service utilization (as indicated by a comparison of the frequency of doctor visits 6 months before vs. 6 months after treatment).

One case study and an uncontrolled trial suggest that explanatory therapy can reduce excessive health anxiety (Kellner, 1982; Romanik & Kellner, 1985). However, it remains to be investigated whether inclusion of reassurance in this treatment is helpful or harmful. The benefits of explanatory therapy may be primarily due to the use of psychoeducation.

Case studies and uncontrolled trials further suggest that excessive health anxiety is reduced by exposure and response prevention (Logsdail, Lovell, Warwick, & Marks, 1991; Visser & Bouman, 1992; H. M. Warwick & Marks, 1988) and by CBT (Furer, Walker, & Freeston, 2001; House, 1989; D. Miller, Acton, & Hedge, 1988; Stern & Fernandez, 1991). The treatments, in these and other studies, were administered in either individual (one-to-one) or group formats. It is not known whether the formats differ in efficacy or patient acceptability. Bouman's (2002) clinical impression is that group treatment for excessive health anxiety can foster a sense of acceptance and social support.

Pharmacotherapies

Case studies and a small number of open trials suggest that the following medications can be helpful in reducing excessive health anxiety: Clomipramine (Kamlana & Gray, 1988; Stone, 1993), imipramine (Lippert, 1986; Wesner & Noyes, 1991), fluoxetine (e.g., Fallon et al., 1996; Viswanathan & Paradis, 1991), fluvoxamine (e.g., Fallon et al., 2003), paroxetine (Oosterbaan, van Balkom, van Boeijen, de Meij, & van Dyck, 2001), and duloxetine (Politi & Emanuele, 2007). Little is known about the long-term effects. There have been reports of patients relapsing when medications are discontinued (e.g., Viswanathan & Paradis, 1991). Moreover, in some cases, health anxiety worsens during drug treatment, as patients become alarmed by side effects like gastrointestinal discomfort (Fallon, 2001; Oosterbaan et al., 2001).

RANDOMIZED CONTROLLED TRIALS

CBT and Related Treatments

There have been several randomized controlled trials in which cognitive behavioral and related treatments were compared to a wait-list control or to one another. Two studies have compared group psychoeducation to a wait-list control (Avia et al., 1996; Lidbeck, 1997). Using a mixed sample of participants with full and abridged hypochondriasis, Avia et al. (1996) found that psychoeducation led to significant reductions in illness fears and attitudes, somatic symptoms, and dysfunctional beliefs. Gains were maintained at 1-year follow-up. There was little change in the wait-list control. Lidbeck's (1997) group psychoeducation was administered to patients with medically unexplained symptoms, most of whom had hypochondriacal features (full or abridged hypochondriasis). Psychoeducation emphasized the role of stress in producing bodily sensations, and included relaxation training. Treatment completers tended to report reductions in somatic complaints and health anxiety. There were no changes in the wait-list control.

Buwalda, Bouman, and van Duijn (2006) compared two 6-week psychoeducational courses for full hypochondriasis; one based on the cognitive behavioral approach (as described earlier) and the other based on a problem-solving approach (similar to behavioral stress management). Both interventions were associated with a reduction in hypochondriasis features, depression, and trait anxiety, with gains maintained at 6-month follow-up. There were no significant differences in the efficacy of the interventions.

One wait-list controlled study of patients with full hypochondriasis suggests that explanatory therapy can reduce health anxiety (Fava, Grandi, Rafanelli, Fabbri, & Cazzaro, 2000). Other wait-list controlled studies of hypochondriasis have shown that the following treatments are effective in reducing health anxiety: exposure and response prevention (Visser & Bouman, 2001), CBT (Clark et al., 1998; H. M. C. Warwick, Clark, Cobb, & Salkovskis, 1996), and behavioral stress management (Clark et al., 1998). CBT is also more effective than treatment as usual, delivered mainly by primary care physicians (Barsky & Ahern, 2004). Treatment-related benefits in these studies were maintained at follow-ups ranging from 3 to 12 months.

Studies comparing different treatment packages have found few differences in terms of efficacy and patient acceptability. This includes studies comparing the following treatments: (a) exposure and response prevention versus cognitive therapy (Bouman & Visser, 1998), (b) exposure and response prevention versus CBT (Visser & Bouman, 2001), (c) CBT versus behavioral stress management (Clark et al., 1998), and (d) CBT versus paroxetine (Greeven et al., 2007). All of these treatments were associated with reductions in the various facets of hypochondriasis, including anxiety, somatic symptoms, dysfunctional beliefs, reassurance seeking, and checking. The treatments were also associated with reductions in depression.

An advantage of CBT over the related treatments is that it has been evaluated in a larger number of randomized controlled trials, and so has a stronger empirical foundation.

Moreover, in the studies comparing CBT to other treatments, the few differences that have emerged have tended to favor CBT. Clark et al. (1998), for example, found that CBT was more effective than behavioral stress management at posttreatment, although there was no difference at 12 month follow up. Greeven et al. (2007) found that for some outcome variables, there was a slight (but mostly statistically nonsignificant) advantage of CBT over paroxetine. For example, for classification of treatment responders (defined by at least a 1 SD reduction in health anxiety, as assessed by questionnaire), the percentage of responses tended to favor CBT. Completer analysis: CBT (54% responders), paroxetine

(38%), placebo (12%). Intent-to-treat analysis: CBT (45%), paroxetine (30%), and placebo (14%).

Pharmacotherapies

At the time of writing this chapter (September, 2008), there had only been two published placebo-controlled drug studies of excessive health anxiety (Fallon et al., 1996; Greeven et al., 2007). The full report of the Fallon et al. study has not yet been published, but the 1996 interim report stated that 20 patients with full hypochondriasis were randomized either to fluoxetine or placebo. There was no significant difference in the proportion of responders in either condition, although there were trends favoring fluoxetine. For patients completing 12 weeks of treatment, 80% of fluoxetine patients were classified as responders, compared to 60% of placebo patients. Fallon's more recent results, based on an increased sample size, apparently indicate that fluoxetine is superior to placebo, both in terms of outcome after 12 weeks and at 9 month follow up (B. A. Fallon, personal communication, September 10, 2002).

Greeven et al. (2007) compared 16 weeks of treatment with either CBT, paroxetine, or pill placebo. As noted earlier, CBT and paroxetine were equally effective. Both were significantly more effective at reducing hypochondriasis (and depression) than pill placebo. Unfortunately, outcome in the Greeven et al. study outcome was assessed only at posttreatment; no follow up assessment was reported. Previous studies suggest that treatment gains are maintained for CBT at follow up (e.g., Clark et al., 1998), whereas there have been some reports of patients relapsing when their medications are discontinued (as previously noted). This suggests that any advantages of CBT over medication may be especially apparent at follow up, when patients have discontinued their medications. Further research is needed to investigate this possibility.

META-ANALYTIC RESEARCH

At the time of writing there has been only one published meta-analysis of psychosocial and pharmacologic treatments for hypochondriasis (Taylor, Asmundson, & Coons, 2005). Twenty-five trials from 15 studies contained sufficient data for the purpose of computing pre-post effect sizes (Cohen's *d* for treatment completers) on self-report measures of hypochondriasis and/or for assessing the proportion of treatment dropouts. Participants in these studies had either full or abridged hypochondriasis. Patients in drug trials were on medication at the time of the posttreatment assessment. Treatment durations were typically between 6 and 12 weeks, and psychosocial treatments typically involved about 12 hours of therapy contact.

Table 26.2 summarizes the main results for each of the treatments included in the meta-analysis. As the table shows, there were few trials per treatment condition and samples sizes per trial tended to be small. Accordingly, results need to be interpreted with caution. The effect sizes for the treatments listed in the table were all larger than the effect size for wait-list control. CBT and fluoxetine tended to yield the largest effects, and these were broadly similar to one another. Cognitive therapy, CBT, and behavioral stress management tended to have the lowest proportions of dropouts.

For studies using mixed samples of full and abridged hypochondriasis, the results suggested that psychoeducation and CBT had similar effect sizes (0.74 vs. 0.51), which were larger than wait-list (0.19) and medical care from a primary care physician (0.20). For this mixed group of full and abridged hypochondriasis, psychoeducation tended to have a lower proportion of dropouts than CBT (2 vs. 13%).

In terms of follow-up data, pretreatment to follow-up effect sizes for measures of hypochondriasis could not be calculated for drug studies because follow-ups were not conducted. For studies reporting follow-up data (3–12 months), results indicated that CBT had the largest effect sizes in studies of full hypochondriasis, and psychoeducation and CBT had the largest effects in studies of mixed, full, and abridged hypochondriasis. When treatment effect size, attrition, breadth of effects on outcome measures, and durability of effects are taken into consideration, the results suggest that CBT is the treatment of choice for full hypochondriasis.

Psychoeducation and CBT are efficacious for comparatively milder samples (i.e., samples including patients with abridged hypochondriasis).

There were insufficient data to include other treatments in the meta-analysis, such as psychodynamic psychotherapies. There was also insufficient information to assess the merits of treatment modality (group vs. individual) and treatment setting (e.g., mental health clinic vs. community or general medical settings). Group treatment may be more economical, and treatments based outside of mental health settings may be less stigmatizing. The merits of combining drug and psychosocial treatments also remain to be investigated. Given the pattern of results in Table 26.2, it would be particularly important to see whether outcome is improved when CBT is combined with serotonergic medication. Combination treatments might be especially useful for very severe hypochondriasis.

CONSENSUS PANEL RECOMMENDATIONS

To our knowledge there have been no published consensus panel recommendations concerning the treatment of health anxiety. However, there is a consensus among clinical investigators that cognitive behavioral interventions are the most efficacious treatments available, although there is ample room for improving treatment acceptability and efficacy (Salkovskis et al., 2003; Stuart, Noyes, Starcevic, & Barsky, 2008; Taylor & Asmundson, 2004).

TABLE 20.2 Meta-Analysis of Comparative Efficacy of Treatments for Hypochondriasis

Treatment Groups	No. Trials	Mean No. Treatment Completers	Mean Treatment Duration Weeks	Mean No. Therapy Hours	Mean % Dropout	Mean Follow-up Duration (Months)	Mean Pre-post Effect Size: Hypochon.	Mean Pre-follow-up Effect Size: Hypochon.	Mean Pre-post Effect Size: Anxiety	Mean Pre-post Effect Size: Depression
Studies of hypochondriasis patients										
Control conditions										
				–	0	–	0.29	–	0.23	0.10
				–	25	–	–	–	–	–
Psychosocial treatments										
				12	22	6	1.05	1.27	0.08	0.89
				4	16	6	0.91	0.88	–	–
				12	11	1	0.83	0.96	–	0.37
				12	14	4	1.00	1.19	–	0.42
				15	10	–	2.05	1.74	1.90	1.36
				15	4	12	1.59	1.25	1.75	1.44
Drug treatments										
				–	18	–	1.34	–	–	–
				–	15	–	1.92	–	–	–
				–	21	–	–	–	–	–
				–	18	–	1.07	–	–	1.01

(*Continued*)

TABLE 26.2 Meta-Analysis of Comparative Efficacy of Treatments for Hypochondriasis (*Continued*)

Treatment Condition	No. Trials	Mean No. Treatment Completers	Mean Treatment Duration (Weeks)	Mean No. Therapy Hours	Mean % Dropout	Mean Follow-up Duration (Months)	Mean Pre-post Effect Size: Hypochon.	Mean Pre-follow-up Effect Size: Hypochon.	Mean Pre-post Effect Size: Anxiety	Mean Pre-post Effect Size: Depression
Studies of mixed samples: Full and abridged Hypochondriasis										
Wait-list control	1	17	8	–	0	3	0.19	0.18	0.00	0.03
Optimized medical care*	1	40	21	–	0	6	0.20	0.30	0.02	−0.06
Psychoeducation	2	23	7	17	2	8	0.74	0.87	0.19	0.05
Cognitive behavior therapy	1	39	21	21	13	6	0.51	0.61	0.31	0.41

*Consisting of routine medical care administered by primary care physician who received extra training to identify psychiatric disorders

—: not applicable or not reported

Source: From "Current Directions in the Treatment of Hypochondriasis," by S. Taylor, G. J. G. Asmundson, and M. J. Coons, *Journal of Cognitive Psychotherapy, 19,* pp. 291–310. Reprinted by permission of Springer Publishing.

PREDICTING TREATMENT OUTCOME

The research reviewed earlier suggests that for mild (abridged) forms of hypochondriasis, psychoeducation may be sufficient, delivered either by the primary care physician or in the form of educational courses. If that does not prove effective, or if the patient has full hypochondriasis, then more intensive interventions could be considered, such as CBT or serotonergic medications.

Not all patients with full hypochondriasis benefit equally from a given form of therapy. Regardless of the type of treatment, the following are the most reliably identified predictors of good outcome, as obtained from a variety of sources (e.g., APA, 2000; Barsky, Fama, Bailey, & Ahern, 1998; Hiller, Leibbrand, Rief, & Fichter, 2002): Hypochondriasis that is mild, short lived, and not associated with complicating factors such as personality disorders, comorbid general medical conditions, or contingencies (secondary gains) that reinforce health anxiety or sick role behavior. In other words, a good prognosis is associated with the milder forms of hypochondriasis, and the absence of complicating factors. (See Taylor & Asmundson, 2004, for a detailed review.) Such findings underscore the importance of findings ways of improving treatment outcome for severe cases.

Research is also needed to determine if a patient is more likely to benefit more from one treatment (e.g., pharmacotherapy) than another (e.g., CBT). If a patient has a strong preference for one type of treatment, then he or she may be more likely to drop out if allocated to a nonpreferred treatment. Evidence so far suggests that no form of treatment is inherently more acceptable to patients than other treatments. Walker, Vincent, Furer, Cox, and Kjernsted (1999) presented written descriptions of CBT and pharmacotherapy for intense illness worries to a community based sample of 23 treatment seeking people suffering from hypochondriasis. The descriptions outlined the time commitment and the major advantages

and disadvantages of each treatment. Most participants (74%) preferred CBT and almost half said they would only accept this treatment.

IMPROVING TREATMENT OUTCOME

Additional research on the efficacy of various treatment strategies, alone and in combination, is also required. In addition to further studies of cognitive behavioral and serotonergic treatments, researchers could also evaluate novel treatments for excessive health anxiety. Interpersonal psychotherapy has been shown to be effective in treating other disorders, such as major depression and bulimia nervosa (Nathan & Gorman, 2007). Stuart et al. (2008) suggested that this type of therapy, in combination with CBT, may be effective for excessive health anxiety, with a focus on the interpersonal consequences of health preoccupation. Methods from motivational enhancement therapy, which have been shown to be effective in treating substance use disorders (W. R. Miller & Rollnick, 2002), have been increasingly used in anxiety disorders, and may also be usefully integrated into cognitive behavioral treatment for hypochondriasis (Taylor & Asmundson, 2004). The merits of such possibilities remain to be empirically investigated.

Pharmacologic treatments also need to be further investigated. For example, studies of medications that show promise for enhancing the effects of behavioral treatment for anxiety disorders, such as D cycloserine (Norberg, Krystal, & Tolin, 2008), or augmenting strategies (e.g., combining serotonergic medications with atypical antipsychotics such as risperidone, Cottraux, Bouvard, & Milliery, 2005) are warranted. Another important area for improving treatment outcome involves treatment acceptability. Results from Barsky and Ahern's (2004) comparison of CBT versus treatment as usual, suggests that there is much room for improvement in this regard.

The treatment offered in this study was not attractive to many hypochondriacal patients.

and only 30% of those eligible entered the trial. Hypochondriacal individuals are by definition convinced of the medical nature of their condition and therefore psychosocial treatment seems nonsensical to them. Although a major problem, this should not detract from the fact that those patients who did undergo treatment benefited from it. And since hypochondriasis is a prevalent problem in ambulatory medical practice . . . this fraction of hypochondriacal patients still represents a sizeable population. The treatment must be made more attractive in the future by seamlessly integrating it into the primary care process and conducting it in the medical setting (as our treatment was not). (Barsky & Ahern, 2004, pp. 1469–1470)

Consistent with some of these recommendations, recent research suggests that CBT for hypochondriasis may be more acceptable for patients if it is delivered in a medical, rather than mental health, setting (Seivewright et al., 2008; Tyrer, Seivewright, & Behr, 1999).

Little is known about how treatment protocols need to be adapted or modified for special populations of health-anxious people, such as particular age groups, cultural groups, or groups with severe general medical conditions. Such individuals need to be considered on a case-by-case basis. For children with elevated health anxiety, interventions should be consistent with the child's developmental level (e.g., cognitive restructuring exercises would be simplified or omitted). For cognitively impaired (e.g., dementing) patients, simple contingency management programs that reinforce (reward) adaptive behaviors (e.g., talking about topics other than their health) but not maladaptive ones (e.g., reassurance seeking) might be most effective (Williamson, 1984).

CONCLUSIONS

Contemporary research suggests that there are effective methods for treating full and abridged hypochondriasis. For the latter

disorder, psychoeducation may be sufficient, delivered either by the primary care physician or in the form of educational courses. If that does not prove effective, or if the patient has full hypochondriasis, then more intensive interventions could be considered. To date, the treatment with the strongest base of empirical support is CBT. For patients with a strong preference for medication, preliminary evidence suggests that fluoxetine or paroxetine should be considered. However, it is unclear whether the gains from medications are maintained once drugs are discontinued. Research suggests that the gains from psychosocial treatments tend to be maintained at follow-ups of up to a year. Although the current psychosocial and pharmacologic treatments are often effective, they are far from completely efficacious. Further research is needed to develop ways of improving patient adherence and increasing treatment efficacy.

EVIDENCE-BASED PRACTICES

- When the quality and quantity of treatment research is considered, CBT emerges at the treatment with the strongest empirical basis for treating patients with full hypochondriasis.
- Psychoeducation may be sufficient for milder cases.
- Published psychotherapy research has only examined CBT and related treatments. There are no published studies on the effects of other treatments such as psychodynamic psychotherapy. CBT and related treatments are the only psychosocial interventions with empirical support.
- The relative benefits of group versus individual treatment are unknown.
- Preliminary evidence suggests that fluoxetine or paroxetine may be useful for treating full hypochondriasis.
- Long-term effects of medication, such relapse rates once medications are withdrawn, are unknown.

- The effects of combining CBT with medications are unknown.
- Little is known about the best way of selecting the type of treatment (e.g., CBT vs. medication) for a given patient. Patient preference, once they receive information about the nature and effects of the various treatments, is an important factor to consider.

REFERENCES

Altamura, A. C., Carta, M. G., Tacchini, G., Musazzi, A., & Pioli, M. R. (1998). Prevalence of somatoform disorders in a psychiatric population: An Italian nationwide survey. *European Archives of Psychiatry and Clinical Neuroscience, 248*, 267–271.

American Psychiatric Association. (2000). *Diagnostic and statistical manual of mental disorders* (4th ed.). Washington, DC: Author.

Avia, M. D., Ruiz, M. A., Olivares, M. E., Crespo, M., Guisado, A. B., Sanchez, A., . . . Varela, A. (1996). The meaning of psychological symptoms: Effectiveness of a group intervention with hypochondriacal patients. *Behaviour Research and Therapy, 34*, 23–31.

Barsky, A. J. (1996). Hypochondriasis: Medical management and psychiatric treatment. *Psychosomatics, 37*, 48–56.

Barsky, A. J., & Ahern, D. K. (2004). Cognitive behavior therapy for hypochondriasis: A randomized controlled trial. *Journal of the American Medical Association, 291*, 1464–1470.

Barsky, A. J., Cleary, P. D., Sarnie, M. K., & Klerman, G. L. (1993). The course of transient hypochondriasis. *American Journal of Psychiatry, 150*, 484–488.

Barsky, A. J., Ettner, S. L., Horsky, J., & Bates, D. W. (2001). Resource utilization of patients with hypochondriacal health anxiety and somatization. *Medical Care, 39*, 705–715.

Barsky, A. J., Fama, J. M., Bailey, E. D., & Ahern, D. K. (1998). A prospective 4- to 5-year study of DSM-III-R hypochondriasis. *Archives of General Psychiatry, 55*, 737–744.

Barsky, A. J., Frank, C. B., Cleary, P. D., Wyshak, G., & Klerman, G. L. (1991). The relation between hypochondriasis and age. *American Journal of Psychiatry, 148*, 923–928.

Barsky, A. J., & Klerman, G. L. (1983). Overview: Hypochondriasis, bodily complaints, and somatic styles. *American Journal of Psychiatry, 140*, 273–283.

Barsky, A. J., Orav, E. J., & Bates, D. W. (2006). Distinctive patterns of medical care utilization in patients who somatize. *Medical Care, 44*, 803–811.

Bouman, T. K. (2002). A community-based psychoeducational group approach to hypochondriasis. *Psychotherapy and Psychosomatics, 71*, 326–332.

Bouman, T. K., & Visser, S. (1998). Cognitive and behavioural treatment of hypochondriasis. *Psychotherapy and Psychosomatics, 67*, 214–221.

Buwalda, F. M., Bouman, T. K., & van Duijn, M. A. J. (2006). Psychoeducation for hypochondriasis: A comparison of a cognitive-behavioural approach and a problem-solving approach. *Behaviour Research and Therapy, 45*, 887–899.

Clark, D. M., Salkovskis, P. M., Hackmann, A., Wells, A., Fennell, M., Ludgate, J., . . . Gelder, M. (1998). Two psychological treatments for hypochondriasis: A randomised controlled trial. *British Journal of Psychiatry, 173*, 218–225.

Cottraux, J., Bouvard, M. A., & Milliery, M. (2005). Combining pharmacotherapy with cognitive behavioral interventions for obsessive-compulsive disorder. *Cognitive Behaviour Therapy, 34*, 185–192.

Creed, F. (2006). Can DSM-V facilitate productive research into the somatoform disorders? *Journal of Psychosomatic Research, 60*, 331–334.

Creed, F., & Barsky, A. (2004). A systematic review of the epidemiology of somatization disorder and hypochondriasis. *Journal of Psychosomatic Research, 56*, 391–408.

Eastin, M. S., & Guinsler, N. M. (2006). Worried and wired: Effects of health anxiety on information seeking and health care utilization behaviors. *CyberPsychology & Behavior, 9*, 494–498.

Escobar, J. I., Gara, M., Waitzkin, H., Silver, R. C., Holman, A., & Compton, W. (1998). DSM-IV hypochondriasis in primary care. *General Hospital Psychiatry, 20*, 155–159.

Fallon, B. A. (2001). Pharmacologic strategies for hypochondriasis. In V. Starcevic & D. R. Lipsitt (Eds.), *Hypochondriasis: Modern perspectives on an ancient malady* (pp. 329–351). New York, NY: Oxford University Press.

Fallon, B. A., Schneier, F. R., Marshall, R., Campeas, R., Vermes, D., Goetz, D., . . . Liebowitz, M. R. (1996). The pharmacotherapy of hypochondriasis. *Psychopharmacology Bulletin, 32*, 607–611.

Fallon, B. A., Qureshi, A. I., Schneier, F. R., Sanchez-Lacay, A., Vermes, D., Feinstein, R., . . . Liebowitz, M. R. (2003). An open trial of fluvoxamine for hypochondriasis. *Psychosomatics, 44*, 298–303.

Fava, G. A., Grandi, S., Rafanelli, C., Fabbri, S., & Cazzaro, M. (2000). Explanatory therapy in hypochondriasis. *Journal of Clinical Psychiatry, 61*, 317–322.

Fink, P., Ørnbøl, E., Toft, T., Sparle, K. C., Frostholm, L., & Olesen, F. (2004). A new, empirically established hypochondriasis diagnosis. *American Journal of Psychiatry, 161*, 1680–1691.

Furer, P., Walker, J. R., & Freeston, M. H. (2001). Integrated approach to cognitive-behavioral therapy for intense illness worries. In G. J. G. Asmundson, S. Taylor, & B. J. Cox (Eds.), *Health anxiety: Clinical and research perspectives on hypochondriasis and related conditions* (pp. 161–192). New York, NY: Wiley.

Greeven, A., van Balkom, A. J. L. M., Visser, S., Merkelbach, J. W., van Rood, Y. R., van Dyck, R., . . . Spinhoven, P (2007). Cognitive behavior therapy and paroxetine in the treatment of hypochondriasis: A randomized controlled trial. *American Journal of Psychiatry, 164,* 91–99.

Gureje, O., Üstün, T. B., & Simon, G. E. (1997). The syndrome of hypochondriasis: A cross-national study in primary care. *Psychological Medicine, 27,* 1001–1010.

Haenen, M. A., de Jong, P. J., Schmidt, A. J. M., Stevens, S., & Visser, L. (2000). Hypochondriacs' estimation of negative outcomes: Domain-specificity and responsiveness to reassuring and alarming information. *Behaviour Research and Therapy, 38,* 819–833.

Hiller, W., Leibbrand, R., Rief, W., & Fichter, M. M. (2002). Predictors of course and outcome in hypochondriasis after cognitive-behavioral treatment. *Psychotherapy and Psychosomatics, 71,* 318–325.

Hollifield, M., Paine, S., Tuttle, L., & Kellner, R. (1999). Hypochondriasis, somatization, and perceived health and utilization of health care services. *Psychosomatics, 40,* 380–386.

House, A. (1989). Hypochondriasis and related disorders: Assessment and management of patients referred for a psychiatric opinion. *General Hospital Psychiatry, 11,* 156–165.

Kamlana, S. H., & Gray, P. (1988). Fear of AIDS. *British Journal of Psychiatry, 15,* 1291.

Kellner, R. (1979). Psychotherapeutic strategies in the treatment of psychophysiologic disorders. *Psychotherapy and Psychosomatics, 32*(Suppl. 4), 91–100.

Kellner, R. (1982). Psychotherapeutic strategies in hypochondriasis: A clinical study. *American Journal of Psychotherapy, 36,* 146–157.

Kellner, R. (1992). The treatment of hypochondriasis: To reassure or not to reassure? *International Review of Psychiatry, 4,* 71–75.

Kirmayer, L. J., & Robbins, J. M. (1991). Three forms of somatization in primary care: Prevalence, co-occurrence, and sociodemographic characteristics. *Journal of Nervous and Mental Disease, 179,* 647–655.

Knight, R. O. (1941). Evaluation of the results of psychoanalytic therapy. *American Journal of Psychiatry, 98,* 434–446.

Kroenke, K. (2007a). Efficacy of treatment for somatoform disorders: A review of randomized controlled trials. *Psychosomatic Medicine, 69,* 881–888.

Kroenke, K. (2007b). Somatoform disorders and recent diagnostic controversies. *Psychiatric Clinics of North America, 30,* 593–619.

Kroenke, K., Sharpe, M., & Sykes, R. (2007). Revising the classification of somatoform disorders: Key questions and preliminary recommendations. *Psychosomatics, 48,* 277–285.

Ladee, G. A. (1966). *Hypochondriacal syndromes.* Amsterdam, The Netherlands: Elsevier.

Lidbeck, J. (1997). Group therapy for somatization disorders in general practice: Effectiveness of a short cognitive-behavioural treatment model. *Acta Psychiatrica Scandinavica, 96,* 14–24.

Lippert, G. P. (1986). Excessive concern about AIDS in two bisexual men. *Canadian Journal of Psychiatry, 31,* 63–65.

Logsdail, S., Lovell, K., Warwick, H., & Marks, I. (1991). Behavioural treatment of AIDS-focused illness phobia. *British Journal of Psychiatry, 159,* 422–425.

Looper, K. J., & Kirmayer, L. J. (2001). Hypochondriacal concerns in a community population. *Psychological Medicine, 31,* 577–584.

Lucock, M. P., White, C., Peake, M. D., & Morley, S. (1998). Biased perception and recall of reassurance in medical patients. *British Journal of Health Psychology, 3,* 237–243.

Marcus, D. K., Gurley, J. R., Marchi, M. M., & Bauer, C. (2007). Cognitive and perceptual variables in hypochondriasis and health anxiety: A systematic review. *Clinical Psychology Review, 27,* 127–139.

Martin, A., & Jacobi, F. (2006). Features of hypochondriasis and illness worry in the general population in Germany. *Psychosomatic Medicine, 68,* 770–777.

Mayou, R., Kirmayer, L. J., Simon, G., Kroenke, K., & Sharpe, M. (2005). Somatoform disorders: Time for a new approach in *DSM-V. American Journal of Psychiatry, 162,* 847–855.

Miller, D., Acton, T. M. G., & Hedge, B. (1988). The worried well: Their identification and management. *Journal of the Royal College of Physicians of London, 22,* 158–165.

Miller, W. R., & Rollnick, S. (2002). *Motivational interviewing: Preparing people for change* (2nd ed.). New York, NY: Guilford Press.

Nathan, P. E., & Gorman, J. M. (2007). *A guide to treatments that work* (3rd ed.). New York, NY: Oxford University Press.

Norberg, M. M., Krystal, J. H., & Tolin, D. F. (2008). A meta-analysis of D-cycloserine and the facilitation of fear extinction and exposure therapy. *Biological Psychiatry, 63,* 1118–1126.

Oosterbaan, D. B., van Balkom, A. J. L. M., van Boeijen, C. A., de Meij, T. G. J., & van Dyck, R. (2001). An open study of paroxetine in hypochondriasis. *Progress in Neuro-Psychopharmacology and Biological Psychiatry, 25,* 1023–1033.

Pennebaker, J. W. (1982). *The psychology of physical symptoms.* New York, NY: Springer.

Politi, P., & Emanuele, E. (2007). Successful treatment of refractory hypochondriasis with duloxetine. *Progress in Neuro-Psychopharmacology & Biological Psychiatry, 31,* 1145–1146.

Rief, W., & Rojas, G. (2007). Stability of somatoform symptoms: Implications for classification. *Psychosomatic Medicine, 69,* 864–869.

Romanik, R. L., & Kellner, R. (1985). Case study: Treatment of herpes genitalis phobia and agoraphobia with panic attacks. *Psychotherapy, 22,* 542–546.

Salkovskis, P. M., & Warwick, H. M. (1986). Morbid preoccupations, health anxiety and reassurance: A cognitive-behavioural approach to hypochondriasis. *Behaviour Research and Therapy, 24,* 597–602.

Salkovskis, P. M., Warwick, H. M., & Deale, A. C. (2003). Cognitive-behavioral treatment for severe and persistent health anxiety (hypochondriasis). *Brief Treatment and Crisis Intervention, 3,* 353–367.

Schweickhardt, A., Larisch, A., & Fritzsche, K. (2005). Differentiation of somatizing patients in primary care: Why the effects of treatment are always moderate. *Journal of Nervous and Mental Disease, 193,* 813–819.

Seivewright, H., Green, J., Salkovskis, P. M., Barrett, B., Nur, U., & Tyrer, P. (2008). Cognitive behavioural therapy for health anxiety in a genitourinary medicine clinic: Randomised controlled trial. *British Journal of Psychiatry, 193,* 332–337.

Stern, R., & Fernandez, M. (1991). Group cognitive and behavioural treatment for hypochondriasis. *British Medical Journal, 303,* 1229–1231.

Stone, A. B. (1993). Treatment of hypochondriasis with clomipramine. *Journal of Clinical Psychiatry, 54,* 200–201.

Stuart, S., Noyes, R., Starcevic, V., & Barsky, A. (2008). An integrative approach to somatoform disorders combining interpersonal and cognitive behavioral theory and techniques. *Journal of Contemporary Psychotherapy, 38,* 45–53.

Taylor, S., & Asmundson, G. J. G. (2004). *Treating health anxiety: A cognitive-behavioral approach.* New York, NY: Guilford Press.

Taylor, S., Asmundson, G. J. G., & Coons, M. J. (2005). Current directions in the treatment of hypochondriasis. *Journal of Cognitive Psychotherapy, 19,* 291–310.

Taylor, S., Thordarson, D. S., Jang, K. L., & Asmundson, G. J. G. (2006). Genetic and environmental origins of health anxiety: A twin study. *World Psychiatry, 5,* 47–50.

Tyrer, P., Seivewright, N., & Behr, G. (1999). A specific treatment for hypochondriasis? *Lancet, 353,* 672–673.

Verhaak, P. F. M., Meijer, S. A., Visser, A. P., & Wolters, G. (2006). Persistent presentation of medically unexplained symptoms in general practice. *Family Practice, 23,* 414–420.

Visser, S., & Bouman, T. K. (1992). Cognitive-behavioural approaches in the treatment of hypochondriasis: Six single case cross-over studies. *Behaviour Research and Therapy, 30,* 301–306.

Visser, S., & Bouman, T. K. (2001). The treatment of hypochondriasis: Exposure plus response prevention vs cognitive therapy. *Behaviour Research and Therapy, 39,* 423–442.

Viswanathan, R., & Paradis, C. (1991). Treatment of cancer phobia with fluoxetine. *American Journal of Psychiatry, 148,* 1090.

Walker, J., Vincent, N., Furer, P., Cox, B., & Kjernisted, K. (1999). Treatment preference in hypochondriasis. *Journal of Behavior Therapy and Experimental Psychiatry, 30,* 251–258.

Warwick, H. M., & Marks, I. M. (1988). Behavioural treatment of illness phobia and hypochondriasis: A pilot study of 17 cases. *British Journal of Psychiatry, 152,* 239–241.

Warwick, H. M., & Salkovskis, P. M. (1985). Reassurance. *British Medical Journal, 290,* 1028.

Warwick, H. M., & Salkovskis, P. M. (1990). Hypochondriasis. *Behaviour Research and Therapy, 28,* 105–117.

Warwick, H. M. C., Clark, D. M., Cobb, A. M., & Salkovskis, P. M. (1996). A controlled trial of cognitive-behavioural treatment of hypochondriasis. *British Journal of Psychiatry, 169,* 189–195.

Warwick, H. M. C., & Salkovskis, P. M. (2001). Cognitive behavioral treatment of hypochondriasis. In V. Starcevic & D. R. Lipsitt (Eds.), *Hypochondriasis: Modern perspectives on an ancient malady* (pp. 314–328). New York, NY: Oxford University Press.

Wesner, R. B., & Noyes, R. (1991). Imipramine: An effective treatment for illness phobia. *Journal of Affective Disorders, 22,* 43–48.

Williamson, P. N. (1984). An intervention for hypochondriacal complaints. *Clinical Gerontologist, 3,* 64–68.

27

Social Anxiety Disorder

JUDY WONG, ELIZABETH A. GORDON, AND RICHARD G. HEIMBERG

OVERVIEW OF THE DISORDER

Diagnostic Criteria

Social anxiety disorder, also known as social phobia, is a disorder characterized by "a marked or persistent fear of one or more social or performance situations" (American Psychiatric Association, 1994, p. 411). Individuals with social anxiety disorder are concerned that they will do something or display visible signs of anxiety that will lead to embarrassment or humiliation when exposed to the scrutiny of others. This fear is often accompanied by physiological symptoms common to other anxiety disorders, such as perspiring, heart palpitations, and blushing, and exposure to feared situations almost invariably provokes anxiety, which may be extreme or take the form of a panic attack. Such situations are either avoided or endured with great distress, and the individual must recognize that his or her fear is excessive. Furthermore, the fear must not be better accounted for by a general medical condition or another mental disorder, although we maintain that it may be more productive to consider social anxiety in certain situations as meeting criteria for diagnosis if it is disproportionate to that experienced by others with the same condition (e.g., a person who stutters and fears the negative evaluation of his stuttering by others to such a degree that he avoids social interaction and lives a life of

extreme isolation). In addition, the current diagnostic system describes two subtypes of social anxiety disorder: Socially anxious individuals who experience anxiety in most social situations are referred to as having the generalized subtype of social anxiety disorder, whereas individuals who fear one or a few specific social situations (e.g., public speaking or eating in public) are referred to as having the nongeneralized subtype. Compared to the nongeneralized subtype, generalized social anxiety disorder is associated with more severe symptoms of social anxiety and greater functional impairment (Heimberg, Holt, Schneier, Spitzer, & Liebowitz, 1993). However, recent research suggests that there is no clear demarcation between subtypes; rather, the current subtyping scheme may represent a means of indexing the severity of social anxiety disorder and may not present a true advantage over a simple count of the number of assessed situations in which the person demonstrates clinically significant fear (El-Gabalawy, Cox, Clara, & Mackenzie, 2010; Vriends, Becker, Meyer, Michael, & Margraf, 2007).

Demographic Variables

Social anxiety disorder is a highly prevalent condition. Data from the National Comorbidity Survey Replication, for instance, show that it is the fourth most common psychiatric disorder in the United States, with an estimated lifetime prevalence of 12.1% (Kessler, Berglund, et al., 2005), less prevalent only than specific phobia, major depressive disorder, and alcohol abuse. When considered on a past-year basis, the prevalence of social anxiety disorder is 6.8%, second only to specific phobia (Kessler, Chiu, Demler, Merikangas, & Walters, 2005). Social anxiety disorder is also characterized by an earlier age of onset compared to other psychiatric disorders (Kessler, Berglund, et al., 2005); however, individuals with social anxiety suffer from clinically significant symptoms for 15–25 years before they seek treatment (Rapee, 1995) and often report that it is their fear of being evaluated by others that keeps them away from the consulting office (Olfson et al., 2000).

Epidemiological studies also suggest that social anxiety disorder is more common in women than in men (Magee, Eaton, Wittchen, McGonagle, & Kessler, 1996), but in clinical samples, men slightly outnumber women (Chapman, Mannuzza, & Fyer, 1995; Stein, 1997). Among those seeking treatment, women score higher than men on several measures of the severity of social anxiety (Turk et al., 1998), suggesting a higher threshold for women before they seek treatment for social anxiety disorder. It has been postulated that it is more costly for men than for women to go untreated because men are typically expected to be more outgoing and assertive in both their personal and professional lives (Weinstock, 1999).

There is currently very little information as to the prevalence or nature of social anxiety disorder as a function of race, ethnicity, or culture in the United States. However, in the National Epidemiologic Survey on Alcohol and Related Conditionsbeing Native American was associated with an increased risk for developing social anxiety disorder, whereas being of Asian, Hispanic, or Black race/ ethnicity reduced this risk (Grant et al., 2005). Prevalence rates of social anxiety disorder in different countries vary widely, although it is unclear whether this represents true difference in prevalence, differences in cultural expression, or the suitability of assessment instruments cross-culturally.

Impact of Social Anxiety Disorder

Social anxiety disorder is thought by some (e.g., Marshall & Lipsett, 1994) to represent the extreme end on a continuum of shyness. However, although shyness and social anxiety are related constructs, they may differ qualitatively, with shyness being a broader and more heterogeneous construct than social anxiety (Heiser, Turner, & Beidel, 2003). In support of this conceptualization, research has demonstrated that, whereas highly shy individuals are more likely to be diagnosed with social anxiety disorder than nonshy or normatively shy individuals, individuals can be classified as being highly shy *without* experiencing the functional impairment and distress associated with social anxiety disorder (Chavira, Stein, & Malcarne, 2002; Heiser et al., 2003; Heiser, Turner, Beidel, & Roberson-Nay, 2009).

Social anxiety disorder is a debilitating disorder, characterized by a chronic, unremitting course (Chartier, Hazen, & Stein, 1998; Reich, Goldenberg, Vasile, Goisman, & Keller, 1994). One 12-year study of clients seeking treatment for anxiety disorders found that, compared to panic disorder with agoraphobia and generalized anxiety disorder, social anxiety disorder was associated with the lowest probability of remittance (Bruce et al., 2005). Social anxiety disorder is associated with significant impairment in social, educational, and occupational functioning (Schneier et al., 1994). Specifically, individuals with social anxiety are more likely to receive public assistance (Schneier, Johnson, Hornig, Liebowitz, & Weissman, 1992), have fewer friends and dating partners (Rodebaugh, 2009; Wenzel, 2002; Whisman, Sheldon, & Goering, 2000), and are less likely to get married compared to individuals with other anxiety disorders (Schneier et al., 1992). A recent study showed that social anxiety was associated with less time worked among female recipients of public assistance (Tolman et al., 2009). In addition to being associated with an overall lower quality of life (Safren, Heimberg, Brown, & Holle, 1997), social anxiety disorder is also often comorbid with other psychiatric disorders, including other anxiety disorders, depression, and alcohol abuse and dependence (Magee et al., 1996). Socially anxious individuals are also more likely to attempt suicide and to use medications to control symptoms (Katzelnick et al., 2001). As the number of social fears increases, comorbidity and service utilization increases, and quality of life decreases.

COGNITIVE MODELS OF SOCIAL ANXIETY DISORDER

According to cognitive models of social anxiety proposed by Rapee and Heimberg (1997) and by Clark and Wells (1995), the core cognitive feature of the disorder is a fear of negative evaluation. This fear leads the individual to perceive social situations as being inherently threatening, producing anxiety that is then maintained by distorted perceptions, avoidance of social situations, and other maladaptive behaviors. Specifically, Rapee and Heimberg posit that the cycle of social anxiety begins with the person's assumption that the perceived audience whether real or imagined is likely to evaluate him/her negatively, the result of which is assumed to have great consequences. In addition to such heightened perception of threat in social situations, individuals with social anxiety form a mental representation of themselves as imagined from the perspective of the audience. Though it is often negatively distorted, this mental self representation is compared to the perceived standard of expectations of the audience. Discrepancy between the individual's perceived performance and the perceived expectations of performance is exacerbated by biased cognitive processes, as a result, individuals with social anxiety come to believe that they will not live up to the audience's expectations and that negative

evaluation is inevitable. Furthermore, socially anxious individuals engage in a process of monitoring threatening external cues (e.g., signs of boredom among audience members) and internal cues (e.g., physiological symptoms of anxiety and negative cognitions about the self). This hypervigilance demands attentional resources, which ironically can lead to actual impairment in behavioral performance. More importantly, external cues are perceived to be evidence for the negative mental self-representation, resulting in the cycle of social anxiety beginning anew.

Similar to the Rapee and Heimberg model, Clark and Wells (1995) propose that social anxiety disorder is marked by a discrepancy between an individual's desire to perform to audience's expectations and her belief that she is unable to do so (Schlenker & Leary, 1982). The Clark and Wells model differs in its relative emphasis on the role of internal cues as one's source of evidence for negative self-representations. In addition, Clark and Wells emphasize the role of safety behaviors in maintaining social anxiety. Safety behaviors refer to any behaviors an individual performs in order to feel less anxious or to avoid feared outcomes. For example, someone who fears being evaluated as a poor public speaker may rehearse extensively for a speech as a safety behavior. Although some safety behaviors may indeed enhance performance, individuals may credit their successes to these behaviors and discount information that disconfirm their negative beliefs about themselves. Thus, engagement in safety behaviors prevents the socially anxious individual from disconfirming unrealistic beliefs about the consequences of their performance in social situations. (Interested readers are referred to a paper by Schultz & Heimberg, 2008, for a comparison of the Rapee-Heimberg and Clark-Wells models.)

Consistent with these cognitive models, cognitive behavior therapies for social anxiety disorder address individuals' patterns of avoidance and provide them with opportunities to reevaluate maladaptive or irrational beliefs related to social and performance situations. Cognitive behavior therapies are a family of techniques derived from the behavioral and cognitive traditions. Techniques that have been empirically examined include exposure, alone and in combination with cognitive restructuring, social skills training, and applied relaxation. We review the evidence regarding the efficacy of these techniques in the next section.

EXPOSURE TREATMENTS

Exposure treatments were found to be successful in the treatment of other anxiety disorders before they were adapted for treatment of social anxiety disorder (Barlow & Wolfe, 1981). In exposure therapy, socially anxious patients are exposed to feared situations through imagery (imaginal exposure) or, more commonly, through direct confrontation in session (in vitro exposure) and/or as homework assignments completed outside of therapy (in vivo exposure). Exposures to feared situations are usually completed in a graded manner, in which patients begin with exposure to less anxiety-evoking situations and gradually progress to more difficult situations. Based on classical conditioning theories, exposure to feared stimuli is thought to reduce anxiety through a process of extinction and habituation. Exposure techniques are hypothesized to be most effective at reducing anxiety when patients are fully engaged with the emotional and physiological arousal evoked by the feared situation (Foa & Kozak, 1986). Research has suggested that exposure effects change by producing new learning that competes with previously learned fear responses (Bouton, 2002).

Randomized Controlled Trials

Comparison to Control Conditions. There is ample evidence to suggest that exposure techniques are efficacious in treating social anxiety disorder. Among the earliest controlled trials of exposure therapy was one conducted by Butler,

Cullington, Munby, Amies, and Gelder (1984), in which they randomly assigned 45 socially anxious patients to either therapist-guided exposure treatment, combined exposure and anxiety management treatment, or a wait-list control group. Patients receiving the anxiety management component were instructed in progressive muscle relaxation, distraction from physiological symptoms, and rational self-talk. To assure that both active treatment groups received equal amounts of exposure time, patients in the exposure treatment received a nonspecific control treatment component that took up the same amount of time as the anxiety management component. Both exposure and exposure with anxiety management treatments were efficacious in reducing social anxiety compared to the wait-list control. In addition, the combined exposure with anxiety management treatment group showed greater gains than the exposure group at 6-month follow-up. It should be noted that, although Butler and colleagues characterized anxiety management as a cognitive restructuring component, anxiety management did not involve instruction on formal cognitive restructuring as characterized by treatments later developed for social anxiety disorder. Therefore, caution should be taken in interpreting results of this study as demonstrating the enhancing effect of adding cognitive restructuring to exposure therapy. Furthermore, the combined treatment condition was associated with more positive expectations for treatment outcome than the exposure alone condition, providing an alternative explanation for the difference between the active treatments.

Alström, Nordlund, Persson, Hårding, and Ljungqvist (1984) also found therapist-guided exposure therapy to be superior to a control condition. Rather than employing a wait-list control group, they administered to all patients a *basal treatment* that included psychoeducation, self-exposure instruction, and unspecified anxiolytic medication; those who only received this basal treatment comprised the control group. Active treatments were therapist-guided in vivo and imaginal exposure, supportive therapy, and relaxation therapy. At posttreatment, the exposure group made significant gains in reducing social anxiety symptoms compared to all other groups. At 3-month follow-up, exposure was superior to the basal treatment, though not statistically different from supportive therapy and relaxation therapy.

Though convinced that exposure therapy was effective at treating social anxiety disorder, Al-Kubaisy and colleagues (1992) wanted to examine whether presence of a therapist during exposures enhanced exposure effects. They compared 8-week treatments involving daily self-exposure homework, daily self-exposure homework combined with therapist-guided exposure, and daily self-relaxation homework. Patients in all conditions met with therapists for 6 hourly sessions to discuss homework and to monitor progress, and patients in the therapist-guided exposure group received nine additional hours to complete in-session exposures with therapists. Both exposure groups were more efficacious at reducing anxiety symptoms than the relaxation group at posttreatment and at 26-week follow-up. However, contrary to the authors' hypothesis, the therapist-guided exposure group was not superior to the group who received only self-exposure homework. Based on these results, the researchers suggested that clinician-accompanied exposures do not enhance the benefits of self-exposure homework.

Comparison to/combination with medications. Three studies have examined efficacy of exposure therapy in comparison to medication treatments. Turner, Beidel, and Jacob (1994) found a treatment that combined imaginal and in vivo exposure to be more efficacious at reducing social anxiety than a pill placebo or the beta-adrenergic blocker atenolol. This was demonstrated across a variety of outcome measures, including self-report social anxiety symptom measures, clinician ratings, and patient self-rated anxiety during a speech task. However, significance of this finding may be called into question because beta-adrenergic blockers have not been shown to surpass placebo, either in the study by Turner et al. (1994)

or another by Liebowitz et al. (1992). Six-month follow-up data suggested that treatment gains were maintained.

Blomhoff and colleagues (2001) conducted a controlled trial examining the selective serotonin reuptake inhibitor (SSRI) sertraline and exposure therapy administered by primary care physicians. A total of 387 patients were randomly assigned to one of four conditions: (1) sertraline with no exposure (medication only), (2) sertraline with exposure (combined treatment), (3) exposure with pill placebo (exposure only), and (4) pill placebo with no exposure (control). All treatments were administered for 24 weeks. However, patients in the exposure groups only met with physicians for exposure training for the first 12 weeks and were then instructed to continue exposing themselves to feared situations in the second 12 weeks. At the 12-week assessment point, all active treatment groups were superior to placebo. After 24 weeks, only the sertraline group was superior to placebo. However, at a 1-year follow-up, patients in the exposure therapy group showed further improvement, whereas patients receiving sertraline or sertraline combined with exposure deteriorated on some measures (Haug et al., 2003).

More recently, Hofmann and colleagues (2006) examined the effects of augmenting exposure therapy with D-cycloserine, a partial agonist of N-methyl-d-aspartate. D-cycloserine is believed to facilitate the extinction of learned fear when administered immediately before or even shortly after extinction training and may strengthen extinction memories so they might be more easily retrieved during subsequent exposures to fear-relevant cues, and these hypotheses have been supported in both animal and human studies (Davis, Ressler, Rothbaum, & Richardson, 2006). In this pilot study, 27 patients were randomly assigned to receive five sessions of group or individual exposure therapy specifically focused on public-speaking situations in addition to either D-cycloserine or pill placebo. At posttreatment and at 1-month follow-up, patients who received exposure augmented with D-cycloserine reported significantly less social anxiety than patients who received exposure with pill placebo, though differences between groups on a clinician-rated measure were not significant. Similar results were reported in a replication study by Guastella et al. (2008), although patients in this study demonstrated broader change in symptom severity, dysfunctional cognitions, and life satisfaction.

Meta-Analyses of Group Designs

Comparison to control conditions. The earliest meta-analysis examining effectiveness of exposure alone was conducted by Feske and Chambless (1995), who compared 9 trials of exposure alone to 12 trials of cognitive behavior therapy (CBT) with a pooled total of 344 participants. Of the nine exposure-alone trials, five involved therapist-assisted in vivo exposures with instructions for self-directed exposure homework, and three involved homework only. One trial directly compared therapist-assisted exposure with homework to homework only. In all trials, treatments were compared to wait-list control groups. Feske and Chambless found that the controlled effect size for exposure-only treatments was large at 0.99. Several meta-analytic studies have subsequently replicated Feske and Chambless's findings that exposure therapies are superior to wait-list control conditions in reducing social anxiety symptoms, with effect sizes ranging from moderate to large (Acarturk, Cuijpers, van Straten, & de Graaf, 2009; Gould, Buckminster, Pollack, Otto, & Yap, 1997; Powers, Sigmarsson, & Emmelkamp, 2008; S. Taylor, 1996). However, in their meta-analysis of various pharmacological and cognitive behavioral treatments, Federoff and Taylor (2001) found that exposure alone was not superior to wait-list control at posttreatment. At follow-up, exposure-alone showed some efficacy, but its effect size was not significantly different from the effect size for a single attention control condition included in the analysis. It is unclear why results of this study were inconsistent with other meta-analytic studies.

Comparison to/combination with medications. The study by Federoff and Taylor (2001) is also the only meta-analysis to examine the effect of exposure-only treatments in comparison to medication. Pharmacological treatments were found to be more efficacious at posttreatment than exposure alone. However, because follow-up data were scarce among medication treatment studies, the authors were unable to compare follow-up effect sizes for medication to those for any of the psychological treatments. Federoff and Taylor caution that because posttreatment assessments for medication studies usually occurred before discontinuation of medication, it was unclear whether gains made with medication would be maintained following treatment.

Conclusions

Exposure therapy, as a stand-alone treatment, is an efficacious treatment for social anxiety disorder. Although the meta-analysis of Federoff and Taylor (2001) suggests that exposure is not superior to treatment with medications at posttreatment, other evidence also suggests that exposure produces gains at follow-up not seen with medications (Haug et al., 2003). Though exposure alone is efficacious, there is reason to believe that exposure in conjunction with cognitive restructuring techniques—which is the most typical CBT practice—may be even more so. As the core feature of social anxiety disorder is thought to be a cognitive one—fear of negative evaluation—combining exposure and cognitive restructuring techniques is thought to increase the efficacy of treatment. Evidence for the efficacy of combined exposure and cognitive restructuring treatments is discussed below.

COMBINED EXPOSURE AND COGNITIVE RESTRUCTURING TREATMENTS

The rationale behind cognitive restructuring is that social situations are not inherently anxiety-evoking, but rather that it is one's thoughts about the situation that produce anxiety (Beck & Emery, 1985; Rodebaugh, Holaway, & Heimberg, 2004). Cognitive behavioral treatments that combine exposure techniques with cognitive restructuring address both the maladaptive thought patterns and avoidance behaviors that may play a maintaining role in social anxiety. A prediction that arises from the cognitive models discussed earlier is that exposure alone would be insufficient to challenge faulty mental representations of the self and others. Furthermore, exposure therapy may be less effective at producing habituation in individuals with social anxiety disorder compared to other anxiety disorders due to the nature of the feared stimuli. Butler (1985) notes that social situations are variable and unpredictable compared to other phobic stimuli, making habituation difficult to achieve. In addition, she points out that there are very few social situations that socially anxious individuals fully avoid in their day to day lives, and their anxiety persists despite frequent exposure to feared stimuli. This suggests that exposure to the feared stimuli alone cannot account for the reduction in anxiety achieved in treatment. Rodebaugh et al. (2004) argue that informal cognitive restructuring in exposure treatments may facilitate anxiety reduction; even when cognitive restructuring is not a formal component of the treatment, the discussion between the therapist and patient about the nature of feared situations provides an opportunity for the patient's beliefs to be challenged, and discussion of the outcomes of exposures in later sessions provides the opportunity for assimilation of information disconfirmatory of irrational, inaccurate, or unhelpful beliefs. In the following sections, we discuss evidence for the efficacy of cognitive behavioral treatments that combine exposure with cognitive restructuring. In addition, we discuss studies comparing exposure treatment to cognitive behavioral treatment.

Randomized Controlled Trials

Comparison to control conditions. Among the first studies of social anxiety treatment to include a credible control condition was the study conducted by Heimberg and colleagues (1990) evaluating the efficacy of a combined cognitive restructuring and exposure treatment package. They randomly assigned 49 patients to cognitive behavioral group therapy (CBGT) or to an educational-supportive group. Patients in CBGT received psychoeducation and training in the use of cognitive restructuring skills, as well as opportunities to use these skills in association with in-session and homework exposures. In the educational-supportive groups, patients were presented with lectures on and discussions of topics related to social anxiety disorder; they were also given opportunities to discuss with other group members anxiety about upcoming social situations. As in CBGT, patients in educational-supportive groups also received homework assignments. In contrast to the study by Butler et al. (1984) described earlier, the groups did not differ in treatment credibility and outcome expectancy. Although both groups showed significant pretreatment to posttreatment decrease in clinician-rated symptom severity, CBGT was superior to the educational-supportive comparison group at posttreatment and at 6-month follow-up. On self-report measures of social anxiety, both groups showed significant and similar improvement at posttreatment. Notably, a 5-year follow-up study conducted with a subset of the original sample revealed that CBGT patients had maintained their gains and remained less anxious than patients in the educational-supportive group (Heimberg, Salzman, Holt, & Blendell, 1993).

Ledley et al. (2009) examined efficacy of an individual cognitive behavioral treatment (I-CBT) for social anxiety disorder that was derived from CBGT originally developed by our group (Heimberg et al., 1990; Heimberg & Becker, 2002). This treatment protocol was conducted with the use of a commercially available client workbook and therapist guide (Hope, Heimberg, Juster, & Turk, 2000; Hope, Heimberg & Turk, 2006) and administered to a sample of 38 patients with social anxiety disorder. There was little attrition from the immediate treatment condition ($N = 1$), and ratings of session tapes revealed a high degree of protocol adherence. I-CBT resulted in a highly significant differential in response rate (73% vs. 6% of completers) and greater decreases on both self-report and clinician-administered measures of social anxiety. Gains were maintained at 3-month follow-up.

Comparison of exposure plus cognitive restructuring to exposure alone, cognitive restructuring alone, or enhanced treatment. A few studies have directly compared exposure treatment to treatment combining exposure and cognitive restructuring. Mattick and Peters (1988) compared 26 patients randomly assigned to therapist-guided exposure to 25 patients assigned to combined exposure and cognitive restructuring. Exposures took place during group sessions and as homework assignments. In the combined treatment, patients were taught cognitive restructuring skills and instructed to use these skills during exposures. At posttreatment, 48% of the patients in the exposure group reported definite avoidance of their target phobic situations, compared to only 14% of the combined treatment patients. Although self-reported anxiety on a performance task decreased from pretreatment to posttreatment for both groups, the groups did not differ significantly. In this study, the combined treatment group was just as efficacious as exposure treatment in reducing anxiety and was superior in reducing avoidance of feared situations. Mattick, Peters, and Clarke (1989) replicated some of these findings in a subsequent study of 43 patients randomly assigned to wait-list control or to one of three active treatment conditions. As in their previous study, they compared exposure to combined exposure and cognitive restructuring; in addition, they examined a treatment of cognitive restructuring without exposure—one

of the few studies to examine cognitive restructuring as a stand-alone treatment. The combined treatment was superior to exposure on two measures of social anxiety, and both were superior to cognitive restructuring alone in reducing avoidance.

Another study directly comparing exposure alone to cognitive restructuring alone was conducted by Emmelkamp, Mersch, Vissia, and van der Helm (1985). In an uncontrolled trial, 34 patients were randomly assigned to exposure alone or to one of two cognitive treatments without in vivo exposure: rational emotive therapy (RET) (Ellis, 1962) or self-instructional training (SIT). One of the earlier cognitive therapies developed, RET targets patients' irrational thoughts and attempts to modify these thoughts through discussion and persuasion. Similarly, in many versions of SIT, which are based on Meichenbaum's (1985) SIT, patients work with their therapists to develop coping thoughts in problematic situations and practice using these thoughts in exposures. However, in the version of SIT used by Emmelkamp et al., no attempts were made to challenge irrational beliefs, and only imaginal exposures were employed. All treatments were equally effective in reducing social anxiety symptoms at posttest. However, these results are difficult to interpret because of small sample size and alterations made to the basic treatment components for the sake of experimental design. Furthermore, although both Mattick et al. (1989) and Emmelkamp et al. (1985) examined cognitive restructuring without exposure conditions, we see little utility to these comparisons as there is little justification for the use of such treatments in real-world clinical settings.

A more recent attempt to examine the efficacy of exposure plus cognitive restructuring for social anxiety disorder was conducted by Rapee, Gaston, and Abbott (2009). Exposure plus cognitive restructuring in this study was based loosely on the work of Heimberg et al. (1990) and Mattick and Peters (1988) but was restricted to cognitive restructuring and in vivo exposure. Cognitive restructuring followed principles described by Beck and Emery (1985) and focused on refutation of unrealistic beliefs through consideration of evidence. In vivo exposure exercises, based on the principles of habituation, were conducted between sessions in a graduated and systematic fashion and were individually tailored to target the social fears of each participant. This *standard treatment* was compared to an *enhanced treatment*. Cognitive restructuring and in vivo exposure were conducted in a similar manner to the standard treatment, although the overlap between cognitive restructuring and in vivo exposure was emphasized through use of hypothesis testing. Furthermore, according to the authors,

> Data gathering was extended to incorporate identification and refutation of underlying beliefs and overarching life scripts by identification of these broader beliefs followed by examination of evidence from across the individual's life. In vivo exercises also included elimination of safety behaviors and subtle avoidance as well as realistic appraisal and feedback of performance. Participants also practiced exercises to train controlled attentional resources away from negative evaluation and the self and toward the task at hand through meditation type exercises and in vivo practice of focusing of attention to different features of the environment (p. 320)

These treatment conditions were compared to a stress management control, which consisted of training in relaxation skills, problem solving, time management, and healthy lifestyle habits. Both standard and enhanced treatments showed good efficacy and outperformed the stress management control on the percent of patients meeting diagnostic criteria after treatment, self report measures of social anxiety symptoms, and life interference. Enhanced treatment, however, resulted in greater improvements than standard treatment on measures of diagnostic severity and clinically significant change. Enhanced treatment also showed significantly greater

effects on measures of cost of negative evaluation and negative views of one's skills and appearance. Changes on these latter variables mediated differences between the treatments on changes in diagnostic severity.

Comparison to/combination with medications. Several studies have examined the efficacy of CBT in comparison to various pharmacological treatments. Heimberg and colleagues (1998) randomly assigned 133 patients from two sites to 12 weeks of CBGT, phenelzine, pill placebo, or the educational-supportive group therapy control used by Heimberg et al. (1990). At posttreatment, 75% of patients who completed CBGT and 77% of patients who completed phenelzine treatment were classified as treatment responders (58% and 64% of the intent-to-treat sample, respectively). Although the response rate did not differ significantly between the two active treatment groups, phenelzine patients were less symptomatic at posttreatment; both treatments were superior to pill placebo and educational supportive conditions. Following the initial 12 week period of acute treatment, patients in both control conditions were removed from the study, as well as patients who were classified as nonresponders to phenelzine or CBGT (Liebowitz et al., 1999). Maintenance treatment was administered to treatment responders for 6 months. Twenty of the initial 31 phenelzine patients were maintained on medication, meeting with their physicians monthly; 21 of the initial 36 CBGT patients met monthly for 2.5 hour group sessions during the maintenance phase. At the end of this maintenance phase, the pattern of differences between phenelzine and CBGT shown after the acute treatment continued. Among those who did not relapse or drop out of the study, phenelzine patients continued to be less symptomatic than CBGT patients. However, another follow up assessment 6 months after the end of maintenance treatment revealed greater relapse among patients with generalized social anxiety disorder receiving phenelzine compared to those receiving CBGT

CBGT may confer greater protection against relapse after treatment has terminated, though the authors note that replication with larger samples is warranted.

A follow-up to the study by Heimberg et al. (1998) was recently reported by Blanco et al. (2010), who compared CBGT, phenelzine, the combination of CBGT and phenelzine, and pill placebo in a sample of 128 patients with social anxiety disorder. Analysis of response and remission rates suggests that combined treatment was more efficacious than placebo, but this was not the case for the monotherapies. Most analyses revealed a patten of combined treatment surpassing both monotherapies and placebo, with a general ordering (from most to least efficacious) of combined treatment > phenelzine > CBGT > placebo.

One study of 45 patients found CBGT to be as efficacious as clonazepam (Otto et al., 2000). It should be noted that patients in the clonazepam treatment were encouraged to face feared situations; this encouragement to engage in self-exposure may have enhanced the effects of clonazepam and provided a more stringent comparison for the cognitive behavioral treatment.

Two separate research groups have compared the efficacy of cognitive behavior therapies to that of the SSRI fluoxetine. Clark and colleagues (2003) randomly assigned 60 socially anxious patients to individual cognitive behavior therapy, fluoxetine plus self-exposure treatment, or placebo plus self-exposure. The cognitive behavior therapy protocol used was based on Clark and Wells's (1995) cognitive model of social anxiety and focused on identifying safety behaviors, shifting the focus of attention away from internal cues during social situations, using video feedback to modify distorted self-perceptions, and engaging in exposures to feared social situations. Following 16 weeks of treatment, the cognitive behavioral treatment was superior to both fluoxetine plus self-exposure and placebo plus self-exposure on measures of social anxiety. At 1-year

follow-up, this difference was maintained. In a large controlled trial of 295 patients with generalized social anxiety disorder, Davidson and colleagues (2004) compared cognitive behavior therapy to fluoxetine, fluoxetine plus cognitive behavior therapy, cognitive behavior therapy plus placebo, and placebo. The cognitive behavior therapy protocol was administered in a group format over a course of 14 weeks and was derived in large part from the therapy protocol developed by the Heimberg group (Heimberg & Becker, 2002), differing mainly in its inclusion of a social skills training component. All active treatments were superior to placebo, but they did not differ in efficacy. Thus, contrary to the findings of Clark and colleagues (2003), results of this trial indicated that CBT was not superior to fluoxetine.

Meta-Analyses of Group Designs

Comparison to control conditions. Feske and Chambless (1995) examined effectiveness of various types of CBT, including RET, SIT, and CBGT, with CBGT comprising half of the CBT trials evaluated in the meta-analysis. The controlled effect size for CBT for symptoms of social anxiety disorder was 0.38, excluding two studies considered to be outliers with effect sizes greater than 1 (with the outliers, the average effect size equaled 0.77). Feske and Chambless explained such variability in effect sizes as a result of differences in the nature control comparisons across studies, as smaller effect sizes were calculated for trials with more stringent control comparisons (e.g., comparisons to an educational-supportive or pill placebo group) and the largest effect sizes for studies utilizing wait-list control comparisons. Similarly, Powers and colleagues (2008) found that CBT and exposure treatments, when compared to wait-list control groups, yielded larger effect sizes than when compared to psychological or pill placebo groups. Despite this variability across studies, several meta-analytic reviews have subsequently replicated Feske and Chambless's findings indicating that cognitive behavior therapies are superior to control conditions in reducing social anxiety symptoms (Acarturk et al., 2009; Federoff & Taylor, 2001; Gould et al., 1997; Hofmann & Smits, 2008; Powers et al., 2008; S. Taylor, 1996).

In addition, some studies have examined the effect of CBT on other psychological symptoms. Feske and Chambless (1995) found that effect sizes for cognitive measures and general mood and anxiety measures were moderate (0.47 and 0.51, respectively). A more recent meta-analysis by Acarturk, de Graaf, van Straten, ten Have, and Cuijpers (2008) of 29 randomized controlled trials (with the majority of trials examining exposure alone or combined CBT treatments) found that psychological treatments produced large effects on cognitive measures (0.80), measures of depression (0.70), and measures of general anxiety (0.70).

Furthermore, CBT has been associated with continued improvement at follow-up. S. Taylor (1996) found that, at 3-month follow-up, effect sizes tended to increase. However, Taylor notes that most studies did not report whether or not patients received further treatment during the follow-up period. Gould et al. (1997) also calculated follow-up uncontrolled effect sizes by comparing within-group changes from posttreatment to follow-up. Their results suggested that at 3 months, CBT patients made modest additional improvements.

Comparison of exposure to exposure plus cognitive restructuring. Meta-analyses have shown mixed support for the superiority of CBT over stand-alone exposure treatments. Feske and Chambless (1995) and Powers et al. (2008) found that combined CBT was not significantly different from exposure alone at posttreatment. S. Taylor (1996) also found that combined CBT was not significantly different from exposure; however, his study showed that CBT was superior to both wait-list and placebo controls, whereas exposure alone was superior only to wait-list controls. This led Taylor to conclude that adding cognitive restructuring to exposure yielded increased benefit. Similarly, Federoff and Taylor (2001) found that

combined CBT was superior to wait-list control and pill placebo, but exposure alone was not superior to either control condition. At follow-up, all the meta-analytic studies found that uncontrolled effect sizes were similar between both exposure and combined CBT (Federoff & Taylor, 2001; Feske & Chambless, 1995; Powers et al., 2008; S. Taylor, 1996).

Comparison to/combination with medications. Two meta-analyses have compared the effects of CBT to pharmacological treatments. Gould and colleagues (1997) examined 24 controlled trials of CBT and pharmacological treatments for a pooled total of 1,079 patients. Effect sizes for CBT (ES = 0.74) and pharmacological treatments (ES = 0.62) were statistically similar, and both treatments were superior to placebo at posttreatment. Compared to CBT, fewer pharmacological trials examined treatment effects at 3- to 6-month follow-up; uncontrolled effect sizes indicated that patients in CBT continued to show modest improvement after treatment (ES = 0.23) and that patients who received pharmacological treatments maintained gains after the discontinuation of medication (ES = 0.07). Gould et al. also calculated a posttreatment effect size for two trials evaluating treatments combining CBT with medication (ES = 0.49), but the number of trials was too small to make conclusions about efficacy. Federoff and Taylor (2001) analyzed data from 108 trials and also found that pharmacological treatments and CBT were both superior to wait-list and pill placebo conditions at posttreatment and that there was a trend (based on a very small number of trials) for the effect size of benzodiazepines to be larger than for CBT. Follow-up analyses were not conducted for pharmacological treatments due to a small number of pharmacological trials that assessed effects at follow-up. CBT continued to show moderate effects at follow-up.

Conclusions

Research has consistently shown cognitive-behavioral treatments that combine exposure with cognitive restructuring to be efficacious in the treatment of social anxiety disorder. In addition, CBT appears to produce greater long-term gains following the active treatment period than pharmacological treatments. On the basis of the results of the meta-analytic studies, it would appear that exposure alone is an efficacious therapy for social anxiety disorder and that adding a cognitive component to the treatment does not offer additional benefit. However, one must consider the differences in control conditions across studies. Exposure-only studies tend to compare the active treatment condition to wait-list controls, whereas several CBT studies compare the treatment group to more stringent placebo control groups. As a result, the effect sizes from CBT studies might be artifactually smaller.

Rodebaugh et al. (2004) argue that it is difficult to interpret studies that compare exposure to cognitive restructuring and claim that one component is more essential than another. For one, informal cognitive restructuring may occur in exposure-alone treatments as therapists talk with clients about the exposure situations; as a result, the clients' expectations about feared situations may be repeatedly challenged even in the absence of formal cognitive restructuring techniques. This hypothesis is consistent with the findings of Feske and Chambless (1995), who found some evidence in their meta-analytic study that active guidance by therapists yielded greater improvement than treatments without active therapist guidance. In addition, Rodebaugh et al. argue that exposure can happen in the context of cognitive restructuring; merely talking to the therapist is a social interaction and a behavior. Therefore, they argue that trying to administer a cognitive restructuring alone treatment is impossible.

SOCIAL SKILLS TRAINING

Social Skills Training (SST) gives socially anxious patients the opportunity to practice engaging in social behaviors with the aid of instruction and corrective feedback from their therapist. Sometimes administered as a stand-alone treatment and sometimes used in conjunction with other cognitive behavioral techniques, SST aims to improve patients' verbal and nonverbal communication skills and to broaden interpersonal repertoires. Some of the specific skills taught and practiced in SST include giving and receiving compliments, stating positive self-assertions, giving and receiving criticism, expressing opinions, and standing up for one's rights (van Dam-Baggen & Kraaimaat, 2000). One of the difficulties of examining the efficacy of SST as a stand-alone treatment is that, by engaging in the practice of social skills, patients will likely be informally exposed to feared social situations; meanwhile, exposure treatment in its formal form is well established as an efficacious treatment for social anxiety disorder.

Use of SST is based on the premise that social anxiety stems from insufficient interpersonal skills, a notion that has mixed support in the literature. Some studies demonstrate that socially anxious individuals perform more poorly than healthy controls in some social situations, for example, by exhibiting poorer eye contact, disclosing less information, and engaging in safety behaviors (Glass & Arnkoff, 1989; Stopa & Clark, 1993). Meanwhile, contradicting evidence suggests that socially anxious individuals perform adequately in social interactions but exhibit a negative interpretation bias in evaluating their own performance (Rapee & Lim, 1992; C. T. Taylor & Alden, 2005). Self-perceived social skills deficits of socially anxious individuals may often be exaggerated, although actual deficits are certainly demonstrated by a subset of individuals with the disorder. Furthermore, impairment in social behavior exhibited by socially anxious individuals may be due to difficulty applying social knowledge or skill in a distressing social context rather than (or in addition to) a lack of knowledge or social skill deficit *per se* (Rapee, 1995; Rodebaugh et al., 2004).

RANDOMIZED CONTROLLED TRIALS

Several open-trial and quasi-experimental studies have lent support for the efficacy of SST in improving the behavioral, cognitive, and affective components of social anxiety disorder (Falloon, Lloyd, & Harpin, 1981; Lucock & Salkovskis, 1988; Stravynski, Marks, & Yule, 1982; Wlazlo, Schroeder-Hartwig, Hand, Kaiser, & Münchau, 1990). One study provided evidence that group skills training may be more efficacious than a certain type of cognitive group therapy for particular patients (van Dam-Baggen & Kraaimaat, 2000). The study assigned 48 patients with either a primary or secondary diagnosis of generalized social anxiety disorder to either group SST or group cognitive therapy derived from RET. Participants in the SST condition improved more in terms of social anxiety and social skills than RET participants during and after treatment. Moreover, at follow-up, the SST group yielded social anxiety and social skills scores that reached the level of a reference healthy population. Notably, random assignment to conditions was not utilized, nor was there any control condition. Further, the cognitive therapy used in this study differs considerably from more comprehensive cognitive behavior therapy typically applied to social anxiety disorder, as it eliminated all behavioral techniques including exposure.

More recently, a randomized trial examined SST as an augmentation to CBGT (Herbert et al., 2005). Researchers randomly assigned 65 participants with generalized social anxiety disorder to CBGT with or without SST augmentation. Both conditions consisted of twelve 2 hour weekly sessions. The SST condition incorporated behavioral modeling, education, identification of performance impairments, and practicing specific skills during exposures and in between sessions. Patients were also educated about three social skill domains including speech content, speech quality (e.g., tone, timing), and nonverbal behaviors (e.g., facial expressions, eye contact). As sessions in both conditions involved equal total time and

equal time in exposure, the SST group received slightly less cognitive restructuring. The group that received SST made significantly greater improvements as assessed by both self-report measures and observer ratings of social behavior. These results make a good case for the augmentation of CBGT with SST as the effect sizes at posttreatment and follow-up were in the large and moderate range, respectively.

To date there have been ample studies that have incorporated SST into their design, but no randomized controlled trials of SST as a standalone treatment for patients with social anxiety disorder as currently defined. In one study conducted prior to the inclusion of social anxiety disorder in the *DSM*, Marzillier, Lambert, and Kellett (1976) randomly assigned socially inadequate psychiatric patients to social skills training, systematic desensitization, or a control group, with mixed results. Patients in both active treatments made significant gains in their social lives, which were maintained at 6 month follow up for the SST group. However, neither treatment group demonstrated superior anxiety reduction, improved social skill, or overall clinical adjustment than the control group. As this study is the sole RCT exploring efficacy of SST as a stand alone treatment for social anxiety symptoms, there is no evidence to support the efficacy of SST as a stand alone treatment for social anxiety disorder (Ponniah & Hollon, 2008).

Meta-Analyses of Group Designs

Few meta analyses have examined efficacy of SST as a stand alone treatment. In 1996, Taylor compared six conditions including wait list control, placebo, exposure, cognitive restructuring with and without exposure, and social skills training. All active conditions yielded reductions in self reported symptoms of social anxiety that were maintained several months after treatment. SST yielded moderate to large within group effect sizes (0.65 at posttreatment and 0.99 at 3 month follow up).

which were qualitatively, but not significantly lower, than most other active treatments, including cognitive restructuring with exposure. All interventions, including placebo, had larger effect sizes than the wait-list condition; however, only cognitive restructuring with exposure yielded significantly larger effect sizes than placebo (S. Taylor, 1996). Effect sizes for SST were examined in two additional meta-analyses and were also nonsignificantly smaller than those for cognitive restructuring with exposure (Federoff & Taylor, 2001; Gould et al., 1997).

More recent meta-analyses have examined SST as a component of larger treatment packages. For example, Acarturk and colleagues (2009) looked at 29 randomized studies examining the effects of psychological treatments, with a total of 1,628 subjects. Using subgroup analyses to examine the differential effects of treatment components and characteristics, the researchers found no indication that the inclusion of social skills training resulted in larger effect sizes. However, this trend applied across most of the subgroup analyses. As most of the studies combined several methods, the lack of power made it difficult to draw conclusions regarding the efficacy of specific components.

Conclusions

There has been ample research examining efficacy of SST, with mixed results. Overall, most studies suggest that SST as a stand-alone treatment is less efficacious than more comprehensive cognitive behavioral treatments, as it tends to yield lower effect sizes and efficacy rates. However, when used in conjunction with other approaches, SST has been a part of a number of programs that have demonstrated efficacy. It is difficult to determine whether SST specifically can account for this success as few studies have included dismantling procedures. Augmenting CBT with SST for patients with demonstrated skill deficits appears to be a well-informed treatment option.

APPLIED RELAXATION

Applied Relaxation (AR) is a specific application of Progressive Muscle Relaxation (PMR) (Bernstein, Borkovec, & Hazlett-Stevens, 2000), a technique employed to manage the physiological arousal and muscle tension often associated with anxiety. When used alone, PMR demonstrates little ability to reduce symptoms of social anxiety and is insufficient as a stand-alone treatment for the disorder (Alström et al., 1984). However, applying PMR within the context of feared situations (PMR + exposure = AR) shows more promise, as discussed later. AR first has patients practice PMR twice daily and then gradually shifts the practice so that one is taught to bring about relaxation quickly when confronting feared situations (Öst, 1987). Patients learn to recognize the early signals of anxiety and to cope with them rather than feeling overwhelmed. Applied Relaxation is a skill that patients can bring with them and use in nearly any situation that induces anxiety.

Randomized Controlled Trials

Quasi-experimental research has explored whether AR may be particularly helpful to a specific subgroup of patients based on their preexisting traits. Öst, Jerremalm, and Johansson (1981) classified 40 outpatients with social anxiety disorder as either *behavioral reactors* or *physiological reactors* based on their performance and heart rate during a social interaction task. Participants within each group were subsequently randomly assigned to one of two 12-week treatment conditions, a behavioral treatment (SST) or a physiological treatment (AR). Participants in both treatment conditions demonstrated improvement at posttreatment on most measures. Further, consistent with study hypotheses, social skills training was significantly better than applied relaxation for the behavioral reactors on 6 of 10 measures whereas AR was significantly better than SST on three measures among the physiological reactors.

A subsequent randomized controlled trial classified 39 outpatients with social anxiety disorder as either physiological or cognitive reactors based on heart rate and cognitions during a social interaction task. Participants were then assigned to one of three conditions, including AR, SIT, or a wait-list control. As with the prior study, active treatments consisted of 10 sessions of individual therapy. Both treatments yielded significant improvements on most measures and performed better than the wait-list condition. However, counter to study hypotheses, both physiological and cognitive reactors in the SIT condition demonstrated superior results on several measures than those in the AR condition (Jerremalm, Jansson, & Öst, 1986).

A more recent randomized controlled trial compared Clark's cognitive therapy to AR and a wait-list condition (Clark et al., 2006). Sixty individuals with generalized social anxiety disorder completed 12 weeks of active treatment or remained on a wait-list for that duration. Both active treatments were superior to wait-list on most measures of distress and psychopathology, but cognitive therapy was superior to AR on measures of social anxiety. The difference was clinically quite meaningful as twice as many patients receiving cognitive therapy were characterized as treatment responders. Differences in treatment outcome were maintained at follow up 1 year later.

Meta-Analyses of Group Designs

Federoff and Taylor (2001) examined a variety of psychotherapeutic and psychopharmacological interventions for social anxiety disorder including AR. Among the active treatments studied, AR demonstrated the lowest within group effect size (moderate effect size, 0.51, for improvement on self report measures pre to posttreatment). Consistent with this, a more recent meta analyses found that treatments that incorporated AR produced a similar effect size (0.55), which was significantly different from placebo and yet lower than other treatments

that did not include relaxation as a component (Acarturk et al., 2009).

Conclusions

Although empirical support suggests that AR is efficacious in the treatment of social anxiety disorder, its use as a sole approach may not be prudent. The literature demonstrates that other treatments, including various forms of CBT, are associated with greater reductions in the affective, cognitive, and behavioral symptoms of social anxiety disorder. Use of AR may be particularly appropriate for individuals who express their anxiety via physiological distress, although the literature provides mixed support for making treatment decisions based on these criteria. If chosen, AR should be used in conjunction with additional approaches that have yielded more robust effect sizes and efficacy rates.

MINDFULNESS AND ACCEPTANCE-BASED THERAPIES

Mindfulness and acceptance-based therapies such as Acceptance and Commitment Therapy (ACT) (Hayes, Strosahl, & Wilson, 1999) and Mindfulness Based Cognitive Therapy (MBCT) (Segal, Teasdale, & Williams, 2002; Teasdale et al., 2000) are increasingly being used to treat a range of psychological disorders including social anxiety disorder. These approaches encompass elements of traditional cognitive behavioral treatments (such as exposure work) but encourage a different relationship with one's thoughts and feelings. Traditional CBT gives patients the option of evaluating and challenging automatic thoughts whereas acceptance based strategies encourage a willingness to experience thoughts and feelings as they are, fully and non judgmentally. Acceptance based models posit that it is the struggle to control and eliminate distressing thoughts and feelings (experiential avoidance) rather than the unpleasant thoughts and feelings themselves that interferes with living a meaningful and fulfilling life. These approaches often incorporate *mindfulness*— the practice of intentionally paying attention to one's internal experiences in a nonjudgmental way (Kabat-Zinn, 1990)—as a means to create room for experiential acceptance.

Among the mindfulness and acceptance-based strategies for treating social anxiety disorder, ACT is one of the more well-known. Acceptance and Commitment Therapy emphasizes six core processes to enhance psychological flexibility. These include accepting difficult emotional states as part of the human condition, differentiating oneself from one's thoughts (cognitive defusion), practicing mindfulness, developing a sense of self as an observer of one's experience (self-as-context), clarifying values, and committing to valued action (Hayes et al., 1999; Hayes & Strosahl, 2004). When applied to social anxiety, ACT typically incorporates systematic exposure exercises to feared social situations, which is an opportunity for patients to engage in committed action and to let go of experiential avoidance. Exposures completed within the context of ACT differ slightly from those of traditional CBT in that they emphasize a willingness to experience anxiety while engaging in valued social situations, rather than on achieving decreased anxiety by the end of the exposure exercise.

Mindfulness-Based Stress Reduction (MBSR) (Kabat-Zinn, 1990) and MBCT have also been applied to the treatment of social anxiety disorder. Mindfulness-Based Stress Reduction aims to promote stress reduction in general rather than on reducing symptoms of social anxiety disorder specifically. This approach encompasses psychoeducation about stress and meditation techniques, the practice of mindful yoga, and sitting meditation. Mindfulness-Based Cognitive Therapy grew from this work and was originally applied to the treatment of recurrent depression. Here, mindfulness practice was used to help patients relate to their thoughts, feelings, and bodily sensations in a new way, for example, as passing events rather than as accurate perceptions of reality (Teasdale et al., 2000). When applied to the treatment of social anxiety disorder, MBCT seeks to lessen preoccupation with negative self appraisals and to enhance attention to current social situations. Techniques, such as body scanning, mindfulness of breathing, staying in the present moment, and mindfully allowing anxious thoughts and physical sensations of anxiety, are incorporated (Kocovski, Fleming, & Rector, 2009).

OPEN TRIALS

Two open trials examining efficacy of ACT for social anxiety disorder show promising results. Ossman, Wilson, Storaasli and McNeill (2006) conducted a small uncontrolled trial of 10 sessions of ACT-based group therapy at a university outpatient clinic. Although reduction of anxiety *per se* was not the primary target for change, patients reported significant decreases in social anxiety as well as experiential avoidance at posttreatment and follow-up with large effect sizes (follow-up effect sizes: 0.83 and 1.71, respectively). Furthermore, treatment completers rated themselves as more effective in living, especially within the domain of social relationships and friendships. One limitation of the study was its high attrition rate, as only 12 of the original 22 participants completed the full course. The authors speculated this may have been due to liberal inclusion criteria (e.g., involving only a brief phone screen for diagnostic criteria for social anxiety disorder), among other factors.

Dalrymple and Herbert (2007) explored integration of ACT with more traditional behavioral techniques including in vivo exposure and social skills training for patients with social anxiety disorder. Nineteen participants completed 12 weekly sessions that emphasized futility of trying to control anxiety and fostered a willingness to endure uncomfortable feelings and thoughts while being exposed to social situations. Participants showed significant decreases in social anxiety, fear of negative evaluation, experiential avoidance, and significant increases in quality of life at posttreatment and follow-up. Experiential avoidance at midtreatment was a key predictor of reduced anxiety at posttreatment. Although this study did not include a control condition, participants were required to remain in a no treatment baseline period for four weeks prior to starting treatment, and no improvements were made during this time.

More recently, Kocovski et al. (2009) conducted an open trial of mindfulness and acceptance-based group therapy for outpatients with generalized social anxiety disorder. Treatment consisted of twelve 2-hour group sessions; it drew largely from ACT and MBCT and also incorporated exposure to feared social situations. Participants demonstrated significant decreases in social anxiety, depression, and rumination as well as significant increases in mindfulness. Effect sizes for changes in social anxiety measures were large for treatment completers; intent-to-treat analysis also demonstrated moderate to large effect sizes. Consistent with previous findings (Dalrymple & Herbert, 2007), acceptance emerged as a possible mediator of change and individuals experienced a significant decrease in social anxiety prior to the introduction of exposure. Weaknesses of the study include lack of independent assessment and a moderate attrition rate (31%; although the authors note that this is consistent with other group treatment studies).

These results are consistent with an earlier study of mindfulness and task concentration (Bogels, Sijbers, & Voncken, 2006) with 10 socially anxious individuals. This treatment consisted of nine sessions, including six of MBCT and three that focused specifically on task concentration exercises, which were utilized to counteract the self-focused attentional bias associated with social anxiety disorder. Participants demonstrated significant reductions in social anxiety, particularly as measured by the Brief Fear of Negative Evaluation Scale (Leary, 1983). Improvements were maintained at 2 month follow-up.

Randomized Controlled Trials

Only one randomized controlled trial examining the efficacy of acceptance and mindfulness-based therapies for the treatment of social anxiety disorder has been conducted. Koszycki, Benger, Shlik, and Bradwejn (2007) compared MBSR to CBGT in the treatment of generalized social anxiety disorder. Fifty-three participants were assigned randomly to a course of MBSR or 12 weekly sessions of CBGT (Heimberg & Becker, 2002). The MBSR course consisted of eight 2.5-hour weekly group sessions and one all-day meditation retreat. The MBSR treatment did not target social anxiety disorder specifically, but rather stress reduction in general via psychoeducation and meditation. Patients in both treatment groups improved; however, patients receiving CBGT demonstrated significantly lower scores on participant and clinician ratings of social anxiety. The CBGT group also demonstrated significantly greater response and remission rates. Although the study supports the conclusion that CBGT is a preferable choice for the treatment of social anxiety, it also demonstrates the potential strength of mindfulness-based strategies. In particular, the MBSR condition showed comparable improvements in mood, functionality, and quality of life even though it did not target specifically social anxiety disorder and included no use of exposure.

Conclusions

The variety of psychotherapies that incorporates mindfulness and acceptance-based techniques is growing and with this has come a growing base of research examining their efficacy. Several open trials have yielded promising results, and some of these studies suggest willingness or acceptance may be mediators of change. The single controlled trial yielded results that were encouraging but somewhat less than those produced by CBGT. Mindfulness and acceptance-based therapies for the treatment of social anxiety disorder cannot be considered empirically supported as of yet, but in the future, they may very well be. Combinations of these techniques with other cognitive behavioral approaches may well prove beneficial.

INTERPERSONAL PSYCHOTHERAPY

Interpersonal Psychotherapy (IPT) is grounded in the central tenet of interpersonal theory that healthy social relationships are essential to maintaining psychological health (Bowlby, 1988; Sullivan, 1953). The goal of IPT is to improve the patient's engagement in close relationships and to strengthen social networks in order to broadly enhance psychological functioning and to promote symptom abatement.

Interpersonal Psychotherapy was first developed to treat unipolar depression among outpatients but was soon adapted and applied to various psychological disorders after its efficacy in treating depression was established via randomized controlled trials (Elkin et al., 1989; Weissman, Klerman, Prusoff, Sholomskas, & Padian, 1981). Interpersonal Therapy has been adapted for the treatment of posttraumatic stress disorder (Bleiberg & Markowitz, 2005), bulimia nervosa (Fairburn, 1998; Fairburn, Jones, & Peveler, 1991), substance abuse (Carroll, Rounsaville, & Gawin, 1991), and bipolar disorder (Craighead, Miklowitz, Vajk, & Frank, 1998), among others. Extending IPT to treatment of social anxiety disorder is fairly intuitive given the interpersonal nature of feared situations. Further, growing literature documenting impaired interpersonal functioning among socially anxious individuals highlights this area as a highly relevant domain for intervention (Alden & Taylor, 2004; Bodinger et al., 2002; Rodebaugh, 2009).

Similar to CBT in structure, IPT has a time-limited course (usually 12–16 weeks) and focuses on an individual's current life circumstances. Therapy typically focuses on exploring and resolving one interpersonal problem area rather than targeting intrapsychic or cognitive aspects of the disorder directly. In the first phase, the therapist and patient identify one problematic interpersonal area on which to focus, which often falls into one of four categories: grief (e.g., complicated bereavement), role disputes (e.g., conflict with a spouse or other significant other stemming from differing role expectations), role transitions (e.g., starting or ending a new relationship or job), and interpersonal deficits (e.g., social isolation, lack of close relationships). The second and third phases of therapy involve addressing the interpersonal problem area and consolidating gains to extend beyond treatment. The therapist's role is to help patients increase flexibility in their interpersonal interactions and to expand upon their repertoire of behaviors. Techniques include reassurance, clarification of emotional states, and role playing.

There are also several key distinctions between IPT and other treatment approaches. Although techniques used in IPT are not unique to this modality, IPT is well defined by its use of these techniques in combination, the active stance of the therapist, and the conceptualization of the problem from an interpersonal perspective. IPT differs from CBT by its focus on interpersonal dynamics as well as its emphasis on exploring affect within therapy. Unlike many other therapies used for social anxiety, IPT does not include exposure exercises as part of the treatment. Furthermore, IPT contrasts with psychodynamic approaches as it emphasizes neither the exploration of childhood antecedents nor transference interpretations and aims to create concrete immediate behavioral and relational change rather than deeper characterological change.

Randomized Controlled Trials

To date, the two randomized clinical trials examining the efficacy of IPT for SAD have offered mixed results. In 1997, Lipsitz, Markowitz, and Cherry modified IPT for the treatment of social anxiety disorder, keeping its same basic structure but incorporating content relevant to social fears. Lipsitz, Markowitz, Cherry, and Fyer (1999) first conducted an open trial in which they administered 14 weeks of IPT to nine individuals with social anxiety disorder. The majority (78%) was classified by independent evaluators as treatment responders and reported meaningful life changes, such as obtaining work, returning to school, and initiating dating. In a follow-up controlled trial, Lipsitz and colleagues (2008) randomly assigned 70 patients to 14 weeks of IPT or supportive therapy (ST). Patients in both groups showed significant improvement from pretreatment to posttreatment, but there were generally few distinctions between those treated with IPT and those treated with ST. The proportion of responders was similar across groups, and participants demonstrated similar improvements on measures of social anxiety. Follow-up analysis similarly failed to differentiate between these groups across measures. Thus, results failed to replicate the previous open trial. The authors note that the two therapies were administered by an overlapping set of clinicians, which may have contributed to a lack of differentiation between treatments. The authors also suggest that because IPT does not incorporate exposure as so many social anxiety treatments do, a longer treatment period might have allowed patients to enter and negotiate new social situations as the opportunities presented themselves.

The second randomized trial (Borge et al., 2008) provides stronger support for the use of IPT for social anxiety disorder, albeit under very specific circumstances. Conducted in an inpatient setting at a national Norwegian clinic, the study involved nonpsychotic patients with highly comorbid and chronic social anxiety disorder. Many of these patients had already tried alternative treatments without success. Eighty individuals were randomized to 10 weeks of residential cognitive therapy (RCT) (based on individual treatment from Clark, 1997) or residential interpersonal therapy (RIPT) (based on the manual of Lipsitz, Markowitz, and Cherry, 1997). Both treatments were modified to fit the inpatient setting and ultimately involved integrated

group, individual, and residential components. Individuals in both conditions responded equally well to treatment, making significant gains across several assessments with medium to large effect sizes and large effect sizes at 1-year follow-up. Just one difference on a secondary outcome measure resulted: Those in the RCT condition demonstrated increased social role security. Both groups reported continued gains from posttreatment to 1-year follow-up. Overall, the study suggests that IPT may be roughly as effective as CBT in some circumstances. It is difficult to generalize these results, however, given the distinct population and setting for treatment. Further, as administered in this study, the two treatments were not as differentiated from each other as they might have been within an outpatient setting.

Conclusions

To date the empirical basis for use of IPT for the treatment of social anxiety disorder is mixed. Of the two randomized trials, one demonstrated that IPT was no more efficacious than supportive therapy, whereas the other demonstrated efficacy on par with CBT but with a population and environment so specific that it is not prudent to generalize to other populations. Research on the interpersonal underpinnings and ramifications of social anxiety disorder make a compelling theoretical case for the use of interpersonal treatment; however, to date the evidence does not demonstrate that this form of treatment is equal to CBT in efficacy. Given promising open trial data and strong theoretical justification for such an approach, future research may be well directed to the study and refinement of this treatment for social anxiety disorder.

PSYCHODYNAMIC APPROACHES

The empirical basis for using psychodynamic therapy for treatment of social anxiety is quite limited. Most of what is known comes from individual case studies or uncontrolled studies, and even these are scarce. However, two recent studies have examined in a more systematic manner a form of focused, short-term psychoanalytic psychotherapy developed by Malan (1976). Malan's treatment is based on the theory that symptoms of social anxiety disorder are connected with recurrent and unconscious internal conflicts. According to this theory, developmental experiences lead socially anxious individuals to internalize representations of important others as shaming and embarrassing. The anxious person later projects these representations onto others, which results in an exaggerated fear of rejection and criticism. Treatment involves obtaining a detailed developmental history of the individual and developing an understanding of the connection between internalized conflicts and symptoms of social anxiety.

Randomized Controlled Trials

A study by a Brazilian research team (Knijnik, Kapczinski, Chachamovich, Margis, & Eizirik, 2004) randomized 40 patients with generalized social anxiety disorder to 12 weeks of psychodynamic group therapy (PGT) based on Malan's (1976) model or the educational supportive psychotherapy control employed in studies by Heimberg et al. (1990, 1998) (credible placebo control group [CPC]). Participants completed measures of general anxiety, social anxiety, and depression at three time-points (pre-, mid-, and posttreatment) and were also assessed by clinicians for global improvement. Attrition did not differ between conditions. Although both groups improved on most measures, patients randomized to PGT were rated as more improved than controls on one measure of social anxiety, the Liebowitz Social Anxiety Scale (Liebowitz, 1987), and this effect appeared to be carried by greater improvement on the avoidance subscale of this measure. Meanwhile, patients in the control condition showed greater improvements on a measure of general anxiety. The authors

interpret these findings as consistent with the idea that psychodynamic therapies can be anxiety-provoking in the short term but eventually lead to longer term change and suggest that a longer course may have yielded a different pattern.

A recent study by the same research team (Knijnik et al., 2008) examined efficacy of adding PGT to treatment with the benzodiazepine clonazepam, which had previously been demonstrated to be more efficacious for social anxiety disorder than placebo medication (Davidson et al., 1993). Fifty-eight adult outpatients with social anxiety disorder were randomized to PGT plus clonazepam or clonazepam alone. The primary outcome measure was a clinician-rated scale of global improvement; secondary outcomes measured social anxiety, quality of life, and depression. Whereas both groups made significant gains, the PGT plus clonazepam group showed significantly greater improvement than the clonazepam only group as measured by clinician ratings of global improvement. There were no differences between groups on secondary outcome measures. The authors suggest that the discrepancy between patient and clinician ratings of change may reflect the better ability of clinicians to detect progress, among other factors.

Conclusions

To date there has been little systematic research evaluating psychodynamic therapies for social anxiety disorder. The two randomized controlled trials discussed earlier provide some evidence that PGT reduces social avoidance more than a stringent control condition (although it was less efficacious than the control on a measure of general anxiety) and that it may provide a significant increment when augmenting therapy with clonazepam. Additional research is needed to determine specific mechanisms involved in improvement and whether specific benefits—such as helping patients with avoidance—can be replicated.

One important point to consider is that the psychodynamic therapy under investigation was administered in a group format, which provided a vehicle for exposure. It may be that the process of conducting psychodynamic therapy within this setting provides patients with the opportunity to practice having conversations with other patients, to become more familiar with talking about personal topics with others, and to habituate to group contexts. Ultimately, these processes may mediate the ability of this treatment to improve symptoms of social anxiety.

EVIDENCE-BASED PRACTICES

Cognitive behavioral treatments that have combined exposure with cognitive restructuring have been the most widely researched treatments for social anxiety disorder. Thus far, this form of CBT has been the only treatment consistently found to be efficacious at posttreatment compared to stringent control conditions, with some evidence showing that it is also associated with the long-term maintenance of gains. One recent study (Rapee et al., 2009) suggests that additional focus on attentional training, elimination of safety behaviors, and specific focus on core beliefs may also enhance the efficacy of this standard approach to CBT. There has been debate in the literature whether adding cognitive restructuring techniques to exposure results in increased efficacy over exposure as a stand-alone treatment. Meta-analyses comparing the two forms of treatment have yielded inconsistent results, with some researchers concluding that adding cognitive restructuring results in no increased benefits. However, the fact that CBT studies tend to employ more stringent placebo control groups might explain why the effect sizes are smaller than effect sizes found in studies of exposure as a stand-alone treatment. Furthermore, it may be impossible to employ one technique without informally employing the other (Rodebaugh

et al., 2004), and the amount of time devoted to cognitive restructuring activities may be associated with a reduction in the amount of time spent in exposure without loss of efficacy; thus, the debate over the added benefits of cognitive restructuring may be an unproductive one.

The current state of the literature supports the conclusion that no alternative psychological treatments for social anxiety disorder are more efficacious than exposure plus cognitive restructuring. However, this does not mean that therapists should refrain from considering these alternative treatments in all cases. It is still important to consider them, as exposure plus cognitive restructuring does not work for everyone, and many therapists do not use it; thus, these alternative treatments have the potential to broaden the pool of treatment responders even if their degree of empirical support is less than that of exposure plus cognitive restructuring. Further, augmentation of exposure plus cognitive restructuring with treatments that address particular client needs should be considered on a per-patient basis. For example, although the use of social skills training as a stand-alone treatment is not supported by the literature (Ponniah & Hollon, 2008), it may be an important addition for patients who present with evident social skill deficits. Use of CBT in conjunction with SST, applied relaxation, or other techniques may further expand our ability to tailor treatment to the particular needs of our individual patients.

When considering other alternatives to CBT for the treatment of social anxiety disorder, mindfulness and acceptance-based therapies have the most extensive support, followed by interpersonal therapies and psychodynamic therapies, respectively. Psychodynamic therapies have very little support and should not be considered as promising as the former two approaches. Mindfulness and acceptance-based approaches are not yet empirically supported for social anxiety disorder, but they may be in the near future. Multiple open trials evaluating efficacy of these therapies have produced moderate to large effect sizes. When considering such open-trial data, it may be kept in mind that social anxiety disorder follows a chronic and unremitting course without treatment. Further, the effect sizes and efficacy rates of standard treatments (e.g., CBGT) have been well established. Therefore, evidence from some of the open trials that lack a control condition may be interpreted with this in mind. There are no RCTs examining ACT or MBCT for treatment of social anxiety disorder, but one randomized trial comparing MBSR to CBGT showed comparable improvements across groups in mood, functionality, and quality of life, although it was less efficacious than CBGT on other measures.

Although too early in the stages of empirical study to be considered empirically supported, some researchers speculate that mindfulness and acceptance-based therapies bring important new perspectives to the discussion of how therapy should be conducted for the socially anxious patient. By fostering a willingness to experience negative emotional states, these strategies may increase the likelihood that patients will participate in anxiety-provoking social exposures, which may ultimately lead to improvement. Further, the emphasis on identifying and living consistently with one's values may lead to more comprehensive improvement in the quality of life than traditional CBT, which has targeted anxiety symptoms more narrowly (Dalrymple & Herbert, 2007). Although reduction of anxiety symptoms is not typically the central focus of mindfulness and acceptance-based therapies, symptom abatement is considered a likely result of embracing one's experiences fully and the behavioral change that comes with it. We have commented elsewhere (Heimberg & Ritter, 2008) that the focus on values in acceptance-based treatments is an important contribution and should be incorporated into CBT. We also note that in CBT, it is possible to teach patients to make an active distinction between thoughts that require attention and modification and those that are best handled in

a more mindful way (Heimberg & Ritter, 2008; Pontoski & Heimberg, 2010).

Acceptability of Treatment

Attrition rates in CBT treatments are fairly low, with estimates ranging from 10% to 18% across meta-analytic studies, with no significant differences found between exposure-only and combined CBT treatments (Federoff & Taylor, 2001; Feske & Chambless, 1995; Gould et al., 1997; S. Taylor, 1996). In addition to examining the efficacy of alternative treatments to CBT, future research on alternative treatments should pay particular attention to rates of attrition.

Comparison of Group Treatment to Individual Treatment

Both group and individual treatments for social anxiety disorder have been developed across treatments of different theoretical orientations. Advantages and disadvantages exist for each format. Advantages of group CBT include the built-in exposure of the kinds of social interactions that many clients with social anxiety disorder fear, including casual interactions with other group members, sharing personal information, and performing in front of others (Ledley et al., 2009). In addition, the group members may benefit from learning from other people's experiences, and by receiving support and encouragement from fellow group members (Heimberg & Becker, 2002). In small clinics or private practices, arranging for in-session exposures may be difficult for individual treatment. Another advantage of the group format is that it may be more cost-effective (Gould et al., 1997); however, some clients may benefit from the greater individual attention available from individual treatment. Disadvantages of the group format include the difficultly in organizing groups and the decreased flexibility in scheduling; in addition, clients may wait longer for treatment as they wait for groups to be assembled (Stangier, Heidenreich, Peitz, Lauterbach, & Clark, 2003).

Comparisons of group and individual treatments have only been conducted for CBT. Most studies have not found a difference in the efficacy of group treatments and individual treatments (e.g., Wlazlo et al., 1990). Meta-analyses have revealed the same (Gould et al., 1997; Powers et al., 2008). Stangier et al. (2003), however, did find a significant difference between the formats in their evaluation of Clark's CBT protocol. Patients in the individual format showed significantly greater improvement than those in the group format on one measure of social anxiety at posttreatment, and significantly fewer patients in the individual format met criteria for the diagnosis of social anxiety disorder following treatment. At the 6-month follow-up, the difference between the groups on the measure of social anxiety was maintained. It should be noted, however, that the Clark's protocol was originally developed to be administered individually and had never been previously evaluated as a group intervention; it is therefore not known whether it simply may not have translated well to the group format. In summary, research suggests that both formats are efficacious in the treatment of social anxiety disorder. We could potentially benefit from learning more about the advantages and disadvantages of each approach, and whether certain patient characteristics make one format better than another. Researchers examining alternative treatments to CBT might also consider examining the efficacy of the different formats.

Alternative Measure of Treatment Success

Treatment efficacy in social anxiety research has typically been based on self-report (and to a lesser extent, clinician-administered) measures assessing social anxiety symptoms. Though the focus on symptoms is necessary for determining improvement, our understanding of treatment effects may be improved through examination of other outcome measures. For instance, given that socially anxious individuals report lower quality of life compared to nonanxious controls (Safren et al., 1997), and given the documented functional impairments associated with social anxiety disorder described earlier, it would be reasonable to evaluate whether treatments succeed in improving overall quality of life. At least one study has found that socially anxious patients who completed a course of CBGT reported an increase in the quality of life following treatment (Eng, Coles, Heimberg, & Safren, 2001). Assessments of quality of life and functional impairment should be routinely included in future treatment outcome studies of social anxiety disorder.

Dissemination of Findings

Although there is abundant literature providing evidence of efficacy of CBT for social anxiety disorder, there is much more evidence for efficacy than effectiveness. Most studies have been conducted in university or other specialty settings in which a structured treatment manual requiring strict adherence is followed and study participants are carefully screened. Patients with comorbid major depression, comorbid alcohol or substance abuse or dependence, or who fall outside a certain age range are often excluded (Lincoln et al., 2003). Thus, it has been argued that patients who receive treatments in nonresearch settings may not achieve outcomes comparable to those obtained in a research setting (Barlow, Levitt, & Bufka, 1999). Therefore, studies examining the generalizability and transportability of empirically supported treatments for social anxiety disorder to outpatient community or private practice settings are needed.

Only three studies of this nature have been conducted so far, all concerning CBT for social anxiety disorder, but the results are quite encouraging. The first benchmarking study (i.e., a study that compares the effectiveness of a treatment as administered in the community to its efficacy as administered in the laboratory) included 217 patients in four outpatient clinics in Germany (Lincoln et al., 2003). Patients were unselected and all had a primary diagnosis of social anxiety disorder. There were significant reductions in social anxiety and avoidance, general anxiety, and depression 6 weeks following the end of treatment. Effect sizes were comparable to the average effect sizes reported in published meta-analyses. Another study (Gaston, Abbott, Rapee, & Neary, 2006) compared outcome of CBGT for 58 clients treated in a university clinic with those for 54 patients treated in a private practice clinic. There were no significant differences in outcome posttreatment, and both groups maintained their gains 3 months later. The most recent benchmarking study (McEvoy, 2007) investigated CBGT for 153 patients with social anxiety disorder in a community mental health clinic. Again, effect sizes were comparable to those reported in previously published efficacy studies for social anxiety disorder. Thus far the evidence suggests that CBT for social anxiety disorder is transportable to and effective in outpatient, private practice, and community mental health clinics.

Conclusion

A range of psychological treatments for social anxiety disorder has been developed since it was first recognized as a significant clinical disorder. These include techniques within the traditional CBT family (exposure with or without cognitive restructuring, social skills training, applied relaxation) as well as newer mindfulness and acceptance-based techniques, and techniques derived from interpersonal therapy and psychodynamic approaches. At this writing, the best evidence supports the use of exposure techniques, with a strong nod to the addition of cognitive restructuring. Other newer techniques, such as attention training and decrease in reliance on safety behaviors may further increase the efficacy of this package, although this statement is based on only one study (Rapee et al., 2009). SST and AR have less empirical support but may certainly have application with specific patients. Mindfulness and acceptance-based techniques hold substantial promise, both on their own and in combination with CBT, whereas IPT and psychodynamic techniques require additional study.

REFERENCES

Acarturk, C., Cuijpers, P., van Straten, A., & de Graaf, R. (2009). Psychological treatments of social anxiety disorder: A meta-analysis. *Psychological Medicine, 39,* 241–254.

Acarturk, C., de Graaf, R., van Straten, A., ten Have, M., & Cuijpers, P. (2008). Social phobia and number of social fears, and their association with comorbidity, health-related quality of life and help seeking: A population-based study. *Social Psychiatry and Psychiatric Epidemiology, 43,* 273–279.

Alden, L. E., & Taylor, C. T. (2004). Interpersonal processes in social phobia. *Clinical Psychology Review, 24,* 857–882.

Al-Kubaisy, T., Marks, I. M., Logsdail, S., Marks, M. P., Lovell, K., Sungur, M., & Araya, R. (1992). Role of exposure homework in phobia reduction: A controlled study. *Behavior Therapy, 23,* 599–621.

Alström, J. E., Nordlund, C. L., Persson, G., Hårding, M., & Ljungqvist, C. (1984). Effects of four treatment methods on social phobia patients not suitable for insight-oriented psychotherapy. *Acta Psychiatrica Scandinavica, 70,* 97–110.

American Psychiatric Association. (1994). *Diagnostic and statistical manual of mental disorders* (4th ed.). Washington, DC: Author.

Barlow, D. H., Levitt, J. T., & Bufka, L. F. (1999). The dissemination of empirically supported treatments: A view to the future. *Behaviour Research and Therapy, 37,* S147–62.

Barlow, D. H., & Wolfe, B. E. (1981). Behavioral approaches to anxiety disorders: A report on the NIMH-SUNY, Albany research conference. *Journal of Consulting and Clinical Psychology, 49,* 448–454.

Beck, A. T., & Emery, G. (1985). *Anxiety disorders and phobias: A cognitive perspective.* New York, NY: Basic Books.

Bernstein, D. A., Borkovec, T. D., & Hazlett-Stevens, H. (2000). *New directions in progressive relaxation training: A guidebook for helping professionals.* Westport, CT: Greenwood Publishing.

Blanco, C., Heimberg, R. G., Schneier, F. R., Fresco, D. M., Chen, H., Turk, C. L., . . . Liebowitz, M. R. (2010). A placebo-controlled trial of phenelzine, cognitive behavioral group therapy and their combination for social anxiety disorder. *Archives of General Psychiatry,67*, 286–295.

Bleiberg, K. L., & Markowitz, J. C. (2005). Interpersonal psychotherapy for posttraumatic stress disorder. *American Journal of Psychiatry, 162*, 181–183.

Blomhoff, S., Haug, T. T., Hellström, K., Holme, I., Humble, M., Madsbu, H. P., & Wold, J. E. (2001). Randomised controlled general practice trial of sertraline, exposure therapy and combined treatment in generalised social phobia. *British Journal of Psychiatry, 179*, 23–30.

Bodinger, L., Hermesh, H., Aizenberg, D., Valevski, A., Marom, S., Shiloh, R., . . . Weizman, A. (2002). Sexual function and behavior in social phobia. *Journal of Clinical Psychiatry, 63*, 874–879.

Bögels SM, Sijbers G, & Voncken M. (2006). Mindfulness and task-concentration training for generalized social phobia. *Journal of Cognitive Psychotherapy, 20*, 33–44.

Borge, F.-M., Hoffart, A., Sexton, H., Clark, D. M., Markowitz, J. C., & McManus, F. (2008). Residential cognitive therapy versus residential interpersonal therapy for social phobia: A randomized clinical trial. *Journal of Anxiety Disorders, 22*, 991–1010.

Bouton, M. E. (2002). Context, ambiguity, and unlearning: Sources of relapse after behavioral extinction. *Biological Psychiatry, 52*, 976–986.

Bowlby, J. (1988). *A secure base: Parent-child attachment and health human development.* New York, NY: Basic Books.

Bruce, S. E., Yonkers, K. A., Otto, M. W., Eisen, J. L., Weisberg, R. B., Pagano, M., . . . Keller, M. B. (2005). Influence of psychiatric comorbidity on recovery and recurrence in generalized anxiety disorder, social phobia, and panic disorder: A 12-year prospective study. *American Journal of Psychiatry, 162*, 1179–1187.

Butler, G. (1985). Exposure as treatment for social phobia: Some instructive difficulties. *Behaviour Research and Therapy, 23*, 651–657.

Butler, G., Cullington, A., Munby, M., Amies, P., & Gelder, M. (1984). Exposure and anxiety management in the treatment of social phobia. *Journal of Consulting and Clinical Psychology, 52*, 642–650.

Carroll, K. M., Rounsaville, B. J., & Gawin, F. H. (1991). A comparative trial of psychotherapies for ambulatory cocaine abusers: Relapse prevention and interpersonal psychotherapy. *American Journal of Drug and Alcohol Abuse, 17*, 229–247.

Chapman, T. F., Mannuzza, S., & Fyer, A. J. (1995). Epidemiology and family studies of social phobia. In R. G. Heimberg, M. R. Liebowitz, D. A. Hope, & F. R. Schneier (Eds.), *Social phobia: Diagnosis, assessment, and treatment* (pp. 21–40). New York, NY: Guilford Press.

Chartier, M. J., Hazen, A. L., & Stein, M. B. (1998). Lifetime patterns of social phobia: A retrospective study of the course of social phobia in a nonclinical population. *Depression and Anxiety, 7*, 113–121.

Chavira, D. A., Stein, M. B., & Malcarne, V. L. (2002). Scrutinizing the relationship between shyness and social phobia. *Journal of Anxiety Disorders, 16*, 585–598.

Clark, D. M. (1997). *Cognitive therapy for social phobia: Some notes for therapists.* Unpublished manuscript.

Clark, D. M., Ehlers, A., Hackmann, A., McManus, F., Fennell, M., Grey, N. . . . Wild, J. (2006). Cognitive therapy versus exposure plus applied relaxation in social phobia: A randomized controlled trial. *Journal of Consulting and Clinical Psychology, 74*, 568–578.

Clark, D. M., Ehlers, A., McManus, F., Hackmann, A., Fennell, M., Campbell, H., . . . Louis, B. (2003). Cognitive therapy versus fluoxetine in generalized social phobia: A randomized placebo-controlled trial. *Journal of Consulting and Clinical Psychology, 71*, 1058–1067.

Clark, D. M., & Wells, A. (1995). A cognitive model of social phobia. In R. G. Heimberg, M. R. Liebowitz, D. A. Hope, & F. R. Schneier (Eds.), *Social phobia: Diagnosis, assessment, and treatment* (pp. 69–93). New York, NY: Guilford Press.

Craighead, W. E., Miklowitz, D. J., Vajk, F. C., & Frank, E. (1998). Psychosocial treatments for bipolar disorder. In P. E. Nathan & J. M. Gorman (Eds.), *A guide to treatments that work* (pp. 240–248). New York, NY: Oxford University Press.

Dalrymple, K. L., & Herbert, J. D. (2007). Acceptance and commitment therapy for generalized social anxiety disorder. *Behavior Modification, 31*, 543–568.

Davidson, J. R. T., Foa, E. B., Huppert, J. D., Keefe, F. J., Franklin, M. E., Compton, J. S., . . . Gadde, K. M. (2004). Fluoxetine, comprehensive cognitive behavioral therapy, and placebo in generalized social phobia. *Archives of General Psychiatry, 61*, 1005–1013.

Davidson, J. R. T., Potts, N., Richichi, E., Krishnan, R., Ford, S. M., Smith, R., & Wilson, W. H. (1993). Treatment of social phobia with clonazepam and placebo. *Journal of Clinical Psychopharmacology, 13*, 423–428.

Davis, M., Ressler, K., Rothbaum, B. O., & Richardson, R. (2006). Effects of D-cycloserine on extinction: Translation from preclinical to clinical work. *Biological Psychiatry, 60*, 369–375.

El-Gabalawy, R., Cox, B., Clara, I., & Mackenzie, C. (2010). Assessing the validity of social anxiety disorder subtypes using a nationally representative sample. *Journal of Anxiety Disorders, 24*, 244–249.

Elkin, I., Shea, M. T., Watkins, J. T., Imber, S. D., Sotsky, S. M., Collins, J. F., . . . Parloff, M. B. (1989). National institute of mental health treatment of depression collaborative research program: General effectiveness of treatments. *Archives of General Psychiatry, 46*, 971–982.

Ellis, A. (1962). *Reason and emotion in psychotherapy.* New York, NY: Lyle Stuart.

Emmelkamp, P. M., Mersch, P. P., Vissia, E., & van der Helm, M. (1985). Social phobia: A comparative evaluation of cognitive and behavioral interventions. *Behaviour Research and Therapy, 23*, 365–369.

Eng, W., Coles, M. E., Heimberg, R. G., & Safren, S. A. (2001). Quality of life following cognitive behavioral treatment for social anxiety disorder: Preliminary findings. *Depression and Anxiety, 13*, 192–193.

Fairburn, C. G. (1998). Interpersonal psychotherapy for bulimia nervosa. In J. C. Markowitz (Ed.), *Interpersonal psychotherapy* (pp. 99–128). Washington, DC: American Psychiatric Press.

Fairburn, C. G., Jones, R., & Peveler, R. C. (1991). Three psychological treatments for bulimia nervosa: A comparative trial. *Archives of General Psychiatry, 48*, 463–469.

Falloon, I. R. H., Lloyd, G. G., & Harpin, R. E. (1981). The treatment of social phobia: Real-life rehearsal with nonprofessional therapists. *Journal of Nervous and Mental Disease, 169*, 180–184.

Federoff, I. C., & Taylor, S. (2001). Psychological and pharmacological treatments of social phobia: A meta-analysis. *Journal of Clinical Psychiopharmacology, 21*, 311–324.

Feske, U., & Chambless, D. L. (1995). Cognitive behavioral versus exposure only treatment for social phobia: A meta-analysis. *Behavior Therapy, 26*, 695–720.

Foa, E. B., & Kozak, M. J. (1986). Emotional processing of fear: Exposure to corrective information. *Psychological Bulletin, 99*, 20–35.

Gaston, J. E., Abbott, M. J., Rapee, R. M., & Neary, S. A. (2006). Do empirically supported treatments generalize to private practice? A benchmark study of a cognitive-behavioural group treatment programme for social phobia. *British Journal of Clinical Psychology, 45*, 33–48.

Glass, C. R., & Arnkoff, D. B. (1989). Behavioral assessment of social anxiety and social phobia. *Clinical Psychology Review, 9*, 75–90.

Gould, R. A., Buckminster, S., Pollack, M. H., Otto, M. W., & Yap, L. (1997). Cognitive-behavioral and pharmacological treatment for social phobia: A meta-analysis. *Clinical Psychology: Science and Practice, 4*, 291–306.

Grant, B. F., Hasin, D. S., Blanco, C., Stinson, F. S., Chou, S. P., Goldstein, R. B., . . . Huang B. (2005). The epidemiology of social anxiety disorder in the United States: Results from the National Epidemiologic Survey on Alcohol and Related Conditions. *Journal of Clinical Psychiatry, 66*, 1351–1361.

Guastella, A. J., Richardson, R., Lovibond, P. F., Rapee, R. M., Gaston, J. E., Mitchell, P., & Dadds, M. R. (2008). A randomized controlled trial of D-cycloserine enhancement of exposure therapy for social anxiety disorder. *Biolical Psychiatry, 63*, 544–549.

Haug, T. T., Blomhoff, S., Hellström, K., Holme, I., Humble, M., Madsbu, H. P., & Wold, J. E. (2003).

Exposure therapy and sertraline in social phobia: 1-year follow up of a randomized controlled trial. *British Journal of Psychiatry, 182*, 312–318.

Hayes, S. C., & Strosahl, K. D. (2004). *A practical guide to acceptance and commitment therapy.* New York, NY: Springer.

Hayes, S. C., Strosahl, K., & Wilson, K. G. (1999). *Acceptance and commitment therapy: An experimental approach to behavior change.* New York, NY: Guilford Press.

Heimberg, R. G., & Becker, R. E. (2002). *Cognitive-behavioral group therapy for social phobia: Basic mechanisms and clinical strategies.* New York, NY: Guilford Press.

Heimberg, R. G., Dodge, C. S., Hope, D. A., Kennedy, C. R., Zollo, L. J., & Becker, R. E. (1990). Cognitive behavioral group therapy for social phobia: Comparison with a credible placebo control. *Cognitive Therapy and Research, 14*, 1–23.

Heimberg, R. G., Holt, C. S., Schneier, F. R., Spitzer, R. L., & Liebowitz, M. R. (1993). The issue of subtypes in the diagnosis of social phobia. *Journal of Anxiety Disorders, 7*, 249–269.

Heimberg, R. G., Liebowitz, M. R., Hope, D. A., Schneier, F. R., Holt, C. S., Welkowitz, L. A., . . . Klein, D. F. (1998). Cognitive behavioral group therapy vs. phenelzine therapy for social phobia: 12-week outcome. *Archives of General Psychiatry, 55*, 1133–1141.

Heimberg, R. G., & Ritter, M. R. (2008). CBT and ACT for the anxiety disorders: Two approaches with much to offer. *Clinical Psychology: Science and Practice, 15*, 296–298.

Heimberg, R. G., Salzman, D. G., Holt, C. S., & Blendell, K. A. (1993). Cognitive-behavioral group treatment for social phobia: Effectiveness at five-year followup. *Cognitive Therapy and Research, 17*, 325–339.

Heiser, N. A., Turner, S. M., & Beidel, D. C. (2003). Shyness: Relationship to social phobia and other psychiatric disorders. *Behaviour Research and Therapy, 41*, 209–221.

Heiser, N. A., Turner, S. M., Beidel, D. C., & Roberson-Nay, R. (2009). Differentiating social phobia from shyness. *Journal of Anxiety Disorders, 23*, 469–476.

Herbert, J. D., Gaudiano, B. A., Rheingold, A. A., Myers, V. H., Dalrymple, K., & Nolan, E. M. 2005). Social skills training augments the effectiveness of cognitive behavioral group therapy for social anxiety disorder. *Behavior Therapy, 36*, 25–138.

Hofmann, S. G., Meuret, A. E., Smits, J. A. J., Simon, N. M., Pollack, M. H., Eisenmenger, K., . . . Otto, M. W. (2006). Augmentation of exposure therapy with D-cycloserine for social anxiety disorder. *Archives of General Psychiatry, 63*, 298–304.

Hofmann, S. G., & Smits, J. A. J. (2008). Cognitive-behavioral therapy for adult anxiety disorders: A meta-analysis of randomized placebo-controlled trials. *Journal of Clinical Psychiatry, 69*, 621–632.

Hope, D. A., Heimberg, R. G., Juster, H., & Turk, C. L. (2000). *Managing social anxiety: A cognitive-behavioral therapy approach* (Client workbook). New York, NY: Oxford University Press.

Hope, D. A., Heimberg, R. G., & Turk, C.L. (2006). *Therapist guide for managing social anxiety: A cognitive-behavioral therapy approach.* New York, NY: Oxford University Press.

Jerremalm, A., Jansson, L., & Öst, L. G. (1986). Cognitive and physiological reactivity and the effects of different behavioral methods in the treatment of social phobia. *Behaviour Research and Therapy, 24*, 171–180.

Kabat-Zinn, J. (1990). *Full catastrophe living: Using the wisdom of your mind and body to face stress, pain, and illness.* New York, NY: Delacorte.

Katzelnick, D. J., Kobak, K. A., DeLeire, T., Henk, H. J., Greist, J. H., Davidson, J. R. T., . . . Helstad, C. P. (2001). Impact of generalized social anxiety disorder in managed care. *American Journal of Psychiatry, 158*, 1999–2007.

Kessler, R. C., Berglund, P., Demler, O., Jin, R., Merikangas, K. R., & Walters, E. E. (2005). Lifetime prevalence and age-of-onset distributions of *DSM-IV* disorders in the national comorbidity survey replication. *Archives of General Psychiatry, 62*, 593–768.

Kessler, R. C., Chiu, W. T., Demler, O., Merikangas, K., & Walters, E. E. (2005). Prevalence, severity, and comorbidity of 12-month *DSM-IV* disorders in the national comorbidity survey replication. *Archives of General Psychiatry, 62*, 617–627.

Knijnik, D. Z., Blanco, C., Salum, G. A., Moraes, C. U., Mombach, C., Almeida, E., . . . Eizirik, C. L. (2008). A pilot study of clonazepam versus psychodynamic group therapy plus clonazepam in the treatment of generalized social anxiety disorder. *European Psychiatry, 23*, 567–574.

Knijnik, D. Z., Kapczinski, F., Chachamovich, E., Margis, R., & Eizirik, C. L. (2004). Psychodynamic group treatment for generalized social phobia. *Revista Brasileira de Psiquiatria, 26*, 77–81.

Kocovski, N. L., Fleming, J. E., & Rector, N. A. (2009). Mindfulness and acceptance-based group therapy for social anxiety disorder: An open trial. *Cognitive and Behavioral Practice, 16*, 276–289.

Koszycki, D., Benger, M., Shlik, J., & Bradwejn, J. (2007). Randomized trial of a meditation-based stress reduction program and cognitive behavior therapy in generalized social anxiety disorder. *Behaviour Research and Therapy, 45*, 2518–2526.

Leary, M. R. (1983). A brief version of the fear of negative evaluation scale. *Personality and Social Psychology Bulletin, 9*, 371–376.

Ledley, D. R., Heimberg, R. G., Hope, D. A., Hayes, S. A., Zaider, T. I., Van Dyke, M., . . . Fresco, D. M.

(2009). Efficacy of a manualized and workbook-driven individual treatment for social anxiety disorder. *Behavior Therapy, 40*, 414–424.

Liebowitz, M. R. (1987). Social phobia. *Modern Problems in Pharmacopsychiatry, 22*, 141–173.

Liebowitz, M. R., Heimberg, R. G., Schneier, F. R., Hope, D. A., Davies, S., Holt, C. S., . . . Klein, D. F. (1999). Cognitive-behavioral group therapy versus phenelzine in social phobia: Long-term outcome. *Depression and Anxiety, 10*, 89–98.

Liebowitz, M. R., Schneier, F., Campeas, R., Hollander, E., Hatterer, J., Fyer, A., . . . Klein, D. F. (1992). Phenelzine vs atenolol in social phobia. A placebo controlled comparison. *Archives of General Psychiatry, 49*, 290–300.

Lincoln, T. M., Rief, W., Hahlweg, K., Frank, M., von Witzleben, I., Schroeder, B., & Fiegenbaum, W. (2003). Effectiveness of an empirically supported treatment for social phobia in the field. *Behaviour Research and Therapy, 41*, 1251–1269.

Lipsitz, J. D., Gur, M., Vermes, D., Petkova, E., Cheng, J., Miller, N., . . . Fyer, A. J. (2008). A randomized trial of interpersonal therapy versus supportive therapy for social anxiety disorder. *Depression and Anxiety, 25*, 542–553.

Lipsitz, J. D., Markowitz, J. C., & Cherry, S. (1997). *Manual for interpersonal psychotherapy of social phobia.* Unpublished manuscript, Columbia University College of Physicians and Surgeons, New York, NY.

Lipsitz, J. D., Markowitz, J. C., Cherry, S., & Fyer, A. J. (1999). Open trial of interpersonal psychotherapy for the treatment of social phobia. *American Journal of Psychiatry, 156*, 1814–1816.

Lucock, M. P., & Salkovskis, P. M. (1988). Cognitive factors in social anxiety and its treatment. *Behaviour Research and Therapy, 26*, 297–302.

Magee, W. J., Eaton, W. W., Wittchen, H. U., McGonagle, K. A., & Kessler, R. C. (1996). Agoraphobia, simple phobia, and social phobia in the National Comorbidity Survey. *Archives of General Psychiatry, 53*, 159–168.

Malan, D. H. (1976). *The frontier of brief psychotherapy.* New York, NY: Plenum Press.

Marshall, J. R., & Lipsett, S. (1994). *Social phobia: From shyness to stage fright.* New York, NY: Basic Books.

Marzillier, J. S., Lambert, C., & Kellett, J. (1976). A controlled evaluation of systematic desensitization and social skills training for socially inadequate psychiatric patients. *Behaviour Research and Therapy, 14*, 225–238.

Mattick, R. P., & Peters, L. (1988). Treatment of severe social phobia: Effects of guided exposure with and without cognitive restructuring. *Journal of Consulting and Clinical Psychology, 56*, 251–260.

Mattick, R. P., Peters, L., & Clarke, J. C. (1989). Exposure and cognitive restructuring for social phobia: A controlled study. *Behavior Therapy, 20*, 3–23.

McEvoy, P. M. (2007). Effectiveness of cognitive behavioural group therapy for social phobia in a community clinic: A benchmarking study. *Behaviour Research and Therapy, 45,* 3030–3040.

Meichenbaum, D. (1985). *Stress inoculation training.* Elmsford, NY: Pergamon Press.

Olfson, M., Guardino, M., Struening, E., Schneier, F. R., Hellman, F., & Klein, D. F. (2000). Barriers to treatment of social anxiety. *American Journal of Psychiatry, 157,* 521–527.

Ossman, W. A., Wilson, K. G., Storaasli, R. D., & McNeill, J. W. (2006). A preliminary investigation of the use of acceptance and commitment therapy in a group treatment for social phobia. *International Journal of Psychology and Psychological Therapy, 6,* 397–416.

Öst, L. G. (1987). Applied relaxation: Description of a coping technique and review of controlled studies. *Behaviour Research and Therapy, 25,* 397–409.

Öst, L. G., Jerremalm, A., & Johansson, J. (1981). Individual response patterns and the effects of different behavioral methods in the treatment of social phobia. *Behaviour Research and Therapy, 19,* 1–16.

Otto, M. W., Pollack, M. H., Gould, R. A., Worthington, J. J., McArdle, E. T., Rosenbaum, J. F., & Heimberg, R. G. (2000). A comparison of the efficacy of clonazepam and cognitive-behavioral group therapy for the treatment of social phobia. *Journal of Anxiety Disorders, 14,* 345–358.

Ponniah, K., & Hollon, S. D. (2008). Empirically supported psychological interventions for social phobia in adults: A qualitative review of randomized controlled trials. *Psychological Medicine, 38,* 3–14.

Pontoski, K. E., & Heimberg, R. G. (2010). The myth of the superiority of concurrent combined treatments for anxiety disorders. *Clinical Psychology: Science and Practice, 17,* 107–111.

Powers, M. B., Sigmarsson, S. R., & Emmelkamp, P. M. G. (2008). A meta-analytic review of psychological treatments for social anxiety disorder. *International Journal of Cognitive Therapy, 1,* 94–113.

Rapee, R. M. (1995). Descriptive psychopathology of social phobia. In R. G. Heimberg, M. R. Liebowitz, D. A. Hope, & F. R. Schneier (Eds.), *Social phobia: Diagnosis, assessment, and treatment* (pp. 41–66). New York, NY: Guilford Press.

Rapee, R. M., Gaston, J. E., & Abbott, M. J. (2009). Testing the efficacy of theoretically derived improvements in the treatment of social phobia. *Journal of Consulting and Clinical Psychology, 77,* 317–327.

Rapee, R. M., & Heimberg, R. G. (1997). A cognitive-behavioral model of anxiety in social phobia. *Behaviour Research and Therapy, 35,* 741–756.

Rapee, R. M., & Lim, L. (1992). Discrepancy between self-and observer ratings of performance in social phobics. *Journal of Abnormal Psychology, 101,* 728–731.

Reich, J., Goldenberg, I., Vasile, R., Goisman, R., & Keller, M. (1994). A prospective follow-along study of the course of social phobia. *Psychiatry Research, 54,* 249–258.

Rodebaugh, T. L. (2009). Social phobia and perceived friendship quality. *Journal of Anxiety Disorders, 23,* 872–878.

Rodebaugh, T. L., Holaway, R. M., & Heimberg, R. G. (2004). The treatment of social anxiety disorder. *Clinical Psychology Review, 24,* 883–908.

Safren, S. A., Heimberg, R. G., Brown, E. J., & Holle, C. (1997). Quality of life in social phobia. *Depression and Anxiety, 4,* 126–133.

Schlenker, B. R., & Leary, M. R. (1982). Social anxiety and self-presentation: A conceptualization and model. *Psychological Bulletin, 92,* 641–669.

Schneier, F. R., Heckelman, L. R., Garfinkel, R., Campeas, R., Fallon, B. A., Gitow, A., . . . Liebowitz, M. R. (1994). Functional impairment in social phobia. *Journal of Clinical Psychiatry, 55,* 322–331.

Schneier, F. R., Johnson, J., Hornig, C. D., Liebowitz, M. R., & Weissman, M. M. (1992). Social phobia: Comorbidity and morbidity in an epidemiologic sample. *Archives of General Psychiatry, 49,* 282–288.

Schultz, L. T., & Heimberg, R. G. (2008). Attentional focus in social anxiety disorder: Potential for interactive processes. *Clinical Psychology Review, 28,* 1206–1221.

Segal, Z., Teasdale, J., & Williams, M. (2002). *Mindfulness-based cognitive therapy for depression.* New York, NY: Guilford Press.

Stangier, U., Heidenreich, T., Peitz, M., Lauterbach, W., & Clark, D. M. (2003). Cognitive therapy for social phobia: Individual versus group treatment. *Behaviour Research and Therapy, 41,* 991–1007.

Stein, M. B. (1997). Phenomenology and epidemiology of social phobia. *International Clinical Psychopharmacology, 12,* S23–S26.

Stopa, L., & Clark, D. M. (1993). Cognitive processes in social phobia. *Behaviour Research and Therapy, 31,* 255–267.

Stravynski, A., Marks, I., & Yule, W. (1982). Social skills problems in neurotic outpatients: Social skills training with and without cognitive modification. *Archives of General Psychiatry, 39,* 1378–1385.

Sullivan, H. S. (1953). *The interpersonal theory of psychiatry.* New York, NY: Norton.

Taylor, C. T., & Alden, L. E. (2005). Social interpretation bias and generalized social phobia: The influence of developmental experiences. *Behaviour Research and Therapy, 43,* 759–777.

Taylor, S. (1996). Meta-analysis of cognitive-behavioral treatments for social phobia. *Journal of Behavior Therapy and Experimental Psychiatry, 27,* 1–9.

Teasdale, J. D., Segal, Z. V., Williams, J. M. G., Ridgeway, V. A., Soulsby, J. M., & Lau, M. A. (2000). Prevention of relapse/recurrence in major depression by mindfulness-based cognitive therapy. *Journal of Consulting and Clinical Psychology, 68,* 615–623.

Tolman, R. M., Himle, J., Bybee, D., Abelson, J. L., Hoffman, J., & Van Etten-Lee, M. (2009). Impact of social anxiety disorder on employment among women receiving welfare benefits. *Psychiatric Services, 60,* 61–66.

Turk, C. L., Heimberg, R. G., Orsillo, S. M., Holt, C. S., Gitow, A., Street, L. L., . . . Liebowitz, M. R. (1998). An investigation of gender differences in social phobia. *Journal of Anxiety Disorders, 12,* 209–223.

Turner, S. M., Beidel, D. C., & Jacob, R. G. (1994). Social phobia: A comparison of behavior therapy and atenolol. *Journal of Consulting and Clinical Psychology, 62,* 350–358.

Van Dam-Baggen, R., & Kraaimaat, F. (2000). Group social skills training or cognitive group therapy as the clinical treatment of choice for generalized social phobia? *Journal of Anxiety Disorders, 14,* 437–451.

Vriends, N., Becker, E. S., Meyer, A., Michael, T., & Margraf, J. (2007). Subtypes of social phobia: Are they of any use? *Journal of Anxiety Disorders, 21,* 59–75.

Weinstock, L. S. (1999). Gender differences in the presentation and management of social anxiety disorder. *Journal of Clinical Psychiatry, 60,* 9–13.

Weissman, M. M., Klerman, G. L., Prusoff, B. A., Sholomskas, D., & Padian, N. (1981). Depressed outpatients: Results one year after treatment with drugs and/or interpersonal psychotherapy *Archives of General Psychiatry, 38,* 51–55.

Wenzel, A. (2002). Characteristics of close relationships in individuals with social phobia: A preliminary comparison with nonanxious individuals. In J. H. Harvey & A. Wenzel (Eds.), *A clinician's guide to maintaining and enhancing close relationships* (pp. 199–213). Mahwah, NJ: Erlbaum.

Whisman, M., Sheldon, C., & Goering, P. (2000). Psychiatric disorders and dissatisfaction with social relationships: Does type of relationship matter? *Journal of Abnormal Psychology, 109,* 803–808.

Wlazlo, Z., Schroeder-Hartwig, K., Hand, I., Kaiser, G., & Münchau, N. (1990). Exposure in vivo vs. social skills training for social phobia: Long-term outcome and differential effects. *Behaviour Research and Therapy, 28,* 181–193.

28

Generalized Anxiety Disorder

ALLISON J. OUIMET, ROGER COVIN, AND DAVID J. A. DOZOIS

OVERVIEW OF DISORDER

Diagnostic Criteria

The objective of this chapter is to critically review the empirical evidence relevant to the treatment of generalized anxiety disorder (GAD) and provide a contemporary view of what can be considered *best practice*. Following a brief summary of the nature of the disorder, including diagnostic criteria, general characteristics, and overall burden, we provide a comprehensive review of the treatment outcome literature, with the primary goal of identifying current empirically supported treatments. Our hope is that this critical review can serve as a useful reference for professionals in both the research and clinical domains.

The diagnostic criteria for GAD have changed dramatically over the years, as the *Diagnostic and Statistical Manual of Mental Disorders* (*DSM*) has been revised. Consequently, understanding of the disorder has seemingly lagged behind that of other anxiety disorders. In *DSM-III* (American Psychiatric Association [APA], 1980), GAD was constructed as a residual anxiety diagnosis, meaning that a person was considered to have this disorder if he or she did not meet criteria for another anxiety disorder. This obviously made the clinical construct both vague and unspecified. It was not until

publication of *DSM-III-R* (APA, 1987) that GAD was given more of an identity, as the criteria were significantly modified and pathological worry was considered the key criterion. Changes in the diagnostic criteria for GAD, which also occurred in the most recent version of *DSM* (i.e., *DSM-IV*; APA, 1994), have resulted in far greater reliability in diagnoses of this disorder (Turk, Heimberg, & Mennin, 2004).

Notwithstanding significant improvements in reliability, shifting of nosology throughout the *DSM* revisions, coupled with the fact that the current criteria for GAD has only been in place for approximately 15 years, has likely impeded progress in this area of research. Dugas (2000) noted that GAD has received considerably less research attention than have other anxiety disorders, and that a considerable proportion of GAD studies up to 1997 were primarily focused on building a basic understanding of the qualities and characteristics of the disorder. Nevertheless, several prominent theories of GAD have emerged over the past 10–15 years, each of which focuses on the role of worry. These theories are reviewed in a later section of this chapter.

As mentioned, current *DSM* criteria for GAD make worry the centerpiece of the disorder. Specifically, in order to be diagnosed with GAD, individuals must experience persistent anxiety and worry over a period of at least six months, about a number of events or activities (e.g., health, finances, career). Furthermore, the worry must be considered difficult to control, and must not be due to another disorder (e.g., worrying primarily about health may warrant a diagnosis of hypochondriasis as opposed to GAD).

When assessing for GAD, it is often helpful to determine whether the individual's worry is normal or pathological. Everyone worries to some degree, and the content of worries among individuals with GAD tends to differ very little from those without GAD (Dugas & Robichaud, 2007; Turk et al., 2004). Although the content of worries may be similar, frequency and intensity of worry over an extended period of time, including the level of difficulty controlling the worried thoughts, are factors that usually distinguish pathological worry from normal worry. Borkovec, Ray, and Stober (1998) articulate the distinction between normal and pathological worry well—pathological worry is chronic, excessive, uncontrollable, and essentially takes the joy out of people's lives.

If a person meets the worry criteria, he or she must also persistently experience at least three of six additional symptoms to be diagnosed with GAD. These symptoms include restlessness or feeling *keyed up*, being easily fatigued, irritability, problems with concentration, muscle tension, and sleep disturbance. Sleep disturbance may manifest itself as difficulty falling or staying asleep, or having a restless and unsatisfying sleep. As with the worry criterion, some of these symptoms must be reliably present for at least six months. Despite the fact that worry is the central feature in the disorder, patients in primary care settings are actually more likely to present with bodily complaints and problems with sleep, than worry (Wittchen & Hoyer, 2001).

Demographic Variables

The aforementioned diagnostic changes to the GAD criteria have also complicated gathering of accurate epidemiological data (Kessler, Walters, & Wittchen, 2004). Nevertheless, enough research has been conducted, including the large National Comorbidity Survey (NCS) studies (e.g., Kessler et al., 2005; Kessler et al., 1994), to have confidence in the available epidemiological statistics on GAD. These studies tend to show that GAD has a lifetime prevalence of ~5% and a 12-month prevalence of ~3% (Kessler et al., 2005; Kessler, Chiu, Demler, & Walters, 2005; Kessler et al., 1994; Wittchen & Hoyer, 2001). These data also tend to show that twice as many women are diagnosed with GAD than are men (Kessler et al., 1994). Unfortunately, there is little available research that seeks to identify the causes of this gender difference (Robichaud, Dugas, & Conway, 2003).

In terms of typical age of onset, there have been varying reports in the literature; some researchers state that onset tends to be relatively early (i.e., adolescence/early adulthood; Brown, Barlow, & Liebowitz, 1994; Kessler et al., 2004), whereas others assert that onset tends to occur in early to middle adulthood (Sexton, Francis, & Dugas, 2008; Wittchen & Hoyer, 2001). Based on their review of the literature, Dugas and Robichaud (2007) posited a bimodal distribution, with peaks occurring between ages 11–20 and then again later in life. Clearly, there is a lack of consistency in our understanding of epidemiology of GAD, perhaps attributable, at least in part, to changing diagnostic criteria. Fairly recent data from the NCS studies suggest that GAD has a later onset than most other anxiety disorders, and that the prevalence of GAD increases across age groups until age 60 (Kessler et al., 2005). In their review, Wittchen and Hoyer (2001) also noted that risk of onset seemed to increase with age. Regardless of age of onset, research indicates that the condition tends to be fairly chronic, with only a minority of patients experiencing spontaneous remission (Brown et al., 1994; Wittchen & Hoyer, 2001), and many cases lasting a decade or longer (Kessler & Wittchen, 2002).

Both clinicians and researchers alike have observed that GAD often co-occurs with other psychological disorders (Kessler & Wittchen, 2002; Stein, 2001). The most common comorbid condition is depression, although it is not uncommon for GAD to also occur in conjunction with other anxiety disorders. The NCS data from 1994 indicate that 90% of individuals with a lifetime diagnosis of GAD had another lifetime psychiatric diagnosis, most commonly depression and dysthymia (Stein, 2001). Indeed, it is typically the rule, rather than the exception, that individuals with GAD will either have another concurrent disorder or will meet criteria for at least a second disorder at one point in their lives. This information is particularly important for the examination of outcome studies, as exclusion criteria often vary from study to study on the extent to which comorbidity is permitted.

Impact of Disorder

Unfortunately, a reputation seems to have developed about GAD that it causes less functional impairment among its sufferers than do other anxiety disorders (Dugas & Robichaud, 2007; Koerner et al., 2004). However, a recent comprehensive review of the personal and economic burden of GAD contradicts such beliefs (Hoffman, Dukes, & Wittchen, 2008). Hoffman et al. reviewed 34 studies from around the world. Significant variation existed in the methodologies used across studies, with most research examining the *human* burden of GAD (i.e., impairments in role functioning and quality of life), and a minority (3) studying its economic impact. Hoffman et al. found that individuals with comorbid GAD tended to be more impaired than did individuals without comorbidity. However, those with pure GAD exhibited impairments that were at least comparable to individuals with major depressive disorder (MDD) and other anxiety disorders.

The economic burden of GAD (including both direct and indirect costs) is also sizeable.

A European study, for instance, found that the 3-month cost of having GAD was $733 US per person for those without comorbidity and $1,208 for individuals with a co-occurring condition (Souêtre, Lozet, Cimarosti, & Martin, 1994). It is clear from Hoffman et al.'s review that previous beliefs about GAD patients being the worried well are quite inaccurate.

Because of inconsistent diagnostic criteria and consequent delays to research focusing on etiological and maintaining factors of GAD, outcome research has also lagged behind that of other anxiety disorders. Recently, however, several cognitive behavioral conceptualizations of GAD have been advanced, and have led to exciting treatment packages (e.g., Wells et al., 2010). The remainder of the chapter focuses on extant research examining efficacy and effectiveness of available treatment options, with the goal of providing an up-to-date analysis of best practices in the treatment of GAD.

COGNITIVE BEHAVIOR THERAPY

Consensus Panel Recommendations

Recently, several different agencies have put forth guidelines regarding best practices in the treatment of anxiety disorders. Overwhelmingly, the psychological therapy most recommended for GAD is cognitive behavior therapy (CBT). Whereas some agencies offer specific guidelines regarding how CBT should be implemented (e.g., McIntosh et al., 2004), others are less precise and suggest only that behavioral and cognitive therapies are helpful for anxiety disorders (National Institute of Mental Health, 2009).

The National Institute for Health and Clinical Excellence (NICE) developed detailed treatment protocols for Panic Disorder (PD) and GAD (McIntosh et al., 2004), wherein they reviewed extant research evidence for pharmacological and psychological interventions in these disorders. These guidelines suggest that the first line of treatment for GAD should be brief, weekly CBT (16–20 hours in total), offered in a primary care setting only by appropriately trained and supervised professionals. Following proper monitoring of care, nonresponders should be offered an alternative form of treatment (e.g., medication, bibliotherapy) and subsequently referred to care through specialist mental health services.

Similarly, the Canadian Psychiatric Association's guidelines advocate for use of CBT in the treatment of GAD (Swinson et al., 2006). Additionally, recent research cited in this report has demonstrated that the addition of cognitive techniques focused on intolerance of uncertainty, poor problem solving, positive beliefs about worry (Dugas, Marchand, & Ladouceur, 2005), as well as elements designed to improve interpersonal functioning (Borkovec, Newman, & Castonguay, 2003) and the sense of psychological well-being (Fava et al., 2005), may lead to improved outcome over and above traditional components of CBT (education, relaxation training, exposure, etc.). According to this report, no research exists at present to justify the combination of CBT with pharmacological treatments; however, consistent with the NICE recommendations, individuals who do not improve with CBT should be offered effective medicinal therapies. Moreover, Swinson et al. (2006) emphasize that the particular components of CBT that are used should be tailored to the particular context of each individual client.

Although the National Institute for Mental Health (NIMH) proposes that the choice between pharmacotherapy and psychotherapy (or combinatory approaches) in the treatment of anxiety disorders should be made depending on the specific problem and the individual's preference following a rigorous and detailed assessment, CBT is the only psychotherapy described in this report (National Institute of Mental Health, 2009). It should be noted, however, that the NIMH does not list effective psychological treatments specifically for GAD, but rather for the full spectrum of anxiety disorders.

Finally, Chambless and colleagues published several documents that arose out of a review of empirically supported treatments (ESTs) conducted by the American Psychological Association Division 12, Society of Clinical Psychology (Chambless et al., 1998; Chambless et al., 1996; Task Force on Promotion and Dissemination of Psychological Procedures, 1995). The goal of the task force was to examine the evidence for ESTs for various disorders, to encourage training for students and professionals in these treatments, and to disseminate information about these treatments to the public and to third-party payers. The authors classified treatments as either: (a) well-established treatments, or (b) probably efficacious treatments, based on the amount and type of existing research evidence (see Chambless & Ollendick, 2001, for a discussion of EST research methodology and classification). For example, treatments that had not been compared to psychological placebo or other treatments could not be considered well established but were considered probably efficacious as long as two or more studies showed that the treatment was more effective than a wait-list control. While acknowledging the incompleteness of their reports, the task force concluded that only CBT was a well-established treatment for individuals suffering from GAD. Applied relaxation (AR), a component of some CBT treatment packages, was classified as probably efficacious (Chambless et al., 1998; Chambless et al., 1996; Task Force on Promotion and Dissemination of Psychological Procedures, 1995).

Randomized Controlled Trials

A number of problems arise when examining existing research about efficacy of CBT for individuals suffering from GAD. First, differences in the diagnostic criteria of GAD over the past three decades have made it difficult to compare outcome studies that have been carried out years apart (Covin, Ouimet, Seeds, & Dozois, 2008). Second, although several studies testing efficacy of CBT exist, they utilize different components, and indeed are based on distinct theoretical models of GAD. For example, Borkovec's cognitive avoidance model (CAM) (e.g., Borkovec & Costello, 1993) has been tested most frequently in the empirical literature. This approach incorporates applied relaxation (AR) during anxiety-provoking mental imagery as described by Bernstein and Borkovec (1973; see also Öst, 1987) with cognitive therapy following Beck and Emery's (1985) methods (e.g., belief identification, evidence review, behavioral experimentation, etc.). More recent models of GAD have given rise to new testable forms of CBT focusing on intolerance of uncertainty (IUM) (e.g., Ladouceur et al., 2000), meta-cognitive variables (MCM) (e.g., Wells & King, 2006), and negative reactions to internal experiences (acceptance-based behavior therapy [ABBT]; e.g., Roemer & Orsillo, 2007). As such, blanket statements regarding the efficacy of CBT may be inappropriate given the variety of techniques employed across studies (also see K. S. Dobson & Dozois, 2010).

Finally, although several studies exist that evaluate the efficacy of current treatments for GAD, they vary methodologically. Indeed, randomized controlled trials (RCTs), which compare the treatment in question to a placebo condition or to another active treatment, provide the most rigorous test of a treatment's efficacy. Although extant research provides several examples of well conducted research, many RCTs have relied solely on wait list controls (WLCs) as comparison groups, limiting the conclusions that can be drawn about a treatment's efficacy over and above common treatment variables. Additionally, different studies have used different outcome measures. Whereas some experiments have utilized broad measures of anxiety (e.g., State Trait Anxiety Inventory [STAI], Spielberger, Gorsuch, Lushene, Vagg, & Jacobs, 1983), others have relied on diagnostic thresholds (e.g., Clinical Severity Rating [CSR] greater than 4 on the Anxiety Disorders Interview Schedule IV [ADIS IV], Brown, DiNardo, &

Barlow, 1994), and/or elevations on self-report scales reflecting pathological worry, the central feature of GAD (e.g., Penn State Worry Questionnaire [PSWQ]; Meyer, Miller, Metzger, & Borkovec, 1990). This diversity of outcome measurement complicates the comparison of efficacy studies.

Importantly, in two separate reviews, Fisher (Fisher, 2006; Fisher & Durham, 1999) reanalyzed data from RCTs conducted since the advent of *DSM-III-R* by applying standardized criteria for clinically significant change to extant data. Although most RCTs report indices of change other than traditional significance measures (e.g., percent recovered, percent achieving high end-state functioning, percent exhibiting clinically significant change), the criteria for these indices are often divergent across studies and outcome measures. By applying consistent definitions of clinically significant change to existing research, individual studies for a given treatment package (e.g., CAM) can be compared to one another. Moreover, although there is a paucity of research examining the relative efficacies of current treatment packages (van der Heiden, 2008), by reviewing clinically significant change achieved by each type of CBT, we can begin to address the question of whether one package is superior to another. According to Jacobson's criteria, (Jacobson, Follette, & Revenstorf, 1984; Jacobson & Truax, 1991), clinically significant change was achieved by participants whose posttest score on the STAI-T was less than or equal to 45 and represented a decrease from pretest of at least 8 points (Fisher, 2006; Fisher & Durham, 1999). Similar criteria have also been utilized for PSWQ scores, where the cutoff score was 47, and the change score was 7 (Fisher, 2006). This type of analysis allows for the comparison of extant research, and therefore, the comparison of different treatment packages.

All published RCTs that have examined efficacy of CBT for GAD and that employed clinical samples diagnosed according to criteria from *DSM-III-R* or later are reviewed in this section of the chapter. Additionally, any study that utilized either behavioral or cognitive techniques in the treatment of GAD are categorized under the rubric of CBT (D. Dobson & Dobson, 2009). Special attention is also paid to which treatment manual (if any) was used, thereby providing a preliminary comparison of the efficacy of current treatment packages. Finally, methodologically sound RCTs that compared CBT to an active treatment are given the most weight, followed by comparisons to placebo (PL) treatments, and ultimately to WLCs.

Cognitive Avoidance Model

Several studies have tested efficacy of a CBT package based on Borkovec and colleagues' cognitive avoidance model (CAM) (Borkovec, 1994, 2006; Borkovec & Costello, 1993; Sibrava & Borkovec, 2006). This model centers around the idea that worry is predominantly a verbal attempt to problem-solve possible future negative events, which further serves to reduce or inhibit aversive mental imagery, emotional experience, and physiological sensations (see Sibrava & Borkovec, 2006, for a detailed review). As such, worry is (consciously or unconsciously) self-reinforcing. Treatment, therefore, consists of typical cognitive therapy (CT) components (e.g., examining the accuracy of dysfunctional thoughts/ beliefs, generating alternative and more accurate thoughts/beliefs, and testing both sets of beliefs using experimental methods; Beck & Emery, 1985) as well as applied relaxation (AR) (Bernstein & Borkovec, 1973; Öst, 1987) implemented during exposure to anxiety-provoking, worry-related mental imagery (Borkovec, 2006).

Since the arrival of *DSM-III-R*, several RCTs have tested the efficacy of the CAM treatment versus active treatments (e.g., Durham, Murphy, Allan, & Richard, 1994), placebo treatments (e.g., Stanley, Beck, & Glassco, 1996), wait-list controls (WLCs) (e.g., Barlow, Rapee, & Brown, 1992), and specific CBT components (e.g., Borkovec, Newman, Pincus,

& Lytle, 2002) in participants diagnosed with GAD (see Table 28.1). Barlow et al. (1992) conducted the first of these experiments[1] by randomly assigning participants to receive either: (a) AR, (b) CT, (c) CBT, a combination of conditions one and two, or (d) WLC.

Following fifteen 1-hour sessions, outcome was assessed using several clinician-rated and self-report measures. All three active treatments resulted in significant reductions in anxious symptoms as measured by the clinical severity rating on the Anxiety Disorders Interview Schedule-Revised (ADIS-R) (DiNardo & Barlow, 1988), the Hamilton Anxiety Rating Scale (HAM-A) (Hamilton, 1959), percent of day spent worrying, and self-monitoring of daily anxiety levels. Moreover, when compared to the WLC, the CBT group showed significantly greater improvement on the ADIS-R, and the HAM-A; whereas the AR and CT groups demonstrated significantly reduced scores on all of the previously listed measures. Intent-to-treat analyses indicated that a significantly greater proportion of individuals in the active treatment groups were classified as treatment responders (33%–50%). A statistical trend also indicated that a higher percentage of individuals in these groups demonstrated high end-state functioning (19%–33%). No individuals in the WLC met criteria for clinically significant change. These gains were largely maintained at 6-, 12-, and 24-month follow-up (Barlow et al., 1992). As reported by Fisher (2006), the recovery rates on the STAI-T at posttreatment for the AR, CT, and CBT groups were 17%, 0%, and 11%, respectively. Of particular importance were results that indicated continued reduction of anxiolytic medication in all treated participants over the follow-up period, suggesting that CBT (and its components alone) may be useful in the

---

[1]Previous experiments have examined the efficacy of CBT in the treatment of GAD; however, Barlow et al. (1992) were the first to test the CAM treatment's utility with a clinical sample diagnosed according to *DSM-III-R* criteria.

TABLE 28.1 Summary of RCTs Evaluating the Efficacy of CBT for GAD

Study	N randomized per treatment	Tx Duration in Total Number of Hours	Reported % Who No Longer Met Diagnostic Criteria at Post-tx and longest follow-up interval	Fisher (2006) Indices of Clinically Significant Change Using Jacobson's Criteria STAI-T (PSWQ)			Outcome Summary
				Posttreatment	6-Month Follow-up	12-Month Follow-up	
GAD							
Borkovec et al.							
CBT			—	11 (—)	—	—	CBT. CT. AR > WL on most measures
CT			—	0 (—)	—	—	
AR			—	17 (—)	—	—	
WL			—		—	—	
Borkovec & Costello							
CBT			—	63 (53)	61 (—)	77 (47)	CBT. AR > SC at post-tx and follow-up
AR			—	56 (47)	77 (—)	53 (50)	
SC			—	17 (22)	38 (—)	39 (39)	
Durham et al.							
CBT			—	30 (—)	20 (—)	35 (—)	CT > AP at post-tx
CBT			—				
AP			—	27 (—)	15 (—)	40 (—)	CT ≫ AP. AMT > AP at follow-up
AP			—	7 (—)	15 (—)	7 (—)	
AMT			—	— (—)	14 (0)	0 (—)	
Stanley et al.			—	7 (—)	16 (—)	6 (—)	
Group CBT			—	—	—	—	CBT = SC at post-tx and follow-up
Group SC			—	—	—	—	

(*Continued*)

TABLE 28.1 Summary of RCTs Evaluating the Efficacy of CBT for GAD (*Continued*)

Study	N (intent-to-treat)	Tx Duration in Total Number of Hours	Reported % Who No Longer Met Diagnostic Criteria at Post-tx (and longest follow-up interval)	Fisher (2006) Indices of Clinically Significant Change Using Jacobson's Criteria STAI-T (PSWQ)			Outcome Summary
				Posttreatment	6-Month Follow-up	12-Month Follow-up	
Ost and Breitholtz (2000)*							
CT	17 (18)	12	—	17 (28)	—	22 (22)	CT > AR on STAI-T
AR	16 (18)		—	7 (13)	—	13 (27)	AR > CT on PSWQ Maintained at follow-up
Borkovec et al. (2002)							
CBT	23 (24)	23	8.69 (19.05)	57 (44)	52 (—)	52 (47)	CBT = CT = AR at post-tx and follow-up
CT	23 (25)		8.69 (19.05)	61 (44)	48 (—)	43 (43)	
AR	23 (27)		8.69 (14.29)	48 (56)	46 (—)	67 (43)	
Stanley et al. (2003)							
CBT	29 (39)	22.5	45 (64)	—	—	—	CBT > MCC at post-tx Gains maintained at follow-up
MCC	37 (41)	15	19 (—)	—	—	—	
Wetherell et al. (2003)							
CBT	18 (26)	12	78 (73)	—	—	—	CBT = DG CBT ≫ WL DG > WL
DG	18 (26)		61 (53)	—	—	—	
WL	2 (23)		14 (—)	—	—	—	Gains maintained at follow-up
Arntz (2003)				—	—	—	CT = AR at post-tx and follow-up

CBT > WL
Gains maintained at follow-up

CBT > MCC at post-tx
Gains maintained at follow-up

CBT > WL at post-tx
Gains maintained at follow-up

CBT > WL
Gains improved at follow-up

CBT > SC at post-tx and follow-up

(Continued)

TABLE 28.1 Summary of RCTs Evaluating the Efficacy of CBT for GAD (*Continued*)

Study	N (intent-to-treat)	Tx Duration in Total Number of Hours	Reported % Who No Longer Met Diagnostic Criteria at Post-tx (and longest follow-up interval)	Fisher (2006) Indices of Clinically Significant Change Using Jacobson's Criteria STAI-T (PSWQ)			Outcome Summary
				Posttreatment	6-Month Follow-up	12-Month Follow-up	
van der Heiden (2008)		14					
MCT	45 (52)		88 (–)	–	–	–	MCT = IUM CBT
IUM CBT	33 (52)		80 (–)	–	–	–	MCT > WL at post-tx and follow-up
WL	19 (52)		5 (–)	–	–	–	
Dugas et al. (2010)		12					
CBT	21 (23)		70 (77)	–	–	–	CBT, AR > WL at post-tx
AR	17 (22)		55 (61)	–	–	–	CBT > AR at post-tx and follow-up
WL	20 (20)		–	–	–	–	
MCT							
van der Heiden (2008)	See above						
Wells (2009)		8–12					
MCT	10 (10)		100 (90)	80 (80)	70 (–)	70 (80)	MCT > AR at post-tx and follow-up
AR	10 (10)		50 (50)	10 (10)	29 (–)	33 (17)	
ABBT							
Roemer & Orsillo (2008)		18					
ABBT	13 (15)		76.92	–	–	–	ABBT > WL at post-tx
WL	12 (16)		16.67	–	–	–	Gains maintained at follow-up

Note: CAM = Cognitive Avoidance Model; IUM = Intolerance of Uncertainty Model; MCT = Metacognitive Therapy; ABBT = Acceptance Based Behavior Therapy. Because intent-to-treat analyses were not always included, this table reports data obtained from completer analyses. For experiments using a WLC, percentages of participants no longer meeting diagnostic criteria were based on analyses of data following treatment of individuals in the WLC.

* Sample sizes were calculated assuming that the original number of participants were evenly assigned to the conditions.

** Because no significant differences were observed between high and low contact conditions, results were collapsed in RCT section.

reduction of benzodiazepine use (see Ahmed, Westra, & Stewart, 2008; Barlow et al., 1992). More recently, Linden, Zubraegel, Baer, Franke, and Schlattmann (2005) confirmed efficacy of CBT (compared to a WLC) in the reduction of anxious symptoms among individuals with non-comorbid GAD.

Two studies have compared CBT to non-directive supportive counseling (SC) with divergent results. Whereas Borkovec and Costello (1993) demonstrated that both CBT and AR alone were superior (clinically significant change rates on the STAI-T according to Fisher [2006] were 63% and 56%, respectively) treatments to SC (17%), Stanley et al. (1996) reported equivalent positive outcome in the reduction of GAD symptom severity, worry, and global measures of anxiety for CBT and SC. Close inspection of the methodology of these studies reveals two major differences: (1) mean sample age (37.5 years in Borkovec & Costello, 1993; 68.3 years in Stanley et al., 1996), and (2) treatment modality (individual in Borkovec & Costello, 1993; group in Stanley et al., 1996). It may be, therefore, that group CBT is less efficacious than its individual counterpart in the treatment of GAD, and moreover that variables such as duration of symptomatology (longer in elderly samples), executive functioning difficulties (Caudle et al., 2007), and the structure of affect (e.g., differences between older and younger samples on frequency of affective factors such as hostility, contentment, etc.; Lawton, Kleban, & Dean, 1993) make more difficult the treatment of older adults with GAD (see Covin et al., 2008).

Indeed, Stanley et al. (1996) used a version of CBT that was adapted for use in elderly samples (presenting material more slowly, using more visual and written aids, using less jargon). Subsequent experiments employing the adapted CAM group treatment package with older adults diagnosed with GAD demonstrated significantly better treatment outcome than a WLC, with possible advantages over a discussion group condition (DG) on reported time spent worrying (Wetherell, Gatz,

& Craske, 2003), and significantly reduced scores on measures of worry and anxiety (with gains maintained at follow-up) compared to a minimal contact control (MCC) group in community (Stanley et al., 2003) and primary care samples (Stanley et al., 2009). Moreover, recent research suggests that supplementing CBT with executive skills training may lead to improved outcome in older adults with GAD (Mohlman, 2008).

Despite the large number of studies using placebo and wait-list controls, to date only one study has tested efficacy of the CAM treatment package against another active treatment for individuals diagnosed with GAD according to DSM-III-R or later (Durham et al., 1994). Participants were randomly assigned to either (a) CT (without the AR component; i.e., Beck & Emery, 1985), (b) analytical psychotherapy (AP) (no specific manual cited), or (c) anxiety management training (AMT) (D. M. Clark, 1989), which consisted largely of psychoeducation and a focus on adaptive coping. The CT was clearly superior to AP at post-treatment and at 6-month follow-up as evidenced by reduced scores on measures of anxious symptoms and double the percentage of individuals meeting Jacobson's criteria (Jacobson et al., 1984) for clinically significant change in the CT group than in the AP group. Although there were no significant differences in outcome between the CT and AMT groups, only CT showed a clear advantage over AP.

In a long-term (8-year) follow-up to this study, CT and AMT groups were amalgamated because of low sample size and compared to the AP group (Durham, Chambers, MacDonald, Power, & Major, 2003). Results indicated that there was generally no significant outcome difference between the two conditions. Issues related to follow-up sample size, diagnostic comorbidity, and psychotherapy received in between posttreatment and long-term follow-up, however, make the interpretation of these results difficult (Durham et al., 2003).

Evidence reviewed earlier reveals that Borkovec et al.'s CAM treatment package (e.g., Borkovec, 1994, 2006; Borkovec & Costello, 1993; Sibrava & Borkovec, 2006) has shown efficacy in the treatment of GAD when compared to WLCs (e.g., Linden et al., 2005), some placebo treatments (e.g., Wetherell et al., 2003), and one active treatment (Durham et al., 1994). Research examining the distinct and combined impact of the components of the CAM treatment package has, however, been equivocal. A further review of studies specifically investigating the contributions of CBT components may help to clarify what role is played by CT, AR, and their combination.

Five studies have examined efficacy of CBT and its components in the treatment of GAD in individuals who have been diagnosed subsequent to *DSM-III-R* (Arntz, 2003; Barlow et al., 1992; Borkovec & Costello, 1993; Borkovec et al., 2002; Öst & Breitholtz, 2000). Although participants in all active CBT conditions (CT, AR, or CBT) improved on measures of anxiety and worry, no important significant differences emerged between components on treatment efficacy, with the exception of one study. In their comparison of CT and AR, Öst and Breitholtz (2000) demonstrated that both conditions showed improvement, but treatment change appeared to vary contingent upon the measure. Only individuals in the CT group showed reduced global anxiety symptoms as measured by the state and trait version of the STAI (Spielberger et al., 1983), whereas only the AR group evidenced less worry as measured by the PSWQ (Meyer et al., 1990). Other experiments investigating the differential efficacy of CBT components have also used a combination of global anxiety and worry-specific measures but did not reveal significant group differences. As such, although CBT according to the CAM model is well supported as an efficacious treatment for GAD, it remains unclear which components are responsible for symptom change, or whether a combination of components is necessary. Further research examining the specific effects of CBT components is warranted.

Intolerance of Uncertainty Model (IUM)

A more recent theory on the etiology and maintenance of GAD focuses on the construct of intolerance of uncertainty (e.g., Dugas, Buhr, & Ladouceur, 2004). Essentially, individuals with GAD are more likely to react negatively to uncertain events or situations, regardless of whether that event is likely or the consequences are severe (Dugas et al., 2005; Freeston, Rhéaume, Letarte, & Dugas, 1994; Ladouceur et al., 1999). This model also posits that individuals with GAD believe that their chronic worry either helps them to prevent negative events from happening in the first place or, at least, prepares them to cope in the event that adverse circumstances arise. This worry, in turn, is associated with poor problem solving and cognitive avoidance, which, similar to the CAM, serve to perpetuate symptoms of anxiety (Dugas, Gagnon, Ladouceur, & Freeston, 1998).

The CBT based on this model, therefore, consists of: (a) increasing tolerance of uncertainty, (b) reevaluating the usefulness of worry, (c) improving problem orientation and problem-solving ability, and (d) processing core fears through imaginal exposure (Robichaud & Dugas, 2006). A unique early stage of this CBT package involves working with the client to separate worries into one of two categories: current problems (i.e., solvable), or hypothetical situations (i.e., unsolvable). Different interventions are then applied to each type of worry; problem-solving training focuses on the solvable worries, whereas worries about hypothetical situations are dealt with through cognitive exposure (Provencher, Dugas, & Ladouceur, 2004). It is important to note that although both the CAM and IUM treatment packages have a cognitive exposure component, the IUM treatment package does not contain a relaxation component. Instead, therapists encourage clients to vividly experience their worries though mental imagery while noting their levels of anxiety until the core fear is processed and the worry is reduced over time (Robichaud & Dugas, 2006).

As such, although AR was considered as an element of CBT in the previous section, it functions as an alternative active treatment to the IUM package.

Four RCTs have tested the efficacy of CBT as described by the IUM in the treatment of GAD (see Table 28.1). Results have demonstrated significantly improved symptoms for the CBT conditions when compared to WLCs in both individual (Dugas et al., 2010; Ladouceur et al., 2000) and group formats (Dugas et al., 2003). These treatment gains were maintained at follow-up (Ladouceur et al., 2000) and, in two of the experiments, improvement in the CBT groups actually continued over time (Dugas et al., 2010; Dugas et al., 2003). In his review of clinically significant change, Fisher (2006) noted that data collected by Dugas et al. (2003) indicated that 48% of participants in the group CT condition were recovered following treatment (as measured by the PSWQ) compared to 4% of individuals in the WLC. At 6-month follow-up, treatment gains improved further, evidencing a recovery rate of 64% (Fisher, 2006).

The only study to examine effects of CBT compared to a placebo treatment focused on benzodiazepine reduction in a sample of individuals diagnosed with GAD who were interested in terminating the use of anxiolytic medication (Gosselin, Ladouceur, Morin, Dugas, & Baillargeon, 2006). Participants were randomly assigned to 12 sessions of either CBT with gradual tapering or SC with gradual tapering. Results demonstrated that the proportion of participants in the CBT group who discontinued benzodiazepine at posttreatment was double that of the SC group. This significant difference was maintained at 3-, 6-, and 12-month follow-up. Moreover, the CBT group showed significantly decreased worry and negative problem orientation following treatment.

Finally, two studies have recently been conducted using an active treatment as a control group. One of these experiments compared the treatment efficacy of CBT to AR and (as described earlier) a WLC (Dugas et al., 2010).

Both CBT and AR showed improvement on all measures from pre- to posttest as well as significant reductions in clinical severity ratings on the ADIS-IV compared to the WLC. However, only the CBT group evidenced reduced self-reported worry and somatic symptoms associated with GAD. Moreover, whereas treatment gains for the AR condition were maintained over time, only the CBT group demonstrated continued improvement on the PSWQ, STAI-T, and Clinical Global Impression-Improvement Scale (CGI-I) (Guy, 1976) from posttreatment to 24-month follow-up (Dugas et al., 2010). Van der Heiden (2008) reported preliminary findings from an experiment examining the relative efficacies of the IUM and the metacognitive model treatment packages, which are reviewed in the next section.

Metacognitive Model

Similar to the IUM, the metacognitive model (MCM) (e.g., Wells, 2005) divides worry into two separate categories. Whereas the IUM distinguishes solvable from unsolvable worries, the MCM classifies worries as either Type 1, worry about life events or situations such as work, family, finances, and so forth, or Type 2, worry about cognitive events such as thought processes or worry about worry (Wells, 1995). According to this model, individuals with GAD worry about worry because of their negative beliefs about the uncontrollability of worry and the dangerous mental, physical, and/or social consequences that may result from their worry. In contrast, positive beliefs about worry, in their role as coping and preparatory strategies, serve to maintain Type 1 worry (Wells & Carter, 2006). The treatment package based on the MCM — metacognitive therapy (MCT) — focuses largely on Type 2 worry. Therapy involves forming a detailed case conceptualization where the nature and depth of the metacognitive beliefs are determined so that they can subsequently be challenged and modified, and alternative strategies for dealing with the what-ifs characteristic of worry can be adopted.

Two RCTs have compared efficacy of MCT to alternative treatments. In a recent pilot study 20 participants diagnosed with GAD according to *DSM-IV-TR* were randomly assigned to receive 8–12 sessions of either MCT or AR (Wells et al., 2010). Compared to the AR condition, results demonstrated significantly greater decreases on measures of worry and trait anxiety, as well as positive and negative beliefs about worry for participants in the MCT condition. An examination of effect sizes reveals 2–6 times greater effects for the MCT condition than for the AR group. At 6- and 12-month follow-up, these differences remained significant for all but one measure related to anxiety (Beck Anxiety Inventory [BAI]; Beck, Epstein, Brown, & Steer, 1988). Moreover, clinically significant change as defined by Jacobson and Truax (1991) was obtained at posttreatment for 70%–80% of participants in the MCT group, as compared to 10% in the AR group. These proportions were largely maintained at 6- and 12-month follow-up. Finally, Wells et al. (2010) reported that, whereas at posttreatment and 12-month follow-up 50% of participants in the AR group no longer met criteria for GAD, the proportions of recovered participants were much higher for the MCT group at 100% and 90%, respectively. Rates of reported clinically significant change for MCT in Wells et al.'s (2010) study are remarkable. Indeed, they are substantially higher than the average rates obtained for CBT (and/or its components) in previous experiments utilizing other treatment packages (34%–46% at posttreatment, 46%–63% at 1-year follow-up; Fisher, 2006). The potential of treatments modeled after cognitive conceptualizations specific to GAD is exciting. Future research aimed at replication, however, is needed.

In the only study to compare two contemporary active CBT packages, van der Heiden (2008) randomly assigned individuals diagnosed with primary GAD to either MCT ($N = 52$), IUM treatment ($N = 52$), or a WLC ($N = 52$). Preliminary analyses included only data obtained from the PSWQ and Structured Clinical Interview for *DSM-IV-TR* Axis I disorders (SCID-I) (First, Spitzer, Gibbon, & Williams, 2001) for treatment completers (MCT, $N = 45$; IUM, $N = 33$; WLC, $N = 19$). Recovery rates for participants in both the MCT and IUM groups were very high (88% and 80%, respectively); however, clinically significant change rates for the PSWQ were less comparable (71% and 46%, respectively). Additionally, although scores on the PSWQ at posttreatment were lowest for MCT, followed by IUM, and then WLC, the only difference that reached statistical significance was that of MCT versus WLC. Both MCT and IUM evidenced maintenance of treatment gains at follow-up (interval not reported) with large effect sizes. Therefore, although both IUM and MCT are efficacious treatments, the preliminary results of van der Heiden's (2008) study indicate that MCT may offer an advantage over IUM in terms of clinical significance. Additional research is needed to examine the relative efficacies of these recent treatment packages.

Acceptance-Based Behavior Therapy

The acceptance-based model posits that individuals with GAD react negatively to internal experiences, and use worry as a mechanism to avoid these experiences (Roemer & Orsillo, 2005). Moreover, as threat (e.g., relationship problems) becomes associated with these internal experiences, individuals may begin to avoid valued actions, such as spending time with their families, thus reducing their quality of life. Acceptance-based behavior therapy (ABBT), therefore, involves increasing acceptance (rather than avoidance) of internal experiences through acceptance and mindfulness-based strategies (e.g., Hayes, Strosahl, & Wilson, 1999; Kabat-Zinn, 2003) and encouraging increased connectedness with people and activities that they personally value (Roemer & Orsillo, 2005).

To date, only one RCT has been conducted to evaluate ABBT in the treatment of GAD (Roemer, Orsillo, & Salters-Pedneault, 2008). Compared to clients in the WLC, individuals in the ABBT condition showed significantly reduced scores on assessor- and self-reported indices of GAD severity, worry, and stress, and significantly increased scores on a measure of quality of life. Following treatment, 77% of people in the ABBT group no longer met criteria for GAD (compared to 17% in the WLC), and 75% met criteria for high end-state functioning (compared to 8% in the WLC). Treatment gains were maintained at 3- and 9-month follow-up. A study comparing the efficacy of ABBT to that of AR in the treatment of GAD is currently underway (L. Roemer, personal communication, July 2009).

Meta-Analyses of Group Designs

To date, nine meta-analyses (MAs) have been conducted that examine efficacy of CBT for GAD. Although these MAs have largely produced positive results, different methodologies, inclusion/exclusion criteria, and timeframes (i.e., diagnoses according to different versions of the *DSM*) have led to some equivocation in their conclusions. Close inspection of the methodologies used in each MA may help to clarify the overall efficacy of CBT for GAD.

The earliest conducted MA included seven studies (Chambless & Gillis, 1993), all of which were published in or before 1993. With one exception (Borkovec & Costello, 1993), the experiments relied on GAD diagnoses according to *DSM III* or earlier. As mentioned, worry was not identified as the core feature of GAD until *DSM III R*, which limits the generalizability of results based on studies conducted before this time to our current understanding of treatment efficacy. Although this MA reported large effect sizes for CBT compared to WLCs and pill placebo treatments, its results may have little bearing on the efficacy of current CBT packages in the treatment of worry and anxiety symptoms characteristic of GAD.

In their comparison of CBT and pharmacotherapy in the treatment of GAD, Gould, Otto, Pollack, and Yap (1997) reported an overall between-groups effect size of 0.70 for

CBT—which consisted of any cognitive, behavioral, or combined treatment compared to a no treatment or placebo control condition—with treatment gains maintained over time. Pharmacotherapy and CBT were equally efficacious at posttreatment, when compared to their relative control groups. However, there was some evidence that effects of pharmacotherapy on anxious symptoms dissipated at follow-up. Additionally, the largest effect sizes among the cognitive behavioral treatments were observed for the full CBT packages (ES = 0.91), followed by their components (0.34 < ESs < 0.64). A follow-up MA, which included three additional studies, demonstrated similar results and indicated that CBT is an efficacious treatment for GAD in both the short- and long-term (Gould, Safren, Washington, & Otto, 2004). It is worth noting that the studies included in these MAs were published between the years of 1975 and 1993. As such, participants were diagnosed across three different versions of the *DSM*, and may have represented fairly distinct clinical samples.

Borkovec and Ruscio (2001) conducted a MA that examined the efficacy of CBT compared not only to no treatment and placebo/alternative treatment conditions, but also to its components. Of the 13 RCTs included (1984–1996), the largest within-groups effect sizes for posttreatment and 6- to 12-month follow-up were observed for the CBT treatments (2.48, 2.44), followed by placebo/alternative (2.09, 2.00), CT or BT components (1.72, 1.71), and finally no treatment (0.01). Moreover, CBT demonstrated large between-groups effect sizes when compared to no treatment controls, small to large effect sizes relative to placebo treatments, and small to moderate effect sizes when contrasted with CT and BT components.

Interestingly, for MAs that compared CBT to its components in the treatment of GAD, larger effect sizes emerged for the combined treatments than for behavioral (including AR) or cognitive elements alone (Borkovec & Ruscio, 2001; Gould, Otto, Pollack, & Yap, 1997;

Gould et al., 2004). This finding is in stark contrast to the evidence described in the section on RCTs that suggests that the components are equally efficacious. Such equivocation is likely attributable to two factors. First, whereas the studies reviewed in the RCT section were conducted only with samples diagnosed according to *DSM-III-R* or later criteria, all three MAs summarized experiments across various versions of the *DSM*, and therefore, various GAD diagnoses. As such, the MAs included studies not described in the RCT section, which may have demonstrated significantly better outcome for combined CBT. Second, a major limitation of many treatment outcome studies is their typically small sample sizes, which can result in reduced power. Similarly, a major advantage of MAs is their reliance on samples collapsed across studies, which increases the likelihood of finding significant effects should they exist. As such, it is possible that the individual RCTs described earlier did not have sufficient statistical power to reveal significant differences between CBT and its' components, whereas MAs, because of their combined increased sample size, uncovered such differences.

Haby, Donnelly, Corry, and Vos (2006) reported a medium to large effect size in their MA that included only RCTs that used samples diagnosed according to *DSM-III-R* or later criteria. Additionally, one MA that investigated efficacy of CBT in comparison to pharmacological treatments for GAD reported medium and large between-groups effect sizes for CBT versus WLC and placebo treatments, respectively (Mitte, 2005). Although the results were equivocal with respect to the superiority of either CBT or pharmacotherapy, attrition rates for CBT (9%) were significantly lower than were those for pharmacotherapy (25%), providing evidence that CBT may be a more tolerable treatment.

The MAs previously described have documented efficacy of CBT for GAD symptoms. In contrast, Westen and Morrison (2001) concluded in their MA that, although empirically supported treatments appear to provide relief immediately following treatment, the paucity of evidence with respect to long-term treatment change indicates that the majority of GAD sufferers likely do not achieve sustained recovery. Closer examination of the differences between this and other MAs may help clarify these discrepant findings.

Westen and Morrison (2001) employed strict inclusion criteria to maximize the experimental integrity of the MA. As such, they included only RCTs that compared a primarily face-to-face standardized treatment to a waiting list control, alternative psychotherapy, pharmacotherapy, or some combination thereof. Moreover, studies were excluded if they did not employ blind assessors, or if their sample consisted of small subsets of a population (e.g., elderly participants). Importantly, only follow-up intervals of 12 months or longer were included. Finally, because the authors wanted a current picture of the efficacy of standardized treatments, they included only studies published between 1990 and 1998. These criteria yielded only five studies pertaining to the treatment of GAD.

For studies including more than one active treatment (e.g., relaxation training and cognitive therapy), effects were collapsed across treatments. As such, the between-groups effect sizes reported in this MA were calculated using data from studies of CBT (and/or its components), brief supportive/expressive psychotherapy (BS/EP), analytic psychotherapy (AP), and anxiety management training (AMT). This combination of theoretically distinct treatment packages may attenuate findings of symptom change (and maintenance of such change) attributable to specific therapeutic factors. Indeed, as noted by Aikins, Hazlett-Stevens, and Craske (2001), the effect size estimated from only the four CBT conditions included in Westen and Morrison's (2001) MA is larger (1.18) than that reported for all the active conditions collapsed (0.90). Moreover, because of their strict inclusion criteria, the authors included no studies conducted after 1998, despite the fact that experiments conducted after this date were based largely on important conceptual advancements (e.g., intolerance of uncertainty) of CBT treatment models (see Aikins et al., 2001).

Additionally, Westen and Morrison (2001) utilized the HAM-A and the STAI-T as outcome variables. Although these measures are well supported in their assessment of global anxiety symptoms, they do not measure the central diagnostic feature of GAD—worry. Similarly, all of the MAs discussed earlier have used composite indices of anxiety calculated by computing the mean effect size across several measures, which reflect symptoms related to trait anxiety, specific phobias, somatic symptoms, and worry, to assess the efficacy of CBT in the treatment of GAD.

To account for this gap in the literature, Covin et al. (2008) published a MA investigating the efficacy of CBT in the reduction of worry among individuals suffering from GAD. By including only studies conducted with samples diagnosed according to *DSM III R* or later criteria who utilized the PSWQ as an outcome measure to compare the efficacy of CBT to placebo treatment or no treatment control groups, the authors were able to obtain a contemporary index of the efficacy of current CBT treatment for GAD. All of the included studies used CBT according to the CAM or IUM treatment packages. The effect size reported for CBT was large (1.18), and fail safe N analyses indicated that for the results to become nonsignificant, 18 studies with null results would have to be conducted. Moreover, closer examination of the data revealed larger effect sizes for individual (1.72) versus group treatment (0.91) modalities, and for younger (1.69) versus older adults (0.82; Covin et al., 2008). Within groups analyses demonstrated that treatment gains were maintained at 6- and 12-month follow-up.

Importantly, prior to treatment, participants with GAD fell within the clinical range on the PSWQ, and at least 1 standard deviation outside of the normative range (Covin et al., 2008). At posttreatment and follow-up, the average PSWQ score of participants fell within the

normative range, and at least 1 standard deviation outside of the clinical range. These results indicate that CBT is an efficacious treatment for worry, which is the central feature of GAD. Furthermore, although studies utilizing global measures of anxiety have indicated high rates of continued symptomatology (i.e., low proportions of participants who meet high end-state functioning) following treatment (e.g., Stanley et al., 2003), Covin et al. (2008) have demonstrated remittance of worry attributable to CBT in the short- and long-term. Finally, the authors suggested that the IUM treatment package may produce larger effect sizes than the CAM treatment package, but acknowledged that this suggestion was based on a very limited number of studies, and therefore remains an empirical question for future research.

Finally, Stewart and Chambless (2009) conducted a MA to examine the effectiveness of CBT across the anxiety disorders. Whereas efficacy studies employ strict inclusion/exclusion criteria, randomization, and treatment manuals, some researchers believe that their results do not generalize to those that would be obtained in real-life practice (e.g., Sanderson, Raue, & Wetzler, 1998; Seligman, 1995; Westen & Morrison, 2001). As such, studies that fit certain criteria such as the use of clinically representative samples, clinically representative structure, and flexible number of sessions (see Shadish, Navarro, Matt, & Phillips, 2000; Weisz, Donenberg, Han, & Weiss, 1995 for a detailed list), were included in Stewart and Chambless' (2009) MA. Results demonstrated large within participants' effect sizes (0.92) for CBT in the treatment of GAD, which falls within the range found in efficacy studies. It appears, therefore, that overall, CBT is an efficacious and effective treatment for GAD.

Single Case Designs

Single case designs typically involve symptom assessment pre- and posttreatment in a small sample of participants, without a control group comparison. Although the information gleaned from this type of design is severely limited by confounding factors (e.g., nonspecific treatment effects, spontaneous remission, etc.), it provides preliminary support for potential treatments that should subsequently be tested in RCTs, as well as additional evidence regarding the efficacy of treatment packages that have already been evaluated using more stringent methods. The following section briefly reviews open trials that have been conducted on recent treatment packages with the goal of providing a comprehensive overview of research examining the efficacy of CBT for GAD.

Cognitive Avoidance Model/Integrative Model

In a recent investigation of the CAM treatment package, benchmarking—comparing outcome data from previously conducted RCTs (for this study Borkovec & Costello, 1993) with that of research conducted in frontline settings (e.g., Wade, Treat, & Stuart, 1998)—was conducted to examine whether the already documented efficacy of this treatment among highly controlled GAD samples would generalize to treatment effectiveness in a real-world setting without the use of experimental controls (Kehle, 2008). Because the authors were examining generalizability of CBT in a frontline setting, patients ($N = 29$) were not screened for a GAD diagnosis, but rather were offered treatment if they suffered from debilitating worry. No experimental exclusion criteria were enforced (e.g., alcohol abuse, psychosis, severe comorbidity, medication use/stability). Results demonstrated a significantly higher dropout rate (72%) in the frontline sample than the benchmark sample (19%; Borkovec & Costello, 1993). This attrition rate had a large impact upon the further results of the study, as demonstrated by nonsignificant pre- to posttreatment decreases on the PSWQ among intent-to-treat participants, and significant improvement on the same measure among treatment completers. The effect size among treatment completers was large

($d = 0.96$) but substantially lower than what was reported by Borkovec and Costello ($d = 1.86$; Borkovec & Costello, 1993). These results suggest that, although the CAM treatment package is efficacious for GAD, its effectiveness is more limited. It should be noted, however, that although Kehle's (2008) findings are supported by similar results obtained in the only other (albeit large-scale) effectiveness trial of CBT for GAD (Westbrook & Kirk, 2005), limitations, such as lack of GAD diagnosis, considerably elevated attrition rate, and nonexpert therapists muddle the conclusions that may be drawn from this research.

Interestingly, effect size obtained using the completer data was identical to the effect size reported in Stewart and Chambless' (2009) MA of effectiveness studies. Moreover, whereas Kehle (2008) offered eight sessions of CBT in a frontline setting to any patient who wanted to reduce debilitating worry and enforced no exclusion criteria, Stewart and Chambless included several studies that fell on a continuum of experimental control, and therefore may not be an accurate representation of strict effectiveness methodology, per se. It is evident from these discrepant findings, however, that future research should focus on evaluating the effectiveness of different CBT packages (or indeed, CBT as a whole, given the treatment flexibility inherent in real-life settings) in the treatment of GAD.

Recently, the CAM treatment package has been combined with interpersonal psychotherapy to form what has been termed integrative psychotherapy (IP) (Borkovec, Alcaine, & Behar, 2004; Newman, Castonguay, Borkovec, & Molnar, 2004). The IP posits that early trauma, insecure attachment, and poor interpersonal skills may be important factors in the etiology and maintenance of GAD (Borkovec et al., 2004; Sibrava & Borkovec, 2006). As such, in addition to CBT, IP includes a focus on interpersonal functioning and emotional processing. Recently, an open trial tested efficacy of this treatment in 18 participants diagnosed with GAD (Newman, Castonguay,

Borkovec, Fisher, & Nordberg, 2008). Results demonstrated significant decreases on measures of anxiety, worry, fear of relaxation, and interpersonal problems, with treatment gains maintained at 1-year follow-up. Moreover, over three quarters of participants demonstrated clinically significant change at follow-up. Although these results are promising, RCTs evaluating the efficacy of IP in comparison to no treatment and alternative treatment control groups are warranted.

Intolerance of Uncertainty Model

Although the IUM treatment package has been examined in fewer studies than has the CAM model (largely because it is a more recent model), results from four RCTs have supported its efficacy. In addition to those trials, three single case designs have been conducted in recent years (Dugas & Ladouceur, 2000; Ladouceur, Leger, Dugas, & Freeston, 2004; Provencher et al., 2004). Results supported the efficacy of the IUM treatment package for the treatment of GAD in younger (Dugas & Ladouceur, 2000; Provencher et al., 2004) and older adults (Ladouceur et al., 2004), with recovery rates (percentage of participants no longer meeting *DSM-IV* [1994] criteria for GAD) ranging from 67.7% to 87.5%. Although all three studies reported maintenance of treatment gains at 6-month follow-up, 12-month follow-up results were equivocal. Dugas and Ladouceur described partial recurrence among two of the three recovered participants, whereas Ladouceur et al. reported sustained treatment effects. Provencher et al. did not report 12-month follow-up data.

Metacognitive Model

In addition to studies described in the RCT section, one single-case experiment has been conducted to test the efficacy of MCT for GAD (Wells & King, 2006). Results demonstrated significantly reduced symptoms of global anxiety according to the BAI and STAI-T, as well as social worry, health worry, and meta-worry as measured by the anxious thoughts

inventory (Wells, 1994). Moreover, Wells and King reported that 88% recovered on the STAI-T as defined by Jacobson's criteria, with 75% of the total sample maintaining recovery at 6- and 12-month follow-up. These results, combined with positive outcome described in two RCTs (van der Heiden 2008; Wells et al., 2009) indicate that MCT is a promising new treatment for GAD.

Acceptance-Based Behavior Therapy

Roemer and Orsillo (2007) first tested ABBT with 19 subjects diagnosed with primary GAD. Results for the 16 participants who completed treatment indicated significant improvement with large effect sizes on several measures of worry, anxiety, and fear and avoidance of internal experiences. These effects were maintained for the 12 participants who were available at 3-month follow-up. With respect to clinical significance, three quarters of participants were classified as treatment responders, and 63% met criteria for high end state functioning. Follow-up analyses including data from the four unavailable participants (at posttreatment, two were classified as nonresponders) revealed that clinical significance rates had dropped: 50% met criteria for treatment response, and 50% maintained high end state functioning. These rates are similar to those documented by Fisher (2006) for other types of CBT in his reanalysis of extant data using Jacobson's criteria (e.g., Jacobson & Truax, 1991).

Conclusions

Several different treatment packages falling under the heading of CBT have been tested since the advent of *DSM-III-R*. Although these packages share many similarities (e.g., focus on cognitive avoidance), they are also differentiated by basic underlying tenets (e.g., intolerance of uncertainty versus worry about worry; Behar, Dimarco, Hekler, Mohlman, & Staples, 2009). Despite theoretical and practical distinctions between these approaches (e.g., use of relaxation, focus on worry vs. acceptance of worry), they have largely shown efficacy in the treatment of GAD, when compared to WLCs, placebos, and alternative treatments. Recovery rates, however, have been low in comparison to other anxiety disorders (e.g., 50% according to Borkovec & Newman, 1998; 80%–85% according to D. A. Clark, 1996). Indeed, when stringent criteria were applied across studies, the percentage of participants classified as recovered on the STAI-T following CBT, AR, and/or CT were 46%, 34%, and 36%, respectively (Fisher, 2006). Treatment gains improved further for the AR and CBT conditions, but not for the CT group at 12-month follow-up. Clinically significant change rates were similar for the PSWQ at posttreatment (AR = 37%, CT = 37%, CBT = 48%), with continued improvement demonstrated by the CBT group at 12-month follow-up.

Importantly, in his review, Fisher (2006) examined efficacy of more recent models of GAD separately. In particular, he reported higher rates of clinically significant change obtained on the PSWQ by the IUM and MCT treatment packages at posttreatment (48% and 80%, respectively) and 12-month follow-up (64% and 80%, respectively). At the time that his review was published, however, raw data were available for only one study testing the IUM, and one manuscript in preparation that described the investigation of MCT. As such, Fisher's (2006) conclusions about the relative efficacies of these two treatment packages were preliminary. A brief examination of clinically significant change in recent studies may provide additional information.

Indeed, data were not available for Ladouceur et al.'s (2000) study that compared individual IUM-type CBT to a WLC (Fisher, 2006). However, the authors did conclude that at posttreatment, 6-month, and 12-month follow-up, the percentage of participants in the CBT condition who scored within 1 standard deviation of the mean of normative samples was 81%, 73%, and 69%, respectively. Moreover, at all three test points, 77% of participants no longer met diagnostic criteria for GAD. These

rates, along with those reported by Dugas et al. (Dugas et al., 2010) are similar to those obtained by Dugas et al. (2003), whose data were included in Fisher's (2006) review. Finally, a recent MA that included only studies using *DSM-III-R* criteria that assessed outcome as a decrease in worry, the central symptom of GAD, demonstrated that the average participant fell within the average range of PSWQ scores following CBT (Covin et al., 2008). Additionally, the authors indicated that the IUM treatment package may offer an advantage in outcome over the CAM package.

In part because mindfulness and acceptance theories are considered by some to be distinct from CBT conceptualizations (e.g., Eifert & Forsyth, 2005; Hayes, 2008), ABBT has not been compared, in terms of clinical significance, to other CBT packages. As mentioned, in the only completed RCT examining the efficacy of ABBT, 77% of people in the ABBT group no longer met criteria for GAD (compared to 17% in the WLC) following treatment, with similar proportions observed at 3- and 9-month follow-up. These results are comparable to those obtained for the IUM treatment package (Dugas et al., 2010; Dugas et al., 2003; Ladouceur et al., 2000).

It is important to note that, with the exception of the CAM treatment package, each form of CBT has primarily been tested by only one research group (i.e., IUM: Dugas, Ladouceur, and colleagues; MCT: Wells, King, and colleagues; ABBT: Roemer, Orsillo, and colleagues). Indeed, the only study that compared extant treatment packages found a slight advantage for MCT over IUM, but presented only preliminary results (van der Heiden 2008).

Overall, existing research evidence supports the use of CBT in the treatment of GAD. That being said, it appears that differing treatment packages may underlie varying levels of efficacy. To date, however, the conclusion that treatments derived from contemporary conceptual models specific to GAD (i.e., IUM, MCT, ABBT, IP) offer improved recovery rates over well-established treatment packages (i.e., CAM) are preliminary, at best. Indeed, the results of outcome studies using newer treatment packages are promising, in particular because of increased rates of clinically significant change (e.g., Wells et al., 2009) and evidence supporting improved symptom change over follow-up (e.g., Dugas et al., 2010). However, future research conducted by outside laboratories and updated analyses of standardized clinically significant change are warranted. Moreover, experiments that directly compare treatment packages may provide clearer indications of what constitutes clinically best practice.

ANALYTICAL PSYCHOTHERAPY

Although analytical psychotherapy (AP) has a long history, research on its efficacy in the treatment of GAD is limited. Moreover, of the studies published in peer-reviewed journals (see further on), the exact nature of the treatment packages varies from study to study. Newer manualized versions of AP, however, have shown some promise in the literature (e.g., Crits-Christoph, Gibbons, Narducci, Schamberger, & Gallop, 2005). A review of the available research pertaining to the efficacy of AP in the reduction of GAD symptoms is presented next.

Randomized Controlled Trials

Very few studies have been conducted to examine efficacy of analytical psychotherapy (AP) in the treatment of GAD. Moreover, of the studies conducted, very few have used a manualized form of AP. To date, it appears that only four RCTs have investigated AP's ability to reduce anxious symptoms among participants diagnosed with GAD, each of which utilized a different version of AP.

As described in the CBT section, Durham et al. (1994) compared relative efficacies of CT, AP, and anxiety management training (AMT) for treatment of GAD. Although AP resulted in significant differences on some measures of anxiety at posttreatment, it was clearly less

efficacious than was CT, as evidenced by substantially lower rates of clinically significant change. Moreover, this difference increased at 6-month follow-up. Importantly, no manual was described to define the treatment of AP, therapists were not trained in AP prior to the experiment's commencement, and the authors did not assess treatment adherence (Crits-Christoph, Connolly, Azarian, Crits-Christoph, & Shappell, 1996). As such, it may be that although the AP condition followed general psychoanalytic concepts (e.g., transference and resistance, relationships, development, etc.), it functioned more as a control treatment for the CT and AMT conditions than as an active treatment in its own right.

In response to this methodology, Crits-Christoph et al., (2005) investigated the efficacy of a brief manualized AP treatment package, brief supportive-expressive psychotherapy (BSEP) (Crits-Christoph, Crits-Christoph, Wolf-Palacio, Fichter, & Rudick, 1995), in comparison to that of SC. The BSEP is an integrative therapy that combines an early version of supportive-expressive therapy (Luborsky, 1984) with a technique designed to uncover the patient's Core Conflictual Relationship Theme (CCRT) (Luborsky & Crits-Christoph, 1989). The CCRT includes the patient's needs/wishes, the responses of others to those needs/wishes, and the self's resultant responses. The BSEP therapist seeks to examine the CCRT as it functions in the client's current relationships, past relationships, and therapeutic relationship with the goal of reducing anxiety symptoms that stem from such conflicts, and encouraging better methods of coping with emotions, expressing needs/wishes, and responding to others. Following 16 weekly sessions, both groups evidenced reduced scores on measures of anxiety and worry, with no significant differences between treatment conditions (Crits-Christoph et al., 2005). Moreover, 79% of participants were classified as recovered at posttreatment. Of particular relevance to the theoretical underpinnings of BSEP, individuals who endorsed problematic schemas related to love and affiliation exhibited less worry remission following treatment. As such, a focus on interpersonal issues may constitute an important role in psychotherapy for GAD (e.g., Crits-Christoph et al., 2005; Newman et al., 2008).

Ferrero et al. (2007) also demonstrated significant pre-post effects for Brief Adlerian Psychoanalytic Psychotherapy (A-BPP) (e.g., Fassino et al., 2005), but failed to find evidence that supported its advantage over pharmacotherapy in the treatment of GAD within a community mental health sample. Moreover, although participants in all three conditions (A-BPP, pharmacotherapy, combined) demonstrated high recovery rates (80%, 67%, and 63%, respectively) on the HAM-A, neither trait anxiety nor worry was assessed.

Indeed, the only study to our knowledge that has supported use of AP over a separate treatment reported decreased scores on two composite scores of the Symptoms Checklist-90 (SCL-90) (Derogatis, Lipman, Rickels, Uhlenhuth, & Covi, 1974), which reflected global anxiety and global distress other than anxiety (Levy Berg, Sandell, & Sandahl, 2009). The type of AP described in this study was referred to as Affect Based Psychotherapy (ABP), which integrates physiotherapy and emotional awareness training with a psychodynamic framework (e.g., Monsen & Monsen, 1999). Importantly, the control group for this study was psychiatric treatment as usual (TAU), which consisted of either formalized psychotherapy other than ABP, regular (but not frequent) doctor appointments, or unsystematic intermittent contacts. As such, it is difficult to assess whether the differences that emerged between treatments reflected advantages of ABP over an active treatment, a placebo treatment, or a no treatment control.

The most important information that arises from the present review of RCTs investigating the efficacy of AP for GAD is the notable lack of consistency of treatment type across studies. Although CBT is an umbrella term that incorporates several different treatment packages based on distinct conceptual models of GAD,

they share several basic tenets (Behar et al., 2009). More importantly, each theoretical model is well supported by research examining its underlying core constructs (e.g., intolerance of uncertainty distinguishes patients with GAD from their nonclinical counterparts; Dugas et al., 1998), and has used appropriate outcome measures to assess efficacy of its associated treatment package (e.g., PSWQ to assess worry, the central feature of GAD). Studies assessing AP, however, vary considerably in their approach, and are based on discrete areas of research.

That being said, a distinction must be made between unvalidated and invalidated treatments (Westen & Morrison, 2001). Outcome research to date has not indicated that AP is not efficacious in the treatment of GAD, but only that evidence does not presently support its use over other active treatments. With the development of more structured treatment manuals (e.g., BSEP; Crits-Christoph et al., 1995), subsequent empirical investigation of efficacy of AP may provide more conclusive results.

Single Case Designs

As mentioned previously, although conclusions derived from single case designs are limited, they can provide additional support to treatment packages that have also been tested in a RCT format. Crits-Cristoph et al. (1996) conducted an open trial of BSEP in a sample of 26 individuals diagnosed with primary GAD. Results demonstrated significant decreases at posttreatment on measures of trait anxiety and worry. Moreover, over three quarters of participants no longer met criteria for GAD following 16 sessions of treatment. This recovery rate is similar to that obtained in studies of CBT; however, no follow-up data were reported. Future studies should examine the efficacy of BSEP as it compares to other validated treatments (e.g., CAM treatment) in both the short- and long-term.

Conclusions

Although results of some studies examining efficacy of AP in the treatment of GAD are promising (e.g., Crits-Christoph et al., 1996), RCTs have largely failed to demonstrate its usefulness over placebo and alternative treatments. Moreover, the lack of consistent manualized treatments makes it difficult to compare results across studies. As such, we cannot currently endorse the use of AP in the treatment of GAD in lieu of other empirically supported treatments. We do, however, encourage both outcome and theoretical studies designed to increase the efficacy of AP treatment packages.

EVIDENCE-BASED PRACTICE

Based on the literature reviewed in this chapter, CBT is the only treatment that has been well supported both in terms of efficacy and effectiveness. This conclusion is complicated, however, by the variety of treatment packages that fall under this heading. Of these, the CAM model bears the most evidence because it has been tested the most frequently, and by different research groups. The IUM treatment package has also been frequently tested, yet, with the exception of one study (van der Heiden 2008), has only been investigated by its developers. Indeed, preliminary results presented by van der Heiden (2008) indicated that although participants with GAD in the IUM condition evidenced reduced symptomatology, they did not demonstrate a significantly better outcome than a WLC. In contrast, the same study revealed significantly reduced scores on the PSWQ for MCT as compared to a WLC. No significant differences emerged between MCT and IUM. Although it is tempting, given these findings, to conclude that MCT is more efficacious than is IUM, the recency of this model necessarily precludes an abundance of research supporting its usefulness. Indeed, it has only been tested in two RCTs.

Because the CAM approach has been tested in multiple studies by independent research groups, it passes the threshold for evidence-based practice. Although newer treatment packages (IUM, CBT, ABBT, IP) are lacking in evidence from studies conducted by outside research groups, they are clearly promising in their ability to increase the proportion of individuals with GAD who obtain clinically significant improvement. Indeed, due to their empirically supported theoretical bases, which are specific to the cognitive underpinnings of GAD symptomatology, these more recent treatment packages will likely demonstrate greater efficacy and effectiveness than the CAM treatment package. This statement, obviously, is preliminary, and research aimed at examining the relative efficacies of contemporary CBT treatments is required to determine which CBT packages and/or components will be most useful in the treatment of GAD.

The AP does not, at present, have sufficient research with which to categorize it as an empirically supported treatment. This is not to say that such an approach is not valid, but rather that it has not yet received enough empirical support. Therefore, its use in place of CBT cannot be considered best practice. Moreover, a closer examination of existing studies reveals that duration of therapy in AP studies varied from 10 sessions to weekly sessions spanning a year's time, whereas studies of CBT typically fell within much shorter durations (see Table 28.1). As such, it appears that CBT is also more cost effective than is AP.

Historically, CBT treatments have been developed according to our understanding of the primary components of GAD. Whereas early treatments focused on somatic complaints (EMG feedback and progressive relaxation; Canter, Kondo, & Knott, 1975; LeBoeuf & Lodge, 1980) and methods of coping with chronic anxiety (AMT; Blowers, Cobb, & Mathews, 1987; Butler, Cullington, Hibbert, & Klimes, 1987), the focus on worry as the central feature of GAD in DSM-III-R resulted in more cognitive conceptualizations of the disorder (e.g., Borkovec & Costello, 1993). In the decades that followed, increased research into the etiology and maintenance of GAD produced advanced conceptualizations (and subsequent treatments) that focused on worry-specific cognitive components (e.g., intolerance of uncertainty, Dugas, Freeston, & Ladouceur, 1997; negative reactions to worry, Roemer & Orsillo, 2005; worry about worry, Wells, 1995), and interpersonal factors believed to impede the efficacy of other CBT packages (e.g., Newman et al., 2008).

Although it is premature to conclude definitively that these new approaches (IUM, MCT, ABBT, IP) constitute best practice, results supporting their efficacy have consistently supported their use, regardless of methodology (RCT, single case studies, etc.). Moreover, rates of clinically significant change obtained in trials of these treatments are compelling in that they are largely substantially higher than those obtained by earlier treatments. As such, it is likely that these approaches will eventually become the treatments of choice for GAD. It is our hope that the next decade of research will clarify these questions both in terms of which treatments consistently demonstrate efficacy and effectiveness (in the short- and long-term) and also which components and/or mechanisms of change are the most salient ingredients for symptom reduction.

REFERENCES

Ahmed, M., Westra, H. A., & Stewart, S. H. (2008). A self-help handout for benzodiazepine discontinuation using cognitive behavioral therapy. *Cognitive and Behavioral Practice, 15*, 317–324.

Aikins, D. E., Hazlett-Stevens, H., & Craske, M. G. (2001). Issues of measurement and mechanism in meta-analyses: Comment on Westen and Morrison (2001). *Journal of Consulting and Clinical Psychology, 69*, 904–907.

American Psychiatric Association. (1980). *Diagnostic and statistical manual of mental disorders* (3rd ed.) Washington, DC: Author.

American Psychiatric Association. (1987). *Diagnostic and statistical manual of mental disorders* (3rd ed., rev.). Washington, DC: Author.

American Psychiatric Association. (1994). *Diagnostic and statistical manual of mental disorders*. (4th ed.) Washington, DC: Author.

Arntz, A. (2003). Cognitive therapy versus applied relaxation as treatment of generalized anxiety disorder. *Behaviour Research and Therapy, 41*, 633–646.

Barlow, D. H., Rapee, R. M., & Brown, T. A. (1992). Behavioral treatment of generalized anxiety disorder. *Behavior Therapy, 23*, 551–570.

Beck, A. T., & Emery, G. (1985). *Anxiety disorders and phobias: A cognitive perspective*. New York, NY: Basic Books.

Beck, A. T., Epstein, N., Brown, G., & Steer, R. A. (1988). An inventory for measuring clinical anxiety: Psychometric properties. *Journal of Consulting and Clinical Psychology, 56*, 893–897.

Behar, E., Dimarco, I. D., Hekler, E. B., Mohlman, J., & Staples, A. M. (2009). Current theoretical models of generalized anxiety disorder (GAD): Conceptual review and treatment implications. *Journal of Anxiety Disorders, 23*(8), 1011–1023.

Bernstein, D. A., & Borkovec, T. D. (1973). *Progressive relaxation training: A manual for the helping professions*. Champaign, IL: Research Press.

Blowers, C., Cobb, J., & Mathews, A. (1987). Generalised anxiety: A controlled treatment study. *Behaviour Research and Therapy, 25*, 493–502.

Borkovec, T. D. (1994). The nature, functions, and origins of worry. In G. C. Davey & F. Tallis (Eds.), *Worrying: Perspectives on theory, assessment and treatment* (pp. 5–33). Oxford, England: Wiley.

Borkovec, T. D. (2006). Applied relaxation and cognitive therapy for pathological worry and generalized anxiety disorder. In G. C. L. Davey & A. Wells (Eds.), *Worry and its psychological disorders: Theory, assessment and treatment* (pp. 273–287). Hoboken, NJ: Wiley.

Borkovec, T. D., Alcaine, O. M., & Behar, E. (2004). Avoidance theory of worry and generalized anxiety disorder. In R. G. Heimberg, C. L. Turk, & D. S. Mennin (Eds.), *Generalized anxiety disorder: Advances in research and practice* (pp. 77–108). New York, NY: Guilford Press.

Borkovec, T. D., & Costello, E. (1993). Efficacy of applied relaxation and cognitive-behavioral therapy in the treatment of generalized anxiety disorder. *Journal of Consulting and Clinical Psychology, 61*, 611–619.

Borkovec, T. D., & Newman, M. G. (1998). Worry and generalized anxiety disorder. In P. M. Salkovskis (Ed.), *Adults: Clinical formulation and treatment* (pp. 439–459). Oxford, England: Pergamon Press.

Borkovec, T. D., Newman, M. G., & Castonguay, L. G. (2003). Cognitive- behavioral therapy for generalized anxiety disorder with integrations from interpersonal and experiential therapies. *CNS Spectrums, 8*, 382–389.

Borkovec, T. D., Newman, M. G., Pincus, A. L., & Lytle, R. (2002). A component analysis of cognitive-behavioral therapy for generalized anxiety disorder and the role of interpersonal problems. *Journal of Consulting and Clinical Psychology, 70*, 288–298.

Borkovec, T. D., Ray, W. J., & Stober, J. (1998). Worry: A cognitive phenomenon intimately linked to affective, physiological, and interpersonal behavioral processes. *Cognitive Therapy and Research, Special Issue: Cognition and anxiety, 22*, 561–576.

Borkovec, T. D., & Ruscio, A. M. (2001). Psychotherapy for generalized anxiety disorder. *Journal of Clinical Psychiatry, 62*, 37–42.

Brown, T. A., Barlow, D. H., & Liebowitz, M. R. (1994). The empirical basis of generalized anxiety disorder. *American Journal of Psychiatry, 151*, 1272–1280.

Brown, T. A., DiNardo, P. A., & Barlow, D. H. (1994). *Anxiety disorders interview schedule* (4th ed.). Boulder, CO: Graywing Publications.

Butler, G., Cullington, A., Hibbert, G., & Klimes, I. (1987). Anxiety management for persistent generalised anxiety. *British Journal of Psychiatry, 151*, 535–542.

Canter, A., Kondo, C. Y., & Knott, J. R. (1975). A comparison of EMG feedback and progressive muscle relaxation training in anxiety neurosis. *British Journal of Psychiatry, 127*, 470–477.

Caudle, D. D., Senior, A. C., Wetherell, J. L., Rhoades, H. M., Beck, J. G., Kunik, M. E., . . . Stanley, M. A. (2007). Cognitive errors, symptom severity, and response to cognitive behavior therapy in older adults with generalized anxiety disorder. *American Journal of Geriatric Psychiatry, 15*, 680–689.

Chambless, D. L., Baker, M. J., Baucom, D. H., Beutler, L. E., Calhoun, K. S., Crits-Christoph, P., . . . Woody, S. R. (1998). Update on empirically validated therapies, II. *Clinical Psychologist, 51*, 3–16.

Chambless, D. L., & Gillis, M. M. (1993). Cognitive therapy of anxiety disorders. *Journal of Consulting and Clinical Psychology, 61*, 248–260.

Chambless, D. L., & Ollendick, T. H. (2001). Empirically supported psychological interventions: Controversies and evidence. *Annual Review of Psychology, 52*, 685–7166.

Chambless, D. L., Sanderson, W. C., Shoham, V., Bennett Johnson, S., Pope, K. S., Crits-Christoph, P., McCurry, S. (1996). An update on empirically validated therapies. *Clinical Psychologist, 49*, 5–18.

Clark, D. A. (1996). Panic disorder: From theory to therapy. In P. M. Salkovskis (Ed.), *Frontiers of cognitive therapy* (pp. 318–343). New York, NY: Guilford Press.

Clark, D. M. (1989). Anxiety states: Panic and generalized anxiety. In K. Hawton, P. M. Salkovskis, J. Kirk, & D. M. Clark (Eds.), *Cognitive behaviour therapy for psychiatric problems: A practical guide. Oxford medical publications.* New York, NY: Oxford

Covin, R., Ouimet, A. J., Seeds, P. M., & Dozois, D. J. A. (2008). A meta-analysis of CBT for pathological worry among clients with GAD. *Journal of Anxiety Disorders, 22*, 108–116.

Crits-Christoph, P., Connolly, M. B., Azarian, K., Crits-Christoph, K., & Shappell, S. (1996). An open trial of

brief supportive-expressive psychotherapy in the treatment of generalized anxiety disorder. *Psychotherapy: Theory, Research, Practice, Training, 33*, 418–430.

Crits-Christoph, P., Crits-Christoph, K., Wolf-Palacio, D., Fichter, M., & Rudick, D. (1995). Brief supportive-expressive psychodynamic therapy for generalized anxiety disorder. In J. P. Barber & P. Crits-Christoph (Eds.), *Dynamic therapies for psychiatric disorders* (pp. 43–83). New York, NY: Basic Books.

Crits-Christoph, P., Gibbons, M. B. C., Narducci, J., Schamberger, M., & Gallop, R. (2005). Interpersonal problems and the outcome of interpersonally oriented psychodynamic treatment of GAD. *Psychotherapy: Theory, Research, Practice, Training, 42*, 211–224.

Derogatis, L. R., Lipman, R. S., Rickels, K., Uhlenhuth, E. H., & Covi, L. (1974). The Hopkins symptom checklist (HSCL): A self-report symptom inventory. *Behavioral Science, 19*, 1–15.

DiNardo, P. A., & Barlow, D. H. (1988). *Anxiety disorders interview schedule revised (ADIS-R)*. Albany: Phobia and Anxiety Disorders Clinic, State University of New York.

Dobson, D., & Dobson, K. S. (2009). *Evidence based practice of cognitive behavioral therapy*. New York, NY: Guilford Press.

Dobson, K. S., & Dozois, D. J. A. (2010). Historical and philosophical bases of the cognitive behavioral therapies. In K. S. Dobson (Ed.), *Handbook of cognitive behavioral therapies* (pp. 3–38). New York, NY: Guilford Press.

Dugas, M. J. (2000). Generalized anxiety disorder publications: So where do we stand? *Journal of Anxiety Disorders, 14*, 31–40.

Dugas, M. J., Brillon, P., Savard, P., Turcotte, J., Gaudet, A., Ladouceur, R., . . . Gervais, N. J. (2010). A randomized clinical trial of cognitive-behavioral therapy and applied relaxation for adults with generalized anxiety disorder. *Behavior Therapy, 41*, 46–58.

Dugas, M. J., Buhr, K., & Ladouceur, R. (2004). The role of intolerance of uncertainty in etiology and maintenance. In R. G. Heimberg, C. L. Turk, & D. S. Mennin (Eds.), *Generalized anxiety disorder: Advances in research and practice* (pp. 143–163). New York, NY: Guilford Press.

Dugas, M. J., Freeston, M. H., & Ladouceur, R. (1997). Intolerance of uncertainty and problem orientation in worry. *Cognitive Therapy and Research, 21*, 593–606.

Dugas, M. J., Gagnon, F., Ladouceur, R., & Freeston, M. H. (1998). Generalized anxiety disorder: A preliminary test of a conceptual model. *Behaviour Research and Therapy, 36*, 215–226.

Dugas, M. J., & Ladouceur, R. (2000). Treatment of GAD: Targeting intolerance of uncertainty in two types of worry. *Behavior Modification, 24*, 635–657.

Dugas, M. J., Ladouceur, R., Leger, E., Freeston, M. H., Langlois, F., Provencher, M. D., & Boisvert, J.-M.

(2003). Group cognitive-behavioral therapy for generalized anxiety disorder: Treatment outcome and long-term follow-up. *Journal of Consulting and Clinical Psychology, 71*, 821–825.

Dugas, M. J., Marchand, A., & Ladouceur, R. (2005). Further validation of a cognitive-behavioral model of generalized anxiety disorder: Diagnostic and symptom specificity. *Journal of Anxiety Disorders, 19*, 329–343.

Dugas, M. J., & Robichaud, M. (2007). *Cognitive-behavioral treatment for generalized anxiety disorder: From science to practice.* New York, NY: Routledge/ Taylor & Francis Group.

Durham, R. C., Chambers, J. A., MacDonald, R. R., Power, K. G., & Major, K. (2003). Does cognitive-behavioural therapy influence the long-term outcome of generalized anxiety disorder? An 8–14 year follow-up of two clinical trials. *Psychological Medicine, 33*, 499–509.

Durham, R. C., Murphy, T., Allan, T., & Richard, K. (1994). Cognitive therapy, analytic psychotherapy and anxiety management training for generalised anxiety disorder. *British Journal of Psychiatry, 165*, 315–323.

Eifert, G. H., & Forsyth, J. P. (2005). *Acceptance and commitment therapy for anxiety disorders: A practitioner's treatment guide to using mindfulness, acceptance, and values-based behavior change strategies.* Oakland, CA: New Harbinger.

Fassino, S., Daga, G. A., Delsedime, N., Busso, F., Pierò, A., & Overa, G. G. (2005). Baseline personality characteristics of responders to 6-month psychotherapy in eating disorders: Preliminary data. *Eating and Weight Disorders, 10*, 40–50.

Fava, G. A., Ruini, C., Rafanelli, C., Finos, L., Salmaso, L., Mangelli, L., & Sirigatti, S. (2005). Well-being therapy of generalized anxiety disorder. *Psychotherapy and Psychosomatics, 74*, 26–30.

Ferrero, A., Pierò, A., Fassina, S., Massola, T., Lanteri, A., Daga, G. A., & Fassino, S. (2007). A 12-month comparison of brief psychodynamic psychotherapy and pharmacotherapy treatment in subjects with generalised anxiety disorders in a community setting. *European Psychiatry, 22*, 530–539.

First, M., Spitzer, R., Gibbon, M., & Williams, J. (2001). *Structured clinical interview for DSM-IV-TR axis I disorders.* New York: Biometrics Research, New York State Psychiatric Institute.

Fisher, P. L. (2006). The efficacy of psychological treatments for generalized anxiety disorder? In G. C. L. Davey & A. Wells (Eds.), *Worry and its psychological disorders: Theory, assessment and treatment* (pp. 359–377). Hoboken, NJ: John Wiley & Sons.

Fisher, P. L., & Durham, R. C. (1999). Recovery rates in generalized anxiety disorder following psychological therapy: An analysis of clinically significant change in the STAI-T across outcome studies since 1990. *Psychological Medicine, 29*, 1425–1434.

Freeston, M. H., Rhéaume, J., Letarte, H., & Dugas, M. J. (1994). Why do people worry? *Personality and Individual Differences, 17*, 791-8–02.

Gosselin, P., Ladouceur, R., Morin, C. M., Dugas, M. J., & Baillargeon, L. (2006). Benzodiazepine discontinuation among adults with GAD: A randomized trial of cognitive-behavioral therapy. *Journal of Consulting and Clinical Psychology, Special Issue: Benefit-Finding. 74*, 908–919.

Gould, R. A., Otto, M. W., Pollack, M. H., & Yap, L. (1997). Cognitive behavioral and pharmacological treatment of generalized anxiety disorder: A preliminary meta-analyis. *Behavior Therapy, 28*, 285–305.

Gould, R. A., Safren, S. A., Washington, D. O., & Otto, M. W. (2004). A meta-analytic review of cognitive-behavioral treatments. In R. G. Heimberg, C. L. Turk, & D. S. Mennin (Eds.), *Generalized anxiety disorder: Advances in research and practice* (pp. 248–264). New York, NY: Guilford Press.

Guy, W. (1976). *ECDEU assessment manual for psychopharmacology* (Rev.). Rockville, MD: U.S. Department of Mental Health and Human Services, Public Health Service, Alcohol, Drug Abuse, and Mental Health Administration, NIMH Psychopharmacology Research Branch.

Haby, M. M., Donnelly, M., Corry, J., & Vos, T. (2006). Cognitive behavioural therapy for depression, panic disorder and generalized anxiety disorder: A meta-regression of factors that may predict outcome. *Australian and New Zealand Journal of Psychiatry, 40*, 9–19.

Hamilton, M. (1959). The measurement of anxiety states by rating. *British Journal of Medical Psychology, 32*, 50–55.

Hayes, S. C. (2008). Climbing our hills: A beginning conversation on the comparison of acceptance and commitment therapy and traditional cognitive behavioral therapy. *Clinical Psychology: Science and Practice, 15*, 286–295.

Hayes, S. C., Strosahl, K. D., & Wilson, K. G. (1999). *Acceptance and commitment therapy: An experiential approach to behavior change.* New York, NY: Guilford Press.

Hoffman, D. L., Dukes, E. M., & Wittchen, H.-U. (2008). Human and economic burden of generalized anxiety disorder. *Depression and Anxiety, 25*, 72–90.

Jacobson, N. S., Follette, W. C., & Revenstorf, D. (1984). Psychotherapy outcome research: Methods for reporting variability and evaluating clinical significance. *Behavior Therapy, 15*, 336–352.

Jacobson, N. S., & Truax, P. (1991). Clinical significance: A statistical approach to defining meaningful change in psychotherapy research. *Journal of Consulting and Clinical Psychology, 59*, 12–19.

Kabat-Zinn, J. (2003). Mindfulness-based stress reduction (MBSR). *Constructivism in the Human Sciences, 8*, 73–107.

Kehle, S. M. (2008). The effectiveness of cognitive behavioral therapy for generalized anxiety disorder in a frontline service setting. *Cognitive Behaviour Therapy, 37,* 192–198.

Kessler, R. C., Berglund, P., Demler, O., Jin, R., Merikangas, K. R., & Walters, E. E. (2005). Lifetime prevalence and age-of-onset distributions of *DSM-IV* disorders in the national comorbidity survey replication. *Archives of General Psychiatry, 62,* 593–602.

Kessler, R. C., Chiu, W. T., Demler, O., & Walters, E. E. (2005). Prevalence, severity, and comorbidity of 12-month *DSM-IV* disorders in the national comorbidity survey replication. *Archives of General Psychiatry, 62,* 617–627.

Kessler, R. C., McGonagle, K. A., Zhao, S., Nelson, C. B., Hughes, M., Eshleman, S., . . . Kendler, K. S. (1994). Lifetime and 12 month prevalence of *DSM-III-R* psychiatric disorders in the United States: Results from the national comorbidity study. *Archives of General Psychiatry, 51,* 8–19.

Kessler, R. C., Walters, E. E., & Wittchen, H. U. (2004). Epidemiology. In R. G. Heimberg, C. L. Turk, & D. S. Menin (Eds.), *Generalized anxiety disorder: Advances in research and practice* (pp. 29–50). New York, NY: Guilford Press.

Kessler, R. C., & Wittchen, H. U. (2002). Patterns and correlates of generalized anxiety disorder in community samples. *Journal of Clinical Psychiatry, Special Issue: Generalized anxiety disorder: New trends in diagnosis, management, and treatment, 63,* 4–10.

Koerner, N., Dugas, M. J., Savard, P., Gaudet, A., Turcotte, J., & Marchand, A. (2004). The economic burden of anxiety disorders in Canada. *Canadian Psychology/Psychologie Canadienne, 45,* 191–201.

Ladouceur, R., Dugas, M. J., Freeston, M. H., Leger, E., Gagnon, F., & Thibodeau, N. (2000). Efficacy of a cognitive-behavioral treatment for generalized anxiety disorder: Evaluation in a controlled clinical trial. *Journal of Consulting and Clinical Psychology, 68,* 957–964.

Ladouceur, R., Dugas, M. J., Freeston, M. H., Rheaume, J., Blais, F., Boisvert, J. M., . . . Thibodeau, N. (1999). Specificity of generalized anxiety disorder symptoms and processes. *Behavior Therapy, 30,* 191–207.

Ladouceur, R., Leger, E., Dugas, M., & Freeston, M. H. (2004). Cognitive-behavioral treatment of generalized anxiety disorder (GAD) for older adults. *International Psychogeriatrics, 16,* 195–207.

Lawton, M. P., Kleban, M. H., & Dean, J. (1993). Affect and age: Cross-sectional comparisons of structure and prevalence. *Psychology and Aging, 8,* 165–175.

LeBoeuf, A., & Lodge, J. (1980). A comparison of frontalis EMG feedback training and progressive relaxation in the treatment of chronic anxiety. *British Journal of Psychiatry, 137,* 279–284.

Levy Berg, A., Sandell, R., & Sandahl, C. (2009). Affect-focused body psychotherapy in patients with

generalized anxiety disorder: Evaluation of an integrative method. *Journal of Psychotherapy Integration, 19,* 67–85.

Linden, M., Zubraegel, D., Baer, T., Franke, U., & Schlattmann, P. (2005). Efficacy of cognitive behaviour therapy in generalized anxiety disorders. *Psychotherapy and Psychosomatics, 74,* 36–42.

Luborsky, L. (1984). *Principles of psychoanalytic psychotherapy: A manual for supportive-expressive treatment.* New York, NY: Basic Books.

Luborsky, L., & Crits-Christoph, P. (1989). A relationship pattern measure: The core conflictual relationship theme. *Psychiatry: Journal for the Study of Interpersonal Processes, 52,* 250–259.

McIntosh, A., Cohen, A., Turnbull, N., Esmonde, L., Dennis, P., Eatock, J., . . . & Salkovskis, P. M. (2004). *Clinical guidelines and evidence review for panic disorder and generalised anxiety disorder.* Sheffield/London, England: University of Sheffield/National Collaborating Centre for Primary Care.

Meyer, T. J., Miller, M. L., Metzger, R. L., & Borkovec, T. D. (1990). Development and validation of the Penn State worry questionnaire. *Behaviour Research and Therapy, 28,* 487–495.

Mitte, K. (2005). Meta-analysis of cognitive-behavioral treatments for generalized anxiety disorder: A comparison with pharmacotherapy. *Psychological Bulletin, 131,* 785–795.

Mohlman, J. (2008). More power to the executive? A preliminary test of CBT plus executive skills training for treatment of late-life GAD. *Cognitive and Behavioral Practice, 15,* 306–316.

Monsen, J. T., & Monsen, K. (1999). Affects and affect consciousness: A psychotherapy model integrating Silvan Tomkins's affect and script theory within the framework of self psychology. In A. Goldberg (Ed.), *Pluralism in self psychology: Progress in self psychology* (Vol. 15, pp. 287–306). Mahwah, NJ: Analytic Press.

National Institute of Mental Health. (2009). *Anxiety Disorders.* Washington, DC: U.S. Department of Health and Human Services.

Newman, M. G., Castonguay, L. G., Borkovec, T. D., Fisher, A. J., & Nordberg, S. S. (2008). An open trial of integrative therapy for generalized anxiety disorder. *Psychotherapy: Theory, Research, Practice, Training. Special Issue: New treatments in psychotherapy, 45,* 135–147.

Newman, M. G., Castonguay, L. G., Borkovec, T. D., & Molnar, C. (2004). Integrative psychotherapy. In R. G. Heimberg, C. L. Turk, & D. S. Menin (Eds.), *Generalized anxiety disorder: Advances in research and practice.* New York, NY: Guilford Press.

Öst, L. G. (1987). Applied relaxation: Description of a coping technique and review of controlled studies. *Behaviour Research and Therapy, 25,* 397–409.

Öst, L. G., & Breitholtz, E. (2000). Applied relaxation vs. cognitive therapy in the treatment of generalized anxiety disorder. *Behaviour Research and Therapy, 38*, 777–790.

Provencher, M. D., Dugas, M. J., & Ladouceur, R. (2004). Efficacy of problem-solving training and cognitive exposure in the treatment of generalized anxiety disorder: A case replication series. *Cognitive and Behavioral Practice, 11*, 404–414.

Robichaud, M., & Dugas, M. J. (2006). A cognitive-behavioral treatment targeting intolerance of uncertainty. In G. C. L. Davey & A. Wells (Eds.), *Worry and its psychological disorders: Theory, assessment and treatment* (pp. 289–304). Hoboken, NJ: John Wiley & Sons.

Robichaud, M., Dugas, M. J., & Conway, M. (2003). Gender differences in worry and associated cognitive-behavioral variables. *Journal of Anxiety Disorders, 17*, 501–516.

Roemer, L., & Orsillo, S. M. (2005). An acceptance-based behavior therapy for generalized anxiety disorder. In S. M. Orsillo & L. Roemer (Eds.), *Acceptance and mindfulness-based approaches to anxiety: Conceptualization and treatment* (pp. 213–240). New York, NY: Springer Science.

Roemer, L., & Orsillo, S. M. (2007). An open trial of an acceptance-based behavior therapy for generalized anxiety disorder. *Behavior Therapy, 38*, 72–85.

Roemer, L., Orsillo, S. M., & Salters-Pedneault, K. (2008). Efficacy of an acceptance-based behavior therapy for generalized anxiety disorder: Evaluation in a randomized controlled trial. *Journal of Consulting and Clinical Psychology, 76*, 1083–1089.

Sanderson, W. C., Raue, P. J., & Wetzler, S. (1998). The generalizability of cognitive behavior therapy for panic disorder. *Journal of Cognitive Psychotherapy, 12*, 323–330.

Seligman, M. E. P. (1995). The effectiveness of psychotherapy: The consumer reports study. *American Psychologist, 50*, 965–974.

Sexton, K. A., Francis, K., & Dugas, M. J. (2008). Generalized anxiety disorder. In M. Hersen & J. Rosqvist (Eds.), *Handbook of psychological assessment, case conceptualization, and treatment, 1: Adults* (pp. 291–318). Hoboken, NJ: Wiley.

Shadish, W. R., Navarro, A. M., Matt, G. E., & Phillips, G. (2000). The effects of psychological therapies under clinically representative conditions: A meta-analysis. *Psychological Bulletin, 126*, 512–529.

Sibrava, N. J., & Borkovec, T. D. (2006). The cognitive avoidance theory of worry. In G. C. Davey & A. Wells (Eds.), *Worry and its psychological disorders: Theory, assessment and treatment* (pp. 239–256). Hoboken, NJ: Wiley.

Souêtre, E., Lozet, H., Cimarosti, I., & Martin, P. (1994). Cost of anxiety disorders: Impact of comorbidity. *Journal of Psychosomatic Research, 38*, 151–160.

Spielberger, C. D., Gorusch, R. L., Lushene, R., Vagg, P. R., & Jacobs, G. A. (1983). *Manual for the state-trait anxiety inventory*. Palo Alto, CA: Consulting Psychologists Press.

Stanley, M. A., Beck, J. G., & Glassco, J. D. (1996). Treatment of generalized anxiety in older adults: A preliminary comparison of cognitive-behavioral and supportive approaches. *Behavior Therapy, 27*, 565–581.

Stanley, M. A., Beck, J. G., Novy, D. M., Averill, P. M., Swann, A. C., Diefenbach, G. J., & Hopko, D. R. (2003). Cognitive-behavioral treatment of late-life generalized anxiety disorder. *Journal of Consulting and Clinical Psychology, 71*, 309–319.

Stanley, M. A., Wilson, N. L., Novy, D. M., Rhoades, H. M., Wagener, P. D., Greisinger, A. J., . . . Kunik, M. E. (2009). Cognitive behavior therapy for generalized anxiety disorder among older adults in primary care: A randomized clinical trial. *Journal of the American Medical Association, 301*, 1460–1467.

Stein, D. J. (2001). Comorbidity in generalized anxiety disorder: Impact and implications. *Journal of Clinical Psychiatry, 62*, 29–34.

Stewart, R. E., & Chambless, D. L. (2009). Cognitive-behavioral therapy for adult anxiety disorders in clinical practice: A meta-analysis of effectiveness studies. *Journal of Consulting and Clinical Psychology, 77*, 595–606.

Swinson, R. P., Antony, M. M., Bleau, P., Chokka, P., Craven, M., Fallu, A., . . . Walker, J. R. (2006). Clinical practice guidelines: Management of anxiety disorders. *Canadian Journal of Psychiatry, 51* (Suppl. 2), 1S–92S.

Task Force on Promotion and Dissemination of Psychological Procedures.(1995). Training in and dissemination of empirically-validated psychological treatments. *Clinical Psychologist, 48*, 3–23.

Turk, C. L., Heimberg, R. G., & Mennin, D. S. (2004). Assessment. In R. G. Heimberg, C. L. Turk, & D. S. Mennin (Eds.), *Generalized anxiety disorder: Advances in research and practice* (pp. 219–247). New York, NY: Guilford Press.

van der Heiden, C. (2008, September). *Treating generalized anxiety disorder with two types of cognitive behavioral therapy: A randomized controlled trial*. Paper presented at the annual meeting of the European Association for Behavioural and Cognitive Therapy, Helsinki, Finland.

Wade, W. A., Treat, T. A., & Stuart, G. L. (1998). Transporting an empirically supported treatment for panic disorder to a service clinic setting: A benchmarking strategy. *Journal of Consulting and Clinical Psychology, 66*, 231–239.

Weisz, J. R., Donenberg, G. R., Han, S. S., & Weiss, B. (1995). Bridging the gap between laboratory and clinic in child and adolescent psychotherapy. *Journal of Consulting and Clinical Psychology, 63*, 688–701.

Wells, A. (1994). A multi-dimensional measure of worry: Development and preliminary validation of the anxious thoughts inventory. *Anxiety, Stress & Coping: An International Journal, 6*, 289–299.

Wells, A. (1995). Meta-cognition and worry: A cognitive model of generalized anxiety disorder. *Behavioural and Cognitive Psychotherapy, 23*, 301–320.

Wells, A. (2005). Worry, intrusive thoughts, and generalized anxiety disorder: The metacognitive theory and treatment. In D. A. Clark (Ed.), *Intrusive thoughts in clinical disorders: Theory, research, and treatment* (pp. 119–144). New York, NY: Guilford Press.

Wells, A., & Carter, K. (2006). Generalized anxiety disorder. In A. Carr & M. McNulty (Eds.), *The handbook of adult clinical psychology: An evidence-based practice approach* (pp. 423–457). New York, NY: Routledge/Taylor & Francis Group.

Wells, A., & King, P. (2006). Metacognitive therapy for generalized anxiety disorder: An open trial. *Journal of Behavior Therapy and Experimental Psychiatry, 37*, 206–212.

Wells, A., Welford, M., King, P., Papageorgiou, C., Wisely, J., & Mendel, E. (2010). A pilot randomized trial of metacognitive therapy vs applied relaxation in the treatment of adults with generalized anxiety disorder. *Behaviour Research and Therapy, 48*, 429–434.

Westbrook, D., & Kirk, J. (2005). The clinical effectiveness of cognitive behaviour therapy: Outcome for a large sample of adults treated in routine practice. *Behaviour Research and Therapy, 43*, 1243–1261.

Westen, D., & Morrison, K. (2001). A multidimensional meta-analysis of treatments for depression, panic, and generalized anxiety disorder: An empirical examination of the status of empirically supported therapies. *Journal of Consulting and Clinical Psychology, 69*, 875–899.

Wetherell, J. L., Gatz, M., & Craske, M. G. (2003). Treatment of generalized anxiety disorder in older adults. *Journal of Consulting and Clinical Psychology, 71*, 31–40.

Wittchen, H. U., & Hoyer, J. A. (2001). Generalized anxiety disorder: Nature and course. *Journal of Clinical Psychiatry, 62*, 15–19.

Author Index

Subject Index